The Oxford Companion to the

BOOK

The Oxford Companion to the

BOOK

EDITED BY MICHAEL F. SUAREZ, S.J. AND
H. R. WOUDHUYSEN

Volume 1

ESSAYS

A–C

OXFORD

UNIVERSITY PRESS

OXFORD

UNIVERSITY PRESS

Great Clarendon Street, Oxford ox2 6DP

Oxford University Press is a department of the University of Oxford.
It furthers the University's objective of excellence in research, scholarship,
and education by publishing worldwide in

Oxford New York

Auckland Cape Town Dar es Salaam Hong Kong Karachi
Kuala Lumpur Madrid Melbourne Mexico City Nairobi
New Delhi Shanghai Taipei Toronto

With offices in

Argentina Austria Brazil Chile Czech Republic France Greece
Guatemala Hungary Italy Japan Poland Portugal Singapore
South Korea Switzerland Thailand Turkey Ukraine Vietnam

Oxford is a registered trade mark of Oxford University Press
in the UK and in certain other countries

Published in the United States
by Oxford University Press Inc., New York

© Oxford University Press 2010

The moral rights of the authors have been asserted
Database right Oxford University Press (maker)

First published 2010

British Library Cataloguing in Publication Data

Data available

Library of Congress Cataloging in Publication Data

Data available

Typeset by Graphicraft Limited, Hong Kong
Printed in China
by C&C Offset Printing Co., Ltd.

ISBN 978-0-19-860653-6

3 5 7 9 10 8 6 4 2

Contents

Associate Editors

Scott E. Casper
THE BOOK IN THE UNITED STATES—
18ᵀᴴ- AND 19ᵀᴴ-CENTURY AMERICA
University of Nevada, Reno

J. S. Edgren
THE BOOK IN EAST ASIA AND
SOUTHEAST ASIA
Princeton University

A. S. G. Edwards
MANUSCRIPTS, COLLECTORS,
LIBRARIES, AND THE BOOK TRADE
De Montfort University

Christine Ferdinand
THE BOOK IN BRITAIN 1501–1780
Magdalen College, Oxford

Vincent Giroud
THE BOOK IN FRANCE
Université de Franche-Comté

Abhijit Gupta
THE BOOK IN SOUTH ASIA
Jadavpur University, Kolkata

Neil Harris
THE BOOK IN ITALY
University of Udine

Lotte Hellinga
TRANSITION TO PRINT CULTURE
1455–*c.*1550
*formerly British Library and
Consortium of European Research
Libraries*

Paul Hoftijzer
THE BOOK IN THE LOW COUNTRIES
Leiden University

Craig Kallendorf
THE BOOK IN THE ANCIENT WORLD
AND RENAISSANCE ITALY
Texas A&M University

David Pearson
THE PHYSICAL BOOK
Guildhall Art Gallery

Ekaterina Rogatchevskaia
THE BOOK IN THE SLAVONIC AND THE
EAST EUROPEAN WORLD
British Library

Geoffrey Roper
THE BOOK IN THE MUSLIM WORLD
Bibliographical consultant

Joan Shelley Rubin
THE BOOK IN THE UNITED STATES
POST 1891
University of Rochester

Peter L. Shillingsburg
THE BOOK IN BRITAIN 1780–1900
Loyola University, Chicago

Margaret M. Smith
PRINTING AND REPRODUCTION
TECHNOLOGIES
University of Reading

Claire Squires
THE BOOK IN 20ᵀᴴ-CENTURY BRITAIN
University of Stirling

Andrew van der Vlies
SUB-SAHARAN AFRICA;
POSTCOLONIAL PERSPECTIVES ON
BOOK HISTORY
University of Sheffield

Marcus Walsh
BIBLIOGRAPHICAL SCHOLARSHIP
University of Liverpool

David R. Whitesell
THE BOOK IN SPAIN, PORTUGAL,
AND LATIN AMERICA
American Antiquarian Society

Reinhard Wittmann
THE BOOK IN CENTRAL EUROPE
University of Munich

Assistant Editors

Charlotte Appel
THE BOOK IN THE NORDIC COUNTRIES
Roskilde University, Denmark

Patricia Lockhart Fleming
THE BOOK IN CANADA
University of Toronto

Ian Morrison
THE BOOK IN AUSTRALIA AND
NEW ZEALAND
State Library of Tasmania

Niall Ó Ciosáin
THE BOOK IN IRELAND
National University of Ireland

Emile G. L. Schrijver
HEBRAICA
Amsterdam University

Karen Skovgaard-Petersen
THE BOOK IN THE NORDIC COUNTRIES
Royal Library, Copenhagen

N. G. Wilson
THE BOOK IN GREEK AND THE
BYZANTINE WORLD
Lincoln College, Oxford

Preface and Acknowledgements

Like so many reference books, the *Oxford Companion to the Book* was initially a publisher's idea. The late Michael Cox at OUP conceived of the project, albeit in a somewhat different form, in the mid-1990s. His enterprising and far-sighted vision was first entrusted to Simon Eliot, who became General Editor of the *OCB* when Anglo-American book history was perhaps still too much in its early stages for the undertaking to come to fruition. Jonathan Rose subsequently took the helm, bringing energy and enthusiasm to the project, and doing important groundwork that was of genuine benefit to the present General Editors when we began planning the *OCB* in 2004. It is no mere coincidence that both Simon Eliot and Jonathan Rose are past-Presidents of the Society for the History of Authorship, Reading and Publishing (SHARP); from its beginnings, the *OCB* has been a highly collaborative, international enterprise.

The form in which it now appears owes an enormous amount to the vigilance and wise guidance of Pam Coote, formerly general editor of reference books at OUP, whose experience and steadfast support have been a constant source of encouragement to both editors from the start to the end of the project. Jo Spillane has stayed the whole course, dealing with thousands of emails and files with rare wit, good humour, and exact attention, ably disguising the fact that the *OCB* was only one among a large number of projects for whose daily management she was responsible.

It would be invidious to single out any of the Associate or Assistant Editors, contributors of essays or of entries (ranging from single entries to many) for special praise. We are grateful to them all for their enthusiasm, expertise, and willingness to contribute to the project. In editing and preparing their work for publication, we have been assisted by a number of colleagues who have played a large but largely invisible part in the creation of the *Companion*. We would particularly like to thank Rebecca Stark-Gendrano, Megan Burke Witzleben, and Kathleen Urda, all graduates of Fordham University. We very much regret the deaths of various contributors and would-be contributors and would like particularly to mention Harold Love and John Klier.

At OUP, in addition to Pam Coote and Jo Spillane, the book has been principally in the hands of Joanna Harris, Clare Jenkins, and Nick Clarke: we are grateful to them for the care they have taken with it and for the support they have offered to us. The general editors selected pictures for the illustrations, with the advice of the Associate and Assistant Editors, and supplied captions for them: the picture research was undertaken by Carrie Hickman. Stephen Roe at Sotheby's provided generous help with the plates. The book was copy-edited by Sarah Barrett whose good sense and knowledge improved it in many ways. Our proofreader, Penny Trumble, found and efficiently corrected much that had escaped our bleary eyes. The index was compiled by Philip Aslett, who evidenced great patience and professionalism. Leofranc Holford-Strevens cast an expert eye over the proofs and saved us from many gross errors, especially in relation to foreign languages.

The General Editors would like to thank the following for help with particular matters: Jason Ashlock, James N. Green, Jasper Griffin, Simon Hornblower, Jamie Mahoney, Ian Michael, Sarah Ogilvie, and Irene Tichenor.

A book of this kind has an immediate story in relation to its writing and production, but it also has a longer history. In reflecting this, the General Editors would like to thank various people and institutions.

Michael Suarez, S.J.: Hugh Amory, John Barnard, Anna Battigelli, John Bidwell, Thomas Bonnell, Rina Capicotto and Joseph Lee, Nick Coote, Robert Darnton, Paul and Mary Giordano, Anne Gorielly and Peter D. McDonald, Lesley Higgins, Kate Kirkpatrick, Roger Lonsdale, Don McKenzie, James McLaverty, Andrew McNeillie, Richard Ovenden, Jan Palmowski, Amanda Paxton, James Raven, Bruce Redford, Tore Rem, Isabel Rivers, Stuart Sherman, Mia Spiro, Dan Traister, David Vander Meulen, Bart Van Es, Sarah Zimmerman; the American Council of Learned Societies; the Center of Theological Inquiry, Princeton; Fordham University; the National Endowment for the Humanities; the Radcliffe Institute for Advanced Study, Harvard University; and Campion Hall, Oxford.

Henry Woudhuysen: Peter Beal, Eileen Boden, Christopher Edwards, John Feather, David Fleeman, Arthur and Janet Ing Freeman, Carter Hailey, Arnold Hunt, John Jolliffe, Danny Karlin, Nicolas Kiessling, Jim McCue, Giles Mandelbrote, Paul Morgan, Angus O'Neill, Richard Ovenden, Richard Proudfoot, Bryan Robson, Keith Walker, and Paul Woudhuysen.

Above all, I would like to thank my family for their generous support and extraordinary tolerance during the course of this (and other) projects.

Introduction

Books in every language testify to the truth that most large-scale scholarly projects fall short of their ambitious design. This *Oxford Companion* treating manifold aspects of 'the book'—a shorthand for any recorded text—is a fitting object lesson. To undertake the editing of a million-word reference work spanning the centuries from the invention of writing to the global dominance of publishing conglomerates, and seeking to reach into every region and many nations, is to attempt what even the most starry-eyed scholars must know themselves unable to perform. More than once we have recalled Robert Southey's words when he withdrew from editing the *Bibliotheca Britannica* proposed by *Longmans in 1803, describing the plan as 'quite beyond my powers'. Yet, firm in the conviction of such a work's potential usefulness to those who attend closely to books and libraries, manuscripts, and archives, we have for six years made this enterprise our daily care. Knowing full well that catching perfection was out of the question, we have simply attempted to bring into the world a work worthy of its subject. Supported by the hope that *The Oxford Companion to the Book* (OCB) might give pleasure and prove a helpful work of reference to its future users—readers and raiders alike—we have endeavoured to produce a book that reflects a passion for the artefact, a fascination with the many aspects of bibliography and book history, and a deep regard for the archive. The reader need not look far to apprehend in these pages the desire to recognize the many men and women—from Pieter van der Aa to Stefan Zweig—whose lives have been variously sustained by 'the book' in its rich pluriformity and diverse contributions to our common humanity. Yet, in this respect, as in many others, we have been forced to be highly selective.

Crucially, we have not laboured alone. Vital to this enterprise has been an editorial team of 28 expert and generous Associate and Assistant Editors, who have repeatedly remedied our ignorance and added their industry to our own. Another 33 scholars who were not editors wrote some of the essays that comprise the first part of the *Companion*. Taken together, these 61 constitute a prime number in more than one sense; added to the general editors, the complete group makes up a team of 63 companions in all, a cohort significantly short of the 72 scribes famously summoned by Ptolemy II, but no less intent on their making. An additional 335 specialist authors also contributed entries to the A–Z that constitutes the second part of the *OCB*. In the late 17th century, the editor of the *Dictionnaire des arts et des sciences* (Paris, 1694), was criticized for too freely crediting the intelligences that had come to him from those who had lived in distant lands, but we have been delighted to rely on a remarkable network of reliable knowledge: in all, 398 scholars from 27 countries, spanning the globe from Helsinki to Dunedin and from Tokyo to Nuuk, have contributed to this *Companion* consisting of 51 essays and 5,160 A–Z entries. Animate with the labours of scholars both living and long deceased, the *OCB* seeks to represent in a single work the world of the book as it is known at the close of the first decade of the 21st century.

The practice of assembling a company of experts in their specialist fields to produce a volume of reference is commonly believed to have been initiated in John Harris's *Lexicon Technicum* (London, 1704), though Harris nowhere acknowledged their contributions. In all likelihood this strategy began much earlier. The topics in the *Companion*, like those in Harris's volume, vary in their treatment from concise definitions to extended essays of some 13,000 words. All but the very shortest entries are signed with their author's initials, for which, see the list of Editors and Contributors and the Index of Contributor Initials, below. Regrettably, what must remain forever inaccessible to the reader are the many conversations (some in person, others by telephone, most via email) that have enriched particular essays and A–Z entries as well as the architecture and content of the *Companion* more generally. Nevertheless, it is our ardent hope that these cross-border dialogues, these discussions among bibliographers, librarians, codicologists, and book historians across time zones have here left their traces in ways that will stimulate future conversations and further research. Perhaps the double columns of this *Companion*'s *mise-en-page might stand as a fitting emblem of thoughtful and animating exchanges translated into print.

In another sense too as General Editors we have been accompanied in our editorial efforts. 'A large work is difficult because it is large', explained Samuel *Johnson in the Preface to his great *Dictionary* (London, 1755). In the midst of inevitable obstacles and problems, we have been sustained by keeping in mind the librarians and antiquarian booksellers, the collectors and scholars, archivists and bibliographers, the general readers and advanced specialists who will, we hope, consult this work, sometimes for purposes beyond our imagining. It is to no small degree through such companionship that we have summoned the resolution to try to encompass the domain of 'the book' in some detail from the cuneiform *tablet to the *telephone directory and beyond in a mere million words. We have ventured to produce a global work, taking the reader to Mount *Athos, Mainz, and Shanghai, to *polar libraries and to Mexico's Biblioteca *Palafoxiana, the first *public library in the Americas. Writing of Pyramus and Thisbe, Ovid declares that 'propinquity brought them together', in time creating a relationship in which the obstacle of a wall was no lasting barrier. In an analogous way, through the juxtaposition of elements the *Companion* is intended to lead readers to forge creative and serendipitous connections more powerful than the boundaries that have thus far kept them separate. Proximity may generate productive associations; typographic contiguity might in some felicitous instances help transcend distances of geography, or even the demarcations of intellectual disciplines. The purpose behind this companion, then, is not merely to supply information, but to promote new knowledge.

Although book history is a relatively recent arrival in the academy, the history of books has been a subject of inquiry for a very long time. It appears that Demetrius of Phaleron and his successors at the *Alexandrian Library were careful to purchase or copy the best versions of the works they sought; thus, the Library's agents had to attempt to ascertain each composition's *authorship (*see also* ATTRIBUTION), transmission (or publishing history), and reception (*see* READING AND RECEPTION). The use of 'the book' to designate the great diversity of textual forms considered in the '*history of the book', or indeed *The Oxford Companion to the Book*, is a kind of synecdoche, a single example to represent the many. Yet, because 'book history' is, necessarily, about far more than the history of books, 'the book' as a category or abstraction encompassing everything from stelae inscriptions (*see* EPIGRAPHY) to *laser-printed sheets is not a formation that comes naturally in English, as it does in French (*Le Livre*; *l'histoire du livre*), or in German (*Buchwesen*). Naturally, the use of the term 'book' in our title does not exclude *newspapers, prints, *sheet music, *maps, or manuscripts, but merely suggests a degree of emphasis. Mindful that in every major European language the word for 'book' is traceable to the word for 'bark', the 'book' might profitably be thought of as originally signifying the surface on which any text is written and, hence, as a fitting shorthand for all recorded texts.

Nevertheless, in several respects, the label 'the book' is an unfortunate one; even when perceived as an archetypal part of a larger whole, the Western *codex, much less the printed book, is not really an adequate emblem of many material manifestations of text—say, *ink-squeeze rubbings, or the *Dead Sea Scrolls. More importantly still, 'history of the book' and 'book history' can carry with them the unfortunate idea that this area of study is restricted to texts as physical objects—the province of analytical (or physical) *bibliography—whereas it encompasses much more besides. 'By its very nature', Robert *Darnton argued, 'the history of books must be . . . interdisciplinary in method.' For these reasons, perhaps the wide-ranging spectrum of inquiry commonly packaged as 'history of the book' might usefully be thought of more extensively as 'historical bibliography', which neither carries with it the cognitive strictures of 'the book', nor suggests a purview limited to artefacts in isolation from the highly contingent circumstances of their production, transmission, and reception over time. Yet, *The Oxford Companion to Historical Bibliography* seemed a bridge too far, even if 'bibliography' is etymologically 'book writing'—i.e. the writing out of books, the writing in books, or writing about books—which may be read broadly. In practice, 'bibliography' typically appears with the modifiers 'historical', 'enumerative', 'descriptive', 'textual' (also called 'textual criticism'), and 'analytical'; as G. Thomas *Tanselle has noted, 'bibliography is not "a subject" but a related group of subjects that happen to be commonly referred to by the same term'.

In both the design and the execution of the *OCB*, we have tried to emphasize the multiplicity of book-historical scholarship—from recognizing the totemic functions of texts to the economic analysis of their production and sale—and to represent the diversity of approaches reflected in modern bibliography and textual criticism (*see*, for example, **18**). Hence, in addition to national and regional histories of the book, the *OCB* seeks to cover a broad spectrum of areas including: authorship; bibliography and textual studies; book collecting and collectors; censorship, pornography, and control; children's books; copyright; the electronic book; ephemera; forgers and forgery; illustration; librarianship and archives; libraries; the MS book; maps and cartography; the material book;

music; news, newspapers, and journals; patronage and prizes; printers and publishers; reading; reproduction; sacred books; scholars, scholarly organizations, scholarship, and writers; and various types of books and writing. (*See* the Thematic Index of Entries.) The idea that bibliography and book history are not inimical, as is sometimes imagined, but mutually enriching and deeply interrelated undertakings has been one of this project's primary foundations. Throughout the pages of the *Companion*, particular attention has been paid to how different societies shape books and how books shape societies.

Ephraim Chambers employed an extensive system of cross-references in his *Cyclopaedia* (London, 1728 [1727]), believing that it would help stitch together its various parts, according his book 'most of the advantages of a continued treatise'. Without wishing to limit what Isaac D'Israeli called the 'interstitial pleasures' of miscellaneity, three practical helps have been introduced into the *OCB* to create a measure of unity and to aid the reader's navigation. At the front of Volume 1, there is a Thematic Index of Entries, which functions as both cognitive map and practical guide. In addition, an extensive system of cross references among essays, from essays to entries, among entries, and from entries to essays has been employed—see the Notes to the Reader. Finally, there is a General Index at the end of Volume 2; indexes are not a common feature of Oxford Companions, but the scope of this project and the mix of long essays and short entries (as opposed to the more usual exclusively A–Z format) suggested the need for additional guidance for readers. Intended to be both a work of ready reference and a vehicle for more systematic study, the *OCB* is designed and written to promote links of various kinds between thematic essays and shorter entries, although its volumes can also be speedily ransacked for needed facts.

The *Companion* seeks to provide an accurate, balanced, comprehensive, and authoritative view of a large subject that is still developing, based on the present state of knowledge. All the essays and many of the entries have accompanying secondary references, generally proportionate to the length at which each subject is treated; these are meant to direct the reader to the most relevant and useful sources for further study. In most cases, the secondary references also represent the principal works consulted by the authors themselves. URLs (Uniform Resource Locators, or Web addresses) have been included whenever particularly important and reliable resources are to be found on the *World Wide Web. Undoubtedly, some of these

will migrate or expire over time, but most readers will agree that, when judiciously used, the WWW is too valuable an asset for research and teaching to neglect merely because a small number of sites will present future difficulties, many of which can be easily remedied.

The idea of a book serving as a companion—a humane presence in whose company one takes nourishment, a trustworthy guide on pilgrimage or expedition, a close associate whose society one prizes—dates back to the classical world. Horace refers to copies of Plato and the comic poets as 'comites', whom one can take along on a journey. Recalling an excursion to a country villa, he asks, 'What was the use of packing Plato with Menander, / of taking out of town Eupolis and Archilochus, such valued comrades? ('quorsum pertinuit stipare Platona Menandro, / Eupolin, Archilochum, comites educere tantos?', *Sermones* 2.3.11–12). In much the same vein, the 14th-century Renaissance humanist Francesco *Petrarca writes, 'I myself am very far from all my books and I find this the only burden of my trip. Having left home, I hear no sound of the Latin tongue, and when I return home I have not the books which are my companions and with which I am accustomed to speak' (*Epistolae de Rebus Familiaribus* 3.1). Taking this idea of companionship still further, Petrarca even composes personal letters to Cicero—whom he calls 'dear friend', 'my familiar', and 'a man whom I cherish beyond all my other friends'. (He also writes, though less intimately, to Seneca, Varro, Homer, Quintilian, Livy, Horace, Pollio, and Virgil.)

Surprisingly, the word 'companion' does not appear as a substantive part of an English printed book title until 1576 and does not figure more than sporadically until the 17th century. The highly popular *Vade Mecum: or, A Companion for a Chyrurgion* (London, 1652 [1651]) of Thomas Brugis (*fl.* 1640?) is among the first to go through multiple editions, although it is not until the Restoration that the *Companion* becomes a publishing trend. Even so, many early companions were essentially *ready reckoners, with tables of interest, duties, fairs, tides, and the like, almost invariably in small *formats, and occasionally including *writing tables or abridged forms of *almanacs. Some sought to dignify their pragmatic function by bearing such titles as *Socius Mercatoris: or The Merchant's Companion* (London, 1674), or *Comes Commercii: or, The Trader's Companion* (London, 1699); the many works styled '*pocket-companion*' emphasized their portability and ease of use. Almost all were either spiritual or practical guides, such as *The Compleat

Cook; or, The Accomplished Serving-maids Companion (London, [*c*.1685]), which promised 'the newest directions for dressing . . . flesh, foul, fish, and performing pastry after divers kinds'.

By the early decades of the 18th century, there were companions for the afflicted and the sick, dancing-masters and those who would be merry, shepherds, corn-dealers, penmen, sailors, Holland-merchants, farmers, songsters, clergymen, mathematicians, travellers, justices of the peace, cooks and confectioners, gardeners, foreigners, painters, sportsmen, midwives, court-keepers, psalm-singers, freemasons, land-purchasers, exact-dealers and accountants, accomplished housewives, devout Christians, sinful souls, swordsmen, florists, navigators, farriers, architects and carpenters, apprentices, carriers, choristers, communicants, men of fashion, schoolmasters, secular 'temple-builders', bucks, ladies, attorneys and solicitors, children, dissenting ministers, spouters, and singers of varying degrees of glee. There were companions for the close-stool, the post-chaise, the altar, the fireside, winter evenings, and almost any tourist destination then imaginable. Among this profusion, the title that the *OCB* might most reasonably aspire to is *A Thousand Notable Things: or, A Useful Companion for All People* (London, 1701). Of course, the value of any companion depends upon one's preferences in friends.

Perhaps inevitably, *A Companion to the Guide, and a Guide to the Companion* (London, [1760]) found its way into print. A corrective and supplement to a *Companion to Oxford* and a *Guide to Oxford*, it was written *anonymously by no less a literary figure than Thomas *Warton. Often there is an aspirational aspect in these titles, reflecting their close kinship with the *self-help book: the Christian is 'devout'; the story-teller 'interesting'; and the swordsman 'expert'. Companions of innumerable variety continued to be popular throughout the 19th century, but it was only in the 20th century that the first Oxford Companion was published. Sir Paul Harvey's *Oxford Companion to English Literature* (Oxford, 1932) inaugurated a tradition that includes some 70 titles currently in print.

The editorial caution of Antoine Furetière led him to avoid advocating heliocentrism in his *Dictionnaire universel* (The Hague and Rotterdam, 1690 [1689]), lest he upset ecclesiastical authorities and risk the penalties of *censorship. As editors of the *OCB*, we have been rather more venturesome, hazarding the possible censure of our contemporaries in the Republic of Letters by including living scholars among those in the firmament of our bibliocentric cosmos.

To those who might object to this decision, we would ask: how could a work purportedly representing important features of the history and current state of bibliography, book history, and textual criticism fail to include such luminaries as Roger *Chartier, Robert Darnton, Mirjam *Foot, Gérard *Genette, Lotte *Hellinga, Jerome *McGann, G. Thomas Tanselle, or W. B. *Todd?

When Walter Map wrote the witty and popular satire *Dissuasio Valerii ad Rufinum Philosophum ne Uxorem Ducat* (A Dissuasion of Valerius to Rufinus the Philosopher that He Should not Take a Wife) in the late 12th century, and some of his contemporaries suggested that it was too good to be actually his, Map complained, 'My only fault is that I am alive; I have no intention, however, of correcting this fault by my death.' Similarly, it would be misguided to produce a book in which mortality, rather than merit alone, was an absolute criterion for inclusion. Book history, in particular, is such a young and evolving enterprise that to ignore a basic protocol of the *ODNB* and most other biographical dictionaries seemed altogether warranted. Yet, the inclusion of particular scholars no more implies a personal endorsement of their work than having entries on individual collectors suggests an enthusiasm for the kinds of books that they enjoy. Conversely, readers will look in vain for excoriating biographical material akin to Pierre Bayle's treatment of King David in the first edition of the *Dictionnaire historique et critique* (Rotterdam, 1696). Throughout, the *Companion*'s persistent aim has been to render its subjects without imposing ethical judgements on persons or things, whether they be *patrons or *forgers, sacred books (*see* **2**) or *Mein Kampf*.

This is not to say, however, that this book is free from judgements, many of them subjective. Rather, the *OCB* is a *critical* work in the root sense of that word: as General Editors we have perforce made thousands of discriminations, many in consultation with our editorial team, but for which we alone are finally responsible. All histories come into being by means of their makers' selections and interpretations that reflect particular interests, partial understandings, and limited perspectives; ours is no exception. A different pair of General Editors would have produced a different, perhaps better, *Oxford Companion to the Book*.

The *OCB* is by no means the first substantial work of reference on 'the book'; nor, we trust, will it be the last. (Of the making of books there is no end.) The *Lexikon des gesamten Buchwesens*, edited by Karl Löffler and Joachim Kirchner (Leipzig, 1935–7) in three large folio volumes was for many years the most important work of its kind. A four-volume version, edited by Joachim Kirchner (Stuttgart, 1952–3, 1955–6), with omissions from and additions to the original, further solidified the *LGB*'s status. The first volume of the new *Lexikon des gesamten Buchwesens* (*LGB*), edited by Severin Corsten, Günther Pflug, and Friedrich Adolf Schmidt-Künsemüller was published in 1985. Described as the second, completely revised edition of the original *LGB*, it now runs to seven volumes, with the eighth and final volume yet to come.

The *Dictionnaire encyclopédique du livre*, edited by Pascal Fouché, Daniel Péchoin, and Philippe Schuwer, is also a work of major importance. The first volume was published in Paris in 2002, the second in 2005; the third and final volume is still in progress. Other comprehensive works of this kind, although they may be less accessible to our readership, are nevertheless worthy of note: *Zusetsu hon to hito no rekishi jiten*, edited by Toshiyuki *Takamiya (Tokyo, 1997); *Kniga: entsiklopediia* edited by V. M. Zharkov (Moscow, 1999); and *Encyklopedie knihy* edited by Petr Voit (Prague, 2006), although this last only covers the 15th to the 19th centuries.

Books frequently cited in this *Companion* are found under 'Abbreviations' in the *preliminaries and should prove useful as a fundamental, if wide-ranging, further reading list for those wishing to deepen their knowledge of some standard works in bibliography and book history. Among them, two classic works, *ABC for Book Collectors* by John *Carter and Nicolas *Barker (8e, London, 2004) and Philip *Gaskell's *A New Introduction to Bibliography* (Oxford, 1972; reprinted with corrections, Oxford, 1974) remain excellent places to begin. Also particularly useful in this regard are R. B. *McKerrow's *An Introduction to Bibliography for Literary Students* (Oxford, 1927) and *An Introduction to Bibliographical and Textual Studies* (4e, New York, 2009) by William Proctor Williams and Craig S. Abbott. The *Companion* makes no attempt to replace G. A. Glaister's *Encyclopedia of the Book* (2e, London, 1979; reissued, Newcastle, Del. and London 1996), a work we have found consistently useful. Other recommended books of this kind include *Wörterbuch des Buches* (6e, 'fundamentally revised', Frankfurt am Main, 2002) by Helmut Hiller and Stephan Füssell; Elsevier's *Dictionary of the Printing and Allied Industries* (in English, French, German, and Dutch; Amsterdam, 1967; 2e, Amsterdam, 1983) by F. J. M. Wijnekus; and Philippe Schuwer's *Dictionnaire bilingue de l'édition / Bilingual Dictionary of Book Publishing* (Paris, 1993). Readers who have difficulties with some of the specialist vocabulary in the *OCB* might profitably resort to Imre Móra's *Wörterbuch des Verlagswesens: In 20 Sprachen / The Publisher's Practical Dictionary: in 20 Languages* (2e, Munich, 1977).

Most publishing projects chafe under the constraints of time, money, and space; this *Companion* is no exception—with five more years and another million words, more could have been done. Like Samuel Johnson, we know that, inevitably, the *Companion* must contain 'a few wild blunders and risible absurdities, from which no work of such multiplicity was ever free', and with him believe that to make it perfect, 'even a whole life would not be sufficient'. Few general editors can forget the errors committed by their encyclopaedic forebears. The entry on Shakespeare in Louis Moréri's *Le Grand Dictionnaire historique* (Lyons, 1674), for example, omits his birth-date, fails to mention any of his plays by name, and gets his date of death wrong. (Shakespeare's crime, obviously, is that he is not Pierre Corneille.) At least Moréri knew that Shakespeare was worthy of inclusion. The article, 'Methodus Plantar', or plant classification, in Johann Heinrich Zedler's *Universal Lexicon* (Halle and Leipzig, 1732–50) omits any mention of Carolus Linnaeus, whose *Systema Naturae* was currently revolutionizing the systematic taxonomy and nomenclature of European botany. Such is the stuff of which our nightmares have been made.

In his Preface to the *Cyclopaedia*, Ephraim Chambers acknowledged the failings of his book, including 'breaches of method', 'errors', 'irregularities', and 'redundancies', while excusing himself by asserting that such defects are inevitable in any considerable work. Despite the sedulous efforts of all those involved in this project, this *Companion* undoubtedly suffers from all these shortcomings—and many others as well. We offer no exculpatory words, but apologize for any errors or omissions and hope that we will have the opportunity of correcting them in the second edition.

MICHAEL F. SUAREZ, S.J.
H. R. WOUDHUYSEN

Charlottesville and London
18 June 2009

Editors and Contributors

Editors and Contributors

General Editors

Michael F. Suarez, S.J. is University Professor and Director of the Rare Book School at the University of Virginia. Formerly the J. A. Kavanaugh Professor of English at Fordham University in New York and Fellow & Tutor in English at Campion Hall, Oxford, he is co-editor of *The Cambridge History of the Book in Britain, Volume 5, 1695–1830* (2009) and co-general editor of *The Collected Works of Gerard Manley Hopkins*, (8 vols, 2006–). (MFS)

H. R. Woudhuysen is Professor of English at University College London. He has edited *The Penguin Book of Renaissance Verse* (1992) with David Norbrook; *Love's Labour's Lost* (1998) and, with Katherine Duncan-Jones, *Shakespeare's Poems* (2007) for the Arden Shakespeare third series. His book *Sir Philip Sidney and the Circulation of Manuscripts, 1558–1640* was published in 1996. (HRW)

Associate Editors

Scott E. Casper (THE BOOK IN THE UNITED STATES—18TH- AND 19TH-CENTURY AMERICA) is Professor of History, University of Nevada, Reno, where he studies and teaches 19th-century American history. He is the author of *Sarah Johnson's Mount Vernon: The Forgotten History of an American Shrine* (2008) and co-editor of *A History of the Book in America, Volume 3, The Industrial Book, 1840–1880* (2007). (SEC)

J. S. Edgren (THE BOOK IN EAST ASIA AND SOUTHEAST ASIA) is Editorial Director of the Chinese Rare Books Project, an online union catalogue based at Princeton University. (JSE)

A. S. G. Edwards (MANUSCRIPTS, COLLECTORS, LIBRARIES, AND THE BOOK TRADE) is Professor of Textual Studies, De Montfort University. He works mainly on medieval and early modern literature, bibliography, and the history of book collecting. (ASGE)

Christine Ferdinand (THE BOOK IN BRITAIN 1501–1780) is Fellow Librarian, Magdalen College, Oxford. Her current research interests are in the economics of the 18th-century book and newspaper trade. (CYF)

Vincent Giroud (THE BOOK IN FRANCE) is a Professor at the Université de Franche-Comté. He has taught at the Sorbonne and at Johns Hopkins, Vassar, Bard, and Yale, where he also served as curator of modern books and manuscripts at the Beinecke Library. (VAG)

Abhijit Gupta (THE BOOK IN SOUTH ASIA) is Reader in English at Jadavpur University, Kolkata. He is the co-editor of *Print Areas* (2004) and *Moveable Type* (2008) in the Book History in India series. (AG)

Neil Harris (THE BOOK IN ITALY) teaches bibliography at the University of Udine. He currently specializes in the history of Italian Renaissance publishing and in the field of early book cataloguing. (NH)

Lotte Hellinga (TRANSITION TO PRINT CULTURE 1455–c.1550) is formerly a Deputy Keeper at the British Library and General Secretary of the Consortium of European Research Libraries. Her area of expertise is the history of the book in the first century of printing. (LH)

Paul Hoftijzer (THE BOOK IN THE LOW COUNTRIES) holds the P. A. Tiele Chair in book history at Leiden University. He publishes on the history of the Dutch book in the early modern period. (PGH)

Craig Kallendorf (THE BOOK IN THE ANCIENT WORLD AND RENAISSANCE ITALY) is Professor of Classics and English at Texas A&M University. He is the author of *The Other Virgil* (2007), *The Virgilian Tradition: Book History and the History of Reading in Early Modern Europe* (2007), and several book-length bibliographies of Virgil, as well as the co-editor of *The Books of Venice / Il libro veneziano* (2009). (CWK)

David Pearson (THE PHYSICAL BOOK) Director, Libraries, Archives, and Guildhall Art Gallery at the City of London, has worked and published extensively on the post-production history of books, with particular reference to bookbinding, and book ownership. (DRSP)

Ekaterina Rogatchevskaia (THE BOOK IN THE SLAVONIC AND THE EAST EUROPEAN WORLD) is Head of Russian collections, British Library. She has published widely on early Russian literature, Russian émigré literature, and the history of the British Library Russian collections. (ER)

Geoffrey Roper (THE BOOK IN THE MUSLIM WORLD) is a bibliographical consultant. He was head of the Islamic Bibliography Unit at Cambridge University Library, 1982–2003, and editor of *Index Islamicus* and of the *World Survey of Islamic Manuscripts*. (GJR)

Joan Shelley Rubin (THE BOOK IN THE UNITED STATES POST 1891) is Professor of History at the University of Rochester, specializing in American culture since 1865. (JSR)

Peter L. Shillingsburg (THE BOOK IN BRITAIN 1780–1900) is Martin J. Svaglic Chair of Textual Studies at Loyola University, Chicago. (PLS)

Margaret M. Smith (PRINTING AND REPRODUCTION TECHNOLOGIES) is formerly Reader in Book Design History, Department of Typography and Graphic Communication, University of Reading. She studies changes in book design and *mise en page* after the introduction of printing. Her publications include: *The Title-Page: Its Early Development 1460–1510* (2000), 'Space-saving Techniques in Early Printed Books' (2003), and 'Printing Red Underlines in the Incunable Period' (2007). (MMS)

Claire Squires (THE BOOK IN 20TH-CENTURY BRITAIN) is Professor of Publishing Studies and Director of The Stirling Centre for International Publishing and Communication at the University of Stirling. (CMS)

Andrew van der Vlies (SUB-SAHARAN AFRICA; POSTCOLONIAL PERSPECTIVES ON BOOK HISTORY) is at the School of English, University of Sheffield. His research areas include colonial and postcolonial print cultures, anglophone postcolonial literatures and theory (especially Southern African literatures), aesthetics and the 'obscene'. He is the author of *South African Textual Cultures* (2007). (AEV)

Marcus Walsh (BIBLIOGRAPHICAL SCHOLARSHIP) is Kenneth Allott Professor of English Literature, University of Liverpool. He has written on Swift, Johnson, and Sterne, biblical scholarship, and the history and theory of editing. (MW)

David R. Whitesell (THE BOOK IN SPAIN, PORTUGAL, AND LATIN AMERICA) is Curator of Books, American Antiquarian Society. Currently Secretary of the Bibliographical Society of America, he has taught descriptive bibliography at the University of Virginia's Rare Book School since 1998. (DRW)

Reinhard Wittmann (THE BOOK IN CENTRAL EUROPE) is Professor for the History of the Book, University of Munich, chairman of Gesellschaft der Bibliophilen, and vice-chairman of Historische Kommission des Börsenvereins des Deutschen Buchhandels. (RW)

Assistant Editors

Charlotte Appel (THE BOOK IN THE NORDIC COUNTRIES) is Assistant Professor of early modern history at Roskilde University, Denmark. Her principal research interests are the history of books, reading, and education, as well as church history. (CA)

Patricia Lockhart Fleming (THE BOOK IN CANADA) is Professor Emeritus, Faculty of Information Studies, University of Toronto, where she served as founding director of the collaborative graduate programme in book history. She is co-general editor and co-editor of Volumes 1 and 2 of *History of the Book in Canada* (*Histoire du livre et de l'imprimé au Canada*) (3 vols, 2004–7). (PLF)

Ian Morrison (THE BOOK IN AUSTRALIA AND NEW ZEALAND) State Library of Tasmania, previously Curator of Special Collections at the University of Melbourne, is a past editor of the *Bibliographical Society of Australia & New Zealand Bulletin* (now *Script & Print*) and has published widely on aspects of Australian book and library history. (IM)

Niall Ó Ciosáin (THE BOOK IN IRELAND) teaches in the Department of History, National University of Ireland, Galway. His current research focuses on the relationship between literacy, print, and language shift in the Celtic language areas in the 18th and 19th centuries. (NOC)

Emile G. L. Schrijver (HEBRAICA) is Curator of the Bibliotheca Rosenthaliana, one of the Special Collections at Amsterdam University Library and the editor-in-chief of *Studia Rosenthaliana*. He has published extensively on Jewish books, in particular on Hebrew manuscripts of the post-medieval period, and has contributed to numerous exhibition and auction catalogues. (EGLS)

Karen Skovgaard-Petersen (THE BOOK IN THE NORDIC COUNTRIES) is Senior Researcher, Curator of Rare Books in the Department of Manuscripts and Rare Books, The Royal Library, Copenhagen. Her fields of research are early modern historiography, and early modern book and library history. (KSP)

N. G. Wilson, FBA (THE BOOK IN GREEK AND THE BYZANTINE WORLD) Fellow and Tutor in Classics (Emeritus), Lincoln College, Oxford, is a specialist in Greek palaeography, the transmission of texts, and the history of scholarship. (NGW)

Contributors

Jane Aikin, National Endowment for the Humanities, has research interests in the history of libraries, federal cultural institutions, and public policy. She is co-editor of the *Encyclopedia of the Library of Congress: For Congress, the Nation & the World* (2005). (JA)

Pablo Alvarez is Curator of Rare Books at the University of Rochester, and History of the Book Instructor in the Department of History, University of Rochester. His research interests include history of the book, incunables, printing manuals, and book iconography. (PA)

Martin Andrews is a Senior Lecturer in the Department of Typography and Graphic Communication, University of Reading. He is also Printing historian and Deputy Director of the Centre for Ephemera Studies at Reading and a graphic designer with a specialism in museum and exhibition design. (MJA)

Anita Ankarcrona is a Lecturer in the Department of History at Stockholm University and a book historian. (AAa)

Martin Antonetti is the Curator of Rare Books at Smith College, where he also teaches courses in the history of the book and in contemporary artists' books. (MA)

Charlotte Appel Assistant Editor. See above.

Catherine Armstrong is a Lecturer in American History at Manchester Metropolitan University. Her research interests include 17th- and 18th-century English and American print culture. Her first monograph, *Writing North America in the Seventeenth Century* was published in 2007. (CMA)

Karen Attar is the Rare Books Librarian at Senate House Library, University of London (formerly the University of London Library). Her research interests are in book collectors and collections, and library history. (KEA)

Paul Baines is Professor of English at the University of Liverpool. He works on 18th-century literature, crime, and book history, and his most recent book is *Edmund Curll, Bookseller* (2007, co-authored with Pat Rogers). (PTB)

Nicolas Barker was Production Manager, Oxford University Press (1971–6) and Deputy Keeper at the British Library (1976–92). He has been the editor of *The Book Collector* since 1965. He is author of *The Complete Calligraphic Work of Francesco Alunno* (2009). (NJB)

Vincent Barnett is a post-doctoral researcher at Bedfordshire University. He is the author of many books and journal articles exploring the history of Russian economics, and is also pursuing research on the economic and aesthetic history of film. (VB)

Virginia L. Bartow is the Curator of the George Arents Collection and Head of Special Collections Cataloging at The New York Public Library. An adjunct faculty member at Pratt Institute, School of Information and Library Services, she teaches 'Knowledge Organization'. (VLB)

Matthew Battles lives in Boston, Massachusetts, where he writes about the history of ideas. He teaches in the Harvard Extension School, and is the author of *Library: An Unquiet History* (2003) and *Widener: Biography of a Library* (2004). (MBa)

Peter Beal, FBA, FSA, was for 25 years English Manuscript Expert at Sotheby's, London. His publications include *Index of English Literary Manuscripts 1450–1700* (4 vols, 1980–93); *In Praise of Scribes: Manuscripts and their Makers in Seventeenth-Century England* (1998); and *A Dictionary of English Manuscript Terminology 1450–2000* (2008). His database Catalogue of English Literary Manuscripts 1450–1700 (CELM) will be launched on the World Wide Web in July 2010. (PB)

Margaret E. Becket is Bibliographer for American History and Mass Media at the University of Rochester. She has contributed several articles to *American Literary Publishing Houses, 1638–1899* and *American Literary Publishing Houses, 1900–1980* (both 1986). (MEB)

Philip D. Beidler is Professor of English at the University of Alabama, where he has worked since 1974. His most recent book is

American Wars, American Peace: Notes from a Son of the Empire (2007). (PDB)

Alan Bell is formerly Librarian of the London Library. (ASB)

Maureen Bell is Honorary Reader in English Literature at the University of Birmingham. She is Director of the British Book Trade Index and has published widely on printing and publishing in early modern England. (MB)

Suzanne S. Bell is the bibliographer for economics and social science data at the University of Rochester; she is the author of the *Librarian's Guide to Online Searching*, 2e (2009). Her research/teaching interest is database searching. (SSB)

Charles Benson is the Keeper of Early Printed Books at Trinity College Dublin. (CB)

Varuni Bhatia is Assistant Professor/Faculty Fellow at New York University. She works on issues of religion and modernity in colonial South Asia. Her interests include modern South Asian intellectual histories, with a focus on social and religious transformations in the subcontinent during the 19th century and the imbrication of the political therein. (VBh)

Margareta Björkman is Professor Emerita of the Sociology of Literature, University of Uppsala. She has published on 18th-century topics including libraries, journalism, translations, and novels. (MBj)

Alistair Black is Professor of Library and Information History at Leeds Metropolitan University. His publications include *A New History of the English Public Library* (1996), *The Public Library in Britain* (2000), and *The Early Information Society* (2007). (AMB)

Elleke Boehmer has published numerous books and articles on colonial and postcolonial criticism and theory, including *Stories of Women* (2005) and a book on Nelson Mandela (2006). She is the author of three novels and is Professor of World Writing in English at the University of Oxford. (EB)

Theo Bögels is a Lecturer in the English Department of the Vrije Universiteit, Amsterdam. His research centres on the literature of the early modern period. His publications stem from an interest in British-Netherlandish relations and the history of the book. (TB)

Mary Ann Bolger is Design History coordinator at Waterford Institute of Technology, Ireland. (MAB)

Elizabethanne Boran is Assistant Librarian of the Edward Worth Library, Dr Steevens' Hospital, Dublin. (EAB)

Alixe Bovey is a Lecturer in Medieval History at the University of Kent, where she specializes in the visual culture of the later Middle Ages. Her work focuses especially on manuscript illumination. (AB)

J. H. Bowman was a Lecturer in Library and Information Studies, University College London. His research interests include Greek type; history of library catalogues and classification; and Robert Proctor. (JHBo)

John Hassett Brady is American and British History Bibliographer and the Director of Reader Services at the Newberry Library. (JHBr)

Sarah Brouillette is an Assistant Professor in the Literature Faculty at the Massachusetts Institute of Technology, where she researches and teaches contemporary British, Irish, and postcolonial literatures, and topics in media history. (SEB)

Matthew P. Brown directs the Center for the Book at the University of Iowa, where he is Associate Professor in the Center and the English department. He is the author of *The Pilgrim and the Bee: Reading Rituals and Book Culture in Early New England* (2007). (MPB)

Megan Burke is a doctoral student at Fordham University. Specializing in material aspects of Victorian literature, including 19th-century book history, she primarily focuses on the role of commodities in character formation. (MDB)

Martin Butler is Professor of English Renaissance Drama at the University of Leeds. He has written *The Stuart Court Masque and Political Culture* (2008), and is a general editor of the *Cambridge Edition of the Works of Ben Jonson* (forthcoming). (MHB)

Michael Caines is Bibliography Editor of the *Times Literary Supplement*. He has edited an anthology of plays by 18th-century women (2004) and a book about the actor David Garrick (2008), and co-edited anthologies on Shakespeare (2003) and the Romantics (2004). (MSC)

M. G. Carter, recently retired Professor of Arabic at Oslo University, is now Honorary Professor in the Centre for Medieval Studies at Sydney University. His main area of research is the history of Arabic grammatical theory and its relationship to law and theology. (MGC)

Sebastian Carter, a graduate of King's College, Cambridge, is a letterpress printer at the Rampant Lions Press. He is the author of *Twentieth-Century Type Designers* (1987; revised paperback 2002), a regular contributor to *Matrix*, and the editor of *Parenthesis*. (SC)

Scott E. Casper Associate Editor. See above.

Joanne Chaison retired in 2008 as research librarian at the American Antiquarian Society, where her career spanned 27 years. She is co-editor, with Scott Casper and Jeffrey Groves, of *Perspectives on American Book History: Artifacts and Commentary* (2002). (JDC)

Swapan Chakravorty is Professor of English and Joint Director, School of Cultural Texts and Records, Jadavpur University, Kolkata. He writes in English and Bengali on Renaissance and early modern European literature, book history, and the history and literature of Bengal. (SKC)

Daven Christopher Chamberlain obtained degrees in Chemistry (Bath) and Paper Physics (Manchester). He worked at Arjowiggins Research and Development for seventeen years, first as a research scientist, later as Head of Testing and Printing. Currently a consultant specializing in forensic analysis of paper and printing, he is editor of *The Quarterly* (Journal of the British Association of Paper Historians). (DCC)

Rimi B. Chatterjee is a novelist and academic. Her novel *The City of Love* (2007) was shortlisted for the Vodafone Crossword Book Award, while her academic book *Empires of the Mind* (2006), won the SHARP de Long Book Prize for that year. She is Senior Lecturer in English at Jadavpur University, Kolkata. (RBC)

Gail Chester is researching publishers' readers at Royal Holloway, University of London. She is widely published on general and academic topics, mainly about publishing, feminism, and the history of both. Recent articles have covered feminist anthologies and the Hawthornden Prize. (GFC)

Sud Chonchirdsin received his Ph.D. in history from the University of London in 1995. He taught Vietnamese history and language at Chulalongkorn University and is currently curator of the Vietnamese collection at the British Library; he also teaches at the University of London. (SCH)

Federica Ciccolella is Assistant Professor of Classics and Italian at Texas A&M University. Her fields of interest and research include Greek and Byzantine poetry, Renaissance Greek grammar, and the reception of antiquity in Byzantium and in the Renaissance. (FC)

Ralph Cleminson is Professor of Slavonic Studies at the University of Portsmouth, and has published catalogues of Cyrillic manuscripts and early printed books in Britain, Ireland, Slovakia, and Hungary. His other research activities include textual criticism and the application of new technology to the description and editing of such material. (RMC)

John Y. Cole is the founding director of the Center for the Book in the Library of Congress. He has published widely about books and libraries in society, with an emphasis on the history of the Library of Congress. (JYC)

Kathleen Coleridge was the Special Materials Librarian at Victoria University of Wellington until her retirement in 2001. She worked on the Turnbull Library's Milton Collection and, since 1980, has published on aspects of the book trades in early Wellington. (KAC)

Christian Coppens is Curator of Rare Books and Manuscripts at Leuven University Library. His research deals mainly with book trade and (private) libraries during the 16th century. (CC)

Helen Cordell worked for over twenty years as South East Asian Bibliographer at the School of Oriental and African Studies, University of London, before becoming Deputy Librarian. Currently she is Hon. Librarian of the Royal Asiatic Society. (HC)

Cecil Patrick Courtney is Emeritus Reader in French intellectual history, and bibliography, University of Cambridge, and Fellow of Christ's College. (CPC)

Matthew Creasy is a Lecturer in the Department of English Literature at Glasgow University. He is a graduate of Cambridge and Oxford and a Kennedy Scholar. (MHC)

Laurence S. Creider is Special Collections Librarian at the University Library of New Mexico State University. His research interests include cataloguing theory and rules, the Venerable Bede, and St Godric of Finchale. (LSC)

Justin Croft is an antiquarian bookseller. (JPC)

Brian Cummings is Professor of English at the University of Sussex and Director of the Centre for Early Modern Studies. He is the author of *The Literary Culture of the Reformation: Grammar and Grace* (2007) and is currently working on the Oxford World's Classics edition of *The Book of Common Prayer*. (BAC)

Bernadette Cunningham is the assistant librarian at the Royal Irish Academy, Dublin. (SBC)

Phyllis Dain is Professor Emerita of Library Service, Columbia University. Her research and writing have focused on the history of American libraries and librarianship, and on the contemporary library scene, especially the public library. (PDa)

Sophy Dale is an editor and arts project-manager based in Edinburgh. Previously, she was Literature Officer at the Scottish Arts Council. (SD)

Jos Damen studied Dutch language and literature at Leiden University. A former head of the Lending Department of Leiden University Library, he is currently librarian of the Leiden Africa Study Centre. (JD)

Nandini Das is a Lecturer in Renaissance English Literature at the University of Liverpool. She specializes in Renaissance romance, prose fiction, and early travel writing, as well as the development of early 18th-century Orientalism. (ND)

Martin Davies was formerly Head of Incunabula at the British Library and editor of *The Library*, 1993–8. He is now Associate Editor of the Villa I Tatti Renaissance Library. (MCD)

Susan Davies is a Lecturer (retired) from the Department of History and Welsh History, Aberystwyth University. A specialist in manuscript and archive studies, she has taught postgraduates in archive administration, history, and humanities. Other activities include peer review and public service in archive and museum matters. (SJD)

Christopher de Hamel is Donnelley Fellow Librarian, Corpus Christi College, Cambridge. He was for many years responsible for sales of illuminated manuscripts at Sotheby's. He has published very extensively on medieval manuscripts and book collectors.

Marieke van Delft is Curator of Early Printed Collections at the Koninklijke Bibliotheek

(The Hague) and general editor of the Bibliopolis Project. She publishes on the history of the printed book in The Netherlands in different periods. (MVD)

Pierre Delsaerdt is Professor of Book and Library History at the universities of Antwerp and Leuven. His research focuses on the history of the book trade and libraries in Belgium, mainly during the early modern period. (PD)

Ian Desai recently completed his doctorate in South Asian History at Merton College, Oxford. (IRBD)

Martin Dewhirst lectured on Russian literature and language from 1964 to 2000 at the University of Glasgow, and is now an Honorary Research Fellow in the Department of Slavonic Studies at that university. He is particularly interested in Russian and Soviet censorship and in Samizdat. (MD)

Archie Leonard Dick holds a Ph.D. in library and information science, and is a Professor in the Department of Information Science at the University of Pretoria in South Africa. His main research interest is the history of reading. (ALD)

Robert Dingley is an Honorary Research Fellow in the School of English, University of New England, New South Wales. He has published extensively on 18th- and 19th-century literary history and co-edits the *Australasian Victorian Studies Journal*. (RJD)

Cristina Dondi was Lyell Research Fellow in the History of the Early Modern Printed Book, University of Oxford, 2002–05, and is one of the editors of the Bodleian Library catalogue of incunabula (6 vols, 2005). Her research focuses on the history of printing in Italy in the 15th century, provenance research as evidence for economic and social history, and on liturgical texts, both manuscript and printed.

Berry Dongelmans is a Lecturer in Book History at the Faculty of Arts of Leiden University. He writes on various aspects of Dutch book history of the 19th and 20th centuries. (BPMD)

Judy Donnelly is a librarian/archivist. She was project manager for the *History of the Book in Canada* (*Histoire du livre et de l'imprimé au Canada*), and project specialist and co-editor of the Historical Perspectives on Canadian Publishing website at McMaster University, Canada. (JAD)

Ian Dougherty is a public historian who has written extensively on New Zealand society and culture, including a biography of Sir Alfred Reed, the founder of the publishing firm of A. H. and A. W. Reed. (IMD)

A. I. Doyle, FBA, is Honorary Reader in Bibliography, Durham University Library and former Keeper of Rare Books. (AID)

Jacalyn Eddy, the author of *Bookwomen: Creating an Empire in Children's Book Publishing, 1919–1939* (2006), teaches history and humanities at SUNY Geneseo. (JE)

J. S. Edgren Associate Editor. See above.

A. S. G. Edwards Associate Editor. See above.

Rachel Anne Edwards holds a BA in English Literature from the University of Victoria and an MLitt in Shakespearean printing from the University of St Andrews. Formerly at the National Library of Scotland, she now works for the Scottish Parliament. (RAE)

Gabriel Egan is Reader in Shakespeare Studies at Loughborough University. He is one of the co-editors of the journals *Shakespeare* and *Theatre Notebook*, and is working on a history of the 20th-century theory and practice of editing Shakespeare. (GIE)

Paul Eggert, FAHA, is an Australian Research Council professorial fellow, general editor of the *Academy Editions of Australian Literature* and author of *Securing the Past: Conservation in Art, Architecture and Literature* (2009): www.unsw.adfa.edu.au/ASEC. (PE)

Marco van Egmond is Map Curator of the Map Collection in the University Library of Utrecht. He wrote a thesis on the Amsterdam map-trading company of Covens & Mortier (1685–1866). (MVE)

Elisabeth S. Eide is a Research Librarian at the National Library, Norway. Her current research interest is Norwegian 19th-century book collections. (EEi)

Evelyn Ellerman is an Associate Professor of Communication Studies at Athabasca University in Canada. She is a literary historian who publishes in the fields of indigenous African and South Pacific literatures. She is interested in the processes of decolonization in the British Empire in general, and in the role of women's groups, adult education, and literature during decolonization in particular. (EME)

David Emblidge edited *The Appalachian Trail Reader* (1996), *My Day: The Best of Eleanor Roosevelt's Acclaimed Newspaper Columns* (2001), *Beneath the Metropolis: The Secret Lives of Cities* (2006). Formerly Editor-in-Chief Mountaineers Books, he is now Associate Professor, Emerson College (MA, Publishing) and is currently writing a narrative history of American bookstores. (DE)

James F. English is Professor and Chair of the English Department at the University of Pennsylvania. His more recent work focuses on the sociology of literature and especially on its institutional and transnational dimensions. He is currently at work on a study of the American importation and translation of contemporary British culture. (JFE)

Lukas Erne is Professor in the English Department at the University of Geneva. He is the author of *Shakespeare's Modern Collaborators* (2008), *Shakespeare as Literary Dramatist* (2003), and *Beyond 'The Spanish Tragedy': A Study of the Works of Thomas Kyd* (2001), and the editor of *The First Quarto of Romeo and Juliet* (2007) and *Textual Performances: The Modern Reproduction of Shakespeare's Drama* (2004). (LE)

Pablo Andrés Escapa has a BA from the University of Salamanca and is a member of the research staff at the Real Biblioteca (Madrid). He is cataloguing manager of early printed collections, with interests in the history of the book, visual and material culture of the text in 17th-century Spain, printing in early modern Europe, and cultural reports between Spain and England. He is editor of *Avisos: Noticias de la Real Biblioteca* (1996–) and *Syntagma: Revista de Historia del Libro y la Lectura* (2002–). (PAE)

Kambiz Eslami is a Librarian at Princeton University Library. He is a contributor to *Encyclopædia Iranica* (1982–), *The Encyclopaedia of Islam Three* (2007–), and is the editor of *Iran and Iranian Studies* (1998). His current project is a major work of reference on the Iranian writer Sadegh Hedayat. (KE)

Monika Estermann, in charge of the Historical Commission of the German Booksellers and Publishers Association, is researching the German book trade, especially the 18th to the 20th centuries. (ME)

Beatrice Fannon is a postgraduate research student at Cardiff University writing a thesis on 'Pastoral Virginity', examining the work of Sidney and Spenser in the light of classical and biblical traditions. (BEF)

Iain Fenlon is Professor of Historical Musicology at the University of Cambridge, and a Fellow of King's College. His most recent book is *The Ceremonial City: History, Memory, and Myth in Renaissance Venice* (2008). (IF)

Christine Ferdinand Associate Editor. See above.

James Fergusson is a writer and antiquarian bookseller. He sits on the editorial board of *The Book Collector* and was founding obituaries editor of the *Independent*, 1986–2007. (JF)

Brian Findlay was a pupil and then a colleague of Don McKenzie. He now serves as parish priest to five small West Suffolk villages. (BJF)

Barbara Laning Fitzpatrick is Associate Professor of English at the University of New Orleans, and teaches 18th-century British literature. She was the textual editor for the Georgia Edition of Tobias Smollett's *Sir Launcelot Greaves* and is currently investigating Smollett's anonymous short fiction. (BLF)

Patrick Denman Flanery holds a D.Phil. in English Literature from the University of Oxford, and a BFA in Film & Television Production from New York University's Tisch School of the Arts. He has published on J. M. Coetzee and Evelyn Waugh, is a regular contributor to *The Times Literary Supplement*, and is writing a book on film adaptation and canonicity. He co-guest edited a special issue of the journal *scrutiny2*, entitled 'South African Cultural Texts and the Global Mediascape' (2008). (PDF)

Patricia Lockhart Fleming Assistant Editor. See above.

John L. Flood is Emeritus Professor of German in the University of London, Past President of the Bibliographical Society, and specializes in German book history. His publications include *The German Book 1450–1750* (1995) and *Poets Laureate of the Holy Roman Empire* (2006). (JLF)

Mirjam M. Foot is Emerita Professor of Library and Archive Studies, University College London and former Director of Collections and Preservation, British Library. Her main interest is the history of bookbinding and book structures, on which she has published extensively. (MMF)

Chris Fowler is Subject Librarian for Publishing, Fine Art, and Arts Management at Oxford Brookes University. She is a chartered member of CILIP and an active member of ARLIS/UK & Ireland, for whom she organizes conferences, workshops, and visits. (CBF)

Peter R. Frank from Heidelberg/Wien, is an editor in German publishing houses (S. Fischer, Luchterhand) and Curator Emeritus at Stanford University Libraries. He is the editor of Grillparzer's works, and author with J. Frimmel of *Buchwesen in Wien 1750–1850* (2008). His interests include book research in Central Europe. (PRF)

Adam Gacek is Faculty Lecturer in Arabic Manuscript Studies and Islamic Studies Librarian at McGill University, Montreal, and the author of a number of catalogues and a wide range of articles on Islamic manuscripts and rare books. His most recent publication is *The Arabic Manuscript Tradition: A Glossary of Technical Terms and Bibliography—Supplement* (2008). (AGa)

Ian Gadd is a Senior Lecturer in English at Bath Spa University. He is Textual Advisor to the Cambridge Edition of the *Works of Jonathan Swift* (2008–), and a volume editor for the *History of Oxford University Press*. (IG)

Jill E. Gage is Reference Librarian, Roger and Julie Baskes Department of Special Collections, the Newberry Library. Her main research interests are English literature, history of the book, and disability studies. (JEGa)

Francis Galloway is the Co-ordinator of Publishing Studies at the University of Pretoria, South Africa. She leads a research team that conducts annual surveys of the country's contemporary book-publishing industry. Her research interests also include the history of individual publishing houses and authors. (FCG)

Eileen Gardiner is co-director of ACLS Humanities E-Book and president and co-founder of Italica Press. She holds a Ph.D. in English literature with a specialization in medieval comparative literature, and is the editor of Hell-on-Line.org. (EG)

Victoria Gardner is a D.Phil. candidate at St John's College, Oxford. She is engaged in writing a social and economic history of English provincial newspapers and their proprietors, 1760–1820. (VEMG)

Simon Gatrell is Professor of English at the University of Georgia, and the editor of three of the novels of Thomas Hardy and author of numerous studies of Hardy and other Victorian writers. (SJG)

Paul F. Gehl is Custodian of the John M. Wing Foundation on the History of Printing at the Newberry Library, Chicago. His principal research interests are in the history of education and publishing history. (PFG)

James Gibbs was educated in the UK and US, and has taught at universities in Ghana, Malawi, Nigeria, Belgium, and the UK. He is reviews editor for *African Literature Today* and joint editor of *James Currey's African Theatre* series. He has published extensively on African literature and drama, and has edited two handbooks for African writers. He is currently a Senior Lecturer at the University of the West of England (Bristol). (JMG)

Ellen D. Gilbert has a DLS from Columbia University and has worked as a librarian, archivist, and editor in academia and for non-profit educational and professional organizations. (EDG)

Vincent Giroud Associate Editor. See above.

Lisa Gitelman is Associate Professor of Media Studies at the Catholic University of America. She is the author most recently of *Always Already New: Media, History, and the Data of Culture* (2006). (LG)

Barbara K. Gold is Professor of Classics at Hamilton College, editor of the *American Journal of Philology*, and Vice-President for Outreach of the American Philological Association. Her areas of research include literary patronage, satire, gender in medieval and renaissance literature, Roman lyric and elegy, Roman comedy. (BKG)

John Goldfinch is Curator of Incunabula at the British Library. (JEGo)

Paul Goldman is currently Associate Fellow, Institute of English Studies, University of London and Honorary Professor, School of English, Communication, and Philosophy, Cardiff University. He is the author of works on 19th-century British art and illustration including *Beyond Decoration: The Illustrations of John Everett Millais* (2005) and *Looking at Prints, Drawings and Watercolours: A Guide to Technical Terms*, 2e (2006). (PHJG)

Magdalena Gram, Ph.D., is a Senior Director, Collections Department, National Library of Sweden. Her main areas of research are art history, especially graphic design and book illustration, and history of the book, including library history. (MGr)

John Gray is Librarian of the Linen Hall Library, Belfast. (JCG)

Milan Grba is a Curator of the Southeast European Collections in the British Library. His main research interests are in the social and cultural history of Southeast Europe in the 20th century and in Anglo-Serbian relations and contacts. (MVG)

Albert Greco is a Professor of Marketing at Fordham University. His research centres on the business of book and scholarly publishing. The author or editor of ten books, his research has been presented at Harvard University, the Library of Congress, and the World Bank. (ANG)

Susan Green is editor of the *Huntington Library Quarterly*, an interdisciplinary journal of early modern studies. (SG)

Nick Groom is Professor of English at the University of Exeter (Cornwall campus). He has written books on the ballad revival, literary forgery, and national identity, and has edited Percy's *Reliques* and the poetry of Thomas Chatterton. (NGr)

Heinz Grotzfeld is Emeritus Professor of Semitic Philology and Islamic Studies, Westfälische Wilhelms-Universität Münster. His main areas of research are Arabic literature and linguistics, including Arabic dialects, Middle Arabic, and Arabic oral literature; Alf Layla wa-Layla; and everyday life in the Middle East. (HG)

Jeffrey D. Groves is Professor of Literature at Harvey Mudd College, Claremont, California. He is a co-editor of and contributor to *A History of the Book in America, Volume 3: The Industrial Book, 1840–1880* (2007). (JDG)

Óskár Guðmundsson is a historian, scholar, and Research Fellow at Snorrastofa, a culture and research centre in Icelandic and European medieval studies. He is the author of many books, especially on the field of medieval history. (ÓG)

Nadja Guggi is a typographic designer with an interest in printing history. She holds a degree from the Department of Typography and Graphic Communication at the University of Reading, and developed the database of the Department's Lettering, Printing, and Graphic Design Collections. (NG)

Abhijit Gupta Associate Editor. See above.

Paul C. Gutjahr is Associate Professor of English, American Studies, and Religious Studies at Indiana University. His primary teaching and research interests include religious print culture in the US and 19th-century American popular literature. (PCG)

Bridget Guzner was Curator of the Hungarian and Romanian Collections in the British Library, responsible for the selection and acquisition of current and antiquarian material, exploring, and describing the collections. Since her recent retirement, her research interests continue to include all aspects of Hungarian and Romanian culture, as well as the history and development of the above-mentioned collections in the British Library. (BG)

Nancy E. Gwinn is Director, Smithsonian Institution Libraries. She has an AMLS from the University of Michigan and a Ph.D. in American Civilization from George Washington University. Her research interests are in library history, international publication exchange, and the Smithsonian Institution. (NEG)

Esko Häkli, Professor, is a former National Librarian of Finland. (EHi)

Steve Hare is a freelance author and journalist, writing on the visual arts, and a lecturer in publishing history with a particular expertise in Penguin history. He compiled *Penguin Portrait* (1995) and several other books on Penguin design, series, and personalities. (SJH)

Michael Harris worked at Birkbeck College, London University. His main research interest is in the history of print generally and of newspapers in particular. He founded a major conference on book-trade history, which continues to be held in London and has been involved in editing and contributing to the annual publication of the papers (30 titles). He is currently working on a full-length study of printed serials published in London on either side of 1700.

Neil Harris Associate Editor. See above.

Charles Hatfield is Associate Professor of English at California State University, Northridge, and specializes in comic art, word and image studies, and children's literature and culture. He is the author of *Alternative Comics: An Emerging Literature* (2005), and he is now writing a monograph on the cartoonist Jack Kirby. (CWH)

Earle Havens is Curator of Rare Books and an affiliate of the Singleton Center for Premodern Studies at Johns Hopkins University. His work concentrates on the history of the book and manuscript culture from the Middle Ages to the 18th century. (EAH)

Jos van Heel is Curator of Manuscripts and Early Printed Books at the Museum Meermanno-Westreenianum in The Hague. He is also attached to the Special Collections Department of the University Library of the Vrije Universiteit, Amsterdam. His publications are concerned mainly with the history of Dutch book collecting in the 18th and 19th centuries. (JVH)

Martin J. Heijdra, Chinese bibliographer at the East Asian Library, Princeton University, has published on the socio-economic history of China, and is currently working on the history of character design and typography in the whole of East Asia. (MH)

Lotte Hellinga Associate Editor. See above.

Peter Hellyer is Russian curator in the British Library. He studied Russian at Nottingham University and compiled *A Catalogue of Russian Avant-Garde Books*, 2e (2006). He curated the Russian section of the exhibition Breaking the Rules: The Printed Face of the European Avant Garde (2007). (PH)

John B. Hench retired in 2006 after 33 years at the American Antiquarian Society, where, among other duties, he administered the Society's book history programmes. He is writing a book on American book publishing and world markets in the 1940s. (JBH)

Ian Higgins is Reader in English at the Australian National University and author of books and articles on Jonathan Swift and

his contexts. He is a general editor of the Cambridge Edition of the *Works of Jonathan Swift* (2008–). (IH)

Richard L. Hills is an Honorary Reader at the University of Manchester, History of Technology, covering steam power, textiles, and papermaking. His latest published works include a three-volume biography of James Watt and the development of power in the textile industry. (RLH)

John Hinks is an Honorary Fellow at the Centre for Urban History, University of Leicester, researching English book-trade networks. At the University of Birmingham, he edits the British Book Trade Index website and is a Visiting Lecturer in early modern English print culture. (JH)

David Hirsch has been Librarian for Middle Eastern and Islamic Studies at the Charles E. Young Library, UCLA since 1989. He is also an Adjunct Assistant Professor in the Department of Near Eastern Languages and Cultures. He is a past president of the Middle East Librarians Association. (DGH)

Barbara Hochman is Chair of the Department of Foreign Literatures and Linguistics, Ben-Gurion University, Israel. She has published widely on American fiction, generic conventions, and reading practices. Current work-in-progress includes the project *Uncle Tom's Cabin and the Reading Revolution*. (BH)

Paul Hoftijzer Associate Editor. See above.

Melissa J. Homestead is Associate Professor of English at the University of Nebraska-Lincoln, author of *American Women Authors and Literary Property, 1822–1869* (2005), and is currently working on Catharine Sedgwick and on Willa Cather's creative partnership with Edith Lewis. (MJH)

David M. Hovde is the Research and Instruction Librarian in the Archives and Special Collections, Purdue University Libraries. He is also an Associate Professor of Library Science. His research has primarily focused on organizations that provided library services to non-traditional users. (DMH)

Leslie Howsam is the author of *Cheap Bibles* (1991) and *Old Books & New Histories* (2006). Her 2006 Lyell lectures discussed research on the correspondence of historians and publishers. She is University Professor at the University of Windsor in Canada.

Arnold Hunt is a Curator of Manuscripts at the British Library. His book *The Art of Hearing: English Preachers and their Audiences 1590–1640* is forthcoming. (AH)

Clare Hutton is Lecturer in English at Loughborough University, and the editor of volume 5 of *The Oxford History of the Irish Book* (2009). (CLH)

David Ibbetson, FBA, is Regius Professor of Civil Law, University of Cambridge. His research covers the history of English and European law; among his publications is *A Historical Introduction to the Law of Obligations* (1999). (DIb)

Jana Igunma is Curator of Thai, Lao, and Cambodian Collections at the British Library. She graduated from Humboldt-University, Berlin in Southeast Asian History (1996), Library and Information Science (2003), and worked as curatorial assistant for Thai, Lao, Cambodian, and Burmese Collections at the Staatsbibliothek zu Berlin. (JDI)

Dirk Imhof is Keeper of Rare Books and Archives of the Plantin-Moretus Museum in Antwerp. His research focuses on publications by the Plantin Press. (DI)

Andrea Immel is Curator of the Cotsen Children's Library at Princeton University. She co-edited the *Cambridge Companion to Children's Literature* (2009) and *Childhood and Children's Books in Early Modern Europe 1550–1800* (2005), and contributed chapters to the *Cambridge History of the Book in Britain*, volumes 5 and 6.

Judy Crosby Ivy is an art historian currently compiling a catalogue raisoné of the works of David Lucas, a mezzotint engraver best known for his collaboration with the landscape painter John Constable. (JCI)

Leon E. Jackson is an Associate Professor of English at the University of South Carolina and author of *The Business of Letters: Authorial Economies in Antebellum America* (2007). (LEJ)

David James is the former Curator of Khalili Collection of Islamic Art, London. He has written several works on Islamic manuscripts, calligraphy, and the arts of the Islamic book. He now lives in Spain and has recently published *Early Islamic Spain* (2009). (DLJ)

Frans A. Janssen is Professor Emeritus of Book and Library History, University of Amsterdam, and retired director of the Bibliotheca Philosophica Hermetica, Amsterdam. A recent publication is *Technique and Design in the History of Printing* (2004). (FAJ)

Ann Rosalind Jones is Esther Cloudman Dunn Professor of Comparative Literature at Smith College (USA). With Margaret Rosenthal, she recently completed a translation of Cesare Vecellio's 1590 costume book, *Degli Habiti antichi et moderni di diverse parti del mondo* (2008). (ARJ)

Barbara M. Jones is Caleb T. Winchester University Librarian, Wesleyan University, Middletown. (BMJ)

Peter Murray Jones is Fellow and Librarian at King's College, Cambridge. He is the author of *Medieval Medicine in Illuminated Manuscripts* (1998), and interested in the communication of practical medical knowledge in late medieval and early modern Europe. (PMJ)

Karen Junod completed her D.Phil. at Oxford in 2005, held a fellowship at Yale's Beinecke Library, and, subsequently, a British Academy Postdoctoral Fellowship. Her research and teaching interests include Anglo-German relations in the 18th and early 19th centuries, the interactions between British literature and visual culture; biography; history of the book. (KJ)

Craig Kallendorf Associate Editor. See above.

Stephen Karian is Assistant Professor of English, Marquette University, Milwaukee, Wisconsin. He specializes in Jonathan Swift, print and manuscript culture, bibliography, textual criticism, and attribution. He is co-editor of the *Swift Poems Project*. (SK)

Lauren Kassell is a Senior Lecturer in the Department of History and Philosophy of Science and a Fellow of Pembroke College at the University of Cambridge. Her first book was on Simon Forman (2005) and she is now writing a history of magical ideas and practices in early modern England. (LK)

Marika Keblusek is Professor of Book History at the University of Amsterdam and lecturer in the Department of Art History of Leiden University. She is also director of the Scaliger Institute of Leiden University Library. (MK)

Raffael Keller is a Librarian at the rare books department of Zürich Central Library and a translator of Chinese literature. His main research area is in the history of the book in Switzerland since 1600. (RAK)

Maire Kennedy is Librarian of the Gilbert Library, Dublin. (MKe)

Donald Kerr is Special Collections Librarian at the University of Otago, Dunedin, New Zealand. His research topics include book collectors, the phenomenon of collecting, and the formation of private libraries. (DJK)

Tim Killick is a Research Associate at Cardiff University. His research and teaching interests include the history of the short story and Victorian illustration. His broader academic interests cover 19th-century textual production, visual culture and theory, and digital humanities. (TK)

Melanie A. Kimball is an Assistant Professor in the Department of Library and Information Studies at the University at Buffalo, State University of New York. Her research centres on the history of public library service to children and children's literature. (MAK)

Eric Kindel is a Lecturer in the Department of Typography and Graphic Communication, University of Reading. His research encompasses stencil-making and the use of stencils during the past six centuries, with particular emphasis on the production of letters, words, and texts. (ETK)

Rositsa Krasteva Kirilova is an Archivist at the Department of Manuscripts and Old Printed Books, National Library SS. Cyril and Methodius, Sofia, Bulgaria. Her research interests are in the field of book studies and book printing. Her publications are connected mainly with the problems of Slavonic Cyrillic printed books, Bulgarian old printed books, and Bulgarian Revival periodicals (1806–78). (RK)

Thorkild Kjærgaard is Head of the Department of Cultural and Social History, Ilisimatusarfik/University of Greenland. He is the author of *The Danish Revolution, 1500–1800* (paperback, 2006). (TKj)

Elizabeth Knowles is a historical lexicographer who worked on the *Supplement* to the *Oxford English Dictionary* and the *New Shorter Oxford Dictionary*, 4e (1983). She is currently editor of the *Oxford Dictionary of Quotations*, 7e (2009). (EMK)

Dilwyn Knox is Reader in Renaissance Studies in the Italian Department, University College London. He is currently working on Copernicus and Renaissance cosmology. (DK)

Shira M. Kohn is a doctoral candidate in New York University's Joint Program in History and Hebrew & Judaic Studies. Her dissertation is entitled 'A Gentleman's Agreement: Jewish Sororities in Postwar America, 1947–1968'. (SMK)

Marie Elena Korey is Librarian of the Robertson Davies Library at Massey College and a member of the Department of English at the University of Toronto. Her research has focused on the history of printing, publishing, and collecting. (MEK)

Peter Kornicki is Professor of East Asian studies at the University of Cambridge. He is the author of *The Book in Japan* (1998), has published catalogues of early Japanese books in European libraries, and is working on Japanese, Korean, and Vietnamese editions of Chinese texts. (PFK)

Joel Kuortti is a researcher at the University of Joensuu, Finland, and an Adjunct Professor at the University of Jyväskylä, Finland. His current research is on postcolonial theory, postcolonial translation, hybridity, and diasporic Indian women writing in English. (JJK)

Julie Anne Lambert is Librarian of the John Johnson Collection, Bodleian Library, Oxford. Her publications include: *Motoring in Britain, 1895–1940* (co-authored with Nick Baldwin (1998) and *A Nation of Shopkeepers* (exhibition catalogue) (2001). (JALa)

Yvan Lamonde is James McGill professor of History and Literature at McGill University and co-editor of *History of the Book in Canada* (*Histoire du livre et de l'imprimé au Canada*). (YL)

Richard Landon is the Director of the Thomas Fisher Rare Book Library and a Professor of English at the University of Toronto. He has taught courses on book history and bibliography for many years and has published widely in these fields. (RL)

Jeanine De Landtsheer is a Research Fellow at Leuven University. Her publications are focused on Justus Lipsius's life and works, and on the edition of his correspondence. She is also involved in translating a selection of the works of Erasmus into Dutch. (JDL)

John A. Lane writes books and articles on the history of printing types, punchcutters, typefounding, type specimens, and analytical bibliography. He has received Guggenheim, PHS, APHA, and American Bibliographical Society fellowships, and works for libraries, museums, type manufacturers, and book dealers. (JAL)

Otto S. Lankhorst is Librarian of the Klooster Sint Aegten, Erfgoedcentrum Nederlands Kloosterleven at Cuyk-St. Agatha, The Netherlands. He publishes on Dutch book history. (OSL)

Edward Larkin is Assistant Professor of English at the University of Delaware. He is the author of *Thomas Paine and the Literature of Revolution* (2005), and editor of the Broadview edition of *Common Sense* (2004). (EJL)

Vivienne Larminie is a research fellow at the History of Parliament Trust, London, working on biographies of Oxfordshire and Wiltshire MPs (1640–60). Other interests include: religion, society, and culture in francophone Switzerland, 1536–1798; European travel and migration. (VML)

Graham Law specializes in 19th-century media and literary history. A professor at Waseda University, Tokyo, he is the author of *Serializing Fiction in the Victorian Press* (2000) and a co-editor of *The Public Face of Wilkie Collins: The Collected Letters* (4 vols, 2005). (GL)

Frederica Law-Turner is an independent scholar and lecturer working on English manuscript illumination. She holds a Ph.D. from the Courtauld Institute, has catalogued medieval manuscripts for Sotheby's, and taught at the University of Kent. Her forthcoming book, *The Ormesby Psalter*, is due for publication by the Bodleian Library. (FL-T)

Urs B. Leu has pursued studies in history, church history, and medieval Latin at the universities of Zurich, Frankfurt, and Heidelberg. He is Scientific Librarian and Director of the rare book department of the Zentralbibliothek in Zurich. His main research areas are the history of the book to 1800 and the history of the Reformation. (UBL)

Andrew J. Lewis is Assistant Professor of History at American University in Washington DC, where he researches and teaches the history of science and early American history. (AJL)

Scott Lewis, Senior Research Fellow, De Montfort University, Leicester, is editor of the Brownings' Correspondence. (SL)

Richard A. Linenthal is an antiquarian bookseller and was for 25 years a director of Bernard Quaritch Ltd. (RAL)

Theo Maarten van Lint (Ph.D., Leiden 1996) is Calouste Gulbenkian Professor of Armenian Studies at the University of Oxford. His main research interest is in medieval Armenian literature, particularly in poetry. He is currently working on a 10th-century interpretation of the *Throne Vision of Ezekiel* by Vardan of Ani. (TMVL)

Geoffrey Little is Communications Coordinator and Selector for Library Science at Yale University Library. His research interests include library history and collections of Canadiana in the US. He has degrees in English Literature and Library Science from the University of Toronto. (GRLL)

Gerard Long is an Assistant Keeper in the Department of Printed and Visual Collections of the National Library of Ireland. (GJML)

Kate Longworth is a doctoral student at Magdalen College, Oxford. She is completing a study of the poetic drama movement in 20th-century England, and is in the early stages of research into the history of the British National Book Council/League. (KL)

María Luisa López-Vidriero is Director of the Real Biblioteca (Madrid) and Co-Director of the Instituto de Historia del Libro y de la Lectura.

Chris Louttit teaches at Radboud University Nijmegen in The Netherlands. His research focuses on Victorian literature and culture. He has published work on Dickens, Gaskell, and Mayhew, and is also interested in the illustration and popular reception of Victorian texts. (CL)

Erin Louttit's current research project is about Rudyard Kipling and late-Victorian Indian religions. Her research interests include Victorian literature and culture, book history, and children's literature. (EBL)

*Harold Love (1937–2007) was an Australian literary historian, critic, and editor. Among his many publications are *Scribal Publication in Seventeenth-Century England* (1993); *English Clandestine Satire 1660–1702* (2004); and *Attributing Authorship* (2002). He also produced editions of Thomas Southerne (with R. J. Jordan; 2 vols, 1988); John Wilmot, earl of Rochester (1999); and George Villiers, 2nd duke of Buckingham (with R. D. Hume; 2 vols, 2007).

Helen Loveday is an independent paper conservator, specializing in the care and preservation of MSS from the Middle East. Her particular area of research is the study of the nature and characteristics of papers from across the Muslim world. (HLL)

Stephen Lovell is Reader in Modern European History at King's College London and the author of *The Russian Reading Revolution: Print Culture in the Soviet and Post-Soviet Eras* (2000). (SLo)

Kathryn A. Lowe is a Senior Lecturer in the Department of English Language, University of Glasgow. Her research and teaching interests include Old and Middle English language and literature, manuscript studies, editing, and historical literacy. (KAL)

Wulf-Dieter von Lucius is an academic publisher in Stuttgart, producing works on publishing, book history, and book aesthetics, being himself a book collector. He is also Honorary Professor at the University of Hohenheim. (WDL)

Beth E. Luey is the founding Director Emerita of the Scholarly Publishing Program at Arizona State University, and author of *Handbook for Academic Authors*, 4e (2002) and *Revising Your Dissertation*, 2e (2008). She is an editorial consultant in Fairhaven, Massachusetts. (BEL)

Mary Niles Maack is professor of Information Studies at UCLA. She is the co-author of

the book *Aspirations and Mentoring in an Academic Environment* (1994), and has written numerous articles that deal with the history of women in librarianship. (MNM)

Joseph McAleer, an independent scholar, holds a doctorate in history from Oxford University. Specializing in the history of publishing and reading habits, he is the author of two books, including *Passion's Fortune: The Story of Mills & Boon* (1999). (JMc)

Marcus McCorison is President Emeritus and sometime Librarian of the American Antiquarian Society, as well as being a former president of the Bibliographical Society of America. He is the compiler of *Vermont Imprints, 1778–1820* (1963). (MAMcC)

John J. McCusker, FRHistS, is the Ewing Halsell Distinguished Professor of American History and Professor of Economics at Trinity University, San Antonio, Texas, and Adjunct Professor of Early American History at the University of Texas, Austin. (JJM)

Beth McKillop has been Keeper of Asia at the V&A since 2004. Earlier a Curator in the British Library, she researches the MS and book history of Korea. Her publications include *Korean Art and Design* (1992). (EDM)

Roberta Magnani has recently completed a Ph.D. on late medieval manuscripts and early printed editions of Geoffrey Chaucer's works. She is currently working on a monograph on 19th-century editions of Chaucer's oeuvre. She teaches Medieval and Renaissance Literature at Cardiff University. (RMa)

Jeffrey Makala is Assistant Special Collections Librarian at the University of South Carolina. He is interested in the history of the book in America, the modern fine press movement, letterpress printing, and contemporary book arts. (JMa)

Ilkka Mäkinen, Ph.D., is a university lecturer in the Department of Information Studies, University of Tampere, Finland and is also the Editor of *Finnish Public Libraries in the 20th Century* (2001). (IJM)

Yasuko Makino is the Japanese Bibliographer at the East Asian Library of Princeton University and is interested in Japanese bibliography and reference works. She has written *Japan Through Children's Literature*, 2e (1985), *A Student Guide to Japanese Sources in the Humanities* (1995), and other works. (YHM)

Cheryl Knott Malone is on the faculty of the University of Arizona School of Information Resources and Library Science. She researches the history of racially segregated public libraries in the US South and the social tagging of images of reading. (CKM)

Keith Maslen, Honorary Fellow, English Department, University of Otago, New Zealand, has, since 1952, published on bibliographical topics, mainly concerning the 18th-century London printers William Bowyer, father and son, and Samuel Richardson, but also on early Dunedin printers. (KIDM)

Samantha Matthews is a Lecturer in Victorian literature at the University of Sheffield. She is the author of *Poetical Remains: Poets' Graves, Bodies, and Books in the Nineteenth Century* (2004). (SM)

Hope Mayo is Philip Hofer Curator of Printing and Graphic Arts, Houghton Library, Harvard University, and writes on topics related to palaeography, bibliography, book history, and the history of scholarship. (HM)

Carol M. Meale is Senior Research Fellow, University of Bristol. Her research interests include the production, dissemination, ownership, and readership of manuscripts and early printed books. She has published widely in these fields. (CMM)

David L. Vander Meulen is Professor of English at the University of Virginia and editor of *Studies in Bibliography*. His research focuses on bibliography and 18th-century English literature, especially the works of Alexander Pope. (DLVM)

Dirk van Miert is a Scaliger Fellow at the Warburg Institute in London. He publishes on Northern humanism, Neo-Latin texts, and the history of universities. (DVM)

Judith Milhous is Distinguished Professor of Theatre at the Graduate Center of the City University of New York. Her research interests lie in theatre, opera, and dance in the culture of England in the 17th and 18th centuries. (JMi)

Laura J. Miller is Assistant Professor of Sociology at Brandeis University. Her research interests include the book industry, the natural foods industry, and the cultural meanings attached to marketing and consumption. (LJM)

Jane Millgate, Professor Emerita University of Toronto, is the author of *Macaulay* (1973), *Walter Scott: The Making of the Novelist* (1984), and *Scott's Last Edition: A Study in Publishing History* (1987). Her Union Catalogue of the Correspondence of Sir Walter Scott is available on the National Library of Scotland website. (JM)

Peta Mitchell is a Lecturer in Writing, Editing, and Publishing at the University of Queensland, Australia. She is author of *Cartographic Strategies of Post-modernity* (2007), and her current research is in online publishing, public intellectualism, and metaphors of contagion. (PRM)

Dennis J. Mizzi holds a doctorate from the University of Oxford. His main areas of interest include the site of Qumran, the sectarian literature among the Dead Sea Scrolls, and the Hebrew language (biblical and post-biblical Hebrew). (DJM)

Charles Monaghan researches the history of American literacy textbooks. He is the author of *The Murrays of Murray Hill* (1998), a study of the social and intellectual background of Lindley Murray, the largest-selling American author in the first half of the 19th century. (CM)

E. Jennifer Monaghan, an alumna of Lady Margaret Hall, Oxford, is a Professor Emerita of Brooklyn College of the City University of New York. Her work on the history of literacy has won 'best article' awards from the American Studies Association and the History of Education Society and includes her *Learning to Read and Write in Colonial America* (2005). (EJM)

Nickianne Moody is Principal Lecturer in Media and Cultural Studies at Liverpool John Moores University. Her main research interests are in comparative, historical, and contemporary popular narrative media. She is the convenor of the Association for Research in Popular Fictions. (NAM)

Nicole Moore is a Senior Lecturer in the Department of English at Macquarie University in Sydney. She is a specialist in Australian literary and cultural history, with a broader interest in the comparative history of publications censorship as a consequence of Empire. Her book *The Censor's Library: Literary Censorship in Twentieth Century Australia* is forthcoming. (NRM)

Leslie A. Morris is Curator of Modern Books and Manuscripts, Houghton Library, Harvard University, and publishes on 19th- and 20th-century American and British bookselling and collecting. She is currently working on the American collector Amy Lowell. (LAM)

Ian Morrison Assistant Editor. See above.

Kevin A. Morrison teaches and writes about the Victorian period in Britain. His publications include essays in *European Romantic Review*, *Victorian Literature and Culture*, *Comparative Literature*, and *Comparative Literature Studies*. (KAM)

James Mosley is Visiting Professor in the Department of Typography and Graphic Communication, University of Reading. He was Librarian of St Bride Library, London, from 1958 until 2000. He has written and lectured widely on the history of printing type and letter forms. (JMo)

Elissaveta Vladimirova Moussakova has a Ph.D. in Art History, and is a Senior Research Fellow and Head of the Manuscripts and Old Printed Books Department at the Bulgarian National Library. She works in the field of manuscript illumination and Bulgarian contemporary art. (EVM)

John Mullan is Professor of English at University College London. His main research interests are in 18th-century English Literature. (JDM)

Andrew Murphy is Professor of English at the University of St Andrews. He is the author, most recently, of *Shakespeare for the People: Working-class Readers, 1800–1900* (2008) and *Shakespeare in Print: A History and Chronology of Shakespeare Publishing* (2003).

Sara Yontan Musnik is Conservateur de bibliothèques at the Bibliothèque nationale de France in Paris where she works as Turkish area specialist. She is also secretary of MELCom International. (SYM)

Ronald G. Musto is co-director of ACLS Humanities E-Book and co-publisher of

Italica Press. He holds a Ph.D. in History, specializing in 14th-century Italy. (RGM)

Robin Myers is Archivist Emerita of the Stationers' Company, and co-founder of the London book trade history conferences and proceedings. Her numerous publications include *The Stationers' Company Archive: An Account of the Records 1554–1984* (1990) and *The Stationers' Company: A History of the Later Years, 1800–2000* (2001). (RM)

Atalanta Myerson is a book historian whose Ph.D. thesis focused on the wartime activities of OUP. She is a research fellow for The History of Oxford University Press project. (AGM)

Martin Næs is Head of Department, the Faroese Ministry of Education, Research, and Culture. He has written extensively on the history of Faroese literature and on the culture of the islands. (MaN)

Paul W. Nash is an independent scholar in the fields of printing history and bibliography. He has written on private presses and early architectural books and is editor of *Printing History News* and joint-editor of *The Private Library*. (PWN)

Lorri Neilsen is Professor of Literacy and Literary studies at Mount Saint Vincent University in Halifax, Nova Scotia. She is the author and contributing editor of six books on literacy, research, and gender and the author of four collections of poetry. As Lorri Neilsen Glenn, she was Poet Laureate for Halifax for 2005–09. She is currently completing a manuscript of essays on literacy entitled *Lyric Inquiry*. (LN)

Steven M. Oberhelman is Professor of Classics at Texas A&M University. His research interests are ancient medicine and medieval Greek and Arabic dreams. (SMO)

Niall Ó Ciosáin Assistant Editor. See above.

Dáibhí Ó Cróinín is Associate Professor of History in the National University of Ireland, Galway. (DOC)

Adri K. Offenberg was Curator of the Bibliotheca Rosenthaliana at Amsterdam University Library until 2004. He has published mainly in the field of Jewish bibliography, especially Hebrew incunabula and Amsterdam Jewish printing, such as *Hebrew Incunabula in Public Collections: A First International Census* (1990); *A Choice of Corals: Facets of Fifteenth-Century Hebrew Printing* (1992), and *BMC 13: Hebrew* (2004). He also was Editor-in-Chief of the journal *Studia Rosenthaliana* and of *Bibliotheca Rosenthaliana: Treasures of Jewish Booklore* (1994; 2e, 1996). (AKO)

Carl Olson is Professor of Religious Studies at Allegheny College. Besides numerous essays published in journals, books, and encyclopaedias, his latest books include the following: *The Different Paths of Buddhism: A Narrative-Historical Introduction* (2005); *Original Buddhist Sources: A Reader* (2005); *The Many Colors of Hinduism: A Thematic-Historical Introduction* (2007); *Hindu Primary Sources: A Sectarian Reader*

(2007); and *Celibacy and Religious Traditions* (2007).

Richard Ovenden is Associate Director and Keeper of Special Collections at the Bodleian Library, University of Oxford, and a Professorial fellow of St Hugh's College. (RWO)

Jan Pauwels is on the staff of the Royal Library of Belgium in Brussels. His research interests include the book trade and book collecting in the 19th and 20th centuries. (JP)

Devana Pavlik graduated from the School of Librarianship in Prague and worked in the State Library of Czechoslovakia while continuing externally with library studies at the Charles University in Prague. She came to England in 1967 and worked in the National Central Library in London and, from 1974, in the British Library. Her 1976 FLA thesis was on the history of scholarly libraries in Bohemia. From 1983 until her retirement in 2003 she was the British Library's Curator of the Czech, Slovak, and Lusatian Collection. (DP)

Christine Pawley directs the Center for the History of Print Culture in Modern America at the University of Wisconsin-Madison, where she is Professor of Library and Information Studies. She is the author of *Reading on the Middle Border* (2001). (CJP)

Denis Paz, FRHistS, is Professor of Modern British History, University of North Texas, and has written books on Victorian administration, anti-Catholicism, and Dickens and the Chartist Movement. He is studying the career of Martin Tupper as poet, trans-Atlantic celebrity, and friend of Gladstone. (DGP)

Derek Pearsall was formerly Professor and Director of the Centre for Medieval Studies at the University of York (until 1985), and subsequently Gurney Professor of English at Harvard. He retired in 2000. His books include *Old English and Middle English Poetry* (1978); *The Canterbury Tales: A Critical Study* (1985); *Chaucer: A Critical Biography* (1992); *Gothic Europe* (2000); and *William Langland, 'Piers Plowman': A New Edition of the C-Text* (2008). (DAP)

David Pearson Associate Editor. See above.

Meliné Pehlivanian is Africa and Armenia specialist at the Oriental Department of the Staatsbibliothek zu Berlin, Preußischer Kulturbesitz. (MP)

Anna Perälä is a researcher on book history (publishers' bindings) at the Svenska litteratursällskapet i Finland (Society of Swedish Literature in Finland). She is the author of *Suomen typografinen atlas 1642–1827; Finsk typografisk atlas 1642–1827; Typographischer Atlas Finnlands 1642–1827* (2 vols, 2000). (APä)

Michael Perkin is retired Curator of Special Collections, Liverpool University Library; his research interests include history of the provincial book trade; history of libraries. His most recent publication is *A Directory of the Parochial Libraries of the Church of England and the Church in Wales* (2004). (MRP)

John G. Peters, Associate Professor of English at the University of North Texas, is author of *Conrad and Impressionism* (2001), *The Cambridge Introduction to Joseph Conrad* (2006), and articles on Oscar Wilde and other authors of the late 19th and early 20th centuries. (JGP)

Angus Phillips is Director of the Oxford International Centre for Publishing Studies and Head of the Publishing Department at Oxford Brookes University. (AGP)

Oliver Pickering recently retired from the Special Collections department of Leeds University Library, and is now Honorary Fellow in the School of English, University of Leeds. He has published widely on Middle English texts and manuscripts, and edited *The Library* from 1999 to 2008. (OSP)

Susan Pickford is a Lecturer at the University of Paris XIII. Her main research interests are issues of atypical paratext, particularly in travel writing, and the cultural and social history of literary translation. (SLP)

Alexis Politis is Professor of Modern Greek Literature at the University of Crete. His main research interests are in the history of modern Greek literature (especially of the 19th century), the history of mentalities, folksongs, and the history of Greek printing and publishing. (AP)

Jane Potter is a Senior Lecturer at the Oxford International Centre for Publishing Studies, Oxford Brookes University. Her book *Boys in Khaki, Girls in Print: Women's Literary Responses to the Great War 1914–1918* was published in 2005. (JEP)

Robert L. Pounder, Professor Emeritus of Classics at Vassar College, received his Ph.D. from Brown University. An archaeologist, he has excavated at Corinth, the Athenian Agora, and Samothrace and published in, among others, *Hesperia*, *American Journal of Archaeology*, *American Historical Review*, and the *Yale Review*. (RLP)

Susan Powell is Chair in Medieval Texts and Culture, University of Salford. Her academic interests include manuscripts and early printed books, with particular relation to late medieval and Tudor sermons and devotional texts. (SP)

Wilfrid Prest is Professor Emeritus in the Law School and School of History and Politics at the University of Adelaide. He is the author of *Albion Ascendant: English History 1660–1815* (1998) and *William Blackstone: Law and Letters in the Eighteenth Century* (2008). (WRP)

Hugh Price was born in Wellington in 1929, and graduated from Victoria University (MA History) in 1953. He managed a bookshop and worked for several general publishers before becoming founder-manager of Sydney University Press in 1963. After 1968 he managed Price Milburn publishers until his retirement. (HCLP)

Leah Price is Professor of English at Harvard University and author of *The Anthology and the Rise of the Novel* (2000). (LP)

Georgia Prince is the Team Leader and Printed Collections Librarian of Special Collections, Auckland City Libraries. She has worked with the Library's heritage collections since 1979, and took up her present position in 2002. (GP)

Goran Proot, Keeper of Historical Collections at the Universiteit Antwerpen, is lead editor of the Short Title Catalogus Vlaanderen and a member of the board of the *Jaarboek voor Nederlandse Boekgeschiedenis*. His doctoral thesis is on Jesuit theatre. (GPr)

Mark Purcell is Libraries Curator to the National Trust, has a special interest in the history of private libraries, and is currently working on the history of country house libraries in Ireland. (MEP)

Katherine Mary Quinn is a Ph.D. student at the University of Birmingham, researching the potential influence of feminism on the editing of Early Modern texts. She has also conducted a biographical research project on the 17th-century printer Anne Maxwell. (KMQ)

Kari Anne Rand is Professor of Older English at the University of Oslo. Her most recent work has been on the transmission of scientific texts in late medieval England. Among her books are *The Authorship of 'The Equatorie of the Planetis'* (1993) and several volumes on Cambridge MS collections in the Index of Middle English Prose series. (KAR)

Gautham Rao is a Golieb Fellow of Legal History at New York University School of Law, and a Ph.D. candidate at the University of Chicago. He is completing a dissertation on the state and the market in early America. (GR)

Donald Rayfield is Emeritus Professor of Russian and Georgian, Queen Mary University of London, author of *The Literature of Georgia: A History*, 2e (2000), *Anton Chekhov: A Life* (1997), and *Stalin and his Hangmen* (2004), and chief editor of *A Comprehensive Georgian-English Dictionary* (2006). (DR)

Joad Raymond is Professor of English Literature at the University of East Anglia. His research interests include early modern book history, pamphlets, newspapers, poetry, and politics. He is currently writing a study of angels and the imagination in early modern Britain. (JR)

Christopher A. Reed, Associate Professor of Modern Chinese History at the Ohio State University, is the author of *Gutenberg in Shanghai: Chinese Print Capitalism, 1876–1937* (2004). He is currently conducting research for a book on the Nationalist Party's propaganda system prior to 1949. (CAR)

Christoph Reske has a Ph.D. in printing technology and is a lecturer and researcher at the Institute of the History of the Book, University of Mainz. He is particularly interested in incunabula, history of printing and types, production and design of books. (CHR)

Suzanne Reynolds is Curator of Manuscripts at Holkham Hall, Norfolk. (SR)

Christine L. Ridarsky is a Ph.D. candidate in the Department of History, University of

Rochester. Her primary research interests are in late 19th- and early 20th-century US rural and agricultural history and American women's history. (CLR)

Per S. Ridderstad is Emeritus Professor in Book and Library History, Lund University, Sweden. (PSR)

R. M. Ritter had a career in US and UK publishing before taking a doctorate at Oxford. He is an authority on editing, with an interest in analytical bibliography and writing technologies. He is author of the *Oxford Style Manual* (2003). (RMR)

Andrew Robinson is a Visiting Fellow of Wolfson College, Cambridge, and a full-time writer. His books include *The Story of Writing: Alphabets, Hieroglyphs and Pictograms* (1995); *The Man Who Deciphered Linear B: The Story of Michael Ventris* (2002); *Lost Languages: The Enigma of the World's Undeciphered Scripts* (2002); and *Writing and Script: A Very Short Introduction* (2009).

Jan Erik Røed is a former Director, University of Oslo library. (JER)

Ekaterina Rogatchevskaia Associate Editor. See above.

Andrei Rogatchevski is a Senior Lecturer in Russian, University of Glasgow; he has also taught in Finland, Germany, and the Czech Republic. His publications include *Bribery and Blat in Russia* (2000; co-edited) and *A Biographical and Critical Study of Eduard Limonov* (2003). (ARog)

Shef Rogers is a Senior Lecturer in English at the University of Otago, Dunedin, New Zealand. He is completing a bibliography of English travel writing 1700–1800 and is working with four Otago colleagues to compile a one-volume history of the book in New Zealand. (CSR)

Eugenia Roldán Vera is Professor-Researcher at the Department of Education of the Centre for Advanced Research and Studies (DIE/CINVESTAV), Mexico. Her fields of research are the history of education and the history of the book in 19th- and 20th-century Latin America. She is the author of *The British Book Trade and Spanish American Independence* (2003).

Paul W. Romaine is a consultant librarian in New York. He is a Vice-President of the American Printing History Association and past curator of the Gilder Lehrman Collection. He studies the history of printing and handwriting 1750–1920. (PWR)

Geoffrey Roper Associate Editor. See above.

Fiona G. Ross is a type-designer, typographic consultant, and part-time lecturer at Reading University, specializing in non-Latin typeforms (particularly Indic and Arabic): their history in relation to cultural and political influences, and with regard to typefounding and composing practices. (FGR)

John C. Ross is an Honorary Research Fellow, School of English and Media Studies, Massey University, Palmerston North, New Zealand. He is currently working on a study of an early 18th-century London printer, and on a critical study of some New Zealand novels. Recent publications include bibliographical histories of George Eliot and of Harold Pinter, in collaboration with William Baker. (JCR)

Adam Rounce is AHRC Research Fellow for the Cambridge Edition of the *Works of Jonathan Swift* at Keele University. He has edited and published articles on various writers, most of whom are connected with the mid- or later 18th century. (ASR)

Nicola Royan is a Lecturer in Medieval and Early Modern Literature, School of English Studies, University of Nottingham, and Editorial Secretary of the Scottish Text Society. (NR)

Joan Shelley Rubin Associate Editor. See above.

David Rundle is a member of the History Faculty of the University of Oxford and was formerly J. P. R. Lyell Research Fellow in Manuscript Studies. He is the Executive Officer of the Society for the Study of Medieval Languages and Literature, and one of the General Editors of the publications of the Oxford Bibliographical Society. (DGR)

Paul Ruxin is Chairman of the Board of Governors of the Folger Shakespeare Library, and a member of the Editorial Committee of the Yale Editions of the Private Papers of James Boswell, the Association Internationale de Bibliophilie, and the Rowfant, Caxton, and Grolier Clubs. (PTR)

Johannes Saltzwedel studied German literature in Tübingen and Oxford. He works for *Der Spiegel* in Hamburg, writing chiefly on the history of ideas and on classical music. His special interests include literary tradition, philology, and book-collecting.

Christa Sammons joined the staff of the Beinecke Rare Book and Manuscript Library, Yale University, in 1968. She currently serves as Curator of the Yale Collection of German Literature and has edited several Beinecke Library publications. (CAS)

Jay Satterfield is the Special Collections Librarian for Rauner Special Collections Library at Dartmouth College. He is the author of *The World's Best Books: Taste, Culture and the Modern Library* (2002). (JCS)

Jamie C. Saucier is a Ph.D. candidate in American history at the University of Rochester, New York. His primary interests are intellectual and cultural history, and he is currently researching his dissertation on suburbanization and post-war social thought. (JCSa)

David Saunders is Professor Emeritus and Adjunct Professor, Socio-Legal Research Centre, Griffith University; and Honorary Professor, Centre for the History of European Discourses, University of Queensland. His publications and research explore the cultural consequences of early modern political settlements and legal arrangements. (DS)

Jef Schaeps is Curator of Prints and Drawings at Leiden University Library. (JS)

Wybren Scheepsma works as a postdoctoral researcher at Leiden University. His research concentrates on medieval religious literature in the vernacular, especially in the Low Countries. (WS)

Christian Scheidegger has pursued studies in history, church history, and Hebrew at the University of Zurich. He is Librarian of the rare book department of the Zentralbibliothek in Zurich. His main research areas are the history of the book to 1600 and the history of the Reformation. (CS)

Marcus de Schepper is Editor of the *Bibliography of Dutch Language and Literature* (BNTL) at the Royal Library of Belgium, Brussels, and secretary of the Society of Antwerp Bibliophiles at the Museum Plantin-Moretus. He publishes widely on 16th- and 17th-century humanism, neo-Latin poetry, and book history. (MDS)

Frieder Schmidt is a historian and Curator of the Paper Historical Collections, Deutsches Buch- und Schriftmuseum of the Deutsche Nationalbibliothek in Leipzig. He is also the co-ordinator of Deutscher Arbeitskreis für Papiergeschichte. (FSt)

Ute Schneider is an Associate Professor at the Gutenberg Institute for Book Science of the University of Mainz. Her main fields of research are the interdependencies between book history and the history of science; the history of publishing houses from the 18th to the 20th century; and the history of readership in the 20th century. (US)

Fred Schreiber holds a Ph.D. in classical philology from Harvard; after teaching classics at CUNY for several years, he founded his own rare book firm, E. K. Schreiber, specializing in Renaissance humanism and early editions of the classics. (FS)

Emile G. L. Schrijver Assistant Editor. See above.

Patrick Scott is Professor of English, University of South Carolina, and Director of Special Collections, Thomas Cooper Library, teaching Victorian literature and the history of the book, with recent publications on Burns, Tennyson, Clough, and Stevenson. (PGS)

David J. Shaw is Secretary, Consortium of European Research Libraries (2002–09); he was formerly Senior Lecturer in French, University of Kent, Editor-in-Chief, Cathedral Libraries Catalogue, and President of The Bibliographical Society (2002–04). He is a specialist in the 16th-century book trade, especially in France. (DJS)

William H. Sherman is Professor of Renaissance/Early Modern Studies at the University of York. His *Used Books: Marking Readers in Renaissance England* was published in 2007. (WHS)

Peter L. Shillingsburg Associate Editor. See above.

Daniel Simon is founding editor and publisher of Seven Stories Press. (DMS)

Sylva Simsova is a refugee from Czechoslovakia. Now retired, she worked

in public libraries (1951–64), lectured in librarianship and information science (1964–85), and served as an information systems consultant (1986–2001). Her publications have focused on librarianship, information science, the psychology of reading, ethnic minorities, comparative librarianship, and the history of Czechoslovak exile. (SS)

Karen Skovgaard-Petersen Assistant Editor. See above.

Madeline Slaven is a book conservator at the Bodleian Library, Oxford. (MRS)

Audrey Holdhus Small is a lecturer in French and francophone studies. Her main interests lie in the problematic nature of the post-colonial, especially the politics and economics of publishing in former colonies. (AHS)

Helen Smith is a Lecturer in English Literature at the University of York. Her research interests include history of the book, Renaissance literature, feminist theory, US Armed Services Editions, and *Tristram Shandy*. (HS)

Margaret M. Smith Associate Editor. See above.

Martha Nell Smith is Professor of English and Founding Director of the Maryland Institute for Technology in the Humanities (www.mith.umd.edu/mnsmith) at the University of Maryland, and Executive Editor of the Dickinson Electronic Archives (emilydickinson.org). (MNS)

Marja Smolenaars is one of the editors of the Short Title Catalogue Netherlands and conducts research into early modern Anglo-Dutch book trade relations. (MS)

Jennifer Snead is an Assistant Professor of English at Texas Tech University. She is currently researching and publishing work on the 18th-century transatlantic evangelical revival, reading publics, and popular literacy. (JES)

Elizabeth Solopova works in the Department of Special Collections and Western Manuscripts at the Bodleian Library, Oxford. Her research focuses on medieval manuscripts, literature, and historical linguistics. She is currently working on a catalogue of medieval psalters at the Bodleian Library. (ES)

Henry S. Sommerville is a doctoral candidate in history at the University of Rochester. (HSS)

Richard Southall has been involved with type and typography since the early 1960s. He has worked at the University of Reading and Stanford University, and at the Xerox Palo Alto Research Center. His book *Printer's Type in the Twentieth Century: Manufacturing and Design Methods* was published in 2005. (RFS)

Jennifer Speake is an independent scholar, writer, and reference book editor specializing in the Renaissance period. She is editor of *Literature of Travel and Exploration: An Encyclopedia* (2003) and *Encyclopedia of the Renaissance and Reformation* (rev. ed. 2004). (JAS)

Claire Squires Associate Editor. See above.

Konstantinos Staikos is an architect who has written on the history of Greek printing and publishing, including Greek editors during the Renaissance. His book *The Great Libraries* (1996; English edition, 2000) covers the subject from 3000 BC to AD 1600. (KS)

David H. Stam is University Librarian Emeritus at Syracuse University and Senior Scholar in the History Department of the Maxwell School. His current research is centred on the history of the polar regions. (DHS)

Rebecca Stark-Gendrano is a doctoral candidate at Fordham University, New York. She is completing a study of fragmentary and unfinished texts by 17th-century English writers. Her research interests include editorial theory, the history of editing, theatrical adaptations, and female authorship. (RSG)

Kathleen Steeden studied Printing and Book Design History at the University of Reading with a focus on 19th-century wood-engraving. She is currently working as a library assistant and as a publications advisor for a national charity. (KES)

Ann Marika Steiner is a Lecturer in Comparative Literature at Lund University, Sweden. Her main research interest is in the 20th century and the contemporary book trade. Her book on subscription book clubs was published in 2006, and she is currently working on the post-war book trade in Sweden. (AMS)

William P. Stoneman is the Florence Fearrington Librarian of the Houghton Library at Harvard University. His research interests include medieval and Renaissance manuscripts and early printed books, and the history of collecting in these areas. (WPS)

Martijn Storms is curator of maps and atlases at Leiden University Library. He studied human geography at Utrecht University where he is working on his doctoral thesis on Dutch estate atlases. (MSt)

Stuart Strachan was Hocken Librarian at the University of Otago, New Zealand, from 1985 to 2008, and has a continuing research interest in his country's archives and library history. He recently edited *Treasures from the Hocken Collections* (2007). (SRS)

Michael F. Suarez, S.J. General Editor. See above.

Anne F. Sutton is Historian Emerita of the Mercery's Company of London. She is editor of *The Book of Privileges of the Merchant Adventurers of England 1296–1483* (2009), author of *The Mercery of London 1130–1578* (2005), and works on medieval London and on Richard III. (AFS)

Ittai Joseph Tamari lectures at the Department of Jewish History and Culture, Ludwig-Maximilians-University, Munich. He researches the history of books printed with Hebrew letters in German-speaking territories in Europe since the 16th century. (IJT)

Barry Taylor is Curator, Hispanic Printed Collections 1501–1850, at the British Library and editor of the *Electronic British Library Journal* (www.bl.uk/eblj). He has published on the 1599 edition of St Isidore, Ramon Miquel y Planas, and Henry Spencer Ashbee. (BT)

Christine Thomas was formerly the Head of Slavonic and East European Collections in the British Library. She has published on the history of Russian printing, the formation of the Russian collections of the British Museum Library, and on Slavonic early printed books. She is also editor of *Solanus: International Journal for Russian and East European Bibliographic, Library, and Publishing Studies*. (CGT)

Elizabeth Susan Tilley is a Lecturer in the Department of English, National University of Ireland, Galway. (EST)

Margaret Timmers was formerly Head of Prints in the V&A's Word and Image Department. She specializes in posters and curated the V&A exhibition, The Power of the Poster, in 1998. (MWT)

Trysh Travis is an Assistant Professor of Women's Studies at the University of Florida, specializing in the gendered history of book publishing and reading. (TT)

Gary A. Tubb is Professor in the Department of South Asian Languages and Civilizations at the University of Chicago. His principal interests include Sanskrit literature, literary theory, grammar, and philosophy. (GAT)

Catherine Cornelia Turner is Associate Professor of English at College Misericordia. She is the author of *Marketing Modernism between the Two Wars* (2003) and writes on the 20th-century publishing and bookselling industries. (CCT)

M. Antoni J. Üçerler, S.J. is a member of the Jesuit Historical Institute in Rome and a tutor at Campion Hall, University of Oxford. His main area of research is the history of Christianity in Japan and China. (MAU)

Ton Croiset van Uchelen was attached to Amsterdam University Library from 1962 to 1997 as Keeper of Rare Books and, from 1987, as Chief Curator/Deputy Librarian. He has been Senior Editor of *Quaerendo* since 1970. (ARACVU)

Wolfgang Undorf has a Masters degree in book studies from Cologne University, and is a Librarian at the National Library of Sweden. His recent research in the field of book history covers the pre-Reformation period in Scandinavia. (WUn)

Eduardo Urbina, Ph.D. from the University of California, Berkeley (1979), is Professor of Hispanic Studies, Texas A&M University, Director of the Cátedra Cervantes, University of Castilla-La Mancha. He is also Director of the Cervantes Project (cervantes.tamu.edu), and editor both of the *Anuario Bibliográfico Cervantino* and the *Anuario de Estudios Cervantinos*. (EU)

Kathleen E. Urda is an Assistant Professor of English at Bronx Community College CUNY in New York City. Her research focuses on 18th- and 19th-century British literature, particularly prose fiction, and on the relationship between the novel and other genres. (KU)

Elena Georgieva Uzunova from SS. Cyril and Methodius National Library, Manuscripts and Rare Books Department, has a Ph.D. in archival science and is a Senior Research Fellow (2006), with particular interests in the Slavic and Bulgarian manuscript tradition (11th–19th centuries), notes as sources for Bulgarian cultural history, archaeography, language, and literature. (EGU)

A. R. Venkatachalapathy is Professor at the Madras Institute of Development Studies. He is also a Tamil writer. His research focuses on the social and cultural history of colonial south India. He has worked extensively on Tamil print culture. (ARV)

Andrew van der Vlies Associate Editor. See above.

Rietje van Vliet is a freelance research journalist. She has published on Elie Luzac, Marc-Michel Rey, and topics concerning the Dutch book in the 18th century. (RVV)

Peter Vodosek is Emeritus Professor of Library Science at Hochschule der Medien/University of Applied Sciences Stuttgart. He has published in the fields of library history, library policy, and library education. (PV)

Aleksandra B. Vraneš is Professor of Philology, University of Belgrade, and President of the Serbian Library Association. Her fields of interest include library science, bibliography, ethics in science, and the methodology of research. Her publications include *Serbian Bibliography in Periodicals: From Orphelin to 1941* (1996), *Basis of Bibliography* (2001), *Academic Libraries* (2004), and *From the Manuscript to the Library: Dictionary* (2006). (ABV)

Bettina Wagner is an Academic Librarian at the Bayerische Staatsbibliothek München, head of manuscript and incunable cataloguing. Her publications are on textual transmission, provenance studies, and book bindings. (BW)

Noel Waite is a Senior Lecturer in the Design Studies Department, University of Otago, and researches in the areas of design history, exhibition design, and print culture. He is the author of *Books for a Nation: The Whitcoulls Story* (2008) and is an editor of a forthcoming *History of the Book in New Zealand* (www.otago.ac.nz/crni/research/print.html). (NDW)

Muhammad Isa Waley has been Curator of Persian and Turkish Collections at the British Library since 1971. His research interests include Islamic palaeography, codicology, illumination, and calligraphy and medieval verse and prose literature on Sufism. (MIW)

Kathleen Walkup is Professor of Book Art at Mills College in Oakland, California, where she directs the Book Art Program. Her research interests include the history of women and books. Her ongoing artists' book project is entitled *Library of Discards*. (KAW)

Marcus Walsh Associate Editor. See above.

Jürgen M. Warmbrunn, Ph.D., is a Slavicist, historian, and academic librarian with a particular interest in East European and Baltic library history and book culture. He is Deputy Director of the Herder-Institut, Marburg, a centre for historical research on East Central Europe, and Director of the research library of the Herder-Institut. (JMW)

Rowan Watson is a Senior Curator in the Word and Image Department of the V&A. His interests include the medieval book trade and illuminated manuscripts in the post-medieval period. (RWa)

Teresa Webber is Senior Lecturer in Palaeography at Cambridge, and Fellow of Trinity College. She has published on medieval handwriting, books and libraries, and co-edited volume one of the *Cambridge History of Libraries in Britain and Ireland.* (MTJW)

Alexis Weedon is Professor of Publishing Studies and Director of the Research Institute for Media Art and Design, University of Bedfordshire. Specializing in publishing economics, quantification, and cross-media production, she is co-editor of *Convergence* and author of *Victorian Publishing* (2003). (AAW)

Adriaan van der Weel holds the Bohn Chair in Modern Dutch Book History at Leiden University. His research interests focus on the history of the 19th- and 20th-century book and the growing use in the 21st century of digital media for the transmission of texts. (AHVDW)

A. B. R. Weiner is a British typographer specializing in electronic documents and information design. He devotes spare time to the activities of the Friends of St Bride Library. (ABRW)

Anthony James West has focused his research and writing since 1989 on the Shakespeare First Folio. He is Honorary Research Fellow, University College London, and Senior Research Fellow, Institute of English Studies, School of Advanced Study, University of London. (AJW)

James L. W. West III is Sparks Professor of English at Pennsylvania State University, where he directs the Penn State Center for the History of the Book. He is general editor of the Cambridge Fitzgerald Edition and past president of SHARP. (JLWW)

Bart Westerweel is Professor Emeritus of early modern English literature at Leiden University. He publishes on 16th- and 17th-century poetry and drama, with a special focus on Shakespeare, Herbert, and emblems. (BWe)

Eric Marshall White, Ph.D., is Curator of Special Collections at Bridwell Library, Southern Methodist University (Dallas). His articles and exhibition catalogues have

focused mainly on 15th-century printing in Mainz and the history of early book ownership, illumination, and binding. (EW)

D. Bruce Whiteman is Head Librarian at the William Andrews Clark Memorial Library, UCLA. He was co-curator of The World From Here: Treasures of the Great Libraries of Los Angeles (2002), and is currently a Ph.D. candidate in Musicology at UCLA. (DBW)

David R. Whitesell, Associate Editor. See above.

David J. Whittaker is Curator, 19th-century Western and Mormon Manuscripts, Harold B. Lee Library, and Associate Professor of History, Brigham Young University. He has co-authored *Studies in Mormon History, 1830–1997: An Indexed Bibliography* (2000) and *Mormon History* (2001). (DJW)

Wayne A. Wiegand is F. William Summers Professor of Library and Information Studies and Professor of American Studies at Florida State University. He served as co-editor of *Library Quarterly* (2003–08), and currently directs the Florida Best Books Awards. (WAW)

Edwin Paul Wieringa was educated in Indonesian Languages and Literatures at the University of Leiden (MA 1988, Ph.D. 1994). Since 2004, he has been Professor of Indonesian Philology and Islamic Studies at the University of Cologne. He is the author of a two-volume *Catalogue of Malay and Minangkabau Manuscripts in the Library of Leiden University* (1998, 2007).

N. G. Wilson Assistant Editor. See above.

Michael B. Winship is Professor of English at the University of Texas. He co-edited and contributed to *The Industrial Book*, volume 3 (2007) of *A History of the Book in America*, and has published widely on 19th-century American literary publishing. (MBW)

Reinhard Wittmann Associate Editor. See above.

Clemens de Wolf is former Keeper of Rare Books and Head of Collections and Research at the Koninklijke Bibliotheek, The Hague. He is one of the initiators of the Short-Title Catalogue Netherlands and the Bibliopolis Project. (CDW)

S. J. Wolfe, MLS, is a senior cataloguer and serials specialist at the American Antiquarian Society. A lecturer and author of a book and numerous articles on Egyptian mummies in 19th-century America, her other research interests include the American iron industry, papermaking, and Civil War medicine. (SJW)

Laurence Worms is an antiquarian bookseller (Ash Rare Books, London). A course tutor at the London Rare Books School, he is also a contributor to the *Oxford Dictionary of National Biography* and *The Cambridge History of the Book in Britain.* (LJW)

H. R. Woudhuysen General Editor. See above.

Paul M. Wright retired in 2006 after nearly 40 years in scholarly publishing, the last

eighteen at the University of Massachusetts Press, where he founded and edited its print culture series. He has a special interest in American publishing history. (PMW)

David Wykes is Director of Dr Williams's Library, London, and Honorary Reader in English at Queen Mary, University of London. (DLW)

Richard Yeo is a Professorial Fellow in the Centre for Public Culture and Ideas, Griffith University, Brisbane, and a Fellow of the Australian Academy of the Humanities. His publications include *Defining Science* (1993) and *Encyclopaedic Visions* (2001). (RY)

William Zachs is the author of *The First John Murray and the Late Eighteenth-century London Book Trade* (1998). He lives in Edinburgh. (WZ)

Jan M. Ziolkowski, Arthur Kingsley Porter Professor of Medieval Latin at Harvard, directs Dumbarton Oaks. He has recent books on fairy tales, Abelard's letters, Solomon and Marcolf, musical notation of classics, and, collaboratively, a 12th-century anthology, and the Virgilian tradition. (JZ)

Janet Zmroczek is Head of European Collections at the British Library. Her research interests include the history of the British Library Polish and Baltic collections and the cultural, social, and literary activities of the Polish community in 19th-century Britain. Her articles on these subjects have been published in a range of British, European, and American scholarly journals. (JSZ)

Johan de Zoete is Curator of the Museum Enschedé in Haarlem, The Netherlands. He publishes on the history and technique of printing. In 2003 he was co-author of a six-volume company history of Joh. Enschedé, *Voor stad en staat. Joh. Enschedé 2003–1703*. (JDZ)

* Deceased

Index of Contributor Initials

APä	Anna Perälä	EAB	Elizabethanne Boran	JDZ	Johan de Zoete
ARACVU	Ton Croiset van Uchelen	EAH	Earle Havens	JE	Jacalyn Eddy
ARJ	Ann Rosalind Jones	EB	Elleke Boehmer	JEGa	Jill E. Gage
ARog	Andrei Rogatchevski	EBL	Erin Louttit	JEGo	John Goldfinch
ARV	A. R. Venkatachalapathy	EDG	Ellen D. Gilbert	JEP	Jane Potter
ASB	Alan Bell	EDM	Beth McKillop	JER	Jan Erik Røed
ASGE	A. S. G. Edwards	EEi	Elisabeth S. Eide	JES	Jennifer Snead
ASR	Adam Rounce	EG	Eileen Gardiner	JF	James Fergusson
BAC	Brian Cummings	EGLS	Emile G. L. Schrijver	JFE	James F. English
BEF	Beatrice Fannon	EGU	Elena Georgieva Uzunova	JGP	John G. Peters
BEL	Beth E. Luey	EHi	Esko Häkli	JH	John Hinks
BG	Bridget Guzner	EJL	Edward Larkin	JHBo	J. H. Bowman
BH	Barbara Hochman	EJM	E. Jennifer Monaghan	JHBr	John Hassett Brady
BJF	Brian Findlay	EME	Evelyn Ellerman	JJK	Joel Kuortti
BKG	Barbara K. Gold	EMK	Elizabeth Knowles	JJM	John J. McCusker
BLF	Barbara Laning Fitzpatrick	ER	Ekaterina Rogatchevskaia	JLF	John L. Flood
BMJ	Barbara M. Jones	ES	Elizabeth Solopova	JLWW	James L. W. West III
BPMD	Berry Dongelmans	EST	Elizabeth Susan Tilley	JM	Jane Millgate
BT	Barry Taylor	ETK	Eric Kindel	JMa	Jeffrey Makala
BW	Bettina Wagner	EU	Eduardo Urbina	JMc	Joseph McAleer
BWe	Bart Westerweel	EVM	Elissaveta Vladimirova	JMG	James Gibbs
CA	Charlotte Appel		Moussakova	JMi	Judith Milhous
CAR	Christopher A. Reed	EW	Eric Marshall White	JMo	James Mosley
CAS	Christa Sammons	FAJ	Frans A. Janssen	JMW	Jürgen M. Warmbrunn
CB	Charles Benson	FC	Federica Ciccolella	JP	Jan Pauwels
CBF	Chris Fowler	FCG	Francis Galloway	JPC	Justin Croft
CC	Christian Coppens	FGR	Fiona G. Ross	JR	Joad Raymond
CCT	Catherine Cornelia Turner	FL-T	Frederica Law-Turner	JS	Jef Schaeps
CDW	Clemens de Wolf	FS	Fred Schreiber	JSE	J. S. Edgren
CGT	Christine Thomas	FSt	Frieder Schmidt	JSR	Joan Shelley Rubin
CHR	Christoph Reske	GAT	Gary A. Tubb	JSZ	Janet Zmroczek
CJP	Christine Pawley	GFC	Gail Chester	JVH	Jos van Heel
CKM	Cheryl Knott Malone	GIE	Gabriel Egan	JWUS	Johannes Saltzwedel
CL	Chris Louttit	GJML	Gerard Long	JYC	John Y. Cole
CLH	Clare Hutton	GJR	Geoffrey Roper	JZ	Jan M. Ziolkowski
CLR	Christine L. Ridarsky	GL	Graham Law	KAC	Kathleen Coleridge
CM	Charles Monaghan	GP	Georgia Prince	KAL	Kathryn A. Lowe
CMA	Catherine Armstrong	GPr	Goran Proot	KAM	Kevin A. Morrison
CMM	Carol M. Meale	GR	Gautham Rao	KAR	Kari Anne Rand
CMS	Claire Squires	GRLL	Geoffrey Little	KAW	Kathleen Walkup
CPC	Cecil Patrick Courtney	HC	Helen Cordell	KE	Kambiz Eslami
CS	Christian Scheidegger	HCLP	Hugh Price	KEA	Karen Attar
CSR	Shef Rogers	HG	Heinz Grotzfeld	KES	Kathleen Steeden
CWH	Charles Hatfield	HLL	Helen Loveday	KIDM	Keith Maslen
CWK	Craig Kallendorf	HM	Hope Mayo	KJ	Karen Junod
CYF	Christine Ferdinand	HRW	H. R. Woudhuysen	KL	Kate Longworth
DAP	Derek Pearsall	HS	Helen Smith	KMQ	Katherine Mary Quinn
DBW	D. Bruce Whiteman	HSS	Henry S. Sommerville	KS	Konstantinos Staikos
DCC	Daven Christopher Chamberlain	IF	Iain Fenlon	KSP	Karen Skovgaard-Petersen
DE	David Emblidge	IG	Ian Gadd	KU	Kathleen E. Urda
DGH	David Hirsch	IH	Ian Higgins	LAM	Leslie A. Morris
DGP	Denis Paz	IJM	Ilkka Mäkinen	LE	Lukas Erne
DGR	David Rundle	IJT	Ittai Joseph Tamari	LEJ	Leon E. Jackson
DHS	David H. Stam	IM	Ian Morrison	LG	Lisa Gitelman
DI	Dirk Imhof	IMD	Ian Dougherty	LH	Lotte Hellinga
DIb	David Ibbetson	IRBD	Ian Desai	LJM	Laura J. Miller
DJK	Donald Kerr	JA	Jane Aikin	LJW	Laurence Worms
DJM	Dennis J. Mizzi	JAD	Judy Donnelly	LK	Lauren Kassell
DJS	David J. Shaw	JAL	John A. Lane	LN	Lorri Neilsen
DJW	David J. Whittaker	JALa	Julie Anne Lambert	LP	Leah Price
DK	Dilwyn Knox	JAS	Jennifer Speake	LSC	Laurence S. Creider
DLJ	David James	JBH	John B. Hench	MA	Martin Antonetti
DLVM	David L. Vander Meulen	JCG	John Gray	MAB	Mary Ann Bolger
DLW	David Wykes	JCI	Judy Crosby Ivy	MAK	Melanie A. Kimball
DMH	David M. Hovde	JCR	John C. Ross	MAMcC	Marcus McCorison
DMS	Daniel Simon	JCS	Jay Satterfield	MaN	Martin Næs
DOC	Dáibhí Ó Cróinín	JCSa	Jamie C. Saucier	MB	Maureen Bell
DP	Devana Pavlik	JD	Jos Damen	MBa	Matthew Battles
DR	Donald Rayfield	JDC	Joanne Chaison	MBj	Margareta Björkman
DRSP	David Pearson	JDG	Jeffrey D. Groves	MBW	Michael B. Winship
DRW	David R. Whitesell	JDI	Jana Igunma	MCD	Martin Davies
DS	David Saunders	JDL	Jeanine De Landtsheer	MD	Martin Dewhirst
DVM	Dirk van Miert	JDM	John Mullan	MDB	Megan Burke

MDS	Marcus de Schepper	PA	Pablo Alvarez	SBC	Bernadette Cunningham
ME	Monika Estermann	PAE	Pablo Andrés Escapa	SC	Sebastian Carter
MEB	Margaret E. Becket	PB	Peter Beal	SCH	Sud Chonchirdsin
MEK	Marie Elena Korey	PCG	Paul C. Gutjahr	SD	Sophy Dale
MEP	Mark Purcell	PD	Pierre Delsaerdt	SEB	Sarah Brouillette
MFS	Michael F. Suarez, S.J.	PDa	Phyllis Dain	SEC	Scott E. Casper
MGC	M. G. Carter	PDB	Philip D. Beidler	SG	Susan Green
MGr	Magdalena Gram	PDF	Patrick Denman Flanery	SJD	Susan Davies
MH	Martin J. Heijdra	PE	Paul Eggert	SJG	Simon Gatrell
MHB	Martin Butler	PFG	Paul F. Gehl	SJH	Steve Hare
MHC	Matthew Creasy	PFK	Peter Kornicki	SJW	S. J. Wolfe
MIW	Muhammad Isa Waley	PGH	Paul Hoftijzer	SK	Stephen Karian
MJA	Martin Andrews	PGS	Patrick Scott	SKC	Swapan Chakravorty
MJH	Melissa J. Homestead	PH	Peter Hellyer	SL	Scott Lewis
MK	Marika Keblusek	PHJG	Paul Goldman	SLo	Stephen Lovell
MKe	Maire Kennedy	PLF	Patricia Lockhart Fleming	SLP	Susan Pickford
MMF	Mirjam M. Foot	PLS	Peter L. Shillingsburg	SM	Samantha Matthews
MMS	Margaret M. Smith	PMJ	Peter Murray Jones	SMK	Shira M. Kohn
MNM	Mary Niles Maack	PMW	Paul M. Wright	SMO	Steven M. Oberhelman
MNS	Martha Nell Smith	PRF	Peter R. Frank	SP	Susan Powell
MP	Meliné Pehlivanian	PRM	Peta Mitchell	SR	Suzanne Reynolds
MPB	Matthew P. Brown	PSR	Per S. Ridderstad	SRS	Stuart Strachan
MRP	Michael Perkin	PTB	Paul Baines	SS	Sylva Simsova
MRS	Madeline Slaven	PTR	Paul Ruxin	SSB	Suzanne S. Bell
MS	Marja Smolenaars	PV	Peter Vodosek	SYM	Sara Yontan Musnik
MSC	Michael Caines	PWN	Paul W. Nash	TB	Theo Bögels
MSt	Martijn Storms	PWR	Paul W. Romaine	TK	Tim Killick
MTJW	Teresa Webber	RAE	Rachel Anne Edwards	TKj	Thorkild Kjærgaard
MVD	Marieke van Delft	RAK	Raffael Keller	TMVL	Theo Maarten van Lint
MVE	Marco van Egmond	RAL	Richard A. Linenthal	TT	Trysh Travis
MVG	Milan Grba	RBC	Rimi B. Chatterjee	UBL	Urs B. Leu
MW	Marcus Walsh	RFS	Richard Southall	US	Ute Schneider
MWT	Margaret Timmers	RGM	Ronald G. Musto	VAG	Vincent Giroud
NAM	Nickianne Moody	RJD	Robert Dingley	VB	Vincent Barnett
ND	Nandini Das	RK	Rositsa Krasteva Kirilova	VBh	Varuni Bhatia
NDW	Noel Waite	RL	Richard Landon	VEMG	Victoria Gardner
NEG	Nancy E. Gwinn	RLH	Richard L. Hills	VLB	Virginia L. Bartow
NG	Nadja Guggi	RLP	Robert L. Pounder	VML	Vivienne Larminie
NGr	Nick Groom	RM	Robin Myers	WAW	Wayne A. Wiegand
NGW	N. G. Wilson	RMa	Roberta Magnani	WDL	Wulf-Dieter von Lucius
NH	Neil Harris	RMC	Ralph Cleminson	WHS	William H. Sherman
NJB	Nicolas Barker	RMR	R. M. Ritter	WPS	William P. Stoneman
NOC	Niall Ó Ciosáin	RSG	Rebecca Stark-Gendrano	WRP	Wilfrid Prest
NR	Nicola Royan	RVV	Rietje van Vliet	WS	Wybren Scheepsma
NRM	Nicole Moore	RW	Reinhard Wittmann	WUn	Wolfgang Undorf
ÓG	Óskár Guðmundsson	RWa	Rowan Watson	WZ	William Zachs
OSL	Otto S. Lankhorst	RWO	Richard Ovenden	YHM	Yasuko Makino
OSP	Oliver Pickering	RY	Richard Yeo	YL	Yvan Lamonde

Thematic Index of Entries

The main headings used in this index, which covers both the essays and the A–Z entries, are listed immediately below. In the index itself, the essays are cited by their number and title; the A–Z entries are referred to by their headword. The index includes coverage of the book in various regional and national areas, using those categories adopted for the essays. However, for reasons of space and because they are so extensively covered throughout the *Companion*, it has been necessary to exclude thematic listings of the book in the different countries of Western Europe (Austria, Belgium, France, Germany, Italy, the Low Countries, Portugal, Spain, Switzerland, but not the Nordic Countries), and in the US. It should be noted that many headwords and some essays appear in more than one place.

Decisions about where to put entries in relation to nations have been governed by a sense of where most users will expect to find them: thus there are entries at various points and in various combinations for Czechoslovakia, the Czech Republic, and Slovakia, for Belgium, the Low Countries, and The Netherlands. Similarly, in assigning entries to centuries it has generally been thought best to place them in the century with which they are usually associated, rather than strictly in relation to the subject's birth or an institution's creation. A number of these decisions may appear to be arbitrary: the reader is therefore advised to look at preceding and/or succeeding centuries for a particular entry or for a sense of the general background relating to it.

THEMATIC INDEX OF ENTRIES

Notes to the Reader

Structure: This book consists of two distinct but interrelated elements. The first (pp. 1–442) is a series of 51 essays: nineteen thematic studies (e.g. Missionary Printing; Paper), followed by 32 national and regional histories of 'the book' (*see* the Introduction). The second (pp. 443–1282) comprises 5,160 A–Z entries, ranging in length from short definitions to longer treatments of up to 2,000 words. These entries cover a broad spectrum of individuals (e.g. collectors, scholars, librarians, printers, booksellers, type designers, and the like) and institutions (e.g. monasteries and libraries, printing offices and publishing houses), as well as a variety of special subjects (such as authorship, forgers and forgery, and the material book)—see the Introduction and the Thematic Index of Entries. Two indexes and a system of cross-references, both explained below, link the two parts and point to salient connections throughout the entire text.

Cross-References: Three kinds of cross-references are used throughout the *Companion*. An asterisk designates the subject of an A–Z entry: 'J. *Ballantyne was an Edinburgh *literary agent and publisher of *novels and magazines.' A bold numeral sends the reader to one of the numbered essays: 'In Korea, metal type was used from early days in just such cases (*see* **41**)'—in this instance, to essay 41, 'The History of the Book in Korea'. A word or phrase in small capitals suggests that the reader consult a related topic: thus, at the end of the entry for **orphan** we read, '*See also* WIDOW.'

In instances where a topic might reasonably be found under another name, we have included a signpost (e.g. **page spread** *See* OPENING; **Sanskrit Press** *See* VIDYĀSĀGAR, ĪŚVARACANDRA) to direct the reader to the entry where it is located. Similarly, when a topic does not have an entry in the A–Z because it is treated at length in the essays, a signpost guides the reader to the appropriate essay, for example: **Qur'ān** *See* **2, 38**; **paper** *See* **10**.

Indexes: Unusually for an Oxford Companion, both the prelims and the endmatter of the *Companion* include indexes to help the reader. The Thematic Index of Entries at the front of Volume 1 (pp. xxix–lx) serves not only as a finding aid but also as a kind of intellectual cartography for the *Companion*. This index makes it possible to read the A–Z entries systematically in clusters (e.g. 19th-century American

publishers; Censorship, Pornography, and Control) and, we trust, readily enables the inquiring reader to perceive a network of connections that might otherwise go unrecognized. Using the Thematic Index, readers may navigate a course that has already been charted, or may more easily discover the way towards new explorations of their own.

The General Index at the end of Volume 2 (pp. 1283–1325) covers both parts of the *Companion* and includes the names of people, book businesses (e.g. publishing firms), and titles of books and MSS, except where these have their own entry in the A–Z. Such entries may be located in the first instance by consulting the alphabetical sequence (see below) and may also be found in the Thematic Index of Entries.

An additional aid for navigating the text of the *Companion* is the numbered contents immediately following the title of every essay. Longer entries in the A–Z also follow this scheme, making it easier for the reader to locate information efficiently.

Alphabetical sequence: A–Z entries are organized in alphabetical sequence letter by letter except 'Mc' and 'St' are treated as if spelled out in full as 'Mac' and 'Saint'. Arabic names with the definite article 'al-' as a prefix are arranged under the second element without being inverted—for example, **al-Muthanná** is found under 'M'. Knights are sequenced by first names rather than titles (e.g. **Nicholson, Sir Charles** comes before **Nicholson, E. W. B.**).

Some special cases: National libraries are sequenced under their respective countries and not under 'National'. Unless an institution is best known in the Anglophone world by its original name (e.g. Bibliothèque nationale), we use English with the original name immediately following, transliterating non-Roman alphabets according to established protocols (see below). When the libraries of institutions include an individual's name, their entries are sequenced under the form of the library name most commonly used—for example, the Bancroft Library at the University of California, Berkeley appears under '**Bancroft**', rather than 'California' or 'Berkeley'. Entries treating publishers, printers, and other book businesses are sequenced under the relevant surname, rather than the first word of the company name; thus, the former German publishing house of the Nazi Party (NSDAP) appears as '**Eher Nachf., F.**', rather than under 'Franz' or 'Verlag'. Similarly, literary prizes are found under the element of the name most commonly used: the **Man Booker Prize** is sequenced under 'B', and the **Samuel Johnson Prize** under 'J'.

Transliteration: Because much of the material in the *Companion* treats subjects from around the globe, we have employed various systems of transliteration for names and terms in non-roman alphabets to make them accessible to English-language readers. For Chinese, we have used the Pinyin system of transliteration. For established Westernized names, we include the Pinyin version in parenthesis after the Westernized version. For Japanese, we use the standard modified Hepburn system, although words that have been naturalized into English are spelled in the anglicized manner. Korean has been transliterated according to the standard McCune and Reischauer system. Throughout the text, we have maintained traditional word order for Asian proper names. For Russian and other Cyrillic languages, we use Library of Congress System II; in cases where names are well known in English, the reader will find the anglicized spelling common in Britain.

Non-English titles: We have not ordinarily translated the titles of works in major European languages other than English, but have provided translations where relevant for languages more likely to present significant difficulties for the majority of our readers. Throughout the *Companion*, book titles follow the capitalization rules of the languages in which they are given.

Dates: Dates for individuals referred to in the text are only given when it is not clear what period is being referred to. The General Index supplies dates for all named individuals except for those with their own entries in the A–Z. For biographical entries, when only one date is known, we have used 'b.' and 'd.' for birth and death dates; '*c.*' for *circa* and '*fl.*' for *floruit*. Alternative dates are indicated by an oblique slash (solidus): e.g. '1694/8' signifies 1694 or 1698. To indicate a sequence of dates, we have employed a hyphen in the standard manner, thus: 1753–7; 1853–1902. A range of dates is represented by a multiplication sign—'b. 1530×39' means born between 1530 and 1539; hence, '1842×7–1890' indicates that an individual was born between 1842 and 1847, and died in 1890. Attempting to be as accurate as possible, we have used two prefixes to indicate different kinds of uncertainty: '1743?', meaning it might have been in 1743, and '*c.*1743' indicating it was around the year 1743.

Secondary references: All the essays conclude with a highly selective list of secondary references including only the most important works available (often, but not necessarily, the author's sources for the essay itself), with a preference where appropriate for studies in English and major European languages. If a title has been translated into English, we give the English title only, including the translator's name. All URLs (www addresses) include a consultation date; unless otherwise specified, these web addresses carry the initial prefix 'http://', the default setting on most web browsers. The A–Z entries typically include secondary references proportionate to their length, providing the most essential references. Readers should consult the List of Abbreviations when perplexed.

Illustrations: The *Companion* includes about 170 pictures and drawings, nearly all of which were chosen not merely to illustrate but also to enhance the information provided in the essays and A–Z entries. Because texts are objects and their reproduction and transmission involve physical processes, the images in the *Companion* are not simply ornaments to the book, but are integral to its intellectual design. Accordingly, captions accompanying images are treated as an important part of the *Companion*'s text and are cross-referenced and indexed in the same manner as the essays and entries so that text and context will be mutually informing.

Assigning authorship: Authorship and the concomitant activity of attribution are important aspects of modern scholarship; hence, all but the shortest definitional entries in the *Companion* are signed by those who created them: full names for the 54 scholars who wrote essays and initials for those contributing A–Z entries—see the Index of Contributor Initials (pp. xxvi–xxviii). Brief biographies of all 398 authors (including the 28 Associate and Assistant Editors) may be found in the list of Editors and Contributors (pp. xiv–xxvi).

List of Abbreviations

1. Bibliographical abbreviations

ADB	*Australian Dictionary of Biography* Online Edition, www.adb.online.anu.edu.au/adbonline.htm
ADeuB	*Allgemeine Deutsche Biographie, 1875–1912*
AGB	*Archiv für Geschichte des Büchwesens*
AHR	*American Historical Review*
ALIAS	*ALIAS: Australia's Library, Information and Archives Services: An Encyclopaedia of Practice and Practitioners*, ed. H. Brian (3 vols, 1988–91)
Altick	R. D. Altick, *The English Common Reader* (1957; 2e, 1998)
ANB	*American National Biography* Online, www.anb.org/articles/home.html
Ascarelli and Menato	F. Ascarelli and M. Menato, *La tipografia del '500 in Italia* (1989)
BB	*Bulletin du Bibliophile*
BC	*Book Collector*
BH	*Book History*
BHR	*Bibliothèque d'humanisme et renaissance*
Bischoff	B. Bischoff, *Latin Palaeography*, tr. D. Ó Cróinín and D. Ganz (1990)
BJRL	*Bulletin of the John Rylands University Library of Manchester*
BLJ	*British Library Journal* (see also eBLJ)
Bloomfield, Directory	B. C. Bloomfield, *A Directory of Rare Book and Special Collections in the United Kingdom and the Republic of Ireland*, 2e (1997)
BLR	*Bodleian Library Record*
BMC	*Catalogue of Books Printed in the XVth Century now in the British Museum* (11 vols, 1908–2007; vols 1–9 repr. 1963)
BMQ	*British Museum Quarterly*
BNYPL	*Bulletin of the New York Public Library*
Bowers, Principles	F. Bowers, *Principles of Bibliographical Description* (1949)
BPPB	*Book Production and Publishing in Britain 1375–1475*, ed. J. Griffiths and D. A. Pearsall (1989)
BSANZ	*Bibliographical Society of Australia and New Zealand*
Butcher	J. Butcher, *Copy-Editing*, 4e (2006)
CBMLC	*Corpus of British Medieval Library Catalogues*, gen. ed. R. Sharpe (1990–)
CHB	*The Cambridge History of the Bible* (3 vols, 1963–70): 1: *From the Beginnings to Jerome*, ed.

	P. R. Ackroyd and C. F. Evans; 2: *The West, from the Fathers to the Reformation*, ed. G. W. H. Lampe; 3: *The West, from the Reformation to the Present Day*, ed. S. L. Greenslade
CHBB	*The Cambridge History of the Book in Britain*, 3: *1400–1557* (1999), ed. L. Hellinga and J. Trapp; 4: *1557–1695* (2002), ed. J. Barnard *et al.*; 5: *1695–1830* (2009), ed. M. F. Suarez, S.J., and M. Turner; 6: *1830–1914*, ed. D. McKitterick (2009)
CHLBI	*The Cambridge History of Libraries in Britain and Ireland*, ed. P. Hoare (3 vols, 2006)
DABC	D. C. Dickinson, *Dictionary of American Book Collectors* (1986)
DBF	*Dictionnaire de biographie française*
DBI	*Dizionario biografico degli italiani*
DCB	*Dictionary of Canadian Biography* Online, www.biographi.ca
DEL	P. Fouché *et al.*, eds., *Dictionnaire encyclopédique du livre* (2 vols, 2002–)
de Ricci	S. de Ricci, *English Collectors of Books and Manuscripts 1530–1930* (1930)
DLB	*Dictionary of Literary Biography*
DNZB	*Dictionary of New Zealand Biography*
DTEI	*Dizionario dei tipografi e degli editori italiani. Il Cinquecento*, ed. M. Menato *et al.*, vol. 1 (1997)
eBLJ	*British Library Journal:* www.bl.uk/eblj/index.html
EIDO	*Editori italiani dell'ottocento. Repertorio*, ed. A. Gigli Marchetti *et al.* (2004)
EMS	*English Manuscript Studies 1100–1700*
Enschedé, Typefoundries	C. Enschedé, *Typefoundries in the Netherlands*, tr., rev., and annotated by H. Carter (1978)
ESTC	*English Short Title Catalogue*
Fletcher	W. Y. Fletcher, *English Book Collectors* (1902)
Foot Festschrift	D. Pearson, ed., *For the Love of the Binding* (2000)
Gaskell, *NI*	P. Gaskell, *A New Introduction to Bibliography* (1972, repr. 1974)
Geldner	F. Geldner, *Die deutschen Inkunabeldrucker* (2 vols, 1968–70)
GJ	*Gutenberg-Jahrbuch*
GP	*De Gulden Passer*
Grove, *Music*	*The New Grove Dictionary of Music and Musicians*, ed. S. Sadie (29 vols, 2001)
GW	*Gesamtkatalog der Wiegendrucke* (1925–)

HBA	A History of the Book in America, 1: The Colonial Book in the Atlantic World, ed. H. Amory and D. D. Hall (2000); 2: An Extensive Republic: Print, Culture, and Society in the New Nation, ed. R. A. Gross and M. Kelley (2010); 3: The Industrial Book, 1840–1880, ed. S. E. Casper et al. (2007); 4: Print in Motion: The Expansion of Publishing and Reading in the United States, 1880–1940, ed. C. F. Kaestle and J. A. Radway (2009); 5: The Enduring Book: Print Culture in Postwar America, ed. D. Nord et al. (2009)	LGB	Lexikon des gesamten Buchwesens, ed. S. Corsten et al., 2e (1985–)
		Lowry	M. Lowry, The World of Aldus Manutius (1979)
		McKerrow, Introduction	R. B. McKerrow, An Introduction to Bibliography for Literary Students (1927)
		Middleton	B. Middleton, A History of English Craft Bookbinding Technique, 4e (1996)
		Moxon	J. Moxon, Mechanick Exercises of the Whole Art of Printing, ed. H. Davis and H. Carter, 2e (1962)
		NDB	Neue Deutsche Biographie (1953–)
HBC	History of the Book in Canada/ Histoire du livre et de l'imprimé au Canada, ed. P. L. Fleming and Y. Lamonde (3 vols, 2004–7)	Nixon and Foot	H. Nixon and M. Foot, The History of Decorated Bookbinding in England (1992)
		Norrie	I. Norrie, Mumby's Publishing and Bookselling in the 20th Century, 6e (1982)
HBPUS	J. Tebbel, A History of Book Publishing in the United States (4 vols, 1972–81)	OBS	Oxford Bibliographical Society
HDHB	Handbuch deutscher historischer Buchbestände in Europa (4 vols, 1999–2000)	ODCC	The Oxford Dictionary of the Christian Church, 3e (1997); rev. edn (2005)
		ODNB	The Oxford Dictionary of National Biography
Heal	A. Heal, The English Writing-Masters and their Copy-Books, 1570–1800 (1931)	OED	The Oxford English Dictionary
		PAAS	Proceedings of the American Antiquarian Society
HHBS	Handbuch der historischen Buchbestände in der Schweiz/ Répertoire des fonds imprimés anciens de la Suisse, www.zb.uzh.ch/hbhch/webpages/ hhch/index.html	PBA	Proceedings of the British Academy
		PBSA	Papers of the Bibliographical Society of America
		PBSC	Papers of the Bibliographical Society of Canada
Hills	R. L. Hills, Papermaking in Britain 1488–1988 (1988)	Pearson, Bookbinding	D. Pearson, English Bookbinding Styles 1450–1800 (2005)
HLB	Harvard Library Bulletin	Pearson, Provenance	D. Pearson, Provenance Research in Book History, 2e (1998)
Hunter	D. Hunter, Papermaking: The History and Technique of an Ancient Craft, 2e (1978)	PH	Publishing History
		PL	Private Library
IDLH	International Dictionary of Library Histories, ed. D. Stam (2001)	PMLA	Publications of the Modern Language Association of America
IEILS	J. Feather and P. Sturges, eds., International Encyclopedia of Information and Library Science, 2e (2003)	PULC	Princeton University Library Chronicle
		RES	Review of English Studies
		Reynolds and Wilson	L. D. Reynolds and N. G. Wilson, Scribes and Scholars, 3e (1991)
IGI	Indice Generale degli Incunaboli delle Biblioteche d'Italia (6 vols, 1943–81)	RFHL	Revue française d'histoire du livre
		Rose	J. Rose, The Intellectual Life of the British Working Classes (1991)
ISTC	Incunabula Short-Title Catalogue	RQ	Renaissance Quarterly
Italian Book	The Italian Book 1465–1800: Studies Presented to Dennis E. Rhodes on his 70th Birthday, ed. D. V. Reidy (1993)	SB	Studies in Bibliography
		SBTI	Scottish Book Trade Index, www.nls.uk/catalogues/resources/sbti
JPHS	Journal of the Printing Historical Society	SQ	Shakespeare Quarterly
JWCI	Journal of the Warburg and Courtauld Institutes	STC	A. W. Pollard and G. R. Redgrave, A Short-Title Catalogue of Books Printed in England, Scotland, & Ireland, 1475–1640, completed by Katharine F. Pantzer, begun by W. A. Jackson and F. S. Ferguson, 2e (3 vols, 1976–91)
LaB	La Bibliofilía	
Labarre	E. J. Labarre, Dictionary and Encyclopædia of Paper and Paper-Making (1952)	
		TCBS	Transactions of the Cambridge Bibliographical Society
Lavigne	J. R. Lavigne, Pulp & Paper Dictionary, 3e (1998)	TLS	Times Literary Supplement

TQ	*The Quarterly* (Journal of the British Association of Paper Historians)	g	gram(s)
		Ger.	German
Verfasserlexicon	*Die Deutsche Literatur des Mittelalters: Verfasserlexicon*, ed. W. Stammler *et al.*, 2e (14 vols, 1977–2008)	Gk	Greek
		Heb.	Hebrew
		Huntington	Henry E. Huntington Library, San Marino, Calif.
Vervliet, Sixteenth-Century	H. D. L. Vervliet, *Sixteenth-Century Printing Types of the Low Countries* (1968)	in.	inch(es)
		It.	Italian
Wiegand and Davis	W. A. Wiegand and D. G. Davis, eds., *Encyclopedia of Library History* (1994)	JRUL	John Rylands University Library, Manchester
Wing	D. F. Wing, *A Short-Title Catalogue of Books Printed in England, Scotland, Ireland, Wales and British America*, 2e (3 vols, 1972–88)	km	kilometre(s)
		Lambeth	Lambeth Palace Library, London
		Lat.	Latin
		LC	Library of Congress
YULG	*Yale University Library Gazette*	lit.	literally
ZfB	*Zeitschrift für Bücherfreunde*	ME	Middle English
		m	metre(s)
		mm	millimetre(s)
2. Other abbreviations		MS(S)	manuscript(s)
		NA	London, National Archives (formerly Public Record Office)
AD	*anno Domini*		
b.	born	NLS	National Library of Scotland, Edinburgh
bap.	baptized		
BC	before Christ	NLW	National Library of Wales, Aberystwyth
BCE	before the Common Era		
BL	British Library	no.	number
BnF	Bibliothèque nationale de France, Paris	NS	new series
Bodleian	Bodleian Library, Oxford	OE	Old English
c.	*circa*; cent(s)	Ph.D.	Doctor of Philosophy
CE	Common Era	pl.	plural
cm	centimetre(s)	PML	Pierpont Morgan Library, New York
col.	column (cited as 'a', 'b', and so on)	*pseud.*	pseudonym
cols	columns	r	recto
CUL	Cambridge University Library	r.	reigned, ruled
d.	died	repr.	reprint(ed)
d.	penny, pence	rev.	revised (by); reviewed by
diss.	dissertation	Revd	Reverend
D.Phil.	Doctor of Philosophy	*s.*	shilling(s)
Dr	Doctor	ser.	series
Du.	Dutch	sig.	signature
e	edition (e.g. 2e, 'second edition')	sing.	singular
ed.	editor(s)	s.n.	*sub nomine*
edn	edition	Sp.	Spanish
Eng.	English	St	Saint
et al.	*et alii* (and others)	suppl.	Supplement
f.	and following	s.v.	*sub verbo*
ff.	and following (plural)	TCD	Trinity College, Dublin
fig.	figure	tr.	translated by, translation, translator
fl.	*floruit*	UL	University Library
fo.	folio	v	verso
Folger	Folger Shakespeare Library, Washington, DC	V&A	National Art Library, Victoria and Albert Museum, London
fos.	folios	vol.	volume
Fr.	French	vols	volumes

1 Writing Systems

Andrew Robinson

1 The emergence of writing

Without writing, there would be no recording, no history, and of course no books. The creation of writing permitted the command of a ruler and his seal to extend far beyond his sight and voice, and even to survive his death. If the Rosetta Stone did not exist, for example, the world would be virtually unaware of the nondescript Egyptian king Ptolemy V Epiphanes, whose priests promulgated his decree upon the stone in three *scripts: hieroglyphic, demotic, and (Greek) alphabetic.

How did writing begin? The favoured explanation, until the Enlightenment in the 18th century, was divine origin. Today, many—probably most—scholars accept that the earliest writing evolved from accountancy, though it is puzzling that such accounts are little in evidence in the surviving writing of ancient Egypt, India, China, and Central America (which does not preclude commercial record-keeping on perishable materials such as bamboo in these early civilizations). In other words, some time in the late 4th millennium BC, in the cities of Sumer in Mesopotamia, the 'cradle of civilization', the complexity of trade and administration reached a point where it outstripped the power of memory among the governing elite. To record transactions in an indisputable, permanent form became essential.

Some scholars believe that a conscious search for a solution to this problem by an unknown Sumerian individual in the city of Uruk (biblical Erech), c.3300 BC, produced writing. Others posit that writing was the work of a group, presumably of clever admin-istrators and merchants. Still others think it was not an invention at all, but an accidental discovery. Many regard it as the result of evolution over a long period, rather than a flash of inspiration. One particularly well-aired theory holds that writing grew out of a long-standing counting system of clay 'tokens'. Such 'tokens'—varying from simple, plain discs to more complex, incised shapes whose exact purpose is unknown—have been found in many Middle Eastern archaeological sites, and have been dated from 8000 to 1500 BC. The substitution of two-dimensional symbols in clay for these three-dimensional tokens was a first step towards writing, according to this theory. One major difficulty is that the 'tokens' continued to exist long after the emergence of Sumerian cuneiform writing; another is that a two-dimensional symbol on a clay *tablet might be thought to be a less, not a more, advanced concept than a three-dimensional clay 'token'. It seems more likely that 'tokens' accompanied the emergence of writing, rather than giving rise to writing.

Apart from the 'tokens', numerous examples exist of what might be termed 'proto-writing'. They include the Ice Age symbols found in caves in southern France, which are probably 20,000 years old. A cave at Peche Merle, in the Lot, contains a lively Ice Age graffito showing a stencilled hand and a pattern of red dots. This may simply mean: 'I was here, with my animals'—or perhaps the symbolism is deeper. Other prehistoric images show animals such as horses, a stag's head, and bison, overlaid with signs; and notched bones have been found that apparently served as lunar calendars.

1

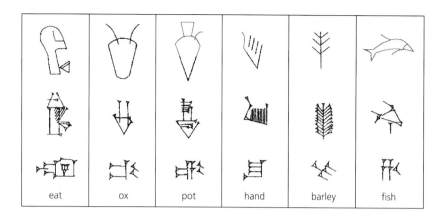

Fig. 1 Some cuneiform signs, showing the pictographic form (c.3000 BC), an early cuneiform representation (c.2400 BC), and the late Assyrian form (c.650 BC), now turned through 90 degrees, with the meaning.

eat ox pot hand barley fish

'Proto-writing' is not writing in the full sense of the word. A scholar of writing, the Sinologist John DeFrancis, has defined 'full' writing as a 'system of graphic symbols that can be used to convey any and all thought'—a concise and influential definition. According to this, 'proto-writing' would include, in addition to Ice Age cave symbols and Middle Eastern clay 'tokens', the Pictish symbol stones and tallies such as the fascinating knotted Inca quipus, but also contemporary sign systems such as international transportation symbols, highway code signs, computer icons, and mathematical and musical notation. None of these ancient or modern systems is capable of expressing 'any and all thought', but each is good at specialized communication (DeFrancis, *Visible Speech*, 4).

2 Development and diffusion of writing systems

To express the full range of human thought requires a writing system intimately linked with spoken language. For, as the founder of modern linguistics, Ferdinand de Saussure, wrote, language may be compared to a sheet of paper: 'Thought is on one side of the sheet and sound on the reverse side. Just as it is impossible to take a pair of scissors and cut one side of the paper without at the same time cutting the other, so it is impossible in a language to isolate sound from thought, or thought from sound' (Saussure, 111).

The symbols of what may have become the first 'full' writing system are generally thought to have been pictograms: iconic drawings of, say, a pot, or a fish, or a head with an open jaw (representing the concept of eating). These have been found in Mesopotamia and Egypt dating to the mid-4th millennium BC, in the Indus Valley dating to the 3rd millennium, and in China dating to as early as the 5th millennium, accord-

ing to the (doubtful) claims of some Chinese archaeologists. In many cases, their iconicity soon became so abstract that it is barely perceptible to us. Fig. 1 shows how the Sumerian pictograms developed into the wedge-shaped cuneiform signs that went on to dominate Middle Eastern writing for some 3,000 years.

Yet pictograms were insufficient to express the kinds of words, and their constituent parts, that cannot be depicted. Essential to the development of 'full' writing, as opposed to limited, purely pictographic, 'proto-writing', was the discovery of the *rebus principle. This radical idea, from the Latin meaning 'by things', enables phonetic values to be represented by pictographic symbols. Thus in English, a picture of a bee beside the figure 4 might (if one were so minded) represent 'before', and a bee with a picture of a tray might stand for 'betray', while a picture of an ant next to a buzzing beehive full of honey, might (less obviously) represent 'Anthony'. Egyptian hieroglyphs are full of rebuses, for instance the 'sun' sign, ☉, pronounced $R(a)$ or $R(e)$, is the first symbol in the hieroglyphic spelling of the pharaoh Ramesses. In an early Sumerian tablet, the abstract word 'reimburse' is represented by a picture of a reed, because 'reimburse' and 'reed' shared the same phonetic value, *gi*, in the Sumerian language.

Once writing of this 'full' kind, capable of expressing the complete range of speech and thought, was invented, accidentally discovered, or evolved, did it then diffuse throughout the globe from Mesopotamia? It appears that the earliest such writing in Egypt dates from 3100 BC, that in the Indus Valley (undeciphered seal stones) from 2500 BC, that in Crete (the undeciphered Linear A script) from 1750 BC, that in China (the 'oracle bones') from 1200 BC, and that in Mexico (the undeciphered Olmec script) from 900 BC—all dates are approximate and subject to new archaeological discoveries. On this basis, it seems reasonable that the *idea* of writing, but not the signs of a particular script, could have spread gradually from culture to distant culture. After all, 600 or 700 years were required for the idea of printing to reach Europe from China (if we discount the isolated and enigmatic Phaistos disc of *c.*1700 BC, found in Crete in 1908, which appears to be 'printed'), and even longer for the idea of paper to spread to Europe (*see* **10**): why should writing not have reached China from Mesopotamia over an even longer period?

Nevertheless, in the absence of solid evidence for transmission of the idea (even in the case of the much more proximate civilizations of Mesopotamia and Egypt), a majority of scholars prefer to think that writing developed independently in the major civilizations of the ancient world. The optimist, or at any rate the anti-imperialist, will choose to emphasize the intelligence and inventiveness of human societies; the pessimist, who takes a more conservative view of history, will tend to assume that humans prefer to copy what already exists, as faithfully as they can, restricting their innovations to cases of absolute necessity. The latter is the favoured explanation for how the Greeks (at the beginning of the 1ˢᵗ millennium BC) borrowed the alphabet from the Phoenicians, adding in the process signs for the vowels not written in the Phoenician script (*see* **3**). There are many other examples of script borrowings, such as the Japanese taking the Chinese characters in the 1ˢᵗ millennium AD and incorporating them into a highly complex writing system that mixes several thousand Chinese characters with slightly fewer than 100, much simpler, syllabic symbols of Japanese origin. If ever the Rongorongo script of Easter Island—the most isolated inhabited spot on earth—is deciphered, it may shed light on the intriguing question of whether the Easter Islanders invented Rongorongo unaided, brought the idea of writing from Polynesia in their canoes, or borrowed it from Europeans who first visited Easter Island in the 18ᵗʰ century. If Rongorongo could be proved to have been invented unaided on Easter Island, this would at last guarantee that writing must have had multiple origins, rather than radiating from a single source.

3 Decipherment

In ordinary conversation, to decipher someone's 'indecipherable' handwriting means to make sense of the meaning; it does not imply that one can read every single word. In its more technical sense, as applied to ancient scripts, 'deciphered' means different things to different scholars. At one extreme, everyone agrees that the Egyptian hieroglyphs have been deciphered—because every trained Egyptologist would make the same sense of virtually every word of a given hieroglyphic inscription (though their individual translations would still differ, as do all independent translations of the same work from one language into another). At the other extreme, (almost) every scholar agrees that the script of the Indus Valley civilization is undeciphered—because no one can make sense of its seals and other inscriptions to the satisfaction of anyone else. Between these extremes lies a vast spectrum of opinion. In the case of the Mayan hieroglyphic writing of Central America, for example, most scholars agree that a high proportion, as much as 85 per cent, of the inscriptions can be meaningfully read, and yet there remain large numbers of individual Mayan glyphs that are contentious or obscure. No absolute distinction exists by which a script can be judged to be deciphered or undeciphered; we should instead speak of *degrees* of *decipherment. The most useful criterion is that a proposed decipherment can generate consistent readings from new samples of the script, preferably produced by persons other than the original decipherer.

In this sense, the Egyptian hieroglyphs were deciphered in the 1820s by Jean-François Champollion and others; Babylonian cuneiform in the 1850s by Henry Creswicke Rawlinson and others; Mycenaean Linear B in 1952–3 by Michael Ventris; and the Mayan hieroglyphs by Yuri Knorozov and others in the 1950s and after—to name only the most important of the successful decipherments. This leaves a number of significant undeciphered scripts, such as the Etruscan script from Italy, the Indus Valley script from Pakistan/India, Linear A from Crete, the Meroitic script from Sudan, the Proto-Elamite script from Iran/Iraq, Rongorongo from Easter Island, and the Olmec, Zapotec, and Isthmian scripts from Mexico. They may be resolved into three basic categories: an unknown script writing a known language; a known script writing an unknown language; and an unknown script writing an unknown language. The Mayan hieroglyphs were until their decipherment an example of the first category, since the Mayan languages are still spoken, and the Zapotec script may be, too, if it writes a language related to modern Zapotec; Etruscan writing is an example of the second category, since the Etruscan script is basically the same as the Greek alphabet, but the Etruscan language is not related to Indo-European or other languages; while the Indus Valley script is an example of the last category, since the script bears

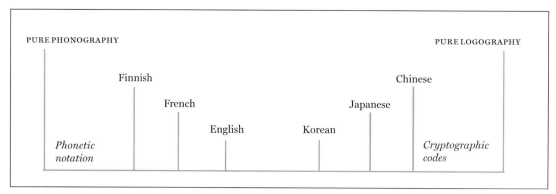

Fig. 2 A schematic diagram of phonography and logography in writing systems.

no resemblance to any other script and the language of the civilization does not appear to have survived (unless, as some scholars speculate, it is related to the Dravidian languages of south India).

In each undeciphered case, the techniques used in successful decipherments have been applied, with varying results. Ventris—perhaps the most ingenious of all the decipherers, since he alone had no help from a bilingual aid like the Rosetta Stone—gave a masterly summary of the science and art of decipherment:

Each operation needs to be planned in three phases: an exhaustive *analysis* of the signs, words, and contexts in all the available inscriptions, designed to extract every possible clue as to the spelling system, meaning and language structure; an experimental *substitution* of phonetic values to give possible words and inflections in a known or postulated language; and a decisive *check*, preferably with the aid of virgin material, to ensure that the apparent results are not due to fantasy, coincidence or circular reasoning. (Ventris, 200)

4 Classification of writing systems

Europeans and Americans of ordinary *literacy must recognize and write around 52 alphabetic signs (26 capital letters and their lower-case equivalents), and sundry other signs, such as numerals, punctuation marks, and 'whole-word' semantic signs, for example +, =, &, %, £, $, which are generally called logograms or *analphabetics. Japanese readers, by contrast, are supposed to know and be able to write some 2,000 signs, and, if they are highly educated, must recognize 5,000 signs or more. The two situations, in Europe/America and in Japan, appear to be poles apart. In fact, however, the different writing systems resemble each other more than at first appears.

Contrary to what many people think, all scripts that are 'full' writing (in the sense defined by DeFrancis

above) operate on one basic principle. Both alphabets and the Chinese and Japanese scripts use symbols to represent sounds (i.e. phonetic signs); and all writing systems mix such phonetic symbols with logographic symbols (i.e. semantic signs). What differs between writing systems—apart from the forms of the signs, of course—is the *proportion* of phonetic to semantic signs. The higher the proportion of phonetic representation in a script, the easier it is to guess the pronunciation of a word. In English the proportion is high, in Chinese it is low. Thus, English spelling represents English speech sound by sound more accurately than Chinese characters represent Mandarin speech; but Finnish spelling represents the Finnish language better than English spelling represents spoken English. The Finnish script is highly efficient phonetically, while the Chinese (and Japanese) script is phonetically seriously deficient—as indicated in Fig. 2.

There is thus no such thing as a 'pure' writing system, that is, a 'full' writing system capable of expressing meaning entirely through alphabetic letters or syllabic signs or logograms—because all 'full' writing systems are a mixture of phonetic and semantic signs. How best to classify writing systems is therefore a controversial matter. For example, some scholars deny the existence of alphabets prior to the Greek alphabet, on the grounds that the Phoenician script marked only consonants, no vowels (like the early *Arabic script). Nevertheless, classifying labels are useful to remind us of the predominant nature of different systems. The tree shown in Fig. 3 divides writing systems according to this criterion, not according to their age; it does *not* show how one writing system may have given rise to another historically. (The broken lines indicate possible influences of one system upon another, for example Chinese characters on the Japanese syllabic 'kana'.) Thus, the Phoenician script is labelled a 'consonantal alphabet', with the emphasis

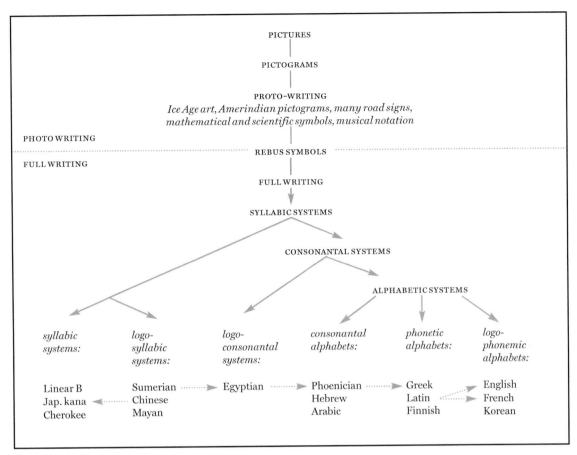

Fig. 3 The classification of writing systems.

on its consonants and without significant *logography, in contrast to the 'logo-consonantal' system of Egyptian hieroglyphs, where logography dominates but there is also a phonetic element based on the consonants—24 signs, each representing a consonant. The tree's terminology is self-explanatory, except perhaps for 'phonemic': the phoneme is the smallest contrastive unit in the sound system of a language, for example the English vowel phonemes /e/ and /a/ in *set* and *sat*, and the consonantal phonemes /b/ and /p/ in *bat* and *pat*.

5 The origin of the alphabet

If the emergence of writing is full of riddles, then the enigma of the first alphabet is even more perplexing. That the alphabet reached the modern world via the ancient Greeks is well known—the word 'alphabet' comes from the first two of the Greek letters, alpha and beta—but we have no clear idea of how and when the alphabet appeared in Greece; how the Greeks thought of adding letters standing for the vowels as well as the consonants; and how, even more fundamentally, the idea of an alphabet occurred to the pre-Greek societies at the eastern end of the Mediterranean during the 2nd millennium BC. The first well-attested alphabets belong to ancient Ugarit, today's Ras Shamra on the coast of Syria, where a 30-sign cuneiform alphabet was used in the 14th century BC; and to the Phoenicians in Canaan in the late 2nd millennium BC, who used 22 consonantal letters.

Scholars have devoted their lives to these questions, but the evidence is too scanty for firm conclusions. It is not known whether the alphabet evolved from the scripts of Mesopotamia (cuneiform), Egypt (hieroglyphs), and Crete (Linear A and B)—or whether it struck a single unknown individual 'in a flash'. Nor is it known why an alphabet was thought necessary. It seems most likely that it was the result of commercial imperatives. In other words, commerce demanded a simpler and quicker means of recording transactions than, say, Babylonian cuneiform or Egyptian hieroglyphs, and also a convenient way to note the babel of languages of the various empires and groups trading with each other around the Mediterranean. If so, then it is surprising that there is no evidence of trade and commerce in the early alphabetic inscriptions of Greece. This, and other considerations, have led a few scholars to postulate, controversially, that the Greek alphabet was invented to record the oral epics of Homer in the 8th century BC.

In the absence of proof, anecdote and myth have filled the vacuum. Children are often evoked as inventors of the alphabet, because they would not have had the preconceptions of adult writers and their elders' investment in existing scripts. One possibility is that a bright Canaanite child in northern Syria, fed up with having to learn cuneiform and hieroglyphs, borrowed from the hieroglyphs the familiar idea of a small number of signs standing for single consonants and then invented some new signs for the basic consonantal sounds of his own Semitic language. Perhaps the child first doodled the signs in the dust of some ancient street: a simple outline of a house, Semitic 'beth' (the 'bet' in 'alphabet'), became the sign for 'b'. In the 20th century, Rudyard Kipling's child protagonist in 'How the Alphabet Was Made', Taffimai, designs what she calls 'noise-pictures'. The letter 'A' is a picture of a carp with its barbelled mouth wide open; this, Taffimai tells her father, looks like his open mouth when he utters the sound *ah*. The letter 'O' matches the egg-or-stone shape and resembles her father's mouth saying *oh*. The letter 'S' represents a snake, and stands for the hissing sound of the snake. In this somewhat far-fetched way, a whole alphabet is created by Taffimai.

To quote an earlier poet, William Blake wrote in *Jerusalem*: 'God ... in mysterious Sinai's awful cave / To Man the wond'rous art of writing gave'. A small sphinx in the British Museum at one time seemed to show that Blake was right, at least about the origin of the alphabet. The sphinx was found in 1905 at Serabit el-Khadim in Sinai, a desolate place remote from civilization, by the famous Egyptologist Flinders Petrie. He was excavating some old turquoise mines that were active in ancient Egyptian times. Petrie dated the sphinx to the middle of the 18th Dynasty; today, its date is thought to be *c*.1500 BC. On one side of it is a strange inscription; on the other, and between the paws, there are further inscriptions of the same kind, plus some Egyptian hieroglyphs that read: 'beloved of Hathor, mistress of turquoise'. Similar inscriptions were written on the rocks of this remote area.

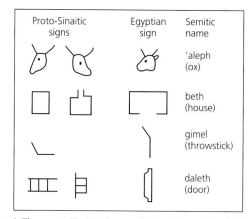

Fig. 4 The proto-Sinaitic theory of the origin of the alphabet.

Petrie guessed that the unknown script was probably an alphabet, because it comprised fewer than 30 signs (out of a much larger number of text characters); and he thought that its language was probably Semitic, since he knew that Semites from Canaan—modern Israel and Lebanon—had worked these mines, in many cases as slaves. Ten years later another distinguished Egyptologist, Alan Gardiner, studied the 'proto-Sinaitic' signs and noted resemblances between some of them and certain pictographic Egyptian hieroglyphs. Gardiner now named each sign with the Semitic word equivalent to the sign's meaning in Egyptian (the Semitic words were known from biblical scholarship) (*see* Fig. 4). These Semitic names are the same as the names of the letters of the Hebrew alphabet—a fact that did not surprise Gardiner, since he knew that the Hebrews had lived in Canaan in the late 2nd millennium BC. However, although the names are the same, the shapes of the Hebrew letters are different from the proto-Sinaitic signs, suggesting that any link between them cannot be a straightforward one.

Gardiner's hypothesis enabled him to translate one of the inscriptions that occurred on the sphinx from Serabit el-Khadim as 'Baalat'—in English transcription with the vowels spelt out. (Hebrew and other Semitic scripts do not directly indicate vowels; readers guess them from their knowledge of the language, as explained in 'The family of alphabets' below.) Gardiner's reading made sense: Baalat means 'the Lady' and is a recognized Semitic name for the goddess Hathor in the Sinai region. Accordingly, the inscription on the sphinx seemed to be an Egyptian-Semitic bilingual. Unfortunately, no further decipherment proved tenable, mainly because of lack of material and the fact that many of the proto-Sinaitic signs had no hieroglyphic equivalents. Scholarly hopes of finding the story of the Exodus in these scratchings were scotched. Nevertheless, it is conceivable that a script similar to the proto-Sinaitic script was used by Moses to write the Ten Commandments on the tablets of stone.

It is still not known whether Gardiner's 1916 guess was correct, plausible though it is. For some decades after Petrie's discoveries in Sinai, the inscriptions were taken to be the 'missing link' between the Egyptian hieroglyphs and the cuneiform alphabet at Ugarit and the Phoenician alphabet. But it seems unconvincing that lowly—and presumably illiterate—miners in out-of-the-way Sinai should have created an alphabet; prima facie, they seem to be unlikely inventors. Subsequent discoveries in Lebanon and Israel have shown the Sinaitic theory of the alphabet to be a romantic fiction. These inscriptions, dated to the 17th and 16th centuries BC—a little earlier than the proto-Sinaitic inscriptions—suggest that the people then living in the land of Canaan were the inventors of the alphabet, which would be reasonable. They were cosmopolitan traders at the crossroads of the Egyptian, Hittite, Babylonian, and Cretan empires; they were not wedded to an existing writing system; they needed a script that was easy to learn, quick to write, and unambiguous. Although unproven, it is probable that the (proto-)Canaanites were the first to use an alphabet.

In the late 1990s, however, the picture was further complicated by new discoveries in Egypt itself; and a revised version of the Gardiner theory now seems plausible. In 1999, two Egyptologists, John Coleman Darnell and his wife, Deborah, announced that they had found examples of what appeared to be alphabetic writing at Wadi el-Hol, west of Thebes, while they were surveying ancient travel routes in the southern Egyptian desert. The date of the inscriptions is c.1900–1800 BC, which places them considerably earlier than the inscriptions from Lebanon and Israel, and makes them the earliest known alphabetic writings.

The two short inscriptions are written in a Semitic script and, according to the experts, the letters were most probably developed in a fashion similar to a semi-*cursive form of the Egyptian script. The writer is thought to have been a scribe travelling with a group of mercenaries (there were many such mercenaries working for the pharaohs). If the Darnell theory turns out to be correct, then it appears that the alphabetic idea was after all inspired by the Egyptian hieroglyphs and invented in Egypt, rather than in Palestine. This latest evidence is by no means conclusive, however, and the search for more alphabetic inscriptions in Egypt continues.

6 The family of alphabets

From its unclear origins on the eastern shores of the Mediterranean, writing employing the alphabetic principle spread—westwards (via Greek) to the Romans and thence to modern Europe, eastwards (via Aramaic, in all probability) to India and thence to Southeast Asia. By the 20th century, as a consequence of colonial empires, most of the world's peoples except the Chinese and Japanese were writing in alphabetic scripts. These employ on average between 20 and 40 basic signs; the smallest, Rotokas, used in Papua New Guinea, has 12 letters, the largest, Khmer, used in Cambodia, has 74 letters.

The western alphabetic link between the Greeks and the Romans was Etruscan—as is clear from the early Greek letter-forms inscribed on Etruscan objects dating from the 7th century BC, which were then borrowed for early Latin inscriptions. This early acquisition from Greek accounts for the differences between some modern European letter forms and the modern Greek letters, which are based on a later Greek alphabet known as Ionian that became standard in Greece in 403–2 BC. The eastern alphabetic link is indicated by the fact that in Mesopotamia, by the 5th century BC, many cuneiform documents carried a notation of their substance in the 22 letters of the Aramaic alphabet, inked onto the tablet with a *writing brush. From the time of Alexander the Great onwards, cuneiform was increasingly superseded by Aramaic; it eventually fell into disuse around the beginning of the Christian era, with the last cuneiform inscription dated AD 75. In Egypt, fairly soon after that, the Coptic alphabet (consisting of 24 Greek letters plus 6 letters borrowed from Egyptian demotic script) supplanted Egyptian hieroglyphs; the last Egyptian hieroglyphic inscription is dated AD 394.

The Aramaic script is the ancestor of modern Arabic, the sacred script of Islam, and of modern ('square') Hebrew script, as used in Israel (see **8**). (A second Hebrew script, known as 'old Hebrew', evolved from the Phoenician script and disappeared from secular use with the dispersion of the Jews in the 6th century BC.) The first independent Arab kingdom, that of the Nabataeans, centred on Petra in modern Jordan, spoke a form of Arabic but wrote in the Aramaic script. The presence of certain distinctively Arabic forms and words in these Aramaic inscriptions eventually gave way to the writing of the Arabic language in Nabataean Aramaic script. This was the precursor of the Arabic script, which arose during the first half of the 1st millennium AD and replaced the Aramaic script (see **38**).

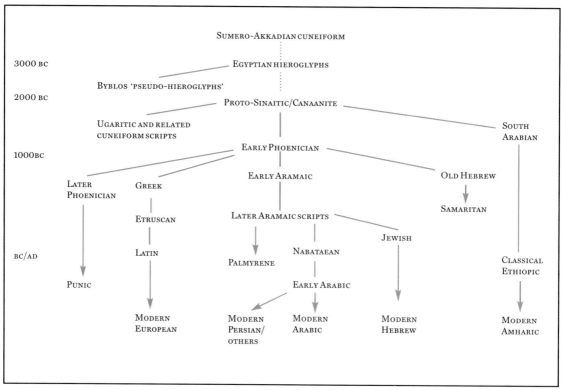

SUMERO-AKKADIAN CUNEIFORM

3000 BC   EGYPTIAN HIEROGLYPHS

BYBLOS 'PSEUDO-HIEROGLYPHS'

2000 BC   PROTO-SINAITIC/CANAANITE

UGARITIC AND RELATED   SOUTH
CUNEIFORM SCRIPTS   ARABIAN

1000BC   EARLY PHOENICIAN

       LATER   GREEK   EARLY ARAMAIC   OLD HEBREW
       PHOENICIAN

                                     SAMARITAN
         ETRUSCAN   LATER ARAMAIC SCRIPTS

                                   JEWISH
         LATIN   NABATAEAN
BC/AD   PALMYRENE   CLASSICAL
                                        ETHIOPIC
    PUNIC   EARLY ARABIC

MODERN   MODERN   MODERN   MODERN   MODERN
EUROPEAN   PERSIAN/   ARABIC   HEBREW   AMHARIC
             OTHERS

Fig. 5 The evolution of the main European alphabetic scripts.

Both the Arabic and Hebrew scripts write only the consonants, not the vowels, in their respective Semitic languages, using 28 letters in Arabic and 22 in Hebrew. Thus, the three letters in modern Hebrew that stand for *ktb* or *ktv* can take the meanings: 'katav' (I wrote), 'kotav' (I write, a writer), 'katoov' (written), 'kitav' (letters, script), and even 'kitovet' (address), 'kitoobah' (marriage certificate), or 'katban' (scribe). In practice, however, various additional signs have been developed to aid the reader in pronouncing the Hebrew and Arabic vowels. The commonest of these is a system of dots placed above and below a letter, referred to as 'vowel points' or *matres lectionis* (Latin for 'mothers of reading').

The time chart in Fig. 5 shows the main lines of emergence of the modern alphabetic scripts from the Proto-Sinaitic/Canaanite scripts of the 2nd millennium BC. It does not include the Indian scripts and their Southeast Asian derivatives, since their connection with Aramaic is problematic and, strictly speaking, unproven. (The earliest Indian scripts, leaving aside the undeciphered Indus Valley writing, are Kharosthi and Brahmi, used in the rock edicts of the emperor Ashoka in the 3rd century BC.) Nor does the chart show later alphabets such as the Cyrillic alphabet used in Russia, which was adapted from the Greek alphabet in the 9th century AD (*see* **35**), the Korean Hangul alphabet invented by King Sejong in the 15th century (*see* **41**), or the so-called Cherokee alphabet (really a syllabary), invented by a Native American, Sequoya, in the US around 1821. Also excluded are runes, since the origin of the runic alphabet, in the 2nd century AD or earlier, though clearly influenced by the Roman alphabet, is not known (*see* **26**).

7 Chinese and Japanese writing

If great claims are made for the power of the alphabet, even greater ones attach to Chinese writing. The evident complexity of the system encourages the notion that it operates quite differently from other modern writing systems. The obscurity of its origins—which may or may not have involved foreign stimulus from, for example, Mesopotamian writing—reinforces its apparent uniqueness. The antiquity of the modern Chinese characters, many of which are clearly recognizable in the Shang 'oracle bone' inscriptions of about 1200 BC, further supports this view, abetted by nationalist pride in the system's exceptional longevity, which exceeds that of cuneiform and equals that of the Egyptian hieroglyphs.

The most important claim is that Chinese characters are 'ideographic'—a word now generally avoided by scholars in favour of the more specific 'logographic'. That is, the characters are thought to be capable of communicating ideas without the intervention of phoneticism or indeed spoken language. Thus, Chinese speakers of Mandarin and Cantonese who do not know each other's 'dialect' and cannot talk to each other are said to be able to communicate in writing through Chinese characters. Some scholars (both Chinese and westerners) have even claimed that the same scenario applies to Chinese, Japanese, Korean, and Vietnamese speakers, whose languages differ greatly but who have shared the use of Chinese characters in their scripts. This, of course, would be inconceivable for equivalent English, French, German, and Italian speakers, who also share one (Roman) script. The implication is that the Chinese writing system works in a completely different way from scripts with a large phonographic component: writing systems are therefore said to come in two fundamental varieties, one ideographic (e.g. Chinese), the other phonographic (e.g. alphabets).

Each of these claims is false. No 'full' writing system, as already explained, can be divorced from the sounds of a spoken language. Written Chinese is based on Mandarin, also known as Putonghua ('common speech'), a language spoken by over 70 per cent of Chinese—hence the myth of the universal intelligibility of Chinese characters. A speaker of Cantonese wishing to communicate in writing with a speaker of Mandarin must learn Mandarin as well as the characters. The characters have both a phonetic and a semantic component, which readers must learn to recognize. The former gives a clue to the pronunciation of the character, the latter to its meaning. Generally, the phonetic component proves a better guide to pronunciation than the semantic does to meaning—contrary to predictions based on the ideographic notion of Chinese.

The Japanese language differs greatly from the Chinese, phonologically, grammatically, and syntactically. Even so, the Japanese based their writing system on the Chinese characters, as remarked earlier. In borrowing the thousands of Chinese signs during the early centuries of the 1st millennium AD, the Japanese altered the original Chinese pronunciation in particular ways corresponding to the sounds of the Japanese language. (Indeed 'kanji', the Japanese word for Chinese character, is an approximation of the Mandarin term 'hanzi'.) Eventually, they invented two fairly small sets of supplementary phonetic signs, the syllabic 'kana' (46 'hiragana' and 46 'katakana')—the forms of which are actually simplified versions of the Chinese characters—in order to make clear how the characters were to be pronounced in Japanese and how to transcribe native words. It would have been simpler, one might reasonably think, if the Japanese had used *only* these invented signs and had abandoned the Chinese characters altogether—but this would have entailed the rejection of an ancient writing system of huge prestige. Just as a knowledge of Latin was until quite recently a *sine qua non* for the educated European, so a familiarity with Chinese has always been considered essential by the Japanese literati.

8 Electronic writing

As the 6th millennium of recorded civilization opened, Mesopotamia was again at the centre of historical events. Where once, at the birth of writing, the statecraft of absolute rulers like Hammurabi and Darius was recorded in Sumerian, Babylonian, Assyrian, and Old Persian cuneiform on clay and stone, now the Iraq wars against Saddam Hussein generated millions of mainly alphabetic words on paper and on the *World Wide Web written in a babel of world languages.

Yet, although today's technologies of writing are immeasurably different from those of the 3rd millennium BC, its linguistic principles have not changed very much since the composition of the Sumerian epic of Gilgamesh (*see* **19**). However, the seismic impact of electronic writing and archiving on information distribution and research has polarized the debate about the correct definition of 'writing'. Must 'full' writing depend on a spoken language, as maintained in this essay? Or can it float free of its phonetic anchor?

Although some people persist in thinking that the digital revolution since the 1990s has made little or no difference to what happens in their minds when they actually read, write, and think, others as stoutly maintain that the *digitization of writing is radically altering our absorption of knowledge and will at last usher in the ideographic utopia imagined by the philosopher Gottfried Wilhelm Leibniz in the 1690s: 'As regards signs, I see … clearly that it is to the interest of the Republic of Letters and especially of students, that learned men should reach agreement on signs' (Mead and Modley, 58). Moreover, this faith in the increasing intelligence of computers—with their ubiquitous pictographic and logographic icons—chimes with many scholars' growing respect for the intelligence behind ancient scripts. Down with the monolithic 'triumph of

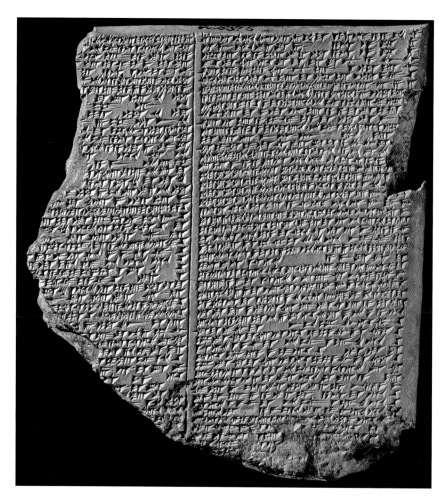

Fig. 6 A clay tablet in cuneiform script from Nineveh, in northern Iraq, written in the 7th century BC, showing part of the epic of Gilgamesh. Associated with *Ashurbanipal, king of Assyria, the *tablets were identified in 1872 by George Smith in the British Museum's collections.

the alphabet', they say, and up with Chinese characters, Egyptian hieroglyphs, and Mayan glyphs, with their hybrid mixtures of pictographic, logographic, and phonetic signs. This conviction has in turn encouraged a belief in the need to see each writing system as enmeshed within a whole culture, instead of viewing it simply as a technical solution to a problem of efficient visual representation of the culture's language. Although one may or may not share the belief in the power of digitization, and one may remain sceptical about the expressive virtues of logography, this holistic view of writing systems is surely a healthy development that reflects the real relationship between writing and society in all its subtlety and complexity.

BIBLIOGRAPHY
[British Museum,] *Reading the Past* (1990)
M. Coe, *Breaking the Maya Code*, 2e (1999)
P. Daniels and W. Bright, eds., *The World's Writing Systems* (1996)
J. Darnell, ed., *Two Early Alphabetic Inscriptions from the Wadi El-Hol* (2006)
J. DeFrancis, *The Chinese Language* (1984)
— *Visible Speech* (1989)
A. Gardiner, 'The Egyptian Origin of the Semitic Alphabet', *Journal of Egyptian Archaeology*, 3 (1916), 1–6
R. Harris, *The Origin of Writing* (1986)
S. Houston, ed., *The First Writing* (2004)
M. Mead and R. Modley, 'Communication Among All People, Everywhere', *Natural History*, 77.7 (1968), 56–63
M. Pope, *The Story of Decipherment*, 2e (1999)
A. Robinson, *The Story of Writing*, 2e (2007)
— *Lost Languages*, 2e (2009)
— *Writing and Script* (2009)
F. de Saussure, *Course in General Linguistics* (1983)
J. M. Unger, *Ideogram* (2004)
M. Ventris, 'A Note on Decipherment Methods', *Antiquity*, 27 (1953), 200–206

2 The Sacred Book

Carl Olson

1 Introduction

Adherents recognize a book as sacred in hindsight after compilers and editors have assembled its parts. A particular book is considered sacred when adherents acknowledge the authoritative nature of the source of the book, which they may believe to be divine or human. When a collection of messages is considered sacred, it is set apart from other types of literature, which are often considered profane or mundane. A sacred book is complete and does not need to be complemented by anything else, although it may invite a commentary to expound its inner meaning. By its very nature, a sacred book represents order, unity, and perfection. A sacred book is also powerful because it can overawe, overwhelm, or inspire a reader or hearer with its message. Although such power is ambivalent because it is both creative and destructive, it also possesses the ability to affect things or persons by forcing them to move or behave in a certain manner, which is indicative of the book's dynamic power to transform people and events. The power inherent within a sacred book contains, moreover, a compulsive aspect because it can coerce and prohibit actions; in short, it exercises control over people and their behaviour. Because of its foundation in an authoritative source—divine or human—readers or listeners are persuaded by the sacred book's message, and they are convinced by its truthfulness to accept it and to live their lives according to its injunctions.

Since a sacred book postulates a fundamental religious message, or makes claims without demonstration, it can function as a performative act in the sense of making something happen, which can assume the guise of faith discovered, knowledge gained, or salvation secured. If to postulate is to take an action that is grounded in a social context, it involves performing a sacred utterance. Lacking material significata (on some levels at least), the sacred book is invulnerable to falsification by reference to natural data within the world. Although a sacred book cannot be falsified by empirical or logical means, it also cannot be objectively or logically verified. Instead of looking at the book as an object that is sacred, it is preferable to concentrate on the sanctity of its religious discourse. It is thus, for instance, not Jesus or the Buddha who are sacred; rather, the discourse proclaiming them respectively divine or enlightened is sacred. This does not preclude the sacred book from being treated with respect and even reverence as a sacred object by its adherents, but it refocuses the notion of the sacred book onto its discourse. Although the sacred book can be discovered in many religious traditions, this essay, for reasons of economy, only considers the formative periods of the major monotheistic traditions (Judaism, Christianity, and Islam), Hinduism, and Buddhism.

Because of the large number of sacred books throughout the world, it is impossible to cover all the worthy candidates. Among the sacred books excluded from this survey are: the *Book of Mormon* revealed to Joseph Smith of the Latter-Day Saints, which shares its status with the Bible for Mormons; the sacred texts of Zoroastrianism: the *Yasna*, *Yashts*, and *Venidad*; the Confucian classics, the products of sages, which include the following five classics: *I-Ching* (Book of Changes); *Shih-Ching* (Book of Poetry); *Shu-Ching*

(Book of History); *Li-Chi* (Book of Rites); and *Ch'un-Ch'iu* (Spring and Autumn Annals); the sacred books of Taoism contained in the *Tao Tsang*, a depository of texts that contains such classics as the *Tao Te Ching*, attributed to Lao Tzu, and the *Chuang Tzu*, named for the sage of the text.

2 Formative Judaic tradition

Passed by oral tradition from one generation to another over centuries, the sacred writings of the ancient Jews did not constitute a single sacred scripture: their literature represented a collection of 24 separate books that they came to call the Bible (Gk *biblia*, 'books')—not the Old Testament, which was assembled later by Christians from a prejudicial and theological position. The separate books of the ancient Jews represented a narrative about God's interaction with His chosen people. Within this dramatic narrative, the major themes of Israel's faith were related, which included the promise of the ancient patriarchs to be faithful to their deity, the divine deliverance of Israel from Egypt, divine guidance while wandering in the wilderness, the bestowing of the law at Sinai to the prophet Moses, and the inheritance of the promised land. This narrative is often shortened to and summarized as 'the Exodus event', which depicts God's redemptive work for his people, and not simply a matter of political liberation from servitude. The Exodus event, during which God acted in history, functions as the sign of His revelation and divine presence. Divine intervention for the benefit of His chosen people means that history becomes the acts of God and thus meaningful. Therefore, the narrative of God's active intervention in history informs the Jewish community about what God has done (past), what God is doing (present), and what God will do (future), which unifies the three moments of time into a meaningful configuration.

The ancient Jews referred to their collection of books as *Tanakh*, an acronym for its three major divisions (*see* **8**). The term *Tanakh* is derived from the first letters of all three divisions: Torah (Law), Nevi'im (prophets), and Kituvim (hagiographa). The initial, most important, and authoritative division is the Torah (Law, also meaning 'instruction', 'teaching'), which includes the so-called Five Books of Moses or the Pentateuch: Genesis, Exodus, Leviticus, Numbers, and Deuteronomy. Scholars refer to the Pentateuch as the Hexateuch, which is derived from the Greek term meaning 'five scrolls' (five books plus Joshua). The Torah represented God's gift to the people of Israel.

This gift was, however, conditional upon the people's acceptance of the divine commandments and their obedience to them as the chosen people.

God's scriptural gift to his chosen people was given in Hebrew, a divine language. However, that the Jews lost the language before the Bible was finalized is evident in the Book of Daniel, which was composed in Aramaic. By the post-Exilic period, Aramaic had become the preferred language for translating the Jewish scriptures, and the 2nd century BC marked a time when many Jews read a Greek Septuagint or an Aramaic version. An oral tradition which preceded the Jewish scriptures assumed the form of the *scroll (Isa. 34:4) or a roll made of *papyrus, *leather, or parchment (Jer. 36:14; Ezek. 2:9). Hebrew writing used Canaanite characters, which were eventually replaced with an Aramaic form of script known as the 'square script'. The process of writing was accomplished by using metal implements for the hard surfaces of stone and metal. A stylus was used for writing on clay or wax, a brush for various materials with paint or ink, and a reed pen with ink.

The prophetic literature is divided into the earlier prophets of Joshua, Judges, Samuel, and Kings, while the later prophets are Isaiah, Jeremiah, Ezekiel, and the twelve minor prophets. Finally, the mixed collection called Ketubim (writings) includes works such as the Psalms, the Song of Solomon, and the moral stories of Job, Ruth, and Esther. The writings also include the wisdom of Proverbs and Ecclesiastes, and the historical Ezra-Nehemiah and Chronicles, with both sets of works representing two texts in a single collection. The final collecting, fixing, preservation, and canonization of the Pentateuch occurred during the Babylonian Exile (Ezra 7:14, 25), which was a period centuries removed from the events recounted in the books.

Modern biblical scholars view the Pentateuch as a composite work representing several major traditions that have been artfully woven together. Scholars have identified four main literary strands, signified by the letters J, E, D, and P. The J literary contribution represents the earliest source originating from the period of the early monarchy (950 BC), whereas the E sources can be dated to the time of the Northern Kingdom (about 750 BC). The D literary strand's best example is the book of Deuteronomy, which dates from the period of the Southern Kingdom (about 650 BC or even later). The P source refers to priestly influence, and dates from the time of the fall of the nation in 587 BC. The entire Pentateuch assumed its present shape around 400 BC. The Pentateuch's written stage was preceded by at least three centuries of oral transmission, and it came to be recognized as the written Law (Torah). The prophets and hagiographa became canonized after the destruction of the Second Temple.

Along with the written Law, Jews recognized an oral law that was developed by the Pharisaic teachers and their successors. The oral law took the form of scriptural exegesis. Rabbinic law was summarized in the Mishnah, while the *gemara* consisted of reports of broad discussions about the Mishnaic text, which was the basic text of the oral Torah. Dating to around the 3rd century AD and containing the legal teachings of the Tannaim, or earliest rabbinic authorities, the Mishnah is a collection of originally oral laws divided into six orders according to subject-matter, devoid of direct reference to the Pentateuch (written Torah). In addition, Rabbinic Judaism gave birth to the Talmud, containing analysis and elaboration of rabbinic lore (*aggadah*), which is prominent in the collection known as the Midrash that originated in the academies of Palestine and Babylonia. Within the Talmud, legal (*halakhah*) aspects dominate the text.

3 Formative Christian tradition

The early Christian community did not possess its own sacred book, and any such notion would have probably struck its members as strange. It did, however, make use of the Hebrew Bible, although it tended to read predictions of the Christ figure into the text. From the perspective of his followers, Jesus did not bring a scripture. His actions, charismatic persona, and message represent his revelation, or 'Good News', to the faithful. When a Christian scripture began to evolve its development was uneven, because of a lack of self-conscious effort and a consistent deliberation about what constituted a scripture.

The letters of Paul are the earliest extant Christian literature, dating from around the mid-1st century, and preserved and gathered into a collection by its end. These letters were called 'letters to the seven churches', because seven was a symbol of wholeness in the ancient world and in this context implied the entire Church. Although the letters are addressed to particular congregations and their problems, Paul's message is intended for a wider audience, an evolving community, and considers its struggle to survive in the hostile sociocultural environment of the Graeco-Roman world. For his message, Paul claimed that his authority came directly from Jesus, the resurrected Lord and Saviour.

Paul's letters were intended to be read aloud to an audience, which was also true of the Hebrew Bible and other documents of the New Testament. Within the context of the ancient Graeco-Roman world, all reading was performed aloud, as Paul instructed his letters should be read (1 Thess. 5:27). The sense of a text was thus to be gained by listening to its being proclaimed. When Paul's letters were read aloud, for instance to a church community, the letters evoked the apostle's presence.

In contrast to Paul's letters, the Gospels are more narratives and interpretations of the life and teachings of Jesus. The word 'gospel' is derived from the Greek word *evangelion*, which means 'good news'—in the New Testament this becomes the good news of salvation, rather than its prior meaning associated with the welfare of the emperor. The authority of these texts was grounded in the words and deeds of Jesus, which were preserved by memory and transmitted orally. The Gospels were composed by anonymous authors, who named their works after a disciple of Jesus, and they consisted of Mark (composed *c.*65–70), Matthew and Luke (*c.*80–90), and John (*c.*90–100). In an effort to collect and codify various traditions about Jesus and sayings attributed to him, each Gospel writer sought to interpret the meaning of Christianity for his specific constituencies. The anonymous authors derived their authority from the various communal traditions rooted in the teaching and deeds of Jesus. During their formative period, the Gospels were considered valuable historical testimonies; it was not until later that they were considered scripture. The traditions about Jesus were preserved by memory and circulated orally.

If the four Gospels are compared with each other, striking differences emerge between John and the *synoptic (meaning that they present a common view) Gospels. Few of the events in Jesus' life recorded, for instance, in the synoptic Gospels are discovered in John. Besides missing events, the location and chronology of Jesus' ministry are different in John, along with style and language. The close literary relationship of the synoptics reflects another problem associated with their similarities. There is general agreement among scholars that Mark is the earliest and that Matthew and Luke used it as a foundation for their Gospels. In addition, the writer of Mark was not precisely an author but rather a redactor, connecting units of an oral tradition. Scholars tend to agree that much of Mark is discovered in Matthew and Luke: the arrangement and sequence of material support a theory of dependence on Mark, and numerous parallel passages indicate that Matthew and Luke tried to improve on Mark's literary style and language. Material missing in Mark is also found in Matthew and Luke. What accounts for the absent material in Mark? Scholars have rejected the possibility that they borrowed from each other, and have concluded that it would be more reasonable to assume they used an independent source. German scholars dubbed this source *quelle*, which was abbreviated to 'Q'. This means that Matthew and Luke used two sources: Mark and Q. Scholars think that Q was probably a written document because of the verbal agreements between the two Gospels. Scholars also tend to think that Q (dated around 50 AD) existed prior to Mark. In addition to Mark and Q, Matthew and Luke both had access to oral or written traditions independent of Mark: these are called the M and L sources.

Scholars arrived at this general consensus about the Gospels by using three types of criticism: source, form, and redaction. Source criticism examines the origins of the texts, whereas form criticism is a discipline that goes behind the written sources to examine the period of the oral tradition. Redaction criticism is an analysis of the editorial work in relation to sources.

In addition to the four Gospels and the letters of Paul, what came to be called the New Testament also included the Acts of the Apostles, letters of Peter, James, and Jude, and the Book of Revelation, which was attributed to John, author of the Gospel. As the Christian Church developed, numerous prescriptive lists of authentic texts existed in many Christian assemblies (*ekklesiai*). These various lists were called canons (Gk *kanones*, 'measures', 'standards'), so called because connected with criteria associated with authenticity. The formation of the fourfold Gospels occurred, for instance, by the late 2ⁿᵈ century, and was generally accepted by the faithful in the 3ʳᵈ. The Gospels gained scriptural status as a group rather than as individual texts—a development suggesting that their authority was grounded in their collective nature.

If the early period of the primitive Christian Church emphasized the oral nature of Jesus' message, why were the Gospels committed to writing? New Testament scholars have offered several plausible reasons for a turn to writing the Gospels. The death of the apostles, or those closest to Jesus during his life, induced a fear about losing the tradition of Jesus. The developing Church wanted to know how to deal with persecution by learning from Jesus. The primitive Church also struggled to define and understand itself separately from Judaism. And it wondered how it could appeal to the Gentiles without losing its original Jewish identity. Finally, the problem associated with

the delay of the *parousia* (second coming of Jesus) and the end of the world served as motivating factors in committing Jesus' message to writing.

Although Christianity was an apocalyptic sect within Palestinian Judaism and Jesus was a Palestinian Jew, the world of the New Testament was dominated by Greek language and culture; the language itself had been transformed from classical Attic Greek into *koinē* (common) or Hellenistic Greek, which became the language of the New Testament. Using material such as papyrus, parchment, or wooden *tablets, Christians preferred the *codex (book-like form), previously used for letter-writing and record-keeping, over the scroll employed in Judaism or for Greek literature. Scholars have offered several reasons for the adoption of the codex, such as economy, compactness, convenience, ease of reference, or usage of an already familiar medium and practical means of communication. A four-Gospel codex was used to preserve the best-known and most widely accepted texts for everyday usage as handbooks for the Christian community.

As New Testament texts gained canonical status, the issue of a sacred language never really developed because Christian scripture spread quickly and into a variety of vernaculars. This situation changed when Jerome translated the Bible into Latin during the 4ᵗʰ century. The Latin version of the scriptures became the sacred language of the Roman Catholic Church until *Luther, a former Catholic priest turned Protestant reformer, translated the Bible into German with the purpose of making the text more accessible to ordinary people in the 16ᵗʰ century.

4 Formative Islamic tradition

Fifteen years after his marriage to an older woman, the prophet Muḥammad, then 40 years old, began to have strange experiences in a cave on Mount Hira, located outside the city of Mecca in Arabia. Some experiences came to him as visions, others as vivid dreams, and some as words on his heart, without his imagining that he had heard anything. An early vision was that of a glorious being standing erect in the sky, who Muḥammad thought was God. Muḥammad later interpreted a voice which spoke to him from behind a veil as being an angel that he finally identified with the angel Gabriel.

When he received his first revelation (96.1–5), Muḥammad was commanded by the heavenly messenger to speak, and he refused at first. After a second command, he asked what he should recite; at the third command, he spoke the 96th *sūra* of the Qur'ān. The term 'recite' (*iqra*) is derived from the same Arabic root as *Qur'ān*, which implies a verbal revelation that is closely related to inspiration. Although the command to recite implies that public worship was to be instituted, when Muḥammad began his public preaching in 613 and presented himself to the people of Mecca as God's messenger, his message was met with opposition. Yet he eventually won adherents to his message about the power and goodness of God, the coming final day of judgement, the need to respond to God with gratitude and worship, and his own vocation as the final prophet.

The process of revelation is called *wahy* in Arabic; it embodies the connotation of verbal inspiration through the mind or heart (26.193–5). Muslims believe that the revelation of the Qur'ān is based on a 'heavenly book' that is preserved in the presence of God, and it is called the 'Mother of the Book' (43.1–4) (*see* **38**). The aim of the revelation (6.19) is intended to be a warning to hearers, and what is revealed is the order (*amr*) or command of God. The command is revealed in Arabic in order to facilitate understanding. The best way for a person to receive the message is to memorize it, a practice that keeps the revelation in one's mind.

According to the orthodox understanding of its origin, the Qur'ān represents the eternal word of God in book form. The prophet Muḥammad was not the author of the uncreated word; he was only its recipient. In fact, Muḥammad is referred to as 'the illiterate prophet' (7.157–8) in order to emphasize that it would have been impossible for him to compose it. The Qur'ān was revealed periodically over a period of about twenty years, not all at one time. The angel Gabriel gave the words of the revelation, although Muḥammad did not write the words himself. There are Islamic traditions that refer to others writing the revelation on available material—such as stones, bones, *parchment, *leather, *palm leaves, and the hearts of men—which led to diverse writings inviting assembly into a coherent collection. According to a traditional account of the collection of the pieces of the revelation, after the battle of Yamanah, not long after Muḥammad's death, many reciters of the revelation were killed. 'Umar ibn al-Khattāb, who was to become the second caliph, became alarmed about preserving the contents of the revelation, and suggested to Abū Bakr, the first caliph, that it be collected and written down. Zayd ibn Thābit, who was commissioned by Abū Bakr, began to collect the revelation, and the efforts that he initiated led to four early

collections in different locations; but none of these texts has survived. Because of serious differences among these four collections, the third caliph, 'Uthmān, urged an end to disputes caused by textual variations by commissioning a revised text. A guiding principle in resolving disputed versions was the preference given to the Quraish tribal dialect of the prophet Muḥammad.

There is a twofold separation of the Qur'ān into a ritual division of 30 approximately equal portions; it is also divided into 114 *sūras* (a term of Syrian origin, meaning 'writing' or 'text of scripture'). As a general rule, the title of a *sūra* has no reference to the subject matter of the text. The heading is instead taken from some prominent term in the *sūra*, such as 'The Bees' (16) or 'The Cave' (18). Each *sūra* is dated to either the Meccan or Medinan period, according to where the prophet was living at the time of the revelation. With the exception of *sūra* 11, all *sūras* begin with the *bismillah* phrase: 'In the name of God, the Merciful, the Compassionate'. In 29 of the *sūras*, this is followed by mysterious letters or a letter of the alphabet. Each *sūra* is divided into verses (*āyāt*, 'sign'). The *sūras* are written in rhymed prose in verses without metre or definitely fixed length; they end with a rhyme or assonance. The Qur'ān itself acknowledges the composite nature of the *sūras* when it refers to the piecemeal nature of its delivery (17.106).

Within the *sūras*, Allah speaks often in the first person singular (51.56). Sometimes God is referred to in the third person, and some passages are clearly spoken by angels (19.65), but only in a few passages does Muḥammad actually speak (27.93). The orthodox position is that the Qur'ān is the literal word of Allah, because it is believed that God is speaking through the angels and the prophet.

A puzzling feature of the Qur'ān to outsiders is its doctrine of abrogation, which stipulates that a later verse might nullify an earlier one. This doctrine fits into a cultural context in which people accepted the existence of spirits and a satanic being that might have deluded Muḥammad into believing that he had received a revelation when in fact he received a demonic message. Such a false passage could be corrected by a later revelation that nullifies the earlier revelation and replaces it with a corrected version in some cases.

The revelation was given in Arabic, or the language of God, according to Muslim tradition, and it was collected in the form of the codex. Arabic presented linguistic challenges for readers because of a lack of vowel signs, diacritical marks, and other orthographic signs, which were necessary in order to differentiate similarly formed consonants. The Qur'ān's language is pre-Islamic Arabic.

A non-revelatory body of literature distinct from the Qur'ān is the *ḥadīth* (a term that embodies the connotation of something 'new', 'coming to pass', and 'occurrence'). It developed to mean 'tradition' in the form of a brief report about what the prophet said, did, approved, or disapproved, although it may also include information in Arabic and preserved in codices about his companions. Besides its textual aspect, the *ḥadīth* consisted of a transmissional chain (*isnād*), such as the following example: A says that he heard it from B, who received it on the authority of C, who said this on the authority of D that the prophet said. These reports were accepted as authoritative secondary sources of Islam by the middle of the 9th century. Scholars collected, sifted, and systematized the traditions until six collections became authoritative. When deciding which reports were authentic, scholars focused on the transmissional chain in an attempt to assess the character and reliability of the transmitters' memories. They also considered the continuity of the transmission and whether or not each link in the transmission was strong and whether any links were broken. The *ḥadīth* is considered coeval and consubstantial with the *sunnah* (lit. 'travelled path') of the prophet, which embodies his exemplary conduct. The prophetic *sunnah* represents reports of Muḥammad's being asked to decide a problem for which no precedent existed. It thereby represents a living tradition for each generation of Muslims, and serves as the norm of the community in the sense of functioning as agreed social practice and social consensus (*ijmā'*). It is possible to differentiate *sunnah* and *ḥadīth* because the latter represents a report and something theoretical, whereas the former is the same report after it acquires a normative quality and becomes a practical principle as the non-verbal transmission of tradition. Besides the revelation, the Islamic tradition thus recognizes the *sunnah*, or exemplary conduct, of the prophet as a standard for behaviour.

5 Formative Hindu tradition

Ancient Indian religious literature can be distinguished as the revealed (*śruti*) and that which is remembered (*smṛti*). The revealed literature includes the Vedas, whereas the remembered body of literature includes the following: Dharma Sūtras (approximate dates of composition 600–200 BC), the epic *Mahābhārata* (composed between approximately 300 BC and AD

300), the epic *Rāmāyaṇa* (composed between 200 BC and AD 200), and Purāṇas, which began to be composed around AD 400 (*see* **39**).

The Vedic literature consists of four collections: Rig, Sāma, Yajur, and Atharva. Each of these collections of hymns is further divided into four revealed (*śruti*) sections: Saṃhita (*mantra* or sacred formula/utterance collection), Brāhmaṇa (theological and ritual commentary), Āraṇyaka (forest or wilderness texts), and Upaniṣad (speculative and secret philosophical texts). It is believed that divine beings revealed this literature orally to ancient sages (*rishis*), who heard them, preserved them within their memory, and passed the revealed hymns on to further generations by oral transmission. Eventually, the revealed hymns were written down in order to preserve and protect them from faulty memory and the vicissitudes of time. Although some Vedic seers attached their names to poems, readers should not construe this signature as a claim of authorship. It is merely an acknowledgement of the identity of the person who received the revelation. The divinely revealed origin of the Vedas gives this body of literature an unquestionable authenticity and authority over other bodies of literature that historically followed it.

The Rig Veda is the oldest collection of verses, consisting of 1,028 hymns, arranged in ten books called *maṇḍalas* (circles). Parts of Books 1 and 10 are the latest additions to the entire corpus followed by Book 9, which embodies hymns recited during the Soma sacrifice. The other books (2–7) are designated the family collections because they were preserved within family clans that memorized and transmitted them for future generations. Book 8 contains several more short family collections, representing the literary products of ancient sages or their patrilinear descendants. In fact, the various books are arranged according to author (i.e. family or clan), deity, and metre. In addition, hymns to specific deities are arranged according to length, with the longest at the beginning of the book. If hymns are of equal length, the hymn with a longer metre is placed first.

It is possible that the Rig Veda antedates the introduction and common use of iron, which means that its origin can be dated to around 1200 BC. According to internal textual evidence, the Vedas originated in northern India and spread to the Punjab and more eastern regions between *c.*1500 and *c.*400 BC. Members of the Angirasa and Kāṇva clans formed the bulk of its poets, who treated the hymns as the clans' private property. In time, Vedic schools called *Śākhās* (branches) developed to control and protect the transmission of texts, which usually resulted in a school adhering to a specific text. These various schools created an interpretive body of literature as reflected in various Brāhmaṇic and *sūtra* types of literature.

The Sāma Veda, for instance, represents material drawn from the Rig Veda with the exception of 75 hymns. This collection of hymns is named for the chants (*sāmans*), which represent the earliest written form of music in Indian history, and is recited during the Soma sacrifice. As the priests recite these verses during the rite, they modify the verses. Finally, the Sāma Veda consists of two parts: an actual text (*arcika*) and the melodies (*gāna*).

The sacred formulas (*mantras*, lit. 'instruments of the mind') repeated by priests in rituals form the bulk of the Yajur Veda, or third Vedic collection. The sacred formulas are arranged according to ritual usage, not numerically. By reciting the sacred *mantras* (syllables, words, or verses), the chanter expresses eternal wisdom and the pre-existent sacred word itself. There were four major types of *mantra* chant: *ṛcs*, *yajuses*, *sāmans*, and *atharvans*, which conformed respectively to each of the major Vedic collections. The importance of *mantras* can be partially grasped by examining Hinduism's two types of speech. The first type was that of the Asuras, or demonic beings: it was without form or order, uncontrollable and inarticulate, similar to the nature of the demonic forces of existence. The Vedic *mantra* was its exact opposite.

The Atharva Veda, or fourth Veda, consists of a collection of hymns focusing on magical and healing rites. In addition, there are hymns related to harmful sorcery and to speculative subjects; others are concerned with rites of passage (e.g. initiation and marriage); there are also two appendices. In sharp contrast to the Rig Veda, the collection begins with short works and increases to longer hymns.

Ancient Indian deities gave the Vedic poets a visionary insight that was conceived as a heart/mind transmission from a superior party to another inferior receiver. After receiving it from higher beings, the poet recites/chants the hymn. By orally reciting a hymn, the poet sends his inner spirit back to the realm of the divine beings who originally inspired the poet. Moreover, the uttering of a hymn about a particular deity sends that hymn back to its source, completing the cycle.

Because the ancient Vedic schools represented a priestly family or clan from a specific geographical area, tribe, or kingdom, and the schools distinguished themselves by their ritual procedures and pronunciation of words, there was no single or original canon of texts established and authenticated by an authoritative body of religious leaders. What we have are plural textual canons of different schools. Thus, the Vedic canon was a collective entity of Vedic texts used by various schools. Vedic literature became a canon by about 400 BC. There is evidence that it was acknowledged by the two grammarians: Pāṇini and Patañjali around 150 BC. Prior to this acknowledgement, the Vedas were also mentioned in the Pāli canon of Buddhism around 250 BC.

Attached to each of the four collections of the Vedas were Brāhmaṇas that explained the complex ritual system. Texts were added to various Brāhmaṇas to explain further the esoteric aspects of the rites. Some of these additional texts were called Āraṇyakas, others were called Upaniṣads, although there was no sharp distinction between these new kinds of text. In addition to treating the ritual system, these esoteric texts also engaged in forms of cosmological and metaphysical speculation. Much like the four Vedas, these esoteric teachings were preserved orally for generations before assuming a written form. As with the Brāhmaṇic texts, particular Upaniṣads are associated with one of the four collections of the Vedas. The Aitareya and Kauṣītakī Upaniṣads are directly connected, for instance, with the Rig Veda, whereas the Kaṭha and Maitrāyaṇī Upaniṣads are associated with the Black Yajur Veda, and the Bṛhadāraṇyaka and Īśa Upaniṣads with the White Yajur Veda.

The Hindu religious tradition acknowledges the existence of 108 Upaniṣads, but it is generally agreed that there are thirteen major texts. Although it appears that the Upaniṣads evolved from the Āraṇyakas (forest texts) and it is difficult to distinguish between them, the oldest Upaniṣads are the Bṛhadāraṇyaka and Chāndogya. The Aitareya, Taittirīya, and Kauṣītaka followed these texts historically. This second group was subsequently followed by the composition of the following examples: Kena, Īśa, Kaṭha, Śvetāśvatara, Praśna Muṇḍaka, Mahānārayana, Māṇḍūkya, and Maitrī. After the appearance of these thirteen major texts, many later Upaniṣads manifested a sectarian character by focusing on deities such as Śiva and Viṣṇu.

The meaning of the term *Upaniṣad* suggests sitting down near a teacher to receive secret instructions characteristic of an intimate student-teacher relationship. In addition to being secret and personal, the teaching context was characterized as relational and dialogical. Overall, the Upaniṣads are not the result of a single mind, but rather represent the pedagogical efforts of many ancient Indian teachers during a historical period of great social, economic, and religious change.

The Upaniṣads are called *Vedānta* (not to be confused with the historically later philosophical school of thought), because they represent the deepest secrets of the Vedas. Although the Upaniṣads develop some notions of the Vedas, they also introduce new ideas (at least in a primitive form) that shape Indian religious culture, and they transform some of the old notions into something fresh and innovative, such as karma (law of cause and effect), rebirth, immortal self (Ātman), ultimate reality (Brahman), and path to liberation (*mokṣa*).

A prevalent theme in the Upaniṣads is the importance of knowing. Although there are some Upaniṣads that discuss the centrality of devotion to a deity and the necessity of divine grace for salvation, such as the Śvetāśvatara Upaniṣad, most Upaniṣads emphasize the importance of knowledge for attaining liberation, which is to be recovered, because the truth—the object of knowledge—is always present; it has been merely lost, and needs to be recovered and rediscovered. This is not an empirical or rational mode of knowledge, but instead an intuitive insight into the true nature of reality, which is a self-validating, transcendent, and infinite kind of knowledge.

The claim that the Vedic hymns were revealed oral literature suggests that the poets did not create the hymns themselves. They saw or heard the hymns from a deep, mysterious force, and received these messages with their mind and/or heart, which enabled them to grasp the true nature of things. The subtle structure of knowing symbolized by the human mind represented a transformative force that could effect change, produce desired results, and establish connections between humans and divine beings. Likewise, the human heart, which was considered similar to the mind, enabled a person to see what was not normally observable or knowable by ordinary social beings. These gifted, visionary poets were able to receive the revelation because they possessed an insight (*dhī*) or ability to see concealed truths. Once they possessed their visions, the poets were able to express these truths in the perfect language of Sanskrit, which allowed them an opportunity to conform themselves to the divine forces giving the messages. The visionary message received by the inspired Vedic poets also enabled them to view the cosmos as an integrated totality held together by a hidden structure (*ṛta*) that was closely associated with the truth (*satya*) and *tapas* (creative heat), that ushered into being the cosmos

and continuously renewed life. Therefore, the inspired Vedic poets were in close touch with the very fabric of the cosmos and the creative forces that sustained it.

These Vedic poets were also the masters and custodians of Sanskrit, which was the language of the revealed hymns and thereby sacred. Sanskrit was inextricably linked with the inspired poets because it was associated with perfection. Sanskrit embodied *brahman*, a mysterious and hidden power that was not only contained within the words of the sacred language, but also functioned to hold the universe together. The power of *brahman* was revealed to the visionary poets. This was considered a sacred power that was directly associated with the sanctity of the scripture preserved in Sanskrit. Nonetheless, the scripture's sanctity was not directly related to its intelligibility to either its hearer or its reciter. The words' holiness was more probably inversely related to their comprehensibility. In other words, strange, mysterious, and unintelligible terms were considered more powerful. Moreover, the sanctity of a term was not something extra added to a word; rather, the holiness of a term was intrinsic to the word.

The importance of poetic inspiration and knowledge is further evident in the Sanskrit term *veda*, because it possesses the root meaning of 'to see', 'vision', and 'knowing'. A master of the *veda* is a person able to see that which is concealed. In short, such a person can witness the eternal, powerful, divine forces of the universe. When the term *veda* is used as a noun, it signifies sacred knowledge. Becoming master or recipient of the *veda* is a transforming experience, because knowing the truth radically changes a person. This points to the powerful nature of knowledge—a conviction that runs like a thread throughout Indian cultural history.

Because of its nature and ramifications, revealed literature takes precedence over literature based on human memory. When there is a discrepancy between the two bodies of literature, a person must rely on revealed literature for guidance because it possesses greater authority than remembered literature. Holding revealed literature in higher regard than remembered literature because of its source in divine revelation and inspiration does not imply that the meaning of revealed literature is readily apparent and easy to discern. Scholarly commentaries are necessary to elicit a hymn's meaning. Within the history of Indian culture, there is a long tradition of textual commentary and interpretation by learned individuals.

The revealed and remembered bodies of literature originated within the cultural context of an oral tradition, which means that the hymns of the Vedas were passed down from one generation to the next via oral transmission after the particular hymns were memorized. In this sense, much of Indian classical literature is related to memory, regardless of its revealed nature. In order to enhance memory and preserve the sacred hymns, priestly scholars devised elaborate methods to assist memory, and particular persons specialized in specific groups of texts to enhance the accuracy of their oral preservation. A person might, for instance, memorize each odd-numbered word of a hymn or every even-numbered term to enhance the correct transmission of the hymn.

Emphasis on the oral nature of ancient Indian sacred literature necessarily implies that scripture is not something written that can be reified. This suggests that scripture in India is not a well-defined entity with clearly established boundaries. The significance of and emphasis upon the oral transmission of hymns can be partially understood by the traditionally negative attitude towards writing in Indian culture. According to the ancient *Aitareya Āraṇyaka* (5.5.3), which originates in an esoteric section of a ritualistic Brahmanical text, the activity of writing is designated as ritually polluting and a person thus stained should avoid reciting the Vedas along with other polluting actions such as eating meat, seeing blood or a dead body, or after sexual intercourse. This attitude helps to explain the traditionally low social status of scribes in the culture.

Despite this negative attitude towards writing and the emphasis on oral transmission that continues into the present, the Vedas were written down around 1000 BC, according to Alberuni (973–1048), a learned scholar of Indian culture of his time period, in Kashmir. In the north, the earliest Indian MSS were composed on palm leaves using black ink; in the south, a stylus was used to scratch letters onto a leaf, which was subsequently blackened with soot. In Kashmir, birch bark was used, whereas other plant materials were used occasionally in Assam. Leather or parchment was avoided because their use involved the killing of animals and pollution, although Kashmiri Brahmins bound their birch bark books with leather. The words of the Vedas were written in the *devanāgiri* script (literally, the writing of the 'city of the gods').

6 Formative Buddhist tradition

There is basic agreement among scholars of Buddhism that an extraordinary and charismatic man lived around the 6th to 5th centuries BC in India, during a period of profound political, social, and economic change. This man is Siddhārtha Gautama, who became known as the Buddha (enlightened one). Distressed by the fundamental problems of human existence, he discovered a solution to these difficulties, spent his life wandering from one place to another teaching, established a monastic community that preserved and expounded his teachings for future generations, and died at around the age of 80. A substantial literature based on his teachings evolved after his death (*see* **39**). Much of this claims to capture his actual teachings that were preserved in an oral tradition two centuries before being written down on pieces of bark, palm leaves, or other available material.

Because the Buddha gave instructions in local dialects, it would be inaccurate to refer to an original Buddhist language, although the closest thing was probably Old Māgadhī, which was the primary language for his teaching. Pāli preserves Old Māgadhī, and it was the language used by missionaries when they took the Buddha's message to Sri Lanka, where it became accepted as a textual language. According to Sinhalese chronicles, writing of the Pāli canon began in the middle of the 1st century BC because of the decline of reciters, war, and famine; the monastic community preserved the canon on wood products bound together by leather strips.

The religious message contained in this literature is not very complicated: the Buddha provides some simple summaries of his basic teachings. These summaries were called the *dhamma* (Sanskrit *dharma*). The first summary of his teaching and analysis of human existence is embodied in the Four Noble Truths: (1) all life is suffering; (2) ignorant craving is the cause of suffering; (3) the attainment of *Nibbāna* (Sanskrit *Nirvāṇa*) ends suffering; (4) the Eightfold Path is the means of attaining the goal. This path is an interdependent way of wisdom, ethical/moral action, and meditation. The other summary of the Buddha's teachings is contained in the three marks of existence: (1) impermanence due to the cycle of causation that creates a constant state of flux; (2) suffering; (3) nonself. Since everything within the world is subject to the cycle of causation, there is nothing within the empirical realm that is permanent. Moreover, there is nothing permanent about the self, ego, or soul to which humans can cling. The Buddha's basic teaching is that it is important to cut out our love of self, which functions as a means of keeping us confined to this realm of suffering, cyclic causation, ignorance, rebirth, and suffering. The teachings are intended to carry a person to a non-empirical realm beyond the cycle of causation and rebirth, freedom from ignorant craving, and liberation from suffering. This transcendent state of *Nibbāna*, which represents the exact opposite of the characteristics of the world, can only be achieved while one is alive, with an enlightened person gaining a permanent state of liberation after death.

After the Buddha's death, a series of councils sought to establish the authenticity of his teachings and to create a canon of sacred literature. Buddhism was able to thrive, find stability, and expand within the social, political, and cultural context created by the Mauryan Dynasty (322–183 BC), which advocated tolerance and support for many religious groups. King Aśoka gave royal support for Buddhism, converting to it late in his life. He transformed it into a missionary religion, which helped it to expand to countries in South Asia, and north to Central Asia and into China, whence it spread to Korea and then to Japan.

Ancient Buddhism traces the origin of its scripture to the personal insights of a human being. Moreover, as the historical Buddha became more revered and exalted in the minds and hearts of his followers, his words became a sacred body of literature due to its origin in the utterances of this historical person. There is thus nothing divinely unique about Buddhist scripture—it is not something that occurred once in history. From the Buddhist perspective, its scriptures are facts about the nature of human existence and the world: they are not the revelation of some deity. This lack of uniqueness should not be construed as a negative characteristic. Rather, Buddhists have tended to place the Buddha's teachings within a broader context because his discourses, based on his personal religious quest and discovery, occurred repeatedly during the lives of previous Buddhas. The historical Buddha merely rediscovered what was known by prior enlightened beings. Thus, the achievement of the historical Buddha represented an awareness of an eternal body of truths that had also been realized by prior figures. This type of belief undermines any possible claim about the uniqueness of the Buddha's achievement. Consequently, what the Buddha taught is fundamentally the same as that taught by other, prior Buddhas. This teaching is always present as a realized possibility for others. Furthermore, the long line of sequential teaching by Buddhas of the past means that enlightenment is not merely an ever-present possibility, but an actuality. The possibility and actuality of enlightenment suggest that there is always the potential for a newer awakening to the eternal truth that can take place within the Buddhist community. Moreover, this suggests that a sacred Buddhist text possesses no intrinsic value. It is only valuable if someone uses it as a guide. Once such a person attains enlightenment, the sacred text can be abandoned and even rejected because it possesses no further utility.

The Buddhist attitude towards scripture is grounded in its understanding of language, which it views as an impermanent human product. Since it is a basic Buddhist philosophical presupposition that everything within the world is impermanent, the impermanent and non-absolute nature of language means that it does not possess an enduring structure or metaphysical status. Lacking any intrinsic value, words are only valuable in an instrumental way. Thus, the value of words resides in their ability to accomplish something.

During the formative period of the historical evolution of Buddhism, its literature was organized into two baskets: *Vinaya-piṭaka* (basket of monastic discipline) and *Sutta-piṭaka* (basket of discourses). According to tradition, this occurred at the first council at Rājagrha, the capital of Magadha, immediately following the Buddha's death around 486 BC when monks met to recite from memory the words of the Buddha. In order to assure accuracy, the monks chanted the remembered teachings in unison. The teaching (*dhamma*) of the Buddha was called *āgama* (lit. 'that which has been transmitted'). After a period of oral transmission from teacher to disciple, the teachings were collected and organized into *suttas* and *gāthās* (verses). Around the 2nd century BC a third basket was added, the *Abhidhamma-piṭaka* (basket of additional teachings). Before these three collections were written down to preserve them, oral reciters preserved them through memory, typically by specializing in a particular subject-matter.

The basket of monastic discipline contains the rules and precepts that guide monastic life. This basket of literature is divided into three major categories: *Sutta-vibhanga*, *Khandhaka*, and *Parivāra*. The first category consists of the *Pāṭimokkha* and its 227 rules, which are arranged according to the degree of seriousness of violating them. The *Pāṭimokkha* developed from a simple confession of faith made by monks and nuns into a basic code used to guarantee proper monastic behaviour. After it became established in this way, it functioned as a monastic liturgy. Monks and nuns periodically chanted these rules within their respective communities as entire groups, which worked to unify the communities and functioned as a reminder of the rules that bound them together. The group recitation of the *Pāṭimokkha* occurred twice a month in connection with fast days (*Poṣadha*) that were historically connected to the religious significance of the new and full moon days in ancient Indian religion. Certain literary features were added to the text as it evolved historically. These included introductory and concluding verses praising monastic virtue and discipline. An introduction (*nidāna*) to the text functioned to summon the monastic community together, and served as a means of conducting the proper confessional procedure. Finally, after each category of violations, the text contained an interrogatory procedure with the purpose of determining violators of the monastic code and distinguishing pure from impure members.

The *Sutta-vibhanga* can be literally translated as 'analysis of a *sutta*' (thread/text). (The root derivation of the term *sutta* or *sutra* connotes the warp of a woven cloth, metaphorically suggesting that the teachings were made into phrases that could be memorized.) The text in this case is the *Pāṭimokkha*, which forms the basis of the regulations for monastic life. There are four parts to the *Sutta-vibhanga*. The initial part is a narrative or narratives that present the actual human circumstances for a particular rule. Secondly, there is the actual rule. Then, there is a commentary on each term of the rule. It concludes with a narrative indicative of any mitigating circumstances, which exemplify exceptions to the rule, and may also relate any changes that could be made regarding punishments. This last aspect suggests the introduction of some latitude into the monastic code. Flexibility is also evident in the use of terms such as 'grave offence', 'light offence', or 'offence of improper conduct'. This introduction of elasticity probably reflects the historical development of the *Pāṭimokkha* into a fixed and closed body of rules. If new rules became inadmissible into the code of conduct, monastic communities discovered that they needed some suppleness in order to respond properly to new incidents that were without much precedent in the established code.

In contrast to the *Sutta-vibhanga*, the *Khandhaka* represents a broader body of rules that serves as a supplement to the basic rules of the *Pāṭimokkha*. The *Khandhaka* also deals with broader issues of communal disharmony and actions by the larger monastic order, along with procedures for the ceremonial life of the community and regulations for dealing with a schism or the threat of a split within the order. It also treats more mundane issues like the use of shoes and leather objects, proper and improper clothing, correct and incorrect behaviour during probationary periods, procedures for settling disputes, and rules specifically for nuns. Finally, the third major category is the *Parivāra*, which is a collection of auxiliary texts of different dates or origin.

The discourses of the Buddha are contained in the *Sutta-piṭaka*, *piṭaka* (basket) connoting something that is capable of holding items. Besides its connection to the metaphor of weaving, the term *sutta* (Sanskrit, *sūtra*) refers to the thread or thong of leather or string used to hold the pages of a text together. In this metaphorical sense, the *sutta* suggests something that binds pages of a discourse together. A *sutta* follows a specific form that starts with the words 'Thus have I heard. At one time ...'. This introduction is followed by the name of the location of the discourse, which is followed in turn by a list of names of those in the audience, and concludes with the sermon of the Buddha. This basic format of the text suggests particular historical circumstances after the death of the Buddha. At that time, monks gathered to share and recite from memory the sermons that they had heard and could remember. The disciples of the Buddha were attempting to construct the authentic tradition in order to establish the actual teachings and orthodox tradition. Specifically, the disciples were concerned to transmit accurately their enlightened master's teachings. They were not concerned about proving or verifying his statements: they thought that any person listening to the message could either accept or reject it.

The *Sutta-piṭaka* texts are arranged according to length. Among the five major collections of these texts are the long sayings (*Dīgha-nikāya*), middle-length sayings (*Majjhima-nikāya*), works connected by their contents (*Saṃyutta-nikāya*), texts arranged by numerical groupings of items (*Aṅguttara-nikāya*) in an ascending order culminating with a list of eleven things, and a collection of minor works (*Khuddaka-nikāya*). This Pāli canon became fixed and closed by 100 BC.

The final basket to be added historically to the Pāli canon was the *Abhidhamma-piṭaka*, the prefix *abhi* meaning 'above'. This prefix suggests what is beyond or superior to the *dhamma* (doctrine/teaching) that it is analysing. The meaning of the term *Abhidhamma* implies that it possesses more authority than the explanations to be discovered in the *suttas* themselves. Thus, this basket consisted of scholastic analysis of material from the *Sutta-piṭaka*, suggesting that its meaning embodies 'understanding the teachings' or 'analysis of the teachings'. This basket of frequently technical literature probably originated from lists of doctrinal topics that were used to collect and preserve concepts and teachings of the Buddha. This literature reflects an excellent example of Buddhist scholasticism that attempted to analyse the teachings of the Buddha from a variety of viewpoints.

After the establishment of the *Tipiṭaka* (triple basket), learned monks wrote commentaries on the texts. During the 5th century AD, Buddhaghosa consolidated, for instance, previous commentaries, and wrote five commentaries on the *Nikāya* texts. This great Buddhist scholar also composed several works on the *Abhidhamma* literature. Other scholars followed in the footsteps of Buddhaghosa with their own commentaries.

7 Brief comparison of the five traditions

Each of the five religious traditions considered here uses its sacred book in a performative way in order to make something happen by the reciting of words. The ritual repetition of the monastic regulations periodically by Buddhist monks, for instance, is a performative function of scripture because it unites the members of the monastery into a brotherhood. The performative nature of *mantras* in Hinduism and Buddhism and prayer in the monotheistic traditions are indicative of the performative aspects of the sacred book that embody *mantras* and prayers. The oral performance of Paul's letters evoked his presence in the early churches. It is also obvious that the psalms of the Hebrew Bible were to be read aloud. Similarly, rabbis of Judaism, Muslim mullahs, and Qur'ānic reciters performed their scriptures.

The sacred language of ancient Hinduism is Sanskrit, Arabic for Islam, and Hebrew for Judaism; but there is no single sacred language for Buddhism or Christianity, although Latin played such a role for some centuries for the Catholic Christian tradition. By surveying the historical expansion of Buddhism throughout the east, it is possible to find that it used the languages of different cultures: Pāli, Tibetan, Sanskrit, Chinese, Korean, Japanese, and others. Beliefs about the impermanent nature of language and lack of a divine revelation within the religious tradition probably formed the context for the use of many languages in Buddhism. Contrary to common presuppositions, the multiple languages for Buddhist scripture did not compromise its authenticity or authority.

These religious traditions also exhibited differences with respect to the issue of the canon, the authoritative and official body of writings of a religious tradition. From a cross-cultural perspective, a canon can be considered closed, as in the cases of Judaism, Islam, Christianity, and Hinduism. In the Muslim tradition, the revelation to the prophet Muḥammad ended with his life, and it was accepted as the final perfect revelation. The Qur'ān anoints itself as scripture and confirms its own canonicity, whereas other traditions experienced a long process before individual tradition reached the status of a canon. With respect to Judaism, there can be levels of the canon formed by Talmudic, legal, ritual, and exegetical commentary. In order for a religious literature to reach canonical status, there must be a strong social consensus about the formation of scripture, and the gradualness of this process has been indicated. In the cases of Buddhism and Christianity, a social consensus was reached by a series of learned councils. Muslims call themselves, Jews, and Christians 'People of the Book' because the three sacred books had the same source, even though the books are very different. Nonetheless, the Qur'ān and the Hebrew Bible have eternal and invariable heavenly prototypes. Muslims stress the uncreated nature of their text and Jews the created nature of it, whereas the Christ himself is seen as the uncreated Word.

In each of the five religious traditions, the original oral nature of their scriptures played an important role in their historical development into sacred books. This process included making decisions about what was authentic and trustworthy—and what was not. The major criterion for inclusion into a canon was whether or not a discourse of the Buddha, for instance, or a saying attributed to Muḥammad, could be traced directly to that figure, or to one or more authoritative witnesses.

These five religious traditions manifest differences with respect to revelation. For Jews and Muslims, scripture is revelation, whereas Christians encounter revelation in scripture. Hindus are closer to the Jewish and Muslim understanding of the relationship between revelation and scripture, while Buddhist scriptures are sacred because of their source in a historical person who achieved enlightenment, which is the source of his authority. This suggests that a sacred book depends on its source, and often a long historical process, until it reaches social consensus and canonicity.

The revelations of the three monotheistic religions represent a historical act that occurred at a particular time and place. There is no divine revelation in Buddhism, although the Buddha did achieve enlightenment within history. For the Vedic sages, their inspiration was an internal process occurring within the mind or heart of an individual sage, who initiated the process of inspiration by ascending and calling upon the gods for assistance, whereas God takes the initiative in the monotheistic traditions.

There are some important differences between writing and the oral transmission of a text. Writing claims an authority the oral cannot, although such authority does not end the importance of the oral tradition, as is evident in Judaism. Writing encourages textual features that make language an object of aesthetic awareness and an artefact to be decoded, which are features that go beyond the oral text. Finally, writing renders possible the creation of a history different from that produced by an oral tradition.

BIBLIOGRAPHY

R. Alter, *The Art of Biblical Narrative* (1981)

J. Barr, *Holy Scripture* (1983)

A. Cole, *Text as Father* (2005)

F. M. Denny and R. L. Taylor, eds., *The Holy Book in Comparative Perspective* (1985)

W. Eichrodt, *Theology of the Old Testament*, tr. J. A. Baker (2 vols, 1961, 1967)

E. Frauwallner, *The Earliest Vinaya and the Beginnings of Buddhist Literature* (1956)

J. Gonda, *The Vision of Vedic Poets* (1963)

— *Vedic Literature* (1975)

B. A. Holdrege, *Veda and Torah* (1996)

M. Levering, ed., *Rethinking Scripture* (1989)

K. R. Norman, *Pāli Literature* (1983)

C. Olson, ed., *Original Buddhist Sources* (2005)

— *Hindu Primary Sources* (2007)

L. Patton, ed., *Authority, Anxiety, and Canon* (1994)

E. F. Peters, *The Monotheists* (2003)

S. Pollock, *The Language of the Gods in the World of Men: Sanskrit, Culture, and Power in Premodern India* (2006)

G. von Rad, *Old Testament Theology*, tr. D. M. G. Stalker (2 vols, 1962, 1965)

C. K. Roberts and T. C. Skeat, *The Birth of the Codex* (1987)

M. Witzel, ed., *Inside the Texts Beyond the Texts: New Approaches to the Study of the Vedas* (1997)

משֶׁה
רְעֻם אֶת
וַיַּעַל הַ
וַיִּשָּׂא אֶ
אַל מָה
וַיַּרְנְמֹי
וַיָּבֹא מֹשֶׁה אֲשֶׁר
יְהוָה אֶת מֹשֶׁ
יְהוָה אֵל כִּ

3 The Ancient Book

CRAIG KALLENDORF

1 Introduction

While the main line of descent traces the printed book in the West back through the medieval *codex to the *scrolls of ancient Greece and Rome, it is important to remember that these latter civilizations arose after, and alongside, a number of other ancient cultures that also had writing. Although it is likely that writing arose independently in the Near East, China, and Central America, Greece and Rome interacted regularly with the cultures of Mesopotamia, Egypt, the Germanic tribes, and Israel, so that a full consideration of the book in the ancient world must take into account all of these areas and their interrelationships.

The earliest writing is logographic (picture writing), beginning with a simple drawing (pictogram), then developing to a sign that represents a number of concepts associated with the original object (ideogram). When the sign represents the sound of an object's name, the logogram has become a phonogram; only when the sign comes to represent consonants, or consonants and vowels, does the system become phonetic. Most early writing systems were mixed, and some have remained that way (*see* **1**).

2 Mesopotamia

By the 4th millennium BC, ancient Mesopotamia had developed the world's first fully developed writing system, a mixed approach of some 2,000 logograms (later reduced to about 800), somewhat over 100 phonograms, and some semantic indicators and syllabic signs. By 2800 BC the signs in this system had taken on a characteristic wedge shape that was easily impressed into the wet clay in which they were usually written, giving the system its name: cuneiform (Lat. *cuneus*, 'wedge-shaped'). This system was developed initially by the Sumerians, but by the middle of the 3rd millennium BC it had been adapted to Akkadian, which became the common language of the Near East, and it was later taken up by the Elamites, Hurrians, Hittites, and Persians.

Ancient Mesopotamian writing is occasionally found on stone, seals, metal weapons and craft objects, *leather, and the wax *tablets that were ubiquitous in the ancient world for note-taking, letter-writing, etc. The classic Near Eastern book, however, was made of clay. The most common shape was oblong, flat on the top with a convex underside, written on while wet with a reed in horizontal rows, starting at the top-left corner on the flat side and continuing to the lower-right corner, then on to the convex side if necessary, where the writing then went from right to left. The tablets were dried in the sun, or kiln-fired in later periods. Important documents were sometimes put into a protective clay envelope. Several tablets could be joined together to make books, which were collected into libraries. The largest of these was the *Ashurbanipal (r. 668–27 BC) Library at Nineveh; the archive at Ebla was notable for its systematic organization, and that of Nippur for its catalogues.

Writing was taught in palace, temple, and home; because the system was complex, the literacy rate remained fairly low (2–5 per cent), but scribes came from a variety of classes, ranging from petty book-keepers to high officials. A significant part of all cunei-form finds are tied to writing instruction (e.g. word lists), and examples of various literary genres also survive, often as schoolboy exercises. Best known are the *Enuma Elish* ('When on High …'), the Babylonian creation poem, and the Gilgamesh epic. Editions of the literary classics were not illustrated, although mathematical figures and diagrams were entered on documentary tablets, and even the legal Code of Hammurabi (1780 BC) contains a picture of Shamash, the god of justice. Books of magic, medicine, and tech-nology, along with maps, astronomical calculations, and building plans, survive, but 90 per cent of what the ancient Mesopotamians wrote is economic and administrative.

3 Egypt

Beginning around 3000 BC, Sumerian influence on Egypt appears to have stimulated a mixed writing system which eventually evolved into around 600 logograms, 100 phonograms, and 24 alphabet-like signs that represent one consonantal sound. In addi-tion to the formal version of this script, called hiero-glyphs (Gk *hieros*, 'sacred' and *glyphein*, 'to carve'), two non-pictorial scripts derived from it—hieratic and demotic—also appeared, to meet the demand for symbols that were faster and easier to write.

The Egyptians wrote on wooden tablets, ostraca (pottery sherds), linen mummy wrappings, monu-ments, and temples, even occasionally on animal skins, but most often on *papyrus, which came from the marshy delta of the lower Nile. The precise details of the production process remain debatable, but it is commonly agreed that the stalks of reeds were opened out and sheets of papyrus were placed on top of one another at right angles, then pressed so that their sap would hold them together. Sheets were next dried and bleached in the sun, then pasted together into scrolls. The pen was cut from the same reed, with its tip pounded into a sort of brush initially, then cut into a split nib in Hellenistic times. Black ink alternated with red to distinguish a second section of text, espe-cially a heading, from which the term '*rubric' (Lat. *ruber*, 'red') is derived. Egyptian scrolls had wide mar-gins, with hieroglyphics being written initially in ver-tical rows from right to left, generally on the inside only of a roll without handles. The outside of the roll

sometimes contained the title, the author's name, and a summary or the opening words of the text, informa-tion that could also be written inside as a *colophon. The Egyptian book bequeathed several things to its successors: writing in columns, illustrations to accom-pany a text, and rubrication for headings, titles, and colophons.

In the Old Kingdom, prayers and lists of a deceased person's accomplishments written on tomb walls evolved into catalogues of virtues and maxims that were transferred to papyrus as 'Instructions to the Dead', to which hymns, prophecies, and warnings were later added. Short stories and ballads, then his-torical inscriptions and narrative poems became common in the New Kingdom, with non-literary writ-ings like astronomical texts, calendars, magical incan-tations, treatises on practical medicine, and court proceedings being copied as well. The best-known genre, however, is the *Egyptian Book of the Dead, which contained burial ceremonies, prayers for the deceased, and speculations about what life beyond the grave held. Illustrations, which were added separately and are sometimes not integrated perfectly with the text, show scenes like the weighing of the deceased's soul and the presentation of the deceased to Osiris by Horus.

4 The Hebrew book

The earliest Hebrew writing goes back to the 15th or 14th centuries BC and is found on metal, pottery bowls, and an ostracon used as an abecedary. By the 10th century, royal records were being kept, and Deuteronomy 6:4–9 presents an early commandment that sacred texts were to be written on doorposts (*mezuza*) and in boxes bound on to the head and arms (*tefellin*). The Bible also refers to seals and signet rings that go back to the 8th century BC, and writing on ivory goes back to the same period, while the earliest frag-ments of the Bible (Num. 6:24–6) are found on two silver scrolls that date from slightly later. Inscribed stones with the teachings of Moses were displayed publicly (Josh. 8:32), and Ezekiel was commanded to write on pieces of wood (Ezek. 37:15–20). Baked clay ostraca were used for receipts, lists, tax records, and drafts. The *Dead Sea Scrolls, fragments found between 1947 and 1956 in caves near Qumran, include the earliest surviving biblical texts written on animal skins.

The Jewish religion has its basis in the Torah, which kept the Hebrews together through exile and persecu-tion; no other book has survived as long with the same physical form and textual stability, nor does any other religious book come with such constraints on its layout, materials, and preparation. The Torah contains the Pentateuch, the first five books of the Bible. It is written on parchment, on the flesh side only, in 248 to 252 columns, with two or three columns per sheet. Mistakes can be corrected, but too many errors condemn the page to the *genizah, the burial ground for damaged, worn, or error-filled Torahs. The sheets are sewn together at the end, and each end is attached to a roller. In addition to the Torah, the other parts of the Old Testament (the Prophets and the Hagiographa, or sacred writings) are important, as is the Talmud, the effort to harmonize the Torah with the commands of everyday life. The Talmud was passed down orally until the 4th or 5th centuries AD, so it is written in codex form, since this was what was common when the text was committed to writing (*see* **8**).

*Parchment appears to have been used in Hebrew scrolls before it was used widely elsewhere in the Graeco-Roman world. Word spacing and justified margins also first appear regularly in Hebrew books.

5 Greece

5.1 The physical book

A good number of charred Greek MSS have been recovered from Herculaneum, and thousands of papyrus fragments have emerged from the graveyards and rubbish dumps of Egyptian towns like Oxyrhynchus. This material has generated fragments of previously *lost books by Alcman, Herodas, Menander, Aristotle, and Philodemus, while lines from other lost works have survived in *florilegia, but what has perished is still immeasurable: over 95 per cent of Sappho, over 90 per cent of Sophocles, and almost all astronomical works prior to Ptolemy, for example.

Writing in ancient Greece evolved through several forms. The Minoan civilization on Crete was contemporary with those in Mesopotamia and Egypt and similar to them in many ways, producing writing on a number of surfaces in two distinct types of pictogram, then in two cursive syllabic scripts. Linear A, found mostly in Crete in the 17th and 16th centuries BC, was engraved on stone, metal, and clay pottery. From around 1600 to 1200 BC mainland cities like Mycenae and Pylos rose to power as well, producing an official script, Linear B, that was related to Linear A but different from it. When the Mycenean civilization was destroyed around 1200 BC, the knowledge of writing perished with it. Around the middle of the 8th century

BC, the Greeks borrowed an alphabetic writing system from the Phoenicians, who also served as intermediaries in the papyrus trade (the Phoenician port of Byblos may have provided the Greeks with their word for book, *biblos*), adapting it to their language. This script began in a monumental version, which evolved into a rounded, more compressed *uncial form as a bookhand, then into a *cursive form for business purposes.

Within a few generations the Greeks were writing on a variety of surfaces: coins, introduced by the Lydians *c*.630 BC; bronze weapons and utensils; seals, of ivory or stone; gems; and stone slabs, for laws and treaties. Wax tablets, held together by thongs into groups of two (*diptycha*), three (*triptycha*), or more (*polyptycha*), were used for note-taking and schoolwork. Pottery often contained the names of figures in a story or the people to whom the vessels were to be given, and ostraca were inscribed in the assembly with the names of political leaders whom the Athenian citizens wished to send into temporary exile (i.e. to ostracize). Parchment, named from an early production centre in Asia Minor (Lat. (*charta*) *Pergamena*, '(paper of) Pergamum'), was used as well, but not extensively during the classical period. The main writing surface for the ancient Greeks was papyrus, obtained (directly or indirectly) from Egypt and written on with a pen (*kalamos*). Writing was in columns, sufficient for 16–25 letters in prose or a line of *poetry, with 25–35 lines per column and two or three columns per sheet, on one side only except for private note-taking. No space was left between words, and there was no systematic *punctuation system, although marks like the *paragraphos*, a horizontal stroke indicating a change of speakers in drama or a break in sense in prose, are sometimes found. Standard 20-foot rolls could be glued together into scrolls of up to 100 feet in length, although anything over 35 feet (the length of two or three books of the *Iliad*) was rare because it was so hard to handle. The scroll could be preserved with saffron or cedar oil and its edges were sometimes coloured; often it had a single handle (*omphalos*), around which the papyrus was rolled. Basic information like the name of the owner, the size and source of the text, and perhaps the price could either hang from the middle of the lower edge or be added in a note at the end of the text (colophon), where it would be equally accessible, since scrolls were generally not rewound for the convenience of the next reader. The scroll could then be covered with fabric or leather and stored in a bucket, case, or on shelves.

*Engraving of a lost piece of Roman sculpture (c.100 AD) of rolled and ticketed *scrolls from Neumagen, near Treves, in C. Browerus and J. Masenius, *Antiquitatum et Annalium Trevirensium Libri XXV* (Lyons, 1670).

5.2 Book trade

Initially 'publication' in the Greek world meant an author reading from a single roll containing his works. This was succeeded by copying for and among friends, but there was no *copyright: an author 'published' a book by seeing to it that correct copies, which were prized more highly than unauthorized ones, were in circulation. In the 6th century BC the tyrant Pisistratus organized competitive recitations of *Homer, whose works he also had edited and copied, and later Lycurgus required that an official copy of the works of the three great tragedians be placed in the public record office of Athens. By the 5th century BC a book trade existed in Athens. A semi-circular recess in the marketplace (the orchestra) had been set aside for booksellers, and Plato says that a second-hand copy of the works of the philosopher Anaxagoras could be had there for one drachma, less than a day's wage for an unskilled worker.

5.3 Reading

By the 6th century BC Athenian graffiti show that writing was common, and by 490 BC vases showed people reading from scrolls of literary authors. The average Athenian male citizen knew his alphabet, girls could get enough of an education to run a household, and slaves were also sometimes literate. With wealth and leisure, education could continue, from the elementary level through more advanced study of language, composition, history, and myth, to the *gymnasia* that eventually spread Greek physical and intellectual values throughout the Hellenized world. People wrote *letters, contracts, and wills, and court cases depended on written documents.

It is not safe, however, to assume that people in ancient Greece read in precisely the same way that modern Europeans do. The fact that texts were written without word division (*scripta continua*) made vocalization almost imperative, so that reading aloud remained normative throughout Greek culture. In time, some Greeks developed the ability to read silently, in a process that is tied to the rise of Socrates' *daimonion*, the inner voice that would later be called one's 'conscience'. Aristophanes' *Knights* (produced in 424 BC, when Plato was 5 years old) has a scene in which a character reads silently, confusing another character who does not recognize this practice, confirming that it was by no means ubiquitous.

5.4 Libraries

The tyrant Pisistratus, an early book collector himself, founded the first public library in Athens, although the books were carried off by Xerxes when he sacked the city in 480 BC. No public libraries are mentioned in the 5th and 4th centuries, but significant private collections were alluded to by Xenophon in the first half of the 4th century BC, and Aristotle's library in particular was notable for its size and breadth. After the death of Alexander the Great, the Ptolemies in Egypt developed a plan to set up a research institute (a Museum) with a small group of residential scholars and substantial library resources to support their work. Books were collected from throughout the Greek world for the *Alexandrian Library, and no expense was spared: after having left fifteen talents (a huge sum) on deposit to borrow the official copy of the plays of the three tragedians, the library opted to forfeit the sum in order to keep the original. The result was the greatest library the world had ever known—by one estimate it contained at least 400,000 books in the main collection, with the 3rd-century catalogue (the *Pinakes*) of Callimachus alone taking up 120 scrolls. The other major Hellenistic library was founded by the Attalids, with the holdings of the *Pergamum Library being large enough that, in the 1st century BC, Mark Antony supposedly gave 200,000 books from it to Cleopatra. Other cities often had libraries suited to their special strengths: in Rhodes, a centre for rhetorical studies, the library of the local gymnasium was rich in speeches and works of politics and history. Inscriptions show that these libraries depended heavily on their donors.

5.5 Textual criticism

Since Greek scrolls were copied by hand, the threat of textual corruption was always high. This threat was addressed in a systematic way by scholars associated with the library in Alexandria, with Zenodotus, Aristophanes, and Aristarchus developing a system of critical signs like the *obelos*, a horizontal stroke in the left margin that signalled a verse as spurious. These same scholars advanced the principle that the best guide to an author's usage is what can be found in his other works. Actors' interpolations were identified in Euripides, and the metrical patterns in Pindar were understood well enough to allow for emendation. The earliest fragments of Homer that have emerged from the sands of Egypt are not significantly different from the textual tradition that derives from Alexandrian scholarship, suggesting that Zenodotus and his successors did their job well. (*See also* **4, 18**.)

6 Rome

6.1 The physical book

Books were present early on in Rome: it is said that in the 6th century BC Lucius Tarquinius Superbus eventually purchased the magical records in the *Sibylline Books*, which were written on linen (*libri lintei*), as were the consular records of the 5th century BC that are also mentioned by Livy. Other writing materials were used in early Rome as well. The Latin word for 'book', *liber*, serves as a reminder that the inside bark of trees (the root meaning of the word) was written on, while Virgil mentions writing on leaves. Inscriptions were made on stone and coloured, usually in red, sometimes in gold. Wax tablets had a variety of uses, from note-taking to deeds and tax receipts, to the production of prose summaries, then first drafts for poetic composition. In the empire, discharged soldiers received a bronze diptychon called a *diploma, awarding them citizenship, land, and the right to marry. Inscriptions are also found on mosaics, coins, pottery, and gems. Parchment was known, but its use was widespread only among the Jews, then the Christians.

From the early republic the basic Roman book was the papyrus scroll, developed along the Greek model. The papyrus was attached to a rod (*umbilicus*) of ivory, ebony, even gold, with handles (*bullae* or *cornua*); the scroll was held in the right hand and unrolled with the left. Originally only one side was written on, and mistakes could be scraped off—indeed, entire MSS, called *codices rescripti* (*palimpsesta* in Greek), were scraped or washed off and reused, with several important texts (e.g. Cicero's *De Re Publica* and the 2nd-century BC *Institutiones* of Gaius) surviving only as the lower text on a *palimpsest. Illustrated books are found only from the 4th century AD, but their existence before that can be inferred: Vitruvius refers to the drawings that accompanied his work, and it is known that the biographical studies of Varro were accompanied by 700 portraits. Travellers' itineraries required maps (e.g. the *Peutinger Table). Several famous *Virgil MSS (e.g. Vat. lat. 3225 and 3867, the Codex Romanus) exemplify the achievements of late Roman illumination.

A variety of writing styles were employed. Square capitals (*capitalis quadrata*), used during the first five centuries after the birth of Christ, began as inscriptional lettering, but were quickly transferred to papyrus. Slow and therefore expensive to produce, they offered an elegant contrast of thick and thin strokes with pronounced *serifs, or finishing strokes. *Rustic capitals, common on monuments from Iberia and the Near East, on less formal public notices, and in many of the earliest surviving MSS of Roman literature, are a more compact *majuscule script that originated in square capitals but shows some cursive influence as well. Uncial (Lat. *uncia*, 'one-twelfth of a foot', i.e. an inch, a derisive term applied to these letters by Jerome, who claimed that such large writing was wasteful) results from a rounding-off of square capital forms, with several distinctive new shapes (e.g. a, d, e, and m) evolving from cursive influence; this script flourished from approximately 300 to 900 among the Christians, who preferred it as a new form of writing that was free of pagan overtones. Under greater pressure from cursive, parts of letters came to be left off and *ascenders and descenders were exaggerated, resulting in the first true *minuscule script: *half-uncial or semi-uncial, which appeared in the 5th century AD and flourished in the 6th, again primarily for Christian works. Punctuation was spotty; word division was initially found in inscriptional square capitals, disappeared under Greek influence, and eventually reappeared, beginning in cursive MSS.

6.2 Book trade

A Roman author began the process of publication with a *recitatio*, a public reading, designed to introduce a new work. Virgil and Horace quickly achieved a level of attention which they found embarrassing, and the practice got even more out of hand in the empire, with the younger Pliny complaining that there was a recitation almost every day. There were advantages to the system: a 'bravo' from the audience must have encouraged the author, critics could point to defects while they could still be easily corrected, and the audience had its appetite whetted. *Patronage was a key part of the Roman literary system, with Maecenas, Augustus' unofficial minister of culture, being the most famous example of a wealthy man who financed the production and distribution of literature in exchange for having the work dedicated to him.

The primary responsibility for getting a work circulated in written form lay with the author, although precisely how this happened has become debatable. The traditional explanation holds that a writer could have the work copied by his own slaves or could rely on a large-scale 'publisher', someone like Cicero's friend and correspondent Atticus (110–32 BC). Atticus and other publishers like Q. Pollius Valerianus, Tryphon, Atrectus, Secundus, and the Sosii brothers had readers dictating to scribes, who produced copies that were disseminated all over the Roman world. The author and his publisher agreed how the book would look (e.g. what type and colour of wrapping the scroll would have), but there was no copyright protection and the author received no *royalties: the advantage of using a publisher was that a writer would not have to have more copies produced under his own supervision, at his own expense. Booksellers (*librarii*) were concentrated near the forum and often specialized, some in rare items, some in contemporary authors, and some in antiquarian goods. Recently, however, parts of this picture have been challenged. W. A. Johnson has noted that the consistent way in which scrolls were prepared suggests a professionalized training among scribes. R. J. Starr and others have urged that the picture of mass-production *scriptoria be replaced with one focused on a series of concentric circles, in which an author made copies for his friends, who had copies made for their friends, with the personal connection to the author being gradually dissolved, but with a bookshop coming into play only as a last resort in aristocratic circles (although it may well have been the first, indeed only, choice for lower-class readers). Cicero and Atticus, according to this argument, may well have had copying done in house, but this was not the norm; more commonly, someone who needed a copy made would resort to a *librarius*, seen here primarily as a copyist who was relatively indifferent about whether the original came from the customer, the handful of books in his stock, or a library.

6.3 Reading

Although the upper classes took more care to educate their children than the lower classes, education was not simply a function of class, as the number of writers of humble origin confirms: Terence came to Rome as a slave, and Augustus' freedman Hyginus became librarian at the Palatine library and wrote learned encyclopaedic works. Books were necessary, as one might expect, at every level of Roman education. The alphabet, then syllables, and basic reading were taught at the beginning, on wax tablets, then later on writing boards. At the secondary level, under the *grammaticus*, *grammar and the interpretation of literature were taught, in Greek and Latin, with reference to many school texts. The third level focused on rhetoric and required both theoretical treatises and sample speeches, and the final level, philosophy, again required access to many books.

Most reading was still done aloud, which required one to learn when to breathe, to raise or lower the voice, and to gesture; it had its physical component, so that reading was commonly positioned in medical books among those exercises that promote good health. Some reading was silent, but usually for texts, like a letter, that did not seem to lend themselves to public consumption. Catullus and Cicero were the first to distinguish kinds of reader, adding to the aristocrats and the teachers traditionally associated with them a new, broad middle group that read more for pleasure than utility, that preferred a simple style, and that was indifferent to the physical qualities of the book. Among them were government employees, soldiers, merchants, tradesmen, and an increasing number of women—indeed, Ovid was especially conscious of this last group. The extensive use of writing within the military suggests that especially in the empire, some level of literacy was widespread, but the poor spelling and grammar of many of the graffiti in Pompeii warn that many of the 'new readers' had absorbed little beyond the basics.

6.4 Libraries

The first significant private libraries came to Rome as the spoils of war: in the 2nd century BC Aemilius Paulus brought back the books of Perseus, king of Macedonia, and Sulla looted from Athens the library of Apellicon of Teos, which included many of Aristotle's books. It quickly became fashionable to have a library in noble villas, with aristocrats like Cicero having books at home but also freely using the libraries of their friends. The library in the Villa of the Papyri in Herculaneum, probably owned in the 1st century BC by Caesar's father-in-law, L. Calpurnius Piso, exemplifies this trend, although its focus on philosophers from Epicurus to Philodemus was probably atypical.

Julius Caesar's plans for a public library in Rome were not carried out, so that it fell to G. Asinius Pollio to found the first public library in Rome. Augustus founded two more, in the Temple of Apollo on the Palatine and in the Portico of Octavia at the Campus Martius. Later emperors built others; beginning with Trajan, libraries were often incorporated into the public baths, until by AD 350 there were 29 in Rome. Libraries were built in the provinces as well, often with the aid of wealthy donors like the younger Pliny, who endowed the library in his native Como. The eastern provinces had a number of famous libraries (e.g. the library of Celsus at Ephesus and, in Athens, the libraries established by Pantainos—built between AD 98 and 102—and by Hadrian), but curiously, the western half of the empire outside Italy has only two securely attested libraries, at Carthage in Tunisia and Timgad in Algeria.

Roman libraries were laid out differently from Greek ones. The Greek library generally contained books in Greek only, stored in small rooms that basically served as stacks and opened onto a colonnade where readers consulted the scrolls. Roman culture was bilingual, so libraries were divided into two sections, one for books in Greek and one for Latin. Scrolls were stored in wooden bookcases (*armaria*), with the centre of the room kept free for readers. Libraries were generally open in the mornings only, but borrowing was occasionally permitted.

6.5 Textual criticism

The initial transmission of texts in ancient Rome was casual, with Cicero complaining that his speeches were mangled and the plays of Plautus being adapted freely by actors. Stability began with the early grammarians. Varro, for example, established a corpus of genuine Plautine plays and worked on the interpretation of obsolete or difficult words. Adoption as a school text helped to preserve a work but also subjected it to poor copying and second-rate scholarly intervention. Among a group of 1st-century AD scholars, the

most famous was M. Valerius Probus, who applied Alexandrian methods, correcting transcription errors, punctuating, and adding critical signs for Virgil, Horace, and Lucretius. Later, Fronto and Gellius studied the early republican authors, attempting to recover readings from old MSS to correct the texts. From late antiquity some 27 subscriptions—formulaic expressions at the end of a book indicating the circumstances under which it was revised and copied—attest to the interest of such important families as the Nicomachi and the Symmachi in correcting and preserving key works of Roman culture like the first decade of Livy's histories.

6.6 From roll to codex

The term *codex* was originally the Roman name for the wooden tablet *notebook. Before the end of the 1st century AD, the Romans began replacing the wood with parchment, and Martial indicates that standard authors were available in this format in his day. Papyrus was not an appropriate substitute for wood in the codex format, since folding and sewing weakened it at the key point, the spine. Parchment had not worked well for scrolls, since it made the MS too heavy, but it was admirably suited to the codex.

The rise of the parchment codex is linked to the rise of Christianity: all of the Christian works found in 2nd-century AD Egypt are in codex form, while 98 per cent of the non-Christian works are not. A number of reasons have been suggested for this. Initially Christianity spread among the lower and middle classes, who had known the codex as a school notebook, a notepad, or a professional manual. It was easier to find a passage in a codex than in a scroll—an important point for a new religion in which textual authority was important. In addition, the parchment codex was free from the pagan overtones that went with the papyrus scroll. Whatever the reason, by the 4th century AD large bibles like the Codex *Sinaiticus were being produced in codex form, which ended up being the dominant model even for pagan texts as antiquity came to an end.

7 Runes

The earliest known example of writing in runes comes from the Danish island of Funen during the second half of the 1st century AD. Often inelegant, runes are associated with peoples not known for their cultural achievements in other areas.

Runes are alphabetic, though without taking full advantage of that system (e.g. consonants do not double) (*see* **1**). They seem to be drawn from the Roman alphabet, adapted to a non-Latin language: five 'unnecessary' letters (K, Q, X, Y, and Z) are used for phonemes and language clusters that have no Latin equivalent, while one rune has no equal in the Roman alphabet. Runes began in the Romanized centres of northern Germany and spread from there, appearing on high-prestige artefacts to record the owner's or giver's name. The only function that goes beyond this is naming a spear 'Prober', which may indicate a certain awareness of the metaphorical but does not suggest magical overtones. The most likely explanation is that runes were developed from Roman writing in the 2nd century AD by Germanic people who had had some contact with the Romans, to mark the donor or maker, ownership or function. Objects so marked became a good way to indicate group membership and forge alliances, something for which the Romans themselves at the same time used language.

8 China

The earliest writing in China appeared *c.*1200 BC in Anyang, the last capital of the Shang dynasty (*see* **1**, **40**). It is sometimes said that this writing was stimulated by contact with Mesopotamia, but there is no archaeological evidence to confirm this assumption. Early Chinese writing appears as a fully developed system, and reasoning from analogy suggests that what has been found at Anyang must be a later version of a writing system whose lost early stages would have resembled early Mesopotamian tablets and Linear A and B remains. Here the problem may revolve around the fact that some writing materials survive longer than others. Early Chinese writing is also found on bones (as souvenirs of royal hunts), turtle shells (as records of the delivery of goods), jade and other precious stones (as marks of ownership), and pottery, but not on the mats of wood or bamboo slips which served as books from the 5th century BC. Letters written on silk were mentioned by writers several centuries before the time to which the earliest surviving examples can be dated. If the early stages of Chinese writing also appeared on surfaces as fragile as these, their disappearance would make sense.

Early Chinese script is often said to be pictographic, but here, each character is part of a real writing system with both a signifier and a signified; in addition, many Chinese pictographs could represent more than one word, so that by evoking a sound as well as an image, they were used as phonograms as well. Abstract signs exist, as do compounds, but only one quarter to one third of the approximately 4,500 surviving signs have been deciphered. These symbols appear most often on animal bones that were heated and cracked for the purpose of divination, with the date and the name of the diviner given first, then the question to which an answer was desired; occasionally the answer is present as well. Fewer examples survive of the bronze ritual vessels in which the elite presented offerings to their dead ancestors, with the name either of the person who commissioned the bowl or of the dead ancestor written on it.

Chinese books written on thin slips of wood begin to be found with some regularity in excavations from the 2nd century BC. The slip (*ce* or *jian*), generally made of bamboo, is 9–9½ inches long and a quarter- to half-an-inch long, with one column per side but often with writing on both sides. Writing in vertical columns seems to be an accommodation to the shape of the bamboo slip. Fan-fold paper books and scrolls became common beginning in the 2nd century AD. The book was covered with a case, a title was pasted on the corner of the cover, and the book was stored vertically. Characters were formed with a hair brush—an appropriate instrument for writing on silk and bamboo, but one which also helped stimulate the straightening of the curves in the old characters, so that their resemblances to pictorial symbols diminished. Chinese writing was linked to painting through *calligraphy, so that by the 3rd century AD the traditional concern for careful letter-making had been extended to book illustration. Imperial edicts and government reports in turn were written on rectangular tablets (*fang*), and writing is also found on triangular prisms (*kie*).

Among the earliest Chinese books is the Book of Odes (*Shijing*), some 300 poems depicting life in the 8th and 7th centuries BC. The works of Confucius (*c.*551–479 BC) were also copied frequently. Around AD 100 Xu Shen wrote a lexicon, and Cao Pei (AD 187–226) produced an encyclopaedia. The Chinese also had scholars investigating the authenticity of works, revising and *collating texts, and commenting upon early books at roughly the same time as the Alexandrian scholars were active in the West. Emperor Wu-ti (157–87/6 BC) set up a body to collect and copy books, and in 26 BC Liu Xiang organized a thorough survey of the book holdings in the Chinese empire.

9 Mesoamerica

Beginning as early as 500 BC, the peoples of Mesoamerica created writing systems in isolation from the Old World (*see* **1**, **46**). The earliest of these scripts in particular remain difficult, if not impossible, to read; as iconic, hieroglyphic systems, they preserved a sense of union between spirit and matter that is fundamentally non-European.

A system of prewriting begins with the Olmec civilization around 900 BC. Mesoamerican writing proper began in the glyphic markers of personal identity: people were identified by signs in headdresses, and captors differentiated from captives by gestures and positioning. Initially the headdresses were lexemic, with signified and signifier still coupled, but beginning around 900 BC the lexical identifier was separated from the representation of the body associated with it. This separation remained porous throughout the scripts of Mesoamerica, however, making them iconic in ways that resemble Egyptian hieroglyphs more than cuneiform and early Chinese writing, which moved towards abstraction more quickly and definitively. Actual writing, in which language is represented graphically, detached from the body of the referent, and arranged sequentially to accommodate greater syntactic complexity, appeared around 500 BC in the Zapotec area of Oaxaca, Mexico, but unfortunately much of it cannot be understood with certainty. A handful of texts also survive from the first few centuries after Christ from the area in and around the Isthmus of Tehuantepec. This writing contains relatively few icons; whether it is decipherable or not remains debatable.

The best-known and best-understood Mesoamerican writing is Mayan, for which thousands of texts ranging from the time of Christ to the 16th century survive. The earliest examples remain difficult to decipher, but examples from the classical period contain comprehensible symbols that changed over time. Mayan script was a relative latecomer in Mesoamerica, using the dating system and column format that had become standard in the other scripts by this time. The earliest examples appear on small objects like carved greenstones and heirlooms, with a tendency for one glyph to fill a block first, then for the block to contain several glyphs. Mayan writing is often said to be tied to the administrative and propaganda needs of the complex society from which it originated; but given the relatively small number of people who could read, this assumption is difficult to prove.

The Mayan script remained tied to the society in which it was created and closed to external influences, ultimately dying with the Spanish conquest. Beginning about AD 350–450, however, the civilization around Teotihuacan began to exert its influence, using an open script that was easily adaptable to the languages and cultures with which it came in contact. The more open writing systems continued among the indigenous peoples of Mexico even after the conquest, appearing in court documents alongside Spanish, then eventually giving way to the Roman script of the Europeans.

BIBLIOGRAPHY

L. Avrin, *Scribes, Script, and Books* (1991)

T. Birt, *Das antike Buchwesen in seinem Verhältniss zur Litteratur* (1882)

H. Blanck, *Das Buch in der Antike* (1992)

W. G. Boltz, *The Origin and Early Development of the Chinese Writing System* (1994)

E. H. Boone *et al.*, eds., *Writing Without Words* (1994)

L. Casson, *Libraries in the Ancient World* (2001)

G. Cavallo, *Libri, scribi, scritture a Ercolano* (1983)

— 'Between *Volumen* and Codex: Reading in the Roman World', in *A History of Reading in the West*, ed. G. Cavallo *et al.*, tr. L. G. Cochrane (1999; French original, 1995)

E. Chiera, *They Wrote on Clay*, ed. G. C. Cameron, 2e (1969)

J. Černý, *Paper and Books in Ancient Egypt* (1952)

P. T. Daniels *et al.*, eds., *The World's Writing Systems* (1996)

O. A. W. Dilke, *Roman Books and their Impact* (1977)

D. Diringer, *The Book before Printing* (1982)

R. W. V. Elliott, *Runes* (1989)

[Galleries Nationales du Grand Palais,] *Naissance de l'écriture* (1982)

H. Gamble, *Books and Readers in the Early Church* (1995)

J.-J. Glassner, *The Invention of Cuneiform*, tr. and ed. Z. Bahrani *et al.* (2003; French original, 2000)

A. Grafton *et al.*, *Christianity and the Transformation of the Book* (2006)

W. Harris, *Ancient Literacy* (1989)

S. D. Houston, ed., *The First Writing* (2004)

M. A. Hussein, *Origins of the Book* (1970)

W. A. Johnson, *Bookrolls and Scribes in Oxyrhynchus* (2004)

F. Kenyon, *Books and Readers in Ancient Greece and Rome*, 2e (1951)

T. Kleberg, *Buchhandel und Verlagswesen in der Antike* (1967)

R. Pfeiffer, *History of Classical Scholarship from the Beginnings to the End of the Hellenistic Age* (1968)

M. Pope, *The Story of Archaeological Decipherment* (1975)

R. Posner *et al.*, *The Hebrew Book* (1975)

Reynolds and Wilson

C. H. Roberts *et al.*, 'Books in the Graeco-Roman World and in the New Testament', in *CHB* 1

W. Schubart, *Das Buch bei den Griechen und Römern*, 3e (1961)

D. Sider, *The Library of the Villa dei Papiri at Herculaneum* (2005)

R. J. Starr, 'The Circulation of Literary Texts in the Roman World', *Classical Quarterly*, 7 (1987), 213–23

J. Svenbro, *Phrasikleia* (1993)

E. Turner *et al.*, *Greek Manuscripts of the Ancient World*, 2e (1987)

B. L. Ullman, *Ancient Writing and its Influence* (1963)

G. Vermes, *The Dead Sea Scrolls* (1977)

D. J. Wiseman, 'Books in the Ancient Near East and in the Old Testament', in *CHB* 1

4 The History of the Book in Byzantium

N. G. WILSON

In the early years of the 4th century AD, the literary world of Greece and Rome experienced the completion of a revolution that had begun some 200 years earlier: from now on the form of the book was no longer the *scroll (Lat. *volumen*), with the text arranged in a series of columns on one side of the papyrus only, but the *codex, with pages. The new format had advantages. If one were searching for a particular passage, it was often quicker to find the right page than to unwind a scroll to the appropriate point, and the use of both sides of the leaves meant that more text could be written on a given quantity of *papyrus or on *parchment, which now became available as an alternative. This increased capacity ought to have facilitated the preservation of a large proportion of the vast range of Greek literature, especially as papyrus had traditionally been inexpensive and probably still was. Evidently, however, the book trade was not sufficiently organized to deploy the necessary resources. What can now be read is a minute percentage of the texts that were probably still available. The codex format, however, if the *margins were fully used, did permit the preservation of material culled from a wide variety of secondary literature, i.e. ancient scholarly monographs and commentaries, almost none of which have descended as independent texts.

During the millennium of its existence the extent of the Byzantine empire fluctuated greatly, but even after the loss of political control it retained varying degrees of cultural influence in such areas as southern Italy, Sicily, Egypt, the Levant, and the Balkans. From the beginning of the period parchment was adopted with increasing frequency as a more durable, if more expensive, writing material than papyrus. Various scripts were in use for literary texts. Of these, the most calligraphic is the type generally known as biblical *uncial or *majuscule, seen at its best in the Codex *Sinaiticus of the Bible, which can be dated to the middle of the 4th century; but, despite its name, the use of this script was not confined to biblical texts. With the decline of the empire resulting from the Arab conquests, book production suffered; it is not clear, however, to what extent the loss of Egypt in 641 affected the supply of papyrus nor, supposing that it did, whether this was the only or the major factor leading to reduced production. Very few books (or fragments) survive that can plausibly be dated to the second half of the 7th century or any time in the 8th. When signs of a revival appear *c.*800, it seems likely that the Byzantines were no longer using papyrus in large quantities, but that they were soon able to avail themselves of the introduction of paper, now being produced in the Levant. Nevertheless, information about the supply and price of writing material at this date is almost entirely lacking. A likely conjecture is that shortages led to experiments with styles of script that had hitherto been used in documents rather than literary texts and that could be written with smaller letters. One of these experiments was eventually found to be satisfactory and generally adopted; it has been suggested that this adaptation of *cursive script with numerous *ligatures combining two or three letters was invented or popularized by monks of the *Stoudios monastery in Constantinople, which was noted for its *scriptorium from the 9th century onwards. Uncial was gradually abandoned except for a few luxury copies of texts destined for liturgical use.

Book production was determined to a very large extent by religious requirements: copies of the Bible, liturgical texts, lives of saints and sermons by the Cappadocian Fathers and St John Chrysostom survive in considerable numbers. There was also a steady production of texts for use in school, most of which were the classics of ancient pagan literature. Some of these have come down to us in numerous copies, but this is not true of all—the frequently made assumption that each pupil owned a copy of every text in the syllabus is by no means secure. Members of the professions needed their manuals and specialized treatises; higher education, however, was much less well organized than in western Europe and did not develop a *pecia system to provide students with copies of essential texts. An educated class that read literature for pleasure scarcely existed. Books seem to have been very expensive. The prices paid by the bibliophile Arethas *c.*900 for a few admittedly calligraphic copies on good-quality parchment prove that a year's salary of a low-ranking civil servant would hardly suffice for the purchase of half-a-dozen volumes. Costs may have been reduced as the production of paper increased;

Marginal note by Archbishop Arethas (c.860–c.940) expressing his disgust at Lucian's apparent confession of homosexuality in his *Amores*.

paper was fairly widely used in Byzantium as early as the 11th century, though it probably all had to be imported (*see* **10**). Yet the re-use of parchment in *palimpsests continued and was not confined to remote or backward regions of the empire—a fact demonstrating that cheap and readily available writing material could not be taken for granted. In these circumstances, one would expect most scribes to save space by using the comprehensive set of *abbreviations that was available for grammatical inflections and certain common words or technical terms. For marginal *commentaries the use of the abbreviations was an unavoidable necessity, but generally scribes did not resort to this solution for the main text. They tended to use the abbreviations at the end of a line to achieve *justification of the margin, which may be a hint that on aesthetic grounds they preferred to avoid them elsewhere.

Scribes were not organized as a guild. It is clear that many individuals made their own copies rather than employing a professional. There were some professionals, as can be seen from the occasional *colophon in which the writer describes himself (women copyists are almost unknown) as a calligrapher; it was possible to earn one's living in this way, but probably not many did so. Some large monasteries (e.g. the Stoudios monastery) had a scriptorium and presumably accepted commissions from external customers; many colophons state that the copyist was a monk. Colophons by Greek scribes are not as frequent or informative as those found in Armenian MSS, however, and so we know relatively little about Greek scribes. A further consequence of this is that it is often impossible to determine in which part of the empire a book was written, because there are only a limited number of cases in which the script gives a clear indication, whereas with Latin MSS it is usually not very

difficult to identify the country of origin, and sometimes much greater precision about a MS's provenance can be achieved.

A tantalizing glimpse of the workings of a scriptorium is provided by the rules drawn up for the Stoudios monastery by St Theodore (759–826). There is mention of a chief calligrapher, who is responsible for assigning tasks fairly, preparing the parchment for use, and maintaining the binder's tools in good order. There are penalties for him and for monks who misbehave or fail to perform their duties, e.g. if a scribe breaks a pen in a fit of anger. Inter alia the scribe is required to take care over *spelling, *punctuation, and *diacritics, to stick to his own task, and not to alter the text he is copying. What is not stated is whether a scribe was expected to copy a certain number of pages each day, and how much the house charged external purchasers. There is no reference to illuminators, but scanty evidence from other sources suggests that they may have had independent workshops.

*Calligraphy does not appear to have been appreciated in Byzantium as an art in the same way as in some other cultures; but the use of the term by scribes is proof that some clients had a high regard for their services, and many extant MSS are marvels of elegant script with a uniformly high standard maintained for several hundred pages—a striking example is the Euclid written for Arethas in 888 by Stephen the cleric (who as it happens does not call himself a calligrapher in the colophon). It is also clear that, for biblical and other religious texts, there was an expectation that formal script would be used, and generally such books, even if not elegantly written, exhibit a presentable standard of penmanship. This requirement went hand in hand with a conservative tradition characteristic of Byzantine culture: an archaizing tendency detectable in the Palaeologan period (c.1280–c.1320) led to the production of many copies, mainly but not exclusively of religious texts, that at first sight look a good deal earlier and as a result used to be incorrectly dated to the 12th century. Nevertheless, schoolteachers and other professionals making copies intended primarily for personal use were often content to write a less formal hand with many cursive elements and abbreviations; these scripts too have often been wrongly dated. In many cases, there is enough individual character in them to permit identification of the writer. A very neat example of this type of script with lavish use of abbreviations is seen in various volumes penned by Eustathius, the lecturer at the patriarch's seminary in the capital, who c.1178 became archbishop of Salonica. Much less legible is the protean hand of a 12th-century grammarian called Ioannikios, who can be identified as the scribe of nearly twenty extant MSS, containing predominantly works by Galen and Aristotle, some of which were probably commissioned from him by the Italian translator Burgundio of Pisa.

Circulation and trade are topics about which information is inadequate. The 6th-century lawyer and historian Agathias speaks of bookshops in the capital and there are occasional later references to booksellers. Yet it is curious that a society which attached great importance to the written word and devoted care to the education of imperial and ecclesiastical administrators capable of drafting documents has left so little record of this and other related matters. It is fairly clear, however, that a desire to obtain unusual texts could not normally be satisfied by a visit to a neighbouring shop, even if one lived in the capital of the empire.

The Byzantines called themselves Romans, but understood that they were custodians of the Greek literary heritage; in their formal writings they did their best to imitate the language and style of the Greek classics. One has to ask how far they succeeded in preserving the stock of Greek literature they inherited in late antiquity. It is fairly certain that already by this date a number of classical texts were no longer in circulation; the destruction of the library at the Serapeum in Alexandria in 391 will no doubt have led to further losses. Though there is very little historical evidence on these matters, it seems that the emperors never succeeded in maintaining a substantial library comparable to those found in the great cultural centres of the ancient world; a monastery with a collection of several hundred volumes such as St John on Patmos was unusually well provided for, and a library of fewer than 100 books might be reckoned perfectly satisfactory. The Byzantines would have needed much greater resources than they disposed of in order to conserve a high proportion of the texts that were still extant. For a time they had partial success: Photius in the middle of the 9th century was still able to locate—it is not known how or where—copies of many important works, especially historical texts that no longer survive today. Probably the copies he consulted were already unique, and if they were not texts of orthodox theological content, there was always a risk that they might be discarded by a reader anxious to make a palimpsest copy of some work of seemingly greater relevance (a notorious example is the palimpsest in which liturgical texts have been written over unique treatises by Archimedes, fragments of the Athenian orator Hyperides, and a hitherto unknown commentary on an ancient philosophical text). Copies of rare works that had not suffered such a fate or been destroyed by accident mostly disappeared in 1204 when the Fourth Crusade sacked Constantinople. After that date, the range of works available was essentially the same as can now be read in medieval copies. When the Turks took the Byzantine capital in 1453, there were few if any texts, the loss of which we should now regret, lurking in the libraries in Constantinople.

BIBLIOGRAPHY
[Dumbarton Oaks Colloquium,] *Byzantine Books and Bookmen* (1975)
N. Wilson, 'The Libraries of the Byzantine World', *Greek Roman and Byzantine Studies*, 8 (1967) 53–80 (repr. with addenda in *Griechische Kodikologie und Textüberlieferung*, ed. D. Harlfinger (1980), and further addenda (in Italian translation) in *Le biblioteche nel mondo antico e medievale*, ed. G. Cavallo (1988))
— 'The Manuscripts of the Greek Classics in the Middle Ages and Renaissance', *Classica et Medievalia*, 47 (1996), 379–89
— *The Oxford Handbook of Byzantine Studies* (2008)

5 The European Medieval Book

Christopher de Hamel

1 The Dark Ages

For more than a thousand years, between the adoption of the *codex as the normal format for MSS in the late Roman empire and the invention of printing in Europe around 1450, all Western books were copied by hand. This is the period that is now called the Middle Ages. Medieval Europe evolved out of the collapse of the Roman empire (Rome finally fell in 476) and emerged in the early kingdoms of Lombardy and in the provinces of Germany, Frankish Gaul, Visigothic Spain, and Anglo-Saxon England. This era is intimately tied up with the history of Christianity, which is a literate religion, like Judaism and Islam. Books—manuscripts (MSS)—were essential to Christianity's success and consolidation. The Scriptures, with written commentaries and interpretations, were fundamental to medieval religious life, and the Christian liturgy was inconceivable without readings and recitations from books. Every church and monastery in Europe inevitably required and used books of some kind. Moreover, Christianity entered into a world where books had been known and valued. The nostalgic and lingering respect for Greek and Roman classical learning survived through the Middle Ages, carrying an uneasy sense that ancient knowledge was somehow unusually special and was even intellectually superior to that of later times. This theme winds in and out of the history of Christian book culture, sometimes in direct conflict and often in an uneasy partnership. The earliest adherents of Christianity grew up in a civilization familiar with Greek and Latin texts of poetry, philosophy, history, and science. Early Christian writers such as Boethius (*c*.480–*c*.524) and Cassiodorus (*c*.490–*c*.580) worked and wrote within this tradition. Boethius was the author of commentaries on Aristotle as well as a work on the Trinity. Cassiodorus, a former Roman civil servant, assembled the *Variae*, a collection of imperial laws, before establishing a monastery near Naples and compiling works on the Psalms and other Christian subjects. Christianity and classical learning were not necessarily contradictory, and the books that emerged around the Mediterranean show debts to both cultures.

A crucial legacy of early Christianity in a Roman context was the invention and adoption of the *codex format. Books in the ancient world had mostly been produced on continuous *scrolls, but the codex was ideal for texts that needed constant consultation at different places, especially law and the Bible. Biblical texts, such as *gospel books, *psalters, and the letters of St Paul, are among the most fundamental of early medieval MSS, for they were used in the liturgy as well as in private study. With these came the biblical commentaries, homilies, and explanations of theology and the religious life with which the ever-expanding Christian Church prepared and defended itself against the assaults on the Roman empire from beyond its fragile borders. Many primitive MSS were prepared, probably mostly by monks, of patristic authors such as Ambrose of Milan (*c*.339–97), Jerome (*c*.345–420), Augustine of Hippo (354–430), Gregory the Great (*c*.540–604), and Isidore of Seville (*c*.560–636).

Early Christian books from southern Europe in what are sometimes called the Dark Ages are usually squarish in shape, on *parchment (*papyrus gradually died out, except in Egypt), and are commonly written in *uncial script or *rustic capitals, generally with enlarged opening initials often in an orange-red colour, and sometimes with pictures in rather sketchy painterly styles not unlike those of ancient Roman frescos. There must have been sites of book production in places like Ravenna, Lyons (a major Roman town in Gaul), and in Rome itself. On the fringes of the old Roman empire, from former provinces such as Gaul and Spain, informal *cursive scripts developed too, derived from the bureaucratic hands of regional imperial administration. Some of these eventually become very distinctive of certain areas, such as Visigothic *minuscule in Spain, *Beneventan minuscule in southern Italy, and a variety of localizable Merovingian cursive hands in France.

By the late 6th century, the papacy had consolidated its position sufficiently to institute a new, Christian form of Roman imperialism. Gregory the Great sent missionaries to England in 597 bringing, according to Bede, 'all the books that would be necessary' for the conversion of the English. The Roman monks, working northwards in Britain, encountered the Irish or Celtic Christians coming south, carrying their own very different style of books. The ultimate sources of Irish Christianity and MS decoration are elusive, but perhaps both had reached the Western Isles through northern Africa, where the ornament of Coptic books resembles some aspects of what is now known as the Irish or 'insular' style, with its *half-uncial script, large interlaced initials, and carpet pages formed of the extremely elaborate decorative interlace of swirling plant stems and incorporating dragons and birds. Famous examples are the Book of *Durrow, late 7th century (Dublin, Trinity College, MS 57), the *Lindisfarne Gospels, early 8th century (London, BL, Cotton MS Nero D. IV), and the Book of *Kells, c.800 (Dublin, Trinity College, MS 58). In the course of the 7th and 8th centuries, the Irish and Roman strands of Christianity merged in Britain, and books were created in a fusion of the two styles. A good example is the *Vespasian Psalter (London, BL, Cotton MS Vespasian A. I), made probably in Canterbury, which included innovations like *historiated initials, or pictures enclosed within letters. Some MSS created in England, such as the Codex *Amiatinus (Florence, Biblioteca Medicea Laurenziana, cod. Amiat.1), a vast single-volume bible in uncial script, are as sophisticated and as classical as anything made in southern Europe.

From England, then, Christianity and insular books moved with missionaries like Willibrord and Boniface to Germany and to other parts of northern Europe. Descendants of the old insular styles are found in MSS made in monasteries and churches founded in Cologne, Fulda, *St Gall, Freising, Würzburg, and elsewhere. By the 8th century, there were certainly major centres of book production across southern Germany and Austria; in France at *Luxeuil, Autun, Corbie, Fleury, and St-Denis, for example; and in Italy in Monte Cassino, Lucca, Bobbio, Rome, Verona, and elsewhere. The earliest surviving book lists—such as that of St-Wandrille in France in the time of Abbot Wando (742–7)—include *gospel books, saints' lives, monastic rules, history, collections of letters from Augustine and Jerome, sermons, and biblical commentaries. The volumes themselves doubtless varied immensely from crowded little tracts in cramped cursive scripts to stately volumes with zoomorphic decoration and bindings ornamented with jewels and precious metal.

2 Carolingian Europe

Charlemagne (c.742–814) took control of the vast Franco-German dominions in the late 8th century. He brought Alcuin (c.740–804) from England to establish a palace library and to reform education in the court. Under circumstances that are hard to document but are graphically visible in the MSS, the script was standardized into a new and (to modern eyes) extremely legible round style, known as *Carolingian (or Caroline) minuscule. By the early 9th century, most books being made in Charlemagne's empire conformed to a remarkably consistent style, often beautifully laid out with spacious *margins prepared according to mathematically precise proportions. Some books had very fine pictures, modelled (probably deliberately) on late antique prototypes. Devotional books made for the royal family and other principal figures of the Church and nobility sometimes had large initials or even whole pages executed in burnished gold. Some very grand books were evidently commissioned for use as symbolic gifts within the royal families, such as the *Dagulf Psalter commissioned by Charlemagne for the pope (Vienna, Österreichisches Nationalbibliothek, Cod. 1861).

There were centres of book production in the great monasteries in Aachen, Tours, Auxerre, St-Amand, Reichenau, and elsewhere, making books for their own use and sometimes also for outsiders. The monastery of St-Martin in Tours, for example, produced Latin bibles for export, such as the spectacular and massive First Bible of Charles the Bald, written c.846 (Paris, BNF, ms. lat. 1). Major MSS were made in and around Rheims, including the *Utrecht Psalter, c.820–40, which has dynamic and frenzied drawings clearly derived from ancient Roman models (Utrecht, University Library, MS 32). It is commonly associated with Ebo (d. 851), archbishop of Rheims 816–35, who had previously been court librarian in Aachen. Another book from Rheims is the vast Bible of San Paolo fuori le Mura—still in the monastery of that name on the outskirts of Rome—c.870, perhaps brought to Italy by Charles the Bald at the time of his coronation by the pope in 875. The 9th century is the first period from which MSS survive from France, Italy, and Germany in any reasonable quantity, including the earliest copies of many classical texts. The handsome appearance of many Carolingian books is a reflection of European prosperity and an evident desire for order and legibility.

In England, however, book production fell off dramatically during the Viking invasions of the 9th century. In a reversal of Charlemagne and Alcuin, Alfred the Great, king of Wessex 871–99, brought scholars from France—such as Grimbald of St-Bertin (d. 901)—to revive learning in England. The Carolingian script was promoted in England, especially in Winchester under Aethelwold, bishop 963–84, and was also practised in Canterbury, Abingdon, and Worcester. Important Anglo-Saxon books include the Benedictional of St Aethelwold himself (London, BL, Add. MS 49598); the Eadui Gospels, early 11th century, signed by the Canterbury scribe Eadui surnamed Basan, 'the fat' (Hanover, Kestner Museum, WM. xxiᵃ 36); and the Harley Psalter, copied in mid-11th-century Canterbury from the 9th-century Utrecht Psalter, mentioned above (London, BL, Harley MS 603).

The Carolingian legacy was taken up by the Ottonian emperors in Germany, and magnificent MSS were made for Otto III, emperor 983–1002, including a gospel book of quite exceptional splendour in a lavish jewelled binding (Munich, Bayerische Staatsbibliothek, Clm. 4453). Centres such as Bamberg, Reichenau (probably), Trier, and Echternach produced books with very fine illumination, including work by the important Trier artist of the late 10th century known as the Master of the Registrum Gregorii. Some Ottonian imperial MSS were written in gold on purple parchment, a symbolic device

believed to go back to the libraries of the emperors of ancient Rome and Constantinople.

In the meantime, MSS were being made in monasteries and churches in Greece and the eastern Mediterranean (see 4). Most Greek texts of the Middle Ages were religious, rather than the secular texts of the ancient world. The most common were the different parts of the Bible (the original language of the New Testament) and patristic and liturgical books. Some were finely illuminated, such as the 6th-century Vienna Genesis (Vienna, Österreichisches Nationalbibliothek, Cod. theol. gr. 31). From 726 until about 842, the period of Iconoclasm, MS illustrations were banned in the eastern empire. Until about the 9th century, most Greek MSS were written in uncial script; minuscule was adopted especially following the initiative of Theodore of Stoudios (759–826), who re-founded the monastery and scriptorium of *Stoudios in Constantinople in 799.

3 Romanesque Europe

In western Europe, religious life was reformed under Gregory VII, pope 1073–85, whose papacy marked the beginning of a century or more of vigorous monastic fervour, the building and re-endowing of many Benedictine houses, and the foundation and spread of new orders, including the Cluniacs, Augustinians, Cistercians, and Carthusians. This was a most intensive period of book production in European monasteries and priories. Library inventories and very large numbers of surviving Romanesque books attest to vigorous attempts to make monastic collections as comprehensive as possible. Chronicles often record that an abbot or bishop had given great sets of books, which may often mean that the benefactor had sponsored their production in high-profile campaigns of building up libraries. Some records survive, showing monasteries seeking *exemplars from elsewhere and lending books to each other. After the Norman Conquest of England in 1066, MSS and scribes were sent from Normandy to English cathedrals, and strong cultural links with French Benedictine monasteries such as Jumièges and Mont-St-Michel are reflected in books made for English cathedral priories, especially Christ Church in Canterbury, Exeter, and Durham. Echoes of Norman forms of script and decoration can be seen too in late 11th-century books made in Sicily, similarly occupied by the Normans from about 1060. A generation later, remarkable homogeneity may be observed in Cistercian MSS. Their austere and elegant style, with prickly script and monochrome initials, may have begun in the mother house of Cîteaux in Burgundy, but the style is easily recognizable in Cistercian books made as far away as monasteries of the order in eastern and southern Europe. The centralized administration of the Cistercian houses has left clear traces in the books they made.

The number of texts in circulation at any period was cumulative. Each generation added new authors and titles to an ever-expanding corpus of required books. The librarian of a late 11th-century monastery might want copies of the Bible—including one of the new, vast many-volumed *lectern bibles initially popular in Italy—with the fundamental biblical commentaries, such as Gregory on the books of Ezekiel and Job, Augustine on the Psalms and John, Jerome on the Prophets, Ambrose on Luke, and Bede on Acts. He would want basic theology and philosophy, such as the *Consolatio Philosophiae* of Boethius and Augustine's *De Civitate Dei*, and some works of Carolingian authors such as Claudius of Turin (d. *c.*827), Rabanus Maurus (d. 856), Pascasius Radbertus (d. 865), and Remigius of Auxerre (d. *c.*908); monastic rules and canons of church councils; early Christian history, including Eusebius, Orosius, and perhaps Bede, and selected saints' lives; some mathematics, music, and science; basic medicine (a herbal perhaps); a few classical texts used for teaching grammar, such as Virgil; and liturgy, of course. It is a good list, but ultimately a finite one. By the early 12th century a monastery would want all these books, and many more, for there were new texts now by Lanfranc (d. 1089), Anselm of Canterbury (d. 1109), Ivo of Chartres (d. 1115), Anselm of Laon (d. 1117), and many others. By the second quarter of the century, learning had begun to move away from the exclusive monopolies of the monasteries, into the schools which eventually evolved into medieval universities, and into the domain of literate laity, both aristocratic and administrative. The number of authors had multiplied further, including Gilbert of Nogent (d. 1124), Rupert of Deutz (d. *c.*1129), Gilbert of Auxerre (d. 1134), Peter Abelard (d. 1142/3), Hugh of St-Victor (d. 1142), William of Malmesbury (d. *c.*1143), Bernard of Clairvaux (d. 1153), Gilbert de la Porrée (d. 1154), William of Conches (d. *c.*1154), Thierry of Chartres (d. *c.*1155), Zachary of Besançon (mid-12th century), and Peter Lombard (d. 1160). There was an almost relentless stream of new titles in the lists of desiderata, in theology, history, politics, geography, natural history (*bestiaries, for example), liturgy (*missals rather than the older *sacramentaries), and the first ancient Greek works translated into Latin from Arabic

intermediaries. At the same time, monasteries were increasingly being expected to produce books for lay patrons as well, including luxury psalters. It was too much. What was laudable and mostly achievable for many monastic *scriptoria in 1050 was simply impossible a century later. This has significant implications.

The mid-12th century was probably the most important watershed in medieval European book production. It affected what books looked like and how they were made. These two points can be taken in turn. Before the 12th century, monks would generally read books aloud to themselves, from end to end, slowly meditating and ruminating on the text. A monk could spend several months or even years studying a single book and could still hope to master most of his monastery's library in a lifetime. By about 1150, however, the number of works in circulation had rapidly become far too great for any person to manage. New kinds of books were therefore devised: glossed texts with selected marginal quotations for quick reference, *encyclopaedias (such as Peter Lombard's *Sententiae* for theology and Gratian's *Decretum* for canon law), *concordances, *florilegia, digests, and *indexes. Scribes devised ways of looking things up, with devices such as alphabetical order, chapter numbers for the Bible and other texts, tables of contents, coloured *paragraph-marks, *running titles along the top of pages, sometimes even *folio numbers, all of which were the result of a sudden excess of knowledge. This phenomenon has some parallels with the information explosion of the 21st century, with innovations in the ways of searching texts. For the first time, books became resources to be consulted, frequently at speed, rather than merely to be read at leisure. The changes were also due to an increase in the lay readership of books, including literate administrators and lawyers. Unlike monks, these were often people in a hurry. A MS of about 1200, usually in two columns, bristling with many carefully graded coloured initials, its margins packed with forms of *apparatus for rapid reference, is very different in appearance from a typical book of 150 years earlier, commonly written as a single column of dense text, elegant but austere, with few initials and scarcely any division between words and almost none between paragraphs.

It is reasonable to assume that most MSS earlier than the 12th century were copied by monks (and sometimes nuns), or at least by members of the Church, mostly in leisure time or in periods set aside among other daily duties of the religious life. Where there is historical or architectural evidence, it seems that scribes commonly worked in the cloisters, where the light was good. Sometimes several monks collaborated on a single book, writing and decorating different sections of the (still unbound) volume. The script and the associated decoration were often executed by the same people. All this began to change around 1100. The sudden and rapid increase in the number of books meant that many monasteries simply no longer had the resources or the time to keep up. Some were also under additional pressure to supply luxurious devotional books, like psalters, for local lords and their families. The first evidence emerges of professional scribes, called in by a scriptorium to help with book production, and of secular artists and craftsmen, who evidently travelled from place to place, employed to decorate and illuminate books. A well-known and documented example in England is Master Hugo, whose name suggests that he was not a monk, who was engaged for various artistic projects at Bury St Edmunds Abbey in the 1130s, including the illumination of the *Bury Bible (Cambridge, Corpus Christi College, MS 2). It may be that the increased professionalism and specialization of artists might help explain the increasingly lavish quality of many 12th-century books, often using expensive pigments, such as lapis and burnished gold. Probably too this marks the gradual transference of the place of working from the cloister, which was open to the weather (which would make manipulating gold leaf almost impossible), to some dedicated studio indoors.

By the mid-12th century, professional scribes and illuminators were beginning to set up commercial and urban businesses independent of monasteries. The earliest city in which this certainly occurred was probably Paris, where potential clients were attracted by the royal court and by attendance at the schools of Notre-Dame and St-Victor, forerunners of the university. There were probably also professional workshops at Sens and possibly at Troyes in France within the 12th century, and at Bologna and Oxford by about 1200. The secular book trade in western Europe is well documented in the 13th century. With certain notable exceptions (like the work of Matthew *Paris, monk of St Albans), few MSS were still being made in monasteries or churches by 1250. A late medieval monastery, wanting a book (for many did, of course), would usually have resorted to a professional craftsman, or urban workshop.

4 Script and decoration

The style of medieval script and book illumination varied immensely throughout the 1,500 years or so of the Middle Ages. The graceful and spacious Carolingian minuscule, first adopted around 800, gradually became heavier with the passage of time, losing its roundness (except in Italy) and fusing laterally about the 1180s into what is usually called 'Gothic' script, or '*textura'. This, in turn, split off into formal display hands, beautiful to look at but slow to write, and the quick *cursive scripts of many less grand late medieval books. These hands too constantly diverged and re-crossed, spawning their own unexpected descendants, reflected in the intriguing medieval term lettre bâtarde of the 15th century. Pictorial styles too in MSS conform to the general trends of other contemporaneous arts and architecture. Close parallels can be found between jaunty 7th-century MS decoration of northern Europe and barbarian metalwork and enamels; between sombre and monumental 12th-century miniatures and Romanesque wall-paintings; between sparkling 13th-century illumination and Gothic stained-glass windows, infused with blue and red; between graceful 14th-century Italian book illustration and the panel paintings and frescos of the early Renaissance; and between the homely, engaging, and sometimes comic miniatures of southern Netherlandish books of around 1500 and the paintings of the Flemish primitives, from the Van Eycks to the Bruegels. That is as one would expect. Often, in fact, they were the same actual craftsmen, working in different media.

Most MSS are transcribed from other MSS, and absorb something of their exemplars and of their creator's own time. The lines of textual transmission can be immensely complicated, for a book may be copied from one source and corrected or corrupted against several others, wisely or carelessly, or may have been taken from a very recent exemplar or one which was already many centuries old, or both. The lines of textual descent are predicated by—and are sometimes actually evidence of—trade routes and cultural exchanges of extreme and fascinating complexity. The universality of Latin, the principal language of most west European MSS before (and even after) the 13th century, accorded an internationalism to the book trade which it has never really recovered, even today.

If the differences in physical appearance of medieval books had to be categorized, it would not be that styles change over various periods and places of production, for that is obvious and as expected, but that the books vary according to their kind of text, even at the same period. This is crucial, and is more marked in MSS than in any period of printed books. A missal, the most formal of liturgical books, would be of a very different size and shape from a utilitarian *cartulary, for example, and would be written in a very different script and ornamented in an entirely different way. These would both, in turn, be quite unlike a volume of classical poetry, probably in a tall narrow format with the first letters of each line slightly separated to the left of the *text block, or a heavy lectern bible, in two columns marked for public reading, or a genealogical *chronicle, strung together like washing on a line, or a pocket-sized book of friars' sermons in tiny abbreviated script, and yet all might have been made at the same period, perhaps even by the same scribe. The hierarchy of MSS, like much of medieval social life, was very pronounced.

5 The Gothic book trade

The best-documented early professional book trade was in Paris. This was mainly, but not exclusively, because of the emerging university, which had been formed into a legally distinct corporation by about 1215, attracting students and literate laity from all over Europe. Many booksellers, or *libraires*, were established in the rue Neuve Notre-Dame, the street created around 1164 leading directly out from the west door of the cathedral on the Île de la Cité (now a pedestrian precinct, with the medieval street-plan marked on its flagstones). Here second-hand books could be bought, and new MSS could be commissioned. The actual work was subcontracted. The parchmenters, scribes, and illuminators often lived on the left bank, in the rue des Ecrivains (already so named by 1209) and the rue Erembourg de Brie, both in the parish of St-Séverin beside the rue St-Jacques, which runs south from the Petit Pont. The names of many such workers are recoverable from documentary sources such as taxation records—at least before 1307, when registered booksellers secured exemption from the *taille*, or royal tax. No fewer than 58 booksellers and 68 parchmenters are known by name from 13th-century Paris.

The university exercised considerable control over the book trade in Paris, ostensibly to prevent overcharging and exploitation of a market on which scholarship depended. From 1275, as far as we know, booksellers were first licensed by swearing oaths of obedience to the university, against the security of a bond of 100 *livres*, limiting the profits which they might make in the buying and selling of books. No one except a sworn bookseller, however, could legally practise his trade in Paris, apart from market traders offering used books valued at no more than 30 sous.

There were also strict regulations governing the hiring out of *peciae. The registered booksellers would own unbound exemplars of specific university textbooks, checked and confirmed as accurate (or meant to be) by the university authorities. These they would then hire out in separate sections, a gathering or pecia at a time, so that students or others could copy out the texts themselves, rather like a lending library for scribes. When one section had been copied, the borrower would return the pecia to the bookseller, collect the next in sequence, and so on. It meant that many scribes could in theory be making their own copies of the same book at once, and each transcript was taken directly from a corrected and approved exemplar. These official exemplars are listed in the university regulations of 1275 and repeated in 1304.

Something very similar, although so far not as well documented, occurred in the University of Bologna, where there were also official pecia lists, mainly for law books, in which that university was supreme. Sometimes the MSS themselves still contain discreet notes in the margins where the scribe has jotted down the number of the pecia being copied, which is clear and satisfying evidence of a book being made in a university context. There are huge numbers of extant 13th- and 14th-century MSS from the university towns of Europe. Those from Paris include many texts of scholastic theology and biblical commentary. Among these are works by the great Dominican masters (such as Hugh of St-Cher, d. 1263, Thomas Aquinas, d. 1274, and Albertus Magnus, d. 1280), and the Franciscans, including Bonaventure (d. 1274), Duns Scotus (d. 1308), and Nicholas of Lyra (d. 1349). There were also textbooks of mathematics and science, especially new Latin versions of Aristotle, derived from medieval translations into Arabic. MSS from Bologna included books of Roman law, both secular and religious, often with extensive commentaries. The corpus of civil law was centred on the late Roman legal codes of Justinian and its various imperial supplements. Canon law included huge compilations of papal or episcopal letters known as decretals, of which the best-known collections circulated under the names of Popes Gregory IX (1234), Boniface VIII (1298), and Clement V (1317).

With notable exceptions, university MSS are often big, chunky volumes, written on brownish parchment in highly compressed and abbreviated book-hands, decorated with simple trailing initials in red and blue, and with wide margins crammed with readers' notes and glosses. Some have small sparkling illuminations, evidently by professional artists. Apart from those made in Paris and Bologna, there are recognizably university books attributable to Montpellier, Toulouse, Oxford, and Padua, and later to Cambridge, Erfurt, and elsewhere.

The principal university towns were a focus not merely for students, but also for royal and ecclesiastical administrators, wealthy aristocratic families, and communities of urban friars (or, put differently, the great administrative and religious cities were not merely a focus for civil servants, noblemen, and friars, but also for universities). It is very clear that the early book trade in Paris, Bologna, and Oxford, especially, was not only catering for an academic market but also had a local clientele that was both lower and higher than the university in the hierarchy of customers. At the bottom end—this is not insulting: they would ask to be there—were the friars. The Dominican and Franciscan convents in Paris, Bologna, and Oxford were among the largest and oldest in Europe. Friars were mendicants, travelling and preaching in public. Their books had to be small and portable. There evolved quite rapidly a distinctive class of MSS of appropriate texts, such as sermon collections, theological florilegia, treatises on virtues and vices, and guides to confession. These are written on very thin parchment in minute scripts, within bindings that were often of limp parchment or *leather, rather than great pieces of wood, all small and light enough to slip into a pocket or mendicant's travelling pouch. It is from this direction that we must look at 13th-century Latin bibles. These little one-volume portable bibles represent one of the supreme success stories of book production in the Middle Ages. They are extremely common. Almost for the first time, they contained the entire Bible, from beginning to end, as we know it now, in a single volume. The components are in a standard and logical order (something almost unknown before 1200); they are divided into chapters and are supplied with alphabetical indices of Hebrew names. The whole volume can fit into the palm of one's hand. Bibles of the 13th century are often illuminated with tiny *historiated initials, no bigger than the smallest of fingernails, marking the beginning of each of their 84 or so books and prologues. They are sometimes called 'university bibles', but it is increasingly clear that their inspiration, format, and extraordinary success were due to the patronage of the Dominicans and Franciscans. So many were made in the 13th century that they evidently furnished the need for Latin bibles for the rest of the Middle Ages, in copies sold and resold for hundreds of years. Bibles as physical books have hardly evolved in shape, size, and

arrangement ever since: many of the innovations designed for the friars by the booksellers of Paris in the 1230s are still found in any traditional modern printed bible today.

6 Lay literacy

If the small-format friars' bibles represent the first moment of the mass publication of popular books in Europe, there was also a constantly increasing and important market for books at the other end of the social spectrum. The relentless advance of lay literacy is a consistent theme throughout most of the history of Europe in the last thousand years, even now. The Ottonian and Carolingian emperors had owned books. By the late 12th century, some exceedingly grand MSS were being made for members of the European royal houses—such as *gospels for Henry the Lion, duke of Saxony (c.1188, Wolfenbüttel, Herzog August Bibliothek, Cod. Guelf. 105 Noviss. 2° and Munich, Clm. 30055), and psalters for Geoffrey Plantagenet, son of Henry II of England (c.1190, later owned by Louis IX, Leiden, Bibliotheek der Rijksuniversiteit, MS. lat. 76A), Ingeborg of Denmark, wife of Philippe Auguste (c.1195, Chantilly, Musée Condé, ms. 9), and Blanche of Castile, wife of Louis VIII (c.1200, Paris, Bibliothèque de l'Arsenal, ms. 1186). These are illuminated MSS of extraordinary splendour, filled with dozens of full-page pictures, and they must have been phenomenally expensive to make. They are eclipsed, however, by even more extravagant copies of the *Bible moralisée*, of which four principal sets were made for Louis IX and members of his family in France, c.1220–c.1240 (Vienna, Österreichische Nationalbibliothek, cod. 2554 and cod. 1179; Toledo Cathedral and New York, Pierpont Morgan Library, M. 240; and Oxford, Bodleian Library, MS Bodley 270b, Paris, BNF, ms. lat. 11560, and London, BL, Harley MSS 1526–7). It is hard to convey the extreme opulence of these vast, illustrated, royal MSS, originally with more than 13,000 pictures each, in brilliant colours and shimmering burnished gold. The precise circumstances of their production are still unclear, but they were doubtless the work of professional artists, even if the books were not actually made in the kind of workshop to which the public would normally have access.

Fashions trickle downwards. Literacy moves sideways. The 13th-century booksellers of Paris, who were coordinating the production of textbooks for students and bibles for friars, were also selling illuminated psalters and other luxury books to the lesser aristocracy and upper middle classes. It is not always easy to identify the original patrons, for heraldry was not yet as precise or as widespread an art as it became in the 14th century, and lay literacy frustratingly seldom extended to writing names on endpapers. Furthermore, many psalters have survived only because they were later given or bequeathed to religious communities, for which (as careful examination reveals) they were not originally intended. In the course of the 13th century, psalters for the possession and private devotion of the laity became more and more common. A smaller format and the numbers and subjects of the pictures became more routine.

The proliferation of lay psalters was not restricted to Paris, and clear clusters of production can be identified in places like Artois (perhaps in St-Omer), Bruges, Oxford, Alsace (probably in Strasbourg), Würzburg, Regensburg, and elsewhere. The usual format was a *calendar at the front, listing the saints' days for the year, followed by a sequence of full-page pictures; then came the psalter itself, with the 150 psalms, usually divided into eight sections, each marked with a large initial, continuing without a break into the biblical canticles, and a Litany; at the end was the Office of the Dead followed by additional prayers to the Virgin Mary and the saints. The supplementary section at the very end gradually assumed ever-greater importance, consistent with the growing cult of the Virgin. It evolved into a series of eight daily occasions for devotion to the Virgin, with selections of appropriate psalms and short hymns. These were named 'hours' after the eight daily services of the monks: Matins, Lauds, Prime, Terce, Sext, None, Vespers, and Compline. By the third quarter of the 13th century this part had become so extensive that, as the metaphor goes, the tail began wagging the dog. For many clients, the whole psalter became superfluous and so scribes omitted it, leaving instead a calendar, the new Hours of the Virgin, the seven Penitential Psalms with Litany, and the Office of the Dead. This was the *book of hours, the most famous and the most common MS of the last part of the Middle Ages. It was entirely a lay creation, for private use at home.

A second major result of increasing lay literacy was the production of MSS in the vernacular. With a few and rare exceptions (most notably in late Anglo-Saxon England), almost all books made in Europe before about 1180 had been in Latin. Although it was no longer spoken as a native tongue, Latin was the language of formal education and of the Church. By the early 13th century, however, literacy was beginning

to overtake learning, at least among the classes who could afford illuminated MSS. The first booksellers in Paris also undertook MSS of literary romances, either in verse or prose, often loosely linked to the recurring themes of chivalry, which are the war and fall of Troy, the court of King Arthur (including the popular *Lancelot* romances), and the wars of Charlemagne against the Saracens. The allegorical *Roman de la Rose* was begun by Guillaume de Lorris around 1230–35 and finished by Jean de Meun in the early 1270s. Vernacular texts of simple science or self-improvement included the *L'Image du monde* (1246) of Gossuin de Metz, the *Livres dou trésor* (1266–8) of Brunetto Latini, the *Livre de Sydrach: La Fontaine de toutes sciences* (c.1270), and others.

There were also translations of classical and religious texts, including the popular *Bible Historiale*, translated by Guyart des Moulins in the early 1290s (revised in 1312) from the 12th-century *Historia Scholastica* of Peter Comestor. All these were produced in fine MSS for an aristocratic and upper middle-class market, often richly illuminated and illustrated in accordance with the client's wealth or desire to impress his family or neighbours. Similar texts were produced in the Holy Roman Empire, in the different dialects of German. A famous example is the *Manesse Codex of Middle High German romantic verse, written probably on the Swiss side of Lake Constance in the early 14th century (Heidelberg, Universitätsbibliothek, Cod. Pal. Germ. 848). Devotional texts were quite often copied in the German vernacular, a fact that has some interest for the history of spirituality. It can be argued that the professionalism of the book trade had considerable significance in the spread and stabilization of vernacular languages. The dominance of the Tuscan dialect in Italy is commonly attributed to the enormous success and circulation of Dante's *Divina Commedia, composed between 1308 and the author's death in 1321, which survives in more than 600 MSS from the 14th century alone. MSS of the *Vite dei Sancti Padri*, translated into Italian by Domenico Cavalca (d. 1342), are far more common than the original text had been in Latin. In England, the development of the vernacular was complicated by the existence of two spoken languages, as well as written Latin. People of Norman descent and the major landowners—those likely to commission MSS—all spoke French, or its Anglo-Norman dialect. The peasants and lower bourgeoisie spoke Middle English, but would seldom have been literate or wealthy enough before the late 14th century to own books. The result is that the very grandest aristocratic books made in

England, like the famous and lavishly illustrated 13th- and early 14th-century Apocalypses, are mostly in French. The finest of all were probably made for the English royal family, who spoke French exclusively, including Cambridge, Trinity College, MS R.16.2, and Oxford, Bodleian Library, MS Douce 180. Not until the publication of the *Canterbury Tales* after Chaucer's death in 1400 had the English language really moved up the scale far enough to have become socially acceptable.

It is reasonable to assume that by the mid- to late 13th century most countries of western Europe had organized facilities, if not settled urban workshops, for the writing and illuminating of books. In England, the best evidence of a secular book trade is from Oxford and, as in Paris, MSS attributable to that centre include not only academic texts but also friars' one-volume bibles, lay psalters, and works of vernacular literature. The illuminator who signed two MSS 'W. de Brailes' (Cambridge, Fitzwilliam Museum, MS 330, and London BL, Add. MS 49999) is generally accepted as being William de *Brailes, documented in Oxford between 1238 and 1252. It is likely that there was some kind of commercial book production in Salisbury, York, Westminster, perhaps Lincoln, and (but not certainly) Cambridge, all within the 13th century. The first documented bookseller in London is, curiously, as late as 1311. Later still, London came to dominate English book production, as decisively as Paris did in France. Until that happened, some illuminators probably still travelled from place to place, picking up work and moving on. Others may have been members of the households of their employers, as doubtless the scribes and illuminators of Edward I were in Westminster Palace, or wherever the court was in residence. The Bohun family, major patrons of book production in 14th-century England, employed at least two illuminators at Pleshey Castle in Essex, both Augustinian friars (they probably doubled as family chaplains)—John de la Teye, recorded in 1361 and 1384, and Henry Hood, recorded in 1384 and 1390.

Unlike medieval France and England, Italy was still a mass of small independent principalities, dukedoms, and republics, associated only loosely by proximity to each other and by a similar language. There was none of the centralized administration that helped concentrate the French book trade in Paris, or that of the Holy Roman Empire in Prague and Vienna. Even the papacy was exiled from Rome, and the best-documented trade in MS production for the papal court is at Avignon, in southern France, where the

popes lived from 1309 to 1377. Certain regions of Italy developed characteristic styles of illumination. Bologna has already been mentioned, and the dominance of legal studies at its university brings it as near to a cultural capital as any by 1300. Very fine bibles and liturgical books, as well as legal MSS and secular romances, are all attributable to Bologna in the late 13th and early 14th centuries. The early Bolognese style, however, is remarkably similar to that of MSS from Padua and Venice, and without supporting evidence, illumination from those three cities is not always easy to separate. Central Italian MSS are usually recognizable, especially Umbrian book production (Perugia was clearly a principal place of production). Southern Italy produced fine books too, particularly Naples. A spectacular example is the hunting book of Frederick II, *De Arte Venandi cum Avibus*, illuminated in Naples c.1258–61, with about 660 miniatures (Rome, Biblioteca Vaticana Apostolica, cod. Pal. lat. 1071). Although the evidence is scanty and still in need of research, it is likely too that Liguria was important for book production before 1300, and Genoa may yet prove to have been a major centre.

7 The late Middle Ages and the Renaissance

By the 14th century Italy had already embarked on that cultural rollercoaster later known as the Renaissance. One practical result of the new recognition of the human being as a free and individual spirit is that the names of artists and illuminators begin to be recorded in considerable numbers, and the distinctive hands of specific painters can be recognized, rather than the mere workshop styles by which medieval artists had tried to conceal their personal traits. Some Italian illuminators are extremely famous, and were already celebrated in their own time. Others have modern names assigned from distinctive pieces of work. In Bologna, a series of illuminators are designated after work on dated guild statutes as the Masters of 1285, 1311, 1314, 1328, and so on, to the Master of 1446. There are also: Nerio, early 14th century; the prolific Nicolò di Giacomo di Nascimbene, documented 1345 to c.1403, known as Nicolò da Bologna; and the Master of the Brussels Initials, c.1400, named after his work in France on the Brussels Hours of the duc de *Berry (Brussels, Bibliothèque Royale, MSS 11060–1). In Siena, there are Lippo Vanni, *fl. c.*1340–*c.*1375, and Sano di Pietro (1405–81). In Florence, many illuminators are known, including Pacino do Bonaguida, also a panel painter, early 14th century; the 'Maestro Daddesco' (*fl. c.*1320–*c.*1360), a sobriquet that may conceal the identity of more than one illuminator, named from similarity of style to the work of the panel painter Bernardo Daddi (d. 1348); the Master of the Dominican Effigies (*fl. c.*1325–*c.*1355); don Silvestro dei Gherarducci (1339–99), also a panel painter and a monk, prior of Camaldoli from 1398; don Simone Camaldolese; Lorenzo Monaco (*c.*1370–*c.*1424), perhaps originally from Siena, also a monk from 1390 at the Camaldolese monastery of Santa Maria degli Angeli in Florence; Zanobi Strozzi (1412–68), who worked also with Fra Angelico; ser Ricciardo di Nanni, *fl.* 1445–80; Bartolomeo d'Antonio Varnucci (1410–79); Francesco d'Antonio del Chierico (1433–84); Gherardo di Giovanni (*c.*1446–97); Monte de Giovanni (1448–1532/3); and Vante di Gabriello di Vanti Attavanti (1452–1520/25, known as Attavante).

Many MSS were produced in Milan and other places in Lombardy. Important illuminators there included Giovannino de Grassi (d. 1398, documented in Milan from 1389, illuminator of the Visconti Hours: Florence, Biblioteca Nazionale Centrale, Landau Finaly cod. 22); Michelino da Besozzo (*fl.* in Pavia, 1388 to after 1450); the prolific and engaging Master of the *Vitae Imperatorum*, early to mid-15th century; the Master of the Franciscan Breviary, *fl. c.*1440–*c.*1460, and the related Master of the Budapest Antiphoner, *fl. c.*1444–*c.*1450, named after Budapest (Orságos Széchényi Könyvtár (library of the National Museum), c.l.m.ae. 462); the Master of Ippolita Sforza, *fl.* 1450–75; Cristoforo de' Predis, *fl. c.*1450–87; Giovan Pietro Birago, from about 1490 to *c.*1518 (also in Brescia); and the Master 'B.F.', as he signs himself (*fl. c.*1495–*c.*1545). In Rimini there was Neri da Rimini (*fl. c.*1300–*c.*1338); in Perugia, Matteo di ser Cambio (*c.*1320–1424); and in Verona, Felice Feliciano (1443–*c.*1480), Liberale da Verona (1445–*c.*1529), Francesco Dai Libri (*c.*1450–*c.*1506), and his son Girolamo Dai Libri (*c.*1475–1555). These last three are especially known for monumental choirbooks.

Illuminators in Venice included Cristoforo Cortese from the last decade of the 14th century until his death in 1445, and the Master of the Putti (*fl. c.*1466–74), who also worked on printed books. Important names in Naples are Gioacchino di Giovanni de' Gigantibus, *fl.* 1450–85, born in Rottemberg in Bavaria (he also worked in Rome); Matteo Felice, *fl.* 1467–93; and Cola Rapicano and Cristoforo Majorana, both second half of the 15th century. Their style, not surprisingly, seems almost indistinguishable from MSS from Catalonia, across the sea in Spain. Perhaps they travelled. Ferrara and Este court patronage attracted illuminators who worked elsewhere too, including

Taddeo Crivelli (*c.*1420–30 to *c.*1476–9, also known in Bologna), Giorgio d'Alemagna (d. 1479), documented in Ferrara 1441–62 and in Modena 1473–6; Guglielmo Giraldi, recorded 1441–94; Franco dei Russi, *fl.* 1455–*c.*1482, born in Mantua but documented in Ferrara, Padua, Venice, and Urbino; Girolamo da Cremona, documented 1460–83 in Ferrara, Padua, Mantua, Siena, Florence, and Venice; and Cosmè Tura (*c.*1430–95). Rome and the papal court seduced many of the best illuminators of all, but not really until the mid-15th century. They included the master scribe and Renaissance book designer from Padua, Bartolomeo Sanvito (1435–1511), and his sometime collaborator, Gaspare da Padova (*fl. c.*1466–*c.*1493, also called the Master of the Vatican Homer), and several of the last great practitioners of MS illumination, including Antonio da Monza, *fl. c.*1490–*c.*1518, from Lombardy, and one of the most famous of all, the Croatian Giorgio Giulio Clovio (1498–1578), painted by El Greco, eulogized by Vasari.

Although there were certainly regional styles of book illumination in 14th-century France (Metz and Cambrai come to mind), Paris continued to dominate the northern book trade and to attract the best craftsmen. It was by far the largest city in medieval Europe. Identifiable illuminators included Honoré d'Amiens, recorded 1289–1312, who was working for the royal family by 1296. Among his MSS was the Breviary of Philippe le Bel (Paris, BNF, ms. lat. 1023). Another illuminator was Jean *Pucelle (d. 1334, documented from *c.*1319), known for the two-volume Belleville Breviary (Paris, BNF, ms. lat. 10483–4) and the tiny Hours of Jeanne d'Évreux (New York, Metropolitan Museum of Art, The Cloisters, Acc.54.1.2). He and his workshop clearly had some business association with the Dominicans, especially with the royal convent of Poissy, downstream on the Seine. French royal patronage achieved its greatest height in the commissions of Charles V (1338–80, king of France from 1364) and his successor Charles VI (1368–1422, r. from 1380), and Charles VI's younger brothers, Jean, duc de Berry, and Philippe le Hardi, duke of Burgundy (1342–1404), and, in time, Philippe's own son and successor, Jean sans Peur (1371–1419). The king and the royal dukes all formed magnificent libraries, many of which are documented in detailed inventories, with histories and chronicles, chivalric romances, allegories, texts of theology and saints' lives, classical texts, moral instruction, poetry, music, politics, warfare, hunting, and alchemy—many of them in specially commissioned translations into French—together with bibles (sometimes also in French), breviaries and missals, and the increasingly popular books of hours, in which they seem to have competed in luxury and refinement. Those made for the duc de Berry include a psalter, c.1380, illuminated by André Beauneveu (Paris, BNF, ms. fr. 13091), the *Petites Heures*, c.1390 (ibid., ms. lat. 18014), the Brussels Hours, c.1400, by Jacquemart de Hesdin and others (Brussels, Bibliothèque royale, ms. 719 (11060-1)), the *Grandes Heures*, 1409 (Paris, BNF, ms. lat. 919), and the two supreme MSS painted by the *Limbourg brothers: the *Belles Heures*, 1408–9 (New York, Metropolitan Museum of Art, The Cloisters, Acc.54.1.1), and the greatest of all, the *Très Riches Heures*, left unfinished at the duc's death in 1416 (Chantilly, Musée Condé, ms. 65). MSS in the royal and ducal collections often had dozens or even hundreds of miniatures, and they were bound in coloured leather or textile, fitted with enamelled and jewelled clasps. Books were clearly a very visible part of a courtly culture; they were exchanged as New Year gifts, and were displayed, shared, and copied. Aspiring authors presented dedication MSS in the hope of further publication under royal patronage. Naturally this affected the fashion for book collecting in France. Stately libraries were formed by noblemen and upwardly mobile courtiers. Wealthy visitors to Paris returned home with MSS or an ambition to own them. Books of hours, at the very least, became almost essential possessions in families of almost any means or literacy.

The Parisian book trade—still principally located around the rue Neuve Notre-Dame—enjoyed a golden period in the decades on either side of 1400, producing many of the most refined and beautiful MSS of the Middle Ages. Some of the illuminators are known only from their best-known books, such as the Master of the *Épître d'Othéa*, the Master of the *Cité des Dames*, the Master of Berry's *Claires Femmes*, the Egerton Master, and the Harvard Hannibal Master. Others—like the *Boucicaut Master (named after a very large book of hours made for the maréchal de Boucicaut, Paris, Musée Jacquemart-André, ms. 2), and the *Bedford Master (named after a book of hours in London, BL, Add. MS 18850, and a breviary in Paris, BNF, ms. lat. 17294)—can be identified with some plausibility. The former was perhaps Jacques Coene, documented in Paris, 1398–1407. The latter was almost certainly Haincelin de Haguenau, documented in Paris from 1403 and still active in the 1420s. Each of these illuminators had assistants and followers (and probably often family members) producing MSS, especially books of hours, to well-practised formulas and in considerable quantities. Most MSS were presumably commissioned by clients from the booksellers in advance; some artists may even have prepared books on speculation, in anticipation of a ready market.

This halcyon period ended quite suddenly in 1420, when the English armies of Henry V, having defeated the French at Agincourt in 1415, now occupied Paris. For 30 years, business came to a virtual halt in the capital. A few illuminators remained, catering to the new rulers, including the Bedford Master, who is named after his patron, the duke of Bedford, English regent in France from 1422 until his death in 1435. Most illuminators left Paris and established themselves in the provinces. This exodus marks the beginning of a widely scattered book trade which became the principal characteristic of MS production in France in the last 80 years of its life. Artists and scribes arrived from Paris, many of them evidently bringing experience and recognizable pattern-sheets with them. They set themselves up in Rouen (the most famous workshops there are associated with the Master of the Geneva Latini, also called the Master of the Échevinage de Rouen); and in Tours (where the painters included *Fouquet, no less, outstanding illuminator of the now-dispersed Hours of Etienne Chevalier, mostly in Chantilly, Musée Condé, ms. 71, Jean Poyer, and Jean Bourdichon, court illuminator to Anne of Brittany and Louis XII); in Bourges (Jean Colombe, who finished the *Très Riches Heures* of the duc de Berry); Poitiers (Robinet Testard); Lyons (the Master of Guillaume Lambert, and Jean Perréal); Nantes; Angers; Rennes; Dijon (probable location of the Master of the Burgundian Prelates); Besançon; and Amiens (birthplace of Simon Marmion). Most of these cities were still making MSS until at least the end of the century. By the 1460s, illuminators were drifting back to Paris. The best-known artists there are Maître François, mentioned in 1473, and Jacques de Besançon, who was in the rue Neuve Notre-Dame from 1472 to 1494. Some flashy and unrefined books were still being written and illuminated by hand in Paris in the 1520s, but the book trade there never really regained the unsurpassed dominance it had enjoyed a century earlier. The relatively late arrival of printing in Paris (1470) is some indication of how far the business of book production in the capital had slipped in European importance.

The political turmoils of 15th-century France undoubtedly played into the hands of the book trade in The Netherlands, southern and northern. By the Treaty of Arras in 1435, the dukes of Burgundy moved the seat of their vast dominions to Flanders. Grand

The 15th-century scribe Jean Miélot at work, from *Le Débat de l'honneur*: he employs *pens, a *stylus, *book weight, book desk, and inkhorn, with a *book chest behind him. The MS was made for Philip the Good; this miniature may be by Jean le Tavernier.

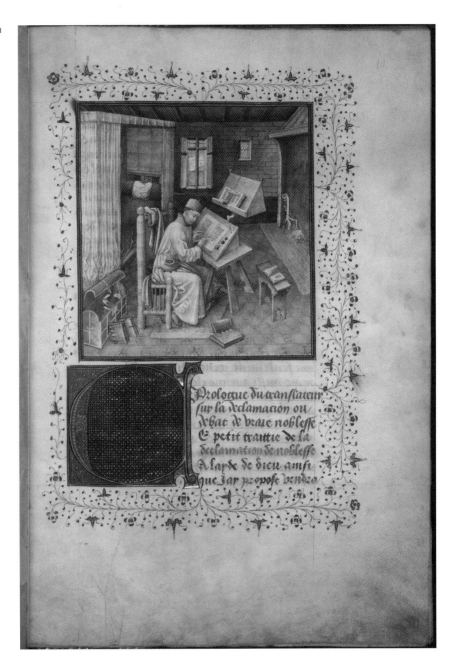

and aristocratic MSS were made in towns such as Lille and Valenciennes, but it was the bourgeois merchant towns that profited most. Bruges, still with shipping access to the open sea, was exporting huge numbers of books of hours to England by the middle of the first half of the 15th century. By 1450, at least as many books of hours for the English market were prepared in Bruges as were made in all of England itself. Very many MSS were sold locally too. The trade was highly organized and illuminators were required to be members of the painters' and saddlemakers' guild of Saint Luke. Alliances with England—including the marriage of Edward IV's youngest sister, Margaret, to Charles, duke of Burgundy—brought Edward himself to Bruges, when forced into exile in 1470–71. He stayed there with a local businessman and major book collector, Louis de Gruuthuse (c.1427–92), who convinced his guest to begin commissioning his own luxurious MSS. This event marks not only the true beginning of the English royal library, but also the consolidation of Bruges as the principal centre of the book trade in the southern Netherlands.

*Caxton, aiming for an exclusively English market, established his first press in Bruges, not England, in 1475. With nearby Ghent, where a prominent MS patron was the late duke's illegitimate son, Raphael de Mercatellis (c.1437–1508), Bruges dominated MS production in northern Europe for 50 years, until at least 1530. A distinctive 'Ghent/Bruges' style included borders formed of naturalistic flowers scattered in *trompe l'œil* designs across painted gold grounds, sometimes with snails and insects rendered with extreme precision. Miniatures, often set in realistic, hazy landscapes, reflect the paintings of the Flemish primitives, such as Jan Van Eyck (who had almost certainly contributed to MSS himself) and Gerard David. The great MS illuminators of Bruges and its environs included the Vienna Master of Mary of Burgundy (painter of Vienna, Österreichische Nationalbibliothek, Cod. 1857), Alexander Bening (d. 1518, known from c.1469) and, above all, Simon *Bening, who was famous across Europe.

In the northern Netherlands, there was almost no book illumination before 1400. Utrecht, like Bruges, became important from about the 1430s, with painters such as the Masters of Zweder van Culemborg and the supreme, but not prolific, Master of Catherine of Cleves, illuminator of the eponymous book of hours (New York, Pierpont Morgan Library, M. 917 and M. 945). Later in the century, distinctive styles of Dutch illumination and coloured penwork point to notable production in Delft, Haarlem, and almost certainly Zwolle, in the eastern Netherlands. At its boundaries, the Dutch style merges with that of the Rhineland, in a line of book production from Cologne at least as far south as Mainz. Although there are exceptions, it is striking to note the strong religious themes of many northern Netherlandish and Rhenish MSS of the very end of the Middle Ages, dominated by books of hours (often in the vernacular), breviaries, psalters, choirbooks, and large institutional bibles. It is a setting that not only anticipates the religious Reformation of the 16th century but also, and more importantly in the present context, it is a world known and exploited by *Gutenberg and his colleagues in Mainz in the 1450s.

This was not the case in Italy. Choirbooks and bibles were certainly still being illuminated in the Italian Renaissance courts, often of princely grandeur (and unexpected secularism), but the distinctive theme was humanism, the Renaissance, and a return to the books and texts of classical antiquity, which is where this essay began. The Florentine humanists, such as *Niccoli and Poggio *Bracciolini, reinvented and promoted a neat, rounded script, resembling Carolingian minuscule but believed by them to be an authentic classical style, ornamented with 'whitevine' initials, as Roman in appearance as the capitals on marble columns. The joyful and infectious rediscovery of classical learning is a familiar tale, and was fed by forays into ancient and neglected monastic libraries and by the exodus of Greek learning into the West following the fall of Constantinople to the Turks in 1453. Italian humanistic MSS are immediately recognizable, wide-margined, elegant, and graceful. The illuminators, many of whom are cited above, supplied appropriate initials and borders, with white vine interlace inhabited by putti, classical urns, butterflies, and—especially in Rome and Naples—long-tailed parrots. MSS are frequently signed and often dated by their scribes. Booksellers, such as *Vespasiano da Bisticci, of Florence, created libraries of such books for the princes and collectors— the Medicis, Estes, Gonzagas, Sforzas, and the popes —and for visitors to Italy. When printing was introduced into Italy, around 1465, the early typographers recognized this new and last manifestation of MS handwriting and copied it, later calling it 'Roman' or, in its cursive form, 'italic'. That moment, more than dynasties or battles, marks the cultural end of the Middle Ages.

BIBLIOGRAPHY

J. J. G. Alexander, *Medieval Illuminators and their Methods of Work* (1992)

F. Avril and N. Reynaud, *Les Manuscrits à peintures en France, 1440–1520* (1993)

Bischoff

M. Bollati, ed., *Dizionario biografico dei miniatori italiani: secoli IX–XVI* (2004)

L. E. Boyle, *Medieval Latin Palaeography* (1984)

R. Clemens and T. Graham, *Introduction to Manuscript Studies* (2007)

C. de Hamel, *A History of Illuminated Manuscripts*, 2e (1994)

A. Derolez, *The Palaeography of Gothic Manuscript Books* (2003)

N. R. Ker, *English Manuscripts in the Century after the Norman Conquest* (1960)

T. Kren and S. McKendrick, eds., *Illuminating the Renaissance: The Triumph of Flemish Manuscript Painting in Europe* (2003)

E. A. Lowe, *Codices Latini Antiquiores: A Palaeographical Guide to Latin Manuscripts Prior to the Ninth Century* (12 vols, 1934–71)

J. Plummer with G. Clark, *The Last Flowering: French Painting in Manuscripts, 1420–1530: From American Collections* (1982)

R. H. Rouse and M. A. Rouse, *Manuscripts and their Makers: Commercial Book Producers in Medieval Paris, 1200–1500* (2 vols, 2000)

Incipit liber tertius a septuagesima

vsch ad pascha dominice resurrectionis.

CDe septuagesima. Capitulõ.i.

Eptuagesima significat tempus deulationis: τ inchoatur a dominica: in qua cantatur officium Circundederunt me. et terminatur in sabbato post pascha. est autem instituta propter tres rationes: vt dicit Johannes belerh in summa: videlicet CPrimo propter redemptioné. Nam qz sancti patres statuerant: vt propter veneratione dñiec ascenfionis quinta feria sicut τ dies dominica solennis esset: τin ipsa nullus penitus ieiunaret: τ sic de diebus quadragesime septem dies diminuebátur. s. oës quinte ferie. Ideo in redéptione illox sancti patres vnam septimaná quadragesime in ieiunis premiserunt: qua τ septuagesimá vocauerunt. CSecúdo propter significatione. Nam hoc tempus significatur deulatio exiliu: τ tribulatio generis húani ab Adá vsch ad finé múdi. Quod quidé exiliu sub reuolutione septé dierú agit: τ sub septé miliú annozú tpe includitur. Ab initio aút múdi vsch ad ascensioném fm quosdaz sex miliú annozú computat. Et nunc vo quicqd tpis sequit sub septimo millenario cópzehendit: cui9 terminu solus deus nouit. Nos igit tps in sexta múdi etate abhoc exilio in spe eterne retributionis innocentie stolla reddita: p baptismú eripuit: sed cósumato exiliu tpe nos vtrach stola decozabit. Hinc est qz in hoc exiliu tpe cática leticie deponim9. Sed in sabbato pasche vnú alla decátam9: tan ch in spe patrie gratulátes τ stolá innocentie sexta etate per tpm recuperátes. Cui etiá tractus subijcit: quo fignatur labor: qué adhuc in mandatox adimpletione retinem9. In sabbato vo post pascha vbi septuagesima terminat: dus alla cátamus: qz cópleto exiliu terminio duplicé stolá glozie cósequemur. Tertio ppter repzesentationé: qm hoc tps.lxx.dierú repzesentat. lxx. annos qb9 filiú israel sub captiuitate babylonica seruierút. Et deponim9cantica leticie quéadmodú τ illi depofuerút dicétes. Quó cárabim9 canticú dñi in terra aliena. In sabbato vo pasche alla cantamus: quia τ illi anno sexagesimo data sibi redeundi licentia letari ceperunt. Sed statim tractú subiúgim9: qz τ illi ab edificatione tépli vsch ad annos.lxx.cópletos pzhibiti fuerút. Ideoch sabbato quo septuagesima terminat: duplex canim9 alla: eozú plená leticiam postch venerút in patriá figurátes. Hoc etiá tps exiliu τ captiuitatis iudeozú repzesentat tps nostre deulationis in qua stetit hu

6 The European Printing Revolution

CRISTINA DONDI

1 Introduction

Printing with movable *type, a European invention of the mid-15th century, revolutionized the making and use of books. The innovative nature of the invention and its implications were felt and discussed from the 15th century onwards; however, a comprehensive and systematic analysis of the phenomenon is largely a product of *book history as a distinct discipline. In the 20th century, authors such as *McLuhan, *Febvre and H.-J. *Martin, and *Eisenstein proposed the idea of a European printing 'revolution' as an all-encompassing intellectual, social, scientific, economic, religious, and cultural revolution. Their arguments, methodologies, and conclusions have been challenged by later scholars (especially in the case of Eisenstein by Needham [review], Grafton, and Johns). Although many bibliographers and book historians now understand printed texts and MSS as coexisting, and even sometimes having a mutually complementary relationship—especially during the *incunable period—it is a fact that within a generation the role of the MS book and of *manuscript culture was fundamentally changed. The continuing existence of MS publication, in certain fields, is a historical phenomenon amply documented by *Love (see 13).

2 MS production and use in Europe in the second half of the 15th century

The appearance of typographic printing coincided with a period when the production of books in MS was everywhere on the increase and the book market, as a consequence, was rapidly expanding. MS production peaked in the late 1460s in Germany and in the early 1470s in France and Italy, entering into decline immediately afterwards. For the average book user of the second half of the 15th century, the printed book gradually took the place of the MS as a natural vehicle for text (see 5).

The reasons for the increasing demand and production of books lie in a number of interrelated factors, chiefly the spread of literacy in urban centres. This process had begun in the 13th century with the foundation of new lay schools next to the religious ones generally attached to cathedral chapters. In Italy, humanist schools were opened for scholars and *scuole d'abbaco*, where teaching was carried out in the vernacular, were founded to train merchants. New universities were established (ten in Germany between 1402 and 1498), and existing ones grew substantially.

Participants in this spread of literacy were part of an expanded middle class, lay professionals who were

53

neither members of the aristocracy nor artisans or peasants. This class included civil servants employed at the numerous lay and religious courts of Europe, such as ambassadors, judges, bailiffs, and their secretaries; professionals such as lawyers, notaries, physicians, and university professors; and even schoolteachers, merchants, and traders.

Many clergymen and members of monasteries and convents were traditionally also purchasers of books. Reformed congregations—e.g. Windesheim among the Augustinian Canons; Monte Cassino, Bursfeld, and Melk among the Benedictines; the Observant Franciscans; the Reformed Dominicans; the Fratres Vitae Communis (see DEVOTIO MODERNA), and Christian humanists of the Netherlands—emphasized university education for their members, rebuilt their libraries, produced new literary works in both the vernacular and Latin to instruct the laity, and paid more attention to the uniformity of their liturgical texts. Naturally, such congregations attached great importance to their book collections.

3 The technical invention

The need to reproduce small images quickly, or to reproduce images with text, was evident by the beginning of the 15th century: representations of saints, with or without accompanying text, and playing cards were reproduced by *woodcut. *Blockbooks produced using the same method appeared around the middle of the century, their letters carved in *woodblocks.

Screw-driven olive and wine presses were common at the period. *Punches, with letters and symbols cut in relief on their ends, were used by seal and coin engravers and by goldsmiths to mark their wares to satisfy guild regulations; the mechanical precision necessary for matrix and mould production was also needed to make arms, armour, clocks, and watches. By the middle of the 15th century these skills were concentrated in large cities. Belonging to this milieu, the first printers, such as *Ratdolt in Augsburg and Venice, *Jenson in Venice, Bernardo Cennini in Florence, and Filippo da Lavagna in Milan, were expert metalworkers and jewellers able to cut their own punches (see 11).

Typographic printing was introduced by *Gutenberg around 1450 in Mainz. The first printing experiments—*indulgences and Donatus' antique Latin *primer, Ars Minor—appear to have been conducted on materials small in size and of saleable interest, often ecclesiastical and educational in nature. The first substantial book printed with movable type is the 42-line or *Gutenberg Bible. The work of Gutenberg at Mainz was continued by other printers in the city, *Fust and Schoeffer.

After the first wave of printer-typographers, printing enterprises were undertaken by individuals familiar with the book as an object, such as *scribes (Schoeffer in Mainz, *Vérard in Paris), schoolteachers (the early printers of Verona, Brescia, Mantua, and Treviso), priests (Lorenzo Morgiani in Florence), and *stationers and binders (Benedictus Hectoris in Bologna).

Between 1460 and 1470, printing expanded in Germany—at Strasbourg (1459–60), Bamberg (c.1459), Eltville (1464), Cologne (c.1465), Basel (1468), Augsburg (1468), Nuremberg (1470), and Beromünster (1470)—and in Italy: at Subiaco (1465), Rome (1467), Venice (1469), Foligno, Naples, Milan, and Trevi (1470–71). By 1480 the industry extended even further: to Paris (1470) and Lyons (1473), Barcelona (c.1473), Louvain (1473, *Martens and *Johannes de Westfalia), Cracow (1473), Gouda (1477, *Leeu), and Westminster (1476, *Caxton). Altogether, presses were set up in more than 100 towns between 1471 and 1480, in almost 90 further places between 1481 and 1490, and in approximately 50 more towns between 1491 and 1500.

The social groups responsible for the increase in the demand for books also became directly involved in their production and use. The many university graduates and humanists who gravitated towards centres of learning found employment as advisers, editors, and *correctors. The spread of *literacy and the increased affordability of books secured them new users, further expanding the market. From its very beginnings, clergymen and religious welcomed and participated in the development of printing. Finally, the wealth of the merchant classes brought the capital investment necessary for the new craft.

For the first time, a group of literate merchants, later defined as *publishers, were willing to invest in book production as a commercial activity. The great increase in the quantity of circulating books, made possible by the new method of mechanical production, resulted in the availability of a larger variety of titles, to more people, in different locations, generally at a cheaper price.

The establishment of printing in about 250 towns, most of which hosted more than one *printing office, is characterized by an enormous amount of entrepreneurial experimentation. A more detailed analysis of the presses' output and period of activity would show that a number of cases involved the work of an itinerant printer or of temporary or short-lived establishments. Printers moved in and out of a profession not yet perceived as such, nor yet clearly defined by regulations, statutes, or guilds; they moved around, sometimes following an invitation, often because they felt they had exploited a limited market's capacity. Surviving business contracts, records of legal disputes, *wills, and *colophons are the main sources of evidence for this migratory working pattern.

There appears to have been a division between the commercially successful printers, who tended not to move, and the itinerant ones, pushed towards the exploration of new markets and opportunities by the absence of medium- to long-term prospects in the small towns, villages, or isolated abbeys and university towns where they stopped to operate. Why some printers did not succeed in establishing themselves even in large centres is a question that has to be analysed case by case. Finally, a comparison may be drawn between the high level of mobility shown by the early printers and that of professions such as teachers and university professors, whose wandering habits were determined sometimes by their fame, sometimes by economic need.

The unique socio-economic-cultural circumstances surrounding the establishment of printing offices and their subsequent activities varied from place to place and from printer to printer: proximity to the papal curia or to paper mills; the involvement of humanists, university professors, or schools; favourable trading location; the local commercial tradition; access to *patronage or commissions—all played a determining role. Scholar printer-publishers, such as *Aldus in Venice and *Froben and *Amerbach in Basle, were very influential. They were driven by the desire to make available to the international scholarly community works that they deemed important—chiefly classical for Aldus, biblical and theological for Froben and Amerbach—in philologically sound and aesthetically pleasing editions.

4 The physical appearance and textual content of early printed books

The MS lies behind each phase of the history of early printing, not only as a source for texts, but also as a model for the printed book's physical appearance, as reflected in choice of type, *format, *layout, *initials, and *rubrication. Types reproduced the *scripts most widely used at the time. Gothic *textura type had special variants according to different locations (more square in northern Germany and The Netherlands, rounder in southern Germany and Italy) and different uses (for liturgical works, legal and school texts, etc.). *Roman, like *italic (from 1501), was developed for classical texts, *bastarda and *Schwabacher founts were cut for printing French and German vernacular works. In the 16th century, a simplification of *letterforms was brought about by the growth and organization of the typefounding business, by the commercialization of matrices, and by the spread of specialist punch-cutting as a profession (e.g. by *Granjon). The only technical difference in the production of printed over MS books, beyond the use of types and a press, lies in the process of the *imposition of the pages to be reproduced on an unfolded *sheet. This involved *casting off the *printer's copy to determine which parts of it would come where on the respective sheets.

During the 15th century, three types of MS were prevalent: the academic book, generally written in two columns on *folio pages, for theological and legal works, and normally confined to library use; the humanistic and student's book, of medium (*quarto) to small *format; and the popular book, whether lay or religious, generally quarto or smaller (in Italy, even pocket-size). Each had its natural continuation in printed form. Data from the *Incunabula Short-Title Catalogue (ISTC) shows continuity with the period before printing was introduced: 8,662 editions in folio (29 per cent, although the incidence is concentrated more in the first decades of production and falls away in the last twenty years of the 15th century); 15,195 editions in quarto (52 per cent); 3,020 in *octavo (10 per cent, mostly printed in the last two decades and increasing after 1501); and 232 in sextodecimo.

The use of large capital initials, *paragraph marks, rubrication (titles, *running heads, running volume numbers, etc.), *decoration, and *illustration was introduced gradually to the set page. During the first decades, printing offices drew on the same craftsmen employed by the MS book trade as rubricators, illuminators, and scribes. Far from finding themselves with less work, they saw their skills required as never before for finishing printed books. It is possible to determine whether a printing office had in-house decorators or regularly employed the services of a nearby artist, by examining copies of the same edition or of a number of editions and analysing their handiwork. Generally, rubrication was carried out at point of sale, sometimes near the place of production before distribution (Jenson in Venice, *Koberger in Nuremberg). Substantial illumination was mostly added after distribution (with the exception of *presentation copies), at the owner's request.

From the 1480s, there appears a substantial increase in the printed component of the page and a falling-off in the need for hand-finishing: woodcut initials and borders, printed running heads, and page or folio numbers are the inevitable consequence of more sophisticated *textual articulation, increased *press runs, and economic policies. The use of hand-applied colour disappears almost entirely in the 16th century, its visual appeal replaced in part by *engravings. The appearance of the printed book had initially been determined by the reading public's habits and tastes, which had developed during the MS period; but from the 16th century onwards, the exigencies of printing would eventually change that public's taste and perceptions.

Books were almost always sold unbound. Most book-shops were, however, able to bind items according to the customer's requirements. There were instances of large-scale importers (e.g. Schoeffer in Mainz) who supplied the binding before offering it for retail. Bindings were provided before distribution only occasionally. *Dedication copies sometimes received such bindings, as did books intended for markets known not to be capable of providing them, as was the case for the *Glagolitic Breviary, printed in Venice c.1491 for the churches of Dalmatia.

A large percentage of the books printed in the first 50 years of printing contained works used during the Middle Ages, particularly within the ecclesiastical and academic worlds, such as bibles and liturgical books, patristics, theology and philosophy, law and science, certain Latin classics (Cicero and Virgil) and vernacular ones (*Dante, *Petrarch, and Chaucer). However, the publication of works relating to contemporary events or written by contemporary authors is a clear sign of the extent to which printing quickly became a common aspect of 15th-century society. Such works included the writings of the humanists, of authors such as Sebastian Brant and Girolamo Savonarola, diplomatic and funeral orations, *sacre rappresentazioni*, indulgences, and calendars.

An analysis of the titles available to the late 15th-century market has been prepared by Hermand *et al.*, using data from the 1998 illustrated ISTC. It shows that almost one third of the total output was in the category of literature, of which 53 per cent were lay texts and 47 per cent religious. Law supplied almost 15 per cent of the total, evenly divided between civil and canon law. Liberal arts (dialectic, grammar and philology, music, and rhetoric) accounted for almost 11 per cent; theology slightly more than 10 per cent; and liturgy almost 9 per cent. Ephemera (advertising,

heraldry, practical astronomy and astrology, commerce, guides, documents pertaining to political and administrative life) supplied slightly more than 6 per cent of the total; history (including biography and hagiography) comprised more than 5 per cent, of which 51 per cent was lay history and the rest religious. Philosophy represented almost 5 per cent; medicine more than 3 per cent. Scientific subjects—alchemy, astronomy and astrology, geography, mathematics and geometry, optics, physics, and natural sciences—account for almost 3 per cent of the total. The smallest categories, each comprising less than 1 per cent of the total output (by numbers of titles, not by *sheets, nor *ens), are the Bible (text only), and works pertaining to the mechanical arts, such as agriculture, architecture, the art of war, cookery, and dance.

Classical texts, distributed among these categories, represent more than 9 per cent of the total. This percentage can be further broken down according to periods of publication, production within large geographical areas, or according to locale. More than 30 per cent of the total Italian output is made up of editions of the classics, almost 17 per cent of which were printed in Venice alone. In France, classics constituted 7 per cent of the total publication; in Germany more than 6 per cent; in Belgium almost 7 per cent; and in The Netherlands approximately 12 per cent. At present, it is not possible to offer data for the percentage of medieval or contemporary authors published in the 15th century, as a biographical profile of all authors is not yet available.

Continuity with MS production is also evident where language is concerned. Out of some 29,000 editions recorded in the *online version of the ISTC database (consulted April 2007), almost three-quarters were printed in the ancient languages: 21,122 were printed in Latin (72 per cent), 154 in Hebrew, 65 in Greek, and 14 in Church Slavonic. As for modern languages, 3,141 editions were printed in German (10 per cent), 2,391 in Italian (8 per cent), 1,611 in French (5 per cent), 566 in Dutch (1 per cent), 421 in Spanish (1 per cent), 234 in English, 134 in Catalan, 33 in Czech, 11 in Portuguese, 2 in Swedish, one edition each in Breton, Danish, Frisian, Provençal, and Sardinian. The editions for which no percentage figure is supplied together represent 3 per cent of the total.

If a country's vernacular output is related to its total output, the extent of modern-language printing by geographical areas can be better understood. In Germany, a total of 9,859 editions were printed, of which 2,897 (29 per cent) were German texts. In Italy, 2,374 of 10,417 editions were in Italian (22 per cent); in France, 1,485 out of 5,167 editions were in French (28 per cent); and in the Low Countries, 554 out of 2,328 editions were in Dutch (23 per cent). Spain shows a higher rate of vernacular printing: of the 882 editions known to have been printed in Spain, 336 were in Spanish (38 per cent). In England, for which more elaborate calculations were carried out by Hellinga, 395 editions are known, of which 63 per cent of the total production was in English, against 9 per cent in legal French, and only 28 per cent in Latin (*BMC* 11.43). Coq observed that at centres where printers had limited commercial power, such as at Florence, or with a number of French and English presses, they tended to specialize in the production of vernacular texts, while the great export centres, such as Venice, published primarily in Latin for a wider European readership.

5 The contribution of the Church and religious orders

From its beginning, members of the Church were very actively involved with the new medium. They acted as benefactors (Nicholas of Cusa, *Bessarion, Pope Sixtus IV), as editors and correctors (Franciscan and Augustinian editors of liturgical texts, mathematics, logic, and literature), as authors of lay as well as religious works (Werner Rolewinck), as translators (Niccolò Malermi of the Camaldoli order translated the Bible into Italian), as printers (Benedictines in Augsburg, Erfurt, Subiaco near Rome; Augustinian Hermits in Nuremberg; Cistercians in Zinna; the Dominican nuns of *Ripoli at Florence; Fratres Vitae Communis in Marienthal, Rostock, Brussels, and Cologne; Franciscans of Santa Maria Gloriosa in Venice), and finally, as book users and owners, both privately (Jacopo Zeno, bishop of Padua, Cardinal Grimani in Venice) and institutionally (the Dominicans of San Marco in Florence). The preservation of thousands of incunables for posterity has to be credited in large part to the libraries of religious institutions.

6 New aspects

Unlike writing a MS, a private individual could not casually print a book, nor could a printer produce a book by himself without establishing a printing office. Moreover, printing required capital investment, principally for the purchase of paper. In addition, it generally required some knowledge of the subject to be printed, to help in the selection and correction of what was printed. Finally, printing called for marketing knowledge: although texts were initially produced with an ideal customer in mind, in order to be profitable a diverse range of buyers had to be reached. In sum, what distinguishes the production of printed books from that of MSS is the necessary collaboration of individuals, each contributing his or her own skills or assets. Behind the publication of most editions lay the joint efforts of artisan printers, financial backers, commercial dealers, and scholars. Never before had these different segments of society worked so closely together.

The 15th-century printer normally operated in an office where a team of people with different skills was assigned to various aspects of the technical process. The few exceptions, such as wandering printers, would necessarily have had to find support wherever they temporarily set up a press: for example, the assistance of members of an aristocratic household might be needed, or of monks and lay brothers if the printer had been called to print a liturgical book in a monastery.

Financial backing frequently came from the commercial sector, quite often from the Church, occasionally from the aristocracy. The financier would generally supply the cost of paper—equal to approximately half the total investment required to produce a book—and could also have an important role relating to the distribution of copies. The number of sheets per copy and the total press run had to be calculated in advance so as to buy enough paper; sufficient money had to be set aside for that part of the investment. Press runs in the 15th century varied substantially according to the technical and financial capabilities of the printers and publishers. Among the important elements in determining the print run were: production costs, anticipated demand, ability to reach the market, the work's genre, and the printing office's commercial practices. For the first two decades, the typical press run seems to have been between 200 and 300 copies: 180 for the 42-line bible, 275 to 300 for the editions of *Sweynheym and Pannartz in Rome. Yet, there are exceptions: 1,025 copies of Pliny were printed (on commission) by Jenson in Venice in 1476; 930 copies of the Bible were printed by Leonardus Wild, also in Venice, in 1478. *Zarotto in Milan always produced around 1,000 copies.

A mistake in the calculation of the print run could compromise the business, and the great variety of runs in this period seems to reflect the search for a balance between conflicting needs. Numbers grew substantially—sometimes to above the level of

1,000 copies—when there were better prospects for distribution, either because the edition had been commissioned or because of the work's great popularity. The popular sermons of Roberto Caracciolo were printed by Mathias Moravus in Naples in 1489 in 2,000 copies. In 1492, Bartholomaeus Ghotan in Lübeck produced 800 paper copies and sixteen *vellum copies of the *Revelations* of St Birgitta, commissioned by the monastery of Vadstena, Sweden. The work of Savonarola was printed in Florence in 1500 in a run of between 2,000 and 3,000 copies.

The printer's reader or proof corrector, a key figure in the process, had to be an educated person. Different publications demanded different skills from the corrector. He prepared the text for the *compositor, marking corrections, spaces to leave blank, and parts of the text to omit. The liberty a compositor ultimately took with a text should not be underestimated: to justify the right-hand margin, he might vary the number and width of blank spaces, introduce or expand abbreviations, intervene in the *spelling and *punctuation, and sometimes even alter the text. This sort of compositorial intervention is often investigated by *analytical bibliography.

Printers frequently used correctors to oversee their editions: Giovanni Andrea Bussi was the editor of Sweynheym and Pannartz's classical editions in Rome. When German printers arrived in Italy, they were helped by local humanists in the selection of works that passed into print; humanists did the same for the presses established in the university towns of Bologna and Paris. The corrector's new professional role involved turning MS into print, paying especial attention to the text's linguistic features.

A further round of collaborative effort is evident at the editorial level. A 15th-century edition commonly contained much more than what was announced in the title. Other works by the same author, by different authors, and excerpts from anonymous works, may all be found before or after the principal work. Moreover, the *paratext might contain a number of letters from and to the editor, and verses in praise of the author, of the text, of the editor, or of the printer are also quite commonly present; their authors were generally contemporaries of the editor—perhaps a student, a colleague, or a local worthy. This historical evidence is, in part, what makes each edition unique—yet it is habitually ignored. The exact content of the surviving c.29,000 editions published in the last 50 years of the 15th century is still not known, despite the important position they occupy within the transmission of the West's cultural heritage.

It is erroneous to assume that incunable editions of any given text were all similar, depending ultimately on the *editio princeps*. In cases where an edition's position within the textual transmission of incunabula (often of the 1470s) has been established, results have shown substantial variation, as would be expected in editions published in different places and, therefore, most probably based on different MSS. In this respect the work of the Leonine Commission on the early editions of Thomas Aquinas, and of Lotte *Hellinga on the tradition of Poggio *Bracciolini's *Facetiae*, are exemplary. In later years, a successful or influential edition of a frequently reprinted text, not necessarily the first edition, tended to be reproduced again and again: the main text would be retained, the paratext often changed and additional material inserted. These later editions may appear to be of little philological importance; nonetheless, for someone pursuing 'the study of texts as historical phenomena reflecting social, intellectual, and economic circumstances in which they were produced' (Jensen, 138), they have an important bearing on the transmission and reception of the specific text during the Renaissance. The establishment of an editorial *stemma, still carried out too rarely, allows the fundamental distinction to be drawn between those texts that were based on previous editions and those based on a MS *exemplar.

The fact that print caused so many more texts to become widely available had the effect of stimulating their critical assessment. MSS gained a new significance as independent sources of earlier authority, a basis for *collation, or simply a better alternative to already printed versions. Indeed, the work of 16th-century scholars such as *Erasmus broke away from the established textual tradition by returning to earlier MSS, which provided fresh evidence for the study of the Bible and the Church Fathers. The wider availability of texts in print did much to foster this critical spirit.

7 Distribution

To distribute their new product, printers initially relied on the same commercial networks in place during the MS period, one that centred on the *stationer's shop, traditionally the supplier of writing materials and books. The famous Florentine bookseller and stationer *Vespasiano da Bisticci—purveyor of grand MSS to the likes of the Medici of Florence (*see* LAURENTIAN LIBRARY, FLORENCE), *Federico da Montefeltro of Urbino, and Matthias *Corvinus, king of Hungary—refused to accept the new invention of printing with movable type and ended his commercial activities in 1478. His main rival in Florence, Zanobi di Mariano, managed to stay in business as he started to deal in printed books as well. In Florence, the number of stationers' shops rose from 12 to 30 during the first half century following the advent of the printing press. The stationers were immediately involved in the new business of printing: by finishing or selling books, occasionally by becoming typographers themselves, but in particular by editing and publishing. Knowing the public's taste and with an established clientele, their contribution to printing was in many instances essential, if never generally substantiated by large financial investments.

The production and distribution of MSS took place almost invariably for local markets, but a successful printer had to have established networks of distribution that went far beyond the boundaries of the town where the printing actually took place. The need to move from a known public to an unknown, potentially larger one strengthened the printer's connection with merchants and traders. The printed book entered the market as a saleable commodity, one not dissimilar to others that were traded in the Middle Ages and during the early modern period. The book trade made the transition from a local to an international business; but because the book was usually not an essential possession, this trade had its own peculiarities. Surviving documents testify to the many problems encountered by the early printers. Relying on the work of agents and on a network of warehouses and bookshops, they only gradually achieved a stable trading pattern, developing a tendency to share risks and costs by creating joint business ventures. The establishment of a family business with branches abroad (e.g. the *Giunta and *Giolito firms) was one natural way of ensuring reliable distribution across borders. The circulation of many thousands of printed books throughout Europe—a further new aspect in the transmission of knowledge and information—was inherent in the rise of printing.

8 The Venetian success

The largest and most successful place for printing in the 15th century was Venice, which boasted a cosmopolitan, entrepreneurial, and merchant tradition, the rich libraries and widespread learning of the patriciate and the religious orders, and a large population of professional and non-professional readers. The 233 presses set up in the city before 1500—some transient, others among the most distinguished in Europe—offered the Italian and international markets a full range of printed products.

The state maintained a non-interventionist attitude. After granting a five-year *privilege to Johannes de Spira in 1469, which expired with the printer's death in 1470, privileges were issued only ad hoc for specific publications, the first to Marcantonio Sabellico in 1486. Until well into the following century, printers were not required to join a guild or conform to established regulations, as was common in most other longer established professions. However, from the very beginning printers in Venice joined confraternities, which helped their integration into the city's social network, bringing obvious benefits.

The first ten years of Venetian printing were dominated by foreign printers, working alone or in syndicates; their success was determined by their advanced distribution networks (often by exploiting their links with fellow foreign traders), as well as by the production side of the business. The following two decades saw the establishment and consolidation of Italian firms, such as *Arrivabene, Giunta, *Torresano, *Scotto, Aldus, and many others. Venetian printers and publishers became market leaders in the production (often on commission and, therefore, at low risk) of *missals and *breviaries for dioceses and religious orders throughout Europe. Many technical innovations originated in Venice, something that again reflects the city's attention to different cultures as a potential market: Glagolitic type for the Slav communities, type for musical notation (for whose invention Ottaviano de' *Petrucci obtained a privilege in 1498), and Greek printing for Greece (Venice being the leading place of publication for such works until the 19th century), as well as *Armenian, *Hebrew, and *Arabic types (see 8, 38).

Of the 1,123 Venetian editions represented in 1,387 copies now in the *Bodleian, 481 (34 per cent) were distributed and used in the 15th and 16th centuries in Italy; almost the equivalent number, 446 (32 per cent), ended up being used either in England (183, 13 per cent) or in Germany (263, 19 per cent). Indeed, England and Spain remained dependent on the importation of foreign books until the following century (see Ford, Needham, 'Customs Rolls'). Latin *textbooks used in schools arrived in England mostly from Germany and the Low Countries, until English printers started to print them towards the end of the century. Textbooks for university students and teachers and for professionals came from Italy, mainly Venice, which was only challenged in the field by Lyons towards the end of the century. Research on this fundamental aspect of the international book trade, and its impact on economic and intellectual history, can be advanced by the discovery and study of archival documents and by the physical examination of the thousands of surviving incunabula.

9 Loss and survival

From the Renaissance to the present day, incunabula have been lost in very large quantities: 'a single copy is by far the commonest survival state for incunable editions' (Needham, 'Late Use', 36). From archival and early bibliographical sources, we know of the existence of editions printed before 1500 that do not survive today in even a single copy; more editions must have existed of which we know absolutely nothing. To assess when and how, and possibly why, the loss of incunabula occurred is as important as understanding how, where, and why copies managed to survive to this day. Scholars such as Needham and Harris have recently engaged with this problem.

Among the direct or indirect agents that destroyed editions and copies are reckless consumption—common with school books, some popular vernacular literature such as *romances, and, occasionally, devotional books such as *books of hours—and obsolescence (typically the publication of more complete and up-to-date works on the same subject). Survival rates are also affected by a book's physical size (small-format books, or books with few leaves are more likely to be lost), its language (Greek and Latin works were more highly valued than vernacular ones), and provenance (institutionally owned books are more likely to survive than individually owned books). Titles may be lost to war, political and administrative changes, *censorship, and occasional floods and fires.

10 The outlook now

At the present time, the great majority of known incunable editions have been included in the ISTC. Practically all 15th-century editions have been surveyed and included in some form of national, local, or subject catalogue. However, the historical evidence, which is so important for contextualizing each edition and each copy, is far from being systematically recorded: copy-specific information from thousands of incunabula in US and Italian libraries is still lacking. For many other European libraries, what there is remains patchy.

No serious analysis of the impact of printing on Renaissance and early modern society can be comprehensive until the historical information is gathered from the extant books to assess where and when they were used, by whom, and how. As with archaeological objects, scholars need to interpret the material clues they retain (decoration, binding, MS notes), and identify ownership inscriptions, which may be contemporary or from later periods, institutional or private, male or female, lay or religious. Much has been discovered and published since Febvre and Martin half a century ago attempted a similar analysis, but much remains to be done.

BIBLIOGRAPHY

BMC

C. Bozzolo *et al.*, 'La Production du livre en quelques pays d'Europe occidentale aux XIVᵉ et XVᵉ siècles', *Scrittura e civiltà*, 8 (1984), 129–76

A. Carelli *et al.*, 'I codici miscellanei nel basso medioevo', *Segno e testo*, 2 (2004), 245–309

H. Carter, *A View of Early Typography up to About 1600* (1969; repr. with an introduction by J. Mosley, 2002)

D. Coq, 'Les Débuts de l'édition en langue vulgaire en France: publics et politiques éditoriales', *GJ* 62 (1987), 59–72

E. L. Eisenstein, *The Printing Press as an Agent of Change* (2 vols, 1979)

L. Febvre and H.-J. Martin, *The Coming of the Book* (French original, 1958; tr. D. Gerard, 1976)

M. L. Ford, 'Importation of Printed Books into England and Scotland', in *CHBB 3*

F. Geldner, *Inkunabelkunde* (1978)

E. Ph. Goldschmidt, *Medieval Texts and Their First Appearance in Print* (1943)

A. Grafton, [review of Eisenstein,] *Journal of Interdisciplinary History*, 11 (1980), 265–86

N. Harris, 'Sopravvivenze e scomparse delle testimonianze del Morgante di Luigi Pulci', *Rinascimento*, 45 (2005), 179–245

L. Hellinga, 'The Codex in the Fifteenth Century: Manuscript and Print', in *A Potencie of Life*, ed. N. Barker (1993)

X. Hermand *et al.*, 'Les Politiques éditoriales dans l'Europe des imprimeurs au XVᵉ siècle: un projet de recherches, en cours', *Archives et bibliothèques de Belgique*, 87 (2009), 75–82

R. Hirsch, *Printing, Selling and Reading 1450–1550*, 2e (1974)

ISTC

K. Jensen, 'Printing the Bible in the Fifteenth Century: Devotion, Philology and Commerce', in *Incunabula and Their Readers*, ed. K. Jensen (2003)

A. Johns, *The Nature of the Book* (1998)

H.-J. Martin *et al.*, eds., *Histoire de l'édition française* (4 vols, 1982–6)

P. Needham, [review of Eisenstein,] *Fine Print*, 6 (1980), 23–35

— 'The Customs Rolls as Documents for the Printed-Book Trade in England', in *CHBB* 3

— 'The Late Use of Incunables and the Paths of Book Survival', *Wolfenbütteler Notizien zur Buchgeschichte*, 29 (2004), 35–59

P. Nieto, 'Géographie des impressions européennes du XVe siècle', in *Le Berceau du livre: autour des incunables*, ed. F. Barbier, *Revue française d'histoire du livre*, 118–21 (2004), 125–73

A. Nuovo, *Il commercio librario nell'Italia del Rinascimento*, 3e (2003)

THE BOOK of COMMON PRAYER, AND Administration of the

Sacraments, and other Rites and Ceremonies,

of the Church of *England;* with the *Psalter* or *Psalms* of DAVID,

7 The Book as Symbol

Brian Cummings

'Books are not absolutely dead things,' wrote John Milton in 1644 in *Areopagitica*. A book is a physical object, yet it also signifies something abstract, the words and the meanings collected within it. Thus, a book is both less and more than its contents alone. A book is a metonym for the words that we read or for the thoughts that we have as we read them. At one level, like any domestic object, a book takes on the imprint of its producer and its users. Old books have further value as containing the presence of many other readers in the past. Yet, more than other objects, a book is felt to embody not only a physical memory but also a record of past thoughts. The book contains both its reader and its author. In Milton's more poetic terms, books 'contain a potency of life in them', because they 'preserve as in a vial the purest efficacy and extraction of that living intellect that bred them'. The book thus achieves a further mystery, of transforming what appears to be purely immaterial and conceptual into something with a concrete form. It is therefore not entirely extravagant for Milton to claim that a book possesses 'a life beyond life'. Destroying a book, then, Milton says, is like an act of homicide—indeed it is worse than that, since a book encloses the life of more than one person and exists in more than one time. Paradoxically, regardless of the material survival of a physical copy or artefact, a book is something immortal and imperishable.

Curtius found the origin of the idea of the book as a sacred object in the ancient Near East and Egypt, where the production of books was cultic and their possession restricted to a priestly caste. Writing is a mystical act, and scribes are accorded a corresponding status as its masters and interpreters. The ancient Egyptian word for the script now known as hiero-glyphs meant 'words of god'. The earliest inscriptions in the tombs of kings acted not only as a literary record but also as physical totems for the pharaoh to avert danger in the afterlife and to communicate with the gods. In contrast, Curtius asserted, in classical Greece there was 'hardly any idea of the sacredness of the book' (Curtius, 304). Indeed in the notorious formula-tion in Plato's *Phaedrus* (274C–276A), writing is purely functional, and fails even to perform properly that function. Knowledge exists in the mind of the philosopher: writing is a mere aide-memoire, and an untrustworthy and ephemeral one at that. Only in the Hellenistic period do the Greeks acquire a 'culture of books'. In the later grammarians, indeed, things come full circle, and Homer, in whose writing no figure of the book appears, comes to be regarded as a sacred writing. Roman literature repeats the pattern, favour-ing the idea of a *rhetor* as a speaker not a writer, until the birth of the *codex produces a new configuration of sensibility.

The material form given to a book has a great deal to do with the symbolic value that is ascribed to it. The Greek word *Pentateuch*, which the Christian Church used to describe the most sacred part of the ancient Scriptures, the Jewish Torah, means literally the 'five containers' in which the scrolls of the text were kept. The *scroll early became a metaphor for what the scroll contained—and perhaps in an extended sense also for the mystery of the relation between the phys-ical text in which God's words were contained and the spiritual sense of what those words were taken to mean. The laws given to Moses were written on stone tables, which in turn are taken to stand as the embodi-ment of divine ordinance. The law is then said to be 'written with the finger of God' (Exod. 31:18). Those who are of God are written into His 'book' (Exod. 32:32); those who have sinned are blotted out. Job reinvents the metaphor to refer to the engraving of an iron pen in lead (with wonderful anachronism, but in the same spirit of applying new media to God's work, the Authorized Version translated this as 'printed in a book', Job 19:23). At other times God writes in wax. But most of all, God discloses Himself in a scroll, the dominant written technology of the ancient world. God bears witness to His purposes in a scroll (Isa. 8:1). At the end of time, 'the heavens shall be rolled together as a scroll' (Isa. 34:4).

These Hebraic metaphors carried over into the Greek New Testament. In the vision of the end of the world in Revelation, 'the heaven departed as a scroll when it is rolled together' (6:14). The passage of time in the created world is conceived as a book which opens and which finally is closed. It is here that what Curtius calls 'the magnificent religious metaphorics of the book' reach their symbolic apotheosis. God's entire intervention in creation is imagined as a book. Just as Ezekiel begins his life as a prophet by eating the book of the divine word (Ezek. 3:1), so it is as a book that St John the Divine imagines the enunciation of the apocalypse (Rev. 5:1). When the dead come before God at the end of things, the books are opened, 'and whosoever was not found in the book of life was cast into the lake of fire' (Rev. 20:15).

It is not difficult to see how the symbolic meaning of the book might translate also into the mystical value of the book as artefact. The idea within the Kabbalah of the secret significance of the very letters in which the Torah is transcribed has been traced back to the 1st century BC. The idea of a magical power inscribed into the very letters of the text finds graphic form in the tradition of illuminating letters. The *Lindisfarne Gospels and the Book of *Kells are now among the best-known artefacts in the Western world, with their extravagant extensions of the individual letter of Scripture to fill out a whole page in a dazzling display of line, colour, and gilt. The metamorphosis of script into abstract geometry or equally into zoomorphic improvisation transforms the book into an object that is hard to summarize in terms of mere text, even though the initials retain their function at the literal level. The book is a figure of itself as much as it is a figure for the contents that it represents.

The book as symbol, then, can be seen to mediate between a number of features of the life of books, both material and abstract. The sense of the book as a sacred object gives rise to a particular kind of artefactual production which manifests in physical form the status of the book as an object. Even in its textual form, the book becomes more than itself, a visual representation not only of the contents within but of the idea of the book altogether. At least in the case of the Semitic religions of Judaism, Christianity, and Islam, this valorization of the book at least partly occurs because of the continual skirmish with iconoclasm. An extraordinary side-effect of this has been the tendency in all three religions towards what can only be described as fetishistic practices of preservation or worship of the material form of the sacred book. The incorporation of the holy book into ritual—the raising of the book, or the carrying of it in procession, or the kissing of the book or kneeling before it—is only the most obvious example of this. Equally widespread is the use of portions of text or even of whole books as amulets or talismans. Hebrew inscriptions worn as amulets are very ancient. Particularly fascinating are the *kimiyah* or 'angel-texts'—names of angels or extracts from the Torah written out on *parchment

and then encased in a silver or other precious container and worn around the neck or elsewhere on the body. Miniature copies of the Qur'ān were copied using a special script known as *ghudar* or 'dust'—so tiny as to be practically illegible—and encased in small jewelled boxes. Although Christian theology often frowned on the use of talismans, the practice of burying a copy of Scripture with the dead was retained. A beautiful example is the *Stonyhurst Gospel—placed inside the coffin of St Cuthbert at Lindisfarne in 698, and discovered intact inside when the saint's body was translated to Durham Cathedral in 1104. Later archbishops wore it round the neck during ceremonial occasions. *Amory has documented a case of a native American being interred with a medicine ball partially made with a page from a printed bible.

Alongside this exceptional investment in the preservation of the book perhaps also should be placed the corresponding urge to destruction. The practice of *book burning goes back at least to the Qing dynasty in China in the 2nd century BC. In Christianity, burning physical books is virtually synonymous with the pronouncement of bans on heretical ideas. The books of Priscillian of Ávila were burned in 383, and those of Nestorius within a generation. The simultaneous combustion of the heretic's works with the consumption of his body on the stake was a material symbol of the purging of abstract ideas: Jan Hus was burned with his books at the Council of Constance in 1415, and the same council ordered Wyclif's bones to be exhumed and burned alongside his writings. Such practices survived the Reformation and transferred into nascent Protestantism: Michael Servetus was burned at Geneva in 1553 with several portions of manuscript and one of his printed works bound around his waist. In the new confessional divisions, the Bible itself came under threat: Tyndale's New Testament was burned in England in the 1520s by official order. In such turmoil, a book could be found miraculously to survive even as the authorities strove to extinguish it. Just as Pedro Berruguete's 1480 painting (now in the Prado) of such proceedings against the Cathars showed St Dominic's works preserved intact alongside the charred detritus of the Cathar texts, so *Foxe reports a burning of Tyndale's Testaments in 1526 in which the precious books simply refused to catch fire.

The power of the book as a sacred object is bound up with its capacity to be rendered as a symbol. When Dante comes to the summit of heaven, he learns that all the *leaves (the loose *gatherings, *quaderni*) that have been scattered by sin are now bound together in one volume by love: *Legato con amore in un volume* (*Paradiso*, 33.86). Shakespeare frequently has recourse to the image of the world as a book. In *Hamlet*, the book of memory becomes the symbol of a person's mortality; *Macbeth* abounds with metaphors of the book as the repository of time and a figure for death.

At iconic moments in the history of the 20th century, the power of the book as symbolic object has been especially apparent. In 1933, the Nazis infamously burned 'degenerate' books in Berlin's Opernplatz. Conversely, in China during the Cultural Revolution, Mao's Little *Red Book was carried on the body or held aloft in staged acts of ideological affirmation. Disseminated on a scale to rival even the great religious sacred texts—740 million are believed to have been printed between the first publication in 1961 and the height of the Cultural Revolution in 1969—the Little Red Book gained its value largely from its status as a political icon. Even as the book is demystified and deconsecrated in the modern world, its symbolic value endures. (*See also* **2**, **8**, **38**.)

BIBLIOGRAPHY
H. Amory, 'The Trout and the Milk: An Ethnobibliographical Talk', *HLB* NS 7 (1996), 50–65
E. R. Curtius, *European Literature and the Latin Middle Ages* (1953)
J. Milton, *Areopagitica* (1644)

8 The Transmission of Jewish Knowledge through MSS and Printed Books

EMILE G. L. SCHRIJVER

1 Introduction

> A beautiful yellow bookcase stood in the house of my deceased grandfather. On the lower shelf were the Holy Scriptures and its commentaries; above these were prayer-books, and what the soul is in need of otherwise; above these were books of customs and of Jewish law; and above these was the Talmud. Like gold coins that shine from a leather purse the golden names of the tractates shone on the leather spines of the Talmud.

This is one of the earliest childhood memories of Samuel Agnon (1888–1970), the first and only Israeli to win the *Nobel Prize for Literature (1966). It shows, above all, a young child's fascination with the religious books of his grandfather, but upon further reading it becomes clear that Agnon's fascination would develop into deep piety in the course of his youth:

> When my father or grandfather were in the house I would sit there and study. When, however, my father and grandfather were in the store, I taught my hand the art to write the books of the Talmud. At times, I would trace the frame of the title-page or the contours of the first letters of the Talmud, and I would write myself a *Mizrah* [a wall decoration indicating the east] with those. Had, in those days, someone told me that there exist more beautiful images than these, I would not have believed him … My grandfather, of blessed memory, left many things … but hardly anything survived in the hands of his children, as the enemy came and plundered everything. But this Talmud was preserved and I still study from it, and at times, when I am writing my stories to kindle the hearts of Israel to the service of the Blessed One, I take a volume from the shelves and read in it and establish a bond with our sages, of blessed memory, and with their holy words.

These quotations from Agnon underline the central role played by the book in traditional daily Jewish life. At least since the Middle Ages Jews have identified strongly with their traditional literature and have laid great emphasis on studying these texts through MSS and printed books in Hebrew and Aramaic and in all other languages employed by Jews in the Diaspora. Agnon's words also stress the importance of the book in religious education, and it may perhaps be said that in a way the history of the Jewish book is a chapter in the history of Jewish education. Here an attempt will be made to present the history of Hebrew books by concentrating on the role they played in the transmission of Jewish knowledge.

2 Transmission of the Hebrew Bible

The central book in Jewish tradition is obviously the Pentateuch, the Torah (*see* **2**). It is traditionally written as a *scroll and read on Shabbat in synagogue in a yearly or three-yearly cycle. The writing of the Torah scroll is guided by set rules which were laid down in a number of treatises, the most famous being the extra-canonical Talmudic tractate *Soferim* (Scribes). This tractate served as the starting point for a number of commentators and legislators who expanded on it, the first and foremost being the great medieval scholar *Maimonides in his legal code *Mishneh Torah*. The high esteem for the holy craft of writing Hebrew Scriptures is actually already clear from the Babylonian Talmud. In the tractates *Eruvin* and *Sota* two similar passages occur, wherein Rabbi Ishmael, a 2nd-century CE sage, is quoted as saying to a learned scribe:

'My son, what is your occupation?' I told him, 'I am a scribe', and he said to me, 'Be meticulous in your work, for your occupation is a sacred one; should you perchance omit or add one single letter you would thereby destroy all the universe.' (*Eruvin*, 13a)

The first surviving biblical texts are found in the scrolls discovered from 1947 onwards in eleven caves near Khirbet Qumran (south of Jericho), the *Dead Sea Scrolls. The greater part of these finds have been published in the last few decades, and they provide a treasure trove of information on early Jewish book culture and the transmission of the text of the Hebrew Bible. For this introduction, two of the most interesting texts among the Dead Sea Scrolls are the so-called Genesis Apocryphon and the Isaiah scroll, both found in Cave 1. Although of a completely different literary character, both provide a fascinating glimpse into the textual variety that existed in these earlier days of the transmission of the Hebrew Bible.

After the period of the Dead Sea Scrolls the textual transmission of the Hebrew Bible is much more blurred because of the absence of written source material. This absence is the result of natural decay, of the hostile destruction of Jewish books, and most probably also of the prominence of the oral tradition within Judaism, which may have been responsible for a general reluctance to write down religious texts.

It was exactly during these dark days of textual transmission that the so-called *Masoretes* (*see* MASO-RAH) developed detailed systems of vowel and *dia-critic signs that were meant to counter the threat of faulty copying that existed in the Jews' largely oral culture. The systems, of which various forms exist, were included in later bible *codices and in the large majority of early printed editions.

The first bible codices emerge as late as the early 10th century: these are indeed the earliest dated Hebrew MSS of the medieval period. The codices were all copied in the Orient, which is most probably the result both of the presence of the necessary know-ledge of its textual intricacies and of the favourably dry climatological circumstances under which they have been kept there in the centuries that followed. The most prominent early bible codices are the *Moses ben Asher Codex, the Leningrad Codex, and the *Aleppo Codex.

The Moses ben Asher codex contains the earliest date mentioned in a *colophon of a Hebrew MS, 895 CE. Now housed in the Karaite Synagogue of Cairo, it was copied in Tiberias and contains the text of the

Prophets. A detailed codicological analysis of the MS published by Glatzer in 1988, however, has proved quite convincingly that the codex, with its colophon, was copied at least a century later from an older *exemplar. Since then a MS with fragments of the text of Nehemiah, kept in the *Genizah Collection of *Cambridge University Library and written in Da Gunbadan, Persia, in 904, is considered the earliest known dated Hebrew MS. The earliest dated Hebrew MS larger than a fragment is a codex of the Latter Prophets with Babylonian vocalization, finished in 916, now held in the National Library of *Russia in St Petersburg.

The National Library of Russia also holds another early codex of the Hebrew Bible, copied in 1008 (MS Firkovich B 19A). This text, also known as the Codex Leningradensis, has served as the basis for the two most important critical editions of the 20th century, the Biblia Hebraica of Rudolf Kittel, first published in 1906, and the Biblia Hebraica Stuttgartensia, first published in 1966. Facsimile reproductions of the MS appeared in 1971 and 1998.

The Aleppo Codex is another early, undated MS of the Hebrew Bible. It is now kept in the Ben Zvi Institute in Jerusalem and was copied more than a millennium ago by Solomon ben Buya'a and vocalized most probably by Aaron ben Asher. The synagogue in Aleppo, Syria, where it had been for centuries, was burned down in 1947 and about one third of the MS was lost. Its remaining part was smuggled to Israel a few years later.

The Jewish preoccupation with the quality of textual transmission is also evident from the high regard accorded to a number of old codices with apparently exceedingly correct biblical texts, which still existed during the Middle Ages but have since disappeared. The most famous is the so-called Hilleli Codex. In his chronicle *Sefer Yuhasin*, written around 1500, Abraham Zacuto reported that the MS was still in existence, but since then no trace of it has been found. Its legendary status confirms the Jewish obses-sion with a correct text, and, as Zacuto put it, 'all other codices were revised after it'.

3 Oral and written transmission

The oral transmission of Jewish knowledge is best known through the concept of the written and the oral Torah, which were both received by Moses on Mount Sinai and assigned equal value as expressions of Divine Revelation. The oral laws were written down for the first time around the year 200 CE in the so-called

Mishnah. The oral traditions that were developed around this *Mishnah* were once again written down in the course of the 4th and 5th centuries CE in the so-called *Gemara*, which, together with the *Mishnah*, constitute the Talmud. Two versions of the Talmud exist: a smaller Palestinian version, and a much more elaborate one, the Babylonian Talmud, the version most commonly referred to. This tradition of orality persisted well into the high Middle Ages and even afterwards and, as already indicated, it may account in part for the lack of early medieval written sources.

It is especially the so-called halakhic or legal literature that provides a fascinating glimpse into the specific nature of Jewish textual transmission. The Israeli scholar Israel Ta-Shma coined the term 'open book' for this:

A long and intensive review of the medieval Hebrew book indicates that quite often books were not meant by their authors to serve as final statements, but rather as presentations of an interim state of knowledge or opinion, somewhat like our computerized databases, which are constantly updated and which give the user a summary of the data known at the time of the latest updating. In a similar way, the medieval book was sometimes conceived of as no more than a solid basis for possible future alterations by the author himself. There were many reasons—some philosophical and psychological, others purely technical—for this profound phenomenon, which can give rise to serious problems as to finality, authorship and authority of a given work. (Ta-Shma, 17)

A fine example of this, among many others, is Isaac ben Moses of Vienna's (*c.*1180–*c.*1250) halakhic code *Or Zarua*. This is a huge work, containing abundant halakhic as well as historical material. There are explicit references within the text to the author 'of blessed memory', and to later additions by the author himself, which prove that both during his life and afterwards paragraphs were added to it. One may even doubt whether he ever considered his composition as finished at all. It has been suggested that the author constantly added to his own words in the margins of his own MSS of the text, and that these additions were included in subsequent versions of it. The same process may account for the inclusion of his students' notes.

Interestingly, the very layout of halakhic MSS, especially in the Germanic lands, confirms the open-book nature of texts like *Or Zarua*. In these MSS 'central' texts are often surrounded by all sorts of smaller, commentary-like texts in creative ad hoc layouts. These surrounding texts would afterwards be incorporated into the next, equally authoritative MS witness of the text.

There are, as well, many testimonies of scribal intervention, correction, and editing, especially in colophons. An interesting example is the colophon of the famous Leiden University MS of the Palestinian Talmud, the only surviving complete medieval MS of this work. The scribe reports that he saw himself as forced to correct the text according to the best of his knowledge, since his copy was full of mistakes. He apologizes for any mistakes of his own. The Leiden MS was finished on Thursday, 17 February 1289 in Rome:

I, Jehiel, son of Rabbi Jekutiel, son of Rabbi Benjamin Harofeh, of blessed memory, have copied this Talmud Yerushalmi ... and I copied it from a corrupt and faulty exemplar and what I was able to understand and comprehend I corrected to the best of my knowledge. And I am fully aware that I did not reach at all the corruptions and faults I found in that copy, and not even half of them. And may therefore the reader of this book who will find corruptions and faults therein judge me according to my merit and not blame me for all of them. And may the Lord, in His mercy, forgive me my sins and cleanse me from my errors, as it is said [Ps. 19:13]: 'Who can be aware of errors, clear me of unperceived guilt.' (Leiden University, MS Or. 4720 (Scal. 3), vol. 2, fo. 303ᵛ)

It is important here to emphasize a particular characteristic of Hebrew books of the Middle Ages. This characteristic also permits a more generic focus on textual transmission during the Jewish Middle Ages, i.e. not on biblical or halakhic texts only, but on literary texts as they appear in medieval MSS. As a result of the comparatively very high level of literacy among Jewish men (and a few women), more than half of all the extant medieval Hebrew codices are the product of the work of a learned copyist who copied for his own use, and not of a professional scribe. It goes without saying that this has had a strong influence on the nature of textual transmission, which was formulated by Malachi Beit-Arié as follows:

Contrary to what one might expect, the high ratio of user-produced manuscripts and the critical reproduction of texts in Jewish society did not necessarily improve the transmission of literary works by eliminating their scribal mistakes and restoring their authentic versions, but often engendered scholarly modifications, revisions and re-creations of the copied text that may very well have distorted and transformed the original work ... Versions created by learned copyists on the basis of several exemplars or by scholarly conjecture ... mixed inextricably disparate channels of transmission or conflated different authorial stages of the text and were dominated by personal choices and judgments. (Beit-Arié, *Unveiled Faces*, 65–6)

Beit-Arié's position is that of a modern scholar here. In most cases, earlier users of the 'distorted' and 'transformed' MSS he describes must have considered the texts before them as authoritative and reliable textual witnesses and have worked with them as such. A striking example of the problems involved here is provided by the text of the *Mishnah*—which, as already indicated, together with the so-called *Gemara* constitutes the text of the Talmud—as it is preserved in the only known complete medieval MS of the Babylonian Talmud, now in the Bavarian State Library in *Munich (Cod. Hebr. 95). Copied in Paris in 1343, its Mishnaic text shows significant textual differences, far beyond the realm of variant spellings or even wordings, from MSS that are considered to represent a reliable textual tradition of the *Mishnah* (such as the famous Kaufmann *Mishnah* MS in the Hungarian Academy of Sciences in Budapest). The rarity of medieval MSS, even fragments, of the Talmud is generally believed to be the combined result of its enormous size, the strength of oral transmission within Judaism, and, notably, Christian aggression, which resulted (for example) in book burnings in Paris in 1242 and, in 1553, in the prohibition against printing the Talmud in Italy. It is therefore difficult to make any final statement about the reliability of the transmission of the text of the Babylonian Talmud. And yet, in the light of the relative quality of its Mishnaic text, it is hard to believe that the text of the Gemara as it appears in the only known complete medieval MS of its text represents anything else but one of Beit-Arié's 're-creations of the copied text that may very well have distorted and transformed the original work'.

In spite of the active copying by individuals, books were generally rare during the Jewish Middle Ages. As a result, scholars and students saw themselves forced to borrow books, often, to make copies for their own use in the process. In the Talmudic academy of Rabbi Israel ben Petahiah Isserlein (1390–1460), the spiritual leader of 15th-century Austrian Jewry, it was customary for students who possessed books to study them during the day, whereas students without books would borrow them to study at night. It is therefore not at all surprising that the lending of books was considered a great merit. In the medieval Ashkenazic *Sefer Hasidim*, or Book of the Pious, it is even stated that when lending books one should prefer a student who uses them on a daily basis over someone who does not. It further states that the greater the number of copies taken from a book, the greater the merit of the owner, and that a fear of possible damage inflicted on a book should never prevent one from lending it. The most striking expression of this attitude is the statement that one should rather sell a book to a Christian who lends it to others, than to one's brother, who does not do so. This general lack of books—in the Middle Ages a larger collection of MSS consisted of some dozens of volumes—would only come to a halt after the invention of printing; even then the relative poverty of the great majority of Jews prevented most of them from building more substantial collections.

4 From MS to printed text

Between 1469 and 1473 the first six Hebrew books were printed by three printers, Obadiah, Manasseh, and Benjamin of Rome. The most likely order of production of these books was established by Offenberg in *BMC* 13 (2005) on the basis of careful typographical and paper analyses of the holdings of the BL and the Bibliotheca *Rosenthaliana in Amsterdam. This analysis does not permit a more precise dating of the individual books.

1. David ben Joseph Kimhi's dictionary *Sefer ha-*shorashim*;
2. Solomon ben Abraham ibn Adret's collection of responsa;
3. Rashi's (Solomon ben Isaac) Commentary on the Pentateuch;
4. Levi ben Gershom's Commentary on the Book of Daniel;
5. Nathan ben Jehiel of Rome's Talmudic dictionary *Arukh*;
6. Moses ben Nahman's Commentary on the Pentateuch.

It must be emphasized that the world's second specialist in the field, Shimon Iakerson of St Petersburg, in his catalogue of the Hebrew incunabula in the Library of the *Jewish Theological Seminary of America in New York (2004–5), is less certain about the exact order of printing. A quick look at the nature of the first six texts ever printed in Hebrew is interesting: two dictionaries, three bible commentaries, and a book of rabbinical responsa (replies to questions about Jewish law); no bibles, no prayer books, no Talmud, no scientific books. Although this would soon be corrected in the course of the 15th century—rather unexpectedly,

Avicenna's medical *Canon* printed in Naples in 1491 is the largest of all Hebrew incunabula—and other genres would appear in print as well, the rarity (for example) of copies of the earliest editions of Rashi's commentaries is a clear indication of the popularity of Bible commentaries. Offenberg has even gone so far as to assume that more early editions have existed, of which no copies remain.

The six Rome imprints precede the book that many non-specialists continue to quote erroneously as the first printed Hebrew book, Solomon ben Isaac's commentary on the Pentateuch (*see* RASHI); finished on 17 February 1475 in Reggio di Calabria, it is the first printed Hebrew book mentioning a date. There were at least 140 Hebrew books printed in the incunable period. These books were produced by approximately 40 presses active in Italy, Spain, and Portugal, and by one in Turkey.

After the expulsion of the Jews from the Iberian peninsula at the end of the 15th century, Italy became the primary centre of Hebrew printing in the Mediterranean world, with Venice, Mantua, Sabbioneta, and Cremona having the most important presses. A particularly significant chapter in the history of the transmission of Jewish texts is the activity of the famous Venetian press of van *Bomberghen, a Christian printer from Antwerp. He had close contacts with Christopher *Plantin; his cousin Cornelius van Bomberghen was one of Plantin's partners. Van Bomberghen (just 'Bomberg' in Hebrew) established his printing press in Venice in 1516 and was active there until his return in 1548 to Antwerp, where he died in 1553. He published first-class editions of the *Biblia Rabbinica*, i.e. the Hebrew Bible with relevant translations and commentaries, and of the Palestinian and Babylonian Talmudim. For his 1522–4 edition of the Palestinian Talmud he claimed to have used a number of MSS in order to achieve the best possible text. Although it is not entirely certain that he really used more than the one MS that is now known as the Leiden MS (its colophon was quoted earlier), his text shows an awareness of textual criticism and a sense of editorial responsibility that would remain the standard for many generations. His was also one of the first *printing offices in which Jewish and non-Jewish specialists worked closely together—an example that would soon be followed in other centres of humanist printing such as Basle, Constance, and Isny.

Other important centres of Hebrew printing in the Mediterranean area were Constantinople and Salonika. An interesting aspect of the history of Hebrew printing in the Balkan lands (*see* **36**) is the sale of books in weekly instalments of one or more *quires, which would be sold after the Shabbat service on Saturday night. This phenomenon, certainly the result of limited funds, may account for the high number of incomplete surviving copies of books published in these cities. Important centres of printing in the Ashkenazi world were Prague, Cracow, and Augsburg. In these a relatively high number of books for everyday use, especially prayer books, were produced: with these, the issue of *textual criticism does not seem to have been very prominent (at least judging from the title-pages). Further Humanist centres of Hebrew printing were Paris, Geneva, Antwerp, and, later, Leiden.

Starting in the second half of the 16th century and on into the 18th century in Italy, the censors of the Office of the *Inquisition used to check and expurgate the large majority of Hebrew books in private and community collections (*see* CENSORSHIP, EXPURGATION). They would often even charge the Jews for their 'holy' work. The Inquisition's special attention to the activity of the Italian Jewish printing presses found its most dramatic expression in the prohibition in 1553 against printing the Talmud. This led to a dramatic decrease in Hebrew book production in general and to all sorts of Jewish *self-censorship, either through the active changing of texts in order to make them 'clean' for the Inquisition, or through the decision simply not to print certain works that would not avoid the censors' criticism.

The 17th century is the century of Amsterdam. The first Jew to print Hebrew in Amsterdam was Menasseh ben Israel, who started printing in 1627. Other important Amsterdam Hebrew printers were Immanoel Benveniste, Uri Fayvesh ben Aaron Halevi, David de Castro Tartas, and the members of the printing dynasties of Athias and *Proops. Although most printers did have a number of major projects through which they would try to establish their name, judging from their productions most Amsterdam printers were willing to print any book that came with proper funding and reliable rabbinical approbations. For their special projects, however, they would invest considerably, either with their own or with external funds, and would do their utmost to produce the best possible text. An interesting case in point are the two competing *Yiddish translations of the Bible that were printed more or less simultaneously in 1678 and 1679. The printer Uri Fayvesh ordered Jekuthiel ben Isaac Blitz to make a Yiddish translation. The translator appeared not to be able to deliver the quality that one of the partners in the project, the printer *Athias, had expected. Athias therefore decided to withdraw from the project, ordering a better translation from Joseph ben Alexander Witzenhausen and publishing it himself. Although both editions were printed in *press runs of more than 6,000 copies, neither was a commercial success. On a more general level it may be stated that the Amsterdam printing business, with its vast international network of authors and readers, its high-quality output, and its close contacts with the surrounding non-Jewish world, constituted the last stage in the industrialization and professionalization of Hebrew printing.

5 The emergence of publishing

The second half of the 18th century was dominated by a major development in the intellectual history of Jewish Europe. The Jewish Enlightenment, or *Haskalah movement, would dominate the world of the book in the late 18th and early 19th centuries and, alongside more traditional presses that catered for the needs of the religious communities, would become responsible for a series of new, critical editions of traditional Jewish texts, textbooks, satirical works, and a number of influential journals. The most important journal was *Ha-me'asef (the Gatherer), issued originally by the Society of Promoters of the Hebrew Language and published in various places between 1784 and 1811. The journal soon became the voice of the Jewish Enlightenment. *Haskalah* goals included getting Jews to adopt the German language and to give up Yiddish, to assimilate into the local culture, and, for literary use, to write biblical ('classical') Hebrew instead of what they considered the inferior Rabbinic Hebrew. The best way to implement these ideals was by means of education. Interestingly, fables were considered especially effective for education, which explains why *Ha-me'asef* contains no fewer than 55 fables.

In the course of the 19th and in the beginning of the 20th century ever more belles-lettres were published, both in Hebrew and in Hebrew and Yiddish translations. This illustrates the continuing emancipation of the Jewish intellectual classes, as well as the development of what has been called 'a vigorous, effective, and dynamic publishing apparatus' (Grunberger, 124). Emerging Zionism was an influential factor as well, since it stimulated the publication of historical novels that connected contemporary Jews with their historical ancestors. One publisher has been particularly important in the development of this 'publishing apparatus', Abraham Leib Shalkovich, or Ben-Avigdor. He started off in Warsaw with a series of 'penny books'

in 1891, and established two conventional publishing houses, one in 1893 and one in 1896. Ben-Avigdor formulated his deeper motivation as follows:

> Upon examining the poverty of our Hebrew literature in all its aspects, we recognize that one of the main factors preventing it from developing as it should is the absence from our midst of well-financed publishers who could pay authors and scholars a just recompense for their labor … (Grunberger, 120)

Ben-Avigdor's and a number of his successor's efforts paved the way for the development of a national, modern Hebrew literature, publishing the works of such authors as Hayyim Nahman Bialik (1873–1934) and Saul Tchernichovski (1875–1943).

The emigration of these authors and many of their colleagues to Palestine in the first decades of the 20th century signalled the emergence of Palestine as the centre of Hebrew literature. This shift to Palestine was further strengthened by the major political events of the 20th century, the rise of Communism in Eastern Europe, the mass destruction of European Jews by the Nazis, and the foundation of the State of Israel in 1948. Modern Israeli authors such as Abraham Yehoshua (1936–), David Grossman (1954–), and Amos Oz (1939–), are published in Israel and widely translated, read, and appreciated in all modern languages. Oz's monumental and highly erudite novel *A Tale of Love and Darkness* (2004) recounts his own family saga and covers Jewish history and intellectual life of the 19th, 20th, and 21st centuries: while writing about himself and his family, he is also telling the story of the Jews. As such his work is both an integral part of a millennium-old tradition and a worthy representative of the promising future of the Hebrew (for which now read Israeli) book.

BIBLIOGRAPHY

S. J. Agnon, *Das Schaß meines Großvaters* (1925)
M. Beit-Arié, *Hebrew Manuscripts of East and West* (1993)
— *The Makings of the Medieval Hebrew Book* (1993)
— *Unveiled Faces of Medieval Hebrew Books* (2003)
M. Glatzer, 'The Aleppo-Codex: Codicological and Paleographical Aspects', *Sefunot*, 4.19 (1988), 167–276 (in Hebrew)
Z. Gries, *The Book in the Jewish World, 1700–1900* (2007)
M. W. Grunberger, 'Publishing and the Rise of Modern Hebrew Literature', in *A Sign and a Witness*, ed. L. S. Gold (1988)
M. J. Heller, *Printing the Talmud* (1992)
— *Studies in the Making of the Early Hebrew Book* (2008)
B. S. Hill, *Incunabula, Hebraica and Judaica* (1981)
— *Hebraica (Saec. X ad Saec. XVI)* (1989)

S. Iakerson, *Catalogue of Hebrew Incunabula from the Collection of the Library of the Jewish Theological Seminary* (2 vols, 2004–5)

S. Liberman Mintz and G. M. Goldstein, *Printing the Talmud* (2005)

A. K. Offenberg, *Hebrew Incunabula in Public Collections* (1990)

— *BMC* 13: *Hebraica* (2005)

D. W. Parry *et al.*, eds., *The Dead Sea Scrolls Reader* (2004)

R. Posner and I. Ta-Shma, eds., *The Hebrew Book* (1975)

B. Richler, *Guide to Hebrew Manuscript Collections* (1994)

E. G. L. Schrijver, 'The Hebraic Book', in *A Companion to the History of the Book*, ed. S. Eliot and J. Rose (2007)

C. Sirat, *Hebrew Manuscripts of the Middle Ages* (2002)

I. Ta-Shma, 'The "Open" Book in Medieval Literature: the Problem of Authorized Editions', *BJRL* 75 (1993) 17–24

E. Tov, *Textual Transmission of the Hebrew Bible* (1992)

— ed., *The Dead Sea Scrolls on Microfiche* (1993)

Y. Vinograd, *Thesaurus of the Hebrew Book* (1993)

9 Missionary Printing

M. Antoni J. Üçerler, S.J.

1 Introduction

The history of printing and the history of the book would be incomplete without an understanding of the key role played by printing presses that were established by missionaries, Roman Catholic and Protestant, in countries throughout East and Southeast Asia, Oceania (*see* **44**, **45**), Africa (*see* **37**), the Middle East (*see* **38**), and the Americas (*see* **46**, **47**, **48**). The missionaries soon discovered that both the propagation of Christian doctrine and the inculcation of its ethical precepts could be greatly aided by the mass production and distribution of books and *pamphlets. The earliest missionary presses were established in the 16th and 17th centuries and were linked for the most part to the Roman Catholic religious orders—Franciscans, Dominicans, Augustinians, and Jesuits—that were engaged in activities throughout the New World and Asia.

Protestant missionary presses first appeared on the Asian scene in India in the 17th century. Over the following 100 years, foundations such as the London Missionary Society, the *British and Foreign Bible Society (BFBS), and the American Board of Commissioners for Foreign Missions were established on both sides of the Atlantic. A common characteristic of their method of evangelization was the strategic use of the printing press.

Missionary printing has taken place throughout the world from the 16th century onwards. This essay provides a preliminary sketch of the most significant developments in South, Southeast, and East Asia: for the Americas, see **46**, **47**, and **48**.

2 India

The story of missionary presses begins on the west coast of India 46 years after the Portuguese first conquered and established a strategic commercial entrepôt in the port city of Goa in 1510. João Nunes Barreto, the patriarch designate of Ethiopia, brought a printing press from Portugal to Goa on 6 September 1556. This press was originally destined for use in Africa, but in view of strained relations between the missionaries and the Emperor of Abyssinia, it remained in Goa. One of the Jesuits who accompanied Barreto to India was Juan de *Bustamente (also known from the 1560s as João Rodrigues), who became master printer at the Jesuit College of St Paul. The press was first used on 19 October 1556, when lists of theses (*conclusões*) in logic and philosophy were printed as *broadsides for students of the College to defend publicly (Wicki, iii. 514, 574). The following year saw the publication of the first book, a compendium of Christian doctrine, composed several years before by Francis Xavier for the catechesis of local children.

Juan Gonsalves (or Gonçálvez), another Spanish Jesuit, is credited with having produced in Goa, in 1577, the earliest metal type in Tamil. Pero Luis, a Brahmin and the first Indian Jesuit, and João de Faria, who helped to improve the *fount, assisted Gonsalves. The result was the first book printed with movable type in an Indian language, namely an emended version of Xavier's original Tamil *catechism, revised by Henrique Henriques, who was the first systematic lexicographer of the language. The 16-page booklet was produced in Quilon (Kollam) in 1578. The *colophon on the last page includes text printed from the type made in Goa the previous year. Another catechism (*Doutrina christã*) by Marcos Jorge, originally published in Lisbon in 1561 and 1566, was translated into Tamil and printed with Faria's type in Cochin on 14 November 1579 (Shaw, '"Lost" Work', 27). A guide to how to make one's confession (*Confessionairo*) and a collection of the lives of the saints (*Flos Sanctorum*) in Tamil followed in 1580 and 1586 respectively. All these books were prepared in accordance with instructions issued in 1575 by Alessandro Valignano, who was responsible for all Jesuit missions in Southeast and East Asia between 1573 and 1606 (Wicki, x. 269, 334). He would also play a crucial role in the beginnings of missionary printing in China and Japan.

The first publication in an Indian language other than Tamil was printed in Konkani some time before 1561 at the College of St Paul. In a letter from Goa on 1 December 1561, Luís Fróis reports that a printed summary of Christian doctrine was read to the local people 'in their own language' (Wicki, v. 273; Saldanha, 7–9). No copy of this work (probably a small booklet) is known to have survived. There are copies, however, of the books written by Thomas Stephens, an English Jesuit and pioneer in the study of Indian languages. The first was his 'Story of Christ' (*Krista purāna*) in literary Marathi, printed in 1616, 1649, and 1654. The second work was a Christian doctrine (*Doutrina christam em lingoa bramana canarim*) in Konkani, the language spoken by the Brahmins in Goa; it was printed posthumously in 1622 (Priolkar, 17–18). Stephens also composed the first *grammar of Konkani, which came off the press in 1640. Although the missionaries had made attempts to produce *Indian type in Marathi-Devanāgarī script or 'lengoa canarina' as early as 1577, they gave up their efforts on account of the difficulty of producing so many *matrices. As a result, they printed Stephens's works in Roman transliteration only (Wicki, x. 1006–7). A total of 37 titles in Portuguese, Latin, Marathi, Konkani, and Chinese were printed between 1556 and 1674 (Boxer, 1–19). The promulgation of a decree in 1684 by the Portuguese authorities in Goa banning the use of Konkani, in a move to root out all local languages, brought Roman Catholic missionary printing in India to an abrupt end. Two centuries would pass before it could be revived.

Meanwhile *Ziegenbalg, a Lutheran from Germany and the first Protestant missionary in India, travelled in 1706 to the Danish East India Company's coastal mission at Tranquebar (Tharangambadi), north of Nagappattinam, where he soon became proficient in Tamil. A library of Jesuit publications, including Henriques' grammar, was available to Ziegenbalg, who found them useful in avoiding pitfalls in the translation of his own works. He wrote to Denmark requesting a printing press in 1709. His Danish patrons then appealed to the *Society for Promoting Christian Knowledge in London, which shipped a press to India in 1712. On 17 October of that year, a Christian doctrine in Portuguese and Tamil was printed in roman letters. Many other works followed and were printed with Tamil type, which he arranged to be cast in Germany on the basis of drawings he had prepared. The type was produced at Halle in Saxony and sent to India in 1713 with Johann Gottlieb Adler, a German printer who established a type foundry in Porayur just outside Tranquebar. Ziegenbalg's translation of the New Testament into Tamil was printed in two parts (1714–15) with a new smaller *typeface cast by Adler. A second edition followed in 1724, with further editions in 1758, 1788, and 1810 (Rosenkilde, 186). To counter the constant shortage of paper and ink, Ziegenbalg also helped establish a local *paper mill and a factory to produce *ink.

After Ziegenbalg, the most famous Protestant missionary printer in India was William *Carey, who founded the Baptist Missionary Society in 1792 and arrived in West Bengal the following year. In 1800, he succeeded in establishing a missionary press at Serampore (Shrirampur), a Danish settlement 20 km north of Calcutta (Kolkata), which was supervised by his fellow missionary and printer, William Ward. Carey then published the Gospel of Matthew, the earliest *imprint produced with Bengali type. The following year saw his first complete translation of the New Testament in that language. Working with his fellow missionary, Joshua Marshman, and with learned Indian converts, he produced further translations of the Bible into Sanskrit, Hindi, Oriya, Marathi, Assamese, and many other languages. The *Serampore press, in operation until 1855, became the most prolific Christian printing concern in India, producing works in more than 40 different languages and dialects (*see* **39**).

3 China, Malaysia, and Singapore

The Chinese stage on which missionaries made their appearance in the 16th century was very different from that of India. Most significant was the integrity of China's territory, free from any form of colonial coercion that might include foreign attempts to control or *censor the printed word. Although records show evidence of the use of movable type made from an amalgam of clay and glue as early as the 11th century, the technology that dominated the Chinese world of printing until the 19th century remained xylography or *woodblock printing, first employed in China around AD 220 (*see* **40**). The bureaucracy of the Middle Kingdom, which was based on a highly centralized civil service examination, depended on the ready availability and wide distribution of books. This in turn created the need for thousands of printers and bookshops throughout the realm. Thus, when Michele Ruggieri and Matteo Ricci, the first two Italian Jesuit missionaries to compose works in literary Chinese, wished to have their books published, they turned to their friends among the literati, who made arrangements to have the printing done either in their own private *printing office or by another local printer.

In a way similar to their counterparts in India, the missionaries in China concentrated their early efforts on producing summaries of Christian doctrine. In 1584, they succeeded in printing at Zhaoqing Ruggieri's *Tianzhu shilu* (The True Record of the Lord of Heaven), the earliest translation of a catechism into Chinese. The *Tianzhu shiyi* (The True Meaning of the Lord of Heaven), a completely revised catechism in dialogue form, was composed by Matteo Ricci and printed in Peking (Beijing) for the first time in 1603. These catechisms, which encompassed a wide range of genres, mark the beginning of the prolific production of works composed in Chinese by several generations of missionaries and printed throughout China on private presses and at printing offices using woodblocks. In addition to expositions of Christian doctrine and liturgical texts, there were works introducing adaptations of Western classical books in the humanities—especially in moral philosophy—as well as numerous scientific treatises on astronomy, mathematics, physics, and geography. In this enterprise the foreign missionaries were often aided by erudite Chinese converts, the most prominent of whom were Xu Guangqi, Yang Tingyun, and Li Zhizao. Approximately 470 works on religious and moral topics composed by missionaries in China and Chinese Christians were printed between 1584 and 1700. Another 120 titles dealt with the West and science (Standaert, 600). These books represent an extraordinary bridge between the canons of classical literature in China and Europe, and they provide both the East and the West with a literary window into each other's ancient cultures and traditions.

Jesuit printing in China: Michele Ruggieri's *Tianzhu shilu* (The True Record of the Lord of Heaven), printed at Zhaoqing in 1584.

The first Protestant missionary in China was Robert Morrison, who arrived in Canton (Guangzhou) in 1807 as a member of the London Missionary Society (LMS). Together with his fellow missionary, William Milne, he subsequently founded the Anglo-Chinese (*Yingwa*) College in the 'Ultra-Ganges Mission' in Malacca (Melaka) in 1818 and completed a translation of the Bible into Chinese in 1819 (printed in 1823). The mission press of the LMS, however, began operations in Malacca as early as 1815. Among the early imprints of 1817 are 'The Ten Commandments' and 'The Lord's Prayer' in Malay, produced in Arabic-Jawi script (Rony, 129). From Malacca, Milne sent Thomas Beighton in 1819 to establish a school for the education of Malays and Chinese in Penang and to work as a printer. Samuel Dyer, Morrison's former student and also an LMS member, arrived in Penang in 1827. An expert in *punchcutting, he worked on a new steel typeface for Chinese characters.

In Singapore, the BFBS had been printing works in Malay since 1822, just three years after Sir Stamford Raffles founded the free trading post. There were also other mission presses that produced a variety of imprints in the 1830s and 1840s and were administered by the LMS and the American Board of Commissioners for Foreign Missions (ABCFM). Two men deserve special mention in this regard. The first is Benjamin Peach Keasberry, a pioneer in Malay education who had perfected his printing skills at Batavia (Java). He learned the language from Abdullah bin Abdul Kadir (or Munshi Abdullah), the father of modern Malay literature, who helped him to produce a new translation of the New Testament into Malay (after the earlier partial Amsterdam and Oxford editions of 1651 and 1677). The second was Alfred North, a Presbyterian minister from Exeter, NH, who was head of the printing division until 1843, the year the American Mission in Singapore was closed. When the 1842 Treaty of Nanking allowed the British to take up residence in China, Walter Henry Medhurst established a new LMS Press in Shanghai, which soon became the most prolific in modern China, printing works in English, Chinese, and Malay on a wide range of topics, sacred and secular. An accomplished polyglot and pioneer lexicographer, Medhurst also published numerous *dictionaries, including the first English–Japanese, Japanese–English vocabulary, printed in Batavia in 1830.

4 The Philippines

Dominican missionaries, who would lead early missionary printing in the Philippine archipelago, built their church and convent of San Gabriel among the Chinese merchants in the Parián, or market district of Manila after their arrival in 1587. The missionaries soon set about preparing Christian texts for the native Filipino as well as the mixed Chinese (or *sangley*) populations. A number of catechisms circulated in MS as early as the 1580s. Some time before 20 June 1593, Gómez Pérez Dasmariñas (governor, 1590–93) authorized the printing of two Christian doctrines, one in Spanish and Tagalog, and another in Chinese. The Tagalog text was prepared by the Franciscans working under Juan de Plasencia, whereas the Chinese doctrine was composed by the Dominicans supervised by Juan Cobo. Both were printed with woodblocks prepared by a Chinese convert and printer, Geng Yong (or Keng Yong), whose Spanish name was Juan de Vera. Cobo composed another summary of Christian doctrine along with a synopsis of Western natural sciences (*Shilu*), which was printed posthumously in 1593. It is noteworthy that Cobo mentions having read Ruggieri's printed catechism of 1584 (Wolf, 37).

Other devotional works followed in movable type between 1602 and 1640 from the Binondo (or Binondoc) quarter of Manila. Of these, the first imprint was probably a booklet with the mysteries of the rosary, printed in 1602, composed by a Dominican, Francisco Blancas de San José, who set up the press at the convent. This was followed by a pamphlet containing the ordinances of the Dominican Order in the Philippines (*Ordinationes Generales*) and another treatise by Blancas de San José, entitled *Libro de las quatro postrimerías del hombre en lengua tagala, y letra española*. Both were printed by Juan de Vera in 1604–5. Other works, printed by de Vera's brother, Pedro, began to appear in 1606. He printed a grammar, *Arte y reglas de la lengua tagala* (1610), compiled by Blancas de San José, and a book in Tagalog to teach the native population Spanish. Pedro de Vera printed these works in Abucay, part of Bataan province where Tomas Pinpin and Domingo Laog, regarded as the first native Filipino typesetters and printers, were active for several decades. The Franciscans also had a press as early as 1606, but no evidence remains of its productions prior to 1655, after which it was transferred to Tayabas (Quezon) in 1702 and to Manila in 1705. The Jesuits, on the other hand, established a press in 1610 at their college in Manila, and the Augustinians were printing at their own convent in Manila as early as 1618. Thus, several hundred titles were published at missionary presses in the Philippines before the 19th century.

5 Japan

The story of missionary printing in Japan is linked to Alessandro Valignano, who was also instrumental in early printing in India. The Jesuits, who first landed in Japan in 1549, soon realized the need for books in order to carry out their work, especially among the learned elites. Unlike China, Japan during the so-called era of Warring States (1467–1568) did not provide them with a readily accessible network of printers on whom they could rely. Valignano therefore instructed Diogo de Mesquita, a Portuguese Jesuit, to procure a press in Europe and to have Japanese typefaces cut in Portugal or in Flanders. The press was acquired in Lisbon in 1586 and first used to print a small booklet, *Oratio Habita à Fara D. Martino*, in 1588 in Goa. There, a number of young Japanese, including Constantino Dourado and Jorge de Loyola, learned punchcutting from Bustamente, the master printer at the College of St Paul. The press was employed again later that year in Macao to print

Christiani Pueri Institutio, a popular treatise in Latin by Juan Bonifacio, before it reached its destination further east.

The first imprints of the new Jesuit mission press were prepared at their college at Kazusa in 1590–91 and included summaries of Christian doctrine, broadsides with prayers, and an abridged version of saints' lives (*Sanctos no gosagueo no uchi nuqigaqi*). This last work was the first book printed in Japanese with movable type. These early imprints employed roman script with a few unsuccessful attempts to produce Japanese type. Other works printed with *roman type include the *Feiqe no monogatari* (Tale of the Heike) (1592), a translation of Aesop's *Fables* (*Esopo no fabulas*) (1593), as well as the trilingual Latin–Portuguese–Japanese dictionary of 1595. A Japanese–Portuguese dictionary (*Vocabulario da lingoa de Japam*) and the first grammar of Japanese (*Arte da lingoa de Japam*) were printed between 1603 and 1608. Major improvements to the *wooden type were made in the early 1590s; metal type of high quality in *cursive script (*sōsho*) was finally perfected in 1598–9 and used in the printing of several important works, including a translation of the *Guía de peccadores* by Luis de Granada and the *Rakuyōshū*, a Chinese–Japanese dictionary.

The Jesuits and their converts were instrumental in effecting a number of innovations in printing in Japan, including the first recorded use of movable type to print in Japanese itself (as opposed to the romanized form of the language); the introduction of furigana (i.e. hiragana or katakana, syllabic characters printed in a smaller fount, to indicate the correct reading of the individual Chinese characters); the carving of two or more characters on a single piece of type; and the use of hiragana-script *ligatures. By 1600, the Jesuits had handed over the day-to-day operations of the press—which had been moved from Kazusa to Amakusa to Nagasaki—to a prominent Japanese Christian layman, Thomé Sōin Gotō. Another layman, Antonio Harada, began printing Christian works in Miyako (Kyoto) in 1610 at the latest. It is uncertain whether he used traditional woodblocks or movable type in his printing office. When the missionaries were expelled from the country in 1614, the press was shipped to Macao, where it was unpacked in 1620 to print an abridged grammar of Japanese composed by João Rodrigues 'Tçuzzu' ('the Interpreter'). Although some sources claim that the press was subsequently sold to the Augustinians in Manila, no conclusive evidence can be adduced to identify the press used in the Philippines with that of the Jesuits from the Japanese mission.

In the aftermath of Toyotomi Hideyoshi's invasion of Korea, where movable type had been in use since the 13th century (*see* **41**), the Japanese regent brought back Korean printing materials in 1592. As a result, the Emperor Goyōzei and Tokugawa Ieyasu published a number of books between 1593 and 1613 using both wooden and copper type (*see* **42**). Whether either of these two independent developments in the history of Japanese movable-type printing exerted any influence on the other remains unclear.

After Japan closed her doors to the West in 1639, missionary printing ceased altogether. It would begin again in earnest only in the 1870s in Nagasaki and Yokohama, under the aegis of prominent members of the Foreign Paris Missions (MEP) in Japan, including Bernard Petitjean, Pierre Mounicou, and Louis Théodore Furet. Even before the proclamation of religious freedom by the Meiji government in 1873, the French missionaries had succeeded in printing catechisms in Japanese as early as 1865.

6 Conclusion

As Europeans began to travel to all corners of the earth beginning in the 15th century, they were determined not only to conquer new lands but also to spread their faith. From *Gutenberg they had learned the power of the printed word, and were determined to use this revolutionary new technology to Christianize Asia. The impact of these efforts varied depending on a number of circumstances. The two most significant variables were the ability to wield control as a colonial power (e.g. in the Philippines, but not in Japan or China) and the pre-existence of a widespread *print culture (e.g. in China), or lack thereof (e.g. in India and Malaya).

This summary account of missionary printing in Asia also suggests that the principal difference between Roman Catholic and Protestant presses was the emphasis placed by the former on the exposition of Christian doctrine and the printing of catechetical treatises, and the early concentration by the latter on the preparation of partial or complete versions of the Bible in local languages. In either case, the missionaries made efforts to learn the local languages and pioneered the production of numerous dictionaries and grammars.

BIBLIOGRAPHY

C. R. Boxer, *A Tentative Check-List of Indo-Portuguese Imprints, 1556–1674* (1956)

C. J. Brokaw, 'On the History of the Book in China', in *Printing and Book Culture in Late Imperial China*, ed. C. J. Brokaw and K. Chow (2005)

T. F. Carter, *The Invention of Printing in China and its Spread Westward*, 2e (1955; repr. 1988)

A. Chan, *Chinese Books and Documents in the Jesuit Archives in Rome* (2002)

C. Clair, *A Chronology of Printing* (1969)

H. Cordier, *L'Imprimerie sino-européenne en Chine* (1901)

T. Doi, 'Das Sprachstudium der Gesellschaft Jesu in Japan im 16. und 17. Jahrhundert', *Monumenta Nipponica*, 2 (1939), 437–65

W. Farge, *The Japanese Translations of the Jesuit Mission Press, 1590-1614* (2002)

R. P. Hsia, 'The Catholic Mission and Translations in China, 1583-1700', in *Cultural Translation in Early Modern Europe*, ed. P. Burke and R. P. Hsia (2007)

J. Laures, *Kirishitan Bunko: A Manual of Books and Documents on the Early Christian Mission in Japan*, 3e (1957; repr. 1985)

J. Toribio Medina, *Biblioteca hispano-americana (1493-1810)* (7 vols, 1898–1907)

— *Historia de la imprenta en los antiguos dominios españoles de América y Oceanía* (2 vols, 1958)

J. Muller and E. Roth, *Aussereuropäische Druckereien im 16. Jahrhundert* (1969)

D. Pacheco, 'Diogo de Mesquita, S. J. and the Jesuit Mission Press', *Monumenta Nipponica*, 26 (1971), 431–43

J. Pan, 'A Comparative Research of Early Movable Metal-Type Printing Technique in China, Korea, and Europe', *GJ* 73 (1998), 36–41

— *A History of Movable Metal-Type Printing Technique in China* (2001)

A. K. Priolkar, *The Printing Press in India* (1958)

W. E. Retana, *Orígenes de la imprenta filipina* (1911)

A. Kohar Rony, 'Malay Manuscripts and Early Printed Books in the Library of Congress', *Indonesia*, 52 (1991), 123–34

V. Rosenkilde, 'Printing at Tranquebar', *Library*, 5/4 (1949–50), 179–95

M. Saldanha, *Doutrina Cristã em língua concani* (1945)

E. Satow, *The Jesuit Mission Press* (1898)

D. Schilling, 'Vorgeschichte des Typendrucks auf den Philippinen', *GJ* 12 (1937), 202–16

— 'Christliche Druckereien in Japan (1590–1614)', *GJ* 15 (1940), 356–95

G. Schurhammer and G. W. Cottrell, 'The First Printing in Indic Characters', *HLB* 6 (1952), 147–60

J. F. Schütte, 'Drei Unterrichtsbücher für japanische Jesuitenprediger aus dem XVI. Jahrhundert', *Archivum Historicum Societatis Iesu*, 8 (1939), 223–56

— 'Christliche japanische Literatur, Bilder, und Druckblätter in einem unbekannten vatikanischen Codex aus dem Jahre 1591', *Archivum Historicum Societatis Iesu*, 9 (1940), 226–80

G. W. Shaw, 'A "Lost" Work of Henrique Henriques: The Tamil Confessionary of 1580', *BLR* 11 (1982–5), 26–34

— *The South Asia and Burma Retrospective Bibliography* (1987)

N. Standaert, ed., *Handbook of Christianity in China* (2001)

R. Streit and J. Dindinger, *Bibliotheca Missionum* (30 vols, 1916–75)

M. A. J. Üçerler and S. Tsutsui, eds., *Laures Rare Book Database and Virtual Library*, www.133.12.23.145:8080/html/, consulted Apr. 2008

J. Wicki, ed., *Documenta Indica* (18 vols, 1944–88)

E. Wolf, 2nd, *Doctrina Christiana: The First Book Printed in the Philippines. Manila 1593* (1947)

10 Paper

DAVEN CHRISTOPHER CHAMBERLAIN

1 Introduction

Paper is a sheet material consisting of overlapping vegetable fibres that bond together to form a compact mat. Its origin can be traced to China, where a court official named Cai Lun is said to have invented it *c.* AD 105. Paper remained exclusive to the Middle East and East Asia until around 1151, when there is evidence of its being made in Spain during the Moorish occupation. Slowly, the craft spread across Europe, from Italy in 1276 to France in 1348, Germany in 1390, and eventually into England by 1495.

Each sheet of paper bears physical signs of the manufacturing process it has undergone. Coupled with analysis of its constituents, these can be used to provide evidence of provenance. This essay presents information on paper as an historical source; although it is chiefly concerned with occidental manufacture from its inception to the present day, its generalities can be applied, with due consideration, to paper from any period or origin.

2 Paper manufacture

Paper can be made from all manner of vegetable fibres, in a process that has remained largely the same for two millennia. Early Asiatic papermakers used various specially harvested and prepared plants as their fibre sources. By contrast, the first European papermakers used textile waste, cordage (rope), and other pre-processed material. It was only in the 18th century that occidental papermakers and scientists investig-

ated raw plants for their papermaking potential; full commercialization of suitable materials did not start until at least the 19th century.

Regardless of which source of fibrous raw material is used, the same basic steps are followed to turn it into paper. The first process involves cleaning and purification. For *rags and cordage this means cutting them into small pieces, dusting them to remove fine matter, cleaning, and softening. The earliest cleaning method involved steeping in water and allowing them to rot partially, and then washing them. Adding alkali, such as lime, helped to speed the disintegration, though this was banned at various times because of the detrimental effect it could have on fibre quality. More recently, processing involved boiling the shredded textile with alkali. The shade of the pulp produced by these methods depended upon the initial textile colour and water quality; by the 1790s, to improve colour and to remove dyes, chemical bleaching was applied in papermaking.

Processing of raw plant matter follows a similar path, except that the unwanted constituents need to be dissolved rather than washed away. Strong alkali or acid is used as a chemical treatment, sometimes following a retting (or soaking) stage in which biological pre-treatment softens the fibres. Again, bleaching may follow before the pulp is ready for use.

Plant or textile fibres prepared in this way are still not suitable for papermaking; they need mechanical treatment to separate the individual fibres, modify their length, alter their flexibility, and increase their surface area to promote bonding. In the earliest

European mills, this process was performed using either kollergangs or stamping mills. Kollergangs were large millstones set on their rims, running in a stone trough; they twisted and crushed batches of fibres without cutting them, in a way similar to milling grain or pressing oilseed. The other process involved pounding the wet fibres with large wooden hammers shod with nails; these 'stampers' tended to flatten fibres and break their outer layers, resulting in more fibrillation than kollergangs. Both processing methods resulted in a strong, very long-fibred pulp. The main change in macerating techniques occurred in the late 17th century, when the *Hollander beater was introduced. This processed larger batches of fibre faster than either of the previous machines, and by the late 18th century its use was widespread. It could produce in hours what took days in a stamper or kollergang; however, there was a trade-off. The rapid processing resulted in more stress to the fibres, causing significant breakage and a consequent reduction in their length and strength; there were also more fibres of varying length, including many very short fibres. In the late 19th century, as continuous machine production became dominant, the last fibre-processing method, refining, gained prominence. Beating is a batch process, whereas refining is continuous, with the fibres being fed by pipeline through a series of rotating barred discs or cones; the end result is more homogeneous than beating, with much more uniform fibre lengths.

After mechanical processing, the fibre suspension is diluted to the required consistency, mixed with chemicals, and introduced to the forming stage. In a handmaking operation, the *vatman uses a *mould to scoop a quantity of the stock, which drains through the porous wire mesh at the bottom to form a sheet. This is then passed to a second worker, the *coucher, who transfers the wet fibre mat on to a textile, usually of felt, to support it during the next process, pressing. A stack of alternating wet mats and felts, called a *post, is introduced into a mechanical press, which expels much of the surplus water. Pressing may be repeated further times with the paper sheets placed together rather than with felts interleaved, before they pass to the drying stage.

The still-damp sheets are then separated from the pile in 'spurs' of four or five, which are dried as a group, as this produces a flatter sheet than if they are dried singly, when excessive curl and cockling can result. The commonest drying method involves draping the spur over ropes in lofts, where air flow regulated by louvres allows them to dry over a period of days. Other methods include pegging the spurs by the corners and hanging them in a loft, and 'sail drying', where the spurs are laid horizontally upon canvas. Draping the sheets over ropes results in a 'back', and pegging produces localized compression at the corners; both of these methods leave tell-tale signs in sheets.

If *sized paper was required, it was made traditionally in a separate process: the dried waterleaf (unsized) sheet was passed through a solution of size, such as animal glue or starch, before being pressed and re-dried. The sheets were then left in stacks to mature, during which time the dried-in stresses relaxed and flattened. By contrast, some modern hand-mills have employed reactive sizes, that are mixed with the fibres prior to forming; in such cases the sheets are fully sized after drying and do not pass through a separate sizing process.

The machine manufacturing process is very similar to that outlined above. The macerated fibre is diluted and mixed with required additives, including sizing chemicals, after which it passes to a moving mesh on which it drains, then through a press section, where it is supported by felts. On early machines the pressed wet web was wound on to a drum, then slit by hand, and the wet sheets were taken to a drying loft; in 1820, however, steam-heated drying cylinders were invented, which allowed the web to be dried prior to reel-up. During this process, the web is pressed against the heated cylinders by stretched textiles, which help maintain contact between paper and hot surface, and exert restraint that helps counteract lateral *shrinkage.

Finally, it should be noted that some sheets are made from a multitude of layers. They can be formed from plies brought together in the wet state and glued or pressed to form a single entity, or from previously dried sheets glued together to form a board. Multi-ply sheets made on hand-moulds are usually of board weights; those made on paper machines could be of board or paper weights. A recent invention in machine manufacture allows the various *furnish fractions to be separated, then recombined at the forming stage to create a multi-layer product in which the properties of the outer plies are tailored to the needs of the final paper, while the inner section contains cheaper components. An example of this is a printing paper whose outer layers consist of virgin chemical *wood fibre, and the inner layer of cheaper recycled fibre.

Although this description of the process of fibre preparation and sheet formation, as practised over almost 900 years, is highly simplified, it should be

Hand papermaking from G. A. Böckler's *Theatrum Machinarum Novum* (Nuremberg, 1661). With water-powered hammers, the linen rags are pulped. The *vatman stands at the *vat with a *mould; the *coucher presses the *post; the drying *sheets hang on ropes above, ready to be *sized, calendared, gathered into *reams, and packaged.

obvious that practices have developed so much during this period that clues will reside in each sheet to aid its identification. The following sections describe various ways that such clues may be read.

3 Sheet structure

The heterogeneous nature of paper can be observed by holding a sheet to a light source and looking at its cloudy appearance; this is known as formation. It is a measure of how evenly the various furnish components are distributed throughout the sheet. Distinction depends mainly upon the fibres, their length, and how well they were macerated and individually separated; it also indicates the degree of their dilution and agitation prior to forming. The presence of undispersed fibre bundles, filler agglomerates, dirt, and other contaminants will also be disclosed by looking through the sheet, as will any fault caused during forming, pressing, or sizing operations—air bubbles and pinholes, which disturb formation, and bloom of sizing, which gives a milky sheen to the sheet.

The condition of the mould is also apparent at this point. For example, Bower has noted a case where a sheet showed a preponderance of fibre in the centre compared to the edges; he attributed this to poor attachment between the mesh and frame of the mould, resulting in sagging of the forming surface.

If one sheet is being compared with another, the degree of similarity between them may also be ascertained. In general, if they have been machine-made, the inter-sheet variability will be much less than for hand-made paper. Furthermore, in machine-made papers, especially those made by modern machines, the presence of dirt should be minimal, because efficient cleaners are used before the forming stage; however, a notable exception is with sheets made from recycled fibre, which may have dirt as a contaminant even with current methods.

Looking through the sheet will also reveal the impression of any relief surface upon which the wet fibre mat was laid prior to drying, or that was pressed into the damp or dry web or sheet after forming; these include: *watermarks; wire or mesh impressions; laid (*wire) and *chain lines; and press, felt, rope, and emboss marks. This last group are formed by compaction of the sheet rather than by lateral movement of mass.

Wire marks are the imprint of the mesh through which the water drained as the sheet was formed; they are further enhanced during couching, when the wet sheet is pressed against a textile material and the wire is pushed into the wet fibre mat. The shape of the mark will not be an exact representation of the original wire, because the sheet shrinks as it dries. This is especially significant for machine-made paper, where lateral shrinkage is high—especially at the web edges—typically leading to the formation of a diamond-shape for the wire mark. Even two hand-made sheets from the same batch can also appear dissimilar, however, if they experience different degrees of shrinkage during drying.

The gross nature of the forming surface will also be visible during drying. In particular, the presence of laid and chain lines will be apparent; wove moulds only became available after 1756. Shadows around the laid lines give information on the barring pattern under the forming mesh, including the presence of *tranchefiles, which were added at the edges of *deckles to improve drainage. Papers made on *Fourdrinier machines have laid lines imparted by a *dandy roll pressing on to the *felt side of the sheet; on cylinder machines and in hand-made products, these lines come directly from the forming wire and are a feature of the wire side of the sheet. A patent for a dandy roll to impart laid lines was granted in 1825; before that date, all paper from Fourdrinier machines was wove.

Felt marks come from the textile on which the wet sheet is couched. They are enhanced during pressing, when both sides take on some of the surface characteristics of the felts. Sometimes this is exacerbated by using heavily textured fabrics for the final pressing, which impart specific characteristics to the sheet surface. For example, some sheets are given a '*linen' finish by pressing against a coarse-textured fabric with a square weave. Alternatively, some machine-made papers are textured on-machine by having various materials attached to the press fabrics; this is called felt-marking. Use of a textured sleeve on a press roll produces a press-mark.

Prominent wire and felt marks are typically not found on very modern machine-made papers, as recent industrial developments have resulted in machine clothing that minimizes marking of the finished sheet. Rope marks come from the cord over which wet sheets were draped during drying. Occasionally, hairs from the rope can also be found embedded in this area. Emboss marks are imparted to a plain wove material when dry, by passing the sheet through a calender (a machine for smoothing or glazing paper) containing a textured roll.

In hand-made paper, watermarks from adjacent sheets may transfer when they are pressed without intervening felts. This is more likely with bulky sheets, and is generally less problematic with lightweight papers. Hand-made sheets more commonly suffer from occasional random imperfections, such as the slur of laid lines, caused by the coucher slipping during the act of couching, or spots of water from the vatman's hands flicking on to the newly formed sheet.

Marks made while the sheet was still very wet, such as laid and chain lines and watermarks, are permanent. Although some relaxation may occur during humidification or re-wetting, such as happens during wet conservation treatment, they remain largely unchanged because their formation involved physical displacement of fibre. By contrast, marks made when the sheet was drier, such as emboss marks, can be removed almost completely by wetting or humidification. One way of differentiating a 'true' watermark from those formed in the press section, or by printing or embossing techniques, is by imaging, using *beta-radiography rather than optical techniques; only a 'true' watermark is visible to radiographic processes.

This discussion concerns the distribution of materials within the plane of the sheet. There also tends to be stratification of material through the thickness of the sheet, however, though this is less obvious during simple visual inspection. Microscopic examination shows quite conclusively that fine materials tend to be concentrated more at the top and in the middle of the sheet, with far less at the surface that contacted the mesh of the forming stage. This is most notable on machine-made paper—especially that made on fast, modern machines where high suction is used to remove water rapidly during sheet formation. The construction of multi-ply sheets is also only revealed by microscopic investigation.

4 Watermarks

Watermarks are one of the main means of identification for assessing paper provenance. Technology follows a simple chronology whereby early examples consisted of bent pieces of wire, tied to the mould face by thinner bits of wire that leave *sewing dots. When watermarking was first started on Fourdrinier machines (c.1826), the same procedure was used, with bent wire being tied to the dandy roll cover in a similar manner. Embossed mould covers were invented c.1848; these allowed the development of more complex watermark designs, with a wider optical density range, resulting in complex pictures that are known as light-and-shade or shadow marks. Eventually, this technology was transferred to dandy roll covers. By 1870, soldering was introduced as a means of

attaching the bent wire that formed the simple binary watermark image; soldering often replaced sewing because it was quicker. Finally, in more recent years electrotyping was developed as a means of mass-producing the raised designs for binary watermarks; these images could be attached either by sewing or soldering.

Watermark imagery and design are also important. Before the 19th century, watermarks were simple binary line-marks that *Hunter divided into four main categories: simple images, such as crosses or circles; human forms and works, such as heads and hands, keys and pottery; animals, including mythological beasts; and flora and images from nature. Eventually, some items from the second category, depicting human creativity, became synonymous with various paper sizes: beakers and pots (*pot), and the fool's cap (*foolscap). By the era of machine-manufactured watermarks, only these images were commonly in use. Some decades later, the trademark was devised: manufacturers, stationers, and latterly customers, introduced named grades of paper to the marketplace, the most famous being Conqueror from Wiggins Teape. Today, trademarks and geometric designs are undoubtedly the commonest form of watermarks from machine-makers; by comparison, hand-makers produce all manner of images, the main requirement being that the design is not too intricate to reproduce and that the image can be fixed to the mesh cover without danger of removal or fouling during normal working practice.

Many catalogues have been produced in which the general imagery of watermarks can be studied. However, it must be remembered that many of these catalogues (such as *Briquet's or *Heawood's) were developed from rather limited sources, and that altogether they contain only a small portion of the whole canon of marks produced since the earliest Western examples, from Fabriano, Italy, in c.1282. Furthermore, most watermark publications contain simple tracings that supply insufficient detail for full identification.

*Countermarks, often found associated with watermarks, give added information such as dates, mill, and maker identification. Their uses have varied through history, but they are probably the main method by which papers from certain periods are assigned to specific mills. However, the best any watermark or countermark can actually do is identify the original mould or dandy cover used to make a specific sheet, since both are portable and can be used at sites other than their origin. Cases in point include the removal of dandy rolls used to mark postage stamp paper, from

Chafford Mill to Roughway Mill in 1878, and the various mills from which *Whatman watermarks originate, especially prior to the opening of *Springfield Mill in 1807.

Dates in countermarks are another common source of problems, since the apparently simple information they convey may not always be correct. For example, a French ordinance of 1741 required all paper makers in the country to include a date in the countermark; many manufacturers complied by using the date '1742' for a number of years, since it was not stated in the original directive that the date should change every year. A similar order, this time containing the stipulation that dates should change annually, was issued in England, in 1794. This should mean the date in English paper from this period is more reliable; Kelliher, however, has highlighted an intriguing publication printed in 1806 on paper dated 1807. In addition, Hunter described the case of Joseph Willcox, an American hand-maker known to have continued using a mould dated 1810 many decades later. In sum, then, the date in a countermark must be treated with as much caution as any other mark in a sheet.

The formal comparison of watermarks and countermarks can be performed on two levels. Superficial comparison requires the imagery and countermark information in the sheet under examination to agree with either a catalogue picture or other reference sheet of paper. For catalogue images, exact agreement is rarely possible, because most published images are low-quality reproductions. Detailed comparison requires the exact size, orientation, position relative to chain and laid lines and sheet edges, and points of attachment, to be assessed and recorded. These permit greater certainty as to the similarity or differences between two sheets. They also allow the identification of *twins, which are pairs of moulds used in tandem to make a single post of paper. Information regarding points of wear and signs of repair to the mould should also be sought. During the working life of a watermark design, parts are subject to abrasion and wear, with sharp edges becoming rounded; *Stevenson analysed the chronology of paper used in the *Missale Speciale by looking at such deterioration. Parts may occasionally need to be removed and replaced; for example, it was common to change the last digit in a date when this became necessary.

Lastly, the watermark's clarity should be noted. The thickness of wire used for producing the image, and its cross-sectional shape, have a bearing on this, as do the condition both of the mould and of the furnish. Good watermark quality requires a short-fibred, well-beaten stock, which is able to conform closely to the watermark design during couching. Insufficient beating—and hence a preponderance of long fibres—significantly affects clarity.

5 Surface characteristics

The sheet surface carries a huge amount of information about its manufacture and processing. Initial investigation can be performed by holding the sheet up to a diffuse light source and viewing it by glancing illumination.

The first features to be noted are whether the individual fibres can be seen, and how glossy the surface looks. If no fibres are visible, the sheet has been coated; this can be confirmed by rubbing the surface with a fingernail or coin, so that the affected area becomes polished and more glossy. If no coating is present, the fibres and filler materials should be visible as shiny filamentous or particulate constituents of the surface. For paper made on a fast machine, especially of Fourdrinier design, the fibres will tend to align in the direction of travel on the forming wire; this allows the grain direction to be assessed. Slower machines, such as cylinder moulds, show less obvious orientation, and hand-made paper shows little or none.

For uncoated papers, the degree of gloss shows whether the surfaces have been calendered, or for older papers, subject to friction- or plate-glazing. Generally this is performed in a *paper mill; however, *Baskerville developed a secret process that involved hot-pressing a sheet after printing, which also resulted in a glazed appearance. A gloss finish can also be imparted to embossed paper; however, embossing leaves a gloss effect only in the troughs of the pattern, whereas the other methods only polish the peaks, while the deep parts of any surface pattern remain matt. Finally, if only one surface is gloss, and the other is both matt and rough, the sheet has been machine-glazed—formed on a paper-machine and pressed against a large highly polished cylinder to smooth one surface preferentially.

If a coating has been applied, several other factors can also be deduced by using low-angle illumination. The degree of gloss is a measure of calendering; highly glossed papers have been super-calendered, while matt papers tend to be calendered lightly. Secondly, the relative thickness of coating can be deduced by whether any fibre shapes are visible. If none can be seen, the sheet has probably had two or three applications of coating; where they are partially visible a single application is more likely; if they are fully visible, but are indistinct, it is likely a thin coating—applied by a size-press or other applicator—which is termed a 'lick-coating', is present. Finally, the method used to apply the coat may be discernible in some circumstances: a series of well-defined evenly spaced lines, running mainly in the machine direction, indicates a wire-wound bar applicator (introduced in the mid-1980s); defects such as thin, straight scratches, again running parallel to the sheet grain, suggest a blade applicator. Other methods can be deduced by microscopic examination.

Careful observation of the surface by glancing illumination from diffuse light will often show the wire side, on which a repeating pattern of geometric marks should be visible; turning the paper whilst viewing it helps to highlight their presence. The side to which the watermark was applied should also be apparent by this method; on hand-made and cylinder-mould-made paper, this will also be the wire side, while on paper from a Fourdrinier machine it will be the felt side.

Visual observation reveals much information about the surface, but detailed measurement, especially of repeating marks, is only possible using image capture and mathematical analysis; the basic methodology for this is described by I'Anson.

6 Other characteristics

First, the type of paper should be noted, because grades were introduced to the market at different times: for example very thin *India paper was introduced into Europe *c*.1750; coated paper was produced and patented in 1827, as was transparent paper.

The weight of a paper can be gauged by hand, as can other aesthetics, often grouped together as 'handle'. These are judged by gripping the sheet firmly, shaking it, and listening to the timbre of the rattle. Assessing paper by this method requires some experience, but it can give information on the degree of beating, possible furnish composition, and extent of surface sizing, all of which contribute to sheet bonding and rigidity. The process used for cleaning fibres may also have a bearing on handle: Bower attributes the softness of 18th-century French papers to their makers' use of alkali, rather than soap, to clean rags before maceration.

Colour should be examined. In most early cases this was a compromise between the collection of rags used, their treatment during pulping, and water quality. Indeed, water quality may vary with the season: heavy rains churn up sediment, making it impossible at times to produce white paper. The colour of early handmade sheets was never very uniform; even colouration only became possible after synthetic dyestuffs were introduced, along with full chemical bleaching.

Determining the size of the original sheet is difficult, but it can be estimated by carefully measuring the existing trimmed sheet. First, a book's gathering that corresponds to a single sheet needs to be identified; the orientation of chain lines in bound, laid paper helps determine this (*see* FORMAT). In a sheet folded in half, the chain lines run parallel to the fold and book spine, producing a *folio. A second fold, perpendicular to the first, will produce chain lines running perpendicular to the spine, and thus a *quarto. A third fold restores the original orientation, producing an *octavo, and so on. Once a single sheet has been identified, any watermark and countermark can be noted, and their relative positions in the sheet assigned. This should allow the sheet's original dimensions to be estimated from a knowledge of common commercial sheet sizes, taking into account the trimming that is necessary during the book-binding process, and the fact that printing papers were generally slightly larger than their equivalent writing-paper sizes, in addition to being more softly sized.

Finally, the edges of the sheet give information on sheet formation and finishing. Rough borders can

Sheet edges (from left to right): hand-made; machine-made cylinder mould; hand-torn; guillotined or cut edge.

be a sign of deckle edges, as from a hand-mould or cylinder-mould machine; equally, however, they could be due to having been torn, in an attempt to simulate the raw edges of a mould. A deckle edge from a hand-mould is generally not straight, and shows an uneven gradation of fibre at the very edge; cylinder-mould machines produce much straighter edges, with a wide fringe of thin fibre at the edge; torn edges are generally straightest and show a preponderance of fibrous filaments along the entire edge. Cut edges can be due to guillotining, die-cutting, or slitting and chopping of the web on a sheeting machine. Guillotined or die-cut edges tend to have a pronounced slur caused by the blade pushing through a mass of sheets; this can be felt by gripping a sheet between thumb and forefinger and pulling it so that the edge is drawn though the digits. Guillotine blades also tend to slice at an angle, which can leave a diagonal scratch on the book edge; die-cutters only move perpendicular to the sheet. Slitting produces a finish known as 'mill' edges.

7 Composition

Analysis of the furnish used for a particular paper requires both specialist knowledge and equipment, but is often necessary to verify what has been deduced from visual observation.

Fibre analysis is the most obvious point at which to start. For occidental papers made prior to the 1750s this should yield only linen or hemp, perhaps with some non-vegetable fibre included, such as wool. Cotton only started to make headway thanks to the introduction of mechanized cotton spinning in the last quarter of the 18th century. By 1800, *straw was used; wood in various forms was introduced by 1845, but did not become popular until much later; esparto was used from 1857, with bagasse (refuse from sugar-making) added c.1884. Pulping methods for wood can sometimes be assigned by means of stain tests: soda wood came first; mechanical groundwood next, from 1851; sulphite from 1872; kraft from 1884, with various semi-mechanical methods starting in the early 20th century. The exact date for the introduction of any fibre is subject to revision, as early trials certainly antedate the years given, which are when their use was commercialized.

Sizing chemistry is probably of next greatest importance. Early papers used gelatine or starch, which was applied as a post-manufacturing surface treatment; smell will often allow gelatine to be detected, and iodine will indicate the presence of starch. The introduction of machine manufacture coincided with a new method, internal sizing, which used rosin precipitated on the fibre surfaces by alum prior to sheet formation. For machine-made papers, however, coating with starch is also a common post-forming treatment, accomplished at a size-press; in addition, some specialist machine grades produced into the second half of the 20th century were 'tub-sized' by running the waterleaf web through a vat of gelatine solution prior to drying and reel-up. Synthetic internal sizes, such as Alkyl Ketene Dimer (AKD) and Alkyl Succinic Anhydride (ASA), were introduced in the 1950s and 1980s, respectively; these are very popular today in most modern mills.

Inorganic pigments were added to paper from the early 19th century, although they were at first used mainly as cheap extenders to the fibre, and as such were viewed with suspicion by many papermakers and customers. Indeed, concern about their detrimental effect on paper strength was so great that in some countries they were banned. In England, for example, before c.1800 no pigments could be added, since they were considered adulterants. However, the benefits of adding some amount of pigment were eventually recognized: pigments increase opacity and improve ink transfer during printing; they also increase ink hold-out, maintaining it at the surface and decreasing its penetration into the sheet during printing, resulting in a better-printed image. The earliest (c.1820) common filler was barium sulphate; gypsum was added soon after, while clay, which had been tested before barium sulphate, was used from 1870. Titanium dioxide, calcium carbonate, and various zinc compounds all came into use during the early 20th century.

The final class of major additives worth assessing are colourants and optical whiteners. Early papers used the intrinsic fibre colour, or natural dyestuffs, such as ultramarine or indigo, or coloured earths like ochre. Indeed, Whatman is credited with the innovation of adding blue dyes to 'whiten' paper, when in 1765 he started to use indigo; however, continental makers from the 16th century had already developed this practice, adding smalts (an oxide of cobalt), indigo, or even small amounts of blue rag to the furnish for the same reason. Synthetic dyestuffs became available after W. H. Perkin's pioneering work—aniline dyes were used from around 1870, with synthetic pigments added by 1901. Optical brightening agents, which fluoresce under ultraviolet light and give paper a bluish tinge, were introduced around the 1950s, and are particularly common in modern papers, where they are used to enhance whiteness. Indeed, fluorescence due to use of such reagents was a major factor in Julius Grant's exposure of the *Hitler Diaries as fraudulent; these chemicals were not introduced to the paper industry until after the Führer's death.

Compared to these four classes, other additives are minor. However, detailed chemical analysis can also reveal traces of bleach residues, formation aids, biocides, fungicides, adhesives, and anti-foam agents, to name but a few chemicals that might be added, intentionally or otherwise, to the furnish. These minor additives, alongside detailed analysis of trace elements found as contaminants in pigments, can be used to provide a paper's chemical 'fingerprint', which may be unique to a locality, mill, or even batch, and which is useful for comparing with other samples of unknown origin.

8 Provenance

Determining the provenance of paper is a complex problem that can be approached on a number of different levels, all with varying degrees of certainty.

If there is no sheet for comparison, assessment involves comparing watermark images with those contained in catalogues or trade listings. Inspection of the surface, looking for coatings or telltale signs of various production processes, should also be undertaken. By these means it may be possible to pinpoint a probable period of manufacture. Chemical and fibre analysis can then be used to identify whether the constituents match those anticipated for the date and origin suggested by visual inspection.

Comparison with a sheet of known origin is far more successful, and is capable of yielding a more exact identification. In this case, visual or instrumental comparison of the two sheet surfaces, markings, structures, and chemistries can be undertaken. In particular, for watermarked paper, an exact comparison of the watermark shape, placement, attachment points, and general quality can be made. However, in many ways this is actually a more difficult analysis to undertake than when no comparison sheet exists, because there is the temptation to look for exact replication of all aspects of the two sheets. Yet, as has been suggested, papermaking is not a wholly controllable process. For sheets made on the same machine

or mould at different times, variations in furnish or process conditions can alter appearance significantly. For sheets made from the same batch, differences can also exist for legitimate reasons. Even more importantly, storage and treatment conditions can have a significant bearing on how a sheet looks: two identical sheets, subject to different handling, can appear quite dissimilar.

To conclude, determining provenance is not an exact science. A great deal can be done to analyse paper as bibliographical evidence, but the sheet is only one part of the story and should never be used alone. Evidence from other sources such as printing, typography, and binding should be included, before experience comes into play. Experience, intuition, and judgement must all be used in the final analysis of how the paper helps to determine the provenance of a work of which it is but one part.

BIBLIOGRAPHY
J. Balston, *The Whatmans and Wove (Velin) Paper* (1998)
S. Barcham-Green, 'An Illusive Image: Some Thoughts about Watermarking Handmade Papers', *TQ* 62 (2007), 1–9
P. Bower, *Turner's Papers* (1990)
— *Turner's Later Papers* (1999)
— 'Watermark Catalogues and Related Texts: A Personal Recommendation', *TQ* 56 (2005), 42–4
B. L. Browning, *Analysis of Paper*, 2e (1977)
N. Harris, *Analytical Bibliography*, www.ihl.enssib.fr/siteihl.php?page=55&aflng=en, consulted June 2007
D. Hunter, *Papermaking: The History and Technique of an Ancient Craft*, 2e (1978)
S. I'Anson, 'Identification of Periodic Marks in Paper and Board by Image Analysis Using Two-Dimensional Fast Fourier Transforms, Part 1: The Basics', *Tappi Journal*, 78.3 (1995), 113–19
— 'Part 2: Forming and Press Section Marks', *Tappi Journal*, 78.7 (1995), 97–106
H. Kelliher, 'Early Dated Watermarks in English Papers: A Cautionary Note', in *Essays in Paper Analysis*, ed. S. Spector (1987)
B. J. McMullin, 'Machine-Made Paper, Seam Marks, and Bibliographical Analysis', *Library*, 7/9 (2008), 62–88
D. W. Mosser *et al.*, eds., *Puzzles in Paper* (2000)
S. Spector, ed., *Essays in Paper Analysis* (1987)
A. H. Stevenson, *The Problem of the Missale Speciale* (1967)
S. Tanner and D. Chamberlain, 'Chafford Mill: A Short History', *TQ* 57 (2006), 37–43

11 The Technologies of Print

James Mosley

1 Introduction

Printing was introduced to a world in which the status of the book and its makers was changing. A professional book trade existed well before printing with movable *types was introduced in Europe during the 15th century. The *pecia system allowed students at the universities of Bologna, Padua, and Paris in the 12th century to hire an authenticated text, or a part of it, to be copied either by themselves or by professional writers. During the early 15th century, *Vespasiano da Bisticci of Florence acquired a reputation as an employer of professional calligraphers and *miniature painters who made beautiful manuscript books for rich clients. Such systems and professions point to the opportunities that encouraged the emergence in the 15th century of the printer and publisher who—gambling on the likelihood that a market existed for multiple copies of texts—was willing to invest in the materials and labour necessary to make many identical books (in advance of sales) by mechanical processes.

The terms that were eventually adopted in modern European languages for the 'printing' of texts and pictures had a long history: words (such as 'impression' and 'stampa') typically signified the application of pressure, most often to leave a visible mark. As Shakespeare writes in the Prologue to *Henry V*: 'Think when we talk of horses, that you see them / Printing their proud hoofs i' th' receiving earth.' Indeed, the principle of using an engraved stone to make repeated characters in a soft material, such as clay, is displayed in many surviving early artefacts, from official Mesopotamian seals (3rd millennium BC) to Roman bricks and tiles stamped before they were fired with their makers' names.

2 Origins

In the Middle Ages, western books and documents were commonly written on *vellum, a prepared animal skin; although some printed books were also made on vellum, there is no doubt that paper (a product consisting of vegetable fibres reconstituted in the form of thin white sheets of a uniform size and thickness (*see* **10**) was necessary for the development of printing in the West. By the 13th century, paper was sufficiently common in western Europe that a decree forbidding its use for the writing of public records was issued in 1231 by the German Emperor Frederick II.

Techniques for making paper evolved in China and spread along the land routes that brought silk and other goods to the West. The traditional date for the invention of paper made from mulberry bark, hemp, and rags is the start of the 2nd century AD (although some scholars maintain that the actual date is between 200 and 100 BC); by the 3rd century, such paper was commonly used in China to write documents. In 1276, *paper mills were operating at Fabriano in Italy, and in 1390 the first paper mill in Germany was established at Nuremberg.

It is not known whether awareness of the processes used in China and neighbouring countries to make multiple copies of books had penetrated to the West before a complete system for printing books evolved in Germany c.1450. These, briefly, were the stages of their development in the East (*see* **40**, **41**, **42**, **43**). By the 7th century, inked *relief seals, cut on wood and pressed by hand, were used in China to authenticate documents written on paper. *Ink-squeeze rubbings were made to provide multiple paper copies of the Confucian texts that were cut on stone and displayed in temples for public reading. A sacred Buddhist text, the *Diamond Sutra (868), a *scroll made up of strips of paper pasted together (see SCROLL BINDING), is the earliest datable instance of the use of engraved relief wood blocks to print many copies of an extensive text and an image with *ink. The technique of *woodblock printing that finally evolved to make printed books required several steps. The text was written by a professional calligrapher on thin sheets of paper and pasted in reverse on a block of wood, so that the writing was visible. Superfluous wood was cut away, leaving a facsimile of the reversed text in relief. Ink was dabbed on the block, and sheets of paper were pressed to it with stiff brushes, thus transferring an image of the writing to the paper. The paper, which tended to absorb the ink, was printed on one side of the sheet only, folded and sewn into books. Until western methods were introduced in the 19th century, this was the usual method of printing texts and pictures in China and neighbouring countries. In 12th-century Korea, movable types reproducing Chinese characters were made from wooden patterns by casting with copper in sand (see 41); such separate types continued in use to some extent in the East, but without displacing engraved woodblocks. The reasons for the very limited use of movable types in the East, compared with the rapidity of their adoption in the West, are complex. The high respect accorded to *calligraphy in China, Korea, and Japan, the fluidity and complexity of the forms of Chinese characters when written by hand, and the very large number of characters probably all contributed.

The mid-15th century 'invention of printing' in the West involved the bringing together of several techniques, devices, and materials. Some of these had long existed but others, such as the paper and the ink, were relatively recent. There may have been several experimenters working at about the same time. Procopius Waldfoghel, born in Prague and established in Avignon in the 1440s, is named in contemporary documents as using a process of 'artificial writing' employing alphabets made in steel, but his method did not necessarily involve the printing of texts. During the 16th century, a claim was made on behalf of *Coster of Haarlem as the inventor of printing, but none of the surviving early fragments of printing that originate in the Low Countries bears Coster's name, nor are there convincing biographical details. In the

Cronica van Koellen, the 'Cologne Chronicle', printed by *Zell (1499)—in which there is some reference to a 'prefiguration' of printing in the Low Countries—unequivocal credit for the invention of printing with movable type in the West is given to *Gutenberg (d. 1468), whose life is well documented; the claim is not seriously disputed today (but see modifications to the traditional account of Gutenberg's invention in the work of *Needham and Blaise Agüera y Arcas). From 1454, when the *folio *Gutenberg Bible of 1,200 pages is known to have been in production, and when the texts of *indulgences were also printed on single *sheets, a technology existed for the making of multiple copies of books and other documents of an acceptable quality. The use of similar techniques spread very rapidly to European countries, and, although MSS continued to be important (see 13), printed texts gradually began taking the place of handwritten ones.

Gutenberg was born c.1400 into a patrician family in Mainz with interests in banking, but there is no evidence that he had direct contact with the technologies of making coins or working in precious metals. In the 1430s he was compelled for political reasons to move to Strasbourg, where he became involved in a partnership that made cast-metal items. Later he returned to Mainz, where he borrowed money from *Fust, a lawyer, to develop a project described in legal documents as *werck der bücher* ('the work of books'). In 1455 Fust foreclosed on the debt and took over the materials developed by Gutenberg. Schoeffer, Gutenberg's former business partner, joined Fust and married his daughter; the names of Fust and Schoeffer appear on several of the earliest printed books beginning in 1457. Schoeffer inherited the business, remaining an important and an active printer in Mainz until his death in 1502/3. Gutenberg stayed in the same district until his death, still in possession of the printing materials mentioned in his will; yet he is not named in any printed book as its maker.

Gutenberg's partnership in Strasbourg, which became the subject of acrimonious litigation in 1436, produced, among other goods, mirrors cast in metal for sale to pilgrims. It is sometimes suggested that experiments towards the making of type and the printing of books began in Strasbourg before Gutenberg returned to Mainz. There is no direct evidence to support this idea, but if the mirrors were made from lead or an alloy using lead, their makers may have developed some of the expertise that would be needed for making type. The earliest surviving fragments of printing that can be associated with

Gutenberg appear to date from about 1450, and make use of a type that is less well finished and printed than that of the folio bible (the so-called 42-line bible) known to have been in production in 1454. This bible and the large 1457 psalter, bearing the names of Fust and Schoeffer, are the products of a printing system capable of making fine books that would command a high price, even if some of its elements may still have needed refinement. The constituents of that system are type, ink, paper or vellum, and a press for making an *impression on them.

Paper had long been in use in Europe for the writing of correspondence and documents, and to some extent for books, as a substitute for the more durable vellum. However, whereas eastern paper was written on with a *writing brush on one side of the sheet, western paper had been adapted to the use of a relatively hard *quill pen to write with a liquid, water-based ink on both sides of the sheet. The materials of paper were still vegetable fibres, mostly in the form of rags, discarded woven linen that had served as clothing or for domestic use. To prevent the penetration of the surface by the liquid ink, the sheet was made relatively hard and firm in its substance, an effect sometimes reinforced by adding size (a diluted solution of colloids made from animal skin and bones) to its surface.

The ink used on metal type was a thin film of stiff, coloured varnish, made by boiling and sometimes setting fire to one of the drying oils, generally linseed or walnut: the process was too dangerous to be carried out in a confined urban space. The substance set firmly and permanently, even without exposure to air. To make black ink, soot was added to the clear varnish; red or other pigments made coloured ink. In fact, printing ink is a version of the oil paint that had become widely adopted by European painters by about 1400.

In order to make a satisfactory print on the hard-surfaced paper that was designed for use with the pen, it was necessary to soften its fibres (by dampening it) and to apply firm pressure. After the sheets were printed, they were hung up on poles or lines to dry. The drying sheets, dangerously flammable, must have been one of the most common sources of the fires that destroyed the premises of many printers during the hand press period.

The printing press was no doubt derived from the screw presses that had evolved in the period of the late Roman empire (see COMMON PRESS). They were routinely used for pressing out the juice of grapes and also for squeezing the surplus water from newly made paper. It seems likely that such presses would have been adapted for delivering the pressure needed to make a sharp, clear impression from pages of inked type on paper.

The element that was wholly new (if the possibility can be discounted that news of the Korean practice of some centuries earlier had penetrated to Europe) was the making of 'movable type': a supply of small metal blocks bearing letters and signs in relief, from which multiple impressions could be taken.

How the early types were made is a subject that has been much discussed, although no definitive conclusions have been reached. It is possible that a slow process requiring much hand finishing, or *dressing, was used initially (perhaps by *sand casting, as was done in Korea). Whatever the first system may have been, it was quite rapidly succeeded by one in which relief steel *punches, filed and engraved with the form of the letter, were hardened and used to stamp impressions in a softer metal, copper, to make *matrices. Matrices were used together with a type *mould that formed the *body of the type. As later surviving examples demonstrate, such moulds were simple hand-held devices, formed from two L-shaped pieces that slid against each other to open and close laterally. Accurate castings about one inch high could be made from a sequence of matrices of letters, with each letter being the same *height from top to bottom, but varying according to the different widths required for narrow letters such as 'i' and wide ones such as 'M'. Eventually, the manual processes for making types and assembling them into words and lines were mechanized (see LINOTYPE; MONOTYPE), and alternative methods of placing words and images on paper were devised. Nonetheless, until the second half of the 20th century, most printed texts were produced using printing surfaces cast in lead alloys from matrices stamped with punches.

3 The hand press period, 1450–1830

The analysis of early fragments of printing attributed to Gutenberg has suggested that some early types may have been made in ways that do not correspond with traditional methods. However, the comparison of multiple scanned images of the pages of different copies of the Gutenberg Bible has revealed that the setting of its type was often altered during the course of printing, sometimes in ways that are hardly visible to the eye. The latter observations confirm beyond doubt that this work was set with and printed from single movable types.

The method of printing at the hand press seems to have undergone a slow evolution. It can be shown that, at least until the later years of the 15th century and often long after, the dominant technique was printing by *formes, in which the first and last pages of one side of a single sheet or of a *gathering made up of several inset sheets (the outer forme) were set in type and printed before the other side of the sheet (the inner forme) or those that came inside the section. The process of *casting off copy to determine on which page it should come required painstaking calculation, and the *compositors who *set the type frequently needed to alter the text—shortening it by resorting to *abbreviations, contractions, or omissions, or expanding it by adding various kinds of spacing such as *quads or *leading—in order to maintain the continuity of the text in the formes which were set and printed later. This technique of printing by formes may help to explain one enduring feature of the traditional wooden press: its *platen (the wooden or metal plate that delivers pressure to the paper) is the size of only one folio page, or half the full forme of type that was later placed on the press.

Some slight qualifications aside, there was a long period from the 1480s until around 1800 when the technology of printing was very stable. Type was made by hand and was set, formed by hand into words, lines, and pages. Presses were operated by hand at a rate that did not—indeed could not comfortably—exceed a certain speed. Paper was made, sheet by sheet, by hand: the maximum width of the mould (see MOULD, PAPER), and therefore of the sheet it made, was limited by the maker's natural arm span, typically about 30in. or 76cm.

The earliest datable image of a *printing office is a woodcut in a book printed in 1499. During the first part of the 16th century, representations of the printing office were symbolic of the trade, and appear on several *title-pages. The images differ in some small details, but, taken together, they confirm that, once established, the equipment and the actions of the printers did not essentially change until 1800 or so. At that point, slight alterations that had begun as refinements of traditional methods and materials gave way to radical developments as printing was mechanized, production speed increased, and the unit cost of books fell.

During the hand press period, printing offices were generally normal houses, like the work places of weavers, joiners, and other tradesmen. The printer, with his family and *apprentices, occupied some of its rooms, and the presses and type occupied others.

Some printing offices were designed to impress visitors, such as the new Clarendon Building (completed 1713) of the *Oxford University Press, but these were exceptions. Most premises were like that of printer and novelist Samuel *Richardson, whose medium-size London printing office in Salisbury Square was also his dwelling, until the weight of the stock of type began to threaten the building's structure, compelling him to move.

The office's equipment comprised one or more presses and a quantity of type. The type was held in open *type cases, subdivided in divisions each of which held multiple *sorts of one character. These smaller compartments of the case varied in size according to the frequency with which each letter, number, or mark of *punctuation was used, the letter 'e' being the largest of them. The compositor or type setter who had learned the arrangement or *lay of the case could pick up each letter without looking at it. Early images show compositors sitting at their work; later it became usual to stand. In some countries, there was a single case, holding both capital and *minuscule letters, but in France, and countries such as Britain which followed French practice, capitals and minuscules had a case each, arranged one above the other, so that capital letters became known as *upper case and the minuscules as *lower case. Whatever its configuration, the case, which held 20–30lb of type (9–14kg), was commonly (like the papermaker's mould) no more than an arm-span wide, so it could be readily lifted and placed on a *frame at a convenient height for setting.

The compositor held a *composing stick, a tool that allowed several lines of type to be set to a given width. The *copy or text for setting was placed where it could be seen clearly, sometimes held in a special device called a *visorium, or simply placed on the right-hand side of the upper case, which in France or England held the *small capitals that were needed only occasionally. The compositor picked up letter after letter and placed them one at a time in the stick, putting spaces between words, and working from left to right, reading the line in the stick to check that it was correct. To *justify or fill each line, the spaces were added or reduced between words until the line filled the stick firmly. The lines were transferred from the stick to a *galley, an open tray, until there were enough for a page. The page of type was tied up with thin cord and placed with other pages on a large flat *imposing stone. A *chase, an open iron frame, was placed over the pages, along with *furniture, pieces of wood cut to size, which filled it exactly and made up the forme for

Printers and compositor in a Dutch *printing office: *engraving after a drawing by P. Saenredam for P. Schrijver's *Laure-kranz voor Laurens Koster* in Samuel Ampsing's *Beschryvinge ende lof der stad Haerlem* (Haarlem, 1628). *Coster was wrongly supposed to anticipate *Gutenberg as the inventor of printing.

A composing *frame with two sets of cases of *type: the *upper case lies at a steeper angle than the *lower case.

Diagram of the parts of a common press.

printing. Wooden *quoins or wedges were driven against long wedge-shaped sidesticks or footsticks to hold pages and furniture together. If properly assembled, the *locked-up forme—made from some thousands of pieces of metal type—was solid and could be safely picked up and placed on the press.

The press in use until the early 19th century was a structure about six feet (two metres) high, made of a solid wood (oak was favoured), and consisting of two uprights with lateral beams. The lower beam received the force of the impression and, accordingly, was fixed; it supported rails on which the *carriage, a flat surface bearing the forme, slid in and out under the platen, a solid, flat piece of wood or metal that hung from the *screw, which delivered the impression and worked in the beam above. The screw appears in early images to have been wooden, but later was normally made of iron or brass, as was the platen (except in Britain, where it was commonly of wood). The platen hung from the *hose, a box or framework that served to keep the platen steady while the screw turned within it. A *bar set in the screw turned it in an arc of about 90 degrees when pulled, lowering the platen by about half an inch (1.2cm) on to the *tympan and the forme beneath it.

The stiff ink was worked out evenly on a flat surface with a pair of leather balls stuffed with wool; the *ink balls transferred a thin film to the type of the forme. The tympan, a hinged framework with vellum or cloth stretched tightly over it (as the name implies), was attached to the carriage. The sheet of paper to be printed was fixed on the tympan with adjustable *points that pierced it and gave an exact location for the second impression on the reverse of the sheet (see PERFECTING). A layer of cloth designed to spread the impression filled the space evenly within an inner tympan that fitted into the outer one. The *frisket, a light wrought-iron frame covered with paper, from which spaces for the pages were cut, was hinged over the tympan; it held the paper to it as it was brought down over the inked forme and protected the areas of the paper which were not to be printed from being soiled. A *rounce or windlass brought the carriage beneath the platen and out again.

Two men worked the press: the *puller, who placed the paper on the tympan, wound the carriage under the platen, and pulled the bar; and the *beater, who worked out the ink and applied it to the forme. They were paid for a notional production of 250 sheets in the hour, one every 15 seconds or 2,500 impressions in a ten-hour working day. Printing office accounts confirm that this output could be achieved, but the figure does not reflect stops for any reason, nor the preliminary time spent in *making ready (preparing the press for printing by pasting paper on the tympan or beneath parts of the text or wood cuts to make them print evenly). The text was sometimes corrected during the course of printing, which meant unlocking the forme (see LOCKING UP) to remove type and make the necessary changes to it: this was known as *stop-press correction. The viscous ink on the balls could sometimes extract a loose piece of type, which was reinserted. For all these reasons, as well as the vagaries of human labour, the daily target of 2,500 impressions per press crew was seldom reached. The second side of the sheet was printed from another forme, made up within a chase that was the same size as the first one.

A proof sheet was printed by placing the made-up forme on the press and pulling one or more impressions (see PROOFS AND PROOFREADING). To make corrections, it was necessary to loosen the quoins and thus to unlock the forme. If a passage needed to be inserted or deleted, the text in question might overrun the page or cause it to be too short, and many succeeding pages might need to be altered. Late in the 18th century, in order to reduce this need, the practice began of pulling proofs on long slips of paper from type that was held in a long *galley (hence *galley proofs), and of making corrections before the type was made up into pages.

This was the equipment of the printing office during the hand press period. The basic unit was one press and one frame, and a case or cases of type. The only essential difference between big and small offices was that the large ones had more presses and type and thus could manage the flow of work more efficiently.

3.1 Materials

Paper was bought by the printer from the mill or from an agent ahead of production. The most expensive single element in the cost of printed books, paper also represented the highest risk, since it could not generally be reused once printed. Another consumable commodity was ink, which could be stored in barrels, and was commonly bought from specialist makers.

Unlike paper and ink, type was not wholly consumed by production. However, type gradually wore out in use or was damaged (known as *type batter) and needed to be replaced: this was done at a rate that reflected the printer's standards and the economics of his operation. Surviving records from the early 16th

century show that some printers bought sets of matrices for the types they used and a mould to go with them, hiring a specialist founder or caster to make a *fount or 'casting' from them—at this date a *fount* (Fr. *fonte*, from *fondre*, 'to melt, cast') was the quantity of type made at one session of casting. This commercial practice was common even in major printing offices such as *Plantin's in Antwerp, which had a big collection of matrices for *roman and *italic as well as many special types for scholarly and liturgical printing. By the 18th century, the founts held by some major printers weighed half a ton or more. From the later 16th century, specialist typefoundries were established in the principal centres of printing, and it became more usual for printers to buy all their founts of type.

Type was cast by hand. First, the matrix for each letter was placed in succession in a two-part mould, which expanded or contracted to suit the letter's width. Next, a ladle was used to pour molten metal into the mould; a rapid upward thrust of the hands while holding the mould ensured that the metal reached the image of the type stamped in the matrix before it cooled. The process of typefounding involved diecasting in an alloy of lead, a cheap and plentiful metal with a low melting-point, which enabled it to be safely used with hand-held devices. The alloy itself was complex, sometimes including more or less tin to aid the flow, and invariably a quantity of antimony, which not only toughened the metal and gave a sharper cast but eliminated shrinkage after casting.

Punches were cut with files and gravers in steel that had been annealed or softened. The punches were then hardened and tempered in order to survive the hammer blow of striking; each punch would serve to make many sets of identical copper matrices. For bigger types, matrices were sometimes struck in lead from punches cut in brass, or were made in brass by casting replicas from big steel punches. The choice of the style of types was governed by the same conventions as styles of writing. Gothic *scripts were used for the vernaculars of the northern languages; gradually, however, the use of the new humanistic upright and cursive forms (roman and italic) spread from Italy and tended to displace the gothic forms, except in Germany. New fashions in *typography were influenced by shifts in calligraphic styles. When they were used to cast type by hand, copper matrices did not noticeably wear out. Thus, there is a long period from the second half of the 16th century to the first half of the 18th century when the same types, derived from matrices struck from the same punches, were used by many printers in different European countries.

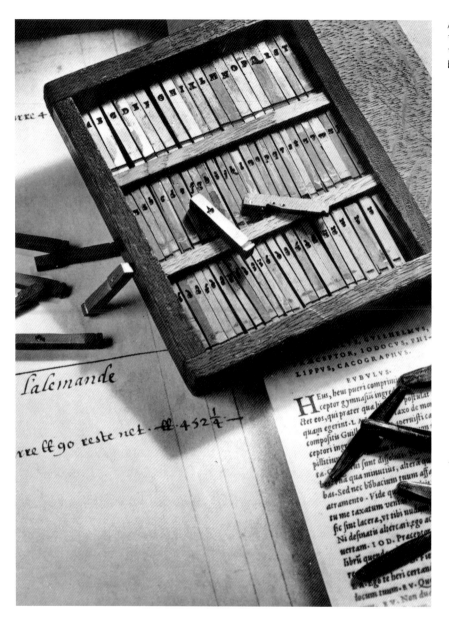

A box of *Fell's *pica italic *matrices, with some steel *punches for larger capitals beneath them.

3.2 *Illustration*

Images were cut on wood at an early date and used with type to make *illustrations or decorations, and sometimes even whole words. Large words on title-pages were commonly cut in wood. *Block printing, which combines images and text cut on a single block of wood, appears to have been introduced during the later 15th century as a simpler imitation of the new books that had been made by using movable type. Any close-grained wood (e.g. apple or pear) could be used, but fine-grained boxwood was especially favoured for smaller images. At an uncertain date, possibly towards the end of the 17th century, engravers began to work on the end grain of the wood, a technique that sometimes achieved finer detail. Its products are known as wood *engravings rather than *woodcut illustrations (*see* **16**).

By the 17th century, however, the woodcut was increasingly supplanted by images made in a wholly different medium and printed on a different kind of press: the incised or etched *copper plate. The making of printed images from copper plates developed at about the same date as printing from type, but the first *intaglio prints were circulated independently and were not incorporated in printed books. To print the fine engraved line, the plate was inked and its surface wiped clean again. When the inked *plate, the dampened paper, and a cloth blanket were passed between the two cylinders of a *rolling press, the pressure of the rollers and the blanket transferred the ink held in the recessed engraved line to the paper. Since the rolling press applied much greater pressure than the press used for type, its operation was correspondingly slow. The pressure also caused wear to the plate, limiting the number of images that could be made before it needed to be re-engraved. The early market for copperplate engravings was generally for independently published images sold singly, such as *maps, reproductions of paintings, and satirical *prints. During the 17th and 18th centuries, however, intaglio prints became widely used for illustrations in books, as well as for adding ornaments and decorative initials to sheets already printed from type. The combination of intaglio and letterpress called for coordination between two different kinds of printer, because the *letterpress printer appears rarely to have had the means to print from plates.

3.3 Preserving and duplicating the text

During the hand press period, type was commonly set for only a sheet or two of a book, and then distributed back in the case after the sheet was printed; thus the same type was used several times in the course of printing a book. Very few printers had enough type to set the whole of a text or, if they had, could afford to leave the type idle while waiting to read and correct one work and finding a press free to print it. If a work sold well, the printing of a new *edition required the setting, proofing, and *correction of the whole text again.

Nevertheless, if a book had a large or reliable market, the heavy financial burden of buying and printing all of the paper at once to produce a large edition could be reduced by spreading it over time, using the return from the sale of the first printing to buy new stock. With enough type, the whole text could be kept in *standing type for years and reprinted many times. There are a few documented cases where this is known to have been done.

Towards the end of the 17th century, a means was found of casting duplicate plates from whole typeset pages; several works, including bibles, were printed from such plates in The Netherlands. This method of duplication was used from a very early period to make reproductions of woodblocks. Most casts of typeset pages were probably made from a mould of fine plaster, although a German work of the 1690s describes a method employing *papier mâché. The practice lapsed for some time, although it may well have continued unobtrusively—if such techniques are well used, there is no easy way of detecting them. At the end of the 18th century, however, interest in the duplication of already composed text revived strongly. Experiments with various processes resulted in one, developed by the *Didot family, called *stéréotypie*, or *stereotyping in English. Another name coined at the same time, and mostly applied to the duplicating of wood-engraved illustrations and ornaments, was 'clichage', known in English as 'dabbing'; its product, the cliché, passed into French and English as a metaphor for phrases repeated unthinkingly.

Reintroduced in the 19th century, papier mâché moulds were sometimes used to make stereotyped casts of the pages of books. Since these moulds were light and relatively durable compared with those of fragile plaster, they could be more safely and easily stored, and were sometimes sent to distant printers to make duplicate plates for printing the same text somewhere else.

3.4 Improvements to existing technology

During the second half of the 18th century, shifts in taste and economic prosperity, which expanded the market for books, encouraged greater aesthetic refinement of the printed page (see MISE EN PAGE). *Baskerville, a rich Birmingham industrialist, former professional *writing-master, and printer, sought to make books in which the type would reflect the elegance of the work of professional calligraphers; his pages show a smoothness resembling the paper of prints from plates that had passed through the rolling press. This effect was achieved partly by pressing the printed sheets between smooth, heated plates, but also by using *Whatman's new *wove paper, which was made in a mould constructed from a fabric of woven brass wires so fine that they left no visible mark.

The expanding market for more visually elegant books led to further improvements to existing technologies and materials. The conventional wooden printing press was adapted in ways that enabled it to deliver a more powerful and consistent impression. Around 1800, Charles *Stanhope, 3rd earl Stanhope, designed a cast iron press (the *Stanhope press), using a system of linked levers to increase its power. Many other iron hand presses using similar systems were developed during the 19th century (e.g. the *Columbian

Wood engraving by Thomas Kelly of printers and compositors at work using a *Columbian press in an English *printing office of the 1820s or 1830s.

and the *Albion). They had greater power and durability than the wooden hand press, and were capable of more refined *presswork, but they did not print significantly faster. Other improvements in existing processes, such as the *aquatint, a means of printing graded tones from a copper plate, assisted the production of expensive books or of single prints for sale to collectors. Nonetheless, they did not affect the basic processes of printing.

3.5 Lithography

The growing market for separately sold prints and for illustrated books encouraged the development of a new method for placing letters or images on paper. *Lithography, the first truly innovative reproduction system to appear for several centuries, would ultimately supersede both relief (letterpress) and intaglio (copperplate) printing. Its development into a practical process lay in the understanding of chemical reactions, a field of scientific research that developed rapidly at the end of the 18th century. Words or images —indeed both together—were drawn with greasy crayon on a polished block of absorbent limestone. The stone was dampened with water, then received an application of printing ink that adhered to the areas drawn with the crayon but was repelled by the dampened parts, which remained clean. The inked image on the stone could then be transferred to paper by putting pressure on it using a specially designed press. Lithography, or 'stone writing', was initially conceived as a means of transferring handwritten texts or drawings to paper without the intervention of typesetting or *copying by professional engravers. Its inventor, *Senefelder, seeking a means of copying music, hit by

accident on the rare variety of limestone, found at Solenhofen in Bavaria, that most suited the method. In time, a metal plate of zinc was developed as a substitute for the heavy and fragile stone. Other developments included a specially treated paper on which text could be written, and the image transferred to the stone. Later in the 19th century, another chemical process, photography, would enable both images and typeset text to be transferred to the stone or plate. A further process, initially designed for printing on tinplate employed for packaging, used a rubber cylinder interposed between the plate and the printing surface. This method enabled the image to be *offset and transferred more efficiently to the surface to be printed. This technique was subsequently developed for lithographic printing on paper. During the second half of the 20th century, offset lithography displaced other processes to become the normal method of printing text and images in books and periodicals and on *posters and packaging.

4 Mechanization

The mechanization of printing was largely driven by the possibilities offered by the development in Britain of new power-driven machinery, which enabled the rapid printing of larger quantities of material by fewer workers. Consequently, the unit cost of the printed item was reduced. During the first decades of the 19th century, methods of mass production were applied to the printing of newspapers and journals, most significantly with the printing in 1814 of *The Times*—the newspaper with the largest daily circulation—on a steam-powered machine (*see* STEAM PRESS). *The*

First made c.1860 at Otley, Yorkshire, by the River Wharfe, for over a century the 'Wharfedale' *cylinder press was used for all kinds of printing: from F. J. F. Wilson and D. Grey, *A Practical Treatise Upon Modern Printing Machinery and Letterpress Printing* (1888).

Times needed to print some 7,000 copies of the complete four-page newspaper overnight, something that was hardly possible with the use of the hand press. Using hand press technology, the outer forme for pages 1 and 4 (consisting only of *advertisements) was printed during the previous day, and the inner forme for pages 2 and 3 (with news and comment) was printed during the night. At *The Times*, multiple copies of this inner forme were set so that the printing could be completed at several hand presses, whose individual output could not exceed 300 impressions in an hour. This arrangement of contents, with advertisements on the front and back pages and news and comment across the centre spread, survived in newspapers long after the technical need for it had ceased.

With the advent of the new printing machine, the sheet was placed on a rotating iron cylinder under which the flat *bed carrying the type, inked automatically with rollers, was carried to and fro (*see* CYLINDER PRESS). It was invented by Friedrich König of Saxony, an engineer who had established a partnership in London in order to develop his machine with the use of British venture capital. The initial speed of impression was 1,000 copies an hour. One of the early investors in König's machine was *The Times*'s proprietor John Walter. However, disagreement with his English investors led König to leave England and set up his own factory at Würzburg with his business partner, Andreas Bauer. König's design was further developed during the 1820s by English engineers, notably the partnership of Applegath and Cowper, who introduced the principle of printing a second impression and delivering a sheet printed on both sides.

A comparable search for venture capital and for purchasers of machinery motivated the Parisian engineer Nicolas-Louis Robert to bring his designs for a paper-making machine to Britain. In this case, the critical innovation was to abandon the mould that made single sheets of paper, and to pour the pulp in a controlled stream on to a long, continuous, rotating band of woven wire. As the pulp dried out, it became paper, which was cut into separate sheets or stored in a roll at the so-called dry end of the machine. Machine-made paper was made and sold from the first decade of the 19th century.

Such innovations transformed the economics of newspaper and periodical printing at a period when the rapid growth in the population and urbanization of industrial nations was expanding markets greatly. Some of the fastest machinery developed at the time employed a principle that was well understood but difficult to apply in practice: namely, passing a continuous band of paper between two cylinders, one bearing the inked text and images, the other applying pressure. After printing, the paper was cut and folded. This process avoided reversing the direction of the heavy flat forme of type—as occurred in the cylinder printing machine—which practically limited the speed of output to about 3,000 sheets an hour. Yet such machines remained in use until the later 20th century for book printing that required relatively short runs and used single sheets of paper.

The principle of rotary printing, as printing from cylinders is known, had been employed by calico printers in Lancashire in the 1780s, where multiple colours were printed simultaneously on a continuous 'web' of fabric from engraved copper plates curved to fit cylinders. Ink was added continuously from rollers and the surplus was removed with a 'ductor' or 'doctor' blade against which the plate rotated before transferring the engraved image to the cloth. This practice of printing on a continuous web was adapted in due course to letterpress, lithographic, and intaglio printing on paper.

The basic requirement of rotary printing was the conversion of the flat printing surface of typeset text to the curved surface of the cylinder. A crude compromise was to lock the type in narrow galleys to the external surface of a cylinder with a radius so big that the lack of curvature was less of an impediment to getting a good impression. This was done during the 1840s on a machine designed for printing the *Illustrated London News*, a magazine that sold 250,000 copies weekly. Multiple stations were set up around the periphery of the cylinder, at each of which was an operator feeding a sheet to be printed with the inked surface. When used for newspaper printing, such presses employed very large sheets of paper, which were delivered folded to the purchaser, who either used a paper knife or struggled with the unopened sheet, like the reader shown in Benjamin Robert Haydon's painting *Waiting for 'The Times'* (1831).

The logical development, when the technical difficulties could be overcome, was a *rotary press, printing on a continuous web or roll of paper. This was realized in the 1860s and used initially for newspapers, but the arrangement has become normal for high volume printing of any kind. A mould was made from the flat surface of the forme of type in flexible papier mâché (called the *flong, from the French *flan*), then dried and curved so that a cast could be made in the form of a half cylinder. Paper from a continuous roll was fed through inked cylinders, to which pairs of such semi-cylindrical casts had been attached. Having been printed on both sides, the paper was cut and folded at the end of the press. In the early 20th century, the casting process and the machining of the plates to fit the cylinders was made faster and more automatic. With the addition of extra printing units, newspapers with more pages could be produced at speeds reaching 80,000–100,000 copies an hour. To speed production still further, multiple moulds could be made and used to cast plates intended for additional presses in the same location or a distant one. Rotary presses fitted with curved stereotype plates were used until the second half of the 20th century for printing newspapers and, in cases where long *press runs were required, for magazine and book production.

4.1 Electrolytic processes

The electrotype, developed *c*.1840, would for some purposes supersede the cast stereotype, both for the duplication of typeset texts and for the reproduction of wood engravings. In *electrotyping, a wax impression was taken from the surface to be duplicated. Then, having been coated with fine graphite to make the surface conduct, the wax was immersed in a bath of copper sulphate solution; as a current was passed through it, particles of copper built up gradually. The resulting copper shell, backed with lead to give it solidity, was capable of a very fine reproduction of the original. It became the standard practice for publishers to keep the original blocks of wood-engraved illustrations (such as those engraved by *Dalziel after *Tenniel's drawings for Carroll's *Alice's Adventures in Wonderland*, 1865) and to supply electrotypes ('electros') to the printer. As they wore out, these were replaced with new plates made from the original wood blocks. Whether stereotyped or electrotyped, plates were made for all books that were frequently reprinted, such as reference works and popular series of inexpensive classic texts.

4.2 Machines for typecasting

Using the traditional hand mould, between 3,000 and 5,000 types could be cast in a working day, depending on the type's body size. In the smaller sizes, equivalent to 10 or 12 point (*points are the unit of linear measure for type), the metal solidified as fast as the caster could throw in the metal and open the mould to eject the type. At the beginning of the 19th century, a significant improvement to the hand mould was introduced. A lever at the side enabled the caster to raise the matrix and eject the cast type without opening the mould. This device is credibly said to have raised the daily production by hand to as many as 8,000 small types. Another mechanical aid was the expedient of fixing a pump to the pot containing molten metal, so that the hand mould could be rapidly and more evenly fed. The powered injection of the metal also made it easier to cast finely ornamented types, introduced to rival the lettering drawn by lithographers, who competed for the more elaborate and profitable work of letterpress printers.

In the 1830s, David Bruce, who had emigrated from Scotland to the US where he became a typefounder, invented a machine that incorporated the two halves of the type mould. Using cams mounted on a single shaft, the machine brought the halves together in front of a pump nozzle, mounted on a metal pot, at the moment when it discharged a *jet of metal. This 'pivotal' typecaster worked by hand or by power, producing 6,000 pieces of the smaller-bodied types in an hour. They were not finished types, however; as in hand-cast type, the work of breaking off the tang or jet of surplus metal, ploughing the foot, rubbing the edges, and undercutting *kerned sorts, had to be done before the type was ready for use. In the 1880s, a new generation of more complex typecasting machines (Barth in the US, Küsterman in Germany) was developed that also cast type in the larger sizes, and delivered the type finished for printing.

The most significant single invention in the field of typefounding was the *pantographic machine punch-cutter, patented in 1885 by Linn Boyd Benton, an American typefounder. The principle of a rotating cutter, mounted on a pantographic frame and tracing the outline of a relief pattern, had been used since the 1830s to cut big types in wood for use on posters (*see* WOODEN TYPE). Its application to the making of steel punches made possible the realization of typesetting machines that changed the market for type for hand setting. It also made possible the creation of types from a drawn alphabet, without the intervention of the hand punchcutter.

4.3 Mechanized typesetting

Much attention was given during the second half of the 19th century to the development of machines for setting type. There were two different approaches to the problem. The first system, widely used, stored cast type and delivered it as unjustified text to a composing stick, where a compositor inserted spaces and justified the line by hand. Such a composing machine, with a keyboard similar to that of a piano, was produced by Young & Delcambre in the late 1840s. More sophisticated machines of this kind were marketed successfully and used well into the 20th century (*see* COMPOSING MACHINES).

The second system, which overtook the first, was for a machine that cast a new printing surface. Several machines of this kind were invented and produced between the 1880s and World War I, but only two of them effectively survived; these divided the larger part of the market between them during the 20th century. In 1887, the Linotype machine was launched by *Mergenthaler, a German immigrant to the US. A supply of brass matrices was stored in a magazine, from which they were released by keyboard in sequence to form the line of text. The words having been spaced with wedges, the line was cast as a solid bar or *slug, the 'line of type' to which its name referred. At first,

the Linotype was bought for newspaper composition, but in the US it eventually came to dominate the machine composition of text for all printed matter, including that of books.

A decade later, in 1897, Tolbert Lanston, who as a clerk had seen the potential of punched cards for sorting data, invented the *Monotype machine. Its keyboard was separate and freestanding: the operation of the keys punched holes in a paper tape that recorded the characters and added a code to calculate the line's spacing. The tape was read by an automated casting machine, which cast each character and space separately and delivered lines that were ready for placing on the printing machine.

The casting of separate type enabled corrections to lines cast on the Monotype to be made by hand. In the Linotype, a line needing correction was reset and recast. This could be done quickly, however, and Linotype slugs were more stable than single types when they were made up into formes on the composing stone. Accordingly, the Linotype, together with some related machines, retained its hold on the market for newspaper and periodical composition. For the composition of books, the Monotype, which was capable of certain typographical refinements, was often favoured.

4.4 Photomechanical processes

During the later 19th century, highly complex processes were developed for the reproduction of images, some of which had a profound effect on printing processes generally. The principle was simple, although in practice great technical skill was needed. A photographic image of a black-and-white drawing was printed on to a zinc plate with a substance that formed a resist, and the rest of the metal was etched away to leave an accurate relief facsimile of the drawing, ready for printing, without the intervention of a professional engraver to interpret it on wood (*see* **16**).

During the 1880s, images for reproduction in books and magazines (a fast-growing market) were increasingly derived from photographs, but these were necessarily interpreted by professional wood engravers who simulated the continuous tone of the photograph by creating the perceived shades of grey with the skilled use of their tools. The mechanical reproduction of photographs was achieved by breaking up the image with a regular screen of fine crossed lines to create *half-tones (comprising dots of varying size) and *etching the image in relief on copper. The drawback of the half-tone block was that properly printing its fine detail required the use of a specially prepared smooth paper, ideally one that was coated with china clay, and known as 'art paper'.

Similar techniques were employed to treat photographs to produce a printing surface for lithographic or intaglio printing. The latter process led to the development of *photogravure, printed either from flat etched plates or from copper cylinders from which both photograph and text could be printed on large web-fed rotary presses. The process of photogravure printed on rotary machines, which at that date produced a denser image than either letterpress or offset lithography, enabled the production of large-circulation pictorial magazines in the years between the two world wars; it was also used for some books of photographs.

4.5 Colour printing for the commercial and popular market

To print in more than one colour, the same sheet must be printed repeatedly; this adds to the cost and demands accuracy in placing the paper, so that the colours print over each other in *register. During the 19th century, multiple colours were increasingly used to increase the effectiveness of new kinds of printing: e.g. posters and packaging, and books for children (see 15). In the 20th century, that market would also include large-circulation periodicals. At first, colours were mixed by specialist printers to make tints that worked in harmonious combinations. With the development of colour theory at the end of the 19th century, processes were introduced that could reproduce all possible colours from the superimposition of three successive printed colours (cyan, magenta, and yellow). However, with experience it became evident that, in addition to the three colours, an additional black printing was needed to give added density to dark hues, thus making a four-colour process.

4.6 Photocomposition of text

A system for setting type by photography was patented in Britain in 1896, and experimental devices for small-scale typesetting were invented and used during the 1930s. It was not until after World War II, however, that systems for text setting were manufactured and marketed on any scale.

One obstacle to the use of photography was that letterpress relief printing was still the dominant means of producing texts. The product of *photocomposition was an image on film; using it for letterpress printing required the making of an etched relief on zinc or magnesium, an expensive process that risked some loss of quality. Although photogravure was too

small a part of the market, offset lithography was more promising. It generally employed text that had been set in metal, then photographed to make the lithographic plate, so direct photocomposition of the text could eliminate this detour. It is not surprising, therefore, that the early photocomposing machines were designed and made in the US, where offset lithography was gaining a steadily increasing share of the market for printing. For printing books, the process had an additional advantage over letterpress, one that it shared with photogravure: photographs could be printed alongside text on the same paper, rather than segregated in a separate section of plates.

Some early photocomposing or filmsetting machines were based on existing machines for making metal type, and produced by their manufacturers in order to gain a share of the future market. Such machines included the Fotosetter of Intertype (makers of a version of the Linotype) and the Monofoto, made by Monotype. In these, photographic negatives were, in effect, substituted for the brass matrices in which metal had been cast; a beam of light created the text, letter by letter, building up lines and pages on film that was then developed. The most innovative machine, designed from first principles rather than adapted from existing models, was the Photon (called the Lumitype by its French inventors, Higonnet and Moyroud, and marketed under that name in France). On the Lumitype, letters were picked out in rapid sequence from images on a spinning glass disk with an electronic flash and the capacity for multiple sets of types or fonts. (During the middle years of the 20th century, the designs of the printing types sold by typefounders or provided by the makers of composing machines were widely known as *typefaces. With the development of photocomposition and digital typography, for which many of the older designs were adapted and redrawn, the term 'font'—the US spelling of the term more commonly spelt 'fount' in Britain—became routinely used for individual designs.)

The first generation of these machines all posed the same problem: to make a correction, it was necessary to set a new line or paragraph and physically strip it into the existing film. It became apparent that the only way of working around this difficulty was to read and correct the text before, rather than after, the type was set and almost ready for printing, as had hitherto been the practice. In the new generation of typesetting machines, the text was entered on a keyboard, coded for such instructions as size of type and *bold type and italics, and held on magnetic tape in order to permit correction and alteration that could be viewed on a screen and checked on an intermediate print. The *computer had entered the printing office and, within a generation—having irrevocably altered the relationship of author, publisher, and printer—it would change the meaning of 'text'. During the 1970s, a third generation of typesetting devices moved away from photocomposition on film, substituting the generation of type in digital form.

4.7 Digital typography

The Apple Macintosh computer, with its mouse and GUI (Graphics User Interface), was launched in San Francisco on 24 January 1984, a date that is often cited as marking the beginning of the digital revolution in printing and publishing (*see* **19**). In addition to the Apple Macintosh computer ('Mac'), four other products marketed in 1984 and 1985 may together be seen as having initiated the practices that ultimately became a normal part of the process of making books and all kinds of printed matter. The page description language Adobe PostScript enabled the integration of text and images on a range of different computers and printers. The LaserWriter, introduced in 1985, was a *laser printer with a raster image processor (*see* OFFSET PRINTING) that incorporated the Adobe PostScript interpreter. Macropedia's Fontographer was a program for drawing new digital fonts, and for adapting existing ones (*see* DIGITAL TYPE DESIGN). Aldus PageMaker was a program that facilitated the setting of type, the handling of images, and their placing on a page. Thus, the design and assembly of a publication's parts—originally the printer's responsibility and, during the 20th century, increasingly shared with a design or production department within a publisher's office—could now be performed by one person with a small computer on a desk. By providing their text in digital form, authors became the primary typesetters of their own books. The advent of the electronic book was in many respects an outgrowth of these new, computerized production technologies.

5 Conclusion

The printed book as an object has not changed radically since its introduction in the 15th century. To be sure, the varieties of its form are now very great indeed, with images integrated into text, an abundance of colour, and a wide range of formats. Yet, in order to convey straightforward texts, lines of black words are still placed on white paper, arranged in a sequence of pages, and made up into a book that can be placed at a comfortable distance for reading. The

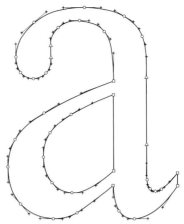

The 'a' of a TrueType font of Times Roman, with all the points that govern its Bézier curves and straight lines.

shapes of the letters may vary from time to time under the influence of changing preferences, but many types in current use are derived directly from those created during the 20th century for machine composition in metal. Indeed, it is generally agreed that—although the appearance of offset lithography is subtly different from that of letterpress printing—digital types and typesetting have on the whole enhanced the look of printing without altering it noticeably.

Nevertheless, the underlying technical processes employed to produce the printed page have changed tremendously. The widespread use of metal type had effectively ceased by about 1980: such type is now employed only rarely, to make special kinds of books (*see* PRIVATE PRESSES). Words are still generally placed on paper with ink, but carbon particles (or *toner) fused by an electrostatic process are more likely to be used to generate copies of digitized books that are printed on *demand. So too, many works are designed to be read directly from a screen without ever being printed on paper. The processes of making and diffusing texts are still developing in directions that are not easy to predict.

BIBLIOGRAPHY

B. Agüera y Arcas, 'Temporary Matrices and Elemental Punches in Gutenberg's DK Type', in *Incunabula and Their Readers*, ed. K. Jensen (2003)

J. M. Funcke, *Kurtze Anleitung von Form- und Stahlschneiden, Erfurt 1740*, intro. J. Mosley (1998)

Gaskell, *NI*

R. Gaskell, 'Printing House and Engraving Shop, a Mysterious Collaboration', *BC* 53 (2004), 213–51

R. E. Huss, *The Development of Printers' Mechanical Typesetting Methods, 1822–1925* (1973)

G. A. Kubler, *A New History of Stereotyping* (1941)

McKerrow, *Introduction*

J. Moran, *Printing Presses* (1973)

R.-G. Rummonds, *Printing on the Iron Handpress* (2 vols, 1997)

R. Southall, *Printer's Type in the Twentieth Century* (2005)

M. Twyman, *Early Lithographed Books* (1990)

12 The Economics of Print

ALEXIS WEEDON

1 The economic value of a book

Four essential factors determine the economic value of a book: its worth as literary property, the cost of its manufacture, regulatory and institutional controls, and its price in the market. The history of the book trade can be read as the economic development of these four key areas. Tracing the development of these factors, this essay's chief focus is on 19th-century Britain, when commercial and technological innovations changed the economic status of the book from a luxury item to an affordable product for the majority of the British population (see **20b**).

2 The Stationers' Company and early institutional structures of the British book trade

Even before the invention of printing, book production was regulated through the craft guild of the Company of *Scriveners in the City of London. By the mid-16th century the guild controlled the economic organization of book production, which was limited to London. The technical importance of printing and its economic advantage over hand copying gradually gave printers status and influence within the guild. However, printing increased the demand for paper which was imported by wealthy merchants—*stationers—who were effectively the capitalists of the trade and held greatest sway within the Company. In 1557, the *Stationers' Company was granted a Royal Charter giving it corporate legal status and the right to self-regulation. The Company gained powers to regulate *apprentices and apprenticeships and to seize illegal books (see CENSORSHIP), and it prohibited printing by non-members. This largely confined printing to London, centralizing the trade until the end of the 17th century (see **20a**).

The Company's custom of recording permission to print a book—a practice inaugurated in part to forestall adverse competition between its members—became regularized, and in 1559 the *Stationers' Register became the authoritative record within the trade of who had the right to print copies of a work. By Elizabeth I's reign, registration had become the mechanism for recording the legal right to publish a work, and in 1637 this was confirmed in law (see COPYRIGHT).

Certain characteristics of the book business in Britain are evident in the early history of the Stationers' Company: there is a strong institutional structure focused on London, an economic interdependence between the elements of the trade that emphasized their mutual business interests above rivalries, and a mechanism to assign and record the right to print copies of books. The Stationers' Register and *patents were early forms of copyright protection. Patents had been assigned by Henry VIII, and they gave the right to print the most profitable books to particular court favourites and their appointed printers. This concentrated economic power in an oligarchy, as the lucrative trade in educational and religious books (*ABCs, *almanacs, *catechisms, *psalters, and *primers) was given to a few favoured members of the Company. Protests ensued, and as a result the patents were shared more widely amongst the members and became jointly owned property. In 1603 this arrangement was formalized into the Company's *English Stock. The Stock was divided into shares with a notional capital of £9,000. Fifteen Court Assistants purchased shares of £320 each, 30 Liverymen purchased shares worth £160, and 60 freemen or yeomen purchased shares worth £80 each. In the early 17th century, shareholders received a remarkable annual dividend of around 12.5 per cent. A large proportion of these co-owners were *booksellers and paper merchants who had the capital to invest in the English Stock. The long-term effect of this arrangement was to separate the printing and publishing functions of book production—an outcome that was crucial to the parallel development of the printing industry and of publishing houses in the 19th century.

In 1637, however, the book trade was still small. There were approximately 26 active *printing offices in London, and a printer might have two or three hand presses with a couple of *journeymen and an apprentice. Essentially, they were small-scale family businesses. By 1730 the size of typical printing offices had increased, while the biggest firms became very large indeed: *Tonson and Watts, for example, employed over 50 men. In the 1750s, Samuel *Richardson had three such establishments with more than 40 men in each. These were printing and bookselling enterprises, fuelled in part by the growing popularity of the *novel and the 18th-century *circulating library market.

The *Printing Act (1662) confirmed the main elements of the trade after the chaos of the Civil War: it was almost exclusively confined to London, limited the number of presses, and ratified that entry in the Stationers' Register was the proof of copyright ownership. The only significant change was that a Licenser, responsible for books and *newspapers, replaced the Elizabethan system of approval by two religious or educational authorities.

The Civil War stimulated *literacy and a growth in demand for news conveyed through print. In 1668, to gain access to this new market, the trade published the first *term catalogues, or lists of new publications for booksellers. It was a significant innovation, which later became the basis of the national bibliography (see *ESTC). During this time, wholesalers came to play a key part in the distribution of books. To recoup the expense of manufacture, copy-owners sold a portion of their *press run at a discount to wholesalers, who then sold them on to booksellers. Significantly, the discount was calculated on the notional retail price of the book, foreshadowing the rise of the *Net Book Agreement (1900), which regulated book prices for nearly the whole of the 20th century.

3 The origins of legal copyright

In 1695, the Printing Act lapsed and the value of English Stock declined, thereby eroding the control of the Stationers' Company over the trade. Copy-owners feared the loss of protection of their copyright and an increase in *piracy, so they replaced the institutional control of the Stationers' Company by trade agreements directly with members of *congers, associations of booksellers or printers who increased their power in the market by pooling their resources in a kind of joint-stock partnership. Such associations not only helped to ensure greater financial stability for their members, they also extended their range of distribution and provided a measure of protection from piracy. Such amalgamations of businesses are indicative of the tightness of the trade and the mutuality of interests in the production and sale of books. Similarly, shared ownership of a book was kept within the group of shareholders through *trade sales. When shares in copyrights became available for sale, often through the estate of a former copy-owner, an auction was typically conducted exclusively for members of the book trade. After the legal protection of the Printing Act lapsed in 1695, this form of trade protection was all that was available until the first Copyright Act came into being.

During the 18th century, various legal remedies were tried to regulate the trade, including laws on copyright, trade protectionism, and taxation (see TAXES ON KNOWLEDGE; STAMP ACTS). The lapse of the Printing Act was also the end of licensing, and taxes on printed matter, introduced in 1711 and later extended, became the means of regulating access to print. They continued until the mid-19th century. By raising the price of newspapers and print, they effectively circumscribed their readership, excluding the poorer classes. Taxes could be claimed back on books sent abroad, however; for some publishers such as H. G. *Bohn, this had the unintended benefit of supporting the growing export trade in books. The 18th century saw the first copyright Act—'for the Encouragement of Learning' (1710)—which gave protection to copy-owners of existing literary property for 21 years and of all new copies after the Act for 14 years. However, it was somewhat hastily drafted, and hence badly worded, leaving open the notion of perpetual copyright. Copy-owners were anxious about the extent of the protection it gave, especially after the initial 21 years had expired, and were concerned about the threat of imported books from emerging centres of printing in Edinburgh and Dublin. Thus, the booksellers put pressure on the government to protect the trade, and in 1739 the Crown passed an act that prohibited the import of English books. It was not to last, and in 1774 a legal judgement ruled that this protectionism was illegal, effectively ending the stranglehold of the London trade. This case (*Donaldson vs Becket) was significant for another reason: it ruled against perpetual copyright. From then on copyright acts have set and adjusted fixed terms for copyright protection.

Authors hardly featured in the 1710 copyright Act, although they soon began to see how it gave them more of an economic stake in their work (*see* AUTHORSHIP). In the 18th century, the author typically received a lump sum for the number of *sheets the work would fill in exchange for its copyright. By 1800 limited-duration copyright was an economic reality, and profit-sharing agreements gradually became more common. During the 19th century the *Society of Authors campaigned for *royalty agreements so that writers might share in the financial reward of their success. Publishers turned their attention to creating markets within a growing and increasingly literate population. Some were able to make a good living from out-of-copyright books. For example, Bohn's Libraries became renowned for their quality and affordability and opened up a market for other such series, which included books in copyright. Other publishers, such as *Smith, Elder, paid highly for the right to publish fashionable works and to capture the tide of popular interest in a genre or author.

4 Nineteenth-century economic history and innovations in the book trade

Industrialization and the consequent economic prosperity of 19th-century Britain significantly changed the costs of book production. Steam-powered machines revolutionized printing and paper manufacture (*see* **10, 11**). The growth in population and improvements in general welfare and education increased the market for print, and there was an unprecedented growth in output. Print was the first mass media, and in the second half of the 19th century printed matter became ubiquitous—it was on hoardings in the street and on packaging in shops and homes (*see* **14**). Booksellers and *newsagents supplied a burgeoning number and variety of books, newspapers, and periodicals. This was the result of falling manufacturing costs, increased demand, and a freedom from the institutional and regulatory controls that had hitherto restricted access.

The market for books expanded as the population grew and the proportion of adults able to read also increased. Market growth meant that, from the 1860s to the 1890s, the industry was financially under pressure to increase productivity without raising costs. This drive for greater economy was achieved though a reduction in the factor costs of production, including: the price of paper, the mechanization of printing, the development of *lithography, and limiting *composition costs through the use of *stereotyping, or taking plate moulds of set type.

Nevertheless, the book trade was not immune from the ups and downs of the economy. Some declines were peculiar to the trade, such as the crisis of 1826 when *Constable, Walter *Scott's publisher, and a number of other publishers and printers failed. Yet, the trade recovered by the 1830s. Other crises were international: following the Napoleonic wars, there were economic downturns in 1819, 1829–32, 1837–42, and 1847–8; similarly, optimism in the revival of trade after the American Civil War was short-lived. The 1864–6 monetary crisis in Britain was perhaps the most severe: it had been caused by a number of London discounting houses borrowing short and lending long. Several failed, including the greatest of the lenders, Overend, Gurney, & Co, pushing many businesses that relied on bills of exchange into bankruptcy, including Samuel *Beeton, husband and publisher of Mrs Beeton. The ensuing financial emergency continued until 1867, reaching its most critical point on 12 May 1866, when the bank lending rate soared to 10 per cent. It was not to reach that level again until the outbreak of World War I.

J. Barnes has argued that such monetary crises spurred innovation in publishing. Certainly, many successes arose from experiments begun in economic depression. For example, *Knight and the Society for the Diffusion of Useful Knowledge (SDUK) launched the *Library of Useful Knowledge in the turbulent post-Napoleonic era. Each fortnightly issue cost 6*d.*, and sales, often to the working or lower-middle classes, sometimes reached 20,000 per issue. Another publisher who profited from economic downturns was *Tegg & Son. It dominated the *remaindering market, and during 1825–7 made a successful business from buying at 'vastly reduced prices the copyrights of works that had not sold well or whose proprietors had gone bankrupt' (Barnes, 235). Innovative formats were another method of stimulating the market, as W. H. *Smith found when he began his first railway bookstall in the depression of 1848. He tempted middle-class readers with the earliest of many *railway libraries; *Routledge, *Colburn, and other publishers followed. The success of Smith and his competitors was fuelled by a 19ᵗʰ-century vogue for publishers' series or 'libraries', which supplied a market for self-education, for book collecting, and, in the latter half of the century, for schoolbooks.

The success of a format could also bring its own difficulties, however. When J. M. *Dent launched *Everyman's Library in 1904, he set aside £10,000 to finance it. The initial volumes sold so well that he reprinted, tying up much of his capital in stock. Dent's bindery did not have enough space to cope with the demand, so he moved his works to Hertfordshire, installed his printing machinery in the basement, and built new houses for his workers. These expenses cost him an additional £20,000, compelling him to go to his papermakers and to his bank for credit. As a major customer with a secure business, he was able to get it, but as Barnes has pointed out: 'innovation depends on solvency, whether the times are prosperous or hard' (Barnes, 239).

From 1876 to 1886 there was a considerable increase in the quantity of books produced in Britain. Economic historians have shown that the depression of 1873–96 had been of greater political than economic significance; although Britain lost her predominant position as the leading manufacturing country and growth was not as rapid as before, the economy also slowed in the US and Germany. Britain came to take a new pivotal role in international trade and financial services. In the publishing industry, trade to the empire was strongest during periods of colonial expansion. Customs figures for the declared value of book exports indicate that there was a strong early market in India from the 1820s to the 1840s (see **39**). In the early 1850s, however, Australia became a significant consumer of British books: by 1868 the weight of books being shipped to Australia was five times greater than the weight to India (see **44**). The export trade suffered reversals in the Australian financial crises of 1883 and 1890. Exports to British North America (later the Canadian Federation) grew in the late 1860s, so that by 1868 the tonnage to North America was double the Indian trade (see **47**). From the 1890s, however,

British publishers felt the effects of competition from indigenous publishing houses and sought to establish branches abroad to handle their trade in the colonies. *Macmillan, for instance, opened offices in India in 1901. Their export trade had been developing over several decades, and from 1873 they had been designing specific editions for the Indian market. Similarly, *Collins opened a warehouse and showroom in Sydney, Australia, in 1874, and in New Zealand in 1888, and the firm also had travellers in India seeking out markets in Bombay, Calcutta, Madras, and Colombo. Such expansion was a typical feature of the internationalization of British book publishing.

5 Reducing the cost of paper

On the manufacturing side of book production—paper and printing—capital investment in printing equipment was needed initially to fund powered presses from the 1830s to the 1850s, and subsequently to replace those presses with improved versions. From the 1860s printers, such as William *Clowes, were investing in patents and were experimenting with composition machines and new photographic and *platemaking processes. Similarly, in the papermaking trade, the *Fourdrinier machine and its later improvements substantially increased output.

The invention of the papermaking machine had a profound effect on the book trade (see **10**). As early as 1804, the Fourdrinier brothers registered a patent for such a machine; their invention was subsequently modified and improved by others. By 1825, over half of all paper in England was made by machine. Machine-made paper had the advantages of speed, flexibility, size, and quality. Testifying to the significance of the Fourdriniers' invention, the book printer George Clowes explained the knock-on result of machine-made paper for the whole of the printing industry: it 'has effected a complete revolution in our business; where we used to go to press with an edition of 500 copies, we now print 5,000' (Plant, 331). Clowes's works at that time was the biggest and most modern in the country; it printed on double-sized paper at a time when only about a fifth of book paper used was double. By 1886, however, this figure had risen to three-quarters. *Quad papers succeeded double and by 1906 were the norm. This doubling-up of sheet sizes corresponded with the increase in the size of presses.

In the 30 years following 1866, paper costs were reduced by approximately two-thirds. This substantial decrease had a significant effect on cost of production.

Contemporary sources explaining the decline in the cost of paper as a proportion of book manufacturing in the 19th century as a whole cite the earlier abolition of duty and the use of *esparto grass and *wood pulp in the manufacture of paper as two major causes. However, other variables also effected this fall: the mechanization of the process of paper manufacture; the availability and affordability of the raw materials for paper; and more economical presses and *imposition schemes. Probably all these factors contributed to helping printers reap the benefits of mechanization, and ensured the more economical use of larger presses.

6 Mechanization of printing

Although Clowes had already experimented with steam power in his printing office in 1823, it was a while before the printing machine itself was commonplace. Before 1820, the steam press was in use by five London printers: *The Times*, Charles Baldwin, Andrew Strahan, Richard Taylor, and Richard Bensley. Not all of these had double-size presses, and it was not until 1828 that the use of double sheets for book work was possible though the introduction of the improved Applegath and Cowper machine. *The Times* had printed its 29 November 1814 edition on König's steam press, and later used Applegath and Cowper's improved version, which could print double-sized sheets at the rate of 1,000 an hour, four times the speed of the hand presses. Throughout the 1830s and 1840s, other printers began to install steam engines and invest in powered presses. Steam-powered double-*platen presses manufactured first by Hopkinson and Cope, then produced to an improved design by Napier, generally came into use during the 1830s. Running at up to 800 impressions per hour, their maximum size was double *royal. This increased capacity fuelled experiments in cheap periodicals. Following the Library of Useful Knowledge, for example, the SDUK published its famous *Penny Magazine* and *Penny Cyclopaedia*. This was a boom period in periodical publishing. In 1836, Dickens published *Pickwick Papers* in part *numbers. The novel was so successful that *Chapman & Hall, Dickens's publishers, had to use stereotypes to print multiple *impressions. The stereotyping process enabled type to be cast to fit a curved surface, and this led to faster cylinder and rotary presses coming on to the market. During the 1860s and 1870s, the Napier steam presses were replaced by these fast, but initially less accurate, single-sided cylinder presses. Wharfedales, used in book work, could take the much larger quad demy sheets. In 1858 *The Times* moved to using stereoplates on cylinders; ten years later, taking advantage of the mechanization of paper manufacture, it dispensed with sheets and employed a rotary press that could take a continuous web of paper. This measure doubled its printing capacity.

Such machines made labour more productive. Both the double platens and the double royal Wharfedales used two operators, but the latter's output was greater. The operators were usually boys, overseen by a machine-minder who made ready the press—that is, imposed the *forme and put it on the press, adjusted the *height of the type by inserting *overlays, and packed cuts where necessary (*see* MAKING READY). When reprinting a work, fitting stereoplates saved time, as the initial labour of levelling the type was preserved in the cast. This reduced the making-ready, and hence production costs. Often some repair work was needed to the stereoplates, but it usually amounted to no more than a few shillings' worth of labour. Such savings meant that it was cost-effective to reprint in shorter runs, though the effort of setting up the press and washing it down afterwards resulted in the fact that the unit cost for editions of fewer than 500 was markedly higher than for editions above that number. This partly explains why, from the 1860s to the 1880s, the most frequent quantity printed was 1,000 books.

As machining, make-ready, and paper costs varied over the century, so too did the unit cost for printing a book. Unit costs fell when the initial fixed set-up cost could be divided among a larger number of books. As more books were printed, the fraction of the set-up cost was reduced until it was less than the combined cost of paper and machining for each unit. At this point the optimum press run was reached. By the 1890s, the optimum run for the publisher was as high as 30,000 copies, although this was obviously not the longest possible print run. It was not unusual for cheap fiction, for instance, to be printed in numbers of 100,000 or more on cylinder presses, although most quality book work was done on sheet-fed machines. Above the optimum press run, the unit cost consisted of the price of the paper, running the machine, and the wages and overtime of the machine-minder and his boys. For magazine publishers, such as *Newnes, using faster *perfecting cylinder and rotary presses, much longer press runs were economical, but initial set-up costs meant that runs had to be over 5,000 to be cost-effective. Publishers used these new, highly economical technologies in the penny market. Newnes, John Dicks, and others published editions of

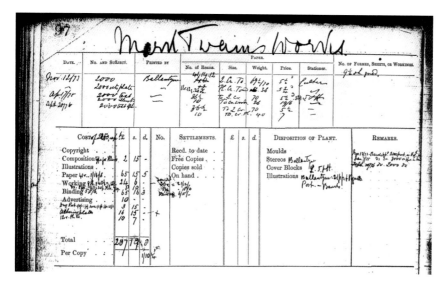

*Chatto & Windus publish *Choice Humorous Works of Mark Twain* (1873); it was followed by a series of *stereotype reprints, all produced by Ballantyne, Hanson, & Co. The publication ledger shows the growing importance of documenting and controlling costs.

popular works, often printed in double columns, magazine-style, on cheap paper; they cost a few pence and were read by the working classes.

Although in the 40 years between 1836 and 1876 the average cost of machining gradually rose at a rate of approximately 7 per cent each decade, between 1876 and 1886 the average cost fell by 29 per cent, and in real terms by nearer half; it remained low until the turn of the century. The fall in paper costs after the abolition of the paper tax, then the replacement of the platen-powered presses by the larger cylinder ones in the 1860s and 1870s, meant that the real reduction in the cost of machining came after the beginning of the fall in paper costs. The percentage fall in the expense of machining cannot be wholly attributed to the incremental increase in paper size. The new machinery was more economical.

7 The wages of compositors and cost of composition

The main reason for the fall in the cost of book production was the move from double- to quad-sized paper and presses, and the use of stereoplates. Composition, for nearly the whole of the 19th century, meant hand composition. Experiments with mechanical means for the selection of type and its *distribution were on the whole unsuccessful. When labour was plentiful, the main concern was the amount of available type. With the spread of stereoplates and typecasting machines in the 1850s, the quantity of type became less of a problem, and what concerned publishers and printers more was the extent of revisions which added to the rising cost of labour.

*Correction represented on average 35 per cent of the composition costs of books between 1836 and 1916, although the proportion varied considerably from title to title. The occasional text needed complete *resetting, whereas others needed very little alteration.

Throughout the 19th century wage levels gradually increased, making labour more expensive. The main period of rising wages was from 1869 to 1876. However, compositors' wages did not rise so sharply. Bowley's and Wood's studies show that compositors' average wages—which in 1800–1810 had been much higher than their fellow workers in cotton factories, the building trade, and the shipbuilding and engineering industries—were by the 1880s at a similar level. Although there were wide geographical differences in the wages of union labour, non-union labour, and piece-work, a comparison of compositors' earnings with Wood's calculation of the mean wage of the period shows that compositors' wages were falling relative to those of other wage earners. Rates of pay and employment levels varied considerably from county to county, causing concern among the typographical societies. In the crisis of 1826, for example, many compositors lost their jobs, and every London printing house allegedly had notices saying that compositors and pressmen need not apply. Even two years later, 800 out of 3,500 compositors and pressmen in the capital were out of work.

With the mechanization of paper manufacture and the adoption of printing machines, the labour-intensive work of composition was the next logical task to mechanize. However, typographical associations and print unions, which were concerned for the continuing employment of their members and for industry standards, resisted the introduction of *composing machines. Their concern over quality was echoed by the printers. The *Linotype machine used in America for book work had been gradually introduced into newspaper offices in Britain in the late 1870s, but the printer W. C. K. Clowes judged that although the Linotype was the right principle, 'at present he did not think it was the machine for bookwork' (Southward, 82). Clowes's firm invested in *Monotype machines when they came into commercial use in 1897, pioneering many of their own modifications. The interval between the technology's invention and its perfection meant that any effect on wages and employment patterns for compositors was deferred until the 20th century, when World War I pushed both prices and wages higher.

When printers moved to an industrialized system of setting and printing, replaced double- with quad-sized presses, and bought machine-made paper, they passed on to publishers the benefits of large-scale manufacturing through the reduction of basic unit costs. By adopting stereoplates (see STEREOTYPING), which conserved labour and allowed for a more flexible mode of production, they enabled publishers to tailor their product more effectively to the market. The most significant factor in the reduction of unit costs, however, was the reduction in paper prices (combined with its greater availability).

8 Types of publishing firm

At the end of the 19th century, the newspaper and publishing industry consisted mainly of family businesses and partnerships. In the book trade, partnerships were often turned into family businesses when partners were bought out or lists were sold, and the business was handed down to the founder's sons and grandsons. Printers apprenticed their sons to their clients' businesses, and publishers found their sons places in fellow publishers' and printers' firms. In this manner, the trade was close-knit. However, after the trade crisis of 1866–7, it became increasingly common to adopt the form of a limited liability company and retain the family's interest through their shareholding and by holding seats on the corporation's board.

The publishing industry became an increasingly attractive field for investment, not least because the taxes on knowledge that had inhibited the growth of newspapers were abated, political control of the press was relaxed, and prosperity increased. The spread of industrialization, which affected printers and paper manufacturers, caused some concern to producers of books for export as by the mid-century European countries began to emulate Britain and became able to manufacture paper more cheaply. The commissioning and sale of books—the province of publishers and booksellers—was largely dependent on trading conditions in Britain and abroad. Tariff barriers were imposed to differentiate markets, and this affected both supply factors and, to a lesser extent, distribution; however, there were no barriers within the empire, and publishers' *colonial editions appear to have sold in good numbers. Perhaps more significant to the trade was the gradual extension of copyright protection. Although copyright law varied throughout the century, efforts to gain international agreements within Europe (by way e.g. of the *Berne Convention) and, most significantly for British publishers, with the US, eventually paid off.

The economic, political, and legal framework that dictated the structure of the newspaper industry also affected book and magazine publishing, though not to the same extent. The mid-century pressures for political reform stimulated the proliferation of newspapers throughout the country. Politics, legal reform, and growing urbanization were agents of change. In the same way as the 19th-century book, periodical, and general publishing firms, so too was the newspaper industry built largely on the model of the family business. Ties between the industries were close, as Lee has stated: 'Newspaper proprietors had customarily been recruited from the ranks of printers and publishers, and the tradition of proprietorship was deeply rooted and long-lived' (Lee, 84).

In the book publishing industry, family firms and partnerships predominated. Such firms were typically valued prior to changing hands, which was either when a firm was being handed on to the next generation, or when a partner left and wanted to release his equity in the stock and good will. As sons (rarely daughters) came into the trade, they were placed in friends' firms to learn the business, sometimes becoming partners, or else setting up partnerships independently when of age. Thus, a close study of 19th-century *imprints often leads to tracing the kinship of publishers. Firms tied by blood, friendship, or the supply chain were also linked through capital investment, long-term loans, shares, and bills of exchange. Towards the end of the century, it became usual in both industries to adopt some form of joint-stock company, which necessitated returning a balance sheet with accurate statements of turnover and capital.

The registrations and returns of joint-stock companies were recorded annually in the parliamentary *blue books that also noted if they had been wound up or were still in operation at the time they made their return. Although some 18th-century newspapers were organized as joint-stock companies, the real expansion came after the Companies Acts of 1854 and 1862, which offered the security of limited liability. From 1856, the details of their corporate finances were recorded in the blue books. Shannon has shown that the early companies invariably made a loss, causing many investors to be understandably cautious of the new system. Certainly, it seems that many printers and the vast majority of publishing companies remained in private hands. Lee has counted some 420 newspaper companies formed between 1856 and 1885. Only 247 'book, magazine, journal, art or general publishing or bookselling' companies were registered in the same period: 38 in the first decade, 58 in the second, and 151 in the third. This rate of increase was below that of newspaper companies; yet, it reflected the expansion of joint-stock companies at the time. 'Infant mortality' in the first decade was 38 per cent among publishing companies, compared with 20 per cent among newspaper companies, though such early corporate demises too fell swiftly to 7 per cent and 10 per cent in the following two decades, slightly above Lee's newspaper figures of 7 and 6 per cent.

In contrast with the newspaper trade, the number of publishing companies formed remained relatively low until the mid-1870s. In the early 1880s, the rate of formation increased as it did in the newspaper trade, with 26 new companies in 1885. It appears that the economic reversals of the mid-1860s did not affect the number of publishing companies registering, although it does seem to have made them more reluctant to submit returns and more cautious about estimating the company's liability.

Much of the capital held by publishing companies is tied up in their copyrights, in contrast with printers, who invest in machinery and presses. Nevertheless, the industries were closely intertwined, and many of the companies' statements describing their 'object or business' cross the boundaries between printer, publisher, and newspaper proprietor; for example, the Kilgore Newspaper and Publishing Company Ltd included as its business 'newspaper and general printing & publishing'. Book printers such as Clowes partially or wholly owned copyrights as well as holding shares in publishing companies. By 1883, however, categories used in the returns make the distinction between newspaper proprietors and printers and publishers, and this may well reflect an increase in the industry's specialization. From the blue books, it is evident that a larger percentage of publishing than of newspaper companies were medium to large (with a nominal capital £10,000 or above), although in the potentially dangerous period between 1866 and 1875 they were more cautious, and limited their liability to lower amounts. It seems too that more of the nominal capital was called in at this time than during the decades before or after.

Many companies were, of course, established to buy an existing enterprise, and a number of firms were formed for the purpose either of turning partnerships and family businesses into private companies or of buying copyrights in order to establish their own business. Between 1856 and 1865, 70 per cent of publishing companies had fewer than ten shareholders. This pattern was reversed in the following (economically troubled) decade when the risk was spread among a greater number of shareholders. Many of these larger companies were educational suppliers or providers of Christian literature ranging from newspapers to schoolbooks. Others were stationers, printers, or periodical publishers first and foremost, and listed publishing or bookselling as a part of their business. By the end of the 1880s there were many more moderate-to-large businesses whose main object was publishing and bookselling, such as Isbister & Company Ltd (1879) with £32,000 nominal capital and 18 shareholders; *Chapman & Hall Ltd (1880) with £150,000 nominal capital and 104 shareholders; and Collins & Sons Ltd (1880) with £200,000 and 17 shareholders. All these publishers called on a fair proportion of their nominal capital: Isbister called in 90 per cent, Chapman & Hall 70 per cent, and Collins 88 per cent.

The hegemonic structure of the publishing industry was challenged by public investment in companies, alternative distribution systems, foreign competition in colonial markets, and ultimately by the reduction in the unit cost of the book. These factors led to a restructuring of the book trades, a phenomenon that had important commercial and cultural implications. Fundamental structural changes paved the way for the future direction of the publishing industry and became integral to 20th-century developments in the horizontal integration of the industry, by which smaller firms merged to form larger publishing houses that commanded a greater market share.

9 The 20th century

The growth in book production in the 50 years before World War I was higher than the growth in the reading public—a 'catching-up' after the setbacks of the mid-1860s. The increase in reading and book buying mirrored the rate of rising literacy. With World War I, both production and labour costs became more expensive. At the same time, however, composition machines—commonly Monotype machines for books and Linotypes for periodicals—were deemed of acceptable quality.

Price structuring, which from the 1870s had become a significant force in differentiating the fiction markets and had taken on greater significance after the collapse of the *three-decker novel market, led to greater price specialization among publishers. In the 1920s and 1930s, some publishers concentrated on cheap reprint editions (e.g. Newnes, Rich, & Cowan) and others on inexpensive tie-ins with films—such as the Readers Library. In the middle price range *Hodder & Stoughton sold genre fiction at 6s. and their '*yellow backs' at 2s. or 2s. 6d. Increasingly, authors' contracts were for specific editions or price bands; other *rights were sold separately. It was also the era of *Penguin's successful launch into the sixpenny market.

The great depression of the 1930s saw some lasting innovations. In 1932 Harold Raymond of *Chatto & Windus initiated *book tokens. Often given as gifts, the tokens were exchanged towards the purchase of a book, and customers usually spent more than the value of the tokens. The scheme thrived in the difficult economic times of the 1930s and consolidated membership of the *Booksellers' Association, since the bookseller had to be a member to claim his proportion of the value of the token. Similarly, the *Left Book Club and *Book Society's book club, the British counterparts to the *Book-of-the-Month Club and the *Literary Guild in America, had considerable success, as they were able to offer new titles more cheaply by buying in bulk for their membership.

From the 1890s, literary agencies had grown to become a separate and profitable business. In 1935, Curtis Brown, the international *literary agent, wrote that the days of the 'good, kind, old-fashioned publisher who used to take over all of his author's rights and re-sell at 50 per cent' had gone. Successful literary properties commanded 'so many widely varied markets and such intricate contracts' that successful authors needed a business manager (Brown, 239–40). In the 1920s, *serialization rights and *translation rights usually brought in a lump sum, while royalty agreements for the differently priced book editions were often on a percentage return, depending on how many were sold (see ROYALTIES). Options on novels

and plays were eagerly sought as a source of stories for films; such rights could bring in a fixed amount, or be related to box office receipts. Agents found a business niche in negotiating and monitoring such contracts for a return of 10 per cent commission on what they brought the author.

World War I and then World War II profoundly affected the book trade. They imposed, if only for the duration of the conflicts, constraints which the trade had been free of for more than 50 years, ranging from restrictions on what could be published to shortages of labour and paper. However, the industry also supplied news of the war, *propaganda, explanatory material, and advice through *pamphlets and books. Stereoplates which had been stored for years in printers' warehouses were melted down in the war effort, signalling the end of an era—and a welcome new beginning for those who wanted to put Victorian literature and its values behind them. The Census of Production revealed that the monetary value of the paper, print, and stationery trades increased by £3,481,000 between the first (1907) and the fourth (1930) censuses. Inflation accounts for some of the rise, but not all. The number of titles published annually rose, causing murmurings of 'over-production' from those in the trade. The four essential factors in the value of a book were well embedded, however. Copyright law was underpinned through international agreement; the printing and book-manufacturing industries were mechanized and competitive; the professional associations representing the booksellers, publishers, and authors cooperated in their members' economic interests; and, significantly, the financial basis of this close-knit industry, the Net Book Agreement, had survived the two world wars.

BIBLIOGRAPHY
Altick
J. Barnes, 'Depression and Innovation in the British and American Book Trade, 1819–1939', in *Books and Society in History*, ed. K. Carpenter (1983)
A. L. Bowley, *Wages in the United Kingdom in the Nineteenth Century* (1900)
A. C. Brown, *Contacts* (1935)
D. C. Coleman, *The British Paper Industry, 1495–1860* (1958)
S. Eliot, *Some Patterns and Trends in British Publishing, 1800–1919* (1994)
J. Feather, *A History of British Publishing* (2006)
R. Floud and D. N. McCloskey, *The Economic History of Britain since 1700* (1994)

E. Howe and H. E. Waite, *The London Society of Compositors* (1948)

D. Keir, *The House of Collins* (1952)

A. J. Lee, *The Origins of the Popular Press in England, 1855–1914* (1976)

B. R. Mitchell, *British Historical Statistics* (1988)

C. Morgan, *The House of Macmillan (1843–1943)* (1943)

A. E. Musson, *The Typographical Association* (1954)

M. Plant, *The English Book Trade* (1939; 3e, 1974)

J. Rose, *The Intellectual Life of the British Working Classes* (2001)

R. S. Schofield, 'Dimensions of Illiteracy, 1750–1850', *Explorations in Economic History*, 10 (1973), 437–54

H. A. Shannon, 'The First Five Thousand Limited Companies', *Economic History*, supplement to *Economic Journal*, 2 (1932), 396–424

— 'The Limited Companies of 1866–1883', *Economic History Review*, 4 (1932–4), 290–316

J. Southward, 'Machines for Composing Letterpress Printing Surfaces', *Journal of the Society of Arts* (20 Dec. 1895), 74–84

A. D. Spicer, *The Paper Trade* (1907)

J. Sutherland, 'The Book Trade Crash of 1826', *Library*, 6/9 (1987), 148–61

S. S. Unwin, *The Truth about Publishing* (1926)

D. Vincent, *Literacy and Popular Culture: England, 1750–1914* (1989)

— *The Rise of Mass Literacy: Reading and Writing in Modern Europe* (2000)

A. Weedon, 'The Press and Publishing: Technology and Business 1855 to 1885', in *We, The Other 'Victorians'*, ed. S. C. Bizzini (2003)

— *Victorian Publishing: The Economics of Book Production for a Mass Market, 1836–1916* (2003)

G. H. Wood, 'Real Wages and the Standard', in *British Economic Growth 1688–1955*, ed. P. Deane and W. A. Cole (1962)

13 The Manuscript after the Coming of Print

Harold Love

1 Introduction

A century ago there were still many inky-fingered individuals, who in Britain were called clerks, whose job was to prepare handwritten records—usually in large volumes called ledgers—of transactions in business, the law, and science. Their forerunners had been active since the first *stylus incised the first clay *tablet. Much of their work, like that of Melville's Bartleby, Gogol's Akaky Akakevich, and Flaubert's Bouvard and Pécuchet, was the soul-destroying creation of duplicate records. In Shaw's *Misalliance*, a copy-clerk is driven to attempted murder by the monotony and pointlessness of his job. Most inscriptional tasks have now moved via *typewriting to the computer. Handwriting today is used to create evanescent records such as shopping lists, lecture notes, or postcards; to fill in crosswords and sudokus; or to complete questionnaires. Even the personal letter is most likely to pass by email. Only the sometimes threatened demise of the keyboard seems likely to modify this situation.

Certainly, there cannot be many important cultural records in the Western world that are conveyed solely by means of handwriting. Under Soviet rule, *samizdat* copies of dissident texts were circulated in typed copies for works in Russian and in handwritten copies for works in Western languages—this was not a question of choice, but dictated by the limitations for that purpose of the Cyrillic typewriter. In China and Japan, where writing systems are much less amenable to keyboarding, the handwritten exemplar retains its prominence, though its multiplication is likely to be performed by the photocopier. Thus that miracle of technology, the Japanese automatic pencil with extrudable eraser, used with the same upwards and downwards alternation as the ancient stylus writing on wax tablets. But a century and a half ago, work by

a handful of major writers and thinkers was still being circulated in MS as a matter of preference. The verse of Emily *Dickinson and Gerard Manley Hopkins received nearly all its circulation in this way, as did the lucubrations of many humbler authors who sought no audience beyond immediate friends and family, or whose themes were unacceptable to the press. The Brontës' juvenilia are a far from unique example of a family writing exclusively for its own enjoyment. The handwritten work was still prized as a gift to a friend or close relative. Travellers would send letter-diaries to their loved ones with a list of others to whom they were to be circulated, who might in turn make personal copies. Someone requiring an out-of-print book, especially one from an earlier century, would see nothing unusual about making a handwritten copy: many antiquarian records passed in this way from scholar to scholar. At universities, well-off students would buy MS books summarizing the lectures of their professors. Poorer students earned money by inscribing these. And then as now, there were *calligraphers, creators of writing as a thing of beauty.

2 From the Enlightenment to the 16th century

A century earlier still, the Europe of the Enlightenment witnessed the closing stages of a tradition of professional MS book production that had been maintained unbroken since the Middle Ages. In countries subject to draconian state *censorship, philosophically heterodox and politically oppositional texts were still copied for sale by scribes working for booksellers. While surreptitious publication through the press was certainly common, the handwritten copy of a suspect work retained a cachet that made it a desirable form of luxury product. It was also written to order with sale assured. Music circulated principally through MS, or through a mixed mode in which partbooks might need to be consolidated into a handwritten score, or a published score supplemented by hand-written parts. J. S. Bach in his lifetime published only a relatively small body of music, chiefly for the key-board. His liturgical and instrumental music with few exceptions remained in MS; and yet much of the latter was widely circulated through copies and copies of copies. Work by his more popular contemporary, Telemann, travelled in MS to all corners of Europe. In early 18th-century Britain, there was a covert market in sumptuously bound *folio and large-*quarto vol-umes of MS satires and lampoons, some with their contents arranged in alphabetical order so as to con-stitute a kind of secret history of the nation since the Restoration of Charles II. Country parsons might purchase collections of MS sermons to see them through the year; lawyers might buy professionally written collections of writs, precedents, or reports.

Moving even further backwards, to the early 17th century, we find scribal production still competitive with the press whenever the ability to create large numbers of copies in a short time was not an issue, or when there were obstacles to the printing of a given work. In Britain, one of these obstacles was the reluct-ance of many authors, especially women, to have their works appear as articles of sale—what Saunders chris-tened 'the stigma of print', though unwillingness gave little protection when booksellers were free to print any fortuitously encountered MS without permission. Yet, Donne was able to restrict the printing of his poems during a lifetime in which they circulated freely in MS, often in large collections. Carew's and, later, Rochester's verse first appeared in print immediately after their deaths, in pirated *editions based on already current MS *anthologies. Sidney may never have seen any of his writings in printed form. Writers would woo patrons with works in MS, which were seen to possess a greater exclusivity than print: Shakespeare's Sonnets give every appearance of such an origin.

At a time when Parliament jealously guarded the privacy of its deliberations, there was a roaring trade in sessional diaries and the texts of speeches—either noted down, reconstructed from memory by fellow members, or provided by the members themselves to entrepreneurial *scriveners. From the same agencies came a wide variety of political commentaries of a kind often unwelcome to the Crown. The tracts of the great antiquary *Cotton fall into this category. *Selden, too, circulated a number of his writings only through the scribal medium. After his death, his free-speaking *Table Talk*, compiled by his chaplain Richard Milward, was reproduced for sale by a *scriptorium, not being

judged fit for the press until after the Glorious Revolution. One body of early 17th-century material of this kind is linked by the easily recognizable hand of Beal's '*Feathery Scribe'. Even plays, when withheld from the press by acting companies, might be acquired in MS, Middleton's *A Game at Chess* being a famous example. *Crane, a scribe with links to Shakespeare's company, left several play *transcripts apparently made for readers.

All these British practices had their counterparts in continental Europe. In addition, there was a lively international exchange of scientific, *alchemical, and astrological MSS in Latin. Alchemy, as an occult sci-ence, was particularly hostile to the press. Latin epi-grams originally exchanged between the statues of *Pasquino and Marforio in Rome, or celebrating or burlesqueing Louis XIV's rebuilding of the Louvre, travelled both singly and in bulk along mazelike chan-nels of erudite correspondence. Religious persecution encouraged organized scribal circulation of opposi-tional writings—in England, Catholic and Puritan, in France, Huguenot and Jansenist. In Spain and Italy, where the *Inquisition reigned and suspicious books were confiscated from travellers, what penetration there was of Protestant, heterodox, and freethinking texts was largely through MS. To move even further into the past is to arrive at the Reformation and then to the founding decades of print in the late 15th cen-tury, prior to which all texts circulated in either oral or handwritten form. For monks and nuns of that tran-sitional age, copying remained a regular duty pre-scribed under the rule of St Benedict. For many scholars and churchmen of a humanist persuasion, the beauty of a fine hand and the exclusiveness of a handwritten Horace or *book of hours outweighed considerations of price and convenience. In other fields of text production, there is a surprising (but on reflection perfectly predictable) confluence of the media. *McKitterick has pointed to the prevalence of printed books with handwritten elements and of handwritten works containing printed components. Nor were printed books and MSS rigidly shelved apart from each other as happens in today's libraries. Instead, they might well be bound together into larger assemblages, now usually dismembered. It was also common for printed books to be heavily annotated and interleaved by their owners. The note-taking scholars studied by Blair worked in order to return print to MS in the form of vast accumula-tions of excerpts. Manuals were available on how information was to be assigned to and retrieved from these.

3 Production and dissemination

Reversing the direction of this passage through time, the process by which the handwritten word perpetuated its ancient traditions in the face of competition from the press needs to be considered. It did this chiefly by specialization. Once a bible, a Latin grammar, or the text of a royal proclamation could be reproduced more cheaply and in a shorter time by a printer than by a scribe, there was little point in trying to compete in that field; but in the case of a smaller text, these advantages were not so pronounced and might be offset by others. A scribe could make several copies of a 1,000-word document during the time taken up by the cumbersome print processes of *casting off, setting, *proofreading, *presswork, and *collating; in cases where fewer than 50 copies were required, print publication might well prove wasteful. (Even today, as Amory has observed, a large part of print production remains unsold, and much that is sold unread.) A handwritten copy could also claim a greater exclusivity, which often led to it being more carefully read and preserved. It was a much better way of reaching a narrow niche audience. Scribal technology was cheap and portable.

A bundle of *quills, a supply of paper and ink, sufficient light, and a table was all that was required to set such work in motion. The time of a clerk came cheaply enough. A team of scribes, gathered together in a scriptorium or contracting individually to write batches for a bookseller or scrivener, was also capable of quite high levels of output when that was necessary. Even for scribal editions of 100 or more documented in the 17th century for newsletters, the economic advantages were probably pretty equally balanced with those of print. Organized production of this kind minimized the textual deterioration that is the bane of seriatim copying while permitting changes to be made at any time to a master copy—a luxury denied the press. Serial publication could also be a way of exploiting otherwise underused labour. Legal offices employed large numbers of clerks whose regular duties would peak when courts were in session and decline during vacations. To take on copying for booksellers offered a solution. Professional scribal services could also be engaged by an aspiring but print-shy author—although this could prove dangerous, since the scribe or scrivener by retaining an extra copy was in a position to commence production on his own behalf. It was usually safer for authors wishing to distribute a text in MS to entrust production to a secretary, family member, or reliable amanuensis—or

to copy it themselves—though many were reluctant to have their words appear in their own, recognizable handwriting.

The other mode by which texts proliferated in MS was through copies successively made by readers. It is astounding with what rapidity and in what quantities this method could spread a short work. The fact that each was in effect an 'edition' of one could lead, as mentioned earlier, to rapid textual change. Yet there were also disciplines of textual recuperation (not least *emendation), well known to experienced transcribers, and for a popular piece there might well be more than one copy available for consultation. The fragile 'separates', often transported in pockets, in which these texts passed suffered an enormous loss rate, since apart from simple wear and tear, paper was in constant demand for domestic uses. Instead, what has generally survived are copies made from these separates in personal *miscellanies and often misnamed *commonplace books. The surviving MS heritage of a really popular short piece is usually a mixture of both reader-inscribed and professionally written separates (when any survive at all), copies from personal miscellanies, and copies in scribal anthologies compiled for sale.

Once in the hands of the professionals, a piece might first be gathered into a 'linked group' or relatively small sub-collection that then became absorbed into larger and larger collections whose relationships can be established by a study of the order of their contents. In many cases, the larger collections reveal an aspiration to comprehensive record-keeping of an antiquarian kind. English examples include the MS records (published by Notestein and Relf) of the proceedings of the 1628 Parliament and the collections (mentioned earlier) written c.1700 of political satires and libertine lampoons dating from 1660, some of which extend to over 600 pages and have their contents dated and in chronological order. These large and expensive volumes were intended for the homes of wealthy buyers, where their chances of survival were greatly enhanced, though the 9th earl of Derby did hide a volume of potentially treasonable satires in a chimney, where it was only found when the house was demolished. What began as topical, quickly became historical and was respected as such in a medium that antiquarians were often more at home with than they were with the press.

By the early 18th century, the professional arm of scribal publication still enjoyed the advantages of efficiency over very short runs, rapid response time, flexibility in its handling of texts, freedom from censorship, and controlled availability. These were enough to keep a small cadre of booksellers' scribes at work for some decades (just how long would need to be determined by a systematic survey of surviving MSS that has yet to be attempted). MSS of this kind were certainly expensive, but so too were printed books. Yet professional *chirographical bookmaking had undoubtedly retreated to an assemblage of niche markets that was to be further eroded by advances in printing—particularly the arrival of the *steam press in the early 19th century and a concurrent sharp decline in the cost of printing paper (*see* **10, 11**)—and then by the transfer of many scribal functions from the male clerk to the female typist. Music copyists survived longer, but even they nowadays are to be found at a computer keyboard. The theatre prompter continued with his copying of *promptbooks and actors' 'sides' until well into the 19th century, by which time, in Britain, most of the standard repertoire could be acquired in cheap multiple sets from various booksellers such as Lacy's, *French's, and Dicks's. What continued, as already mentioned, was the preparation and circulation of texts by their authors in small handwritten editions or single copies circulated under supervision. A vast amount of writing between the 18th and 20th centuries still reached its readers in exactly this way, sometimes because it was not acceptable to the press, but more often because that was the way authors or transcribers preferred it.

One not atypical career was that of Roger North (1653–1734), a prolific author of biographies and works on music, whose magnum opus is his vast historiographical *Examen*. North continually returned to and revised his writings and held many in multiple copies; yet, he seems to have had no desire to see them in print. Those that did appear were published in edited form by family members after his death. This may have been what he wanted, but it makes more sense to see that family as his intended audience, or to classify him as an author who wrote primarily for himself with no particular desire for readers, except just possibly a generalized 'posterity'. Around 1703 Celia Fiennes opened her account of her travels: 'As this was never designed, soe not likely to fall into the hands of any but my near relations, there needs not much to be said to excuse or recommend it' (Fiennes, 1). Newton's alchemical and theological writings were preserved for private use in careful MS copies: only his scientific ones went to the press. Perhaps the purest examples of composing for personal gratification are writers of diaries. In many recorded cases, the diary, however laboriously compiled, is destroyed before death, having always been intended for the writer alone. There are also cases of writing consciously performed for ritual sacrifice. At Spenser's funeral, fellow poets threw elegies into the grave, together with the quills with which they had been written. D. G. Rossetti buried MS poems with his wife, Elizabeth Siddal, but later thought better of it and had them retrieved.

Moreover, it should not be forgotten that for many writers the preferred form of publication was performance. This was the norm in the ancient world, when the public reading was the means by which most work became known, and only a small proportion was ever available in published form. In the theatre, this has always been the case. Shakespeare is often held to have had little concern for any written dissemination of his plays, though this view has recently been challenged. Clearly, there have always been authors in other genres who preferred the classical tradition. Kafka saw hardly any of his work in print during his lifetime, but he enjoyed reading it aloud to his circle of close friends. Kafka's first printed texts were largely compiled by one of those friends (Max Brod) from his disorganized MSS after his death. Members of the clergy have always devoted a great deal of their energy to the writing of sermons, often on a weekly basis. Although those by recognized stars of the pulpit—or those produced for some shining occasion—might then be printed or recorded in *shorthand, and some might be lent or sold on to colleagues, the vast bulk were discarded, if not immediately after delivery, at least on the retirement or death of their authors. Most academic and public lectures suffered the same fate. In some cases those of great philosophers, such as Wittgenstein, or writers, such as Coleridge, and scientists are known only from the notes taken by their students or members of their audience.

Other writers were keen to be read, but wanted to choose by whom and under what circumstances—what Ezell has conceptualized for early modern Britain as 'social authorship'. This would include the more literary stratum of letter writers, such as *Walpole. He cultivated correspondence as an art form intended for preservation, but always directed to particular recipients and their immediate circles, with whom they would be assumed to share the pleasures of the epistolary text. It is most unlikely that Walpole foresaw the accumulative passion of W. S. *Lewis. Hopkins, mentioned earlier, circulated new work through the post to a small circle of friends who were mostly fellow poets. For him, as for many other non-professional writers of his and earlier times, authorship was a vital means of intellectual and aesthetic exchange. Thomas Campion's Latin epigrams contain several pieces chiding fellow neo-Latin poets for refusing to circulate their verse except to intimates. In the 18th century, the works of his distinguished successor Anthony Alsop had to be retrieved after his death from copies sent to friends.

For some writers, the management and circulation of their MSS required them to acquire the skills of both the librarian and the publisher. Bach must have filled a good-sized room of his home in Leipzig with the scores and parts for his cantatas alone. In other cases, one detects an almost fetishistic devotion to the handwritten word, often evident in the care involved in its presentation and preservation. Emily Dickinson is one famous example of a hoarder and decorator of her MSS. Other writers surprise by the care taken with their MSS, even when intended for the press. Kipling would write in a special *Indian ink on a sheet of high-quality paper and tie the sheets together with a ribbon. It was clearly the initial inscription, not the printed outcome, that represented for him the perfect embodiment of the imagined word.

4 Conclusion

The transition of textual work from the handwritten word to various forms of mechanical and electronic reproduction did not, in many cases, make much difference either to the attitudes of the worker or to how the product was used by its purchaser; but there are ways in which the effect of the 'meaningful surface' of MSS differs from that created by *typography or electronography. The most ambitious attempt to theorize those differences is that of the Jesuit scholar *Ong, for whom the chirographic text embodies a presence-rich 'secondary orality', anchoring it firmly in the world of human interaction. In contrast, the printed text reduces language to a 'thing-like status' and living knowledge to 'cold non-human facts' in a way that is inherently authoritarian. Certainly, there are degrees of overlap in both cases. A perfectly formed Renaissance italic hand or a flawlessly rounded 19th-century *copperplate achieves a suppression of individuality far greater than that of the freewheeling typography of *L'Estrange's late 17th-century *Observators* with their idiosyncratic intermingling of capitals, italic, and *black letter and free use of brackets and of capitalization for emphasis. Yet Ong's general point is a fair one.

There is something remote and impersonal about a well-constructed typographic page that is the price it exacts for permitting us to read it at high speed. Few reading experiences can, on the other hand, be more intense than that of a great poem or musical work written out in the script of its creator. The late Patrick O'Brian's last, uncompleted novel was brought out in an edition with a reproduction of the MS and a type transcript on facing pages. The MS is a corrected working draft, not a fair *copy, but instinct with the human face of authorship. The corresponding typography, by contrast, is sober and inexpressive, but of course much clearer—and one suspects that most readers of the volume quickly revert to it once they become engrossed in the narrative.

BIBLIOGRAPHY

H. Amory, 'The Trout and the Milk: An Ethnobibliographical Talk', *HLB* NS 7 (1996), 50–65

P. Beal, *Index of English Literary Manuscripts*, vol. 1: *1450–1625* (2 parts); vol. 2: *1625–1700* (2 parts) (1980–93)

— *In Praise of Scribes* (1998)

A. Blair, 'Note Taking as an Art of Transmission', *Critical Inquiry*, 31 (2004–5), 85–107

S. Colclough, '"A Grey Goose Quill and an Album": The Manuscript Book and Text Transmission 1820–1850', in *Owners, Annotators and the Signs of Reading*, ed. R. Myers *et al.* (2005)

M. Ezell, *Social Authorship and the Advent of Print* (1999)

C. Fiennes, *The Journeys*, ed. C. Morris (1947)

E. Havens, *Commonplace Books* (2001)

H. Love, *Scribal Publication in Seventeenth-Century England* (1993)

— 'Oral and Scribal Texts in Early Modern England', in *CHBB* 4

A. F. Marotti, *Manuscript, Print and the English Renaissance Lyric* (1995)

D. F. McKenzie, 'Speech–manuscript–print', in *New Directions in Textual Studies*, ed. D. Oliphant and R. Bradford (1990)

D. McKitterick, *Print, Manuscript and the Search for Order, 1450–1830* (2003)

W. Notestein and F. H. Relf, *Commons Debates for 1629* (1921)

P. O'Brian, *The Final Unfinished Voyage of Jack Aubrey* (2004)

W. J. Ong, SJ, *Orality and Literacy* (1982)

J. W. Saunders, '"The Stigma of Print": A Note on the Social Bases of Tudor Poetry', *Essays in Criticism*, 1 (1951), 139–64

H. R. Woudhuysen, *Sir Philip Sidney and the Circulation of Manuscripts, 1558–1640* (1996)

14 Printed Ephemera

MICHAEL HARRIS

1 Introduction

The category of ephemera forms an elusive, sometimes contentious, element in the output of print. The aim of this essay is not to attempt to describe everything that can be identified as ephemera, but rather to trace the category's porous boundaries and, in particular, to suggest how different forms have, over time, changed in their relationship to the book. Ephemera challenges definition, and studies have tended to locate the material at the fringes of everyday life. The general sense of marginality is reinforced by the flux of *advertisements and notices, concerned for example with pizza delivery and weight-loss clinics, which clog up the postal services. Indeed, whatever the extent of the electronic revolution (see **19**), it has not undermined, and in many respects has multiplied, the variety of fugitive or ephemeral print.

Implicit in the definition of printed ephemera as marginal is the notion of a great sea of flimsy print continuously washing up against the sturdy breakwaters of the book—that the book and the printed non-book are two aspects of the same thing. In this notion, the book, as the *codex, identified by its binding, its bulk, and its capacity and manufacture for indefinite preservation, is a distinct entity. It is a pragmatic view that has clear benefits to the individuals and institutions seeking to construct a library and preserve its contents. One of the problems with the dialectic between ephemera and books, however, is that the book, though obviously distinct on the shelf, is itself an inherently insecure component of *print culture. The book as a form is usually placed at the top of a hierarchy of print, standing at the pinnacle of a pyramid of output that broadens out to the flat base of printed ephemera. However, this seems less than realistic, given the ephemeral nature of many books (see SURVIVAL RATES); moreover, their own boundaries with other forms are often insecure, blurring and fading over time. Within print culture, there has been a continuous process of reassessment, which (mainly through collection) has brought a range of non-book material into a new conceptual alignment with the book and suggested the limitations of the current use of the term 'ephemera'.

2 Some definitions

As currently formulated, ephemera are usually identified in terms of their physical characteristics. Their primary form is as a single piece of paper, although this can be extended to a *sheet folded into a limited, but not usually defined, number of pages. However, this is not a hard and fast rule over the historical period of print; *telephone directories or *railway timetables may also be identified as ephemera in book form on the basis of their content. Typically unbound though often in *wrappers, ephemera were usually limited to a day-to-day use and had disposal or destruction as their likely end. This applied particularly to the enormous category of printed advertisements. Even so, the characteristic of disposability has its own problems. Printed ephemera were sometimes produced to be collected and even preserved. This was the case, for example, with cigarette cards as well as with the memorials of such historic events as the battle of Blenheim, the death of Nelson, or the Great Exhibition of 1851. The durability of ephemera through a growing range of individual collections is discussed below.

If the physical characteristics of material lumped under the heading of ephemera are hard to identify,

The spread of ephemera and *display types: *playbills, *posters, and *broadsides painted by John Orlando Parry in his *London Street Scene* (1835), also known as *The Posterman*.

establishing the chronology of ephemeral print's production is equally problematic. Much writing on the subject has emphasized the material's production side. In this context, the business of the *jobbing printer and developments in printing and paper technology are crucial (*see* **10, 11**). Both these elements offer a way into the history of the subject and a framework for its analysis; however, they also create a tendency to push the development of forms of ephemeral material into the 19th and 20th centuries, which become, by implication, an age of ephemera. Nobody suggests that such material was not produced before 1800; but the almost total loss of many or most of the early forms—whose rarity is marked by the high commercial value of such items as advertisements for night soil removal—has created some distortion. Similarly, a historical focus on the business organization of printers engaged in the mixed production of books, serials, and jobbing printing has done little, if anything, to augment our understanding of the ephemeral materials themselves.

The modern chronology of the output of ephemeral print must be weighed against the huge scale of material produced across the early modern period. One factor that drove the increase in printed ephemera was the erratic but continuous move from MS to print (*see* **13**). From the early 17th century, serial information, including news, moved from handwritten copies to a printed equivalent (*see* CORANTO; MAGAZINE, ORIGINS OF; NEWSBOOK; NEWSLETTERS). For other kinds of pragmatic material, both freely distributed and paid for, it is extremely difficult to follow the process that changed their character. Advertisements in late 17th-century newspapers indicate that several members of the book trade specialized in the production and supply of printed *forms geared to tax collection and other kinds of bureaucratic organization. By 1700, print was the natural medium for *handbills and *posters, at least in London, and the lines of serial print were beginning to extend across the nation. When Ned Ward visited the Royal Exchange in 1699 during the course of his ramble, he found the pillars and every available wall space covered with posters and advertisements, the bulk probably in printed form. There are no pictorial representations of this scene complete with its burden of fly-posting. In fact, the general exclusion of ephemeral print is a feature of illustrations of London's built environment at this time. Set against this are the views offered in 19th-century prints. In this period, the fascination with the output of the developing technology of print, combined with a growing interest in the lower levels of print culture, supported the production of some striking images depicting the mass of print displayed in public spaces.

Across the entire modern period, a huge and expanding volume of print in all its forms was in circulation. In the attempt to get some sort of *bibliographical control over the composition and character of ephemera, scholars have undertaken a process of listing. This has usually been done by constructing sequences made up of main physical forms and of the themes around which ephemeral print has clustered, for example, business, transport, leisure and entertainment, and home life. The *Encyclopedia of Ephemera* originally compiled by Maurice Rickards, and edited and completed by Michael Twyman, offers a long alphabetical list made up of categories and describes, among other items, 'Fly-paper', 'Quack advertising', 'Telephone card', and 'Zoëtrope strip/disc' (an early method of creating the illusion of movement through revolving pictures). If the *Encyclopedia* does not define the field, at least it makes a heroic attempt at laying out an impressive range of representative samples and at providing a useful, inevitably selective, series of bibliographies. An underlying problem with this and alternative listings is that they tend to create an artificial homogeneity in which all the selected non-book materials have an equivalent importance. An alternative approach maintains the interest in form, but focuses on the ways in which the separation of blocks of material has come about, in particular through the process of collection.

In its raw state, printed ephemera can be seen as a huge and alarming heap of materials—the trivial and the profound, the commercial and the exhortatory—jumbled together in the context of the confused variety of everyday life. Supply-side analysis emphasizes this diversity and invariably highlights the technology of production and its relation to what could be done in the *printing office. Ephemeral print cannot be defined through the character of the organization or business through which it was produced, however. Any analysis of collecting ephemera, on the other hand, begins with the idea of consumption and indicates the ways in which the conditions for the identification and classification of non-book materials were created. Across the entire period in which the proliferation and diversification of print was taking place, collectors began to offer a gloss on the meanings and uses of an apparently inchoate mass of individual items. Through their intervention, large areas of what is still included with printed ephemera have moved out of the shadowy hinterland of the trivial and disposable to another level where a new set of definitions is required. A few examples follow, each of them having a flexible link to the general category of street literature.

3 Collecting ephemera: ballads, chapbooks, almanacs, and newspapers

The street was and remains one of the most dynamic sites for the dispersal of ephemeral printed products. During the Victorian period, the average metropolitan *flâneur* could expect to be offered dozens of printed items, advertisements, and handbills during a stroll along Oxford Street in London. In the 17th and 18th centuries, huge quantities of handbills—medical, political (in vast numbers during elections), or commercial—were passed around the streets of London and its suburbs; much of the material was entirely free, and so it remains in the 21st century. The wastage was almost total and the survival of single copies, used as bookmarks or wrapping paper, is almost miraculously unusual. The same can be said of posters, which were once a prominent feature of the urban environment but have since largely disappeared. Even so, some of the materials distributed at street level have survived to become part of the historical printed *archive.

All of the street-based material noted above was free and instantly disposable, and hence had an exceedingly short life expectancy. At the same time, within the flow of street-based print was to be found the commercial presence of paid-for material, such as *ballads, *almanacs, newspapers, and *chapbooks; these represented a significant link between the respectable book trade and the popular consumer. Such products satisfy the definitions of ephemerality: their distribution matched the output of handbills in scale and informality, and their survival was just as uncertain. They formed part of the retail process that ran through the street. The presence of this paid-for material and of its *hawkers as part of the notorious hyperactivity of the London streets took on a respectable visual dimension through the publication of a series of images representing a cross-section of street traders. From the 1690s, the most frequently reprinted images were those produced by Marcellus Laroon the elder. His lifelike portraits of street dealers, probably from around Covent Garden, published in *The Cryes of the City of London Drawne after the Life* (1687), included some of those whose uncertain livelihood was drawn from the open-air sale of ephemeral forms of print. They included a pair of ballad sellers, an almanac dealer, a newspaper seller and a pedlar whose tray, filled with 'knicknackatories', probably contained a selection of chapbooks. It is this range of generally disposable material that provides the focus of what follows.

Ballads, chapbooks, almanacs, and newspapers were issued under the direction of core members of the book trade working within the orbit of the *Stationers' Company. The trade had a presence in the street through the booths and stalls long established in London, while at least some of the hawkers were full or part-time employees of booksellers. Despite these formal arrangements, the products the hawkers sold were, in form and character, intended for the medium of the street, and as such were cheap, short term, and disposable. Though they were produced in very large quantities, their survival was far from assured. Indeed, at the point of purchase and use, it was hard to distinguish them from the other paper items that ebbed and flowed within most urban centres. The question is: how did some components of this material take on an aggregate status over time that has required a different formulation in relation to the book?

The first collectors of ephemeral print were attracted to the street-based, popular character of the material. Individuals—influenced by a variety of cultural and commercial motives—began the process of gathering and preservation, which gradually gave elements of ephemera a place within contemporary private and public collections. Collectors' ideas about popular print were inevitably affected by changing social, political, and economic forces. However, the initial impulse to accumulate and safeguard this material formed part of a more general phenomenon of collecting that, during the 17th century, characterized the activities of the endlessly curious and acquisitive sector of middling society known as virtuosos.

The cultural importance of this amorphous group in the construction of what has been described as a bourgeois public sphere was manifested most fully in the social environment of the *coffee house. Such public spaces helped develop the shared interests of its patrons, most notably through serial print, which formed an integral part of coffee house culture. That culture gave rise to the circumstances in which individuals collected and preserved forms of printed material that would otherwise have been destroyed (often by being put to other uses, such as wrapping food or doing service in the lavatory) along with the mass of free promotional material handed about in the street. Collectors in the 17th and 18th centuries created the conditions for an expanded interest in ephemeral print, which is only now moving into the mainstream of respectable scholarship.

Indeed, the act of collecting became a mechanism for repositioning cultural value of the slight and disposable literature of the streets: this is most evident with regard to two popular forms, ballads and chapbooks. Both were produced on a substantial scale at very low cost, and as such might have been thought unlikely to form part of the collecting interests of the book-centred library owner within the social elite. Ballads and chapbooks were published during the 17th century under a monopoly grant by a group of publishers, partners in the *Ballad Stock, organized through the Stationers' Company. However, because the grant did not prevent the intervention of others in this profitable and accessible area of the market, the ballad became the focus of long-running commercial struggles. The *broadside ballad was printed in *black letter on one or both sides of the sheet, usually in double columns, and sold for 1d. Ballad verse, often related to current events and combining information with entertainment, was usually printed under a *woodcut pictorial heading. The scale of output was vast: about 3,000 titles were recorded in the *Stationers' Register during the 17th century; many were frequently reprinted and *press runs were large. At his death in 1664 one publisher, Charles Tias, had about 37,500 ballad sheets at his house and shop on London Bridge. Such materials were eminently disposable. Although, among the lower social levels, their short-term destruction might be delayed because such publications were commonly used for decoration or to teach reading, their ultimate fate was almost certain.

The same might be said of chapbooks, which increased in number over the 17th century and probably overtook ballads in the scale of their distribution. Sold on the street, chapbooks came in a range of *formats varying from *duodecimos of 4 pages to *quartos of 24 or more; the books sold for between 2d. and 6d. Also published by partners in the Ballad Stock and their competitors, chapbooks reached a prodigious level of output. For example, a 1707 inventory of the goods of the publisher Josiah Blare identified his holdings of 31,002 'great and small books', kept in his shop at the sign of the Looking Glass on London

Bridge. Blare was one of the group of printers and publishers involved in the chapbook market: the identity of members of the group is often obscure, but they may have numbered around twenty. Their commercial activity suggests the distribution of an enormous volume of material, mostly produced in London and sold throughout the nation by long-distance pedlars, commonly called *chapmen, as well as urban hawkers and *colporteurs. The chapbook was cheap, ubiquitous, and highly ephemeral. Copies from the 17th and 18th centuries have survived in very small numbers; by the 19th century, the form and its sellers, as recorded by Henry Mayhew, were disappearing as new social and economic conditions overtook the street trade.

A scattering of ballads and chapbooks, along with other kinds of ephemeral print, would have survived in miscellaneous private and public collections; however, because these holdings were constantly dislocated by death or changes in collecting policy, the historical analysis of print relies heavily on the survival of focused accumulations of such material by private individuals. The most important of the early collectors was *Pepys, whose broad interest in printed material extended to the products hawked around the streets of London. His collection of ballads, which he added to the collection made by *Selden, contained at his death 1,775 sheets bound up in volumes and organized by subject. His collection of chapbooks numbered 215 titles, in a variety of formats, bound in eight volumes classified according to trade usage as 'Penny godlinesses', 'Penny merriments', and 'Vulgaria'. Pepys's collection of street literature comprises only a very small part of the total output, but it represents a means by which the ephemeral literature of the period can begin to be identified and assessed. The collection remained intact and passed, at the death of his heir in 1724, to his old college, Magdalene at Cambridge, where it has remained. As one historian put it, 'The convoy of wagons which took the 3000 books and their twelve presses to Cambridge was a sealed train carrying Pepys's reputation to posterity' (*ODNB*). Among the books in the presses or *book cases were the popular ephemeral items he had so carefully preserved.

Another important collector of street literature was *Bagford, a shoemaker turned bookseller, antiquary, and pioneering bibliographer. From his base in Holborn in London, he supplied the leading collectors of the day, including Pepys and the omnivorous Robert *Harley, with ballads and more conventional forms of print. His own interests as a scholar centred on a never-completed history of printing and printed books. His own collecting was geared to this project: he acquired a large quantity of title- and other pages from derelict books (later used by *Ames for his *Typographical Antiquities*), as well as a steady flow of black-letter ballads published from the Restoration onwards. At his death, the two volumes of ballads were acquired by Harley; they subsequently passed through a series of private collections, including that of John *Ker, the 3rd duke of Roxburghe, before the *British Museum Library purchased the collection, now in four volumes, in 1845.

Ballads had been entering the principal public collections from early in the 18th century, as libraries acquired quantities of other material in which many forms of ephemeral print were embedded. The collections of *Wood, Richard *Rawlinson, *Douce, and *Percy were among those acquired by the *Bodleian Library in Oxford. By the 19th century, institutions secured a critical mass of material (not always permanently), creating the conditions for research into it. The formation of societies (such as the *Percy Society) and the publication of lists and *bibliographies of street ballads began to move this genre of ephemera into a new relation with the printed archive.

A related category of highly ephemeral street literature was the almanac. Possessing a broader social appeal, it stood midway between recurrent forms, produced to supply an apparently continuous demand, and serial commodities, such as the newspaper. Among the most perennial products of print culture, the almanac was constructed around the calendar of saints' days and holidays laid out in the preliminaries to the Bible or to the *Book of Common Prayer. By the mid-17th century, it was produced and sold either as a small-format leaflet of up to 24 pages or as a *folio broadside printed on one side of a sheet for public display. The Stationers' Company held the monopoly for the calendar, and it licensed production of a changing list of almanacs under approximately fifteen different titles. These were sold in November each year in very large quantities. By the 1660s, an annual total of 300,000 to 400,000 copies were printed, enough for one in every three families in the nation. The numbers exceeded the production of even ballads and chapbooks, suggesting a pattern of consumption that reached far across the social scale. The Stationers' commercial interest in this huge output was sustained throughout the 18th century and defended by a continuous and partially successful rearguard action against a variety of street-level interlopers.

The almanac was essentially ephemeral. Owners would most likely have got rid of it at the end of the year it covered, which meant the almost inevitable destruction of most copies. Aside from the earliest issues, out-of-date almanacs were not sought out by collectors; the relocation of this highly disposable form from the street to the library was tied to changing characteristics of its content and use. First, the calendar was supplemented by an increasing amount of material on a range of practical or entertaining subjects. Predictions of all sorts, the dates of local fairs, historical lists, timetables for gardeners, and medical information became part of the genre's collective and individual appeal. Such material did not lose its currency every year, and it became common for all of the Stationers' Company almanac titles to be bound up together in a decorative binding to be added to the library shelf. Some stationers themselves may have sold cumulative volumes in book form as a commercial enterprise. Secondly, from the late 17th century it became increasingly common for copies to be interleaved with blank pages for use as a *diary or a personal record of events. This practice extended from the middling and elite to shopkeepers and farmers—indeed, to anyone with business to transact. Many surviving 17th- and 18th-century diaries were entered in the convenient framework of the almanac. The ephemeral form therefore took on a dual character, both as a throwaway item and as a durable component of the library. Nowadays, this duality can be identified in the publication of *Old Moore's Almanac* on one hand and **Whitaker's* and **Wisden Cricketers'* almanacs on the other.

The transmission of street materials through collections, and the potential duality of such items, also characterize the newspaper. The most complex of the forms still (curiously) considered as printed ephemera, the newspaper poses a number of problems aggravated by the tendency to conceive of ephemera as constituting virtually all non-book print. The difficulty of locating the newspaper within the printed archive is related to the defensive position adopted by librarians hoping to secure themselves from the onset of an avalanche of print. Newspapers' demands in terms of collection, storage, and access are, it must be admitted, almost too much to bear. But problems also arise from the difficulty of conceptualizing an alternative to the established hierarchy of book-down print. The idea that the newspaper is simply a disposable item along with, say, a knitting pattern, railway ticket, or bumper sticker is, regrettably entrenched.

Although the *Encyclopedia of Ephemera* is a useful guide to a wide range of obscure material, it nevertheless does have some significant limitations that reflect common problems in the study of ephemeral print. Ballads, chapbooks, and almanacs each have an entry, as does the newspaper. Its entry states that 'a study of the subject as a whole is virtually impossible', then provides a series of sub-headings: 'First and last issues', 'Mastheads', 'Headlines/front pages', 'Commemoratives', 'Improvised newspapers', 'Mock newspapers', 'Language minority newspapers', 'Ships' newspapers', and 'Curiosities'. The entry embodies the idea of the newspaper as a heap of discrete copies and fits it into a conventionally subordinate position in the hierarchy of print. There is no doubt that, at the point of consumption, the newspaper is an entirely ephemeral product. Created for the day, or some other limited period, it is produced for immediate use and, to some extent, predicated on equally immediate disposal. Its content is as current as possible and its format, geared to cheapness and the exigencies of competition, has a built-in disposability. This sense of immediacy is heightened by the presence of an increasing load of advertising of all sorts. After fulfilling their initial purposes, newspaper copies were applied to a range of mixed and largely non-literary purposes. By the early 18th century, these conventionally included lighting pipes, lining pie dishes, and fulfilling the needs of the jakes. As the scale of output grew and costs fell (following the repeal of mid-19th-century taxes), the newspaper began to manifest itself more clearly as litter. Victorian commuters arriving at the main London stations left behind huge quantities of cast-off copies to be thrown away or recycled. In this context, the association of newspapers with printed ephemera seems hard to resist.

However, the notion of instant disposability misses the point. To its early producers, the newspaper was a collectable form. Pages were numbered consecutively from issue to issue, and annual *indexes and cumulative *title-pages were often given away to encourage people to collect them. The inescapable fact about the newspaper is that it is a serial product and, in this respect, cannot be disposed of. Throw one away and the periodical flow will bring another one along behind. Periodicity is the mechanism and time the dimension within which the newspaper functions; these are the core characteristics that put the form at the heart of print culture. Continuously present since the first such London publication in 1620, the proliferation and expansion of newspapers have overtaken and dwarfed all the other forms of print put together. The numbers themselves are complex, and indeed alarming. By 1700, about 30 serial titles were in publication, producing a yearly total of more than 1,400 issues. If each is taken to have been printed in the low average of 300 copies per issue, the total annual output would have amounted to just below half a million copies. In 1750, the proprietors of the London titles, with the representatives of a widening circle of local papers, purchased about 7.5 million tax stamps, a number rising annually (see STAMP ACTS; TAXES ON KNOWLEDGE). The acceleration of output in the 19th century—linked directly to developments in the technology of print (see 11), as well as to the repeal of taxes—ushered in the mass market of the next century. The *Daily Mail* became the first *Fleet Street paper to achieve circulation of a million copies for a single issue. At the same time, the newspaper moved beyond the orbit of the relatively conventional and sluggish book trade into its own industrial system. It was a sign of the times when, in 1937, the book trade's much-venerated business organization was retitled the Worshipful Company of Stationers and Newspaper Makers.

Despite this remarkable growth in output, the status and importance of the newspaper remained contested issues. At the end of the 19th century, for example, the idea of the newspaper press as the Fourth Estate was undermined by forms of commercialism rooted in the populist techniques of the new journalism. This undermining promoted the newspaper's identification with ephemera. The fact that there is still no general, comprehensive history of English newspapers suggests that the process by which the newspaper was brought into the orbit of collectors and collections was more problematic than in the case of the less bulky and challenging forms of street print.

Collections of newspapers began to be formed in the mid-17th century when their importance as a contemporary record of events was first recognized. At the outbreak of the English Civil War, the bookseller *Thomason was pressed by Charles I in 1640 to compile an archive of contemporary materials by collecting *newsbooks and related current materials as they appeared. Thomason continued the work until the Restoration, by which time he had collected some 30,000 *tracts bound up in more than 2,000 volumes. Thomason died without receiving his commercial reward, but his cumbersome collection remained intact, passing through a variety of hands before its purchase in 1762 for the library of *George III. It subsequently formed a part of the king's gift of that library to the British Museum.

The wholesale collection of newspapers by a private individual became an increasingly hopeless enterprise; nonetheless, during the late 17th century, runs of the *London Gazette* (1665 to date) were occasionally advertised for sale to the public, and the binding up of selected titles seems to have remained fairly common. A few individuals have succumbed to the mania of general newspaper collecting. For the most part, however, private collections have usually had a specific purpose. *Burney—schoolmaster, book collector, and noted classical scholar—maintained an interest in the theatre, filling 400 volumes with newspaper cuttings, *playbills, and prints on theatrical matters. From 1781, he filled a further 700 volumes with a retrospective collection of newspapers obtained at first from coffee houses. Similarly, the antiquary and printer *Nichols developed a particular interest in biography, publishing obituaries in the *Gentleman's Magazine* of which he was the proprietor. By the time of his own death, he had built up a collection of newspapers that filled 238 volumes. Such projects indicated the engagement of a later generation of middling virtuosos with the serial publication of news and information. At the same time, from the 18th century, increasing numbers of people developed more limited collections of cuttings, adapted to their own personal use and assembled as part of their private record-keeping.

Although the personal collection of newspapers remained a fairly quixotic enterprise, a semi-automatic accumulation of this material was taking place in London and across the kingdom. From the late 17th century, the tendency for newspapers to pile up in public spaces (such as coffee houses), where access was offered to large numbers of readers, created drifts of serials. Without an active policy of disposal, serial collection was almost unavoidable. When, in the 1850s, Peele's coffee house and hotel in Fleet Street attempted to sell its runs of major titles dating back to the 1770s, the collection weighed about six tons. It was eventually sold as waste. In political departments, lawyers' offices, and businesses and institutions of all sorts, the steady increase in semi-automatic collection continued to take place.

However, for the newspaper and related serials to become more closely identified with the printed archive, a great deal more than the isolated action of individuals and casual, often unwitting, accumulation by institutions was needed. A major development in the formation of a comprehensive and systematic collection came when the British Museum was established in 1753. Even so, the process by which newspapers were incorporated into the library was long and painful. As with other forms of non-book material, the initial intake was both retrospective and marginal to the concerns of the Trustees. The Thomason collection of newsbooks and related items entered the library through royal bequest. Similarly, in 1818, the reluctant acceptance of the Burney newspapers was predicated on the purchase of his huge library of classical texts in book form. The Trustees refused to buy the Nichols newspapers, and, although some part eventually came to the British Museum, the bulk was not acquired by the Bodleian Library until 1865, the same year that the library's Hope Collection of Newspapers—formed by John Thomas Hope (1761–1854) and bequeathed to the Bodleian by Frederick William Hope (1797–1862)—had its first published catalogue.

During the early decades of the 19th century, the British Museum library became partially reconciled to housing the current output of newspapers, and made arrangements with the Stamp Office to receive copies of papers deposited at Somerset House in London for tax purposes. As the volume of output increased, conflict arose among British Museum officials over the handling of newspapers within their book-centred collections. As the whole collection was extended and overhauled, *Panizzi's appointment led to disagreements over the purchase of foreign newspapers (and over much else as well). In 1873, however, as the arrangements for taking in current titles were becoming problematic, the legal requirement for the deposit of books was extended to newspapers. The huge build-up in library holdings that accompanied this decision rapidly filled the Museum's newspaper reading room, initially opened in 1885. The imbalance between the scale of the collections of newspapers and of books was becoming critical, and, at the end of the century the Trustees sought powers to disperse the foreign and local papers to their places of origin. A bill in 1899 proposing this measure failed, and a new solution was devised to remove the threat of the rising tide of newspapers and related materials. Land in Hendon at Colindale in North London was purchased; in 1910 it became the base for what is now the British Library Newspaper Library. It was a symbolic as well as an actual separation. On one hand, the split tended to emphasize the division between print in serial and book form. The two could not easily cohabit in a library setting, and the division lent credence to the idea of non-book ephemera. On the other hand, the creation of the Newspaper Library gave a new emphasis to the whole range of serial output as part of the national collection. Over time, the relocated material became a focal point within the printed archive, with its own storage and reading space as well as a specialist staff, and increasingly sophisticated mechanisms for collection and access.

4 Other collections

This sort of redefinition through collection and integration gave serials, along with other forms of street material, a distinct identity. The notion of 'printed ephemera' could no longer accommodate materials that had become major elements in the printed archive. At the same time, from the 19th century, the view of what material was collectable and susceptible to cultural analysis had expanded. The vast, amorphous heap of print—generated over five centuries and relating to nearly every form of human activity—began to take on a clearer definition. The very act of identifying such selected elements within material generally regarded as ephemeral created a mechanism for the continuous reassessment of its value and use.

Pepys had included tobacco labels and trade cards in his London collection, and Bagford had a variety of similar scraps in his volumes. By 1800, a widening spectrum of individuals was becoming involved in collecting ephemeral material. *Grangerizing, the extra-illustration of books, encouraged publishers to produce, and collectors to seek out, printed materials, drawn from an eclectic range of sources, to augment and personalize their volumes. Such items might include not only pictures of people and of places, but also oddities such as the printed labels once sold by booksellers and printers at winter fairs on the ice of the frozen river Thames. Contemporary and historic material was also sought after during the middle-class vogue for making *scrapbooks and *albums. Increasingly, more focused collections of ephemeral printed pieces were also assembled around such items as playing cards, *bookplates, stamps, matchbox labels, *bill heads, and trade cards, some of which came to be housed in major libraries.

The recognition in the 19th and early 20th centuries of the cultural and historical value of the vast and increasing range of print led to a more generalized identification of the scale and character of printed ephemera. This shift of perspective was encouraged by the creation of huge, open-ended collections in Britain and America. In England, the main line of interest was generated by John *Johnson, 'printer, ephemerist, and classical scholar' (ODNB). Johnson started working at the *Oxford University Press in 1915 and, in 1925, was appointed printer to the university, a post he held until his retirement in 1946. His contribution to the Oxford Press was considerable, but his long-term achievement as a collector of printed ephemera was equally great, if not greater. Taking an entirely open-ended approach, he sought out every form of fugitive print that was part of the 'paraphernalia of our day-to-day lives' and destined for the waste-paper basket after use (*ODNB*). His huge collection came to include more than a million items, mainly dating from the 18th century to his final cut-off date of 1939, though he had 16th-century material as well. It has been incorporated with several large specialist collections of watch papers, valentines, cigarette cards, and bank notes, which have remained intact as subsets within the collection. Johnson himself devised 700 headings for his material, which was already well known by the 1930s. Holbrook Jackson described it in *Signature* in 1935 as 'a Sanctuary of Printing' (*ODNB*).

Part of Johnson's definition of ephemeral print was that it included anything a library would not accept as a gift; the Bodleian Library adopted a position in relation to anything identified as ephemera that echoed the British Museum's response to the newspaper. Collections that included ephemera—such as those accumulated by *Burton, Wood, and *Hearne—had long been identified as acceptable acquisitions. However, even in the 1930s a policy of exclusion continued to be applied, and moves were made to clear out calendars, advertisements, and modern illuminated items such as certificates and commendations as unwanted ephemera. The John Johnson collection, as it became known, remained in a semi-detached state in two rooms at Oxford University Press. It was only in 1968 that the Bodleian was reconciled to its existence and the whole mighty accumulation was transferred to new accommodation within the library under a specified curator, in the first instance the scholar and librarian Michael L. Turner.

The metamorphosis of the John Johnson collection both represented and contributed to a flowering of interest in the fugitive output of the press, both as an area of research in its own right and as an increasingly integrated component of academic studies. The collection offered a line of systematic access to the many varieties of print. General studies of the material in it started in the 1960s, and the collection itself has contributed directly to the flow of published information, most recently through a catalogue of its holdings of commercial ephemera (*A Nation of Shopkeepers*, 2001).

In 1975 Maurice Rickards set up the Ephemera Society in London; subsequently, national groups have been formed in America (1980), Australia (1985), and Canada (1988). Exhibitions, lectures, and publications have ensued. At the same time, a wide range of academic and other institutions have become involved in assembling and organizing their own collections. The *Encyclopedia* (2000) provided a list of 116 known holdings and, in a few cases, including *Reading University and the *Rare Book School at the University of Virginia, courses on printed ephemera have been incorporated into the study of the *history of the book. Part of this spread of interest in all areas of fugitive print has been the formation of an international network of ephemera dealers. In England, one of the most active was Andrew Block, who first opened a shop in northwest London early in the 20th century where he sold penny *comic books for a halfpenny. In many parts of the world, ephemera fairs in various guises now run in tandem with their book-centred equivalents. *Digitization is beginning to change the subject and its study.

5 Conclusion

'Printed ephemera' is an unstable concept, one that shifts according to the chronology of print, the circumstances of production and consumption, and the status of forms within established collections. The separation of books from the rest of the printed archive and the privileging of the codex—not only as a product intended to be preserved and stored, but also as the primary mechanism for cultural formation—seem increasingly untenable. Major libraries have become more aware of the value and interest of alternative varieties of print, and many artificial boundaries have begun to blur. Books are, in many cases, created from the materials that were produced and distributed in forms usually identified as ephemeral. The ebb and flow of their content in and out of serial publications, for example, gives print a much more fluid character than the serried rows of volumes on the library shelf seem to suggest. Similarly, books are surrounded by concentric circles of print relating to every aspect of their production, sale, and ownership, without which their content can hardly make sense. Book history has moved towards an interest in the reception and social context of print, making the issue of daily experience—and, therefore, of ephemerality—an integral part of its remit. It seems increasingly realistic to consider the products of the press as stretched along a spectrum of print, within which the book has (in physical terms at least) a modest place. In many ways the serial form has primacy in such a reconfiguration, mainly through the force of periodicity and the nature of a continuous sequence of production and consumption. The term 'printed ephemera' still has a value, but it should be used with care.

BIBLIOGRAPHY

[Bodleian Library, Oxford,] *The John Johnson Collection: Catalogue of an Exhibition* (1971)

— *A Nation of Shopkeepers* (2001)

B. Capp, *Astrology and the Popular Press* (1979)

F. Doherty, *A Study in Eighteenth-Century Advertising Method* (1992)

J. W. Ebsworth, ed., *The Bagford Ballads* (2 vols, 1876–8; repr. 1968)

G. K. Fortescue *et al.*, eds., *Catalogue of the Pamphlets, Books, Newspapers and Manuscripts Relating to the Civil War, Commonwealth and Restoration Collected by George Thomason, 1641–1661* (2 vols, 1908)

M. Harris, 'Collecting Newspapers', in *Bibliophily*, ed. M. Harris and R. Myers (1986)

A. Heal, *The Signboards of Old London Shops* (1957)

L. James, *Print and the People, 1819–1951* (1976)

J. Lewis, *Ephemera* (1962)

ODNB

M. Rickards, *Collecting Printed Ephemera* (1988)

— *The Encyclopedia of Ephemera*, ed. M. Twyman *et al.* (2000)

S. Shesgreen, ed., *The Criers and Hawkers of London* (1990)

M. Spufford, *Small Books and Pleasant Histories* (1981)

M. Twyman, *Printing, 1770–1970* (1970; repr. 1998)

E. Ward, *The London-Spy*, intro. R. Straus (1924)

T. Watt, *Cheap Print and Popular Piety, 1550–1640* (1991)

15 Children's Books

ANDREA IMMEL

1 Introduction

The children's book—a work conceived, produced, and marketed for the consumption of a young audience—appeared relatively late in the history of the western European printed book. Although its development is thought to be symptomatic of the so-called discovery of childhood, the emergence of the children's book after the invention of printing in the late 15th century cannot be understood without reference to the history of European education. Improvements in children's reading materials are sparked by educational reforms and by advances in cognitive psychology, as well as by shifts in *literacy rates or by sociopolitical change. Similarly, the evolution of literary works reflecting the way childhood experiences help form children's minds elevated the status of leisure reading. This much-expanded role for imaginative literature in the 19th century became a powerful stimulus to develop the children's market across genres. Finally, advances in the technologies of book production—especially methods for reproducing images and manufacturing edition bindings—made it possible to transform the presentation and packaging of text for children via the *codex and related non-book products (*see* **11, 16, 17**). With the development of an extensive network of special collections of historical children's print and material culture, a comprehensive history of the children's book has become feasible. This essay is intended as a prolegomenon to the enterprise. Focusing on the English-speaking world—the home of one of the oldest and most diverse traditions of publishing for children—the following discussion identifies a range of issues with which a full history of the children's book might engage.

2 Origins and development

Most accounts of Western children's books begin with the genre's 'invention' in the mid-18th century; the dramatic increase in production of juvenile books after that date is said to demonstrate that children were being taken seriously as an audience with special requirements. Nevertheless, previous generations of children not only learned to read, but became highly literate, without such luxury of choice. Examining evidence about children's reading experiences before 1700 contributes to the identification and contextualization of forces that subsequently shaped the genre. To understand the shift in attitudes regarding the child reader's requirements—specifically the displacement of the classical curriculum by new kinds of books—consideration must be given to the changes that occurred long before the 18th century in the cultural construction of childhood, educational provision, class dynamics, family structure, and printing technology.

The long history of the children's book properly begins with the invention of printing, by which time parts of English society had been collectively literate for around a century. Many children learned to read at home, instructed by either a parent or an employer. Because literacy had long been linked with religion, learning the alphabet was an act of devotion. After mastering letters, children were taught how to combine letters into syllables, and syllables into words, then encountered their first texts: basic Latin prayers such as the Paternoster and Creed, the psalms, and the hours. At this stage, boys destined for the ministry, trade, or administration attended school to learn Latin grammar; other children learned to read in their mother tongue. *Ballads and *chansons de geste* might be given to children to spark their interest in reading, although the practice was generally frowned upon. Social reading—that is, reading aloud to an audience—was a favourite form of entertainment and edification (at least in wealthy households). In a society where books were relatively uncommon, the ability to read was highly variable, and works were often intended for audiences of all ages.

During the late 15th and 16th centuries, much of what children read had been in circulation before the invention of printing. By modern standards, few concessions were made to children as readers. Production was dominated by didactic works, including Latin *grammars (by Donatus and others), courtesy literature or *conduct books (e.g. Robert Grosseteste's *Puer ad Mensam*), moral instruction (e.g. *Disticha Catonis*), or *anthologies (e.g. Geoffroy de la Tour Landry's *Book of the Knight of the Tower*, which *Caxton printed in 1484). In time, illustrated abridgements and adaptations of adult texts intended to teach children began to appear. Notable examples include Charles *Estienne's series of illustrated booklets based on Lazare de Baïf's scholarly treatises on Roman antiquities, including *De Re Vestiaria Libellus* (Paris, 1535), and *Holbein's picture bible, *Icones Historiarum Veteris Testamenti* (Lyons, 1547). *Erasmus, Cordier, and Vives attempted to enliven Latin instruction with colloquial dialogues about experiences in the classroom, schoolyard, and street in which the child's voice can be plainly heard. Narrative vernacular fictions were aimed principally at adults, but children almost certainly enjoyed the many works in wide circulation that featured the adventures of young characters, from saints' lives to didactic romances such as the *Seven Sages of Rome*. Some of those popular works, among them the Robin Hood ballads, *Bevis of Southampton*, and *Guy of Warwick*, continued to circulate in *chapbook adaptations, *picture-book versions, and retellings well into the 19th century.

The most notable 17th-century works for children were produced by Puritans and dissenters, who distinguished little children from youth in order to accommodate their actual capabilities and to ensure that children would not be excluded from God's grace should they die before becoming capable of true faith. Yet the Puritans also shaped texts in ways that respected children's autonomy and preserved their freedom of conscience. The result was revolutionary works whose pedagogy was surprisingly child-centred. For example, the *Ludus Literarius* (1612) of John Brinsley, Master of Ashby-de-la-Zouche School,

incorporates progressive teaching techniques for the youngest learners. Among the most influential Western children's books was the *Orbis Sensualium Pictus* (1658) of *Comenius, an advocate of universal education who used his years of pedagogical experience to develop the book's method of teaching Latin via a pictorial *encyclopaedia. In *A Token for Children* (1672), the minister James Janeway held up young saints who died before reaching adolescence as examples for the emulation of his readers, while Bunyan composed emblems for children on familiar, homely subjects.

The rise of the modern children's book is generally seen as coinciding with the Enlightenment, when advances in science, technology, and manufacturing held out the promise of rationally restructuring society for the improvement of mankind. Educational issues were central to discussions of moral and political philosophy during the period; *Locke held that education was the best means of ensuring the continuity of prevailing values from generation to generation, and *Rousseau argued that education should transform society by effecting radical change in the attitudes and behaviour of young people. Early childhood was increasingly viewed as the critical stage of life for shaping the future adult, so that ensuring the quality of elementary instruction took on a new urgency. Yet Isaac Watts is a rare example of an important early 18th-century author who condescended to write for young people and to put his name on the title-pages of his books: most preferred *anonymity, regarding themselves as philanthropists laying the foundations on which a mind could be built. By the 1790s, well-educated literary women such as Anna Letitia Barbauld, Sarah Trimmer, Ellenor Fenn, Lady Fenn, Maria Edgeworth, and Mary Wollstonecraft carved out a space where women writers might exercise their talents in the nation's service. Idealistic (and shrewd) entrepreneurs such as John *Newbery, John *Harris, and Joseph *Johnson ensured that they also turned a profit. Enterprising book-, map-, and print-sellers drove the expansion of the juvenile market, developing an unprecedented range of illustrated materials adapted from existing print formats—from the harlequinade to the jigsaw puzzle and board game —for the pleasurable instruction of children.

The market for children's books expanded and diversified exponentially during the 19th century, due to the ever-increasing numbers of young British subjects being tutored privately at home or educated in Sunday or board schools. Children's publishers who entered the market's fray during this period battled for hearts, minds, and money. Publishers claimed their part of the market by identifying a constituency and providing it with suitable material at a reasonable price, while keeping an eye on the competition. The *Religious Tract Society, Edwin J. Brett, publisher of the blood-and-thunder magazine *Boys of England*, and Henry Cole, in his attempts to elevate the imagination and taste of young readers with the Home Treasury series, all did this. Such major authors as Ruskin and Thackeray wrote original books for children, and Continental writers such as Heinrich Hoffmann and Hans Christian Andersen attained international reputations in translation. Similarly, writers from Captain Marryat to Frances Hodgson Burnett produced narrative fiction (*tract, historical novel, school or adventure story, *Kunstmärchen*, etc.) for periodicals or as separate volumes, and in the process earned handsome livings and won popular acclaim, even celebrity. At the same time, enterprising publishers such as *Routledge and Frederick *Warne built up extensive *backlists of toy books, consisting chiefly of material in the public domain, such as fairy tales and nursery rhymes, reprinted with stylish illustrations (usually without acknowledgement to the artists) and colourfully repackaged in eyecatching covers, thanks to the technological improvements in book production. A parallel trend was the reprinting of modern classics as series of school *prize books.

By World War I, the children's book had developed into a diverse, complex subsystem of fiction and non-fiction genres that paralleled the adult book world. Youngsters in Western industrialized nations could now be provided with specialized books through to their adolescence. Readers could be categorized by age (and by class, sex, ethnicity, disability, and religion as well) to assist in the production of materials that drew young people into appropriate reading communities. These might reflect the educational priorities of institutions or represent groups of varying tastes or socioeconomic classes. This period also marked the beginning of the literary institutionalization of children's books as a genre. Public *lending libraries and publishing houses organized children's departments. National and international prizes, such as the *Newbery, Caldecott, *Carnegie, Hans Christian Andersen, and Astrid Lindgren awards, recognizing achievement in children's books, were established, along with specialized journals to review new publications and analyse contemporary trends (e.g. *The Horn Book*; 1924–) or to provide a forum for academic criticism of children's literature (e.g. *The Lion and the Unicorn*; 1977–). Collectors began to take a serious interest in antiquarian children's books, and major collections were created in public and research libraries (e.g. the *Osborne Collection in Toronto, the *Opie collection in the *Bodleian, and the *National Art Library, Victoria & Albert Museum).

With institutionalization has also come the increasing commercialization of children's classics—and relatively short-lived fads such as the Goosebumps series—by international corporations (e.g. Walt Disney Enterprises) and publishers (e.g. *HarperCollins, *Scholastic) on a scale not envisioned by the Victorians. Dr Seuss, Potter's *Peter Rabbit books, Milne's Winnie the Pooh stories, C. S. Lewis's Chronicles of Narnia, and J. K. Rowling's *Harry Potter series have all become the basis for literary brands. These books are then periodically repackaged, exploited for merchandizing spin-offs, adapted for television and film versions, and promoted through highly sophisticated interactive websites.

3 Children's texts as printed books

In the late 17th century, the growing interest in the workings of the human mind stressed the training of the senses, rather than the memory, and led to a new emphasis on the visual aspect of children's books. The relations that have persisted since the 18th century between educational, artistic, technological, and commercial considerations have allowed great creative scope in the presentation of material to the child reader. A book's intended audience can be discerned usually from its packaging: the younger the reader, the more features are used to interpret, decorate, or promote the text. As the child matures, the book incorporates fewer such elements.

Children's books have been sold in *edition bindings since the late 17th century; the materials of the binding and its decoration typically distinguish a book for younger readers from one for older children, or a school book from one for leisure reading. During the 18th century, school books for vernacular reading instruction, such as James Greenwood's *London Vocabulary* (1711?), were typically bound in tanned *sheepskin stretched over *boards (with or without *endleaves), in undyed *canvas boards, or in sheepskin with a row of scallops stamped parallel to the *spine. Colourful embossed *Dutch gilt-paper *wrappers or boards are the hallmark of 'entertaining little books' for younger children, such as *The History of Little Goody Two Shoes* (1765). Works of serious fiction, history, natural history, and school anthologies would be edition bound in *sheep- or *calfskin (plain or *sprinkled), with panelled gilt spines similar to those for adult bindings.

In the 19th and 20th centuries, artists and publishers followed much the same formula, but took advantage of new materials and technologies. The upper cover often featured a striking illustration to attract the readers' eye, while the lower cover served some promotional purpose, typically featuring book lists or *blurbs. *Crane's four series of toy books—Aunt Mavor's Toy Books, Routledge's New Sixpenny Toy Books, Walter Crane's Sixpenny, and Shilling Toy Books—all feature distinctive cover designs and advertisements for the publisher. Crane also adapted his style to what he was illustrating, using wrappers for the socialist *The Dale Readers: First Primer* (1899) and decorated cloth for Mrs Molesworth's fantasy *The Tapestry Room* (1879) and Otto Goldschmidt's *Echoes of Hellas* (1887–8).

Like bindings, the *text block is not purely utilitarian, but may be adapted to meet the audience's special requirements or add a playful element. Durability, for instance, was crucial. The first untearable book was the *hornbook, a wooden paddle upon which a printed *leaf was mounted under a thin layer of horn, from which children learned their letters. Later, printers used pages of cloth, *cardboard, plywood, and plastic (*see* BATH BOOK) that can withstand rough treatment by very small children: those printed on fabric are known as rag or *cloth books, while those on heavy card stock are called board books. The leaves of the text block may be folded in various ways. The *battledore, an 18th- and 19th-century alternative to the hornbook, consists of a sheet folded into two panels and a narrow flap, similar to an envelope that has been opened up. The accordion-pleated strip, called a panorama or leporello, displays collections of images (familiar domestic objects, for instance) accompanied by minimal text. The folded strip can also advance the narrative, as in Aliquis's *The Flight of the Old Woman Who Was Tossed Up in a Basket* (1844). *Shaped books are those where the text block is die-cut in the shape of the figure on the cover, such as Lydia Very's *Little Red Riding Hood* (1863). To create changing pictures, flap-transformation and split-leaf books have leaves that are divided vertically into graduated pages, as in John Goodall's Paddy Pork series, or horizontally into multiple sections as in Walter Trier's *8192 Crazy People* (c.1950). Holes may also be cut through the text block and integrated into the story line, as in Eric Carle's *The Very Hungry Caterpillar* (1969).

Modified text blocks are almost always found in works where illustrations are integral to their concepts. A survey of the history of children's book illustration is beyond this essay's scope (*see* **16**), but brief mention may be made of the ways visual schemata in children's books become instructive: by training the eye to observe and analyse, by stimulating the imagination, by encouraging the assimilation of information, and by teaching children how to interpret images in different formats and styles. For example, grids filled with small illustrations are traditionally associated with the teaching of vocabulary and grammar. The pictorial language of isotypes (pictographic images), such as those by Gerd Arntz in *Die bunte Welt* (1929), helps children to visualize enormous quantities of specific things. Numbered tableaux depict animals, things, people, and activities on one page, and their relationships are explained in the facing commentary. This technique, originated by Comenius, gave rise to what is called in German the *Anschauulehrebuch*. Such illustrations lend themselves to visual play (sometimes called the armchair scavenger hunt) in which children search for objects described in the text, which are concealed in the illustration's complex compositions. Henry Anelay's *The Mother's Picture Alphabet* (1862) is a sophisticated Victorian example. In the 20th century, the so-called hidden picture puzzle-book has developed into a category in its own right, with popular series such as *I Spy* by Jean Marzollo and Walter Wick, or Martin Handford's *Where's Wally?*

Illustrations in children's books may also be designed to direct artistic play. Colouring and drawing books allow children to copy figures or colour the outlines for models, while patterns for making paper toys are featured in Ebenezer Landells's *Girl's Own Toy-Maker* (1859). The activity book, developed in response to the 19th-century educator Friedrich Fröbel's art curriculum, is frequently consumed in the creation of objects for recreation or display. Paul Faucher's Père Castor series, issued between 1930 and the 1960s, is the most ingenious and distinguished of the activity book genre. Faucher's illustrators, many of them émigrés who had been members of the 1920s Soviet avant-garde, conceived illustrations that could be cut out to make stained-glass windows, magic lantern slides, tangrams, masks, and model gardens.

Related to the activity book are publications in which the illustrations include cut-out figures that engage the child in dramatic play. The earliest examples are the S. and J. Fuller paper doll books issued in the 1810s: the head of the main character can be inserted on six or seven costumed figures, reflecting his or her changing circumstances during the story's progress. A slot book, such as Else Wenz-Viëtor's *Nürnberger Puppenstubenspielbuch* (1919), consists of backgrounds printed on cardboard pages in which slits are cut for the insertion of figures. Nancy Pritchard White's *Nursery Rhyme Puppet Book* (1957) is conceived as a miniature theatre, complete with scripts, sets, and puppets.

Illustrations may also try to bring the other senses into play as in a *scratch-and-sniff book. Dorothy Kunhardt's *Pat the Bunny* (1940) encourages preschool children to touch the pages, by stroking, for example, a piece of sandpaper cut in the shape of Daddy's unshaven cheek. Sound was added to books as early as 1865: *The Speaking Picture Book* featured a sound box with nine cords which, when pulled, produced animal noises. Sound recordings may accompany books, whether on phonodisc (e.g. Ralph Mayhew's Bubble Book series, 1917–22) or cassette (e.g. the 1990s Children's Classics from the Stars series produced by Rabbit Ears Productions), or a compact disc (e.g. John Lithgow's 2004 *The Carnival of the Animals*). In *movable and *pop-up books mechanical illustrations use sophisticated paper-engineering in order to create the illusion of movement and passage of time, to metamorphose an image, or to reveal the differences between the insides and outsides of things and bodies. Almost anything can now be grafted on to a *codex to encourage a more interactive reading experience, as the title of David A. Carter's *Jingle Bugs: A Merry Pop-up Book with Lights and Music!* (1992) suggests.

4 The MS book

The almost exclusive focus of the history of the children's book on the printed work has led to the neglect of the long tradition of MS books made by and for youngsters. Whatever the period in which they were produced, the majority of surviving MSS for children are instructional. The most common MSS are those created by a parent or relative (usually a mother or aunt) for a particular child's use: for example the 1814 *Cayer d'instruction pour Alfred, Bourdier de Beauregard* (published by Charles Plante in 2007), a charmingly illustrated compendium of the things encountered within the vicinity of the family chateau by Alfred's uncle, the artist C. P. Arnaud. Many MSS of this type were never intended to circulate outside the family circle. Perhaps the most extensive of these MSS are the 400 reading instruction aids created by Jane Johnson, a minister's wife, for her children in the early 1740s, complete with hand-lettered picture cards

illustrated either with cut-outs from *engravings or her own lively drawings: these now are in the *Lilly Library of Indiana University. Sometimes women published MSS that proved effective in the school room in the hope that others with less time or experience teaching young children would find them helpful. Lady Fenn made books for her nephews, with text composed of cut-out letters and accompanied by her pictures, one of which was the precursor of her easy reader *Cobwebs to Catch Flies* (1783–4), which remained in print for 80 years.

At the other end of the spectrum are instructional MSS commissioned from professional artists for children from privileged backgrounds. The contents and quality of the illuminations in certain books of hours, such as the Winchester Hours, Use of Sarum, *c.*1490 (*Pierpont Morgan Library, MS M.487), suggest that they were intended for the religious instruction of young children. Sumptuous works, such the Medici Aesop of *c.*1480 (*New York Public Library, Spencer MS 50) compiled for little Piero de' Medici by his tutor, the Florentine humanist *Poliziano, were also produced for foreign language teaching. Similar works have been created in the 20th century: the Rose family have commissioned a series of Haggadahs by famous artists for use in family observances of Passover.

The other most important category of MS book is that created as a gift to a child for leisure reading. Like instructional MSS, they are most often produced by parents or close family friends, sometimes for a particular occasion or as a consolation for an extended separation between parent and child. A notable example is John Lockwood Kipling's album of drawings and photographs, *Picture Bubbles Blown for Ruddy by Papa*, produced for Rudyard and his little sister in 1868. Many famous children's books originated in such private productions, whether first conceived as a bedtime story (Helen Bannerman's *Little Black Sambo*), as a story spun out to pass the time during a summer's outing (Lewis Carroll's *Alice's Adventures in Wonderland*), as a picture letter to amuse a sick child (Potter's *Tale of Peter Rabbit*), or as a Christmas present (Heinrich Hoffmann's *Struwwelpeter*).

Children themselves are great makers of MS books, both for their own pleasure and to fulfil assignments. For instance, Jane Austen and her sister Cassandra wrote and illustrated *A Short History of England* while they were children. The juvenilia of famous writers tend to attract the lion's share of attention, but books made by children who did not attain great distinction later in life also deserve study as a legitimate form of literary production. *Commonplace books or family magazines made by young people have attracted serious scholarly attention. More ephemeral works—including *scrapbooks like the one assembled by Frederick and Amelia Lock (*Princeton University Library, Cotsen 20613), the MS describing everyday occupations by the young cousins of the novelist Frances Burney (Pierpont Morgan Library, MS MA 4166), or the frequently elaborately decorated *copy books of apprentices or pupils in writing schools—can be studied as forms of children's self-expression. Such MS books are also testimony to the ways, aside from reading, that children assimilate print culture during work or leisure.

5 Defining the children's book

Defining children's books primarily by audience still raises points of contention a century after the genre's integration into the print networks for publication, consumption, and reception. Compared with most other readers, dependent children have relatively little control over what they read; most of their critical early experiences with books are mediated by the adults who create, publish, distribute, assign, teach, and pay for them. That youngsters need assistance and guidance is indisputable, but they must also be granted agency appropriate to their own development. This tension between adult and child is at the forefront of modern discussions of the genre's definition.

There is consensus that it is too imprecise—because too inclusive—to define a children's book simply as any text that a child happens to read. Youngsters may not restrict their reading to works approved by adults, but range into forbidden territory—chapbooks, ballads, blood and thunders, series fiction, *comic books, and *manga. Although accounts of childhood reading, almost always reconstructed later in life, may be highly selective or wildly inaccurate, it is clear that children often read indiscriminately, including works far above their capabilities (Gibbon 'rioted' in his father's library; Benjamin *Franklin relished speculative divinity and *Crouch's sixpenny compilations). Children may also 'adopt' adult works not intended for them, the most famous examples being *Robinson Crusoe* and the first two books of *Gulliver's Travels*.

Central to the definition of the children's book is the traditional desire to inculcate good reading habits as the best way to exploit educational opportunities and to secure a productive and fulfilled future. Thus, the book stands both as the primary means of instruction and as a potent symbol of literacy, promising the

possession of cultural capital and the prospect of social advancement. Yet at the same time the school book also represents compulsory reading, to be associated with the regimentation of the classroom. Often, in the elementary school book, cultural expectations, social realities, and teleologies underlying developmental psychology collide. A book adopted for use in a system of national compulsory education is likely to promote the values of the established religion, ruling class, or dominant ethnic group. To minorities, however, school books may look more like instruments of colonization or hegemony than disinterested conveyers of knowledge.

Countervailing such concerns is the powerful image of the solitary child engrossed in a book, cultivating the pleasures of the imagination. Predicated on oppositions between private and public, reason and the imagination, instruction and delight, this construction of the young reader embodies the Romantic paradigm of childhood reading articulated by Wordsworth in Book 5 of *The Prelude* (1805). Attempting to lift the child above the clash of cultural politics, the Romantics privileged such genres as fairy tales, poetry from popular oral traditions, and chapbook abridgements of medieval chivalric *romances as true children's books. This narrowly belletristic definition of the children's book has discouraged the careful contextualization of much writing for children, encouraging instead the dismissal of 'didactic' works—including fictions as diverse as Maria Edgeworth's tales, Hesba Stretton's tracts, or Charlotte Yonge's novels—because the authors' designs upon the child are considered too transparent. It has also helped to reinforce a bias against books that were popular with previous generations of children, but which no longer connect with a contemporary audience. Once a children's book is no longer read by its primary audience, it is usually discarded as a curiosity, whose appeal is difficult to conceive.

Given the complexity of the issues surrounding children's books, it may be impossible to arrive at a definition of the genre that allows educators, parents, and critics confidently to sort the sheep from the goats. For example, is a book such as Edgard Tytgat's illustrated version of Perrault's *Le Petit Chaperon rouge*, published by Cyril *Beaumont in an edition of 50 copies in 1918, a book for children or adults? The status of Rosemary Wells's board book *Max's First Word* (1998), designed to be read to very small children by an adult or older child, is similarly unclear. *Textbooks are generally composed with an eye both to the ideal student, who is supposed to master its contents, and to instructors, who must convey its matter to classes of widely diverging backgrounds and abilities. Because so many books for young readers are arguably cross-written texts (i.e. composed for a multi-generational audience), it may beg the question to put too high a priority on purity or exclusivity in defining the genre. If the children's book is a form that lends itself to hybridity and experimentation in ways whereby boundaries between audiences are constantly subverted, then that reality should be accepted, rather than explained away. That the lines between child and adult readers are frequently blurred should be regarded as normal, rather than an aberration, and perhaps one of the deepest wellsprings of creativity.

BIBLIOGRAPHY

G. Adams, 'The *Medici Aesop*: A Homosocial Renaissance Picture Book', *The Lion and the Unicorn*, 23 (1999), 313–35

B. Alderson, 'Novelty Books and Movables: Questions of Terminology', *Children's Books History Society Newsletter*, 61 (July 1998), 14–22

— and F. de Marez Oyens, *Be Merry and Wise* (2006)

— and A. Immel, 'Children's Books', in *CHBB* 6 (2009)

C. Alexander and J. McMaster, eds., *The Child Writer from Austen to Woolf* (2002)

G. Avery and J. Briggs, eds., *Children and Their Books* (1989)

B. Bader, *American Picture Books from Noah's Ark to The Beast Within* (1976)

S. Bennett, *Trade Bookbinding in the British Isles 1660–1800* (2004)

E. Booth and D. Hayes, 'Authoring the Brand: Literary Licensing', *Young Consumers*, 7 (2005), 43–5

R. Bottigheimer, *The Bible for Children* (1996)

F. J. H. Darton, *Children's Books in England* (1999)

K. Drotner, *English Children and Their Magazines, 1751-1945* (1988)

M. O. Grenby, 'Chapbooks, Children, and Children's Literature', *Library*, 7/8 (2007), 279–303

A. Horodisch, 'Die Geburt eines Kinderbuches im 16. Jahrhundert', *GJ* 35 (1960), 211–22

F. Hughes, 'Children's Literature: Theory and Practice', *English Literary History*, 45 (1978), 542–61

P. Hunt, ed., *Children's Literature: An Illustrated History* (1995)

B. Hürlimann, *Three Centuries of Children's Books in Europe* (1968)

A. Immel, 'Frederick Lock's Scrapbook: Patterns in the Pictures and Writings in Margins', *The Lion and the Unicorn*, 29 (2005), 65–86

— 'Children's and School Books', in *CHBB* 5

L. Marcus, *Minders of Make-Believe* (2008)

J. Morgenstern, 'The Rise of Children's Literature Reconsidered', *Children's Literature Association Quarterly*, 26 (2001), 64–73

N. Orme, *Medieval Children* (2001)

A. Powers, *Children's Book Covers* (2003)

K. Reynolds and N. Tucker, eds., *Children's Book Publishing in Britain since 1945* (1998)

A. Richardson, *Literature, Education, and Romanticism* (1994)

J. Shefrin, *Neatly Dissected* (1999)

C. Sommerville, *The Discovery of Childhood in Puritan England* (1992)

J. I. Whalley and T. R. Chester, *A History of Children's Book Illustration* (1988)

16 The History of Illustration and its Technologies

Paul Goldman

1 Introduction

The impulse to illustrate text is of great antiquity and antedates the printed book by thousands of years. It is known that there were books written on wood in China datable to about the 13th or 14th century BC, and it may be assumed that at least some of these were illustrated. The age and fragile nature of the materials has meant that enormous quantities of material, whether illustrated or not, have been lost from the classical periods of Greece and Rome and most other early civilizations, with the notable exception of ancient Egypt. There, the relative durability of *papyrus and the fact that items were deliberately and carefully buried has ensured some remarkable survivals. Among the more regularly illustrated works was the *Egyptian Book of the Dead: one of the most celebrated examples is the British Museum's Hunefer Papyrus, datable to about 1300 BC.

During the 2nd century AD, as the *codex began to be introduced, radical changes in the somewhat static style of illustrative designs might have been expected, but there were few striking developments, at least in the early years. Notable illustrated MS codices from about the 4th century AD are the Milan *Iliad* (Milan, *Ambrosiana) and the *Vatican Virgil. Of necessity, these books were illustrated by hand but, within perhaps as little as three centuries, the first technology to produce designs that could be multiplied had been

discovered and successfully employed. This was the making of woodblocks for the printing of both text and image together; it was in use in China by the 7th century AD—initially, it appears, for printing on textiles. Although this process was also current at about the same time in Egypt, it seems not to have developed there to encompass illustration. The blockbooks of China, then, antedate by several hundred years the Western printing of books from movable type, which was discovered, apparently independently, without knowledge of the Oriental achievement. The *Diamond Sutra (British Library)—arguably the earliest dated printed book (AD 868)—contains a remarkable woodcut *frontispiece. The printing was done by rubbing the paper against the block, since there appears to have been no handpress in this period.

Both Byzantine and Western MS illumination developed from at least the 6th century AD, attaining ever higher levels of artistry and refinement. Among the outstanding MSS of this period are the Book of *Kells (Trinity College, Dublin), datable to about the end of the 8th century, and the *Lindisfarne Gospels (British Library), datable to about 710. All such works may be seen as vehicles for illustration, albeit entirely hand-drawn and *illuminated. In Europe, printing from woodblocks was known by the 12th century, but it was originally employed only for stamping designs on to textiles. The earliest surviving prints on paper are not datable before the final years of the 14th century.

2 The age of woodcut

Among the earliest European woodcuts to bear a date is a Madonna of 1418, but it is probable that the somewhat crude surviving image-prints of religious subjects date from the final years of the preceding century. These were probably sold as devotional images within churches, or were distributed by travelling *chapmen. Although not requiring a press, *block printing produced books that combined text and illustrations and helped pave the way for illustrated books printed with movable type. A notable example is the *Biblia Pauperum, produced in The Netherlands and datable to the middle of the 15th century. Other similar books, mostly of a devotional nature, were printed at about the same time, but almost inevitably the names of their authors, artists, and woodcutters remain unknown. Such books continued to be produced into the 16th century and, when superseded by books printed in a press, their cuts went on being reused for illustrations, sometimes for hundreds of years.

Woodcuts were employed almost as soon as books began to be printed from movable type. It is now believed that *Schoeffer's *Mainz Psalter of 1457 was the first printed book in the West to contain woodcut decoration—remarkably, some of these cuts were printed in colour. It is possible, however, that the book's colour initials were printed either directly from wood or, conceivably, from metal cast from wood, so that the Psalter could be viewed as a type of illustrated book. The earliest true woodcut-illustrated books seem to have been produced at Bamberg by *Pfister. The first of these was probably Ulrich Boner's Der Edelstein (1461), notable also on account of its being apparently the earliest dated book in the German language. Pfister printed some nine editions of five books; most copies of these rare books are hand-coloured. Ulm and Augsburg also saw rapid development in the publication of books illustrated with woodcuts: two especially significant works were the Cologne Bible of about 1478–9, and *Schedel's Weltchronik, better known as the *Nuremberg Chronicle, of 1493. Michael Wolgemut and Wilhelm Pleydenwurff are known to have contributed designs for the Chronicle, which perhaps marks the starting point for book illustrations undertaken by major artists, with their contributions being recorded. Wolgemut is significant for another reason: he was the master of *Dürer, one of the greatest woodcut designers for book illustration. Among his achievements in this regard are the *Apocalypse, the Great Passion, the Life of the Virgin, and the Little Passion,

which were all published between 1498 and 1511. Despite their thin textual content, they should be viewed not merely as vehicles for a genius, but as genuine illustrated books. Dürer's contribution to the medium also seemed to signal the decline in the hand-colouring of woodcuts in books—his work never required hand-colouring.

The other major designer of woodcut illustration in this period was Hans *Holbein, arguably the only artist in Europe to rival Dürer. Most of Holbein's work was done in Basel, where the blocks were cut, although many of the books themselves were printed in France. The various cities with which he was associated indicate that the trade in his books was international. The Trechsel brothers of Lyons printed the Icones Historiarum Veteris Testamenti (1547), largely derived from *Froschauer's folio Bible (Zurich, 1538), containing Holbein's designs. In the same year the firm also published the celebrated and influential Dance of Death.

The great advantage of woodcut (a relief method of printmaking) was that illustration and text could be printed together in the same press—a feature not provided by *intaglio and printing from metal. Generally, with 15th- and 16th-century European woodcut printing, artists such as Dürer and Holbein drew designs that were then cut by members of guilds; hence the cuts were not, strictly speaking, autograph. This division of labour was to be repeated in the 19th century, especially in England, where large firms employed wood engravers to interpret artists' drawings. In both cases, the names of the woodcutters and the wood engravers were only occasionally recorded.

3 The age of metal

Following the advent of the woodcut, copper engraving and *etching were the two most important techniques for producing images for illustrations. Both were *intaglio methods and used a press exerting heavy pressure to force the dampened paper into the lines holding the ink, and hence transfer them to the surface. Etching had been invented first as a means of decorating armour, and the earliest dated print from an etched plate is of 1513 by Urs Graf. Although engraving on metal had been used by the Greeks, Etruscans, and Romans to ornament items such as bronze mirror-backs, it was not until the 15th century that goldsmiths in Germany employed engraved copper plates, initially to record their designs. The earliest such impressions were made in the 1430s, some 50 years after the first Western woodcuts. Many

A copper plate and its print: *Rana piscatrix* ('The Toad Fish or Fishing Frog') from Walter Charleton's *Exercitationes de Differentiis et Nominibus Animalium* (Oxford, 1677).

leading artists in Italy, Germany, and The Netherlands took swift advantage of the new techniques, chiefly to produce single-sheet prints. The benefits of sharper lines and enhanced delicacy also encouraged publishers to explore the medium for their own purposes. However, unlike woodcuts, which can be printed at the same time as letterpress, engravings and etchings—both requiring separate, individual printing—had to be inserted into books when they were bound. This was, inevitably, a slower and more laborious process.

Antwerp became an important centre for book production largely through the entrepreneurial French printer Christopher *Plantin, who operated his press there from 1535 until his death in 1589. Illustrated books and separate engravings printed in Antwerp circulated in large numbers throughout Europe, and Plantin ensured the success of his engravings by employing many of the finest practitioners. Books by authors such as Alciati with engravings of emblems (his *Emblematum Liber* was first published in 1531) proved enduringly popular. In 1568 Plantin produced what is generally considered to be his most important publication, an eight-volume *polyglot bible which contained both copper engravings and woodcuts. Also highly significant was Hieronymus Natalis's *Evangelicae Historiae Imagines*, posthumously published at Antwerp in 1593–5: its engravings were chiefly the work of the three Wierix brothers, who both designed and engraved the plates.

Peter Paul Rubens, himself an Antwerp man, was responsible for some of the most distinguished designs for title-pages that emanated from Plantin's press, then run by his friend *Moretus who was also Plantin's grandson. Although making drawings for book illustrations was essentially a part-time activity for Rubens, he produced several which included allegorical figures and motifs, often depicting complex iconographic ideas. One of the most important of such books is the *Breviarium Romanum* of 1614, in which the engraving work was entrusted to Theodoor *Galle.

In France too, especially in the two main publishing centres of Paris and Lyons, copper engraving was becoming popular for illustrations. The greatest Lyons publisher in the mid-16th century was *Tournes, and from his shop in 1561 came *L'Apocalypse figurée*, with engravings by Jean Duvet, a faulty though undeniably charming draughtsman, much influenced by Italian mannerist artists, notably Pontormo and Rosso Fiorentino.

Etching also began to find favour with French publishers, and a leading illustrator in the medium was Jacques Callot, celebrated for his disturbing plates on the subject of war, *Les Petites Misères* (1632) and *Les Grandes Misères* (1633). Issued in *carnet* or notebook form, their relative lack of text renders their status as illustrated books doubtful. His two books of emblems—*Vie de la Mère de Dieu* (1646) and *Lux Claustri* (1646)—belong more securely to the category.

In England at around the same time, *Hollar dominated etching and was responsible for more than 2,500 plates. Some of these were for books, and the 44 he made for Virgil's *Georgics* after Francis Clein's designs constitute what was probably the most ambitious illustrated volume yet published in the country. Commissioned by the publisher *Ogilby, it appeared in 1654. Such was the success of this luxurious publication that Ogilby followed it with an edition of Aesop in 1665 for which Hollar etched 58 plates, once again based on drawings by Clein. The year 1688 saw a significant fourth edition of Milton's *Paradise Lost*, printed by Miles Flesher for *Tonson. This work contained just twelve engraved plates of which eight were after John Baptiste de Medina. The unsigned images for Books 1 and 2 were of most significance, however. Now revealed to have been derived from prints by old masters, they form a bridge between those artists and the future generation of Blake and Fuseli.

Just as the Goncourts understood the 17th century in France as 'the century of the frontispiece', so too did they name the 18th 'the century of the *vignette'. However, nearly all of the finest productions were made between 1750 and 1780; and it is fair to say that almost no major illustrated books appeared in the country during the first half of the century. Among the finest was La Fontaine's *Contes et nouvelles*—published at Paris in 1762 and commissioned by the Fermiers Généraux, which formed 'the first financial company in the kingdom'; the Goncourts called the edition 'the great monument and triumph of the vignette, which dominates and crowns all the illustrations of the age' (Ray, *French Illustrated Book*, 31, 54, 55). Charles Eisen made 80 designs for the book, considered to be some of the most vivacious and accomplished he ever drew. There were also 53 *tailpieces and four vignette-*fleurons by Pierre-Philippe Choffard which complement the more earthy plates by Eisen.

Another equally distinguished but utterly different venture was the appearance of one of the most ambitious and successful travel books ever published. This was *Voyage pittoresque ou Description des royaumes de Naples et de Sicile*, published in Paris between 1781 and 1786, with outstanding designs by several important artists, notably Fragonard and Hubert Robert. The entire undertaking was really the brainchild and the obsession of Jean-Claude Richard, abbé de Saint-Non. He visited Italy for the first time in 1759 and the country, and especially Rome, entranced him. He then devoted his life and most of his wealth to ensuring that this large-scale project was completed to his satisfaction. It is far more than a mere topographical

record, since the plates are full of drama, including sections devoted to volcanoes—the plate by Robert of Vesuvius erupting in 1779 is especially striking. Some of the plates were engraved after Saint-Non's own designs, and something of his devotion to creating this book can be gauged by his motto: 'What flowers are to our gardens, the arts are to life.'

In 18th-century England, black-and-white illustration in books became increasingly sophisticated with the growing mastery of the various metal techniques. In the first half of the century, the *Opera* of Horace illustrated by *Pine deserves special note. The book appeared between 1733 and 1737 and is significant because both text and designs were engraved. A pupil of Bernard Picart, Pine created a unity in the volume which is elegant and pleasing, and his use of the vignette makes it virtually the only English production worthy to be compared with the books that were shortly to be produced in such abundance on the other side of the Channel.

Several later works also demand mention: one of the most significant involved the reproduction, in various forms of engraving, of oil paintings. This was the Shakespeare (1791–1804) commissioned by *Boydell, an entrepreneurial and influential print-seller in London. He launched his grandiose scheme in 1786 and invited most of the leading artists of the day to paint large canvases on subjects from the plays. Among those who contributed were Reynolds, Benjamin West, Fuseli, Romney, William Hamilton, Northcote, Opie, Wheatley, and Wright of Derby. Boydell's intention was to promote the British school of history painting and encourage a choice of serious subjects by native authors. The idea was first to exhibit the paintings in his own gallery and then, in order to recoup some of the enormous sums involved, to produce engraved versions for a monumental publishing enterprise. Although the project was an abject failure and was mercilessly lampooned by Gillray in his 1791 cartoon, *Alderman Boydell or a Peep into the Shakespeare Gallery*, it was important as a showcase for most of the current metal techniques. It is, for example, one of the few books in which *mezzotint was extensively employed. This essentially tonal method had been first mentioned by the German Ludwig von Siegen in 1642; it was mastered by Prince Rupert, who developed the required 'rocking' tool at around the same time. Its principal virtue is a remarkable softness of texture, enabling it to imbue 'colour' to fabrics, especially satin, so that it was used to great effect in the reproduction of portraits, particularly those of Reynolds and Gainsborough. Its chief drawback is the limitation of numbers—only comparatively few impressions can be taken before the plate begins to deteriorate, thus rendering it unsuitable as a method for illustrating books.

Perhaps the greatest book to combine anatomy and art published in England in the late 18th century is *The Anatomy of the Horse* by George Stubbs, which appeared in 1799. Technically complex—involving various intaglio methods—the 24 plates were intended not only for artists and designers, but for farriers and horse dealers. Additionally, the book demonstrates that illustration could be used for works of imaginative literature and for non-fiction. From the earliest years of printing, science, medicine, and invention, as well as virtually every other subject based on observations that needed recording, provided ideal matter for illustration in Europe and beyond.

*Blake is an isolated genius in the field of illustration. His first significant original work (until late in life he worked as a reproductive engraver) was *Songs of Innocence* of 1789, in which both the text and the illustrations were etched in relief and coloured by hand. He followed this with several more 'Illuminated Books' before the turn of the century; later came two monumental achievements, produced by this method, *Milton* (1801–8) and *Jerusalem* (1804–20). Although Blake had disciples (notably Samuel *Palmer), he created no school of illustration. His extraordinary and technically complex publications remain unrivalled and unchallenged, and his unique method of printmaking was rarely emulated.

Turner and Constable, though both primarily painters in oils, nevertheless saw the opportunities illustrated books offered to disseminate their ideas. Turner made nearly 900 designs for reproduction: in his middle years, the larger plates were chiefly produced in the form of copper engravings, but later in life he made many smaller drawings (often vignettes) which appeared as steel engravings. This is a confusing term, since steel is so hard that it is almost impossible to engrave. Instead, where steel was used, the lines were almost invariably etched, although they were laid in the regular manner of a copper engraving. Since Turner was trained in the workshop of the mezzotint engraver John Raphael Smith, he understood the art of engraving almost better than the engravers did themselves, and hence was painstaking in ensuring his watercolours were reproduced in black-and-white prints to the highest possible standards. One of his best books is *Picturesque Views on the Southern Coast of England*, which appeared in parts between 1814 and 1826. Employing several brilliantly talented

engravers, notably W. B. and George Cooke, the book encouraged an interest in the beauties of the country in much the same way as William Daniell's *A Voyage Round Great Britain*, which was published at almost exactly the same time. Constable's paintings were splendidly recorded in mezzotint by David Lucas in *Various Subjects of Landscape, Characteristic of English Scenery* (1833). The artist's aim was to bring for himself the same kind of recognition Turner had obtained on the publication of his *Liber Studiorum* (1807–19). In this he was unsuccessful, for both the part-issue (1832–3) and the book itself both sold poorly.

4 Advances in colour

Stipple engraving, which involves a large number of dots as opposed to lines, and *aquatint (a variety of etching) are two essentially tonal techniques, which were important, since both could be printed in colours, and also could have colour added by hand. Stipple was never ideal for use within books, however, although one or two notable examples were produced. Perhaps the most magnificent work containing early English stipple colour-printing is *Imitations of Original Drawings by Hans Holbein*, which was published in *folio between 1792 and 1800. Francesco Bartolozzi provided all but four of the numerous plates, which are highly sophisticated essays in the form, faithfully recording the appearance of the original designs in the Royal collection.

Perhaps the greatest master of the aquatint method was Goya, but his disturbing plates such as the *Caprichos* (1799), although intended to be issued in sets or in albums, scarcely qualify as illustrations in the accepted sense, since there is little textual matter. Additionally, he did not employ colour with aquatint. In Britain, however, aquatint, which had been pioneered in France in the 1760s, began to be increasingly used for volumes of topography, travel, sport, and humour.

The Microcosm of London (1808–10) combined a detailed record both of the interiors and exteriors of the major buildings in the city and of the animated figures which bring them to life. The architectural drawings were the work of Auguste Pugin and the people were the responsibility of *Rowlandson— arguably the greatest British comic draughtsman, who drew in an inimitable cursive style. The aquatint plates were undertaken by several of the finest practitioners of the period after the designs of the two artists. These volumes, like so many others conceived and executed on a grand scale, were routinely broken up, in order for the plates to be sold separately. Complete volumes are scarce today, but individual plates taken from them appear frequently on the market. Rowlandson was himself an accomplished etcher and aquatinter, and his masterpieces in this manner are probably the three volumes devoted to the travels of that aged pedant, Dr Syntax, published between 1812 and 1821. Although William Combe's text is tedious in the extreme, Rowlandson's quirky images remain forever fresh and amusing.

Aquatint, as its name suggests, imitates watercolour closely, and its rise in popularity coincided, not surprisingly, with the development of the English school of watercolour painting, which was one of the richest and most distinguished movements in the history of art. Travel, botany, and sport were just three of the subjects for which coloured aquatints proved ideal.

Between 1814 and 1825 Daniell produced eight volumes of one of the most sumptuous of such *colour-plate books. For *A Voyage Round Great Britain* (with a diverting text by Richard Ayton), Daniell both drew the original designs and made the aquatints from them. The result is a view of the country which is gentle and harmonious: most, if not all, industrial ugliness is rendered with restraint and delicacy. In many such books, the plates were first printed in just two colours and were then augmented by hand-colouring, invariably meticulously done. Almost none of the names of these talented colourists, who often were women, are recorded.

Flowers too attracted the aquatint artists: arguably the most outstanding printed specimen of the time is Robert John Thornton's *The Temple of Flora* (1807), which formed the concluding section of the author's *New Illustration of the Sexual System of Linnaeus*. Although the grandiose nature of the publication seems somewhat risible today, the quality of the plates, exquisitely coloured and finished, after both Thornton and Philip Reinagle (and others), is staggering, and the volume as a whole is a tour de force.

The love of sport, so much a British obsession, was a further area suitable for the attentions of the aquatinters. In 1838, R. S. Surtees published *Jorrocks's Jaunts and Jollities*, with delightful monochrome etched plates by Phiz (H. K. *Browne), but it was with the second edition of 1843, published by *Ackermann, and containing broadly comic colour aquatints by Henry Alken, that the book became celebrated. Alken continued to use aquatint far longer than most other artists, but he was unable to prevent the relentless march of *lithography, which by the late 1830s began to dominate colour illustration.

5 The age of stone

Lithography was invented, or perhaps more correctly, discovered in 1798 by *Senefelder in Munich. This was the first entirely new printing process since the invention of intaglio in the 15th century, and provided great opportunities to use colour in books, together with a hitherto unmatched softness and delicacy of texture. Lithography proved particularly suitable for large books, especially in Britain for topography and travel, while in France the technique was used to illustrate major works of Romantic literature in which artists such as Daumier, Delacroix, Gavarni, and Géricault chiefly employed black and white.

Delacroix found inspiration in *Faust*; his version, with a translation by Albert Stapfer, appeared in 1828. (Goethe himself was pleased with the lithographs.) Although it initially met with a hostile reception from a public astounded by the daring, fantastic medievalism of the designs, the book created a distinguished tradition in French illustration. Daumier, however, was perhaps the greatest artist to use lithography, and much of his best work appeared in periodicals. It is in *La Caricature* (1830–35) that many of his most memorable satires can be sampled: of the 91 images he made for it, 50 were published in the last year before its suppression. The scenes in which he epitomized the oppressive practices of the July Monarchy were especially acerbic.

In contrast, the colour lithographed books in Britain at the same period dealt in the main with very different topics. In *The Holy Land* (1842–[45]), completed by *Egypt and Nubia* (1846–9), David Roberts produced probably the most remarkable and imposing of English travel books illustrated by lithography. The prints were the work of Louis Haghe, and they were almost exactly the same size as Roberts's deft watercolours. The combination of topographical accuracy, aesthetic sensitivity, and delicate colours ensured enormous popularity for these volumes and, needless to say, most fell victim to '*breakers'. *Lear similarly published several important books of his tours: in *Views in Rome and its Environs* (1841) he produced panoramic lithographs of a large size, concentrating more on the countryside than the monuments of the city itself; *Illustrated Excursions in Italy* (1846) combined lithographs and wood-engraved vignettes. His more celebrated *Book of Nonsense* (1846) used lithography both for text and image. Lithographic colour printing, or *chromolithography, provided Owen *Jones, an architect and ornamental designer, with a suitable medium for his work: perhaps his greatest achievement using it is *The Grammar of Ornament* (1856). His ideas proved influential on the design of wallpapers, carpets, and furnishings, and his approach to book illustration culminated in the work of William *Morris.

6 The age of wood engraving and mass production

At the end of the 18th century and in the early years of the 19th, *Bewick was the first leading exponent of wood engraving. Not only did he illustrate delightful books—chiefly of natural history, such as *A General History of Quadrupeds* (1790), with vignettes frequently drawn from life—but he was an influential teacher. Among his pupils were William Harvey, John Jackson, and Ebenezer Landells. Luke Clennell was also taught by Bewick, and one of his best books is undoubtedly Samuel Rogers's *The Pleasures of Memory* (1810), for which he engraved 34 delicate vignettes after *Stothard.

Wood engraving, like the woodcut of a previous age, had the same advantage over all other methods of printmaking: blocks could be set up and printed with the letterpress at the same time. This led in mid-19th century Britain to the mass production of illustrated books and, in a significant expansion of activity, of periodicals. Etching, which was very much the province of comic artists such as *Cruikshank and Phiz, was coming to the end of its life as a mass method of communication, but one of its last gasps was also, paradoxically, hugely influential. This occurred when Phiz was asked to take over the illustration of some 'Sporting Sketches' by Charles Dickens, following the death of the originator of the project, Robert Seymour, who had completed just seven designs before his suicide. Phiz contributed 35 etched plates to what Dickens termed merely 'a monthly something', which became *The Posthumous Papers of the Pickwick Club*. Issued in parts (or *numbers) from 31 March 1836 to 30 October 1837, the work has genuine claims to being the first illustrated English novel of stature. In other words, it is probably the first such publication where original illustrations accompany a true first edition, as opposed to a reprint.

Wood engraving soon began to overtake etching in Britain and in France, both on account of its convenience and because of the excellence of the engravers. Across the Channel, a landmark was *Paul et Virginie*

A wood-engraved block and its print: 'The Night Heron' by Thomas *Bewick for *A History of British Birds* (Newcastle, 1804).

(1838), published in Paris by Curmer. This lavish edition of Bernardin de Saint-Pierre's classic tale of natural love in Mauritius was illustrated with numerous wood engravings—after artists such as Tony Johannot, Paul Huet, Isabey, and others—that integrated happily with the text. Equally significant is the fact that most of the engravers were English, demonstrating their superiority in the field. Within a year, an English translation was published in London by W. S. Orr in almost as fine an edition, although it lacked four of Curmer's plates. Other English publishers soon followed, bringing to the public the wood-engraved illustrations of artists such as Grandville and Gigoux in English-language editions.

Stylistically, many British artists of the 1840s betray the influence of German designers such as Julius Schnorr von Carolsfeld and Moritz Retzsch. A notable publication in this manner was Samuel Carter Hall's *The Book of British Ballads* (1842, 1844), which was notable for a consciously Teutonic layout—where the designs often encircle the text or run in panels next to it—and was the sole work with illustrations by the uniquely disturbing Richard Dadd.

The year 1848 saw the foundation in London of the Pre-Raphaelite Brotherhood, and although the movement itself was short-lived, its influence on illustration was momentous. In 1855, *Routledge published *The Music Master* by the Irish poet William Allingham, with wood engravings after John Millais, Dante Gabriel Rossetti, and Arthur Hughes. Almost at a stroke a new kind of illustration, which was powerful in execution, intellectual in approach, and essentially realistic in the way faces and bodies were depicted, came to the fore. Rossetti's beautiful image 'Maids of Elfen-Mere' set the standard, not only encouraging other Pre-Raphaelites, such as Holman Hunt and Edward Burne-Jones, to make increasingly bold designs, but also spurring the group known today as the 'Idyllic School' to produce distinguished work. Among these practitioners were George John Pinwell, John William North, Frederick Walker, and Robert Barnes. In 1857, *Moxon published an edition of Tennyson's poems, now known as the Moxon Tennyson, containing designs by Millais, Rosssetti, and Hunt in the new style, and others by artists such as J. C. Horsley and William Mulready, still highly reminiscent of the 1840s. The book was a commercial failure, partly because of its lack of artistic unity, but it was a significant achievement. From this date, there was an explosion in the publication both of illustrated books and also of periodicals. Three of the most important magazines for illustrations in the 1860s were the *Cornhill Magazine*, *Good Words*, and *Once a Week*. The wood engraving for them was largely undertaken by large London firms, notably the *Dalziel brothers and Joseph Swain. The names of the highly skilled people who worked at speed and often overnight to meet deadlines are rarely recorded. Many of them are likely to have been women who worked in a sweatshop economy. Long *press runs from wood engravings were often achieved by the use of metal *electrotypes, which were faithful *facsimiles of the boxwood blocks.

In *The Pencil of Nature* (1844–6), W. H. Fox Talbot produced the first published book illustrated photographically. It was not until the 1880s that *photomechanical processes such as line-block, *half-tone, and *photogravure began to supplant wood engraving, then in decline.

The subject of illustrated children's books is so vast that it can only be touched on here (*see* **15**). By the latter half of the 19th century, more and more books were being published specifically for children to enjoy and read on their own. It was soon realized that colour was an essential ingredient for them, and sophisticated effects were achieved by artists such as *Caldecott, *Greenaway, and *Crane.

7 The book beautiful, *livre d'artiste*, and the private press

As a reaction to the decay in production values prevalent in the 1880s, William Morris began a movement to produce beautiful books that were consciously medieval both in style and means of production. Paradoxically, however, in his *Kelmscott Press books he did not entirely outlaw mechanical means for producing them. Other presses that made illustrated books of distinction included the *Vale and *Eragny presses, vehicles for *Ricketts and Pissarro respectively. By definition, their books were published in *limited editions and were aimed at wealthy collectors. At about the same time in France, the concept of the *livre d'artiste* (*artist's book) emerged, led by entrepreneurial publishers such as *Vollard. These were luxury publications, containing woodcuts and lithographs by major artists such as Bonnard, Rodin, *Picasso, *Matisse, and Dufy. Similar publications appeared also in Germany and Austria featuring artists of the stature of Paul Klee and Franz Marc.

Significant and striking though these volumes are, they are fundamentally portfolios of master prints: they are not books in the traditional sense and are certainly not designed for reading. Since the impressions were not invariably bound in, they encouraged the removal and framing of individual sheets. In Britain in the 1920s and 1930s, a few books were published containing original copper engravings, etchings, and even *pochoir designs (hand-coloured through stencils). However, it was in autograph wood engraving that the British *private press movement excelled. The *Golden Cockerel Press was one of the best; it hosted the talents of, among others, *Gibbings, Clifford Webb, and Gwenda Morgan. Towards the end of the century several private presses—notably Whittington, Gwasg *Gregynog, and the Fleece—continued to thrive using original wood engravings, invariably printed from the wood and published in limited editions and to very high standards.

8 Contemporary illustration and the digital revolution

While the limited edition artist's book continued to flourish throughout the 20th century and beyond, perhaps most notably in the US and UK, becoming ever more experimental and avant-garde, nearly all non-fiction trade books were routinely illustrated by photographic means. The only genre of imaginative book to attract illustration today as a matter of course is that of young children's books, while works aimed at teenagers, such as J. K. Rowling's *Harry Potter series, remain unillustrated. Some publishers like the *Folio Society still commission new illustrations for their high-quality reprints. Such books are printed in commercial numbers, though theoretically limited, and hence are available relatively inexpensively.

With digital technology, the appetite for illustrated books seems inexhaustible, as the means of meeting it becomes simpler both for the self-publisher and for the professional. In the world of the adult trade novel, an interesting development has been the recent use of digital images by writers such as W. G. Sebald and Michel Houellebecq. Their skilful combining of word and image may presage developments soon to come.

BIBLIOGRAPHY

D. Bland, *A History of Book Illustration* (1958)

A. M. Hind, *An Introduction to a History of Woodcut* (1935)

P. Hofer, *Baroque Book Illustration* (1951)

C. Hogben and R. Watson, eds., *From Manet to Hockney: Modern Artists' Illustrated Books* (1985)

S. Houfe, *Fin de Siècle: The Illustrators of the Nineties* (1992)

G. N. Ray, *The Illustrator and the Book in England from 1790 to 1914* (1976)

— *The Art of the French Illustrated Book 1700 to 1914* (1982)

F. Reid, *Illustrators of the Sixties* (1928)

J. Selborne, *British Wood-Engraved Book Illustration 1904–1940* (1998)

T. Watt, *Cheap Print and Popular Piety, 1550–1640* (1991)

J. I. Whalley and T. R. Chester, *A History of Children's Book Illustration* (1988)

17 Bookbinding

David Pearson

1 Introduction

Books have needed outer covers and a means of holding them together for as long as they have existed, partly to keep their pages in the intended order, and partly to provide protection. Bookbinding embraces all the techniques that have evolved to achieve these ends, including the materials and structures employed, and the many ways in which the covers have been decorated. It is a subject of study in its own right, with an extensive literature; bookbindings have been admired and collected for their artistic qualities, but their intrinsic interest goes beyond this. Before mechanization was introduced in the 19th century, all bookbindings were individually handmade objects and the choices exercised in deciding how elaborate or simple a binding should be became part of the history of every book. The introduction of paperback binding, coupled with rising exploitation of the pictorial possibilities of outer covers, is a significant element in modern publishing history and in the dissemination of books to ever greater markets during the 20th century.

2 Early history

*Papyrus, which could be glued together into long *scrolls that might be stored in protective wooden cases, was the preferred writing medium in ancient Egypt and its use spread across the Graeco-Roman world during the pre-Christian era (*see* **3**). The *codex—the form of the book as we know it—emerged from this tradition during the first few centuries AD when leaves of *papyrus began to be folded and sewn into *leather covers. Structures like this, originating in the near east, known from the 2nd century, are particularly associated with the emerging Christian sects; they gradually replaced scrolls as the preferred method for recording and storing texts during the succeeding centuries.

The Roman statesman Cassiodorus (*c*.490–*c*.580), in his *Institutiones* (written *c*.560), refers to bookbinders trained to produce bindings in various styles, and an 8th-century English MS illustration is generally believed to depict him with his nine-volume Bible, bound as recognizable codices with decorated covers. The *Stonyhurst Gospel, made *c*.700, is the oldest surviving European decorated binding; with folded and sewn quires, covered with decorated leather over boards, it brings together essential characteristics that would remain constant in bookbinding practice for the following millennium and more.

3 Western bookbinding structures (pre-mechanization)

Most bookbindings made in Europe between *c*.800 (when the sewing style developed) and 1800 conform structurally to a standard model, sometimes called flexible sewing. The leaves are folded into *gatherings

147

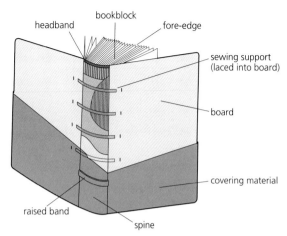

The basic structural features of a European bookbinding in the medieval and hand press periods.

the end of the 18th century, rising leather costs, combined with ever-growing book production, led to greater experimentation with cloth and paper as alternative materials. During the 1820s and 1830s, books were increasingly issued with cloth-covered boards, secured to the text block using glued strips of canvas, rather than laced-in sewing supports. Cloth covers, decorated and lettered, could be prefabricated and *case binding quickly became established as the standard technique. Whole editions of books therefore began to be issued in identical bindings, another major change from the practice of the handpress era.

These essential structural features of casebound books have continued largely unchanged to the present time, although the processes involved have undergone progressive mechanization (see section 8, below). While many 'hardback' books still conform to this style, modern books often rely on glue rather than sewing to hold them together, an alternative (and cheaper) binding technique that dates back to 1836 when William Hancock was granted a patent for what were then called caoutchouc bindings. After gathering the text block in the usual way, the spine folds were cut off (leaving each leaf a *singleton, not attached to any other) before being coated with a flexible rubber solution that when set held all the leaves together. As the rubber perished over time, the leaves fell out, and the technique was largely abandoned commercially around 1870. It was revived in the 20th century and the introduction of new *thermoplastic glues from

which are sewn through the central folds on to a number of supports running horizontally across these folded edges. The projecting ends of the supports are laced and secured into stiff boards, which are then covered with an outer skin (typically leather or parchment, but possibly paper or fabric); this is decorated to create the finished product. Additional leaves (*endleaves) are commonly added at each end of the *text block before attaching the boards; the *spine is rounded; endbands may be added at head and foot; and the leaf edges are trimmed with a sharp blade (sometimes called a plough) to create an even surface. In bookbinding terminology, the construction stages are known as *forwarding, and the decoration as *finishing.

These processes remained essentially constant throughout the medieval and handpress periods; the relatively few changes that evolved over time were commonly associated with a wish to expedite or economize on labour and materials as more books came to be produced. Once printing was established, the double-thickness sewing supports typically used in medieval bindings gave way to single ones, and various techniques were developed to speed up sewing by running the needle between gatherings as it ran up and down the spine. An alternative practice widely used for *pamphlets and temporary, cheap bindings was *stabbing and stab-stitching, running a thread through the whole text block near the spine edge.

4 Post-mechanization structures

Bookbinding practices, like all other aspects of the book-production and distribution industries, underwent major changes during the 19th century. Towards

Diagram of the structural features of a modern casebound book ready for casing in (adapted from Gaskell, *NI*).

about 1950 onwards led to increased production of what are variously called unsewn or *perfect bindings, much used particularly for *paperback books. The failure of the glue over time remains a problem, and bindings based on sewing continue to provide the strongest and most permanent structures.

5 Non-Western bookbinding structures

The earliest codex bindings, from North Africa and the surrounding area, followed a different sewing technique using a chain stitch sewn across the gatherings, instead of running the thread up and down the quires. This method, sometimes called *Coptic sewing, was initially used across Europe, but was abandoned there in favour of *flexible sewing around the beginning of the 9ᵗʰ century. The Coptic method continued to be used in the Near East, including the Byzantine and Islamic cultures where bookbinding flourished throughout the Middle Ages and beyond. Coptic sewing produces books that open well, but whose spines tend to become concave over time, and whose board attachment may be weaker than that produced by Western methods of laced-in supports.

In Asia, a variety of binding styles developed, influenced by the shapes and characteristics of the writing materials. In India and other parts of Southeast Asia, *palm leaves, cut into long thin strips, were commonly held together with string passed through holes in each leaf, fastened at each end to a wooden cover; this *pothi* format, an ancient tradition, remained in common use down to the 19ᵗʰ century (*see* **39**). Chinese and Japanese binding (*see* **40, 42**) evolved differently, following the invention of paper in China around AD 100 and its widespread adoption for documentary purposes (although bamboo and wood, in thin strips tied together, were also used, and *pothi*-type structures

*Thread, four-hole, or Japanese binding: this characteristic binding format developed in China during the Ming period and has been extensively used in East Asia.

using paper leaves are known in China from the 7ᵗʰ century onwards).

The Chinese made extensive use of scrolls during the first millennium AD and their earliest printed books (using *block printing) were scroll-based, like the *Diamond Sutra (dated to 868). The concertina format, made by pasting sheets together in one long continuous sequence, but folding it rather than rolling so as to create a rectangular book-shaped object when closed, was a natural evolution from the scroll, and began to emerge during the Tang dynasty (618–907). During the Song dynasty (960–1279), scroll-based formats were increasingly replaced by ones based on folded leaves, more like Western book structures. Various kinds of stitching techniques are known to have been used, as well as paste-based ones such as butterfly binding, in which single bifolia are pasted together at the spine fold. The *bifolia would typically be printed or written on one side only, leaving alternate blank *openings corresponding to the pasted folds. By folding the other way, and binding along the open edge rather than the folded one, it was possible to create a book of continuous text without blanks, and it was this development, together with the emergence of new sewing methods, around the 12ᵗʰ–14ᵗʰ centuries that led to the format most commonly recognized today as a typical oriental binding. Sometimes called four-hole binding or Japanese binding (although it developed in China), such books are sewn through the open folds that make the spine edge, stabbing through the whole text block and running the thread over the head and tail as well as round the back. This format became established during the Ming dynasty (1368–1644) and has continued in use, although Western bookbinding methods also became increasingly common in East Asia after the 19ᵗʰ century.

6 Materials used in bookbinding

In European practice, leather-covered boards were the typical choice, over many centuries, for bindings

*Coptic sewing differs from western *flexible sewing technique in that the *quires are sewn together with a chain stitch, rather than being sewn on to separate sewing supports run across the *spine.

intended to be permanent. From the earliest times to the end of the Middle Ages, boards were usually made of wood (in England, oak or beech), cut in thin slices with the grain running parallel to the spine. During the 16th century, wood was gradually replaced by pasteboard and other paper-based boards, being both lighter and cheaper, as books became smaller and more numerous. Millboard (made from waste hemp materials) was introduced in the 17th century and strawboard (based on pulped straw) in the 18th. Modern bookbindings typically use some kind of machine-made paper-based *cardboard. Medieval bindings commonly had metal clasps across their edges to prevent the *vellum leaves from cockling, a tradition which died out (other than for ornamental purposes) during the 16th and 17th centuries as pasteboard and paper replaced wood and vellum.

Leather used for bookbinding has come from a range of animals, prepared in different ways. Leather is made from animal skins either by tanning—treating the dehaired skin with tannic acid—or tawing, when the chemical used is potassium aluminium sulphate (alum). The former creates a smoother, harder leather which can take and retain impressed decoration. Medieval bookbinders typically used tawed leather, made not only from domestic animals but from deerskin and sealskin. In most European countries, tanned leather replaced tawed for bookbinding during the 15th century, although tawed pigskin continued to be popular in and around Germany into the 17th century.

Tanned *calfskin, dyed a shade of brown, is the covering material most commonly found on postmedieval British bindings. Calf produced a durable but lightweight leather, with a smooth and pleasing surface. Tanned *sheepskin, which has a coarser grain and is less hard-wearing, was used for cheaper work. Tanned *goatskin was the leather of choice for the best-quality bindings; it was increasingly used in Europe from the 16th century onwards, having been developed for bookbinding by Islamic craftsmen in the Near East well before then. Most of the goatskin used in England during the hand press period was imported from Turkey or Morocco and, hence, was commonly called '*Turkey' or '*Morocco'.

Vellum or parchment, made by soaking calfskin or sheepskin and drying it under tension, without chemical tanning, was also extensively used as a covering material in early modern Europe, often for cheaper bindings when a vellum wrapper, without boards, might provide sufficient protection for a pamphlet or small book. In Britain, the use of vellum for binding work dwindled after the mid-17th century, except for *stationery binding, but it continued to be much used in Germany and the Low Countries well into the 18th century. Paper, or paper over thin boards, was also sometimes used for cheap or temporary bindings, and this practice increased as time progressed; there are a few extant examples of printed-paper wrappers from the early centuries of printing (there must once have been very many more, which have perished), but 18th-century pamphlets in *wrappers of blue or *marbled paper are relatively common. Towards the end of that century books increasingly came to be issued in paper-covered boards, a trend that continued throughout the 19th century with a growth in printed paper covers. During the hand press period, paper or card-based binding options were generally more common in continental Europe than in Britain; wrappers of rough plain card (sometimes called *cartonnage) began to be used in Italy during the 16th century and can also be found from France or Germany around that time and later.

The use of fabric as a covering material dates back to medieval times, originally as a luxury option, using velvet or embroidered textiles. Many elaborately decorated velvet bindings from the 16th and 17th centuries survive, and in early 17th-century England there was a vogue for devotional books with embroidered linen or satin covers. The use of fabric as the default option for bindings dates from the early 19th century, when binders began to experiment with cotton cloth, although rough canvas was used for schoolbooks and similar cheap household books from c.1770. Cloth was quickly established during the second quarter of the 19th century as a standard covering material for the prefabricated binding cases which were then transforming bookbinding production. *Bookcloth is typically cotton-based, coated or filled with starch or an equivalent synthetic chemical to make it hardwearing, water-resistant, and capable of being *blocked with lettering or pictorial designs.

7 Bookbinding decoration

Decoration has long been the aspect of bookbindings and their history that has attracted most interest, both among those who were producing and owning them at the time of their creation and among their successors. The outside of a book is its first and most immediately visible aspect, the part that can be seen even when it is closed and on a shelf: it thus bears the greatest potential to attract or impress users. Down the ages, handsomely decorated bookbindings have been commissioned, collected, valued, sold, and displayed, appreciated not only for their beauty but for the statements they may make about the importance of the book's contents, or the status of the owner. Much of the published literature on bookbindings is dedicated to these kinds of bindings, but it is important to recognize that all bindings have some kind of decoration, however minimal, and that it is worth studying and understanding the full range of options produced over the centuries.

Bookbinding decoration, like every other kind of art form, has always been subject to ever-shifting tastes and fashions, and each generation had its own ornamental vocabulary within which patterns and styles were created. A 16th-century binding will look different from an 18th-century one because the tool shapes and layout designs belong distinctively to their own time. This applies to plain bindings as well as fancy ones; bookbinders always offered their customers a range of options from the simplest and cheapest to the most luxurious and expensive, with many possibilities in between. Understanding the full picture allows one to recognize bindings of all kinds, to place them within the spectrum of options available, to compare them with other bindings of their time, and to interpret the choices that were made in their creation.

The development of bookbinding design, like all aesthetic fashions, is a process of continual change, dependent partly on the potential of the materials available and partly on the creation and dissemination of new artistic ideas. Styles typically began in one place and spread across continents; English bookbinding was influenced by what was being produced in France and Holland, which in turn was influenced by designs from Italy or other European artistic centres. Across Europe, countries developed variations and characteristics of their own, but at any one time there was a broad commonality of design conventions. In America, where bookbinding began soon after European settlers arrived (the first North American bookbinder is recorded in 1636), styles and techniques followed European, particularly British, models. Bookbinding tools always belonged within the wider ornamental fashions of their time—the neoclassical motifs of 18th-century bindings, for example, are mirrored in contemporary architecture, woodwork, and other decorative arts—but usually with a distinctive twist of their own, making them recognizably intended for binding decoration.

Tanned leather bindings have usually been decorated by building up patterns with heated metal tools, leaving a permanent impression in the surface. Tools may be small individual stamps, large blocks, or wheels with an engraved design around the rim, and are run along a cover to create a continuous line of ornament (*fillets and rolls). For greater visual impact, tools can be applied through a thin layer of gold leaf, leaving a gilt rather than a *blind impression; this was an Islamic invention, known from at least the 13th century, and many handsome gilt-tooled bindings from Persia and North Africa survive from the 14th and 15th centuries. The technique travelled to Italy and Spain in the 15th century, and gilt-tooled bindings began to be produced in quantity all over Europe from the 16th. The great majority of the countless thousands of tanned leather bindings produced during the hand press period carried some degree of blind- or gilt-tooled decoration, varying from a few lines or simple tools to elaborate designs. At the top end of the market, skilled craftsmen like *Planche, *Mearne, or Roger *Payne produced striking and sophisticated bindings; many examples, showing the ways in which styles developed by time and place, will be found in the extensive literature on bookbinding.

Decorative effects on leather bindings could be further enhanced by using *inlays or *onlays of differently coloured leather, or by applying paint as well as

A 16th-century strapwork binding: brown calf, *gold tooling, and black paint. The lower cover of Xenophon's *La Cyropédie* (Paris, 1547), bound for Edward VI.

tooling. Leather could also have patterns cut into it (*cuir ciselé*); this was popular in and around Germany in the late medieval period, but was otherwise uncommon in binding practice. Many of the decorative techniques used on leather were also shared with vellum bindings. Decoration was commonly placed not only on covers and spines, but on board edges, using narrow rolls; leaf edges were usually coloured or sprinkled, or gilded in the case of better-quality bindings. Spine-labelling, using lettered leather labels, became common from the late 17th century; before then, books might have their titles written on their leaf edges or elsewhere, reflecting different storage methods before it became common practice to shelve books upright, spine outwards.

Medieval leather bindings, typically covered with tawed rather than tanned leather, were often largely undecorated, although a vogue for tool-stamped, tanned leather bindings (*see* ROMANESQUE BINDINGS) developed in the later 12th century. Special bindings of the Middle Ages tended to rely on other techniques, using covers of ivory, enamel, or jewelled metalwork, made separately and nailed on to the wooden boards. Many medieval abbeys and large churches had *treasure bindings like this for bibles and important devotional books, although relatively few have survived.

The introduction of cloth as the standard covering material for bindings, in the second quarter of the 19th century, saw attention rapidly paid to developing its decorative capabilities. Gold blocking on cloth began in 1832, initially for spine lettering, but quickly adapted to be applied to covers as well. Experimentation during the following decade with abstract and pictorial designs, using gold and coloured inks, led to the production from mid-century of a wide variety of striking *publishers' bindings in decorated cloth. This tradition declined towards the end of the century, as *dust jackets evolved; these became increasingly common from the 1880s, initially with printed text but gradually becoming the more pictorial and actively designed covers we are familiar with today. The story of dust jackets and pictorial covers for paperbacks belongs more to design history than bookbinding history, but the importance of these contemporary methods of drawing attention to books by their covers is self-evident.

The growth of machine-made cloth binding in the 19th century led to a corresponding decline in the making and decoration of leather bindings, although the trade never died out. A reaction against a feeling that artistic standards in bookbinding had fallen was initiated in the 1880s by *Cobden-Sanderson, whose

A 19th-century decorated binding: according to contemporary advertisements, L. M. Budgen's *Episodes of Insect Life* (London, 1849), published under the pseudonym 'Acheta Domestica', was 'Elegantly bound in fancy cloth' and sold for 16s.

beautifully crafted bindings, produced to his own designs, inspired a revival of interest in handcrafted bookbinding. A tradition of fine bookbinding flourished in many countries during the 20th century; in England, the formation of the Guild of Contemporary Bookbinders in 1955 (subsequently renamed *Designer Bookbinders) provided a focus for this movement, within which numerous contemporary binders have continued to produce bindings combining the highest quality of craftsmanship with artistic flair, and experimentation with the possibilities of bookbinding as an art form.

Nineteenth- and 20th-century bookbindings commonly have decoration on their covers or dust jackets that reflects the content of the book. This is a modern development; throughout the medieval and hand press periods, bookbinding decoration was normally abstract, with no attempt to use designs to represent content. There are exceptions, but they are very few in proportion to the bulk of what was produced.

An 18th-century binder's workshop: a relatively small number of people carry out the various operations involved in *forwarding and *finishing; from C. E. Prediger, *Der Buchbinder und Futteralmacher*, vol. 2 (1745).

A 20th-century binding by Edgar *Mansfield, an influential figure in the development of the *Designer Bookbinder movement in the later 20th century: *blind-tooling on yellow *goatskin. The upper cover of H. E. Bates's *Through the Woods* (London, 1936).

8 The bookbinding trade

Bookbinding was generally carried out as a professional activity within the broader umbrella of the book trade. During medieval times, some bookbinding was undertaken within monasteries as a logical adjunct to the writing and copying of MSS, but as soon as a secular trade in making and selling books developed (around the 12th century), binders emerged as one subset alongside parchment makers, *scribes, and *stationers.

The organization of binding work varied a little from country to country according to local custom, but throughout the early modern period binders generally entered the trade through *apprenticeship to an established practitioner, followed by formal membership of a guild or similar trade association. In England, there was never a separate bookbinders' guild, and London binders (where much of the trade was concentrated) belonged to the *Stationers' Company, which also embraced printers and booksellers. Binders were typically the poor relations within this framework, in terms of both earnings and social status, and many binders who succeeded financially did so by diversifying their activities into selling books, stationery, or other wares. The relationship between booksellers and binders in the early modern period—the extent to which binders had independent business relationships, or were employed by the booksellers—is not well documented. It is increasingly recognized that books were often bound before being put on sale, but there is little evidence to suggest that *edition binding in any deliberate sense was carried out much before the 19th century. Selling books ready-bound seems to have been more common in Britain than in continental Europe, where the tradition of issuing books in paper wrappers, to be bound to a customer's specification, continued well into the 20th century.

Before the 19th century, binderies were typically small establishments run by a master with a handful of assistants (who might be apprentices, journeymen, or members of his family; women were often involved in some of the operations, such as folding and sewing). In France, there was a recognized distinction between forwarders (*relieurs*) and finishers (*doreurs*); in Britain, Germany, and elsewhere these roles were less formally identified, although individuals within workshops are likely to have specialized. Representations of European binding workshops between the 16th and 18th centuries, of which a number survive, commonly show something between two and eight people at work in one or two rooms carrying out the various activities of sewing, beating, covering, and decorating involved in binding production.

All this changed during the 19th century, when the trade was gradually transformed by mechanization. Growing book production, the development of cloth casing, and the invention of machines to carry out binding processes led to binderies becoming much bigger operations with factory-like assembly lines. During the first half of the century, many of the operations such as folding, sewing, and attaching cases were still carried out by hand, but the second half saw the introduction of steam-powered folding machines (from 1856), sewing machines (from 1856), rounding and backing machines (from 1876), case-making machines (from 1891), gathering machines (from 1900), and casing-in machines (from 1903). Many of these were first introduced in America. Bookbinding today, for the great majority of the books issued through normal publishing trade channels, is carried out as an automated industrial process, whose capacity has been enhanced since the 1950s by the development of new fast-drying inks and glues.

9 The collecting, study, and importance of bookbindings

Bookbindings play an important functional role in the life of every book, but their impact and potential to affect the values associated with books goes beyond this. The statement that a luxuriously bound book can make about the importance of its contents, or its owner, is a tradition that stretches back through generations of wealthy bibliophiles to the treasure bindings displayed on medieval altars. Queen Elizabeth I liked her books bound in velvet; her royal library presented a rich and colourful display to impress visitors, and drew together a collection of books that she found individually satisfying to look at and to handle. Less wealthy owners have also taken active delight in the aesthetic satisfaction which bindings can bring. *Pepys recorded in his diary (15 May 1660) that he purchased books 'for the love of the binding', and had many of his books rebound to create a uniform image. Finely bound books have often been created as gifts, sometimes in the hope of influencing potential patrons. The admiration and expense of fine bindings have also generated criticism; *Naudé lamented 'the superfluous expenses, which many prodigally and to no purpose bestow upon the binding of their books ... it becoming the ignorant only to esteem a book for its cover' (Naudé, 61). Many early purchasers were at least as concerned about functionality as decoration—they wanted their books sound and well made, without missing leaves—and wealthy owners did not necessarily have fancy bindings.

Early bookbinding practice is not well documented; contemporary manuals or archival sources on binders and their lives are relatively scarce before the 19th century. The bindings themselves constitute the largest body of evidence for exploring bookbinding history. The serious study of the subject began in the late 19th century, initially with a focus on the artistic qualities of fine bindings, maturing into a tradition of comparative study of surviving bindings to identify sets of tools used together, from which workshops and their dates of operation may be deduced. Bindings can therefore be attributed to particular binders, times, and places. Towards the end of the 20th century increasing attention was paid to structural aspects as well as decorative ones, with a growing emphasis on the full range of bindings produced, the plain and the everyday as well as the upmarket and the fine. The idea of systematically collecting bindings for their own sake is similarly a relatively recent development, and a number of important collections of fine bindings were formed in the 20th century.

Bookbinding studies have in the past been regarded as having a rather peripheral role in the overall canon of historical *bibliography, compared with printing and publishing history, or work more directly focused on textual or enumerative bibliography. Bookbindings have been thought to be incidental to and unconnected with the works they cover, and the past emphasis on fine bindings has lent the subject an art-historical flavour that can veer towards dilettantism. More recent developments in book history, concerned with the ways that books were circulated, owned, and read, have created a framework in which it is easier to see bindings as an integral part of that whole. It is now widely recognized that the reception of works is influenced by the physical form in which they are experienced—an area where bindings play an important role. A reader's expectations may be conditioned by the permanence, quality, or other features of a book's exterior. Bindings may reveal ways in which books were used—how they were shelved or stored, how much wear and tear they have received—and the rebinding of books by later generations of owners may reflect changing values (contemporary bindings of Shakespeare are typically much simpler than the elaborate gilded goatskin in which 19th-century owners rebound early editions of his works). Cheap and temporary bindings, or bindings whose internal structure shows corner-cutting techniques, may indicate likely original audiences.

More obviously, knowledge of binding history allows us to recognize when and where bindings were made, and therefore where they first circulated. In the early modern period, books were not necessarily bound and first sold where they were printed, as printed sheets often travelled significant distances before being bound. Imprints should not be taken as an indicator of place or date of binding, for which decorative, structural, and other material evidence, interpreted by comparison with other bindings, is a surer guide. Bindings may also incorporate direct evidence of early ownership, in the form of names, initials, or *armorial stamps on the covers or spine, practices that have been common in Europe since the 16th century. *See also* BOOK CLOTH; GOLD TOOLING; TOOLING; TRADE BINDING.

BIBLIOGRAPHY
D. Ball, *Victorian Publishers' Bindings* (1985)
C. Chinnery, 'Bookbinding [in China]', www.idp.bl.uk/ education/bookbinding/bookbinding.a4d, consulted Mar. 2006
M. M. Foot, *The History of Bookbinding as a Mirror of Society* (1998)
E. P. Goldschmidt, *Gothic and Renaissance Rookbindings* (1928)
D. Haldane, *Islamic Bookbindings* (1983)
H. Lehmann-Haupt, ed., *Bookbinding in America* (1941)
R. H. Lewis, *Fine Bookbinding in the Twentieth Century* (1984)
Middleton
G. Naudé, *Instructions Concerning Erecting a Library* (1661)
H. M. Nixon, *English Restoration Bookbindings* (1974)
Nixon and Foot
J. B. Oldham, *English Blind-Stamped Bindings* (1952)
D. Pearson, *English Bookbinding Styles 1450–1800* (2005)
N. Pickwoad, 'Onward and Downward: How Binders Coped with the Printing Press before 1800', in *A Millennium of the Book*, ed. R. Myers *et al.* (1994)
E. Potter, 'The London Bookbinding Trade: From Craft to Industry', *Library*, 6/15 (1993), 259–80
J. Szirmai, *The Archaeology of Medieval Bookbinding* (1999)
M. Tidcombe, *Women Bookbinders 1880–1920* (1996)

18 Theories of Text, Editorial Theory, and Textual Criticism

Marcus Walsh

1 Issues for textual scholarship and theory

The book as a form has enabled the expression, transmission, and multiplication of knowledge. Written words are more stable than speech. Printed words are more stable and, equally important, more replicable than spoken or written words. Nevertheless, the permanence of the book is undercut regularly by various processes of change.

Texts have been embodied in a number of physical forms: handwritten on *papyrus, *vellum, or paper (*see* **10**), or scribally copied (occasionally derived in both cases from oral *dictation); printed in hand-set *type, machine-set type, or *stereotype; composed at a keyboard, electronically processed, and output to an electronic printing device; or electronically processed and sent as a file direct to a local visual display or to the *World Wide Web. Texts are products of human agency, composed by individuals and copied and processed—in MS, printed, and electronic forms—by a variety of technologies, all embodying human crafts and decisions.

Through these processes, texts are subject to innumerable types of variation and mistake. A dictating voice may be misheard; an author's or a *scribe's hand may be illegible and, hence, misread. Transcription always involves change and error, as well as a conscious or unconscious process of editing. *Composition (the setting of type) adds technically specific issues: the wrong case, the wrong *fount, the *turned letter. Performance texts may be transcribed or printed from faulty memorial reconstruction (*see* BAD QUARTOS OF SHAKESPEARE'S PLAYS). Type and typeset *formes are subject to 'batter', type movement, and loss. Etched or engraved plates are prone to wear and damage. Authors emend and revise, before, during, and after the publication process. A text may be subject to imposed change, *censorship by the publisher, by external authority, or *self-censorship. Unique MSS may be lost, destroyed, or damaged by interpolation, fire, flood, or vermin. Transmission from any medium to another—printed, photographic, electronic—may be affected by various types of interference. Electronic texts have their own characteristic modes of variation: misconversion between character sets, or locally unintended effects of global search and replace operations (*see* **19**).

Theorists of text and of editing have thus confronted many practical questions: the construing of foreign letter forms (e.g. Greek or Hebrew) and historical scripts (e.g. *secretary hand); consideration of the errors that might arise from misconstruction during the production process; the practices of printing houses and *compositors; the possible priorities and relations among multiple witnesses of a text; the historical *bibliography of printed texts; and lexical and semantic change.

There are larger issues of philosophical definition and choice, arising from conceptions of textual identity, textual meaning, and textual function. Conceptions of textual editing vary in the regard paid to *diplomatic and bibliographical evidence, and to considerations of putative *authorial intention and semantic coherence. Should editors base their work on the assumption that the text replicates the words intended by the author? Or should they assume that the text reflects a broader process of interaction among or negotiation between the original author (or authors), sponsors, publishers, printers, and audience? Should editors privilege a particular source document, and, if so, should that document be a MS or a copy of a printed edition? Should they consciously present the text in relation to contemporary audience tastes? These alternatives—variously prioritizing the author, the documentary witness, the sociological circumstances of production, or taste as a principle of authority—respond to different disciplinary and social sources and functions in the edition. For most of the 20th century, literary scholarship, particularly in English, privileged the author and used bibliographical and critical processes in order to reach a putative authorial text hidden or corrupted by subsequent error. Historians, by contrast, have generally preferred *diplomatic editions (i.e. a text faithfully transcribed from its appearance in a particular document) or a type- or photographic *facsimile of a particular document. In recent years, some theorists have advocated a more sociological approach to editing, and sought textual versions reflecting the complexities of social production. For centuries, texts have been adapted according to the perceived taste or capabilities of their target audience. *Pope, for example, purged *Shakespeare of comic improprieties in his 1723–5 edition, and the *Bowdlers produced an expurgated *Family Shakespeare* (1818).

2 Early classical and biblical textual scholarship

Textual study and textual editing began with the most ancient Western texts: the Greek classics and the Bible (*see* **2**, **3**). Classical textual scholarship originated, as far as is known, in the *Alexandrian Library, in the 2nd and 3rd centuries BC. Here, scholars undertook the huge task of ordering some hundreds of thousands of MSS—none of them original authorial documents—to produce from fragmented and widely diverse copies more reliable and complete texts of authors such as Homer. Scholars developed a system of marginal critical signs for such apparent errors as incorrect repetitions, interpolations, misorderings of lines, and spurious lines or passages. Corrections were normally not entered in the text itself, but made and justified in extended *scholia. Here, already, is an editorial practice founded on the exercise of critical judgment, in relation to issues of authorial style and usage.

After the decline of Alexandrian scholarship, the copying and editing of Greek and Latin literary MSS continued at Pergamum, where Crates (*c*.200–*c*.140 BC) examined and emended the text of Homer, and at Rome, where Aelius and Varro worked on issues of authenticity and textual corruption in the writings of Plautus and of others. In the later Roman empire, Hyginus wrote on the text of Virgil, M. Valerius Probus

applied Alexandrian methods to the texts of Virgil, Terence, and others, and Aelius Donatus and Servius commented on Terence and Virgil. After the empire's fall, classical texts continued to be copied in monastic *scriptoria. Although textual activity lapsed from the 6th to the 8th centuries, a marked renaissance occurred in the Carolingian era and the 11th and 12th centuries.

In the Renaissance, the classics of Rome and Greece were rediscovered, collected, edited, and *annotated by a succession of scholars, from *Petrarca and Poggio *Bracciolini onwards. Lorenzo Valla (1406–57) and *Poliziano were key figures in the development of textual criticism and historical scholarship. Valla influentially demonstrated, from linguistic and historical evidence, that the Donation of *Constantine was a *forgery, and wrote a ground-breaking study of Latin usage, the *Elegantiae Linguae Latinae* (1471). Poliziano used Greek sources to illuminate Latin texts, and argued for the superior authority of the earliest MSS. *Aldus's press issued a stream of Latin and Greek texts edited by a team of scholars, including *Musurus, who used the best available MSS and applied their linguistic knowledge to amend the MSS for the printer. Francesco Robortello edited Longinus (1552) and wrote the first developed study of the methodology of textual criticism, *De Arte Critica sive Ratione Corrigendi Antiquorum Libros Disputatio* (1557), which insisted on *palaeography, usage, and sense as criteria for *emendation. Major textual scholars in France and The Netherlands—notably Lucretius' editor *Lambin; Manilius' editor J. J. *Scaliger; Tacitus' editor *Lipsius; *Vossius; and Daniel *Heinsius—made significant contributions both to the methodology of editorial emendation and to essential areas of knowledge for informed editing, including chronology, the usage and lexis of the ancient languages, and literary contexts.

The earliest biblical textual scholars also had to deal with a plethora of non-original documents. The New Testament existed, in whole or in part, in some 5,000 Greek MSS, as well as in Latin versions and patristic quotation. St Jerome, author of the Vulgate Latin translation, was apparently conscious of the problems that arise in MS transcription, including the confusion of letters and of *abbreviations, transpositions, dittography, and scribal emendation. Humanist textual scholarship antedated printing. Valla, for instance, amended the Vulgate on the bases of the Greek original and patristic texts (1449; published by *Erasmus, 1505). The first printed bibles, by *Gutenberg and other presses, were in Latin. The Hebrew Old Testament was not printed until 1488, at the *Soncino

Press; and the first Greek New Testament, the *Complutensian Polygot, was printed in 1514 but not published until 1522. It was narrowly beaten to the market by Erasmus's edition, which, despite being hurriedly edited from the few MSS readily to hand, became the basis of the *textus receptus* that would dominate for four centuries, underlying Robert *Estienne's editions (1546 and 1549), Beza's Greek testaments (1565–1604), the *Authorized Version (1611), and the *Elzeviers' Greek testament (1624).

3 After the Renaissance: beginnings of rational methods

In France, Richard Simon's monumental study of the Old and New Testaments was the first full-scale analysis of the textual transmission of an ancient text. Investigating Greek MSS of the New Testament and surveying printed texts from Valla onwards, Simon examined critically the inconsistencies and repetitions of the Old Testament, especially of Genesis, imputing them not to the first penmen, but to scribal error. In England, Walton's *polyglot Bible (6 vols, 1655–7) included for the first time a systematic *apparatus of variant readings. *Fell issued a small-format Greek Testament with apparatus giving variants from dozens of MSS (1675). John Mill undertook an extensive study of the text of the New Testament; his examination of numerous MSS and printed editions culminated in an innovative edition (1707) with enormously detailed prolegomena, listing some 30,000 variants.

However, the overwhelmingly significant figure of the time, for European and English textual method, was Richard *Bentley (1662–1742). In his *Dissertation upon the Epistles of Phalaris* (published in the second edition of William Wotton's *Reflections upon Ancient and Modern Learning*, 1697)—one of the most devastating interventions in a long and pugnacious scholarly career—Bentley emphatically demonstrated that the letters attributed to the ancient tyrant Phalaris were spurious, and thus demolished Sir William Temple's adduction of Phalaris as evidence for the superiority of ancient writers. Bentley's argument was based on extraordinarily extensive literary, etymological, and historical evidence. His imposing scholarship and formidable methodology are in evidence throughout his editions of Horace (Cambridge, 1711; Amsterdam, 1713) and Manilius (1739). Familiar with the MS tradition, Bentley was aware of the distance of all surviving documents of classical writings from their originals. He was prepared both to diagnose errors that had, through many possible routes, entered

the text and to make emendations with or without the MSS' supporting authority. For Bentley, editorial choices, though informed by the documentary tradition, must advert to the sense of the text, as constrained by cultural and linguistic possibility: 'to us reason and common sense are better than a hundred codices' (note on Horace, *Odes*, 3. 27. 15).

Bentley also contributed to New Testament editing, publishing *Proposals for Printing a New Edition of the Greek Testament* (1721), to be based on the Vulgate and the oldest MSS of the Greek text, in both English and European libraries. He intended thereby to produce a text, not identical with the irredeemably lost original autographs, but representative of the state of the New Testament at the time of the Council of Nicaea (AD 325)—thus obviating a huge proportion of the tens of thousands of variants amongst later, and generally less authoritative, MSS. On the basis of his collations he claimed: 'I find that by taking 2,000 errors out of the Pope's Vulgate, and as many out of the Protestant Pope Stephens' [i.e. Estienne's 1546 New Testament], I can set out an edition of each in columns, without using any book under 900 years old, that shall ... exactly agree.' Aware that he was treading on sensitive ground, Bentley took a more reverent approach to the extant documentary witnesses, avowing that 'in the Sacred Writings there's no place for Conjectures ... Diligence and Fidelity ... are the Characters here requisite' (Bentley, *Proposals*, sig. A2ᵛ).

Bentley's work had a huge effect on classical editing in Europe and England, where his numerous disciples included Jeremiah Markland (1693–1776) and *Porson. His influence also extended into the expanding field of the editing of secular, modern, and early modern literary writing, particularly to *Theobald. For Theobald—editor of Shakespeare (1733) and the critic, in *Shakespeare Restored* (1726), of Pope's earlier, aesthetically driven edition of the playwright's works—the Shakespearean textual situation resembled that of the ancient classics. No 'authentic Manuscript' survived, and 'for near a Century, his Works were republish'd from the faulty Copies without the Assistance of any intelligent Editor ... *Shakespeare*'s Case has ... resembled That of a corrupt *Classic*; and, consequently, the Method of Cure was likewise to bear a Resemblance' (Smith, 74, 75). Theobald, as an 'intelligent' editor, was prepared, like Bentley, to venture conjectural emendation and to do so through careful reasoning based on a remarkably thorough knowledge of his author's writings, language, and broader cultural and linguistic context. The 'want of Originals' may require us to guess, but 'these Guesses turn into

Something of a more *substantial* Nature, when they are tolerably supported by *Reason* or *Authorities'* (Theobald, 133). Theobald's 18th-century successors followed him in their almost universal agreement that textual choices should be made on the basis of interpretive, as well as documentary, arguments. Nevertheless, as the century wore on, editors more fully recognized the status and authority of the *folio and *quarto texts, found better access to copies of both, and benefited from increasing understanding of Shakespeare and his times. Critical divination became a less significant part of an editor's methods: 'As I practised conjecture more, I learned to trust it less,' Samuel *Johnson famously wrote in the Preface to his 1765 edition (Smith, 145).

Theobald and Johnson, for all their textual care, followed the *textus receptus* of Shakespeare, based on the Fourth Folio and inherited through the publishing house of *Tonson, which owned the Shakespearean *copyright. In a significant move, *Capell not only bypassed traditional textual corruption, but applied a sophisticated editorial practice. Having collected virtually all the early printed editions of Shakespeare, Capell proceeded to *collation, adhering 'invariably to the old editions, (that is, the best of them) which hold now the place of manuscripts' (Shakespeare, 1. 20). From those early editions, he chose one as the 'groundwork' of his own text, never to be 'departed from, but in places where some other edition had a reading most apparently better; or in such other places as were very plainly corrupt but, assistance of books failing, were to be amended by conjecture' (Capell, i). Capell's use of the earliest texts, his relatively sophisticated understanding of textual authority, and his willingness to apply conjecture where the documents were demonstrably corrupt (i.e. resistant to interpretation by appeal to contextual knowledge) anticipates key features of the *Greg–*Bowers position in 20th-century textual theory.

The most important contribution to classical and biblical editing was the extended formulation of stemmatics by *Lachmann (1793–1853), and his forerunners F. A. Wolf, K. G. Zumpt, and F. W. Ritschl. For textual traditions where the original MSS are lost, even sophisticated practitioners lacked a clear and overriding principle for understanding relations amongst derivative MSS (and printed texts), and were thus limited in the extent to which they could provide bibliographical arguments for editorial choice. Lachmann's genealogical method transformed classical editing, and retains some value today. The editor, by this method, begins with a process of *recensio*,

analysing the MS evidence and constructing a *stemma codicum*, a family tree of surviving MSS deriving from an *archetype. The enabling principle is that 'community of error implies community of origin', i.e. if two or more MSS share a set of 'variants', they may be assumed to derive from a common source. MSS that can be shown to derive from other extant MSS may be excluded from editorial consideration. From the extant later MSS, it is possible to reconstruct an archetype, usually a lost but sometimes a surviving MS. On the basis of the *recensio* results, an editor may construct a text (*examinatio*), choosing between witnessed readings on the basis of the *stemma*, and making conjectural changes (*emendatio*) at points in the text where the MS tradition fails to provide a credible authorial original.

Lachmann's procedure provided some solid methodological ground for textual editing where originary documents were lost. Nonetheless, it has several limitations. It assumes that each witness derives from only one exemplar, although scribes since antiquity have attempted to improve their work with readings from second or further sources, producing conflated, or *contaminated, texts. It assumes that a derivative text can only produce new errors, not introduce corrections. Constructing the guiding stemma also involves judgements about the number and nature of variant readings. Lachmann's method assumes a single authoritative source, not allowing for such complexities as authorial revision. *Bédier alleged that textual critics overwhelmingly construct stemmata with two branches, which does not constitute a historically probable result; in his own work, Bédier rejected eclectic choice among witnessed readings and preferred the conservative policy of selecting a 'bon manuscrit', chosen on such grounds as coherence and regularity, minimally amended.

At the beginning of the 20th century, the most forceful theoretical writings on classical textual editing were those by *Housman. Their lasting import is in no way weakened by their frequent acerbity. For Housman, Lachmann's method was essential; it had properly removed from consideration 'hundreds of MSS., once deemed authorities' (*Manilius*, 1. xxxiii). Nonetheless, textual criticism 'is not a branch of mathematics, nor indeed an exact science at all. It deals with a matter … fluid and variable; namely the frailties and aberrations of the human mind, and of its insubordinate servants, the human fingers' ('Application', 69). Its subject is to be found in 'phenomena which are the results of the play of the human mind' (*Confines*, 38). Textual problems are individual; they require particular solutions. Textual criticism cannot be reduced to hard rules and fixed procedures; it requires 'the application of thought'. Housman had particular contempt for editors who, bewildered by the rival merit of multiple witnesses, retreated from critical judgment into reliance on 'the best MS.' Such a method 'saves lazy editors from working and stupid editors from thinking', but it inevitably begets 'indifference to the author himself', whose original words may not be found in such a MS (*Manilius*, 1. xxxii; *Lucan*, vi). Nor can it be assumed that the correction of obvious errors in a single witness will restore authorial readings: 'Chance and the common course of nature will not bring it to pass that the readings of a MS. are right wherever they are possible and impossible wherever they are wrong' (*Manilius*, 1. xxxii). It is the textual critic's responsibility to identify error, on the basis of the most extensive knowledge of 'literary culture', grammar, and metre, and by the exercise of 'clear wits and right thinking' (*Confines*, 43). The knowledgeable editor will know enough to recognize possible readings, and find 'that many verses hastily altered by some editors and absurdly defended by others can be made to yield a just sense without either changing the text or inventing a new Latinity'. However, Housman was equally alert to the dangers of 'the art of explaining corrupt passages instead of correcting them' (*Manilius*, 1. xl, xli). Behind all these propositions stands Housman's invariable insistence that textual editing should start with the author's thought.

4 Twentieth-century theories and practices of textual editing

As secular classics became increasingly the focus of scholarship in the humanities at the start of the 20th century, so a new methodological sophistication was applied to their textual criticism. The so-called *New Bibliography was developed by *McKerrow and Greg. McKerrow was first to use the phrase '*copy text'. The concept of using a particular text as the basis of an edition was not new, but in McKerrow's thinking it is specifically theorized as the text that best represents the author's intentions. In his earlier work, McKerrow argued that the editor should accept such later texts as incorporated authorial revisions and corrections (Nashe, 2. 197). Subsequently believing that a later edition would 'deviate more widely than the earliest print from the author's original manuscript', he argued that editors should base their text on 'the earliest "good" print', and insert 'from the first [later] edition

which contains them, such corrections as appear to us to be derived from the author'. Even at this stage, however, McKerrow's position remained essentially conservative. Resisting eclectic choice, he insisted that where a later edition contained demonstrably authorial substantive variants the editor must adopt them all: 'We are not to regard the "goodness" of a reading in and by itself ... we are to consider whether a particular edition taken *as a whole* contains variants from the edition from which it was otherwise printed which could not reasonably be attributed to an ordinary press-corrector, but ... seem likely to be the work of the author' (McKerrow, *Prolegomena*, 18). McKerrow's position remains here perilously close to the 'best MS' approach.

New Bibliographical theory reached its classic development in Greg's influential article 'The Rationale of Copy-Text'. Here Greg, in answer to McKerrow, mounted a powerful argument for critical editing. Rejecting 'the old fallacy of the "best text"' (Greg, 'Rationale', 24), by which an editor thinks himself obliged to adopt all the readings of his exemplar, he distinguished between *substantive readings ('those namely that affect the author's meaning') and *accidentals ('such in general as spelling, punctuation, word-division ... affecting mainly ... formal presentation') (p. 21). He argued that 'the copy-text should govern (generally) in the matter of accidentals, but that the choice between substantive readings belongs to the general theory of textual criticism and lies altogether beyond the narrow principle of the copy-text' (p. 26). In Greg's recommended procedure, the editor (where extant texts 'form an ancestral series') normally chooses the earliest text, which will 'not only come nearest to the author's original in accidentals, but also (revision apart) most faithfully preserve the correct readings where substantive variants are in question' (pp. 22, 29). Having chosen the copy text, the editor will follow it regarding accidentals. Where there is more than one text of comparable authority, however, 'copy-text can be allowed no over-riding or even preponderant authority so far as substantive readings are concerned' (p. 29). For Greg, as for McKerrow, the editor seeks the author's intended text, and is thus obliged to 'exercise his judgement' rather than fall back on 'some arbitrary canon' (p. 28). By applying critical discrimination amongst substantive readings in the quest for authorial readings, Greg belongs to an English lineage that includes Bentley, Housman, and Theobald.

It is an exaggeration to say that all subsequent textual critical theory consists of footnotes to Greg;

nonetheless, a high proportion of writing on the subject over the last half century has elaborated and developed Greg's thinking, or positioned itself in opposition to his tenets or their implications. Greg's rationale continues to provide a vital framework for editors working on English literary texts. Greg's most notable expositors and followers have been *Bowers and *Tanselle. Greg's expertise (like McKerrow's, and that of their ally A. W. *Pollard) lay chiefly in the field of 16th- and 17th-century literature, but Bowers insisted that Greg's was 'the most workable editorial principle yet contrived to produce a critical text that is authoritative in the maximum of its details ... The principle is sound without regard for the literary period' (Bowers, 'Multiple Authority', 86). Indeed, Bowers's own extraordinary editorial output included authors from Marlowe and Dekker, through Dryden and Fielding, to Whitman, Crane, and Nabokov. The Modern Language Association of America adopted the Greg–Bowers position as the basis for its *Statement of Editorial Principles and Procedures* (1967), which guided the work of the *Center for Editions of American Authors (established 1963). Bowers's major statements of bibliographical and editorial principle and method may be found in *Principles of Bibliographical Description* (1949), *On Editing Shakespeare and the Elizabethan Dramatists* (1955), *Textual and Literary Criticism* (1959), and *Bibliography and Textual Criticism* (1964).

A major predicate of the work of McKerrow, Greg, Bowers, and Tanselle is that the goal of literary editorial enquiry is the text intended finally by the author. In an age where the concept of authorial intention, or rather its knowability and reconstructability, has itself come under serious attack, this predicate has required sophisticated justification. A key document in this process has been Tanselle's 'The Editorial Problem of Final Authorial Intention', which draws on an extensive range of theoretical writing, including E. D. Hirsch's *Validity in Interpretation* (1967). Editors, Tanselle suggests, 'are in general agreement that their goal is to discover exactly what an author wrote and to determine what form of his work he wished the public to have'. Editorial choice depends upon a critical determination of intended authorial wording and meaning: 'of the meanings which the editor sees in the work, he will determine, through a weighing of all the information at his command, the one which he regards as most likely to have been the author's; and that determination will influence his decisions regarding variant readings' (Tanselle, 'Editorial Problem', 167, 210).

Authorial intention as a basis for textual editing is nevertheless a complex 'problem', and it has been interrogated from many points of view. Some have seen the privileging of authorial intention not as a rational choice, but determined by ideologies of individualism. Morse Peckham has complained that to privilege authorial intention is a form of 'hagiolatry', attributing to the author divine inspiration or charisma (Peckham, 136). Others, such as Greetham, have represented the project of reconstruction of an authorially intended text as an impossible Platonizing attempt to find a nonexistent ideal, a 'text that never was' (Greetham, *Theories*, 40). Texts raising particularly complex questions of intention and revision have given rise to significant shifts or innovations in the editorial paradigm. One controversial exemplar has been George Kane and E. Talbot Donaldson's edition of the B-text of *Piers Plowman* (1975), in which the editors insistently privileged the interpretation of variants based on internal evidence, rather than prior recension. Another, yet more contested, has been *Gabler's edition of Joyce's *Ulysses* (1984), in which a clean 'reading' text was printed in parallel with a *synoptic text and its apparatus, which documented in detail the diachronic processes of Joyce's alterations. The necessity of extensive textual apparatuses that provide full evidence for editorial deviations from the documentary witnesses has exercised both critical editors and their opponents. Issues raised by authorial revision, already present in writings within the Greg–Bowers tradition, have been a continuing matter of editorial concern. Authorial revision may produce distinct versions, of which no conflated edition can be properly representative. This argument—persuasive in the case of *Piers Plowman* and unimpeachable in the case of Wordsworth's *Prelude*, which grew from a two-book poem (1799) to a thirteen-book poem (1805)—has had force too for less obviously extensive revisions. In Shakespearean textual criticism, it has resulted in discrete editions of the 1608 quarto *History of King Lear* and the 1623 Folio *Tragedy of King Lear*. Parker has argued that relatively small-scale authorial revisions may have partly or wholly unintended consequences for large-scale textual meaning. Greg's textual discriminations have come under fire, as mechanisms of selection and control, in recent arguments for '*uwnediting' that dismiss cases for textual choice (on interpretive or bibliographical grounds) as arbitrary and ideologically driven, and prefer previously rejected texts, readings, and variants.

The argument for uwnediting may arise out of an informed insistence on bibliographical particularity, which conscientiously eschews semantic reading and the editorial process of discrimination arising from it (as with *McLeod), or from a rejection, itself ideologically compromised, of the historical reliance of critical editors on evidence and reason (as with Marcus). The radical scepticism of postmodern theory has also found its way into textual thinking. Goldberg, for instance, has argued that the multiple forms taken by texts mean 'that there is no text itself ... that a text cannot be fixed in terms of original or final intentions'. Hence, Goldberg concludes, 'no word in the text is sacred. If this is true, all criticism that has based itself on the text, all forms of formalism, all close reading, is given the lie' (Goldberg, 214, 215). This is a conclusion that, taken seriously, would disable not only the Greg–Bowers rationale but all text-based academic disciplines, and the book itself.

One of the most significant movements in text critical theory of the last three decades has been a sense amongst some thinkers—notably *McKenzie and *McGann—that the Greg–Bowers line reduced bibliography and textual editing to 'a sharply restricted analytic field' in 'desocializing' the understanding of textual production. Rejecting authorial autonomy and the possibility of an uninfluenced intention, McGann insisted that 'literary works are fundamentally social rather than personal or psychological products, they do not even acquire an artistic form of being until their engagement with an audience has been determined ... literary works must be produced within some appropriate set of social institutions' (McGann, *Critique*, 119, 121, 43–4). Those social institutions include scribes, collaborators, editors, censors, the *printing office, publishers, and the theatre. The production of the literary work, as well as its meanings, is significantly shaped, on this account, by multiple human agents and the forms of presentation with which those agents endow the work. The social argument has been persuasive for many areas of textual work—especially for modern Shakespeare editors, who would shift the emphasis from the book focus of the Greg–Bowers school towards the negotiation amongst playwright, playhouse, players, and audience.

The extent and consequences of these challenges are real, though it has been argued that the breadth and flexibility of the Greg–Bowers position has not always been fully comprehended and that it remains a competent rationale. It has not been refuted by the historical facts of authorial revision and distinct versions, or the social circumstances of literary creativity and production; none of these factors is wholly new to the debate. As Tanselle puts it, 'critical editors interested in authors' final intentions are not trying to mix versions but to recreate one ... critical editors ... all must rely on surviving documents ... and strive to reconstruct from them the texts that were intended by particular persons (whether authors alone, or authors in collaboration with others) at particular points in the past' (Tanselle, 'Textual Criticism and Literary Sociology', 120, 126).

The book-based edition itself faces a challenge from the most consequential recent development in textual criticism: the exploitation of computational resources (*see* **19**). A straightforward and powerful example is the full-text electronic database (e.g. Early English Books Online or Eighteenth-Century Collections Online), which provides users with facsimile pages of an astonishing range of early books. More complex, multimedia hypertextual resources are available on the *World Wide Web. Though the printed *critical edition has been itself a *hypertext of a sophisticated kind, it is certainly true that electronic hypertext can do much that the book cannot. Electronic memory allows for the presentation of multiple particular versions of the text of any particular work. Hyperlinks enable flexible connections among those texts, and among an essentially unlimited range of contexts, in video, audio, and textual formats. Software applications allow for seemingly infinite varieties of search and comparison among the resources of the hypertextual database. There are parallels and synergies here with postmodern tendencies in recent contemporary critical theory. Major hypertextual archives (e.g. the Rossetti Archive at the University of Virginia) already exist, and a number of writers—Landow, Lanham, McGann (*Radiant Textuality*)—have begun to develop the theory of hypertext, mostly in positive terms.

Electronic forms are inherently inclusive, and are thus powerful and valuable in themselves. However, either they do not make discriminations, or they make discriminations in hidden and unarticulated ways. Because of their very plenitude, hypertext *archives are not editions. Books are crafted objects, embodying critical intelligence, made by the normally irreversible decisions of their authors, printers, and publishers. The book-based *scholarly edition embodies its maker's ethical choices amongst texts, variants, and understandings. *Love has argued that 'the electronic medium with its infinite capacity to manufacture increasingly meaningless "choices" and its unwillingness to accept closure is almost by definition post-ethical or even anti-ethical' (Love, 274–5). Editors and textual critics, as they embrace some of the pleasures of an electronic future, will need more than ever to create central and transparent roles for agency, responsibility, and critical intelligence.

BIBLIOGRAPHY

J. H. Bentley, *Humanists and Holy Writ* (1983)

R. Bentley, ed., *Q. Horatius Flaccus* (1711)

— *Proposals for Printing a New Edition of the Greek Testament* (1721)

F. Bowers, 'Some Principles for Scholarly Editions of Nineteenth-Century American Authors', *SB* 17 (1964), 223–8

— 'Multiple Authority: New Problems and Concepts of Copy-Text', *Library*, 5/27 (1972), 81–115

E. Capell, *Prolusions; or, Select Pieces of Antient Poetry* (1760)

W. Chernaik *et al.*, eds., *The Politics of the Electronic Text* (1993)

T. Davis, 'The CEAA and Modern Textual Editing', *Library*, 5/32 (1977), 61–74

P. Delany and G. Landow, eds., *Hypermedia and Literary Studies* (1991)

J. Goldberg, 'Textual Properties', *SQ* 37 (1986), 213–17

A. Grafton, *Defenders of the Text* (1991)

D. C. Greetham, *Scholarly Editing* (1995)

— *Theories of the Text* (1999)

W. W. Greg, 'The Rationale of Copy-Text', *SB* (1950–51), 19–36

A. E. Housman, ed., *M. Manilii Astronomicon* (5 vols, 1903–30)

— 'The Application of Thought to Textual Criticism', *Proceedings of the Classical Association*, 18 (1921), 67–84

— ed., *Lucan Bellum Civile* (1926)

— *Selected Prose*, ed. J. Carter (1961)

— *The Confines of Criticism*, ed. J. Carter (1969)

G. Landow, *Hypertext* (1992)

R. A. Lanham, *The Electronic Word* (1993)

H. Love, 'The Intellectual Heritage of Donald Francis McKenzie', *Library*, 7/2 (2001), 266–80

L. Marcus, *Unediting the Renaissance* (1996)

R. Markley, ed., *Virtual Realities and their Discontents* (1996)

J. McGann, *A Critique of Modern Textual Criticism* (1983)

— *The Beauty of Inflections* (1985)

— *Textual Criticism and Literary Interpretation* (1985)

— *The Textual Condition* (1991)

— 'Textual Criticism and Literary Sociology', *SB* 44 (1991), 84–143

— *Radiant Textuality* (2001)

D. F. McKenzie, *Bibliography and the Sociology of Texts* (1986)

McKerrow, *Introduction*

R. B. McKerrow, *Prolegomena for the Oxford Shakespeare* (1939)

R. McLeod, 'UN *Editing* Shak-speare', *Sub-Stance*, 10 (1982), 26–55

Metzger, *The Text of the New Testament* (1992)

G. Most, 'Classical Scholarship and Literary Criticism', in *The Cambridge History of Literary Criticism*, vol. 4: *The Eighteenth Century*, ed. H. B. Nisbet and C. Rawson, (1997)

T. Nashe, *The Works of Thomas Nashe*, ed. R. B. McKerrow (5 vols, 1904–10; 2e, rev. F. P. Wilson, 1958)

H. Parker, *Flawed Texts and Verbal Icons* (1984)

M. Peckham, 'Reflections on the Foundations of Modern Textual Editing', *Proof*, 1 (1971), 122–55

Reynolds and Wilson

W. Shakespeare, *Mr William Shakespeare his Comedies, Histories, and Tragedies*, ed. E. Capell (10 vols, 1767–8)

P. Shillingsburg, *Scholarly Editing in the Computer Age* (1996)

D. N. Smith, ed., *Eighteenth Century Essays on Shakespeare*, 2e (1963)

G. Tanselle, 'Greg's Theory of Copy-Text and the Editing of American Literature', *SB* 28 (1975), 167–230

— 'The Editorial Problem of Final Authorial Intention', *SB* 29 (1976), 167–211

— 'The Editing of Historical Documents', *SB* 31 (1978), 2–57

— 'The Concept of *Ideal Copy*', *SB* 33 (1980), 18–53

— 'Recent Editorial Discussion and the Central Questions of Editing', *SB* 34 (1981), 23–65

— 'Classical, Biblical, and Medieval Textual Criticism and Modern Editing', *SB* 36 (1983), 21–68

— 'Historicism and Critical Editing', *SB* 39 (1986), 1–46

— *A Rationale of Textual Criticism* (1989)

— 'Textual Criticism and Deconstruction', *SB* 43 (1990), 1–33

— 'Textual Criticism and Literary Sociology', *SB* 44 (1991), 83–143

L. Theobald, *Shakespeare Restored* (1726)

U. von Wilamowitz-Moellendorff, *History of Classical Scholarship*, ed. H. Lloyd-Jones (1982)

W. Williams and C. Abbott, *An Introduction to Bibliographical and Textual Studies* (1999)

F. Wolf, *Prolegomena to Homer 1795*, tr. A. Grafton *et al.* (1985)

19 The Electronic Book

EILEEN GARDINER AND RONALD G. MUSTO

1 Definition

An electronic book (also e-book, ebook, digital book) is a text- and image-based publication in digital form produced on, published by, and readable on computers or other digital devices. E-books are presented visually or aurally, with the *audio book as a precursor to, and limited exemplum of, electronic publishing's potential. Components other than text have been considered enhancements, including multimedia (sound, images, film/video/animated graphics). The e-book is a young medium and its definition is a work in progress, emerging from the history of the print book and evolving technology. In this context it is less useful to consider the book as object—particularly as commercial object—than to view it as cultural practice, with the e-book as one manifestation of this practice.

2 History

2.1 Print antecedents

From the mid-1970s, text- and image-based publications were being produced by computer. The first developments took place in the newspaper industry, and the book business followed. Some segments of the book trades, particularly *scholarly publishing and other economically marginal areas, had experimented in the 1970s and 1980s with author-generated books.

Following complex instructions from their publishers, authors would produce *camera-ready copy that could be used to create *plates for printing. When authors began to have desktop *computers, they produced *copy that could compete with the quality of typeset pages. Within ten years, books were being produced on desktop machines, and innovators in book production had harnessed the power of these small computers to produce books inexpensively from electronic MSS or by simple rekeying, using word-processing software—the era of *desktop publishing had begun. By the early 1990s, these capacities were expanded by sophisticated page-makeup programs like PageMaker and Quark.

Large commercial publishers had invested heavily in the traditional forms of production and were slow at first to adopt new methods. Typesetters, however, were often using computers before the publishers who contracted out to them were aware of it. From the mid-1990s publishers understood the power of exploiting this technology themselves, which had a significant impact on the cost and speed of book production and resulted in the nearly fourfold growth in the number of US titles produced annually between 1994 (52,000) and 2004 (195,000).

The files used to produce books could be read on a computer screen, but paper was still the medium of presentation. Electronic files alone were not enough to initiate a revolution in reading. Many factors had to be in place before the era of e-books arrived.

164

2.2 Digital development

In July 1945 Vannevar Bush, a pioneering engineer in the development of analog computing, published an article in which he introduced the Memex: a hypothetical instrument to control the ever-accumulating body of scientific literature. He envisioned an active desk that performed as a storage and retrieval system. A Memex user would consult a book by tapping a code on a keyboard, bringing up the text. The Memex had many features that are now familiar components of e-books: pages, page turners, annotation capability, internal and external linking, and the potential for storage, retrieval, and transmittal. However, Bush imagined that all this would be accomplished through the miracle of microfilm.

It would be another twenty years before the development of one of the essential elements of the electronic book: hyperlinking. In 1965 Ted (Theodor Holm) Nelson first published the terms '*hypertext' and 'hypermedia'. These two sides of hyperlinking were developed by teams of engineers working throughout the 1960s and 1970s. On 9 December 1968, Douglas Engelbart made a presentation, now known as 'The Mother of All Demos', of the oNLine System (or NLS), developed at the Stanford Research Institute. This event introduced many of the elements of today's digital world: e-mail, tele-conferencing, video-conferencing, and the mouse. Most importantly for the future of the book, it demonstrated hypertext and introduced the 'paper paradigm', which embodied the current standard experience of a computer: windows, black text on white background, files, folders, and a desktop.

At the same time, Andries van Dam was working with colleagues at the Brown University Center for Computer & Information Sciences, developing the Hypertext Editing System, unveiled in April 1969. This spawned a variety of hypermedia and hypertext experiments during the 1970s and 1980s. Between 1978 and 1980, students at the Massachusetts Institute of Technology produced the first significant hypermedia application, the Aspen Moviemap, which used a stop-frame camera to create an interactive map of Aspen, Colorado, based on actual photos. These experiments culminated in the development of HyperCard at Apple Computer by Bill Atkinson in 1987. Apple released this software as freeware on its new Macintosh computer. Content creators immediately embraced the program's promise.

Although many early works were no doubt lost, one has long endured. In 1988, Brian Thomas, along with Philip A. Mohr, Jr., released *If Monks Had Macs ...* from their company, riverText. It was first published as a collection of games and serious ideas constructed in HyperCard using the pre-print metaphor of a *monastic library, complete with music and the sound of a cloister's fountain. It came on 800K diskettes as Macintosh freeware, thus establishing an early precedent that would resonate in the later open-access movement. It also included what Thomas said 'might be called the first real or widely read e-book', *The *Imitation of Christ*, one of the first bestsellers of the *Gutenberg revolution (*see* **6**). *If Monks ...* also included an introduction to the White Rose, a clandestine group of young German students who were hunted down and summarily executed for distributing anti-Nazi *pamphlets they printed on a secret press.

The choices in *If Monks Had Macs ...* were prophetic: its metaphors of pre-print MS, early print, and marginal publishing not only introduced a new medium, but also set the intellectual and cultural paradoxes within which the e-book still operates: an essentially nonlinear, multiple medium that most readers and producers approach with the cultural apparatus developed for the *codex. It was also both retrospective and prescient in terms of production and distribution: like early print, it was produced and distributed outside the mainstream of academic and large business institutions.

In 1993, the small independent firm, Italica Press, published its first e-book, also on HyperCard on two 800K diskettes: *The Marvels of Rome for the Macintosh* was an electronic edition of the celebrated medieval guide to the city. In a 1994 review, *Architronic* remarked: 'it is an enjoyable demonstration of the future of HyperCard programming, when interactive layers will make innovative approaches to thinking about texts possible'. In 1995, *If Monks Had Macs ...* was commercially released by Voyager, which had previously released an annotated, disk-based version of the Beatles' *A Hard Day's Night*—a marvel of electronic publishing, if only a curiosity of cinema.

2.3 The CD-ROM

Although tours de force, these early experiments were cumbersome, slow, and nearly unviewable. Things began to change with the introduction of the CD-ROM in 1987. Already in use in the music industry by 1982, the CD-ROM was first widely integrated into consumer computers as a storage device in the 1991 Apple Macintosh. A CD could hold nearly 800MB and was far more convenient to handle, store, and transport than an 800K diskette. By 1992, the first e-book titles began to arrive on CD-ROM, again as freeware, but intended to encourage consumers to purchase computers with new CD-ROM drives.

By 1993, 4 million CD-ROM players had been sold in the US market; large publishers, which had hesitated to enter the market as long as e-books were diskette-based and limited in size, now jumped in. CD-ROM book sales reached nearly $1 billion by 1994, with more than 8,000 titles, ranging from the Bible to reference and business books, and from fiction to children's literature. Bookshop chains were encouraged to set aside CD-ROM sections for the new e-books, and the industry began to float the first of many pronouncements of the end of print. By late 1994, however, sagging sales and a stagnating user base of individual computer owners with CD-ROM drives (5 million)—coupled with a widespread discontent within the library community over the difficulty of cataloguing, and providing storage and access for, the new medium—sent CD-ROM titles tumbling from most publishers' lists. The Library of *Congress's decision not to catalogue CD-ROMs confirmed their end for all but large reference collections, archival use, or supplemental material in *textbooks, instructors' manuals, or study guides. By the late 1990s, most narrative titles on CD had become audio books: a return not to the codex but to pre-codex oral traditions.

2.4 The World Wide Web

Although disk-based e-books proved as ephemeral to the development of the electronic book as *block printing and the block book in the ultimate development of the print revolution, the lessons learned during the years of developing digital content were not lost. Large corporate investments in the digitization of content, improvements in delivery software, and the vital experience in conceptualizing hypertext and in obtaining and then protecting digital rights, had profound effects on the development of the e-book, even if the largest stakeholders ultimately decided to stand on the sidelines and await further signs of progress.

The invention and growth of the *World Wide Web was particularly important for e-books, because the Internet provided enormous advantages in storage, retrieval, and delivery. Yet the first library of e-books antedates this technological leap by almost 25 years. In 1971 Michael Hart at the University of Illinois began Project Gutenberg (PG) by creating electronic texts of small, public-domain works, beginning with the *Declaration of Independence, the Bill of Rights, and the US Constitution. These were hand-keyed: a

labour-intensive, and volunteer, effort. When the capacity of storage media increased, PG digitized larger books, including *Alice in Wonderland*, *Peter Pan*, and the Bible; and with the development of affordable optical character recognition (*OCR) technology by the mid-1990s, PG could rely on a speedier processing method, which eventually had nearly the same accuracy as rekeying. This pioneer initiative continues on 40 mirror sites with thousands of books that can be read on any computer, personal digital assistant (PDA), or reading device.

3 Scale and commercialization

Technologically, commercially, and culturally, the e-book remained essentially a digital version of print; yet by 2003 virtually all content was being produced digitally, either originally created or retrospectively converted. To accomplish this conversion, most enterprises relied either on automated digitization or on the low wages and long working hours of thousands of centres in the Global South (primarily in India), where an enormous new workforce could produce encoded text, images, and links. This raised ethical and economic issues that were virtually nonexistent for the print book, which grew out of the highly skilled guild and other craft enterprises of the late Middle Ages and remained the realm of expert and relatively well-compensated craftsmen.

As early as the 1980s, computer servers were developed with the capacity to store and distribute digital content consistently and widely; from 1991, Gophers and listservs (*see* SEARCH ENGINES) began to establish networks of both scholarly and non-commercial communication. With the emergence of CompuServe and AOL in 1995, widespread commercial delivery systems had begun to take advantage of the web's broad interconnectedness, and its ability to store and serve up content independent of client machines and physical media like diskettes or the CD-ROM.

The development of independent web-browsing software took these disparate elements and brought the possibilities of the e-book one step forward. There were several early examples, but Mosaic, the first 'user-friendly' browser, was not released until 1993. It was developed at the National Center for Supercomputing Applications (NCSA) at the University of Illinois at Urbana-Champaign. Mosaic changed the face of the Internet with the integration of text and image in the same window. Marc Andreessen, the leader of the team that developed it with funding from the National Science Foundation, soon turned Mosaic into a commercial venture that developed into Netscape, which introduced Navigator in 1994. In the same year Microsoft introduced Explorer, also based on Mosaic. In 1993 there were 500 web servers; in 1994 there were 10,000, and by June 2007 there were over 125 million websites—the alteration from counting servers to sites reflecting an enormous growth and change in hosting, from discrete peripheral networks to colossal aggregated data centres.

Such developments meant that libraries of e-books emulating PG began to appear with frequency in the late 1990s. Some mimicked libraries of printed materials by providing a searchable catalogue of available works; others offered searchability of the full text across the collection. Some, such as netLibrary, offered digital downloads; others, including *Perseus, Questia, ACLS Humanities E-Book, and Oxford Scholarship Online, offered online access through institutional or individual subscription. Still others—ranging from large-print booksellers (e.g. *Barnes & Noble and *amazon.com), to publishers' own online stores, to dedicated online electronic booksellers—followed a retail model, selling one e-book at a time. A commercial avatar of PG appeared in Google Book Search, which promised vast amounts of content free to users, but its approach to copyrighted material proved controversial and slowed its full public release.

4 Characteristics

Certain characteristics of e-books are unlikely to change. These are associated with the codex: *title, contributors, table of *contents, list of illustrations and tables, *front matter, *chapters, pages, page or paragraph numbers, *running heads, *book marks, *annotations, back matter (*index, *glossary, references, notes, *bibliography, etc.), *copyright notice, *cataloguing information, and *International Standard Book Number. Although these elements have the same taxonomies in print and electronic media, they may sometimes have a different form and function. For instance, the table of contents in an e-book, instead of being on its own page or pages, is often located in a separate cell to the left of the text and is viewable throughout the book. 'Pages' or 'screens' need not be all the same size and can function organically in relation to the relative size of portions of the text. A page might contain a paragraph or as much as a whole chapter, although for ease of reading and navigation, the chapter is often broken into subsections, each presented on a separate page. In an e-book, pages or paragraphs are often numbered for identification and referencing. Annotations need not be either footnotes or endnotes. They can appear in a separate (pop-up or parallel) window, giving the reader the opportunity to look at the text and the annotation simultaneously. They can also appear in the separate window with all the other notes, so that the reader can see them in context. Cross-references hyperlinked within a book can bring a reader to other locations in the text, as well as to reference materials, such as *glossaries, *dictionaries, and *gazetteers.

5 Reading practices and authorship

To understand what components of an e-book make it a 'book' is only half the subject at hand. The other half is to understand what components make it electronic. By definition it is in digital form: produced on, published by, and readable on a computer or other device, but special attributes accrue to the book by this form. The principal feature of an e-book is hyperlinking, or moving seamlessly from one place to another designated place or 'target' by clicking on text or image (hypertext and hypermedia respectively). Most of the navigation features of e-books are the result of hyperlinking, whether the table of contents, annotations, cross references, or bookmarks. A related capability is scripting: like hyperlinking, scripting initiates an action, but rather than simply bringing the reader to another place, it can trigger complex automated actions simultaneously, like opening additional windows, playing music or video, or enlarging images.

Searchability is another key feature of the e-book, and functions to identify word or other object occurrences. Searching does not replace an index, but augments it, since indexes provide a sense of the topics, questions, and concerns of the text regardless of the keywords an author uses. Here one encounters one of the chief issues in electronic publishing: *authorial intention and control over the reader's experience of the text. Hyperlinking, non-linear and multipolar connections, and vast quantities of supplemental materials open up myriad paths to reading and interpretation: deconstruction and reassembly of an author's argument and ultimate sense may be central to the online experience; authorial voice and point of view are contested far more actively than in print.

The e-book also allows a publisher or distributor to control access to a title in ways unimagined even by the *Index Librorum Prohibitorum. It can encrypt the book and apply a digital-rights management (DRM) scheme to any book, chapter, article, image, video clip, or sound file. It can control printing, copying, and alterations. It can—depending on legal issues—track usage, preferences, even the rate of reading.

6 Coding: approaches and functions

All e-books rely on systems of encoding text and images to deliver consistent and reliable results to a reader. While it is possible to create e-books from proprietary software packages—for example, *word processing programs, page-makeup programs, extensions of such programs (Immedia), or hypertext programs—this approach relies on having the proper software to read the e-books installed on the end user's machine. Solutions to this issue take various forms. The earliest and perhaps still most universal has been ASCII (*American Standard Code for Information Interchange). Because of its universal readability, sites such as PG began with, and still make available, ASCII versions of their texts as well as other formats. Another solution has been the various versions of 'portable document format' or *PDF files first developed by Adobe for its Acrobat software in 1993 and adopted by other commercial and open-source content creators (Common Ground, Envoy). PDFs allow content to be shared with other devices regardless of platform or software. As PDF software has evolved, it has enabled creators to incorporate not only text and images but also multiple viewing options, searchability, sound, music, video, hyperlinking, and scripting. The chief limitation of collections of PDF documents, however, remains the lack of cross-searchability among titles.

The development of the Web went hand in hand with the creation of its fundamental component, Hypertext Markup Language, or *HTML. This coding language is the universal engine of the Web and allows most of its basic functions. Although simple to learn and deploy, HTML has certain drawbacks, most noticeably a lack of predictable results in formatting and presenting anything but basic design layouts and text formats. To refine HTML, various other approaches have been developed, including *SGML (Standard Generalized Markup Language) and *XML (Extensible Markup Language). The last is currently the standard for e-book development because it offers greater control over text, images, and other e-book components. Also, and more importantly, it establishes the overall structure of e-books in an open-source, replicable, scalable, and predictable manner. The basic language structure is a subset of SGML and was developed in the 1980s (with version 3 published in 1994) for the parsing, presentation, and preservation of early texts. From SGML derived the conventions of the TEI (Text Encoding Initiative) consortium, from which derive most document architectures (document type definitions or DTDs). Although developers continue to offer more sophisticated variations on page layout, hypertext, and parsing programs, the widespread international adoption of TEI in the world of libraries, archives, and publishing continued to assure its dominance.

7 Models and aesthetics

E-books are extremely adaptable and functional; when the proper coding language and syntax are applied, they can be formatted and designed to mirror the best print traditions and practices. Yet this very comparison with print models raises issues of technological dependence and transition; every new model of digital innovation for the book seems to look back to historical precedents from the age of the codex and early print. After Gutenberg's revolution, the various forms of book production—MS, block printing, or movable type—coexisted for almost two centuries with no readily apparent fitness of any one mode to survive the others.

Ultimately, movable type outstripped both the MS and the block book for reasons which are obvious today but which, at the time, seemed its very weaknesses: standardization; the reorganization of the page to clearly defined zones of type, margin, and image; the inflexibility of its glossing and other annotation systems; the paring down of *de luxe features like elaborately illuminated capitals, flourishes,

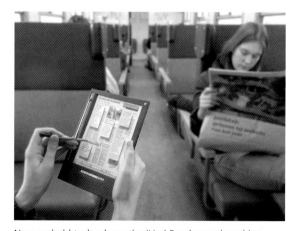

New and old technology: the iLiad Reader marketed by Libresco. Just as the characteristics of *newspapers changed people's reading habits and the railway revolutionized the distribution of print, so e-books may change how, what, when, and where material is read.

colouring, variation of typeface and *point sizes; and even limitations on the physical dimensions and media of the book—all in the name of sustainability. In the end, however, movable type's modularity offered convenience, economy, and consistency.

In the same way, the creation of standardized online tools and coding modules today may appear to limit the creative freedom of website authors, whose works remain unique artistic creations, akin to the *artist's book: beautiful works, like those by *Picasso or *Matisse, that are not intended to be duplicated but stand alone to present us with the freshness of the state of the art. Like the MSS of the classics and scriptures with their endless variants of text, layout, and *apparatus bemoaned by Renaissance scholars and printers, these websites lack common standards and common norms for reading and review. These characteristics make them unamenable to common publishing or scholarly practices of fixed revisions and editions. Although often collaborative, these websites are also frequently individually maintained. Like the MSS scattered in monastic libraries throughout Europe that the humanists sought to recover and transform into standardized print before they disappeared, such websites are also difficult to sustain and preserve.

These lessons and precedents of the codex's past remain cogent in the digital realm. As in print, the best e-books are formatted with sufficient borders and a line length constrained by the eye's gaze—not more than ten to twelve words per line. Although online choices are more limited, founts and sizes are applied with the same care: primarily *serif for text and *sans serif for display. Colour is used sparingly in text, as it may distract from the flow of reading.

Coding languages, editorial skills, and historical precedent aside, some of the more significant disadvantages of the e-book remain aesthetic. Most have been the result of current reading devices. The surface that substitutes for paper has not enhanced the reading experience. Both the texture and lighting of most screens had been mediocre. In addition, the space of the reading display was often small, and it was usually horizontal, whereas the print book and its cultural habitus have customarily favoured a vertical format.

Presentation and reading remain highly dependent on the device and software used. There are two current alternatives: devoted readers and PDAs with dedicated software as against conventional computers with web browsers and other general-reader software. PDAs have constrained the format and potential of e-books, whereas computers have offered more user-friendly display space, usability, and compatibility.

Between 1999 and 2002 a concerted effort was launched to capture the term 'electronic book' or 'e-book' and associate it with the devices themselves rather than with content. This effort emanated from a 'book as object' perspective, particularly 'the book as commercial object', weighing mass and price against cultural practice. The market saw the rapid rise and decline of the devices: Franklin eBookMan, Gemstar and RCA eBooks, PalmPilots, RocketeBooks, all missing the mark.

What did emerge from the effort to produce such devices was the development of e-book reader software, such as Adobe, Microsoft, Palm, Mobipocket, and Kindle. Initially, many were device-specific; but as desktop and laptop computers became the most widely used reading devices, browsers began to function seamlessly with reader software, thus piggybacking on an installed base of available devices, which also had the advantage of not being single-purpose or dedicated. Each year brings new efforts, and the technology improves so that the electronic reader will one day function like a full computer while emulating or improving upon the look and feel of the attractively bound codex. Apple iPhone (multifunction), Amazon Kindle (dedicated), and Sony Reader (dedicated and allied with Google Book) are taking three new directions.

Meanwhile, there are several advantages to e-books over their print counterparts. Convenience is one. Having neither weight nor volume, electronic books are easy to store and transport. They offer greater flexibility in format: colour, size, founts, layouts are all tremendously variable, even within the parameters of good taste. They offer a richer reading experience through hyperlinking to sound, video, images, and text. E-books can also incorporate a remarkable timeliness: they can be scripted to gain access to current information from online resources, or information can be updated on devices as required.

8 State of the art: three visions

In March 1999, *Darnton described a model for the e-book as a six-layered pyramid, with the lightest piece of interpretation at the top, and the material becoming broader and heavier with commentary and primary sources as the reader delved towards the bottom. The e-book was a self-contained construct produced by author and reader together, with comments, interpretive essays, and exchanges all holding up the piece at the top. Darnton's article had an immediate and profound impact and became an important theoretical model. Darnton also engaged the culture of reading in the electronic environment. He believed that 'the computer screen would be used for sampling and searching, whereas concentrated, long-term reading would take place by means of the conventional printed book or downloaded text'.

In 2001, Clifford Lynch of the Coalition for Networked Information offered his own definition of the e-book: 'just a large structured collection of bits that can be transported on CD-ROM or other storage media or delivered over a network connection, and which is designed to be viewed on some combination of hardware and software ranging from dumb terminals to web browsers on personal computers to the new book reading appliances'. Lynch wondered if the tradition of the book, as either cultural practice or commercial object, would be discarded in favour of some new model. Lynch's bare-boned and catholic definition reflected his throughgoing familiarity with the field and its most important players. He dared to look forward to the end of print culture.

At the same time, and with greater fanfare, the editor and publisher Jason Epstein offered in the *New York Review of Books* his own vision of the e-book and its future: most digital files will be printed and bound on demand by ubiquitous ATM-style machines. Epstein's view was utopian, not because of any grand vision of a digital future, but precisely because of its negation of technological and cultural developments. Like More's original *Utopia*, it was as much a critique of current practice and a nostalgic glance at a lost past as a blueprint for the future. As late as 2008 he continued to promote an alliance of publishers that would essentially link the future of the e-book to that of print: relying on myriad points of sale and assuming a widespread competence of retail delivery.

9 Conclusion

As the e-book entered its second decade, all options remained viable, ranging from scanned print, to print on demand, and digital downloads, to born-digital works existing on and delivered through the World Wide Web. No model had as yet attained the level of an industry, much less a cultural, standard; and issues of open access, copyright, and reading devices remained thorny. But enormous changes had occurred in the culture of reading and production: the electronic realm was firmly in the ascendant; an entire generation had been educated and reared on various electronic formats; and the amounts of data, including the book produced in electronic form, had long overwhelmed that produced by print.

What is a book? If a series of discrete cuneiform texts recording grain or cattle stocks were placed in some edited order inside a container, would they constitute a 'book'? Are all the MS books and other documents catalogued and uncatalogued in an archive, one large book? Are games, *telephone directories, interactive narratives, or the results of data mining, books? What roles do the author, the reader, and the medium play? For example, does the ever-changing content, bookmarks, and hyperlinks in an iPhone constitute a new, irreplicable book? Have we reached a stage in the development and organization of information where human agency is becoming increasingly irrelevant to the creation and consumption of objects of knowledge? Or will individual choice and taste become all important? The radical dismemberment and reassociation of content in the digital realm force us to look at these questions in a new light, with a newly focused urgency. As Lynch notes, physical objects and cultural practice stand together in a dynamic dialogue. Are all these forms of communication part of the future of 'the book' in which we still play a role, assume an agency, or are they part of some other future? *See also* ELECTRONIC EDITING AND MARKUP LANGUAGES; ELECTRONIC BOOKS AND HYPERTEXT.

BIBLIOGRAPHY

V. Bush, 'As We May Think', *Atlantic Monthly*, July 1945, www.theatlantic.com/doc/194507/bush, consulted July 2007

C. M. Christensen, *The Innovator's Dilemma: When New Technologies Cause Great Firms to Fail* (1999)

R. Darnton, 'The New Age of the Book', *New York Review of Books*, 46 (18 Mar. 1999), www.nybooks.com/articles/546, consulted July 2007

D. Edgerton, *The Shock of the Old: Technology and Global History since 1900* (2006)

— The Demo, video.google.com/videoplay?docid=8734787622017763097&q=engelbart, consulted July 2007

J. Epstein, 'Reading: The Digital Future', *New York Review of Books*, 48 (5 July 2001), www.nybooks.com/articles/14318, consulted July 2007

M. Hart, 'The History and Philosophy of Project Gutenberg', www.gutenberg.org/wiki/Gutenberg:The_History_and_Philosophy_of_Project_Gutenberg_by_Michael_Hart, consulted July 2007

Knowledge Worker: A Conversation with Brian Thomas, members.aol.com/hcheaven/interviews/thomas/thomas1.html, consulted July 2007

C. Lynch, 'The Battle to Define the Future of the Book in the Digital World', *First Monday*, May 2001, www.firstmonday.org/issues/issue6_6/lynch, consulted July 2007

Mosaic: The First Global Web Browser, www.livinginternet.com/w/wi_mosaic.htm, consulted July 2007

V. Mosco, *The Digital Sublime: Myth, Power, and Cyberspace* (2005)

M. Naimark, Aspen Moviemap, www.naimark.net/projects/aspen.html, consulted July 2007

20a The History of the Book in Britain, c.1475–1800

ANDREW MURPHY

1 Origins

The history of the book in Britain begins, in fact, on the Continent. In 1471, the Kent-born merchant *Caxton travelled from Bruges to Cologne, where he formed a partnership with the printer and *punchcutter Johannes Veldener. Having mastered the art of printing, Caxton returned to Bruges in the following year, probably accompanied by Veldener and by an assistant, de *Worde. At Bruges, the merchant set up a press and issued the first English-language printed book, the *Histories of Troy* (1473/4), his own translation of Raoul Le Fèvre's *Le Recueil des histoires de Troyes*. Caxton eventually returned to England (probably in 1476) and established a press in the precincts of Westminster Abbey, assisted again by de Worde. The first piece of printing to be completed at Caxton's English press was an *indulgence produced for the abbot of Abingdon—an early indication of how important *jobbing printing would prove to be within the trade. In 1477, Caxton issued the first printed edition of The *Canterbury Tales. In the same year, he published *The Dictes or Sayengis of the Philosophres*, an 11th-century Arabic work by Mubashshir ibn Fatik, Abu al-Wafa, which had been translated (from a French-language version) by Earl Rivers, brother-in-law of Edward IV. Over the course of his career, Caxton published works by Boethius, Cato, Cicero, Higden, Lydgate, Virgil, and others.

On Caxton's death in 1492, de Worde took over the business. A native of Alsace, he was typical of the printers who helped to expand the trade in its earliest decades. Government legislation in 1484, intended to restrict the conditions under which aliens could conduct business in England, specifically exempted printers and other members of the publishing trade from its terms in order to promote the growth and development of the industry at a time when few natives had the necessary training or equipment to set themselves up as printers. De Worde soon found himself competing for business against the Normans *Pynson and Guillaume Faques (who changed his name to William Fawkes and was appointed *King's Printer in 1503), along with the Belgian de *Machlinia and his partner *Lettou, who may have been a Lithuanian. Gradually, more native printers entered the trade, and in 1534 the government repealed the exemption that foreign printers had enjoyed since the 1484 Act.

As the trade expanded, competition caused printers to move toward specialization. De Worde, one of the first to recognize the value of the *textbook trade, aimed a substantial percentage of his output squarely at the grammar school market. Pynson (who succeeded Fawkes as King's Printer in 1506) specialized in legal printing, producing volumes of statutes, law codes, and handbooks for lawyers. Other identifiable popular classes of books in the first century of printing included *herbals and medical works, most notably Sir Thomas Elyot's *Castel of Helth*, issued in several editions from 1539; *translations of the classics, such as Arthur Golding's version of Ovid's *Metamorphoses* (first four books, 1565; fifteen books, 1567); *chronicles and histories (e.g. Holinshed's *Chronicles of England, Scotlande, and Irelande*, 1577) and ephemeral works of various kinds, including *ballads, *almanacs, and *pamphlets purporting to provide the last words of executed criminals. Religious publishing was also particularly important in the period.

2 The Stationers' Company

Over time, the publishing trade became more highly organized. A trade company for *scribes, illuminators, and those involved in the binding and sale of MS books had existed in London since 1403. The earliest printers tended not to affiliate themselves with this company, largely because they were generally based in parts of the capital that lay beyond the City of London's jurisdiction. This was Caxton's situation, as his original base in Westminster was not within the City boundaries (and, in any case, having started life as a merchant, he was a long-standing member of the Mercers' Company). As time went on and more printers began to locate themselves within the city (particularly in the area around *St Paul's), the *Stationers' Company gradually came to be the publishing trade's representative organization. The Company's importance was recognized in 1557, when Queen Mary granted it a charter establishing it as a fully fledged corporation. The charter decreed that printing was to be confined to those who were freemen of the Company, thus giving them, as *Blayney has put it, 'a virtual monopoly of printing in England' (Blayney, *Stationers' Company*, 47). In return for the powers granted to it, the Stationers' Company was expected to play a role in what amounted to government *censorship. Company officers were empowered to search the premises of all printers and other members of the trade and to seize any seditious or heretical material. The Company regulated publishing and enforced an early system of *copyright (though the word itself is an 18th-century coinage) by requiring that new titles be registered in advance of being printed.

By the close of the 16th century, the Stationers' Company was beginning to lay the groundwork for consolidating the *rights in certain standard works into a portfolio controlled by its most senior members. A royal grant by James I in 1603 added to this portfolio a further range of works, including books of private prayers, *psalters, psalms, and almanacs. The '*English Stock', as it became known, confirmed the prosperity of the Company, although the running of the scheme also had the effect of alienating many among the most junior ranks of the profession, who felt excluded from the profits generated by the staple works that formed the core of the English Stock. Efforts in the early decades of the 17th century to create a Latin Stock and an Irish Stock proved unsuccessful.

At the same time as the Stationers' Company was consolidating its power, the book trade itself was also undergoing a process of division and specialization. When Caxton printed a book, he bore the up-front costs—such as buying paper—himself (though he also relied on the frequent support of aristocratic patrons). He then printed the book using his own press and sold at least some copies directly to the buying public. As the 16th century progressed, these three aspects of the book trade—financing the production costs, producing the book, and selling it—gradually diverged into the distinctive roles of publisher, printer, and retailer. At the end of the century, there was still a high degree of overlap between the three, and it was not uncommon for individual members of the trade to serve, effectively, as publisher-printers: purchasing the rights to print a book, financing the costs, and then printing it themselves. Thus, the *title-page for Edmund Spenser's *The Shepheardes Calender* (1579) indicates that it was 'Printed by Hugh Singleton, dwelling in Creede Lane neere vnto Ludgate at the signe of the gylden Tunne, and are there to be solde.' Increasingly, however, title-pages came to bear a standard formula, which indicated that a book was printed 'By X for Y.' Thus, for example, when Thomas Middleton's *Microcynicon* appeared in 1599, the title-page noted that it had been 'Imprinted at London by Thomas Creede, for Thomas Bushell' and that it was 'to be sold' at Bushell's 'shop at the North Doore of Paules Church'. Here Bushell was the publisher, employing Creede as his printer; by now, the publisher's address was being provided largely for the benefit of those seeking to buy copies of the book wholesale (Blayney, 'Publication', 390).

Early in the 17th century, *Bodley prevailed upon the Stationers' Company to enter into an unusual agreement with Oxford University. He set himself the task of resuscitating the University's library and oversaw the opening of a new building—named in his honour—in 1602. Bodley had considerable success in convincing antiquarians, scholars, and other benefactors to donate books and MSS to the library. He also persuaded the Stationers' Company to arrange for the library to be provided with one free copy of every work registered at Stationers' Hall. Although the library's holdings increased considerably as a result of Bodley's efforts, in truth the collection remained quite limited by modern standards. Almost half a century after it had opened its doors, the Bodleian held a mere 15,975 volumes (Benson, 113). The Oxford holdings were not, however, unusually small: all British universities had very limited collections at the time. Beyond the

173

universities, libraries tended to be smaller still and were mostly confined to religious institutions of one sort or another. The high cost of books throughout this early period tended to restrict private ownership of significant numbers of books to those with substantial incomes.

3 Beyond London

The concentration of power in the hands of the Stationers' Company had the effect of retarding the development of printing elsewhere in the country. Some printing had been carried out at the abbey of St Albans late in the 15th century, where the output of the Press at *St Albans included the *Book of Hawking* (compiled 1486). There were also early attempts to establish publishing enterprises in the English university towns. *Rood began printing at Oxford in 1481 and *Siberch commenced work at Cambridge in 1519; neither venture was particularly successful. In the 1580s, Joseph Barnes and Thomas *Thomas carried out some printing at, respectively, Oxford and Cambridge, but it was not until the late 17th century in Oxford and the very early 18th century in Cambridge that the university presses were established in something approximating their modern form. At Oxford, the key figure was the vice-chancellor *Fell, who put into practice the kind of ambitious scholarly publishing project that Archbishop Laud had originally envisaged earlier in the 17th century. At Cambridge, *Bentley, Master of Trinity College, advanced the University Press as a serious business concern from the beginning of the 18th century. Notable volumes published by the Press at this time included Bentley's own edition of Horace (1711) and the second edition of Newton's *Philosophiæ Naturalis Principia Mathematica* (1713). In 1662, York was also granted the right to have printers operate there.

The development of printing in other parts of Britain was similarly fitful. Wales lacked the concentrated population necessary to sustain a native industry. In the early modern period, the largest town in the principality was Carmarthen, with a population of just 2,000. A clandestine Catholic press operated fleetingly from a cave in Little Orme in 1587, but the first successful printing press in Wales was not established until 1718, when Isaac Carter set up a business in Trefhedyn in Cardiganshire. From the early 18th century onwards, a reasonably well-rooted print industry did take hold in the principality. Outside Wales, however, a relatively vigorous tradition of Welsh-language publishing had been established long before this

period. In 1546, Edward Whitchurch published *Yny Lhyvyr Hwnn y Traethir* in London. Written by John Prise, secretary of the King's Council in Wales and the Marches, the book was aimed partly at popularizing the basic tenets of the Christian faith; it included an alphabet, basic Welsh reading lessons, and a selection of prayers and other elementary religious texts. The Welsh scholar William Salesbury published a Welsh–English dictionary in the following year; he also wrote Protestant polemics in both languages. A Welsh New Testament was published in 1567 and a Welsh Bible in 1588. The success of the Reformation in Wales played a significant role in establishing a Welsh-language publishing tradition. Williams, for example, has observed that the widespread use of Welsh translations of the scriptures 'enabled the Welsh, alone among the Celtic-speaking peoples, to move on—to some degree at least—from the oral and manuscript tradition of the Middle Ages to the printed-book culture of the sixteenth and seventeenth centuries' (Williams, 49).

The first printer to operate in Scotland was Andrew Myllar, who seems to have been born in Fife and to have studied at the University of St Andrews (without completing his degree). Myllar learned the art of printing in Rouen, and on returning to Scotland entered into a partnership with *Chepman. Granted a printing patent by James IV in 1507, the two men set up a press in Edinburgh. Their publications included a *Book of Good Counsel to the Scots King* (1508), poems by Dunbar and Henryson and, perhaps most famously, the *Breviarium Aberdonense* (1509–10). Through the middle decades of the 16th century, Scottish *imprints remained relatively uncommon, but, in the 1570s, *Bassandyne and Alexander Arbuthnet collaborated in producing an English-language Bible that was widely used throughout Scotland. Like its southern neighbour, Scotland had its royal printers, with *Waldegrave, printer of the Marprelate tracts, serving James VI in this capacity from 1590.

The first work printed in Scots Gaelic was the *Foirm na nUrrnuidheadh*, a translation by John Carswell of the Book of Common Order (generally known as 'Knox's Liturgy'), published by *Lekpreuik in 1567. The text has an interesting 'archipelagic' context, in that, as Mac Craith has noted, Carswell chose 'classical common Gaelic as his medium, with relatively few concessions to Scotticisms' (Mac Craith, 143), signalling that the book was intended for Irish speakers as well as speakers of Scots Gaelic.

Attempts to foster the Protestant Reformation in Ireland through publications in the Irish language were less than convincing and met with little success. Elizabeth I provided funding for the casting of a *fount of Irish type in 1567, but the first Irish printed work did not appear until 1571, when a trial piece entitled *Tuar Ferge Foighide* (a religious ballad by Philip Ó hUiginn) was produced. Shortly afterwards, Seán Ó Cearnaigh (John Kearney) printed the *Abidil Gaoidheilge agus Caiticiosma*, a Protestant *primer. These proselytizing efforts prompted a Catholic counter-move in which Irish Franciscan friars initiated a programme of Irish-language publishing from a base located first at Antwerp and, subsequently, at St Anthony's College in Louvain. The Franciscans commissioned a fount that more closely matched the distinctive characteristics of the Irish alphabet.

4 MS circulation and playbooks

In addition to continental printing ventures, the MS circulation of texts—particularly Geoffrey Keating's *Foras Feasa ar Éirinn* (1634/5)—also remained an important part of Irish-language textual culture until the end of the 18th century. The Irish tradition was not, however, exceptional in this, and, as *Love, Woudhuysen, and others have shown, MS circulation remained an important part of the textual scene in England as well (*see* **13**). From the closing decades of the 16th century onwards, a dual culture developed whereby literary works, in particular, often circulated both to a coterie MS audience and to a broader and more anonymous print audience. Shakespeare's sonnets may serve as an emblematic instance here. In his *Palladis Tamia* (1598), Francis Meres praised his contemporary for his work in the theatre, and commented favourably on Shakespeare's 'sugred sonnets', then in circulation only among the poet's 'private friends'. These private texts became a public commodity a little more than a decade later when *Thorpe—with or without the poet's consent—published *Shake-speares Sonnets* (1609), thus circulating the poems to a wholly new audience. For some writers, MS circulation was the dominant mode of publication for much of their work. Indeed, although Donne's poetry was well known within his own extended social network during his lifetime, a substantial collection of his poems was not issued in print until 1633, two years after his death.

The persistence of MS circulation also highlights the fact that many of the pieces now considered masterworks of the English Renaissance may not have had such elevated status (at least from a publishing point of view) in their own time. This is particularly true of Renaissance drama. In the early 20th century, some bibliographical scholars plotted scenarios in which unscrupulous publishers sought out bit-part actors and paid them to reconstruct the text of popular plays from memory so that they could rush them into print (as '*bad' quartos) and turn a quick profit. Blayney challenged this view in 1997, arguing that the publishing and reprint histories of Renaissance plays indicate that they were unlikely to have made any publisher's fortune. Thus, *Hamlet*, which in its first 25 years appeared in no more than four editions (excluding the *First Folio collection of 1623), might be contrasted with Arthur Dent's *Sermon of Repentance* (first published in 1582), which achieved nineteen editions over an equivalent span of time (Blayney, 'Publication'; Farmer and Lesser; Blayney 'Alleged Popularity').

5 Religious publishing

Dent's outselling of Shakespeare by a factor of almost five to one (not even taking into account that the *press runs of the *Sermon* were probably larger than of *Hamlet*) draws attention to the central importance of religious material to the publishing trade in this period. The output of the majority of publishers in the first century or so of printing was heavily dominated by religious works of one sort or another. Indeed, in his influential study of English books and readers, Bennett estimated that, in this period, 'printers, as a body, gave something like half their output to this side of their business' (Bennett, 65). Once the Reformation—with its emphasis on reading scripture in the vernacular—firmly took hold in England, there was a high demand for English-language bibles, *prayer books, and *catechisms. In 1571, the Convocation of Canterbury ordered that a copy of the Bishops' Bible (first published in 1568) should be placed in every cathedral and, if possible, in every church. It was subsequently issued in scores of editions. The *Authorized Version of the Bible, first published in 1611 under the sponsorship of King James I, was one of the signal achievements of the early modern era.

If the state sponsorship of Protestantism helped to drive forward vernacular religious publishing, then the emergence towards the end of the 16th century of more radical types of Protestant belief, which were opposed to what they perceived as the compromising doctrines and policies of the state Church, had the effect of accelerating such publishing still further. The Marprelate *tracts provide an early example of this process. The pseudonymous '*Martin Marprelate' took 'ecclesiological battle out of the study and into the street' (*ODNB*). The Marprelate attacks on the episcopacy first began to appear in 1588, clandestinely printed by Waldegrave. The pamphlets' wit and energy generated considerable public interest, as did the cat-and-mouse game that the producers of the tracts played with the authorities. The first pamphlet was printed at East Molesey, near Kingston-on-Thames. For the second, Waldegrave moved to Fawsley House in Northamptonshire, after which he moved again, this time to Coventry, where two further works were produced. Then, Waldegrave bowed out and John Hodgkins took over as printer, working at Wolston Priory. Hodgkins subsequently moved the operation to Newton Lane, near Manchester, but here he and his workmen were finally arrested by the earl of Derby's men and taken to London to be tortured and imprisoned. (Nevertheless, one final tract was produced at Wolston Priory.) The anti-episcopal polemics prompted a number of replies and counter-attacks from the government side, indicating how printed matter tends to generate still more print.

6 Copyright and control

The battles between the Puritans on one hand and the government and the state Church on the other did not come to an end with the silencing of the Martinists. Religion and politics became ever more closely entwined in the run-up to the Civil War, prompting further pamphlet exchanges that persisted throughout the War and Interregnum. This period witnessed an extraordinary efflorescence in the number of titles published, as indicated by the remarkable collection of some 22,000 printed items gathered together by the bookseller *Thomason between 1640 and 1661 (preserved in the *British Library). As the Thomason collection's large number of *newsbooks indicate, the era has become closely associated with the emergence of the newspaper as a distinctive form in Britain.

The structures of authorization and control instituted by the government authorities and the Stationers' Company in the mid-16th century fractured irretrievably in the face of the proliferation of publishing activity prompted by the Civil War and its aftermath. Throughout the Interregnum, Parliament struggled to reimpose some form of order and control on the publishing trade, but with steadily diminishing results over time. In the wake of the Restoration, an attempt was made to return to the status quo. An Act passed in 1662 sought to reinstate the old order, with one notable innovation: the appointment of an official surveyor and licenser of the press. This role was initially filled by *L'Estrange, who claimed to have suppressed more than 600 publications during his licensing career. The 1662 legislation was renewed in 1664 and 1665, lapsed in 1679, was revived in 1685, and then finally lapsed again without any further renewal in 1695. Government authorities seem not to have been unduly troubled by the loss of the licensing provisions that had been included in the legislation. Treadwell has noted that, in 1693, the Jacobite printer William Anderton was tried and executed under the law of treason—suggesting that, in taking forward the case, the government was seeking to reassure itself that 'there were other and more effective means than licensing to control the press' (Treadwell, 776).

The lapsing of the 1662 legislation signalled the final shattering of the mid-16th century dispensation that had granted such a high degree of control over the publishing trade to the Stationers' Company. With the geographical and other limitations on printing effectively withdrawn in 1695, the number of presses increased both in London and throughout the country. As Treadwell has noted, London had about 45 *printing offices in 1695, but by 1705 that number had risen to close to 70. During that ten-year period, printers set up presses in numerous towns including Bristol (1695), Shrewsbury (1696), Exeter (1698), and Norwich (1701). The Stationers' Company never really recovered from the loss of power that resulted from the lapse of the licensing Act, and it would never again be quite the same force in British publishing.

From the late 17th century onward, many leading publishers avoided relying on the Company to protect their interests; instead, they banded together into smaller-scale, semi-formal trade alliances. Thus, when Richard Royston—who had himself served as Warden and Master of the Company—drew up his will in 1682, he advised the beneficiaries that new editions of the works to which he held the rights should be undertaken by six or eight members of the trade (Blagden, *Stationers' Company*, 174–5). The logic of his proposal implied that multiple investors would have the effect of spreading the risk of any new undertaking; such a plan would also help to draw in potential competitors and thereby guard against possible rival editions, at a time when the enforceability of ownership rights could not be legally guaranteed.

The kind of collaboration that Royston proposed became standard practice in the 18th century (extending even into the early decades of the 19th), and the groups of publishers which came together in such arrangements were known as 'printing *congers'. The title-page of Samuel *Johnson's *Dictionary* (1755) indicates that it was printed for 'J. and P. *Knapton; T. and T. *Longman; C. Hitch and L. Hawes; A. *Millar; and R. and J. *Dodsley.' Such ad hoc conglomerations were essentially joint-stock companies; each member bought shares in a book and divided the profits according to his initial investment. Such joint ventures spread the financial risk of publishing; for a large work such as the *Dictionary* in two substantial *folio volumes, a considerable amount of capital was required. Another tactic adopted by publishers to minimize the investment risk involved in undertaking larger-scale projects was to seek out subscribers who paid (or sometimes part-paid) for their copy of a new work in advance, with their names then being included among the list of subscribers in the opening pages of the book. *Theobald's edition of Shakespeare's *Works* (1733), issued in seven *octavo volumes, included a *subscription list running to just under 430 names, headed by the Prince of Wales and the Princess Royal.

In the wake of the definitive lapse of the 1662 Act in 1695, the publishing trade persistently lobbied Parliament to pass some form of legislation that would afford legal protection of their interests. What emerged from this process was an *Act for the Encouragement of Learning, by Vesting the Copies of Printed Books in the Authors or Purchasers of such Copies (8 Anne, c. 19), passed by Parliament in 1709 to take effect in 1710. Feather has observed that, to the trade, the legislation 'represented a substantial victory, granting them the rights they sought while not reimposing the irksome requirements of pre-publication censorship' (Feather, 5). The Act, however, contained a set of far-reaching provisions, whose implications seem not to have been fully registered by the publishing trade when it was passed. The legislation introduced a modern concept of copyright as being vested in the author and, crucially, restricted in duration. Copyright on works already in print was to be limited to 21 years; new works were to be protected for 14 years, renewable for a further 14 if the author were still alive. The copyright provisions of the Act were a radical departure from standard practice within the industry. Traditionally, authors sold their work outright to a publisher, who then owned the rights to reproduce the text in perpetuity. The 'property' of a book was, therefore, treated in much the same way as real property: publishers could buy and sell such rights and they could pass them on in their wills.

The London publishing trade largely ignored the time limitations introduced by the 'Statute of Anne', or

'Copyright Act', as it is commonly called, and proceeded as if copyright continued to be perpetual. Throughout the 18th century, trading in shares in the most lucrative titles continued, even beyond the point when the new legislation dictated that these shares had effectively been rendered worthless. Thus, for example, when the *Tonson publishing firm—one of the foremost London houses of the 18th century—was wound up following the death of Jacob Tonson III in 1767, the rights held by the company were sold at auction for £9,550 19s. 6d., despite the fact that the copyright on many of the 600 lots being offered for sale had expired. A notable example is the Tonson rights in Shakespeare, which fetched £1,200 at the *trade sale, even though Shakespeare's works had effectively been out of copyright for more than three decades (Belanger, 195; Blagden, 'Trade Sales', 250).

The London trade's insistence that the 1710 Act had not changed the traditional practice of perpetual copyright did not go unchallenged over the course of the century, however. Some less well-established members of the trade in England did, from time to time, attempt to assert their entitlement to print works whose copyright had expired. In general the London publishing elite were able to counter such moves, either by exploiting the law courts' uncertainty over the issue or by simply buying off the publishers concerned. A more determined challenge developed, however, from outside England. In the 18th century, Scottish and Irish publishing came into their own and the number of printers operating in both countries increased very considerably. Some, such as the *Foulis brothers, who were based at the *Glasgow University Printing Office, aimed at producing work of the very highest quality; others, such as Patrick Neill of Belfast, had rather more fleeting and less ambitious careers in the trade. The Scots and the Irish undercut their London rivals and often exported their wares into the English market. English publishers complained bitterly of *piracies, with the novelist *Richardson, himself a printer, railing against cut-price editions of his work, which arrived from Dublin virtually before he had finished printing them himself in London (Ward, 18–20).

However, the more significant battle to be fought in the 18th century was not over works such as Richardson's, which were still in copyright, but rather over those works where copyright had lapsed, but which the London trade still treated as if they were private property (see *Millar vs Taylor). It was a Scottish publisher, *Donaldson, who forced the issue of the unrestricted reprinting of these works, setting up a branch of his Edinburgh firm in London and challenging the established trade all the way to the House of Lords. In 1774, the Lords confirmed Donaldson's assertion that the time limits placed on copyright by the 1710 Act effectively negated traditional practice. The 1774 ruling in Donaldson vs Becket had the result of dramatically opening up the publishing trade in Britain. As Mark Rose has observed, the 'works of Shakespeare, Bacon, Milton, Bunyan, and others, all the perennials of the book trade that the booksellers had been accustomed to treat as if they were private landed estates, were suddenly declared open commons' (Rose, 53). W. Forbes Gray has characterized the ruling as 'the Magna Charta of literary property', since it helped to establish the notion of a 'public domain' of works that were available to any publisher who wished to produce an edition at a competitive price (Gray, 197).

Among those who took immediate advantage of the new dispensation was John *Bell, proprietor of the 'British Library' bookshop on the Strand in London. In 1776, Bell initiated his 'Poets of Great Britain Complete from Chaucer to Churchill', a series running to a total of 109 volumes, priced at 1*s.* 6*d.* each. He also launched '*Bell's British Theatre' in 21 volumes, published in 6*d.* weekly *numbers, or parts (Altick, 54). These volumes were inexpensive by the standards of the 18th century, and Bell's efforts prompted others, such as John Cooke and James Harrison, to enter the field with competitively priced series of their own. As a result books became cheaper, and a much wider range of works became available to the less well-off sectors of society (although St Clair has argued that this range narrowed progressively as the limits on copyright were extended over time).

One other legacy of the 1710 Copyright Act was the formalization of the entitlement of certain libraries to receive copies of new publications without charge—and this was not altered by the 1774 Lords' decision. Where Bodley, in a private arrangement, had persuaded the Stationers' Company to supply his Oxford library with one copy of every book registered at Stationers' Hall, in 1662 this agreement was extended by law to include *Cambridge University Library and the Royal Library. The Act further extended and codified the arrangement, with the four Scottish universities, the library of Sion College in London, and the Faculty of Advocates' Library in Edinburgh gaining *legal deposit status. The range of institutions benefiting from this provision was narrowed early in the 18th century, but it is in the 1710 Act that the seeds of the great copyright deposit collections can be found. The

British Museum was established in 1753; four years later, it took possession of the Royal Library collection (*see* GEORGE III), which served as the foundation of what has since become the *British Library. The Faculty of Advocates' Library formed the starting point of the National Library of *Scotland collection.

Outside these great libraries, more modest institutions were slowly beginning to emerge, dedicated to serving the needs of the general reader. In 1725, Allan Ramsay opened the first British *circulating library, in Edinburgh. Sixteen years later, the miners of Ramsay's own birthplace, Leadhills, in Lanarkshire, came together to establish the Leadhills Reading Society, setting up a library and assembling a significant collection of books on a wide variety of topics. Local initiatives of this kind proliferated throughout Britain during the course of the 18th century, serving the needs of less well-off general readers until the institution of the public *lending library system from the middle of the following century.

7 Conclusion

In the closing decades of the 15th century, Caxton offered his customers a luxury product, of interest largely to wealthy members of the aristocratic circles in which he moved. In the centuries that followed, books remained expensive commodities, with prices held artificially high, partly as a result of the restrictive practices employed by a London-based publishing elite. The 1774 Lords ruling was an early step towards making books less expensive and more readily available to a wider social spectrum. As the 18th century drew to a close, further steps in this direction were being taken.

If Caxton could have been plucked from his Westminster printing office and dropped into its late 18th-century equivalent, he would have been able to work as a *compositor or printer with very little adjustment. The *common presses being manufactured in the 18th century differed very little from the first press that Caxton had brought with him from the Continent in the mid-1470s (*see* 11). In the final years of the 18th century, however, printing technology began to change. In 1727, the Edinburgh goldsmith *Ged began experimenting with *stereotype printing—taking impressions of the completed *formes of type and using the moulds to produce metal *plates that could be used repeatedly, without the need for recomposition. Ged never managed to make the process commercially viable (largely because of the resistance of typefounders and compositors who feared for their livelihood), but at the very end of the century, earl *Stanhope revived the technique, eventually making it a commercial success and opening the way for extended press runs and cheap reprints. The earl also, around 1800, introduced the iron *Stanhope press, which significantly reduced the amount of labour involved in the printing process. If Caxton could have stood on the threshold of the 19th century and looked forward, he would have seen a future that would surely have astonished him: the hand-crafted printed book of his day gradually turning into a genuinely mass-produced object passing into the hands of even some of the poorer members of society.

BIBLIOGRAPHY

Altick

T. Belanger, 'Tonson, Wellington and the Shakespeare Copyrights', in *Studies in the Book Trade in Honour of Graham Pollard*, OBS, NS 18 (1975)

H. S. Bennett, *English Books and Readers 1475 to 1557*, 2e (1969)

C. Benson, 'Libraries in University Towns', in *CHLBI* 2

C. Blagden, 'Booksellers' Trade Sales 1718–1768', *Library*, 5/5 (1950–51), 243–57

— *The Stationers' Company: A History, 1403–1959* (1960)

P. W. M. Blayney, 'The Publication of Playbooks', in *A New History of Early English Drama*, ed. J. D. Cox and D. S. Kastan (1997)

— *The Stationers' Company before the Charter, 1403–1557* (2003)

— 'The Alleged Popularity of Playbooks', *SQ* 56 (2005), 33–50

H. Carter, *A History of Oxford University Press* (1975)

B. Cunningham, *The World of Geoffrey Keating* (2000)

A. B. Farmer and Z. Lesser, 'The Popularity of Playbooks Revisited', *SQ* 56 (2005), 206–13

J. Feather, 'The Publishers and the Pirates: British Copyright Law in Theory and Practice, 1710–1755', *PH* 22 (1987), 5–32

W. F. Gray, 'Alexander Donaldson and His Fight for Cheap Books', *Judicial Review*, 38 (1926), 180–202

R. G. Gruffydd, 'The First Printed Books, 1546–1604', in *A Nation and its Books*, ed. P. H. Jones and E. Rees (1998)

H. Love, *Scribal Publication in Seventeenth-Century England* (1993)

E. W. Lynam, *The Irish Character in Print, 1571–1923* (1968)

M. Mac Craith, 'The Gaelic Reaction to the Reformation', in *Conquest and Union*, ed. S. G. Ellis and S. Barber (1995)

D. McKitterick, *A History of Cambridge University Press* (3 vols, 1992–2004)

A. J. Mann, *The Scottish Book Trade 1500–1720* (2000)

M. Plant, *The English Book Trade* (1939; 3e, 1974)

J. Raymond, *The Invention of the Newspaper* (1996)

M. Rose, *Authors and Owners* (1993)

W. St Clair, *The Reading Nation in the Romantic Period* (2004)

M. Treadwell, 'The Stationers and the Printing Acts at the End of the Seventeenth Century', in *CHBB* 4 (2002)

R. E. Ward, *Prince of Dublin Printers* (1972)

G. Williams, 'The Renaissance and Reformation', in *A Nation and its Books*, ed. P. H. Jones and E. Rees (1998)

H. R. Woudhuysen, *Sir Philip Sidney and the Circulation of Manuscripts, 1558–1640* (1996)

20b The History of the Book in Britain, 1801–1914

Leslie Howsam

1 A book culture

Print was the principal medium of written communication in Britain during the 19th and early 20th centuries. In that era of rapid population increase and concentrated industrial, urban, and imperial expansion, MS circulation was minimal and broadcasting lay in the future. Along with *periodicals and *newspapers, books and *pamphlets constituted the material culture of print in a rapidly changing society. Much of that change was painful, and for many the experience of reading was a source of comfort or consolation; for others it was an opportunity to acquire useful knowledge or adhere to a system of belief. Men and women of all social ranks were readers, writers, and publishers, but a passion for the acquisition of literacy was particularly conspicuous in the working class. William Lovett (1800–1877) characterized his 'life and struggles' in terms of 'the pursuit of bread, knowledge and freedom'. In *printing offices and *booksellers' shops, and on the streets where vendors cried their wares, ideas and arguments jostled together. Evangelical religious enthusiasm, liberal political economy, and radical egalitarianism were only the most prominent of many competing ideologies. Pious people of the middle class eschewed the theatre and frivolous amusements, but enjoyed respectable *novels read aloud in the family circle, while *conduct books taught young people how to behave in polite society. Meanwhile, more secular spirits sought to break free of the prevailing culture's unofficial *censorship by seeking out cheap, sometimes disreputable, editions of works of science and politics as well as of fiction and poetry.

*Literacy measured by the ability to sign one's name (which normally implied at least minimal skills with reading) sat at about 50 per cent in 1801 and had risen to almost 100 per cent by 1914. Percentages, however, are of less interest than the way in which people used their literacy: for maintaining relationships with family at a time of increasing social mobility; for engaging with the natural world, with employers and colleagues in factories and other workplaces; and for engaging with religion or politics. The balance of work and leisure changed too, as the economic misery of the Napoleonic wars (until 1815) and their aftermath (until about 1850) gave way to a period of relative prosperity. Governments mandated a reduction in working hours for adults as well as educational provision for children. Both policies affected the practices of writing and publishing books, as well as the experience of reading.

The spread of reading and the dissemination of print can be credited both to broad socio-economic forces and to specific technological and cultural changes. Religious and political ideals competed vigorously and prosperity increased unevenly. At the same time, the mechanical capacity of printing and bookbinding equipment improved, along with readers' ability to illuminate their books or journals by something stronger than candlelight. As a society, Britain had been moderately pious, but people's reading of bibles and *tracts increased significantly as a result of the evangelical publishing activities of the *British and Foreign Bible Society and the *Religious Tract Society. Strict sabbatarianism gave rise to Sunday newspapers and to programmes of respectable reading for boys and girls. Similarly, the secular utilitarian ideologies of free trade and political economy, espoused by the Society for the Diffusion of Useful Knowledge (SDUK), were widely promoted in its *Penny Magazine* and other publications. At the other end of the political spectrum, radical political ideas circulating in the first two decades of the 19th century grew out of a profoundly literate working-class culture, steeped in the notion of human rights expounded by Paine in *Rights of Man*. Despite the variety of ideologies in the politics of reading, all these people and organizations shared two things: they believed in the power of print to create change, and they were deeply suspicious of merely entertaining literature.

The book trade was based in the growing urban centres of Britain, primarily in London and Edinburgh. Indeed, there were strong business and personal relationships between publishers in the two cities. Yet printing, bookselling, and *circulating libraries all flourished in Wales, and in Scottish and English provincial cities and towns as well. In the comfortable middle class, as among the struggling labourers, books were the mass medium through which culture was constructed. Children learned from print both directly and indirectly (*see* **15**). Women readers, and indeed writers, found in books and periodicals a respectable place from which to approach the wider world, despite the social constraints that operated throughout most of the period. Men and boys could explore their masculinity and women and girls their femininity, and Britons of both sexes and all classes could use print to position themselves in relation to the imperial and colonial possessions that their nation claimed.

2 Economics

From the consumers' and producers' points of view, the economics of the book in Britain went through a dramatic transformation (*see* **12**). Identified in the first half of the 19th century as a luxury commodity (short *press runs offered at high prices), the book became a commonplace cultural product (manufactured on an industrial scale and priced for middle- and working-class budgets). This distinction is complicated, however, by two major exceptions. Commercial circulating libraries (of which *Mudie's was the largest) purchased the expensive volumes and rented them to readers at a manageable rate; and various publishers circumvented the high cost of a complete book by making it available to readers on a week-by-week or monthly basis. Bible and tract societies saw

social utility in collecting penny subscriptions until a book was paid for, and Dickens's first publishers, *Chapman & Hall, discovered the benefits of selling books in *numbers, or parts. They could always be collected up and repackaged as a new edition—or various editions—after the author had finished the tale and the first cohort of readers had followed in his or her wake.

In the early decades of the 19th century the rate of publication rose, from a few hundred titles annually at the beginning, to 3,000 or 4,000 by the mid-1840s. New technologies (*see* **11**) meant new economies of scale for the book trade, and entrepreneurs also took advantage of changes in the banking and insurance sectors. In 1814, *The Times* first used a *steam press to print the newspaper, and although the use of steam for book printing was not commonplace until later, the new technology was perceived as a watershed. In the 1840s there arose a 'passionate argument about the future of publishing and bookselling' (Raven, 321). The debates revolved around *intellectual property and *taxes on knowledge, often pitting the interests of publishers against those of authors and of readers. The Copyright Act of 1842 extended protection of an author's rights to 42 years (or seven years after his or her death, whichever was greater). Yet it was publishers and star authors, more than readers or the majority of writers, who benefited most from the change. Further legislation concerned international *copyright, but British authors remained unprotected in the colonial and American markets for most of the century. The British government derived income from the book trade by means of the stamp tax (*see* STAMP ACTS). Increasingly, this was seen to stifle the freedom of the press and the circulation of knowledge. The last stamp tax was repealed in 1855 and the excise tax on paper in 1861.

The economics of the book in the second half of the 19th century have been succinctly characterized: 'the period from 1846 to 1916 saw a fourfold increase in production and a halving of book prices' (Weedon, 57). By 1914 there were some 10,000 titles a year being published, and prices for books had plummeted from the luxury level into the range of modest family budgets. The circulating libraries, which had benefited from the *three-decker format when prices were high, now forced it out of the market. The publishing business, which for most of the 19th century had been one where powerful individual literary entrepreneurs were succeeded by their sons and nephews, now began to be reorganized as limited-liability companies.

3 Production and publishing

As in other parts of the industrialized world, most of the technologies of book production in Britain advanced dramatically between 1800 and 1914. Paper made by hand from rags gave way to paper made by *machine, and, later, from *esparto grass and, eventually, wood pulp as raw material (*see* **10**). The craft of setting movable *type by hand, which had changed little since *Caxton's time, was supplemented by making *stereotype (from the 1820s) and later *electrotype (from the 1890s) plates that captured whole pages at once. Yet *composition itself was not mechanized until the introduction of *Linotype in the 1870s and *Monotype in the 1890s. Hand presses remained ubiquitous in local printing offices and for small jobs for many years, but the larger printers adopted steam presses by the 1830s and 1840s. Twyman has characterized the transformation of illustrations (first from copper and later from steel *engravings, then electrotype) as a complex and multilayered process (*see* **16**). At the end of the century, photography was in use and colour was enriching printed pages for the first time. The practice of supplying expensive books in flimsy paper covers or boards, so that they could be rebound for the purchaser's private collection, began to give way to *edition binding in the 1830s (*see* **17**). *Leather was used only for *bibles and special works, while the use of *book cloth for a whole edition could be made attractive with colour and design. Over the course of the century, the cost of labour as a proportion in the cost of producing a book increased, while that of raw materials decreased.

The culture of book production was transformed along with the technology. During the first quarter of the 19th century, the bible and tract societies were among the few publishers interested in keeping the price of books low. Their concern was with saving souls, while a few other specialists in cheap books churned out reprints of the classics for the school and popular working-class markets. The leading London firms, meanwhile, provided luxurious volumes for the leisured upper-class reader and used copyright law to protect their investment in works. The firms included the *Rivington, *Longman, and *Murray families as well as *Bentley and others in London. *Blackwood, the *Chambers brothers, and *Strahan operated in Edinburgh. These booksellers—the term was still in use whether or not the firm engaged in the retail trade—were conservative men of business to whom the luxury price of two guineas for a work in *quarto seemed appropriate. *Knight likened their strategy to that of fishmongers who destroyed their stock in the late afternoon, rather than reducing its price after servants had purchased enough for the gentry's midday meals. Like reprinting in cheap editions, this policy would have allowed the fish merchants to take advantage of a second class of customers, poorer families preparing supper, without any risk to the market earlier in the day. Similarly, the top London and Edinburgh publishers were slow to recognize that the market for reprinted works of literature in cheap editions would not spoil that for fresh originals in good bindings at high prices. Exacerbating the effects of this commercial outlook, the price of paper was high during the Napoleonic wars, and printing and bookbinding (*see* **17**) remained labour-intensive crafts. Even stereotype was only practical for those few works that would be very widely circulated. These included not only spiritual and educational books, but the novels and poetry of *Scott, whose influence on book prices was profound. His popular novels, beginning with *Kenilworth* in 1821, were the first to achieve the exorbitantly high price of 31*s*. 6*d*. and to expand to three volumes. A noticeable but brief dip in booktrade fortunes occurred in 1826 when the firm of *Constable went bankrupt despite owning the profitable copyrights to Scott's works as well as publishing the *Edinburgh Review* and the *Encyclopaedia Britannica*.

During the 1830s and 1840s, the book trade's leaders maintained their conservative approach, but experiments in social engineering by means of print culture were nevertheless under way. *Railway books and booksellers appeared later, along with trains and stations. Under Knight's leadership, the SDUK published series of works in both 'useful' and 'entertaining' knowledge, issued in affordably priced *part-issue format, rather than full-scale volumes. Later, they developed their periodical, the *Penny Magazine*; in *Crotchet Castle* (1831), Thomas Love Peacock captured the SDUK's timeliness when he caricatured it as the 'Steam Intellect Society'. Knight campaigned vigorously for the stamp duty on paper to be repealed. The tax, determined by the *Stamp Act, was also the focus of working-class political activity, which flourished in the 1830s as a campaign for the publication and sale of *The Poor Man's Guardian* and other *unstamped periodicals. It was in 1836 that the formidable partnership of Chapman & Hall as publishers and Dickens as author initiated *The Pickwick Papers* and hit upon the idea of part-issue. The combination of a negligible unit price and a cliffhanger ending proved irresistible. This format became part of the infrastructure of publishing and remained so until the 1870s, when magazine serialization and one-volume reprints took over.

Dickens's huge income from authorship in mid-century was scarcely typical; also unusual were the complex business, literary, and indeed social relationships with his publishers that Patten has recorded. Most authors had to be content with a modest one-off payment for the copyright, so that if their work became popular it was the publisher who benefited. The usual alternative method of payment, a system of *half-profits, was equally unsatisfactory for authors. There were numerous instances of unfair accounting practices by publishers that occasioned vociferous objections, both from individual writers and from the *Society of Authors. The system of paying a percentage *royalty, popular in the US, was slow to be adopted in Britain. Meanwhile, publishers acquired works for their list not only in the form of new MSS by unknown (and untried) authors, but by purchasing stereotype plates and producing reprints. By the 1860s, the practice of reprinting was finally reducing the price of books. Publishers issued 6s. editions of works they had originally published at much higher prices. Sometimes this happened quickly, but in other cases so slowly that the crusade for cheap literature continued to flourish.

The railway boom of the 1840s and 1850s transformed the distribution of books and periodicals and affected patterns of publishing and of reading. W. H. *Smith and other booksellers profited from the railway novel that could be purchased at a station stall and that could be consumed comfortably on a train journey. The leading publisher here was *Routledge. Their shilling *Railway Library editions, known as *yellow backs, were bound in coloured paper and furnished with an illustration on the upper cover and advertisements on the lower. Smith and Routledge, however, never competed directly with the major publishers that had survived from the 18th century into the Victorian age. *Macmillan was different. Founded in 1843 at Cambridge, it moved to London in 1858 and became a leading publisher with a general list that included history, literature and criticism, and science (with periodicals such as *Nature*), as well as heavyweight new books and cheap reprints of older ones. Alexander Macmillan once told a correspondent, 'I don't think that *paying* things need be done in a slovenly way', a remark that combined his commercial ambitions with his literary and bibliophilic ones (Freeman Archive 1/7, fo. 495). Although his 'tobacco parliaments' were at the very centre of London's

literary culture, Macmillan was also one of the Victorian publishers most active in reaching out to customers and colleagues throughout the British world, establishing offices not only in the colonies but in North America.

The book culture at the turn of the 20th century was very different from the mid-Victorian trade. The three-decker novel format came to an end, while the *penny dreadful flourished. A Society of Authors was founded in 1883 to protect its members' literary property. Authors' *literary agents began to undertake the filtering services previously handled by *publishers' readers. A *Net Book Agreement in 1890 ensured that price competition would not damage the infrastructure of the trade. New firms and new series appeared: John *Lane founded the *Bodley Head in 1894, establishing ambitious aesthetic standards for the book trade; and *Dent initiated *Everyman's Library in 1906. Everyman offered Edwardian readers many of the works, as standards or classics, that had been seen as risky a few decades earlier. Philological and literary scholars combined forces to initiate the *New* (later *Oxford*) *English Dictionary*, while other men of letters joined together to produce and publish the *Dictionary of National Biography* under the auspices of G. M. *Smith in 1900.

4 Circulation and preservation

Authors, readers, and publishers have been seen as the three central constituencies in the culture of books from 1800 to 1914, but the institutions of circulation and preservation—periodicals, booksellers, and *libraries both public and private—were essential supporters of their interdependent relationship. The periodical press benefited even more than the book trade from the changes in technology, literacy, and leisure that characterized the period (*see* **14**). North estimates the quantity of text published in periodical form to have been at least 100 times that appearing between the covers of books. Moreover, book and periodical formats became closely interrelated. An alternative to the part-publication of novels was publication in the weekly or monthly issues of a periodical; once a literary work was brought to completion in a periodical, it could be reissued in one or more volumes. Several major publishers maintained their own periodicals, employing their authors on them, in order to manage this policy: *Thackeray, for example, served as editor of the *Cornhill Magazine*. Conversely, some historians, cultural critics, and other non-fiction authors sought contracts with publishers for volumes of their collected essays, works that had first appeared in periodical form. The periodical has been identified, by Beetham and Brake among others, as a hybrid form that was enormously influential in the print culture of Victorian Britain.

Periodicals arrived through the *postal system, or were purchased alongside books or newspapers. Books could also be ordered from the publisher (or the circulating library) to be delivered by post to the country; cities and provincial towns had bookshops, where sellers were entitled to discounts on set prices. In the earlier decades of the 19th century, street vendors supplemented the established shops, particularly for politically radical pamphlets and evangelical tracts. In rural areas, *colporteurs carried print from house to house. Especially when the price of new books was exceptionally high, *second-hand bookshops and market stalls were a crucial source for working-class and lower-middle-class readers.

Libraries ranged from the small number of great copyright libraries, through the innovative subscription-supported *London Library, to modest and well-meaning local institutions as well as private collections large and small. State-funded public *lending libraries were slow to develop, despite the support of Edward *Edwards and the passage of enabling legislation in 1850. *Mechanics' institutes were furnished with libraries that provided much of the material for the reading lists of working-class autodidacts. In both public and mechanics' institute libraries, the provision of fiction was discouraged. Meanwhile the commercial circulating libraries, whose existence was so central to the structure of the publishing trade, filled the need for entertainment. By the late 19th century, however, readers and writers were increasingly frustrated by the restrictions imposed by Mudie's and other circulating libraries, which many perceived as a form of *censorship.

5 Subjects and genres

The 19th century saw the appearance of a rich body of fiction and poetry that has become part of the English literary canon. Among the principal authors of the day were Austen, Scott, the Brontës, Tennyson, the Rossettis, Dickens, Elizabeth Gaskell, Thackeray, Trollope, George Eliot, Meredith, Gissing, Stevenson, Hardy, and Wilde. In the *history of the book, however, these great names take their place among the vast number of unknown writers who contributed to the market for fiction and poetry. Those categories, in turn, exist in relation to religion, history, philosophy,

science, and all the other subdivisions of the publishing trade's vast output. The material is difficult to count and categorize, partly because it so far outpaced that of the 18th century and partly because the sources from which statistical and subject analysis can be drawn were not consistently organized throughout the period.

Religion, not fiction, was still the dominant subject of the early 19th century, although literary writing was already growing fast. Bibles, tracts, and commentaries made up some 20 per cent of the books published between 1814 and 1846. The second- and third-largest categories were almost equal: a catch-all, combining works on geography, *travel, history, and biography came in at 17 per cent, while fiction and juvenile literature measured about 16 per cent. A little over half of the latter category, 8.9 per cent or 3,180 entries over 32 years, constituted *novels, romances, and tales as distinct from moral tales and books for *children. *Poetry and drama, however, were a separate category in the booktrade press's calculations. They were sixth at about 8 per cent, after education (12 per cent) and the jumble of arts, science, mathematics, and illustrated works (9 per cent). Works on medicine and law amounted to 6 per cent and 4 per cent respectively. Another unhelpful combination category was politics, social science, economics, and military and naval (4 per cent—but some works that would now be included under those headings no doubt found themselves in geography, travel, and so forth). Finally, works of logic and philosophy, and belles-lettres amounted to only 1 per cent; a further 3 per cent of works defied categorization as miscellaneous (Eliot, *Patterns and Trends*, 44–6). These figures must be treated with caution, however, as they are based on counting titles only, and take into account neither the sizes of works (best measured by counting *sheets), nor the extent of press runs. In the absence of edition quantities, especially, such numbers can be used only as general markers.

Another snapshot of the reading public's preferences in terms of genre and subject is available for the end of the period, 1870–1919. By then, the fiction and juvenile category was highest at 23 per cent, followed by religion (only 16 per cent), geography, travels, history, and biography (down to 12 per cent) and education (11 per cent). The awkward 'miscellaneous' now amounted to 19 per cent, with arts, science, mathematics, and illustrated works falling to 8 per cent and poetry and drama rising to 7 per cent. Meanwhile logic, philosophy, and belles-lettres rose to 5 per cent. Medicine and law both sat at 3 per cent, with their declining percentage share being attributed to the rise of other categories rather than to any decline in interest or rate of publication. The portmanteau category of politics, social science, economics, and military and naval also came in at 3 per cent of all the many titles published and recorded by the trade (Eliot, *Patterns and Trends*, 46–53). Now it was fiction, or more broadly literature, that was the subject of most new books, not religion.

Percentages can be deceptive: they create artificial disconnections between ways of knowing the world that were tightly twisted together. Religion and science, for example, are often regarded as competing ideologies in the mid-19th century, and Darwin's ideas are seen to counter those of the Bible. A more complex and more interesting perspective is provided by Secord's scholarly examination of the authorship, production, distribution, and reception of all the variations of a single work of evolutionary science that encompassed and challenged religion (as well as phrenology) and that prepared the minds of readers for Darwin's ideas.

School books and *textbooks were part of the 11 or 12 per cent of the titles reckoned as education, but their numbers accounted for a much larger proportion of the total quantity of volumes in print, because their print runs tended to be substantially larger than those for most other kinds of books. Longmans and others began publishing textbooks in the 1830s; Macmillan, George *Bell & Sons, and the *Cambridge and *Oxford university presses all started to compete with them in the 1860s; changes in education law and financing in 1870, 1882, and 1902 greatly increased the demand. School books were exported to the colonies and to the US. Profit margins were small, but the global English-language market was reliable. Boards of Education in Britain and the colonies ordered about 60,000 copies of the compendia known as 'readers' or reading books in a single year, 1860–61 (Weedon, 128).

6 Reading

Scholars from a variety of academic disciplines and cultural commentators of all political stripes have

The *private press movement: the *Kelmscott Press edition of Froissart (1897) in Lord Berners's translation. Printed after W. *Morris's death in two *limited editions of eight and two leaves, the latter on *vellum. The *red printing, elaborate *borders, and *initials provide a luxurious display.

weighed in on the subject of the British reading public between the Napoleonic wars and World War I. Had Britons become irresponsibly frivolous addicts of sensational trash by the end of the century, as Leavis insisted, or were they serious autodidacts devoted to the classics, as J. Rose has maintained? Although a *Reading Experience Database is seeking to collect the transitory and precious evidence, there may ultimately be no satisfactory way to measure or to characterize, for a whole nation, so private and intimate a process as reading. Because many books and newspapers were very widely read, however, the communal aspects of the experience and influence of reading are factors that scholars dare not overlook.

The autodidact experience is important in the early 19th century, when educational provision was spotty and unregulated. Working-class autobiographies disclose how difficult it was to find affordable and engaging reading material. Even the poorest homes had copies of the Bible and *Book of Common Prayer, The *Pilgrim's Progress and, sometimes, Paradise Lost, although it is not clear how often or how intensively those works were read; probably they formed part of most children's preparation in the skills of literacy. The possession and reading of other books depended on chance, on the works of history, science, fiction, or philosophy that happened to be available from a second-hand bookseller or in a mechanics' institute library. Cheap reprints increased the access of humble people to books, but, as St Clair has argued, that access was shaped—and drastically limited—by publishers' control over intellectual property. In the mid- and late 19th century, cheap editions of the 'old canon' of authors were more affordable than contemporary books.

As is invariably the case, throughout the period the material book and the cultural experience of reading it were intertwined. In 1800 literacy was restricted, and only a limited range of engaging reading material was available. Yet as the century progressed, new formats and cheaper prices created new markets and found new readers. By the 1860s publishing had become a major enterprise: books and periodicals were taken for granted as a cultural necessity. In 1914 the stereotype plates that had by that time provided millions with access to novels and poetry at modest prices were melted down to make munitions, and the people who had been brought up on them took their universal literacy into the trenches.

BIBLIOGRAPHY
Altick
J. J. Barnes, Free Trade in Books (1964)
— Authors, Publishers, and Politicians (1974)
M. Beetham, 'Towards a Theory of the Periodical as a Publishing Genre', in Investigating Victorian Journalism, ed. L. Brake et al. (1990)
B. Bell, 'New Directions in Victorian Publishing History', Victorian Literature and Culture (1994), 347–54
L. Brake, Print in Transition, 1850–1910 (2001)
N. Cross, The Common Writer (1985)
A. C. Dooley, Author and Printer in Victorian England (1992)
S. Eliot, 'The Three-Decker Novel and its First Cheap Reprint, 1862–94,' Library, 6/7 (1985), 38–53
— Some Patterns and Trends in British Publishing 1800–1919 (1994)
— 'Patterns and Trends and the NSTC', PH 42 (1997), 79–104; 43 (1998), 71–112
J. Feather, A History of British Publishing, 2e (2006)
N. N. Feltes, Modes of Production of Victorian Novels (1986)
— Literary Capital and the Late Victorian Novel (1993)
D. Finkelstein, The House of Blackwood (2002)
E. A. Freeman Archive, John Rylands University Library
A. Fyfe, Industrialised Conversion (2000)
— 'Societies as Publishers', PH 58 (2005), 5–42
G. L. Griest, Mudie's Circulating Library and the Victorian Novel (1970)
L. Howsam, Cheap Bibles (1991)
— 'Sustained Literary Ventures', PH 32 (1992), 5–26
— et al., 'What the Victorians Learned', Journal of Victorian Culture, 12 (2007), 262–85
E. James, ed., Macmillan (2002)
J. O. Jordan and R. L. Patten, eds., Literature in the Marketplace (1995)
M. E. Korey et al., Vizetelly & Compan(ies) (2003)
R. G. Landon, ed., Book Selling and Book Buying (1978)
P. Leary, 'Googling the Victorians', Journal of Victorian Culture, 10 (2005), 72–86
Q. D. Leavis, Fiction and the Reading Public (1932)
W. Lovett, Life and Struggles (1876)
P. D. McDonald, British Literary Culture and Publishing Practice, 1880–1914 (1997)
J. North, 'Compared to Books', in The Waterloo Directory of English Newspapers and Periodicals, www.victorianperiodicals.com, consulted Sept. 2007
R. L. Patten, Charles Dickens and His Publishers (1978)
M. Plant, The English Book Trade (1939; 3e, 1974)
J. Raven, The Business of Books (2007)
J. Robson, ed., Editing Nineteenth Century Texts (1967)
Rose
M. Rose, Authors and Owners (1993)
W. St Clair, The Reading Nation in the Romantic Period (2004)
J. Secord, Victorian Sensation (2000)
J. Shattock and M. Wolff, eds., The Victorian Periodical Press (1982)
P. L. Shillingsburg, Pegasus in Harness (1992)

J. A. Sutherland, *Victorian Novelists and Publishers* (1976)

— 'The Book Trade Crash of 1826', *Library*, 6/9 (1987), 148–61

J. Topham, 'Scientific Publishing and the Reading of Science in Nineteenth-Century Britain', *Studies in the History and Philosophy of Science*, 31 (2000), 559–612

M. Twyman, *Printing, 1770–1970* (1970; repr. 1998)

D. Vincent, *Bread, Knowledge and Freedom* (1981)

— *Literacy and Popular Culture* (1989)

R. K. Webb, *The British Working-Class Reader* (1971)

A. Weedon, *Victorian Publishing* (2003)

J. H. Wiener, *The War of the Unstamped* (1969)

20c The History of the Book in Britain from 1914

CLAIRE SQUIRES

1 The 20th-century book

What might be distinctive about the book in 20th-century Britain, the publishing industry that produced it, the book trade that circulated it, and the readers that consumed it? The most iconic books of the period, as well as the most indicative of the book's relationship to wider society, were *Penguin *paperbacks. They were cheaply priced and appealed to a mass readership; in addition to fostering innovation in design and being creatively marketed, the series took advantage of developing distribution channels. There is nothing more characteristically 20th-century, or more British, than the Penguin. As historians of Penguin know, however, the launch of the company in the 1930s drew as much from continuity and revival as it did from change and revolution. The post-1914 period has similarly been one of upheaval, but also of evolution: in production techniques; business practices; the culture of publishing; and in books themselves, both in form and in content.

Indeed, a history of the book in 20th-century Britain could be told through some of the publishing industry's individual products and book series, which demonstrate changes and continuities from the preceding era. For a large part of the 20th century, British books continued to exist under a legislative framework that curtailed their production and sale. Radclyffe Hall's The *Well of Loneliness was banned in the 1920s for obscenity; Joyce published *Ulysses overseas. Later in the century, Penguin's publication, in 1960, of Lawrence's *Lady Chatterley's Lover successfully challenged the *Obscene Publications Act, seemingly ushering in a period of freer social mores and publication practices, although the controversies surrounding Rushdie's The *Satanic Verses in the 1980s

and 1990s demonstrated that freedom of speech remained contested. In a different vein, *Dent began production of the first *Everyman's Library books (themselves modelled on earlier reprint series) in the opening decade of the century. These were marketed for the growing population of newly literate readers, which Penguin also sought in the 1940s with its *Penguin Classics. Another instance of change is the global phenomenon of the *Harry Potter series in the 1990s and 2000s. J. K. Rowling's stories illustrated the overwhelming commercial potential of the British book, founded on packaging, brand management, *rights sales, merchandizing, and relations with other media. Yet, some 100 years earlier, Beatrix Potter's *Peter Rabbit books employed the same sorts of strategies to foster their international success.

These examples afford a view of only a few of the patterns and progressions of the British book in the 20th and early 21st centuries. The following sections offer a more comprehensive survey, through an examination of the relationships between British publishing, society, and the rest of the world; its own internal business and culture; and its readers and consumers.

2 Empire, export, and globalization

The shape of a nation's publishing industry reflects and affects the nation itself; the many shifts in British history have no small bearing on book-trade history. At the start of the 20th century, the industry was built upon imperial lines. It was structured around independent, largely family-run, companies; industrialized in terms of production and distribution; and catering to the new mass markets engendered by the Education Acts of the previous century.

In 1914 Britain had the world's largest empire, its vast territories spread throughout the globe. British publishing followed suit, providing books for the empire. *Copyright legislation protected publishers' property overseas, and the *printing offices that had been established originally for colonial and missionary communications now brought a wider print culture to the colonies. Subsequently, publishing companies such as *Oxford University Press, *Heinemann, *Longman, and *Nelson set up branch offices and subsidiaries in Africa, Australia, Canada, New Zealand, and Asia, though the management of these enterprises tended to remain firmly with the British base (*see* **37, 44, 47, 45,** and **39,** respectively). The British book was widely exported, and British publishers benefited greatly from international trade. *Educational publishing was central to the building of the Empire, and in the development of the colonies.

Although World War II inevitably disrupted the patterns of colonial publishing, after 1945, the British government strongly encouraged reconstruction. At the end of the 1940s, 29 per cent of the value of British publishers' book sales derived from exports. By the end of the 1960s, this figure had climbed to almost half of all British publishing revenue. As the empire began to crumble, and successive nations won their independence and joined the Commonwealth, the export trade faced a serious threat. Many decolonized nations worked towards establishing indigenous publishing enterprises, although for many countries, problems with infrastructure, investment, and a lack of skilled workers and of *publishing education, made local publishing problematic. For British publishers, however, the greater threat came in terms of international competition from the increasingly powerful US publishing industry and from an attack on trade agreements and conventions that safeguarded British interests. Territorial rights in the English language were traditionally drawn upon colonial lines, with Britain publishing exclusively throughout the Commonwealth. The Australian and New Zealand markets became particularly contentious, as readers wanted access to inexpensive US editions. The US successfully challenged the British Commonwealth Market Agreement in 1976, and protected markets were forced open, driving down British profits and the value of export sales. Nonetheless, the exclusive territorial rights specified in *contracts meant that worldwide English-language publishing continued to operate along neo-colonial lines, even if the profits derived by Britain were much diminished. The post-colonial era was neither one of completely unfettered free trade nor one which saw the uncomplicated rise of local publishing industries.

In the second half of the 20th century, global economic and business development extended into the publishing industry. A succession of conglomerations produced ever-larger and more internationalized companies, frequently with multimedia portfolios. At the beginning of the 21st century, some of the biggest British publishing groups were ultimately owned by foreign companies: Hodder Headline (originally *Hodder & Stoughton), *Little, Brown, and *Orion (*Hachette); *Macmillan (*Holtzbrinck); and *Random House and *Transworld (*Bertelsmann). Yet the relationship between global ownership and publishing patterns is complex. In the 21st century, British writers and publishers remained important originators and producers of cultural material, with intellectual properties widely translated elsewhere. Although their global dominance was unprecedented, the Harry Potter books demonstrated how the British publishing industry could foster publishing on an extraordinary international scale.

3 Wartime

As with every other area of civilian life, the two great armed struggles of the 20th century had their impact on the British book trade. World War I seriously depressed book production, with title output falling by 1918 to its lowest level since 1902. The book trade lost key workers, first to voluntary recruitment and then to conscription (publishers were not exempted from national service). The cost of raw materials—crucially, that of paper—rose dramatically as imported supplies were restricted, and the cost of books duly followed the upward trend. By 1918, the industry was seriously depressed.

A similar pattern occurred during World War II, although with arguably even greater effects. Publishers had their access to paper stocks rationed as foreign importation was banned. The Book Production War Economy Agreement, negotiated by the *Publishers Association, imposed low production standards as a paper-saving measure. Books produced under the Agreement had thin, low-quality paper covered with small, closely set type. These challenges to the trade were exacerbated by aerial bombardment. During the Blitz, several publishers, including *Unwin, *Ward Lock, Hodder & Stoughton, and Macmillan, were bombed, losing business records and stock. The wholesaler *Simpkin, Marshall, which supplied many of Britain's booksellers, received a direct hit. As a consequence, demand far outstripped publishers' capacity to supply. The issues of supply continued well beyond 1945, and the editor Diana Athill's description of the 'book-hungry days' of the 'post-war book famine' was not exaggerated (Athill, 34).

Wartime inhibited publishers in terms of content, sometimes with overt government *censorship. The Defence of the Realm Act (DORA) of 1914 affected many areas of life, including publishing and the dissemination of information. The Act meant that some publishers engaged in *self-censorship by deciding not to publish potentially controversial works, while others (including the pacifist publisher C. W. Daniel) were prosecuted for publishing books dealing with subjects such as homosexuality and conscientious objection.

Wartime publishing also presented publishers with opportunities, however. In World War I, companies responded to the changed environment by publishing works relating to the new social and political conditions: *pamphlets assessing current affairs; novels with wartime themes; periodicals with articles on the war effort. In the years before and during World War II, publishers' output similarly reflected the changing times. Penguin's 'Specials'—midway between books and pamphlets—were produced rapidly to cater for readers eager for information about the precarious days through which they were living (titles included a guide to identifying combat planes). Penguin also developed schemes to supply books to the troops via the Forces Book Club and to prisoners of war.

During both world wars, some companies operated by publishing works in partnership with, or on behalf of, the government. In 1914–18, these included veiled *propaganda, such as patriotic novels from mainstream publishers (including Hodder & Stoughton, T. Fisher *Unwin, and Macmillan), arranged under the auspices of the propaganda department at Wellington House. In World War II, OUP played a vital role in *government printing and publishing by secretly producing, distributing, and even creating propaganda and informational materials, leading it to be dubbed 'Printing House Number One' by the Admiralty. Although the primary impetus was patriotism, incentives to produce such materials also ranged from the financial to (in World War II) the granting of additional paper rations.

The commercial legacy of both wars was—like much in industrial Britain—depression. The book trade suffered from downturns in production figures; disabled organizational structures; continuing problems with the supply of raw materials; and the knock-on effects of a broader economic malaise. The conservatism of the 1920s and 1930s did not bode well for publishing innovation, although the growing provision of education and the vision of a small number of key interwar publishers—*Allen & Unwin, *Gollancz (and his *Left Book Club), and Penguin among them—militated against this. Paper rationing remained in place until 1949. The prewar output of more than 17,000 new titles in 1937, after reaching the low of c.6,700 in 1943, would not be surpassed until the early 1950s. Depression and austerity were threats to the reconstruction of a strong national publishing industry in both postwar periods. Still, there were opportunities—pre-eminently, the waves of educational reform—which were eagerly seized by some sections of the book trade.

4 Education, access, and the reading public

Substantial British educational reform began in the 19th century, with the 1870 Education Act establishing the principle of free and compulsory primary-level education. In 1902 similar legislation was applied to the provision of secondary-level education, and by 1944 school attendance was made compulsory and free for all children under 15. From the 1960s there was a rapid expansion of the university sector. Publishers sought to cater for this newly literate and expanding mass readership. The ubiquity of the reprint series in the 19th and 20th centuries was indicative of a close marriage between educational reform, *literacy, and *publishers' lists. *World's Classics and Penguin Classics would, in later editions, include critical apparatus such as *introductions and *footnotes or endnotes, increasing their pedagogic usefulness. From the 1930s onwards, the rise and success of the paperback was intimately connected with universal literacy and the production of affordable, quality literature and non-fiction for all. Many of Penguin's non-fiction *Pelicans appealed to readers' self-educative tendencies, and a certain earnestness in the post-1945 book-buying public was echoed by a seriousness in publishing programmes, discussed and analysed in works such as Richard Hoggart's *The Uses of Literacy* (1957)—itself a Pelican title.

Yet, as Hoggart's book emphasized, leisure and entertainment were also important factors in shaping the nature of publishers' output. Between the wars, popular fiction flourished, with genres such as westerns, *detective, and *romance novels having widespread appeal. Emblematic of the popularity of genre fiction is the decision in the 1920s by the general publishing company *Mills & Boon to specialize in romance. Interwar critics of the mass reading public, such as Q. D. Leavis in *Fiction and the Reading Public* (1932), expressed deep concerns about the direction publishing and literature was taking, proclaiming that 'novel-reading is now largely a drug habit' (Leavis, 19). The anxieties displayed by some in the 19th century about the subversive dangers of a newly literate audience developed in the 20th century into fears about the deterioration of literary quality in a democratized marketplace. The ambivalence of the book trade, caught between the demands of capitalism and those of culture, would continue to cause consternation throughout the 20th century. Geoffrey *Faber, publisher of high-modernist authors including Eliot and Pound at his eponymous company, articulated his disdain for a market-focused breed of publishers whom he perceived to be publishing for the 'herd'. Carey has advanced the polemical argument that, as a result of the reading public's expansion, modernist writers intentionally retrenched their art in order to exclude new readers, and to extract themselves from the marketplace. Nevertheless, other historians of the period have maintained that the modernists were as keen to situate themselves in the market as more obviously popular writers, promoting their authorial personae and collaborating and negotiating with publishing intermediaries to produce their work.

Publishers keen to cater to the new reading public did not only have to compete among themselves, however. The increasing numbers and distribution of newspapers and periodicals were in themselves competition for the book (*see* **14**). The development of new technologies led to a widening of cultural and leisure pursuits: in the early 20th century, radio and cinema; post-World War II, television; and at the end of the century, computers and the *World Wide Web. Each of these developments presented real threats to reading as a leisure pursuit and—particularly with the Internet—as a source for information. Yet, at the beginning of the 21st century, the production of print-based books remained buoyant: the development of other mass media, including the advent of the electronic book (*see* **19**), posed a threat, but also presented opportunities. Cross-media interactions created a vibrant market in *subsidiary rights, as publishers, authors, and *literary agents negotiated deals to turn literary content into film and television versions, and new media spawned spin-off publishing activities. Contrary to the expectations of some more pessimistic commentators, new media in the 20th century could also enhance the publishing trade.

The push towards mass education and literacy in Britain developed alongside the growth of public *lending libraries. The 1850 Public Libraries Act enshrined the principle of such libraries, but they did not take substantial hold until the end of the 19th century and the opening decades of the 20th. At the beginning of World War I, 60 per cent of the British population had access to a public library; by the mid-1930s such access had become near-universal. Commercial *circulating libraries were also widespread in the first half of the 20th century, but these largely disappeared after World War II, as the public library system strengthened. Towards the end of the 20th century, however, the public library system suffered from funding cuts and diminishing borrower figures.

Shifting moral attitudes and the changing shape of British society during the 20th century both influenced and was influenced by the materials produced by publishing companies. Throughout the course of the century, the legislative framework and judicial activity surrounding the content of books underwent radical changes with the gradual arrival of a more permissive society. However, although bold and progressive publishers such as *Calder & Boyars continually pushed at social and political boundaries, the courts' role in censorship and publishers' attendant fear of prosecution meant that material about certain topics still struggled to be disseminated.

The *Lady Chatterley* trial gave rise to words much repeated in histories of British publishing. The jury was asked by the prosecution whether Lawrence's work was one that they 'would approve of your young sons, young daughters—because girls can read as well as boys—reading this book ... Is it a book that you would even wish your wife or your servants to read?' (Rolph, 17). The assumption of upper-middle-class male mores was rejected, and Penguin was vindicated. The second half of the 20th century was undeniably a freer environment for the book, although legislation that could be invoked to censor books continued: the Official Secrets Act; Section 28 of the Local Government Act 1988 (which curtailed the 'promotion' of homosexuality within schools); and the Incitement to Racial and Religious Hatred Act 2006. The desire to establish a free society continued to be in conflict with a desire to protect some groups within it.

5 The business of books

The foundations of the 20th-century book business had been laid at the end of the previous century. The *Society of Authors, the *Booksellers Association, the

Publishers Association, and the literary agent, all had their origins in the late 19th century. Their establishment pointed toward a more organized, professionalized industry. As the 20th century wore on, this modernity intensified, as the industry became increasingly corporate and globalized.

The shape of the British publishing industry had already changed substantially in the previous century, with existing and new companies gaining in size, and developing diverse lists. From 1914, several new companies joined their ranks, which, in addition to Allen & Unwin, Gollancz, and Penguin, included firms established by émigrés: *Deutsch, *Hamlyn, and *Weidenfeld & Nicolson, for example. In the 1960s, a concerted wave of mergers and acquisitions began to reform the national publishing industry, with ever-larger publishing groups being subsumed into global corporations, whose interests were much broader than publishing alone. By the beginning of the 21st century, British publishing had come to be dominated by a very small number of very large publishing groups: Bertelsmann, Hachette, *HarperCollins (News International), and *Pearson.

Nonetheless, the second half of the 20th century also allowed for diversity and innovation. The feminist publishers of the 1970s and 1980s, pre-eminently *Virago Press, shook up the male-dominated industry by revising gatekeeping policies, by publishing many more books by and about women (both reprints and originals), and by encouraging exclusively or predominantly female staffing. New computer-based technologies such as *desktop publishing and *print-on-demand meant that smaller companies could be quickly established, with a much lower threshold of required technical expertise. Apart from the wartime periods, annual British book-title production saw a relentless increase—from under 10,000 new titles at the beginning of the 20th century to over 100,000, and rising, at its end.

With all-encompassing changes in organization, structure, and technologies in the 20th century came transformations in the culture of publishing. Publishers became increasingly market-focused, with a concomitant shift in emphasis from the editorial function of publishing houses to their accounting, marketing, and sales departments. Publishing, which had once been seen as an 'occupation for gentlemen', as the title of *Warburg's memoir affirms, had always been more mercantile than some of its participants would have wanted to admit. Yet the growth of the mass market, and the activities by which publishers sought to develop their share of it, meant that, as the

20th century progressed, Warburg's distaste for the 'tradesman' and publishing as a business would come to be deeply anachronistic. At the beginning of the 21st century, British publishers—and their global parent companies—demanded a strong return on investment, and viewed their operations as businesses first, and purveyors of culture and information second.

The *Net Book Agreement, established at the very beginning of the 20th century, but dissolved in its final years, symbolically brought to an end the argument that, compared to other goods, 'books are different', a phrase that was used in an unsuccessful challenge to the agreement in the 1960s. Heavy discounting practices followed the NBA's dissolution. In the competitive environment of the 1990s and 2000s, with chain superstores, supermarket selling, and online retailing, independent booksellers struggled for survival in a market in which price was a key marketing weapon.

At the turn of the new century, the need for publishers to reach their markets nurtured a promotional culture in which authors could become heavily involved with their books' marketing through literary *festivals and meet-the-author events in bookshops, schools, and libraries. The category of *authorship expanded to encompass a substantial celebrity book market, which was reliant on the practice of *ghost-writing to deliver autobiographies and novels. Literary *prizes have proliferated, with the long-established *James Tait Black Memorial Prize joined in the second half of the century by (among many others) the *Booker, *Whitbread, and *Orange. *Reading groups spearhead sales in the general trade market, while in the 2000s a televised book club, *Richard and Judy, became the single most effective maker of bestsellers.

Meanwhile, technological advances have led to rapid changes in the sectors of educational, STM (Science, Technical, and Medical), and reference publishing, with digital publishing pushing new business models (see COMPUTER; 19). The nature of some market sectors has rendered book publishers into information providers, with their products barely recognizable as the traditional *codex. As these technological developments have progressed, however, a reverse trend can be perceived in the enduring activities of *private presses. Their use of hand presses in a globalized, digital environment is undoubtedly nostalgic; nevertheless, the continued resilience of the printed British book in the 21st century suggests that it is far from dead.

The landscape of post-1914 British publishing, and the books that it produced, have thus undergone a series of rapid transformations. These developments have frequently been organic rather than schismatic, growing out of 19th-century trends. Yet, for all its continuities, the British book in the 20th and early 21st centuries has proved itself distinctive: thoroughly engaged with deep changes in society, heavily market-oriented, and occasionally iconic both in form and in content.

BIBLIOGRAPHY

D. Athill, *Stet* (2000)

E. de Bellaigue, *British Book Publishing as a Business since the 1960s* (2004)

C. Bloom, *Bestsellers* (2002)

P. Buitenhuis, *The Great War of Words* (1987)

J. Carey, *The Intellectuals and the Masses* (1992)

G. Clark and A. Phillips, *Inside Book Publishing*, 4e (2008)

P. Delany, *Literature, Money and the Market* (2002)

J. Feather, *A History of British Publishing*, 2e (2006)

D. Finkelstein, 'Globalization of the Book 1800–1970', in *A Companion to the History of the Book*, ed. S. Eliot and J. Rose (2007)

R. Hoggart, *The Uses of Literacy* (1957)

A. Jaffe, *Modernism and the Culture of Celebrity* (2005)

M. Lane, *Books and Publishers* (1980)

Q. D. Leavis, *Fiction and the Reading Public* (1932)

J. McAleer, *Popular Reading and Publishing in Britain, 1914–1950* (1992)

I. Norrie, *Mumby's Publishing and Bookselling in the 20th Century*, 6e (1982)

A. Phillips, 'Does the Book Have a Future?', in *A Companion to the History of the Book*, ed. S. Eliot and J. Rose (2007)

J. Potter, *Boys in Khaki, Girls in Print* (2005)

— 'For Country, Conscience and Commerce', in *Publishing in the First World War*, ed. M. Hammond and S. Towheed (2007)

L. Rainey, *Institutions of Modernism* (1998)

C. H. Rolph, ed., *The Trial of Lady Chatterley* (1961)

Rose

J. Rose, 'Modernity and Print I: Britain 1890–1970', in *A Companion to the History of the Book*, ed. S. Eliot and J. Rose (2007)

— and P. J. Anderson, eds., *British Literary Publishing Houses 1881–1965* (1991)

C. Squires, 'Novelistic Production and the Publishing Industry in Britain and Ireland', in *A Companion to the British and Irish Novel 1945–2000*, ed. B. Shaffer (2005)

— *Marketing Literature* (2007)

J. A. Sutherland, *Bestsellers: Popular Fiction of the 1970s* (1981)

A. Travis, *Bound and Gagged* (2000)

F. Warburg, *An Occupation for Gentlemen* (1959)

J. P. Wexler, *Who Paid for Modernism?* (1997)

21 The History of the Book in Ireland

NIALL Ó CIOSÁIN AND CLARE HUTTON

1 From the coming of print to the Great Famine
2 1850 to the early 21st century

1 From the coming of print to the Great Famine

Although Ireland had a rich MS culture throughout the Middle Ages, it was not until 1551 that the first printed book was produced there, and very little was printed for a century thereafter. It has been estimated that, in 1640, one title was printed in England for every 8,800 people, whereas in Ireland the figure was one for every 190,000. One reason for this is that printing was an urban phenomenon, and Ireland was an overwhelmingly rural country. Its towns were mainly seaports trading with England and, to a lesser extent, with continental Europe. Imported books dominated the market: as late as 1700, only 20 per cent of books bought in Ireland were produced there; of the rest, 75 per cent came from England and 5 per cent from Europe. Ireland was England's largest market for book exports, surpassing both Scotland and Virginia. Most book imports came into Dublin, the capital, but there was also substantial traffic into the south and west, to Waterford, Cork, Limerick, and Galway.

Another reason for the slow development of printing in Ireland was that, as in England, the legal structure of the trade was effectively a monopoly. Printing was introduced by the state and, until 1732, was restricted to the holder of the patent of King's Printer. The first to occupy that office was Humphrey Powell of London, who came to Dublin and produced the first book printed in Ireland, the *Book of Common Prayer, in 1551. Powell is one of only two known printers in 16th-century Ireland. The other, William Kearney, was also a state printer; between them, they are known to have produced eight works, four of which were *broadsides.

The royal patent was granted in 1618 to the London *Stationers' Company, who intended to continue importing their Irish stock as well as producing books in Dublin, but the venture was not a success, and the Company sold the patent in 1639 to William Bladen.

However, the lengthy civil war and the political fragmentation of the 1640s led to a considerable expansion of printing: presses were established for the first time in Waterford, Kilkenny, and Cork. The full monopoly was restored in 1660 and granted to John Crooke, although he allowed other printers to work under licence from him.

The King's Printer's exclusive rights ensured that Ireland's printed output would be entirely Anglican and overwhelmingly in the English language. The vast majority of the population, however, remained Roman Catholic; most of them spoke Irish, although English was well established among the Catholic commercial and political elite. Catholic books, mainly devotional, were imported from Europe; they were not produced in any numbers in Ireland until well into the 18th century. The King's Printers did produce a few books in Irish, including a New Testament in 1602, but this was not followed by other religious works and was not part of a successful Reformation.

From the early 18th century, however, the Irish economy as a whole began to expand and rural areas became more commercialized. The consequent increase in the domestic market for consumer goods, along with the growth in *literacy, created a network of distributors and customers for the book trade. This trend was reinforced by a long period of political stability, in contrast to the wars of the 17th century. The Dublin book trade expanded continually throughout the 18th century; and while the capital retained its overwhelming dominance in book production, the century also saw the establishment of printers and booksellers in provincial towns. Whereas in the 1690s printers were active outside Dublin only in Cork and Belfast, in the 1760s there were presses in some 16 towns, and by the 1790s in 34. The majority of these, however, produced *newspapers and *jobbing printing; significant quantities of books were manufactured only in Cork, Belfast, Newry, Limerick, and Waterford.

In Dublin, expansion began during the 1680s and was rapid after 1700. The number of booksellers increased from 25 in 1700 to 65 in the 1790s. By mid-century, some specialist sellers had emerged. Although the office of King's Printer continued to exist, its privileges had effectively disappeared by the late 17th century. A printers' and stationers' guild, the Guild of St Luke the Evangelist, was established in 1670, but it was confined to Dublin and even there had little effect in regulating the trade, functioning principally as a political club. One feature of the stationers' guild, typical of 18th-century Ireland in general, was that full membership was restricted to adherents of the state Church. Catholics were permitted to have a type of sub- or quarter-membership. This did not inhibit the activities of Catholic printers, however; and since the vast majority of the population outside the towns was Catholic, printers and booksellers serving this market flourished in Dublin, particularly after 1750. Ignatius Kelly and Patrick Wogan, among others, made fortunes from devotional books, schoolbooks, and *chapbooks produced for a mainly rural market.

The 18th-century Dublin book trade's most distinctive feature, however, was that it was a reprint trade. The British Copyright Act of 1710, which protected literary property in a printed work, did not apply to Ireland, and throughout the century many Dublin booksellers were active in reprinting works already published in London. They were typically able to procure *sheets of new books from London quickly enough to be able to produce a Dublin edition within a month or two of its initial publication. Labour costs in Dublin were lower and *copyright costs did not have to be paid, making these editions cheaper than the originals. They also tended to be in smaller *formats and of inferior quality. Until 1739 these reprints could legally be exported to Britain and, after 1783, to the US. Their principal market was domestic, however, and although there are suggestions that Dublin reprints may have been smuggled into Britain after 1739, the level of port surveillance meant that the numbers of books may have been very small. Certainly, domestic reprints dominated the Irish market; the private libraries of Irish elites tended to contain Dublin reprints of authors such as Samuel *Johnson or Gibbon, rather than the original London editions.

One consequence of the lack of copyright in Ireland was that Irish authors, such as Sheridan and Goldsmith, had their work published in London, initiating a trend that continued long after the reprint trade had ended. The main exception was *Swift, whose political *pamphlets of the 1720s and 1730s won him national fame, and whose works were published by *Faulkner, the leading printer of mid-18th-century Dublin.

The buoyancy of the Dublin book trade came to a sudden end at the close of the 18th century. The later 1790s saw serious difficulties in procuring paper; although there were some *paper mills in Ireland, most of the paper used was imported. War with France after 1793 cut off much of this supply, and an increased duty imposed in 1795 meant that Dublin-produced books no longer had a price advantage over London imprints. The reprint industry came to an end with the 1801 Act of Union, through which British copyright law was immediately extended to Ireland. The effect was dramatic: the publication of books in Ireland fell by three-quarters in the early decades of the 19th century. At the same time the economy as a whole continued to grow, with war even accentuating agricultural prosperity, and domestic demand for books remaining high. The result was a huge increase in imports, whose annual value rose from an average of £650 in 1780 to about £6,500 in 1810. This phenomenon reinforced the trend of Irish writers publishing their works in London; during the first half of the 19th century, the only prominent Irish author to be published initially in Dublin was William Carleton.

Some Dublin booksellers survived by becoming agents for London publishers. Others emigrated, resulting in a substantial movement of personnel to the US. This emigration had begun already in the 1760s, and gathered pace with increased contact between the Irish and American trades after 1780. The largest migration came at the turn of the century, produced by economic downturn and political crisis; by the early 19th century, at least 100 booktrade workers had settled in America, mainly in Philadelphia and New York. Many continued their reprinting activities, including Mathew *Carey, who in the early 19th century was the most successful publisher in the US.

The effect of the Act of Union was felt principally at the top of the market. Among the more popular readership, however, the Act had less impact, and a number of developments in the early 19th century provided a good deal of business for printers and publishers. From about 1810 onwards, and particularly in the 1820s and 1830s, a series of Protestant evangelical societies was active in rural Ireland, constituting what has been called 'the Second Reformation'. Although they produced very few converts, these organizations had a major impact by establishing schools (for which they provided *textbooks), and by subsidizing and distributing vast amounts of religious and moral literature, all of which was printed in Dublin. The Catholic response, which included setting up rival schools, along with a mass Catholic political movement in the 1820s, also stimulated popular publishing. The state responded to both groups by establishing a national education system in 1831, ensuring a continued and vibrant business in schoolbooks.

In provincial towns, where the market was local and not dependent on reprints, the effect of Union was not felt very strongly; indeed, printing and publishing in places such as Cork, Limerick, and Belfast was at its height in the decades after 1810. Belfast was the home of one important innovation in book marketing in the 1840s: *Simms & M'Intyre's Parlour Library, which packaged popular novels in a single volume costing 1s. In the towns of the south and southeast, more Irish language publishing occurred during these decades than any other.

Printing in Irish effectively ceased for decades after the Great Famine of the late 1840s, which devastated Irish-speaking areas. The famine was also a turning point for printing and the book trade in Ireland more generally. Printing in provincial towns declined, and the trade began to centre on Dublin. Technological advances such as steam printing (*see* **11**) demanded substantial investment, which favoured larger firms in the capital; improvements in communications, particularly the spread of railways, enabled the Irish rural market to be centrally supplied. In Dublin, the combined effect of the Famine and a commercial crisis in 1847 resulted in a series of bankruptcies of printers and publishers.

2 1850 to the early 21st century

One publisher to survive the profound cultural, social, and economic upheaval of mid-19th century Ireland was James *Duffy, who published the immensely popular and successful 'Library of Ireland' in Dublin between 1845 and 1847. This series of monthly shilling volumes included newly commissioned works of nationalist history and literature and was designed, in Duffy's words, to appeal to the 'increased education and Nationality of the People'.

McGlashan & Gill, established in 1856 by Michael Henry *Gill, a Catholic who worked as the printer for the Protestant stronghold of Trinity's Dublin University Press, followed the example set by Duffy and published titles that appealed more or less exclusively to the local market. As Printer to the University, a post he held until 1875, Gill was able to establish a strong position in the market, coming to his new business with an intimate knowledge and experience of all aspects of the book trade, a solid contact list, and an awareness of the gaps in the market which the University Press could not hope to fill.

By the late 19th century, Gill & Son (as it became) was one of the firmer fixtures within the Irish book trade, with a printing works that backed on to the firm's shop on Dublin's main thoroughfare, O'Connell Street, and which sold *missals, *prayer books, religious statues, priests' vestments, and candles alongside the firm's publications. Duffy and Gill had earlier shown evidence of their interest in the intellectual revival of Irish culture, through the publication of titles such as Eugene O'Curry's *Lectures on the Manuscript Materials of Ancient Irish History* (Duffy, 1861) and John O'Donovan's *annotated *translation of *The Annals of the Kingdom of Ireland by the Four Masters*, a large and beautiful *parallel text edition in seven *quarto volumes, expertly printed by Gill at the University Press (1848–51). By the early 1890s, however, when W. B. Yeats and his peers wished to gain support for their attempts to rejuvenate Irish culture more generally, the editorial response from Irish publishers was decidedly lacklustre. The dynamism and energy associated with the house of Duffy faded quickly when its founder died in 1871. By the 1890s, the publishing arm of the business was doing little more than issuing reprints of titles published decades earlier. Under the guidance of Gill's son, Henry, nationalist and stridently Catholic literature had come to dominate the firm's lists, this being, perhaps, the inevitable consequence of the increasing public confidence of the Catholic Church, which both Duffy and Gill had done much to engender in the 1860s and 1870s.

With such fixed and limited horizons, and in the face of such strong competition from London, the Irish publishing industry had little to offer aspiring and serious authors. Production values were generally poor, distribution networks were dwarfed by those of the London firms, and the chance of an author being paid a competitive rate was all but nonexistent. That the Irish publishing industry was revived in the early decades of the 20th century, and in the face of such inauspicious circumstances, is testimony to the vigour and nationalist commitment of Yeats's generation, which became increasingly aware that it was culturally incongruous for a separatist literary movement to be dependent on the support of British publishers.

In 1903 Yeats, with his sister, the printer and artist Elizabeth Corbet Yeats, established the *Dun Emer Press (later known as the *Cuala Press), a *private press which published *limited and expensive first editions of Yeats's works and those of his friends. Maunsel & Company, established in Dublin in 1905 by a group of literary enthusiasts, also did much to promote the literature of the Irish Literary Revival and the thinking behind the more general cultural revival and political upheavals that took place in Ireland in the period leading up to the foundation of the independent Irish Free State (1922). Yet Maunsel was undercapitalized and poorly managed, and despite achieving standards of literary and typographical excellence, it was bankrupt by 1925. The Talbot Press, founded in 1913 as the cultural imprint of the Educational Company of Ireland (established 1910), ran on a smoother basis. It served some contemporary authors by subsidizing cultural publishing with the steady profits made by the publication of school textbooks, a sector of considerable importance to the Irish publishing business throughout the 20th century.

The status of the Irish language was also transformed by the cultural revival of the early 20th century, with the production of works in Irish growing from perhaps two or three books per decade in the late 19th century to ten or twenty per year in the 1900s. The Irish language movement was self-consciously and deliberately attempting to create a new literature, a new *print culture, and a new readership. In the realm of *typography, a choice had to be made between using roman type or Gaelic type. The vast majority of books in the early 20th century used Gaelic type, chosen probably as a sign of the distinctiveness of Gaelic culture. This meant that a printing trade that had functioned almost exclusively in English needed to procure new *founts, as well as *compositors and proofreaders with the ability to deal with them.

The period leading up to the outbreak of World War II was particularly difficult for publishers in both the Irish Free State and the six counties of what had become, with Partition in 1920, Northern Ireland. Those who survived the violence and political instability accompanying the War of Independence and the Civil War found themselves working in a climate of reaction and cultural caution which developed as the 1920s wore on, culminating, in the Irish Free State, in the Censorship of Publications Act (1929). This notorious Act saw many works by leading writers of British, American, and Irish modern fiction being prohibited for being 'indecent and obscene'. *Censorship was a significant feature of Irish literary culture up to 1967, when the government finally responded to the palpable shift in public opinion and amended legislation to allow prohibitions on books to lapse after

twelve years, a development which, applied retroactively, immediately lifted the ban on over 5,000 titles.

The impact of the 'Economic War', a tariff dispute between Britain and Ireland from 1932 to 1938, was considerable, with Irish producers generally suffering more than British consumers. As British publishers found the books that they wished to export to Ireland becoming subject to duties, the British authorities retaliated by imposing prohibitive taxes on Irish books, including those crossing the border to Northern Ireland. This levy added to the difficulties which censorship had already put in place, and the only significant Irish publishing firms to survive were Gill and Talbot, who worked with caution and diplomacy, serving the steady indigenous religious and educational markets while firmly rejecting anything that threatened to upset the pieties of Irish public life. The deterioration of the international situation in 1939 further disrupted business, with military censorship, paper shortages, and printing firms finding that it was impossible to get replacement parts for their machines.

Under the Irish Free State (Constitution) Act of 1922, Irish was recognized as the state's national language, and Irish became compulsory in schools. The new government set up its own publishing venture, An *Gúm (The Scheme) in 1927. By the mid-1930s it had published more than 400 works, including original material in Irish, modern versions of older Irish classics, and translations of foreign novels, particularly novels in English. In some respects the state's support for Irish-language publishing went hand in hand with its enthusiasm for censorship: both initiatives involved the desire to control and direct the evolution of national book culture. By reducing the supply of largely imported literature, the government inadvertently provided a fillip to the commercial fortunes of the Irish publishing sector, as domestic production expanded to fill the gap. Moreover, the two publishing houses established in the 1940s—a period of intense difficulties for those in the book trade—reflected the Catholic and Gaelicizing tendencies of the State's founders. The Cork-based Mercier Press, founded in 1944, was committed to publishing books that explored 'spiritual and intellectual values over material ones', while *Sáirséal agus Dill, established in 1947, was an Irish-language publishing house that issued over 100 titles before the death of its founder, Seán Sáirséal Ó hÉigeartaigh, in 1967.

From 1949 to 1957, the Republic of Ireland's annual economic growth rate was only 1 per cent, easily the lowest in western Europe. Unemployment was high, and there was mass emigration. Most significant authors continued to seek publication primarily in London, and there was little innovation or dynamism within the Irish book trade, which largely served a limited indigenous market with works that could only achieve a local sale. The one exception to this general pattern was the *Dolmen Press, a small literary publishing house founded by Liam Miller in 1951. A literary enthusiast who was committed to the value of publishing Irish literature in Ireland, Miller's list would eventually include works by writers such as Thomas Kinsella, Flann O'Brien, and John McGahern, whom he numbered as friends. Miller's first interest, however, was book design: he was inspired by the private press ideal espoused by the Cuala Press, and, with his wife Josephine, he printed many of the works on a hand press. Unfortunately, however, Dolmen was not run on a secure financial basis and did not survive beyond Miller's death in 1987.

In the period 1958–64, following the introduction of new economic policies in the Republic, annual growth shot forward to 4 per cent. *Paperback publishing boomed, making access to a wide range of literature easy and affordable. In a dramatic reversal of cultural policy, the government in the Republic became increasingly helpful to both English-language publishers and authors. The Arts Council (An Chomhairle Ealaíon) began to provide grants for individual titles as well as interest-free loans, and profits arising from 'original, creative' work by writers 'solely resident in Ireland' became exempt from income tax in 1969, a move that made the Republic something of a writers' haven. In 1967, the Irish University Press was established, inspired by the worldwide expansion of the university sector, the market for reprints, and the tax-free status of the Shannon Industrial Estate, where the press established a vast modern *printing office. The dramatic collapse of this venture in 1974 had one unexpected consequence: it left a large number of talented young editors, production staff, and promotions people out of work. A number of these went on to found their own publishing businesses, mostly small, editorially led and owner-managed literary presses publishing books on issues of Irish interest; by the early 1980s there was considerable energy in the sector.

The escalation of violence in Northern Ireland from 1969 provided another paradoxical boost to the culture of the Irish book, to the extent that the violence generated responses in the form of histories, autobiographies, polemics, fiction, drama, and poetry. In recent decades, Belfast's Blackstaff Press, established in 1971 and given crucial financial support by the Arts Council of Northern Ireland, has been an important outlet for material of this kind. The Gallery Press, founded in 1970, and now operating from County Meath, in the Republic, is also a significant force in Irish publishing. However, Gallery, like Blackstaff, would long ago have faded from the scene had it not been for significant sponsorship from both the Irish Arts Council and the Arts Council of Northern Ireland.

The contours of Irish life began to change decisively in the mid-1990s, during a period of very rapid economic growth. The 'tiger' years, which saw Ireland become a normal European economy, now appear to have been a period of 'catch-up' rather than the miracle they seemed at the time. Publishers have shared in the increased wealth, and Irish authors are no longer so likely to seek initial publication overseas, owing to the growing size and professionalism of the Irish publishing industry, a more general confidence in Irish business, and—in an ironic sign of globalizing times—the presence of Penguin Ireland and Hodder Headline Ireland, two publishing conglomerates, which set up offices in Dublin in 2003.

BIBLIOGRAPHY

C. Benson, 'Printers and Booksellers in Dublin 1800–1850', in *Spreading The Word: Distribution Networks of Print 1550–1850*, ed. R. Myers and M. Harris (1990)

R. C. Cole, *Irish Booksellers and English Writers, 1740–1800* (1986)

R. Gillespie, *Reading Ireland: Print, Reading, and Social Change in Early Modern Ireland* (2005)

— and A. Hadfield, eds., *The Oxford History of the Irish Book*, vol. 3: *The Irish Book in English, 1550–1800* (2006)

M. Harmon, *The Dolmen Press* (2001)

C. Hutton, ed., *The Irish Book in the Twentieth Century* (2004)

— *The Oxford History of the Irish Book*, vol. 5: *The Irish Book in English, 1891–2000* (forthcoming)

V. Kinane, *A Brief History of Printing and Publishing in Ireland* (2002)

L. Miller, *The Dun Emer Press, Later the Cuala Press* (1973)

N. Ó Ciosáin, *Print and Popular Culture in Ireland, 1750–1850* (1997)

J. W. Phillips, *Printing and Bookselling in Dublin, 1670–1800* (1998)

M. Pollard, *Dublin's Trade in Books, 1550–1800* (1989)

W. Wheeler, 'The Spread of Provincial Printing in Ireland up to 1850', *Irish Booklore*, 4.1 (1978), 7–18

22 The History of the Book in France

Vincent Giroud

1 Introduction

The history of the book in France reflects the peculiar dynamics between culture and power that have characterized the country throughout its history. These dynamics take two principal forms. The first is a constant trend towards centralization, resulting in the supremacy of Paris, always but never successfully challenged. The second is a long tradition, beyond regime changes, of state intervention or control in cultural matters. Yet this situation also carries contradictions and paradoxes, including the perpetual gap between cultural policies, stated or implemented, and a reality that, through inertia or active resistance, counters them.

2 The MS age

Books, in France as everywhere else, preceded printing. By the 2nd century AD in Gaul, dealers in *codices were established in the major Roman cities of the Rhône valley (Vienne, Lyons), indicating that Latin literature was distributed in the country. In the 4th century, as Christianity spread, intellectual centres focusing on the dissemination of sacred texts were formed around the great figures of the period, such as Martin in Tours and Marmoutiers, and Honorat on and off the Mediterranean coast. Three centuries later, under the Merovingian kings, came the first wave of monastic foundations, some in the main cities (Paris, Arras, Limoges, Poitiers, Soissons) but many in isolated areas, mostly in the northern half of what is now France. The majority were founded between 630 and 660: *Luxeuil, near Besançon; Saint-Amand, near *Valenciennes; Jouarre, near Meaux; Saint-Bertin, near Saint-Omer; Saint-Riquier, in Picardy; Fleury (now Saint-Benoît), on the Loire near Orléans; Jumièges, on the Seine south of Rouen; Chelles, to the northeast of Paris; Corbie, near Amiens. These, along with cathedral schools in the cities named above, as well as Arles, Auxerre, Bordeaux, Laon, Lyons, Toulouse, and others, became and remained the principal centres of book production in the country until the creation of universities in the 13th century. Their *scriptoria were among the most important of medieval Europe. While many of these made books for the monastery's use, some became book production centres, specializing—like modern publishing houses—in certain types of MS. Commentaries on the Fathers of the Church came from Corbie, didactic texts from Auxerre and Fleury-sur-Loire. Saint-Amand was famous for its gospels and *sacramentaries. Saint-Martin in Tours became a leading producer of large, complete bibles, of which the Bible of King Charles the Bald (823–77), now in the *Bibliothèque nationale de France (BnF), is an outstanding example. On becoming abbot of the recently founded Cluny in 927, Odon brought with him 100 MSS; their number grew to 570 by the end of the 12th century. The second wave of monastic foundations—in the 11th century, especially under the impulse of St Bernard—resulted in an increase in MS production and in new networks for their dissemination, with the Grande Chartreuse (1084), Cîteaux (1098), and Clairvaux (1115) forming important libraries.

The university of Paris, created in 1215, while opening up the territory of learning beyond the confines of monasteries and cathedral schools, produced an immediate demand for books—as did the foundation by Cardinal Robert de Sorbon, in 1257, of a college for poor theology teachers that was to bear his name. By the late 13th century the *Sorbonne, enriched by donations, had (for the time) a large library. In 1338 it contained 1,722 volumes, 300 of them publicly accessible (though *chained against theft) in the main reference room (*grande librairie*), the remainder locked up in the *petite librairie*, from which they could be made available for consultation and circulation. In addition to academic libraries, a book trade appeared, with *stationers operating workshops in the Latin Quarter to furnish students and teachers with copies of MSS. Laymen, responsible to the university's religious authorities, ran the *pecia system: for a fee, students or professional copyists could borrow MSS established from a model copy (the *exemplar) previously checked by university commissions. The dealers (*libraires-jurés*), affiliated to the university, were to check the new copies for completeness and accuracy. Like the monasteries before them, universities acquired specialisms—Paris in theology and Orléans in civil law—differences that were reflected in the libraries and book trades flourishing around those two centres. With the development of biblical exegesis in the 12th century, new types of bible, incorporating commentaries (some running to fourteen volumes), became a Parisian specialty in the 13th century, as did one-volume 'pocket bibles'. Another speciality, recorded by Dante in the *Divina Commedia (*Purgatorio*, 11.80–81), was illumination, with workshops such as that of the *Limbourg brothers producing luxury volumes of which the spectacular *books of hours of the period remain celebrated examples.

Although lay books *par excellence*, books of hours and *psalters were both in Latin; a genuine vernacular literature appeared in the 12th century, both in the *langue d'oc* spoken in southern France and the *langue d'oïl* spoken in the north. At first the transmission of these texts was oral. Thus, there are no early MSS of the 9th-century *Chanson de Roland*, which began to be written down in the early 11th century. Of the five verse novels of Chrétien de Troyes (*fl.* 1170–85), the most important writer of his age, there are no MSS before 1200. As early as the 13th century, the most widely disseminated French work was the allegorical, didactic *Roman de la Rose* (first part *c.*1230, second part *c.*1270): about 250 complete copies are preserved. Troubadour poems started being collected only during the 14th century. By then, Christine de Pisan, the first real woman of letters, operated the equivalent of a small private scriptorium to disseminate her poems.

Considering that only about 10 per cent of the French population was literate in 1400, books were used and enjoyed by a privileged minority. An even smaller minority within that minority, the first French book collectors, appeared at that time. The famous image of King Charles V among his books, like a monk (BnF, Fr. MS 24287), was a political statement of sorts. The king's library, to be sure, was as much an ancestor of the BnF as a private library. It also served as a model for the aristocracy, a model not only followed but surpassed by some members of the royal family, who were truly the first French bibliophiles—especially Jean, duc de *Berry (the king's brother) and their cousin *Philip the Good, duke of Burgundy: both owned some of the most expensive books of their time. The 15th century also marks the beginnings of urban *patronage, characteristic of the rise of an identifiable bourgeoisie, with well-known instances in Bourges and Rouen.

Humanism, as has often been pointed out, came to France as a result of the sojourn of the popes in Avignon (1309–78), which brought Petrarch (*Petrarca) and Boccaccio (*see* DECAMERON) to the country, while Poggio *Bracciolini toured abbeys (Cluny) and cathedral schools (Langres) in search of MSS of classical authors. Avignon became one of the earliest centres of paper production in France (Champagne was another) as the new material began to replace *parchment. It also figures in the immediate prehistory of the invention of printing, as a certain Procopius Waldfoghel formed an association with local scholars and printers in 1444 to develop a system of 'artificial writing' about which nothing else is known. Other prototypographical experiments may have taken place in Toulouse around that time (*see* **6, 11**).

3 The coming of print

Printed books were introduced into France before printing was established in the country. *Gutenberg's associates *Fust (who died in Paris in 1466) and Schoeffer brought their productions to the French capital, where they were also available through their representative, Hermann de Staboen. Once *Heynlin and Guillaume Fichet had established the first French printing press in a Latin Quarter house owned by the Sorbonne, the new technology spread fairly quickly to the provinces. *Le Roy printed the first book in Lyons in 1473. Presses are recorded at Albi in 1475; at Angers and Toulouse in 1476; at Vienne and Chablis (the northern Burgundy wine village) in 1478; in Poitiers in 1479; at Chambéry and Chartres in 1482; at Rennes and two other Breton cities in 1484 (the first work in the Breton language was printed as early as 1475); at Rouen in 1485; at Abbeville in 1486; at Orléans and Grenoble in 1490; at Angoulême and Narbonne in 1491. Save for a few ephemeral undertakings, like the one Jehan de Rohan ran in his Breton château of Bréhant-Loudéac in 1484–5, most were permanent establishments. Leaving aside the Alsatian region, which was politically and culturally part of the Germanic world, there were presses in about 30 French cities by 1500.

Lyons was not a university town but a major commercial centre with frequent contacts with northern Italy and Germany. It soon became the second most active city for printing in France and, in the 1490s, the third in Europe. Books were sold at its four annual fairs. Of its emergent prosperous, progressive merchant class, Barthélémy Buyer, Le Roy's patron, was an outstanding example. Paper mills operated in Beaujolais nearby and in not-too-distant Auvergne. By 1485 Lyons boasted at least twelve printers, most of them coming from Germany, such as Martin Huss from Wurtemberg, whose *Mirouer de la rédemption de l'humain lignaige* (1478) is the first illustrated book printed in France (using woodcuts from Basel). To the same Huss is owed the first known representation of a printing office, in the 1499 *Grande *danse macabre*, a powerful image showing the emissaries of death grabbing the *compositor, pressmen, and *corrector caught in the middle of their respective tasks. Also in Lyons, Michel Topié and Jacques Heremberck printed von *Breydenbach's *Sainctes peregrinations de Jerusalem* (*Peregrinatio in Terram Sanctam*), the first French book illustrated with *engravings (the plates copied from the woodcuts of the 1486 Mainz edition). Half the titles printed in French before 1500 originated from Lyons, including the very first, the *Légende dorée* which Le Roy issued in 1476.

Although Lyons to a great extent showed the way, Paris was already the capital of the book in France and, after Venice, the second most active publishing centre in Europe in the 15th century. Printers and booksellers soon congregated in the southeastern part of the Latin Quarter, especially along the rue Saint-Jacques (where *Gering and his associates set up shop

after Heynlin left the Sorbonne). Paper and parchment dealers were situated further east, in the Faubourg Saint-Marcel. The book trade established itself mostly along the river and on the Île de la Cité. Most of the early Parisian printers came from abroad, especially the German-speaking world. The first 'native' printing office, the Soufflet Vert, was opened in 1475 by Louis Symonel from Bourges, Richard Blandin from Évreux, and the Parisian Russangis; *Bonhomme, who printed the first French book issued in the capital, probably set up his press in that same year. The university's presence influenced the types of book first printed in the city: pedagogical works like Gasparino Barzizza's letters and spelling manual, Fichet's *Rhétorique*, classical authors in particular favour in schools (Cicero, Sallust), or works popular in the legal and clerical professions, like Montrocher's *Manipulus Curatorum*. The city's long association with illuminated MSS was also a factor: a large part of the Parisian 15th-century output (700 of the 4,600 incunables that originated in France) was printed books of hours, produced at times with blank spaces left so that they could be decorated by hand. These were the specialty of Jean Du Pré and Pierre Pigouchet and, after them, *Vérard, who before becoming a prolific and successful printer ran a workshop of copyists and *enlumineurs*. The continued prestige enjoyed by MSS also explains some of the typographical characteristics of many French incunables: the preference for the so-called gothic *bastarda type, closest to late medieval calligraphy (whereas Gering and his colleagues had initially used an elegant roman type cast from Italian models); and the taste for elaborately decorated *initials also reminiscent of illumination (which recur in French books well into the 17th century).

Other printing cities in France were often university towns, like Angers and Tours. In most cases, however, the Church was the promoter, the resulting products being books needed for religious services: *breviaries were printed at Troyes and at Limoges, and copies of a *missal and psalter at Cluny. The patronage of the Savoy court played an important role in Chambéry, where Antonine Neyret issued his *Livre du roy Modus*, the first French hunting book, in 1486.

Much 15th-century book production was targeted at the academic world or the Church, while books of hours and chivalric *romances were favoured by the rich bourgeoisie. Literature as it might be understood now—including many reprints of the *Roman de la Rose* and rare editions of the greatest poet of the previous generation, François Villon (*fl.* 1450–63)—represented a small percentage of the trade's output. Yet more popular forms of printing appeared and spread in the shape of small *pamphlets printed in French in gothic type, ranging from current news to practical handbooks; many have not survived.

Naturally, the political powers viewed the invention of printing with movable type with interest and encouraged it. There are signs that Heynlin was protected by Louis XI (r. 1461–83); the Italian campaigns of his son Charles VIII in 1495–8 (their spoils leading to the establishment of royal MS collections in Amboise) spurred the spread of humanism in France.

4 The 16th century

Paris, with 25,000 titles, and Lyons, with 15,000, continued to dominate French printing in the 16th century, while Rouen established itself as the country's third printing centre (with Toulouse fourth). The proportion of titles printed in French grew rapidly, the balance relative to Latin tilting towards the vernacular in the 1560s. At the same time, humanism brought to France an unprecedented interest in Greek texts: Gilles de Gourmont printed the first French book in Greek in 1507, while François I gathered at Fontainebleau the best collection of Greek MSS in western Europe, appointing as its curator Guillaume Budé.

Between 1521, when the Paris faculty of theology condemned Luther and obtained from the Paris parliament the right of control over all religious publications, and 1572, the year of the St Bartholomew Massacre, printing was intimately connected with the spread of the Reformation in France, with the king acting at first as an arbiter. His sister, *Marguerite de Navarre, protected the reformist circle formed around Guillaume Briçonnet, bishop of Meaux. The king himself defended the biblical scholar Jacques Lefèvre d'Étaples, whose translation of the New Testament was issued by *Colines in 1523, two years after the faculty of theology had banned biblical translations. But he was powerless to prevent the execution of Louis de Berquin, the translator of *Erasmus, in 1529, and turned to repression when Lyons-printed *broadsides attacking the Catholic mass were posted in 1534, an indirect cause of the condemnation and execution of *Augereau in the same year. For a while, early in 1535, printing was banned altogether. Then came a series of regulations destined to establish royal control over all printing-related matters: the institution of *copyright deposit (the Edict of Montpellier, 1537), the regulation of the printing professions and the

creation of the post of *Imprimeur du Roi* (1539–41), and the tightening of *censorship in 1542. More such measures were adopted by Henri II. The Ordinance of Moulins (1566) made general the obligation to obtain a *privilege, to be granted exclusively by the Chancery. The success of these repressive measures is attested by *Dolet's execution (1546) and the departure of Robert Estienne for Geneva following the deaths of François I (1547) and Marguerite (1549).

The first half of the 16th century, heralded by the publication of Erasmus's *Adagia* at Paris in 1500, is dominated by the great humanist printers: in Paris *Badius, *Tory, Colines, *Morel, *Vascosan, and above all the *Estiennes; in Lyons *Gryphius, Dolet, and de *Tournes. The dissemination of humanism was also facilitated by entrepreneurs like *Petit, the most prominent French publisher of the age, who issued over 1,000 volumes between 1493 and 1530. While the 'archaic', gothic appearance of the previous period was still widespread, humanist printers favoured roman types such as the one Estienne used for Lefèvre's revisionist *Quintuplex Psalterium* (1509)—thus typographic innovation, soon to be codified by Tory in *Champfleury* (1529), typically accompanied progressive thinking. It led to the work of the great French typographers *Garamont, *Granjon, and the *Le Bé dynasty in Troyes, suppliers of *Plantin's Hebrew types. One of the most admired typographical achievements of the period is *Le Songe de Poliphile*, a French version of the *Hypnerotomachia Poliphili*; printed by Jacques Kerver in 1546, it also marked the apogee of the French Renaissance illustrated book with its beautiful woodcuts, attributed to Jean Goujon and Jean Cousin.

Lyons, having neither a university nor a parliament, enjoyed greater political freedom, at least until the early 1570s, to the point of becoming a Calvinist city in 1562–72. At least fifteen editions of the Bible in (banned) French translation appeared there between 1551 and 1565. In 1562 de Tournes published at Lyons the first edition of Marot's translation of the Psalms completed by Beza, 'the most ambitious publishing project of the 16th century' (Chartier and Martin, 1. 321) for which nineteen Parisian printers were contracted (two, Oudin Petit and Charles Périer, were victims of the St Bartholomew Massacre), as well as many in the provinces. After 1572, Geneva (where de Tournes's son and successor moved in 1585) replaced Lyons as the principal centre of dissident religious texts printed in French (*see* **25**).

This ideological effervescence was accompanied by an extraordinary literary flowering: Rabelais

(*Pantagruel* and *Gargantua*, first printed at Lyons in 1532 and 1534), the Lyonnais Maurice Scève (*Délie*, 1544), du Bellay (*Défense et illustration de la langue française*, 1549 and many later editions), Ronsard (*Les Amours*, two editions in 1552), the other poets of the Pléiade group, and Montaigne, whose *Essais* were first printed at Bordeaux. André Thevet popularized voyages of discovery with his *Singularitez de la France antarctique* (1557). Ambroise Paré fostered the renovation of surgery with his *Cinq livres de chirurgie* (1572)—its Huguenot printer, Andreas Wechel, left Paris for Geneva that same year—and Androuet du Cerceau's *Plus excellents bastiments de France* (1566–79) promoted the canons of the Fontainebleau School.

Montaigne's library (described in *Essais*, 2. 10) is that of a cultivated reader of wide intellectual curiosity; it differs from that of a bibliophile like *Grolier, earlier in the century, with his particular interest in bindings. The 16th century can rightly be called the golden age of French binding, with names like Étienne Roffet (named Royal Binder in 1533), Jean Picard, Claude Picques, Gomar Estienne (no relation of the printing dynasty), and Nicolas and Clovis *Eve (the latter active during the 1630s). Progress was also made in printing music, first by *Haultin, then by Pierre Attaingnant of Douai (*fl.* 1525–51), who became the first royal printer of music, to be succeeded by Robert Ballard, whose family retained the office for more than two centuries.

The Wars of Religion, for all their human cost, resulted in relatively little destruction of books (the main casualties were in the libraries of Cluny, Fleury, and Saint-Denis). They generated, on both sides, a mass of propaganda and counter-propaganda (362 pamphlets printed at Paris in 1589 alone). On the Catholic side, they resulted in a revival of liturgical and patristic literature at the end of the century, often involving—in Paris and in Lyons—groups of printers operating as 'companies' to share the publication of particular works. Another, long-term consequence of the Counter-Reformation, the establishment of Jesuit schools throughout the country, produced a rise in literacy and fostered the development of new printing centres in medium-sized cities such as Douai, Pont-à-Mousson, and Dole.

5 The 17th century

Historians of the book who regard the 16th century, especially the reign of Henri II (1547–59), as the apogee in French book arts from both a technical and an aesthetic standpoint, view the 17th century as a period of decline. This applies to the number of titles printed (not, however, to the total output), with Parisian production dropping to 17,500 titles (excluding pamphlets). Lyons, meanwhile, kept its provincial supremacy in absolute terms, but declined in proportion, challenged by other cities, especially Rouen. The development of the paper industry, discouraged by heavy taxes, was further slowed down by the growing shortage of rags, which led to a serious crisis until the 1720s. The quasi-medieval organization of the book trade stifled initiative. Despite Denys Moreau's attempts under Louis XIII, and with the exception of *Grandjean's efforts at the end of the century, the triumph and ubiquity of Garamond type did not stimulate typographical innovation. Nor is the period particularly notable for its illustrated books, though significant exceptions include Jean Chapelain's *Pucelle* with engravings by Abraham Bosse after Claude Vignon (1656) and, in the later period, Israel Silvestre's and Sébastien Leclerc's *festival books documenting Versailles's grandest occasions.

The 17th century is notable for other reasons. First, books and reading habits—the result of a higher literacy rate, which by 1700 averaged 50 per cent—became more general. This applied to men more than to women, to cities more than to the countryside, and to the areas north of a line going from Saint-Malo to Geneva (known as the 'Maggiolo line' after the author of a survey in the late 1870s) more than to western, southwestern, and southern France. Beyond the prestigious collections formed by de *Thou, *Mazarin, *Brienne, *Colbert, and the *Lamoignons, private libraries, even of modest size, became normal among the growing merchant and legal professions in Paris and most French towns. In the lower echelons of society, the spread and lasting success of the *Bibliothèque bleue, which made Troyes the fourth most important printing city in 17th-century France, is a signal phenomenon, highlighting the growing role of non-conventional channels (such as itinerant pedlars) in book distribution.

The second notable factor is the bolstering of political controls over all matters relating to the printing and selling of books after the period of unrest following the relatively liberal reign of Henri IV (1589–1610). Richelieu (prime minister 1624–42) and his successors, suspicious of provincial printing, allied themselves with the Parisian printing oligarchy (Sébastien Cramoisy and Antoine Vitré, among others), rewarding them with privileges (and privilege extensions) for lucrative publications in exchange for their docility:

Vitré was thus among the publishers who denounced the poet Théophile de Viau for freethinking in 1623. Censorship was taken away from the universities and concentrated in the hands of the chancellor, a policy reinforced when Pierre Séguier was appointed to the chancery in 1633. The Imprimerie royale, installed in 1640 at the Louvre, with Cramoisy as its first head, both conferred prestige and exercised control. Even the *Académie française (1635) was intended partly as a group of royal censors. Similar strictures on the rise of *newsletters were maintained by granting an exclusive privilege to Théophraste Renaudot's *Gazette de France* (1631).

As controls grew, however, so did the inability of the authorities to enforce them, as shown by the massive pamphlet literature, printed and disseminated throughout France, that accompanied the revolt known as the Fronde (1649–52)—more than 1,000 titles are recorded in its first and final years, many of them personal attacks on Mazarin, the prime minister, so that the term *mazarinade* was coined to describe them (he himself collected them). Among many glaring indications of the failures of the privilege system is the example of Sully (prime minister under Henri IV), who did not bother to apply for one when publishing his memoirs in 1638. A longer-term phenomenon with far-reaching implications in the publishing world was the Jansenist crisis, which began in 1643 when Arnauld and his Port-Royal allies protested against the papal condemnation of Jansen's *Augustinus*, attacking the Jesuits in return. Not only did the ensuing conflict lead to a vast number of publications, largely unauthorized, on both sides, it also destabilized the Parisian printing establishment. The paradoxes of this period are typified by the fact that Pascal's publisher, Guillaume Desprez, went to the Bastille for printing the immensely successful *Provinciales* (1656–7)—he was also to publish the posthumous *Pensées* (1669)—but became rich in the process.

The policies of Louis XIV—genuine 'cultural policies' ahead of their time—also reveal both great determination to control print and ultimate powerlessness to do so. His measures included the creation of more academies (1663–71), the incorporation of writers (Boileau, Racine, La Fontaine) into an all-encompassing system of court patronage, the reduction and eventual limiting of the number of authorized printers, and imposing a cap on the number of provincial printing offices. In 1667, powers to enforce book controls and exercise censorship were given to the Lieutenant of Police. In 1678–9, local privileges

were suppressed: some parliaments, like Rouen, had taken advantage of their relative autonomy to encourage local business. While these policies, though repressive enough, were unsuccessful in stemming the spread of 'bad' books, their chief victim was provincial printing. By the most conservative estimates, at the end of Louis XIV's reign Paris produced 80 per cent of the national output. Another unintended consequence of French absolutism was the prosperity of foreign printers of French books, who now contributed 20 per cent of the total, a proportion that peaked at 35 per cent in the middle of the 18th century.

The first decades of the 17th century had seen the triumph of the religious revival launched by the Counter-Reformation, St Francis de Sales's *Introduction à la vie dévote*, first printed at Lyons in 1609, being its most famous title. It is contemporary with another publishing phenomenon, the success of Honoré d'Urfé's 5,000-page novel *L'Astrée* (1607–24), the 'first bestseller of modern French literature' (Chartier and Martin, 1. 389). The baroque and classical periods are characterized above all by the enormous development of the theatre, as shown by the careers of Corneille, despite the Académie's strictures on *Le Cid* (1637); *Molière, despite his brush with censorship; and Racine. Typically, printer-publishers (like Augustin Courbé and Claude Barbin) formed groups to issue plays and divided the imprint between themselves. Meanwhile, clandestine reprints appeared almost immediately, originating in the provinces (such as Corneille's native Rouen) or abroad (especially from the *Elzeviers). The success of these piracies also revealed the vast appetite of the market. Barbin, the leading literary publisher of the day, was also responsible for La Fontaine's *Fables* (first edition, 1668) and Mme de La Fayette's novel *La Princesse de Clèves* (1678), published anonymously. In 1699 his widow issued Fénelon's *Télémaque*, which was pirated twenty times that year and went through innumerable editions. Among the century's other notable productions are the first French world atlas, Nicolas Sanson's *Cartes générales de toutes les parties du monde* (1658); the Port-Royal *Grammaire* (1660–64) and *Logique* (1662); and the founding text of French art history, André Félibien's *Entretiens sur les plus excellens peintres anciens et modernes* (1666–88).

6 The 18th century

The early 18th century is dominated by the figure of the Abbé Bignon (1662–1747), appointed in 1699 by Chancellor Pontchartrain, his uncle, to be in charge of all book policies (the title *Directeur de la librairie* became official only in 1737). Bignon was, in fact, a sort of 'minister of literature' (to use Malesherbes's phrase, though he claimed there was no such thing). He organized a countrywide publishing survey in 1700 and spearheaded the development of provincial academies, while proving an inspired leader of the Bibliothèque royale from 1719 until 1741. Although the number of censors increased (there were close to 200 by 1789), and despite a few well-known cases such as the banning of Voltaire's *Lettres philosophiques* in 1734 (they had first come out in English the previous year), Bignon's influence and that of his successors was largely a moderating one. In fact—and this is one of the many paradoxes of the late *ancien régime*—the agents of the repressive policies were chiefly animated by pragmatism. To counter the growing number of illicit imports of French books printed in Germany or Holland, Bignon created a system of 'tacit' or oral permissions to legitimize provincial piracies. Chrétien Guillaume de Lamoignon de Malesherbes, director of the Librairie in 1750–63, was a friend of the *philosophes* and pursued this trend, protecting *Rousseau and tipping off the printers of the *Encyclopédie* against possible arrest. But he was caught in another French 18th-century paradox: although the monarchy was largely sympathetic to the Enlightenment, it had to contend with other traditional sources of censorship, the Church and parliaments, whose interventions (generally after publication) eventually turned into embarrassments for the Crown, as in the case of Helvetius' *De l'esprit* (1758–9).

In 1764, only 60 per cent of the books printed in France were 'legal'. Of the 'illegal' works, most were banned religious books (Protestant, Jansenist, or otherwise unorthodox). The rest were unauthorized provincial reprints, political satires, or *pornographic literature (which boomed in the 18th century, *Sade being one example of this trend among many). A large number of the century's 'great books'—*Candide* may be the most famous—were for one reason or another illegal. The absurdity of this situation, denounced by Diderot in his *Lettre sur le commerce de la librairie* (1763), was partly remedied in 1777 when Miromesnil, Keeper of the Seal, modified the privilege system to legitimize a large portion of provincial, clandestine productions, while recognizing for the first time that literary property belonged to the author. Ultimately, to paraphrase Tocqueville (Malesherbes's great-grandson) in *L'Ancien Régime et la révolution*, the real winners were men of letters, propelled to the rank of major political figures of international stature.

Against this backdrop, the French 18th century rivals the 16th for its accomplishments in the arts of the book. Their prestige was such that Louis XV, as a child, was initiated into printing, while the regent and the marquise de Pompadour published their efforts as amateur book illustrators. Some of the great painters of the age—Oudry, Boucher, Fragonard—contributed to the genre, along with the more specialized book illustrators *Cochin, Charles Eisen (his most celebrated work was the 1762 'Fermiers Généraux' edition of La Fontaine's *Contes*), *Gravelot, and Jean Michel Moreau le Jeune. Louis-René Luce and *Fournier renewed typography early in the period, while the *Didots brilliantly interpreted neo-classical taste during the latter half. Technical innovation came to the paper industry as well: the Annonay mills near Saint-Étienne made the names of Canson, Johannot, and Montgolfier famous, while to the south of Paris the Essonnes mill, purchased by a Didot, became the country's most technologically advanced by the last years of the *ancien régime*. Equally esteemed for their technical mastery and decorative brilliance, the *Deromes, *Padeloups, and Dubuissons produced bindings of unsurpassed elegance. The enlightened aristocracy and princes of the Church—François-Michel Le Tellier, Joseph Dominique d'Inguimbert, *La Vallière, *Soubise, the marquis de Méjanes, the marquis de Paulmy—formed bibliophilic collections, some of which are now the great treasures of Parisian or provincial libraries. There was an expanded market for ambitious editorial projects: the *Encyclopédie*, naturally, the Oudry-Jombert *Fables* of La Fontaine, and Buffon's *Histoire naturelle*, printed by the Imprimerie royale (1749–89). Printed across the river from Strasbourg, the Kehl edition of Voltaire's works (1785–9), launched by *Pancoucke before the writer's death in 1778, was brought to completion by Pierre Augustin Caron de Beaumarchais amidst many difficulties, and sold out despite two concurrent piracies. Pancoucke typifies the growing contemporary awareness of the publisher's role, distinct from the printer's. The book trade also acquired greater professional autonomy. These advances were paralleled by the growth and success of *book auctions. There were between 350 and 400 book dealers in Paris in 1789, most of them established in the traditional area around Notre-Dame and along the river, but many migrating to the Palais-Royal area. Some doubled as *cabinets de lecture* (small lending libraries), institutions that remained in favour throughout the first half of the following century. Meanwhile, the first genuine public libraries appeared: in 1784 there were eighteen in Paris, beginning with the Bibliothèque royale, open twice a week to 'everyone', and sixteen in the provinces; some had begun as private collections, others as religious or institutional collections, others prefigured municipal libraries.

7 The Revolution and afterwards

One of the first initiatives of the Revolution was to abolish royal censorship and to proclaim the freedom of writing and printing, both included in the Declaration of the Rights of Man of 26 August 1789. The office of the Librairie and even copyright deposit, seen as a repressive measure, were terminated, along with printers' and all other guilds. The copyright legislation adopted by the Convention in 1793 (a maximum protection of ten years after the author's death) advanced many titles into the public domain. The nationalization of church properties (decreed in November 1789), the confiscation of works belonging to émigrés and (after 1792) the royal collections, followed by the libraries of all suspects under the Terror of 1793–4 (coinciding with a de facto re-establishment of censorship), displaced vast numbers of books and MSS. To a considerable extent, this benefited the Bibliothèque nationale (BN) and future municipal libraries. The revolutionary book world, especially in Paris, has been aptly compared to a 'supernova' (Hesse, 30), growing to nearly 600 *libraires* and printers, most of them small, precarious units, while 21 traditional houses, having lost their clientele, went bankrupt in four years. The explosion of periodicals and *ephemera was accompanied by a decline in book production, and piracy was rife. Among the many worthy projects launched during that short period, the last king's librarian, Lefèvre d'Ormesson, started a 'Bibliographie universelle de la France' in 1790. He was guillotined in 1794. The same fate was met that year by Malesherbes and by Étienne Anisson-Duperron, head of the Imprimerie royale, where he had been a strong promoter of technical innovation.

The Napoleonic system, so much of which has survived in modern France, restored stability through an approach that was, in fact, the opposite of the free-market model favoured in the first stages of the Revolution. In the short term, its chief beneficiaries were municipal libraries, which in 1803 received (theoretically on deposit) the revolutionary spoils stored in warehouses: many such libraries were actually born out of this decree. In the long term, the chief victims of the Napoleonic system were arguably universities: not only had they lost their libraries,

abolished in 1793 (not to be formally re-established until 1879), but they were regimented once and for all into a state educational structure that gave them neither the opportunity nor the funds to build research collections comparable to their British, Dutch, German, and, later, American counterparts. (*Strasbourg, the only possible exception, is largely indebted in this respect to its having been under German rule between 1871 and 1918.) Until 1810, the surveillance of publications was left to the police, headed by the notorious Fouché, an arrangement that induced a *self-censorship even more effective than outright repression. Nor was there any hesitation to resort to repression when necessary: in 1810, Fouché's successor, Savary, was directed to seize and destroy the entire edition of Mme de Staël's *De l'Allemagne*; its author was exiled. The new set of rules established in 1810 remained in place more or less until 1870. They officially reintroduced censorship, reduced the number of Parisian printers to 60 (later increased to 80), and made authorization to print or sell books subject to a revocable licence or *brevet*. Tight control was exercised by a Direction de la librairie, which proved so zealous that Napoleon had to dissociate himself from it publicly. A more positive and longer-lasting creation was the future *Bibliographie de la France, reviving d'Ormesson's plans. Characteristically, the *Imprimerie nationale ('Impériale' for the time being) grew enormously, involving more than 150 presses and 1,000 printers by 1814. A splendid product of state intervention, the *Description de l'Égypte*, documenting the scientific aspects of Bonaparte's 1798–9 expedition, was commissioned in 1802. The last of its 21 volumes (13 comprising plates), issued in 1,000 copies, came out in 1828.

The period associated with Romanticism witnessed what has been termed 'the second revolution of the book', namely, the appearance of a mass market. This was made possible by the progress of literacy as well as by technical innovation. Mechanization affected the paper industry, printing (with some resistance among workers, as a case of Luddism in the 1830 Revolution attests), and binding (*see* **11**). *Stereotyping became enormously important—Didot, in particular, exploited and systematized the discoveries of 18th-century pioneers such as *Hoffmann and L.-É. Herhan. *Lithography made possible large *press runs of high-quality illustrated texts, while the coloured woodcuts manufactured by Pellerin in Épinal not only remain forever associated with this Vosges city but also played a key role in the dissemination of the Napoleonic legend. Large printing plants flourished:

Chaix in Paris, which prospered by printing *railway timetables; or, in Tours, the equally famous Mame, specializing in religious literature, a field dominated by the figure of the Abbé *Migne. Another mark of progress was the birth of 'industrial' distribution methods, facilitated after 1840 by the spread of railways and the growth of modern publicity methods. One consequence of these developments was the separation of the functions of printer and publisher—still often united in the first decade of the century (as in the case of the Didots), but almost universally kept apart by its end. On the other hand, the tradition of publishing houses owning and operating a bookshop remained alive throughout the century and beyond. Typographically, the only innovator was the Lyonnais Louis Perrin and his *augustaux*, inspired by Roman inscriptions, which in 1856 became the 'Elzévir' type popularized by Alphonse Lemerre's imprints.

Balzac, a sometime printer himself, has left in his 1843 novel *Les Illusions perdues* a memorable account of the book world of the 1820s—from the traditional, family operation of David Séchard in Angoulême, threatened locally by enterprising, commercially minded competitors, to the new type of Parisian publishers and dealers, for whom poetry and the novel were above all a commodity to be bought and sold. The year 1838 typifies the liveliness of the book world: Louis *Hachette, a successful supplier of primary school textbooks now in great demand following Guizot's 1833 education laws, opened a branch in Algiers; the first novel to be serialized in the popular press, Dumas's *Le Capitaine Paul*, appeared in *Le Siècle*; Labrouste drew the plans for the new Bibliothèque *Sainte-Geneviève; and Gervais Charpentier launched his 'Bibliothèque Charpentier', which genuinely prefigures the modern paperback, and whose modest price (3.50 francs) compensated for its dense typography. The 'Charpentier revolution', as it has been called, which did away with the elegant 'Didot style' that had dominated the previous 40 years, was quickly imitated. Bourdilliat & Jacottet dropped the price of their books to 1 fr., as did Michel Lévy, publisher of *Madame Bovary* (his brother Calmann later headed his house). By 1852, only fifteen years after the line from Paris to Saint-Germain opened, Hachette acquired the monopoly on French railway station bookstalls, creating a 'Bibliothèque des chemins de fer' the following year. Other successful careers of the period resulted in the establishment of long-lasting houses: *Dalloz, *Garnier, *Plon, *Dunod, *Larousse. The mechanization of *wood engraving led to a boom in children's literature. Although the best-known names

remain those of the comtesse de Ségur (a Hachette author) and Jules Verne (published by Hetzel), the phenomenon also benefited provincial publishers.

French Romanticism is associated above all with poetry and the novel, and to a lesser extent the theatre; but the greatest success of the period was a religious essay, Lamennais's *Paroles d'un croyant* (1834). Its sales were boosted by its being immediately added to the *Index Librorum Prohibitorum*, a fate it shared with Renan's even more successful *Vie de Jésus* (1863), which sold more than 160,000 copies in its first year. The 'consecration of the writer' (Bénichou) in 19th-century France reached its apex with Hugo's state funeral in 1885. This development began with the founding of the first writers' associations: the Société des auteurs in 1829, followed by the Société des gens de lettres in 1837. Decades before the *Berne Convention on copyright of 1886, these organizations were instrumental in securing the first bilateral agreement against piracy (with Belgium, 1852), and in having copyright extended to the surviving spouse (1866). Similarly, progress was achieved in the book world (including unionization) as a result of the founding of the *Cercle de la librairie in 1847.

The general trend towards democratization that characterizes the 19th century had implications for the illustrated book, which had largely been a *de luxe affair in the previous century. Although Delacroix's lithographs for the second edition of Nerval's translation of Goethe's *Faust* (1828), today considered a landmark in book illustration, were a commercial failure, the technique was popularized in the 1830s by a new kind of illustrated press (*Le Charivari, La Caricature*), where Honoré Daumier and, especially, J. J. Grandville published their work. Grandville dominated the illustrated book of the 1830s and 1840s, much as *Doré did in the 1850s and 1860s. A celebrated achievement of the Romantic period remains the 1838 *Paul et Virginie* published by Léon Curmer, with woodcuts and etchings by Tony Johannot, Louis Français, Eugène Isabey, Ernest Meissonier, Paul Huet, and Charles Marville. The greatest monument of the time, however, and one of *lithography's most beautiful products, is the series of *Voyages pittoresques et romantiques de l'ancienne France* edited by *Nodier and Baron Taylor, published by Didot in ten parts, each devoted to a French province, between 1820 and 1878. Géricault, Ingres, the Vernets, and Viollet-le-Duc, among others, participated in the project. Seven years after H. F. Talbot's *Pencil of Nature*, the French 'photographic incunable' (Brun) was Renard's *Paris photographié* (1853). Nevertheless,

Il n'a plus qu'à filer son cocon et à s'enterrer dans un livre qui lui sert de chrysalide.

A bookworm, by J. J. Grandville, from *Scènes de la vie privée et publique des animaux* (Paris, 1842) by P.-J. Stahl (P.-J. Hetzel) and others.

its appearance was anticipated by the two photographic plates—reproduced via the process invented by A. H. L. Fizeau—that were included in *Excursions dagueriennes* in 1842.

Since the French Revolution put large quantities of early and rare books on the market, the 19th century was the golden age of French bibliophilia, with Nodier, creator of the **Bulletin du bibliophile*, as its patron saint and *Brunet its founding father. The Société des bibliophiles françois was established in 1820. Among the collections dating from the period, few can match in splendour the one formed (largely in England) by the duc d'Aumale and now preserved at *Chantilly.

Considering their rapid rise at the end of the *ancien régime*, French libraries should have enjoyed a golden age in the 19th century as well. With exceptions—the *Arsenal under Nodier (though more as a salon than from a professional viewpoint) and *Sainte-Geneviève—they did not. Even the Bibliothèque nationale suffered from comparative neglect until space problems

forced the renovation begun in the 1850s and completed in the 1870s. Municipal libraries, consolidating their revolutionary gains, did relatively better. Compensating in part for the lack of public investment, lending *cabinets de lecture* flourished in the early 19th century (more than 500 operated in Paris) and several different types of library appeared during the period, especially small, specialized institutional libraries established by learned societies, such as the *Société de l'histoire du protestantisme français; chambers of commerce (created throughout the country between 1825 and 1872); and religious institutions (some of these were confiscated, once more, at the 1905 separation between Church and state). As a result of the parallel rise in industrialization and literacy, a growing concern for popular libraries manifested itself during the Second Empire. The Société Franklin, founded in 1862, devoted itself to this effort. The École des Chartes, possibly the century's greatest legacy to librarianship, was founded in 1821 in order to train *palaeographers and *archivists. It was moved in 1897 to the new Sorbonne buildings.

The period 1870–1914 confirmed and accelerated the trends of the second book revolution. Although around 6,000 titles were printed in 1828, the figure had risen to 15,000 by 1889 and grew to about 25,000 by 1914. The growth was particularly spectacular in the newspaper and periodical press, finally liberalized by the law of 29 July 1881. Newspapers reached a circulation they were never again to equal: Milhaud's *Petit Journal* was selling more than a million copies by 1891. In 1914, *Le Petit Parisien* was issued in 1.5 million copies, with *Le Matin* and *Le Journal* not far behind at 1 million each. After a relative decline in the 1870s, this boom affected nearly all sectors, perhaps most especially the novel. Thus, if the initial volumes of the Rougon-Macquart series sold moderately, the success of *L'Assommoir* in 1876 propelled Zola (a Charpentier author) to the highest print runs of any novelist in his generation (55,000 copies for the first printing of *Nana* in 1879). Yet these figures pale before those achieved by the book that has become synonymous with Third Republic ideology, the *Tour de la France par deux enfants* by 'G. Bruno' (nom de plume of Mme Alfred Fouillée). Published by Belin in 1877 and read by generations of schoolchildren, it sold more than 8 million copies over the course of a century. Another popular genre of the pre-1914 period, detective fiction, was born in 1866, when Émile Gaboriau's *L'Affaire Lerouge* was serialized in *Le Soleil*. Its leading exponents in the early 20th century were Maurice Leblanc (his hero, Arsène Lupin, described as a 'gentleman burglar') and Gaston Leroux with his Rouletabille series.

New publicity methods soon affected literary publishing. They were used by the young Albin Michel to launch his first title, Félicien Champsaur's *L'Arriviste* (1902), and by Arthème Fayard (a house founded in 1857) for its collections 'Modern Bibliothèque' (note the missing 'e' in the adjective) and 'Le Livre populaire', which had considerable success before 1914, thanks to a policy of combining large print runs (100,000 or more) and low *royalties.

At the other end of the spectrum, French *bibliophilia continued to flourish at the fin de siècle, as the names of *Essling, *Rahir, and Henri Béraldi (founder of the Société des amis des livres in 1874) testify. French bibliophiles of the period, however, do not seem to have had much contact with the pictorial avant-garde of their age, which left disappointingly few traces on the book arts of the time. Little notice was given to such landmark works as Manet's illustrations to *Mallarmé's version of Poe's *The Raven* (1875), *L'Après-midi d'un faune* (1876), and Poe's *Poèmes* (1889)—also in Mallarmé's translations—nor to Lautrec's two remarkable productions, Clemenceau's *Au pied du Sinaï* (1898) and *Renard's *Histoires naturelles* (1899). The foresightful *Vollard tried to redress the situation at the end of the century. Mallarmé's death in 1897 having interrupted his tantalizing project of *Un coup de dés* illustrated by Odilon Redon, Vollard's first two books, Verlaine's *Parallèlement* (1900) and Longus' *Daphnis and Chloé* (1902), were both illustrated by Bonnard. Now considered the first masterpieces of the modern *artist's books, they were poorly received at the time. (Vollard printed them both at the Imprimerie nationale, an institution then in such turmoil that the French Parliament debated its abolition.) Vollard's example inspired another pioneer, *Kahnweiler, whose first book, Apollinaire's *L'Enchanteur pourrissant* (1909), with Derain's subtly 'primitivistic' woodcuts, is another landmark; his *Saint Matorel* (1911), derided by contemporary *livres à figures* collectors, inaugurated *Picasso's glorious association with the illustrated book.

8 After 1914

After the expansion of the late 19th and early 20th centuries, the period beginning in 1914 was, in France as elsewhere, a time of crisis and renewal. World War I, during which restrictions halved paper supplies, was followed by a short boom in publishing during the 1920s. The so-called *années folles* were well attuned to the development of modern methods of book promotion. One of their early beneficiaries was Pierre Benoît's novel *L'Atlantide*, a 1919 bestseller (a term soon adopted by the French) published by Albin Michel; the Académie française awarded it the Grand Prix du roman it had established the previous year. This new importance of literary prizes in the publishing world was signalled, also in 1919, by the controversy that ensued when the *Goncourt went to Proust's *À l'ombre des jeunes filles en fleurs* in preference to Roland Dorgelès's war novel *Les Croix de bois*. (A different kind of controversy had surrounded the creation of the Femina Prize in 1904—its all-female jury was a response to the Goncourt Academy's perceived misogyny.) The Renaudot Prize, founded in 1926, was soon seen as open to the avant-garde: its early laureates included Céline and Aragon, whose publisher Denoël thus came close to rivalling *Gallimard and *Grasset. A fifth prize, the Prix Interallié, was created in 1930 and first awarded to Malraux's *La Voie royale*. After more than three-quarters of a century, the same five prizes continue to dominate the French literary landscape.

If the late 19th century had seen a gap between bibliophilia and the artistic avant-garde, the first half of the 20th saw the triumph of the *livre de peintre* or *livre d'artiste* (artist's book), with strong innovators following in Vollard and Kahnweiler's footsteps: *Skira and *Tériade in the 1930s and 1940s, *Iliazd, *Lecuire, Pierre-André Benoît, among others, in the 1950s and after. By contrast with their 19th-century predecessors, *Matisse and Picasso, arguably the century's two most important painters, were each involved in many book projects; Picasso throughout his career (he illustrated more than 150 books), Matisse for a relatively short period in the final part of his, both with magnificent results. No satisfactory discussion of their art—or of the art of the book in France between 1930 and 1970—can ignore their achievements in this field.

The 1920s and 1930s were a time of typographical success, led by the Imprimerie nationale and epitomized by the success of the Futura (or 'Europe') type launched by the foundry of *Deberny & Peignot. The same decades also witnessed a renaissance of bookbinding design in France (which had begun in the art nouveau period), marked by the achievements of Henri Marius-Michel, Victor Prouvé, and Charles Meunier. An even more impressive group—under the aegis of dealers like Auguste Blaizot and collectors gathered in the association Les Amis de la reliure originale—was the generation of Paul Bonet, Henri Creuzevault, Georges Cretté, and Pierre Legrain. They were succeeded, after World War II, by the outstanding trio of Georges Leroux, Pierre-Lucien Martin, and Monique Mathieu. Their successor, Jean de Gonet, has been remarkable both for his efforts to democratize original bindings by using industrial *leather ('revorim') and because, unlike them, he operated his own workshop rather than being strictly a designer.

World War II, when the country was occupied for more than four years, had dramatic consequences for the book world. Censorship was imposed by the Nazis (the notorious 'Otto list'); shortages of paper more than halved production; 'Aryanization' measures affected individuals (such as the general administrator of the BN, Julien Cain, who was sacked by Vichy and later deported by the Nazis) and publishing houses—although *Nathan managed to sell its shares to a group of friends, Calmann-Lévy was purchased and run by a German businessman and Ferenczi was put into the hands of a collaborator. The first two publishers were later revived, but the third never regained its prewar status. Yet, paradoxically, the four years of occupation coincided with a literary flowering, reading having become by necessity the chief cultural activity. The years following liberation confirmed the emergence of a new literary generation—that of Beauvoir, Camus, Queneau, and Sartre—which recaptured the kind of prestige enjoyed by 18th-century *philosophes*, a prestige reflected in their publisher, Gallimard.

For all its aberrations, the Vichy period also marked a return to the long French tradition of intervention in cultural matters, following the relative disengagement that had characterized most of the Third Republic. From this point of view, there was a continuity with the Fourth and Fifth Republics. Already in the 1930s, particularly in the shadow of the Depression, there was a growing concern that the state was not doing enough to support libraries or the book trade and that a *politique de la lecture* was in order. This was accomplished through a variety of government agencies working sometimes in harmony, at other times in competition. The cultural division of the ministry of foreign affairs, established in the early 1920s, subsidized French book exports (and was quickly accused of favouring Gallimard authors). A Caisse nationale des lettres, with representatives of the profession, was created in 1930 with a view to granting loans and subsidies—it became the Centre national des lettres in 1973 and the Centre national du

livre in 1993. It too has not been immune to charges of favouritism. In the wake of the liberation, a Direction des bibliothèques et de la lecture publique was created within the education ministry (with Cain at its head). Since school libraries were not part of its responsibilities, it focused instead on the creation of a network of lending libraries called Bibliothèques centrales (renamed 'départementales' in 1983), which helped to reduce the cultural gap not only between Paris and the provinces but also between large cities and rural areas. School libraries began to receive serious attention in the 1970s. University libraries, however, remained (and still are) the poor relations of the French educational system, even as the French student population doubled over the same decade. The overwhelming success (particularly with students) of the Bibliothèque publique d'information at the Pompidou Centre, which opened in 1977, showed how keenly the lack of research facilities with open stacks and late and Sunday hours was being felt.

The Mitterrand government that came to power in 1981 proclaimed ambitious cultural policies (the official portrait of the president showed him with an open copy of Montaigne in his hands). One of its first measures was the imposition of a 5 per cent cap on book discounts, with a view to protecting independent bookdealers. The Direction du livre (created in 1975) and BN were placed under the authority of an expanded ministry of culture headed by Jack Lang. More subsidies were indeed available, but to what extent any of the official measures have affected continuing economic or cultural trends is debatable. The most enduring legacy of the Mitterrand years and, significantly, the most controversial of his *grands projets* remains the new, high-tech BnF, opened in 1996 after his death and named after him.

Economically, the trend towards greater corporate amalgamation, beginning in the 1950s, led, after the economic crisis of 1973, to the formation of three publishing giants: Hachette, which throughout the century had grown as both publisher and book distributor; the Groupe de la Cité, formed in 1988 and including Larousse, Nathan, the Presses de la Cité, Bordas, and the 4-million-member France-Loisirs book club; and Masson, the medical publisher, which had grown by absorbing Colin in 1987 and Belfond in 1989. The three became two when Masson Belfond was absorbed by CEP/Cité/Havas in 1995—to be resold to a different group six years later. Behind these two groups are larger financial entities, Lagardère for Hachette, Vivendi-Universal (originally a water-supply company) for the other. Following *Rizzoli's purchase of *Flammarion, only five major Parisian firms, which themselves had absorbed smaller houses, remained independent by 2005: Albin Michel, Calmann-Lévy, Fayard, Gallimard, and *Le Seuil. According to 2002 statistics, 80 per cent of all French book production came from the top 15 per cent of a total of 313 publishers. The same statistics revealed a significant decline of the workforce in the publishing sector (about 10,000, down from 13,350 in 1975), while the number of titles published (20,000) is lower than the figure for 1914. A very small number of titles represent a high percentage of the total sales, not necessarily at the lower end: Marguerite Duras's *L'Amant* in 1984 and Yann Arthus-Bertrand's photographic album *La Terre vue du ciel* in 2000 both sold more than 1 million copies each. Corporate mergers have also affected the book trade, with large chains like *FNAC (itself now controlled by a major financial group) or non-traditional outlets ('hypermarkets') occupying a position of growing importance. Despite remarkable exceptions like *Actes Sud—which, however, eventually opened offices in Paris—the trend towards amalgamation has reinforced the position of the capital, which at the beginning of the 21st century controlled about 90 per cent of production. One could qualify this picture, however, by stressing the viability of small or medium-sized specialized houses, such as L'Arche, devoted almost entirely to the theatre; or the relative health of religious publishing, dominated by the three Catholic houses of Bayard, Le Cerf, and Desclée de Brouwer.

Culturally, the most important event in French book history between 1945 and the advent of the Internet was the launching of the 'Livre de poche' series by Hachette and Gallimard (1953). This comparatively belated French answer to *Penguin Books deeply affected book-buying and reading habits—a 20th-century equivalent of the 'Révolution Charpentier' in the 19th. Gallimard and Hachette were 'divorced' in 1972, when Gallimard created the Folio collection to reissue titles from its own considerable list.

Another notable postwar change has been the growth of children's literature and the parallel development of children's libraries since the first, 'L'Heure joyeuse', was opened in Paris in 1924 by a branch of the American Relief Committee. A landmark in this respect was the creation of the association La Joie par les livres in 1963. A private initiative, it led to the opening of a model children's library in the Paris suburb of Clamart in 1965. In addition to specialized houses like L'École des loisirs (also established in 1965), many of the major publishers (Gallimard for one) opened a children's department.

In a different sphere, the postwar period saw a resurgence, followed by a gradual decline, of censorship on moral grounds: *Olympia Press and J.-J. Pauvert, publisher of Sade and L' *Histoire d'O*, were prosecuted in the 1940s and 1950s, while the suppression of Bernard Noël's *Le Château de Cène* was met with a public outcry in 1973. In popular literature, where detective fiction has continued to flourish, perhaps the most striking phenomenon has been the spread of *comic books to the adult population, exemplified by the success of Goscinny and Uderzo's Astérix series in the 1970s. The 'bande dessinée' is now a respectable genre with its museum and annual festival in Angoulême.

Traditional forms of book culture, however, are still very much alive at all levels. Evidence for this can be found at the academic level by the vitality of 'l'histoire du livre' (launched by the publication in 1957 of Lucien *Febvre and H.-J. *Martin's *L'Apparition du livre*); at the bibliophilic level by the health of book collecting, nourished by the seemingly endless supply of material at auction or through the outstanding antiquarian book trade; and, in the population in general, by the qualitatively important place books and reading continue to occupy in the collective perception the French have of their own culture.

BIBLIOGRAPHY

F. Barbier, *Histoire du livre* (2000)

P. Bénichou, *The Consecration of the Writer, 1750–1830*, tr. M. K. Jensen (1999)

[Bibliothèque nationale de France,] *En français dans le texte: dix siècles de lumières par le livre* (1990)

R. Brun, *Le Livre français* (1969)

R. Chartier and H.-J. Martin, eds., *Histoire de l'édition française* (3 vols, 1982)

A. Coron, ed., *Des Livres rares depuis l'invention de l'imprimerie* (1998)

DEL

L. Febvre and H.-J. Martin, *The Coming of the Book*, tr. D. Gerard (1997)

C. Hesse, *Publishing and Cultural Politics in Revolutionary Paris, 1789–1810* (1991)

H.-J. Martin, *Print, Power, and People in 17th-Century France*, tr. D. Gerard (1993)

P. Schuwer, *Dictionnaire de l'édition* (1977)

M.-H. Tesnière and P. Gifford, eds., *Creating French Culture* (1995)

23 The History of the Book in the Low Countries

PAUL HOFTIJZER

1 The Roman period to the Middle Ages

The region that is now roughly The Netherlands, Belgium, Luxemburg, and the upper part of north-western France first came into contact with written culture during the Roman period (1st–4th century AD). Archaeological evidence is scarce, but certainly in larger Gallo-Roman settlements, writing for administrative, commercial, and educational purposes appears to have been used on a regular basis. How much of this practice survived the onslaught of the Migration Period is uncertain, but by the 6th century writing returned at least in the southern Netherlands. In the north, the former border region of the Roman empire, MSS did not appear until the 8th century. The first *codex ever seen there may well have been the book with which the English missionary Boniface tried to defend himself, when he and his 52 companions were slain by heathen Frisians at Dokkum in 754.

For the next few centuries, ecclesiastical and monastic sites, of which the densest concentration was found in the south, were the main centres of book production and consumption in the Low Countries. The books were almost exclusively liturgical and theological works, but there is also evidence for the transmission of classical texts. The 8th-century bishop Theutbert (Theodard) of Utrecht, for instance, possessed a MS of Livy copied two centuries earlier. Little remains of the earliest work of local *scriptoria documented at important Benedictine abbeys such as *Echternach, Elno, St Omer, and Arras. Most MSS in the libraries of churches and monasteries would have been acquired from elsewhere in any case.

The era of Charlemagne (742–814) and his immediate successors—whose policies of political, religious, and cultural reform created more stability in north-west Europe—strongly promoted the making and use of books, aided by the introduction of the *Carolingian minuscule, the dominant form of writing until its ultimate replacement by *gothic-style *scripts in the 13th century. Various schools and traditions existed next to each other, such as the large, sumptuously *illuminated books produced at the court of Charles the Bald (823–77) and the more soberly executed work of monastic scriptoria, which were strongly influenced by English and Irish models. This receptivity of Netherlandish MS production to influences from other regions would remain one of its characteristic features.

During the 10th and 11th centuries, when Viking raids still ravaged the Low Countries, MS production was at a low. The 12th century, however, saw the height of Romanesque illumination, which, although remaining traditional in its concepts, combined a newly found vitality with great plasticity. Bookmaking was still the prerogative of the monasteries, but the Benedictines now had to share their dominance with new monastic orders, such as the Cistercians and Premonstratensians. The main centres of production were located in the present border region with northern France, in Flanders, and along the Meuse valley. Of the output of scriptoria in the north, particularly those at the Benedictine abbey of Egmond and the cathedral school of Utrecht, only a few specimens have survived.

As in architecture, sculpture, and painting, the arrival of the Gothic style in MS production was closely connected to the emergence of cities. Reading and writing turned into a normal feature of many aspects of city life; the making of books became an activity for professional lay artists working for a predominantly urban clientele. This is not to say that monastic scriptoria dwindled, but their output decreased in relative terms. As the Low Countries during the high Middle Ages swiftly developed into one of the most densely populated and urbanized areas of

Europe, the production and use of MSS in cities all over the region expanded substantially. Religious and theological books remained of primary importance, but more and more works on worldly subjects, such as law, medicine, astrology, and history, as well as literary compositions and schoolbooks, were becoming available. In book illumination, highly expressive and elaborate styles emerged, with a typical Netherlandish tendency towards naturalism and realism.

This development reached its peak during the 15th century. The flowering of urban society was reinforced by the incorporation of a large part of the region into the dominions of the dukes of Burgundy, who, having huge resources at their disposal, sought to affirm their power and status by cultural means. In this cross-fertilization of urban and courtly culture, MS making thrived as never before. Ghent and Bruges in particular became the leading centres for the production of luxurious MSS of the highest quality after the fashion of Flemish mannerism. Many of these MSS found their way into collections of highly placed patrons and bibliophiles in the Low Countries as well as abroad, especially in France and England. The names of the artists involved are often unknown; they are referred to by such titles as the 'Master of Mary of Burgundy' or the 'Master of the Dresden Hours'. Their highly specialized art continued well into the 16th century, as can be seen in the work of one of the most accomplished illuminators from Bruges, *Bening. At Louvain, which had become the seat of the first university of the Low Countries in 1425, several *librarii* were soon active in the copying and selling of more functional academic texts.

The new impetus was also felt in the northern Netherlands, which for a long time had lagged behind the far more prosperous south. Under the influence of the spiritual renewal of the *Devotio Moderna and the establishment of the court of the Counts of Holland in The Hague, a remarkable regional flowering occurred. In their striving for piety and spirituality, the Devotionalists attached great value to reading and writing and were very active in copying MSS—for their own use as well as on commission. A large part of their work consists of *books of hours, intended for private devotion and for that reason often written in the vernacular. The courtly milieu of the counts of Holland, who had close connections with the neighbouring bishopric of Utrecht and the dukedom of Guelders, proved a fertile environment for the production of exquisite illuminated MSS, the most famous of which is the *Hours of Catherine of Cleves (c.1440), made by an unknown master.

Under these circumstances, it is not surprising that printing arrived early in the Low Countries. Precisely when, however, is impossible to say, as no dated or otherwise identifiable printed material has survived from before 1473. What now is called 'Dutch prototypography'—fragments of anonymously printed schoolbooks and religious and humanistic works (once attributed to *Coster)—in all likelihood dates from c.1470 and may well be associated with one punchcutter-printer. Of even older origin are a series of xylographic prints or *woodblock-printed books, but again nothing is known about their maker(s).

Most early printers in the southern Netherlands were active in major cities such as Ghent, Bruges, Brussels, Louvain, and Antwerp, while in the north they worked in smaller towns such as Utrecht, Deventer, Zwolle, Gouda, Delft, Leiden, and Haarlem. They had as a rule learned their craft in Germany or northern Italy. Their *printing offices were small and often still combined the entire process of book production and distribution, from casting type to selling books. Although catering for a regional and supraregional market, they very much depended on local conditions for their survival. The economic depression and political instability in the northern Netherlands during the last decades of the century were the cause of a series of bankruptcies and the migration of businesses to the south, particularly to Antwerp.

Early Netherlandish book production, which amounts to some 2,200 *editions before 1501, was mainly religious in character, with an emphasis on works connected to the Devotio Moderna movement. Educational centres such as Deventer, which had a famous Latin school, and the university town of Louvain specialized in schoolbooks and classical and humanist texts. The dominant language was Latin, books in Dutch amounting to only 25 per cent of the total. The common typeface—for Latin texts as well—was a formal gothic letter (*textura); *roman faces were only used occasionally. A large percentage (40 per cent) of Netherlandish *incunables are illustrated with woodcuts, sometimes of exceptional artistic quality.

2 1500–1700

During the 16th century, printing in the Low Countries came into its own. As humanism became the driving force of intellectual life, first in the south and in the second half of the century also in the north, education, and consequently literacy, were considerably enhanced. Large quantities of *textbooks for use in the region's growing number of primary and secondary schools were printed. Supplementing the canon of established classical and medieval knowledge, new scholarly works on a wide range of subjects were published. Although literary expression was still very much the domain of older traditions of medieval drama, rhetoric, and romance, new forms of poetry and prose, inspired by Italian and French Renaissance models, gained popularity, first in Latin, soon also in Dutch. The book trade eagerly tapped into these new trends.

The Reformation provided an equally potent incentive to book production. From the 1520s onwards there was a growing demand for Protestant books, from treatises by Luther and other, often more radical reformers to editions of the Bible in the vernacular. The first complete Dutch edition of the Bible, which was partly based on *Luther's German translation, appeared from the Antwerp press of Jacob van Liesvelt as early as 1526. Many others would follow. The so-called 'Souterliedekens', rhymed translations of the Psalms in Dutch, set on the melodies of secular songs, were very popular too. First published in Antwerp in 1540, they were reprinted over and over again. Although the Catholic Church and the secular authorities reacted vehemently against the Reformation movement by putting increasingly severe sanctions on the making, selling, and reading of heretical works, the storm could not be calmed (see CENSORSHIP). Motivated by religious zeal as much as by commercial gain, some printers did not hesitate to risk their lives by producing Protestant books, often working underground or from exile in places such as Emden just across the border in Germany. A typical example is the Antwerp printer and bookseller Adriaen van Berghen. Having been convicted in 1535 for selling heretical books from his stall in Antwerp, he fled to Holland, where he lived in various places until he finally settled in Delft. When, in 1542, his house was found to contain a stock of forbidden books, he was banned from the city, but this relatively mild punishment was overturned by the Court of Holland and he was beheaded soon after in The Hague.

The undisputed centre of the 16th-century Netherlandish book trade was Antwerp. The city on the Scheldt was a magnet for printers and booksellers from other places, because of its large population, booming economic conditions, and excellent connections to European markets. Book production in Antwerp shows all the characteristics of early capitalist enterprise, such as the participation of external investors, the diversification of production, and adaptation to a mass market. All this can best be seen in the activities of the most renowned printer and publisher of the period, *Plantin. At the height of his career, in the 1570s, he ran a fully equipped type-foundry, a printing office with sixteen presses, and a bookshop with sales all over Europe. His output of some 1,500 publications ranged from the impressive eight-volume *polyglot *Biblia Regia* (1568–72) and ponderous scholarly works to elegant *emblem books, small-*format editions of classical writers, school-books, and *pamphlets. Other Antwerp book trade entrepreneurs chose to concentrate their activities on a specific genre, for instance music books, the speciality of the firm of Jean Bellère, *maps and *atlases, pioneered by *Mercator and *Ortelius, books for the Spanish market, the business of Martinus Nutius, or all sorts of prints and *engravings, made in the workshops of Hieronymus Cock and his successors the *Galle family.

Works in Latin were now printed in a wide range of roman and *italic faces in all sizes, designed by the best French and Flemish punchcutters such as *Garamont, *Granjon, *Le Bé, and van den *Keere. For vernacular books, a growing number of gothic types were available, including the elegant *civilité letter. In book illustration, high-quality images were often executed by *etching or engraving (see **16**). Bookbinding followed the fashion of neighbouring countries, especially France, but during this and later periods, frugal Netherlandish taste on the whole did not allow for much luxury in external ornamentation. The most commonly used type of binding was made of plain, unadorned *vellum (see **17**).

The combination of religious oppression, social and political unrest, and outright war in the second half of the 16th century proved fatal to the cohesion of the Low Countries. Within twenty years the Dutch Revolt—started in 1568 as an uprising against the autocratic rule of Philip II of Spain—divided the region into two political entities: the Roman Catholic southern Netherlands, which remained first under Spanish, then Austrian Habsburg rule, and the northern provinces which became an independent, predominantly Protestant republic. Thousands of religious and economic refugees left the south. Many temporarily went to England and Germany, but in the end most found a permanent home in the newly created United Provinces. Among them were scores of printers and booksellers, the majority of whom settled in the rising cities of Holland and Zeeland: Amsterdam, Haarlem, Leiden, Rotterdam, Dordrecht, Gouda, Delft, and Middelburg. Bringing with them technical skills and commercial expertise, they greatly invigorated the book trade in the north.

Apart from immigration—a phenomenon that would recur on a huge scale at the end of the 17th century when large numbers of Huguenot refugees arrived from France, among them again many printers and booksellers—there were other factors that contributed to the success of printing and bookselling in the Dutch Republic. A loose confederation of seven provinces, of which Holland was the most powerful, the country lacked central political authority, while its largest and most powerful city, Amsterdam, at times acted like a state within a state. A situation existed in which censorship was by no means absent, but could only be practised in a limited manner. Even the system of *privileges, which in other countries served as a means of preventive government control, in the northern Netherlands remained confined to its primary function as a protection of publishers' *copyrights. Combined with long-established traditions of tolerance, these realities earned the Dutch Republic a reputation for being a country where the printing of books that were forbidden elsewhere was openly permitted. As the English naturalist John Ray wrote in his travel journal in 1633: 'The People say and print what they please, and call it Liberty' (Ray, 54). Indeed, during the 17th and 18th centuries many controversial foreign authors, from Galileo to Descartes and from *Comenius to *Rousseau, published their work more or less freely in the United Provinces. Even the most hated of religious sects, the Socinians, had their writings printed without too much difficulty in Amsterdam in a splendid multi-volume *Bibliotheca Fratrum Polonorum* (1665–9).

The book trade in the Dutch Republic equally profited from favourable economic conditions. A good network of roads and waterways made transport easy and inexpensive. Thanks to low interest rates and a well-developed financial market, capital was readily available, and there was abundant skilled labour in all branches of bookmaking. The absence of strict external and internal economic regulation prevented excessive monopolies and market protection. In most cities, restrictive guilds of printers and booksellers did not come into existence until the second half of the 17th century, and their rules were not on the whole very strict. Following in the wake of other merchants, booksellers developed extensive international networks for the distribution of their books. They regularly visited the semi-annual *book fairs at *Frankfurt and later at *Leipzig in order to exchange their latest publications, but also to act as middlemen for colleagues in other countries. Some booksellers had agents and even branches in strategically located

cities such as Paris, London, Florence, Vienna, Gdańsk (Danzig), and Copenhagen. The home market was no less important, thanks to high *literacy levels among men and women and a flourishing cultural and intellectual climate. The foundation of new universities in *Leiden (1574), Franeker (1585), Groningen (1614), and *Utrecht (1636), which all soon attracted many students from abroad, created opportunities for specialized scholarly publishers: thanks to the use of Latin as the language of academic communication, they could easily reach an international clientele. The most famous Dutch academic publishers, the *Elzeviers in Leiden, were active for well over a century and had branch offices in Amsterdam, The Hague, and Utrecht.

Because competition was fierce, Dutch printers and publishers were constantly trying to strengthen their position by finding new niches in the market. For example, *newspaper publishing in various languages and various forms (including the *coranto) became a separate branch of publishing as early as the second decade of the 17th century. Amsterdam firms such as *Blaeu and *Janssonius in the 17th century, and *Mortier and *Van Keulen in the 18th, applied themselves to the publication of high-quality maps and atlases. Jewish printers, often financed by external backers, specialized in the bulk production of religious texts for Jewish communities in Germany and eastern Europe (*see* **8**). In the 1680s, French-language scholarly journals, carrying book *reviews, were introduced, thanks to the contribution of immigrant Huguenot publishers, editors, and journalists. Examples of this highly successful genre include the *Nouvelles de la République des Lettres* (Rotterdam, 1684–7), edited by Pierre Bayle, and the *Bibliothèque choisie* (Amsterdam, 1703–13) of Jean Le Clerc.

There were also technological innovations, such as the application of an improved *hose in printing presses (an invention attributed to the Amsterdam printer Willem Jansz Blaeu) and the introduction of forms of *stereotype printing by the Leiden Lutheran minister Johann Müller, *c.*1710. The widespread use of smaller *formats was made possible by the introduction of compact, yet highly legible roman typefaces. These *founts, cut by Christoffel van *Dijck and others, also found their way to other countries, especially England. The most important innovation in the second-hand book trade was the printed *auction catalogue. The first such catalogue appeared in Leiden in 1599 for the auction by Louis Elzevier of the library of the statesman-scholar Marnix de Sainte-Aldegonde; within a few decades they were common all over the country.

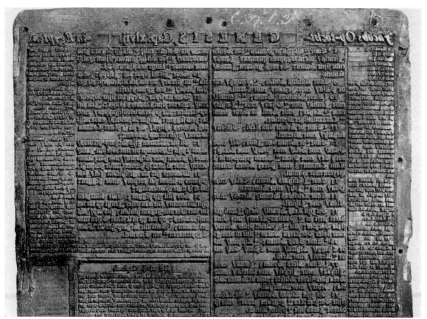

A *stereotype *plate (1) believed to have been made by the process invented by Johann Müller and the corresponding page of a Dutch bible printed by Müller's sons and Samuel Luchtmans at Leiden in 1718.

The large number of auction catalogues from the 17th and 18th centuries that have survived are proof of a very lively book culture in the Dutch Republic. Reading vernacular books was a fairly normal practice among upper- and middle-class sections of the population, and many people, certainly in the cities, owned small to medium-sized book collections. Their contents ranged from religious texts—above all the Bible, but also sermons and treatises of an often moral and pious nature—to practical and educational works, books on history and travel, and a wide variety of literary genres: farcical and anecdotal texts, non-fictional prose, poetry, *song books, *plays, emblematic works, etc. In addition, newspapers, *broadsides, pamphlets, *chapbooks, *almanacs and more ephemeral printing, much of which has not survived, were consumed in vast quantities (see 14). Most of these publications were acquired through regular bookshops, but there also existed a thriving itinerant book trade in spite of restrictions enforced by local booksellers' guilds. Some cities had municipal libraries, although access was normally restricted to the

A 17th-century Dutch bookshop from two drawings by Salomon de Bray, c.1625: the shop, probably in Haarlem, sold prints, pictures, and globes as well as bound books and books in *sheets. On the left an assistant is binding books.

members of the elite. Private book collections of true *bibliophiles were relatively scarce, perhaps partly because of the absence of a strong aristocracy and court. Nevertheless, important libraries were created by individuals such as Thysius (*see* THYSIANA, BIBLIOTHECA, LEIDEN), *Pauw, Hendrick Adriaansz van der Marck, the *Meermans, and *Crevenna.

3 1701–1900

That the book trade in the Dutch Republic was vulnerable became apparent from the end of the 17th century onwards. The succession of continental wars seriously affected international sales, while at the same time competition grew from other countries— France, England, and the German states. Also, the decline of Latin as the scholarly language of the republic of letters and the growing importance of vernacular languages in Europe presented a significant barrier to this Dutch-speaking nation. Even the mass production of pirated editions of foreign bestsellers, which for a long time was one of the mainstays of the early modern Dutch book trade, lost much of its ground, as can be seen in relation to the printing of English bibles. The huge flow of copies of the *Authorized Version with the original London imprint from Amsterdam to Britain in the 1670s and 1680s was reduced to a trickle by the middle of the 18th century. Only the *piracy of French bestsellers continued to thrive; but here too, competition from other countries, in particular the southern Netherlands

and Switzerland, was fierce. Attempts to redress this downward spiral—by the introduction of commission trading and a system of trade correspondents, or by the reduction of entrepreneurial risk through *subscription publishing and the collaboration of multiple publishers—were not sufficient. As the Leiden bookseller Elie Luzac observed in his *Hollands rijkdom* (The Wealth of Holland) published in 1783, when the Dutch Republic was torn apart by political crisis: 'Elsewhere they now have paper of the same quality but cheaper than ours; they print as well but cheaper than we and they produce type as good as ours but cheaper; and although we may have political hack-writers in abundance, our Dutch book trade lacks serious works of scholarship' (Luzac, 4. 425–6).

In stark contrast to the north, the book trade in the southern Netherlands during the 17th and 18th centuries experienced a period of prolonged decline. To the drain of talent and skills at the end of the 16th century were added economic and cultural stagnation and the strict supervision of the printing press by the Catholic Church and the secular authorities. In order to survive, printers and publishers adopted various strategies. The Plantin-*Moretus firm, for example, concentrated its activities on the publication of luxurious and expensive works and on the mass production of all sorts of Catholic Church books intended for the global Spanish market, for which they enjoyed a royal privilege. Some firms, like the Verdussen family of Antwerp, tried to cut back on expenses by outsourcing their printing or restructuring their distribution, while others concentrated their efforts on the manufacturing of cheap devotional booklets, images of saints, tales of chivalry, *romances, almanacs, catchpenny prints, plays, and songs, all in the vernacular and aimed at the domestic market. Piracy and the printing of illicit, particularly French, books provided another route of escape. In the 18th century, Brussels, capital of the Austrian Netherlands, and the autonomous cities of Liège and Bouillon hosted numerous printing offices working exclusively for the French market. Between 1774 and 1783, the French-born publisher Jean-Louis de Boubers at Brussels, for example, printed a splendid *collected edition of Rousseau's works in twelve illustrated volumes with the *false imprint 'Londres', but, needless to say, without the consent of the author, nor of any legitimate publishers.

The transitional period from the 18th to the 19th century was a bleak era for publishing and bookselling in both the northern and southern Netherlands. In addition to the deep economic depression, repeated changes in the political regime of the two countries, growing censorship, and the seemingly endless Napoleonic wars all had a devastating impact on the book trade. Yet there were some redeeming features. Under the influence of the Enlightenment, the emancipation of the middle classes brought about the participation of a greater element of the population in cultural and political life. Many local and national societies and reading circles were founded for the active or passive pursuit of science and literature, and these initiatives stimulated publishing and the consumption of books. The collapse of the political system of the *ancien régime* gave birth for the first time to a free, critical, and opinion-forming periodical press. However short-lived it may have been, it set an example for the future. Where the book trade, under harsh economic circumstances, had become increasingly protective of vested interests, the step-by-step abolition of the guild system contributed to a much-needed liberalization of the market. Finally, the issue of copyright was gradually being addressed by a succession of laws that better protected the rights of publishers and, to a limited extent, of authors.

In 1815 the Congress of Vienna decided to restore the political unity of the Low Countries through the creation of the Kingdom of the Netherlands, headed by the son of the last Dutch stadtholder, King William I (1772–1843). It was an artificial construct destined to fail from the start. Despite some successes in the economic and social sphere, the north and south had been separated too long to be able to form a coherent national community. The Belgian Revolt of 1830 and the ensuing independence of the southern Netherlands under the royal House of Saxe-Coburg meant that each of the two countries would go its own way. A long and difficult process of recovery began, in which more general social developments, such as the growth of the population, the centralization and democratization of government, the liberalization and industrialization of the economy, educational reform, and the emancipation of the underprivileged directly correlated with changes in the world of books. It is worth noting, for example, that printing and publishing for a mass audience in The Netherlands did not come about until the second half of the 19th century. This was the era when, among many other factors, the mechanization and industrialization of production in printing and related activities finally got off the ground (*see* 11), the old stamp duty on newspapers and journals was abolished (1869), the quality of primary and secondary education was drastically improved, working hours of labourers were reduced and their wages increased, and the first steps were taken on the road to the liberation of women.

Annual book production in The Netherlands in this period rose from a few hundred titles at the beginning of the 19th century to some 3,000 by 1900. Foreign-language publication having come to an almost complete standstill, publishers now aimed entirely at the vernacular market. In relative terms, religious books began to lose ground to other genres. Literary works found their way to the public in an increasing variety of guises, as original or translated individual pieces, but also in the shape of serial publications, *anthologies, and contributions to journals and almanacs. They were, moreover, printed in various forms and formats for different readerships. The highly popular *Nederlandsche Muzenalmanak* (1819–47), for instance, could be had in five different versions at prices ranging from three and a half guilders for a copy on ordinary paper, bound in *cardboard, to seven and a half guilders for a *fine paper copy, bound in satin with a *slipcase. At the same time, there was a growing demand for non-specialist books on a wide range of topics—science, medicine, biology, history, and art. Moreover, thanks to innovative techniques in book illustration—such as wood and steel engraving, and *lithography and photography—new types of publications came on the market, including children's books, illustrated magazines, and practical handbooks (*see* 15, 16).

The organization of the Dutch book trade changed with the times. The branch organization Vereeniging ter Bevordering van de Belangen des Boekhandels (the ancestor of the present *Koninklijke Vereniging voor het Boekenvak) was founded in 1815 as a national successor to the local guilds. It was established first and foremost to combat piracy, but gradually took on other tasks as well, such as the regulation and improvement of the trade, the compilation of an annual bibliography of newly published books, the publication of a trade journal (*Nieuwsblad voor den boekhandel*), the organizing of trade fairs, and even the provision of a professional library and documentation centre in Amsterdam (the present Library of the *Royal Netherlands Book Trade Association (KVB)). A prominent role in these activities was played by the Amsterdam publisher and antiquarian bookseller Frederik *Muller. Book distribution was modernized by the creation in 1871 of a central distribution office in Amsterdam, the Bestelhuis, which organized the now generally accepted commission trade. The traditional figure of the bookseller, who combined both publishing and bookselling and often ran a printing office as well, slowly disappeared. Instead, printing, publishing, and modern and antiquarian bookselling became separate activities. The foundation of separate organizations for publishers (Nederlandse Uitgevers Bond, 1880) and booksellers (Nederlandse Boekverkopers Bond, 1907) is an indication of this process of occupational diversification and professionalization. At the other end of the spectrum, by 1866 Dutch typesetters had already achieved a national trade union (Algemene Nederlandse Typografen Bond)—the first such organization in The Netherlands—which successfully campaigned for a reduction of working hours and higher wages in the printing industry. Finally, in 1881, a modern Copyright Act was issued to protect the rights of native authors and publishers, although it would take until 1912 for the Dutch government to sign up to the international *Berne Convention of 1886.

In Belgium, the modernization of printing, publishing, and bookselling was a much longer-drawn-out affair. The main obstacle was the linguistic division of the country between French- and Flemish-speaking regions. French had long been the language of the political and cultural elite of southern Netherlandish society, which in effect meant a lasting dependence on the powerful publishing industry in France. Authors preferred to have their work issued by French publishers, as it guaranteed them better terms and conditions and a larger audience. The Flemish-speaking population, on the other hand, had become culturally backward and provincial. The volume of Flemish books produced at the beginning of the 19th century consisted of little more than, as the Antwerp author Domien Sleeckx recalled in his autobiography, 'almanacs, schoolbooks, church books, and similar pious writings' (Simons, 1. 18–20). It took the protagonists of the Flemish Movement (Vlaamse Beweging), which started as a band of romantic writers and intellectuals after Belgian independence, much time and effort before they were able to use the printing press as an instrument for the promotion of their ideals. The problems they encountered may be illustrated by the publishing history of the first edition (1838) of the most famous Flemish book of the 19th century, the nationalist historical *novel *De leeuw van Vlaanderen* (The Lion of Flanders) by Hendrik Conscience. As no publisher dared to take the risk of issuing it, the book was printed at the author's own expense; to his relief, he had (barely) found a sufficient number of people willing to subscribe to it. (Nearly a third of the subscribers came from The Netherlands.) The novel's eventual success convinced one entrepreneur, Joseph-Ernest Buschmann, of the viability of setting up a publishing firm in Antwerp that specialized in Flemish literary works; throughout the second half of the 19th century, however, it would remain difficult for Flemish writers to get their work published. Although in 1893 a Dutch book trade and publishing company, De Nederlandsche Boekhandel, established itself in Antwerp with the aim of promoting Flemish literature, leading Flemish literary authors by that time had their books published in The Netherlands because in all respects—editorial attention, typography, remuneration, readership—they were better served there than in Flanders.

4 The modern era

It has been said, with some exaggeration, that the modern era in The Netherlands did not begin until after World War II. To an extent this observation also holds true for the book trade. With the exception of a handful of more enterprising firms—*Sijthoff in Leiden, *Enschedé in Haarlem, *Nijhoff in The Hague, *Elsevier in Amsterdam—publishing and bookselling up to the 1950s could be characterized as insular and conservative in their method, scope, and ambition. Most publishing and bookselling businesses were small in size and family-owned. They stuck to their traditional ways and shied away from innovation. Moreover, the rigid segmentation (*Verzuiling*) of society along the lines of religious and political groupings dominated publishing and bookselling. Firmly believing in the principle of 'sovereignty within one's own community', Catholic and Protestant publishers supplied their co-religionists with their own children's literature, schoolbooks, magazines, and newspapers. Even in smaller Dutch towns, it was quite normal up to the 1960s to find one bookshop for Catholics and another for Protestants. On a lesser scale, socialists and communists practised similar forms of media control.

In the prewar years, the demand for books and other reading matter grew enormously, however. Whereas in the 19th century readers often had been dependent on *subscription libraries and on reading rooms to quench their thirst for reading, the improved economic situation of a large part of the population now made it possible to buy books as well. Demand was stimulated by idealistic publishers such as the socialist *Arbeiders Pers and the humanistic Wereldbibliotheek, which offered good books at a low price. Reading was also actively promoted by initiatives such as the annual Boekenweek (Book Week), first organized in 1932. Each year a renowned author was invited to write a short novel which was given away free in bookshops when customers spent a certain amount of money on other items during the Boekenweek.

In Flanders, the situation was rather different. The catastrophe of World War I—as far as books are concerned, best symbolized by the burning of *Louvain University Library by the Germans—was followed by a period of new nationalist confidence and optimism, during which several important publishing houses were founded, such as De *Sikkel (1919), Standaard Uitgeverij (1924), and Manteau (1932). It seemed that Flemish publishers were finally able to free themselves from the Dutch stranglehold. A further indication of the increased self-awareness was the creation in 1929 of the branch organization Vereniging ter Bevordering van het Vlaamse Boekwezen, the counterpart of the Dutch Vereeniging ter Bevordering van de Belangen des Boekhandels, in order to represent better the economic interests of Flemish publishers.

World War II did not stop this development. During the Nazi occupation, Flemish publishers enjoyed remarkably more freedom than their colleagues in the north. This was due in part to differences in their administrative situations. Whereas The Netherlands had a civic government under complete German control, Belgium was governed by a somewhat more tolerant German military administration. But it also had to do with the affinity felt in certain circles of the Flemish Movement for National Socialism. Either

way, while in Belgium book production remained relatively unhindered and stable, in The Netherlands there was harsh censorship and, partly also because of a serious paper shortage, a sharp drop in production. In 1944 only 965 titles were published, against 3,370 in the first year of the war. At the same time, restrictions on Dutch publishing resulted in a flurry of illegal printing activities. All kinds of illicit newspapers, books, and pamphlets were printed, mostly in limited *press runs. One of the best-organized illegal publishers was De *Bezige Bij in Amsterdam. The revenues of its publications, such as the famous poem *De achttien doden* ('The Eighteen Dead') by Jan Campert and the news-sheet *Vrij Nederland*, were used to support people in hiding and to finance the Resistance movement.

Although the end of the war did not bring about the radical change to the old political system desired by many, in both countries a process of reorientation and modernization in many spheres of society soon got under way. The book trade was no exception to this development, although it must be said that changes in Belgium, where the situation remained complicated by the country's linguistic divisions, were slower and less comprehensive than in The Netherlands. Within a few decades, publishing changed from a supply-oriented to a demand-driven industry, resulting in an ever-growing number of books and other publications. By 1980, some 15,000 titles were published annually in The Netherlands alone, a number that by the end of the century would rise to approximately 18,000. The majority of this output consisted of 'general books', including popular fiction and non-specialist works.

In this far more competitive market there was a constant drive for cost reductions, both in production and in management. The introduction of new typesetting (*photo, *computerized), printing (*offset), and binding (paperback) techniques made it possible to handle larger print runs at a lower cost, thereby fulfilling the growing demand of the reading public as well as stimulating it. This development can best be illustrated by the unparalleled success of the *paperback. The first paperback pocket-book in The Netherlands appeared in 1951 as part of the Prisma series of classic literary works from the Utrecht publishing firm Het Spectrum. Print runs of individual volumes soon reached 250,000 or more. The formula was immediately copied, so that by the 1960s most publishers had their own paperback series in a wide range of genres, including literature, popular science, leisure, dictionaries, and children's books.

Rising costs and the increased scale of production necessitated organizational reforms. Mergers and takeovers succeeded each other rapidly, both nationally and internationally. In the 1970s and 1980s in particular, firms like Elsevier and *Kluwer expanded at breakneck speed, both eventually becoming world leaders in their fields. In the course of these events, quite a few Belgian publishers who did not have the necessary financial resources were swallowed by more affluent Dutch publishers, thus counteracting the trend set in Flanders during the interwar period. The few houses that survived as independent enterprises by and large were modest-scale publishers of educational and academic books, such as *Brepols in Turnhout and Peeters in Louvain.

Similar processes of rationalization, concentration, and commercialization can be observed in book distribution. The Dutch Bestelhuis was transformed by a collective effort of the various branch organizations in 1973 into the Centraal Boekhuis, which took care of the storage, distribution, and transport of the constantly growing volume of books. Independent bookshops joined trade syndicates to strengthen their position in relation to publishers. The downside was that bookshops became much more uniform. The first Dutch *book club had been founded in 1937, but the great success of this means of distribution came in the 1960s and 1970s, when two more book clubs were created. Together they achieved a temporary market share of no less than 20 per cent. A characteristic feature of the Dutch book trade was the fixing of book prices, a collective agreement among publishers and retailers enforcing uniform pricing, with the intention of guaranteeing a varied supply of books (cf. NET BOOK AGREEMENT). One undesired effect, however, was overproduction. At the same time, new collective initiatives were adopted by the various branch organizations of the book trade. Book promotion was now organized centrally by the Commissie Collectieve Propaganda van het Nederlandse Boek (CPNB), which has both a commercial and cultural purpose and is responsible for the Boekenweek. In 1960 the Stichting Speurwerk betreffende het Boek was founded, which gathers much-needed statistical information.

In libraries in Belgium and The Netherlands, the postwar trend has been toward professionalization, increases in scale, and automation through the integration of new information technologies. More than its counterpart in Brussels, the *Koninklijke Bibliotheek (KB) in The Hague has deliberately taken on the role of national library: it has set up new projects in centralized cataloguing (Nederlandse Centrale Catalogus; Short-Title Catalogue, Netherlands); acted as a voluntary deposit library for Dutch publishers; and promoted preservation and *digitization. In 1998 the KB initiated the *Bibliopolis-project, an electronic *history of the book which integrates existing and new information systems in the field of Dutch book history. In university libraries, electronic access for all members of the academic community has become a key notion, while there is a growing awareness of the importance of special collections in teaching and research. Public libraries, which experienced an enormous expansion of readers in the 1950s and 1960s, have been liberated from concentrating on specific groups of users, and in both countries now cater to about a quarter of the population, offering a varied supply of materials and services.

BIBLIOGRAPHY
H. Furstner, *Geschichte des niederländischen Buchhandels* (1985)
J. P. Gumbert, *The Dutch and Their Books in the Manuscript Age* (1990)
H. Hasquin, ed., *La Belgique autrichienne, 1713–1794* (1987)
W. Gs. Hellinga, *Copy and Print in the Netherlands* (1962)
L. Hellinga-Querido *et al.*, eds., *The Bookshop of the World: The Role of the Low Countries in the Book-Trade 1473–1941* (2001)
P. G. Hoftijzer and O. S. Lankhorst, *Drukkers, Boekverkopers en Lezers in Nederland tijdens de Republiek* (2000)
P. Janssens, *België in de 17de Eeuw*, vol. 2: *De Cultuur* (2006)
E. Luzac, *Hollands rijkdom* (4 vols, 1780–83)
J. H. Marrow *et al.*, *The Golden Age of Dutch Manuscript Painting* (1989)
P. F. J. Obbema *et al.*, *Boeken in Nederland* (1979)
J. Ray, *Observations Topographical, Moral, & Physiological Made in a Journey Through Part of the Low-Countries* (1673)
P. Schneiders, *Nederlandse Bibliotheekgeschiedenis* (1997)
L. Simons, *Geschiedenis van de Uitgeverij in Vlaanderen* (2 vols, 1984–7)
M. Smeyers, *Flemish Miniatures from the 8th to the mid-16th Century* (1999)
M. van Delft and C. de Wolf, eds., *Bibliopolis: History of the Printed Book in the Netherlands* (2003), www.bibliopolis.nl, consulted Feb. 2008
L. Voet, *The Golden Compasses: A History and Evaluation of the Printing and Publishing Activities of the Officina Plantiniana* (2 vols, 1969–72)

...lich auch blutvergi...

verzeichnet) ward jm

ſonder als einem Biſ

var kein Biſchoff/ ſon

her zum erſtē mal wid

rieg gefürt vmb zeytli

en krieg in die hend ge

z in maſſen widerſetz

hingelegt werden/ biſ

ſt verzert haben. Se

onſere Landsfürſtē/ri

24 The History of the Book in Germany

JOHN L. FLOOD

1 Introduction

Historically, 'Germany' is difficult to define in geographical and political terms. The Roman province of Germania covered only the southern part of what we now call Germany; the area north and east of the Danube, Main, and Rhine was never part of the Roman empire. Whereas around 1200 Germany was thought of as extending 'from the Rhine to Hungary'—and Hoffmann von Fallersleben in the 1840s saw it as stretching 'from the Maas to the Memel, from the Etsch to the Bælt'—modern Germany's borders are more narrowly drawn: the Etsch, the river Adige, is now in Italy, and Germany's eastern frontier is at the Oder. In political terms, German history is essentially the painful story of various German states, sometimes pulling together, sometimes pulling apart, united only by the German language. After 843, the Frankish empire (which under Charlemagne had comprised what is now France, much of Germany, Switzerland, and part of Italy) was divided into three, in essence creating France, Germany, and the buffer state of Lotharingia in between—sowing the seed of future conflicts. Even this 'Germany' was not a unity: the 'Holy Roman Empire of the German Nation' remained a loose conglomeration of territories and municipalities under the notional direction of the Holy Roman Emperor until its dissolution in 1806. Austria then became a nation in its own right (*see* **30**). Whereas countries like Britain and France have for centuries had national capitals exerting a powerful cultural influence, it was not until 1871 that Berlin became the capital of the newly established German Reich. The 20th century saw this unity torn asunder and, in 1990, reassembled. Yet even today, Germany, though it again has a national capital, is a federation of territories, at least some of which (Bavaria and the Hanseatic City of Hamburg, for instance) are exceedingly proud of their own history and distinctive cultural traditions. The regional diversity of Germany helps to explain the relative decentralization of the German book trade and the lack of a single national library. Against such a background the German language—spoken also in Austria, parts of Switzerland, and in some areas of Belgium, and, in earlier times, also used where French (e.g. Alsace) and Slavonic languages now hold sway—has (despite marked regional differences) been a major factor for cultural unification. German book history likewise transcends national boundaries; hence, this survey will address the German-speaking area of past and present Europe as a whole.

2 The Middle Ages

The history of the book in Germany must begin with the early monastic *scriptoria. Two of the most important were those at Fulda, where the monastery was founded in 744 by the English missionary Wynfreth (St Boniface), 'Apostle of the Germans', and *St Gall in Switzerland. It is at St Gall (founded 613) that the oldest German book is preserved, the so-called *Abrogans* (Codex 911), a small late 8th-century *glossary giving the German equivalents of words from the Old

Testament; *Abrogans* ('humble') is the first word in the list. This modest book encapsulates something of the monastic endeavours of the Carolingian period to express Christian terms and other concepts from the world of late antiquity in the vernacular. Indeed, the struggle between Latin and the vernacular would play a major part in the history of the book in Germany. Other early monastic scriptoria, mostly dating from the 8th century, include Freising, *Reichenau, Murbach, *Corvey, Regensburg, Salzburg, and Tegernsee. As elsewhere in Europe, they chiefly produced works of theological interest—but also literary, scientific, and medical MSS—either for their own use or for exchange. By 1200, there were about 700 monastic houses in German-speaking areas, but by then towns were becoming more important, and the emerging secular culture led to the spread of knowledge beyond the cloister's confines. Monastic scriptoria could no longer satisfy the demand for books, so increasingly they were produced by lay scribes, and MSS began to be disseminated through the developing trade in commercial centres and university towns. MS production peaked in the 15th century, when we also find secular scriptoria such as Diebold Lauber's at Hagenau (near Strasburg), which produced illustrated MSS of German literary texts on a commercial basis. Bookbinding now became a lay occupation, too. The turn of the 14th century saw the earliest German paper mills, the first built near Nuremberg in 1389 by the merchant Ulman Stromer, who had learnt the technique in Lombardy (*see* **10**).

3 The 15th century

Roman Germania created a number of major towns in southern and western Germany—Cologne, Mainz, Trier, Strasburg, Augsburg, Regensburg, and Vienna—that would for centuries play important roles as administrative, ecclesiastical, cultural, and commercial centres. Several of them were significant in the rise of the printed book in the 15th century. *Gutenberg from Mainz, the inventor of printing with movable type, spent several years experimenting at Strasburg in the 1430s and 1440s. His achievement was to have combined many pre-existing elements—printing, punch-cutting, the press, paper—into a single effective technical process (*see* **6**, **11**). He invested a considerable sum of borrowed money in developing the technique at Mainz in the early 1450s, and though in effect he bankrupted himself, he completed the printing of the two-volume Latin Bible now known as the *Gutenberg Bible or the 42-line Bible (from the

number of lines of text on the page) by August 1456 at the latest.

Printing soon spread to other towns, in Germany and beyond. From Mainz it was introduced to Bamberg, an important bishopric, *c*.1459; here Heinrich Keffer completed the 36-line Bible by 1461. Initially, the principal centres were generally commercial cities where capital, suitable texts, and readers could be found. At Strasburg, where Gutenberg's invention was introduced in 1459–60, early printers included Heinrich Eggestein, *Mentelin, Johann Prüss, and Johann Grüninger. Cologne (where printing was introduced in *c*.1465), a city of 35,000 inhabitants, was the largest German printing centre in the 15th century, especially for theological books. Here the most productive printer was Heinrich Quentell; the leading publisher was *Birckmann, whose business extended into The Netherlands and Burgundy, and who also had a shop at *St Paul's in London. At Augsburg, the first printer was Günther *Zainer in 1468. The foundation of the University of Basle in 1460 led to this city's early importance as a printing centre from 1468–70, associated with famous humanist printer-publishers like *Amerbach, Johann and Adam Petri, *Froben, Andreas Cratander, and *Oporinus. At Nuremberg (1470), the leading publisher was *Koberger, who had 24 presses working for him.

The all-pervasiveness of the Church and of Latin meant that the book trade throughout Europe was international in scope, relatively little being published in the vernacular. Latin would predominate in the German book market for at least two centuries. Until the Reformation at least, printing did not much favour contemporary writers, publishers preferring the well-tried texts of the past. Among the few contemporary authors whose works were regularly printed in the first decades of printing were Sebastian Brant, whose *Narrenschiff* (Ship of Fools, 1494) became an international success once it had been mediated through Latin into French and English; and the Ulm physician Heinrich Steinhöwel, whose many translations from Latin were printed by Johann Zainer, the first printer at Ulm from 1472 onwards.

The introduction of printing did not mean a sudden break with the MS tradition. As elsewhere in Europe, the handwritten book and the printed book coexisted for some time (*see* **13**). A phenomenon particularly characteristic of The Netherlands and Germany in the mid-15th century was the production of *blockbooks, mostly short devotional texts (**Biblia Pauperum*, *Apocalypse*, *Ars Moriendi*), with text and illustrations carved into blocks of wood, inked, and transferred to paper by rubbing; the method was still being used for *ABCs and similar works in the 1520s. Though the earliest typographic books were modelled on MSS, in time their appearance changed. The *folio format inherited from MS culture increasingly gave way to the handier *quarto and *octavo. The *title-page came into regular use and subsumed the function of the *colophon. The *abbreviations and *ligatures familiar from the MS age largely disappeared from printing *founts. In scholarly books, *footnotes replaced *marginal notes. And although outside Germany *roman typefaces predominated, books in German were generally printed in *gothic and books in Latin in roman.

Of the c.27,000 different books printed in the 15ᵗʰ century, about 11,000 were produced in Germany, with only about 4 per cent in German. Yet works in German figured among the earliest books printed: one of Gutenberg's first trial pieces was a German poem on the Day of Judgment, and in 1461 *Pfister printed Johannes von Tepl's *Ackermann von Böhmen* and Ulrich Boner's *Edelstein* at Bamberg (these two were the first typographic books to contain illustrations, with 5 and 203 woodcuts respectively). It was Augsburg, however, that was particularly noted for books in the vernacular: G. Zainer, J. *Bämler, Anton Sorg, and Schönsperger played leading roles, each often bringing out works that one of the others had already published. Though perhaps initially not a place that one associates particularly strongly with vernacular books, several notable German works appeared in Strasburg as early as 1466–80, including *Mentelin's 1466 Bible (the first printed bible in any vernacular) and his 1477 editions of the Arthurian *romances *Parzival* and *Titurel*. Strasburg's output in this field certainly expanded around 1500 and especially in the early 16ᵗʰ century, when printers like Johann Grüninger, Hans Knobloch, and Bartholomaeus Kistler established reputations for illustrated works. Books in German were also printed at Basle, Nuremberg, Heidelberg, Ulm, and smaller towns like Urach, Esslingen, and Reutlingen; further north, printers at Leipzig, Cologne, Lübeck, Magdeburg, and Stendal issued books in Low German, which was then still the mother tongue of virtually everyone in that area.

Among the chief glories of early German printing were the illustrated books, particularly from Augsburg, Strasburg, Nuremberg, and Ulm. They included devotional works (Cologne Bibles, c.1478; Zainer's 1472 edition of the *Golden Legend* with 120 woodcuts, the first illustrated book from Augsburg), classics (the illustrations in Grüninger's 1496 Terence are constructed from 85 interchangeable woodcut components), practical handbooks (Bämler's 1475 Augsburg edition of Konrad von Megenberg's *Buch der Natur*, containing the earliest known printed botanical illustrations), *chronicles (including Ulrich von Reichenthal's *History of the Council of Constance*, Augsburg, 1483; the *Chronicle of the Saxons*, Mainz, 1492; and Koberger's Latin and German editions of Schedel's *Nuremberg Chronicle*, Nuremberg, 1493, with 1,809 woodcuts), travel accounts (*Breydenbach's *Peregrinatio in Terram Sanctam*, Mainz, 1486), *herbals, didactic works (Brant's *Narrenschiff*, Basle, 1494), heroic poems (*Heldenbuch*, Strasburg c.1479), chivalric romances (*Tristrant*, Augsburg 1484; *Wigoleis vom Rade*, Augsburg 1493), and other popular narratives. More *incunabula illustrated with woodcuts were produced in Germany than anywhere else, and this tradition continued into the 16ᵗʰ century, which saw the *woodcut develop into a major art form in the hands of artists like *Dürer, *Cranach, *Holbein, and *Burgkmair.

By the early 16ᵗʰ century, the market was already oversupplied with books. In 1504, Koberger in Nuremberg lamented that trade was not what it had been, even the Latin Bible Amerbach had printed for him at Basle between 1498 and 1502 (*GW* 4285) proving unsaleable. As books became more plentiful, humanist scholars began to form significant private libraries. Examples include those of Amplonius Ratinck at Erfurt, Hermann and Hartmann Schedel and *Pirckheimer at Nuremberg, Sigismund Gossembrot and *Peutinger at Augsburg. The library of *Rhenanus survives, still intact, at Sélestat in Alsace.

4 The 16ᵗʰ century

Gutenberg's 42-line Bible was the first of 94 Latin bibles printed in Europe in the 15ᵗʰ century. Of these, no fewer than 57 appeared in German-speaking towns. Germany led the way in printed vernacular bibles too, long before the Protestant Reformers, in asserting the priesthood of all believers, contended that all Christians had the right and duty to explore scriptural truth for themselves. Starting with Mentelin's edition of 1466, ten German bibles were already on the market by 1485 when the archbishop of Mainz attempted to ban their printing. By the time *Luther published his New Testament translation—based on *Erasmus's Greek text instead of the Latin Vulgate—at Wittenberg in September 1522, fourteen editions of the complete

Part of the Psalms in German from the first vernacular translation of the Bible, printed at Strassburg by *Mentelin not after 1466 (GW 4295).

Bible had appeared in High German (at Strasburg, Augsburg, and Nuremberg) and four in Low German (at Cologne, Lübeck, and Halberstadt). The first edition of Luther's New Testament quickly sold out, and a revised edition (with Cranach's woodcuts altered for reasons of *censorship) appeared in December 1522; there were many reprints, authorized and unauthorized. Its popularity was such that already in 1527 Hieronymus Emser published at Dresden a rival, 'Catholicized' version of Luther's translation, even though he believed that reading the Bible should be restricted to scholars. Luther's complete Bible translation (based on Hebrew and Greek sources), first published in 1534, has influenced the German literary language just as much as the *Authorized Version has influenced English. By the time of Luther's death, at least 355 editions of his translation, or parts of it (Pentateuch, Prophets, Psalms, New Testament, Apocrypha, etc.), had been published (chiefly at Wittenberg, Augsburg, Strasburg, Nuremberg, Basle, Erfurt, and Leipzig), with at least 90 more in the Low German version (mainly from Magdeburg, Wittenberg, Erfurt, Lübeck, and Rostock).

The press was undeniably a significant factor in the success of the Reformation, but printing, especially in the vernacular, would not have developed as rapidly without its stimulus. In 1525, 60 per cent of everything printed in Germany was in German, but this was a passing phase: for the rest of the century, printing in German was about 40 per cent. Luther himself saw printing as 'the greatest and latest gift of God, for by this means God seeks to extend the cause of true religion to the ends of the earth and to make it available in all languages'. Already by 1500, printing had been attempted in some 60 German-speaking towns and was well established in most of them; but with the torrent of *pamphlets issued after 1517 the industry soon spread to a multitude of small, relatively unimportant towns – some 160 in all by 1600, and 330 by 1700. The main centres of Protestant publishing included Wittenberg, Nuremberg, Frankfurt, and Strasburg, while Catholic books were chiefly produced in Cologne, Ingolstadt, Munich, and Dillingen. By 1530, some 10,000 pamphlets had appeared, totalling nearly 10 million copies, and many more were issued throughout the century. Broadly speaking, these aimed to influence public opinion both on burning social and political issues (such as the Peasants' War and the threat of Turkish expansion) and especially on matters concerning religion and the Church (for instance, Henry VIII's quarrel with Luther). Some 70 per cent of titles published between 1520 and 1526

debate the fundamental importance of the Scriptures for the laity. By 1520, 32 tracts by Luther had been published in more than 500 editions, and within a few years a quarter of all German publications appeared under his name. Before he died, more than 3 million copies of his writings, excluding his Bible translations, had been printed.

The Reformation, and all it entailed, inevitably encouraged reading and stimulated book production generally: a wider range of books was being published, not least in the fields of literature, medicine, and technology. It is, however, difficult to quantify this precisely. Given the lack of exact information about the number of *printing offices, the titles they published, and indeed the vague definition of 'book' (whether, for instance, proclamations, pamphlets, and *calendars are included), estimates are largely speculative. It has been claimed that in the 16th century 150,000 items were published in Germany, while estimates for the 17th century range between 85,000 and 150,000, and for the 18th century between 175,000 and 500,000.

With the growth of the book trade, patterns of business had to change. Whereas MSS were mainly produced on commission, printing was generally a speculative business, stocks being produced in the hope of finding customers for them. Distribution thus acquired a new importance. Until the 18th century, *book fairs, principally at *Frankfurt and *Leipzig, played a major role. Frankfurt, in the centre of Germany and readily accessible by river, was important for the distribution of scholarly books in Latin throughout Europe; books were certainly being traded there in the 1480s, decades before its first press was established. Leipzig, too, lay on major north–south, east–west trade routes. These fairs, held twice a year, around Shrovetide or Easter and at Michaelmas, provided the best opportunity for publishers to sell books in quantity to other book dealers. The book trade expanded so greatly that a guide to what was on offer became a desideratum. The initiative was seized by the Augsburg bookseller Georg Willer, who in the autumn of 1564 issued his first Frankfurt catalogue, *Novorum Librorum, quos Nundinae Autumnales Francofurti Anno 1564 Celebratae Venales Exhiberunt, Catalogus*; thereafter it appeared twice yearly. Books were listed first by language (Latin and Greek, then German) and within each group by subject: theology, law, medicine, the liberal arts. So successful were Willer's catalogues that he soon had rivals. In 1598, the Frankfurt Council decided to ban the publication of private fair catalogues and to issue its own—a sensible precaution, given surveillance by the

Catholic-orientated Imperial Book Commission (established in 1569 to prevent the circulation of seditious and defamatory material). Issuing an official catalogue not only enabled the council to demonstrate to the emperor that it was being vigilant, but helped it exercise stricter control of the trade by keeping a watch on the observance of printers' privileges and ensuring that copies of books were deposited as required. The official catalogue (*Mess Catalog) appeared—latterly somewhat fitfully—until about 1750. A catalogue was issued at Leipzig, too, but there it remained in private hands, being first published by Henning Grosse in 1594 and then by his successors until 1759. Because the Leipzig fairs followed those held at Frankfurt, the Leipzig catalogues generally listed the same books as the Frankfurt ones, though they often included a (sometimes substantial) section of 'books not shown at Frankfurt'. As the first regularly appearing bulletins of recent publications, these catalogues long remained essential reading for scholars. The curators of the *Bodleian Library at Oxford consulted them to select books, though from 1617 they used the London bookseller John Bill's own English version of the Frankfurt catalogue. In 1685, Jean-Paul de La Roque, editor of the *Journal des savants* in Paris, remarked that until then German books had been known in France only through the Frankfurt fair catalogues. The catalogues represent a useful, if far from comprehensive, indicator of the book trade in the early modern period. Their purpose was to advertise and to generate interest, not to serve as comprehensive bibliographical aids: it is reckoned that they include only about 20–25 per cent of the books actually available. Their focus is primarily on books of scholarly interest, especially in Latin, with a potential for wide geographical dissemination, while small works, books of sermons, prayer books, university *theses, and calendars scarcely feature. Fuller coverage was attempted by early efforts at cumulative bibliography such as Conrad *Gessner's *Bibliotheca Universalis* (Zurich, 1545), Johannes Cless's *Unius Seculi Elenchus Librorum* (Frankfurt, 1602), and Georg Draud's *Bibliotheca Classica* (Frankfurt, 1611) and *Bibliotheca Exotica* (Frankfurt, 1625).

5 The 17th century

The Thirty Years War (1618–48) had a devastating effect on Germany: one third of the population is believed to have perished. The economic downturn affected the quality of books, inferior paper and narrow types being used to reduce costs. (The *Endters of Nuremberg were one of the few firms still producing fine books.) During the 1630s, the number of titles listed in the fair catalogues was little more than a third of what it had been in 1619, and even after the cessation of hostilities, slow economic recovery—exacerbated by plague, food shortages, and a prolonged cold spell (the 'little Ice Age')—meant that it was decades before the prewar level was reached again.

Although Vienna and Munich publishers effectively had a monopoly in the Catholic domains of the Habsburgs and the Wittelsbachs, the centre of gravity of the book trade shifted from the south to the centre and north. Even though the Lutheran Reformation had spent its force by the mid-16th century, the Protestant book trade maintained its ascendancy over German intellectual life. The Frankfurt fair, however, lost its dominant role. Many dealers, especially foreigners, failed to resume their activities there after 1648, the restrictions imposed by the Jesuit-dominated Imperial Book Commission proving serious disincentives. The attempts of the Commission and the *Index Librorum Prohibitorum* to control books were largely ineffective, however, in part because their workings were arbitrary. Titles sometimes appeared on the *Index* simply because their authors were non-Catholics. Books in the vernacular were particularly targeted because they were intended for a wider public. One might have expected the Catholic authorities to permit Protestant books dealing with internal theological quarrels as revealing the inadequacies of their cause, but these too appeared on the *Index*. Often it sufficed for a book to have been printed in a Protestant town for it to be listed.

Between 1680 and 1690, publishing at Frankfurt collapsed, and Leipzig moved quickly into the forefront of the German book world. This city was favoured by its accessible position in central Europe and the privileges that the Saxon government bestowed on the trade fairs (and the liberality with which the city council interpreted them), as well as by the importance of its university. The business acumen of members of the book trade there was also a major factor in its success. It was a member of the Leipzig trade, Philipp Erasmus Reich, a partner of the firm of *Weidmann (founded 1680, later Weidmann und Reich), who would eventually put an end to the Frankfurt fair by closing his Frankfurt warehouse in 1764 and encouraging others to do likewise.

As yet there was no attempt to enlarge the reading public by drawing in the bourgeoisie or the lower classes. Commonly, households might possess a bible, Luther's *catechism, an *almanac, perhaps a *herbal or other household medical book, a guide to letter writing, and a popular religious book, but hardly ever any imaginative literature. A great deal of popular religious writing, described on title-pages as 'useful' or 'edifying', was published. In the early 18th century, one of the most widely read books was still *Vom wahren Christenthum* by the Pietist Johann Arndt, first published in 1605. Yet, such reading ensured that literacy was reasonably widespread, especially in Protestant areas.

Among the characteristic forms of publication in the 17th century were popular, illustrated political *broadsides. Thousands still survive, not only dealing with the war (the demise of Tilly, for instance, or Gustavus Adolphus of Sweden as the saviour of Lutheranism) but treating such topics as the Dutch struggle for independence from Spain, the Gunpowder Plot, and hatred for the Jesuits. Another ubiquitous form of ephemeral publication was booklets of occasional verse, often in Latin, marking birthdays, name-days, marriages, promotions, retirements, deaths, and other significant events—well over 160,000 funeral booklets alone survive. The year 1609 saw the appearance of the first two regularly numbered and dated German *newsbooks, the forerunners of modern *newspapers: the Wolfenbüttel *Aviso, Relation oder Zeitung*, and the Strasburg *Relation aller Fürnemen und gedenkwürdigen Historien*. The first German daily newspaper was the *Neueinlaufende Nachricht von Kriegs- und Welthändeln*, published by Timotheus Ritzsch at Leipzig on 1 January 1660; this became the *Leipziger Zeitung* in 1734 and ceased publication only in 1921.

The artistic talents that helped adorn early printed books became rarer after the mid-16th century, and woodcuts more workaday and less imaginative. The 17th century saw increasing use of *engraving. Among the best-known examples are Johann Philipp Abelin's *Theatrum Europaeum* (21 vols, 1635–1738) and various topographical works of Matthäus Merian (1593–1650) from Basle, who took over the Frankfurt business of his father-in-law, de *Bry, in 1624.

6 The 18th century

In the 17th and early 18th centuries, the book market was still dominated by the old-fashioned polyhistor penning enormous tomes (often still in Latin) for a restricted scholarly public. Theology was particularly strongly represented. In 1650, 71 per cent of the books in the Leipzig catalogues were in Latin; in 1701, 55 per cent; but in 1740, only 27 per cent; in 1770, 14 per cent; and only 4 per cent in 1800. The proportion of

books produced in Latin was higher in university towns such as Jena and Tübingen than in commercial centres like Augsburg and Hamburg. The catalogues also show (notwithstanding their limitations) that the proportions of books in the categories of 'religious literature for the layman' (devotional works, sermons) and 'imaginative literature' (including novels, drama, and poetry) were inverted between 1740 and 1800—the former representing nearly 20 per cent and the latter barely 6 per cent of the total books on offer at the earlier date, and under 6 per cent and more than 21 per cent respectively at the end of the period. In general, the book trade expanded fourfold during the 18th century. The mid-century saw the emergence of the popularizing writer who made knowledge available in German for a wider readership. The numbers of books in the fields of philosophy, philology, pedagogy, natural sciences, and economics increased to some 40 per cent, while belles-lettres grew almost tenfold, from 2.8 per cent in 1700 to 21.5 per cent in 1800. At this date, theology represented only about 13 per cent of the total.

By about 1740, the position of writers was changing and the potential public for imaginative literature was expanding. In the 17th century, there had not yet emerged a profession of letters as such. Writers had depended on their main occupations or professions for any social respect they enjoyed; anyone hoping to live by his pen was invariably doomed to contempt and poverty. Writers had been primarily scholars: professors, schoolmasters, or clergymen. Aristocrats would have considered it unseemly to be seen as dependent on their pens, and bourgeois writers would emphasize that their writing was merely the product of their leisure hours. In the 18th century, the role of aristocratic literary patrons declined, and that of the commercial publisher grew.

An important development in the 18th century was the emergence of the novel. Earlier, novels had been of a learned character, intended not for popular consumption but rather for aristocratic or scholarly readers well acquainted with the events and personalities of ancient and contemporary history, classical mythology, and the works of ancient philosophers and poets. A good example is *Die Römische Octavia* by Anton Ulrich, duke of Braunschweig-Wolfenbüttel (1633–1714). Such novels primarily reflected the absolutist court ideal, and served as vehicles for moral or political ideas of the kind young noblemen were expected to imbibe. In the 18th century, however, a market developed for travel novels, love stories, ghost stories, novels about knights and robbers, and more besides.

The epistolary novel became fashionable, Goethe's *Werther* (1774) becoming the best-seller of the century, with authorized editions far outnumbered by piracies and translations. Translated works were also attractive to publishers, who did not need to pay authors an honorarium, only a translator's fee. Foreign authors popular in Germany included *Richardson, Sterne, and (earlier) Defoe. Three translations of *Robinson Crusoe* (1719) appeared within a year: one translation saw five editions in 1720 alone. *Crusoe* precipitated a flood of German imitations, the best of which was Johann Gottfried Schnabel's four-volume *Insel Felsenburg* (1731–43), in which four shipwrecked travellers seek to live in harmony in an ideal social community that contrasts sharply with contemporary German society. This novel, frequently reissued and reprinted in pirated editions, came to be found next to the Bible in all pious middle-class homes. Another, later excrescence of the craze for 'Robinsonades' was *Der schweizerische Robinson* (1812)—written by Johann David Wyss of Berne—known to generations of English readers as *The Swiss Family Robinson*.

Numerous distinguished publishing houses emerged in the 18th century. At Stuttgart, *Cotta is famous for his 60-volume Goethe edition. At Leipzig, Johann Gottlob Immanuel Breitkopf (1719–94) became renowned for innovations in printing complicated music from movable type; the firm's successor, *Breitkopf & Härtel, established in 1796, remains one of the leading names in music publishing. Another Leipzig firm was Georg Joachim Göschen (1752–1828), whose most prominent authors were Schiller, Goethe, and Wieland. His Wieland edition, printed in roman instead of 'monkish' *Fraktur, failed to be the pioneering success it might have been because other printing houses considered it too expensive to re-equip themselves with roman types, and the public was too inured to reading German in Fraktur to want to change. *Unger at Berlin, who published Goethe, Schiller, and also the early Romantics—including August Wilhelm Schlegel's translations of Shakespeare—was likewise interested in typography. He helped promote Firmin *Didot's roman letter in Germany but, faced with continuing opposition to roman, he devised a lighter gothic type, the 'Unger-Fraktur', intended to assist foreign readers unfamiliar with the traditional Fraktur then still generally in use; Unger's type extended the life of Fraktur in Germany.

The growth of the reading public in the 18th century led to reorganization of the book trade. Whereas previously the publisher-bookseller had dominated, with trade being conducted on an exchange basis largely through the book fairs, from the mid-18th century publishing and bookselling evolved into separate activities. The advantage of the exchange system, with printer-publishers and booksellers trading books primarily according to the quantity of paper involved, had been that it obviated the need to hold considerable capital in the form of cash; moreover, it facilitated trade between the various territories in the empire (with their different currencies) as well as the international trade in Latin books. The disadvantages were that many booksellers found themselves sitting on a wide-ranging, unspecialized collection of sometimes quite unsaleable books, without adequate liquid capital to finance new ventures or pay authors who increasingly wanted to be paid in money, not in books.

The lack of an effective central government in Germany meant that publishing was still carried on under exclusive regulations in each individual state. This perhaps worked well enough while the book market was relatively small, but became problematic as it expanded. The most urgent needs were for a general system of copyright and for measures to prevent the production of cheap, shoddily printed unauthorized editions in other territories. Such piracy was not only widely tolerated but, in some states, even encouraged. The demise of the Frankfurt fair and the inconvenience of the long journey to Leipzig meant that piracy particularly flourished in many south German towns, printers there seeing this as a legitimate response to the monopolies and higher prices of Leipzig publishers. The pirate publishers—who paid no authors' fees, printed only successful works, and often used the cheapest paper—contributed in no small measure to making books cheaper and thereby encouraging reading. One of the worst offenders was *Trattner in Vienna, who was abetted even by the imperial court; he employed fifteen presses in a large-scale operation to produce cheap reprints. His leading opponent was Philipp Erasmus Reich in Leipzig, who in 1764 attempted to form a protective organization and found support in most of the large towns in northern Germany, as well as in Nuremberg and Ulm. Leipzig publishers abandoned the old exchange system and began to insist that booksellers pay in cash and maintain no right to return unsold books. While this had some positive effects—publishers flush with cash were now able to contemplate new projects and authors could expect larger fees—it also meant that readers faced higher prices for books. In 1773 the sale of unauthorized editions at Leipzig was prohibited, but the pirates resorted to selling their wares through travelling salesmen who visited localities where books had previously been a rarity. In the absence of central government, there was little authors or publishers could do to remedy the situation. Even after the end of the Holy Roman Empire in 1806, little changed: in 1815 the kingdoms of Württemberg and Bavaria both expressly permitted the reprinting of 'foreign' books, that is, those published beyond their own narrow confines. It was not until well into the 19th century that general protection could be guaranteed. The first work granted full copyright protection, recognized throughout Germany, was *Cotta's Goethe edition (1827–30).

One manifestation of the 18th-century Enlightenment was a tremendous growth in the publishing of *encyclopaedias and reference works and an explosion in the publication of journals and almanacs. The first major German encyclopaedia was *Zedler's 68-volume *Grosses vollständiges Universal-Lexicon aller Wissenschaften und Künste* (Halle and Leipzig, 1732–54). It was innovative in two respects: it was the first such work written by a team of editors, each responsible for a particular field of knowledge, and it included biographies of living persons. The first German periodical, the *Acta Eruditorum*, launched at Leipzig in 1682, was a scholarly journal in the mould of the *Philosophical Transactions* of the Royal Society of London; but Christian Thomasius's *Monatsgespräche*, published from 1688, marked the beginning of a new age with articles on a wide range of topics and reviews of new publications, presented to a broader public in German. By the mid-18th century, hundreds of similar weeklies and monthlies were appearing, mostly in university towns like Halle, Leipzig, and Jena, but also in Frankfurt, Berlin, and Hamburg, addressing themselves not to a scholarly public but to the bourgeoisie, and aiming to instruct in a pleasant and entertaining way. The earlier part of the century also saw the launch of imitations of English moral weeklies: *Der Vernünfftler* (1713), *Der Patriot* (1724), and others were modelled on Addison and Steele's *Tatler* (founded 1709) and *Spectator* (1711). Then came more specifically literary journals such as *Nicolai's *Allgemeine deutsche Bibliothek* (1765–1806) and Christoph Martin Wieland's *Teutscher Merkur* (1773–1810), emulating the *Mercure de France*. Others fostered interest in foreign literature, such as Johann Joachim Eschenburg's *Brittisches Museum für die Deutschen* (1777–80). Noteworthy, too, are some early journals for women readers, including Johann Georg Jacobi's *Iris* (1774–6), Christian Gottfried Schütz's *Akademie der Grazien* (1774–80), and many others, most of them short-lived. By publishing texts

and reviews, these journals encouraged a love of literature and sharpened readers' critical faculties.

Altogether 2,191 journals of all kinds began publication between 1766 and 1790—three times as many as in the previous 25 years. The resonance they found may be gauged from the lively debate engendered by Moses Mendelssohn's and Immanuel Kant's discussion of the question 'What is Enlightenment?' in the *Berlinische Monatsschrift* in 1784. Particularly influential was the *Allgemeine Literatur-Zeitung*, published six times a week by Bertuch in Jena, which reviewed the latest German and foreign books. Bertuch also published the *Journal des Luxus und der Mode*—one of the earliest illustrated magazines—which remains a valuable source of information about men's and women's fashions and the domestic scene around 1800. Another of Bertuch's ventures was *London und Paris*, published until 1815, which informed readers about the social scene in the British and French metropolises. While *London und Paris* merely reported on the French political scene following the Revolution, other journals—such as J. F. Unger's *Deutschland*, with its pronounced republican sympathies, and the conservative *Wiener Zeitschrift*—more actively espoused politics of various hues. By contrast, with *Die Horen* Friedrich Schiller strove 'to unite the politically fragmented world under the flag of truth and beauty'. It called forth a wave of new literary journals, which, though generally short-lived, testified to the vitality of the Romantic Age. The most important of these was *Athenaeum* (1798–1800), edited by Friedrich and A. W. Schlegel.

Almanacs, catering for almost every profession, interest, or taste, were a special feature of 18th-century German publishing. Examples include the *Gothaischer Hofkalender* or *Almanach de Gotha*, first published in 1763, and Schiller's *Historisches Kalender für Damen*, published by Göschen (1790–94). They contained contributions by leading writers and poets and were often illustrated by well-known artists such as *Chodowiecki.

Germany had always been well supplied with libraries, but access was generally privileged. Many religious houses held significant collections, often splendidly housed (as at Ottobeuren, Kremsmünster, Melk, Einsiedeln, St Gall, Schussenried, and Admont). The 17th century had been the age of the great private and court libraries, among them those of the Elector Palatine at Heidelberg, Duke August of Braunschweig-Lüneburg (1579–1666) at *Wolfenbüttel, the imperial court library at Vienna (founded 1493, now the *Austrian National Library), and the Royal Library at *Berlin (founded 1661). Several towns had old-established Ratsbibliotheken, municipal libraries intended for the use of city councillors and other worthies. Such collections had existed since the late 14th century in Nuremberg and Regensburg, while Lüneburg, Braunschweig, Hanover, Leipzig, Lübeck, Hamburg, and Frankfurt followed in the 15th, with others founded in the 16th, often as a direct consequence of Luther's encouragement of town councils to enhance library provision. A few libraries actually called themselves 'public', but they were generally poorly stocked and had extremely restricted opening hours—the one in Bremen was accessible only fortnightly on Wednesdays, for example. Even university libraries were hardly user-friendly: those at Leipzig and Halle were open for only four hours a week, and it was considered a real novelty when Göttingen, on its foundation in 1734, opened its library every day to staff and students and allowed them to borrow books—from the outset, this library was conceived as a research facility. As the reading habit grew, so too did demand for access to books. This resulted in the establishment of lending libraries and 'reading societies', which in turn stimulated the demand for more books. A lending library open to all-comers had been founded in Berlin as early as 1704, but only somewhat later did these proliferate: Braunschweig had one in 1767, Hanau 1774, Munich 1774, Schwäbisch Hall 1784, Giessen 1785, Stuttgart 1791, Bamberg 1795, and Breslau 1800, for instance. One enterprising Leipzig book dealer, Sommer, sold bargain-priced 'starter collections' of up to 500 volumes to people wanting to establish libraries. Reading societies (*Lesegesellschaften*) were established in many towns: 13 by 1770, a further 50 by 1780, and about 370 more by 1800. The one at Stralsund, founded in 1779, specialized in lighter fare such as novels, plays, and poems, but others provided more generally for philosophy, theology, history, and geography. These societies aimed to give members—mostly the better-educated middle class—the opportunity to read as inexpensively as possible. Books and journals might be circulated among members or made available in a common reading room. Contemporary observers, critical of a perceived 'mania' for reading, advocated attempts to direct readers towards what was 'useful', with the aim of fostering good Christians, obedient subjects, and committed workers. A notably successful example of such 'improving' reading-matter, aimed at countryfolk, was Rudolf Zacharias Becker's *Noth- und Hülfsbüchlein für Bauersleute* (1788); by 1811 a million copies had been produced, many of

which had been foisted by territorial princes on their unsuspecting subjects. Other works were targeted at women, servants, children, and young people.

Great libraries have at all times been threatened with plunder and dispersal. The Palatine library at Heidelberg was removed to the *Vatican in 1623; Gustavus Adolphus took many books from Catholic libraries to Sweden at about the same time (*see* **26**). Napoleon is said to have looted 10,000 incunabula from libraries on the west bank of the Rhine; about 100 Jesuit libraries were closed in Germany alone in 1773. From 1783, 1,300 monastic libraries were confiscated, and hundreds more were secularized around 1803. Their MSS and incunabula substantially enriched court and university libraries—thus, what is now the Bavarian State Library (which holds the second largest collection of incunabula in the world) at *Munich became the largest German library in the 19th century. About this time, a number of smaller universities were also closed and their collections were amalgamated with other university libraries. Germany, being decentralized, still has no true national library; instead, it relies on a collaborative network of state and university libraries.

7 The 19th century

The 19th century saw decisive developments in book production. New inventions reduced production costs, and increasing literacy created further demands for books. The writing profession expanded considerably. As early as 1777, Georg Christoph Lichtenberg asserted, 'There are assuredly more writers in Germany than all four continents need for their wellbeing', and in 1785 it was claimed that 'the army of German writers' was 5,500 strong. By 1800, no fewer than 10,648 Germans were calling themselves writers, a figure that, by 1900, rose to 20,000 and included hundreds of women writers, 70 per cent of whom wrote under male pseudonyms. The number of bookshops grew from 300 to 5,000 during the century, and the annual output of titles increased from 3,906 in 1800 to 14,039 in 1843, and 24,792 in 1900. The number of periodicals and newspapers grew from under 1,000 around 1800 to 5,632 in 1902, with the real growth coming in the last third of the century. Music publishing increased by 250 per cent between 1871 and 1900. Growth was further fostered by improvements in communications (railways, telegraph, telephone) and the emergence of railway bookstalls, department stores, and mail order. Series for travellers began to appear in the 1850s (such as *Brockhaus's *Reisebibliothek für Eisenbahn und*

Schiffe, 1856–61) on the model of George *Routledge's *Railway Library (1848). The 19th century was the heyday of serial novels, marketed through itinerant booksellers. Late in the century, there were an estimated 45,000 men peddling books to 20 million readers throughout Germany and Austria. The 19th century also saw the foundation of the earliest book clubs, offering subscribers new books at advantageous prices. The earliest, apparently, was the Verein zur Verbreitung guter katholischer Bücher, founded in 1829. The Litterarischer Verein in Stuttgart, founded in 1839, specialized in scholarly editions of older literary works, many of which have still not been superseded. Later, 20th-century book clubs included the *Büchergilde Gutenberg and the *Deutsche Buchgemeinschaft, both founded in 1924. Among the newcomers after World War II were the Wissenschaftliche Buchgesellschaft with 140,000 members, originally designed to reissue standard works of scholarship that had become unobtainable since the war, and the Bertelsmann Club (with some 4.7 million members and 300 branches in Germany alone).

Among the inventions that led to cheap editions were wood-pulp paper—achieved as a practical process by Friedrich Gottlob Keller in 1843—and the *steam press, devised by Friedrich König. Steam-driven presses were first put to use by *The Times* in 1814 and employed for the printing of books by Brockhaus at Leipzig in 1826. Planographic *lithography, invented by *Senefelder in 1798, represented a major step forward in the reproduction of illustrations. The advantages such innovations conferred went hand in hand with improvements in the organization of the book trade, especially through the *Börsenverein des deutschen Buchhandels, established at Leipzig in 1825 and soon embracing publishers, wholesalers, and retailers of books throughout the German-speaking world. In 1887, the Börsenverein introduced a net price agreement, saving smaller booksellers from being undercut by unscrupulous profiteers. Though the German states lagged behind England and France in introducing *copyright laws, the grand duchy of Saxe-Weimar was the very first, in 1839, to incorporate the principle of a 30-year term of protection after the author's death. Copyright was confirmed throughout Germany in 1871 and internationally by the *Berne Convention in 1886.

An important issue in publishing during the first half of the 19th century was the struggle for freedom of the press. Political journalism expanded spectacularly during the century (200 titles in 1800; 1,012 in 1847; 1,300 in 1862; 2,427 in 1881; 3,405 in 1897; and 4,221

in 1914). Restrictions were somewhat less irksome in Saxony than in Metternich's Austria, but everywhere publishers fought courageous battles against censorship and police control. Concessions were made in 1848, but rescinded in 1851—the situation improving only in 1874, when censorship was finally abolished, though even then the writings of many social democrats were banned (2,592 items between 1878 and 1918).

One vigorous campaigner in the battle for freedom was the Leipzig publisher *Reclam, remembered today above all for *Reclams Universalbibliothek, a series he founded in 1867 (and still going strong) which brought to the masses the works of writers of all periods in good, cheap editions. Reclam had already had a remarkable success with an inexpensive twelve-volume edition of Shakespeare in 1858, reprinted six times within a year and followed by editions of 25 individual plays in 1865. The Universalbibliothek was inaugurated with Goethe's *Faust*, but the most popular title has proved to be Schiller's *Wilhelm Tell*, with well over 2 million copies sold. By 1892 the series comprised 3,000 titles. The texts were reliable but produced as economically as possible—Reclam was one of the first German publishers to use *stereotypes extensively. The paper-covered editions were available singly, and for half a century the price was kept at 20 pfennigs a copy, thus enabling even the most impecunious to gain access to great literature. In 1917 Reclam started selling titles through vending machines on 1,600 railway stations, in hospitals, and even on transatlantic liners. So immediately recognizable was Reclam's design that during the two world wars, *propaganda pamphlets made up to look like Reclams were disseminated among German front-line troops.

Other successful 19th-century Leipzig publishers included Karl Christoph Traugott Tauchnitz. Around 1816, he produced cheap editions of the Greek and Latin classics employing the stereotype process, which he was the first to use in Germany. In 1837, his nephew Christian Bernhard Tauchnitz established his own business, which became famous for its Collection of British and American Authors, founded in 1841: this eventually comprised some 5,400 titles. *Tauchnitz secured the goodwill of authors by voluntarily paying them a royalty and undertaking not to sell the books in Britain or its empire. Another Leipzig publisher was *Teubner, renowned for editions of the Greek and Latin classics, as well as mathematical books and other scholarly works. Teubner, like Cotta and others, sometimes co-published works with Black, Young, & Young of Tavistock Street, London. F. A. Brockhaus, who originally worked under Teubner, established his reputation with his *Conversationslexikon* (1812), which in its present form, *Brockhaus Enzyklopädie* (21e, 2005–6), is still the leading German encyclopaedia. The early success of the *Conversationslexikon* demonstrated the tremendous potential for sales among the middle classes. In 1984 Brockhaus amalgamated with Bibliographisches Institut, Mannheim, publisher of *Meyers Enzyklopädisches Lexikon* (9e, 1971–9), which originated in Meyer's *Großes Lexikon für die gebildeten Stände* (52 vols, 1839–55). Another well-known firm linked with Leipzig, though only after relocating there in 1872, was *Baedeker, publisher of the renowned series of travel guides; the firm began when in 1832 Karl Baedeker acquired the Koblenz publisher Friedrich Rähling and with it J. A. Klein's *Rheinreise von Mainz bis Köln* (1828).

The early 19th century saw the founding of three influential literary journals: *Zeitung für die elegante Welt* (1801–59), August von Kotzebue's *Der Freimüthige* (1803–56), and, most important of all, Cotta's *Morgenblatt für gebildete Stände* (1807–65). The huge growth in publishing is reflected in the need for reviews like the Heidelberg *Jahrbücher der Literatur* (1808–72) and the *Wiener Jahrbücher* (1818–49), while the more popular end of the market was catered for by J. J. Weber's enormously successful *Pfennig-Magazin* (1833–55), modelled on the English *Penny Magazine*. Another of Weber's ventures, launched in 1843, was the *Leipziger Illustrierte Zeitung*, modelled on the *Illustrated London News*. As censorship restrictions were relaxed, ever more periodicals and magazines came on to the market. The *Berliner Illustrierte Zeitung*, which started with an edition of 14,000 copies in the 1890s, had sales of more than a million copies by 1914. Then there were family magazines like *Die Gartenlaube* (from 1853) and *Westermanns illustrirte Monatshefte* (from 1856), both of them long-lived. The satirical journal *Simplicissimus* was founded in 1896. Although they were the forerunners of the magazines we know today, they were not scandal sheets, but were published to inform and educate a broader reading public.

8 The 20th century

Throughout the 19th century Leipzig publishers led the field in Germany, though the quality of their typography, paper, illustrations, and binding was often far from outstanding. The turn of the century, however, saw growing interest in book design based on the traditions of earlier periods. William *Morris's Arts and Crafts movement resonated in Germany, where like-minded people tried to link new artistic forms with an appreciation of materials and craftsmanship to create a harmonious combination of type, paper, illustration, and binding. Notable examples of this trend were the magazines *Pan* and *Jugend* (from which the term *Jugendstil* derives). A number of *private presses on the English model were founded, such as Carl Ernst Poeschel's and Walther Tiemann's Janus-Presse (1907); the *Bremer Presse (1911), influenced by *Cobden-Sanderson; and the *Cranach-Presse, established by Harry Graf Kessler who emulated the *Kelmscott and the *Doves presses. After about 1910, the decorative, flowing forms of *Jugendstil* increasingly contrasted with the hard, broken forms of Expressionism—among whose exponents as book illustrators were *Kokoschka, Max Beckmann, Ernst Barlach, and *Kubin. The growing number of design-conscious mainstream publishers included Anton Kippenberg of the *Insel-Verlag in Leipzig, Eugen Diederichs at Düsseldorf, and Hans von Weber, who founded his Hyperion-Verlag in Munich in 1906.

The momentous political events that overwhelmed Germany in the 20th century inevitably affected the book trade. In 1922–3 it was devastated by galloping inflation. Soon after Hitler's appointment as chancellor, one of the most notorious episodes took place when nationalistically minded students set fire to thousands of Jewish, socialist, and other 'un-German' books in various university towns on 10 May 1933. The works of Freud, Marx, Heinrich Mann, Kurt Tucholsky, and hundreds of others were ceremoniously burnt. These events presaged tighter control of the production and distribution of written material. Authors wanting to continue publishing were obliged to join the Reichsschrifttumkammer, established under the aegis of Goebbels's Reichsministerium für Volksaufklärung und Propaganda in September 1933. Publishers and booksellers were made to toe the line in the same way. Thus, in 1934 the Jewish firm of *Ullstein was 'Aryanized'. While a small number of Jewish publishers such as the *Schocken-Verlag were initially tolerated, from the end of 1938 all Jewish businesses were forbidden. Lists of prohibited books and authors were drawn up, but these were not divulged to the book trade, so that booksellers needed to be extremely circumspect in selecting their stock. The works of émigré authors such as Thomas Mann and 'decadent' writers such as Robert Musil and Joseph Roth were forbidden, and books were removed from libraries or placed under restrictions. Concomitant with such repressive measures were various initiatives to promote officially approved works—couples getting married were presented with Hitler's *Mein Kampf.*

World War II and the postwar division of Germany inevitably had enormous consequences for both library provision and the book trade. Many libraries were destroyed (15–20 million books were lost), though precautions had been taken to evacuate some major collections: the Prussian State Library's stock of 3 million books and 71,600 MSS was dispersed from Berlin to some 30 sites throughout the country. After the war, some material returned to the original building on Unter den Linden in East Berlin, while other parts of the collection formed the nucleus of a new library in West Berlin; much valuable material has still not yet returned from Cracow (Poland). Following the fall of the Berlin Wall in 1989, the two libraries were unified, administratively, though not physically. As for publishing, output—which had stood at 24,792 new titles in 1900, 34,871 in 1913, and 37,886 in 1927—fell to 20,120 in 1938 and 5,304 in 1944. Leipzig, the centre of the industry, was largely destroyed by bombing in December 1943: Reclam's stock was lost, and though their printing works survived unscathed, the equipment was taken by the Russians as war reparations in 1946. After the war, the Occupying Powers (Britain, France, USA, and the Soviet Union) initially forbade the production and dissemination of printed material, confiscated National Socialist and militaristic literature, and introduced censorship. Gradually, the Four Powers issued licences and German publishing burgeoned again, though developments varied somewhat in the different zones of occupation. The first licence for the publication of books in the British Sector of Berlin was granted on 3 October 1945 to Walter *de Gruyter Verlag, whose roots go back to 1749. In the German Democratic Republic (GDR), the former Soviet Zone of Occupation, almost all publishing firms passed into state control. Thus, long-established firms like Breitkopf & Härtel, Brockhaus, Insel, and Reclam at Leipzig, and Niemeyer at Halle, were taken into state ownership as *Volkseigene Betriebe* (VEB), while the same firms re-established themselves as private companies in the West—Breitkopf & Härtel at Kassel, Brockhaus at Wiesbaden, Insel at Frankfurt, Reclam at Stuttgart, and Niemeyer at Tübingen. The West German publishing industry recovered so quickly that the expectations of Swiss publishers that they would be able to step into the breach were scarcely realized (*see* **25**). West German output increased from 14,094 titles in 1951, to 42,957 in 1971, and 63,679 in 1986. In the GDR, production

grew from 1,998 in 1949 to 6,471 in 1985, and publishing was affected by tense power struggles between authors, publishers, the political leadership, and the State Security Service (the 'Stasi'). Since the reunification of Germany, considerable reorganization of the publishing industry has taken place. In 2004, German publishers issued 86,543 titles in 963 million copies. Recent years have seen increasing tendencies towards globalization, in which German publishing houses such as *Bertelsmann and *Springer play major roles. Bertelsmann, which today operates in 63 countries and has 95,000 employees, with a turnover of 17.9 billion euros in 2005, was founded as a small publisher of bibles and religious literature at Gütersloh in 1835. After 1850 it broadened its range, and during World War II it became a leading supplier of reading matter to soldiers at the front. Its premises were destroyed in 1945, but in 1946 it began afresh, receiving a licence to publish from the British Military Government. It launched its book club in 1950, moved into gramophone records in 1958, collaborated with AOL to promote multimedia in 1995, acquired the New York publisher *Random House (which includes such well-known names as *Chatto & Windus, *Bodley Head, Jonathan *Cape, and *Virago) in 1998, and entered into partnership with Sony Corporation to produce music and videos in 2004. Similarly, Springer-Verlag, which was part of the Bertelsmann empire from 1999 to 2003, began in 1842 as a Berlin bookshop founded by Julius Springer, who published a few political and general magazines. Today Springer, based at Heidelberg, is a world leader in the fields of science, medicine, economics, engineering, architecture, construction, and transport.

One of the most obvious changes in the appearance of German books since the middle of the 20th century, the abandoning of Fraktur, is a legacy of National Socialism. German texts had customarily been printed in gothic types since the 16th century, partly rejecting foreign (especially Italian) influence, partly from national pride, and partly from Lutheran rejection of Roman Catholicism. In 1794 the Berlin publisher Nicolai described gothic type as a truly national script that would encourage a wider national ethos. When the Brothers Grimm began publishing their *Deutsches Wörterbuch* in roman type in 1852, some critics were fiercely hostile. After the creation of the Reich in 1871, support grew for Fraktur as a truly German script—Bismarck claimed he would refuse to read a German book that was not printed in gothic type, for 'a German word in Latin letters is as alien as a Greek word in German letters'—and the Reichstag was petitioned on the matter, though in 1911 it decided not to proceed. But the continuing preference for gothic typefaces deterred foreign readers—even conservative Sweden had increasingly adopted roman, largely under the influence of Carolus Linnaeus (1707–78), who induced the government to abolish customs duty on Dutch roman type. For scholars and scientists hoping to reach an international readership, Fraktur was an obstacle, so books intended for such an audience were often printed in roman. Yet domestic readers preferred Fraktur as being more legible and easier on the eyes. In the 1930s, the National Socialists were inclined to enforce its use as an expression of the Nordic soul— only with difficulty were they persuaded by the ministry of transport that it would be unsafe to use Fraktur for road signs at the time of the Berlin Olympic Games in 1936. However, the matter was settled once and for all when on 3 January 1941 Hitler declared gothic type to be a Jewish invention and ordered that henceforth roman should be the norm. 'A century from now,' he said, 'our language will be *the* European language. Countries to the east, north, and west of us will learn our language in order to be able to communicate with us. The prerequisite of this is the replacement of so-called gothic script by the script previously known as Latin script and which we now call normal script.' Thereafter, editions of *Mein Kampf* and of the party newspaper, *Völkischer Beobachter*, were duly printed in roman, and very soon this ousted Fraktur almost entirely except for ornamental purposes. The last major newspaper to adopt roman was the *Neue Zürcher Zeitung*, in 1946.

A recent development that initially occasioned great controversy and even led to lawsuits before the Federal Constitutional Court at Karlsruhe, but which ultimately has had little effect on the appearance of books, was the spelling reform ratified by the governments of Germany, Austria, and Switzerland in 1996, introduced in 1998 and, in theory, finally implemented in 2005.

BIBLIOGRAPHY

N. Bachleitner *et al.*, *Geschichte des Buchhandels in Öster-reich* (2000)

J.-P. Barbian, *Literaturpolitik im 'Dritten Reich'* (1995)

F. Barbier, *L'Empire du livre* (1995)

B. Bischoff *et al.*, eds., *Das älteste deutsche Buch* (1977)

S. Corsten, ed., *Lexikon des gesamten Buchwesens*, 2e (1987)

O. Dann, *Lesegesellschaften und bürgerliche Emanzipation* (1981)

M. U. Edwards, *Printing, Propaganda, and Martin Luther* (1994)

R. Engelsing, *Analphabetentum und Lektüre* (1973)

J. Eyssen, *Buchkunst in Deutschland vom Jugendstil zum Malerbuch* (1980)

S. Fitos, *Zensur als Mißerfolg* (2000)

H. Flachmann, *Martin Luther und das Buch* (1996)

J. L. Flood and W. A. Kelly, eds., *The German Book, 1450–1750* (1995)

M. Giesecke, *Der Buchdruck in der frühen Neuzeit* (1991)

[Gutenberg-Gesellschaft and Gutenberg-Museum,] *Block-bücher des Mittelalters* (1991)

J. Ing, *Johann Gutenberg and his Bible* (1987)

G. Jäger, *Geschichte des deutschen Buchhandels im 19. und 20. Jahrhundert*, pts. 1 and 2, *Das Kaiserreich 1871–1918* (2001–3)

F. Kapp and J. Goldfriedrich, *Geschichte des deutschen Buchhandels* (4 vols, 1886–1913; repr. 1970)

A. Kapr, *Johann Gutenberg*, tr. D. Martin (1996)

H.-J. Künast, 'Getruckt zu Augspurg': Buchdruck und Buchhandel in Augsburg zwischen 1468 und 1555 (1997)

H. Kunze, *Geschichte der Buchillustration in Deutschland: Das 15. Jahrhundert* (1975); *Das 16. und 17. Jahrhundert* (1993)

J. Lehnacker, *Die Bremer Presse* (1964)

A. Martino, *Die deutsche Leihbibliothek* (1990)

B. Müller, ed., *Zensur im modernen deutschen Kulturraum* (2003)

U. Neddermeyer, *Von der Handschrift zum gedruckten Buch* (1998)

F. Ritter, *Histoire de l'imprimerie alsacienne au XVe et XVIe siècles* (1955)

H. Sarkowski, *Springer-Verlag: History of a Scientific Publishing House* (1977)

G. K. Schauer, *Deutsche Buchkunst 1890 bis 1960* (1963)

R. Schenda, *Volk ohne Buch* (1977)

W. Schmitz, *Deutsche Bibliotheksgeschichte* (1984)

R. W. Scribner, *For the Sake of Simple Folk: Popular Propaganda for the German Reformation* (1981)

P. Stein, *Schriftkultur* (2006)

T. Verweyen, *Bücherverbrennungen* (2000)

A. Ward, *Book Production, Fiction, and the German Reading Public 1740–1800* (1974)

L. Winckler, *Autor—Markt—Publikum* (1986)

R. Wittmann, *Geschichte des deutschen Buchhandels*, 2e (1999)

25 The History of the Book in Switzerland

LUKAS ERNE

1 The Middle Ages

Medieval book production in Switzerland chiefly took place in monastic scriptoria. The *St Gall Abbey Library, the country's oldest library, preserves a unique collection of books from the Carolingian period, many of exceptional beauty, with important *miniatures and bindings. The abbey is known to have had a *scriptorium as early as the 8th century, and the first known scribe, Winithar, was active in the years 761–75. From the 10th to the 12th centuries, newly founded monasteries (including the Benedictine houses at Einsiedeln, Engelberg, and Muri) acquired and produced significant collections of theological literature. In the 13th and 14th centuries, Zurich saw the production of splendidly illustrated MSS in German, made for the aristocracy or rich citizens, most notably the *Manesse Codex. Apart from medieval books produced in Switzerland, a few modern libraries house collections consisting chiefly of MSS produced elsewhere. For instance, the Bongarsiana collection, in the Burgerbibliothek in Berne, comprises an important collection of medieval *codices, the St Gall Abbey Library houses significant illustrated Irish MSS from the 8th century, and the Bibliotheca *Bodmeriana in Cologny near Geneva, founded by *Bodmer, contains a number of outstanding works, including the earliest dated MS (1308) of Guillaume de Lorris and Jean de Meun's *Roman de la Rose*.

2 The early modern period

Situated on the borders of Germany and France, on the banks of the Rhine, Basle was ideally placed to become one of Europe's early centres of book production. The Council of Basle (1431–49) brought about important traffic in books from abroad, and the foundation of the country's oldest university (and

university library) in 1460 testified to the city's intellectual life. Berthold Ruppel, who had worked with *Gutenberg in Mainz, introduced the printing trade to Basle in the 1460s; it rose to considerable significance by the 1480s, with more than 70 printers at work by the turn of the century. Among the important *incunables produced in the city was Sebastian Brant's *Narrenschiff* (Ship of Fools, 1494), printed by Johann Bergmann von Olpe, easily the most popular book in German before the Reformation.

Around 1500, humanism and the Basle book trade enjoyed a fruitful relationship which resulted in important works of biblical philology, the Church Fathers, Greek and Latin classics, and neo-Latin literature. Many of these books were of the highest typographic quality, some of them illustrated by leading artists of the time, among them *Holbein the younger. Important printers active in Basle at the time include *Amerbach, *Petri, and J. *Froben, who collaborated on major printing projects up to 1511. Froben's printing house, in which a Latin bible was produced as early as 1491, became a centre of humanist book production (with books printed in Latin and Greek, as well as Hebrew) to which (among others) the humanist scholar *Rhenanus contributed. Froben's close ties to *Erasmus, who lived in Basle in 1514–15 and from 1518 to 1529, led to the publication of almost half of Erasmus's first editions by Froben. The Basle book trade, with its solid network of agents abroad, was also of importance for the rapid spread of *Luther's ideas: as early as 1518, Froben published a Latin edition of his works, followed by a second edition the following year, while Petri published Luther's *Septembertestament* in December 1522, just three months after its original publication.

Although Basle was the earliest and most important centre of book production, the first dated printed book in Switzerland, Johannes Marchesinus's

Mammotrectus super Bibliam of 1470, names not Basle but Beromünster as the place of printing. Other dated incunabula were produced in Burgdorf (1475), Zurich (1479–82), Rougemont (1481), Promenthoux (1482), Lausanne (1493), and Sursee (1499–1500), but since these books were the work of itinerant printers, the locations tell us little about the significance of these places for the early book trade. The place that did become another early centre of book production before the end of the 15th century was Geneva, where printing started in 1478, with the *Livre des saints anges*, printed by Adam Steinschaber (a rare copy of which belongs to the *British Library's strong collection of incunables printed in Geneva). Louis Cruse (from 1479), Jean Belot (from 1497), and Wigand Köln (from 1521) were the chief Geneva printers in the following decades; but the Geneva book trade would no doubt have remained in the shadow of that of Lyons if it had not been for the Reformation. Called to Geneva by Guillaume Farel, Jean Girard (from 1536; d. 1558) became the chief printer of the works of Calvin. As the Protestant Rome, Geneva saw the publication of many important works of reformed religion, particularly bibles and *psalters, although the first French Protestant translation of the Bible (1535), by Pierre-Robert Olivétan, was printed in Serrières (now part of Neuchâtel), by Pierre de Vingle. This translation was revised under the influence of Calvin, leading to the publication of the important versions of 1560 and 1588, both printed in Geneva. An Italian translation of the Bible was also printed in Geneva, in 1555, as was, in 1560, the famous English Geneva Bible as well as the first translation of the New Testament into Romansh, the fourth national language, by Jachiam Bifrun. In the 1550s a number of significant French printers escaped from religious persecution by going to Geneva, including *Crespin, Conrad Badius, and the *Estienne family, Robert and his eldest son, the great scholar-printer Henri *Estienne (whose five-volume *Thesaurus Graecae Linguae* was published at Geneva in 1572–3), establishing work of unprecedented quantity and quality in the Geneva book trade.

Owing to the Reformation, Zurich became the third centre of book production in Switzerland from the 1520s. Hans Hager printed a number of works by Ulrich Zwingli as well as an early edition of Luther's translation of the New Testament. *Froschauer, who published most of Zwingli's writings, printed superb books, including the so-called Froschauerbibel (1524–9), the first Swiss *folio Bible, and the Zürcher Bibel (1531). Froschauer was also long believed to be the printer of the Coverdale Bible (1535), although current scholarly opinion calls this into question. Along with humanism, the Reformation was thus the chief motor of the Swiss book trade in the early modern period. Literacy among the population remained low, however, and the proportion of people reading regularly was probably no higher than 2 per cent before and 4 per cent after the Reformation. Publishers therefore did not primarily aim at local sales, and the *book fairs in *Frankfurt, *Leipzig, Paris, and Lyons remained of great importance for the dissemination of books produced in Switzerland. This may also explain why throughout the 16th and 17th centuries books printed in Switzerland—contrary to other European countries—mostly continued to appear in Latin rather than in the vernacular.

3 The 17th and 18th centuries

In the 16th century, the Catholic parts of Switzerland produced less than 1 per cent of the country's total output, and in Fribourg printing even remained prohibited until 1584. In the 17th century, however, the Counter-Reformation led to sustained book production in Catholic parts of the country, in particular in Einsiedeln, Lucerne, and St Gall. In Einsiedeln Monastery a *printing office was founded in 1664, in which massive, multi-volume works of theology and history were printed. At the same time, the Thirty Years War (1618–48) and its consequences hampered the development of the book trade, until the following century when Enlightenment doctrines led to a significant increase in the demand for secular literature. From early on, the book trade in Switzerland had been catering for an international market, but this proved particularly true in the latter half of the 18th century, when Swiss-French publishers in Geneva, Lausanne, Neuchâtel, and Yverdon flooded the international market with *piracies of recently published literary and philosophical works, notably the *Encyclopédie* (1751–72), but also political and anti-clerical tracts, as well as erotica and *pornographic literature. Of particular importance was the *Société Typographique de Neuchâtel, founded in 1769, whose archives have survived largely intact and constitute an invaluable source of information about the book trade and intellectual life of the 18th century, as demonstrated, most notably, in *Darnton's *The Business of Enlightenment*.

4 From the 19th century to today

In the course of the 19th century, reading spread thanks to newly founded lending libraries, reading groups, and book societies. For instance, the *Geneva Société de lecture was founded in 1818 and acquired as many as 30,000 books within the first twenty years of its existence. In the course of the 20th century, book production in Switzerland increased from about 1,000 titles to almost 14,000 per year. Just over four-fifths of the books published at the end of the 20th century appeared in one of the national languages: 59 per cent in German, 18 per cent in French, 3 per cent in Italian, and 0.6 per cent in Rhaeto-Romanic, much of the rest being published in English. Yet these account for only about 30 per cent of the books on sale in Switzerland, with roughly 70 per cent being of foreign origins. Among Swiss publishing houses established in the 20th century are *Slatkine and *Droz, both based in Geneva, founded in 1918 and 1924, respectively. In the mid-20th century, Switzerland became a centre for high-quality colour book production thanks to publishers such as C. J. Bucher, Conzett & Huber, and *Skira.

With regards to book preservation, a number of public or private libraries today house important collections, notably the chief university libraries, the Public Library of the University of *Basel, the City and University Library of *Berne, the Cantonal and University Library of Fribourg, the Library of *Geneva, the Public and Cantonal Library of *Lausanne, the Public and University Library of *Neuchâtel, and the *Zurich Central Library. The Swiss National Library in *Berne, founded in 1895, collects all publications relating to Switzerland and also houses the Swiss Literary Archives, created in 1989, following the Swiss writer Friedrich Dürrenmatt's donation of his MSS to the Confederation. The Swiss Federal Archives, which build on the archives of the Helvetian Republic founded in 1798, have similarly been housed in Berne since the early 19th century. Several museums display aspects of the history of the book, including the *Basler Papiermühle, the Swiss Gutenberg Museum of Fribourg, founded in 2000, and the new museum of the Bibliotheca Bodmeriana, inaugurated in 2003. *See also* A. FRUTIGER; ORELL, GESSNER, & CO.; SCHWEIZERISCHE BIBLIOPHILENGESELLSCHAFT.

BIBLIOGRAPHY
J. Benzing, *Die Buchdrucker des 16. und 17. Jahrhunderts im deutschen Sprachgebiet*, 2e (1982)
D. Bertholet, *Suisse Romande terre du livre* (2006)
P. G. Bietenholz, *Basle and France in the Sixteenth Century* (1971)
A. Bruckner, *Scriptoria Medii Aevi Helvetica* (14 vols, 1935–78)
E. Büchler, *Die Anfänge des Buchdrucks in der Schweiz*, 2e (1951)
T. Bürger, *Aufklärung in Zürich* (1997)
P. Chaix, *Recherche sur l'imprimerie à Genève* (1954)
R. Darnton, *The Business of Enlightenment* (1979)
— and M. Schlup, eds., *Le Rayonnement d'une maison d'edition dans l'Europe des Lumières* (2005)
R. Diederichs *et al.*, eds., *Buchbranche im Wandel* (1999)
J.-F. Gilmont, *La Réforme et le livre* (1990)
P. L. van der Haegen, *Der frühe Basler Buchdruck* (2001)
U. Joerg and D. M. Hoffmann, eds., *La Bible en Suisse* (1997)
P. Ladner, ed., *Iter Helveticum* (5 vols, 1976–90)
E. C. Rudolphi, *Die Buchdrucker Familie Froschauer in Zürich, 1521-1595* (1963)
P. F. Tschudin, *Handwerk, Handel, Humanismus* (1984)
B. Weber, ed., *Cinq siècles d'imprimerie à Genève* (1978)
M. E. Welti, *Der Basler Buchdruck und Britannien* (1964)

26 The History of the Book in the Nordic Countries

CHARLOTTE APPEL AND KAREN SKOVGAARD-PETERSEN

1 Introduction

When surveying the history of the book in the Nordic countries, a balance needs to be struck between the region as a whole and its individual countries (Sweden, Denmark, Finland, Norway, Iceland, Greenland, and the Faroe Islands). Among the most important unifying factors is language. Swedish, Danish, and Norwegian are closely related and still mutually intelligible, whereas Icelandic and Faroese have stayed closer to Old Norse. Finnish belongs to a different language group (Finno-Ugric), as do the Sami languages, spoken in the north of the Scandinavian peninsula. Greenlandic is an Inuit language. Many people in the outer regions have also been able to communicate in Swedish, Norwegian, or Danish.

The present survey, emphasizing the relationship between book and society, cannot do justice to the region's richness and variousness. Even though societal developments have often been similar or directly shared, different geographical and natural conditions have created diversity across the extensive region and its populations. These numbered in total 24 million people in 2000, compared to 2 million around 1600. Moreover, international orientations have varied (from Finland in the east to the Atlantic Islands in the west), and borders and political alliances have often changed.

2 The Middle Ages

The great majority of medieval books once found in the Nordic countries have disappeared completely. Some were worn out, and some vanished after the Reformation because of general neglect and contempt. Others were lost in fires, notably in Copenhagen (1728) and Åbo/Turku (1827). Among those that have been preserved are a number of invaluable Icelandic *codices. Furthermore, numerous fragments have survived as binding material (e.g. c.10,000 leaves or sheets representing c.1,500 books from Finland), adding considerably to what is known about Nordic medieval book culture.

With the missions and the establishment of churches in the 10th–12th centuries, Scandinavia became part of Christian European culture, being introduced to *parchment books and to the Latin language and alphabet. Reading and writing were not entirely new phenomena. Runes (see 3) had been used for inscriptions on metal, stone, and wood since around AD 200. After the Latin alphabet was introduced, runes remained in use for short inscriptions; in some areas, as indicated by outstanding finds from Bergen, west Norway (c.1100–1400), they may even have become more common for everyday purposes.

The earliest Nordic book production can be traced to Lund, a Danish episcopal seat from c.1060 and a Scandinavian archdiocese from 1104. Monarchs worked closely with church leaders, and Lund was an important centre of both learning and politics in the 12th century, particularly while Absalon was archbishop (1177–1201). He commissioned the writing of *Saxo Grammaticus' *Gesta Danorum*. The Norwegian archbishopric of Nidaros (Trondheim), founded 1153, occupied a similar position. Here the legend of St Olav, Norway's royal saint, was given its written form, an Olav liturgy established, and national historical writing cultivated. By contrast, the establishment of the Swedish archdiocese in Uppsala (1164) did not result in a national historiography, probably owing to the Swedish monarchy's weaker position.

In the 12th and 13th centuries, collections of books were established in connection with churches, particularly cathedrals and monasteries. These were

Latin libraries, containing liturgical books, bibles, collections of sermons, schoolbooks, and, to a lesser degree, classical authors and books on secular subjects such as medicine. Book production took place in the *scriptoria of larger ecclesiastical institutions, although in Iceland there was considerable involvement by lay landowners. Among local ecclesiastical productions were books about the lives and miracles of local saints, annals, and registers of donations.

European influence was also evident in the field of law. Legal books in Latin were imported, providing additional inspiration for the composition of provincial laws in the vernacular. As early as 1117/18, Icelandic laws were recorded in writing. Many vernacular laws from the 12th and 13th centuries bear witness to strong royal powers in mainland Scandinavia; in 1274 King Magnus Lagabøtir ('Law-amender') promulgated a legal revision that provided a uniform law for the whole of Norway.

In Iceland and Norway, the vernacular was central, even within ecclesiastical administration. Here, an extraordinary narrative literature in Old Norse emerged during the 13th and 14th centuries. Hundreds of sagas were recorded in writing, some of them based on oral traditions known in other Scandinavian areas as well. The Icelanders' sagas, e.g. *Njál's Saga*, and *Snorri Sturluson's *Heimskringla*, are justifiably famous. The *Edda* poems are important sources of Nordic mythology. An outstanding treatise is the *King's Mirror*, written in Norway *c.*1250. As early as *c.*1150, the establishment of a written standard of Old Norse was discussed theoretically in the so-called *First Grammatical Treatise*.

In Sweden and Denmark, book culture was primarily a Latin phenomenon until the 14th century, when the vernacular, including Low German, became more common in law books and legal documents, medical manuals, and devotional books. Continental *romances were translated at noble courts. Particularly in towns, the need for reading, writing, and accounting increased, as did the number of schools, scriptoria, and administrative *archives. The introduction of paper *c.*1350 contributed further to more widespread and informal use of writing (private letters, copies of documents) (*see* **10**). Books and documents of particular importance, however, were still written on locally produced parchment.

Around 1500, the majority of books proper were presumably liturgical and devotional volumes in Latin. The richest library was the Swedish monastery of Vadstena, which housed the Order of the Most Holy Saviour, instituted by St *Birgitta. The library comprised *c.*1,400 books, of which *c.*500 are still extant (in *Uppsala and Stockholm).

In order to obtain a university education, increasing numbers of young Scandinavians went abroad. Only in 1425 did it become possible to obtain a bachelor's degree at Lund; the first—and for centuries the only—Scandinavian universities opened in Uppsala (1477) and Copenhagen (1479).

3 1500–1800

During the early modern period, Nordic countries were divided politically in two. The kingdom of Sweden also comprised Finland, while the Danish-Norwegian king ruled Denmark, Norway, Iceland, the Faroe Islands, and Greenland, as well as the mainly German-speaking duchies of Schleswig and Holstein. Post-Reformation Nordic book history is well documented thanks to comprehensive national bibliographies. The first books were printed in Denmark in 1482 and Sweden in 1483 by the German Johann Snell, following invitations from the bishops of Odense and Uppsala. Imported printed books had been on the scene earlier, however. The Dutchman Gotfred of *Ghemen settled briefly in Copenhagen, but otherwise most early 16th-century printers were itinerant Germans. Throughout the early modern period, many craftsmen and tradesmen emigrated from or were trained in Germany. German trends and techniques were followed closely: *black letter was used for vernacular texts, whereas *gotico-antiqua *roman type became the standard for books in Latin; likewise, bookbindings displayed German influence in the use of decorative *roll tools, many of them imported.

After the Lutheran Reformation, the Swedish and Danish kings sought to control imported and domestic publications. A royal printing press, Kungliga Tryckeriet, was founded in Stockholm (1526), establishing an effective monopoly for almost a century. In Denmark, two or three presses were active simultaneously (*see* BENEDICHT), but with a few exceptions (*see* BRAHE), they were situated within the city walls of Copenhagen, effectively tied to the government through *privileges and commissions. In both countries, the Crown ordered and financed important publications, including the first full bibles in the vernacular (Sweden, 1540–41; Denmark, 1550) and national *hymnals. Privileges were also given for the printing of homilies, *prayer books, and other literature regarded as useful or edifying by the authorities.

The first book produced for Finland was the *Missale Aboense* (1488), printed by Bartholomaeus Ghotan in

Lübeck; during the 16th century, almost all books for Finnish use were printed in Stockholm. Of special importance was *Agricola, who translated the New Testament (1548) and composed several religious books in Finnish.

In Iceland, the Catholic bishop invited a Swedish printer c.1530 to Hólar; after the Reformation (1550), *Hólaprent remained the only Icelandic printing press. Many bishops were involved in the production of vernacular religious books. In the late 17th century, the press was moved to the other episcopal see, Skálholt (where Icelandic sagas were also printed), but later returned to Hólar. Much literature continued to be copied and read in MS. Danish was the language of the administration, and many Icelanders read books in Danish.

Copenhagen had three printers c.1600, ten c.1700, and twenty c.1800. A few provincial presses (Elsinore, Sorø, Aarhus, and Odense) operated for short periods, but provincial *printing offices were not established on a more permanent basis until the 1730s, when they often centred on a local newspaper. In 1643, Tyge Nielsen came to Christiania (Oslo) as Norway's first printer. This was the only Norwegian town with a permanent printing office until printing began in Bergen (1721), followed by Trondheim (1739); many authors on the west coast continued to use Copenhagen presses. The Danish and Norwegian book markets formed a whole, not least because Danish was used as the written language in both countries.

Sweden had one (royal) printing house in 1600, but seventeen in 1700, six of them in Stockholm. Other towns with presses were Uppsala (from 1618), Västerås, Strängnäs, Kalmar, Linköping, and Gothenburg. In 1642, the first complete bible in Finnish was printed in Stockholm; in the same year a press was established at the new Finnish Academy in Åbo. Another two presses were founded later in the 17th century, in Åbo (see GEZELIUS) and Viborg.

The increasing number of printers weakened direct royal control, but governmental and ecclesiastical influences remained strong due to official privileges and *censorship regulations. Everyday censorship was fairly lax, but enforced vehemently as soon as suspicions arose. Apart from confessionally dubious books, most attention was directed at criticism of the king (in Denmark particularly after the introduction of absolutism in 1660–61) and at the new medium of the regularly published *newspaper, in Denmark from 1634 and in Sweden from 1645.

The Danish and Swedish governments continued to support the printing of religious and educational books, as well as laws and statutes. Political *pamphlets became increasingly important, especially in Sweden, in connection with its numerous 17th- and early 18th-century wars. After 1658, when Denmark lost the southern parts of the Swedish peninsula, the printed word (especially Swedish *catechisms) was used in a campaign to 'Swedenize' former Danish subjects.

Book production and the book trade became increasingly differentiated during the 17th century. Bookbinders formed special guilds, obtaining in Sweden a monopoly for the selling of bound books. Some of Stockholm's printing houses—Ignatius Meurer, Henrik Keyser, Georg Gottlieb Burchardi—developed into important publishing firms with strong international relations. In Copenhagen, major booksellers, such as Joachim Moltke and Daniel Paulli, became the most important publishers. At international *book fairs, they exchanged scholarly books in Latin with their European colleagues.

Rising production is indicated by extant imprints. According to the bibliography *Bibliotheca Danica*, fewer than twenty different publications survive from the years 1500–1509, 368 from 1600–1609, and 1,164 from 1700–1709. The balance between titles in Latin and Danish fluctuated (though was often close to being equal), until Latin became confined to academic titles during the 18th century. However, *press runs as well as multiple editions indicate that many more copies of books were printed in the vernacular from the late 16th century onwards. Popular religious and entertaining titles were printed in runs of 1,000 or 2,000 copies. Many such editions have not survived.

New genres appeared (household manuals, devotional titles for female readers) along with older ones (*chapbooks, *ballads). Such items, usually printed in *octavo or even smaller *formats, sometimes contained *woodcuts. Copper *engravings (from c.1600) were confined to more expensive *folios. Both Denmark and Sweden saw the appearance of such magnificently illustrated publications as Samuel Pufendorf's *De Rebus a Carolo Gustavo Gestis* (1696) and *Flora Danica* (1761–1883).

Popular literacy was stimulated by many factors. After the Reformation, the teaching of the catechism was given high priority, and clergymen encouraged 'reading in books' to strengthen children's rote-learning. Seventeenth-century reading campaigns were supported by bishops and kings, most directly through the Swedish Church Law of 1686. The rising trade in ballads and 'harmful' stories—an unintended consequence of increasing *literacy standards—was opposed by the same authorities.

By the mid-18th century, according to the extraordinarily detailed information of Swedish and Finnish parish registers, more than 90 per cent of adults could read the required religious texts in print. Writing, by contrast, remained more closely tied to professional needs. Standards in the rest of Scandinavia, Iceland, and—a few decades later—Greenland were probably as high. In Norway and Denmark, governmental regulation was gradually intensified, and more formal schools were established following legislation in the 1730s. In the early 19th century, national laws concerning compulsory school teaching for all children were issued across the region.

Local book supplies varied considerably with population density and infrastructure. In most towns, especially along the coasts, books were permanently available (e.g. in the numerous small-scale Danish boroughs with typically 1,000–5,000 inhabitants and between one and four binders selling books). People in southern Scandinavia's rural areas and along the Norwegian west coast also had frequent contact with urban book markets. Further inland and further north, however, deliveries were few and far between. In addition to the religious context of reading instruction, this meant that for many Nordic people the world of books was confined to a limited selection of (mainly devotional) literature.

Readers interested in a wider range of books had to acquire these in a capital or university city. The populations of Stockholm and Copenhagen grew significantly, from 10,000 and 20,000 inhabitants respectively in 1600 to c.60,000 in 1700. Dutch booksellers were present in Copenhagen from the 1630s and in Stockholm from 1647 (Johannes *Janssonius, the *Elzevier family). Foreign books were also imported by university booksellers. Traditional bookselling in churches ceased, but around 1700 more booksellers and publishers opened shops with their own premises.

In the 18th century, the acquisition of colonies led to a boom in Pietist missionary printing. In Copenhagen, a special press was established in 1714 (from 1727, Vajsenhuset) for both missionary and domestic education. For some years, a printing press was also installed in the colony of Tranquebar, India, and in the West Indies. Swedish missionary publications were printed for North America (including books in the Indian Lanape language). In 1755, the New Testament was translated into Ume-Sami, and a Swedish–Sami dictionary was published (1780) to assist missionary work. *Egede brought a Pietist mission and Danish religious books to Greenland in the 1720s. The Bible was translated into Greenlandic, thus profoundly shaping the written and printed language. The first book was printed in Greenland in 1793, but traditional MS publication survived in this small population until well into the 19th century.

Enlightenment ideas came to Stockholm and Copenhagen at a time when the capitals were experiencing flourishing trade and rising standards of living and education. A key figure was the history professor, playwright, and essayist Ludvig Holberg (1684–1754), regarded as the first Norwegian-Danish author to become rich from the sale of his books. From the 1740s, new societies and journals, particularly concerned with economics and science, were established with royal support.

In the world of libraries, significant developments took place during the early modern period. Medieval clerical book collections were dissolved or destroyed after the Lutheran Reformation, and Protestant church libraries remained modest, although some cathedral libraries and cathedral schools could boast fine collections. From the late 16th century, extensive libraries were built up by nobles (*Rantzau, *De la Gardie, *Karen Brahe, Otto *Thott), some of whom invested in exquisite uniform bindings by trendsetting bookbinders inspired by French and English fashions (e.g. the Reusner, Bergman, and Boppenhausen families).

*Probate inventories and the new trend for public *book auctions (from the mid-17th century) provide documentation for the many scholars and wealthy merchants who owned major libraries. One private collector, P. F. Suhm in Copenhagen, famously opened his library to the public (1778). The universities, particularly *Uppsala and Copenhagen, had considerable collections. The two royal libraries expanded from the mid-17th century, primarily by incorporating private collections and war booty; and bookbinders were attached to the courts. *Legal deposit was formally introduced in Sweden in 1661 and Denmark in 1697. Public access to the National Library of *Sweden in Stockholm was granted from 1713; the Royal Library in *Copenhagen gave limited access to scholars, but otherwise remained closed to the public until 1793.

The first commercial *lending library appeared in Copenhagen in 1725. From the mid-18th century, a variety of private and institutional libraries were established across Scandinavia, in provincial towns and the country. Moreover, private ownership of books became generally more common. One remarkable Norwegian peasant, *Aarflot, even turned his collection into a public lending library.

The market for books changed from the mid-18th century. Newspaper production took permanent hold, especially in towns (*see* BERLINGSKE TIDENDE). Major firms expanded and modernized their businesses, helped by the abolition of old regulations in the different crafts. Among the leading names in Stockholm were *Momma, *Fougt, and *Salvius, the latter reorganizing Swedish bookselling by commissioning provincial booksellers. Similar changes took place in the Danish and Norwegian markets thanks to *Gyldendal (Copenhagen, 1770–). In the 18th century, Finland endured frequent periods of war and Russian occupation, forcing Finnish book production to move to Stockholm; Jacob Merckell and, later, the *Frenckell family dominated the Finnish book trade.

The Enlightenment increasingly challenged censorship. It was relaxed considerably in Sweden (1766), where *freedom of the press became relatively well secured. In Denmark, censorship was abolished during J. F. Struensee's short rule (1770–71), but controls were gradually re-established and tightened in 1799.

4 1800–2000

After the Napoleonic wars, the Nordic political landscape was radically transformed. In 1814 Norway was separated from Denmark and made subject to the Swedish king until 1905. Iceland, Greenland, and the Faroe Islands remained with Denmark; Iceland achieved independence in 1944, and home rule was established in the Faroes and Greenland in 1948 and 1979, respectively. After wars with Germany, Denmark lost Schleswig-Holstein in 1864. Finland, an autonomous grand duchy of Russia 1809–1917, was subject to strict censorship at a time when such control was being dismantled in Sweden, Norway, and Denmark (1810, 1814, 1849) in connection with new democratic constitutions. Around the mid-19th century, liberalization, including the abolition of guild monopolies in trade and manufacturing, was occurring all over Scandinavia.

At the same time, history, mythology, and language were cultivated intensely as part of the formation of national identities. In the 'new' nations—Norway, Finland, Iceland, the Faroes, and Greenland—language became a major issue. Two Norwegian written language forms, *bokmål* (relatively close to Danish) and *nynorsk* (based on western Norwegian dialects with elements from medieval Norse), were created, the latter as a reaction against former Danish rule. Today both are recognized as official written languages

(*bokmål* being more commonly used; *see* NORSKE SAMLAGET).

In Finland, Swedish remained the cultural and administrative language for much of the 19th century, but Finnish gradually gained ground, achieving equal legal status in 1892. Both languages are now officially recognized (Swedish being a minority language). In Iceland, the nationalist movement stressed continuity with medieval Norse. An active language policy strove to replace old and new borrowings from foreign languages with Icelandic words.

The general interest across Scandinavia in national history and popular culture gave rise to numerous important and popular collections of ballads and tales. Examples include the Swedish ballads edited by Geijer and Afzelius, the Norwegian tales collected by Asbjørnsen and Moe, and the monumental Finnish national epic, the *Kalevala*.

Popular religious revivalist movements profoundly influenced 19th-century developments. In Norway, the lay preacher Hans Nielsen Hauge (1771–1824) achieved a tremendous following by distributing huge quantities of religious *tracts across the country. In Denmark, N. F. S. Grundtvig (1783–1872) became the unofficial head of a nationally oriented, non-puritan, religious revival, inspiring the establishment of 'folk high schools' (*folkehøjskoler*), exam-free boarding schools for adults in the countryside. Although preferring the 'living word' to 'bookish learning', these schools motivated generations to further study across Scandinavia and, along with other religious movements of more puritan origin (especially in Norway and Sweden), made inventive use of printed materials such as *newsletters, recruiting pamphlets, and edifying tracts.

New publication strategies were explored by the many recently established societies, associations, political parties, trade unions, cooperatives, temperance societies, and sports clubs. The resulting explosion in *jobbing printing and small editions was assisted by lower printing costs and improved distribution channels (new railway systems revolutionized the transport system, especially in the vast, less densely populated areas of Scandinavia). At the same time, major industries and retail concerns began to print catalogues, and even small shops used print for advertising.

Newspapers were perhaps the single most important media of the 19th and early 20th centuries, stimulating democratic developments and vice versa. From *c*.1830, they could be printed faster and more cheaply, resulting in a dramatic increase in print runs and

Illustrations of runic stones from the Danish scholar Carl Rafn's 'Runic Inscriptions in which the Western Countries are Alluded to', in *Mémoires de la Société Royale des Antiquaires du Nord, 1848–9* (Copenhagen, 1852); the variety of languages is notable.

diversity. In Sweden, L. J. Hierta founded the politically influential *Aftonbladet* in 1830; by 1900, the country had *c*.120 newspapers. In Finland (where the oldest still-published newspaper is *Åbo Underrättelser* (1824–)), both Finnish and Swedish-language newspapers became important organs of public debate. The Atlantic regions saw their first *periodicals in the last half of the 19th century: Iceland's *Þjóðólfur* (1848), Greenland's *Atuagagdliutit* (1861–), and the Faroese *Dimmalætting* (1877–). The first Faroese printing press was established in 1852, when a short-lived attempt at newspaper publishing was made.

From the late 19th century, new political parties were formed, all with their own newspapers. Several Danish provincial towns had four different daily papers, representing different parties. Norway had an abundance of local newspapers and, despite declining readerships, remains—like Finland, Iceland, and Sweden—among the leading newspaper nations worldwide.

As elsewhere in Europe, the book industry in the Nordic countries changed following the introduction of new printing and manufacturing technologies *c*.1830 (*see* **11**). Hitherto, Nordic countries had mainly used imported paper, producing it on a small scale (mainly in Sweden). However, after the development of wood-based paper, Finland and Sweden (and to a lesser extent Norway), with their large areas of forest,

developed significant paper industries. In 2000, Finland was the second largest exporter of paper, after Canada (*see* **10**).

During the 19th century, publishing and the book trade were organized along still recognizable lines. Professional bodies were established. Danish book prices became fixed in 1837—a principle that was relaxed only in about 2000—and regulations were made against the unauthorized sale of books. Of the numerous publishing companies founded in the mid-19th century, many existed well into the 20th century. C. A. Reitzel (1789–1853) published the period's most celebrated Danish authors, including Hans Christian Andersen and Kierkegaard. The largest and most influential firm, however, was *Gyldendal, not least because of its dynamic director Frederik V. Hegel (1817–87).

For most of the 19th century, the Norwegian book market remained strongly influenced by Danish interests. Prominent authors such as Ibsen and Bjørnstjerne Bjørnson published their books with Gyldendal, Copenhagen. Under its director William Nygaard (from 1888), *Aschehoug gave ample opportunity to authors to publish with a Norwegian firm, but it was not until Gyldendal had set up an independent Norwegian company (1925) that it became a matter of course for authors to publish in their own country. Both Aschehoug and Gyldendal Norsk Forlag have remained important elements in Norwegian literary life.

In Finland, a significant role was played by the Finnish Literature Society (1831), which initiated several publications, including the *Kalevala* and Aleksis Kivi's *Seven Brothers*. Major firms did not emerge until the last decades of the 19th century. Werner Söderström's publishing house supported Finnish-language literature, but for moral reasons refrained from publishing modern realism. He was soon rivalled by the more liberal publishing house Otava (1890). Both are prominent in the contemporary Finnish book market (*see* wsoy).

In Sweden, the early establishment of a free press stimulated the rapid expansion of publishing across the country. One particularly influential house was that of *Bonnier, which published Strindberg's works and grew during the 20th century into a major media group.

Technical, economic, and social developments made books widely affordable. Entertaining literature was consumed in large quantities, and new foreign novels by e.g. August Lafontaine, Scott, Dickens, and Dumas were translated. Some were *serialized in newspapers, others launched in cheap editions, often through subscription sales, by major publishing houses.

One successful enterprise (1897–1918) was the Danish-Norwegian series *Frem* (in Swedish, *Ljus*), with *c*.170,000 subscribers in the three countries. It published articles relating to history and science and could be bought in inexpensive instalments. Exceptionally large press runs were also reached by the 'crown' and 'half-crown' editions of classical bestsellers. Such developments arrived later in Scandinavia than in many other parts of Europe; pocketbook series similar to *Penguin's were only introduced in the Nordic countries after World War II. By the 1970s, *book clubs had acquired a dominant position in the market for popular literature.

Another important phenomenon in the decades around 1900 was the multi-volume encyclopaedia (e.g. the Danish *Salmonsen's Leksikon*). In the 1970s, the publication of extensive encyclopaedias and reference works boomed in Finland. Major national encyclopaedic projects were completed in Sweden and Denmark around 2000.

Lending libraries existed in all Nordic countries from the mid- or late 19th century. In rural districts, they were often established within individual parishes; in towns, many were run by societies and organizations. The first public libraries appeared in the 1880s, and during the 1920s and 1930s, the young welfare states took over full responsibility for municipal libraries (*see* PALMGREN). Much money was spent to supply the same variety of books to all citizens, irrespective of location. Local branches were set up in small communities, and *mobile libraries introduced. From the 1960s, *comic books were made available in libraries, followed by tapes, videos, CDs, DVDs, and free Internet access. Special departments for *children's books are found in all public libraries.

Since the 1960s, children's literature has achieved an important position in the Nordic countries, being recognized for both educational value and literary quality. Books by numerous authors (especially Astrid Lindgren) have been widely read by children in all parts of the region, possibly providing more shared reading experiences than any other works of Nordic literature.

In other respects, Nordic book culture has become increasingly international. During the late 19th century, professional standards and artistic aspirations were raised through French and English influences (e.g. *Hendriksen, and later *Kumlien). Around this time, German *Fraktur gradually disappeared as a standard type. Aesthetic concerns were also manifested in bookbinding, with Sweden's Gustaf Hedberg and Denmark's *Kyster as pioneers. Early 20th-century Scandinavian *typography was strongly influenced by Modernism (Hugo Lagerström, Steen Eiler Rasmussen). In the 1940s and 1950s, British axial typography prevailed in fiction (C. Volmer Nordlunde) and Swiss asymmetry in *textbooks (Viggo Naae, *Forsberg). From the 1960s onwards, both lines were typographically improved (*Frederiksen, Carl Fredrik Hultenheim, *Kristensen), and increased *legibility became a major desideratum (Bror Zachrisson). Late 20th-century typographers excelled in imaginative book cover design (Austin Grandjean).

Since World War II, the majority of translated books have come from English-speaking countries; from the late 20th century, globalization and higher standards of English proficiency have resulted in Scandinavians buying and reading increasing numbers of books in English. However, some 'book traffic' has also gone the other way. Several 20th-century Nordic authors have had their works translated into English and other languages, including *Nobel prize-winners Selma Lagerlöf, Knut Hamsum, and Sigrid Undset and crime fiction writers Maj Sjöwall, Per Wahlöö, and Henning Mankell. According to UNESCO's 1998 World Culture Report, the Nordic countries are among the nations with the highest numbers (per capita) of library books and book titles published annually.

BIBLIOGRAPHY

GENERAL

P. Birkelund *et al.*, eds., *Nordisk Leksikon for Bogvæsen* (2 vols, 1951–62)

Royal Library, Denmark, www.kb.dk/en/index.html, consulted Sept. 2007

National Library of Finland, www.lib.helsinki.fi/english/, consulted Sept. 2007

National Library of Iceland, www.bok.hi.is/id/1011633, consulted Sept. 2007

Nordisk tidskrift för bok- och biblioteksväsen (1914–2006; from 2001, *Nordisk tidskrift för bok- och bibliotekshistoria*)

National Library of Norway, www.nb.no/english, consulted Sept. 2007

National Library of Sweden, www.kb.se/ENG/kbstart.htm, consulted Sept. 2007

DENMARK

Bogvennen (1893–)

C. Bruun, *Bibliotheca Danica, 1482-1830* (6 vols, 1877–1914); 2e (5 vols, 1961–3)

H. Ehrencron-Müller, *Forfatterlexikon omfattende Danmark, Norge og Island indtil 1814* (12 vols, 1924–35)

A. Frøland, *Dansk Boghandels historie 1482-1945* (1974)

Fund og Forskning i Det kongelige Biblioteks samlinger (1954–)

Grafiana (1997–)

I. Ilsøe, 'Printing, Book Illustration, Bookbinding, and Book Trade in Denmark, 1482-1914', *GJ* 60 (1985), 258–80

K. B. Jensen, ed., *Dansk Mediehistorie* (4 vols, 1996–2003)

L. Nielsen, *Dansk bibliografi 1482-1600* (3 vols, 1919–35); 2e (5 vols, 1996)

— *Den danske bog* (1941)

E. Petersen, ed., *Living Words and Luminous Pictures* (1999)

FAROE ISLANDS

M. Næs, *Fra spadestik til global udfordring* (2005)

FINLAND

T. Boman *et al.*, eds., *Bibliografi över Finlands bokhistoria 1488-1850 före 1991* (1993)

Fennica: The National Bibliography of Finland, www.fennica.linneanet.fi, consulted Sept. 2007

C.-R. Gardberg, *Boktrycket i Finland* (3 vols, 1948–73)

K. K. Karlsson, *Finlands handpappersbruk* (1981)

A. Perälä, *Typographischer Atlas Finnlands 1642-1827* (2 vols, 2000)

[F. W. Pipping,] *Förteckning öfver i tryck utgifna skrifter på Finska* (1856/7)

GREENLAND

K. Oldendow, *Groenlandica: Conspectus Bibliographicus* (1967)

ICELAND

B. S. Benedikz, *Iceland* (1969)

H. Hermannsson, *Catalogue of the Icelandic Collection Bequeathed by Willard Fiske* [1960]

S. Nordal, ed., *Monumenta Typographica Islandica* (6 vols, 1933–42)

NORWAY

J. B. Halvorsen, *Norsk forfatter-lexikon 1814-1880* (6 vols, 1885–1908)

H. Pettersen, *Bibliotheca Norvegica (1643-1918)* (4 vols, 1899–1924; 2e, 1972–4)

C. Sciøtz and B. Ringstrøm, *Norske førsteutgaver, en hjelpebok for samlere av skjønnlitteratur*, 2e (2006)

H. L. Tveterås, *Den norske bokhandels historie* (4 vols, 1950–96)

SWEDEN

Biblis (1957–97; 1998–)

Bokvännen (1946–97)

J. Brunius, ed., *Medieval Book Fragments in Sweden* (2005)

I. Collijn, *Sveriges bibliografi intill år 1600* (3 vols, 1927–38)

— *Sveriges bibliografi, 1600-talet* (2 vols in 1, 1942–6)

K. E. Gustafsson and P. Rydén, eds., *Den svenska Pressens historia* (5 vols, 2000–03)

H. Järv, ed., *Den svenska boken* (1983)

D. Lindmark, *Reading, Writing, and Schooling, 1650-1880* (2004)

H. Schück, *Den svenska förlagsbokhandelns historia* (1923)

Svensk bibliografi 1700-1829 (*SB* 17), www.kb.se/hjalp/english, consulted Sept. 2007

27 The History of the Book in the Iberian Peninsula

María Luisa López-Vidriero

1 Early printing

Printing arrived late in the Iberian Peninsula, towards 1472 in Spain and 1487 in Portugal; the region's surviving *incunables are characteristically archaic in style. The introduction and subsequent development of the printing press in Spain did not follow the pattern typical in the rest of Europe for three principal reasons: the political organization of Spain into multiple kingdoms; the fact that no one city was identifiable as the national capital; and the coexistence of two main languages, Castilian and Catalan.

Although Saragossa, Logroño, Barcelona, Valencia, and Seville were leading printing centres, the Castilian presses (Salamanca, Burgos, Alcalá de Henares, and Toledo) were especially important in Spain's typographical map. As printing began to develop, Castile was enjoying a golden moment of political and cultural hegemony; the printing press played a crucial role in the policy of national unity promoted by the Catholic Monarchs (1474–1516). Just as the Habsburg and Bourbon dynasties would later, the *Reyos Catholicos* used the press as an instrument for developing both the theory of statecraft and its practical application.

The advent of printing called for the reorganization of bookselling and the circulation of MSS, requiring the introduction of edicts to regulate the book as a commercial and intellectual product. These legislative measures attempted to bring authorized printed materials on to the market during escalating conflicts in 16th-century Europe. Widespread *censorship became one of the gravest intellectual and civil problems of the period. A law of 1502 regulated the intervention of the Crown in the printing industry and tried to resolve conflicts over the importation of 'false and defective' printed books. This was the first of many such measures that were to run alongside developing religious problems in Spain and Europe. Thus, a proclamation of 1558 established administrative and doctrinal control based on a complex formalized system, reinforced by the appearance in 1559 of expurgatory *indices and lists of forbidden books drawn up by Fernando Valdés, *Inquisitor General 1547–66. The reign of Philip II (1556–98) saw increasingly severe legislation: originally it attempted to regulate the printed book as a commercial object, but finally it consisted of a complex web of measures treating the book as an intellectual and ideological product. The consequences were decisive for controlling the publication of spiritual and liturgical literature for laymen.

Imports, opportunism, and service to the Church—already observable in the earliest Spanish incunable, *Parix's *Sinodal de Aguilafuente* (Segovia, 1472)—are three of the chief characteristics of early Spanish printing. The use of *roman type in the first product of the Spanish press distinguishes it from the *gothic type employed in most early Spanish printing. This peculiarity reveals Spain's dependence on foreign models for its printing: prominent workshops employed foreign experts, including Parix, Heinrich Botel, Paul Hurus, Mathaeus Flander, Peter Brun, Nicolaus Spindeler, and Johannes de Salsburga, as printers. Before coming to Spain, European *journeymen printers (principally Germans) passed through Italy and France; as a result, they stocked the *type cases of their new Spanish offices with *founts collected on their travels, their work reflecting their native customs and preferences.

Parix's Spanish output illustrates other printing tendencies. His second series of printed books—e.g. Escobar's *Modus Confitendi* (1471–2), and Pontanus' *Singularia Iuris* (c.1473)—all demonstrate the desire to open up broader geographical markets. These works, associated with university studies, tested possible demand for establishing production centres close to towns where the *studia generalia* (the great medieval universities) flourished. The Church and the universities were the driving forces of publishing and printing in Spain; they provided the texts and a guaranteed market for printers and *stationers. They also financed many editions of religious books.

From 1475, gothic and roman types were both employed in Spanish incunable printing, but gothic dominated production well into the 16th century. Gothic type remained in use for legal printing, and it appeared in popular productions such as *broadsides until well into the 18th century. Spanish gothic founts reveal the foreign influence in type design, and, to a certain extent, that influence lies behind the typographical features common to Castilian *black-letter types.

Three stages of Castilian printing can be distinguished. From 1472 to 1478, there are records of only fifteen *printing offices, of which nine had a printer whose name is known. Spanish printers worked in Seville and Valencia; in the rest of Spain, presses were run by foreign master printers. The names of most printers working in the northern Castilian Meseta remain unknown, except for Parix (at Segovia and perhaps also at Salamanca). Both the language of the works produced (seven in Latin, five in vernaculars) and the types employed (eight in roman, four in gothic) reflect the need to meet the demands of a precise and ready market in the midst of manifest technical limitations.

From 1480 to 1490, presses were distributed more widely. In Castile, they extended over both Mesetas. Printing took root in urban centres with established markets. Workshops were set up in university and commercial towns: Salamanca, Valladolid, Toledo (Juan Vázquez), Huete (Álvaro de Castro), Burgos (de *Basilea), and Zamora (Antonio de Centenera, focusing on university courses at Salamanca). Almost all the printers of the day used a particular international gothic type, even at Coria and León. The quality of the editions improved, incorporating native *engraving and *wood engraving. In *Los doze trabajos de Hércules* (Zamora, 1483), for example, Centenera considerably advanced the illustration of literary works, a practice that would flourish in the 16th century.

From 1491 to 1500, native gothic types were improved and new, foreign types also appeared. The gothic designed by the brothers Baptista and Gregorio de Tortis, for example, became fundamental to Hispanic typography. Fadrique de Basilea at Burgos, the anonymous printing office at Salamanca, and Peter Hagembach in Toledo, all used these Venetian *typefaces. At Valladolid, Juan de Francourt employed a new gothic typeface of Parisian design for *Tratado de confesión* (1492), *Ordenanzas reales de la audiencia y chancillería de Valladolid* (1493), and Díaz de Toledo's *Notas del relator* (1493). Publishing output grew and became more refined: page design began to be richly ornamented, and illustrated editions appeared from workshops whose importance grew. These years also witnessed the appearance of *Brocar, one of the principal printers during the reign of the Catholic Monarchs. He was active or had a commercial presence in Pamplona (Navarre), Logroño (Rioja), Alcalá de Henares, Burgos, Toledo and Salamanca (Castile), Seville (Andalusia), and Saragossa (Aragon).

By European standards, 15th-century Spain had a small printing output, although its presses produced more than Belgian or English workshops. Spanish printing was competitive chiefly because more than half of its publications were in the vernacular (Castilian and Catalan). In this respect, Spain led Europe. Spain's production of liturgical and legal texts was also the highest in Europe. The geographical radius of its printing activity is equally significant: only a quarter of Spain's output emerged from Catalonian and Valencian presses. The Castilian cities, with good communications, relied on long-established commercial fairs and a civic elite active in the import and export business. Castile's commercial prosperity and the growth of its governmental administration and universities ensured that printing became a permanent industry.

The Catholic Monarchs' legal measures to stimulate printing and the book trade were potent weapons in their establishment. Printers' exemption from military service and the reduction of taxes on book imports served to encourage the book trade and turn it into an attractive mercantile sector. These measures also included incentives for citizens to enter the trade, and for foreign printers to consider Spain, and later Portugal, countries with favourable employment prospects, especially during the European economic crisis towards the end of the 15th century.

Seville was well suited to immigrant German printers, and in 1490 a group of them was invited to make the city a typographical centre. The aim was for them to collaborate with the *studia*, a typical arrangement in other European university cities. However, an analysis of Sevillan production shows that publications there went beyond academic matters. Meinardus Ungut and Stanislaus Polonus came from Naples and formed a printing company in Seville to meet the official aim of producing editions of works on civil and ecclesiastical law that previously had been scattered and inaccessible. *El libro en que están compiladas algunas bulas*, printed by Polonus years later in Alcalá de Henares (1503), testifies to the aim of publishing a legal canon to standardize juridical and legislative provision.

Sevillan printers produced the highest proportion of vernacular books in all Spain. Across a broad range of genres—medicine and law, liturgical works, and translations and adaptations of the classics—only a third were in Latin. Moreover, a national literature was developing that included histories of Castile, vernacular devotional works, and books for entertainment. The publication of Ludolf of Saxony's *Vita Christi*, translated by Ambrosio Montesino and printed by Polonus at Alcalá de Henares (1502, 1503), was subsidized by the government, despite its being a religious work. It demonstrates the Spanish monarchy's desire to rival the magnificent illustrated edition (in four volumes, printed by two Germans) financed by the Portuguese monarchs in 1495.

The introduction of printing in Portugal, however, was not associated with royal power, but rather with the Jewish community (*see* **8**). Works printed in Hebrew were the first to appear from 1487 (*Pentateuco*, printed by Samuel Gacon in Faro); these were set in imported types, easily obtained by an international community with commercial ties to Paris, Livorno, Genoa, Naples, Antwerp, and Amsterdam. The type designs found in these incunables reflect a desire to embellish the biblical text. The quality of their execution may be explained by collaboration, before the arrival of printing, between an important centre of Luso-Hebraic *calligraphers and the probably Jewish school of xylography (*see* BLOCK PRINTING) connected to local *scriptoria. The neighbouring *paper mills established in 1411 helped foster the emergence of the main Hebraic printing offices at Faro, Lisbon, and Leiria. The seven incunables from the first press (1489–92) in Lisbon—that of Rabbi Eliezer Toledano—employ characters and ornamental *borders closely related to those created in Hijar (Aragon) by the Hebrew printer Eliezer ben Alantansi (1485–90). The similarity of name and typeface suggests that this printer possibly migrated. Between 1488 and 1495, printing moved from the coastal region to the interior of Portugal, and the spread of Judaic and Christian bibliography connected with biblical exegesis lasted

until the decree expelling the Jews in 1497. The last Hebrew press was that of Samuel Dortas in Leiria, ending its activities in 1496 with three editions of Abraham Zacuto's *Almanach Perpetuum*, now with the text in Latin. These firms began printing in Hebrew, but later in Latin, Castilian, and Portuguese. In Spain, the crisis facing Hebrew printing had already occurred in 1492, the year of the expulsion, causing the disappearance of the presses of Juan de Lucena (1475) at La Puebla de Montalbán (Toledo), Solomon Alkabiz (1476–82) at Guadalajara, and those at Zamora and Hijar that had provided synagogues' liturgical needs, including exegetical readings.

Portuguese incunables, both Latin and vernacular, reveal the importance of the Church and the Crown in such titles as: *Tratado da Confissom* (Chaves, attributed to Randolfo, 1489); *Constituições do Bispado do Porto* (Rodrigo Álvares, 1497); and *Breviarium Bracarense* (Braga, 1494), printed by Johann Gherlinc, an immigrant from Barcelona, where he operated 1486–9. Ludolf of Saxony's *De Vita Christi*, translated into Portuguese by the Alcobaça Cistercians, is a fine example of foreign participation in Portuguese typography. In 1495, the Germans Nicolaus of Saxony and Valentinus of Moravia (who adopted the Portuguese name Valentim *Fernandes under the protection of João II) produced this emblematic work in four volumes, decorated with woodcut borders, chapter-headings, and engravings of German provenance. Fernandes was the first to be granted the royal *privilege to print and sell Marco Polo's *Travels* (1502).

2 From the 16th century to the Baroque period

During the 16th century, Portuguese printing progressed slowly. The Lisbon presses remained in foreign hands: Jakob *Cromberger, a member of a German family established in Seville; Germão *Galharde, a Frenchman; and Giovanni Petro Buonhomini (active 1501–14), an Italian who also worked in association with Fernándes, using the name of João Pedro de Cremona. With João Álvares (1536–c.1587), originally holding the privilege of printer to the University of Coimbra, a group of native printers emerged. Luís Rodrigues (Lisbon 1539–49) improved typography and added the use of italics. In 1564 António Gonçalves, assistant to Duarte Nunes de Leão, obtained his licence and devoted the greater part of his output to religious and moral works; in the *Espejo del Principe Christiano* he appears as printer to the archbishop of Lisbon. The *editio princeps* of *Os Lusíadas* (1572) marks the start of a prolific epoch in Rodrigues's workshop. Camões's influence—based on his experience on the Malabar coast—is reflected in editions from 1573: *Sucesso do Segundo Cerco de Diu* (1574) and *História da provincia de sãta Cruz* (1576). António Ribeiro (1574–90), was the King's Printer from 1580; António Álvares, was printer to the archbishop of Lisbon; and Francisco Correia, the royal printer and printer to Cardinal Don Enrique, rented his printing office from Johannes Blavius in 1564 and continued printing in Lisbon until 1581. From the middle of the century, Lisbon again depended on important foreign master printers. Among these were: Blavius, from Cologne who settled in Lisbon between 1551 and 1563, and Pedro *Craesbeeck, a Flemish disciple of Plantin's, who established his Lisbon printing office in 1597 and produced a fundamental work for the history of the Portuguese language, *Origem da Lingua Portuguesa* (1605) by Nunes de Leão. Craesbeeck and his son António held the title of royal printer until it passed to the Frenchman *Deslandes.

The period of Portugal's annexation to Spain (1580–1640) had repercussions for written culture and for the activities and allegiances of the printing trades. Lourenço de Anvers, printer to the duke of Bragança, and Valente de Oliveira both printed periodicals, *gazetas*, and *mercúrios*. Domingo Lopes de Rosa and António Olivares, through minor and occasional publications, supported the Portuguese political cause. During the 16th century, Spanish presses published works in Portuguese: liturgical books commissioned by the Braga diocese at Salamanca, legal works, and the Manueline *Ordenações* at Seville (Cromberger, 1521, 1525). With the Annexation, both countries published significant works of imperial policy. Political events and permeable frontiers explain the phenomenon of 'flying printers' between Spain and Portugal (e.g. Tanco de Frejenal).

The early years of the 16th-century Spanish printing scene brought increased attention to Seville, where works including Juan del Encina's *Cancionero* and Nebrija's *Introductiones* represented contributions to national literacy and linguistic history. An active family enterprise began with Jakob Cromberger in 1503. The intellectual circle surrounding Seville cathedral and the city's academy—Pedro Núñez Delgado, López de Cortegana, and Jerónimo Pinelo—had their books printed by Cromberger, his son Johann, and above all by the latter's widow, Brígida Maldonado, who supervised the printing of Juan de Cazalla's works (*Lumbre del alma*, 1542), as well as *Doctrina Cristiana* and the *Confesionario* by Domingo de Valtanás (1544). The

Crombergers printed the first Spanish translations of *Erasmus (*Querella de la paz* (1520), *Enchiridion* (1528?), *Los coloquios* (1529), and *La lengua* (1533, 1535, 1542)). Spanish Erasmianism had another active printing office in Castile, that of Miguel de Eguía, Brocar's son-in-law. Eguía's press at Alcalá de Henares, a university city and focus of intellectual reform, issued the monumental *Complutensian Bible (1514–17). In 1529, Eguía also printed an anonymous edition of the *Diálogo de Doctrina Christiana* by Juan de Valdés, whose condemnation by the Inquisition prompted his journey to Italy.

The reformers, including Juan and Alfonso de Valdés, exemplified the supporting role of European presses in the spread of Erasmianism: the *Diálogo de Lactancio* or *Lactancia*, together with the *Diálogo de Mercurio y Carón*, were printed in Spain in 1529. In 1531 the Inquisition banned the publication, and Juan and Alfonso de Valdés appeared in the indexes of prohibited books at Milan and Venice in 1554, and at Portugal in 1581 (*see* INDEX LIBRORUM PROHIBITORUM). The *Lactancio* was printed on its own (bearing a *false imprint) in Spanish at Paris in 1586. Another edition (*Dialogo en que particularmente se tratan las cosas acaecidas en Roma*, Oxford: Joseph Barnes, 1586), was produced by Antonio del Corro, whose Protestantism obliged him to leave Spain. At the insistence of the earl of Leicester, he was appointed theological censor at *Christ Church, Oxford (1578–86); he founded the Spanish Protestant Church. Queen Elizabeth I's protection enabled Spanish exiles to continue their intellectual work; English presses played a fundamental role in publishing books written by Spaniards persecuted for religious and political motives. Spain, for its part, supported English Catholics and, through the Jesuits, encouraged a secret press for the English mission and the establishment of another press in the English College at St Omer to produce Counter-Reformation works for distribution among recusants.

There were also other reasons for European countries to involve themselves energetically in the market for Spanish books. The consequences of the Council of Trent (1545–63) were decisive. The *Nuevo rezado* required the immediate and huge production of liturgical books beyond the capacity of the Spanish presses. Philip II granted the right to print these books to foreigners who possessed the necessary technical and economic means. *Plantin, appointed chief King's Printer in 1570, was the great beneficiary of this measure that proved so adverse for the national book industry. The fact that the Spanish monarchy had possessions outside the Iberian Peninsula explains why presses in the Low Countries (Brussels and Antwerp) or in Italy (Milan and Naples) should have produced Spanish works for sale not only in Spain and America, but for the European trade. From the 15th century, Spain's principal book imports were Latin works from Italy and Germany. There was considerable European involvement in the Spanish book trade, including the financing of occasional publications.

At the beginning of the 16th century in Catalonia, Venetians such as the bookseller Francesco de Moris represented and acted on behalf of a wide network of booksellers from Venice and from Genoa; the latter were also active in the paper trade. In Valencia, Giovanni Battista Riquelme and Lorenzo Ganoto, both merchants from Savona, financed the *Suma de todas las crónicas del mundo* (printed by Gorge Costilla in 1510) and the *Cancionero General* (printed by Christoph Kaufmann in 1511). In Castile, Francesco Dada and Giovanni Tomasso Favario financed Andrés de Burgos in 1505 to print Encina's *Cancionero* on his Burgos presses. Melchior Gorricio subsidized Hagembach's editions in Toledo. From the 1520s, the companies of bookseller-stationers who were related to the great printing houses of Italy or Lyons (*Giunta, Portonariis, Boyer) turned from controlling book imports to book production and publishing through their Castilian sub-offices in Salamanca or Valladolid. They maintained an active presence in the fairs at Medina del Campo; the Giunta family set up in Saragossa, Burgos, Salamanca, and Madrid; Guillaume Rouillé, the outstanding Lyons publisher, created a powerful commercial network. The Lyons publishers—the Cardon brothers, Philippe Borde, and Claude Rigaud—strongly supported Catholic reform by financing Jesuit and Dominican authors in the Iberian Peninsula.

Royal, noble, and patrician book-collecting in Spain provides an excellent vantage point for observing the vitality and shape of the book trade. As the collections and rare items belonging to individual bibliophiles became available, three exceptional libraries were created: the Columbine Library, the Casa del Sol library, and the Royal Library of Philip II, also known as the *Escorial Library. The Columbine Library in Seville houses the collection of the humanist Hernando *Colón (1488–1539), son of Christopher Columbus, while the Casa del Sol library in Valladolid, which is essential for studying the Anglo-Spanish book trade, contains the holdings of the count of Gondomar, who served as Philip III's ambassador in London (1613–18, 1620–22).

The poor quality of paper and ink and the worn types of many later 16th-century books testify to the generally low standards of bookmaking at a time when the world of Spanish letters was reaching its zenith. Although Spanish presses were generally undistinguished, production was increasing considerably, religion, history, law, and cartography being the dominant subjects. Closely linked to Spanish political and economic development during the reigns of the later Habsburg monarchs, there was a proliferation of minor printing in the form of news-sheets, *arbitrios*, and reports. Post-Tridentine spiritual practices led to an increase in sermons and devotional literature consonant with the new urban religious sensibility and sociability. Nevertheless, the printing industry and book trade began to decline in the last quarter of the 16th century. The lack of technical resources and skilled operatives became evident, especially in the early decades of the 17th century, when the wish to publish in Spain still existed. But the decisive causes of the decline were religious and civil censorship, interventions by the Inquisition, royal privileges permitting monopolies of sales and of printing liturgical books, together with the lack of essential materials and means. The shortage of trained professionals is palpable: around 1640 in Madrid there were only ten printing offices with some 50 master printers and pressmen, and 45 people in the bookselling trade.

Madrid, a great printing centre from 1560 to 1580, also boasted the *Imprenta Real (Royal Press), set up by an agreement between Philip II and Julio *Junta (a Florentine printer belonging to the Giunti family, who had started printing at Salamanca). In contrast with more ordinary productions, this workshop's output represented the splendour of the Baroque, creating outstanding illustrated books with characteristic architectural title-pages—portico and altarpiece—designed by important Spanish and foreign artists, especially Flemish engravers (Pedro Perret, Juan Schorquens, Jean de Courbes, Juan de Noort, Pedro de Villafranca), such as João Lavanha's *Viaje a Portugal de Felipe III* (1622). The works of great Spanish authors of the Golden Age—Góngora's *Soledades* (1635) and his *Polifemo* (1629)—were set in type at the Imprenta Real as well as at other Madrid printing offices. Under de la *Cuesta's imprint (1604–25) appeared Cervantes's *Don Quixote*, part I (1605) and *Novelas ejemplares* (1613), Lope de Vega's *Arcadia* (1610) and *Jerusalén conquistada* (1609), and Ercilla's *Araucana* (1610). Luis Sánchez, who had the best pressmen and was also a publisher and bookseller, printed Pedro Mexía's *Silva de varia lección* (1602).

The printing office visited by Alonso Quijano (*Don Quixote*, part II, chapter 62) has been identified with the outstanding firm in Barcelona at that time, owned by *Cormellas. His presses were divided between two establishments, one in El Call and the other in Plaça de Sant Jaume. Before Don Quixote's fictional arrival, he had already brought out *Lazarillo de Tormes* (1599), *Guzmán de Alfarache* (1599), and Montemayor's *La Diana* (1614). The Prologue to *Quixote*, part I, reconstructs in masterly fashion the complexity of the Spanish book during the Golden Age.

On the Spanish Levante, Valencia maintained its leading place as a printing centre; a number of its successful families—Mey, Macé, and Gárriz—demonstrate the benefits to be obtained from the printing trade. In Aragon, the Dormer, Larumbe, and Lanaja families maintained a high level of book production at Saragossa. Seville continued as the main Andalusian centre; the widow of Nicolás Rodríguez is associated with a typical illustrated genre, the *festival book, which reproduces ephemeral architecture (e.g. Torre Farfán, *Las Fiestas de S. Iglesia de Sevilla*, 1671). In Old Castile, the presses remained active at Valladolid, the capital of Spain under Philip III between 1601 and 1606, with established printing offices (*Fernández de Córdoba) and printers such as Luis Sánchez, who operated there and in Madrid, and Godínez de Millis who also had premises at Medina del Campo.

3 From the Enlightenment to the 20th century

The Spanish and Portuguese Enlightenment modernized the legal, industrial, and economic aspects of the printed book. Lisbon reflected this vitality: the number of booksellers swelled to 750, mostly of Portuguese origin. A similar increase occurred among the printers, especially from 1756 onwards. Until José I's death in 1777, the marquis of Pombal's political programme, most notably the expulsion of the Jesuits in 1759, promoted this noteworthy growth. In Spain, a change of dynasty began to take place in 1700 with the death of Charles II. The house of Bourbon entered Spain with Philip V (born at Versailles in 1683), who reigned 1700–1746. Thus began a process of profound modernization and accommodation with the European Enlightenment, which would reach its apogee during the second half of the century and the reign of Philip's nephew Charles III (1759–88). New legislation supported efforts to promote the commercialization of

the book, but the measures sharply divided different sectors of the book trade. In 1752, legislation against the import of books failed because of fierce opposition from Spanish booksellers; but the law of 1754, promulgated by Ferdinand VI (1746–59), successfully regulated trading in imported books. It demanded a special royal authorization for works in Spanish by native authors, and imposed a tax by the Council of State on every foreign printed book imported for sale. The bookbinders opposed imports because they took away their business, and in 1778 they succeeded in obtaining a legal measure that allowed the import only of unbound books, those in paper wrappers, or those with old bindings. The government's strategy of attempting to break the centuries-old dependence of Spanish booksellers on foreign products was designed to promote domestic production by making it difficult to import books and by fostering local trade associations. Between 1758 and 1763, Madrid saw the creation of the *Royal Company of Printers and Booksellers, which principally used *Ibarra's printing office. In 1759 the Compañía de Impresores y Libreros de Valencia was formed, followed four years later by the Royal Company of Printers and Booksellers of Madrid. Supported by the government, this limited company aimed to recover parts of the market traditionally dependent on foreign presses.

With Charles III came approval for the free pricing of books, the first measures to control periodical publications, and recognition of the exclusive rights of authors and their heirs. Responsibility for censorship rested with the cultural institutions of government, such as the royal academies. A law of 1768 enshrined the intervention of the Inquisition in the printing of books. The Imprenta Real collaborated with other institutions such as the Royal Academy of Fine Arts, producing such publications as *Retratos de los españoles ilustres* (1791), a monumental work that engendered pride in the Spanish Enlightenment. This attitude was reflected in the publication of Juan Sempere y Guarinos's six-volume bibliography *Ensayo de una Biblioteca española de los mejores escritores del reynado de Carlos III* (1785–9).

Education was to be encouraged and national pride recovered by publishing the country's historical sources as well as the classical and contemporary works essential for enlightened thought. These texts were to be translated into Spanish by great authors who would help to create a national consciousness and restore the purity of the language. This initiative is represented by such publications as: *Los Diez libros de Architectura de M. Vitruvio Polione, traducidos y* comentados por Don Joseph Ortíz y Sanz (1787) and Conyers Middleton's La vida de Cicerón, translated by Nicolás de Azara (1790). The Biblioteca del *Palacio Real, founded in 1711, collaborated in this undertaking as a supplier of texts and as a publishing house. Nicolás Antonio's national bibliography—Bibliotheca Hispana Nova (Ibarra, 1783–8); Bibliotheca Hispana Vetus (widow and heirs of Ibarra, 1788)—is a product of that cooperation. One indication of Spain's resurgent importance is the fact that both *Baskerville (Specimen of the Word Souverainement in 11 sizes, 1766) and *Bodoni (1776) travelled to Madrid to present samples of their types for the royal press.

The state also sought to make Spanish *de luxe publishing competitive throughout Europe. Books of quality emerged from the Madrid workshops of *Ibarra, *Sancha, and *Cano, and from printing offices in Valencia run by Antonio Bordazar (active 1701–40), *Monfort y Besades, José Orga, father and son (1744–1808), and Salvador Fauli (1742–1800). The engravers from the Academy of Fine Arts worked for these printers on editions that are justly famous today, such as a Sallust (Conjuración de Catalina y Guerra de Yugurta, translated by the Infante Don Gabriel Antonio, son of Charles III, 1772), and the Quixote of the Academy (edited by the *Real Academia Española, 1780), both printed by Ibarra. Bodoni was appointed royal printer, in part because the dukedom of Parma was linked to the Spanish royal family. Typography and the allied book arts improved considerably, to some extent because government grants to printers, engravers, and binders allowed many to have professional training in Paris or London. The type specimen books of the era—by Antonio Espinosa (1766, 1771, and 1780), Gerónimo Antonio Gil (1774), the convent of San José in Barcelona (1777 and 1801), the Palacio Real (1787), the Royal Press (1788 and 1799), the widow of Eudal Paradell (1793), and Francisco Ifern (1795)—bear witness to typographical advances mainly concentrated in Madrid, Barcelona, and Valencia. One of the most interesting and wide-ranging of contemporary bookmen was Antonio de Sancha; a bookseller, printer, publisher, and binder. Among the re-editions of the Spanish Golden Age published by the elder Sancha is the poetic anthology Parnaso español (1768–78), a nine-volume compilation of the best Castilian poets illustrated with their portraits. His son Gabriel produced the exquisite volumes of both parts of Quixote (1797–8, 1798–9).

The chronicles of Spanish history were republished in monumental style by the academic movement: the Crónica de Juan II (Valencia: Monfort, 1779), for example, rivalled in political design the handsome edition printed by Brocar in Logroño in 1517. The Spanish monarchy's links with the Kingdom of the Two Sicilies and the dukedom of Parma widened the ambit of Spanish printing to Italy. From the middle of the 18th century until the death of Ferdinand VII (1833), Spanish binding also enjoyed a period of splendour; and although French and English influences were manifest, royal binders such as the Sanchas, Gabriel Gómez, Carsí y Vidal, Santiago Martín, and Antonio Suárez Jiménez developed techniques in which the mosaic, 'cortina', Valencian, and Spanish *tree calf styles stood out.

From 1808 political problems—royal exile, the Peninsular War (1808–14), constitutionalism, and Ferdinandine absolutism—delayed until the 1840s the modernization of printing that had taken place in the rest of Europe. Nevertheless, the period of transition between the ancien régime and modern society is of great interest for publishing history. Spain, an invaded country that was developing a parliamentary system of government, adopted new uses for printed material, including *propaganda, ephemeral patriotic literature, and *newspapers. The mechanization of book production had a special impact on Madrid and above all Barcelona, which, impelled by Catalonian industrial development, became a powerful urban printing centre during the 19th century. Towards the end of the century, the indianos, or rich colonists returning from America, provided capital, brought new marketing techniques, and favoured the launch of a book industry that relied on the collaboration of the magnificent noucentisme artists.

Espasa-Calpe, a remarkable Spanish publishing house that connects the 19th and 20th centuries, employed a business model favoured by industrial societies. Espasa, the family imprint (Barcelona, 1860), formed an association with Salvat (1869–97) and captured the market in translations of French books. The firm launched a magazine of high quality (El Mundo Ilustrado), bought the rights of *Brockhaus & Meyer (1905), and the plates of Meyers Großes Konversations-Lexikon. Later, with a committee of 33 editors and more than 600 collaborators, the firm published the Enciclopedia Espasa. In 1925, now merged with Calpe and assisted by a favourable contract with Papelera Española, the national papermaking company, Espasa opened an innovative, all-embracing bookshop in the Gran Vía in Madrid. La Casa del Libro was stocked with their older flagship series of scholarly texts: Clásicos Castellanos and their more popular Colección Austral, launched in

1937 by their Buenos Aires office during the Spanish Civil War.

The Second Spanish Republic (1931–6) brought in a policy of promoting books and of integrated publishing that supported education and the diffusion of culture. Intellectuals associated with the Institución Libre de Enseñanza (Free Institute for Teaching) and members of La Generación del 27 (The Generation of 1927) founded important periodicals: the *Revista de Occidente*, directed by the philosopher José Ortega y Gasset between 1923 and 1936; *Litoral*, edited by Emilio Prados and Manuel Altolaguirre; *Gaceta Literaria*, edited by José Bergamín between 1933 and 1936; *Caballo Verde para la Poesía*, edited by Neruda; and *Octubre*, founded by Rafael Alberti and María Teresa León. They also published books of high quality via *private presses (Manuel Altolaguirre-Concha Zardoya). Silverio Aguirre was the Madrid printer most involved with the Silver Age authors, and Signo the most representative publisher.

Argentina and Mexico, countries that welcomed the Spanish Republican exiles from 1939, provided continuity for this intellectual publishing movement (Losada, *Emecé, Séneca, and *Sur) (*see* **46**). In postwar Spain, poetry magazines such as *Garcilaso* or *Vértice* were the heirs, albeit under a Fascist banner, of the aesthetics and high standards of 1930s printing. The annual publishers' prizes awarded by Nadal (1944) and *Planeta (1952) encouraged literary publishing. *Aguilar promoted high production values with its three differently sized series, 'Obra Completa', 'Crisol', and 'Crisolín', all printed on *India paper and bound in *leather. In Valencia, María Amparo and Vicente Soler (Tipografía Moderna) launched their exquisitely produced series for bibliophiles, 'La fonte que mana y corre' (1945–75). Collaboration between Amparo-Soler and the bibliophile Antonio Rodríguez-Moñino saw the launch of Editorial Castalia in Madrid and its flagship series in 1969, Clásicos Castalia, which has since proliferated in series for all ages of reader: Castalia Prima, Castalia Didáctica, and Escritoras Madrileñas, to name a few. This collaboration gave continuity, in the midst of the dreary postwar Spanish publishing scene, to the Republican tradition of careful critical editing.

Francisco Pérez González created the publishing house Taurus in 1955, with Gutiérrez Girardot and Miguel Sánchez. Later on, Santillana, under Jesús Polanco's direction, consolidated and gave security to the publishing industry. Juan Salvat joined the family firm in 1955 and ran Salvat Editores until 1992, when it was sold to *Hachette. He introduced door-to-door

selling of weekly parts or *fascicles; his programme for revolutionizing the distribution system was adopted by Círculo de Lectores and Grupo Zeta. In 1959, Germán Sánchez Ruipérez founded *Anaya, which became a leader in educational texts and is now incorporated into the Santillana Group. Beatriz de Moura founded Editorial Tusquets in 1969 after working at Lumen, created by Esther Tusquets. Their series 'Marginales' and 'Cuadernos Ínfimos' became essential for short-story readers and authors. Jorge Herralde founded Anagrama in 1969 and created the *prizes Ensayo (best essay, 1973) and Herralde de Novela (best novel, 1983). Carlos Barral and Jaime Salinas, promoters of the Formentor Prize at the end of the 1950s, internationalized Spanish publishing at *Seix Barral and introduced the Latin American Boom writers at *Alfaguara. Alianza Editorial (with its pocket editions designed by Daniel Gil), Siglo XX, Taurus, and Cuadernos para el Diálogo, were all symbols of progressive quality of popular publishing in the late Francoist era.

BIBLIOGRAPHY

A. Anselmo, *Origens da imprensa em Portugal* (1981)

— *História da edição em Portugal*, 1 *Das origens até 1536* (1991)

P. Berger, *Libro y lectura en la Valencia del Renacimiento* (1987)

Bibliografia Geral Portuguesa, Século XV (2 vols, 1941–2)

BMC 10

J. Delgado Casado, *Diccionario de impresores españoles (Siglos XV–XVII)* (1966)

— and J. Martín Abad, *Repertorios bibliográficos de impresos del siglo XVI* (1993)

V. Deslandes, *Documentos para a história da tipografia portuguesa nos séculos XVI e XVII*, ed. A. Anselmo (1988)

J. Domínguez Bordona, *Manuscritos con pinturas* (1933)

M. Fernández Valladares, *La imprenta en Burgos, 1501–1600* (2005)

C. Griffin, *The Crombergers of Seville* (1988)

— *Journeymen-Printers, Heresy, and the Inquisition in Sixteenth-Century Spain* (2005)

F. Guedes, *Os livreiros em Portugal e as suas associações desde o século XV até aos nossos dias* (1993)

[*Leituras,*] *O livro antigo em Portugal e Espanha, séculos XVI–XVIII/El libro Antiguo en Portugal y España, Leituras: Revista da Biblioteca Nacional*, 3.9–10 (2002)

M. L. López-Vidriero and P. M. Cátedra, eds., *El libro antiguo español* (3 vols, 1992–6)

J. P. R. Lyell, *Early Book Illustration in Spain* (1926)

M. de la Mano González, *Mercaderes e impresores de libros en la Salamanca del siglo XVI* (1998)

F. J. Norton, *A Descriptive Catalogue of Printing in Spain and Portugal, 1501-1520* (1978)

M. Peña Díaz, *Libro y lectura en Barcelona, 1473–1600* (1995)

— *El laberinto de los libros: historia cultural de la Barcelona del Quinientos* (1997)

W. A. Pettas, *A History and Bibliography of the Giunti (Junta) Printing Family in Spain, 1526–1628* (2005)

J. V. de Pina Martins, *Para a história da cultura portuguesa do Renascimento: A iconografia do livro impresso em Portugal no tempo de Dürer* (1972)

Real Biblioteca (Madrid), *Encuadernaciones de la Real Biblioteca*, www.encuadernacion.realbiblioteca.es, consulted May 2008

28 The History of the Book in Italy

Neil Harris

1 Introduction

Histories of the book in Italy, especially those assessing the impact of printing, often follow a predictable and all too conventional narrative pattern. They open with the German printers—who began publishing the works of antiquity at Subiaco in 1465 and at Rome in 1467—before switching to Venice in 1469, where yet more German printers and a French goldsmith cut the first *roman types. They usually describe the extraordinarily rapid spread of printing through the Italian cities: Trevi and Foligno in 1470; Bologna, Ferrara, Florence, Milan, Naples, and Treviso, and possibly Genoa, Perugia, and Verona in 1471; Cremona, Fivizzano, Mantua, Mondovì, Padua, and Parma in 1472. Indeed, by 1500, presses had operated in almost 80 localities. They next offer detailed accounts of *Aldus from 1495 onwards: his recovery of the Greek and Latin classics, his design of roman type, and his pocket-sized texts in *italic. If space allows, they might say something about Venetian publishing's Renaissance dominance and praise its illustrated books, before jumping to an account of the unique visual achievement of *Bodoni in Parma at the end of the 18th century. The conclusions of such standard accounts often comment on modern publishing in Italy, on the rise of Milan, and (perhaps) on the bestseller all'italiana in the 1950s and 1960s. None of this is wrong, since the salient facts are correct; even so, such a view is at best superficial, and the same pattern can be seen in a different light.

Rather than begin with the itinerant typographers, it may be useful to glance at the state of the book trade in Italy just before the advent of printing. The chief figure is the Florentine bookseller *Vespasiano da Bisticci, who organized on a huge and costly scale the copying and decoration of MSS for such clients as Cosimo de' Medici and Federico da *Montefeltro. Late in life, Vespasiano included in his memoirs a spiteful jab at the printing press, which was putting traditional bookmakers like himself out of business. His jaundiced claim that Federico would never have allowed a printed text in his collection is unfounded, but revealing. It shows that it is misleading to apply to Italy the idea—intrinsic to Lucien *Febvre's and Henri-Jean *Martin's French concept of the *history of the book—of a sharp rupture between printing and the MS tradition (see 13), since, if anything, the two for a while flourished and intermingled.

In 1949, *Ridolfi defined early printers as 'gente di necessità intesa alla moneta' ('people who are obliged to deal with money') (Ridolfi, 6). The German artisans, who hauled their possessions over the Alps on the back of a mule, had their eyes on a book market where fabulous sums were being paid for illuminated MSS on *vellum. Italy was also undergoing a cultural revolution (characterized as 'the Renaissance' by 19th-century scholars) that consisted initially in the rediscovery of ancient Greek and Roman works. This innovation was prompted in part by the Council of Ferrara and Florence in 1438, which attempted a conciliation between the Western and Orthodox churches; although the council ultimately failed, it did establish a direct acquaintance with Greek culture and language, up to that time known to Italian intellectuals

257

principally through medieval Latin. The subsequent fall of Byzantium (Constantinople) in 1453 precipitated a migration of Greek scholars, often with MSS in their baggage, who scraped a living in Italy through teaching. With its position athwart the Mediterranean, governing trade between West and East, with the wealth of its great banking families, and the influx of outside revenue ensured by the Catholic Church, 15th-century Italy (albeit fractured into feuding and sometimes warring states) was the richest and culturally fastest-moving 'country' in Europe. It was ripe, therefore, for a new way of making books.

2 The introduction of printing

Recent years have seen a lively discussion about the Parsons fragment, comprising eight leaves belonging to an *octavo edition in Italian of the *Leiden Christi* (Passion of Christ), a popular German work circulated widely in northern Europe in the 15th century. Discovered in 1925 by the Munich bookseller Jacques *Rosenthal, the fragment was described by *Haebler in 1927, before disappearing the following year into the collection of the Louisiana bibliophile Edward Alexander Parsons (1878–1962); it was forgotten until 1998, when it resurfaced and was sold at auction (*see* BOOK AUCTIONS) by *Christie's in London. The bibliographical excitement it generated stemmed from the large *rotunda type, whose *sorts have been filed to make them fit together, suggesting an early date of printing. Since its metal-cut illustrations were used in southern Germany c.1459–61, the edition may have been printed soon afterwards, almost certainly in Italy; linguistic analysis suggests that the translation was done in or near the triangle formed by Parma, Bologna, and Ferrara. If the assumptions about the date and place are correct, the fragment is unquestionably the first surviving printed Italian artefact. (This same rationale acknowledges, however, that other texts may have been produced even earlier and have been entirely lost; *see* SURVIVAL RATES.) Following its purchase for the *Scheide collection in Princeton, the fragment was connected to a document written in Bondeno, near Ferrara, in February 1463, containing an agreement between a German priest, Paul Moerch, and his compatriot, Ulrich Purschmid (or Bauerschmid), from Baisweil, near Augsburg. The agreement refers to making terracotta figures of a Pietà and of a Virgin and Child; it also discusses shaping formes to produce a Latin grammar ('formam unius Donati'), a child's *psalter ('formam unius Psalterii puerorum'), and an *ABC for learning

purposes ('formam unius Tabule puerorum'). It has been argued that the fragment and the agreement are closely related, so that the dawn of printing in Italy should be antedated to Bondeno, c.1463 (Scapecchi). Yet, however beguiling at first sight, the presumption is a dangerous one. In Latin, *forma* designates any surface used as a *matrix, while the agreement as a whole suggests that Purschmid's expertise is in ceramic (*see* KOREAN TYPE) rather than casting in metal. Moreover, rudimentary printing techniques were employed in Italy in the pre-*Gutenberg era. A Venetian document of 1441 talks of 'carte da zugar' and 'figure stampide' (playing cards and printed images); another of 1447 mentions 'alcune forme da stanpar donadi et salterj' ('some formes to print grammars and psalters')—two of the three items in the Bondeno document (Cecchetti). Although the 1463 agreement may well refer to a primitive process in which sheets were *impressed on one side only from a surface moulded in relief, no verdict is yet possible on the Parsons fragment. Nonetheless, it does support the observation that, following the spread of printing north of the Alps, German artisans (who financed their move by printing small, easily sold books) might plausibly have arrived somewhere in the Po valley.

Unless an earlier example comes to light, it must be concluded that datable printing began in Italy when *Sweynheym and Pannartz set a press up in Subiaco, a small town 70 km east of Rome. Why they settled there, at the Benedictine monastery of Santa Scolastica, unfortunately remains unknown. Their first printed text was a Donatus, which has been lost. The first to have survived, in some twenty copies, was Cicero's *De Oratore*; the *edition is undated, but a copy once in Leipzig, now in Moscow, bears a note written on 30 September 1465. This was followed by a Lactantius in October and, in 1467, by Augustine's *De Civitate Dei*. Thereafter, they sensibly shifted business to Rome. The ups and downs of their subsequent enterprise are delineated in the prefaces and dedications of their editor, the bishop designate of Aleria, Giovanni Andrea Bussi. Far from enjoying an overwhelming success, a combination of factors—including a policy of issuing large, humanist-orientated works, the overprinting of such sure sellers as Cicero, and competition from other Germans such as *Han (who in the meantime had gravitated to Rome)—ensured that, by the early 1470s, there was a book glut (Bussi). The early publishers' pecuniary embarrassment is symptomatic of a wider difficulty: they failed to harness the dynamics of an expanding but largely unknown market.

The standard view of Italian book history states that, by 1500, printing had gained a foothold in numerous cities; what is generally not mentioned is how often that foothold was lost. Usually, a press was set up and operated for a short period of time (sometimes producing only a single edition), before moving elsewhere. One example is Treviso, where printing was introduced by *Geraert van der Lys in 1471; some eleven presses worked there until 1494, after which printing was extinguished until 1589. Geraert also inaugurated printing at Udine in 1484, where it lasted for a couple of years; the next press did not appear there until 1592. Unlike Germany, where printing, once established, in most cases persisted, in Italy it failed to take root just about everywhere. Only five Italian cities (Rome, Venice, Ferrara, Milan, and Bologna) maintained unbroken publishing activity up to and including the 16th century. In another five (Florence, Naples, Parma, Modena, and Turin), printing had a false start, but was introduced a second time and afterwards proceeded steadily. In another two (Brescia and Siena), the new *ars* ran well during the 15th century, once under way, but suffered major setbacks in the 16th century. To understand why the printing seed was often sown but rarely flowered, one episode is particularly instructive, because those involved went to court and left a sheaf of documentation. These legal records tell the story of the partnership between Johannes Vurster, who in 1473 introduced printing at Modena, and a local paper merchant, Cecchino Morano, who saw in it a chance to expand his business. The two turned out several large books aimed at nearby *Bologna University, but failed to find a market. In 1476, after being sued by his partner and narrowly escaping imprisonment, Vurster fled town, leaving behind him a shop full of unsold volumes (Balsamo). Although supporting evidence of this quality is generally lacking, it is plausible that many such early ventures regularly teetered on the brink of financial disaster and sometimes plummeted into the abyss. After all, the foreign prototypographers lacked both the local market knowledge needed to distribute what they printed (hundreds of copies of the same book) and the depth of capital necessary for a more gradual sales policy. Although printing failed to establish itself in 85 per cent of the places it touched, one city rapidly triumphed over all the others: Venice.

3 Venice

Introduced by John of *Speyer in 1469, printing in Venice burgeoned extraordinarily in just a few years.

According to the *Incunabula Short Title Catalogue* (ISTC), Venice produced some 3,500 known editions, putting Italy as a whole—with some 9,900 impressions—just ahead of Germany's 9,300, and far exceeding France's 4,500 items. Venice outstripped Paris, its main European rival, by 25 per cent, and issued double the number of editions produced by Rome, its principal Italian competitor. Yet the editions do not tell the full story. In Venice, half the recorded output was in *folio format and only 9 per cent in *octavo or smaller; in Paris, folio represented only 12 per cent, *quarto 58 per cent, and octavo the rest; in Rome, folio stood at 15 per cent, quarto 68 per cent, octavo 17 per cent, while many items there were orations confined to a single sheet of paper or less. In other words, most Venetian books were big and those of other centres were conversely small. Although the distribution of books has been much disturbed over the course of centuries, censuses of 15th-century books conducted in outlying European districts show the extent of Venice's penetration: 23 per cent of *incunabula now in Poland were printed in Venice, 27 per cent in Spain, 28 per cent in Hungary, 33 per cent in Portugal.

Venice's dominance inside Italy grew constantly, and the city acted as a publishing magnet, attracting other enterprises. Among the presses that disappeared from Treviso, several reappeared in its powerful neighbour a year or so later. Precise counts are never possible, but it is estimated that some 230 printing businesses were active in Venice before 1501. In simple terms, Venetian books were better. Not only were they better designed and better printed, they also used better paper and were usually the first to employ illustrations and *paratextual elements, such as *indexes. At the same time they were less expensive. Not surprisingly, therefore, booksellers and customers in cities all over Europe accorded their preference to Venetian products, so that local printers had to fall back on narrower markets. *Caxton's patriotism was genuine, but by publishing mostly in the vernacular, he tacitly admitted his inability to compete with the elegant Latin imprints of *Jenson and the like. The technical superiority of Venice appears above all in her printers' mastery of the more complex typographical procedures, such as liturgical texts in *red and black. The existence, sometimes fragmentary, of *breviaries and *missals 'ad usum Sarum', for the diocese of Salisbury, bears witness to commissions received from the far-off English market. Once the industry was well established, continuity with the tradition of hand decoration was translated into supremely elegant *woodcut illustrations, inspired by major artists such as Mantegna, which again increased the product's marketability. Likewise, European music printing, in which the staves, the notes, and sometimes the words required separate impressions, was dominated by Venetian firms, beginning with *Petrucci in 1501 and followed later in the century by *Gardano and *Scotto.

The question why this happened in Venice is rarely asked. Naples possessed a larger population, Florence was at the height of its Renaissance glory, while Rome boasted the luxury and splendour of the papal court. Italian cities such as Milan and Ferrara had ruling dynasties offering *patronage, while Bologna, Padua, and Pavia had flourishing universities. Albeit with a mountain range at its back, a city such as Genoa shared many similarities with Venice: a maritime republic, with a papermaking industry at nearby Voltri, and an almost identical political system, in which a doge was elected by a hereditary aristocracy. Yet printing there took several attempts to get off the ground, establishing itself securely only in 1534. What Venice had on a greater scale was a highly ramified mercantile and financial organization, definable as a predisposition to risk, based on the lucrative but financially dangerous trade with the Middle East and East Asia. Even before the time of Marco Polo, luxury commodities such as silk and spices had passed through Venice for distribution elsewhere in Europe. The economy of the city revolved around the *sortes* (shares) purchased in trading ventures, which, if successful, recouped the original investment several times over; if the ship failed to return, as in Shakespeare's *The Merchant of Venice*, the participants lost some or all of their money. The system involved society at all levels, even very small investors, such as widows and orphans; this induced a mentality in which Venetians instinctively grasped the economics of the new publishing business, where a raw commodity (paper) was transformed into a value-enhanced, finished product (printed text) that required further monies in order to distribute it and ensure a profit.

As far as an early concentration of capital is concerned, *Jenson's career provides valuable insights. Known today for the marvellous *mise-en-page* of his editions and for a roman type surpassed only by Aldus, he was the front man for a publishing consortium that included the merchant-bookseller Peter Ugelheimer (Nuovo). The annals of his output can be read in ISTC, but a project worth undertaking would be an exhaustive *census of surviving copies to establish what proportion were printed on *vellum and how many were

*rubricated and/or illuminated. In the one edition subjected to such an inquiry, the 1478 folio Roman Breviary, 24 of the 45 known copies are vellum and almost all exhibit hand-added decoration of the first order (Armstrong). Publishing in the long term went in the opposite direction, as large, high-quality, hand-embellished, polychrome books on parchment (which approximated MSS) were replaced by small, sometimes shoddily printed, monochrome books on paper. Nonetheless, the luxury, high-cost product filled something more than a niche market; holding its own up to the beginning of the 16th century, it was fully exploited by Jenson, who was followed by Aldus and emulated in Paris by *Vérard.

A book industry which produced vastly more than the local market could ever have absorbed had to export on a large scale. Venice's other great advantage was its pre-existent distribution network, allowing it to send goods via water along the Adriatic seaboard and through a system of rivers and canals covering the whole of northern Italy, as well as by road, with trains of mules that crossed the Alps into Germany and France. This same network was exploited in parallel by the paper and textile trades, with which the book trade had many affinities—some publishers are also known to have been cloth merchants. The concentration of commercial expertise from elsewhere in Italy ensured furthermore that, once the publishing industry was fully established, few in it were bona fide Venetians. The places of origin of the city's printers, proudly declared in the *colophons of its Renaissance imprints, mostly form a pinpoint map of the Po valley, with a grouping of dots around Brescia and the Italian lakes (Toscolano on Lake Garda was also the heart of the Venetian papermaking industry) and, further off, the Piedmont town of Trino.

Venice's bookshops and *printing offices were concentrated between the Rialto and St Mark's Square; from the Renaissance to the 18th century, travellers' accounts speak of a vast emporium, where buyers spent hours browsing in dozens and dozens of shops. An early measure of this intense bookselling activity is the *Zornale* of *Maggi, which from 1484 to 1488 provides a record of each day's sales: entries are concise, usually no more than the title, but the ledger scrupulously records prices, which can be compared to other commodities, and the nature of the purchases. Although most items are sold singly, sometimes a buyer takes two, three, even up to twenty books together. At the same time, the book trade perceptible through the *Zornale* remains conservative; for all the speed with which Italian printers mastered the technology, their prime concern was to transfer the textual heritage of the Middle Ages into the new medium. As *Scholderer observed in 1935, 'while Italian incunabula form the most varied and interesting body of books of their class, the culture which they reveal is so fully elaborated as to appear to a large extent static' (*BMC* 7. xxxvii). Rather curiously, when the shake-up came, it was produced largely by a return to an even greater antiquity.

4 Aldus

The importance of being Aldus, to misquote Oscar Wilde, is undeniable. After that of *Gutenberg, his name is probably the best known in the whole of book history. On the other hand, although Gutenberg's claim to fame is established by his invention of the printing press, why precisely has Aldus gained such renown? After all, he was a latecomer to the profession; in 1495, when he opened shop, over 200 other presses had already worked or were working in Venice. While rivers of ink have been lavished on his achievement—and there is no doubt that there was an achievement—its nature is not always clear; indeed, it is necessary to remember that the first, and most diligent, purveyor of the myth of Aldus was Aldus himself. After his death in 1515, the Aldine brand was assiduously marketed for the rest of the century, first by the *Torresani family, later by his direct heirs, so that, matters of *pietas* apart, the legend must have been good business. Consequently, the whole story abounds in pitfalls: even today some bibliographical writers assert that Aldus launched a 16th-century proto-*paperback revolution with low-cost, octavo-format classics, despite the fact that his enchiridions were expensive by contemporary standards, so much so that it was profitable to counterfeit them in Lyons.

A proper assessment of Aldus would concentrate on his personality as a schoolteacher and on the fact that, like another remarkable typographical innovator, *Baskerville, he came to printing late in age by Renaissance terms, in his mid-40s. He did so in the guise of a frustrated intellectual, one who had failed to succeed as a humanist or as a scholar in the mould of his teacher, Battista Guarino. Education, therefore, was the lynchpin of the Aldine project, because he aimed not only at recovering the texts of classical antiquity, but at finding readers for them. He was the right man at the right time, but he also found the right collaborators: Torresani and the aristocrat Pierfrancesco Barbarigo, whose deep purses financed the enterprise; *Griffo, whose extraordinary eye and

hand produced the required *typefaces; *Musurus and *Bembo, whose intellectual prestige and editorial abilities guaranteed the quality of the texts. The central idea was that the study of Greek and, to a lesser extent, Latin should be at the heart of the educational canon; however, the correct printing of Greek, with its numerous combinations of breathings and *accents, presented a considerable obstacle. The first individual to overcome these challenges successfully, Aldus placed at the core of European pedagogical thinking the concept that the education of young gentlemen and of governing elites should be based on the intensive study of a remote dead language. The net outcome was that, for 400 years, students sweated over Aeschylus and Sophocles in the classroom, becoming adults who shared a common *forma mentis*.

Focusing on Aldus's part in this intellectual upheaval allows Italy's role in book history to be better defined. Most of the high moments in the canonical interpretation sketched out in the introduction of this essay have common ground in the same element: in a word, design. Early in 1496, after issuing his first books set entirely in Greek, Aldus published *De Aetna* with a new roman type that elaborated upon and strengthened Jenson's already remarkable character of 1470, and that, with refinements, culminated in the unreadable but visually splendid *Hypnerotomachia Poliphili*. The type's subsequent versions, remodelled by *Garamont, culminate in *Morison's Times New Roman (1932), the common default character on today's *computer screens. Yet, it remains recognizable as Aldus's offspring. Much the same is true of italic; the first Aldine design of 1501 may have no direct modern progeny, but nobody has ever questioned the significance of his innovation.

5 An interlude with factors and causes

By the end of 1500, the Italian publishing industry (mostly in Venice) had taken on a recognizable physiognomy that in many respects would remain unaltered until the fall of the Venetian Republic in 1797. However, its dominance and success simultaneously held the seeds of its own decline, one that would last for centuries. At the cost of some simplification, five interrelated factors are examined in this digression: political structure, new world exploration, religious reform, national language, and readership.

During this period, Italy had no single dominant political entity. The peninsula was broken into small states, of which the two strongest, Venice and the papacy, depended on the election of a gerontocrat ruler. In Venice, the doge was little more than a figure-head: real power generally rested with the faceless aristocrats of the Council of Ten. The system ensured political continuity, but constrained initiative, since the favoured policy was to hedge, block, and wait for the problem to go away. The papacy did elect a real ruler, but usually at an advanced age: an energetic figure, such as Julius II (r. 1503–13), could mould events, but reigns were so short that enemies rode out the storm. The political set-up meant, therefore, not only that there was no single central market represented by a capital (such as Paris or London), but also that, when by the late 18th century the book industry needed vigorous institutional measures, the Italian states were too weak and too divided to supply them.

The second event contributing to the long-term decline of the Italian publishing industry was the discovery of America in 1492 and of the sea route to the East in 1497–9, which gradually shifted the balance of power in Europe from the Mediterranean to the more dynamic nations along the Atlantic seaboard, gradually nullifying Venice's role as an entrepôt for trade with the Orient. The third historical consideration is the religious metamorphosis caused by the success of Protestant reform in northern Europe and by its failure in Italy. The long-term outcome of the Reformation was a gradual closing of the frontiers to the Italian book, linked also to the decline of Latin as a universal means of communication.

Although these first three factors were external to the book trade, the two remaining were internal, and require lengthier treatment, starting with the national language. From the 16th to the middle of the 20th century, an averagely educated Italian was expected to master two languages, apart from what was spoken at home, through schooling and reading. The first was classical Latin (often with the rudiments of Greek)—a dead language, but necessary to understand the importance of Italy's cultural heritage. The second language was Italian, which at that time was neither dead nor living. Outside school, the average Italian employed a dialect whose range of intelligibility varied considerably. In the north and in Tuscany, the same dialects covered large regions; in the agricultural and poverty-stricken regions of the south and in the islands, however, linguistic zones were more restricted, meaning that people living in one village could hardly talk to those 20 miles away. Italian's growth into a national spoken language is that of an artificial tongue, to some extent an ideology, that was largely book-disseminated. Its progress originated in two key periods. First, in the 14th century, three works

written in Tuscan vernacular—Dante's *Divina Commedia*, *Petrarca's Rerum Vulgarium Fragmenta*, and Boccaccio's *Decameron*—set new literary standards and started the long, slow march of European modern languages. Secondly, in the 16th century, Bembo decreed in his *Prose della Volgar Lingua* (1525) that the norm for written Italian should be Petrarca in poetry and Boccaccio in prose. To some extent, he only expressed as theory what had been posited previously by others, such as Fortunio's *Regole Grammaticali della Volgar Lingua* (1516), and what Venetian printers were already doing. What made the difference was his authority as a nobleman, as an editor, and as an author, who in 1539 received a cardinal's hat, in modern parlance 'for services to literature'. Bembo and his fellow theorists were not, however, concerned with whether the establishment of a single written norm would lead to a unified spoken language. That process would not occur for another four centuries, when other media were introduced.

The application of a Tuscan norm based on the literature of the Trecento (i.e. writers of whom the youngest was 30 years older than Chaucer) was facilitated by the example of Renaissance masterpieces such as the *Cortegiano* (1528). Written by the Mantuan career diplomat and papal nuncio Baldassarre Castiglione, the archetypal *conduct book went through several drafts in order to obtain the right linguistic patina; it was seen through the press in the author's absence by a Venetian *corrector, Giovan Francesco Valier, whose final emendations are visible in the *printer's copy kept by the Aldine press and given to *Grolier. The case of the Ferrarese poet Ludovico Ariosto is even more interesting, since his *Orlando Furioso* (1532) continues an earlier poem, the *Orlando Innamorato* by Matteo Maria Boiardo, first published in 1482–3 in a lost *editio princeps, with a third book added in 1495 (Harris). Telling the story of the paladin Roland—who falls in love with the beautiful but evil-intentioned Angelica and thus forsakes his duty to Charlemagne and to Christendom—Boiardo's story enthralled 15th-century readers with its breathtaking adventures and spectacular sword fights; however, it was written in a Po valley cadence, whose rhymes offended the ear of Italian purists. The first version of Ariosto's continuation, in 40 cantos, published in 1516 was a half-way stage that maintained dialect forms and rhymes; a partial revision appeared in 1521, followed by a fully-fledged Tuscanized definitive edition, with the addition of six cantos, in 1532. The 287 press variants and a cancellans sheet (*see* CANCEL) described by *Fahy show the author fiddling with the text up to and even after the last possible moment. The virtuosity of the outcome was hailed as a triumph, and its stature as Italy's Renaissance chef-d'œuvre has rarely been questioned; it also proved to be a commercial success for publishers such as *Giolito and Valgrisi, who turned out editions in multiple *formats augmented with illustrations, commentaries, and other sorts of paratext. In the 1580s it was temporarily eclipsed by the *Gerusalemme Liberata*, initially entitled *Il Goffredo*, which contained a poetical, allegorical account of the First Crusade that profoundly influenced other European writers. Its author, Torquato Tasso, can claim to be the first genuine pan-Italian writer, since in childhood he travelled widely and thus avoided growing up speaking a local dialect. All these writers, who grappled with the task of creating literary works in what was effectively a foreign language, are comparable to a novelist such as Conrad, who wrote in English, his third language after his native Polish and after French.

The last factor bearing on the history of the book in Italy is the absence of a solid middle-class readership. The term 'middle-class' here is a deliberate anachronism, designating a numerically consistent body of users who see the book as an instrument for self-improvement and as an expression of their own upward aspiration. Since Italy had enjoyed a higher level of urban *literacy than elsewhere in Europe during the early Renaissance and has never since lacked erudition nor scholars, to speak of the absence of a whole class of readers appears to be a contradiction. Nevertheless, this is what happened and, though the causes were many and complex, the key moment in this literacy-failure probably occurred in 1559, when the first Roman *Index banned the Bible in Italian. Quite independently of the sacred text's content and import, the Bible is a large book and therefore its removal from circulation had important and damaging consequences for the general standard of literacy. Before that date, reading the scriptures, even by those who knew little or no Latin, was fairly widespread in Italian society. The earliest *volgarizzamento* of the Bible by Nicolò Malermi had appeared in Venice in 1471. The 16th century saw further translations, especially that by Antonio Brucioli (1532) which seemed tainted with heresy. The Catholic Church's fears about uncontrolled and uncontrollable reading of the biblical text thus resulted in a wider clampdown on the circulation of ideas. From 1559 (or rather from 1564, when the definitive Tridentine *Index confirmed the ban), a split emerged in Italian reading practice and habits. At one extreme, an elite educated on the

Aldine model consumed works in both quantity and quality; however, because members of religious orders constituted a significant portion of this category, family reading was generally excluded and women were often discouraged from becoming literate. At the other end, readers with minimal formal education sought out and perused texts, sometimes incurring the wrath of the authorities. For example, at Udine in 1584 and again in 1599, a miller, Domenico Scandella (known as Menocchio), was accused of heresy before an *Inquisition tribunal, which recorded his reading and what he thought he found there (Ginzburg). The trial has a bibliographical import, since the books Menocchio liked best, such as Mandeville's travels, were second-hand and dated back half a century and more. Otherwise, as a direct consequence of the clampdown, the books of the last third of the 16th century are unappetizing fare and there is little to attract a middle-of-the-road reader. Textual *censorship may not have wholly deterred lovers of literature, but episodes such as the *rassettature* of the *Decameron* between 1573 and 1588, in which negative references to the clergy were removed and some tales were substantially rewritten, demonstrate that the conduct of the book trades was materially altered, and not for the better. A sea-change is visible also in the catalogues of firms such as Giolito, which abandoned its predominantly literary output in favour of markedly religious productions. To attribute this metamorphosis merely to publishing timidity is to oversimplify: society was changing, readers were changing, and books merely followed the trend. This crack in social literacy created in the 16th century became a chasm by the 18th century.

6 The 16th century and the supremacy of Venice

The minute tallying of Venetian daily existence in Marin Sanudo's diaries, kept from 1496 to 1533, is silently eloquent when it reaches the last day of 1500. No jubilant throng of printers, publishers, and booksellers gathered in St Mark's Square to cheer the ending of the incunable age and dance into the small hours of the incoming century. This is hardly surprising, since the bibliographical threshold of New Year's Day 1501 is a later demarcation, long recognized as artificial and undesirable; it is, nevertheless, a convenient moment for taking stock (Norton). The ongoing Italian census of 16th-century books (*Edit16*), together with its sister system, Servizio Bibliotecario Nazionale (SBN), shows that, in 1501, slightly more than 200 titles were published in a dozen cities. The lion's share appeared in Venice (64 per cent). Its closest rival was Milan (16 per cent), which had a plethora of small printers and two large publisher-booksellers, *Legnano and *Nicolò da Gorgonzola. Thereafter came Bologna (7 per cent), mainly with large tomes for university use, then Rome (3 per cent) and Brescia (2 per cent). Reggio Emilia (2 per cent) was surprisingly active, publishing its statutes in that year, while token presences mark the output of Turin, Parma, Pavia, Perugia, Ferrara, and Florence. Centres that temporarily appear dormant, however, such as Modena, may have produced ephemera that have not survived (*see* **14**), or undated imprints that have been classified as possible incunabula. A pattern emerges that remained true up to the 17th century: Venice dominated the trade and other centres struggled to compete. Although important literary works might have a first edition elsewhere (e.g. Sannazaro's *Arcadia* in Naples, or Ariosto's *Orlando Furioso* in Ferrara), subsequent editions invariably migrated to Venice.

This dominance was reinforced by legislation and by the lobbying power of the publishers themselves, who from 1549 were organized in their own guild (Brown). John of Speyer's 1469 monopoly concession was followed by a hiatus, but around the turn of the century requests for *privileges came thick and fast. Aldus was especially assiduous: he obtained protection for his Greek texts in 1496 and 1498 and for his new italic type in 1501; the year after, he demanded measures against the *counterfeit printing of his octavo editions. The system was open to abuse, so much so that in 1517 the senate, irritated by the number of blanket applications for authors and titles, cancelled all extant concessions and—recognizing the need for tighter controls—in 1545 placed the book trade under the charge of the Riformatori dello Studio di Padova. Like other Italian states, Venice kept its university in a satellite city, Padua, where, owing to the disastrous war of the League of Cambrai (1508–16), all teaching had ceased; in 1528, therefore, this new magistrature was created to reopen the university and oversee its running. Elective by nature and considered prestigious, the Riformatori became the equivalent of a culture ministry with powers over academies, libraries, and the book trade. Printers had to submit any work they intended to publish for approval, and permission followed swiftly—as long as nothing was found against religion, against princes (i.e. other governments), or against morality in general. With the promulgation of the *Index*, the Inquisition's attempts to impose

censorship led to bitter disputes, not only with publishers but also with the Venetian authorities, who resented and obstructed Roman interference (Grendler). In 1596 a concordat was signed, however, ratifying a system of double approval, in which the inquisitor verified that the book contained nothing against the Catholic faith. However, owing to frequent—and often justified—complaints about his overstepping his jurisdiction, it became increasingly common to obtain only state approval and to evade church control by a *false imprint describing the place of publication (Infelise).

Statistics defining early book output are misleading at the best of times, but evaluating Italian Renaissance production is akin to a blindfold obstacle race. First, a significant percentage of imprints no longer survive. Second, large-scale export at the time and *bibliophile collecting in the interim have ensured that approximately half the surviving copies of pre-1601 books—sometimes the sole witnesses of their respective editions—are now found outside Italy. The largest single collection is in London: rough counts suggest that, if the *British Library took part in *Edit16*, it would hold just under 40 per cent of the total, whereas the National Central Libraries of *Florence and *Rome both average fewer than 30 per cent. Third, inside Italy itself, there is no tradition of concentrating early books in a few major collections. Instead, small towns have collections besides which the well-known public library parameter of one book per inhabitant appears almost absurd: Poppi, in Tuscany, with 5,300 inhabitants boasts 500 incunabula, while not-too-distant San Gimignano, with a population of 7,400, owns 1,600 16th-century books. Up to now, therefore, attempts at quantification—such as those constructed on the BL's holdings—have proved inaccurate. However, the existence of electronic media not only simplifies counting, but also offers new opportunities.

At the time of writing, *Edit16* lists 6,800 entries for 1501–20 (39 per cent from Venice); 6,300 for 1521–40 (54 per cent); 10,800 for 1541–60 (56 per cent); 16,900 for 1561–80 (43 per cent); and 21,100 for 1581–1600 (34 per cent). The sort of plateau in early production is attributable to the anti-Venetian war and to the subsequent sack of Rome in 1527, accompanied by an outbreak of the plague, so that the century's publishing nadir came in 1529. Otherwise, from 1501, inspired by the Aldine model, Venice reversed its earlier practice of publishing large-format books. According to ISTC, in 1465–80 54 per cent of Italian editions were in folio, 41 per cent were quarto, and

5 per cent were octavo or less; in 1481–1500 these proportions have already shifted respectively to 39, 50, and 11 per cent. By comparison in *Edit16*, by 1521–40 folio shrinks to 13 per cent, quarto holds at 32 per cent, octavo reaches 52 per cent, and even smaller formats—mainly *duodecimo—make themselves known at 3 per cent. In 1581–1600, folio remains constant at 10 per cent, though some titles are large, multi-volume publications; quarto climbs again to 46 per cent; octavo drops back to 31 per cent; and smaller formats make inroads to reach 13 per cent. The objective of resorting to smaller formats was to save paper, which in a Renaissance book could lead to savings of up to a third, though paradoxically the first edition in a new format often employs a greater number of sheets than its immediate predecessor. A large work never out of print, such as Boccaccio's *Decameron*, shows a characteristic evolution: after the folio *editio princeps* c.1470 (127 sheets), it reached its maximum size with the *Ripoli edition *c.*1483 (151 sheets), although from 1504 to 1518 a more compact layout reduced the sheets to 63. The first quarto in 1516 contained 91 sheets, reduced to 68 by 1541; the octavo format first introduced in 1525 required 84 sheets, which fell to 56 by 1540; a trial sextodecimo imprint in 1542 has 23½ sheets, although the first duodecimo in 1550 uses 38½.

In this competitive market, books had to be attractive to buyers and Venice pioneered the innovation of the *title-page and the consequent shift of publication-related information from the *colophon to the front of the book. Publishers there swiftly caught on to the importance of clearly recognizable brand names. In incunabula, the traditional sign, or mark, of the medieval *stationarius* (*stationer)—an orb with a double-cross, hanging over the shop door—appeared as a woodcut *printer's device, often with the addition of the proprietor's initials, in conjunction with the colophon. This usage gave way, by the following century, to a more distinctive publisher's mark that visually identified the bookshop, at times with a pun on the owner's name, as with the Tower (Torresani), the St Bernard (Bernardino Stagnino), and the St Nicholas (Nicolò Zoppino). Other establishments employed an easily remembered symbol, such as the Anchor (Aldus), Cat (*Sessa), Dolphin (Garanta), Lily (*Giunta), Mermaid (Ravani), and Phoenix (Giolito). Publisher-printers were also adept at other tricks, such as modifying the date on the title-page, typical of Giolito's output (so that the book would appear to be 'new' for more than a year at a time), or edition-sharing (where the name and mark of one publisher

were substituted in press with those of another). This last habit in particular might cause migraines for those who have to catalogue such books, but it reveals substantial alliances within the Venetian industry, especially in the last part of the 16ᵗʰ century, when the market for large editions of patristic authors experienced an upturn after the regeneration of monastic libraries following the Council of Trent and the creation of a network of seminaries to train priests. A consortium of Venetian publishers, therefore, issued editions where each owned a personalized quota, the most striking example being the eleven-volume quarto edition of the works of St Augustine in 1570 (republished in 1584), split between Giunta, Nicolini, Sessa, Valgrisi, Varisco, and Zenaro.

7 The 17ᵗʰ to the 19ᵗʰ centuries: decline, revival, fall, renewal

The number of titles published in Italy peaked in 1588. The publishing crisis that followed—in full swing by the early 17ᵗʰ century—was mainly Venetian and had various causes, some of which have already been noted, such as the introduction (or often return) of printing to minor centres, usually as a service industry catering for local needs; thus, by 1601 presses were solidly implanted in more than 40 localities. In 1606 the jurisdictional conflict between Venice and Rome reached its height, with the interdict, largely disobeyed, forbidding priests from holding religious events in the city. The opposing factions engaged in a *pamphlet war, in which Venice's spokesman, the Servite friar Paolo Sarpi, demolished the papal arguments. In retaliation the Church intensified its attack on the economic base of the Venetian industry—the publishing of liturgical texts in red and black—by issuing privileges that favoured Roman editions and encouraging Venetian printers to relocate to Rome. With the trade elsewhere in Europe crippled by the Thirty Years War (1618–48), the final blow for a struggling industry came with the 1630 plague, which decimated the population of northern Italy. In the decade that followed, Venetian output dropped to 20 per cent of its former height, overtaken within the Italian market (albeit temporarily) by Rome and within the international market by Paris. Italian dominance of the European market had always been favoured by the role of Latin as the universal language: around mid-century, a different economic and political hegemony imposed French as the new lingua franca.

By the 18th century, a qualitative split is apparent. The top end of the market was occupied by works of notable, if to modern eyes dusty, erudition: the age's leading intellectual was a librarian, Ludovico Antonio Muratori. Just as the *Encyclopédie* was the most important French book of its time, so its Italian counterpart was the immense assemblage of medieval sources Muratori edited as the *Rerum Italicarum Scriptores* (25 vols, 1723–51). Second place on the scale of importance belongs to his later successor at the *Estense Library, Girolamo Tiraboschi, whose *Storia della Letteratura Italiana* (10 vols, 1772–82) imposed a nonexistent national identity on a very existent literature. The publishing trade revived, bolstered by large-scale printing projects and aided both by the decline of traditional rivals Lyons and Antwerp and by the recession caused in France by the War of the Spanish Succession (1701–14). Venice in particular, led by the Baglioni firm, recovered its preeminence in the printing of liturgical texts, which were exported mainly to the Spanish dominions in the New World. Another proof of revival was the success enjoyed by what to all intents and purposes was an academic press, set up in the house of a Padua University professor and managed by the printer *Comino, with an essentially Aldine programme of Greek and Latin classics in elegant typography. The exclusive market for quality printing also sustained and largely justified the remarkable career of Bodoni, who transformed type design more profoundly than anyone since Aldus. But however extraordinary as typographical artefacts, his books are not intended to be read: his best-known publications therefore are his specimens, including the misleadingly titled *Manuale tipografico* issued by his widow in 1818. The steady advance of francophone culture is marked also by editions of the *Encyclopédie* in Lucca (1758–76) and in Livorno (1770–78), as well as by the reprint of the later *Encyclopédie méthodique* undertaken by the Seminary of *Padua.

The other end of the market was formed by a large-scale production, often in minor centres, of *almanacs, *chapbooks, works of popular piety, and so on, much of it anonymous and largely uncharted by bibliographers. To Venetian eyes, the most damaging producer was the Bassano *Remondini firm, which, after opening a branch in Venice, attacked the publishing establishment from 1750 onward by systematically undercutting the price of steady-selling works whose privilege had recently expired. Savings were obtained by crowding half as much text again on to the page, with deleterious results for its quality, so that they

Contorni, printers' *ornaments (*fleurons or *borders), from *Bodoni's widow's celebrated *type specimen book, *Manuale tipografico* (1818).

were accused, rightly, of provoking a lapse in printing standards, in which others followed suit.

The French revolutionary armies that swept through Italy overthrew the Venetian Republic in 1797 and, among other things, turned the book trade inside out. When the dust settled in 1814, much appeared the same, but new ideas were stirring in the north. In particular, there was a growing sense that Italy was more than a geographical expression, and in the Risorgimento (resurgence) that followed, the existence of a national language and literature, however virtual, thrust the country towards unity. The cause was significantly espoused in publishing circles by foreign nationals, such as the Frenchman *Le Monnier and the Swiss *Vieusseux, together with francophone Piedmontese such as *Pomba and *Barbèra, who with their respective series, the 'Biblioteca Italiana' and the

'Collezione Diamante', insisted on the nation's de facto cultural homogeneity. The cities of the north were also more amenable to technological progress; Pomba in Turin was the first to invest in a mechanized printing office, and Milan rapidly became Italy's main publishing centre (Berengo). In the period 1814–1900, book production increased tenfold, leaving aside the growth of newspapers and magazines.

The century was also marked by a search for readers. Now that Italian publishing was confined to Italy, with few opportunities for export elsewhere, the domestic market proved suffocatingly small. The one exception to this rule was music publishing, dominated by *Ricordi, for Italian opera ruled the European stage in the period from Verdi to Puccini. In the 19th century, two important factors emerge regarding the question of the absence of a middle-class readership. The first is the failure of the *circulating library to take root, presumably because not enough native Italians were willing or able to disburse the sums involved: the one splendid exception, Vieusseux in Florence, was funded by foreign tourists. The second is the meagre fortune enjoyed by that archetypal middle-class genre, the novel, with its obligatory happy ending bringing marital, monetary, and social advancement. The first successful European novel, Samuel *Richardson's *Pamela* (1740), was translated into Italian in 1744, whereas the first indigenous attempt, Pietro Chiari's *La Filosofessa* (1753), significantly pretended to be the translation of a French original, made as the sheets came off the press in Paris. Although other titles were produced, for a long time only one was accepted as literature, Manzoni's I *Promessi Sposi* (The Betrothed). Sharing with Richardson a story-line where a young girl is kidnapped in order to be seduced, it involved a significant effort to erase the dialect forms of the first edition and to create the pure contemporary Tuscan of the final version; thus, it established a new standard for the Italian language. The two other most successful fictional works of the 19th century were both aimed at the children's market: De Amicis' *Cuore* (1868) and Collodi's worldwide bestseller *Pinocchio* (1883) (*see* **15**).

Outside the French-reading, educated classes, fictional narrative otherwise struggled with a dearth of readers and with the backwardness of the educational system. For Italy as a whole, 75 per cent of the population was unable to read or write in 1870; in the rural south, this figure reached 90 per cent. Primary schooling became obligatory in 1877, but a lack of resources and the opposition of the clergy meant that the law remained a dead letter in many places; in 1911 the number of Italians with inadequate literacy skills still averaged 38 per cent.

8 The 20th and 21st centuries: two wars, Fascism, and after

In 1901, the Italian book trade presented geographical and cultural anomalies that remain substantially true today. Rome was the political capital; Milan, dominated by the rivalry between *Sonzogno and Treves, was the economic and publishing capital; Florence—with the official home of the Italian language at the Crusca Academy, the country's most important libraries, and publishers such as Barbèra, *Bemporad, Le Monnier, and *Sansoni—was the cultural capital. Although once-glorious Venice had almost disappeared from the map, other cities had publishing houses of considerable standing, such as Utet in Turin and *Zanichelli in Bologna. An important novelty was the arrival of professional booksellers from the German-speaking world, such as Loescher, *Hoepli, and *Olschki, who took over established firms and subsequently broadened their scope. Beyond the handful of large companies, much publishing was local in character, revolving around a network of bookshop-stationers in small centres. Unity had also left the country with a network of libraries, including those of the universities, belonging to the former Italian states. Although enormously wealthy in terms of manuscripts and valuable printed books, most of these collections had little to offer for a population with low-grade reading skills.

Italy entered World War I in 1915 to settle its outstanding account with the Austro-Hungarian empire, suffered a shattering defeat at Caporetto, and obtained little more than crumbs at the Versailles peace table. Resentment opened the door to Mussolini, who took power in 1922. Fascism was not, as Benedetto Croce subsequently claimed, a Hyksos invasion by an external enemy that had to be borne and resisted; it began as a movement of army veterans, led by a man who started his political career on the left and veered to the right; and it happened with the support, outspoken or silent, of many institutions, including the Catholic Church. In the circumstances, the connivance of publishers, who bowed to the regime or actively profited from it, such as *Mondadori and Vallecchi, is comprehensible; it makes the stand of the few who did not, especially *Einaudi and *Laterza, all the more admirable. As a totalitarian dictatorship, Fascism strongly exploited publishing as *propaganda: from

1926, books had to display on the title-page the year in the Fascist era. The government also imposed a central control on the industry, both by censorship, through what in 1937 became the ministry for popular culture (usually known by its Orwellian semi-acronym Minculpop), and by incentives, including substantial loans to modernize printing works. The central figure and intellectual of a regime otherwise notoriously short of brainpower was Giovanni Gentile, a philosopher, university professor, owner of the publishing firm Sansoni, and driving force behind *Treccani in producing the *Enciclopedia Italiana*. Though anti-Semitism was not intrinsic to Fascism but borrowed from its nastier stablemate, with the passing of the racial laws in 1938 lists were compiled of Jewish authors and of writers judged 'decadent', who were banned, while publishing houses with Jewish links were taken over (such as Treves) or renamed (such as Olschki, which became Bibliopolis).

Despite the devastation and the chaos brought by World War II, in the aftermath newspapers, publishing houses, and cinema production companies in Italy remained in substantially the same hands. The Christian Democrat party, after the 1946 referendum transformed Italy into a republic, won a landslide election victory in 1948 and remained in power for the next 50 years. If the institutions and the government were in the hands of the Right, the intelligentsia was synonymous with the Left, and a heady mixture of economic boom, the expansion of university education, a steep rise in the birthrate, and ideas—sometimes music—from across the Alps, the Channel, and the Atlantic, set a cultural revolution in motion. From 1945 until the 1980s, Italy had the most politicized publishing output in Europe. Although the two publishing giants, Mondadori and *Rizzoli, remained middle-of-the-road, thinkers and political activists were catered for by Einaudi and *Feltrinelli; university texts were supplied by Il *Mulino and *Angeli; the dictionary market was covered by Zanichelli and Utet; while specialist academic publishing was the preserve of a renewed Olschki.

In one sense, the paperback revolution had its beginning in Italy in 1932, when *Mardersteig designed the *Albatross layout in Mondadori's Verona printing works; but otherwise the difficulty of finding a mass Italian readership has continued to trouble publishers. The postwar market was dominated by translations of English-language writers, ensuring steady growth for firms such as *Longanesi and *Bompiani; more recently, European authors have been catered for by the elegant *Adelphi. If the novel

is taken as a mirror of the society it depicts, a list of the most successful 20th-century titles whose first edition appeared on Italian soil offers food for thought. The top two works are not Italian at all: *Lady Chatterley's Lover*, which Lawrence self-published in Florence (1928), and Pasternak's *Dr Zhivago* (1957), which Feltrinelli had smuggled out of the USSR. Third on the list is another triumphant Feltrinelli intuition, *Il Gattopardo* by Tomasi di Lampedusa (1958); fourth place goes to Eco's medieval whodunnit *Il Nome della Rosa* (1980). Further places are occupied by a string of 1960 bestsellers *all'italiana*, including Cassola's *La Ragazza di Bube* (1960), Sciascia's *Il Giorno della Civetta* (1961), and Bassani's *Il Giardino dei Finzi Contini* (1962). Several of these have highly successful film versions; indeed, Italian narrative is closely interwoven with cinema, dominated by the neo-realism of De Sica, who in 1960 filmed Moravia's 1957 novel *La Ciociara*, and the luxuriant imaginings of Fellini, who in the same year made *La Dolce Vita*. Successful cinema versions have also reinforced the genuine popular success of Guareschi's Don Camillo stories (1948); although the anti-communist satire was anathematized by left-wing critics, they have sold in the millions and been translated into 20 languages.

Change has also been manifest in librarianship, where the static network of state-owned and municipal collections—with valuable holdings of rare material, but with little to interest the contemporary user—has been challenged by the genesis of numerous libraries in small urban centres, especially those under communist administrations in Emilia Romagna and Tuscany. Here the example of Einaudi—who donated a library to his family's home town, Dogliani, and published the catalogue as a guide to a model collection (1969)—proved hugely influential.

Through the advent of new media (cinema, radio, and television), a sort of linguistic unity was reached—though even in the 21st century dialect is still spoken in the mountains to the north, in the south, and in the islands. The task begun by the Tuscan writers of the Trecento, continued by Bembo and Manzoni, was rounded off through popular TV culture, whose abundant quiz shows—with long-standing comperes such as Mike Bongiorno—regularly oblige contestants to display their knowledge of the Italian language.

Italy remains a complex, contradictory publishing market, with lots of books, lots of bookshops, lots of book lovers, lots of libraries, and few readers. Obligatory secondary education and the freedom of university access have significantly redrawn the literacy map, especially for women, who form up to

90 per cent of arts faculty students. Nonetheless, there remains an unbridged gap between a highly educated intellectual class, often with impressive personal book collections, such as Umberto Eco, and a vaster general public, whose interests are bounded by the sporting newspapers. Nationwide publishing is mostly controlled by larger media corporations, which sustain this relatively unprofitable activity, almost as a front activity, in order to guarantee the circulation of certain ideas and concepts. The media tycoon Silvio Berlusconi, at the time of writing Italy's third-time prime minister, is also the country's largest publisher by virtue of his ownership of the Mondadori group. Lastly, the economic 'miracle' of the 1960s made Italy the world leader in the field of colour printing, both in product packaging (e.g. Barilla pasta) and in advertising material for the luxury goods industry, which exports worldwide such Italian brands as Versace, Ferragamo, and Ferrari. The availability of this technology has an obvious spin-off in the market for glossy, lavishly illustrated exhibition catalogues, where the leading firm is *Electa. Another application for this expertise has been developed by Panini in Modena, which patented collectable cards with pictures of footballers, and which now offers many card albums on diverse subjects, including *Harry Potter. In the 1990s, it applied its skill in polychrome printing to make perfect *facsimiles of Medieval and Renaissance MSS, most notably the Bible of *Borso d'Este, marketed in numbered editions intended for wealthy bibliophiles. The success enjoyed by this and other initiatives shows that in some ways the book market in Italy has little altered in nearly six centuries—or perhaps it is necessary to admit, like the main character in *Il Gattopardo*, that 'for everything to remain the same, everything must change'.

BIBLIOGRAPHY

L. Armstrong, 'Nicolaus Jenson's *Breviarium Romanum*, Venice, 1478: Decoration and Distribution', in *Incunabula: Studies in Fifteenth-Century Printed Books Presented to Lotte Hellinga*, ed. M. Davies (1999)

L. Balsamo, *Produzione e circolazione libraria in Emilia (XV–XVIII sec.)* (1983)

M. Berengo, *Intellettuali e Librai nella Milano della Restaurazione* (1980)

H. F. Brown, *The Venetian Printing Press* (1891)

G. A. Bussi, *Prefazioni alle edizioni di Sweynheym e Pannartz prototipografi romani*, ed. M. Miglio (1978)

B. Cecchetti, 'La stampa tabellare in Venezia nel 1447', *Archivio Veneto*, 29 (1885), 87–91

Edit16 (Edizioni Italiane del XVI secolo), vols A–F (1989–2007), on-line version on SBN site

G. Fragnito, *La Bibbia al Rogo: la Censura Ecclesiastica e i Volgarizzamenti della Scrittura, 1471–1605* (1997)

C. Ginzburg, *The Cheese and the Worms: The Cosmos of a Sixteenth-Century Miller*, tr. J. and A. Tedeschi (1980; Italian original, 1976)

P. Grendler, *The Roman Inquisition and the Venetian Press 1540–1605* (1977)

N. Harris, *Bibliografia dell' 'Orlando Innamorato'* (2 vols, 1988–91)

— 'Ombre della storia del libro italiano', in *The Books of Venice*, ed. L. Pon and C. Kallendorf (2008)

M. Infelise, *L'Editoria Veneziana nel '700* (1989)

P. Needham, 'Venetian Printers and Publishers in the Fifteenth Century', *LaB* 100 (1998), 157–200

F. J. Norton, *Italian Printers 1501–1520* (1958)

A. Nuovo, *Il Commercio Librario nell'Italia del Rinascimento*, 3e (2003)

B. Richardson, *Print Culture in Renaissance Italy* (1994)

— *Printing, Writers and Readers in Renaissance Italy* (1999)

R. Ridolfi, 'Proposta di ricerche sulle stampa e sugli stampatori del Quattrocento', *LaB* 51 (1949), 2–9

SBN (Servizio Bibliotecario Nazionale), www.sbn.it, consulted Sept. 2007

P. Scapecchi, 'Subiaco 1465 oppure [Bondeno 1463]? Analisi del frammento Parsons–Scheide', *LaB* 103 (2001), 1–24

G. Turi, ed., *Storia dell'Editoria nell'Italia Contemporanea* (1997)

29 The History of the Book in Modern Greece, c.1453–2000

ALEXIS POLITIS

1 The 15th century to 1820

The history of modern Greek books can be divided into two periods: before and after 1820. The early printing of Greek books occurred outside Greek territory, on presses partly owned by Greeks. After 1820, numerous presses operated in the Greek state and in eastern Mediterranean towns.

The first modern Greek book—that is, a book written in the Greek language (though not necessarily in the modern tongue) and printed for the Greek public—is Constantinus Lascaris' *grammar (Milan, 1476). Modern Greek society readily adapted to the appearance of printed books, and several Greeks contributed to their development. Greeks cut various *typefaces, and in the late 15th century, *Callierges and Nikolaos Vlastos founded the earliest Greek press. The first Greek books, however, were printed in Italy, and, by the early 16th century, several Italian printers sought to expand into the Orthodox East, starting Greek-interest presses in Venice. Approximately 440 titles had been printed by 1600, mostly for liturgical or educational use; modern Greek literary works were far less numerous.

This pattern persisted during the early 17th century: Greek books were printed by Italian publishers, most appearing in Venice. In 1627, Patriarch Cyril Lukaris attempted to found a press at Constantinople, but ultimately failed; his printer, *Metaxas, was forced to seek refuge on the Ionian Islands. In 1670 the first Greek firm appeared: Nikolaos Glykis bought a Venetian publishing house, which his descendants maintained until 1854. A second Greek press was started by Nikolaos Saros in 1686. Greek publishing almost doubled during this period, bearing witness to significant market demand in the Orthodox East. Liturgical texts, together with religious books, accounted for approximately three-quarters of the output. Only a third of the books were new, the rest being reissues.

In the first half of the 18th century, Venice remained the main centre for Greek books, with output determined by educational and religious requirements. Presses began operating in the semi-autonomous principalities of present-day Romania (*see* **31**), but the *printing office at Moschopolis produced only fifteen books between 1725 and 1755. By the century's end, a press was established on Mount Athos, along with others in Constantinople and Corfu. Little popular literature appeared, although some older works were published, including Georgios Chortatzis's 16th-century *Erophile* and Vicenzos Cornaros's 16th–17th-century *Erotocritos* (1713). After 1750, the coming of the Enlightenment brought rapid change.

The Greek Enlightenment's first book was Eugenios Voulgaris' *Logic* (Leipzig, 1766). By the century's end, the cultural landscape in Ottoman-occupied Greece resembled Europe's: schools proliferated, scientific works were translated, and a small number of people travelled or studied in Europe. This coincided with significant social changes and incipient revolution. As the new merchant class increased in numbers and gained in social power, Rhigas Velestinlis published *pamphlets (Vienna, 1797) calling for a national uprising.

These changes are reflected in book production. In the first two decades of the 19th century, the number of books reached approximately 1,400, or 35 per cent of the total national output of 5,000 titles between 1476 and 1820. Simultaneously, the numbers of reprints and of religious books fell. Production in Venice declined proportionally from 80 per cent to 50 per cent, with 25 per cent being printed in Vienna; production in Constantinople, where a press controlled by the patriarchate was founded in 1798, was insignificant.

Qualitative changes were more marked, with books appearing in the fields of philosophy, science (mostly *translations), classics, and language instruction; literary output, mostly plays in translation, remained insubstantial. As intellectual circles grew, the Vienna-based periodical *Ermis o Logios* (The Learned Hermes, 1811–21) became a rallying point for progressives, whose leading light was *Coray.

The *formats and *press runs of books varied considerably. Ecclesiastical books were generally printed as *quartos, school and scientific works in *octavo, and popular literature in smaller formats. The normal size of editions seems to have been 500–1,000 copies, but larger numbers were not unknown, particularly for liturgical works and school *textbooks.

Bookshops first appeared in early 19ᵗʰ-century Constantinople. Books were sold either by orders placed with general merchants or by *colporteurs at trade fairs. However, the mid-18ᵗʰ century saw the advent and growth of *subscription publishing: handwritten or printed *advertisements for the book were circulated, and once there were enough subscribers, it would be printed, with a *subscription list. Most scientific and new books were published in this manner.

Public libraries were similarly lacking. Several monasteries had libraries, typically formed from bequests by monks or prelates; however, they were rarely used. From the early 19ᵗʰ century onwards, however, school libraries were established in Chios, Smyrna, Milies on Mount Pelion, and Kozani. Private libraries were rarer. By the 16ᵗʰ century, several major libraries survived in Constantinople. The Maurokordatos family established a significant library (*c*.1720), gathering printed books from Europe and attempting to collect the entire modern Greek output by copying monastic MSS; the library was broken up *c*.1765. In the early 19ᵗʰ century, several private Greek libraries were established in Europe and on the Ionian Islands, some of which still survive.

2 1821–1900

Between the Greek declaration of independence in March 1821 and the arrival of the first king of Greece in January 1833, centuries-old assumptions were overturned in every part of life. Printing presses donated by European philhellenic committees were established in the newly free state at Kalamata, Missolonghi, Athens, and Hydra. Although a mere 5–6 per cent of all Greek books printed in 1821–30 were produced on free territory, they redrew the ideological landscape. By 1850 there were more than 50 printing offices in Greek territory and the Ionian Islands, primarily in Athens where the government was based; by 1863, there were 35 more. Although few of the presses were long-lived or prolific, the book market was dynamic.

The most important press was owned by an Athenian, Andreas Coromilas, who specialized in school textbooks and literature. In 1833–6, his presses produced 70,000 copies, overshadowing the 29,000 produced by his four major rivals. He introduced *stereotyping (1840) and opened a branch in Constantinople (1842). He printed more than 300 titles in all, mostly textbooks, dictionaries, or scientific works. The business survived until 1884.

Athens gradually increased its lead in book production. Of the *c*.9,000 Greek books produced in 1828–63, half were printed there; 500 in Constantinople (5.5 per cent); 450 in Smyrna and Hermopolis (5 per cent); and 600 in Venice (6.5 per cent). In 1864–1900, *c*.32,000 Greek books were produced; Athens's and Constantinople's share of the market increased, while that of the other places fell. Annual book production grew tenfold between 1820 and 1900. As the economy improved and population increased, new and better-organized publishing houses appeared, creating distinctive series (*plays, handbooks, *pocket books).

At the end of the War of Independence, bookshops run by foreigners appeared on Greek territory (Nafplio, Hermopolis, Athens); their number increased *c*.1840 in Constantinople and in Athens after 1850. By 1877 Athens had 16 bookshops, Constantinople 8, Smyrna 5, and Hermopolis 4, with another 24 in 11 provincial towns.

Subscription publishing, often used by provincial booksellers, retained wide currency. It peaked *c*.1880 with 153,000 named subscribers to 213,000 copies, but declined after 1890, disappearing by the following century. To facilitate ordering, publishers and booksellers printed catalogues, which are now a primary source of information on book distribution from 1860. After 1850, books (particularly *novels) were sold by serial publication in *numbers with *newspapers. Assisted by the foundation of the press distribution agency in 1877, this practice of issuing *fascicles was also applied to such books as the second edition of the *History of the Greek Nation* (1892), by Constantinos Paparrigopoulos, and the 79-volume scientific series 'Maraslis Library' (1897–1908).

Before 1821, Coray had proposed creating a central National Library; an initial core collection was assembled at Aegina in 1829. The University of Athens

Library was founded in 1838, and housed in a building shared (1842–1903) by the National Library of *Greece. The Parliament Library opened in 1845 and grew rapidly thereafter. Other public or municipal libraries either languished or relied on private donations. An attempt to establish a network of school libraries was bogged down by bureaucracy.

3 1901–2000

Between 1901 and *c*.1925, Greek publishing was dominated by Georgios Fexis' firm, founded in 1888. Initially relying on cheap novels, a 'drama library', and similar series, he bought Venice's last publishing house in 1901, producing more than 300 titles in six years about subjects including law, medicine, language learning, modern history, and practical matters.

During the wars of 1912–22, the reading public grew and Greek territory doubled, allowing the creation of several new publishing houses. The most important were Eleftheroudakis (1877–1962), Sideris (1874–1928), Georgios Vasileiou (1888–1932), Zikakis (1883–1925), Ganiaris (1894–1966), and Govostis (1904–58). Several smaller publishers active in the 1920s created literary or philosophical series, translating 19th-century European works and fostering modern Greek literature. Perhaps the best indicator of financial and intellectual vigour was the publication of the *Great Greek Encyclopaedia* (1926–34), a 24-volume work produced by Paul Drandake. Related developments include the creation of the Aspiotis-ELKA graphic design workshop, which produced major art publications until the 1980s, and the foundation of the *Gennadius Library (1926). In 1926, Greece's second university was founded in Thessaloniki, followed a year later by the Academy of Athens; both formed noteworthy libraries. This period also saw the publication of the twelve-volume Eleftheroudakis *Encyclopaedic Dictionary/Lexicon* (1927–31), followed by the nine-volume *Major Dictionary of the Greek Language* (1936–50) by Demetrios Demetrakos-Mesiskles.

During World War II, literary publishing blossomed. In the absence of European imports, Greek books gained readers, some books generating queues outside bookshops, and some editions selling out in days. New publishing houses appeared on the scene, including the short-lived Glaros (Seagull), Ikaros, headed by Nikos Karydis, and Alpha, run by Ioannis Skazikis.

The 48-volume 'Basic Library', the first series to anthologize a substantial body of modern Greek literature, appeared between 1953 and 1958. In 1955,

Atlantis, the earliest five-colour *rotogravure press, was established. State literature and essay prizes were inaugurated in 1958, as was the National Research Foundation's Centre for Modern Greek Research, which has worked systematically on the history of the Greek book.

In the 1960s the Galaxy Press emerged, producing the first successful series of pocket books featuring quality Greek and foreign literature; its 300 titles were often reprinted, some poetry volumes running to 5,000 copies. Kedros Press, which promoted modern literature, also appeared at this time. The 1967 dictatorship impeded literary activity; in an act of passive resistance, several authors voluntarily stopped publishing until 1970. After that year, there was a miniature publishing boom, comprising small new publishing houses (mostly left-leaning) as well as a new, cheaper series of pocket books: Viper Books (by Papyros Press) numbered 2,650 titles in ten years, selling one million copies in 1971. Other signs of this blossoming include the inauguration of the Modern Greek Library series (by Hermes) and Ekdotiki Athinon's multi-volume *History of the Greek Nation*.

In 1990 books became a trade commodity, sold in supermarkets and attracting the interest of big business. After 1995, most newspapers included a weekly books supplement or dedicated several pages to books. Oddly, the circulation of pocket books dwindled; popular bestsellers appeared in the same format as quality literature, often issued by the same publishing houses. The 21st century has been marked by the establishment of multi-story book 'megastores' (e.g. Eleftheroudakis, Ianos, Fnac) in city centres and suburbs. The explosion in book publishing seems unlikely to abate: the 7,450 titles published in 2001 rose to 9,209 in 2006.

BIBLIOGRAPHY
L. Droulia, *History of the Greek Book* (2001) [in Greek]
D. S. Ginis and V. Mexas, *Greek Bibliography 1800–1863* (3 vols, 1939–57) [in Greek]
P. Iliou, *Additions to the Greek Bibliography (1515–1799)* (1973) [in Greek]
— *Greek Bibliography 1800–1818* (1998) [in Greek]
— and P. Polemi, *Greek Bibliography 1864–1900* (2006) [in Greek]
A. Koumarianou *et al.*, *The Greek Book 1476–1830* (1986) [in Greek]
E. Legrand, *Bibliographie hellénique: XVᵉ–XVIᵉ siècles* (4 vols, 1885–1906)
— *Bibliographie hellénique: XVIIᵉ siècle* (5 vols, 1894–1903)

— *Bibliographie hellénique: XVIIIᵉ siècle* (2 vols, 1918–28)
National Book Centre, www.ekebi.gr, consulted Sept. 2007
National Documentation Centre, www.argo.ekt.gr, consulted Sept. 2007
D. E. Rhodes, *Incunabula in Greece* (1980)

K. S. Staikos, *Charta of Greek Printing* (1998)
— and T. E. Sklavenitis, eds., *The Publishing Centres of the Greeks* (2001)
— *The Printed Greek Book, 15ᵗʰ–19ᵗʰ Centuries* (2004) [in Greek]

30 The History of the Book in Austria

JOHN L. FLOOD

1 Introduction

Given Austria's linguistic and historical ties with Germany, its book culture has inevitably been strongly influenced by its neighbour (*see* **24**). Part of the Holy Roman Empire until 1806, Austria was for centuries dominated by the Habsburgs, who ruled until 1918. Under this dynasty, Bohemia and Hungary were united with Austria in 1526. In 1867 the double monarchy of Austria-Hungary was created, whose multi-ethnic population (51 million in 1910, with 2.1 million in Vienna) embraced not only German-speakers, but also the peoples of most of the now independent states of central Europe. Following World War I, the borders were redrawn, creating the (first) Republic of Austria, with Czechoslovakia and Hungary as independent states. In 1938, Austria was annexed to the German Reich, and in 1945 occupied by American, British, French, and Soviet forces until the Second Republic officially came into being in 1955. Today Austria's population is *c.*8.2 million, of whom 1.6 million live in Vienna.

2 Early history

In the Middle Ages, book culture flourished in such monasteries as Salzburg (then belonging to Bavaria) and *Kremsmünster, both 8th-century foundations, and later at Admont, St Florian, and elsewhere.

In 1500, the population of the area corresponding to present-day Austria was about 1.5 million. Vienna had *c.*20,000 inhabitants, Schwaz 15,000, Salzburg 8,000, Graz 7,000, Steyr 6,000, and Innsbruck 5,000. At that date, Vienna's university (founded 1365), was a centre of humanist scholarship. The first printer in the city was Stephan Koblinger, who arrived from Vicenza in 1482 and stayed until at least 1486. Next came Johann Winterburger (active 1492–1519, producing *c.*165 books, including many editions of

classical authors), Johann Singriener (1510–45, with *c.*400 books in various languages), and his partner, Hieronymus Vietor. In 1505 the brothers Leonhard and Lukas Alantsee established a bookshop in Vienna. The chief places of printing outside Vienna were Innsbruck (1547), Salzburg (1550), Graz (*c.*1559), Brixen (1564), Linz (1615), and Klagenfurt (1640). Yet, compared with Germany, the book trade in Austria was relatively underdeveloped. Austrian readers were principally supplied by booksellers from southern Germany, especially Augsburg.

In the early modern period, Austria experienced a series of crises. The economy (especially mining) was affected by the geo-strategic shift resulting from the discovery of the New World. Vienna and Graz were besieged by the Turks in 1529 and 1532 respectively, and the Turkish wars flared up again in 1593. Vienna was besieged once more in 1683. From the 1520s there was social unrest among the peasants, and religious life was shaken by the Reformation. The fear of Lutheranism led to *censorship being imposed as early as 1528. Unlike in Germany, Protestant printing was never more than peripheral in Austria. The Counter-Reformation brought educational reform and renewal of intellectual life through the Jesuits, who also established printing presses (for example, in 1559 at Vienna), but it also meant the confiscation and burning of Protestant books (for example, 10,000 books at Graz in August 1600). Even in 1712, Salzburg householders had non-Catholic books confiscated during fire inspections of their premises.

Austria was not spared the economic decline associated with the Thirty Years War, and even between 1648 and the Napoleonic era there were more years of war than of peace. Although printer-publishers were found throughout Austria, their importance was generally limited and local; few of them attended the *book fairs in *Frankfurt or *Leipzig. Hence Austrian authors seldom enjoyed European resonance. One exception was the preacher Abraham a Sancta Clara (1644–1709), whose works reached an international audience, chiefly through German reprints produced at Nuremberg and Ulm.

On 8 August 1703, Johann Baptist Schönwetter launched a daily newspaper, the *Wiennerisches Diarium*; renamed the *Wiener Zeitung* in 1780, it became the official gazette of the Austrian government in 1812, and is today one of the oldest continuously published newspapers in the world. In the 18th century, responsibility for censorship in Austria shifted from the Church to the state. Censorship was relaxed under Joseph II (emperor 1765–90), but the Napoleonic wars and the repressive policies of Prince Metternich led to its reimposition. Only after the 1848 revolution did matters improve.

As for the book trade itself, the demise of the exchange system for settling accounts and the insistence of Leipzig publishers on cash payments led to a boom in cheap reprints in southern Germany and Austria. A prominent figure in this regard was *Trattner, court bookseller and printer in Vienna, who was actively encouraged by Empress Maria Theresa to issue reprints of German books.

3 Modern times

Until 1918, the centres of publishing and literary life in the Austrian empire were Vienna and Prague. Writers associated with Vienna at this time include Hugo von Hofmannsthal and Karl Kraus (founder of the most important critical journal of the early 20th century, *Die Fackel*), while Prague produced Kafka, Rilke, and Franz Werfel.

During the 1930s, competition from German publishers became particularly intense. In 1934 the German government decreed that books sold abroad should receive a 25 per cent price subsidy. For Austria, this meant that German imports were now cheaper than home-produced books. In 1936 the Austrian government retaliated with a 3 per cent surcharge on foreign books, to provide a subsidy for Austrian publishers.

Between 1918 and 1938, some 90 publishing houses were founded in Austria, most of them short-lived, not least because of National Socialist policies following the Anschluss in March 1938. Among them were *Phaidon, established in 1923—which became renowned for its large-format, richly illustrated, but modestly priced *art books—and Paul *Zsolnay Verlag, also founded in 1923, which specialized in literature. With the annexation, both these firms moved from Vienna to Britain. Phaidon is now an international concern; Zsolnay was re-established in Vienna in 1946. Other Austrian publishers and booksellers emigrated and built up successful businesses in the US: Friedrich Ungar, who founded the Frederick Ungar Publishing Company in 1940; Wilhelm Schab, who set up in New York in 1939; and *Kraus.

The Nazis took immediate steps to control the book trade. Many Vienna publishers and booksellers quickly fell into line, while Jewish firms were liquidated and undesirable books impounded. More than 2 million books were removed from publishers' stockrooms and bookshops; some were retained for 'official' purposes but most were pulped. Books were removed from libraries, too—only the *Austrian National Library and the university libraries in Vienna, Salzburg, Graz, and Innsbruck were spared.

In 1945, the Allies imposed various denazification measures. A list of more than 2,000 prohibited books and authors was drawn up, and these were removed from public and private libraries—60,000 volumes from municipal libraries in Vienna alone were pulped. Pre-publication censorship was introduced, and schoolbooks were subjected to especially rigorous inspection.

Given that Leipzig, the centre of the German publishing industry, had been largely destroyed, there was initially great optimism in Austria that Vienna might become the centre of German-language publishing. However, paper was in short supply, printing equipment was antiquated, and the books produced had limited appeal. More new publishing ventures were founded on idealism than on a sound commercial basis. Moreover, in the early postwar years exporting to Germany was prohibited, which meant that the largest potential market was closed to Austrian publishers.

Austrian publishers' chief problems continue to be that the local market is too small and competition from powerful German rivals too intense. In the 1970s, while Austrian sales to Germany doubled, German publishers quadrupled theirs to Austria. Today, four out of every five books available in Austrian bookshops have been published in Germany, while German bookshops stock barely any Austrian titles. Of *c*.500 Austrian publishers today, more than half are based in Vienna. Two-thirds of them cater purely for the Austrian or regional market. A distinctive feature of Austrian publishing is the number of firms run by state organizations, the Catholic Church, and other institutions. The Österreichischer Bundesverlag (ÖBV), the largest publisher, is a state enterprise that traces

Prisoner-of-war reading: W. Irving's *Life of Oliver Goldsmith* (New York, 1843–4) sent by the Danish Red Cross, examined by camp officials, and marked with a fine hand-printed bookplate as belonging to international prisoners in Oflag XVIIIa in south Austria.

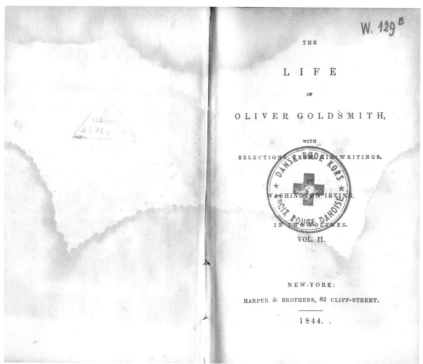

its origin to the schoolbook printing works established by Maria Theresa in 1772 to promote literacy. Firms such as Carinthia, Styria, and Tyrolia belong to the Church. Only three Austrian publishers—the ÖBV, the privately owned Verlag Carl Ueberreuter in Vienna, and the educational publishers Veritas in Linz—figure among the 100 largest German-language publishers. The continued independence of Austrian publishers has become more precarious since the country's accession to the EU in 1995.

BIBLIOGRAPHY

N. Bachleitner *et al.*, *Geschichte des Buchhandels in Österreich* (2000)

A. Durstmüller, *500 Jahre Druck in Österreich* (1982)

H. P. Fritz, *Buchstadt und Buchkrise. Verlagswesen und Literatur in Osterreich 1945–1955* (1989)

M. G. Hall, *Österreichische Verlagsgeschichte 1918–1938* (1985)

— *Der Paul Zsolnay Verlag* (1994)

— and C. Köstner, *"… allerlei für die Nationalbibliothek zu ergattern …": Eine österreichische Institution in der NS-Zeit* (2006)

A. Köllner, *Buchwesen in Prag* (2000)

J.-P. Lavandier, *Le Livre au temps de Marie Thérèse* (1993)

LGB 2

31 The History of the Book in Hungary

BRIDGET GUZNER

1 Book culture in the Middle Ages

The earliest Hungarian written records are closely linked to Christian culture and the Latin language. The first *codices were copied and introduced by travelling monks on their arrival in the country during the 10th century, not long after the Magyar tribes had conquered and settled in the Carpathian Basin. Written records were primarily created in monasteries; however, legal and other official documents were produced by an ecclesiastical body ('loca credibilia') unique to Hungary. This legal institution continued to operate in convents and chapter houses, issuing certified records in *chancery script to laymen and the clergy until 1874. The earliest ecclesiastical library, founded in 996, was that of the Benedictine monastery of Pannonhalma. Its MS holdings included as many as 250 liturgical and classical works by Cicero, Lucan, Donatus, and Cato, but the original library repeatedly fell prey to fire and only one codex survives from it. The cathedral libraries of Pécs (where there had also been a university, founded in 1367 but which closed in 1390), Veszprém, and Esztergom were destroyed following the continuous expansion of the Ottoman empire and the battle of Mohács, where the Turkish army, led by Süleyman I, attacked and defeated Hungarian forces in August 1526.

In the 14th century Hungarian students frequently studied at European universities, especially in Cracow, Vienna, Bologna, and Padua. On their return, they were reported to have owned small libraries, but none of their booklists survives. Information on the origins and subsequent fate of the most significant medieval MSS is scant. The *Gesta Hungarorum* (c.1200)

chronicles the history of the Hungarians from the beginnings till the Árpáds' conquest of Hungary. Written by the unidentified Magister P. (sometimes referred to as 'Anonymus') during the reign of King Béla III (1172–96), the book had been held abroad since its creation, only to be repatriated to the National Library of *Hungary from Vienna in the 20th century. The most impressive historical work of the Hungarian Middle Ages is the chronicle (also called *Gesta Hungarorum*) of Simon Kézai, the court chaplain of Ladislas IV, written in 1282–5. The Leuven Codex of the late 13th century is a collection of MS sermons, including the first fragment of Hungarian literary text, known as *Ómagyar Máriasiralom* (Old Hungarian Lamentations of the Blessed Virgin), written on *vellum at Orvieto by Dominican monks, three of whom were Hungarian. The Belgian university of Leuven (Louvain) finally agreed to give it to Hungary in 1982.

The first Hungarian printed book was produced in the Buda printing house of Andreas Hess at Whitsuntide in 1473, at the invitation of and with financial support from the city's provost, Vice-Chancellor László Karai. Hess, who was probably German, had left Rome for Buda—the spiritual and administrative centre of the Empire formed by the famous collector *Matthias Corvinus—and proceeded to set up his *printing office. Over the next five months, he produced his *Chronica Hungarorum* (also known as the *Buda Chronicle*). He cast his letters from *matrices imported from George Lauer's press in Rome, and used the same paper and *fount in his second, undated book printed in Buda. It comprised two works: Basil the Great's *De Legendis Poetis* and

Xenophon's *Apologia Socratis*, with the *colophon '.A: .H. Bude.' at the end of the first work.

Between 1477 and 1480, an unknown printer produced three more *incunabula, most likely in Hungary, but at an unidentified place of printing. The first was the *Confessionale* of Antoninus Florentinus, archbishop of Florence; the second, Laudivius Zacchia's *Vita Beati Hieronymi*; and the third, a *broadside *indulgence granted by Canon Johannes Han to Agnes de Posonio (dated, by hand, 11 May 1480), was discovered near Pozsony (now Bratislava). All three documents were probably printed by a small itinerant press in Hungary from *type cast from matrices attributed to the press of the Neapolitan Matthias Moravus.

Popular interest in MSS and books continued after the cessation of the two earliest printing offices. Foreign booksellers in Buda supplied the clergy and the royal court with books printed in Venice or MSS commissioned from Germany. Of nine Buda publishers, only two are known to have been Hungarian. Theobald Feger was the first in Hungary to sell Latin and German editions of *Schedel's *Nuremberg Chronicle*, printed by *Koberger. The most notable publication of the age, however, was János Thuróczy's (Johannes de Thwrocz) *Chronica Hungarorum*, printed in March 1488 in Brünn (Brno) for János Filipec, bishop of Olmütz (Olomouc). As Filipec's church press had no suitable type for secular works, his printers, Conrad Stahel and Mathias Preunlein, used the *gothic founts of *missals and a large number of high-quality *woodcut illustrations. The *Chronica* was reprinted in June of the same year in Augsburg by *Ratdolt with a *printer's device designed by Feger. This second edition, dedicated to Matthias Corvinus, was illustrated with more woodcuts, and is still the best-known and most distinguished incunable associated with Hungary, owned by many European and US libraries.

2 The Reformation and the baroque age

For most districts of Royal Hungary, the battle of Mohács (1526) and the subsequent Turkish occupation were followed by 150 years of turmoil, loss of independence, and economic degradation. Hungarian centres of humanist and literary thought were destroyed and Hungarian books came to be printed abroad, mainly in Cracow and Vienna. Thus, the first book printed entirely in Hungarian, an edition of St Paul's Epistles, translated and with a commentary by Benedek Komjáti (a follower of Erasmus), was produced at Cracow in 1533 by Hieronymus Vietor.

The traumatic experience of Mohács was associated with the birth of the Reformation. The reformers' teachings spread in the 1520s, gaining ground in the relatively secure region of Transylvania, the only Hungarian territory to have escaped Turkish occupation. In Braşov, Johannes Honterus (1498–1549), a learned reformer of the Transylvanian Saxons, set up his printing press in the early 1530s and went on to produce more than 35 works in Latin, Greek, and German. Still in Braşov, the first books in Romanian printed with *Cyrillic types were attributed to *Coresi, the deacon, printer, and editor who promoted vernacular Romanian in church as the official written language. More than 30 of his books were circulated throughout the Romanian lands. Another town that played an important role in the printing of Latin and Hungarian books while upholding Protestant reform was Kolozsvár (Cluj). There, Gáspár Heltai, preacher, writer, and pre-eminent theorist of the Hungarian Reformation, founded a famous printing office (originally, with György Hoffgreff) in 1550. Between 1559 and 1575, it produced 45 works in Hungarian, Latin, and Greek, all enriched with attractive woodcut illustrations. Heltai initially printed religious works, but he later turned to more secular genres: *romances, tales, and legends. After his death, his wife continued to print less prestigious but no less entertaining chronicles in verse.

Other printers during the Reformation and Counter-Reformation produced material aimed at serving and supporting Hungarian Protestantism. The most significant of these, Gál Huszár, established his printing office first in Magyaróvár (Mosonmagyaróvár), then in Kassa (Košice). He later settled in Debrecen to print and publish the works of the Reformed bishop Péter Juhász Melius (1532–72). In 1555, Raphael Hoffhalter settled in Vienna, where his printing office produced 123 Latin and Hungarian publications during the following seven years. His Protestantism made him flee, in 1563, to Debrecen, where the quality of his books and *engravings surpassed those of his predecessors. Between 1588 and 1590, Bálint Mantskovits established a printing office in Vizsoly, producing the first complete Hungarian Protestant Bible. The Vizsoly Bible, translated by Gáspár Károlyi, is considered the finest undertaking of 16th-century Hungarian printing.

Under Habsburg domination, there were two noteworthy workshops on Hungarian territory. One was in Nagyszombat (Trnava), the centre of the Counter-Reformation at the time, where the Grand Provost Miklós Telegdi founded his press in 1578 and produced superb examples of baroque printing. The other press was located in Bártfa (Bardejov): its master printer, David Guttgesel, used attractive German types, *borders, and *ornaments in his Latin, Hungarian, and German books.

Most 17th-century Transylvanian Protestant printers, however, learned their art in workshops in The Netherlands. Ábrahám Szenczi Kertész became acquainted with Dutch book production while studying in Leiden. He founded his printing office in Nagyvárad (Oradea) in 1640 and printed more than 100 books, mostly in Hungarian. János Brewer brought his finely cut Dutch types back from Holland to his press at Lőcse (Levoča) to produce, with his brother Samuel, exquisite editions of *Comenius' work, as well as the famous *calendars of Lőcse.

Nicholas *Kis followed the same pattern, starting his apprenticeship with *Blaeu in Amsterdam, improving his type designing, cutting, and printing skills. By 1685 he had produced 3,500 copies of his Amsterdam Bible. In 1686 he published the Book of Psalms, translated by Albert Szenczi Molnár, and the New Testament in the following year. His European fame led to commissions from Holland, Germany, England, Sweden, and Poland. His Georgian, *Greek, *Hebrew, and *Armenian types, cut with meticulous expertise, further enhanced his reputation. On his return to Kolozsvár, he brought together municipal and church presses, and in the next nine years published more than 100 finely printed inexpensive books, including the scholarly works of Ferenc Pápai Páriz, the scientist and compiler of a Latin–Hungarian dictionary. Kis strove to stamp out illiteracy and cultural backwardness and to develop a uniform Hungarian orthography.

In Transylvania the princes Gábor Bethlen (r. 1613–29) and György Rakóczi I (r. 1630–48) sought to deprive indigenous Romanians of their national rights and to convert them to Calvinism. The Romanians responded with a developing sense of patriotism, striving to promote their unified literary language. The Romanian New Testament (Alba Iulia, 1648), printed by its translator, Simion Ştefan, Metropolitan of Transylvania, during the autonomous province's golden age, was part of this process. Romanian printing with Cyrillic characters reappeared in 1733 in a calendar printed in Braşov and produced by the schoolteacher Petcu Şoanul. Enlisting the help of experienced Hungarian printers, Bishop Petru Pavel Aaron refurbished the Blaj printing works with new Cyrillic and Latin founts, as well as high-quality materials and typographic equipment, to produce large numbers of Romanian school *textbooks and *primers. This was a step towards a new age of secular culture.

3 Enlightenment and the Reform era

After the dissolution of the Jesuit order in 1773, the Nagyszombat University and Press, formerly under Jesuit leadership, was moved to Buda in 1777 to be managed by the printer Mátyás Trattner (1745–1828). In 1779, it was licensed to print and distribute textbooks for all Hungarian schools, but it also enthusiastically distributed Reform literature. Reorganizing and expanding production under Sámuel Falka Bikfalvi's direction, Buda's university press employed nineteen typefounders to supply most of the country's presses. Falka's types show the influence of foreign printers and designers, such as *Didot and *Bodoni. As manager of the foundry, Falka renewed his types (much admired by the author Ferenc Kazinczy) while developing and producing beautiful *wood and *copperplate engravings.

Throughout the 18th century, printing offices opened in Eger, Esztergom, Temesvár (Timişoara), Pécs, Nagykároly (Carei), and Kassa (Košice), but none reached the high standards of the Debrecen or Kolozsvár workshops. By the end of the 18th and the beginning of the 19th centuries, competition among the growing number of printers forced prices and quality down. The development of *lithography resulted in the break-up of technical and commercial networks; typographical traditions and aesthetic considerations were disregarded. With the mass production on cheap paper of ephemera, daily *newspapers (see 14), books, and journals, typographic standards sank to low levels.

The 19th-century Reform Movement sought to promote Hungary's economic and cultural progress. To eradicate the country's cultural backwardness, Count István Széchenyi (1791–1860) became the founder and sponsor of various projects and reforming institutions, including the Hungarian Academy of Sciences. His political writings, in which he argued that Hungary should remain loyal to the Austrian empire, were mostly printed by the newly founded Trattner-Károlyi Press. Another representative of the Reform Era was the printer and bookseller Gusztáv Emich (1814–69). During his 26-year publishing career he produced 663 works, of which 629 were in Hungarian. His printing and publishing enterprise effectively created the Athenaeum Literary and Joint Stock Limited Printing Company (1868), which by the end of the century had become the best-equipped printing establishment in the country.

Pallas, the country's largest printing and publishing firm, was founded in 1884. It boasted a modern typefoundry, a lithographic press, a bindery, rotary-*offset and *intaglio printing presses. Besides books, it produced journals as well as commercial and official documents. The eighteen-volume Pallas encyclopaedia (1893–1900) turned the Pallas Literary and Printing Company into Hungary's most prestigious enterprise. As the smaller printing offices gradually replaced their obsolete equipment with modern machinery, they developed advertising techniques and widened their business networks. Towards the end of the 19th century, the spread of *literacy increased the demand for books so rapidly that booksellers became publishers. They sponsored Hungarian literature and produced editions of national classics, large *press runs of popular fiction, cheap newspapers, series of complete works, and *translations of popular authors, making contemporary world literature available to a Hungarian readership. By 1895, there were 104 printing offices in the capital, and their products began to reflect the elements of the eclectic and Art Nouveau styles.

4 The 20th century

The Kner printing and publishing firm at Gyoma, founded in 1882, adopted the theories and practices of earlier typographers and contemporary designers. The family business was at its peak in the 1920s. Following losses suffered in the war, Imre Kner (1890–1945) and Lajos Kozma (1884–1948) revived the typographic traditions of the baroque period, combining them with modern-day typesetting technology. They produced remarkable works such as the 'Monumenta Literarum' and the 'Kner Classics' series. The Kner Press was the first to announce the liberation of Hungary following World War II. It continued to function under the directorship of the designer, printer, and researcher György Haiman (1914–96), until it was nationalized in 1949.

Between the wars, the traditions of prestigious later 19th-century publishers—Athenaeum, Révai Brothers, and Singer & Wolfner—in producing important titles in small editions, with little art or music publishing, were continued. World War II and the Communist takeover in 1948 changed everything virtually overnight. All publishing houses, booksellers, and printers were nationalized. The new *copyright law stripped publishers of their rights; those not closed down were amalgamated with larger socialist enterprises responsible for publishing within rigidly defined fields. Under the general censorship of the Ministry of Culture, which was ruled by the Communist Party, and the Book Commission, their main task was to educate the masses. During the 1950s, publishing houses were based on Soviet patterns and integrated into a strongly centralized system. In 1952, the trade licences of 182 booksellers and 153 stationers were revoked; the subjects assigned to the newly appointed publishing houses remained unchanged for the following 35 years.

Throughout the 1960s and early 1970s, the political authorities chose which literary works were to be supported or tolerated, and which to be banned and their authors silenced by the general Directorate of Publishing. Although this system of ideological control remained unchanged for more than 40 years, censorship gradually became more relaxed; economic difficulties led to dwindling state subsidies; and the 1980s began to see a technically developed and intellectually strong publishing industry able to satisfy a readership that was by now aware of Communism's impending collapse. *Samizdat books did not have the important role in Hungary that they had in other Soviet bloc countries. By the end of the 1980s, there was little to distinguish samizdat from 'official' publications. The Hungarian Writers' Association became a stronghold of dissent as well as a centre of political opposition. Its leaders played an important role in the movement that marked the end of dictatorship. In 1987–8, the Europa publishing house produced Koestler's *Darkness at Noon*, Pasternak's *Dr Zhivago*, and, in 1989, Orwell's *Nineteen Eighty-Four*, all in excellent Hungarian translations.

5 Publishing after 1989

In 1989, censorship and state control over publishing were officially lifted. Legally registered companies were free to engage in publishing. Focusing chiefly on bestselling books and popular fiction, huge editions of previously banned literature were distributed by the burgeoning number of publishers and street vendors throughout the country.

After 1993, two of the previously state-owned distributors were privatized and remodelled to meet modern needs. This resulted in the creation of well-appointed large bookshops and the emergence of a balanced book market. Hungary had been one of the earliest European countries to be admitted into the *International Publishers Association, hosting the first international conference of publishers in 1913.

In 1998, the Hungarian Publishers' and Booksellers' Association (MKKE) joined the prestigious European Publishers' Federation and the European Booksellers' Federation, and in 1999 the country was chosen as guest of honour at the *Frankfurt Book Fair, considerably enhancing its standing on the European cultural scene. In the 2000s, Hungarian publishing has been characterized by trends common throughout Europe: growth in sales volume; better quality production; greater variety of titles; expansion of bookshop chains; the establishment of web-based bookstores; and the expansion of electronic publishing.

BIBLIOGRAPHY

J. Fitz, *A magyar könyv története 1711-ig* (1959)

K. Galli, *A könyv története: I. A kezdetektől a 15. század végéig* (2004)

P. Gulyás, *A Könyvnyomtatás Magyarországon a XV. és XVI. században* (1931)

D. Simionescu and G. Buluță, *Pagini din istoria cărții românești* (1981)

32 The History of the Book in the Czech Republic and Slovakia

Devana Pavlik

1 Historical background

Czechs and Slovaks shared their early history in the Great Moravian Empire, a 9th-century Slavonic state along the middle Danube. The first MSS were brought by missionaries promulgating the Church's Latin rite. Liturgical texts in Old Church Slavonic were introduced and copied by the Byzantine mission of Sts Cyril and Methodius who were invited, in 863, to replace the Latin rite with a language understood by the people. For this purpose, they invented *Glagolitic script, translating liturgical texts and the Bible into Old Church Slavonic. When Great Moravia collapsed in 906/8 the Czech centre of power grew in central Bohemia, while Slovakia was, until 1918, under the rule of Hungary, whose religious, political, and cultural development it followed. The Czech lands of Bohemia and Moravia came under the dominance of the Holy Roman Empire.

Both the Czech lands and Slovakia were part of the Austro-Hungarian empire until its dissolution in 1918, when they co-founded a democratic state: Czechoslovakia. Until 1945, Czech and Slovak printing, publishing, and bookselling did not markedly differ from the rest of Europe. Fundamental changes came with the Communist takeover in 1948, however, when private firms were either liquidated or transferred into state ownership and centralized. Soviet-style organization of publishing and distribution was enforced, together with strict *censorship. Material deemed politically undesirable was withdrawn from libraries. Some free Czech and Slovak émigré publishing continued abroad and was re-energized by the post-1968 wave of exiles. At home, independent underground publishing took off in the 1970s and 1980s (see SAMIZDAT), signalling future developments.

The demise of Communism in November 1989 brought complete transformation: with a market economy came the reorganization of the publishing and distribution industries as well as of libraries and archives. Private publishing ventures started practically overnight, and large print runs of suppressed works by dissident Czech and Slovak writers were produced. *Translations of the latest fiction and popular non-fiction quickly appeared, satisfying demand for previously inaccessible literature. In 1993, Czechoslovakia was divided along its historical borders into the Czech Republic and Slovakia.

2 The Czech Republic

2.1 Early development

The 11th century saw the founding of monasteries and of cathedral and collegiate chapters that began assembling collections of imported and domestically produced MSS. The earliest evidence of biblical *translations into Old Czech comes from the late 11th or early 12th century. Existing Czech texts were finally assembled into the complete Bible around 1380, the Czech translation being the third vernacular rendering of the Scriptures after French and Italian. Surviving MSS include 25 complete *bibles, 27 Old Testaments, 35 New Testaments, 22 *psalters, 17 gospel books, and numerous smaller fragments. Many are beautiful examples of Czech Romanesque and Gothic book *illumination. The most outstanding among the early illuminated examples is the Codex Vysehradensis (1086); the most famous is the Codex *Gigas, or Devil's Bible (1204), over one metre high. The foundation of the university at Prague in 1348 and the existence of the archbishopric there encouraged MS production that reached its zenith during the reign of Wenceslas IV (1378–1419), when only Parisian *scriptoria outshone Prague's in the beauty of their illuminated codices.

Printing in Bohemia is traditionally thought to have begun in 1468 with *Kronika trojánská* (Trojan Chronicle), the first Czech printed book, and the New Testament (with the unclear inscription 'M.4.75'). Because there is no conclusive evidence, however, the Latin *Statuta Synodalia Arnesti*, printed at Pilsen in 1476, is now regarded as the first book printed in the Czech Republic. The majority of *incunables were printed in Prague, but printing also went on at Vimperk in southern Bohemia.

Of the 44 surviving incunabula printed in Bohemia, 39 are in Czech and 5 in Latin. Most Bohemian printers were local craftsmen, but the situation differed in Moravia, where foreign printers worked. Of the 23 extant incunabula produced in the Moravian printing centres of Brno and Olomouc, 2 are in German and the rest in Latin.

Most titles were secular in nature. There were educational works (e.g. Latin *grammars, Donatus' *Ars Minor*), legal works (Latin and vernacular), travelogues, legends, and *chronicles (e.g. the *Trojan Chronicle*, in two *editions; Twinger's *Martimiani* (1488); and the *Chronica Hungarorum* (1488), the first illustrated Brno imprint, printed in Latin). The Severin-Kamp press brought out the first illustrated Prague *imprint, the Czech edition of Aesop's *Fables* (1488?). A Czech version of the popular *Legenda Aurea*, known as *Pasionál*, was printed twice, once lavishly illustrated, but it is the unillustrated edition that represents the height of Czech incunabula *typography. There were *almanacs, *calendars, and other works, including *Von den heissen Bädern* (Brno, 1495), Folz's tract on the medicinal value of bathing in natural hot springs.

Sacred incunabula are dominated by biblical texts. The first complete bible in Czech, a *folio of 610 leaves printed in double columns of 47 lines with titles in red, was printed in 1488 by Severin-Kamp. An illustrated edition, with 116 locally made *woodcuts, was printed a year later in the silver-mining town of Kutná Hora (Kuttenberg) by Martin of Tišnov. The New Testament in Czech was also published in illustrated and plain versions. The Psalter appeared in Czech and Latin; there were also liturgical works, books on church administration, two *missals, and a number of contemporary tracts, Catholic and Protestant.

Incunables in the vernacular were printed using Czech *bastarda types, the earliest being the most ornate (emulating handwritten forms), the later influenced by *rotunda and *Fraktur. *Textura and rotunda *founts were used for Latin works; imported German

*Schwabacher is found in imprints connected with Prague University.

Several incunabula printers from the kingdom of Bohemia and Moravia distinguished themselves abroad, including Johann Sensenschmidt at Nuremberg and Bamberg, Mathias Grossmann Moravus at Naples, and Valentinus de Moravia, who printed the first book in the Portuguese language at Lisbon.

2.2 The 16th century

The 16th century was the golden age of Czech printing, with 4,400 titles printed. Religious controversies stimulated the growth of printing, driven in part by the rapid production of *pamphlets and polemical literature. Humanism began to change the look of the printed book and its contents, and the increasing wealth of burghers brought books to a wider public. As the number of book collectors and readers grew, the libraries of professional men sometimes surpassed those of the nobility. *Printing offices were established in many towns; bookselling was promoted through bookshops, markets, and *book fairs, and via lists of books in print distributed throughout the country and abroad. In addition to printing in Latin (using Roman types), Czech, and German (using Fraktur and Schwabacher), there was also printing in *Cyrillic script: the first bible in Cyrillic was printed in Prague in 1517–19 by *Skaryna. The first book in Hebrew was printed in Prague in 1513, and, by the end of the century, there were several Hebrew presses operating in the city (*see* **8**).

Printing presses were established by scholars and intellectuals promoting humanist literature. Most significant was the press of Daniel Adam of Veleslavín, a Prague University professor who took over from the highly successful *Melantrich in 1584. Publishing 100 titles, Veleslavín was an enthusiastic promoter of the use of the Czech language in scholarly literature and founded modern Czech lexicography, his best work in this sphere being a monumental Latin–Greek–German–Czech dictionary (1598). He used some 50 different founts, employed high-quality *ornaments, and lavished great care on *title-pages, typically executed in black and red. The peak of 16th-century printing was achieved at the *printing offices of the Unity of Brethren, especially at their Moravian locations in Ivančice and Kralice. Founded soon after 1500, the Unity was among the first printers to spread Reformation ideas. Its imprints are characterized by fine typography and design, and by the high standard of their Czech language. The Unity's six-volume *Kralice Bible (1579–94) crowns the impressive sequence of Czech bible printing in this era.

2.3 The 17th and 18th centuries

The victory of the Catholic Habsburgs over the Protestants in 1620 had far-reaching consequences for the development of printing. The Czech language, regarded as a tongue of heretics and rebels, was replaced by German as the official language; printing in Czech was largely confined to prayer books, hymn books, sermons, hagiographies, novels, and folk tales. As exponents of the Counter-Reformation, the Jesuits exercised tight control over printing, which they concentrated in a small number of establishments. The largest of these was their own press at the Klementinum complex in Prague. Lists of prohibited books were compiled, and many books printed in the previous century were taken from their owners and banned and burned. Destroyed books were fast replaced by new material—textbooks, *postils (biblical commentaries), hymn books, and homiletic literature—issued in large numbers by the Jesuits.

Many Czech scholars and artists, such as the educationalist *Comenius or the engraver *Hollar, went abroad to work and publish, while foreign artists began leaving their mark on the baroque book in the Czech lands. *Copperplate *engravings replaced woodcuts in book illustration, and large presentation volumes incorporated engraved *plates, *frontispieces, and title-pages. Marked differences in quality emerged between editions of historical, legal, theological, and scientific works, and cheaply produced editions for the mass market. At the lowest end of the 'paper goods' market were *broadsides, numbering some 6,000 items by the end of the 18th century.

The first *periodicals appeared after 1658, achieving genuine popularity in 1719 with the *Prager Post*, published twice weekly by Carl Franz Rosenmüller, the best Prague printer of the rococo era, whose press issued historical works by Bohuslav Balbín, Václav Hájek, Gelasius Dobner, and others.

Enlightenment ideas and religious and social reforms introduced in the last part of the 18th century heralded the awakening of Czech national consciousness. Scholarly research into Czech history, the revival of Czech as a literary language, and new discoveries in science benefited from the relaxation of printing restrictions. The Royal Czech Society of Sciences was founded in 1770, and works by such eminent scholars as M. A. Voigt, G. Dobner, R. Ungar, J. Dobrovský, J. Jungmann, P. J. Šafařík, and F. Palacký were published. The publisher who best represented the Czech

national awakening was Václav Matěj Kramerius (1753–1808), journalist and translator, who started his renowned *Imperial and Royal Prague Post Newspaper* in 1789. His 'Czech Expedition'—a centre for the publication and distribution of books in Czech, mostly renderings of popular foreign works—issued some 84 titles printed by various presses.

2.4 The 19th century

The first half of the 19th century saw the foundation of many learned societies and libraries, as well as the beginnings of modern Czech literature, especially poetry. The cost of publication, and sometimes distribution, was often borne by authors themselves. In science and the humanities, publishing was subsidized by the Matice česká, founded in 1831, which organized public collections and appeals for donations. With Matice's financial support, scientific illustration and the publication of maps and atlases developed and flourished. It ensured the survival of the *Journal of the Czech Museum*, that started in 1827 and continues to this day, and financed such significant undertakings as Jungmann's five-volume Czech–German dictionary (1835–39) and Šafařík's *Slovanské starožitnosti* (1837).

The second half of the century witnessed considerable developments in the field of Czech belles-lettres as well as science, and a corresponding growth of publishing houses. The largest firm was that of Ignác Leopold Kober (1825–66), which published *c*.300 titles including the first Czech *encyclopaedia, the ten-volume *Slovník naučný* (1860–72), edited by František Ladislav Rieger.

Modern book illustration began in the 1860s with the artists Josef Mánes and Mikoláš Aleš. In the 1890s, *Braunerová pioneered the movement for the book as an aesthetic artefact (see *artist's book); her compatriot artists *Mucha and František Kupka made their name in book art in France. The journal *Moderní revue* became a platform for the Decadent and Symbolist movements. The efforts of late-century graphic artists were summarized by Vojtěch Preissig, who provided the theoretical and practical foundation for the development of 20th-century book design.

2.5 The 20th century and after

The largest publishing house before the foundation of the Czechoslovak Republic in 1918 was that of Jan Otto (1841–1916). It encompassed many fields of knowledge for all levels of readership and price ranges, including prestigious illustrated journals (*Lumír*, *Zlatá Praha*, and *Světozor*) and several ambitious literary series. The firm's efforts culminated in 1888–1909 with the still-unsurpassed 28-volume encyclopaedia *Ottův slovník naučný*.

In typography, great advances were made in the first twenty years of the new century. Important developments in this sphere are connected with the 1908 foundation of the Association of Czech Bibliophiles and with Karel Dyrynk, Method Kaláb, and Oldřich Menhart. Typography was also of great interest to the Czech avant-garde, represented by Josef Šíma, Jindřich Štýrský, and Toyen, together with its theorist, *Teige.

During World War II, the seven-year Nazi occupation of Bohemia and Moravia severely restricted *freedom of the press. These strictures were partly compensated for by publishing abroad, mainly in England, through the efforts of Czechoslovak forces and the exiled government.

The legacy of 40 years of Communism, 1948–89, with its centralized system of publishing, bookselling, libraries, and archives, meant huge changes when its rule ended. By the close of the millennium, economic changes—the rising cost of living and increasing book prices (the average book price rose by 260 per cent between 1990 and 1995)—resulted in a sharp drop in book sales. However, both the fact that quality publications maintained their value and the continuing vitality of the annual Prague Book Fair testify to a buoyant Czech book culture.

3 Slovakia

3.1 Early development

In Slovakia, the Nitra Gospels, dating to the end of the 11th century, were among the Latin MSS that were copied and kept in monasteries and chapter houses. Lay scriptoria arose at the end of the 14th century.

The first Slovak printed books, the work of an unidentified Bratislava printer, date to 1477–80. Lutheranism influenced the development of the first printing presses: 16th-century printers travelled frequently, forced to change their place of work when harassed for their religious beliefs. They set up in Košice, Šintava, Komjatice, Plavecké Podhradie, and Hlohovec, sometimes printing parts of one book in different towns. The Slovak printer *Bakalár worked in Pilsen in Bohemia. The language of the landlord class and most of the urban population was Hungarian; until the end of the 18th century, a large proportion of Slovakian printing was carried out in Hungarian. Books in Czech for the Slovak-speaking population (standard written Slovak did not develop until the 1780s) were mostly imported from Bohemian and Moravian presses, which were better equipped to produce large volumes such as bibles, postils, and hymn books. Such printing in Slovakized Czech as existed in Slovakia concentrated on popular works, e.g. textbooks and calendars. By the last quarter of the 16th century, printing presses were established in Trnava, Bardejov, and Banská Bystrica. Bratislava grew in importance by the century's end when, during the occupation of a large part of Hungary by the Turks, many government bodies and schools moved there from Buda. The foremost Bratislava printing press, that of the archbishopric, flourished 1608–63. Printing grew in Trnava after the foundation of the university in 1635.

Until 1700, the centre of book production was concentrated in Levoča, mainly in the hands of the Breuer family, who produced some 700 titles by the late 17th century. Most of these were in Latin, but some were in the vernacular, including three editions of Juraj Tranovský's popular hymn book *Cithara Sanctorum* (1636, 1639, 1653) and Comenius' *Orbis Pictus* (1685). The first newspaper in Hungary was printed in Levoča and Bardejov in 1705–10; others followed in Bratislava. Košice, the eastern Slovakian metropolis, rose to prominence as a printing centre in the 18th century. The works of Sámuel Timon, printed in Košice in 1733 and 1736, greatly contributed to the national identity of Slovakia, as did *Bel's *Compendium Regnorum Sclavoniae* in 1777. The written Slovak language, based on western Slovak dialect, was codified by Anton Bernolák in 1787.

3.2 The 19th century and after

At the end of the 18th century, the Slovak National Revival, together with Enlightenment ideas, spurred the growth of printing, publishing, bookselling, and the founding of libraries. In 1843, Ľudovít Štúr, leader of the revival movement, introduced written Slovak based on the dialect of central Slovakia: this became the language of the revivalists and was accepted as the standard national language. Slovak revivalist printing was provided by the *Jelinek Press (Trnava) and Škarnicel Press (Skalica), which issued the acclaimed journal *Slovenské pohľady*. Technical progress in the 19th century brought fundamental changes in printing, publishing, and distribution, facilitating further growth.

In 1870, the Book Printing Holding Association in Turčiansky sv. Martin became the leading printer of Slovak language books and periodicals. Vernacular publishing grew, leading to the foundation of the Booksellers and Publishers Holding Association (1885). The two organizations merged in 1908, representing the bulk of Slovak publishing prior to 1918.

Between the two world wars, Slovakia enjoyed unprecedented economic and artistic development. Many cultural and educational institutions were established or renewed, libraries of all types built, and publishing houses established to issue books in Slovak. The end of Communist rule advanced the Slovak quest for complete independence from the Czechs, which was attained in 1993.

In 2000, the *Slovak National Library separated from the cultural body *Matica Slovenská. Large publishing firms that survived the transition into the market economy, such as the SPN-Mladé letá, have been augmented by small independent publishers. The skilfully managed Petrus in Bratislava exemplifies current trends. The Bratislava Biennial of Illustrations (started in 1967) is arguably the most important international exhibition of book illustration for children and young adults worldwide. Under the patronage of *UNESCO and IBBY, it presents several prizes and has exhibited work from some 90 countries.

BIBLIOGRAPHY

M. Bohatcová, *Česká kniha v proměnách staletí* (1990)

V. Breza, *Tlačiarne na Slovensku 1477–1996* (1997)

HDHB

F. Horák, *Pět století* [Five Hundred Years of Czech Printing] (1968)

I. Kotvan, *Inkunábuly na Slovensku* (1979)

Lexikon české literatury (1985–2008)

V. Petrík, *Slovakia and its Literature* (2001)

M. Strhan and D. P. Daniel, eds., *Slovakia and the Slovaks* (1994)

P. Voit, *Encyklopedie knihy* (2006)

33 The History of the Book in Poland

JANET ZMROCZEK

1 The foundations and development of book culture

When the Polish King Mieszko I was baptized in 966, his acceptance of Catholicism set the course of Polish cultural history and the development of the Polish book. Evidence suggests that MS books had come to Poland with Christian missionaries from neighbouring countries and farther lands (Ireland and Italy) even before Mieszko's official conversion. Poles themselves began participating in the development of an indigenous book culture only in the 12th–13th centuries; until this time, books were generally imported from abroad, or created by people from other countries. Annals and chronicles recording Polish history may have been written as early as the 10th century, but the first surviving example is the 12th-century *Rocznik Świętokrzyski*, now held by the National Library of *Poland in Warsaw.

As Poles travelled more frequently to study at Italian and French universities and more monasteries were established on Polish soil, a greater interest in writing led to the development in the 13th century of a wider network of *scriptoria, attracting native Polish clergy. The scriptoria in Silesia were particularly prolific, producing a number of richly *illuminated MSS, including the oldest surviving MS containing a full sentence in Polish: The Chronicle of the Cistercian Monastery at Henryków. From the 14th and early 15th centuries, the book began to spread beyond church and court circles, encouraged in part by the beginning of writing in Polish. Important surviving Polish-language MSS of this period include the Sermons from the Holy Cross Mountain Monastery and *Psałterz Floriański*, a richly illuminated *codex containing psalms in Polish, Latin, and German.

Under the Jagiellonian dynasty (1385–1569), Poland, in union with Lithuania, was the largest and most powerful empire in Europe with a truly multi-ethnic population. It encompassed the Korona (Poland proper) as well as Lithuania, Orthodox Ruthenia, and Lutheran Prussia. Thus, German, Lithuanian, Ruthenian, Yiddish, and other minority languages coexisted with Polish, enabling cross-fertilization between diverse cultures. Political and economic prosperity facilitated *patronage of the arts and an interest in books among royalty, magnates, and prosperous townsfolk, which led to a flowering of the art of illumination in the 15th–16th centuries, led by Cracow. The *Kodeks Behema*, (*c.*1505–6)—a compilation of statutes, privileges, and laws relating to trade and the guilds of Cracow, illustrated with exquisite *miniatures—testifies to this. Cracow, the capital city and a thriving commercial centre, was home to the Akademia Krakowska (precursor of the Jagiellonian University) founded in 1364, where the professors found MS books a vital working tool, which they frequently donated to the Academy's library.

2 Printing to 1600

Printing in Poland began in Cracow, with the arrival of an itinerant Bavarian printer, *Straube, in 1473. *Fiol established the second Cracow *printing office,

288

subsequently printing the first four books in *Cyrillic types (c.1490–91). The first printed text in Polish—daily prayers included in the *Statuta Synodalia Episcoporum Wratislaviensium*—appeared in 1475 at the Wrocław (Breslau) printing office of Kasper Elyan (c.1435–1486). In the 15th century, there were also printers in Malbork (Jakub Karweyse), Gdańsk (Konrad Baumgarten), and probably Chełmno (the anonymous printer of the sermons of Pope Leo I). However, Polish publishers still often used printers from abroad for more complex commissions, as Polish printers frequently lacked up-to-date *types and equipment.

Polish-language printing in Cracow dates from 1503, when the wine merchant Jan Haller established his own printing office, run by the German Kasper Hochfeder. Their *Commune Incliti Poloniae Regni Privilegium*, a collection of Polish legislation compiled by Jan Łaski (1456–1531) was among the first of c.250 items printed by Haller in twenty years of work. He also owned one of Poland's oldest *paper mills, at Prądnik Czerwony near Cracow, founded c.1493. Other prominent printers of early 16th-century Cracow were Hieronymus Vietor, the Szarffenberg family, Florian Ungler, and Maciej Wirzbięta. Both Ungler and Vietor made important contributions to the development of Polish language and its orthography. Ungler printed the first known book in Polish, *Raj duszny* (1513), a prayer book translated from Latin. Ungler's books were richly ornamented and illustrated (e.g. Stefan Falimirz's herbal *O ziołach i o mocy gich* (1534) with 550 fine *woodcut illustrations). Vietor, initially a printer in Vienna, developed close links with humanist intellectuals there; his *printing office in Cracow contributed to the dissemination of humanist thought. He printed works by *Erasmus and acquired *Greek types to print the Greek writings of the Cracow humanists. Hungarians studying at the Akademia Krakowska also worked with Vietor to publish Hungarian *grammars, *dictionaries, and religious works. In the later 16th century, Jan Januszowski introduced new types and improved printing processes. His *Nowy karakter polski* (1594), published using his new types, established the rules of Polish orthography. He printed more than 400 titles, including many works by Jan Kochanowski. Wirzbięta printed most of the works of Mikołaj Rej, the first outstanding author writing exclusively in Polish. In the second half of the 16th century, Cracow had twelve printing offices, including one printing Hebraica (*see* **8**). In all, around 4,200 different titles were printed in Poland during the 16th century.

Both Ungler and Maciej Szarffenberg possessed *Hebrew types, the latter using them in 1530 to print Phillippus Michael Novenianus' *Elementale Hebraicum*. The first Jewish printing house in Poland was founded in Kazimierz near Cracow in 1534 by the Helicz brothers, who learned the craft in Prague. They enjoyed great success until boycotted by their fellow Jews for converting to Christianity. Another early Hebrew printing house dating from 1547 was located in Lublin. Polish Hebrew printers, like Polish Latin printers, always faced competition from printers abroad, particularly in Italy, Bohemia, Germany, and Holland, since the importing of Hebrew books was unrestricted.

As in much of Europe, the Reformation and Counter-Reformation facilitated the spread of literacy and increased demand for print. Printing spread beyond the capital city to small towns and villages where Protestant printers operated presses under the protection of local landowners. In Poland-Lithuania, Lutheranism held sway in the north, whereas Calvinism, antitrinitarianism, and unitarianism took hold amongst the landed gentry, the magnates of Małopolska, the grand duchy of Lithuania, and even Europe's largest landowners, the Radziwiłłs. At first, Polish-language Protestant literature was printed primarily in Königsberg, where Jan Seklucjan published his New Testament (1551–3) in Polish. The first full text of the Bible in Polish, the *Biblia Leopolita* (1561)—published by Cracow Catholics, printed by the Szarffenbergs—was lavishly illustrated, but relied on older translations.

Meanwhile, the Polish Calvinists were working on a completely new translation, the *Biblia Brzeska* (Brest-Litovsk, 1563). The work of some dozen theologians, writers, poets, and translators led by Jan Łaski (1499–1560), it remains one of the great Polish cultural treasures both for its linguistic beauty and its appearance, though most copies were destroyed when Mikołaj Krzysztof Radziwiłł returned to the Catholic fold. The Catholics realized that in order for them to participate fully in the polemical debates raging at the time, a more accurate translation, drawing on the most recent research, was required. The result was Jakub Wujek's bible (Cracow, 1599). For the next three centuries, it was the canonical text of the Polish Bible. In response, other Protestant bibles appeared in the early 17th century, including the Polish Brethren's New Testament (1606), rigorously translated from the Greek, and the *Biblia Gdańska* (1632), the canonical text for Polish Protestants. No significant translations of the Bible into Polish appeared thereafter until 1965.

3 Relations between Polish and European cultures

In the 16ᵗʰ and 17ᵗʰ centuries, Polish writers, thinkers, and theologians were integrated into mainstream European culture. With Latin as the lingua franca of intellectual life, Poles studied and taught at universities in Italy, France, Switzerland, and Germany; many Protestants sought asylum in Poland, where from 1573 non-Catholics were protected by the state. Publishers in Germany, Switzerland, Italy, The Netherlands, France, and England produced works by Polish writers, many of whom were part of the European intellectual network. For example, Jan Zamoyski, founder of the Akademia Zamoyska, was close to *Aldus in Venice. Several influential works of Polish history (e.g. by Marcin Kromer and Maciej z Miechowa) and treatises on government and politics (e.g. Andrzej Frycz Modrzewski's *De Republica Emendanda* and Wawrzyniec Goślicki's *De Optimo Senatore*) enjoyed great acclaim throughout Europe. In the 16ᵗʰ century, 724 titles by Polish authors were printed abroad, and in the 17ᵗʰ century more than 550.

4 The 17ᵗʰ and 18ᵗʰ centuries

By the mid-17ᵗʰ century, disastrous wars with Sweden and Russia, Cossack uprisings, and internal feuding had brought about the demise of Poland-Lithuania's golden age. Polish printing deteriorated, particularly in the second half of the century, as did cultural, economic, and educational life generally. The victory of the Counter-Reformation stifled much of the open debate that had characterized 16ᵗʰ-century Polish intellectual life. Printing became subject to strict *censorship by the Church, which produced *indexes of prohibited books; *book burning became a public spectacle in Cracow. When Sigismund III moved his capital to Warsaw (1596), Cracow lost its supremacy as a printing centre because the *privileges for *government printing ceased. When the royal court moved to Warsaw, this privilege passed from the Piotrkowycz family in Cracow to Jan Rossowski, who had been printing in Poznań 1620–24. The Piotrkowycz family eventually donated all their printing equipment to the Akademia Krakowska, which formed its own printing house at the end of the 17ᵗʰ century. Another notable academic printer at this time was the Akademia Zamoyska in Zamość, which benefited from Januszowski's experience and equipment. Itinerant printers profited from the boom in the printing of ephemera, as in the rest of Europe (*see* **14**). A vogue for popular literature also developed, where the quality of the printing mattered little, if at all.

The Enlightenment reached Poland much later than it did western Europe: Polish culture was not revitalized until the 1730s, after the intellectual and institutional stagnation of the previous century. German influences in Gdańsk led to the first learned societies whose aim was to promote the sciences and humanities, and in Toruń, to developments in the study of Polish language and culture. Enlightenment ideas reached Warsaw considerably later, mainly through French influence, though in 1732 *Załuski announced his intention to form a *public library in Warsaw. Poland's last king, Stanisław August Poniatowski, played a pivotal role in the development of intellectual and cultural life via his support for the arts and reform of the state, including the introduction of state control of the educational system with the Commission of National Education. This necessitated an entirely new set of *textbooks, since Polish replaced Latin as the language of instruction. New Polish terminology was introduced in mathematics, physics, and grammar; important steps were taken in the codification of the language, which reached fruition with the publication in 1807–14 of Samuel Bogusław Linde's six-volume dictionary of the Polish language. The press began to play an important role in public life with the magazine *Monitor* (1765–84), attracting the most significant writers and thinkers of the day. Warsaw supported eleven printing firms in the latter part of the 18ᵗʰ century. The most ambitious were those of Michael Gröll—who arrived in Warsaw in 1759 via Dresden—and Pierre Dufour, a Parisian who established his printing office in 1775 and produced titles in Polish, Hebrew, and Cyrillic. Their work characterized the new trend for simple, cleaner types and a modern design aesthetic enabled by new type foundries, such as that run by Piotr Zawadzki, a printer, publisher, and bookseller in his own right. Gröll also modernized Polish bookselling practice, holding *auction sales, publishing fixed-price catalogues (*see* BOOKSELLERS' CATALOGUES) of his own publications, and promoting books by *reviews. He also marketed Polish books abroad through firms in Amsterdam, Paris, and Berlin, and presented translations of Polish writers at the *Leipzig *book fair.

5 Book culture in partitioned Poland

After 1795, when Poland ceased to be a sovereign state and was partitioned between Russia, Prussia, and

Austria, the fate of the Polish book was subject to the vagaries of the occupying powers. The printed word became a force that united Poles living in the tripartite partition with their fellow countrymen who sought asylum abroad, and kept a Polish national identity alive. Inside partitioned Poland, conditions varied. During the early 19th century, within the Russian partition, Wilno (Vilnius) was the most important cultural centre, largely because of the university where Polish Romanticism developed (with Adam Mickiewicz playing a central role). Józef Zawadzki, the leading printer in Polish, Lithuanian, and Hebrew, did much to modernize Polish bookselling and publishing: his authors were paid *royalties, and he established a chain of bookshops in other cities. Wilno was also home to the Typographical Society, formed in 1818 to promote reading. This early progressive atmosphere came to an end after the November Uprising of 1823. In Warsaw, from 1801 the Society of the Friends of Science played an invaluable role in promoting academic publishing until its closure in 1831. During the later 19th century, without state support, the Polish School Society and the Mianowski Fund supported publishing both for schools and for research and academic communities. Influential private firms included the Glücksbergs for Polish history and literature, and the Arcts for textbooks, *music, *children's books, and, in the 20th century, dictionaries and *encyclopaedias. The other major publisher of reference works was Samuel Orgelbrand, whose 28-volume *Encyklopedia Powszechna* first appeared in 1859–68. Gebethner & Wolff, founded in 1857, was the largest publisher, printer, and bookseller; the firm continued until the Communist authorities closed it in 1960. Among its authors were many of the greatest writers, composers, and historians of the day: Władysław Stanisław Reymont, Henryk Sienkiewicz, Bolesław Prus, Bruckner, and Szymanowski.

A weak economy and intensive Germanization policies subdued the development of Polish cultural life throughout the Austrian partition during the 19th century, though the scope for Polish educational, cultural, and social activities revived after Galicia gained autonomy in 1868, with Cracow and Lvov playing a leading role. Lvov was the site of the *Ossoliński Institute; Cracow was home to the Academy of Sciences (founded 1873) and the Jagiellonian University, which regained its Polish identity in the 1870s and thus resumed its role as the centre for academic publishing. Cracow was also at the heart of the revolution in Polish artistic book design encouraged by the Young Poland movement at the turn of the century.

The artist and dramatist Stanisław Wyspiański, influenced by William *Morris and Walter *Crane, sought to bring to his works a unity of form and content that expressed national characteristics with secessionist and symbolist aesthetics. His work with members of the Polish Applied Arts society, Józef Mehoffer and Zenon Przesmycki (founder of the Warsaw journal *Chimera*), laid the foundation for the modern Polish book arts.

In the Prussian partition, particularly strong pressures to Germanize left no infrastructure for higher education or Polish learned societies until the later 19th century, when the Society for Public Education (1872–9) and the Poznań Society of the Friends of the Sciences (1857–) were formed. Poznań was the regional centre for bookselling, printing, and publishing activity, with many bookshops also operating reading rooms and lending libraries. In Silesia and East Prussia, material was also produced for the Polish-speaking population—chiefly popular and religious literature, *calendars, journals, and practical manuals.

6 Nineteenth-century Polish publishing abroad

Publishing activity both by Polish exile communities of the Great Emigration after the failed Uprising of 1830–31 and by subsequent waves of political refugees was particularly important. The centre of Polish printing abroad was in Paris, where many of the great works of Polish Romanticism were first published. In the period 1831–61, some twenty Polish printers were active in eleven French cities, with significant activity also in the UK, Belgium, and Switzerland. The first Polish-language publications in England were *pamphlets of the utopian socialist organization, the Grudziąż Commune in Portsmouth. The first Polish book printed in London, Antoni Malczewski's *Marja* (1836), was printed at an English press using Polish types. Stanisław Milewski and Aleksander Napoleon Dybowski opened the first Polish printing office in London in 1837 to publish the journal *Republikanin*. Although the Polish community in Great Britain was small compared to that in France, it was politically very active, and published prolifically for its size, with output intended for readers in the UK community, émigré communities elsewhere, and sometimes in partitioned Poland itself. Radical Poles in London had close links with other such groups, including the Russians; 1853 saw the founding of a joint printing house for the Polish Democratic Society and Herzen's *Free Russian Press. Between 1891 and 1903, B. A.

Jędrzejowski (Józef Kaniowski) ran a printing office for the Polish Socialist Party in London.

7 The 20th century

When Poland regained independence in 1918, printing, publishing, and cultural life were reinvigorated, but many obstacles remained for the development of reading and book culture. Literacy levels were low (c.33 per cent in 1921) and book prices were high. There were approximately 500 publishers in Poland in 1935; overall production in terms of titles had nearly trebled from c.3,000 (early 20th century) to c.8,700 (1938). Gebethner & Wolff remained the giants of Polish publishing and bookselling, but the Arcts were still influential, as was the Mianowski Fund for the publishing of scholarly works; however, there was still a preponderance of small and medium-sized firms. There were more than 1,000 bookshops, but these were very unevenly distributed, with many in Warsaw and other large cities and few in the eastern and western provinces. In the 1920s–30s, as in the rest of Europe, there was renewed interest in the art of the book in Polish circles. A number of bibliophilic associations emerged to publish journals such as *Ex Libris* (1917–25) and *Silva Rerum* (1925–31) and to support printers with artistic ambitions. These included Jakub Mortkowicz, who distinguished himself in the early 20th century as a literary publisher of writers such as Cyprian Norwid and Stefan Żeromski; he was influential in setting up Polish booksellers' and publishers' associations. Other producers of acclaimed artistic books were Adam Jerzy Połtawski and Samuel Tyszkiewicz. Tadeusz Makowski and Tytus Czyżewski, both working in Paris, were also renowned Polish illustrators.

World War II resulted in huge losses for Polish culture. Under German occupation, schools and bookshops were closed. Printing houses and libraries came under German administration. Polish publishers were forbidden to operate; three German firms published popular literature, *primers, and *propaganda in Polish. All Jewish bookshops, libraries, and printing offices were destroyed. Soviet occupiers also removed collections of books and whole libraries from Poland's eastern territories, sometimes burning them as they went. There was wholesale destruction of books deemed undesirable by the occupiers; booksellers, librarians, and private individuals heroically endeavoured to hide their collections and so preserve the national printed heritage. An underground publishing infrastructure developed, far more prolific than that in other occupied countries. It produced more than 1,500 journals and 1,400 book titles. During the war, Poles in exile and in military camps abroad also published extensively, producing some 15,000 titles overall.

Immediately after World War II, with the publishing, bookselling, and library infrastructure all but destroyed, many prewar publishers sought to satisfy the hunger for books sparked by the government's education campaign. From 1946, Communist authorities began exerting control, establishing a system of censorship and assuming control over publication rights for the principal twelve classic Polish authors—required reading in schools and thus the largest sellers. Censorship suppressed the publication of works considered harmful to the interests of the Polish People's Republic, including all mention of Polish–Russian relations and other controversial political issues. In reaction to this, London, sometimes called the Polish capital abroad, became the greatest centre of free Polish publishing. Major London publishing houses included Gryf, Veritas, Oficyna Poetów i Malarzy, the Polish Cultural Foundation, and Odnowa. With print runs as high as 2,000, they flourished until the mid-1970s, when the older generation of Poles began to die and émigré literature lost some of its vitality, though later waves of emigration after the political crises of 1968, 1976, and 1981 led to some revitalization. The Instytut Literacki in Paris was also influential, publishing books and the monthly journal *Kultura*. At times in postwar Poland, there were harsh punishments for possessing émigré literature, and its importation was strictly prohibited. However, as clandestine publishing took off in the late 1970s, new generations of Poles were able to read émigré classics and other independent publications (*see* SAMIZDAT AND TAMIZDAT).

In Poland itself, from the late 1940s, private publishers were branded as petty capitalists with no place in the new popular democracy. In 1949–50, printing, bookselling, and distribution were all brought under state control. Before 1950, approximately 300 private publishers were in operation; by 1955, 97 per cent of books were published by 33 publishers heavily centralized in Warsaw. Despite huge subsidies and record *press runs, the needs of the reading public were not met. For example, the thirteen-volume *Works* of Stalin was published in a print run of 1.8 million, while textbooks and belles-lettres were in short supply. The state bookseller, Dom Książki, bought the entire print run of every book published, so publishers had no interest in whether a title sold well. Books often cost less than the paper on which they were printed,

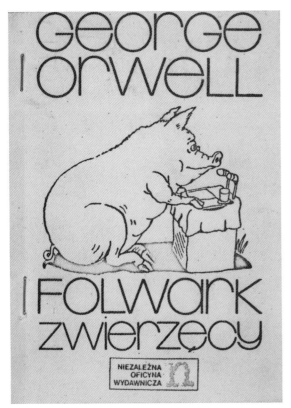

Polish *samizdat publishing: George Orwell's *Folwark Zwierzęcy* (*Animal Farm*; Warsaw, 1979), originally translated by Teresa Jeleńska for the League of Poles Abroad (London, 1947), here illustrated by Andrzej Krauze. The stapled binding is noteworthy.

straining available resources. From 1956, the de-Stalinization of Polish cultural policy led to far fewer titles being published—and these in lower print runs—as well as to more realistic publishing programmes and pricing policies.

Publishers' and booksellers' associations were allowed to operate again and seek out new writers. Policies that kept Polish readers isolated from Western ideas and literature were slightly relaxed, although international links were still fostered primarily within the Soviet bloc. However, the 1960s and 1970s were marked by perennial paper shortages and the inability of Polish publishing to satisfy reader demand. Books were often printed on poor paper with low production standards.

In the late 1970s a new phenomenon began to ripple the stagnating waters of Polish state publishing. Samizdat was known to small, select audiences in a number of Communist countries, but in Poland, the phenomenon of independent publishing reached a mass audience. The organizational strengths of Polish oppositional movements such as KOR (the Committee for the Defence of Workers), coupled with assistance from abroad, meant that many independent publishers could work at a professional level, using materials and equipment from official printing houses or smuggled in from abroad. Some titles had press runs reaching more than 100,000. From 1976 to 1989, more than 6,500 books and 4,300 periodical titles were published, printed, and distributed underground. This breaching of the government's control over the media and publishing played a profound role in the collapse of Communist power.

Since the later 1980s the state monopoly had been progressively weakening, and in May 1990 censorship and state control over publishing were officially lifted. The early 1990s saw a production boom, with thousands of new publishers, many short-lived, making the most of the public's hunger for popular fiction in *translation, *cookbooks, practical manuals, etc. The state publishers were gradually privatized or became cooperatives. Polish readers finally had access to the full range of books, including those by previously banned writers or on taboo subjects. In 1999–2003, the number of book titles published per annum hovered around 20,000. In 2003, not surprisingly, the largest number of titles (500) was published by WSiP, a specialist in textbooks, but a further seven firms produced more than 200 titles each. Of the 20,681 book titles appearing in 2003, just under a quarter were translations. The first decade of the 21st century has been characterized by common global trends: retail book chains, Internet bookselling, and growth in *electronic publications.

BIBLIOGRAPHY
B. Bieńkowska, *Książka na przestrzeni dziejów* (2005)
— and H. Chamerska, *Books in Poland* (1990)
Encyklopedia wiedzy o książce (1972)
J. Sowiński, *Polskie drukarstwo* (1988)

34 The History of the Book in the Baltic States

Jürgen M. Warmbrunn

1 The independent states

The Baltic States comprise the Republics of Estonia, Latvia, and Lithuania. As the so-called Baltic Sea Provinces, all three states formed part of the Russian empire in the 18th and 19th centuries (except for Lithuania Minor, which was under the governance of Prussia and later of Germany). The three states proclaimed their respective independence in 1918, losing it again in 1940 following the Hitler–Stalin pact and annexation by the Soviet Union. After the outbreak of the war between the Soviet Union and Nazi Germany, the Baltic States were briefly occupied by German troops until the Soviet Union reconquered and annexed the republics within the USSR. Under Soviet occupation, the Baltic States suffered severe population loss through deportation and emigration, the latter resulting in a sizeable output of émigré publications (e.g. in Sweden, Germany, the UK, US, and Australia). Following the establishment of strong pro-independence movements during the second half of the 1980s, Estonia, Latvia, and Lithuania formally declared their independence in 1990 and de facto became independent sovereign states again in 1991. In 2004, they became members of the European Union and NATO.

2 Similarities and differences

The historical and cultural development of Estonia and Latvia has been largely influenced by the presence of a German upper class—originally established under the rule of the Teutonic Order and comprising noblemen, academics, clerics, merchants, and craftsmen— as well as by their long affiliation with Russia and later the Soviet Union. Lithuania in turn has strong historical ties to Poland; the two countries formed a 'Republic of two Nations' (Rzeczpospolita Obojga Narodów) between 1569 and 1795, and share a predominantly Catholic faith. Particularly in Estonia and Latvia, the Reformation played a major role in the spread of books and reading in the vernacular. Latvian and Lithuanian are both Baltic languages and form part of the Indo-European linguistic family, whereas Estonian is a Finno-Ugric language, which in part explains the traditionally strong ties between Estonia and Finland.

Under Soviet rule, the Baltic States' printing and publishing industries were nationalized into large state enterprises and tightly controlled to forestall the publication of dissenting opinions. In Latvia, for example, following a 1965 decision by the Central Committee of the Communist Party of the Soviet Union, the issuing of all *newspapers, journals, and other publications was centralized in the Riga Printing House, where editorial staff and production facilities for the whole country were concentrated. During the occupation of the Baltic States, the Soviet authorities nevertheless permitted the publication of a considerable number of works in the three languages.

The library system in the Baltic Soviet republics had been reorganized according to Soviet directives. Since 1990, however, the independent countries have again developed a system of public and academic libraries offering free access to their holdings and information resources. In Estonia in particular, libraries also play a major role in the dissemination of information technology and use of the *World Wide Web.

Following the return to independence, *censorship was abolished in the Baltic States and a new printing, publishing, and bookselling sector has developed under free market conditions with a wide variety of publishers and booksellers. Estonia and Latvia still have significant Russian minorities, a fact that results in a continuing demand for Russian language publications in those countries.

3 Estonia

Fragments of the first surviving work printed in Estonian come from a *catechism printed at Wittenberg in 1535, the Wanradt-Koell Catechism. Printing in Estonia itself developed only in the 17th century: first—from 1631—in Dorpat (Tartu), and later—from 1634, when Cristoph Reusner established his successful enterprise—in Reval (Tallinn). Book publishing in Estonian began in 1637, and periodicals in Estonian followed in 1766. Many printers also worked as booksellers and publishers. From the second half of the 19th century, the numbers of printers and of printed materials in Estonia increased rapidly; toward the end of the first period of independence in 1936, there were 94 printers at work.

The first itinerant booksellers were active in Estonia in the 16th century, while the earliest bookshops recorded in Tallinn and in Tartu date from the 17th. Initially, books were mainly sold by bookbinders, but later, printers also offered their products for sale. Independent bookshops developed in the 18th century (Gauger in Tartu, von Glehn in Tallinn), often operating *subscription libraries simultaneously. In the 19th century the numbers of publishing companies increased, mostly due to the merging of printing and bookselling enterprises.

Publications in Estonian were originally distributed by shops catering for the needs of country people, and later by itinerant booksellers. The first bookshop selling Estonian language publications was established in 1867 by *Laakmann in Tartu. The publication of titles in Estonian, the official language of the new state, increased enormously following its first declaration of independence in 1918.

The development of libraries in Estonia has been strongly influenced by the country's political and social changes. Tallinn has only a few pre-Reformation fragments from monastic libraries, while the library holdings of the Swedish University in Tartu were taken to Stockholm in 1710. The oldest book collection still to be found in Estonia derives from St Olav's Church in Tallinn. Reading societies in Estonia developed toward the end of the 18th century. In 1825 the Estonian Public Library was founded in Tallinn,

and the country's major academic library, the *Tartu University Library, was founded in 1802. From the 1860s, libraries catering for the Estonian-speaking population developed in towns and in the country. In 1918 the Estonian provisional government decided to establish a state library, originally designed mainly to meet the needs of government and parliament; by the 1930s, it began systematically to collect all publications in Estonian and on Estonia.

4 Latvia

The first work in Latvian was most likely printed in Germany in 1525, but the oldest surviving Latvian printed text is a Catholic catechism printed at Vilnius in 1585, closely followed by books printed in Königsberg for Latvian evangelical parishes (1586–7).

In 1588, the Riga town council established the *Riga Printing House, owned by Nicolas Mollyn, who also acted as a bookseller. Following a Swedish initiative, a second *printing office—the Royal Printing House—was established in Riga by J. G. Wilcken, publishing many books in Latvian and Estonian. In Mitau (Jelgava), a printing office existed from 1666–7, but its importance was later overshadowed by J. F. Steffenhagen's printing company (1769–1919). For the region of Latgale (which came under the control of Russia in 1772 through the First Partition of Poland, and underwent a ban on using roman script), books were mostly printed in Vilnius. Although, by the end of the 18th century, there were printers throughout the country, the first printing office run by Latvians was not opened until 1869. During the country's first period of independence, the number of printing firms increased considerably owing to much higher demand, reaching 108 in 1931.

Vernacular works were mostly sold by itinerant booksellers (*colporteurs, or *chapmen) who are documented in Riga from the second half of the 15th century. Bookshops traded mainly in conjunction with printers and bookbinders. Of primary importance is the bookseller J. F. Hartknoch, who also ran a publishing firm, maintained close links with western Europe, and published the most prominent Baltic authors of his day, including Kant and Johann Gottfried von Herder. The first Latvian-language publishing firms set up business in 1867 in Riga and Jelgava. The turn of the century saw a huge expansion of the book industry, which continued to flourish during Latvia's first period of independence.

Despite the loss of the famous collection of the dukes of Courland to St Petersburg in 1714, Latvian libraries have a long history, beginning with the foundation, in 1524, of Riga City Library which was based on the libraries of secularized monasteries. In 1885 the Jānis-Misiņš-Library was founded, with the aim of documenting the history of the Latvian book. The library of the University of Latvia (founded in 1909) took over the holdings of the earlier Polytechnic Institute, and the foundation of the National Library of *Latvia followed the country's first declaration of independence (1919).

5 Lithuania

Printing, publishing, and bookselling in Lithuania were largely influenced by religious divisions. Duke Albrecht of Prussia brought theologians from Lithuania to Königsberg, where works in Lithuanian intended to strengthen the Lutheran faith were printed. Martynas Mažvydas's Lutheran catechism, printed in *roman type in 1547 by Hans Weinreich in Königsberg, is regarded as the first Lithuanian book. Earlier, between 1522 and 1525, the first vernacular editions of the Bible had been printed in Vilnius by *Skaryna. From 1553, printers worked with roman type in Brest-Litovsk. Their printing equipment was later transferred to Vilnius and given to the Jesuits for use in their university by Count Mikolaj Krzysztof Radziwiłł, whose family supported the printing of both Protestant and Catholic books in the 16th and 17th centuries. By 1805 the Vilnius Academic Printing House had produced 3,264 titles, mostly in Latin and Polish, but also in Lithuanian. Among these are the first Lithuanian Catholic books: Mikalojus Daukša's catechism (1595; the unique copy is now in the Vilnius University Library) and *Postilla* (1599), as well as the earliest Lithuanian *dictionary by Konstantinas Sirvydas. The first Lithuanian *grammar, however, was printed in Königsberg (1653). Until the 18th century, there were also 33 smaller printing houses working for Catholics, Protestants, and the Orthodox in Lithuania.

Following the uprising of 1863–4, the Russian governor-general banned the printing of Lithuanian books in roman type in an attempt to Russify the country, a move strongly opposed by the nationalist movement, the Catholic Church, and the general population. As a consequence, Lithuanian Catholic books with roman characters were printed in Prussia at Memel and Tilsit and brought illegally over the border by *knygnešiai* (book-bearers).

In 1900 there were 51 printing houses in Lithuania, producing Russian, Polish, and Jewish publications. Once the printing of Lithuanian books in roman type had been legalized again (1904), there was a significant increase in the number of printing offices, which—as in the other Baltic States—flourished, particularly in the first period of independence; between 1918 and 1940, 110 printing companies operated in Lithuania. The Polish printing firm of Zawadzki, successor to the Academic Printing House, was the most productive in Vilnius, combining publishing, printing, and bookselling activities between 1805 and 1940. Because Kaunas was Lithuania's interwar capital, a large number of publishing houses opened there, among them state, university, ministerial, minority, and private commercial publishers.

The existence of book collections in the Roman Catholic monasteries of Lithuania dates back to the 16th century. The library of the Jesuit Academy in Vilnius later became part of the *Vilnius University Library, but, following the university's closure, its holdings were taken to Kiev, Kharkov, and St Petersburg. During Lithuania's first period of independence, a central library was founded in the capital Kaunas, but its books and MSS were transferred to Vilnius in 1963 to form the State (today National) Library of *Lithuania. Since 1922, Kaunas has also had a university with its own library, which was closed in 1950, but reopened in 1989 following independence. The holdings of the Kaunas Art Institute were among the many losses suffered by official and private libraries in the Baltic States during World War II.

BIBLIOGRAPHY

H. Bosse *et al.*, eds., *Buch und Bildung im Baltikum: Festschrift für Paul Kaegbein* (2005)

K. Garber and M. Klöker, eds., *Kulturgeschichte der baltischen Länder in der Frühen Neuzeit* (2003)

Z. Kiaupa, *The History of the Baltic Countries*, 3e (2002)

L. Kõiv and T. Reimo, eds., *Books and Libraries in the Baltic Sea Region from the 16th to the 18th Century* (2006)

A.-M. Kõll, ed., *The Baltic Countries under Occupation: Soviet and Nazi Rule, 1939–1991* (2003)

P. Lotman and T. Vilberg, eds., *The 20th-Century Libraries in the Baltic Sea Region* (2004)

35 The Slavonic Book in Russia, Ukraine, and Belarus

CHRISTINE THOMAS

1 Early East Slavonic MSS

There is no direct evidence of written documents from East Slavonic lands before the acceptance of Christianity by Prince Vladimir of Kiev c.988. From the 11th century, there are twelve extant MSS (seven of them dated) written in Old Church Slavonic in Cyrillic script. The first MSS are the Novgorod Codex (beginning of 11th century), discovered in 2000; the *Ostromir Gospels (1056–7); and Sviatoslav's Miscellanies (*Izborniki Sviatoslava*) (1073, 1076). These compendia of works by the Church Fathers, parables, riddles, moral instructions, aphorisms, and citations originated in Kiev in the reign of Prince Sviatoslav. Three of the 11th-century MSS (the Ostromir Gospels, the Sviatoslav Miscellany (1073), and the Chudov Psalter) are richly illuminated and contain decorative woodcut headings made of intertwined letters, known as *viaz'*. All surviving pre-14th- century MSS are on *vellum, after which paper came increasingly into use. In Novgorod, archaeologists have unearthed medieval commercial and private texts scratched with a bone *stylus on *birch bark.

2 The beginning of printing

The earliest Cyrillic books, printed in the Balkans and in Crakow by *Fiol, were liturgical and closely modelled on MSS (*see* **36**). They are mostly small *folios (without *title-pages), with elaborate interlaced woodcut *headpieces and *initials, a lavish use of red, and with signed *gatherings but without *foliation. Later products, such as *Skaryna's *Cyrillic imprints, were closer to the central European Renaissance tradition and completely alien to Moscow printing, which began only in the 1550s; they influenced the work of some later Ukrainian and Belarusian printers.

Seven undated liturgical books were printed in Moscow in 1553–67 at the Anonymous Press, which was founded at the instigation of Tsar *Ivan IV and Metropolitan Makarii to ensure both the uniformity and the wider circulation of Orthodox liturgical texts. The earliest dated Moscow *imprint is the famous 1564 folio *Apostol* (liturgical Acts and Epistles), printed by *Fedorov and *Mstislavets. It has elegant and well-set *type and headpieces of white flowing foliage on a black background, typical of Muscovite MSS and later printed books. In 1565, Fedorov and Mstislavets printed two editions of a *book of hours but then, accused of heresy, fled to the grand duchy of Lithuania.

After their departure, printing in Moscow revived in 1568 and continued sporadically until the city's Printing House burned down in 1611, during the Time of Troubles. Five other 16th-century printers are named in surviving Muscovite books: it seems likely that printing expertise came to Muscovy from Poland, with Ukraine and Belarus acting as a conduit. By the end of the century, some twenty editions had been published in Moscow, all Orthodox liturgical texts, the vast majority at one press controlled by Church and state.

3 Printing in 17th-century Moscow

In the 17th century, Moscow became the single greatest producer of Cyrillic books, most coming from the Moscow Printing House (Pechatnyi dvor), reopened in 1614. The House was divided into three 'huts', each under a *master printer and with its own proofreading department, forge, carpenter's shop, typefoundry, block-making shop, and bindery. Its output was almost entirely religious in content, the vast majority of its books being large-format liturgical works, though the largest *press runs were for smaller-format *primers, *psalters, and books of hours. In the 1630s the master printer Vasilii Burtsov Protopopov, who had earlier worked with the Belarusian itinerant printer Spiridon Sobol, began to lease two presses in the Printing House. Burtsov broke new ground for Moscow. In 1634 and 1637 he produced primers in two large editions of 6,000 and 2,400 copies, respectively; the 1637 edition had a woodcut of a schoolroom, the first illustration in a Moscow-printed book. His *Kanonnik* of 1641 was the first Muscovite book to have a title-page.

Under Tsar Alexei (r. 1645–76), the Printing House's repertoire became more varied. Alexei, with aspirations to modernize Russia and to create an orderly and efficient realm, not only attempted to standardize church ritual and liturgical texts but instigated, in a limited way, secular printing. He commissioned codes of civil (1649) and canon law (completed in 1653), and a book on infantry warfare (1647), translated from the German of Johann Jacobi von Wallhausen's *Kriegskunst zu Fuss* (1615).

Yet it was the Church, rather than the government, that provided the main impetus for printing: decrees and other government documents were not printed. The energetic Nikon, appointed Patriarch of Moscow in 1652, set the Printing House the task of standardizing and revising liturgical texts, seeking to ensure their accuracy. Church councils in 1654 and 1656 produced his corrected versions and banned earlier texts and liturgical practices. A group of Old Believers rejected these innovations, continuing to copy in MS and to print the pre-reform texts until well into the 20th century.

In 1663, the first Moscow Bible appeared. It incorporated a number of innovations, such as a woodcut *frontispiece with the national coat of arms, a portrait of the tsar, a *map of Moscow, and Old and New Testament scenes. By the end of the 17th century, about 500 books had been printed in Moscow, almost all religious in content and all in Church Slavonic. The first *grammar of the vernacular (Russian) language was printed at Oxford in 1696.

4 Belarusian and Ukrainian printing, 16th–17th centuries

In contrast with Muscovy book culture, the Ukrainian and Belarusian book developed in an environment where Orthodoxy was not the sole religion. However, printing with Cyrillic type in those lands was influenced by the wish of the Ukrainian and Belarusian Orthodox to keep their religion alive. Although most printers were itinerant, some printers and Orthodox merchants had their own presses. Of the presses financed by merchants, the most famous was that of the Mamonich family in Vilnius. Other presses were set up by magnates, such as the hetman Hryhorii Chodkiewicz and Prince Vasyl Kostiatyn of Ostrih (Konstanty Wasyl Ostrogski). At the *Ostrih (Ostrog) Press on Kostiatyn's estate, Fedorov printed five books, notably the Bible of 1581 that served as an *archetype for the Moscow Bible (1663). The third category of printing houses was those of the Orthodox confraternities whose educational programmes needed grammars and books on poetics, rhetoric, and philosophy as well as polemical works. The most prolific were in Lviv (1591–1788), headed by the distinguished printer *Slezka, and in Vilnius, established in 1591. A fourth category of presses was the monastery presses. For Belarusian book culture, the most important was that of the Vilnius Holy Spirit Monastery, and, for Ukrainian works, the press of the Kiev Monastery of the Caves, founded in 1616. Throughout the 17th century, this press continued to produce books of very high scholarly and technical standards, especially during the tenure of *Mohyla. In the second half of the century, most privately owned presses ceased to exist, and printing was dominated by the monasteries. Although only Vilnius, Kiev, and Lviv developed into major printing and bookselling centres, presses were active in more than 30 locations.

Ukrainian and Belarusian books were closer to mainstream European printing tradition than Muscovite books. For example, dates of printing were given in the Western style from the birth of Christ, whereas Moscow followed the Byzantine tradition of dating from the creation of the world. Even religious books contained secular elements: there was some use of the vernacular and wider use of illustrations, title-pages, *commentaries, and *indexes.

5 Eighteenth-century Russia

The end of the 17th century marked a turning point in the history of Russian printing. In 1698, *Peter the Great hired Dutch printers to establish Russian presses for printing maps, charts, and books on technical subjects, and commissioned the new Civil *founts for secular publications. The state supplanted the Church as the main driving force behind printing. In the tsar's new capital, the St Petersburg Press, established in 1711, became the main publisher of government publications, notably the *Vedomosti* (News), the first printed Russian *newspaper. A new monastic press was established at the Alexander Nevsky Monastery outside St Petersburg in 1719. The Moscow Printing House (known, from 1721, as the Moscow Synodal Press) expanded, and the quantity of religious printing under Peter grew, though not as fast as secular printing.

Twice as many books were published during Peter's reign (1682–1725) as during the whole of the 17th century, with state and legal documents constituting more than 60 per cent of the titles, religious publications totalling less than a quarter, and popular publications (*calendars and primers) forming the third largest category. Fewer than 2 per cent of publications were devoted to history, geography, science, and technology; these, intended for a narrow audience, were issued in small print runs. Between 1727 and 1755, the Russian Academy of Sciences press published about half of all new books and over three-quarters of secular books. Its products, including Russia's first scholarly journal, *Commentarii Academiae Scientarium Imperialis Petropolitanae*, were almost invariably in Latin or German, and so were accessible only to a

International science in 18th-century Russia: the Scottish scientist Matthew Guthrie, living in St Petersburg, publishes his account of the freezing point of mercury.

small readership. The Academy bookshop, opened in 1728, sold Russian and foreign books, and from 1735 it issued a catalogue that also circulated in the provinces.

In 1714, the Russian Academy of Sciences Library opened in St Petersburg to all, free of charge; *Moscow State University Library and press were established in 1755–6. The 1750s saw the expansion of the periodical press, an increase in the publication of literature translated into Russian, and, to a lesser extent, of original works in Russian. These developments were given impetus by the initiatives of Catherine the Great (r. 1762–96). She supported the founding of the Society for the Publication of Foreign Books (1768–83), which was responsible for the publication of 112 separate translations (including Fielding, Tasso, *Rousseau, Montesquieu, Voltaire, and selections from the *Encyclopédie*), and became the leading voice for the Russian Enlightenment. In the wake of Catherine's initiation of the journal *Vsiakaia vsiachina* (Odds and Ends, 1769), a spate of short-lived satirical journals, on the model of English periodicals such as the *Spectator*, came into existence, four of them edited by *Novikov.

6 Private printers in Russia

In the 1770s, leasing agreements were granted to some non-native printers, and in 1771 J. F. Hartung became the first private printer in Russia—for foreign books only. A 1783 decree permitted the free establishment of presses anywhere within the empire, subject to the *censorship of local police. Half a dozen independent presses sprang up in Moscow, including Lopukhin's Masonic press, with which Novikov was closely associated. It published some 50 works before being closed down in 1786. By 1801, 33 private presses had opened in Moscow or St Petersburg, publishing over two-thirds of Russian books. Most private printers were from the merchant class; the majority were non-Russian, and largely German-speakers. There was a smaller group of 'intellectual' publishers. For all private publishers, finances were precarious. State monopolies had been granted to institutions (mainly the Academy) for the few profitable types of publication—*textbooks, calendars, and *almanacs. However, private publishers were able to exploit the growing market for popular adventure stories; the most sought-after was Matvei Komarov's bawdy *Adventures of the English Lord George* (1782).

Only the police, the senate, or the empress had the power to ban books. In the face of the publication of Old Believer texts and a growing number of mystical, including Masonic, works, the Church felt most threatened by relatively unrestricted printing. In 1787 an imperial edict authorized the synod to search all bookshops and publishing houses in the empire. The subsequent 'book raids', especially stringent in Moscow, temporarily paralysed the book trade, although ultimately few books were confiscated. On reopening, bookshops recovered quickly until the outbreak of the French Revolution. In 1790–95 several writers and publishers were arrested, books were confiscated, and printing offices closed down. Imports of French books and newspapers were banned. The first (official) presses had been established in the provinces in 1784; by the end of the century, seventeen provincial capitals had printing offices. The 1795 clampdown provided a stimulus to provincial printing, with a number of printers moving out of the capitals. In September 1796, two months before her death, Catherine issued an edict revoking the right of individuals to operate their own presses. The repression of Catherine's last years was intensified by her son Paul (r. 1796–1801), and by the end of the century, only three active private presses remained.

Alexander I (r. 1801–25) allowed the independent presses, closed under the 1796 law, to reopen. A decree of 1804 established Russia's first systematic censorship legislation, which, although relatively liberal in spirit (operated not by the police but by the ministry of education), introduced the concept of pre-publication censorship. Private publishing, overwhelmingly concentrated in the capitals, revived very slowly, and operated far below the level of the late 1780s. The book market was too small to make unsubsidized publishing a viable enterprise. However, some firms, like that of Semen Ioannikievich Selivanovskii and Ivan Petrovich Glazunov, the most famous representative of the Glazunov dynasty of publishers and booksellers, emerged and were to play an enduring and prominent role. The Academy, kept afloat by its monopoly on calendars, remained the dominant publisher of scholarly monographs and journals. Besides its main journal, *Mémoires de l'Académie* (then in its fifth series), it launched in 1804 the innovative and successful *Tekhnologicheskii zhurnal* (Technological Journal), intended to popularize science. It also continued to publish *Sanktpeterburgskie vedomosti* (St Petersburg News), and produced textbooks for the educational institutions established in the early 1800s.

7 From 19ᵗʰ-century Russia to World War I

In the first half of the 19th century, education expanded and university enrolments grew, stimulating a demand for books among a wider section of society. Printing technology improved, and in the 1830s the first successful commercial publishers and booksellers emerged.

The war against Napoleon had a devastating effect on the trade: the 1812 fire of Moscow destroyed presses (including Moscow University Press), MSS, and thousands of books. The following years saw a steady recovery. The Ekspeditsiia Zagotovleniia gosudarstvennykh bumag, established in St Petersburg in 1818 for the printing of bank notes, incorporated a *paper mill, and by the 1820s Russia was producing much of its own paper. In 1812, the first iron press was imported for use by the Russian branch of the *British and Foreign Bible Society. The first *lithographic presses appeared in St Petersburg (1816) and Moscow (1822). Moscow University Press—which by 1825 had overtaken the Academy in size, with 30 presses—was the main producer of textbooks and modern literature. The skills of a rising school of Russian engravers were used in finely printed books, including about

The third edition of Aleksandr Pushkin's *Eugene Onegin* (St Petersburg, 1837), the last for which he read *proofs. A *thirty-twomo, such *miniature books (it is 11cm tall), were a novelty in Russia at the time.

40 publications devoted to Russian history, commissioned by *Rumiantsev.

Until the 1820s, most elite reading was of works in French, but then a vogue arose for Russian-language almanacs, similar to the *gift books fashionable in Britain and the US; they were popular with a new readership of women educated in institutes for aristocratic girls, boarding schools, or at home. The most famous almanacs of the 1820s (e.g. *Poliarnaia Zvezda* (Polar Star) in 1823–5, and *Mnemozina* in 1824–5), featuring some of the best Russian authors of the day, were literary and commercial successes, stimulating interest in native writing. They also played an important part in the professionalization of authorship, since their publishers paid fees to contributors. In the 1820s and 1830s, an increasing demand for home-grown literature was met by the works of such authors as Ivan Krylov and Aleksandr Pushkin, although all writings were severely censored following the failed Decembrist uprising (1825).

Bookshops and fee-based *circulating libraries had existed in Moscow and St Petersburg from the mid-18th century, owned primarily by foreigners. The bookshop and library opened in St Petersburg in 1788 by the Russian bibliographer Vasilii Stepanovich Sopikov was a notable exception. After 1812, however, the trade was mostly in the hands of Russians. The most outstanding library was that of the bookseller and publisher Vasilii Alekseevich Plavil'shchikov, founded in St Petersburg in 1815. By the 1820s it had a stock of 7,000 titles and had become a meeting place for writers. Upon his death in 1823, Plavil'shchikov left his bookshop and library to his most valued

assistant, *Smirdin, under whose aegis it became one of the richest in Russia.

Some of Smirdin's publications, such as his two-volume *Novosel'e* of 1833–4, are prime examples of the *Didot style of typeface, introduced to Russia by the typefounder Zhorzh Revil'on (Révillon). The press and type foundry of Adol'f Pliushar (Pluchart) was also in demand for fine publications. Other St Petersburg firms that came to prominence include those of the Glazunov family (whose catalogues remain an invaluable bibliographical source), and of Isakov, Bazunov, and Lisenkov. Iakov Alekseevich Isakov was at work from 1829 until his death in 1881, with a lending library for foreign books and an office in Paris for the purchase of French books. One of Smirdin's former salesmen, Fedor Vasil'evich Bazunov, set up the St Petersburg branch of the business, in 1835 (its Moscow branch was run by other family members). After 1854, it expanded under Aleksandr Fedorovich Bazunov until its bankruptcy in the early 1870s; the firm also produced useful catalogues.

In Moscow, the leading figures were the bookseller and publisher Aleksandr Sergeevich Shiriaev and the French publisher and printer Auguste Semen, whose press was considered the finest in Moscow. Among institutional publishers, the Academy's repertoire was broadening. From 1834, its *Mémoires* were divided into four specialized subject series, and in 1836 it launched a *Bulletin scientifique* with more concise articles and announcements. Moscow University Press continued its dominance: by mid-century it was still producing a third of all secular Moscow publications. Religious publications were produced in considerable numbers by the Synod Press.

Provincial publishing, which had seen some expansion from the 1820s onwards, continued to develop very slowly, dominated by local government publications. Provincial readership also grew slowly, poor transport making books 10–12 per cent more expensive in the country. In the 1830s, 'thick' encyclopaedic journals began to find a niche, constituting popular and useful reading for country landowners and their families. Urban publishing in the 1830s saw an increasing readership, larger editions, lower prices, and the expansion of periodical circulation. However, the economic depression of the 1840s was followed by the Crimean War and the 'Seven Years' Gloom' (1848–55), with a tightening of censorship in response to European revolutions. A number of booksellers went out of business.

Between 1855 and 1860, there was a striking increase in the number of periodicals: over 150 new titles appeared. The political climate under Alexander

II (r. 1855–81) allowed the topic of the emancipation of the serfs to be discussed in print. The abolition of serfdom in 1861, economic recovery, the flourishing of trade and industry, and the growth of the railways resulted in a corresponding upturn in the production and distribution of printed material. Despite intensified censorship (responsibility for censorship passed in 1865 from the relatively enlightened ministry of education to the ministry of the interior), this growth continued into the 1870s. Large-scale capitalist enterprises began to emerge, among them the publishing houses of Mavrii Osipovich Vol'f and Aleksei Sergeevich Suvorin in St Petersburg, and *Sytin in Moscow. Suvorin and Sytin became leading newspaper proprietors.

The tsar's reforms also resulted in the development of public *lending libraries in the 1860s. Charitable literacy committees raised funds for the creation of over 100 local libraries. The publisher Florentii Fedorovich Pavlenkov bequeathed his entire fortune to create more than 2,000 public libraries. Following Alexander II's assassination in 1881, censorship became harsher. Numbers of publications, especially those on political topics, declined; but the end of the 1880s saw an increase in scholarly works, and a government drive for economic growth resulted in a proliferation of agricultural and technological materials. Around the turn of the century there was an expansion in mass market publishing, ranging from Marxist publications to cheap editions of Russian and foreign classics and translations of *detective novels.

The material infrastructure for printing expanded and developed; the number both of presses and of technological advances—including the introduction of *rotary presses and the mechanization of typesetting—grew (see **11**). Educational works became a more important strand in popular publishing. A series of inexpensive editions of Russian classics and Western authors in large print runs was launched by Suvorin, who established retail outlets in many provincial towns. The publishing firm Posrednik (Intermediary), established in 1884 as a joint enterprise of Sytin, Tolstoy, and his disciple Vladimir Chertkov, provided wholesome and edifying booklets for the minority of literate peasants (13 per cent), as did some 50 educational organizations. Catering to the higher end of the educational market were the St Petersburg firm Prosveshchenie (Enlightenment, established 1896), and the German-Russian concern *Brokgauz & Efron.

In contrast with the largely utilitarian, mass-produced publications most typical of this time, some lavish illustrated books and magazines also appeared,

exemplified by the journals of the World of Art (Mir iskusstva) movement. The work of some of the best illustrators of the period can also be seen in the short-lived satirical journals that sprang up after the 1905 revolution, when censorship was temporarily in abeyance. From 1910 to 1914, Russian Futurist poets and painters collaborated to produce handmade books, with very limited *press runs, later to become collectors' items.

The first years of the century up to the outbreak of World War I saw an unprecedented expansion in Russian publishing, with a growing emphasis on the commercial mass market. Whereas between 1801 and 1900, c.2,500 titles had been published, some 400,000 appeared between 1901 and 1916. In 1912 and in 1913, Russia produced nearly as many books as Germany. The outbreak of war caused figures to slump; there was a chronic shortage of paper (the huge growth in Russian output had made the country dependent on imported printing supplies, particularly from Germany) and many presses were forced to close. The chief academic publishers, such as the Academy of Sciences and Moscow University, as well as some of the larger commercial publishing houses, survived the war, and the printing of government patriotic literature, as well as of Bolshevik leaflets and *broadsides, continued.

8 Ukraine and Belarus within the Russian and the Austro-Hungarian empires

The 18th century saw a decline in Ukrainian and Belarusian book culture. Russian imperial decrees in the 1720s banning the publication of anything apart from liturgical texts identical to those printed in Moscow and St Petersburg limited the previously distinctive nature of Ukrainian printing. The first work of literature in modern Ukrainian, Ivan Kotliarevs'kyi's burlesque travesty of Virgil's *Aeneid* (in which the Trojan heroes become Cossacks expelled from their homelands by the Russian government), circulated in MS and was eventually published in St Petersburg in 1798. Publications in Ukrainian, or even in the Ukrainian recension of Church Slavonic, were not allowed. No longer permitted to publish new texts, the Kiev Monastery Press did, however, continue to produce books with ornaments and illustrations, including excellent *woodcuts by prominent Ukrainian artists. The presses of the Uniate monasteries—at Pochaiv (1734–1914) and at Univ (1660–1770)—on territory that remained part of Poland-Lithuania, became the most productive centres. Printing for the

Orthodox in Belarus, also part of Poland-Lithuania, was restricted by the Catholic Church. Publishing continued in the (Uniate) Supraśl Monastery and nine other cities.

As a result of the first partition of Poland, Russia gained more Ukrainian and some Belarusian territories. State presses were opened in Elizavetgrad (1764), Kharkiv (1793), Kiev (1787), and Ekaterinoslav (1793), and in the administrative centres of Belarus (Vitebsk, Hrodna, Mohileu, and Polotsk) for the publication of official directives and reports in Russian.

In the first half of the 19th century, there was still no Ukrainian-language publishing. The Ukrainian-language *Istoriia rusiv*, an anonymous history of the Ukrainians, circulated in MS, as did some other books in the language. Several publishers in Ukraine (notably Kharkiv University Press, founded in 1805) touched on Ukrainian themes. Kiev University Press (founded 1835) published some important historical documents on national history in its four-volume *Pamiatniki* (Monuments, 1845–59), and from 1839 the Odessa Society for History and Antiquities began publication of its journal. In 1836 Ivan Timofeevich Lisenkov, a native of Ukraine, established his publishing and bookselling business in St Petersburg, specializing in Ukrainian authors; and in the 1860s, against a background of increasing national cultural awareness, the scope of Ukrainian publishing in Russia widened somewhat. Panteleimon Aleksandrovich Kulish set up a press in St Petersburg, publishing the works of Ukrainian authors, textbooks in Ukrainian for Sunday schools, and, in 1861–2, the only Ukrainian-language periodical in the empire, *Osnova* (The Base). In East Ukraine, centres of printing included Kiev, Odessa, Chernihiv, and Poltava.

Ukrainian-language printing in East Ukraine was again curtailed by the 1876 Edict of Ems, which authorized the publication of only limited subject matter—historical documents, ethnographic materials, and belles-lettres (subject to approval by the censor)—and also required that permission be sought for the importing of Ukrainian-language publications from abroad (e.g. Prague, Vienna, and Geneva, as well as Western Ukraine). From 1875, some underground revolutionary and populist presses were set up in Odessa, Kiev, Kharkiv, and Ekaterinoslav.

One of the results of the 1905 revolution in Russia was the appearance of Ukrainian- and Belarusian-language magazines, newspapers, and educational societies. New Belarusian publishers began work, two in St Petersburg and three in Vilnius, where one, *Nasha Niva* (Our Cornfield) and its newspaper of the same name, came to embody the early 20th-century Belarusian literary renaissance.

A 1906 law established freedom of publication of books for non-Russian nationalities, including the Ukrainians. The Kiev publisher Chas (Time, 1908–20) made a particularly important contribution to the development of Ukrainian culture, producing works by Ukrainian authors, translations from other languages, and textbooks for a mass readership. Nevertheless, Ukrainian publications were censored more strictly than those in other 'minority' languages of the Russian empire. From 1798 to 1916, only about 6,000 books were published in Ukrainian, and fewer than half of those within the Russian empire.

In Western Ukraine, conditions for publishing became more favourable following the 1867 Austro-Hungarian Constitution. Private and institutional presses were founded in Lviv, Chernivtsy, Peremyshl, and Kolomye; the most influential and long-lasting were those of the Prosvita (Enlightenment) society, established in 1868, and the Shevchenko Scientific Society, which set up a press in Lviv in 1873.

During World War I, most Ukrainian publishing was carried out abroad—in Vienna, Canada, and the US. During the short-lived period of Ukrainian statehood (1917–21), 78 Ukrainian titles were published in 1917, and 104 in 1918. In 1918–19, the National Library of *Ukraine and the Ukrainian Book Chamber (centres for *legal deposit and national bibliography) were founded.

9 The Soviet Union

Soon after the October 1917 revolution, all press organs deemed to be counter-revolutionary were closed down. A number of pre-revolutionary publishing houses, including Sytin, were allowed to continue operations. In the civil war years, when publishing reached its lowest ebb, Russian publishers abroad, notably *Grzhebin in Berlin, were enlisted to help supply textbooks for the government's literacy campaign.

The first state publishing enterprises were set up from 1918, among them Vsemirnaia Literatura (*World Literature), the State Publishing House, and Kommunist. The most important, the State Publishing House (Gosizdat), established in 1919, was charged with regulation of other publishing bodies, state and private, and after 1921 was producing one third of all books on Soviet territory. The printing industry was nationalized. In 1922, with the foundation of the Soviet Union, bodies equivalent to Gosizdat were established in East Ukraine and Belarus, now designated 'Soviet Socialist Republics'. Moves were made to build up the library network. All significant private book collections were nationalized, benefiting especially the Petrograd Public Library (later National Library of *Russia) and the Library of the Rumiantsev Museum (later the *Russian State Library). Both had been designated legal deposit libraries in May 1917. The Chief Administration on Publishing Affairs (Glavlit) was established in 1922 and operated as the main organ of censorship until 1990. During the years of the New Economic Policy (1921–9), some relaxation of state control galvanized the publishing industry, leading to a rise in the quantity and quality of publications. By the late 1920s, print runs of a million were not uncommon. Gosizdat, with its subsidies, control over allocation of scarce paper supplies, and right of first refusal of all MSS, retained its favoured position, but private publishers were again allowed to operate. By January 1925 there were 2,055 publishing houses in the Soviet Union, of which around 400 were private. Some of the best avant-garde artists of the time produced remarkable books. Innovation in literature was also tolerated. However, as the 1920s progressed, there was more and more state pressure for 'approved' literature (propaganda, socio-economic and political titles) to be published.

The Soviet government also followed a policy (1925–32) of 'indigenization', promoting the indigenous languages of the Union's non-Russian peoples. There was an initial period of Ukrainianization during which Ukrainian-language book publishing, though state-controlled, increased. A Ukrainian-language-based education system was introduced, dramatically raising the literacy of the Ukrainophone rural population. By 1929 the number of Ukrainian newspapers, of which there were very few in 1922, had reached 373 out of a total of 426 titles published in the republic. Of 118 magazines, 89 were Ukrainian. There was a renaissance of national literature, and book publishing in Ukrainian reached 83 per cent of the total output.

The 1930s brought dramatic strengthening of the powers of censorship, wielded not only by Glavlit but, increasingly, by the Central Committee of the Communist Party and the USSR *Writers' Union. In literature, the doctrine of socialist realism ruled. An attempt was made to eradicate duplication and to rationalize publishing; as a result of mergers and restructuring, a number of specialized state publishing houses were formed under the aegis of the Association of State Publishing Houses (OGIZ). There were parallel developments in Ukraine and Belarus.

However, duplication and inefficiency remained widespread.

Government sales of rare books and MSS (including the Codex *Sinaiticus) abroad for hard currency impoverished Soviet libraries and enriched public and private collections in Europe and North America. The Stalinist terrors of 1934 and 1937–9 resulted in bookshop and library purges: works written by or making reference to condemned people or on forbidden subjects were removed, to be destroyed or placed in libraries' special, restricted-access collections ('spetskhrans'), together with most foreign publications. Writers, bibliographers, and book historians were among those to perish in the purges. In 1939, Western Ukraine (Galicia) was incorporated into the Soviet Union and all its publishing houses were closed down (50 had existed in the interwar period).

World War II brought with it a chronic shortage of paper, the relocation of much publishing away from Moscow and Leningrad, and loss of Soviet control in areas under German occupation. Book production fell from about 40,000 titles in 1941 to about 17,000 in 1944. Rare items from libraries in the western part of the USSR were evacuated to the east, but thousands of books were lost, as a result of bombing or seizure by the Germans, and more than 40,000 Soviet libraries were destroyed. Many libraries managed to function throughout the war, including the Leningrad Public Library (later National Library of Russia), which served readers throughout the 900 days of the siege of Leningrad. There was some underground publishing in the occupied territory of Belarus and Ukraine, and the Belarusian Gosizdat, evacuated to Moscow at the end of 1942, continued to function.

After the war, the Soviet publishing industry recovered relatively quickly: by 1948 output had come close to 1938 levels, and it rose steadily thereafter. The industry retained its prewar structure, and output was very much influenced by the dictates of the Party. Following Stalin's death in 1953, Khrushchev's dismantling of the Stalin cult and selective relaxation of censorship resulted in some liberalization of literature, and diversification in the content of published works. In Russia, a degree of polemical debate appeared in the literary journals, both hard-line (notably *Oktiabr'* (October)) and liberal. Among the latter, *Novyi mir* (New World), edited by Aleksandr Tvardovskii, was in the forefront, publishing Solzhenitsyn's *One Day in the Life of Ivan Denisovich*.

An August 1963 decree initiated a radical reorganization of publishing, printing, and the book trade; by 1964, these had a structure that was to remain in place until the emergence of a market economy in the 1990s. In order to establish more effective government supervision, responsibility for control of the press in the Soviet Union passed to the State Committee for the Press (renamed State Committee for Publishing, Printing, and the Book Trade in 1972), directly subordinate to the USSR Council of Ministers (other republics had separate equivalents). It was charged with reducing the number of publishing houses and rationalizing areas of coverage assigned to those remaining. However, both in the book trade and in library supply, the cumbersome 'administrative command' system, which inhibited publishers' ability to respond to readers' demands, caused a shortage of the books that people wanted to read. Along with *samizdat, a thriving black market emerged not only to disseminate dissident and other forbidden literature but also to make up for the shortage of popular and perfectly legal publications.

During the Brezhnev era, known as the 'period of stagnation', the book industries remained stable. In the 1970s and early 1980s, all printing was censored, and the central control of raw materials and printing continued to influence print runs. Authors were paid to a standard formula, according to genre (e.g. fiction or textbook) and length. Perhaps for this reason, the average length of a Soviet book in 1984 was about 136 octavo pages, in contrast with the average 82 pages during the 1930s.

One of the Soviet media's clichés—that the USSR was 'the world's foremost nation of readers'—could in many ways be justified. The book industry had few rivals worldwide in numbers of titles and copies published. Illiteracy had been virtually eradicated, and more than half the population were users of the extensive network of urban and rural libraries. Yet, for seven decades, the book was essentially the ideological tool of a totalitarian state.

The Gorbachev reforms brought about a loosening of state control, initiated from above and seized upon from below. The Law on State Enterprises (1987) allowed some private initiatives, and the Law on the Press and the Media (1990) guaranteed their freedom. The Law also allowed any organization or individual to register as a publisher and establish mass media publications. State publishers were given more leeway to decide what they would publish, and some were leased to collectives. The first private publishing firms, small cooperatives, appeared in 1988, and a considerable number were established in 1989–90, but most were short-lived. A parallel press emerged, producing thousands of semi-legal leaflets and periodicals of every conceivable kind, among them anarchist, feminist, Green, nationalist, and religious.

10 Post-communist Russia

Following the break-up of the Soviet Union in 1991, the collapse of centralized control brought with it a crumbling of state structures. The political and economic crises of 1990 and 1991 brought the publishing industry to its knees. In 1992 there was an all-time slump, with only about 28,000 books being published, but there were already signs of recovery in 1993. In 2000 the *Russian Book Chamber registered 56,180 titles (surpassing the previous official record of 55,657 titles in 1977). The Book Chamber record is almost certainly an underestimate because of the failure of some publishers to comply with legal deposit. The shape of the industry also changed: by mid-1993, state houses were producing only 30 per cent of books, and in the ensuing years private publishers took over more and more of the market. By 2000, the seven most prolific publishers were all—with the exception of the state-owned textbook publisher, Prosveshchenie—private firms, less than a decade old. Some of the larger ones—EKSMO, Terra, and Olma-Press—had acquired their own printing plants and distribution systems.

With the demise of the state publishers and the appearance of private houses more responsive to demand, the two most popular genres to emerge were crime and *romance novels. In the early 1990s, these were translations of foreign writers, but Russian authors largely superseded them later in the decade. Glossy magazines also began to make an appearance. Another significant growth area was encyclopaedic dictionaries on a wide range of subjects. Scholarly publishing survived, and even flourished, aided by finance from NGOs (non-governmental organizations). Alongside books on previously taboo subjects or by banned authors, works formerly published in centres of Russian publishing abroad—such as Paris, Frankfurt-am-Main, Berlin, Israel, and various cities in the US and Canada—made their first appearance in Russia.

There was considerable democratization in libraries, in spite of difficulties caused by dwindling financial support from the state. By the early 1990s, the considerable task of releasing restricted books from the spetskhrans and entering them in general library catalogues was virtually complete. The 1994 Law on Libraries guaranteed all citizens free access to information through libraries. An Open Society programme, Russian Libraries on the Internet, helped to provide access through the *World Wide Web.

11 Post-Soviet Belarus

At the end of the Soviet period, Belarus was probably the most Russified of all the republics, with a weak sense of national identity. At the very time in early 1989 that a law was passed prohibiting cooperative or private publishing, the first private publishers appeared, circumventing the law by purchasing *ISBNs from Russian publishers in return for giving them 10 per cent of every print run.

In the early years of independence, up to 1994, the government had a policy of Belarusianizing education and reviving the moribund literary language (kept alive in the diaspora). The works of émigré writers were published. Post-1990, more books, booklets, magazines, and newspapers were published in Belarus: 2,823 books (435 in Belarusian) were produced in 1990 compared with 7,686 (761 in Belarusian) issued in 2000.

In 1995 the Russian language was given official status along with Belarusian. Although the situation in Belarus was not conducive to the development of independent publishing, by 1995 private publishers accounted for some 70 per cent of the nation's total output. The second half of the decade, however, saw a decrease in private publishing. The government repressed the independent press, refused registration to private publishers, and closed down newspapers offering a critical perspective. The state-owned press enjoyed more favourable conditions, although it too was in crisis. The beginning of the 21st century saw a significant growth in numbers: there were 490 publishers in 2002, although 80 per cent of them were orientated towards the Russian-language market.

12 Independent Ukraine

Steady Russification throughout the Soviet period had caused a decline in Ukrainian-language publishing. Although in the 1960s some 60 per cent of the books published in Ukraine were in Ukrainian, by 1980 that figure had decreased to 30 per cent. As a consequence, some Ukrainian-language publishing was undertaken abroad. Following its revival in 1947 in western Europe and in the US, the Shevchenko Scientific Society played an important role in publishing: it issued three multi-volume encyclopaedias of Ukraine and, from 1989, operated in Ukraine. Other key publishing

centres were the Harvard Ukrainian Research Institute (founded 1968) and the Canadian Institute of Ukrainian Studies (founded 1976).

Post-independence, political restrictions on publishing were replaced by economic constraints, and publishing grew slowly, from 5,855 books in 1991 to 7,749 in 2000. Russian and Belarusian publishers, who operated under a more favourable tax regime, flooded the Ukrainian market with cheaper Russian-language books, especially in the lucrative area of popular literature. Despite a large number of enterprises (2,000 private and 28 state publishers in 2002), Ukraine produced less than one book per person in 2002, compared to 3.5 in Russia and seven in Belarus. The distribution system broke down, and newly established wholesalers concentrated mainly on popular material. However, in the field of scholarly publishing, both state publishers and institutions, ranging from the Academy and national libraries to small local museums, produced a wealth of historical and bibliographical material on Ukrainian history and culture. Scholarly publishing was assisted by funding from government, NGOs, and Ukrainian centres in the diaspora. The Ukrainian Publishers and Booksellers Association, established in 1994, became an energetic lobbying body, and the Ukrainian Academy of Printing in Lviv established courses in publishing and bookselling. By the end of the 1990s, there was a substantial improvement in typographical standards and in publishing facilities. Electronic publishing developed quickly, and the Vernads'kyi National Library of Ukraine began an active *digitization programme.

BIBLIOGRAPHY

M. R. Barazna, *Belaruskaia knizhnaia hrafika, 1960–1990-kh hadou* (2001)

I. A. Isaievych, *Ukraïns'ke knihovydannia: vytoki, rozvytok, problemy* (2002)

M. N. Kufaev, *Istoriia russkoi knigi v XIX veke* (1927; repr. 2003)

D. Likhachev, ed., *Knizhnye tsentry Drevnei Rusi* (2 vols, 1991–4)

S. Lovell, *The Russian Reading Revolution* (1999)

G. Marker, *Publishing, Printing, and the Origins of Intellectual Life in Russia, 1700–1800* (1985)

E. L. Nemirovskii, *Frantsisk Skorina* (1990)

I. Ohiienko, *Istoriia ukrains'koho drukarstva* (1925; repr. 1994)

M. Remnek, ed., *Books in Russia and the Soviet Union: Past and Present* (1991)

G. P. M. Walker, *Soviet Book Publishing Policy* (1978)

36 The History of the Book in the Balkans

Ekaterina Rogatchevskaia and Aleksandra B. Vraneš

1 Balkan geography

The Balkans, the region in the southeast of Europe, is geographically bounded by the rivers Sava and Danube in the north; the Mediterranean in the south; the Black Sea, the Sea of Marmara, and the Aegean Sea in the east and southeast; and the Adriatic and Ionian seas in the west and southwest. Although the question is disputed, the countries making up the region are generally taken to include: Albania, Bosnia and Herzegovina, Bulgaria, Croatia, Greece, Macedonia, Moldova, Montenegro, Romania, Serbia, Slovenia, and European Turkey. Geographical position defines the Balkan identity, but the region is diverse politically, ethnically, and linguistically. The book culture of the area is characterized by the coexistence in its history of different ethnic groups (e.g. Celts, Illyrians, Romans, Avars, Vlachs, Germans, Slavs, and Turks), languages (e.g. Latin, Greek, Albanian, various Slavonic and Turkic languages), cultures, religions (e.g. paganism, Catholicism, Orthodox Christianity, and Islam), and political systems (e.g. of the Roman, Ottoman, and Austro-Hungarian empires, and the Soviet bloc).

2 South Slavonic MSS and the beginning of printing

The Balkans could be called the birthplace of Slavonic *literacy, which began in the second half of the 9th century with the missionary activities of the brothers Cyril (Constantine) and Methodius, Byzantine Greeks from Thessaloniki. They introduced *Glagolitic and later the *Cyrillic alphabet, translating parts of the Bible and some service books into the Old Church Slavonic understood by all Slavs. The first Slavonic centres of literacy developed at Ohrid (now in Macedonia) and Preslav (the capital of the first Bulgarian empire; now in Bulgaria). Whereas Ohrid cultivated Glagolitic, Cyrillic became the official *script of Bulgaria. Old Church Slavonic gradually assumed vernacular features, laying the basis for the development of other literary Slavonic languages.

Glagolitic script was used in the south Slavonic countries and in Moravia until the 12th century, but then was generally replaced by Cyrillic or Latin, and localized mainly in Croatia. Early examples of Glagolitic script are rare. The first surviving MSS are of the 10th–11th centuries: the Kiev Folia, the Prague

307

Fragments, the Glagolita Clozianus, the Codex *Zographensis, the Codex *Assemanianus, the Codex *Marianus, the *Sinai Psalter, and the Euchologium Sinaiticum. Cyrillic script had three main variants: *uncial ('ustav', in use during the 11ᵗʰ–14ᵗʰ centuries), *half-uncial ('poluustav', 15ᵗʰ–17ᵗʰ centuries), and the *cursive script called 'skoropis' (mainly used in documents since the 14ᵗʰ century). The earliest dated Cyrillic MS is the *Savvina Kniga. Scholars estimate that about 30 other books survive from the 11ᵗʰ century, although not all of them originated in the Balkans.

Before the 18ᵗʰ century, when Peter the Great introduced Civil *founts in Russia (see **35**) and the codifcation of national languages started in some countries, Cyrillic printing—mainly catering for the needs of the Orthodox Church—was widely used. Although the first Cyrillic book was printed by *Fiol in Poland, and highly productive presses also existed in Venice, Prague, Vilno, and elsewhere, the Balkans played an important role in Cyrillic printing, the second Cyrillic press beginning production in Montenegro as early as in 1493. Glagolitic printing was localized in Croatia and Slovenia, although Glagolitic presses also operated in Italy.

3 Bulgaria

The Church Slavonic MSS written in the first Bulgarian empire are richly *illuminated. The earliest Cyrillic MS of Bulgarian origin is the Codex *Suprasliensis. In the 14ᵗʰ century, the Tărnovo school of literature developed a distinct style of handwriting and illumination. One of the best examples of this style is the Gospels of Tsar Ivan Alexander (1356), now in the *British Library. The first printed books were produced outside Bulgaria.

The elements of Modern Bulgarian were first evident in Filip Stanislavov's *Abagar* (Rome, 1651). The leading figure in the Bulgarian National Revival (1762–1878) was Paisius of Hilandar (1722–73), who wrote a Slavonic-Bulgarian history (*Istoriya Slavyanobolgarskaya*). Another person of note was Neofit Rilski, the author of the first Bulgarian *grammar (1835). The National Revival made possible the start of printing in Bulgaria. Having bought a press in Belgrade, Nikola Karastoyanov, who had worked previously in Serbia, founded the first *printing office in Samokov (1828). Commercial publishing and bookselling are associated in Bulgaria with *Danov. The national bibliography was initiated by K. Velichkov in 1897.

Independence from the Ottoman empire meant the revitalization of publishing and bookselling, and there were 80 independent publishers before World War II. In 1939, they produced 2,169 titles with a total *press run of 6.4 million copies.

4 Serbia

Serbian book culture also developed using the Cyrillic alphabet and was shaped by Orthodox Christianity, although it later experienced Arabic and Turkish influence within the Ottoman empire. The most productive *scriptoria were located in monasteries. One of the earliest South Slavonic Cyrillic MSS, the Miroslav Gospels, written c.1185–1190, probably in Kotor (now in Montenegro), was commissioned by Prince Miroslav, brother of Stefan Nemanja (later known as St Simeon), the ruler of the most successful medieval Serbian kingdom of Raška. The richly illuminated gospels are among the most beautiful Slavonic MSS; unsurprisingly, both Montenegrins and Serbs claim them as part of their own written heritage. Stefan Nemanja's youngest son, Rastko Nemanjić (later St Sava), is considered the founder of the independent Serbian Orthodox Church and the author of the *Life of St Simeon*. The father and son were also founders of Hilandar monastery, an Eastern Orthodox monastery on *Mount Athos in Greece; following its foundation in 1198, Hilandar was the principal centre for Serbian medieval book culture. During the Turkish rule that began in the 15ᵗʰ century and lasted for over 300 years, Serbian spirituality and national identity were preserved in monasteries, Hilandar taking the lead.

The printed book evolved in parallel with the MS book in the 16ᵗʰ century (cf. **6**, **13**). Serbia's first press, which produced the Rujan Gospels (1537), was located at the Rujan monastery, close to the Tara Mountain. Presses were established in the monasteries of Gračanica (producing an Octoechos or prayer book, 1539), Mileševa (three books printed, 1544–57), and the Mrkša Church (two imprints, 1562–6). In 1552, Prince Radiša Dmitrović founded a press in Belgrade, and started working on the gospels. As he died shortly afterwards, the work was continued by Trojan Gundulić of Dubrovnik and Mardarios of the church at Mrkša. After this brief period of activity, Serbian printing declined, religious and historical works being printed at Venice. Zaharije Stefanović Orfelin, a Serbian poet and engraver, established the first Serbian periodical in 1766 and wrote a biography of Peter the Great. In the 19ᵗʰ century, Serbian books were published in Leipzig, Novi Sad (the capital of Voedovina, then under Hungarian jurisdiction), and other towns that were situated in territories belonging to the Austro-Hungarian empire. *Matica Srpska played an important role in developing printing in the Serbian language and promoting Serbian book culture. The language reforms introduced by *Karadžić contributed to the landmark events in the history of the Serbian book. These included the foundation of the Royal Serbian Press in Belgrade in 1832 and the opening of the National Library of *Serbia and of the Serbian Literacy Society, the predecessor of the present Serbian Academy of Sciences and Arts (1892).

During World War I, significant numbers of Serbian books and periodicals were published in France, Greece, and Switzerland. The national book industry quickly recovered, only to collapse again during World War II, when the partisans' illegal presses alone were active.

5 Montenegro

In the 8ᵗʰ and 9ᵗʰ centuries the medieval state of Duklja, a predecessor of the modern Montenegro, was under Byzantine, Serbian, and Bulgarian domination. After the Great Schism in 1054, Duklja became predominantly Catholic. Once Stefan Nemanja made the land part of his state of Raška, he converted the population to Orthodoxy, and Latin cultural advancement was effectively stopped by ending the production of Latin books. Since then, Montenegro's book culture has been closely connected with the Serbian book. The second Cyrillic press—founded in 1493 on the initiative of Đurađ Crnojević, the ruler of the independent principality of Zeta—opened in Montenegro. Although its exact location remains unknown, the press, where the hieromonk *Makarije may have worked, most likely operated in Cetinje. The Montenegrin printing tradition was continued in Venice by *Vuković from Podgorica, who had a great influence on Serbian and Montenegrin culture, as well as on the development of printing in other Slavonic countries.

Under Ottoman rule, printing and literary activities were significantly reduced; but one of the first signs of the national revival, Vasilije Petrović Njegoš's *History of Montenegro*, was published in Moscow in 1754. *The Mountain Wreath*, the best-known book by the Montenegrin national poet and philosopher Petar II (Petrović Njegoš), was also published abroad in 1837, although by then he had already established his own press (1834), the second on Montenegrin soil. During a Turkish siege in 1852 its *type had to be melted down for bullets, but in 1858 a new press was obtained.

The establishment of a National Public Library in Cetinje was first proposed in 1879, but implemented only in 1893. From 1905, the library started receiving *legal deposit copies. By 1912, it had more than 10,000 titles, a large number of *incunabula and early printed books, and more than 100 MSS, but the holdings suffered severely from the occupying Austrian troops in 1918. In 1946 the Public Central Library was created at Cetinje, and given its current name in 1964. The library's major published work was *Crnogorska bibliografija 1494–1994*, a national bibliography.

6 Macedonia

Macedonian book culture developed under Bulgarian, Serbian, and Byzantine influence, reflecting the political landscape of southern Europe. Skopje, Macedonia's capital, became the capital of the Serbian empire in 1346, but from the late 14ᵗʰ century, the region was part of the Ottoman empire for about 500 years.

Important Macedonian books were produced outside the country: Jakov of Kamena Reka (the Stone River) had a Cyrillic press in Venice in 1560s; Hristofor Žefarovik's *Stemmatographia*, containing portraits of Bulgarian and Serbian rulers and images of South Slavonic coats of arms, was published at Vienna in 1741. In the 19ᵗʰ century, when publishing in Macedonia largely depended on the requirements of local schools, Teodosij of Sinai owned a press in Salonica, issuing the first *prayer book in a local Macedonian dialect and a short *dictionary. Although Bulgarian, Serbian, and Greek were the languages of instruction, fifteen *primers in a local Macedonian dialect were published between 1857 and 1875. The idea of establishing a Macedonian linguistic and national identity was first mooted in 1870, but was delayed during the interwar period, when local dialects were largely banned. The language was standardized and officially recognized in 1944. At present, materials in three main languages—Macedonian, Albanian, and Turkish—are published to serve the needs of the ethnically diverse population. More than 100 publishing houses issue material in Macedonian, with some twenty publishers catering for the other languages.

7 Bosnia and Herzegovina

Medieval Bosnian literature developed in Bosnian Cyrillic script, a variant of Cyrillic, and in Glagolitic. The oldest work in the Bosnian Cyrillic script is the

Charter, a trade agreement between Bosnia and Dubrovnik (1189), issued by the Bosnian Ban (ruler) Kulin; the oldest book in this script is the Service to St Mary (Ofičje svete dieve Marie), printed by Giorgio de Rusconi at Venice in 1512. The two known copies are held at the *Bibliothèque nationale and at *All Souls College (Oxford).

Cyrillic printing in Bosnia is associated with Božidar Goraždanin. In Goražda (in the east of Bosnia and Herzegovina), he established a press that produced three books in 1519–23. During the entire Ottoman period only four presses operated in Bosnia (three of them in the 19th century), with the total output of four *newspapers and 50 book titles.

For a period of more than 300 years no Bosnian press existed, and all printed materials came from abroad. Even the first periodical, *Bosanski prijatelj*, was founded in Zagreb in 1850. However, following an initiative by the Ottoman authorities, the first modern Bosnian printing office was set up in Sarajevo in 1865. By the end of the 19th century, two offices had been established in Mostar: the Press of the Catholic Mission in Herzegovina, started by the Franciscans, and the Herzegovina vilajet ('province' in the Ottoman empire) press. Under Austro-Hungarian rule, publishing grew, and the number of enterprises reached 40, adding German, Hungarian, and Yiddish to the linguistic landscape of Bosnian publishing. During the 40 years of Austro-Hungarian domination, 1,600 titles were published—Bosnia contributed 2,000 titles to book production for the kingdom of the Serbs, Croats, and Slovenes—and in 1945–51 book production reached 1,750 titles. Bosnian companies did fairly well as part of the publishing industry of the Socialist Federal Republic of Yugoslavia, but the 1992–5 war had a devastating effect not only on the local economy, but on the area's cultural heritage, as the National and University Library of *Bosnia and Herzegovina in Sarajevo was destroyed.

8 Croatia

The earliest works written on Croatian territory were in Glagolitic script. In their union with Hungary, the Croats were mainly Catholics, but Croatia appeared to be the only European nation given special permission by Pope Innocent IV (in 1248) to use its own language in its liturgy and the Glagolitic alphabet for service books. One of the most beautiful Glagolitic MSS is the Missal of Prince Novak (1368), now held in the *Austrian National Library. It contains the famous hymn 'Dies irae' and some musical notation. The

earliest Croatian incunabulum, the *Missale Romanum* (1483; its place of printing is unknown), survives in thirteen copies and eight fragments.

The first dated press in Croatia was opened in 1494 at Senj by Blaž Baromić, Croatia's first printer, who learned the art in Venice. The press was active until 1508 and printed seven books. In Rijeka (Fiume), a press was established in 1530 by the bishop of Modruš, Šimun Kožičić Benja. It published six Glagolitic books in two years. Croatian Cyrillic script was used in the Adriatic city-state of Dubrovnik and in Bosnia and Herzegovina; some scholars consider it the same as the Bosnian Cyrillic script, bosanica or bosančica. From the 15th century, the bulk of Croatian literature appeared in Roman script. In the 17th century, only one printing house operated in Zagreb (1664), but during the 18th and early 19th centuries, seven presses were working on Croatia territory. A Venetian printer, Carlo Antonio Occhi, published 50 books at his press in Dubrovnik in 1783–7.

Croatian Romantic nationalism emerged in the mid-19th century to counteract the apparent Germanization and Magyarization of the country. The Illyrian movement attracted a number of influential figures from the 1830s onward, and produced some important advances in Croatian culture and language. These were promoted by a society, Matica Ilirska (later Matica Hrvatska), formed in February 1842 and based at the National Library of *Croatia. After the fall of the absolute monarchy, the publishing industry revived. Matica published the first literary-scientific magazine *Književnik* (1864–6), and from 1869 the main fiction magazine for 19th-century Croatian literature, *Vijenac*.

9 Slovenia

As Slovenia's history includes its being part of the Roman empire, the Holy Roman Empire, and Austro-Hungary, the development of its book culture was considerably influenced by Latin and by German culture. As in the rest of Europe, scriptoria were mainly based in monasteries. For example, in the late 12th century, the Cistercian monastery of Stična produced the *Collectarium*, a collection of religious lives. Overall, 32 codices and five fragments from Stična have survived. Another scriptorium of note is the former Carthusian abbey at Žiče, the largest Carthusian monastery in this part of Europe and the first charterhouse outside Romance-language countries. The monastic library contained about 2,000 MSS, of which only 120 books and about 100 fragments survived.

310

The first printer of Slovenian origin, Matevž Cerdonis, worked in Padua in 1482–7, but the earliest books in Slovenian, by *Trubar, were produced at Ulrich Morhart's press in Tübingen. The Reformation was especially important for Slovenian culture and the development of the language: the first complete Bible in Slovenian, translated by Jurij Dalmatin, was printed at Johann Krafft's press in Wittenberg in 1584. A press on Slovenian soil opened in 1575 at Ljubljana; it belonged to Janž Mandelc, and produced ten books before it closed in 1580. Another press at Ljubljana was in operation from 1678 until 1801. The largest 19th-century publishers were Druzba Svetega Mohoria (1852), Slovenská matica (1846), and Slovenska knižnica (1876–80). The beginning of the 20th century saw several waves of Slovene publishing, closely linked to the nationalist movement. Publishing and other cultural institutions suffered considerably under the German occupation during World War II, although partisans maintained active underground presses.

10 Albania

The Illyrian tribes that populated the territory of present-day Albania were Christianized in the 1st century AD. The country's central position subsequently made it a battlefield between the western and the eastern halves of the Byzantine empire; at some point in history it was administered by the eastern empire, but ecclesiastically dependent on Rome. In the Middle Ages, the population of the southern and eastern parts of Albania became Orthodox Christians, whereas Roman Catholicism remained strong in the north. During the Ottoman rule that lasted until the beginning of the 20th century, the majority of the Albanian population converted to Islam.

The written Albanian language can be traced back to the 14th or late 15th century. Gjon Buzuku's *Meshari* (*Missal), published in 1555 at Venice, is the first printed work in the language. The Reformation greatly advanced the development of Albanian literature and book culture, and in the 16th–17th centuries, original works of poetry, prose, and philosophy were published. In the 18th century, both Christians and Muslims used the Albanian language to maintain their cultural heritage. However, the works of the most notable Albanians were published abroad (e.g. Pjetër Budi's *Rituale Romanum* and *Speculum Confessionis*, or Pjetër Bogdani's *Cuneus Prophetarum*, a *parallel-text theological *tract in Albanian and Italian). On the other hand, Greek language and culture dominated southeastern Albania. In Voskopojë, a press was set up which produced books in Greek and Aromanian (the vernacular language close to Romanian) in the Greek alphabet. Although Albania was the last Balkan country to gain independence from Ottoman rule, it too had its National Renaissance movement and version of literary Romanticism. The development of printing was, however, slowed because of complications with the Albanian language, which had been written with various alphabets since the 15th century. The roman alphabet for Albanian was standardized in 1909, and a unified literary version of Albanian, based on the Tosk dialect, was established in 1972.

Émigré publishing represented a further distinctive characteristic of Albanian book culture. The Albanians who fled the country because of Enver Hoxha's regime set up their publishing centres in Italy, France, Germany, and the US. In the 1990s, Albanian communities all over the world were enlarged by the Kosovo Albanians, who had produced their printed material in Zagreb, Skopje, and Tirana, but had lost the opportunity to do so at home due to political turbulence.

11 Romania

In the Middle Ages, Romanians lived in two distinct and independent principalities, Wallachia and Moldavia (Moldova), as well as in the Hungarian-ruled principality of Transylvania (*see* **31**). During Ottoman rule, Wallachia and Moldavia had some internal autonomy and external independence, which were finally lost in the 18th century. Christian Orthodox, Latin, and oriental cultures influenced Romania's culture. Tîrgovişte and Braşov became noteworthy centres for early Cyrillic and Romanian printing.

The Romanian language finally established itself as part of written culture in the 17th century. The first collection of laws printed in Wallachia, the *Pravila de la Govora*, appeared at Govora in 1640. Other printing centres of note were Iaşi, where *Varlaam's *Cazania* was printed; Alba Iulia (the Bălgrad New Testament, 1648), and Bucharest (the first Romanian Bible, 1688). In the 18th century, new presses were installed in Buzău, the Snagov monastery, and Râmnicu Vâlcea; a third (which had Greek types) began operating in Bucharest. Arab, Greek, and Turkish books were printed in addition to the Cyrillic and Romanian ones.

The first newspaper, *Curierul românesc* (1829), was started by 'the father of Romanian literature', Ion Heliade Rădulescu. Bucharest was also home to the Library of the Academy (1867) and the Central State

Library (1955; later the National Library of *Romania), while university libraries had been established earlier in Iaşi (1839) and Cluş (or Cluj-Napoca, 1872).

12 The socialist and post-socialist eras

The publishing and bookselling industries in all socialist countries followed the pattern previously established by the Soviet Union: private publishers and printers were closed; the state controlled the production and distribution of printed material; *censorship was introduced. This resulted in an unbalanced book market, with overproduction of *propaganda and severe shortages in popular literature. Large state subsidies led to unnaturally low book prices. On the other hand, communist ideology contributed to creating a cultural infrastructure of schools, public libraries, book clubs, and so on in all the Balkan countries. Having recovered from the devastation of World War II, most of the communist bloc countries reached their highest book production figures by the 1990s, although problems with distribution were much harder to solve: for example, in 1988, 27 per cent of books published in Bulgaria did not find their way to consumers, as demand for them did not exist.

Different political and economic conditions determined the development of publishing in individual countries. In Bulgaria, publishing and censorship were strictly centralized, unlike in Tito's Yugoslavia, where publishing relied on state giants and on private and small enterprises that balanced *self-censorship and profitability. Slovenia was early in learning Western marketing strategies and adopting modern manufacturing techniques.

Not surprisingly, the transition from socialism was difficult, and was accompanied in some cases by military conflict. In Bulgaria, although overall production figures in the early 1990s were lower than at the end of the communist era, the number of publishers grew from 752 in 1993 to 2,000 in 2000, spread equally over the country. In Bosnia and Herzegovina in 1996, 1,800 publishers were operating in the country in a great number of new and well-established places. Romanian publishing activity was still strongly centred around Bucharest, however. In Croatia, 1,828 of more than 3,000 publishers were located in Zagreb, followed by Split with 184 firms. Another common tendency in the transitional market economy was a significant growth of titles produced to satisfy different types of readership, combined with a notable fall in print runs. Many national libraries also found it extremely difficult to exercise their right to receive *legal deposit publications during this period. Such problems were partly caused by political and economic instability and partly by the legal ignorance of new participants in the book market. Links between national libraries across the Balkans were broken. In Serbia, there was a clear reduction in materials printed in the non-Serbian languages of the former Yugoslavia. Montenegro and Macedonia, having lost their Serbo-Croatian-speaking market, concentrated on their national readership. The numbers of bookshops in all the countries fell, as very few survived the early years of a market economy. However, the face of bookselling changed dramatically with the introduction of large book chains and *online shops.

BIBLIOGRAPHY

M. Biggins and J. Crayne, eds., *Publishing in Yugoslavia's Successor States* (2000)

A. Gergova, ed., *Bŭlgarska kniga* (2004)

E. L. Nemirovskii, *Istoriia slavianskogo kirillovskogo knigopechataniia XV–nachala XVII veka* (2003)

D. Tranca, *A General Survey of the Romanian Book* (1968)

37 The History of the Book in Sub-Saharan Africa

ANDREW VAN DER VLIES

1 MS cultures

Although the printing press did not reach sub-Saharan Africa until colonial administrators and Christian missionaries arrived in the 18th and early 19th centuries, the continent's engagement with writing and the economies of text is much older. Scribal cultures thrived in parts of West Africa on early trade routes across the Sahara, and although knowledge of Arabic seems never to have been widespread, a significant literature in African languages transcribed in Arabic script ('Ajami') developed. Important MS libraries survive in Mali, as well as in Ghana, Côte d'Ivoire, Niger, Senegal, and northern Nigeria—whence early Hausa-language Ajami texts date from the 17th century. Most other West African countries also have significant collections, many in private hands. In East Africa, Arabic MSS survive from the 11th century, although Kiswahili, the lingua franca of the coastal region, is now nearly exclusively written and printed using the roman alphabet.

More than 1,500 languages are spoken in Africa, and many sub-Saharan countries possess an extraordinary linguistic richness (Nigeria's 100 million people speak more than 250 languages; the same number occur among Cameroon's population of 20 million). Despite the difficulty of conveying the complexities of some tonal languages in script, most African languages are now written and printed using the roman alphabet. A few languages—notably Egyptian, Berber, and Nubian in North Africa, and Vai in 19th-century Liberia—developed their own, sometimes short-lived writing systems. The Ge'ez syllabary, developed from a consonantal alphabet, is still the basis for the alphabet in use in many printed works in contemporary Ethiopia—a country unique in sub-Saharan Africa for its history of written literary production dating to the first centuries of the Common Era. Early MSS in Ge'ez, which developed as a literary language between the 3rd and 8th centuries and persists as a liturgical language in the Ethiopian Coptic Church, include *translations from Greek and Arabic and an Old Testament with 81 books (to the Catholic Bible's 45 and the Protestant tradition's 39). Most early Ethiopian MSS are theological treatises (e.g. *The Interpretation of Divinity*), lives of saints, and royal chronicles (*Kebra-Negast*, *Lives of the Kings*), although religious poetry and hymns developed in the 14th century. Amharic, the language of the common people rather than the Church and its scribal culture, grew in importance with the ascendancy of the centralizing Shoan dynasty and the influence of Protestant missions in the early 19th century. In 1824, the *British and Foreign Bible Society printed a bilingual Ge'ez-Amharic edition of the Gospels; The *Pilgrim's Progress* appeared in Amharic in 1887, and Afä-Wärq Gäbrä-Iyäsus's *Lebb Wälläd Tarik* (A Story from the Heart, one of Africa's first African-language novels) was published in Amharic in 1908. Shortly after a printing press was installed in Addis Ababa in 1911, catalogues of Ge'ez and Amharic MSS were printed. In 1922, the Berhanena Selam Printing Press began publishing Amharic school texts locally. Soon, the power of the press superseded that of the continent's oldest surviving scribal culture.

ሐ:እምራ:እይ:ነገሮ:ስክል እ.
ዞሎ:ዘኮነ:ለዐሊ ሁ ቀወነስ
ሐ:ባ ቢ የ:ንስ ሐ:ወድ ሳ ን:እም
ሐጉ ል:በ ጸ ሎ ታ:ለ እ ግ ዝ እ
ት ነ:ማርያ ም:ወ ለ ዴ ተ:እ ።
ም ለ ክ ቀ ጸ ሎ ታ:ወ በ ረ ክ ታ;
የ ሀ ሎ:ም ስ ለ:ገ ብ ራ:ኔ ደ ስ ማ
ርያ ም ዓ ለ መ:ዓ ለ ም:አ ሜ ን;
ብ ኪ :ተ መ ይ ጠ:እ ያ ም ፉ ሃ
ገ ጋ ይ:ዘ ኢ መ ፉ ት ው ቀ እ ለ
ጸ ሐ ፉ:ስ መ ኪ:ክ ል ኢ ቴ:እ ን
ው ቀ ጓ ረ ተ:ም ግ በ ር:ማርያ ም
ወ በ ስ ለ:ዞ ስ:እ ፈ ው ቀ ቀ ድ
መ:ወ ና ይ ተ ኪ:ወ ር ሳ ራ ኔ ኩ
ቀ ድ ው ቀ እ ፍ ቀ ሮ:ም ኑ ኑ:ወ
ለ ሀ ይ:ሳ ስ ው ቀ

2 The impact of slavery and evangelism

Seminal 'movements' in the development of African *print cultures include slavery, and the forces that opposed and finally achieved its abolition—Christian evangelism, and the mission-facilitated literacy it spread across broad swathes of the continent (*see* **9**). The arrival of print and the book produced ambivalent results in zones of cultural contact: facilitating productive engagements with modernity yet silencing ancient cultures; promoting new forms of knowledge while functioning as a vehicle for organizing site-specific hierarchies of power.

Early Portuguese settlements were established in West Africa in the 15th century, and the European slave trade—which would transport more than 11.5 million Africans to Europe and the Americas between the 16th and 19th centuries—began with a voyage to Portugal in 1441. The slave trade was banned throughout the British empire in 1807, and slavery itself abolished in 1833, although it persisted elsewhere—notably in the southern US—until significantly later in the century. Narratives produced by slaves forcefully removed from their West African homelands in the 18th and early 19th centuries constitute perhaps the earliest works produced in English by black Africans. Emancipated slaves were often engaged by abolitionists to produce anti-slavery memoirs; some were examples of *ghostwriting, including those by Briton Hammon (Boston, 1760), James Albert Gronniosaw (Bath, *c.*1770), and Venture Smith (New London, CT, 1798). Philip Quaque, sent for his education from the Gold Coast (present-day Ghana) to Britain by the Society for the Propagation of the Gospel in Foreign Parts, corresponded extensively with the London-based Society on his return to Africa to serve as a minister; his late 18th- and early 19th-century letters offer nuanced engagements with *patronage and missionary education. Other notable works in a similar vein include Phillis Wheatley's *Poems on Various*

Subjects (1773), Ignatius Sancho's *Letters* (1782), and Ottabah Cugoano's *Thoughts and Sentiments on the Evil and Wicked Traffic of Slavery* (1787). The most famous remains *The Interesting Narrative of the Life of Olaudah Equiano, or Gustavus Vassa, the African* (1789).

Much of sub-Saharan Africa's indigenous print and publishing history is most deeply marked by the complex consequences of the work of 18th- and 19th-century Christian missionaries. Their idea of the book—and of the Book—as a symbolic marker of a newly configured African engagement with European models of modernity promoted print cultures that interacted with a variety of local cultural attitudes and intellectual traditions, and thus accumulated a range of functions, forms, and symbolic values. Hofmeyr cites a 1931 report in the *Missionary Herald* of a Baptist convert called Ruth, who attached the pages of a bible to a flagpole beside her home in the Belgian Congo, claiming that it marked her family as 'People of the Book', just as the Belgian official flew the Belgian flag when in residence (Hofmeyr, 'Metaphorical Books', 100). The book serves here as literal and figurative flag, a sign of the imbrication of print cultures with local structures of understanding and identification.

Presbyterians were among the first in West Africa to import presses and train local operators, and by the mid-19th century had produced *catechisms, lessons, *almanacs, and schoolbooks. Other missionary and philanthropic societies followed suit, some importing foreign expertise (the American Colonization Society employed a Jamaican printer in Yorubaland in the late 1850s), and many establishing depots to sell imported texts and produce translations into local languages. The Bremen Mission published Ewe *grammars in eastern Gold Coast in the 1850s; others (e.g. the Basel Mission and Wesleyan Methodists) were responsible, in the later 19th century, for early works in languages such as Twi, Ga, and Fante. Missionary activity was fraught with contradictions, often engendering tensions with colonial administrations; in a famous mid-19th century incident in eastern Cape Colony, colonial soldiers melted *Lovedale press type to make bullets.

Missions had a widespread effect, influencing European attitudes towards Africa (through *tracts and other material about evangelical work in Africa distributed in Europe), and encouraging the export of specially produced material to Africa. The London-based Sheldon Press's 'Little Books for Africa' and similar series found their way to the continent before World War II, when missionary-sponsored journals such as *Books for Africa* also flourished. Accounts including Margaret Wrong's *Africa and the Making of Books: Being a Survey of Africa's Need of Literature* (1934), published in London by the International Committee on Christian Literature for Africa, assessed the economic and practical difficulties of producing affordable books for Africans during the global depression. Paradoxically, restrictions on shipping and imports during World War II boosted local book production, much of it then still mission-controlled. After a decline in the 1930s, Ghana's Methodist Book Depot enjoyed a 60 per cent share of the national educational market by 1950, regularly distributing 500,000 copies of individual *textbooks.

Mission presses also facilitated the growth of literate African elites, allowing local writers access to print and distribution networks, and, with the spread of literacy, to audiences for writing in indigenous African, as well as in European, languages. Literary genres encouraged by missionary presses—exemplary lives, conversion narratives, didactic poetry, *self-help manuals, and ethnographic accounts—proved highly adaptable by politically pragmatic African writers. The Liberian Joseph J. Walters's *Guanya Pau: A Story of an African Princess* (1891), for example, argued for improving the condition of women, and Jomo Kenyatta's apparently merely ethnographic *My People of Kikuyu and The Life of Chief Wangombe* (1942) offered critiques of European intervention in East African societies. Mission presses dominated book production in many parts of the continent until the mid-20th century (with a handful of foreign-owned or multinational-affiliated presses controlling much publishing activity during the century's second half). Missionary-facilitated print production, with its own complex traditions, necessarily disseminated European institutional and cultural assumptions. Nevertheless, access to the technologies of print also paved the way for the *pamphlets, books, and journals that would fuel anti-colonial independence movements.

3 West Africa

The British colony of Sierra Leone served, after 1787, as a home for emancipated slaves from Britain and from colonies such as Nova Scotia; after the abolition of the slave trade throughout the empire, in 1807, it provided refuge for freed slaves from the rest of West Africa. Liberia, too, became a home for former slaves from North America after 1822, the American Colonisation Society having been established in 1816 to facilitate their return. West African intellectuals including E. W. Blyden, Samuel Ajayi Crowther, and

J. E. Casely Hayford produced early works central to forging notions of pan-African identity. Crowther's *The Gospel on the Banks of the Niger* (1859) recorded his prescient concern with the importance of written forms in securing the influence of Christianity in the region; his legacy in making the Bible available in Hausa is particularly valuable. Casely Hayford's *Ethiopia Unbound* (1911) was long regarded as the first fictional work in English by an African writer, although credit is now given to the unidentified author of *Marita: or the Folly of Love* (serialized in Gold Coast's *Western Echo*, 1886–8) and to Walters for *Guanya Pau* (1891).

Missionaries and mission-educated Africans were not alone in directing printing and publishing. From the mid-20th century onwards, booksellers operated wherever print flourished, however sporadically; schools, newspaper offices, churches, and clubs all frequently featured small bookshops. There were also notable state interventions, as in the Translation Bureau in Zaria in northern Nigeria, directed by Rupert East. Initially given the task of educating Africans for clerical work in the colonial administration, it soon ran writing competitions, and commissioned works in Hausa, encouraging book production in a roman script—which Ricard noted is called *boko*, from the English 'book', but (not accidentally) sounds like the Hausa for 'trickery' (Ricard, 58–9). Similar enabling work was continued by the Nigerian Northern Region Literature Agency (until 1959), the Hausa Language Board, and, after independence, the Northern Nigeria Publishing Corporation (1967). The state government in Kano later funded a publishing company, Triumph, to produce two *newspapers in Hausa (one printed in Ajami). Such *vernacular literature bureaux and state-sponsored initiatives operated at various times across the continent, with varying degrees of success. Others in West Africa included the United Christian Council Literature Bureau in Bo, Sierra Leone (1946), and the Bureau of Ghana Languages, Accra (1951).

Oxford University Press Nigeria (now University Press plc) opened in Ibadan in 1949. The Ibadan University Press, the first African university press outside South Africa, followed in 1951. The 1950s saw the foundation of a number of new literary magazines—pre-eminently, perhaps, J. P. Clark Bekederemo's *The Horn* and Ulli Beier and Janheinz Jahn's *Black Orpheus*, both in 1957—and the first significant indigenous publishing ventures (including Onibonoje Press & Book Industries Ltd in Ibadan, 1958). They were joined by increasing numbers of presses, commercial or state-sponsored, both locally and foreign owned, as independence spread across West Africa from Ghana (1957) and French Guinea (1958), to Ivory Coast (Côte d'Ivoire), Upper Volta (Burkina Faso), Dahomey (Benin), Mali, Cameroon, Mauritania, Nigeria, Senegal, Togo (all in 1960), and beyond. In 1961, the influential *Mbari press was founded, as well as Longman's Nigerian company, and the *African Universities Press in Lagos in the following year. *Macmillan opened its Nigerian branch in 1965, when the Nigerian Publishers' Association, Africa's first national book trade organization, was also established (Kenya's was second, formed in 1971, with Ghana's following in 1975). In 1968, *UNESCO hosted a regional book development conference in Accra, the first of several such regional initiatives. The International Conference on Publishing and Book Development in Africa was convened at Nigeria's University of Ife in 1973; 1975 saw the establishment of the now-defunct UNESCO co-sponsored Regional Book Promotion Centre for Africa in Yaoundé, as well as the first issue of the influential *African Book Publishing Record*. The *Noma Award for Publishing in Africa was established in 1979, the first award going to the Senegalese author Mariama Bâ, for *Une si longue lettre*.

Landmarks in Francophone book production in the region include the establishment of the journal and publishing house *Présence africaine* by Alioune Diop, Aimé Cesaire, and Leopold Sédar Senghor in 1946, and the publication of standard *anthologies of African and Caribbean writing, including *Poètes d'expression française* (ed. Léon Damas, 1947) and *Anthologie de la poésie nègre et malgache* (ed. Senghor, 1948). Among early Francophone African publishing houses were the Centre d'édition et de diffusion africaines in Abidjan, the Centre d'édition et de production pour l'enseignement et la recherche in Yaoundé (both 1961), and, more significantly, Éditions CLE in Yaoundé, established in 1963 with German and Dutch church funding; the last remained for many years the only significant African publishing venue for local Francophone writers. However, in 1972, the governments of Senegal, Côte d'Ivoire, and Togo, along with French publishing interests, set up Les nouvelles éditions africaines (NEA) in Dakar, with branches in Abidjan and Lomé. NEA Dakar split from the branches in 1991, and smaller firms such as Éditions Khoudia in Dakar (founded by Aminata Sow Fall, the first female publisher in Francophone West Africa), Les Éditions du livre du sud (Abidjan), Le figuier and librairie-éditions Traoré (both Bamako), and Arpakgnon (Lomé), have since come to prominence. The devaluation of the Communauté Financière Africaine (CFA) franc stimulated indigenous presses, now able to compete with increasingly expensive imports from France.

Between the 1930s and 1960s, vibrant popular print cultures developed, exemplified by so-called market literatures, cheaply published and widely circulated works including self-help manuals and popular thrillers, often drawing on local or mission-endorsed narrative models. Another influence was the arrival of cheap Indian pamphlets in the late 1940s (many Nigerian soldiers served in the British army in India and Burma), and of popular American and European *detective fiction and *comics. The best-known market literature is associated with Onitsha in southeastern Nigeria, whose heyday was from the 1950s to the mid-1970s; pamphlet cultures emerging elsewhere include, since the early 1990s, charismatic Christian publications, and northern Nigerian, Hausa-language 'Kano market literature', often written by women and addressing domestic issues pertinent to the predominantly Muslim society. There is a similar 'hawkers' literature' tradition in Francophone West Africa.

4 East and Central Africa

Print cultures in the East African states of Kenya, Tanzania, and Uganda developed comparatively later and more sparsely than in West Africa for a number of reasons: the absence of large-scale resettlement of former slaves (as in Sierra Leone and Liberia); the later and less intensive establishment of missions in the region; and the absence of educational institutions for Africans (such as Sierra Leone's Fourah Bay College) until the early 20th century. Indeed, *Makerere University College, a significant site in the development of a regional community of African writers, was not founded until the 1920s, and was granted university status a decade later. Uganda long enjoyed a vibrant intellectual culture, with elites writing and publishing in Luganda rather than English. In Kenya, however, the case was somewhat different. Kiswahili —a language with significant influence from Arabic, spoken in the coastal regions from Kenya south to northern Mozambique—was perhaps the only indigenous Kenyan language with a written tradition in the 19th century. The first book in English by a black Kenyan, Parmeneo Gĩthendu Mockerie's *An African Speaks for his People*, was published in London by the *Hogarth Press in 1934; Kenyatta's *Facing Mount Kenya* (1938) followed. Early works in Gĩkũyũ were mostly inspired by the oral narrative tradition or were accounts of a society under threat from colonial settler religion and government—e.g. the early landmark book by Stanley Kiãma Gathĩgĩra, *Miikarire ya Agikuyu* (*Customs of the Kikuyu*, 1933), published by the Church of Scotland Mission press, Tumutumu. Vernacular presses, newspapers, and book publishing developed widely after World War II. The East African Literature Bureau, run initially by the Church Mission Society's Nairobi bookshop manager, Charles Roberts, was established in 1947 (with offices in Dar es Salaam, Nairobi, and Kampala) to provide development-related material on agriculture, health, and education, as well as fiction, poetry, and anthropologically inspired titles. From its founding to the beginning of the Mau Mau struggle in 1952, it published more than 900,000 volumes, mostly in Kiswahili (41 per cent), but also English (12 per cent), Luganda, Gĩkũyũ, and Dholuo. The Kenya Literature Bureau resumed its operations in 1980, and numerous government or state-sponsored bodies, such as Kenya's Institute of Education and the *British Council in Nairobi, have also produced important anthologies and publications in a number of languages.

The influence of educational publishing on book production in East Africa, as elsewhere in Africa, cannot be overestimated. Missionary presses published grammars and school books from the earliest days of printing, and literature bureaux and other government agencies continued the trend. Western publishers were quick to see the potential for books in Africa's large post-independence markets, with educational criteria structuring the field of expectation (including standards of aesthetic judgement) and reception in a perhaps unprecedented manner. *Oxford University Press opened its East African branch in Nairobi in 1952; other British firms followed: Longman Kenya, Longman Tanzania, and Longman Uganda in 1965. *Heinemann Educational Books established an East African firm in 1968 (this became Heinemann Kenya, and later East African Educational Publishers). Other local publishers, though markedly fewer than in West Africa, operated sporadically throughout the early post-independence period. Significant presses established in the region in the last decades of the 20th century include the Mzumbe Book Project (Mzumbe, Tanzania, 1988), Phoenix Publishers in Nairobi (1989), Fountain Publishers in Kampala, and Mkuti na Nyota Publishers in Dar es Salaam (both 1991). Educational publishing still accounts for up to 80 per cent of the African publishing industry's economic activity.

Elsewhere, book production has faced greater hurdles. A number of presses have existed in the former Belgian Congo (Zaïre; Democratic Republic of Congo)—including Éditions CEDI (1946), Éditions Saint-Paul Afrique (1957), CEEDA Publications (1965), and Les Éditions Okapi (1966)—but despite landmark early works (including Thadée Badibanga's *L'Éléphant qui marche sur les oeufs*, 1931, and Paul Lomami-Tshibamba's *Ngando*, 1948), literary production did not flourish there until the late 1960s, and has been constrained by recent protracted civil conflicts.

5 Southern Africa

Whereas printing arrived in Batavia in 1625, the first press appears to have reached the Dutch East India Company's settlement at the Cape of Good Hope (established 1652) after 1784, when a German bookbinder, Johan Christiaan Ritter, produced handbills and three almanacs. Repeated requests for a press to serve the official needs of the settlement were refused by the Company's ruling council in Amsterdam until 1795, and were then frustrated by the surrender of the Cape to British rule that year. Some believe an eight-page Dutch translation of a letter from the London Missionary Society (LMS) to believers at the Cape, printed by V. A. Schoonberg in 1799, to be the first 'book' printed at the Cape. A private firm, Walker & Robertson, enjoyed a brief monopoly on printing after August 1800; they issued South Africa's first serial, the *Cape Town Gazette and African Advertiser* (forerunner of the *Government Gazette*), in August 1801. The government took over the press the following October.

Early South African book collections include over 4,000 volumes bequeathed to the Dutch Reformed Church by Joachim von Dessin, a Dutch East India Company soldier at the Cape between 1727 and 1761, and that amassed by *Grey after 1855 (while governor of the Cape Colony), which formed the core of the foundation collection of the *South African National Library.

George Greig, Thomas Pringle, and John Fairbairn published the short-lived *South African Commercial Advertiser* in 1824, sparking confrontation with the Cape Colony's governor, Lord Charles Somerset, and igniting a debate about *freedom of the press in the colonies. Significant other periodicals between the 1830s and 1880s included the *Cape Monthly Magazine*, the pro-settler *Graham's Town Journal*, and *De Zuid-Afrikaan*, sympathetic to the 'Dutch' proto-Afrikaners. Early Afrikaans-language works

include the fascinating case of Abu Bakr Effendi's *Uiteensetting van die Godsdiens* (Exposition of the Religion), compiled in the 1860s as a guide to Islamic law and ritual practice for the Cape's Muslims (predominantly descended from the earlier Malay slave community), printed in Arabic script and published by the Ottoman state press at Istanbul in 1877.

Jan Carl *Juta established a commercial publishing firm in Cape Town as early as 1853; it remains the oldest continuously productive publishing house in the country. Commercial English-language publishing began in earnest with T. M. *Miller in 1893. After World War II, local publishing expanded, with *Timmins, *Balkema, and Struik setting up as trade and Africana publishers. Oxford University Press and Purnell had both entered the local market by the 1960s, and significant local oppositional presses during the apartheid era included the *African Bookman, David *Philip, *Ravan, *Ad Donker, *Skotaville, and *Taurus. Important journals of the period include *The African Drum* (later *Drum*)—the primary venue for 1950s black writers including Lewis Nkosi, Es'kia Mphahlele, and Can Themba—as well as English-language literary organs such as *Contrast, New Coin, Ophir, Purple Renoster*, and *Classic*, some of which heralded the emergence of a generation of Black Consciousness poets.

As elsewhere in Sub-Saharan Africa, missionary activity played an important role in the development of printing cultures. T. J. van der Kemp, of the LMS, may have printed a spelling table in a local Khoi language at Graaff Reinet as early as 1801, and *Tzitzika Thuickwedi mika khwekhwenama* (Principles of the Word of God for the Hottentot Nation) at Bethelsdorp *c*.1804. At Kuruman, in the northern Cape, Robert Moffatt translated the Bible into Setswana, acquired a press from the LMS, and published more than 100 items between the 1830s and 1870. Moshoeshoe invited the Paris Evangelical Missions to his mountain kingdom (Basutoland, now Lesotho, annexed by Britain in 1868) *c*.1833; they printed actively from 1841 (at Morija, after 1860), producing a Sesotho New Testament (1845) and *The Pilgrim's Progress* (1872). In time, the first collections of Basotho customs and proverbs were compiled (Azariele M. Sekese's *Mekhoa le maele a Basotho*, 1907), and important early poetry and creative prose published—notably Thomas Mofolo's *Moeti ao Bochabela* (translated as *The Traveller to the East*; serialized 1906) and *Chaka* (1925). As was common practice, the Morija Press vetted indigenous writing for compliance with Christian orthodoxy, a fate that also befell, for example, Solomon

T. Plaatje's groundbreaking novel, *Mhudi*, at the Lovedale Press in 1930 (the *Heinemann African Writers Series published an unexpurgated version in 1978). Plaatje is also remembered as an influential editor of newspapers—*Koranta ea Becoana*, and *Tsala ea Batho* (or *Tsala ea Bechuana*)—and for his translations of Shakespeare into Setswana.

Scottish missionaries at Chumi and, especially, Lovedale, in the eastern Cape Colony, effectively directed early isiXhosa-language written and printed culture, publishing a *primer (1823), *Systematic Vocabulary* (1825), English–isiXhosa *dictionary (1846), isiXhosa Bible (1857), and Tiyo Soga's translation of *The Pilgrim's Progress* (1867). The Wesleyan Missionary Press in Grahamstown also facilitated important early isiXhosa publications, including a grammar (1834) and journal, *Umshumaydi Wendaba* (Publisher of News, 1837–41). Lovedale published newspapers like *Isigidimi SamaXhosa* (The Xhosa Messenger, 1870–88), edited by such leading black intellectuals as John Knox Bokwe, John Tengo Jabavu, and William Wellington Gqoba. By the end of the 19th century, there were two independent weekly newspapers with black editors: *Imvo zabantsundu* and *Izwi labantu*. In Zululand, annexed by the British Crown in 1887, missionary activity and print cultures were hampered by Shaka's expansionary wars of the early 19th century. American missionaries printed elementary educational and religious texts from 1837, an isiZulu grammar (1859), and a New Testament (1865). An isiZulu grammar in Norwegian was published in 1850. Important early newspapers include *Ilanga lase Natal* (The Natal Sun), published first in April 1903, edited by John Langalibalele Dube; a leading writer and educationalist trained in the US, he would later be the first president of the African National Congress. The earliest printed book in the vernacular by a black author was Magema M. Fuze's *Abantu abamnyamalapha bavela ngakhona* (Black People: Where They Come From), written in the late 19th century but published only in 1922. In the early 20th century, R. R. R. Dhlomo and H. I. E. Dhlomo also produced significant work.

In Rhodesia (Zimbabwe), missionary presses published bible translations into Ndebele (1884) and Shona (1907), and there was an active literary bureau in Salisbury (Harare). Post-independence Zimbabwe has been home to a number of energetic publishers, notably Baobab Books, co-founded and run by Irene Staunton in 1987, which regularly published editions (with *press runs of *c.*2,000 copies) of Zimbabwean and other African authors. In 1999, Staunton left to launch Weaver Press.

Printing began in Lusophone southern Africa in 1843, with the first book, verse by the mestizo writer José da Silva Maia Ferreira, published in present-day Angola in 1849. Portuguese contact with this region's Kongo kingdom had begun in 1493; some 1,540 letters between its Christian convert king, Afonso I, and the king of Portugal are among the earliest Lusophone African texts. An early collection of kiMbundu orature (orally transmitted literature), Joaquim Dias Cordeiro da Matta's *Philosophia popular em provérbios Angolenses*, appeared in 1891. From the 1930s, the Lisbon-based House of Students from the Empire proved crucial in the development of nationalist literary and political elites, many of whom returned home to the colonies (Angola, Mozambique, Cape Verde, Guinea-Bissau, and São Tomé e Príncipe) to fight for the independence that would come after the 1974 coup in Portugal. Communist regimes in newly independent Angola and Mozambique established high levels of state control over publishing, the Instituto Nacional do Livro et do Disco (Maputo, 1976) and Instituto Nacional do Livro (Luanda, 1978) enjoying near-monopolies. However, the end of South African-sponsored insurgencies, and increased support for civil society in these countries in the 1990s, allowed a number of autonomous, commercial publishers (e.g. Editora Escolar, Maputo, 1993) to emerge.

Elsewhere in the Southern African Development Community, printing was introduced to Île de France (Mauritius) by the French in 1767, and subsequently reached Madagascar (where the LMS also established a press, in 1826). Madagascar is its own special case, unusual among former French colonies in having been a unified kingdom with a single written language (Malagasy, related to Malay) before colonization. It also possessed a history of writing in Arabic script. Throughout the early 20th century, French colonial policy was to promote the teaching of French, but after the 1972 revolution, Malagasy literary production and printing have been actively encouraged.

6 Book production in Africa today

Africa generates less than 2 per cent of global book production, and remains unable to satisfy its own book needs, importing some 70 per cent of its books from Europe and North America (and exporting about 5 per cent of its output). Economic crises in the 1980s and 1990s hampered many African governments' abilities to fund book development or subsidize publishing, much less stock libraries; weak currencies across the continent have made imports of foreign-produced books and publishing materials prohibitively expensive. Even in South Africa, which has arguably the most developed publishing industry, fewer than 10 per cent of the population have the money to purchase books regularly. Nonetheless, small presses across the continent—more than 200 were active in 2000—continue to produce material in a variety of forms and languages, both African and European, with initiatives such as the *African Books Collective, and *African Publishers Network, Southern African Book Development Education Trust, and specialist foreign publishers such as James Currey and Hans Zell, seeking to support their endeavours. *See also* AFRICAN LIBRARIES, EAST AND WEST; AHMAD BABA LIBRARY; CENSORSHIP; **23, 25**.

BIBLIOGRAPHY

African Book Publishing Record

E. A. Apeji, 'Book Production in Nigeria: An Historical Survey', *Information Development*, 12 (1996), 210–14

D. Attwell, *Rewriting Modernity* (2005)

F. R. Bradlow, *Printing for Africa* (1987)

M. Chapman, *Southern African Literatures* (1996, 2003)

N. Evans and M. Seeber, eds., *The Politics of Publishing in South Africa* (2000)

A. Gérard, *African Language Literatures* (1981)

J. Gibbs and J. Mapanje, *The African Writers' Handbook* (1999)

S. Gikandi, ed., *Encyclopedia of African Literature* (2003)

G. Griffiths, *African Literatures in English* (2000)

I. Hofmeyr, 'Metaphorical Books', *Current Writing*, 13.2 (2001), 100–108

— *The Portable Bunyan: A Transnational History of 'The Pilgrim's Progress'* (2004)

— and L. Kriel, 'Book History in Southern Africa', *South African Historical Journal*, 55 (2006), 1–19

— *et al.*, eds., 'The Book in Africa', *Current Writing* 13.2 (2001)

C. Holden, 'Early Printing from Africa in the British Library', *BLJ* 23 (1997), 1–11

D. Killam and R. Rowe, *The Companion to African Literatures* (2000)

L. de Kock, *Civilising Barbarians* (1996)

S. I. A. Kotei, *The Book Today in Africa* (1987)

C. R. Larson, *The Ordeal of the African Writer* (2001)

B. Lindfors, *Popular Literatures in Africa* (1991)

S. Mafundikwa, *Afrikan Alphabets* (2004)

R. L. Makotsi and L. K. Nyariki, *Publishing and Book Trade in Kenya* (1997)

C. R. Namponya, 'History and Development of Printing and Publishing in Malawi', *Libri*, 28 (1978), 169–81

S. Newell, *Literary Culture in Colonial Ghana* (2002)

— ed., *Readings in African Popular Fiction* (2002)

— *West African Literatures* (2006)

J. Opland, 'The Image of the Book in Xhosa Oral Poetry', in *Oral Literature and Performance in Southern Africa*, ed. D. Brown (1999)

A. Ricard, *The Languages and Literatures of Africa*, tr. N. Morgan (2004)

A. H. Smith, *The Spread of Printing: South Africa* (1971)

A. van der Vlies, ed., 'Histories of the Book in Southern Africa': *English Studies in Africa*, 47.1 (2004)

— *South African Textual Cultures* (2007)

B. A. Yates, 'Knowledge Brokers: Books and Publishers in Early Colonial Zaire', *History in Africa*, 14 (1987), 311–40

H. Zell, *Publishing, Books and Reading in Sub-Saharan Africa*, 3e (2008)

38 The History of the Book in the Muslim World

Geoffrey Roper

1 The origins of the Arabic book

Arabic is a Semitic language akin to Hebrew and Aramaic. The *Arabic script developed from that of ancient Nabataean Aramaic, and reached only a very imperfect state in the pre-Islamic period. Arabic literature (mainly poetry) was then transmitted almost entirely orally. The written language of the period has survived only in the form of inscriptions on stone (*see* EPIGRAPHY), but there are a few tantalizing references in early Arabic poetry to writing on palm-bark and *parchment, and the use of *reed pens. Arabia also accommodated communities of Jews and Christians with a scriptural tradition in which some Arabs participated. Thus, book culture was not completely alien to pre-Islamic Arabs, even though they have left no surviving physical books. The form of the book was at this stage in a state of transition, from the *scroll to the *codex. By the time the Arabs felt an imperative need to create enduring but portable written texts, in the 7ᵗʰ century, the codex had already emerged as the norm, and it therefore became the prime vehicle for their emerging culture of the book. This need, and its physical expression, resulted from the impact of the new religion of Islam, conveyed through, and embodied in, a great book of revelation in the Arabic language.

2 The Qur'ān: the book seen as divine revelation and redemption

The word *qur'ān* in Arabic means simply 'reading' or 'recitation' but when applied to the founding revelatory scripture of Islam, it may have taken on some of the connotations of the cognate Syriac word *qeryānā*, meaning 'scripture reading' or 'lesson'. In the view of Muslims, the Holy Qur'ān contains the spoken words of the one transcendent God (Allāh), transmitted through the angel Gabriel (Jibrīl) to the Prophet Muḥammad, who lived in the Hijaz (western Arabia), *c.*570–632. These words, comprising 114 unequal *chapters (*sūras*), each divided into verses (*āyas*), were received over a period of about twenty years. They constitute a variety of material, ranging from passages of sublimely poetical quality to narratives, liturgies, and regulations for personal and communal conduct. Together they are regarded as the final revelation and message of the one true God to humankind, providing the ultimate source of belief and behaviour for all people who submit to Him (Muslims). Islam (literally, 'submission') is therefore, above all, a book-centred religion, in which redemption comes through obedience to a sacred text.

The Qur'ān was also regarded as being derived from a transcendent celestial Book (*Kitāb* or *Umm al-Kitāb*,

Mother of the Book), which had previously been revealed to Jews and Christians. Although they were accused by the Muslims of having corrupted their versions of the text, they were nevertheless regarded as the People of the Book (*Ahl al-Kitāb*) and respected as such (*see* **2**).

It is thought that Muḥammad, in the final period of his life, started the process of committing the Qur'ān to writing, probably by dictating it to *scribes who wrote it down on available materials, such as stones, animal bones, or *palm leaves. Oral transmission and memorized versions, however, continued alongside the written texts, which inevitably took varying forms. Eventually a standardized recension emerged, which is traditionally attributed to 'Uthmān ibn 'Affān (d. 656), the third caliph (successor of the Prophet and leader of the Muslim community), who is said to have ordered four or five master copies to be made of the definitive text, to be placed in the main Muslim cities and towns and used as exclusive *exemplars. Historically considered, it is likely that the process actually took much longer, and that, although the standard form of the text may go back to the 7th century, its detailed readings were not standardized for a further three centuries. One important reason for this was the fact that the Arabic script contains only consonants and long vowels, and reading and syntax depend on the insertion of short vowels, for which a consistent orthographical system was not devised until later. Early Qur'ān MSS also often lack even the dots that distinguish consonantal letters of the same basic shapes.

Until the advent of a standard printed version in the 20th century, the making of accurate copies of the Qur'ān (*muṣḥaf*, plural *maṣāḥif*—Muslims never speak of them as 'Qur'āns') was a sacred duty, since they embodied both the divine revelation and the indispensible guide to human life. They moreover became reflections of the sublime beauty of the divine word, through the development of Arabic *calligraphy, which evolved into the highest art form in Muslim societies. Great care was also taken with the design of Qur'ān copies, including the use of *illumination. Nevertheless, educated persons still had to learn the text by heart, and oral transmission continued to be of great importance until the print era, because MSS could not meet the universal demand among Muslims.

Non-Muslims have naturally not shared the Muslim faith in the divine origin and nature of the Qur'ān. European Christians until recent times regarded it as a *forgery, created by an impostor. Nevertheless, because of the challenges presented by Islam, they undertook translations of it into Latin, from the 12th century onwards, and later into European vernaculars. They were also responsible for the first printed versions of the Arabic text, starting with the Venice *Qur'ān of 1537/8. In the Enlightenment period and later, there was a growing appreciation of its literary merits, and even of its spiritual qualities. Modern ecumenism and multiculturalism have continued this tendency. Meanwhile, from the 19th century onwards, the Qur'anic text was subjected to philological, textual, and historical analysis comparable to the 'Higher Criticism' of the Bible, which cast considerable doubt on the integrity and chronology of the text and highlighted its relationship with pre-Islamic, especially Christian, scriptural traditions and terminology (*see* TEXTUAL CRITICISM). For Muslims, however, such treatment was anathema.

Whatever view is taken of these matters, it is hardly possible to overestimate the historical role of the Qur'ān as a book that has influenced and even determined the social, moral, and intellectual life, over many centuries, of about one fifth of the world's population.

3 Arabic scribal culture and its legacy

The Qur'ān also transformed Arab society into a pre-eminently literary culture. Because the overwhelmingly powerful revelation had come in the form of a book, textuality became the predominant characteristic of Arab and Muslim cognitive processes, and came to permeate Muslim society. From the earliest stage, it was necessary for Muslims to supplement the Qur'anic text with further sources of authority. The most important of these were the remembered and recorded sayings of the Prophet, known as *Ḥadīths*. These were eventually systematized and elaborated, together with the regulations in the Qur'ān itself, into bodies of law, which were carefully recorded in writing and continually copied and recopied to serve the needs of the community and its governing authorities. At the same time, the old Arabic poetic tradition was revived, re-examined, and committed to writing in order to provide insights into the meanings of Qur'anic terminology. This in turn stimulated a new Islamic Arabic poetic and literary movement that produced large numbers of new texts, incorporated into MS books over the following centuries.

In a few decades following the death of the Prophet, the Muslims pushed out of Arabia and conquered vast areas from the Atlantic to central Asia. Many of the populations of these areas adopted Islam, and some, especially among the adjacent territories, also adopted the Arabic language. They thereby entered this new Arabic-Islamic book culture, but at the same time they brought their own literary and intellectual heritage into it. Not only older literary traditions, but also philosophy, science, mathematics, geography, historiography, and other disciplines came to flourish in the Muslim environment, which enthusiastically promoted the acquisition of knowledge and learning as a virtue enjoined by the Prophet. The writing and copying of texts was an essential and integral part of this endeavour; during the 8th–15th centuries in Muslim lands it reached a level unprecedented in the history of book production anywhere. In his *Fihrist, the 10th-century bibliographer Ibn al-Nadīm al-Warrāq used his knowledge of the trade and of the contents of important collections to list the works of some 4,300 authors whose writings were then available in Arabic; in the 17th century, the Turkish scholar Kâtib Çelebi (Hacı Halife) enumerated more than 14,500 titles of which he had knowledge. Many texts were, of course, copied repeatedly down the generations.

The number of MSS produced is impossible to compute. Today there are more than 3 million MS texts in the Arabic script, preserved in libraries and institutions throughout the world, as well as an unknown but substantial number still in private hands. A very high proportion of these were written within the last 500 years: this reflects the longevity of the scribal tradition, but it is also a result of the destruction which has overtaken much of the earlier written output of Muslim civilizations in the period of their greatest intellectual vigour. Neglect, decay, and accidental loss by fire and flood have been compounded by the deliberate and belligerent destruction of significant parts of the written heritage, both by Muslims and by their enemies. The Mongol devastations of the 13th century are especially notorious, but the phenomenon has continued into the present era: important Islamic MS collections have been wholly or partly destroyed in and after the wars in Bosnia-Herzegovina, Kosovo, Afghanistan, and Iraq in the late 20th and early 21st centuries.

What remains, however, forms a substantial part of the world's intellectual and textual heritage. Not only is this heritage a vital underpinning of Muslim life and thought, but it has also constituted an essential strand of the European philosophical and scientific tradition. This was partly because Muslims inherited, translated, and transmitted the ancient books of the Greeks, Iranians, and Indians. Equally important were the original intellectual contributions of writers such as Ibn Sīnā ('Avicenna'), Ibn Rushd ('Averroes'), Al-Khwārizmī (whence 'algorithm'), and many others, whose books contributed to the development of thought that led to the European Renaissance. Muslim books entered Christian Europe by two routes: some were studied and translated in the medieval period in former Muslim centres in Spain; others were brought later, from the 17th century onwards, as Arabic MS books from Ottoman and other Muslim territories.

4 Physical aspects of the Muslim MS book

Although the earliest Arabic and Muslim writings may have been on bones and palm leaves, the normal materials in the first two centuries were *papyrus and *parchment. The former entered widespread use after the Muslim conquest of Egypt in the 640s, but chiefly for letters and documents, rather than books. Literary texts and Qur'anic fragments written on papyrus are extant, however, and there is evidence that some of them were assembled into codices. Parchment was the writing material favoured for Qur'āns, for which durability was more important than portability. Some magnificent specimens, usually in *oblong shape, with their width exceeding their height by up to 50 per cent, can be seen in surviving collections.

In the 9th century, a new material was introduced from China, via central Asia: *paper (*see* 10, 40). As a comparatively portable as well as durable medium, this soon became widely adopted both for fine Qur'āns and for more mundane and secular texts. Many centres of paper production were established throughout the Muslim world, and their techniques were eventually transmitted to Christian Europe. Not only was paper convenient to use, transport, and store, it was, most importantly, considerably cheaper than papyrus and parchment, probably partly because of the use of recycled rags as raw material in its manufacture. Whereas an early Qur'ān on parchment is reckoned to have required the skins of about 300 sheep, an equivalent amount of paper could be produced much more rapidly and at much lower cost.

The relative inexpensiveness of paper was a major factor in the explosion of book production and the transmission of knowledge in medieval Muslim societies from the 10th century onwards. Generally, only rulers, officials, and other privileged persons could afford the older materials, but paper put books within reach of a wider class of educated readers. Its availability and use seem also to have been the main reasons for the development of more cursive and legible styles of the Arabic script in that period. It provided a more convenient and readily usable medium for texts other than the Qur'ān, in which functional legibility was more important than hieratic presentation. Later, these styles were themselves calligraphically elaborated and used for fine Qur'āns written on paper.

Further developments in Iran from the 13th century onwards also made available much larger paper sizes, which in turn may have encouraged the development of book *illustration (*miniatures), as well as more lavishly and monumentally written and illuminated Qur'āns. From the 14th century, higher-quality European (especially Italian) paper rapidly displaced the local product in most Muslim lands. This reliance on imports does not seem, however, to have had an adverse effect on book production.

Because both parchment and paper were, by later standards, relatively scarce and expensive commodities, the practice of reusing them was not uncommon. Arabic *palimpsests on parchment exist in a number of collections; paper was also often recycled, both for non-book uses and to make further supplies.

Muslim scribes continued to use the ancient *pen made from reed (Arabic *qalam*, from Greek καλαμος), which was already the normal writing implement in the areas where Islam became predominant, and is mentioned in the Qur'ān itself. It consisted of a tube cut from the stem of a carefully selected reed (those from the marshes of Egypt and Iraq were especially favoured), which was matured by soaking in water and then carefully sharpened to an incised point. The shape and position of the incision varied according to the style of script for which it was intended. There were also distinct regional differences in the shapes of the nibs, especially between Spain and North Africa on the one hand and the central and eastern Muslim lands on the other. The craftsmanship involved in preparing pens was considered an essential and integral part of scribal art. Although there are occasional references in Arabic sources to metal pens, and one 10th-century Egyptian ruler is even said to have designed a gold *fountain pen, the reed remained the *sine qua non* for Muslim penmanship until the 19th century. Pens were protected by being kept in special cases (see PENNER), incorporating inkwells; the cases were often themselves vehicles for artistic decoration.

The *inks used had almost as exalted a status in the literature of penmanship as the pens (one poet called ink 'the perfume of men'). They varied in their recipes. In the earlier period, for writing on parchment, a brownish ink was used, made from combinations of mineral salts and tannins derived from gall-nuts.

After the introduction of paper, however, this was found to have a destructive effect, and black inks made from soot and gum (already used on papyrus) were preferred; they were also considered aesthetically superior. Moreover, they were easier and cheaper to prepare, and this too contributed to the efflorescence of MS book culture. Coloured, especially red, inks were quite often used, and the practice of *rubrication was widespread, helping to clarify the structures of texts and *headings in the absence of *punctuation (see TEXTUAL ARTICULATION). Gilt and silver also appear in some more prestigious MSS, especially Qur'āns, both for script and illumination (see ILLUMINATED MANUSCRIPT, MUSLIM).

The Arabic script, under the impetus of the need to write down the divine text of the Qur'ān, quickly developed from its rudimentary beginnings. By elaborating a system of pointing and *diacritics, it remedied its deficiencies and emerged as a functional means of rendering and recording Arabic texts, although it never became fully phonetic. At the same time, as the vehicle of the divine message, it attracted a spiritual, even mystical, veneration that inspired the desire to transform it into an object of sublime beauty. Calligraphy therefore became the highest art form in Muslim culture, and a great variety of fine script styles emerged, used primarily, but not exclusively, for writing the Qur'anic text. These ranged from the simple and dignified, even monumental, Kufic of the earlier period to intricate, elaborate, and curvaceous compositions in later times. There were also considerable regional variations, reflecting the different civilizations and patrimonies of Muslims across Asia, Africa, and Europe.

The production of more utilitarian MSS, embodying the huge output of devotional, theological, legal, historical, scientific, and other 'secular' knowledge, required more functional styles of script, designed primarily for legibility and communication. Most Arabic MS books are therefore written in smaller and simpler cursive styles, notably *naskh* (which later became the basis of Arabic *typography) and, in the Muslim West, various forms of *Maghribī*. Yet, even in workaday MSS, aesthetic considerations were rarely abandoned altogether, and writing still had sacred connotations, especially since the name of God (Allāh) was always present, if only in the universal opening invocation (*basmala*): 'In the name of God, the Compassionate, the Merciful.'

The complexities of nomenclature for the different script styles, and the lack of consistency and systematic correlation with what appears in extant MSS, has

The six classic hands,
al-aqlām al-sittah, of Arabic
calligraphy, with *nasta'līq*
and the three *Maghribī*
hands.

Tawqī' and *riqā'*

اللّهمّ بنورك اهتدينا وبفضلك استغنينا

وفي كنفك اصبحنا وامسينا انت الاول فلا شئ قبلك وانت

الاخر فلا شئ بعدك نعوذبك من الفشل والكسل

ومن عذاب القبر ومن فتنة الغنى والفقر

Muhaqqaq and *rayhān*

اللّهمّ بنورك اهتدينا وبفضلك استغنينا

وفي كنفك اصبحنا وامسينا انت الاول فلا شئ قبلك

وانت الاخر فلا شئ بعدك نعوذ بك من الفشل والكسل ومن

عذاب القبر ومن فتنة الغنى والفقر

Thulth and *naskh*

اللّهمّ بنورك اهتدينا وبفضلك

استغنينا وفي كنفك اصبحنا

وامسينا انت الاول فلا شئ

قبلك وانت الاخر فلا شئ بعدك

نعوذبك من الفشل والكسل ومن

عذاب القبر ومن فتنة الغنى والفقر

Nasta'līq

اللّهم بنورك اهتدينا و بفضلك استغنينا

كنفك اصحنا والمسينا الاول فلا شئ قبلك

325

Thulth maghribī

اللهم نور لي اهتدينا وبيضك الستغنينا وبك حبك اصحنا

ولامسينا انت الاول ولا شي فبلك وانت الاخر ولا شي بعدك لنعوذ

بك من العثار والكسل ومن عذاب القبر ومن فتنة الغني والفقر

Scribal maghribī

اللهم نور لي اهتدينا وبيضك استغنينا وكبعك اصحبنا ولامسينا انت الا وا ولاشي

فلك واب الا خر ولا شي بعدك نعوذ بك من العثار والكسل ومن عذاب القبر ومن فتنة الغني والفقر

Qur'anic maghribī

اللَّهُمَّ بِنُورِكَ اهْتَدَيْنَا وَبِفَضْلِكَ اسْتَغْنَيْنَا وَفِي

كَنَفِكَ أَصْبَحْنَا وَأَمْسَيْنَا أَنْتَ الأَوَّلُ وَلا شَيْءَ قَبْلَكَ

وَأَنْتَ الآخِرُ وَلا شَيْءَ بَعْدَكَ نَعُوذُ بِكَ مِنَ الكَسَلِ

وَالكَسَلِ وَمِنْ عَذَابِ القَبْرِ وَمِنْ فِتْنَةِ الغِنَى وَالفَقْرِ

The six classic hands, *al-aqlām al-sittah*, of Arabic calligraphy, with *nastaʿlīq* and the three *Maghribī* hands.

rendered the entire field of Arabic *palaeography quite problematic. Much scholarly work remains to be done before a clear picture can emerge of the typology of *bookhands and their chronological and geographical interrelationships.

There is one respect in which the more utilitarian bookhands were less practical than the grander Qur'anic scripts: they were rarely vocalized, whereas Qur'anic MSS, from the 10th century onwards, normally carried the diacritic vowel signs (*ḥarakāt*), to ensure the sacred text's correct reading. The absence of these in more mundane texts undoubtedly speeded up their production, and economized on the use of paper and ink; but it inevitably led to ambiguities in understanding and interpretation, and may have played some part in restricting functional literacy to an elite who knew the full phonetic and semantic values of the literary language through oral transmission. This may in turn have reinforced the still-prevailing division between literary Arabic and the unwritten colloquial dialects spoken by ordinary people.

The presence of pictorial illustrations in Muslim MS books was discouraged by Islamic injunctions against figurative representation. Certainly, they are never found in Qur'ān MSS, but they do appear in some 'secular' books to accompany literary, historical, scientific, and occasionally even erotic texts, especially from the 13th century onward. Schools of miniature painting emerged, mainly to cater to the tastes of ruling elites. Miniatures' exquisite beauty has appealed also to connoisseurs, mostly non-Muslims, in recent times, and they have become sought-after collectors' items; they were, however, for the most part extrinsic to mainstream book culture in the Muslim world.

Other features of book design and *layout are worthy of note. Except in the humbler 'working' MSS, pages were carefully ruled to ensure regular and equal spacing of lines, and to calibrate texts in terms of page numbers. This was done either with a *stylus or, more commonly, with cords assembled in a frame (*misṭara*), which could be used to provide standard rulings throughout a volume (*cf.* PRICKING AND RULING). Although some MS pages were designed to provide a comfortable balance between black and white through generous *margins and interlinear space, the high cost and uncertain availability of paper in many cases imposed cramped layouts making maximum use of space. Sometimes a virtue seems to have been made of this necessity by dividing the *text blocks into columns and/or panels, in some cases with oblique lines of text, arranged in a harmonious manner: poetry MSS offer the best examples of this. Otherwise, margins were often filled with *glosses and *commentaries, sometimes also written obliquely to the main text. Punctuation was rudimentary, consisting only of circles, rosettes, palmettes, groups of dots, or other devices separating verses of the Qur'ān and occasionally clauses, *paragraphs, or sections in other works.

Where they do occur, they rarely follow sentence structure in the modern sense.

*Gatherings (quires) were often (except in the early period) numbered to assist in assembling them in the correct order, using first alphabetic (*abjad*) numeration and later Indo-Arabic numerals or numbers spelt out as words. The numbering of leaves (*foliation) did not become widespread until the 16th century. *Catchwords were also used as a method of ensuring correct sequences as early as the 11th century, and became common from the 13th century onwards.

Texts normally ended with *colophons, which usually gave the date (and occasionally also the place) of copying and the copyist's name, together with thankful invocations and benedictions, and sometimes a recapitulation of the title and/or author of the work. At the beginning of a MS, *title-pages are sometimes found on the blank *recto of the first leaf, or incorporated into an illuminated *frontispiece, but they are not necessarily contemporary with the rest of the book, and their contents may be inaccurate. Details of author and title are normally located within the first page or two of text, after preliminary pious invocations and, sometimes, other prefatory matter. The text nearly always starts on the verso of the first leaf.

The illumination and decoration of MSS was an important Islamic art form, second only to calligraphy. The finest Qur'āns contain magnificent frontispieces and *headpieces (*'unwāns) with gilt and/or multicoloured abstract, floral, and foliate patterns, as well as text *borders, panels for headings, and sometimes interlinear decoration as well. Many lesser MSS were also illuminated, at least at their start. This, and some of the other features previously mentioned, underline the important role of the book in the visual as well as the literary culture of Muslim societies. These features can also provide useful, sometimes vital, evidence for the placing and dating of otherwise unattributed MSS.

One category of MS book in which the Muslim world made a notable contribution to global knowledge is that of *maps and *atlases. Muslims extended the inherited traditions of Ptolemy and other ancient cartographers to create world and regional maps of an accuracy that was not matched until modern times. This development was driven by the official and administrative requirements of the Muslim empires, but it coincided and interacted with the emergence of the new paper-based book culture from the 9th century onwards. Maps and atlases were, however, produced not to meet any widespread demand, but generally in response to rulers' commissions. Many of these maps were schematic rather than realistically scaled, but they reflected a growing visual sophistication that eventually culminated in such cartographical masterpieces as the world map of the 12th-century geographer Al-Idrīsī and the extraordinary atlas entitled *Kitāb Gharā'ib al-Funūn* (Book of Curiosities) now in the *Bodleian Library, Oxford, which has published it on the *World Wide Web.

*Bookbindings in the Muslim world were also vehicles for artistic finesse (*see* **17**). Although isolated examples are recorded of books in scroll form, the codex was the normal form of the book from the very beginning of the Islamic period, and at first wooden *boards, later *leather covers, were used to hold the leaves and gatherings together. Bookbinders emerged as specialized craftsmen by the 9th century, when several of their names were recorded. Yet, although the craft clearly enjoyed a certain prestige, its practitioners are predominantly anonymous, and their status is unclear.

Book covers were generally made of *pasteboard, often containing recycled MS leaves, and wholly or partly covered with leather, which was also pasted directly on to the spine. This unsatisfactory method often caused bindings to become detached, so many MSS were subsequently rebound. The rear cover was normally extended into a folding flap covering the book's *fore-edge. The front cover was usually decorated—in the late medieval period from which most of the earlier surviving examples date—with tooled rectangular panels containing geometric patterns, and borders, sometimes containing Qur'anic quotations. Often, the rear cover was also decorated, with a different design. Gilding was sometimes used. Later, central medallions of various shapes were imposed. In Iran, from the 16th century onwards, there was greater use of *gold, with other colours added. Lacquer was also used to create elaborate pictorial compositions on bindings. Inside the binding, the *endpapers of books of this later period were sometimes adorned with *marbling, using a technique that seems to have originated in Iran and reached its apogee in Ottoman Turkey.

Some MSS, of square or oblong shape, were encased in boxes, often glued to the spine, which served to protect what would otherwise have been a somewhat cumbersome and vulnerable book. Boxes, envelopes, and bags were also used for small portable MSS, especially Qur'āns and prayer books, designed to accompany and to protect travellers.

However important bindings may have become, the central role in the production of MS books was always

A *map of the Gulf of İzmir from a MS dated 1587 of Piri Reis's *Kitāb-i Baḥriyye*: the original work belongs to about 1521 and, like a *portolan, describes the Mediterranean for sailors.

held by the scribes themselves. The profession of scribe soon became established and honourable in Muslim society, and included people of all levels of education. Professional scribes were sometimes also specialized calligraphers, illuminators, or miniature painters operating in palace workshops, or secretaries working in court chanceries with an exalted status. At the other end of the scale, however, they might be market stallholders offering their services to all and sundry. In between, there were many paid copyists working in libraries, colleges, mosques, and other religious institutions. They were employed by wealthy patrons and book collectors, by scholars with particular needs, or by authors. Many MSS, however, were not written by professionals. Some were written by authors themselves: a number of *autograph or *holograph copies of Muslim writings survive in libraries. Impecunious writers and scholars also often resorted to copying in order to sustain themselves; students and other readers frequently made copies, in libraries and elsewhere, simply for their own use; such MSS often fall well short of the standards of calligraphy, or even legibility, found in those made for sale or on commission.

Inevitably in traditional society, most scribes, whether professionals or amateurs, were male. Yet there exist a surprising number of references to women performing this role. Some caliphs and other rulers employed female servants or slaves as calligraphers or as secretaries. Poets and writers also sometimes employed bondwomen to transcribe their works; other Muslim women were themselves poets or scholars who produced their own MSS. Even some fine Qur'āns are known to have been copied by female calligraphers, and in 10th-century Córdoba there were reported to be 170 women occupied in writing Qur'āns in the Kufic script. Much later, in 16th-century Iran, a traveller claimed that 'the women of Shiraz are scribes … in every house in this city the wife is a copyist' (Būdāq Qazwīnī, quoted in Déroche, 192). With all due allowance for exaggeration, these references indicate that book production was by no means an exclusively male domain in traditional Muslim societies.

Scribal activity did not entirely displace oral transmission in the diffusion of texts, however. Written books were often created in the first place by copying from dictation or from memory. The right to transmit the text was frequently granted in the form of a licence (ijāza) given by the author (or, later, an authorized agent in an established chain of transmission) on the basis of a satisfactory reading from the copy, which had to conform to the orally transmitted and memorized version. This system applied especially to religious or legal texts copied in the environment of a madrasa (college), and was prevalent in the 11th–16th centuries, although in some places it continued until much later.

Whatever the immediate source, the maintenance of accuracy has always been a problem in texts reproduced in Muslim MS culture, as elsewhere. Copyists, however well-educated and trained, were always fallible. Sometimes they may have had difficulties reading the source MS, especially if it were in an unfamiliar variety of script. Even if this were not so, they could all too easily lapse into unintentional repetitions, omissions, and other corruptions of the text. Two particular problems arising from the nature of the Arabic script are false transcriptions caused by misreading or misplacing the diacritical points distinguishing different letters (tashīf), and by transposing root letters within a word (tahrīf or ibdāl). Although many MSS were checked and edited before being released, the corruption of texts in this way, an inevitable consequence of scribal culture, was a continual source of anxiety and insecurity in a civilization for which the authenticity and integrity of texts was of paramount importance.

Some books, as already stated, were written to order or for the use of the writer. Many others, however, were produced for sale. The occupation of bookseller and *stationer (warrāq) overlapped with that of scribe. In some ways, this enterprise was comparable to that of publishers in the print era: they received texts from authors, either by dictation or in writing, then transcribed them, or employed others to do so, in sufficient quantities to meet demand, bound them, and sold them at a profit. Occasionally, they restricted the supply in order to keep prices high; sometimes they sold books by auction (see BOOK AUCTIONS). As well as trading in copies made by or for themselves, booksellers dealt in copies bought in from elsewhere; they also acted as purchasing agents, seeking out particular titles or genres on behalf of scholars or collectors. Some booksellers were learned or literary men themselves: one of the most famous was the 10th-century scholar-bibliographer Ibn al-Nadīm al-Warrāq. Bookshops tended to cluster in particular streets or quarters of towns, a pattern (common among many trades) that can still be found today in, for example, the *Sahaflar market in Istanbul. In some cities, a guild structure existed, with the book trade supervised by a shaykh or master.

The high importance and value attached to books and reading in traditional Muslim societies led to the formation of many large *libraries. These belonged to rulers, mosques, educational institutions, and private individuals. Although the quantities of volumes that they contained were undoubtedly exaggerated in literary sources, there can be little doubt that they numbered many tens of thousands in the major centres, such as Baghdad, Cairo, and Córdoba. *Catalogues of libraries were compiled, and some libraries provided facilities, and even personnel, for making new copies of texts. Many libraries in the Muslim world were established as inalienable endowments (waqfs), so that books could not be sold or otherwise dispersed. Yet, borrowing by scholars was generally allowed, and this inevitably led to some losses. Much greater destruction and dispersal, however, resulted from fires, floods, and conflict, often compounded by neglect, misappropriation, and theft—problems that have continued into modern times.

5 The Muslim MS book beyond the Arab world

The Qur'ān gave the Arabic language and script a central importance in Islam. The areas of western Asia, North Africa, and Spain that adopted Arabic became the heartlands of book culture in the heyday or 'classical' period of Muslim civilization, from the 8th to the 13th centuries. As such, they have been the main focus of studies of that culture. But Islam eventually spread over a huge area from the Atlantic to the Pacific, and in later periods other, non-Arab Muslim peoples and empires became predominant. They created their own literary traditions and produced MS books in their own languages; but the powerful influence of Arabic was such that they adopted many Arabic loanwords and, most importantly, the Arabic script, which was adapted to write a variety of languages, most of which are intrinsically unrelated to Arabic. In most of these areas, however, much religious and legal literature was also written in Arabic, and many copies of the Qur'ān were made, always in the original.

Iran had a proud ancient literary tradition and, from the 10th century onwards, in addition to producing magnificent Qur'āns, created a flourishing Persian MS culture. Poetic books were especially noteworthy, and a characteristic oblique and highly artistic form of the Arabic script was developed to write them, known as *nastaʿlīq* ('hanging script'). Rulers and wealthy patrons often commissioned exquisitely decorated and illustrated MSS, and Persian miniatures have become much-treasured *objets d'art*. Unfortunately, this has led to many of them becoming separated from the texts they were created to illustrate.

Ottoman Turkey became the centre of a large empire that by the mid-16th century included most of the Arab world and much of southeastern Europe. Having inherited the Arabic MS tradition, the Turks both continued it and created a Turkish book culture that also borrowed some elements of the Persian. Ottoman calligraphers became especially celebrated, both for Qur'āns and for more humble MSS executed with great elegance. Istanbul became the greatest centre in the world for Islamic books, and remains the largest repository of them to this day. At the same time, the Ottomans extended Muslim book culture into the Balkans. In Bosnia-Herzegovina especially, many MSS in Arabic, Persian, and Turkish were both written and imported, and were preserved in important libraries. The Bosnian language itself was also written in the Arabic script.

Further east, in India (and south Asia generally) there were many centres of Muslim civilization, especially during the period of the Mughal empire (1526–1857), and many of these also became centres of MS production. Apart from Qur'āns, most books were in Persian, including fine illuminated and illustrated MSS, but from the 18th century onwards, there was also some writing in local vernaculars, especially Urdu. In central Asia, many MSS were likewise in Persian, but with increasing use of regional Turkic languages. In southeast Asia, Arabic Qur'āns were written in quite distinct local styles (similarly, in China), and there was also a significant Malay literature in the Arabic script that developed its own MS traditions. Finally, mention must be made of sub-Saharan Africa, where the advent of Islam in large areas of both east and west brought literacy and a distinctive written culture embodied in characteristic MS books both in Arabic and in African languages, using a distinctive style of the Arabic script (*see* **37**). Some of these were preserved in libraries; many more have emerged from private collections in recent years.

6 The longevity of the Muslim MS tradition

Most surviving Muslim MSS date from the 16th century or later. This is only partly due to the loss of older ones. The writing of books by hand continued as the normal method of textual transmission for far longer in the Muslim world than elsewhere. The late arrival of printing was as much the consequence as the cause of this state of affairs. A number of more fundamental reasons can be identified.

One is the extreme reverence felt by Muslims for the handwritten word. Not only was writing regarded as a quasi-divine and mystical activity, but the beauty of the cursive Arabic script aroused an almost physical passion, akin to human love. Annemarie Schimmel has identified numerous passages of Muslim poetry in which books and writing are likened to bodily characteristics of the beloved that arouse desire. Given such feelings, even if they were directed by poetic conceits, it is not surprising that Muslims were reluctant to abandon the handwritten book. Another factor was the widespread engagement of large sections of the educated population in book copying (and associated trades). Many wholly or partly earned their living by it. There was thus a substantial vested interest in retaining this method of production, whatever its limitations. A third reason, arising from the other two, was that Muslims felt supremely comfortable with MSS, which they regarded as an integral part of their culture and society. Even when economic and other conditions created a substantial rise in demand for books among emerging classes of society, as in 18th-century Egypt, it was felt that scribal production was adequate to cope with this phenomenon.

At the same time, patterns of intellectual and religious authority within Muslim society were closely bound up with book production and the limited transmission of texts. Islam has no ecclesiastical organization, and the status of religious leaders, who had great authority but lacked secular power, depended essentially on their role as scholars and producers of texts. This in turn depended on maintaining the sacred character of writing and a degree of exclusiveness in and control over the creation and distribution of books. Accordingly, Muslims went on writing and copying books by hand until the emergence of new patterns of state authority that were associated with modernizing influences coming partly from outside the Muslim world.

7 The origins of printing in the Arabic script

Printing was practised in the Muslim world as early as the 10th century. Block prints on paper, and at least two on parchment, found in Egypt, survive in several collections, notably in Cairo, Vienna, Cambridge, and New York, and further pieces have emerged from excavations. One in private hands may originate in Afghanistan or Iran. However, no literary or historical testimony to the craft of *block printing seems to exist, except for two obscure references in Arabic poems of the 10th and 14th centuries to the use of *tarsh* to produce copies of amulets. It has been suggested that this non-classical Arabic term signified tin plates with *engraved or repoussé lettering used to produce multiple copies of Qur'anic and incantatory texts for sale to the illiterate poor. Certainly, the style of the surviving pieces indicates that they were not intended to gratify any refined literary or artistic taste, since the script is generally far from calligraphic, and there are even errors in the Qur'anic texts. Some have headpieces with designs incorporating bolder lettering and ornamental motifs, sometimes white on black, which may have been printed with separate *woodblocks. Some block-printed patterns have also been found on the endpapers of MS codices. The origin of the processes used is unknown: China or central Asia have been suggested, but there are serious doubts about any connection with Chinese woodblock printing, in view of the marked differences in the techniques and the contrast between these pieces and the luxurious character of other Chinese imports to the Muslim world and their local imitations. A link with the printing of patterns on textiles, also practised in medieval Egypt, cannot be ruled out.

Some scholars have speculated that this Muslim precedent may have played a part in the origins of European printing several centuries later. No evidence of any such link has yet emerged, and definitive answers to this and other outstanding questions concerning medieval Arabic printing must await further discoveries and research.

Muslim block printing of texts seems to have died out in the 15th century, although this or a related technique was evidently employed subsequently to make lattice patterns for use in the decorative arts. There is nothing to suggest that this technique was ever used to produce books or substantial literary texts in any form. These remained the monopoly of scribes in the Muslim world until the 18th century, and the origins of Arabic typography and printed-book production must be sought not in the Muslim world itself, but in Europe.

Arabic script, being cursive, presents problems quite unlike those of the Roman, Greek, and Hebrew *alphabets which preoccupied the first few generations of European typographers. Not only is a higher degree of *punchcutting skill required—especially if calligraphic norms are to be imitated—but *matrices must be justified even more minutely if the breaks between adjacent *sorts are to be disguised. The *compositor likewise must constantly avoid using the wrong letter form. Moreover, as well as different initial, medial, final, and isolated sorts for each letter, an abundance of *ligatures is also needed for pairs or groups of letters. If vowel signs (*harakāt*) are required—for Qur'anic and certain other texts—then even more sorts are needed, as well as huge quantities of quadrats (*see* QUAD (1)) and *leads to be interspersed between the vowel strokes. A full Arabic *fount can therefore contain over 600 sorts. This makes it an expensive investment, and economic factors alone have therefore impeded the development of Arabic typography, as compared with its European counterparts.

Arabic printing with movable type originated in Italy in the early 16th century. The first book was the *Kitāb Ṣalāt al-Sawāʿī* (*Book of Hours), printed by the Venetian printer Gregorio de Gregorii at Fano (or possibly in Venice) in 1514 and sponsored by Pope Julius II for the use of Arab Melkite Christians in Lebanon and Syria. The type design is inelegant, and it was set in a clumsy, disjointed manner. Rather better was the typography of *Paganino, who printed the whole text of the Qur'ān in Venice in 1537/8, probably as a commercial export venture. Nevertheless, it was still so remote from calligraphic norms as to make it quite unacceptable to the Muslims for whom it was intended, especially as its pointing and vocalization were inaccurate and incomplete; it also contained errors in the Qur'anic text. Italy remained the main home of Arabic printing for the rest of the 16th century; it was in Rome that *Granjon produced his elegant Arabic types in the 1580s, which for the first time achieved calligraphic quality, with their liberal use of ligatures and letter forms derived from the best scribal models. They were used principally in the lavish editions of the *Tipografia Medicea Orientale between 1590 and 1610, and they set the standard for nearly all subsequent work. Their influence is notable in the Arabic founts of the Dutch scholar-printer *Raphelengius and his successor, *Erpenius, who produced many Arabic texts with his more practical and workmanlike founts in the early 17th century, and whose type-styles were much used or copied in Germany, England, and elsewhere. A more elegant and beautiful fount was commissioned by the French scholar-diplomat *Savary de Brèves: it was evidently based on Arabic calligraphy seen while he was French ambassador in Istanbul between 1592 and 1604, and/or in MSS in Rome, where the types were cut before 1613. It was later used both there and at the *Imprimerie royale in Paris in the mid-17th century, and again in the Napoleonic period. Subsequently it provided a model for other types, notably that of the Congregatio de *Propaganda Fide, which had a monopoly on Arabic printing in Rome from 1622 onwards, and that of the monastic presses of 18th-century Romania (see 31).

There was a steady flow of Arabic printed books from most of the European centres of learning during the 17th–19th centuries. After *Granjon, other leading typographers, such as *Caslon and *Bodoni, were also involved in the design of Arabic founts. As well as Orientalist editions, the European presses produced biblical and other works for use by Christians in the Middle East, and some polemical literature written with the futile aim of converting Muslims. There were also some 'secular' texts intended as a commercial export commodity for sale to Muslims. These seem to have met at first with some resistance, and were seized and confiscated, but the Ottoman sultan in 1588 issued a decree forbidding any such interference. Nevertheless, these exports of European printed books in Arabic achieved little commercial success, although some copies were used by Muslims, as is shown by owners' *inscriptions in them.

8 Arabic-script book printing in the Muslim world

Printing in the Muslim world originated in the non-Muslim communities living there. Hebrew typographic printing started in the Ottoman empire in 1493, and in Morocco in 1515; *Armenian types were used from 1567 in Turkey, and from 1638 in Iran; *Syriac type was used for both Syriac and Arabic in Lebanon in 1610; Greek books were printed in Istanbul from 1627; *roman types appeared in Izmir in the 17th century. Yet typography in the Arabic script of the Muslim majority was not used in the Muslim world until the 18th century: before then, the few such printed books in use were imported from Europe.

Why was book printing not adopted by Muslims for more than 1000 years after it was invented in China and 250 years after it became widespread in western Europe (in spite of its use by non-Muslims in the Muslim world)? The reasons for this delay must be sought both in the nature of Muslim societies and in the supreme religious and aesthetic role accorded to the written word within them. Some indications of the profound Muslim attachment to MS books and scribal culture have already been given, and there can be no doubt that this was the main reason for the reluctance to embrace printing. Some more specific reasons can also be adduced.

The use of movable type seemed to be the only practical method of printed-book production before the 19th century. This involved creating punches and matrices and casting individual types for all the letters and letter combinations of the Arabic alphabet, in their different forms; then, the compositor had to reassemble these separate sorts to create lines of text and pages of a book. As far as Muslims could see, this was done without regard to the intrinsic subtleties of the processes of calligraphic composition, and its relation to underlying aesthetic and 'spiritual' considerations. Such segmentation and mechanization of the sacred Arabic script seemed tantamount to sacrilege in the eyes of devout Muslims. The production of the Qur'ān by mechanical means was considered unthinkable, but other texts bearing the name of God (as nearly all did) were also regarded by most scholars and readers as not to be violated by the methods of mass production. Rumours were also spread of the use in printing of ink brushes made from hogs' hair, which would automatically defile sacred names; other rumours circulated about impure inks, which might also have the same effect.

Apart from these considerations, the mass production of books by printing challenged the entrenched monopolies of intellectual authority enjoyed by the learned class ('ulamā'), and threatened to upset the balance between that authority and the power of the state. This was indeed one important reason why printing was eventually sponsored, in the 18th and 19th centuries, by modernizing rulers. They wanted to create a new, broader military and administrative class, versed in modern sciences and knowledge, who could bolster the power of the state against both traditional hierarchies within and new threats from outside. The printing press was seen as an indispensable instrument for achieving this new order.

The first printing with Arabic types in the Middle East was at Aleppo in Syria in 1706, by the Christian deacon 'Abd Allāh *Zākhir: the first book was a psalter—*Kitāb al-Zabūr al-Sharīf.* The initiative in setting up this press came from the Melkite Patriarch of Antioch, Athanasius Dabbās, who between 1698 and 1705 had spent some time in Romania, where he arranged for two Arabic liturgical books to be printed at the monastery of Sinagovo (Snagov) near Bucharest, under the auspices of the Voivod of Wallachia, Constantin Brâncoveanu. This cooperation was facilitated by the common religious and political interests of Melkites and Romanians, both being semi-autonomous Orthodox subjects of the Ottoman empire. They were intended for free distribution to Orthodox priests in Arab countries, to overcome the shortage and high price of MS service books. Under Patriarchal auspices, and with the cooperation of the Romanians, this activity was transferred to Syria, and Zākhir went on to print in Aleppo an Arabic New Testament (also in 1706) and other Christian works, until the press ceased operation in 1711. He subsequently embraced Catholicism and moved to the Greek Catholic monastery of St John the Baptist at Shuwayr in Lebanon, where he set up a new press which published a long but intermittent series of biblical and theological works from 1734 to 1899. Its early materials can still be seen in the museum there. Another Orthodox Arabic press was established in Beirut at the beginning of the 1750s, again with help from Romania, but it published only two books, in 1751 and 1753.

Arabic printing in the Arab world remained in the hands of Syrian and Lebanese Christians for more than 100 years. They used types modelled partly on local Christian bookhands, but also influenced by the European tradition of Arabic type design, especially that of Orthodox Romania and of the Propaganda Fide Press in Rome. Their output was too small and intermittent to bring about any revolutionary change in book culture, but some observers, such as the French traveller and intellectual C. F. Volney, observed an increase in reading and writing among the Levantine Christians in that period. In his view, however, the press's potential for such improvement was vitiated by the exclusively religious nature of the books printed there.

Meanwhile, the Ottoman Turks revived Muslim printing in Istanbul in the second decade of the 18th century, when İbrahim *Müteferrika began printing engraved maps, using copper *plates, and probably techniques, imported from Vienna: the earliest extant map is dated 1719/20. This was part of a programme of Westernizing innovations in the Ottoman capital which also led, less than ten years later, to the establishment of Müteferrika's famous book-printing establishment, complete with Arabic types cut and cast locally and modelled on the neat Ottoman *naskhī* bookhand of the period. The first book, an Arabic–Turkish *dictionary, was printed in 1729 in 500 copies and was followed by sixteen others in Ottoman Turkish, in *editions ranging from 500 to 1,200 copies, before the press was closed in 1742. They were all secular works—on history, geography, language, government (including one written by Müteferrika himself), navigation, and chronology—because the printing of the Qur'ān and religious texts was still forbidden. Several were illustrated with maps or pictorial engravings. Apart from a reprint in 1756, the press was not restarted until 1784, after which Ottoman Turkish printing had a continuous history until the adoption of the Latin alphabet in 1928.

It has been claimed that the 18th-century Müteferrika press was a failure, that its printed editions were only marginal phenomena in Turkish literary and scholarly culture, and that most of its limited output remained unsold. Recent research by Orlin Sabev into the book inventories contained in Ottoman probate documents of the period has shown, however, that these printed books achieved a considerable penetration among the contemporary educated classes, especially among administrators and officials, and that 65–75 per cent of the press's output was sold or otherwise distributed before Müteferrika died in 1747. Yet it remains true that 18th-century Turkish book printing and its impact was at a very modest level compared with earlier western European *incunabula (*see* **6**), and that scribal transmission remained prevalent. Print had not yet become an agent of change in the Muslim world, although the way was now open for it.

333

Arabic printing in Egypt began with the presses of the French occupation of 1798–1801. Napoleon took from Paris a fount of the 17th-century Arabic types of Savary de Brèves, and from Rome the Arabic founts of the Propaganda Fide Press. However, these were used only for a relatively insignificant output of proclamations, materials to help the French occupiers to learn Arabic, and a treatise on smallpox. All the equipment was removed when the occupation of Egypt came to an end. The continuous history of Arabic printing in that country, and among Arab Muslims in general, dates from 1822, when the first book emerged from the state press of Muḥammad ʿAlī (ruler of Egypt, 1805–48), known as the *Būlāq Press, after the place near Cairo where it was situated. This undertaking was started by an Italian-trained typographer, Niqūlā Masābikī (d. 1830); the first presses and types were imported from Milan, and are perceptibly European in style. They were soon replaced, however, by a succession of locally cut and cast founts based on indigenous *naskhī* hands. Although somewhat cramped and utilitarian, rather than calligraphic, they set the norm for Arabic typography, both in Egypt and at many other Muslim Arabic presses elsewhere, for the rest of the 19th century. *Nastaʿlīq* types were also occasionally employed, both for Persian texts and for headings in Arabic works. A *Maghribī* fount was also later created, but little used.

In the first twenty years of the Būlāq Press (1822–42) about 250 titles were published, including some religious and literary works—e.g. the *Thousand and One Nights (Alf Layla wa-Layla)*—but most were military and technical books, official decrees, *grammars, manuals of epistolography, and translations of European scientific and historical works. After some vicissitudes in the mid-19th century following the death of Muḥammad ʿAlī, the Būlāq Press again became, from the 1860s onwards, the driving force behind a publishing explosion in Egypt. Between 1866 and 1872, it was thoroughly modernized, with new typefounding equipment and mechanized presses imported from Paris, and greatly improved typefaces. By the end of the century it had published more than 1,600 titles, representing about 20 per cent of total Egyptian book production.

As the first press in the Arab world to produce Arabic (and Turkish) books for Muslims, the Būlāq Press occupies a crucial place in Arabic and Muslim book history. Although some of its early output achieved only a very limited circulation, it nevertheless established printing for the first time as a normal method of producing and diffusing texts. Initially,

technical and educational works, and, then, historical, literary, and religious titles became available to educated people on an unprecedented scale, despite initial resistance. This access to books in turn helped to create a new reading public and a new public sphere. Nor was the influence of the Būlāq Press confined to Egypt: its books were exported to Turkey, Syria, Lebanon, Palestine, and other Muslim countries, and stimulated the establishment or revival of printing far beyond the Nile valley.

In the first half of the 19th century, many Arabic books were imported into the Middle East by Christian missionaries. Most of these were printed at a British-run press in Malta between 1825 and 1842; they included secular educational works as well as religious tracts. The types were at first brought from England, but in the 1830s a new fount was cut and cast locally from calligraphic models, almost certainly prepared by the famous Arab writer *Fāris al-Shidyāq, who had been a scribe in his youth and worked at the Malta press in this period. These set new standards among the Arab (mainly Christian, but also some Muslim and Jewish) pupils who used them, and the tradition was later continued by the American mission press in Beirut, which introduced a new typeface in the late 1840s, again based on calligraphic models: known as 'American Arabic', it has a characteristic attenuated and forward-sloping appearance, and was also used by several other presses in the Arab world. A more orthodox, but clear and workmanlike face, based on Turkish models, was adopted by the press of the Jesuit mission in Beirut about 1870, and also became very popular throughout the Levant (*see* **9**).

Other Catholic mission presses inaugurated Arabic printing in Jerusalem in 1847 and in Mosul in 1856: in both cases, their first founts were brought from Europe (Vienna and Paris, respectively). The first press in Iraq had, however, operated in Baghdad in 1830, using a fount similar to those of the first Persian ones in Iran, established at Tabriz c.1817 and Tehran c.1823: an elegant Persian-style *naskh*, but with some curious idiosyncrasies, such as the shortened top-stroke of the letter *kāf*. *Nastaʿlīq* typography was not and has never been favoured in Iran, despite the prevalence of this style in the scribal tradition (including *lithography). It was, however, used in India as early as 1778 and remained in use there, both for Persian and for Urdu, until the mid-19th century; it was later revived in Hyderabad.

In the Middle East, Arabic typography burgeoned from the mid-19th century onwards, with presses starting at Damascus in 1855, Tunis in 1860, Ṣanʿāʾ in 1877,

Khartoum in 1881, Mecca in 1883, and Medina in 1885. Most of these used local types in the Istanbul and Būlāq traditions, and many of them produced *newspapers as well as books.

From the late 1820s onwards, however, many books and some newspapers, were printed not from type, but by a hybrid method of book production: lithography. This was favoured in many places, especially in Morocco, Iran, and central, south, and southeast Asia, where it almost completely displaced typography for nearly half a century. This phenomenon in Muslim printing history has no counterpart in earlier European experience. Whereas in Europe lithography was used almost entirely for pictorial and cartographical illustration, Muslims used it to reproduce entire texts written by hand. In this way, they could retain most of the familiar features of Islamic MSS, and the calligraphic integrity of the Arabic script, including some styles difficult to reproduce typographically. At the same time, they could also avoid expensive investment in movable types. As a consequence, some of the conscious and subliminal effects of the standardization of text presentation, and the emergence of a new print-induced *esprit de système*, as proposed by *Eisenstein in relation to early modern Europe, do not apply to those societies where this method was prevalent (*see* 6). On the other hand, the low prices and ready acceptability of books printed by this method meant that lithographically reproduced texts—mainly traditional and classical ones—achieved a far wider dissemination. In this way, lithography did much, as Ian Proudfoot has shown, to 'usher in the print revolution' (Proudfoot, 182). At their best, lithographed texts, many complete with pictorial miniatures, could rival well-executed MSS of the period in beauty and clarity; at their worst, they could degenerate into barely legible grey scrawls.

The late 19th and early 20th centuries saw a revival of Arabic typography in the Middle East, with considerable improvements in typefaces, especially in Egypt, where the new founts of *Dār al-Ma'ārif, and of the Būlāq Press itself from 1902 onwards, set higher standards of clarity and elegance. In 1914, the new fount designed there for Aḥmad Zakī Pasha halved the number of sorts by eliminating many ligatures, while retaining some of the calligraphic features of the older Būlāq types. Later, the introduction of *Linotype hot-metal machines further simplified the setting of Arabic-script texts, while inevitably moving the appearance of such works further away from traditional calligraphy and bookhands. However, with the modern decline of metal types and the intro-duction of *photocomposition, latterly *computer-generated, the way was opened for a return to calligraphic norms.

Apart from type styles, other features of the early Muslim printed book must be noted. As with earlier European incunabula, the tendency at first was to imitate MS styles and layouts. Words and lines were set closely, paragraphs and punctuation were lacking, the main type area was often surrounded by *rules, and glosses or even complete commentaries appeared in the margins. Red ink was sometimes used for headings or key words, following the scribal practice of rubrication. Traditional tapered colophons were common. Title-pages were often lacking, but the verso of the first leaf was commonly commenced by a decorative *'unwān* (headpiece), often containing the title and/or *basmala* formula: the earliest were engraved on wood, but later elaborate designs were constructed from *fleurons and other single-type ornaments, following a European printing practice whose aesthetic origins lay in the infinitely repeatable geometric and foliate patterns of Islamic art. In the late 19th century, some elaborate pseudo-Oriental designs were used for headpieces and borders, especially in Ottoman Turkey, perhaps reflecting a European rather than an indigenous taste; later still, other European artistic influences, such as the *Jugendstil* (*see* 24) can be detected in decoration and page-design. By this time, European norms—title-pages, paragraphing, *running heads, etc.—had begun to dominate Muslim book production.

Punctuation was another such modern feature. In Muslim MSS, as has been said, it was rudimentary, and it remained so in printed texts until the end of the 19th century. In the 1830s the celebrated Arab writer Fāris al-Shidyāq had become familiar, while working at the Malta press, with European books and literature, and had observed the usefulness of punctuation marks in clarifying the structure and meaning of passages of prose. In 1839, he published at Malta a *primer and reading book of literary Arabic, and boldly decided to introduce Western punctuation into it, using commas, dashes, colons, exclamation marks, question marks, quotation marks, and full stops (or periods). He set them out in his introduction, explained their use, and urged that they should be generally adopted in Arabic. This proposal was, however, ahead of its time. In the Muslim world, his appeal at first fell on deaf ears, and he himself eventually gave up the idea. In the second edition of his primer, published at his press in Istanbul in 1881, all the punctuation marks were omitted, as well as his introduction to them.

Later, in the 20th century, full punctuation was widely adopted in Arabic.

Fāris al-Shidyāq's Istanbul press (the *Jawā'ib Press) introduced other significant improvements to Arabic book design in the 1870s and 1880s. His books look different from those of most other 19th-century Muslim presses. They largely abandoned the marginal commentaries and glosses with which earlier books were often encumbered. In some cases running heads were introduced, repeating the title or number of the chapter or section at the top of each page as an aid to those referring to the book. They nearly all have title-pages, setting out clearly and systematically not only the title itself, but also the name of the author, and such imprint information as the name of the press, the place and date of publication, and whether it is a first or later edition. This practice, as Eisenstein has pointed out, engendered 'new habits of placing and dating' (Eisenstein, 106); it also aided the subsequent development of more precise *cataloguing and enumerative *bibliography. Another new feature of the print era to be found in most publications of this period is a table of *contents, with page numbers, likewise enabling the reader to make more systematic use of the book.

Page layouts at the Jawā'ib Press also set new standards, being generally more spacious and easier on the eye than most ordinary MSS or earlier printed books from the Muslim world. Margins are reasonably wide and, as already mentioned, unencumbered by glosses or commentaries. The spacing between words tends also to be more generous, leaving a better overall ratio between black and white than on most pages either of ordinary MSS, or of Būlāq and early Turkish printed books. These features made them easier to read and therefore more accessible to a wider public. They eventually became standard aspects of 20th-century Arabic book design.

The character of the Arabic script itself has been remarkably unaffected by its use in printed books. Because Arabic writing was and is regarded by Muslims as sacred, the self-imposed task of typographers has nearly always been to reproduce its calligraphic qualities as faithfully as possible. As already noted, this involved the creation of extensive founts containing all the letter forms and combinations. Thus confronted with considerable difficulties and expense, Arab typographers towards the end of the 19th century began to introduce some simplifications, while for the most part successfully retaining full legibility and a degree of elegance. Yet, the Arabic script, unlike the roman, has never really acquired separate typographic norms, either aesthetic or practical, which could permit a decisive breach with its scribal past. Some radical innovators in the 19th and 20th centuries produced schemes to reform the alphabet by creating entirely discrete 'printed' letters, but there was never any serious prospect of their acceptance.

Illustrations in Muslim printed books, until the introduction of modern *half-tone techniques at the end of the 19th century, can be divided into two categories. First, *woodcuts and engraved or lithographed plates were used in typographic books, mainly for maps, diagrams, and didactic or technical illustrations. These often incorporated perspective, itself an innovation in the visual culture of many areas of the Muslim world. Technical illustrations were sometimes found in Arabic MSS. Before the print era, however, the transmission of technical data in the form of diagrams always depended upon the accuracy of scribes who often regarded them as little more than exotic appendages, frequently misplacing and sometimes omitting them altogether. With the introduction of standard, repeatable, engraved diagrams incorporated into printed books, the presentation of such information became far more accurate and reliable.

The second category of illustration consisted of pictures introduced into the texts of lithographed books; these were often copied from, or in the style of, miniatures in MSS. Such miniatures are a notable feature of Persian lithographed books of the 19th century, where they usually accompany literary works from an earlier period. Although they are broadly in the style of MS miniatures, it has been observed that they belong more to the domain of popular art than to that of the lofty court culture from which illustrated MSS originated. Lithographic miniatures also sometimes feature modern subject matter. A notable example is the depiction, in a work of classical Persian poetry printed at Tehran in 1847, of the process of lithographic printing itself. In an Uzbek lithographed text of 1913 a miniature shows a gramophone of the period.

Both kinds of illustration—in typographic and lithographic books—reproduced pictorial elements in a standard, repeatable form for a much wider readership than that of illustrated MSS, and thus helped to transform the visual and artistic awareness of educated Muslims during the 19th and 20th centuries.

9 Printing the Qur'ān

Apart from short extracts used in medieval block-printed amulets, the Arabic text of the Qur'ān was not printed until the 1530s, when a somewhat inaccurate and defective version was published by Christians in Venice. Subsequent complete editions appeared in Hamburg (1694), Padua (1698), and St Petersburg (1787). This last was personally commissioned by the Russian empress Catherine for the use of her Muslim subjects, and was the first to involve Muslims in its preparation. It represents a curious and unusual amalgamation of European book design, with baroque text borders and ornaments, and traditional Muslim presentation of the vocalized Qur'anic text, with marginal notes on readings and *variants. It was later reprinted a number of times, both in St Petersburg and in Kazan (Russian Tatarstan). In the Muslim world itself, however, printing the sacred text remained firmly off-limits until the 1820s or 1830s, when the first editions were published in Iran. The earliest of these may have been typeset (reliable bibliographical information is not readily available), but it was the advent of lithography that gave the impetus to Qur'ān printing because it enabled the all-important MS conventions and aesthetic/theological ethos to be maintained.

A further incentive was also provided by another European non-Muslim edition, greatly superior to its predecessors, edited by the German orientalist Gustav Flügel, and first published by *Tauchnitz in Leipzig in 1834. This for the first time provided a convenient and affordable text that was reasonably authentic. It was *stereotyped and issued in several subsequent editions, and achieved a considerable circulation, even reaching the Muslim world. However, the verse numbering and some other aspects of this version were not in accordance with orthodox Islamic practice, so there remained a clear need for further Muslim editions. This demand was partly met by subsequent lithographed versions in Iran, India, and Turkey.

In Egypt, the impetus of modernization created a tension between conservatives, who abhorred the idea of profaning God's words with movable types, and more progressive religious educators who wanted to place a copy of the Qur'ān, if not in the hands of every Muslim, then at least of every college pupil. Some attempts were made to publish the text in the 1830s, but the distribution of copies was successfully blocked by the religious authorities. Later, in the 1850s, some were distributed, but only after each individual copy had been read by a Qur'anic scholar and checked for errors, at great expense. From the 1860s onwards, the Būlāq and other Egyptian presses did print more Qur'āns, but generally embedded in the texts of well-known commentaries.

In Istanbul, the Ottoman calligrapher and court chamberlain Osman Zeki Bey (d. 1888) started printing Qur'āns reproducing the handwriting of the famous 17th-century calligrapher *Hafız Osman, using new lithographic equipment capable of an unprecedented, high-quality output. For this publishing venture, he had the express permission of the sultan-caliph—one reason why his editions gained a wide popularity in Turkey and elsewhere. This press also used photolithography, which enabled it to print miniature Qur'āns, small enough to be carried in a locket—no other technique could do this. The Glasgow firm of David Bryce, which specialized in *miniature books, produced a rival version around 1900, and Muslim troops on both sides in World War I carried these amuletic miniatures into battle (see 7).

By the early 20th century, now that reluctance to accept printed Qur'āns had largely been overcome, the need was felt for a new authoritative version that would do full justice to the demands of traditional Islamic scholarship, in respect of both the shape of the text (i.e. the form of the text as it appears in the early MSS without vocalization and diacritics) and the way it was presented. The lead was taken by scholars at Al-Azhar mosque-university in Cairo, the pre-eminent seat of traditional learning in Islam. After seventeen years of preparatory work, their edition was published in 1924, under the auspices of King Fu'ād of Egypt. It was printed orthographically in such a way that the shape of the original 7th-century consonantal text is clearly presented, but at the same time it included all the vocalization and other indications which are required for understanding the meaning and for correct recitation. It is also meticulously executed in conformity with calligraphic norms. The Cairo *Qur'ān quickly established its authority, and was followed by a host of further printed editions reproducing it or based upon it. These have continued to the present day, and even online *digitized versions follow the Azhar text.

The ready availability of inexpensive copies of a standard authorized version of the Qur'ān transformed the attitude of many Muslims to the sacred text, and the uses to which they put it. Its function ceased to be primarily ritual and liturgical, and it came to be regarded as a direct source—not necessarily mediated by scholarly interpretation and authority—of guidance and wisdom in human affairs. This idea was reinforced by the abolition, in that same year (1924), of the Islamic caliphate, which had previously been, at least in theory, a religiously ordained but non-scriptural source of authority. The new accessibility and role of the Qur'ān consequently led some believers to adopt fundamentalist attitudes to Qur'anic doctrine, with considerable consequences in the social and political spheres. Others, in contrast, gradually abandoned traditional scholastic and legal interpretations in favour of their own reconciliations of Qur'anic ethics with modern life and politics. This divergence remains an acute feature of modern Islam, reinforced by outside pressures and new sources of authority in what continues to be above all a book-based system of belief.

10 Muslim book culture in the 20th and 21st centuries

By the beginning of the 20th century, printing had largely displaced the writing of MSS as the normal method of transmitting texts in most of the Muslim world. Only in a few remote areas, such as Yemen, did the scribal profession continue to flourish. In the main centres of literary culture, a new civilization of the book emerged, in which texts were readily available for purchase at affordable prices and were relatively easy to read. Newspapers, periodicals, and other *serials were also widespread. These developments in turn encouraged and facilitated the spread of *literacy. In schools, the availability of printed primers and *textbooks revolutionized education, enabling students to embrace reading as an individual, internalized activity, rather than a ritual adjunct of rote learning. Nevertheless, older practices continued in some places where well-educated teachers were in short supply, or where conservatism or ideology rejected the free understanding of texts.

The rapid transition from MSS to printed books and serials as the normal means of transmitting texts had profound effects on the development of Muslim literary cultures. Insufficient research has been done to enable these effects to be measured or to be traced accurately. It seems likely, however, that the much wider dissemination of texts, both new and old, together with the standardization and systematization of their presentation, and their permanent preservation, played a major role in promoting the cultural and national self-awareness that has led to a renaissance of Arabic, Turkish, Persian, Urdu, Malay, and other Muslim literatures in modern times. This new self-consciousness has also had repercussions in the social and political spheres. In the case of Turkish and Malay, the rejection of the Arabic script in favour of the roman alphabet has reinforced their separate literary and national identities.

In the Arab world, the early 20th century saw a revival in Arabic typography: a development subsequently reinforced by the adoption of Linotype machines in major printing offices, as well as by the greater mechanization of the printing presses themselves. These developments permitted considerable increases in the production of books, magazines, and newspapers. Cairo and Beirut remained the principal publishing centres, as well as the main hubs of literary activity, throughout the transition from Ottoman and European rule to full independence and beyond. Both lost ground, however, in the 1970s and 1980s because of declining quality, lack of investment, rising prices in Egypt, and ruinous strife in Lebanon. Other Arab countries have therefore become relatively more important, notably those of the Maghrib (with an important output in French as well as Arabic), Iraq until 1991, and most recently Saudi Arabia. The lack of a well-developed book trade in these countries has, however, hampered development, as have political and religious *censorship and restrictions in some cases. As elsewhere, the spread of broadcast and electronic media, especially television, video, and the Internet (see WORLD WIDE WEB), has had some adverse impact on the market for printed literature, but this has been largely offset by the rise in rates of literacy. Similar trends are to be found in most other Muslim countries, but there has been a publishing explosion in Turkey and Iran, especially in the late 20th and early 21st centuries.

The advent of electronic texts and the Internet has had a noticeable effect in the Muslim world, as elsewhere (see **19**). In some countries, such as Saudi Arabia, governmental controls and restrictions on Internet access have prevented full use being made of the new opportunities for access to texts in global cyberspace. Even where this was not the case, however, language barriers have created problems, because the *digitization of the Arabic script was a late development, which at first lacked standardization. Since the widespread adoption of Unicode (see ELECTRONIC EDITING AND MARKUP LANGUAGES), however, many websites in Arabic and Persian have been established, some of which provide substantial textual databases, including the Qur'ān, *Ḥadīth*, and other essential Islamic texts, as well as a great deal of secondary material, much of it promoting particular doctrinal, sectarian, and political viewpoints. The Internet has also accelerated a pre-existing tendency to adopt English, rather than Arabic, as an international Muslim language. As in the rest of the world, the long-term effects of the development of electronic textuality on Muslim book culture cannot yet be predicted.

BIBLIOGRAPHY

H. S. AbiFarès, *Arabic Typography* (2001)

G. N. Atiyeh, ed., *The Book in the Islamic World* (1995)

J. Balagna, *L'Imprimerie arabe en occident* (1984)

A. Ben Cheikh, *Production des livres et lecture dans le monde arabe* (1982)

J. M. Bloom, *Paper before Print* (2001)

A. Demeerseman, *Une étape importante de la culture islamique: une parente de l'imprimerie arabe et tunisienne, la lithographie* (1954)

— *L'Imprimerie en Orient et au Maghreb* (1954)

F. Déroche *et al.*, *Islamic Codicology*, tr. D. Dusinberre and D. Radzinowicz, ed. M. I. Waley (2005)

P. Dumont, ed., *Turquie: livres d'hier, livres d'aujourd'hui* (1992)

E. L. Eisenstein, *The Printing Press as an Agent of Change* (2 vols, 1979)

A. Gacek, *The Arabic Manuscript Tradition* (2001)

W. Gdoura, *Le Début de l'imprimerie arabe à Istanbul et en Syrie* (1985)

Y. Gonzalez-Quijano, *Les Gens du livre: édition et champs intellectuel dans l'Egypte républicaine* (1998)

E. Hanebutt-Benz *et al.*, eds., *Middle Eastern Languages and the Print Revolution* (2002)

N. Hanna, *In Praise of Books: A Cultural History of Cairo's Middle Class* (2003)

F. Hitzel, ed., *Livres et lecture dans le monde ottoman*, special issue of *Revue des mondes musulmans et de la Méditerranée*, 87–8 (1999)

K. Kreiser, ed., *The Beginnings of Printing in the Near and Middle East* (2001)

M. Krek, *A Bibliography of Arabic Typography* (1976)

— *A Gazetteer of Arabic Printing* (1977)

U. Marzolph, *Narrative Illustration in Persian Lithographed Books* (2001)

— ed., *Das gedruckte Buch im Vorderen Orient* (2002)

B. Messick, *The Calligraphic State* (1993)

J. Pedersen, *The Arabic Book*, tr. G. French (1984; Danish original, 1946)

I. Proudfoot, 'Mass Producing Houri's Moles, or Aesthetics and Choice of Technology in Early Muslim Book Printing', in *Islam: Essays on Scripture, Thought and Society*, ed. P. G. Riddell and T. Street (1997)

N. A. Rizk and J. Rodenbeck, 'The Book Publishing Industry in Egypt', in *Publishing in the Third World*, ed. P. G. Altbach *et al.* (1985)

G. Roper, ed., *World Survey of Islamic Manuscripts* (4 vols, 1992–4)

P. Sadgrove, ed., *History of Printing and Publishing in the Languages and Countries of the Middle East* (2004)

K. Schaefer, *Enigmatic Charms: Medieval Arabic Block Printed Amulets* (2006)

C. F. de Schnurrer, *Bibliotheca Arabica* (1811)

J. Skovgaard-Petersen, ed., *The Introduction of the Printing Press in the Middle East*, special issue of *Culture and History*, 16 (1997)

39 The History of the Book in the Indian Subcontinent

Abhijit Gupta

1 The MS book

The Indian subcontinent is home to more languages than anywhere else in the world. The Indian constitution recognizes 22 official languages, but the number of mother tongues in India exceeds 1,500, of which 24 are spoken by a million or more people. Any history of such a diverse constituency is bound to be selective and incomplete. This is true for the book as well, especially in the pre-print era. Although the first printing with movable *type in India occurred as early as in 1556, almost two and a half centuries were to pass before print was able to infiltrate the intellectual world configured by the MS book. This should not be surprising, for the history of the MS book in the Indian subcontinent is a long and highly sophisticated one, dating back to at least the 5th century BC. It is beyond the scope of this essay to treat the MS book in any detail, but it is essential to have an understanding of some of its basic features.

The rise of heterodox movements such as Buddhism and Jainism triggered a movement from orality to literacy in India. Orthodox Hinduism set little store by writing, and its key texts, the Vedas, were memorized and transmitted orally (*see* 2). A great deal of significance was attached to the spoken word and the performative aspects of the text. There are some technical terms in later Vedic works that might be taken as evidence for writing, but that task was assigned to the clerical caste of *kayasthas* who did not enjoy any great social prestige. On the other hand, the need to transcribe correctly the teachings of the Buddha and

Mahavira led to a widespread MS tradition from the 5th century BC in which authenticity and canonicity were the chief impulses, as opposed to the more prosaic aims of Hindu MS practice. The Jatakas (collections of stories about the Buddha) mention wooden writing boards (*phalaka*) and wooden pens (*varnaka*), and *lekha* or writing as part of the school curriculum. Buddhist MSS were mostly produced in monasteries and universities. When the Chinese traveller Fa Xian visited India in the 5th century CE, he saw professional copyists at work at Nalanda University; two centuries later, another Chinese visitor to the university, Yi Jing, reportedly carried away 400 Buddhist MSS. Similarly, Jain copyists were monks and novices, sometimes even nuns.

The earliest known substrate for recording texts in ancient India is the talipat or writing palm (*Corypha umbraculifera*), which is native to the Malabar coast of southern India and has palmate leaves folding naturally around a central rib. The tree was extensively cultivated, since the leaves were also used for thatching and the sap fermented to make palm wine. It is believed that there was a rich trade in the leaves from the south to the north, but this also meant that the Buddhist *scriptoria in Bihar and Nepal were heavily dependent on the availability of the leaf. One of the earliest accounts of the general use of the talipat throughout India is from Xuan Zang, who described it in the 7th century CE. In about 1500 CE, the talipat was supplanted by the palmyra, which was easier to cultivate and commercially more valuable, owing to the range of products it yielded. *Reed *pens were used with the talipat, while an iron *stylus was used with the palmyra. After the grooves were scored, they were smeared with ink and then cleaned with sand. In north India, the bark of *birch and aloe seem to have been extensively used, the former in the western Himalayas, the latter in the Assam valley. Birch bark was known as *bhurjapatra*, and is frequently mentioned in northern Buddhist and Brahmanical Sanskrit works (Buhler, 1973). After writing, the finished stack of leaves was strung on a cord through pre-bored holes and protected by a pair of wooden covers. This form of the book—known as the *puthi* or *pothi*—survived until the mid-19ᵗʰ century, with some minor variations. In Nepal, for example, covers of valuable MSS were sometimes made of embossed metal, while Jain MSS were kept in sacks made of white cotton.

Papermaking had been known in China from the beginning of the first millennium CE, but it reached India via the Turks after their conquest of northern India in the early 13ᵗʰ century (*see* **10**). There is some evidence of papermaking in the Himalayan region before this period, especially in Nepal, but it never posed a serious challenge to *palm-leaf MSS. With the beginnings of Muslim rule in India, paper became the substrate of choice, as no material other than paper was considered suitable for writing in Arabic, Persian, and Urdu (*see* **38**). The rich traditions of illumination, illustration, and *calligraphy in these languages required exceptionally high-quality paper, which sometimes had to be imported from places such as Iran. For bindings, *leather and board were used: these could not be used for Hindu MSS. Perhaps the richness and sophistication of the Mughal MS tradition was one reason why printing failed to make much impact in north India, despite the presentation to the Emperor Akbar of a copy of *Plantin's *polyglot Bible in 1580. This historic gift was made when a delegation of Portuguese Jesuits visited the emperor at Fatehpur Sikri (*see* **7**). In a richly symbolic response, the emperor had several of the engravings in the Bible copied by his own painters.

Although the Hindu and Muslim MS traditions took somewhat different routes, they were both instrumental in creating highly evolved communication networks. Access to the production and ownership of MSS was restricted in the Hindu and Buddhist traditions, yet the rise of the vernaculars in the second millennium CE saw a much wider diffusion of the culture of writing and reading. The examples of the great Indian epics *Mahābhārata* and *Rāmāyaṇa* demonstrate how new interpretive communities were formed once the Sanskrit hegemony was challenged,

and created a kind of 'social memory' mediated by the book. On the other hand, the Islamic MS tradition in India was a direct result of court *patronage, and consequently much more opulent. Given the centrality of the Qur'ān to Islam, book arts such as calligraphy and illumination were accorded the highest prestige (*see* ILLUMINATED MS, MUSLIM). Outside court circles, guilds of *scribes acted as purveyors of knowledge and information, leading to the creation of a robust public sphere.

The coming of print did not immediately precipitate a battle of books. More often than not the printed book took its cue from the MS book, and for a while there was space for both forms. Ultimately, however, it was the loss of political power to the British that undermined the cultural and social authority of the MS tradition. Under the new political dispensation, the voice of power would henceforth be articulated through print.

2 Early printing: from Goa to the Malabar coast

Print arrived in India by accident. In 1556, King João III of Portugal despatched a group of Jesuit missionaries and a printing press to Abyssinia, at the request of its emperor. When the ship put in at Goa, a Portuguese colony on the west coast of India, news came that the emperor had changed his mind. The Portuguese authorities in Goa had not been particularly keen to introduce printing to the area, but they now found themselves with not just a press but a printer. He was Juan de *Bustamante, a Jesuit brother from Valencia, reportedly accompanied by an Indian assistant trained in printing at Lisbon (*see* **9**).

The first book to be printed in Goa was *Conclusões e outras coisas*, in 1556. Unfortunately, no copy is extant, a fate shared by most of the early publications from Goa. The first Indian language rendered in the medium of print was Tamil. This might appear odd, given that the lingua franca in and around Goa was Konkani. But the Jesuits, led by Francis Xavier, who died in Goa in 1552, had established an extensive network of Jesuit missions along the Coromandel coast and had baptized more than 10,000 Tamil-speaking Parava fisher-people. A key figure in the new technology was Henrique Henriques, a Portuguese Jew, who produced five books in Tamil script and language, as well as a Tamil *grammar and *dictionary. In 1577 Henriques's first book was printed at Goa: *Doctrina Christam, Tampiran Vanakkam*, a translation of a Portuguese *catechism of 1539. This book was not only the first to be printed with Indian type, but the first with non-*roman, metallic type anywhere in the world. The Tamil type for the book was prepared by the Spaniard Juan Gonsalves, a former blacksmith and clockmaker, with assistance from Father Pero Luis, a Tamil Brahmin, who had entered the Jesuit order in 1562.

Bustamante was asked by the Portuguese Jesuits to set up a press at the College of *St Paul in Goa, and it was under the *imprint of the college that most of the early publications were issued. Other printers who were active in Goa during this period were João de Endem and João Quinquencio. Their output may be described as modest, having little or no impact outside the immediate circle of missionary activity. Printing was too alien and expensive an activity to elicit more than polite interest locally, while the finished product —the printed book—was regarded as part of the paraphernalia of church ritual. Even within missionary circles, the protocols and potential of printing were only partially appreciated. In the context of Goa, it seems that the printed book was seen solely as a tool for evangelizing. According to Priolkar, 'Printing activity continued to prosper so long as the importance of local languages for the purpose of proselytisation was fully appreciated' (Priolkar, 23). This was reinforced by the Concílio Provincial of 1606, which stated that no cleric should be placed in charge of a parish unless he learnt the local language. Yet Priolkar has argued that this stipulation was steadily undermined through the 17th century, until a decree was promulgated in 1684 which required that the local populace abandon the use of their mother tongues and switch to Portuguese within three years. It is therefore not surprising that printing came to a standstill in Goa at about the same time, in 1674. Another century and a half was to pass before it would reappear, in 1821.

The next significant printing initiative took place in Tranquebar (now Tharangambadi), on the east coast of India, and was triggered by the arrival of the Danish Lutheran missionary Bartholomew *Ziegenbalg in 1706. The nearest Jesuit mission at Elakkuricci was less than 50 miles away, and a battle began between the two rival missions to win the hearts and minds of the local people. Ziegenbalg spent long sessions with an Indian pundit learning local language and customs. To his parent body, the *Society for Promoting Christian Knowledge, he wrote:

> I must confess that my School-Master ... has often put such *Philosophical* Questions to me, as really made me believe ... one might discover things very fit to entertain

the curiosity of many a learned Head in *Europe* ... We hope to bring him over to the Christian Knowledge; but he is confident as yet, that one time or other we will all turn *Malabarians*. (Priolkar, 37)

He sent his emissaries far and wide, to buy up books from the widows of scholarly Brahmins, and left detailed descriptions of the MSS:

> As for the *Outside* of these Books, they are of a quite different Dress from those in Europe. There is neither Paper nor Leather, neither Ink nor Pen used by the Natives at all, but the Characters are by *Iron Tools* impressed on a Sort of Leaves of a Certain Tree, which is much like a Palm-Tree. At the End of every Leaf a Hole is made, and through the Hole a String drawn, whereby the whole Sett of Leaves is kept together. (Priolkar, 39)

Between 1706 and 1711, Ziegenbalg wrote a number of letters to the SPCK (*see* SOCIETY FOR PROMOTING CHRISTIAN KNOWLEDGE) asking for a printing press:

> We heartily wish to be supplied with a *Malabarick* and a *Portuguese* printing press to save the expensive charges of getting such books transcribed as are necessary for carrying on this work. I have hitherto employed Six *Malabarick* writers in my house ... 'Tis true those books which we get from the *Malabar* heathens must be entirely transcribed; or brought up for ready money, if people will part with them; but such as lay down the grounds of our holy religion, and are to be dispersed among the heathens, must be carefully printed off for this design. (Priolkar, 40)

In a remarkably shrewd move, Ziegenbalg argued that the book's form and content were indivisible, and the 'superior' technology of printing must be employed to confer an equivalent superiority upon Christian teachings. Convinced by his arguments, the SPCK despatched a press to Ziegenbalg in 1711, with a printer, Jonas Finck. After many vicissitudes the ship arrived, but not Finck, who disappeared off the Cape of Good Hope after the ship had been waylaid by the French and diverted to Rio de Janeiro. A soldier was found to work the press, and printing began in October 1712.

The press's crowning work was Ziegenbalg's 1715 Tamil *translation of the New Testament—the first such translation in any Indian language. The *fount bore a close resemblance to the letters in the palm-leaf MSS, while the language used was a version of demotic Tamil spoken in and around Tranquebar. The type had originally been cast at Halle in Germany, but it became necessary to cast smaller founts for the various publications undertaken by Ziegenbalg. A typefoundry was set up in Poryar, the first in India, and this was followed by the establishment of the first modern *paper mill in the country in 1715. With these, the Lutheran mission attained a degree of self-sufficiency in printing, and was no longer entirely dependent on the long supply chain from Germany. This self-sufficiency can be gauged from the press's high output: 65 titles from 1712 to 1720, 52 more in the next decade, and a total of 338 titles for the 18th century. The mission also received requests from the Dutch in Ceylon to print in Tamil and Sinhalese. A press at Colombo was reportedly set up by Peter Mickelsen, one of the casters of Tranquebar's types. The first book printed in Ceylon was an *octavo Singhalese prayer book produced in 1737–8 for the East India Company.

And what of the Jesuits? In 1717, the controversial and colourful C. G. Beschi arrived in Elakkuricci near Trichinopoly and stayed there for the next three decades. Despite his meddling in local politics and ostentatious habits, he was unable to raise sufficient resources to take on the well-funded Lutherans and was forced to fall back on palm-leaf MSS. The only weapon in his arsenal was his vastly superior knowledge of Tamil: what ensued was a battle of books—MS versus print, Jesuit versus Lutheran, purity versus contamination—in many ways anticipating the clash between the rival intellectual worlds of MS and print in 19th-century Bengal. Though Beschi poured scorn on his rivals for their imperfect knowledge of Tamil and their flawed translations of the scriptures, he was fighting a losing cause, and soon the Jesuits were in retreat in the region, leaving the field clear for Protestants.

After Tranquebar and Colombo, the scene for printing shifted to Madras (now Chennai). In 1726, Benjamin Schultze set up a branch of the SPCK at Vepery, outside Madras. By the middle of the century, it was under the care of Johann Philipp *Fabricius. In 1761, the English under Sir Eyre Coote successfully besieged the French at Pondicherry, and the spoils of war included a printing press seized from the French governor's palace. This press would probably have been used for Jesuit printing, so its loss was a further blow to the Society of Jesus in the region. Coote took the press and its printer to Madras, where Fabricius persuaded him to donate the press to the SPCK, on condition that printing orders from Fort St George—the seat of the Madras presidency—would take precedence over mission work. Soon the SPCK acquired its own press: the English war booty was returned to Fort St George, where it was renamed the Government Press, while the Vepery Press now

became the SPCK Press. It was on this press that Fabricius printed his famous Tamil–English dictionary in 1779. In 1793 the Press produced a Tamil translation of The *Pilgrim's Progress: this was a bilingual edition, with English on the left and Tamil on the right side of every page.

In many ways the fortunes of the Pondicherry press were symbolic of the momentous changes taking place in mid-18th-century India. Coote's military action dealt a decisive blow to French colonial aspirations, leaving the way clear for the British. Just four years earlier, in 1757, Robert Clive had won a historic battle at Plassey in Bengal, defeating the last independent nawab of Bengal, and paving the way for the territorial expansion of the East India Company in India. As centres of administration were set up in the three presidencies of Calcutta, Madras, and Bombay, print became an indispensable component of the engine of colonization. The missionaries, who had thus far championed print, suddenly found their efforts being swiftly outstripped by government printing.

3 Printing in the east: Serampore and Calcutta

If religion was behind the coming of print to west and south India, the initial impulse in Bengal was almost entirely political. In 1778 Nathaniel Brassey Halhed, a civil servant of the East India Company, produced the first printed book in the Bengali language and script, *A Grammar of the Bengal Language*. Initially, William Bolts was asked to design the Bengali type, but his design was not to Halhed's liking. The task was then entrusted to Charles *Wilkins, also a civil servant with the Company, who cast the type with the help of Pancānan Karmakār, a smith, and Joseph Shepherd, a seal- and gem-cutter. The printing was carried out on a press at Hooghly, possibly owned by one John Andrews. The Company itself paid for the printing, in a somewhat miserly manner.

By the end of 1800, there were as many as 40 printers working in Calcutta (now Kolkata). This was unprecedented not just in India, but in the whole of south Asia. Although presses in Madras remained mainly in government hands, Calcutta saw a large number of private entrepreneurs open *printing offices. The almost overnight rise of the periodical press is also remarkable. In the period 1780–90, seventeen weekly and six monthly periodicals were launched in Calcutta; almost all of the city's printers were connected with the periodical press at some time. Chief among them was James Augustus Hicky,

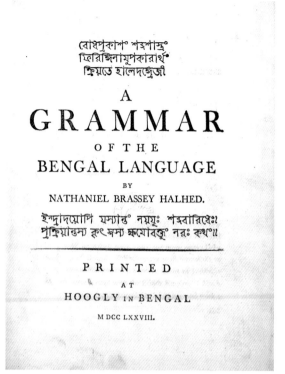

The first British use of Bengali founts: N. B. Halhed, *A Grammar of the Bengal Language* (1778).

who was the editor of the first *newspaper in India, the weekly English-language *Bengal Gazette* (1780), and who went to jail for his fearless—and sometimes scurrilous—criticism of the governing council. As far as book publishing was concerned, Andrews's press had travelled to Calcutta via Malda and had acquired a new name—the Honourable Company's Press—and was now run by Charles Wilkins. This press accounted for a third of all books printed in Calcutta before 1800, including *Asiatick Researches*, the journal of the newly established Asiatic Society. Books and periodicals were, however, not the chief sources of revenue for the Calcutta printing trade. *Stationery, legal and mercantile *forms, *handbills, etc. formed the staple of their survival, a further sign that the trade was coming of age. The most characteristic product of the trade was the *almanac, with three different *calendars: Muslim, Hindu, and Christian. In fact, the trade in almanacs still continues to be a lucrative sector of the Bengali book trade.

Materials and equipment—type, paper, ink, and the presses—had to be imported from Europe. Some type was manufactured locally, notably by Daniel Stuart and Joseph Cooper, who set up a foundry for their

Chronicle Press. Along with Bengali, this foundry also made Devnagari and *nasta'līq* types, the latter being used for printing in Persian. The availability of paper continued to be a problem. Good-quality paper had to be imported from Britain, while Patna supplied the local handmade variety, which was considerably cheaper. There were several unsuccessful attempts to set up paper mills in Calcutta during this period. John Borthwick Gilchrist, principal of *Fort William College in Calcutta and founder of the *Hindustanee Press, was not alone in complaining bitterly about the unscrupulous and fraudulent behaviour of printers, referring to 'typographical quicksands, and whirlpools, on the siren shores of oriental literature' and deploring the 'eternal treacherous behaviour' of his Bengali assistants (Shaw, *Printing*, 24–5).

Two events in 1800 were to have a momentous effect on printing in south and southeast Asia. The first was the establishment in Calcutta of the Fort William College to train the British civilians of the East India Company. The second was the establishment of a Baptist mission at Serampore (25 km from Calcutta) by William *Carey, an ex-cobbler, who arrived at Calcutta in 1793. His first few years in India were spent in Malda, working for an indigo planter, and learning Bengali and Sanskrit from his *munshi* (language teacher), Rām Rām Basu. His early attempts to set up a mission in British India failed, as the Company was hostile towards missionary activity. Eventually, Carey was permitted to establish his mission in Danish-controlled Serampore (then known as Fredericksnagar), where he was joined by two other Baptists, William Ward and Joshua Marshman. In the meantime Carey had acquired a wooden hand press (*see* COMMON PRESS), thanks to the munificence of George Udny, the indigo planter who had supported Carey and his family.

The Serampore mission was founded on 10 January 1800. In August that year, a Bengali translation of St Matthew's Gospel was published by the press. About the same time, Carey joined Fort William College as a teacher of Bengali and Sanskrit, for a salary of Rs. 500. The same mission that had been refused permission by the government now became a partner in training the future elite of the Raj.

The efforts of Carey and his assistants soon made the *Serampore Press the most important centre of printing in Asia. Pancānan Karmakār, the goldsmith trained in type production by Wilkins, was 'borrowed' by Carey from Colebrooke, and then put under virtual house arrest in Serampore. With the help of Pancānan and his son-in-law Manohar, a typefoundry was set up in March 1800. In its first ten years, the foundry produced type in at least thirteen languages. The printing press was in the immediate charge of Ward, who left detailed accounts of its day-to-day running. In a letter of 1811 he wrote:

> As you enter, your see your cousin in a small room, dressed in a white jacket, reading or writing, and looking over the office, which is more than 170 ft. long. There you find Indians translating the scriptures into the different tongues and correcting the proof-sheets. You observe, laid out in cases, types in Arabic, Persian, Nagari, Telugu, Panjabi, Bengali, Marathi, Chinese, Oriya, Burmese, Kanarese, Greek, Hebrew and English. Mussulmans and Christian Indians are busy composing, correcting, distributing. Next are four men throwing off the scripture sheets in different languages, others folding the sheets and delivering them to the large store-room, and six Mussulmans do the binding. Beyond the office are varied type-casters besides a group of men making ink, and in a spacious open-walled round place, our paper-mill, for we manufacture our own paper. (Koschorke, 59–60)

Not surprisingly, translations of the Bible accounted for the bulk of the publications. Between 1800 and 1834, the Serampore Press printed bibles in almost 50 languages, 38 of which were translated at Serampore by Carey and his associates. There were altogether 117 *editions, of which 25 were in Bengali. It seems that the Press supplied bibles to almost all significant Baptist missions in the region, from Indonesia in the east to Afghanistan in the west. From the report for 1813, it appears that a Malay bible in roman characters was in preparation, while a five-volume reprint of the entire Bible in Arabic was being undertaken for the lieutenant-governor of Java. The memorandum of 1816 claims that a Chinese Pentateuch was in the press, and that 'the new moveable metal type, after many experiments, are a complete success'. The 1820 report records the printing of the New Testament in Pashto, and also the setting up of a paper factory: 'After experiments lasting for twelve years, paper equally impervious to the worm with English paper, and of a firmer structure, though inferior in colour, is now made of materials [from] the growth of India' (Grierson, 247).

Perhaps even more significant than the bibles were the Bengali translations of the two great epics *Rāmāyaṇa* and *Mahābhārata*. These were published during 1802–3, and marked the first appearance of the epics in printed form, in any language. The Press also published dictionaries, grammars, dialogues or colloquies, Sanskrit phrasebooks, philosophy, Hindu mythological tales, *tracts, and the first newspaper in

Bengali, the *Samachar Durpun*. The first number of this twice-weekly, bilingual (Bengali and English) paper was published in May 1818. According to a calculation made by the missionaries themselves, a total of 2,120,000 items of print in 40 languages were issued by the Serampore Press from 1800 to 1832.

Along with the mission's own publications, the Press also filled orders from Fort William College. During the first two decades of the 19th century, the college played a crucial role in producing grammars and lexicons in all the major Indian languages, a task carried out by Indian and European scholars. Altogether, 38 such works were produced in Arabic, Persian, Sanskrit, Urdu, Braj, Bengali, Marathi, Oriya, Panjabi, Telugu, and Kannada. Another important category was ancient Indian tales and verses, translated for classroom use into modern languages, especially Urdu and Bengali. The college's publications programme had a twofold aim: to produce *textbooks for its students, and to encourage scholarly editions of books with no immediate pedagogical value. Besides the Mission Press, two other presses printed for the College. The first was the Hindustanee Press of John Gilchrist, which specialized in Persian-Arabic printing, especially in *nastaʿlīq*. The second was the Sanskrit Press of Bāburām Śarmā, the first Indian to own a press in Bengal (he was succeeded by Lallulāl in 1814–15, who was also a teacher at the college). In 1808 the college noted:

> a printing press has been established by learned Hindoos, furnished with complete founts of improved Nagree types of different sizes, for the printing of books in the Sunskrit language. This press has been encouraged by the College to undertake an edition of the best Sunskrit dictionaries, and a compilation of the Sunskrit rules of grammar. (Das, *Sahibs*, 84)

The College's publications did not have much impact beyond the classroom and European circles. This lack was filled by the *Calcutta School-Book Society (founded in 1817), which began to commission and publish some of the earliest secular school textbooks in Bengali and English. Its establishment coincided with that of the Hindu College in the same year. For more than half a century, the CSBS published hundreds of titles for 'cheap or gratuitous supply ... to schools and seminaries of learning'. Significantly, the Society's charter stated that it was not its design 'to furnish religious books: a restriction however very far from being meant to preclude the supply of books of moral tendency' ([Calcutta School Book Society, iii]). From 1821, the Society was assisted by a monthly grant from the government; a few years later it acquired its own press and depository at Lallbazar. In 1823, the *Calcutta Christian Tract and Book Society was set up to supply books to missionary-aided vernacular schools. Within a short time it had published a large number of tracts whose *press runs often went into five figures. A similar role was played by the Christian Vernacular Literature Society. But the man who had the most impact on the textbook trade was the scholar and reformer *Vidyāsāgar. While a teacher at Fort William College, he started the Sanskrit Press in 1847, along with his colleague Madanmohan Tarkālaṅkār. Both men produced Bengali *primers which became legendary: the former's two-part *Barṇaparicay* (1855) and the latter's *Śiśuśikṣā* (1849). Their popularity can be gauged from the fact that in 1890, the 149th and 152nd editions (respectively) of the two primers were issued. Vidyāsāgar reformed Bengali *typography into an alphabet of 12 vowels and 40 consonants and designed the so-called Vidyāsāgar *saat* or type case, for greater ease of *composition.

By the middle of the 19th century, printing had spread to Assam, with Baptist missionaries setting up a press there and starting the first Assamese periodical, *Aruṇoday*, in 1846. After a slow beginning, Dhaka exploded into print in the second half of the century, with the Girish Press printing more than 500 titles by 1900. The trade in Bengal had become sufficiently large to require *bibliographical control. James *Long, a philologist and ethnographer, compiled three bibliographies of printed works in the 1850s, the first of their kind in India. His *Descriptive Catalogue of Bengali Works* (1855) contained 1,400 entries on books and periodicals in Bengali. A high proportion of the titles were accounted for under such categories as textbooks, translations, dictionaries, grammars, *law books, and religious literature, but the trade in popular books flourished as well. This was commonly—and often pejoratively—known as 'the Bat-tala trade', in reference to the north Calcutta location where such books were mostly printed. According to Long,

> Few Bengali books are sold in European shops. A person may be twenty years in Calcutta, and yet scarcely know that any Bengali books are printed by Bengalis themselves. He must visit the native part of the town and the Chitpoor road, their Pater Noster Row, to gain any information on this point. The native presses are generally in by-lanes with little outside to attract, yet they ply a busy trade. (Ghosh, 118)

One of the pioneers of this new literature was Gaṅgakiśor Bhattāchārya, considered the first Bengali printer, publisher, bookseller, and newspaper editor. After beginning his life as a compositor at the Mission Press, in 1818 he set up his own Bangal Gezeti Press, and was also responsible for printing the first illustrated book in Bengal, Bhāratcandra's *Annadā-mangal*, in 1816.

Tales, light verses, and farces were common examples of Bat-tala printing, and Long recorded with disapproval that many of these dealt with erotic themes, 'equal to the worst of the French school' (Ghosh, 87). Long's reservations notwithstanding, the Bat-tala trade was thoroughly indigenous, unmediated by missionary or reformist values. Yet, it was not until the mid-century that the Bat-tala trade assumed a truly commercial character. In 1857, Long listed 46 presses in the area—along the Garanhata, Ahiritola, Chitpur, and Barabazar roads—which printed a wide range of genres such as almanacs, mythological literature, farces, songs, *medical texts, and typographically distinct Muslim-Bengali works. This last category is particularly remarkable for the way in which it retained some of the protocols of the MS book. In fact, many Bat-tala productions show a divided commitment to MS and printed forms of the book, especially in the disposition of the *title-page, whose *paratextual excess seemed to signal some kind of confusion about proprietorship, authority, and entailment. Although the production values of Bat-tala literature often left a lot to be desired, there is no doubting the energy and vitality of its genres. Bat-tala publications consciously distanced themselves from the moralizing and reformist agenda of print, and dealt unabashedly in subgenres such as erotica, scandals, current events, doggerel, and songs. These proved so irksome to the reformist lobby that they pushed for and, in 1856, succeeded in having an Act passed to prevent the public sale or display of obscene books and pictures. Shortly afterwards, Long reported with some satisfaction that three people had been arrested for selling an obscene book of songs by Dāśarathi Roy, and that 30,000 copies of the book had been sold at the price of four annas. The Supreme Court imposed a fine of Rs. 1,300 upon the vendors, then a considerable sum. This post-publication *censorship was in fact the first of a number of official measures to impose some kind of restriction on print—an initiative that would gain urgency after the failed 1857 uprising by the sepoys and the consequent takeover of India by the British Crown. Matters reached a crisis with the furore over the English translation of Dīnabandhu Mitra's *Nīl-darpaṇ* (The Indigo Planting Mirror), a play fiercely critical of indigo planters. Following a successful *libel action by the planters, Long went to jail (for a month) for his role in facilitating the translation. It was therefore not surprising that the Indian Press and Registration of Books Act (1867) mandated that all publications in British India be registered. The Act was a watershed in the history of Indian printing and, in hindsight, an acknowledgement that print had truly become a part of everyday life in India.

4 The other presidencies: Bombay and Madras

Printing came to Goa in as early as 1556, but bypassed Bombay (now Mumbai), fewer than 500 miles away. The Marathas of the Peshwa period did not seem interested in printing, although there is some evidence that Bhīmjī Pārekh, a Gujarati trader, set up a press in 1674. After this, there was a hiatus for more than a century until 1780, when Rustom Caresajee printed the *Calendar for the Year of Our Lord for 1780*, a 34-page publication priced at two rupees.

In the last years of the century, the Courier Press was the most important in Bombay. It printed the periodical *The Bombay Courier*, which was probably started in 1791. An advertisement carried by it in 1797 is thought to be the first in Gujarati characters: its type was cast by a press employee named Jijibhāi Chhāpghar. Robert Drummond, who wrote a *Grammar of the Malabar Language* in 1799 and for whom Jijibhāi also cast type, hailed him as an 'ingenious artist who, without any other help or information than what he gleaned from Chamber's Dictionary of Arts and Sciences, succeeded in completing a font of the Guzzeratty types a few years ago' (Priolkar, 73). The first Maratha characters are likewise thought to have appeared in an advertisement in the *Bombay Courier* in July 1802. The first Gujarati press proper was established in 1812 by *Ferdunji Marzaban, who used to visit his friend Jijibhāi at the Courier Press, and was inspired by his example to start a printing office of his own. The first book to be printed by Ferdunji's press was an almanac, in 1814.

As in Bengal, missionaries were quick to appear on the scene. In 1813, although they had been turned away from Calcutta, a group of Americans were allowed by the governor, Sir Evan Nepean, to open a mission in Bombay. A printing office was started in 1816 with a single wooden press and a single fount of Marathi type, acquired in Calcutta, with which an eight-page scriptural tract was produced in 1817. Over the next two decades, the press steadily grew in size until it employed a staff of 25. It had its own

typefoundry, which could cast type in at least nine languages, a bindery, and a lithographic press. Thanks to the ingenuity of a young apprentice, Thomas Graham, by the mid-1830s the press was able to produce vastly improved Marathi and Gujarati type. The 1840s also saw the beginning of printing in Mangalore, on the west coast. A mission from Basle was established there in 1836; the first newspaper in Kannada came from its press in 1843.

At the end of the third and decisive Anglo-Maratha War in 1818, British power replaced the Peshwas in Maharashtra. The new regime established the Bombay Education Society, whose task was to produce vernacular textbooks. With the help of a group of *shastris*, *pandits*, and *munshis* (teachers) the society produced the first Marathi dictionary (*Shabdakosh*) in 1824. The availability of Marathi type was a recurring problem, so a government lithographic printing unit was inaugurated with six machines. Printing by *lithography was considerably aided by the discovery in 1826 that the Kurnool stone was particularly suitable for lithographic use. For a period, lithography was preferred over typographical printing in government circles, principally owing to the large size and crude contours of the available type. As far as private initiatives were concerned, the Parsi trading community took the lead in setting up printing presses. Consequently, a commercial print culture in western India first developed in Gujarati, rather than in Marathi. Veena Naregal has suggested that the slow growth of a Marathi print culture was largely due to high-caste repugnance towards the manual labour associated with the print trade.

In the mid-19th century, two men changed the face of Marathi printing. In 1840, Gaṇpat Kṛsnājī built a wooden hand press and started experimenting with ink-making and type design. In order to print the Hindu almanacs that were his stock-in-trade, he designed and cast improved type in both Marathi and Gujarati. Until Bhau Mahājan established his press in 1843, Kṛsnājī's press was the sole producer of Marathi books outside government and missionary circles. His 'pioneering efforts to publish sacred and "popular" precolonial texts illustrated many trends that were to characterise the emerging sphere of vernacular production' (Naregal, 185). Bhau Mahājan's Prabhakar Press printed progressive periodicals such as the *Prabhakar* and the *Dhumketu*. The task of typographical reform, on the other hand, was carried on by Jāvjī Dādājī, who had started his career by working at the *American Mission Press, and later joined the staff of the Indu-Prakash Press. In 1864 he opened a small typefoundry, and he established the Nirnaya-Sagara Press in 1869. Along with his friend Ranojī Rāojī Aru, he set a very high standard for Marathi, Gujarati, and Sanskrit typography.

In keeping with the two other presidencies, Madras became the undisputed centre of 19th-century print culture, although mention must also be made of Maharaja Serfoji II of Tanjore. In his palace in 1805, he set up a press that produced eight books in Marathi and Sanskrit. But it was in Madras that a 'nexus between pundits, printing and public patronage was cemented with the establishment of the College of Fort St George in 1812' (Blackburn, 74). This was followed by the establishment of the Madras School Book Society in 1820, to cater for students in missionary-run schools. The SPCK's Vepery Press continued to be active: along with the Madras Male Asylum Press (established in 1789), it accounted for a major share of periodical printing. At the suggestion of the Vepery Press, the government decided to train local goldsmiths in cutting type. This resulted in the creation of the first Telugu type in India. However, advances in Telugu printing were hampered by confusion over competing renderings: the Telugu used by missionaries, for example, was a mishmash of dialects and styles, to which Hindu scholars paid no attention. This confusion delayed the advent of print in the language by almost half a century.

The founding of the College of Fort St George in 1812 marked the entry of the pundits into the world of printing, and initiated a fascinating encounter between the worlds of print and MS. The publishing history of the Tamil epic *Tirukkurāl* in 1812, for instance, shows how the MS book's editorial and textual protocols were being exploited to arrive at an authentic version for print. With the pundits drafted into teaching at the college, in its first two decades the press produced 27 books, mostly in Tamil and Telugu. More importantly, teachers acquired a familiarity with print that would later be employed in a radical reshaping of literary culture. From the third decade of the century, a number of 'pundit-presses' began to appear, such as the Kalvi Vilakkam, founded by the Aiyar brothers in 1834, Tiru Venkatacala Mutāliyār's Sarasvati Press, and the Vidya-anubalana-yantra-sala or the Preservation of Knowledge Press of the famous Jaffna Tamil scholar *Ārumaka Nāvalar, a remnant of which still exists. Many of these presses played an important role in shaping public opinion, especially during the anti-missionary campaigns of the 1840s. Another important development of the period was the rise of journalism in several languages—European and Indian—representing almost all shades of political and social opinion. By the middle of the century, printing in Tamil had encompassed almost all major genres, and a standardized orthography was more or less in place. In 1862, the Revd Miron Winslow of the American Mission Press published his landmark Tamil–English dictionary; three years later, the missionary John Murdoch produced the first bibliography of Tamil printed books. The founts for the dictionary, cut by P. R. Hunt, were a high water mark of Tamil typography.

5 Printing in north India

When printing began to spread westward in the first third of the 19th century, it took the lithographic rather than the typographic route. Lithography was particularly suitable for printing in Urdu and Persian, as it was an inexpensive technology, and 'reproduced the elegant hand of calligraphers, who in turn found cheap employment' (Orsini, 'Detective Novels', 437). The problems associated with the development of Indian types could be bypassed through the new technology of lithography, and by mid-century, Lucknow and Kanpur became the principal centres of lithographic printing in all of South Asia.

That is not to say that there was no typography in Hindi publishing. Printing in Devanagari (the script in which Hindi and many Indian languages is written) dates back to the 17th century, but its appearances were sporadic until the Serampore missionaries began to use Devanagari type to print in a large range of north Indian languages and dialects. Of the 2,120,000 volumes issued from the press in its first three decades, as many as 65,000 were printed in Devanagari. There was a good deal of printing in Devanagari at Bombay as well, but primarily in Marathi and Sanskrit. In Europe too, the rise of Indian studies led to the casting of high-quality Devanagari founts, especially in Germany, where Schlegel and Bopp produced editions of the *Bhagavadgītā* and the *Hitopadeśa* in the 1820s. Thanks to the refinements in Devanagari, printers in Calcutta and Benares (Varanasi) were able print books in the Nepali language as well.

Printing came to Lucknow in 1817 when the Matba-i Sultani, or Royal Press, was established; but printing did not begin in earnest until the coming of lithography in 1830. That year, Henry Archer, superintendent of the Asiatic Lithographic Company in Kanpur, was invited to set up a press in Lucknow. In the beginning, the trade was not commercial, in the sense that books were usually published to an author's or a patron's order. Nevertheless, a score or so of lithographic presses were operating in the city by the 1840s, chief among which was Muṣṭafá Khān's *Mustafai Press, which published expensive books as well as popular genres such as *masnavis* and *qissas*. The *quissas*—moral tales, short anecdotes, fables—were first published at Fort William College in Calcutta for pedagogical purposes, but soon became a staple of commercial publishing in Persian and Urdu. A particularly popular title was the *Tuti nāmā* (Tales of a Parrot) of which at least fifteen different editions appeared in Calcutta, Bombay, Madras, Kanpur, Lucknow, and Delhi between 1804 and 1883.

Largely owing to the activities of schoolbook societies and missionaries, printing also spread to nearby towns and cantonments such as Agra, Allahabad, Meerut, and Lahore. A schoolbook society for the North-Western Provinces, with its headquarters at Agra, was set up in 1838. The same year saw the establishment of a missionary schoolbook society in Benares. Two major blows were subsequently dealt to printing at Lucknow, however. In 1849 the Nawab Wajid Ali Shah imposed a temporary ban on printing, as a result of which many firms shifted to Kanpur. This was followed by the sepoy uprising in 1857, leading to further uncertainty in the trade. The one beneficiary of this state of affairs was Nawal Kishore Bhargava of Agra, who in 1858 set up the *Nawal Kishore Press at Lucknow, in a field virtually devoid of competition. Munshi Nawal Kishore had started his career as an Urdu journalist and had learnt presswork while employed at the Kohinoor Press of Lahore. In Lucknow, he started by printing in Urdu, but soon became the pioneer of Hindi printing in the city. More crucially, he enjoyed English patronage, which meant that the Press received the lion's share of government custom, especially extremely lucrative textbook contracts. In the 1860s the Press issued cheap editions of famous Hindi classics, in printings of several thousands at a time, followed by Hindi translations of Sanskrit scriptures, and bilingual editions of Sanskrit texts with Hindi commentary. Another important centre of printing in Hindi was Benares, although a fully fledged print culture would develop there only in the 1870s. This was largely brought about by the efforts of the remarkable Bhāratendu Hariścandra, who wrote and published in every possible literary genre in his short but extremely productive life. His lead was followed by the likes of Rāmakṛṣṇā Varmā, whose Bharat Jiwan Press (established in 1884) specialized in Brajbhasha poetry, as well as translations of Bengali novels: the latter paved the away 'for the

explosion in fiction writing that took place in Benares in the 1890s' (Orsini, 'Pandits', 120).

6 Print and the nation

By the turn of the century, print had spread to almost every part of the Indian subcontinent, with an elaborate network of production and distribution in place. The rise of public libraries and reading rooms created new spaces for the consumption of print. The Calcutta Public Library (established in 1836) showed the way, by involving its subscribers, both Indian and British, in decision-making, especially with regard to acquisitions. The gradual increase in *literacy and the formation of new interpretive communities created new tastes and reading habits, as embodied most visibly in the phenomenal rise of the Indian *novel. The pioneer in this regard was the Bengali author Bankimcandra Cattopādhyāy, who is credited with having written the first novel in an Indian language, in 1865. The rise of this genre was perhaps the most decisive indication of the extent to which print had penetrated and modified the literary protocols of Indian languages.

The potentially large Indian market now began to attract overseas publishers. The two houses that took the lead in this initiative were *Macmillan and *Oxford University Press. The rapid spread of education made the textbook market in India highly lucrative, and Macmillan entered it with a splash, taking over Peary Churn Sircar's Books of Reading in 1875 from the firm of *Thacker & Spink. Macmillan published F. T. Palgrave's famous *Golden Treasury*, and the algebra and geometry of Hall and Knight, and Hall and Stevens, which are still in use. In 1886, the firm ventured into fiction, with 'Macmillan's Colonial Library' and 'Macmillan's English Classics' for Indian Universities. OUP took a more scholarly route, by publishing the monumental 50-volume *Sacred Books of the East* (edited by F. Max *Müller), as well as the 'Rulers of India' series, although it set up an Indian branch office only in 1912, in Bombay, under E. V. Rieu. Other British firms following their lead included *Longman and *Blackie, the latter publishing the ubiquitous Wren and Martin *Grammar*. In the field of distribution, A. H. *Wheeler obtained the franchise for bookselling at railway stations all over India, and became an essential part of Indian travelling experience. Another bookselling giant was *Higginbotham's of Madras; it started as the Wesleyan Book Depot in 1844 and is currently India's oldest surviving bookshop. The Oxford Book and Stationery Company (not connected to OUP) (*see* OXFORD AND IBH), a chain of bookshops run by the Primlanis, set up business in 1920 and opened bookshops in Calcutta, Bombay, and Allahabad which continue to operate.

By the beginning of the 20th century, print had become an integral part of the public sphere and thoroughly indigenous. The competition between traditional and modern knowledge systems was now firmly enacted in the arena of print. There was an enthusiastic collaboration between print and the rise of regional-language literatures, involving figures such as Subramaṇiya Bhārati, Rabindranath Tagore, *Fakirmohan Senāpati, and Munṣī Premcānd. The beginnings of the freedom movement during this period also saw the emergence of what may be called print nationalism. Print, especially in the periodical press, was widely mobilized in the task of articulating the idea of a nation, and focusing opinion about the evils of colonial rule. The proposed partition of Bengal in 1905, and the *swadeshi* movement in its wake, saw extensive use of print, with leadership provided by men of letters such as Tagore and periodicals such as the *Jugāntar*. Not surprisingly, the hand of the Raj began to come down heavily upon so-called 'seditious' literature, and books were often proscribed and withdrawn from circulation. Raids on bookshops, the interrogation of suspects, and the arrest of authors, publishers, and printers became common. In 1907, Gaṇeś Deśmukh was sentenced to seven years' transportation for distributing a seditious songbook, while the minstrel poet Mukundadās was jailed for three years for performing a *jatra*, or musical drama, critical of the Raj. There were attempts at circumvention, however. After the passage in 1910 of the Indian Press Act, which aimed to prevent the publication and dissemination of seditious literature in all forms, nationalist literature was often circulated via princely states and non-British foreign enclaves such as Pondicherry and Chandannagar. Returning Indian and European sailors provided another conduit for overseas revolutionary literature. The civil disobedience movement brought in its wake the repressive 1931 Indian Press Act, which sought to prevent the distribution of material considered an incitement to violence.

The new century also saw the rise of a number of firms that took the lead in standardizing publishing, and bringing it more into line with international practice. The first attempts to form trade associations took place during this time, notably in the College Street book mart in Calcutta. The passing of the Indian Copyright Act of 1914 ratified the 1911 British Act with minor changes, and helped clarify author–publisher

relations. Another notable development was the rise of specialist publishers, leading to the standardization of editorial and scholarly practices, a task initiated by learned societies such as the *Nagari Pracharini Sabha of Kasi and the *Bangiya Sahitya Parishat in Calcutta. When Tagore set up the publishing arm of his world university, *Visva-Bharati, it became one of the first publishing houses in India to adopt uniform editorial conventions. A similar role was played by the *South India Saiva Siddhanta Works Publishing Society in Madras.

7 Publishing after 1947

The first two decades after Independence saw the coming of age of a number of young firms. Many of them had been loosely associated with the freedom movement, such as Hind Kitab and Renaissance Publishers, set up to publish the works of the revolutionary M. N. Roy. But the field was dominated by *Asia Publishing House of Bombay, founded in 1943 by Peter Jayasinghe, and widely regarded as the first Indian publishing house to be organized along truly professional lines. Over a period of four decades it published nearly 5,000 titles, mostly in the social sciences and politics, and in its heyday was able to maintain branch offices in London and New York. Nevertheless, it may have overreached itself, for its decline in the 1980s was sharp and sudden. Another publisher of serious books was *Popular Prakashan, which was started as a bookshop in 1924 but soon went into publishing, and which distinguished itself by issuing the seminal works of the historian D. D. Kosambi in the 1950s. In fact, many firms that had begun life as booksellers and distributors branched out into publishing after Independence, making intelligent use of their networks. Such was the case with *Rupa, which was founded in 1936 and became one of the largest wholesalers, distributors, and exporters in India before diversifying into publishing. *Allied, established in 1934, took the same route and went into textbook publishing.

In the *paperback sector, two firms led the way: *Jaico, founded in 1946 in anticipation of Independence, was the first publisher of paperbacks in English. *Hind Pocket Books, started in 1958 by D. N. Malhotra, began the paperback revolution by printing ten Hindi titles. It published fiction and non-fiction in Hindi, Urdu, Punjabi, and English, and started two book clubs, one for books in Hindi and one in English. But perhaps the most energetic publisher of the period was a late entrant, Vikas Publishing House (established in 1969), which published in a wide range of subjects, at an average of 500 titles every year. A key factor in the firm's success was the access it had to its sister concern, the UBSPD, which had one of the most sophisticated distribution networks in the country. Alternative models of publishing were provided by the *Sahitya Pravarthaka Cooperative Society, set up as a cooperative for Malayalam authors, and P. Lal's Writers Workshop in Calcutta, which has published over 3,000 young English-language authors since 1958.

A large part of the publishing market was accounted for by the government and its subsidiaries. In 1954 the government founded the *Sahitya Akademi as a national academy of letters, with the mandate of publishing in Indian languages, both in the original and in translations. The Akademi has since published several thousand titles, but its distribution network is practically nonexistent. The National Book Trust was established in 1957 to provide books at cheap prices. Among overseas publishers, OUP India led the field, steadily consolidating its position, while others such as Macmillan, Blackie, and *Orient Longman (the post-Independence avatar of Longman) closed their Indian businesses following restrictions on foreign firms' holding equity. OUP was unaffected because it is a department of the University and enjoys exemption from corporate taxes in many countries. Currently, it is India's leading publisher of scholarly and reference books, with a list of more than 3,000 titles. In the 1960s, the United States' PL 480 programme resulted in more than a thousand American college-level textbooks being registered in India at subsidized prices. Some four million books were distributed through this route. American publishers were late to enter the field and when they did so, it was with higher-level textbooks. *Prentice Hall set up business in 1963, while McGraw-Hill entered the market in collaboration with the Tata family in 1970.

This was roughly the state of the publishing business until economic liberalization was set in motion in the early 1990s. Penguin India started publishing from 1987, and currently publishes 200 titles annually, with a backlist of 750 titles, making it one of the biggest publishers of English books in South Asia. Macmillan returned to India after a period of absence, and has tried to reclaim the prominence it once enjoyed in educational publishing. The loosening of import and equity restrictions led to the entry in recent years of conglomerates such as HarperCollins, Random House, and the Pearson Group: HarperCollins was the first out of the starting gate, and has recently allied with the India Today group. All this portends an imminent boom in publishing in India, and one not merely restricted to the English language. Penguin has plans to enter into regional-language publishing, a market whose full potential is far from being tapped. India is also in the process of becoming the 'back office' for overseas publications, with increasing volumes of editorial and production work being outsourced to it.

According to the Federation of Indian Publishers, there are more than 11,000 publishing firms in India, some four-fifths of which are publishing in regional languages. Unfortunately, most of them seem unable to break out of their outdated business models. There are some exceptions, of course, such as *Ananda, which is the leading publisher of Bengali books, and belongs to the group of companies that includes *Anandabazar Patrika*, the first Bengali daily to have used Linotype. In contrast, English-language and bilingual publishing has seen the entry of a number of independent niche firms, which have brought creativity and energy to publishing. Tara in Madras publishes for the neglected young adult sector, while Kali for Women and Stree have distinguished themselves in women's studies. Permanent Black has set a high standard for scholarly publishing; Seagull is noted for the quality of its theatre and arts books, and Roli publishes expensive art books for an overseas market. Translation is another sector that is beginning to register growth after decades of inexplicable neglect. Thus, with an expanding population, solid businesses, overseas and domestic investment, and a degree of commercial innovation, the future of Indian publishing seems highly promising.

BIBLIOGRAPHY

P. Altbach, *Publishing in India* (1975)

C. Bandyopādhyāy, ed., *Dui śataker bāṅglā mudraṇ o prakāśan* (1981)

S. Blackburn, *Print, Folklore, and Nationalism in Colonial South India* (2003)

— and V. Dalmia, eds., *India's Literary History* (2004)

G. Bühler, *Indian Paleography* (1904; repr. 1987)

[Calcutta School-Book Society,] *The Fifteenth Report of the Proceedings of the Calcutta School Book Society* (1852)

R. B. Chatterjee, 'A Short Account of the Company's Trade with the Subcontinent', in *Macmillan: A Publishing Tradition, 1843–1970*, ed. E. James (2001)

— *Empires of the Mind: A History of Oxford University Press in India Under the Raj* (2006)

R. B. Darnton, 'Literary Surveillance in the British Raj: The Contradictions of Liberal Imperialism', *BH* 4 (2001), 133–76

S. K. Das, *Sahibs and Munshis: An Account of the College of Fort William* (1978)

— *Encyclopaedia of India Literature* (5 vols, 1989)

K. S. Duggal, *Book Publishing in India* (1980)

A. Ghosh, *Power in Print: Popular Publishing and the Politics of Language and Culture in a Colonial Society, 1778–1905* (2006)

G. A. Grierson, 'The Early Publication of the Serampore Mission Press', *The Indian Antiquary*, (1903), 241–54

A. Gupta and S. Chakravorty, eds., *Print Areas: Book History in India* (2004)

— *Moveable Type: Book History in India* (2008)

P. Joshi, *In Another Country: Colonialism, Culture, and the English Novel in India* (2002)

B. S. Kesavan, *History of Printing and Publishing in India* (3 vols, 1985–97)

V. Koilpillai, *The SPCK in India* (1985)

K. Koschorke *et al.*, *History of Christianity in Asia, Africa, and Latin-America, 1450-1990* (2007)

J. P. Losty, *The Art of the Book in India* (1982)

M. Mamoon, *Unish shatake dhakar mudran o prakashana* (2004)

V. Narayana Rao, 'Print and Prose: Pandits, *Karanams*, and the East India Company in the Making of Modern Telugu', in *Literary History: Essays on the Nineteenth Century*, ed. S. Blackburn and V. Dalmia (2004)

V. Naregal, *Language Politics, Elites and the Public Sphere* (2001)

Nikhil Sarkār (Śrīpāntha), *Jakhan chāpākhānā elo* (1977)

F. Orsini, 'Detective Novels: A Commercial Genre in Nineteenth-Century North India', in *India's Literary History*, ed. S. Blackburn and V. Dalmia (2004)

— 'Pandits, Printers and Others: Publishing in Nineteenth-Century Benares', in *Print Areas: Book History in India*, ed. A. Gupta and S. Chakravorty (2004)

R. Pinto, *Between Empires: Print and Politics in Goa* (2007)

S. Pollock, *The Language of Gods in the World of Men: Sanskrit, Culture and Power in Premodern India* (2006)

A. K. Priolkar, *The Printing Press in India* (1958)

G. Shaw, *Printing in Calcutta to 1800* (1981)

— 'On the Wrong End of the Raj: Some Aspects of Censorship in British India and its Circumvention During the 1920s–1940s: Part 1', in *Moveable Type: Book History in India*, ed. A. Gupta and S. Chakravarty (2008)

U. Stark, *An Empire of Books: The Naval Kishore Press and the Diffusion of the Printed Word in Colonial India* (2007)

40 The History of the Book in China

J. S. Edgren

1 The book before paper and printing

Although the early invention of true paper (2nd century BC) and of textual printing (late 7th century) by *woodblock printing profoundly influenced the development of the book in China, the materials and manufacture of books before paper and before printing also left some traces. Preceding the availability of paper as a writing surface, the earliest books in China, known as *jiance* or *jiandu*, were written on thin strips of prepared bamboo and wood, which were usually interlaced in sequence by parallel bands of twisted thongs, hemp string, or silk thread. The text was written with a *writing brush and lampblack *ink in vertical columns from right to left—a *layout retained by later MSS and printed books—after which the strips were rolled up to form a primitive *scroll binding (*see* **17**). The surviving specimens of *jiance* are mostly the result of 20th-century scientific archaeological recovery, and date from around the 6th century BC to the 3rd century AD.

An important and unusual example of *jiance* was discovered in 1959 at Wuwei county, Gansu province. The text of the classic *Yili* (Book of Etiquette and Ceremonial) was found in a Han dynasty (206 BC–AD 220) tomb. The text-bearing strips, mostly of wood, are exceptionally long: they record the number of each column, as well as displaying the name and number of each section of text when rolled up. On the basis of very early inscriptions and citations in ancient texts, there is good reason to believe that this book form existed four or five centuries earlier than the 6th century BC. The subject-matter of *jiance* ranges from mundane archival documents to important historical, philosophical, *medical, and military texts. Some large caches containing thousands of bamboo strips have

been discovered in recent decades, and many such texts have not yet been published or made available for study. Because the binding thongs or strings usually disintegrate, some texts have been difficult to put in order. Others found in tombs in humid regions present serious *conservation problems.

Although its use began later, *silk is mostly contemporaneous with bamboo and wood as an important material for pre-paper MS books. By the early Warring States period (403–221 BC), the philosopher Mozi (*fl.* 400 BC) could state that texts written on bamboo and silk or engraved on metal and stone were thus transmitted for posterity. Silk books also took the form of *scrolls, and the continuous weaving of textiles allowed for drawings or diagrams accompanying the text. The early Han tomb at Mawangdui, Changsha, Hunan province, contained *maps on silk as well as silk books. A highly valuable material, silk was used sparingly. According to the *Hanshu yiwenzhi*, the catalogue of the early Han imperial library, compiled by Ban Gu, only about 25 per cent of its holdings consisted of silk scrolls. In fact, the invention of paper probably came about as an economical alternative to silk.

*Script has a history of more than 4,000 years in China, and text was inscribed on objects of diverse materials and forms before and during the development of scroll books of bamboo and silk. The so-called 'oracle bones' used for divination since the mid-Shang dynasty (*c*.1300–1046 BC) comprise animal bones as well as tortoise shells with brief texts engraved on their surfaces. Mozi's mention of texts engraved (and also cast) on metal chiefly refers to Shang and Zhou (1046–256 BC) bronze ritual vessels; his mention of texts engraved on stone refers to stone monuments such as the so-called 'stone drums' (7th or 8th century BC) still preserved at the Palace Museum in Beijing.

The more familiar flat stone tablets with lengthy inscriptions came into being in the Han dynasty. In Chinese culture, the durability of metal and stone serves as a metaphor for the inscriptions' longevity. Furthermore, inscribed seals of metal (bronze, iron, gold) and stone (especially jade), as well as inscribed stone tablets, probably inspired the invention of printing (*see* SIGILLOGRAPHY).

Commemorative stone tablets (*bei*) have been erected in China for more than 2,000 years. Chinese stele inscriptions also include tomb inscriptions (*muzhi*), inscriptions on natural stone surfaces, and inscriptions on objects such as Buddhist and Daoist stone sculptures. Engraving of the Han 'stone classics' was undertaken in AD 175–183; the tablets were erected in a public place at the capital Luoyang to allow scholars and students to copy standardized versions of the Confucian classics. Three or four centuries later the technique of *ink-squeeze rubbings made from *bei* initiated the primitive duplication of texts that led to the method of xylographic printing.

The *Suishu jingjizhi*, the bibliography of the official history of the Sui dynasty (581–618), includes several ink-squeeze rubbings (*taben*), apparently all in the form of scrolls. Rubbings are also sometimes stored as folded *sheets. The earliest extant ink-squeeze rubbing mounted as a primitive scroll is of an inscription commemorating a hot spring entitled *Wenquan ming*. It was written by the Tang emperor Taizong, and is dated 653. This incomplete scroll discovered in Dunhuang is now in the *Bibliothèque nationale de France (BnF). The vertical orientation of most inscriptions engraved on steles is not directly compatible with the horizontal orientation of scroll and of album binding, which eventually became the favoured form of preserving ink-squeeze rubbings. Rubbings made on large sheets of paper must first be cut into columns of text equal to the height of the scroll or album *leaf, and then arranged to read from right to left by pasting the strips in the correct order. This is a task more often assigned to a scroll-mounter than to a bookbinder. The album binding, which superficially can be mistaken for the *pleated binding, is usually regarded as belonging to the realm of painting and *calligraphy rather than of books. Folding albums of painting or calligraphy are called *ceye* (Japanese *gajō*), and are made from single sheets of stiff paper folded vertically in the centre. The sheets are then bound by consecutively pasting the edges parallel to the centrefold until the *volume is formed. Covers of wood or textile-covered *pasteboard can be attached to the top and bottom surfaces.

Although archaeological evidence shows that paper existed in China two to three centuries earlier, the first formal acknowledgement of papermaking was made in a report to the emperor, in AD 105, by Cai Lun, a eunuch at the Han court. Most importantly, he encouraged the use of a variety of raw materials such as tree bark, hemp, rags, and fishing nets to produce a writing material to replace silk. After its dissemination in China during the first centuries of the Common Era, paper became the dominant material for MS production. Scrolls of paper gradually replaced rolls of silk. The period from Han to Sui witnessed increased circulation of books and the growth of libraries. The introduction of Buddhism to China at about the same time gave added stimulus to these through the promotion of sutra-copying. As the number of translations increased, the Buddhist canon expanded rapidly and demanded countless copies of texts; this is reflected in the hoard of tens of thousands of Buddhist scrolls discovered at Dunhuang, a cave complex in Gansu province, a desert outpost in Chinese central Asia. There, in 1907, while leading a British archaeological expedition from India, Aurel Stein was shown previously sealed caves containing enormous quantities of mostly Buddhist artefacts dating from the 4th to the 10th centuries. Most of the Chinese objects that he acquired entered the *British Museum, including thousands of Buddhist MSS in scroll binding, as well as a small number of books in *codex forms, and some twenty specimens of Tang xylography. A year later, Paul Pelliot arrived at Dunhuang with a French expedition and acquired a smaller quantity of valuable MSS and several examples of printing, now in the BnF. German, Russian, Japanese, and Chinese teams also collected MSS at Dunhuang. Despite limitations of subject-matter and regional provenance, the magnitude of the discovery, and the fact that the MSS and books had been preserved intact for more than eight centuries, profoundly influenced Chinese textual and bibliographical scholarship. The International Dunhuang Project was established in 1994 at the *British Library, where most of the Stein documents are now housed.

In ancient times, textual seals and pictorial seals, cut in relief or *intaglio, were used for identification and authentication. Seals were impressed in soft clay, which was allowed to harden and display its text while sealing a document. Malleable clay was suited to the uneven surface of books made of bamboo and wooden slats. The use of silk as a writing material made it possible to apply *ink to the surface of the seal and stamp it directly on to the silk. The increased use of paper invited innovations such as the use of vermilion ink—made from cinnabar—to replace black ink from soot, or the use of engraved wooden stamps to replace seals cut in metal or stone. Reproducing a brief text or religious votive image by means of an inked stamp impressed on paper is not far removed from transferring text or illustration by pressing paper on to an inked woodblock. Unlike the relief text of seals cut backward in 'mirror' image for stamping, the intaglio text of steles was cut forward and could be read directly. However, at least one stone inscription cut in reverse exists from the first half of the 6th century, implying that it could be treated as a large printing block. The ink-squeeze rubbing method of duplicating the texts of steles, and their assumption of book forms in imitation of MSS, offered further stimulation to the idea of textual printing.

2 Tang to Yuan (7th–14th centuries)

The actual circumstances of the invention of printing in China are not known; however, Tang dynasty (618–907) references to printing and the corpus of undated specimens of printing from Tang tombs all point to an approximate date no later than AD 700. Thanks to datable specimens of printing, such as the *Pure Light Dharani Sutra (*Mugu chŏnggwang tae taranigyŏng*, c.751) from neighbouring Korea and the Empress Shōtoku's printed charms (*Hyakumantō darani*, 764–70) from Japan, printing is known to have spread to both places by the mid-8th century (*see* **41, 42**). Chinese scholars recently have regarded the Pure Light Dharani Sutra as imported into Korea from the Tang capital, Luoyang, but they have not presented satisfactory evidence for this.

There is no doubt that the widespread availability and diverse uses of paper before the 8th century provided the necessary basis for xylographic printing. The corps of artisans skilled at cutting text on seals and steles, as well as workers in decorative architectural wood carving, provided a ready source of labour needed to engrave the wooden blocks for books. The selective inclusion of the names of scribes and block-cutters on the woodblocks used for printing was inherited from the tradition of engraving stone tablets. Among the early single-sheet prints from Dunhuang, a block-cutter is referred to as *jiangren*, a general term for craftsman, together with his personal name.

The names of *patrons and publishers also appeared quite early. The *Jingang jing* (*Diamond Sutra), published in 868 (on the fifteenth day of the fourth month,

i.e. 11 May), is regarded as the world's oldest complete printed book. The dated *colophon by a certain Wang Jie records that he printed the book in honour of his parents. It too was discovered at Dunhuang, and is now in the British Library. In the mid-10th century, large-scale publishing of printed Buddhist texts was sponsored in Hangzhou by Qian Hongchu, fifth prince of the Wu-Yue Kingdom. He published the dharani-sutra text *Baoqieyin tuoluonijing* in 956, 965, and 975, each in a purported edition of 84,000 miniature scrolls. Each version contains a dated colophon before a small *frontispiece woodcut clearly stating his aims. The 956 edition was reprinted in Korea in 1007, which provides further evidence of the early transmission of printed texts from China to Korea (*see* **41**). Around the same time as Qian Hongchu's Buddhist activity in eastern China, two officials in other realms independently completed publication of the Confucian classics. Feng Dao published his canon at the National Academy in Kaifeng in 953, and a little later Wu Zhaoyi published his version in the Shu Kingdom (Sichuan), but specimens of neither exist today. Shortly thereafter, printing of the first Buddhist canon was begun in Sichuan in 971 during the Kaibao reign period (968–75). Called the *Kaibao Tripitaka*, its c.5,000 volumes were in scroll form, and several are still extant. The first *Tripitaka Koreana* of the early 11th century was based on the *Kaibao Tripitaka*, imitating both its printed style and its scroll binding.

Up to the early Northern Song (960–1127), the majority of published books and prints were either religious or official governmental publications. At the same time, there were ephemeral private publications such as dictionaries, *almanacs, and *calendars. Nearly all of the above appeared as unbound single sheets or were bound as scrolls or pleated books. By the mid-11th century there was a new-found growth of secular printing and commercial publishing in China due to the relaxation of government restrictions. Traditional Chinese *bibliography divides publishers into three general categories: *guanke* (official publishing), *sike* or *jiake* (private publishing), and *fangke* (commercial publishing). Although religious publishing might be taken as a type of private publishing, it deserves a category of its own as a significant form of non-governmental institutional publishing.

Buddhist and Daoist books continued to follow the conventions of scroll and of pleated binding; but to serve the new demands of secular publishing, *butterfly binding was conceived, for ease of reading as well as for convenient sales and distribution. In scrolls and pleated books, the right- and left-hand borders of

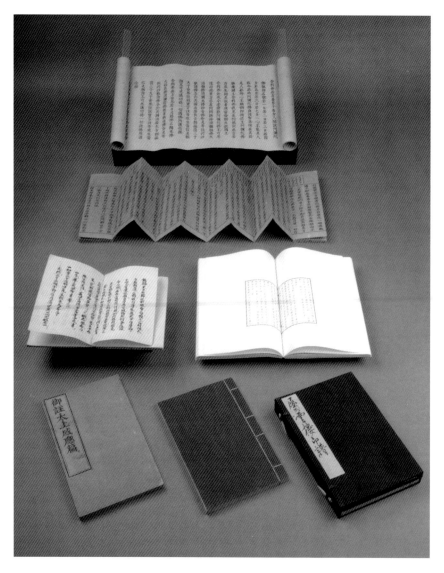

Traditional East Asian book forms. **A** (top): *scroll binding:18ᵗʰ-century printed Buddhist sutra (Japan). **B** (2ⁿᵈ from top): *pleated binding, 17ᵗʰ-century printed Buddhist sutra (Japan). **C** (3ʳᵈ from top left): *butterfly binding: 16ᵗʰ-century Buddhist MS (Japan). **D** (3ʳᵈ from top right): *butterfly binding: contemporary printed book bound in traditional style (China). **E** (bottom left): *wrapped-back binding with original printed title label: 17ᵗʰ-century printed book (China). **F** (bottom centre): *thread binding: 18ᵗʰ-century printed book (China). **G** (bottom right): protective folding case, MS title label: early 20ᵗʰ century (China).

printed sheets were concealed in the course of binding to provide continuous text, but the butterfly binding left all four borders exposed and provided an advanced codex format with conveniently divided units of text. This new format of the Chinese printed book (one leaf to be folded into two pages) that is meant to be bound upright—initially as a butterfly binding, and later as a *wrapped-back binding, or a *thread binding—is always a 'folio' binding in Western terms. Some MS books followed this model from printed sheets, with bordered and lined stationery, but many were written on blank paper without borders or dividing lines.

Tang bibliographies in the official histories—arranged according to the quadripartite classification scheme of *jing* (classics), *shi* (histories), *zi* (philosophers), and *ji* (literature)—contain an immense variety of titles. These and many other works were available to early Song readers and scholars in the form of original and transcribed MSS. In the 11ᵗʰ century, after exposure to limited categories of printed books, and after laws prohibiting the private printing of certain types of book had been rescinded, the concept of printing and distributing multiple copies of all kinds of text took hold. This stimulating environment encouraged the Song polymath Shen Gua to describe in detail the mid-11ᵗʰ-century invention of printing with movable *type made of earthenware. He tells of a commoner named Bi Sheng, who during the Qingli reign (1041–8) made movable type of clay hardened in a kiln. He further explains each step of setting and levelling the type, and finally of printing. It is not known whether this experimental method was used at

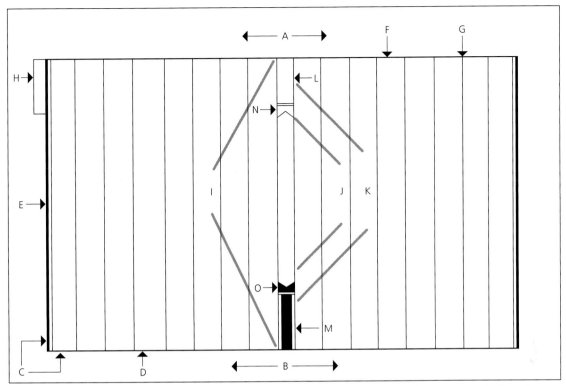

The traditional format of the Chinese printed book (one *leaf to be folded into two pages) that is meant to be bound upright as a *butterfly binding, a *wrapped-back binding, or a *thread binding. Some MS books follow this model, with bordered and lined *stationery, but many are written on blank paper without borders or dividing lines. Books to be bound as *scroll or *pleated bindings share a few of the same elements as the traditional format.

The area of the sheet of paper (one leaf) is called *zhimian* (paper face or surface). The woodblock printed area is called *banmian* (block face or surface). The space above the printed area is called (A) *tiantou* (heavenly head or upper margin). It is also called *shumei* (book eyebrow), and the space below the printed area is called (B) *dijiao* (earthly foot or lower margin).

The border lines (upper, lower, left, right) of the rectangular woodblock are called (C) *bianlan*. A single line is called (D) *danbian* or *danlan*; double lines are called (E) *shuangbian* or *shuanglan*. The columns to accommodate vertical rows of text are called (F) *hang*, and the vertical dividing lines between them are (G) *jie* (boundary lines). The small rectangular box attached to the upper-left or upper-right corner of the woodblock printed area is called (H) *shuer* (book ear), *erge* (ear box), or simply *erzi* (ear).

The column in the centre of the woodblock is called (I) *banxin* (block heart), or *bankou* (block mouth). When the leaf is folded and bound with other leaves as a book, the area is called *shukou* (book mouth). The *banxin* is usually divided into three segments: the middle is called (J) *zhongfeng* (central seam). *Zhongfeng* can also refer to the *shukou*. The upper and lower segments of the *banxin* are called (K) *xiangbi* (elephant trunk). If the space is left blank, it is called (L) *baikou* (white mouth); if it contains a black column of varying width, it is called (M) *heikou* (black mouth). A thin line of black is called *xian heikou* (wire black mouth) or *xi heikou* (fine black mouth); a thick line of black is called *da heikou* (big black mouth) or *cu heikou* (coarse black mouth). Small segments called *yuwei* (fish tails), flat on one side and V-shaped on the other, can appear above the lower *xiangbi* and/or below the upper *xiangbi*. If left blank, they are called (N) *bai yuwei* (white fish tails), and if blank but outlined with double lines, *xian yuwei* (wire fish tails). If they are filled in with black, they are called (O) *hei yuwei* (black fish tails).

the time, but Shen's vivid account has influenced later generations throughout east Asia.

Despite resistance from conservative scholars who feared the wide dissemination of faulty texts by private and commercial publishers, the desire for convenient and cheaper access to texts and the lure of profit from commercial publishing prevailed. Indeed, by all accounts the growth of xylographic printing,

invented 300 years previously, was surprisingly rapid. A level of demand that exceeded the printed output, and the persistence of respected associations attached to MSS, meant that handwritten books continued to coexist with printed books for a long time. Nevertheless, by the end of the century the celebrated statesman and poet Su Shi, among others, commented on the prevalence of printed books in society. However, the Northern

Song's violent demise has resulted in a paucity today of actual examples of secular books that circulated at the end of this dynasty.

Buddhist books from the late Northern Song have survived much better because they often were published in larger quantities, and because two voluminous Tripitaka editions were published in Fujian province in the south of China, where the woodblocks were stored for continual use. The first, called the *Chongning Tripitaka*, was begun at the Dongchansi Temple near Fuzhou around 1080, and the second one, known as the *Pilu Tripitaka*, commenced publication at the Kaiyuansi Temple, also in Fuzhou, about three decades later. When completed, each of these Tripitaka editions contained *c*.6,000 volumes in pleated binding form, and nearly complete sets and many individual volumes are held by major libraries. The names of patrons, block-cutters, and printers appear in most of the volumes, providing valuable material for the study of Song Buddhist books. The *Pilu Tripitaka* was not completely published until the mid-12th century, and the woodblocks for individual titles from both Tripitaka editions continued to be made available as a form of printing on *demand. Unlike these institutional publications, privately published Buddhist books of the Northern Song often have splendid woodcut frontispiece illustrations. The first Daoist canon was published (1113–18) in Fuzhou at the Tianning Wanshou Temple under imperial patronage. Unfortunately, the books and woodblocks were transported to the Northern Song capital, and nothing survived its downfall.

In 1127, when Kaifeng fell to the nomadic Nüzhen, founders of the Jin dynasty (1115–1234), the fleeing Chinese were not able to save many printed books. The printing history of other border states such as the Qidan-Liao (907–1125) and the Tangut-Xia (1038–1227)—as well as of the Tibetans, the Uygurs (Uighurs), and the Mongols, all of whom were interactive contemporary with Song China—needs to be included in any comprehensive understanding of Chinese book culture spanning the period from late Tang to Yuan (1279–1368). Among these peoples there survive unique Chinese texts and editions of books imported to those regions from China proper, but no longer extant in China itself. The influence of Chinese printing technology is apparent; indeed, the Uygurs and the Tangut made early use of movable-type technology. In the cases of the Qidan (Khitan), the Tangut, and the Nüzhen (Jurchen), the influence of Chinese institutions and their need to deal directly with China led all of them to publish Chinese-language

educational and Confucian texts. More importantly, however, they had a great need for Buddhist texts, usually available in Chinese-language translations, and they reprinted many of them. The Liao and Jin editions of the Tripitaka were both based on the *Kaibao Tripitaka* and were published in scroll bindings. Among these three border groups, the Tangut presents an especially interesting case, because its population in the Xi Xia state contained few ethnic Chinese, and because a great number of its printed books exist. Unlike Dunhuang, Xi Xia imprints discovered in 1908–9 by the Russian P. K. Kozlov at Karakhoto greatly outnumber MSS. The books and documents are housed in the Institute of Oriental Studies of the Russian Academy of Sciences, and the works of art and cultural objects are kept in the Hermitage Museum, both in St Petersburg. After the Xi Xia state was established, it quickly created a complex system of script and, for political as well as practical reasons, published a majority of books in its own language.

The style of printing of Chinese script in the border regions depended upon whether the block-cutter was a non-Chinese native or an ethnic Chinese. In the absence of contemporary models to copy, older styles from the Tang appear in books. In addition to the use of non-Chinese languages and scripts in some of the books produced by these border-state peoples, exotic book forms also were employed. The form known in Chinese as *fanjiazhuang* (Sanskrit clamped binding) refers to *pothi* (Indian *palm-leaf MS books) imported to China through Tibet and central Asian territories. Although the horizontal orientation of the palm-leaf books was unsuited to later Chinese books, *fanjiazhuang* was used for Sanskrit and Tibetan books, whose languages were written horizontally, as well as for Mongolian books, which adapted to the form.

After the Southern Song dynasty (1127–1279) established its capital at Hangzhou and gained effective control of all of southern China, it maintained a century-long coexistence with the Jin dynasty in the north. In this relatively peaceful climate, the country prospered and the role of books in society reached new heights. Official publishers at the capital and in the provinces produced editions for the revived political and educational bureaucracies, as well as for the growing number of civil service examination candidates. When their efforts failed to meet demands, commercial publishers eagerly supplied the market with comparable publications. Rong Liulang (12th century) is an example of a commercial publisher who relocated from the former capital of Kaifeng to

Hangzhou. The Southern Song civil service network ensured that locations of official publishing were widespread, and in each of these locations and beyond, private and commercial publishers sprang up. The expanding market for books inspired diversity. Although type design in the conventional sense was not an issue, publishers of high-quality xylographic books were sensitive to the calligraphic style of the text. In addition to models derived from the famous Tang masters, contemporary calligraphers served as scribes for texts to be engraved. Like the *kegong* (block-cutters), the scribes' names often were recorded in the books. A unique characteristic of xylographic printing is the ability to produce accurate *facsimiles of actual handwriting: this was done for prefaces contributed by famous persons. Another characteristic of Song printed books is the use of many varieties of paper, which presumably were produced near places of publication using local raw materials. The regions around Hangzhou in the east, Sichuan in the west, and Fujian in the south were recognized as the three major publishing centres. In addition to the standard classics, histories, and philosophical works produced for the educated classes, popular publications for a wider audience circulated. Literary editions enjoyed a particular vogue. Thanks to informative prefaces and printers' colophons in many Song books, the distribution of places of publication can be clearly understood, and occasionally the particular circumstances of an edition can be established.

Members of the Chen lineage, headed by *Chen Si, published books and ran bookshops in Hangzhou in the Southern Song. Some published the collections of Tang and Song poets with an elegant and distinctive style of printing; their one-line colophons advertised their addresses. An example is the 13th-century edition of the *Tang nülang Yu Xuanji shiji*, the collected poems of the Tang female poet Yu Xuanji, published by the Chen bookshop at the Muqin district in the capital. The last page of text and the one-line colophon are surrounded by more than 40 *ex libris* seal impressions and a couple of collectors' inscriptions. This is a vivid reminder that the proliferation of printed books in the Southern Song stimulated private book-collecting, and that later generations of Ming and Qing book-collectors prized Song editions above all else.

The 1173 edition of *Huaihai ji*, the collected writings of Qin Guan, was published at the local academy of Gaoyoujun in Yangzhou. After the preface, the itemized costs (i.e. sale price) for bound volumes is calculated in great detail:

The Gaoyoujunxue edition of *Huaihai wenji* [i.e. *Huaihai ji*] accounts for 449 woodblocks [i.e. woodblock surfaces, since blocks usually were cut on both sides], which together with blank leaves and endpapers uses altogether 500 sheets of paper. *Sansheng* paper at 20 cash per sheet is 10 strings of cash; *xinguan* paper at 10 cash per sheet is 5 strings of cash; *zhuxia* paper at 5 cash per sheet is 2 strings and 500 cash; ink at 1 cash per woodblock is 500 cash; the binding of 10 volumes with dark blue paper at 70 cash per volume is 700 cash; and the fee for labour and materials is 500 cash. (Nihon Shoshi Gakkai, pl. 38)

The currency cited is the familiar Chinese round coin with a central square hole, commonly called 'cash'. A thousand coins can be strung together as a 'string of cash'. The names of the block-cutters responsible are engraved throughout the book.

Under the great Khubilai Khan, the Mongol-Yuan dynasty was exceptional in thoroughness of its conquest of China; nevertheless, it can be said to have inherited the Song Chinese publishing tradition and other institutions intact. Official government publications were issued from the new capital, Dadu (Beijing), and official editions, as well as many Buddhist books, were printed from existing Song woodblocks in the former Song capital, Hangzhou. Private publishers and academies throughout the empire were also very active. The improvement of transportation networks and the growth of commercial publishing—particularly in Fujian province—resulted in the increased use of cheap bamboo paper, which came to characterize inferior popular printing in later periods. The publishers of Jianyang in northern Fujian developed now familiar *formats such as *shangtu xiawen* (picture above, text below), in which continuous woodcut illustration ran across the top of the pages, with text placed underneath. They also produced many medical books, popular *encyclopaedias, and works of fiction and drama. The travels of Marco Polo included the first decade of the Yuan dynasty, and his book was among the earliest to report on China to the West. Strangely, however, despite his visits to the publishing centres of Hangzhou and Fujian, he failed to mention the existence of printed books in China long before their appearance in Europe.

In the realm of books, one of the outstanding achievements of the Yuan period was the earliest use of two-*colour printing. The Buddhist text of the Diamond Sutra with commentary, published in 1341 at the Zifusi Buddhist Temple in Huguang (Hubei province), has a main text of large characters printed in red with a commentary of smaller characters printed in black. The work also contains a two-colour woodcut which demonstrates good registration (*see* REGISTER (2)). This magnificent publication was produced more than 250 years before the wave of two-colour printing in the late Ming.

Influenced by Bi Sheng's invention, at the end of the 13th century a Yuan man named Wang Zhen carved more than 60,000 pieces of *wood type for printing projects in Anhui province. His detailed description of the type and his method for printing are all that survive: when he published his major work, the *Nongshu* (Book of Agriculture), in 1313, he used xylography. This choice suggests the difficulty private or commercial enterprises had in using native typography successfully to print texts in a language with many thousands of different characters. The Qing court in the 18th century, without regard for cost, produced two *founts (one bronze, the other wood), each of around 250,000 types, to execute its projects. From the end of the 15th century in China, movable-type printing was carried out on a small scale, but it never successfully challenged xylography as a viable method of printing. The principal investment of the traditional Chinese publisher was in suitable wood to be prepared as printing blocks, the commission of the calligraphic transcription of the text on to thin paper to serve as the pattern for engraving, and the necessary labour to cut the blocks. The printing of a small number of copies, *collating, and providing a temporary binding for the volumes, was often performed by the block-cutter. A small outlay for paper and ink for the initial printing was also required. As far as is known, an average initial printing was between 50 and 200 copies, and each subsequent printing may have numbered no more than that. Nevertheless, total print runs were often numbered in the thousands. In the case of certain popular books and religious publications, individual printings of 1,000 or more are not unknown. The cost of paper, ink, and labour would become an extended expense over the blocks' life. This differs from the Western publisher's need to produce the entire edition at once.

3 Ming to Qing (14th–19th centuries)

In 1368, Zhu Yuanzhang declared himself emperor of the Ming dynasty (1368–1644), and China again reverted to native Chinese rule. The Ming capital was established at Nanjing in the south, but the Yongle emperor moved the capital to Beijing in 1420. The first decades of the new regime were rather unsettled, and private and commercial publishing fell into decline. The organs of official publishing were active,

however, and the *Silijian (Directorate of Ceremonial) took a leading role. Throughout the 15th century, the palace published lavish editions of standard works in large formats. The regional academies published the classics and educational works, and the network of princedoms set up in the early years of the Ming produced more than 500 titles. As the economy improved in the 15th century, the number of booksellers and publishers increased, and more illustrated popular literature and religious tracts, especially in the *shangtu xiawen* format, began to appear.

Imperially sponsored projects in the early Ming were conceived on a grand scale. Three Buddhist Tripitaka editions and a Daoist canon were published in the first 75 years of the dynasty. In 1403 the Yongle emperor initiated his most famous enterprise, the *Yongle dadian*. It was a huge MS compilation ordered as a classified encyclopaedia of extant knowledge, based on citations culled from 8,000 works. It was arranged in 22,877 *juan* (the chapter-like division of traditional books) and bound in more than 11,095 *folio-size volumes. Nearly 3,000 scholars and scribes worked full-time to complete the compilation in five years. Printing a work of this size was out of the question, so the encyclopaedia had to be consulted in the imperial library. After centuries of attrition and misfortune, less than 10 per cent of the original exists today. The largest parts are held by the National Library of *China, the Library of *Congress, the *Tōyō Bunko, and the British Library.

By the Jiajing period (1522–66), a significant change had taken place and book-collectors, as well as private and commercial publishers, were laying a foundation for the flourishing of publishing that would occur toward the end of the Ming period. The oldest surviving private library in China was founded in Ningbo in 1561 by Fan Qin, a retired official. The library is called *Tianyige, and in time it came to symbolize the ideal private library. The Jiajing era also witnessed increased official publishing, including the activities of the Southern Academy in Nanjing. Jianyang commercial publishers increased their output, and private publishers in the Jiangnan area of central China began producing editions of the highest quality, especially facsimiles based on Song and Yuan editions. Superior editions of the Jiajing period have always been in great demand. The modern Nanjing book-collector Deng Bangshu went so far as to collect 100 Jiajing editions and provide them with a room of their own in his library. He designated the room as Baijingzhai (studio of 100 Jiajing editions), and ordered a special *ex libris* seal to be stamped in each of them.

Beginning in the Wanli reign (1573–1620), improved economic and social conditions, and increased numbers of candidates sitting imperial examinations, led to an unprecedented offering of books that reached readers across a broad spectrum. Two examples embody this 16th-century trend. First, the *Xuanhe bogu tulu*, a magnificent illustrated catalogue of the Northern Song imperial collection of bronze vessels, was published in the 14th century; in the Jiajing period, a full-size facsimile edition appeared in 1528. In the Wanli period no fewer than five new editions, all illustrated, were published in 1588, 1596, 1599, 1600, and 1603. Secondly, the collected works, entitled *Cangming ji*, of Li Panlong, an official and writer whose poems and essays were greatly admired after his death in 1570, were published in at least ten different editions between 1572 and the early 17th century. A collection of his poetry, published earlier, had at least four editions. Copies of *Cangming ji* also circulated in Korea and Japan, where selections were published.

The period also witnessed the introduction and spread of two important developments in Ming printing: books illustrated with woodcuts and books printed in colour. Suddenly, all China's major works of fiction and drama were available in illustrated editions, and even picture books with minimal text appeared. Polychrome printed books fell into two categories: pictorial and textual. The total colours used on a page or leaf ranged from two to five or six, including black (ink) as one of them. Polychrome textual printing seems to have been limited to the *taoban yinfa* (multi-block) technique, although the 14th-century Diamond Sutra, already described, used the more primitive *shuangyinfa* (double-impression) technique. From around 1615, two lineages (Min and Ling) in Wuxing (Huzhou) published most of these books, in which the main text was printed in black, and punctuation and facsimiles of handwritten annotations and other text appeared in red, blue, and occasionally in one or two additional colours. Fine white paper was used, and these books were undeniably elegant. Polychrome pictorial prints consisted of prints that attempted to imitate the appearance of colourful hand-painted pictures with little or no outlining, as well as narrative pictures with outlined figures containing colours.

A sub-genre of two-colour textual printing is the *yinpu* (seal book), which began to be published in the early Wanli period. Seal books contain collections of seal impressions printed in red, either impressed from actual seals using cinnabar paste or printed in red xylographically, accompanied by seal texts and minimal explanations printed in black. Such books containing the seals of one person or family may be compared with Western books of *heraldry. Collections of ancient seal inscriptions suited the growth of epigraphical studies in the Qing. All editions with actual seal impressions were extremely limited.

The best-known of the pictorial books is the *Shizhuzhai shuhuapu* (Ten Bamboo Studio Manual of Calligraphy and Painting), published by *Hu Zhengyan from 1633 to 1644, although work may have begun earlier. It took more than a decade to complete and employed the refined *douban yinfa* (assembled-block) technique. His *Shizhuzhai jianpu* (Ten Bamboo Studio Collection of Letter Paper) of 1644 moreover used the *gonghuafa* (blind-printing) technique that produced exquisite small units of embossed surface. Other examples of pictorial colour printing are exceedingly rare; arguably the finest instance—the unique illustrations for the Yuan drama *Xixiang ji* (Tale of the West Chamber) in the Museum für Ostasiatische Kunst, Cologne—was published in 1640 by *Min Qiji, the doyen of the Min printers in Wuxing. The recent rediscovery of the Shibui collection of late Ming polychrome editions of erotic picture books will require a reassessment of early colour printing and of the role of *pornography in late Ming society—a role which previously was limited to critical accounts of published pornographic fiction.

The renowned Italian Jesuit missionary Matteo Ricci was involved with the earliest polychrome printing of the *Cheng shi moyuan*, a compilation of decorative designs for Chinese moulded ink sticks, published in 1606. The work contains essays and encomiums, including one by Ricci accompanied by his original phonetic transcription—the first published attempt to romanize Chinese. It is likely that Ricci had met the compiler, Cheng Dayue, in Nanjing, and given him original engravings that were copied into *Cheng shi moyuan* as woodcut facsimiles—the first examples of Western graphics to appear in a Chinese publication. Three images were from *Evangelicae Historiae Imagines* by the Jesuit Gerónimo Nadal, and the fourth was an image of the Madonna and Child produced in Japan in 1597 after a Spanish prototype. In a small number of copies of *Cheng shi moyuan*, Cheng Dayue experimented with the *duoyinfa* (multiple-impression) technique to produce polychrome woodcuts; however, the Western ones from Ricci were printed in black only. Beginning with Ricci, a succession of talented Jesuits in China published books in Chinese until their presence was banned in 1724 (*see* **9**). These books included works on theology, geography, history, science, and mathematics. Works such as *Zhifang waiji*, a geography of the world with six folding maps, compiled and translated into Chinese by Giulio Aleni and others and published in Hangzhou in 1623, had a profound effect on the Chinese intellectual class. This publication was the first of its kind in Chinese, and was intended to explain some of the new concepts of cartography and geography introduced by Ricci a couple of decades earlier.

Publishing in the last four decades of the Ming became frenetic. Besides new editions of the classics and standard titles, often hastily edited in the rush to market, dictionaries, primers, *textbooks, *anthologies, practical handbooks, medical texts, travel *guidebooks, artisan *pattern books, *novels, and *plays circulated. Unauthorized editions, *plagiarized prefaces, and *pirated contents were not uncommon. The growth of titles and subject-matter in this competitive commercial environment encouraged new forms of *advertising. Most commercial editions included a separate leaf called *fengmianye* (cover page), folded and printed on one side and attached to the uppermost bound volume of a work. It resembled a Western *title-page, and likewise seems to have evolved from the printer's colophon. These cover pages—used since the late 13th century, following the introduction of the wrapped-back binding, but especially popular at the end of the Ming—commonly included the title, author's name, publisher's name, and occasionally a date and a brief statement about the book and its contents. The cover page was fundamentally a commercial advertisement with appended statements by the publisher, and many were bound into the books, preserving their valuable data. The cover page sometimes contained a hand-stamped price or a distinctive seal impression meant as a trademark, and it was common to print pseudo-*copyright statements such as *fanke bijiu* ('unauthorized reprints will be investigated'), which were utterly ineffectual. However, it all ended unceremoniously for the most speculative publishers in 1644, when Li Zicheng entered Beijing and the Manchus began their conquest of the entire country.

The first years of the Qing dynasty (1644–1911) included aggressive efforts to stabilize the country: official publishing consisted mostly of moralistic tracts emphasizing the new Manchu rulers' commitment to traditional Confucian values. Scholarly publishers such as *Mao Jin continued into the Qing, private publishers cautiously carried out their projects, and commercial publishers tried to survive without the

flamboyance they had become used to. As Chinese scholars recovered, they looked inward to try to understand the sources of this transformation of power. At the same time, the Manchu ruling class, recognized for its grasp of military matters (*wu*), was eager to demonstrate its support for civil affairs (*wen*) through promotion of literate culture. During the Kangxi emperor's reign (1662–1722), ambitious scholarly publications were initiated, and the *Wuyingdian hall within the Forbidden City was established as the central office for palace publications.

The Kangxi emperor took particular pride in publication of the *Quan Tang Shi* (Complete Poetry of the Tang Dynasty) in 900 *juan* in 1707, which he had commissioned through Cao Yin, head of the salt monopoly at Yangzhou. Over the next decade the palace published two new, classified encyclopaedias plus the eponymous *Kangxi zidian* (Kangxi Dictionary) in 40 volumes. The emperor also ordered the missionary Matteo Ripa to produce the first copperplate prints in China. Completed in 1713 and based on a suite of woodcuts published by the Wuyingdian, 'Thirty-six Views of the Jehol Imperial Gardens' appears to have used both *etching and *engraving. The greatest enterprise sponsored by the emperor, however, was not completed until four years after his death in 1726. The *Qinding Gujin tushu jicheng* is an enormous classified encyclopaedia of 10,000 *juan*, bound in 5,000 volumes. It is the largest printed book of its kind produced in China; only the MS *Yongle dadian* is bigger. What is most remarkable is that the work was printed from a fount of 250,000 bronze types and is profusely illustrated with woodcut illustrations. Whether these types were cut by hand or cast at the Wuyingdian is still debated. During the emperor's lifetime, the palace also published his collected writings and a large illustrated work commemorating his 60th birthday celebrations in Beijing in 1713.

Later in the 18th century, the Qianlong emperor (r. 1736–95) continued this form of imperial patronage and published even more works, including the *Shisanjing zhushu* (Thirteen Classics) from 1739 to 1747 in 115 volumes and the *Ershisi shi* (Twenty-four Dynastic Histories) from 1739 to 1784 in 722 volumes. The MS compilation called *Siku quanshu* (Complete Library of the Four Treasuries) was unquestionably his greatest achievement. Thousands of works from all over the country were sent to an editorial committee in Beijing for consideration. The emperor's aim was not merely to preserve important extant texts by copying; he wanted to exercise the power of *censorship through the committee's review, and lists of proscribed books were issued. The Manchus feared sedition among the majority Chinese population, and they opposed moral turpitude of the sort that was perceived to have led to the fall of the Ming. Names of authors considered critical of Manchu rule were to be deleted from books, and their books and woodblocks were to be burned (*see* BOOK BURNING). In the end, 3,461 titles were selected for inclusion in the *Siku quanshu*, and 6,793 were merely reviewed. Editing and transcription took place between 1773 and 1782. Seven identical MS sets of *c*.36,000 volumes each were produced between 1782 and 1787. The complete bibliographical descriptions for these 10,254 titles were published by the Wuyingdian as the *Qinding siku quanshu zongmu* (Imperially Authorized Annotated Catalogue of the Complete Library of the Four Treasuries), which is still one of the most important Chinese descriptive bibliographies. Another by-product of these activities was the printing of 134 significant titles from the *Siku quanshu*. In 1773 the superintendent of the Wuyingdian, Jin Jian, was appointed to undertake the project. In a persuasive proposal to the throne, which was followed by publication of an illustrated handbook describing the process, Jin recommended that the entire collection, to be named the *Wuyingdian juzhenbanshu*, be printed from wooden types. After the emperor's approval, 253,500 types had to be cut by hand, and the printing of all 134 titles, numbering over 800 volumes, lasted from 1774 to 1794.

The Qianlong emperor's expansion of the palace rare book collections coincided with great interest in book-collecting in society at large. Encouraged by the palace publication projects, many of whose titles were reprinted in the provinces, and buoyed by the improved economy, an upsurge of private and commercial publishing took place in the 18th century, despite threats of censorship emanating from the Qing court. Civil service officials posted throughout the empire were very active, printing local histories and a variety of scholarly works. The Qing period was also noteworthy for the widespread publication of genealogies using native typography. Early in the 19th century, scholars and book-collectors, inspired by the likes of *Huang Pilie and Gu Guangqi, produced numerous bibliographical works and published facsimile reprints of Song and Yuan editions.

The 19th century witnessed the beginning of the end of the dominance of xylography in the history of book and print culture in China. Nevertheless, certain events conspired to prolong that demise. In the West, the year 1800 is a convenient (if approximate) date to divide the era of hand printing from the age of machine printing; in China, the corresponding dividing line would be nearly a century later.

By the end of the 1830s, high-quality private publishing began to decline, probably owing to economic downturns and the foreign incursions leading up to the Opium Wars, and followed by the Taiping Rebellion. The Taiping armies left a swathe of destruction across central and southern China in the 1850s. Book collections were destroyed and book production was interrupted for more than a decade. In the wake of the disaster, voluminous reprint collections of new xylographic editions of standard texts were commissioned to replace the losses. A new demand for printed matter came from Protestant missionaries, and although they promoted letterpress printing, they also turned to xylography as a practical and economic means of producing some of their texts. It was not until the end of the 19th century that alternative technologies such as *lithography and Western-style movable-type printing began to compete successfully with xylography. As the dynasty declined, their use increased, including reprints of the huge reference work *Qinding Gujin tushu jicheng*. The *Shenbaoguan in Shanghai printed a small-format edition with lead type (1884–8), and an official agency, the Zongli Yamen, published a full-size lithographic reprint, printed by *Tongwen Shuju (1895–8). These two reprints were in thread binding, but at the turn of the century Western-style bindings began to appear and would soon become the norm. The century, and before long the dynasty, ended amid an outpouring of publications, new in form and content. Journalism, especially pictorial journals and serial fiction, attracted a wide audience. New publishers using lithography and Western-style movable type sprang up everywhere, but especially in Shanghai.

4 The 20th century

The future course of books and publishing in 20th-century China was set in 1897 with the founding of *Shangwu Yinshuguan (Commercial Press) in Shanghai. After the abolition of the imperial examinations in 1905, traditionally educated scholars such as Zhang Yuanji (1867–1959) encouraged the publishing of new Western-style textbooks, from which the Commercial Press first gained its reputation. The *Zhonghua Shuju, founded in Shanghai in 1912, would become its leading competitor. The first decade of the 20th century also saw the birth of modern libraries in China. Academic and public libraries such as the

*Peking University Library, the *Nanjing Library, and the National Library of China were founded then. The New Library Movement was linked to educational reform and was inspired by the American model. By 1925 the Library Association of China was established, with the reformer Liang Qichao as chairman and *Yuan Tung-li as secretary. In 1927 the new organization became a founding member of the *International Federation of Library Associations.

Increased political activities after the republican revolution of 1911 greatly stimulated the periodical press. *Qingnian zazhi* (Youth Magazine), also titled *La Jeunesse*, was established by Chen Duxiu in 1915 in Shanghai, where it was published by Qunyi Shushe with support from *Yadong Tushuguan. In 1916 the title was changed to *Xin qingnian* (New Youth). The New Culture Movement that followed spawned countless books and periodicals. For the first half of the 20th century, revolution, foreign invasion, and civil war precluded publishing's peaceful development. Publishers changed names and locations, property was destroyed, and writers used many *pseudonyms under threats of censorship and imprisonment. Yet the book survived and flourished.

After 1949, the new Communist government merged and nationalized the publishing industry and book trade. Most of these activities were organized by the distributor *Xinhua Shudian. In the 1950s, important publishing projects benefited from government subsidies and from a large pool of talented writers and editors. At the same time, major publishing houses such as Shangwu Yinshuguan and Zhonghua Shuju, as well as the Nationalist government publisher *Zhengzhong Shuju, were replicated and set up in exile in Taiwan by former managers and editors who had fled the mainland. During the Cultural Revolution (1966–76) publishing and bookselling in China came to a standstill; but since then they have re-emerged very strongly, and the antiquarian book trade has been aided by a vibrant *book auction market. Since 1949, woodblock printing has been extolled as an important Chinese invention and national cultural asset. This historical turn has resulted in the preservation of existing collections of woodblocks and the maintenance of skills such as papermaking, calligraphic transcription, block-cutting, hand printing, and traditional binding.

Like other countries, China has been profoundly affected by the digital revolution. The automation of data brought about by the introduction of computers was first applied to cataloguing and indexing books— catalogues of individual libraries developed into

The inaugural issue of *Qingnian zazhi* (Youth Magazine) or *La Jeunesse* (September 1915).

electronic databases. The *digitization of texts in China has grown exponentially in recent years without reducing the growth of new print publications, and the natural division between modern books and ancient texts has not disappeared. The digitization of new books, of course, is merely a new form of publication, and the digitization of current publications is fraught with legal issues of copyright. On the other hand, the digitization of ancient books and MSS not only provides access to their texts but is closely related to issues of preservation. The future of Chinese digital books and virtual libraries is as unpredictable as the technology that underlies them.

BIBLIOGRAPHY

C. Brokaw, *Commerce in Culture* (2007)

— and K. Chow, eds., *Printing and Book Culture in Late Imperial China* (2005)

T. Carter, *The Invention of Printing in China and Its Spread Westward* (1925; rev. edn. 1955)

L. Chia, *Printing for Profit* (2002)

K. Chow, *Publishing, Culture, and Power in Early Modern China* (2004)

J.-P. Drège, *Les Bibliothèques en Chine au temps des manuscrits* (1991)

J. S. Edgren, 'The *fengmianye* (Cover Page) as a Source for Chinese Publishing History', in *Studies of Publishing Culture in East Asia*, ed. A. Isobe (2004)

M. Heijdra, 'Technology, Culture and Economics: Movable Type Versus Woodblock Printing in East Asia', in *Studies of Publishing Culture in East Asia*, ed. A. Isobe (2004)

P. Hu, *Visible Traces* (2000)

International Dunhuang Project, www.idp.bl.uk, consulted Dec. 2007

J. McDermott, *A Social History of the Chinese Book* (2006)

[Nihon Shoshi Gakkai (Japan Bibliographical Society),] *Naikaku Bunko sôhon shoei* (Illustrations of Song Editions in the Naikaku Bunko Library) (1984)

C. Reed, *Gutenberg in Shanghai: Chinese Print Capitalism, 1876–1937* (2004)

T. H. Tsien, *Paper and Printing* (1985)

— *Written on Bamboo and Silk*, 2e (2004)

K. T. Wu, 'Ming Printing and Printers', *Harvard Journal of Asiatic Studies*, 7 (1943), 203–60

— 'Chinese Printing Under Four Alien Dynasties', *Harvard Journal of Asiatic Studies*, 13 (1950), 447–523

41 The History of the Book in Korea

BETH MCKILLOP

1 Three Kingdoms (*c*.57 BC–AD 668, United Silla 668–935)
2 Koryŏ (918–1392)
3 Chosŏn (1392–1910)
4 Modern (1910–)

1 Three Kingdoms (*c*.57 BC–AD 668, United Silla 668–935)

In Korea and throughout East Asia, engraved *inta-glio seals and texts cut on stone steles were precursors of printing as a widespread technology. In neighbouring China, the fixing of classic texts as engraved stone slabs in AD 175 is an important landmark. Early political groupings on the Korean peninsula also recorded texts on stone and later took black-and-white *ink-squeeze rubbings on *paper from such engraved slabs. Intensive contact with China had led to the spread of Chinese *script and knowledge of the Chinese language in Korea by about the 1st century AD. Chinese characters, which have both a semantic and a phonetic element, were used to write Korean words by following their sounds. Educated Koreans also learned to read and write in Chinese. From about the 6th to the 15th centuries, this complex and confusing system of borrowing Chinese script was the only one used to record the Korean language.

The earliest surviving writings using the native transcription system are poems. Texts from the Three Kingdoms period that survive as physical objects include a massive memorial slab—more than seven metres high and engraved with 18,000 seal-script Chinese characters, praising King Kwanggaet'o (who ruled the northern Kingdom of Koguryŏ, AD 391–413)—and an engraved stele (AD 503) from Yŏngil, North Kyŏngsang Province. It is a slab of granite, polished for engraving on three sides; bearing 231 characters of various sizes, in an archaic style, it records the judgement of a dispute about land ownership. The preservation of written words for posterity has been an enduring preoccupation on the Korean peninsula.

Papermaking had probably reached Korea from China early in the Three Kingdoms period, transmitted through the Chinese commandery at Lelang, which ruled the northwest of the peninsula in 108 BC–AD 313. The spread of the Buddhist faith eastwards into Korea in the 4th to 6th centuries brought the need to provide copies of holy writings, required by monks and believers for their devotions and studies. Sponsors supported hand-copying and, later, printing of scriptures; the names of such benefactors are sometimes recorded in *colophons or other notes to the texts. During the Three Kingdoms, United Silla, and Koryŏ (918–1392) periods, all such copies were in Chinese characters, since classical Chinese was accepted as the written language of palace, court, and temple. Finely produced temple copies of such texts as the *Diamond and Lotus Sutras, stamped images of the Buddha, and copies of incantations and chants were certainly produced in great numbers, although few have survived from before the Koryŏ.

The printed text of the *Mugu chŏnggwang tae taranigyŏng*, (*Pure Light Dharani Sutra), a kind of Buddhist incantation, was discovered in October 1966 in the second storey of the Sŏkkat'ap (Sakyamuni Pagoda) at Pulguksa (Pulguk Temple), Kyŏngju. This text was translated into Chinese in 704, and the temple built in 751; thus, the Dharani was printed and then enclosed inside the pagoda, probably to mark the temple's consecration. This small paper *scroll, measuring 6.5 × 648 cm, was found in a container for Buddhist relics. Its measurements are approximate, since the early sections are in a poor state of conservation. Each of its twelve *sheets of paper contains between 55 and 63 columns of characters; each column has seven to nine characters, measuring 4–5 mm. It was printed on thin mulberry (Korean *tak*) paper from engraved wooden blocks. On the basis of analysis of the graphic style of the characters and the vegetable material used for the paper (*broussonetia kazinoki*), it seems that the Silla kingdom was its probable place of production. The text uses Empress Wu characters, special graphic forms for a small number of terms created in China during her rule (684–705). Given the extent of cultural exchange between Tang China and Silla, it is entirely credible that a text originally cut on to blocks and printed in China could have been re-cut and printed in Korea, to be buried as part of a group of protective holy relics during the consecration of Pulguk Temple.

Another example of the highly developed nature of textual transmission in the Silla period is a fine scroll MS of chapters 1–10 of the Avatamsaka Sutra in the Ho-Am Museum (National Treasure 196 of the Republic of Korea). This document was copied in 754–5 at the behest of High Priest Yŏn'gi Pŏpsa of Hwangnyong Temple, Kyŏngju. The colophon records the date of production, as well as the names and ranks of the nineteen workers who made the copy. They include the sutra copyists, the painter of the cover papers, and the papermakers. The text, in regular sutra-script, is enclosed in a cover of purple-dyed mulberry paper, on which two Bodhisattvas seated in front of a storied, tiled-roof building have been painted in gold. Measuring 14 metres long and 26 cm high, with 34 characters per column, the scroll is composed of 43 sheets of sheer white paper and is rolled around a 24-cm wooden spindle with crystal knobs on both ends.

2 Koryŏ (918–1392)

*Woodblock printing of Buddhist texts grew in volume and extent throughout the period of Koryŏ rule, a time of intense devotion to the Buddhist faith. The Korean printing historian Sohn Pow-Key has estimated that more than 300,000 woodblocks for the texts of Buddhist scriptures were cut. The act of sponsoring sutra-copying was believed to gain spiritual merit for the believer.

Pre-eminent among the printing enterprises of the period were the two sets of woodblocks engraved to print the entire known corpus of Buddhist scriptures, the Tripitaka. In both instances, the enterprise was motivated as much by a desire to secure divine protection for the nation against the succession of continental invaders who attacked it—the Khitan in the 11th century, the Jurchen (founders of the Jin dynasty in China) in the 12th century, and the Mongols in the 13th century—as by a pious concern to preserve and record its sacred sermons, Buddhist rules, and treatises. Mindful of the need for divine protection, the court commissioned artisans to select and prepare wood, to copy the carefully chosen and checked texts, to cut the transferred texts in *relief on both sides of the blocks, and then to print, using charcoal-based *inks, on to locally produced paper.

The Tripitaka was first cut in Korea for printing in its entirety, over a long period between 1011 and 1087; however, the blocks were lost, destroyed by fire during the Mongol invasions of the early 13th century. About 300 printed Tripitaka scrolls (out of some 11,000) survive in the Buddhist temple Nanzenji, Kyoto. Volume 78 of the Avatamsaka Sutra from the same Tripitaka is in the Ho-Am Art Museum (National Treasure 267 of the Republic of Korea). The monk Ŭich'ŏn (1055–1101), fourth son of King Munjong, had travelled to China and collected thousands of Buddhist texts to bring to his native country. He devoted many years to cataloguing the teachings of the different Buddhist schools, and compiled the *Sok changgyŏng* (Supplement to the Canon).

Immediately after the first Korean Tripitaka was lost, the enterprise of cutting a new Tripitaka was undertaken. This re-cut Tripitaka was a project of the highest importance for king and country, the work lasting from 1236 to 1251. The exact number of blocks, made of seasoned woods, has been estimated differently by various scholars. Currently, 81,155 blocks survive: eighteen of the original blocks were lost, 296 were added in the Chosŏn period (1392–1910), and twelve were added during the Japanese occupation (1910–45). The number of blocks has given the name 'P'almangyŏng' (Tripitaka of 80,000) to the 13th-century Tripitaka. The blocks measure 72.6 × 26.4 × 3 cm and are engraved on both sides. The print area, delineated by single-line *borders, is 24.5 cm high, and each block has 23 columns of fourteen 27-mm-high characters. The graphic style of the characters is uniform throughout the entire corpus. Each block carries the name of the sutra, the *chapter and the *folio number. The blocks have been lacquered, and metal reinforcing strips have been applied to the corners to prevent warping. On completion of cutting in 1251, the blocks were used for printing at Namhae, South Kyŏngsang province, and subsequently moved north for storage to a repository on Kanghwa Island.

At the time of the second cutting of the Tripitaka blocks, between 1236 and 1251, the Koryŏ court had fled from the invading Mongols, to take refuge on Kanghwa Island. By the late 14th century, however, even Kanghwa Island was no longer secure against hostile forces. Pirate attacks endangered the security of the scriptures, and there was military unrest throughout the country. This led to the choice of the distant southern mountain fastness of the *Haeinsa Buddhist temple as a safe storage location for the precious double-sided printing blocks, which were moved there in 1398. In 1488, decades after the blocks had arrived at Haeinsa, a set of four special buildings was repaired and adapted to protect the blocks. Located higher than the rest of the temple complex, these structures are rectangular wooden-pillared, hipped-roof buildings, set on granite stones, and arranged in a courtyard formation. Rows of slatted windows punctuate the walls, providing natural ventilation and minimizing the spread of damp. The earthen floors of the stores lie on a layer of charcoal, regulating humidity and temperature, and exposed rafters encourage air circulation. The woodblocks are arranged on five-storey shelf structures. Rare survivals of the wooden architecture of the early Chosŏn dynasty, the repositories have proved a well-ventilated and damp-proof environment to safeguard the precious blocks. Between 1967 and 1976, a set of *impressions of the Korean Tripitaka was made from these blocks and distributed to libraries and universities in Korea and around the world.

Looking more broadly at book production in Koryŏ, it is notable that scholars and officials paid increasing attention to the teachings of the Chinese philosopher Confucius, and thus required copies of definitive versions of Confucian texts and *commentaries by later Chinese scholars. Obtaining books from China was often difficult, because of war or because the Chinese authorities were suspicious of Korea's reasons for seeking copies of Chinese books. Indeed, the Song poet Su Dongpo (1036–1101) wrote several times against the sending of books to Koryŏ. The Korean court was often frustrated in attempts to obtain the goods it needed from China. Gifts of books were sent only with imperial consent, which could not be relied upon. Despite these difficulties, Korean book collecting was so persistent that on three or four occasions during the 10th and 11th centuries, Koryŏ sent back Chinese books that had been lost in Song China and were required there. The Chinese envoy Xu Jing, who visited Korea in 1123, noted in his account of the visit, *Xuanhe fengshi Gaoli tujing* (Illustrated Account of the Xuanhe Emperor's Envoy to Korea), that the 'Royal Library by the riverside stores tens of thousands of books' (Sohn, 'Early Korean Printing', 98).

During the 13th century, experiments with movable *type produced works that have since been lost, but are remembered because of the practice of recording printing information in colophons. From this period, three pieces of evidence survive for the use of movable metal type. One is a collection of Buddhist sermons entitled *Nanmyŏng ch'ŏn hwasang song chŭngdoga*, printed on Kanghwa Island in 1239 using blocks cut from a text originally printed using cast movable types. The colophon states:

> It is impossible to advance to the core of Buddhism without having understood this book. Is it possible for this book to go out of print? Therefore we employ workmen to re-cut the cast-type edition to continue its circulation. Postface written with reverence by Ch'oe I [d. 1249] in the 9th moon [of 1239].

The second piece of evidence for 13th-century movable-type printing is a collection of ritual texts, *Sangjong yemun*, which were reprinted c.1234 during the Kanghwa Island period, using metal types, to replace an original lost during the flight from Kaesŏng. The colophon clearly states, 'here we have now printed 28 copies of the book with the use of movable metal types, to distribute among the various government offices'; it then expresses the hope that officials will not lose it. The third piece of evidence is a number of excavated individual types from the Koryŏ era, now in Korean museum collections. These types have a metallic composition similar to that of Koryŏ coins. An example is the 1 cm-high character for 'return' (*pok*), now in the National Museum of Korea. Scholars believe that the disruptions of the mid-Koryŏ, when the court moved from Kaesŏng to Kanghwa, stimulated the use of metal types, in order to produce small *editions of essential works destroyed during the Mongol invasions. Clearly, Koryŏ printers made significant use of movable type in the mid-13th century.

No dated work printed with movable types survives from the 13th century. For the 14th century, however there is an extant work—the world's earliest—printed by means of metal movable types. *Paegun hwasang ch'orok pulcho Chikchi simch'e yojŏl* (Essentials of Buddha's Teachings Recorded by the Monk Paegun) is a collection of Buddhist biographical and historical excerpts by the Sŏn (Zen) Buddhist master Kyŏnghan (1298–1374), better recognized by his pen name of Paegun. Also known as *Chikchi simch'e yojŏl*, it consisted of two volumes: the lost first volume comprised hymns and poems, and teachings of Buddhist masters; the incomplete second volume is held by the *Bibliothèque nationale de France. The surviving volume bears a colophon dating it to the seventh moon of 1377; it notes that the place of production where

The world's earliest dated printing using movable type, *Paegun hwasang ch'orok pulcho Chikchi simch'e yojŏl* (Essentials of Buddha's Teachings Recorded by the Monk Paegun), printed at Hŭngdŏksa (Ch'ŏngju) in 1377.

movable type was used was Hŭngdŏksa, a temple in Ch'ŏngju. The *verso of the colophon sheet records the names of two Buddhist believers in charge of printing, Sŏkchan and Taldam, as well as a sponsor, the nun Myodŏk. The volume contains 38 sheets, with a print area of 20.2 × 14.3 cm. There are eleven columns of 18–20 characters. Formerly in the collection of the French diplomat Collin de Plancy (1853–1922), the book was recorded by Courant in *Bibliographie coréenne* (no. 3738) before disappearing from view; it reappeared in a 1972 exhibition in Paris. Hŭngdŏksa was excavated in 1984 during the construction of a housing development, revealing bronze vessels bearing the temple name. Subsequently, the Cheongju (Ch'ŏngju) Early Printing Museum was opened at the temple site to celebrate Korea's contribution to printing and to mark the place of production of this, the world's earliest surviving book printed with metal movable type.

To understand the reasons for the adoption of movable type as a method of printing in Korea, it is useful to think of the disadvantages of woodblock printing in a society where the need for books was confined to a small readership. Cutting wooden blocks is relatively wasteful of materials, and requires that the blocks be stored for reuse, with the ever-present danger of destruction through fire. It is striking that evidence of 13th-century metal movable type dates to the period of the Mongol invasions, when fire destroyed countless buildings and their contents. In China, by contrast, *print runs were much larger than the tens of copies normal in Korea; thus, there was little incentive to popularize the use of movable type, because blocks could be used to make dozens of impressions. Sohn has pointed out that, in Korea,

works printed with metal type were printed in relatively small quantities and include a wide variety of titles. On the other hand, works in great demand, such as *calendars, were printed from woodblocks. (Sohn, 'King Sejong's Innovations', 54)

A further consideration must be the availability of raw materials and of skilled metal-working artisans engaged by the foundries of Buddhist temples, which commissioned bronze bells, drums, and utensils for temple services.

3 Chosŏn (1392–1910)

In 1392, after a period of instability and Mongol-dominated rule earlier in the century, the new dynastic house of Chosŏn came to power and established its capital in the centre of the peninsula, in modern-day Seoul. It continued to patronize Confucian studies in an increasingly systematic fashion. The period of Buddhist predominance drew to a conclusion. Indigenous customs and practices had long coexisted with those of the imported religion, but Confucian rites and practices began to exert an ever-stronger influence on family and ritual life. Confucian ideals gradually penetrated beyond the court and aristocratic class. Confucian studies were not an innovation of the Chosŏn period—they had formed the syllabus of the state examinations introduced in Koryŏ in the 10th century—but the early Chosŏn kings and their advisers began to reform social and religious observances and to sweep away heterodox ideas and practices, both those of native Korean origin and the excessive powers of the Buddhist Church. For this, they needed to study many Chinese editions of works of neo-Confucian philosophy. Chosŏn rulers and officials may have known of printing using metal types in Koryŏ times. In the early years of the 15th century, they began attempts to make the technique more efficient.

The third Chosŏn king, T'aejong (r. 1400–1418), is recorded as showing great concern about how books were produced:

> Because our country is located east of China beyond the sea, not many books from China are readily available. Moreover, woodblock imprints are easily defaced, and it is impossible to print all the books in the world using the woodblock method. It is my desire to cast bronze type so that we can print as many books as possible and have them made available widely. This will truly bring infinite benefit to us. (Lee, i. 537)

The types cast at T'aejong's behest, known from the cyclical name of the year 1403 as *kyemi*, were the first of a series of cast types—almost all made of bronze,

but including a number of iron, lead, and even zinc types—produced throughout the long rule of the Chosŏn house.

After the 1403 *fount, the next casting was in 1420, the *kyŏngja* year. Again, the dynastic annals provide a detailed account of royal involvement, in the person of the fourth king, Sejong (r. 1418–50):

> To print books, type used to be placed on copper plates, molten beeswax would be poured on the plates to solidify the type alignments and thereafter a print was made. This required an excessive amount of beeswax and allowed printing of only a few sheets a day. Whereupon His Majesty personally directed the work and ordered Yi Ch'ŏn and Nam Kŭp to improve the casting of copper plates to match the shape of the type. With this improvement the type remained firmly on the plates without using beeswax and the print became more square and correct. It allowed the printing of several sheets in a day. Mindful of the Typecasting Foundry's hard and meritorious work, His Majesty granted wine and food on several occasions. (Lee, i. 538)

The resulting page was well proportioned, with characters whose horizontals slope slightly upwards from left to right. This flat-heeled type could be evenly spaced without wax; it represents an important refinement of the use of movable type.

Sŏng Hyŏn (1439–1504) described the processes involved in printing with metal types in *Yongjae ch'onghwa* (Assorted Writing):

> The person who engraves on wood is called the engraver and the person who casts is called the casting artisan. The finished graphs are stored in boxes and the person responsible for storing type is called the typekeeper. These men were selected from the young servants working in the government. A person who reads manuscript is called the manuscript reader. These people are all literate. The typekeeper lines up the graphs on the manuscript papers and then places them on a plate called the upper plate. The graph levelling artisan fills in all the empty spaces between type on the upper plate with bamboo and torn cloth, and tightens it so that the type cannot be moved. The plate is then handed over to the printing artisan to print. The entire process of printing is supervised by members of the office of editorial review selected from among graduates of the civil service examination. At first no-one knew how to tighten up the type on a printing plate, and beeswax was used to fix type on the plate. As a result each logograph had an awl-like tail, as in the *kyŏngja* type. Only after the technique of filling empty space with bamboo was developed was there no longer a need to use wax. Boundless indeed is the ingenuity of men's intelligence.

In 1434, the type known as *kabin* was cast, and enjoyed such popularity that it was recast seven times over hundreds of years. It is a large fount, with characters measuring 14 × 15 mm (compared to 10 × 11 mm for the 1420 fount), and an elegant and lively calligraphic style. This type is narrower at the base than on the printing surface, and was therefore economical to cast. *Kabin* types for Chinese characters were also used in the first work to be printed using both Chinese characters and Korean *han'gŭl* movable types: the *Sŏkpo sangjŏl* (Episodes from the Life of the Buddha) printed in 1449 from a 1447 fount. *Han'gŭl*, an invented syllabic script, was introduced by King Sejong in 1443 to increase the literacy of the population and to represent the sounds of Korean graphically. In the preface to *Hunmin chŏngŭm* (Correct Sounds to Instruct the People), Sejong wrote:

> The sounds of our language differ from those of Chinese and are not easily communicated by using Chinese graphs. Many among the ignorant, therefore, though they wish to express their sentiments in writing, have been unable to communicate. Considering this situation with compassion, I have newly devised twenty-eight letters. I wish only that the people will learn them easily and use them conveniently in their daily life.

Han'gŭl script from the *Sutra of Filial Piety* in a 16th-century *block printing (1) copy.

The new alphabet was the culmination of years of research by King Sejong and his scholar assistants. The *letterforms have a fascinating origin. Consonants are shown in shapes mirroring the position of oral organs during articulation of each sound: the 'k' sound being shown by ㄱ, reflecting the position of the tongue against the roof of the mouth, while the 'm' sound, a square shape, ㅁ, imitates pursed lips in forming the sound. Closed vowels are represented graphically using horizontals, and open vowels using vertical lines. The Korean alphabet has always been written syllabically, with groups of letters arranged in discrete squares rather than in long strings, reflecting the phonemic structure of the language. This grouping convention is clearly influenced by the appearance of written Chinese characters. The earliest *han'gŭl* letters, in the 15th and 16th centuries, were upright and angular, but with time the practice of brush writing engendered a more fluent style incorporating curved and weighted strokes. The first publications to reproduce *han'gŭl* were produced from woodblocks, but in the centuries that followed, many works were published using types; Sohn listed fourteen *han'gŭl* founts in his 1982 survey of Korean types, *Early Korean Typography*.

The finest editions continued to be court-sponsored works, supervised by the Office of Paper Production, the Office of Movable Type, and the Office for Woodblock Printing. By the late Chosŏn, private individuals, Confucian academies (*sŏwŏn*), local scholars, and authors all sponsored the printing of books, and some commissioned new types.

Despite the close interest of 15th-century Korean kings in printing technology, the early introduction of cast metal-type printing led neither to an expansion of publishing nor to demonstrable increases in literacy. The reasons for this lie in the Confucian values that dominated society. With a strong focus on self-cultivation and virtuous leadership, the government encouraged austerity and deplored commerce. According to Confucius, the ideal man should be 'poor yet delighting in the Way, wealthy yet observant of the rites' (*Analects*, i.15). Korean scholar-officials of the Chosŏn fervently upheld this Confucian ideal, depressing the natural growth of markets and the circulation of traded goods. In this restrictive economy, books were printed for use in tightly controlled circumstances. Technical manuals, children's *textbooks, lists of medical plants, *maps, collections of letters, language *primers, and practical and literary works were available to the officials, teachers, and artisans who required them. Gazetteers recorded the topography, products, population, and significant achievements of the various regions of the land. For lower-class people, and for teachers in schools in different regions of the country, popular and philosophical works were produced to promote the Confucian virtues of loyalty, obedience, chastity, brotherly love, and filial piety. Clan associations issued detailed *genealogies to allow each generation to trace its family lineage, an important component of Confucian ancestor worship. Candidates for the civil service examinations studied the philosophical and literary texts that formed the syllabus of these gruelling, extended tests.

Despite the restrictive nature of the economy and government control of print, then, tens of thousands of hand-copied and printed books from Koryŏ and Chosŏn times survive in Korean and overseas libraries. The Harvard-Yenching Library catalogue alone lists 3,850 titles. Libraries in Japan contain substantial holdings of rare Korean books. Despite the losses caused by time and by war, the national and former royal libraries in South Korea preserve vast repositories of archival and published material, periodically enriched by donations from private collections. Book reading and scholarship were a vital part of Korean life.

With the advent of Japanese and Western political and economic interests c.1880, modern printing technology was introduced. The *Hansŏng Sunbo/Seoul News* was printed using a Western-style press imported from Japan, associating new technology with the reform movement that flourished briefly in the face of strong conservative opposition from the political elite. Christian missionaries were important carriers of printing innovation to Korea (see **9**): the Trilingual Press was established in 1885 by a Methodist, H. G. Appenzeller. French Catholics were also active in the late 19th century, and Father E. J. G. Coste supervised the printing and binding of the pioneering *Dictionnaire coréen* in 1880, introducing the first *han'gŭl* founts used by non-Korean printers. Bibles and language-learning aids were among the early publications of the first English press, which printed James Scott's *English and Corean Dictionary* under the supervision of Bishop C. J. Corfe in 1891. The *Pilgrim's Progress*, Aesop's Fables, and *Gulliver's Travels* were other early Western titles published by missionaries in this period.

4 Modern (1910–)

Japan annexed Korea in 1910, leading to a decline in independent publishing. The period 1910–45 was characterized by some cultural enterprises forcefully resisting the Japanese colonial regime, while others accommodated and collaborated with the Japanese. Writing and publishing in the Korean language was constrained, as the colonizers attempted to shape Korean social and cultural identity in ways that supported Japanese imperialist ambitions. For a time, the future of Korean as a medium of formal communication and education was uncertain. It was against this background of struggle and contested nationhood that modern Korea's influential newspaper and book publishing companies were founded. Writers, academic societies, and newspapers all had to contend with military control and close *censorship. Resentment against Japan continues to colour both of the modern Korean states' commercial and official publishing enterprises.

Following Japan's defeat in 1945 and the Korean War of 1950–53, the peninsula was divided into a communist north and a capitalist south. Since then, the Korean book has had two principal manifestations, which naturally reflect the separate social systems, market models, and graphic identities of North and South Korea. South Korean books have used a mixed script, with a small number of Chinese characters, particularly for place and personal names. The publishing industry, both academic and commercial, is highly developed and integrated into the international community. Bookshops thrive in the major cities. In addition to print publishing, South Korea has become a world leader since the 1990s in electronic publishing and database creation. *Digitized versions of the Korean Tripitaka and the Annals of the Chosŏn Dynasty are pioneering examples of large-scale scholarly digital projects that have revolutionized access to pre-modern textual sources in the humanities (see **19**).

North Korean publishing is dominated by Communist Party doctrine and the cult of the late President Kim Il Sŏng (1912–94) and his son and successor, Kim Jŏng Il (1942–). The quality, circulation, and appearance of North Korean publishing in the early 21st century has changed little since the economic crisis that followed the collapse of the international socialist bloc in 1989. Book circulation in North Korea is low, and subject-matter tightly controlled by the state. Nevertheless, a steady stream of fiction, poetry, historical studies, reference books, *sheet music, cartoons, and educational textbooks is produced. In contrast to the South Korean practice of mixed Chinese and *han'gŭl* script, in North Korea, no Chinese characters are used. There is very little interaction with publishing outside the country; electronic publishing is closely controlled. Generally, North Korean institutions and individuals are not connected to the *World Wide Web. Despite these differences, however, the two Koreas are united by their pride in the 15th-century *han'gŭl* alphabet. They also celebrate Korea's notable achievements in printing culture: the world's earliest datable printed text (*c*.751); the earliest dated work printed with movable type (1377); and the survival of the Korean Tripitaka woodblocks stored at Haeinsa (13th century).

BIBLIOGRAPHY

M. Courant, *Bibliographie coréenne* (3 vols, 1894–1901)

P. Lee, ed., *Sourcebook of Korean Civilization* (2 vols, 1993–6)

B. Park, *Korean Printing* (2003)

Sohn Pow-Key, 'Early Korean Printing', *Journal of the American Oriental Society*, 79 (1959), 96–103

— *Early Korean Printing* (1984)

— 'King Sejong's Innovations in Printing', in *King Sejong the Great*, ed. Y.-K. Kim-Renaud (1992)

— 'Invention of the Movable Metal-type Printing in Koryo: Its Role and Impact on Human Cultural Progress', *GJ* 73 (1998), 25–30

42 The History of the Book in Japan

P. F. KORNICKI

1 Scribal culture

Japan first became acquainted with both writing and the book from China, at some time in the first half of the first millennium AD. There can be no doubt that Chinese, as the language of Buddhism in East Asia, as the language of the intellectual tradition that is now termed Confucianism, and as the language of scholarly discourse in East Asia, was central to book production in Japan from its beginnings right up to the 19th century.

In all likelihood Chinese texts had been transmitted to Japan by the end of the 5th century, and although the dates and details given in Japanese annals are not reliable, it seems clear that books from China were increasingly valued as gifts in Japan. These would have been Confucian and Buddhist texts, and would have taken the form of rolls or *scrolls rather than bound books. Imported works needed to be copied to become accessible, and this was particularly important in the case of Buddhist texts once Buddhism took root in Japan. By the 7th century, therefore, *shakyō*, or sutra copying, was an organized activity, both as a means of reproducing texts for study and devotion and as a pious activity in its own right. In 673, a complete copy of all the Buddhist texts so far transmitted to Japan was made at the Kawaradera Temple for the purpose of preservation, while a sutra copied in 686 was copied primarily to benefit the sponsor's ancestors. By 727, a sutra *scriptorium had been established by the government at Nara with a staff of copyists and proofreaders for the production of sutras to be used in government-sponsored temples. Most of these texts were copied in black *ink on paper that had been dyed with a yellow preservative, but some were luxury copies in gold letters on indigo paper. In addition, a state library had been established in 702 with a staff of twenty copyists who were supposed to copy Confucian as well as Buddhist MSS; the Confucian texts would have been essential for the newly founded university, since the education system was modelled on that of China and required Chinese literacy.

Most of the MSS produced in the Nara period have long since perished, but recent finds of *mokkan* (wooden *tablets used to record bureaucratic texts) and *urushigami* (scraps of paper preserved by lacquer) have over the last 50 years greatly enhanced our knowledge of the texts and the forms of the Chinese language in use in early Japan. A much clearer picture of the Chinese books that were available in Japan at the end of the 9th century is provided by *Nihonkoku genzaisho mokuroku*, a catalogue of extant books compiled at imperial command.

The oldest extant MS produced in Japan is a commentary on the Lotus Sutra which dates from the early 7th century; it is, of course, entirely in Chinese and may indeed have been written by an immigrant from the mainland rather than a native Japanese. By the early 8th century, however, the Japanese had not only written their first Chinese-style chronicle, but also two works in which the Japanese language appears for the first time: *Kojiki* (Record of Ancient Matters) and *Man'yōshū* (Collection of 10,000 Leaves), an anthology of poetry. At this stage the only technique for recording Japanese was, rather clumsily, to use Chinese characters for their sound value alone. In the 9th century, however, this developed into a syllabary of highly abbreviated forms of Chinese characters known as *kana*, which were used to record Japanese texts, such as poetry and, later, prose works such as the poetic diaries of the Heian period (794–1185) and, especially, the *Tale of Genji* and other classic works of court literature. By the late Heian period, *woodblock printing was being used in Japan to print various Buddhist texts, but all works of Japanese literature circulated only in MS until the early 17th century, when the first printed editions were produced. The reasons for this exclusion of Japanese writings from the world of print are complex, but they may be summed up as: the domination of printing by Buddhist monasteries; the importance of *calligraphy in the preparation of MS copies; and the hermetic court milieu in which Japanese literature was produced and consumed. As a result, large numbers of Heian texts—known now only by name—did not survive the centuries of MS tradition and some, such as the *Tosa nikki* (Tosa Diary) of 935, only survived by chance.

Throughout the Heian period, and indeed right to the present day, the practice of copying sutras for devotional reasons continued. The celebrated scholar and poet Fujiwara no Teika (1162–1241), for example, made many copies of the Lotus Sutra in his own hand for this purpose. Sutra decoration assumed ever more elaborate forms, with *frontispieces and beautiful papers—and sometimes the text was superimposed on scenes of secular life. But sutras were also being copied for more scholarly reasons. In the 9th century, six monks were at various times sent to China to procure MSS of Buddhist texts; on their return catalogues were drawn up of the MSS they had managed to acquire. Subsequently, monks came from other temples throughout Japan to copy them and take copies elsewhere. From the 11th century, however, it was increasingly common for printed Buddhist texts to be imported from China or Korea, and from the 12th century Buddhist texts were being printed in Japan, so the imperative to keep making copies by hand weakened, except for devotional purposes.

During the wars of the 12th century and those that followed, many Japanese books were lost: more than half of the 493 works described in *Honchō shojaku mokuroku*, a 13th-century catalogue of Japanese books, are no longer extant. On the other hand, the *Tosa nikki* survived, because the original MS of 935 survived in a palace library until at least 1492 and was copied four times: two 13th-century copies have survived and have made it possible to reconstruct the original text.

Once commercial publishing grew in importance in the 17th century, the scribal traditions, it might be supposed, died away. This was not, however, the case. Scribal production and circulation continued up to the end of the 19th century. This was partly a matter of continuing traditions: sutra copying for devotional reasons continued, and so did the production of luxury editions of classical works of literature with fine

calligraphy, which the samurai elite preferred to printed copies. A new practice was making MS copies of printed books, either for reasons of economy, or because of rarity, or as a way of learning the text: this last purpose was recommended, for example, in the case of the *Onna daigaku* (Greater Learning for Women), a moral primer for girls first published in the early 18th century. Another reason for preferring MS over print was to restrict the circulation of new knowledge: innovative medical techniques or new styles of *ikebana* (flower arrangement), for example, generated an income for the initiators, and it was therefore in their interests to restrict circulation by producing MS accounts for the eyes of their followers only. But the most significant reason for the continued circulation of MSS was the *censorship legislation of the Edo period (1600–1868), which forbade the publication of scandalous or other matters concerning the samurai class as a whole. As a result, accounts of the samurai rebellion of 1651, or of the sex scandal of 1801 which embroiled women of the shogun's household, could not be printed; although bans were placed even on the circulation of MS versions, there was no effective means of policing this practice—and the heavy demand for works of this kind, often written up in a sensational manner or semi-fictionalized, was met by *circulating libraries. This is clear not only from surviving books bearing the seals of these libraries but also from legal documents generated by cases in which circulating libraries were caught with such material in their possession.

In the modern period since 1868, MS production, except for devotional or other private purposes, has diminished considerably. However, it is worth noting that, given the cumbersome nature of the Japanese typewriter, official documents were commonly written by hand until the advent of computer-generated text.

2 Print up to 1600

Woodblock printing is without doubt a Chinese invention, probably of the 7th century, but the oldest extant printed texts in East Asia are to be found in Korea and Japan. The first evidence of printing in Japan is on a stupendous scale: it is reported in the chronicles that between the years 764 and 770 1 million Buddhist invocations (*Hyakumantō darani) were printed and inserted inside miniature pagodas. This was both an exercise in atonement and a monument to the power of the imperial institution that commissioned this exercise. Large numbers of these pagodas and their printed contents have survived, sufficient to show that at the least 100,000 were produced, if not the full million. But this was decidedly not a case of printing for the purpose of reading; it was rather a ritual act, which has other parallels in the treatment of texts in Buddhism, such as prayer wheels, and the texts were not intended for reading. Nevertheless, it is eloquent evidence of the transmission of printing technology to Japan in the 8th century.

There are some records of similar instances of the devotional printing of sutras in the Heian period, but it is not until commentaries and doctrinal works were being printed (the earliest extant one is dated 1088) that printing for the purpose of producing texts to read is encountered. These were, of course, Buddhist texts in Chinese, as was true of almost all printing up to the late 16th century. Most printing at this stage was conducted in Nara at the Kōfukuji, the family temple of the dominant Fujiwara family, but in the Kamakura period (1185–1333) printing spread to other parts of Japan. The monasteries of Mount Kōya began printing works of esoteric Buddhism and the writings of the monk Kūkai (774–835), such as his *Sangō shiiki* (printed in 1253), a comparative study of Buddhism, Confucianism, and Taoism. Kyoto temples began printing works related to their particular sect of Buddhism, sometimes in the form of *facsimile editions of imported Chinese editions. One of the very few works to be printed in the Japanese language in these centuries was *Kurodani shōnin gotōroku* (printed in Kyoto in 1321), a collection of the sayings of the founder of the Pure Land sect of Buddhism in Japan.

Zen temples in Kyoto and Kamakura began printing in the late 13th century, but they were concerned less with the production of sutras than with printing collections of the sayings of Chinese, or occasionally Japanese, Zen masters. In 1367, eight Chinese Zen monks skilled in printing came to Kyoto at the request of Japanese monks and worked for some years as printers. Around a quarter of all the editions produced by Zen temples were of Chinese secular works, starting in 1325 with an edition of a collection of poems by a monk of the Tang dynasty. This, like many other such editions of Chinese works, was a facsimile of an imported Chinese edition.

The first canonical Chinese text printed in Japan was an edition of the Confucian *Analects* printed in the trading community of Sakai, south of Osaka, in 1364, and in 1481 Zhu Xi's commentary on the *Greater Learning* was printed in Kagoshima. However, given the importance of Confucian texts for elite education, it has to be said that surprisingly few were printed

before the 17th century. During the 16th century more and more Chinese secular works were being printed, but these were mostly dictionaries, guides to poetry composition, and medical texts.

Throughout this entire period from the 12th to 16th centuries, very few works of Japanese authorship were printed, with the principal exception of *Ōjō yōshū*, a treatise on the 'essentials for salvation', of which nine editions were printed between 1168 and 1600. The world of print was dominated in fact by Buddhist texts and texts in Chinese, and these required sophisticated Sinological literacy of their readers. There is little sign, therefore, of a book trade or of commercial publication at this stage.

In the late 16th century, Japan was brought into contact with two distinct typographical traditions, those of Europe and of Korea. As early as the 1540s, Francis Xavier had had some of his works translated into Japanese with a view to having them printed, but the printing activities of the Jesuit Mission in Japan did not commence until 1590, when the first European printing press was brought to Japan, to be followed later by others (*see* **9**). Although many of the publications of the Jesuit Mission press were deliberately burnt by Japanese authorities in 1626 in connection with the suppression of Christianity, it is clear that in fewer than 30 years around 100 titles were printed; fewer than 40 survive today, however, many in a single copy. Jesuit Mission printing included annual church calendars and various devotional works and classical authors in Latin—and, remarkably, some devotional works in a romanized transcription of Japanese as well. The casting of a Japanese *fount made Japanese publications possible, too, and in 1592 the Jesuits printed part of the *Heike monogatari* (Tale of the Heike) in romanized transcription: this was the first work of Japanese literature to appear in print.

The Korean tradition of movable type (*see* **41**), which goes back to the 13th century, does not seem to have been transmitted to Japan until force intervened: as a result of the Japanese invasion of Korea in 1592–8, printed books were looted and a printing press with *type was taken back to Japan and presented to Emperor Go-Yōzei. In 1593, the press was immediately put to use to print a Chinese text, the *Classic of Filial Piety*, the first book to be printed typographically in Japan by Japanese artisans.

In a sense, both of these developments stimulated printing in Japan, the Jesuits by printing Japanese literature and the printers working for the emperor or the shogun by printing secular Chinese works. However, since the Jesuit press was located in Kyushu,

Sagabon production in 1608: *Ise monogatari* (The Tales of Ise). The books were the product of a collaboration between the merchant connoisseur Suminokura Soan and the artist and calligrapher Hon'ami Kōetsu.

far from the centre of political power, and since all Christian missionaries were subject to persecution, it has long been assumed that Korean typography had the greater impact. Recent discoveries have nevertheless suggested that Jesuit printing techniques did have an influence that was subsequently denied by contemporaries for fear of being associated with a banned religion. Whatever the case, it is clear that these developments brought print out of the monasteries and gave it a secular purpose in Japan.

3 Print 1600–1868

In the 1590s, both the imperial household and Tokugawa Ieyasu, soon to be shogun, separately sponsored the preparation of large founts of wooden type and, then, the use of these founts for printing books. The *chokuhan*, or imperial editions, produced 1595–1621, were all secular works—at first Chinese works and then some works of Japanese authorship, such as the first two books of the *Nihon shoki* (Chronicles of Japan). Ieyasu, meanwhile, printed other Chinese secular texts and the *Azuma kagami* (Mirror of the East), a 13th-century Japanese chronicle. By this time, monasteries in and around Kyoto were also experimenting with typography (the oldest surviving imprint dates from 1595), and so were some private individuals, such as the physician Oze Hoan, who printed four Chinese medical works in 1596–7.

The most impressive typographic products of these early years were the so-called Sagabon, books printed in Saga, near Kyoto, between 1599 and 1610. The calligraphy and artistic direction were provided by the arbiter of taste Hon'ami Kōetsu; a merchant intellectual, Suminokura Soan (1571–1632), brought the organizational skills. Together they printed mostly Japanese texts, such as the *Ise monogatari* (Tales of Ise), the first Japanese secular book to be illustrated. Through the use of *ligatures, their wooden types sought to reproduce the flow of calligraphy, and aesthetic effects were enhanced by the use of coloured and patterned papers. The art of the Japanese book had its beginnings here.

At what point a book trade can be talked of is unclear. Most of the works mentioned so far seem to have been printed in small numbers, and there is no evidence of commercial distribution. By the 1620s, however, there certainly were commercial publishers in operation, and they were printing for the market.

For the first half of the 17th century, typography and woodblock printing existed in tandem, and sometimes they were used together, as in the case of woodblock illustrations to typographic texts. These were decades of extraordinary productivity as most of the classic works were put into print for the first time. Take the case of the *Tale of Genji*: four typographic editions were printed between 1600 and 1644; in the 1650s the poet Yamamoto Shunshō put out a large-format illustrated edition that went through innumerable reprints and also appeared in other formats; and more than twenty editions of several condensed versions were published between 1651 and 1700. In addition, annotated editions of the *Tale of Genji* and other classics were published, making these difficult texts accessible in a linguistic sense as well. Reprinted classics were far from dominating production, however, and the range of books was vast. Sinological works such as the Four Books of the Confucian tradition, which formed the cornerstone of the education system, were a staple product, but the new printed editions differed from their predecessors and from Chinese editions in being equipped with *kunten* (reading marks) which enabled Japanese readers to construe Chinese as if it were Japanese. In addition to these existing texts, there were also many new books, and increasingly books were being written with a view to being printed. These included new works of fiction, letter-writing manuals, and guide-books; most of them took advantage of the one feature that typography could not supply, namely woodblock illustrations, which became an indispensable part of almost all texts until the late 19th century.

By around 1650, however, all commercial publishers had abandoned typography and operated exclusively with woodblock printing. Was this a technological reversion? Why did it happen? For a number of very good reasons, typography could not at this stage compete. First, given the nature of the Japanese language, vast founts of type were needed to represent all the characters and *kana* signs, and since metallic type was too costly to contemplate for this purpose, wooden type dominated, although it was subject to splitting and movement in the frame; by contrast, woodblocks involved much less capital investment. Secondly, woodblocks suited the slower markets of the 17th century, for extra copies could be printed at will over years or decades, whereas typography proved less flexible. Thirdly, by the 1620s most publishers were producing books laden with *kunten* in the case of Chinese texts or, in the case of Japanese texts, with *kana* *glosses beside the characters to indicate their pronunciation and thus make texts accessible to those with lower levels of literacy. There can be no doubt that it was far easier to incorporate these glosses in woodblock-printed works, to say nothing of the ease of including illustrations within the text. For commercial purposes, then, typography was dead by 1650, and did not revive until the mid-19th century; a small amount of private publishing continued to use wooden type, but the quantities were tiny.

As woodblock printing resumed its pride of place, publishers began to be more innovative and adventurous in their pursuit of the market. Periodicals and *newspapers were unknown, but many types of publication had steady sales and required constant updating. One of these was *maps and another was the samurai directories known as *bukan*. The cartographic knowledge acquired by the shogunal government in connection with its assertion of control over all the land of Japan acquired a commercial life of its own as publishers put out large, block-printed maps of cities, provinces, the whole of Japan, and even the world. One of the most significant maps was that of Japan produced in 1779 by Nagakubo Sekisui, a man of humble origins who achieved fame and position by means of his cartographic skills; his map of 1779 was the first in Japan to show lines of latitude and longitude and thus fix Japan's position on the globe in relation to other countries. Like other maps of Japan before modern times, it did not show Hokkaidō, which at the time was not considered part of Japan proper; the many reprints and cheap versions of this map testify to its lasting popularity as the most accurate map of Japan available. All printed maps carried information in the form of text as well, and labelling included the names of prominent officials; to keep them constantly up to date, therefore, it was necessary to make frequent alterations to the printing blocks by excising text and replacing it with plugs of wood on which the new text was cut.

Bukan, on the other hand, were samurai directories —exhaustive lists of officials, giving details of rank, office, heraldic symbols, notional income, and so on. These details were naturally subject to incessant change, and the publishers usually indicated that they revised the texts every month to keep them up to date. The same applied to other such directories, such as the *Yoshiwara saiken*, or guides to the Yoshiwara-licensed quarter listing all the brothels and the courtesans, and the *unjō meiran*, guides to the Kyoto aristocracy. Print made all this knowledge public and indiscriminately available, but its susceptibility to change made these directories and maps a profitable staple for publishers in Edo.

Most publishers sought to produce a wide variety of wares, with Sinology and Buddhist texts at one end and popular fiction at the other, and in between niche publications like medical textbooks, flower arrangement manuals, poetry collections, and so forth. As early as the 1660s, there was a growing sense that printed books had become a flood, and in an attempt to bring order to the undifferentiated mass of books

A book- and printseller's premises in the Edo period, illustrated in the first volume of *Edo meisho zue* ('The Famous Places of Edo', 1834–6): the project was initiated by Saitō Nagaaki and illustrated by Hasegawa Settan.

already on the market, the booksellers in Kyoto clubbed together to produce catalogues listing books in print according to a number of categories. The first of these appeared in the 1660s, and it was succeeded every five or ten years for over a century. These catalogues became both increasingly sophisticated in their classification systems and more detailed, giving even book prices in some cases. It was at this time that some publishers were appending notices at the end of their publications listing other books they had for sale, indicating a growing awareness of the market. By the late 17th century, there were the beginnings of a booksellers' guild in existence in Kyoto, but it was not recognized by the authorities until 1716. This was followed by the acknowledgement of similar guilds in Osaka in 1723 and Edo in 1725; the only provincial guild was that of Nagoya, which was recognized in 1798. The shogunal government was not enthusiastic about the establishment of trade guilds, but perceived them to be a necessary evil in order to limit the scope for *copyright disputes. Until the late 19th century, copyright lay with publishers, not with authors, and the

most common cause of legal disputes was copyright infringement. The establishment of guilds reduced the number of cases within any one publishing centre, but did not stop disputes between publishers in different cities: thus, when an Osaka publisher put out a collected edition of Tang poetry in 1751, it was found that this replicated a book produced by an Edo publisher, and so he lost not only the copies he had printed but also his printing blocks. The guilds did not prevent such cases occurring, but they did provide a mechanism for resolving inter-city disputes like this. The guilds served one other important function as well, and that was the delegated role of censor.

Until the Edo period, censorship had been virtually unknown in Japan; there were none of the *book burnings or systems of control found in earlier ages in China. There were, it is true, two or three cases of books causing offence in Japan before 1600, but these were MSS, and it is not until the Edo period that printed books began to come under scrutiny. What first prompted this scrutiny was not the development of a publishing industry in Japan, but the importation of Chinese books written by Matteo Ricci and other European missionaries in China. By this time Christianity had been proscribed in Japan, but among the imported books was a book by Ricci refuting Buddhism and justifying Christianity, as well as other books that had nothing to do with Christianity except that they were written by missionaries and concerned Europe, such as a study of European irrigation. In 1630, an edict was issued banning 32 named books of this sort, and the list was later extended. By the end of the century, a bureau was in operation in Nagasaki to check the cargoes of all incoming Chinese ships to make sure that they were not carrying any of the proscribed books or similar works. The efficiency of this bureau kept offending books out of the official trade, but could not prevent smuggling; the detailed bureaucratic records now give a good idea of what books were legally imported to Japan and when. This system of import censorship remained rigidly in force until the 1720s when the Shogun Yoshimune, who was a man of scientific curiosity, relaxed the ban to permit books written by Jesuits to enter Japan so long as they were not about Christianity, so that their writings on astronomy could be of benefit to Japanese scholars.

There was no censorship legislation aimed at domestically published books in the first half of the 17th century, but that does not mean that no censorship was exercised. It is clear from a number of book bannings that the two taboo subjects were Christianity and Toyotomi Hideyoshi (1536–98), the hegemon who had preceded Tokugawa Ieyasu and whose heirs were considered by some to have been cheated by Ieyasu. In 1657 in Kyoto and in 1673 in Edo, the authorities at last took cognizance of the rising tide of publications, and of the possibility that some might have undesirable contents, by issuing the first censorship edicts. These were vaguely worded, prohibiting books that depicted the Shogun and the samurai class (whether favourably or not) and books that dealt with matters 'unusual', meaning scandals and sensational events; nothing was said about policing. By 1682, public notice boards were warning people against handling 'unsound' books, but this did nothing to stem the tide, for news-sheets were gaining in popularity, especially after the sensational case in 1703 of the 47 samurai who avenged their master by slaughtering his high-ranking aggressor and were then forced to commit ritual suicide. An Osaka publisher put out a book on these events in 1719, fully aware that punishment would follow, but convinced that if he could sell half his copies good money could be made; he and the author had to spend some time under house arrest as

a result, but the book reached the public and MS copies were made to satisfy continuing demand.

It was finally in the 1720s that legislation was issued laying down the guidelines that were to govern censorship for the remainder of the Edo period. In future, all publications were to carry the real names of the author and publisher in the *colophon, and the guilds were to be responsible for ensuring that publications by members did not contravene the law. Since the guilds now enjoyed monopolistic publishing privileges recognized by the authorities, they had little choice but to cooperate. Needless to say, these new arrangements did not prevent daring publishers from publishing books without colophons, and erotic books in particular took this strategy, even sometimes ridiculing the law by appending lewd parodic colophons. The major difficulty for the guilds, however, lay in understanding just what constituted 'undesirable' books; for the most part they seem to have erred on the side of caution, but in the 1790s and the 1830s there were crackdowns that caught the guilds unawares and led to punishments not only for the publishers and authors but also for the guild officials responsible.

The censorship system was never effectively policed and many publications slipped under the net, but the timidity of the guilds ensured that few risks were taken with books that went through the normal procedures. On the other hand, some publishers became adept at finding ways around the law, by omitting colophons altogether or resorting to MS publication, for selling books remained their business.

From the early decades of the 17th century, publishers had been striving to make their books more attractive and accessible to readers. One practice that soon became ubiquitous was the inclusion of small *kana* glosses alongside characters to indicate the pronunciation; this initially constituted a service to readers with a limited grasp of characters, but it later became a means for playful or ironic use of the glosses to subvert the sense of the characters. Similarly ubiquitous was the use of illustrations, which formed an indispensable part of all literary works; some authors produced their own illustrations, some made sketches in their MSS to indicate to the artist the kind of illustration required, and others still teamed up with famous artists such as Utamaro (1759–1806) and Hokusai (1760–1849), to produce books in demand both for the text and for the illustrations. Almost all *ukiyoe* (woodblock print) artists undertook book illustration, and so highly was their work regarded that from the middle of the 17th century publishers were already producing *ehon*, books consisting solely or almost entirely of illustrations. By the end of the 18th century the development of *colour printing made it possible to print exquisite books like Utamaro's *Ehon mushi-erami* (Picture Book of a Selection of Insects, 1788) in which close observation made possible by imported microscopes was married with Utamaro's skills as a graphic artist. In the 19th century, artists like Hokusai were as busy with book illustration as they were with single-sheet prints, and Hokusai's illustrations for the historical novels of Kyokutei Bakin were as successful as his own picture books, such as his famous *manga* books.

In the 17th century, books were generally expensive and sales of more than 2,000 indicated a bestselling book. The catalogues produced by the booksellers' guilds in 1681, 1696, and 1709 all provide prices; and although these were subject to variation depending upon the quality of the paper and the covers, they provide a glimpse of the relative cost of books at the end of the century. The *Ise monogatari*, one of the most popular works of classical literature, was usually published with illustrations in two volumes, and these rarely cost more than 2 *monme*; by comparison, the normal daily wage of day-labourers at this time was 1.5 *monme*, so books were becoming more affordable. In the course of the 18th century, some kinds of fiction were being produced in small illustrated booklets with poor calligraphy, and these sold for very low prices. Multi-volume works of fiction, with better calligraphy and finer illustrations, inevitably cost more, but again the price was lower for copies printed on paper of poorer quality.

Readers did not necessarily have to purchase books, however. Diaries, letters, and notations in surviving copies attest to the widespread practice of borrowing books from neighbours. This was particularly common in rural communities or in cities far from Edo or Kyoto where the supply of books could not be relied upon until the 19th century. It was also common for borrowers to make copies by hand of books they did not own, or to hire an amanuensis to do so, and this practice survived until the late 19th century.

A particularly important means of gaining access to books, almost everywhere in Japan, was the circulating library, or *kashihon'ya*. Unlike their European counterparts, these generally consisted of men carrying their stocks around on their backs, visiting their regular customers and collecting payment in arrears. They were definitely operating in Kyoto and Edo by the late 17th century, and it is clear that by the late 18th century they were working in most castle towns throughout Japan and in hot-spring resorts and similar places of leisure. Some of them were independent businesses specializing in book lending, but others were an arm of bookselling firms seeking to extend their customer base by taking books for sale or rent into the rural environs of big cities. For the most part their stock was dominated by current fiction, but they also carried illicit MSS, travel guides, and other non-fiction. The largest of them all, Daisō in Nagoya (founded in 1767), had a stock of 20,000 books with sometimes as many as six copies of a single title in the case of illicit MSS; unusually, Daisō took the form of a shop rather than a delivery service.

Before the Edo period, Japan had made strenuous efforts at various times to maintain the flow of books from the mainland—mostly China, but also Korea. By the early 17th century, the quantity of Chinese works that had already been transmitted to Japan was huge, ranging from Buddhist and Confucian texts to Tang poetry, neo-Confucian texts of the Song dynasty, and the colloquial fiction of the Ming dynasty. This flow of books did not cease in the Edo period, even though there were no direct diplomatic relations between the shogunate and the rulers of the Qing dynasty that assumed power in China in 1644. The trade was conducted at Nagasaki, the only port open to foreign ships, at the initiative of Chinese merchants, and all imports were carefully examined and registered by shogunal officials before being offered for sale. The number of ships varied from year to year, reaching a peak of 193 in 1688, and not all of them carried books.

In the middle of the 19th century, after China's humiliation in the first Opium War (1840–42), imports from China assumed a new importance as Japan sought to avoid China's fate. Particularly important were two works by Wei Yuan on the threats that the Western barbarians posed: they were not only imported, for in the 1850s countless Japanese editions, at first in the original Chinese and then in Japanese translation, were published. These provided information about the Western nations who were encroaching ever more frequently on East Asian waters and about how they might be repulsed—issues which were of prime importance following the arrival in Japan of ships from America and Russia in the summer of 1853.

Of increasing significance, too, were the Dutch books imported into Japan. By the middle of the 17th century, the Dutch were the only Europeans remaining in Japan, the Portuguese and Spanish having been expelled and the English having withdrawn. The Dutch were confined to the man-made island of

Deshima in Nagasaki harbour, and were subject to more stringent controls than the Chinese. Knowledge of Dutch was largely limited, in the 17th century, to the official interpreters, who seem to have had little intellectual curiosity. Nevertheless, it was in that century that the flow of books from Holland to Japan began. As early as 1650, the shogunal government had placed an order with the Dutchmen for a book on dissection, and over the succeeding decades there are records of other books being presented to the shogun, including Rembert Dodoens's herbal in the 1618 Dutch edition and a zoological treatise. In the 18th century, interest in Dutch books gradually spread, to some extent with shogunal encouragement, and a school of learning known as Rangaku (Dutch studies) began to make increasing contributions to Japanese intellectual life.

In 1771 Sugita Genpaku, a doctor with an interest in Western science, was shown an imported copy of a Dutch edition of J. A. Kulmus's *Anatomical Tables* and, although he could not read the text, he was impressed by the detailed illustrations. With a group of like-minded scholars, he proceeded to carry out a dissection to test their accuracy, and having concluded that Chinese and Japanese conceptions of the workings of the body were not empirically based like those of Kulmus, he enlisted the help of Maeno Ryōtaku (1723–1803) and others to produce a translation. This was completed in 1774 and published under the title *Kaitai shinsho* (New Book of Anatomy). This book, of which a copy was tactfully presented to the shogun, legitimized Dutch studies and stimulated interest in Dutch books. (It should be remembered, however, that many of these Dutch books were, like the Kulmus, in fact Dutch translations of books published first in other languages.) Thereafter, the Dutchmen were requested to bring more medical and scientific books, and in the 19th century books on military science as well. In this way, a thin but steady stream of imports introduced empirical science to Japan and familiarized Japanese with European science and medicine well before the so-called opening of Japan in 1854.

From the 1850s onwards, it became easier to acquire Western books as foreigners began to settle and trade in the treaty ports of Yokohama and Kobe. However, the numbers of Japanese with a reading knowledge of any European language other than Dutch was insignificant, and it was only in the late 1870s that proficiency in English, French, German, and Russian grew to the point that it was worthwhile for the *Maruzen bookshop in Tokyo to stock some foreign titles.

4 Print since 1868

The Meiji Restoration of 1868 had no immediate effect on print and publication except in the area of censorship, for the first efforts were made in that year to initiate a rigorous system of pre-publication censorship. A new word, *kankyo* (government permission), was introduced to make it clear that the government, rather than the guilds, was now to determine permission to publish. Already in that year news magazines had vigorously opposed the new government—most of them had been banned and closed down before the end of the year. As the government's authoritarian tendencies became clearer in the 1870s and opposition became more strident, the regulations became ever more severe until in 1875 new laws were drawn up on the French model, which held newspaper editors criminally responsible for the contents of their newspapers and made it impossible to publish books deemed to be damaging to public peace or morals. In the same year, the notorious Libel Law made it an offence to publish matters that reflected badly on members of the government, even if they happened to be true.

The technology of commercial print continued to be dominated by woodblock printing up to the 1880s. Metallic movable type had been reintroduced in the 1850s and was favoured for translations of Western books and for new works of fiction, but in the 1880s it became the dominant technology, except for Buddhist sutras, which continued to be printed with woodblocks. Many of the publishers of the Edo period proved unable to cope with the shift in technology and closed their doors in the 1880s, but some, like *Murakami Kanbei of Kyoto, weathered the storm and survive to this day.

The government reversed the policy of the Tokugawa shoguns and adopted a public presence in the world of print by launching an official gazette, the *Dajōkan nisshi*, in 1868 to make public the texts of government decrees. At first this was printed with woodblocks, but the government then established in the Ministry of Works an office for the casting of type for the use of the agencies of central and local government and the Imperial University (founded in 1877). Following the government's lead, others founded newspapers, too; the first daily was *Kankyo Yokohama Shinbun* (Government-Permitted Yokohama Newspaper), which was founded in 1870 and switched from woodblocks to typography in 1873.

Circulating libraries continued to flourish in the Meiji period and continued to offer customers the fiction of the early 19th century; some, however, began to advertise newspapers, textbooks, and even books in English on scientific or professional subjects with a view to attracting students at the new educational institutions. Japanese who travelled to the West in the 1860s reported on the provision of *public libraries which were free at the point of access; from the desire to emulate Western practices sprang Japan's first public library, which was established by the ministry of education in 1872. Although this institution started charging fees in 1885, public libraries were founded throughout Japan in the early 20th century. Nevertheless, circulating libraries survived by offering their customers fiction, and later *manga* (comics), for the public libraries disdained to stock these categories of book.

The first decades of the Meiji period saw the emergence of a flood of periodicals, including women's literary journals such as *Jogaku zasshi* (Journal of Women's Learning, 1885–1904) and influential political magazines such as *Kokumin no tomo* (The Nation's Friend, 1887–98). Other new forms of publication were translations of Western writings on law and medicine and translations of Western literature, including the novels of Disraeli and *Scott. At the same time, however, the literature of the Edo period had not been forgotten: many works were frequently reprinted typographically, albeit inevitably without the illustrations, testifying to their lasting appeal.

Towards the end of the 1880s, new publishing firms began to replace the older businesses that had failed to adapt to the new world of typography, steam power, and modern business methods. One of these new firms was Hakubunkan (1887–1947), which established a presence with a succession of strikingly new magazines and was soon the leading publishing house in Japan. The first of these magazines was *Nihon taika ronshû* (Essays by Leading Japanese), founded in 1887, in which the issues discussed ranged from literature to medicine and hygiene. In 1894, upon the outbreak of the Sino-Japanese War, Hakubunkan produced the first photo magazine, *Nisshin sensō jikki* (True Record of the Sino-Japanese War), and the following year launched *Taiyō* (Sun), a bestselling general magazine. The firm was also making its mark with major publishing projects, such as an encyclopaedia in 1889 and from 1893 *Teikoku Bunko* (Library of the Empire), a series of 100 volumes containing the major literary works of the Edo period presented without their illustrations as if they conformed to the conventions for current novels.

By the late 19th century, Japanese publishing had caught up technologically with Europe and North

The cover of an 1897 issue of the journal *Kokumin no tomo* (The Nation's Friend).

America, and the reading public's appetite for new journals was unabated. A number of these have enjoyed remarkable longevity, such as *Chūō Kōron*, (The Central Review), which had its origins in a temperance magazine founded in 1887. In 1899, its name was changed and it became a serious journal containing an offering of literature and comment. It took a liberal stance, and in 1944 was suspended at army insistence following the publication of an article that was judged damaging to the war effort; it resumed publication in 1946. Another was *Bungei Shunjū* (Literary Times), founded by the prominent writer Kikuchi Hiroshi in 1923 and still influential today; it supports the *Akutagawa Prize, the most prestigious prize for works of fiction in Japan. There were also important mass-market magazines aimed at women readers, such as *Katei no tomo* (The Family's Friend, from 1903) and *Shufu no tomo* (The Housewife's Friend, from 1917).

In the 1930s, censorship became ever more severe: a left-wing writer, Kobayashi Takiji, was brutally murdered by the police, and all left-wing journals were forced to cease publishing. Under the US occupation, which lasted from 1945 to 1952, wartime censorship controls came to an end, though criticism of the Occupation authorities was not permitted in public media, and left-wingers again came under pressure during the Cold War. Nevertheless, the more liberal atmosphere encouraged a resurgence, and new magazines were launched with information about Western fashions or ways of life.

Two of the leading publishers in Japan today are *Kōdansha and Shōgakukan. Kōdansha was founded in 1909 and continues to dominate the Japanese publishing world, although in 2002 it recorded an overall loss for the first time since 1945. Today, it is known for a clutch of serious magazines as well as for its large stable of *manga* magazines. Kōdansha International publishes books in English and other languages on Japanese culture and society, often translated from Japanese originals. Shōgakukan is also active as a publisher of *manga* and, together with a subsidiary, owns Viz Media, which publishes, among other things, English versions of Japanese *manga*. *Manga* remain a prominent feature of popular culture, and have shrugged off accusations that they are violent, sexist, and racist; the rise of the Japanese animation film, or *anime*, has generated new tie-ins for *manga* publishers.

In spite of the popularity of *manga*, they are by no means all there is to Japanese publishing today. Every bookshop stocks large numbers of the small and modestly priced paperbacks known as *bunkobon*, which provide easy access to Japanese literature old and new, to foreign literature in translation, to books on contemporary issues, and so on. Bunkobon were first introduced to the reading public in 1927 when *Iwanami Shoten launched their series. Iwanami, which was founded in 1913, is now a respected academic publisher responsible for a number of academic journals; the firm has issued the standard editions of many works of classical Japanese literature and has published several editions of the complete works of Natsume Sōseki (1867–1916), one of the leading novelists of modern Japan.

There is much talk of a crisis in Japanese publishing and of a move away from print—the latter is seen to be behind the decreasing circulation figures of daily newspapers. It is also true that there has been a decline in sales of new books and in the number of bookshops (though there are still more than 8,000). On the other hand, the number of new titles published each year has continued to rise (74,000 in 2002), and when a translation of J. K. Rowling's *Harry Potter and the Goblet of Fire* was published in Japan, the first printing was of 2.3 million copies. This may suggest that Japanese publishing follows global trends, but the globalization of Japanese books still has a long way to go. It may be easier to buy them now in London or Seoul, but while many foreign books are published in Japanese translation, very few Japanese books are translated into other languages, except a handful of literary works into European languages and some academic or political books into Korean or Chinese.

BIBLIOGRAPHY

M. E. Berry, *Japan in Print: Information and Nation in the Early Modern Period* (2006)

J. Hillier, *The Art of the Japanese Book* (1988)

P. F. Kornicki, *The Book in Japan* (1998)

— 'Block-Printing in Seventeenth-Century Japan: Evidence from a Newly Discovered Medical Text', in *Print Areas: Book History in India*, ed. A. Gupta and S. Chakravorty (2004)

— 'Manuscript, not Print: Scribal Culture in the Edo Period', *Journal of Japanese Studies*, 32 (2006), 23–52

E. May, *Die Kommerzialisierung der japanischen Literatur in der späten Edo-Zeit* (1983)

R. Mitchell, *Censorship in Imperial Japan* (1983)

G. Richter 1997, 'Entrepreneurship and Culture: the Hakubunkan Publishing Empire in Meiji Japan', in *New Directions in the Study of Meiji Japan*, ed. H. Hardacre and A. L. Kern (1997)

H. Smith, 'The History of the Book in Edo and Paris', in *Edo and Paris: Urban Life and the State in the Early Modern Era*, ed. J. McLain *et al.* (1994)

K. Yamashita, *Japanese Maps of the Edo Period* (1998)

43a The History of the Book in Southeast Asia (1): The Islands

EDWIN PAUL WIERINGA

1 General introduction

The region of insular or maritime Southeast Asia, which today comprises six young nation-states, encompasses not only hundreds of languages and literatures but also quite different cultural and political backgrounds. Indonesia (independence: 1945), Malaysia (independence: 1957), and Brunei (independence: 1984) are countries with Muslim majorities, whereas the populations of East Timor (officially Timor-Leste; independence: 2002) and the Philippines (with the exception of the Islamic South; independence from Spain declared in 1898, but only achieving sovereignty from the US in 1946) are predominantly Roman Catholic. The city-state of Singapore (independence: 1965), previously a British colony and part of Malaysia, is often referred to as a 'Chinese enclave' by its neighbours.

Until the 20th century, the overwhelming majority of the myriad language communities in this region were pre-literate. However, most of them have rich and varied oral traditions. It has been argued that even in the 'literate' societies—such as among the Malay-speaking group—oral habits still persist in written composition. Whereas reading is normally a silent and private activity in present-day Western societies, literature is often still reproduced orally and publicly in maritime Southeast Asia.

This region is home to some of the world's oldest and richest literatures. For example, the earliest inscription in Old Javanese is dated AD 25 March 804, and the first dated poem in Old Javanese idiom, composed in Indian metres, is preserved in a stone inscription, dated AD 856. Probably the longest literary work in the world is found in South Sulawesi: an old

Buginese epic, known as *I La Galigo*, telling the story of the mythical ancestors and founders of the local kingdoms. Its size is estimated at *c.*6,000 folio pages.

The history of the book in maritime Southeast Asia is beset with gaping lacunae, not least because writings on perishable materials of plant origin such as *palm leaf and bamboo rarely survived the centuries. Most pre-19th-century MSS have fallen victim to unfavourable climatic conditions, while fire, floods, and vermin also have taken their toll. Moreover, the tsunami of 26 December 2004 almost completely destroyed several important library holdings in Aceh, North Sumatra.

2 Writing systems

Three kinds of writing system successively entered maritime Southeast Asia: Indic, Arabic, and roman scripts. For the period before the 16th century, the only reliably dated sources of information are haphazard stone and metal-plate inscriptions. The earliest known inscriptions are in Sanskrit on seven stone pillars in what is now the Kutai region in East Kalimantan, dated to the 4th century, and described as (early) Pallawa script. Pallawa script as found in various parts of the archipelago is a lithic script used for monumental purposes.

By the middle of the 8th century, a rounder and more *cursive script, called Kawi or Old Javanese, begins to appear in inscriptions. Apparently, Kawi was intended for writing on palm leaves. Different styles of Indic scripts in the archipelago have been identified, especially for the 13th–15th centuries, but the paucity of inscriptions does not allow an exact reconstruction of the expansion of writing systems.

Around the 16th century, four families of Indic scripts can be distinguished in Indonesia: Batak, South Sumatran, Javanese-Balinese, and Bugis-Makasar. These four related but distinct Indic writing systems are syllabaries, in which the letters represent consonants with the inherent vowel /a/, altered by adding dots or dashes. The interrelationship between them is still shrouded in mystery. In 2002 a Malay tree-bark MS, said to date from the second half of the 14th century, was discovered in Kerinci, South Sumatra. Intriguingly, however, this text—known as 'The Tanjung Tanah Code of Law'—is written in a script strongly resembling 17th- or even 18th-century Javanese script.

Following the advent of Islam in the 13th century, Arabic script was adopted for writing several Austronesian languages (*see* **38**). Malay was almost exclusively written in a modified version of the Arabic script called Jawi, whereas the use of the Javanese version of the Arabic script called Pégon was generally reserved for writing religious texts.

The Europeans, who entered the region in the 16th century, championed the use of roman script. Dedicated to translating the Bible into indigenous languages, Christian missionaries were especially active in employing this script. Its use in printing gave roman script an overpowering advantage, strongly supported in the 19th and 20th centuries by colonial governments. In the 20th century, roman script became the accepted medium for the public sphere throughout the entire region. In the Philippines, Indic syllabaries closely connected to the Indic scripts in Indonesia had been in use before the 16th century, but under the Spanish colonial system roman script rapidly superseded the ancient Philippine alphabets.

3 Dating systems

Ancient systems of chronology—intimately associated with agriculture and astrology—have been identified among several maritime Southeast Asian peoples. These age-old and now obsolete *calendars manifest a strong Indian influence. For example, the Batak possess a chronological system imbued with Sanskrit-derived terminology that is used to find auspicious moments. Regional versions of the octaval calendar, a rather simple system based on an eight-year cycle, have enjoyed great popularity among the Muslim communities of maritime Southeast Asia for ages, but nowadays outside Java its workings are forgotten. The modernization process which forcefully set in around the turn of the 20th century has promoted a globalization of time-reckoning: modern printed books bear

*imprints with dates in the Christian era, whereas Islamic publications follow the calendrical practices of the Middle East.

4 Book forms

Although almost all writings before *c*.1500 are inscriptions engraved in stone or metal (with hardly any surviving MSS), after that date there are only a few inscriptions, but many MSS. In the pre-modern period, two traditions of writing stemming from different cultural sources can readily be discerned: an 'Indianized' tradition, bringing with it a syllabic script and a tradition of using palm leaves; and an Islamic tradition originating in Western Asia, bringing with it an Arabic script and a tradition of writing on paper.

Before paper was introduced, palm leaf was the most popular writing material, and in the Javanese-Balinese tradition its use continues today, especially in Bali. Most widely used are the leaves of the *lontar*-palm (*Borassus flabellifer* or *flabelliformis*); a MS consisting of a bundle of these leaves is also called *lontar*. Both sides of the leaf are incised with a knife, and the script is then blackened with lampblack. The leaves are bound in bundles by string through a central hole. A coin with a hole is knotted at the end of the string, which is then wound around the boards, holding the leaves together. Important texts were kept in wooden boxes, sometimes beautifully painted and carved. The leaf of the *nipah*-palm (*Nipa fruticans*) is thinner than that of the commonly used *lontar*, and is usually inscribed with a pen or *writing brush and ink.

In South Sulawesi the common word for MS is *lontaraq*, clearly a borrowing from Javanese/Malay *lontar*. A few extant palm-leaf MSS from this region have a singular shape in that they look like audio or video cassettes: their contents are written on rolled-up palm leaves, and by unwinding the roll the text 'unfolds' before the reader's eyes between the two reels, not unlike a *scroll. However, such palm-leaf examples are rare; all other MSS from South Sulawesi, written by the Bugis, Makasarese, and Mandarese peoples, are on paper, almost exclusively European.

In Sumatra, the Batak used the inner bark of the *alim* tree (*Acquilaria malaccensis*) for their folding-book MSS, characteristically folded in concertina fashion. The bark books, generally characterized as 'books of divination', used to be compiled by magicians and healers. However, people outside the priestly circle also crafted MSS, using bamboo to write letters and lamentations. South Sumatran MSS, which are written on bark, bamboo, rattan sticks, and goat or buffalo horn, also reflect an ancient writing tradition that antedates Islam in Sumatra. The oldest specimen of a South Sumatran MS is a tree-bark book in Lampung script containing a version of the Malay *Hikayat Nur Muhammad* (Story of the Muhammadan Light), presented to the *Bodleian Library, Oxford, in 1630 (MS Jav. e. 2).

The use of paper is closely associated with the spread of Islam from the 13th century onwards. In this respect it is a telling fact that nearly all Malay MSS have been written on paper, known as *kertas*, a loanword from Arabic. By the 18th and 19th centuries, the high-quality products of European *paper mills were eagerly imported in the archipelago. Today, paper is the most widely used material for all writing. With the advent of printing and machine-made paper (*see* **10**), the age-old traditions of MS writing were practically discontinued.

5 Printed books

The introduction of print in the region is intertwined with European colonial involvement. The first book printed in the Philippines was the *Doctrina Christiana en lengua española y tagala* in 1593, explicating basic Roman Catholic teachings in Spanish and Tagalog, written by Friar Juan de Plasencia, and printed with woodblocks (*xylography) in Manila. The only known surviving copy is in the Library of *Congress (Rosenwald 1302). Until the late 19th century, printing presses were owned and run by Roman Catholic orders. After Spain ceded the Philippines to the US in 1898, English was to become the language of government and education. Books in Tagalog generally have a nationalist outlook.

In the Indonesian archipelago, the Dutch East India Company issued a printed Malay translation of the Bible in 1629, but only from the 19th century onwards would the impact of European printing make itself felt. The puzzling question of the 'delayed' use of printing by Muslims is still unclear. The jealousy of scribes is sometimes mentioned among the reasons for this reticence, as well as an aversion to the mechanical reproduction of books dealing with God's word, but inadequate capital must also have played a considerable role. The invention of *lithography by *Senefelder around 1797 paved the way for a revolution in the Islamic book world (*see* **38**). Lithographed books ideally fitted the traditional views on the art of book production, carefully preserving the form of MSS, while the newly available technique needed

much lower capital investment than printing with movable type.

The British missionary Walter Henry Medhurst (1796–1857) seems to have been the first person to use lithographic printing in maritime Southeast Asia. His lithographic press in Batavia (Jakarta) printed texts in Malay-Arabic, Javanese, and Chinese scripts. The Revd Benjamin Peach Keasberry, who learned about printing from Medhurst, established a *printing office in Singapore in 1839, working together with the Malay language teacher and writer Abdullah bin Abdul Kadir Munshi. Abdullah Munshi has been called the 'father of Malay printing'. During the 1840s and 1850s collaboration between Keasberry and Abdullah Munshi resulted in a number of printed Malay books, of which Abdullah's own autobiography, *Hikayat Abdullah* (Abdullah's Story, 1849), brought its author lasting fame.

The first known Islamic printed book in the archipelago was an edition of the Qur'ān published in Palembang in 1848. A Malay version of a devotional text in praise of the Prophet Muḥammad was printed in Surabaya in 1853. The third lithographic press in the archipelago was established in the 1850s at the Buginese-Malay court on the island of Penyengat in Riau. By the 1860s, Singapore emerged as the region's Muslim printing centre. Its printing industry was run by a few men from the north coast of Java. In Singapore they were not subjected to the highly restrictive Dutch press laws, and could take advantage of the city's strategic position as the most important assembly point for the increasing number of Southeast Asian pilgrims in transit to Mecca.

At the beginning of the 20th century, however, the Singapore book printers' position was challenged by imported, better-quality products from Bombay (Mumbai) and the Middle East. In 1884, the Meccan-based *ulama* (Islamic scholar) Ahmad bin Muḥammad Zayn from Patani became the supervisor of the Malay press established in Mecca under the auspices of the Ottoman government. Understandably, works of Malay scholars from the region of Patani in southern Thailand were most numerously represented in the Meccan editions.

In the gradual transition from MS to print, two decisive streams of printing activity may be distinguished. On the one hand, Islamic printing mainly reproduced texts belonging to the traditional Arabic-script MS literature. On the other hand, the European and Chinese printing presses created a new Malay literature in roman script. In the 20th century, book production was increasingly based on *type. The

Dutch colonial government set up its own bureau for popular literature in 1908, known as Balai Pustaka (Institute of Belles-Lettres), which actively attempted to transform Indonesian writing traditions in accordance with modern Western tastes. This institution had a tremendous influence upon the development of the Malay language used in Indonesia, which came to be known as 'Indonesian' (Bahasa Indonesia). The Malay Translation Bureau, established by the British in the Malay Peninsula at about the same time, was far less successful. However, in independent Malaysia the governmental Dewan Bahasa dan Pustaka (Language and Literature Agency), established in 1956, plays a powerful role in promoting Malay as the national language.

Print caused an explosion in the amount of reading material: already in the 1860s the number of books produced by one Singapore printer in one year equalled the estimated number of all Malay MSS extant (*c.*10,000 items). The mass production and distribution of texts greatly augmented the reading audience and broadened its composition. However, the oft-made claim of the so-called 'literacy thesis'— that literacy, the technology of writing and printing, develops a 'modern' mentality, transforming ways of thinking and representations of tradition—is debatable. Although the proliferation of print is generally regarded as the driving force of 'modernity', the fact that the new print media were not exclusively a 'modernizing' domain is easily overlooked. 'Traditionalists', too, crossed the print threshold, indicating that print *per se* did not necessarily change time-honoured thinking and received wisdom. Undeniably, however, print technology was to play a formative role in shaping public discourse and in forging different 'imagined communities' of people sharing the same world view.

A printing press above a Malay advertisement for the printer in Tanah Abang (a sub-district of Central Jakarta, Indonesia), from Haji Adam's 1926 booklet *Syair Mikraj Nabi Muhammad SAW* ('Poem on the Ascension of the Prophet Muḥammad, peace be upon him').

BIBLIOGRAPHY

B. Anderson, *Imagined Communities* (1983)

T. E. Behrend and W. van der Molen, eds., 'Manuscripts of Indonesia', *Bijdragen tot de Taal-, Land- en Volkenkunde*, 149.3 (1993)

D. D. Buhain, *A History of Publishing in the Philippines* (1998)

P. Herbert and A. Milner, eds., *South-East Asia* (1988)

H. C. Kemp, *Oral Traditions of Southeast Asia and Oceania: A Bibliography* (2004)

A. Kumar and J. H. McGlynn, eds., *Illuminations: The Writing Traditions of Indonesia* (1996)

J. H. McGlynn, ed., *Language and Literature* (1998)

Asmah Haji Omar, ed., *Languages and Literature* (2004)

J. de Plasencia, *Doctrina Christiana en lengua española y tagala* (1593), www.lcweb2.loc.gov/cgibin/ampage?collId=rbc3&fileName=rbc0001_2002rosen1302page.db, consulted Sept. 2007

I. Proudfoot, *Early Malay Printed Books* (1993)

A. Sweeney, *A Full Hearing* (1987)

43b The History of the Book in Southeast Asia (2): The Mainland

JANA IGUNMA

1 Writing systems

The development of writing and dating systems in mainland Southeast Asia is connected with the spread of Hinduism, Buddhism, Confucianism, and Christianity in this area. The first writing system was *chữ' nho'*, Classical Chinese, which was the official writing system when Vietnam was under direct Chinese rule (111 BC–AD 938). In the 13th century, *chữ' nôm*, a system based on *chữ nho*, was developed to write the Vietnamese language. It consisted of orthodox Chinese characters supplemented by a set of new characters specifically created to write Vietnamese words. The situation was complicated, however, as constant close contact with the Chinese produced layers of Chinese vocabulary in varying degrees of Vietnamese naturalization, and the most highly naturalized words were accepted as Vietnamese. In the 19th century, both *chữ' nho'* and *chữ' nôm* were replaced by *quốc ngữ'*, a system developed by Portuguese Jesuit missionaries in the 17th century based on the Latin alphabet. *Quốc ngữ'* is still used to write Vietnamese and several languages of minority subgroups as well.

From the 6th to 8th centuries, a growing Indian cultural influence led to the creation of writing systems based on Indic *scripts belonging to the Brahmi family (*see* **39**). Khmer script is known to date back to the 6th century. Among the several styles of Khmer script are *'aksar chriĕng* (slanted script), *'aksar chhŏr* (upright script), *'aksar mūl* (round script), and *'aksar khŏ'm* (a variation of round script). Khmer script was also used at the Thai royal court until the late 19th century.

Burmese script, as a descendant of the extinct Mon script, has been attested as early as the 12th century. It is used to write the Burmese language, as well as

languages of the Karen, Taungthu, and Mon people in Burma. A variation of Burmese is used to write modern Shan.

Thai script descended from the Brahmi script through its intermediate descendant, Khmer. The development of Thai script is usually attributed to King Ramkhamhaeng in the 13th century. Since then, it has undergone many stylistic changes. In Thailand, Thai script is also used to write Lao and other Tai languages. Historically, most of the Tai groups in Vietnam, Laos, Thailand, and Burma have had their own writing systems based on Indic models of writing.

The Lao script, which exists in different styles (*Lao tham, Lao būhān*, modern Lao), can be traced back to the 14th century. It was used to write the Lao language of Laos and northeast Thailand, and Northern Thai as well. Today, it is also employed in writing several minority languages of Laos. Variations of *Lao tham* were used to write the languages of smaller Tai groups such as Tai Lư' and Tai Khœn.

2 Dating systems

The traditional Vietnamese calendar followed the Chinese model. Years were recorded using a method of cyclical characters and year designations, marking the divisions into different periods or eras of a ruler's reign. The years, in turn, were divided into twelve lunar months of 29 or 30 days. Over a period of nineteen years, seven intercalary months were added in order to bring the lunar cycle into accord with the solar cycle. In the 20th century, the lunar calendar was replaced by the Gregorian calendar and Christian Era (or Common Era) for official purposes. Modern printed books give an imprint in the Christian Era.

In Burma, government and administrative matters are regulated by the Christian Era and Gregorian calendar. Religious and cultural festivals are determined either by the Burmese Era, which is counted from AD 638, or the Buddhist Era, dating from 544 BC. MSS and older books usually are dated according to the Buddhist Era or the Burmese Era. Modern printed books often give an imprint in the Christian Era and/or the Buddhist Era.

The traditional Cambodian calendar is lunar-solar, in which the months are lunar, alternately having 29 or 30 days. The gap between the solar and the lunar years is resolved by adding, every three or four years, an intercalary month. In Buddhist texts, the Buddhist Era is normally used. In *inscriptions and some recent texts, the Saka Era is used, beginning AD 79. Besides that, the Culla Era, dating from AD 639, and the Christian Era are common.

In Thailand, the Buddhist Era was adopted as the official dating system in 1932. Since the beginning of the Bangkok period (AD 1782), the Buddhist Era has been defined as starting at 543 BC. Other eras in use, mainly in MSS and early printed books, are Chunlasakkarāt (beginning AD 638), Mahāsakkarāt (beginning AD 78), and Rattanakōsinsok (beginning AD 1781).

In Laos, the Christian Era, which remains officially in use today, was introduced by the French at the end of the 19th century. Until the mid-20th century, the Buddhist Era (starting 543 BC), the Chunlasakkarāt, and the Mahāsakkarāt eras were also used. Traditionally, the Lao followed a lunar-solar calendar similar to the Cambodian model.

3 Book forms

*Palm-leaf MSS and folding books were produced for a variety of purposes in Buddhist monasteries and at the royal and local courts in Burma, Thailand, Cambodia, and Laos. The production of MSS was regarded as an act to gain merit. They provided teaching material and handbooks for monks and novices, as well as Buddhist literature and historical works to read to the lay people during religious ceremonies. MSS were also important for history writing (by demand of the royal or local courts), the transcription of oral tradition, and the production of professional manuals (including for astrologers, healers, fortune tellers, legal specialists, and artists).

The earliest material for producing MSS in these countries was the palm leaf. Most commonly, the *Corypha umbraculifera* was used. The leaves of MSS are mostly 45–60 cm long and 4.5–6 cm wide; shorter ones are 25–30 cm long. There are usually three to five lines of writing on each leaf. Sometimes, small drawings decorate the text. The writing is incised with a metal *stylus before lampblack is applied to the leaves, and then wiped off, leaving the black in the incisions only. The leaves are then bound in bundles with a string and preserved in wooden covers, which can be lacquered and gilded, or decorated with an inlay of glass or mother-of-pearl (*see* **17**). Infrequently, a similar type of MS was produced from bamboo stems. Because of the late introduction of printing in Laos, palm-leaf MSS are still produced there today.

Other MSS to be found in Burma, Thailand, Laos, and Cambodia are folding books (Thai/Lao *Samut khoi*, Burmese *Parabaik*). The paper, normally made from the bark of the *Streblus asper*, was folded in an accordion fashion to form a book. Folding books are mostly 30–50 cm long and 10–15 cm wide, but longer ones are up to 70 cm long. The paper is usually a natural cream colour and written on with black China ink and a bamboo pen. Alternatively, the surface could be blackened with lacquer and written on with a white steatite (soapstone) pencil, in yellow ink made from gamboges, or from orpiment mixed with the sap of *Feronia elephantium*. The cover pages often were lacquered and gilded.

*Illustrations could be an important part of a folding book. They give a pictorial (and often idealistic) impression of the work's content (or of a topic related to it). Sometimes, however, text and illustrations were unrelated. Lavishly coloured illustrations often accompany folding books on Buddhist themes, especially MSS dealing with the Jātakas and the life of the Buddha, Buddhist cosmologies, treatises on worldly and supernatural beings, and MSS on fortune-telling, astrology, or traditional healing.

Vietnamese MSS were written in standard or *cursive *calligraphy on paper made from the bark of *Streblus asper*. The size of the paper varied considerably, from an oblong format of *c.*14 × 25 cm to a large *format of *c.*22 × 32 cm. If bound, *butterfly and *thread bindings were used. Vietnamese MSS often contained literary and philosophical works, chronicles, and works on administrative and legal issues.

Lacquered MSS or *Kammavaca*, as they are known in Burma, are among the most sacred of Burmese Buddhist texts. These MSS are still used for monastic ritual, most commonly for ordinations in Burma. Containing rules of monastic service, they include scripts (*khandaka*) on ordination and admonitions to the newly ordained monk. *Kammavaca* consist of a number of unbound 'leaves', made from thin wood or bamboo slices, folded layers of cotton, or thin metal sheets, which are then covered thickly with a few coats of red or brown lacquer to create a smooth, pliant surface. Some rare *Kammavaca* MSS are made from ivory. Normally, gold leaf is applied before the words are painted in a stylized fashion with thick black lacquer. Intervening illustrations are often added. The finished MS is protected by covers of brown or orange lacquered teakwood, also decorated with panels of lively freehand gold leaf or relief-moulded lacquer with glass inlay. When boys enter a monastery for a period (a practice that remains obligatory), parents present the presiding monk with a *Kammavaca* concerning ordination.

4 Printed books

The oldest method of printing in mainland Southeast Asia was *woodblock printing (xylography), a limited art confined chiefly to certain temples and villages of northern Vietnam. The beginnings of printing in Vietnam are not precisely known, though it is believed to date back to the 13th century AD, and is especially associated with the efforts of the 15th-century scholar Luong Nhu Hoc. The oldest definitely dated specimen is the 1697 *edition of the Great Official History.

The first publishers in Burma and Thailand were missionary presses, which printed biblical texts and teaching materials for Christian communities (*see* 9). Later, royal and governmental presses printed official papers and materials for administrative purposes; Buddhist institutions printed for the Sangha and lay people; and libraries and public bodies published to promote indigenous literatures and cultures. By the end of the 19th century, Buddhist monasteries played an important role as publishers: their cremation volumes appeared in high numbers and were dedicated to various topics, from Buddhism to linguistics, literature, anthropology, arts, history, and archaeology.

In 1816, the first printing press in Burma was established at Rangoon under the supervision of Adoniram Judson. The press was made and the types cut at the *Serampore Mission of the Baptist Missionary Society, where Burmese texts had been printed since 1810. After the British acquisition of Arakan and Tenasserim, missionary work increased and more presses were established in Tavoy (1837) and Moulmein (1843). These operations pioneered the translation and printing of the Bible in the Karen and Mon languages. King Mindon established the first Royal Printing Press in Mandalay in 1864. By 1870, the Burma Herald Press

started publishing law books, moral tracts, and popular Burmese dramas. Among printing ventures that transferred Burmese MS texts into printed forms was the Haddawaddy Press (founded in 1886), which produced nearly 1,000 titles, including the whole Tripitaka in Burmese script. Another important publisher was the Burma Research Society, which did valuable work in editing and publishing old MS texts under the guidance of U Pe Maung Tin (1888–1973).

In Thailand, the first printing press was established in Bangkok by Roman Catholic missionaries in 1836. Interest in publishing was confined mostly to the foreign missionary organizations, which published numerous translations of biblical tracts, commentaries, and catechisms in Thai languages. The royal court first made use of a press in 1839 to publish a royal proclamation banning the opium trade. In 1858, King Rama IV commanded the government to establish its own press to print *The Royal Gazette* (*Ratkitchanuphēk*), as well as administrative papers and records (*čhotmaihēt*), handbooks, laws, travel reports, speeches, and descriptions of the provinces of Thailand.

Thailand's policy of educational modernization in the first two decades of the 20th century required the mass production of teaching materials, textbooks, and teachers' manuals. The Buddhist community produced pedagogical matter in great quantities, including translations of Buddhist scriptures and commentaries from Pāli into Thai. Cremation volumes appeared in large numbers, and often had the character of research papers or speeches dedicated to religious, cultural, anthropological, linguistic, literary, and social topics. During the reign (1910–25) of King Rama VI, the publishing of literary works reached new heights. The king, a dedicated writer himself, translated numerous literary works from Western languages into Thai.

By the end of the 19th century, some commercial publishing houses had been established in Bangkok, and more followed during the first 30 years of the 20th century. Notable publishers include Bradley's Press, Smith's Press, Union Press, Thai Printers, and Sophon Phiphatthanakon Printers, as well as the Siam Society and the Vajiranana National Library.

In 1892, the first Lao printing press was founded in Chiang Mai, after a Lao *typeface had been acquired from the Lampang Presbyterian Mission. For much of its history, the press was the only body printing in the Lao language and *Tham* script. It produced large quantities of bibles, textbooks, and *tracts, as well as administrative papers and handbooks.

The French introduced modern techniques of printing in Vietnam, Laos, and Cambodia. Western typographic presses were established in Cochinchina in 1862 and Tonkin in 1883. One of the earliest Vietnamese publishers was Imprimerie de l'Union (founded in the late 19th century), which competed with French publishing houses in Saigon. After World War I, a large number of publishing houses were established in Hanoi, Huê, and Saigon. In the first three decades of the 20th century, the French made great efforts to rein in publishing in Chinese characters and successfully promoted printing in *quôc ngũ'* and French.

Although a Khmer type had been developed by the end of the 19th century, the first Khmer text to be printed in Cambodia appeared only in 1908. In the 1920s, modernist monks such as the Venerable Chuon Nath and Huot That promoted the publication of a range of texts with the help of Louis Finot. In Laos, the first press to print Lao script was established only in the late 1930s. After World War II, organizations such as the Comité Littéraire Lao, the Ministère des Cultes, and the Bibliothèque nationale used *photocopying to reproduce texts, whereas the revolutionary Neo Lao Haksat (Lao Patriotic Front) printed large editions of propaganda literature in cave presses until 1975.

BIBLIOGRAPHY

[Cornell University Library,] *The Book in Southeast Asia* (1990)

H. Ginsburg, *Thai Art and Culture: Historic Manuscripts from Western Collections* (2000)

P. Herbert and A. Milner, eds., *Southeast Asia: Languages and Literatures* (1989)

D. E. U. Kratz, ed., *Southeast Asian Languages and Literatures* (1996)

S. F. McHale, *Print and Power: Confucianism, Communism, and Buddhism in the Making of Modern Vietnam* (2004)

E. Rhodes, *The Spread of Printing, Eastern Hemisphere: India, Pakistan, Ceylon, Burma and Thailand* (1969)

B. Siworaphot, *Samut khoi* (1999)

44 The History of the Book in Australia

IAN MORRISON

1 Introduction

At the beginning of the 21ˢᵗ century, Australia is among the most urbanized countries in the world, and one of the most sparsely populated. The three major cities of the eastern seaboard—Sydney, Melbourne, and Brisbane—account for nearly half the country's population of 20 million. Similarly, the book trade is dominated by just a few of the more than 200 active publishers. In 2001, six multinationals—*Penguin, *Random House, *HarperCollins, Pan *Macmillan, Hodder Headline, and *Simon & Schuster—held more than 60 per cent of the general retail market. The largest Australian-owned publisher, *Allen & Unwin, had 9 per cent of the market. Only two other Australian-owned companies—the (now British-owned) travel-guide publisher *Lonely Planet and the directory publisher UBD—featured in the top 25. The general retail market is dominated by chain stores and franchises.

Sales data are more ambiguous, however. The educational and general non-fiction markets are dominated by Australian titles, which in 2004–5 outsold imported titles by more than two to one (84.4 million copies, against 39.5 million). Adult fiction, however, is dominated by imported titles, which in monetary terms outsold Australian titles by more than 50 per cent. Translating this data into an accurate account of what Australians read is complicated by the fact that it reports only mainstream commercial outlets: direct retail sales by small publishers, religious bookselling, and subscription publishing by multinationals such as *Time-Life and *Readers' Digest are not included. Further, a 2001 survey found that as many as one third of books purchased are intended as gifts; that

few of these gifts are actually read; and that about one third of the books that *are* read are borrowed either from friends or from libraries. It is clear that Australian authorship and subject-matter are valued highly by readers of non-fiction, but are largely inconsequential to readers of fiction.

2 First encounters to the gold rushes, 1788–1850

Australia's foundation legends are products of the European Enlightenment: from reports of explorers, scientists, and settlers, beginning with Dutch landfalls in the 17ᵗʰ century, through the scientific voyages mounted by the French and the English in the 18ᵗʰ century, to the 'heroic age' of land exploration in the 19ᵗʰ century. The eleven convict transport ships that set out from England in 1787 to establish a colony in New South Wales brought books of all kinds and a printing press. Although nobody was found to work the press until 1796 (the first professional printer, George *Howe, arrived in 1800), print culture was integral to the colony from the start.

The first book produced specifically for distribution in Australia was a homily directed at transported convicts, Richard Johnson's *Address to the Inhabitants of the Colonies Established in New South Wales and Norfolk Island* (London, 1794). An official account of *The Voyage of Governor Phillip to Botany Bay* was published at London in 1789, and several officers also produced accounts of their experiences. Watkin Tench, John White, John Hunter, and David Collins were all remarkable for their scientific curiosity. Their books went through multiple editions and were widely translated. A number of works attributed to the

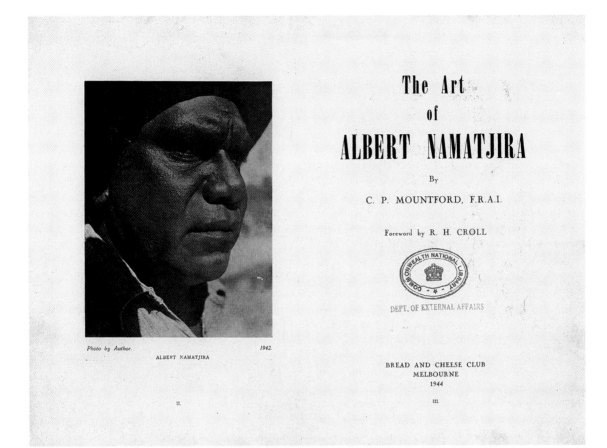

The first monograph on an Aboriginal artist. The Bread and Cheese Club's leading spirit was J. K. Moir, who donated his collection to the State Library of *Victoria. The Commonwealth National Library was the forerunner of the National Library of *Australia.

'gentleman thief' George Barrington (who had been transported in 1790) were compiled by hack writers from these genuine narratives. Long before Europeans began publishing accounts of the continent, however, the Aboriginal Australians had complex oral cultures stretching back tens of thousands of years, with hundreds of different languages. The subtleties of their encounters with European literacy have only recently begun to be explored. David Unaipon (*Native Legends*, 1929) is justly famous as the first published Aboriginal author, but the first Aboriginal to engage actively with European literacy was the Eora leader Bennelong, who dictated a letter in 1796. In the intervening years, Aboriginal publishing was predominately conducted by white missionaries and fell into two main categories: language books directed at Europeans (starting with Lancelot Threlkeld's 1827 *Specimens of a Dialect of the Aborigines of New South Wales*); and scripture texts and *primers for

Aboriginals on mission stations. Penny van Toorn has pointed out that categorizing Aboriginal culture as 'oral' and European as 'literate' is oversimplistic, privileging European concepts of what writing *is* and *does* over other sign systems. Aboriginal culture inscribed meanings on message-sticks, as well as on rocks, bark, human bodies, clothing, and ritual objects. European writing appeared, as van Toorn puts it, 'on objects as diverse as Bibles and flour bags', and 'entered Indigenous life-worlds as part of a foreign invasion' (van Toorn, 14).

Literacy levels among the 'invaders', who included Irish, Scots, and Welsh, as well as West Indians such as Howe, also varied enormously. The culture of many convicts and common soldiers was primarily oral and highly diverse. Nonetheless, Lieutenant Ralph Clark was able to stage a production of Farquhar's *The Recruiting Officer* with a convict cast in 1789.

Howe's appointment as Government Printer around 1800 marked the beginning of local publishing. He started Australia's first newspaper, the *Sydney Gazette*, in 1803 with a *press run of 100 copies. Modelled on the *London Gazette*, it contained official notices, advertisements, and general news. With such a tiny circulation, its survival depended on Howe's government salary and the success of his other business ventures, notably trading in sandalwood. In 1810, Howe replaced the original wooden *common press with an iron *Stanhope. By 1819, the colony's population had grown to 30,000 and the *Gazette*'s circulation to 400. Howe's publishing activities expanded to include missionary works in Pacific languages, some literary titles, and John Lewin's *Birds of New South Wales* (1813).

The next permanent British settlements in Australia were in Van Diemen's Land, now Tasmania, at Hobart in 1803 and at Launceston in 1806. Hobart's first newspaper, the *Derwent Star*, appeared in 1810. It ceased after a few issues, and only three copies have survived. The *Hobart Town Gazette*, established by *Bent in 1816, proved more durable, surviving Bent's imprisonment and sacking by Lieutenant-Governor Arthur in 1825. In 1827 Bent's replacement, a free settler, Dr James Ross, started an independent newspaper, the *Hobart Town Courier*.

The 1820s were a turning point, with the settlements' physical dimensions expanding. Explorers had been pushing west, south, and north: in 1812, the known land of New South Wales consisted of a few dozen miles around Sydney, but by 1827 it extended for hundreds of square miles. The Australian colonies were becoming attractive to free settlers. Hobart and Sydney were no longer prison camps on the edge of the recognized world; they had become proper towns, with churches, schools, and other civilized amenities. Military rule was beginning to give way to civilian councils. During the 1820s, 11,200 out of 43,950 new arrivals were free; in the 1830s, free settlers numbered 66,400 out of 117,090 arrivals. Growing numbers of people born in the colonies were now of an age to become parents themselves.

Many convicts and emancipists had a rudimentary education, but few could afford to spend large sums of money buying books. Libraries and learned societies began to form. Although the Philosophical Society of Australasia (Sydney, 1821–3) and the Van Diemen's Land Scientific Society (Hobart, 1829) were stillborn, the decade saw the opening of the Wesleyan Library in Hobart in 1825 and the Australian *Subscription Library (forerunner of the State Library of *New South Wales) in Sydney in 1826. Independent newspapers were increasing in number, and were less vulnerable to government interference: Bent's defiance had been squashed in 1825; but when Governor Darling imprisoned the proprietors of the *Australian* and the *Monitor* in 1829, the newspapers both continued publishing.

The mid-1820s saw an upsurge of original poetry in Sydney and Hobart newspapers. The first magazine, Robert Howe's *Australian Magazine* (Sydney, 1821), was soon followed by the first book of verse by an Australian-born poet, Charles Tompson's *Wild Notes from the Lyre of a Native Minstrel* (Sydney, 1826) and the first Australian-published novel, Henry Savery's *Quintus Servinton* (Hobart, 1830).

In 1820 there were only two Government Printers, Howe and Bent; *ink and paper were expensive, often unobtainable, and seldom of high quality. The limited capacity of colonial printers and the high costs of raw materials ensured that the book trade continued to be dominated by imports, and most Australian writers sought to have their books produced in England. The colonial market was nevertheless substantial: booksellers' and auctioneers' catalogues from the 1840s show between 10,000 and 30,000 books advertised each year. The London publisher Thomas *Tegg's sons James and Samuel arrived in 1834. James established a business in Sydney, Samuel settled in Hobart. For most of the following decade, they played a dominant role in the Australian book trade. James published more than 100 titles, including two magazines (*Tegg's Monthly Magazine*, 1836, and *Literary News*, 1837–8), *broadside and book *almanacs, political and religious *pamphlets, literary works, and William Bland's account of Hume and Hovell's expedition to Port Phillip (1837).

During the 1830s, newspaper circulation grew and prices fell; the cover price of the *Australian*, for example, was 9*d.* in 1830; by 1835, it was down to 4*d.* The total weekly output of all newspapers in 1827 was 3,700 copies; in 1836 it was 7,800. Sydney readers could choose from seven titles: the staid *Sydney Gazette*, the radical *Australian*, the once outrageous but now stuffy *Monitor*, the conservative *Sydney Herald*, the eccentric *Sydney Times*, the provocative *Colonist*, and—for business news—the *Commercial Journal*. Only the *Herald* (now the *Sydney Morning Herald*) survived the economic depression of the 1840s, but new papers continued to appear, and the overall effect was of continuing expansion. Hobart too had several newspapers, and a provincial press was emerging in the towns around Sydney, as well as in the new settlements of Moreton Bay (Queensland),

Western Australia, South Australia, and Port Phillip (Victoria). Most struggled financially, but their proprietors were motivated more by political power than by financial gain. By the end of the 1850s all the colonies had elected legislatures, and many politicians were newspapermen.

Booksellers were running successful *circulating libraries in the 1830s, and *athenaeums or *mechanics' institutes were established in the larger centres: Hobart (1827), Sydney (1833), Newcastle (1835), Melbourne (1838). By the end of the century, every town of any size had its 'institute'. Free *public libraries were slower to develop. The Melbourne Public Library (now the State Library of *Victoria) opened in 1856, and the other colonies gradually followed suit: New South Wales (1869), Tasmania (1870), South Australia (1886), Western Australia (1887), Queensland (1890).

3 From the gold rushes to Federation, 1850–1901

The great spur to colonial growth in the 1850s was the discovery of gold in Victoria and New South Wales. Early gold finds had been suppressed by administrators fearful of losing control—a reasonable fear in a penal colony. The influx of free settlers, and the economic downturn of the 1840s, made such news more welcome. It is impossible to overstate the effects of the rushes. Between 1851 and 1861, the population of Victoria grew from 77,000 to 538,000; New South Wales from 178,000 to 350,000; South Australia from 63,000 to 126,000; Queensland from 8,000 to 30,000. Tasmania, however, flat-lined; the end of convict transportation in 1855 combined with the pull of the mainland goldfields to cancel out any population growth from free settlers. Universities, too, were being established—at Sydney (1851), Melbourne (1853), Adelaide (1874), and Tasmania (1890)—although higher education remained the exclusive preserve of a tiny minority until well into the 20th century, and university libraries were accordingly slow to develop.

Inflation soared as employers increased wages to keep tradesmen from the diggings. In 1850, skilled tradesmen could earn 5s. or 6s. a day; by 1855, compositors on the Melbourne *Herald* were being paid £1 a day. Melbourne, the city hardest hit, embarked on a series of major public works—a Public Library, an Exhibition Building, a University—to bring a sense of order to what was essentially a frontier town devastated by the stampede to the diggings. By the 1890s, Sydney and Melbourne were comparable in size to many European cities. Melbourne's leading news-

papers, the radical *Age* and the conservative *Argus*, had reputations that extended far beyond Victoria. International Exhibitions brought Sydney (1879) and Melbourne (1880 and 1888) world attention.

The gold rush also accelerated the growth of non-English publishing. The first German newspaper, the *German Australian Post*, appeared in Adelaide in 1848, and numerous other German-language publications were issued in South Australia and Queensland during the second half of the century. German Moravian missionaries were active in publishing works in South Australian Aboriginal languages. Other non-English publications included the French *Journal de Melbourne* (1858), the *English and Chinese Advertiser* (Ballarat, 1850s), the Welsh *Yr Australydd* (Melbourne, 1866–72), and a Hebrew almanac (Hobart, 1853).

Rapid population growth created a steady market for *textbooks and practical treatises, but literary publishing remained fragile. The colonial market was too small to sustain even the most prolific writer. Newspapers were the main outlet for fiction and poetry throughout the 19th century. The country press in particular was extraordinarily literary by 21st-century standards, but it offered only a precarious livelihood. Most colonial writers had other careers—commonly the law or the civil service—or private means. The few who lived by their pens either published in Britain or worked as journalists or newspaper editors.

Given these conditions, the richness and diversity of writing that appeared in the 1860s is remarkable. The instant popular success of the *Australian Journal* (Melbourne, 1865–1962) gave colonial writers a major boost, in morale if not earning power, and the decade saw the emergence of prolific popular writers such as Garnet Walch and R. P. Whitworth. Marcus Clarke and 'Rolf Boldrewood' (Thomas Alexander Brown) began their careers as newspaper columnists, the precocious Clarke writing for Melbourne's *Australasian* and Boldrewood for Sydney's *Australian Town and Country Journal*. *Stenhouse, a Sydney lawyer, became the patron of a coterie of intellectuals that included Daniel Deniehy, editor of the *Southern Cross* (1859–60), and the poet Henry Kendall. Kendall and his contemporaries Charles Harpur and Adam Lindsay Gordon are renowned for their poems of the Australian bush, but each was just as at home with European and biblical mythology.

The major book publishers during this period were all based in Melbourne: *Robertson, *Mullen, and E. W. *Cole. Several of the larger Melbourne printing firms also became successful publishers. Sands &

McDougall, F. F. Bailliere, and Gordon & Gotch all built intercolonial mini-empires based on publishing modest-looking reference books that few could afford to be without. Sands & McDougall's postal *directories (published from the 1850s to the 1970s), Gordon & Gotch's *Australian Handbook and Almanac* (1870–1906), and Bailliere's *atlases, *gazetteers, and directories (1860s to 1880s), have retained their value as sources for historical research.

Among the notable figures in the Sydney trade were: William Maddock (active 1862–96), whose list included practical treatises on topics as diverse as billiards and animal husbandry; William Woolcott and J. R. Clarke (active 1850–95), who published music and scenic views; and J. J. Moore, whose *Moore's Almanack and Hand Book* (1852–1940) quickly established itself as a standard reference work. Unlike its English namesake, the Sydney *Moore's* was a rationalistic compendium of useful knowledge.

The prominent religious publishers were the Catholic Edward Flanagan and J. G. O'Connor (Sydney, 1860s–1880s) and the Anglican Joseph Cook (Sydney, 1850s–1890s). Heterodox publishers included Joseph Wing, publisher of the *Spiritual Enquirer* (Bendigo, 1874–5), the *Reformer* (Melbourne, 1880–83), and numerous spiritualist pamphlets; the atheist Joseph Symes, publisher of the *Liberator* (Melbourne, 1884–1904); and the spiritualist W. H. Terry, publisher of the *Harbinger of Light* (Melbourne, 1870–1956).

Many provincial centres had flourishing printer-publisher-booksellers. Most survived principally as booksellers and *jobbing printers; some, notably Ballarat's F. W. Niven (who developed an innovative crisp *photolithographic process), played a major part in the industry's development.

South Australian and Tasmanian publishers concentrated on localized almanacs, guidebooks, and technical works. In Adelaide, the major figures were E. S. Wigg (active from 1849) and W. C. Rigby (active from 1859); the firms they established flourished well into the 20th century. Hobart publishing was dominated by the Davies family—proprietors of the *Mercury* newspaper (established 1854)—and the *Walches. Besides their *Literary Intelligencer* (1859–1915) and *Tasmanian Almanac* (1862–1980, by far the longest-running Australian almanac), the Walches were significant for promoting the career of the writer and artist Louisa Anne Meredith.

Western Australia and Queensland, both first settled in the 1820s, developed more slowly. Other than government publications, their 19th-century publishing consisted mainly of newspapers and almanacs.

During the 1870s and 1880s, colonial publishers, especially in Melbourne and Sydney, were increasingly active in promoting local authors, but they seldom managed to do more than cover expenses. Writers with serious ambitions looked to Britain. Clarke's *His Natural Life* (1874) and Boldrewood's *Robbery Under Arms* (1888) first appeared as serials in Australian journals, but only achieved 'Australian classic' status after publication in London. The prolific thriller writer Fergus Hume published his first novel, *The Mystery of a Hansom Cab*, in Melbourne in 1886; he returned to England in 1888 and spent the rest of his life there. The careers of such diverse writers as Rosa Praed, Ada Cambridge, and Nat Gould all followed similar trajectories.

To the extent that such writers built their careers on British sales, they might seem irrelevant to Australia. However, the Australasian colonies were, at least in terms of volumes per capita, many British publishers' largest market. The newspaperman James Allen was doubtless bragging when he commented at length in his *History of Australia* (1882) on the wide reading and deep knowledge of contemporary literature, science, and international politics displayed by the people of Victoria; but all the statistical and anecdotal evidence supports the general point that Australians devoured any printed matter they could obtain. British publishers began to produce cut-price '*colonial editions' in the 1840s; by the end of the century, several —notably *Cassell and *Eyre & Spottiswoode—had established branches in the colonies rather than rely on agents, and had become part of the local publishing scene.

By the 1880s colonial publishing was again shifting gears, conscious of the coming centenary of British settlement and of the growing agitation for the Australian colonies' political union. The market for commemorative reference books—such as the *Australian Dictionary of Dates and Men of the Time* (1879), *Cyclopedia of Australasia* (1881), *Picturesque Atlas of Australasia* (1886–9), *Cassell's Picturesque Australasia* (1887–8), *Chronicles of Early Melbourne* (1888), and *Australian Men of Mark* (1889)—seemed inexhaustible. With the success of the aggressively nationalistic Sydney weekly, the *Bulletin*, in the 1880s, it was possible to imagine a future in which Australia had a thriving literary culture all its own.

4 Federation to World War II, 1901–45

By the 1890s, Australian attitudes to Great Britain and the empire were diverse and complex. A series of crises in the Pacific spurred agitation for political union; fears of French and German expansion were exacerbated by reports of Russian plans to attack Melbourne and Sydney. In 1885, Queensland, Tasmania, Western Australia, Victoria, and Fiji formed the Federal Council of Australasia. Sir Henry Parkes, the New South Wales premier and former newspaper proprietor, initiated moves towards full political unification in 1889. Then, leading up to Federation, the Australian colonies contributed troops to Britain's war against Boer separatists in southern Africa. One of the most popular Australian books of this period was the Revd W. H. Fitchett's *Deeds that Won the Empire* (first published as a newspaper serial in 1896), with total sales of more than half a million.

After a decade of negotiations and political campaigning, New South Wales, Victoria, Queensland, South Australia, Tasmania, and Western Australia formed the Commonwealth of Australia in 1901. A strain of populist nationalism—at once egalitarian and xenophobic—found literary expression in the Sydney weekly, the *Bulletin*, which also produced a popular monthly, *Lone Hand* (1907–21). A. G. Stephens, the *Bulletin*'s literary editor (1894–1906), had mixed success with his own magazine, the *Bookfellow* (three series: 1899, 1907, 1911–25).

The success of *Angus & Robertson and the *Bulletin* in promoting populist, nationalistic writers proved there was a viable market for Australian stories told in an Australian idiom. The *New South Wales Bookstall Company—the first great Australian *pulp publisher—offered Australian writers the prospect of a living wage in their own country for the first time. In Melbourne, the bookseller Thomas Lothian began publishing in 1905, setting a more literary tone with poets such as Bernard O'Dowd, John Shaw Neilson, Marie Pitt, and 'Furnley Maurice', as well as the short-lived magazine the *Native Companion* (1907), which published the New Zealand writer Katherine Mansfield's first stories.

When the *Berne Convention on international copyright was signed in 1886, Australia was part of the British empire, and the *Net Book Agreement of 1900 perpetuated British control of the Australian market. Although Australian writers were free to seek out US publishers, British editions of their works took precedence in their home country—and Australian literary history has been framed largely within the history of British publishing. Although US editions were demonstrably superior in their physical presentation, the quality of their texts, and the financial rewards they gave to authors, they have remained largely unknown to Australian audiences. British 'colonial editions' retained a presence in the Australian market until 1972.

Once the initial euphoria of 1901 had passed, the Commonwealth of Australia continued to cling to the British empire. Between the 1890s and the 1940s, Australian culture became increasingly xenophobic. A defining moment for the new Commonwealth was the Immigration Restriction Act of 1901, which effectively prohibited non-European immigration. The 'White Australia Policy' was not formally abandoned by the Australian government until 1973.

Commemorations such as the sesquicentenary of Sydney in 1938 and the centenary of Melbourne in 1934 saw an upsurge in the collecting of Australiana, especially books from the age of British exploration in the 18th and early 19th centuries. This trend reached its apex when the Melbourne businessman Sir Russell Grimwade acquired 'Captain Cook's Cottage' (actually the home of the navigator's parents after their son had gone to sea) for Melbourne's centenary celebrations. That Cook never saw Melbourne, and may not have seen the cottage, was no deterrent. More importantly, large-scale bibliographies were appearing: the *Mitchell Library's *Bibliography of Captain James Cook* (1928); *Miller's *Australian Literature* (1940); and *Ferguson's *Bibliography of Australia 1784–1900* (1941–69). Sir Edward Ford began the collecting that would eventually lead to his *Bibliography of Australian Medicine* (1976).

A key episode in the development of Australian library services was the scathing report in 1935 by Ralph Munn, of the Carnegie Corporation, and Ernest Pitt, head of the State Library of Victoria. The Munn–Pitt report was a political success in promoting the concept of free, municipally funded public libraries; by the 1960s such libraries had replaced, or subsumed, the vast majority of the subscription-funded mechanics' institutes and schools of arts that had been the standard model of library service since the mid-19th century. Circulating libraries, too, began to decline after World War II, and, although some lingered into the 1970s, they ceased to play a significant part.

Robertson's *Monthly Book Circular* came to an end in 1891, and when Walch's *Literary Intelligencer* closed in 1915 the Australian book trade found itself without a local journal. In 1921, D. W. *Thorpe started the *Australian Stationery and Fancy Goods Journal*, forerunner of the *Australian Bookseller and Publisher*.

Art publishing gathered momentum during World War I with Thomas Lothian's production in 1916 of two lavish books, *The Art of Frederick McCubbin* and

Ida Rentoul Outhwaite's *Elves and Fairies*. Sydney Ure Smith established two key journals: *Art in Australia* (1916–42), with its *tipped-in colour plates, provided a forum for the fine arts; *The Home* (1920–42), although focused on interior design and decoration, included articles about contemporary art, and featured covers by such notable artists as Thea Proctor. *Manuscripts* (1931–5) was another notable art journal, promoting the work of such artists as Margaret Preston, Eric Thake, and Christian Waller, although it also included substantial poetry and prose fiction; later issues included bibliographical notes by *Mackaness.

One of the most striking little magazines of the period was *Vision* (1923–4). Edited by Frank C. Johnson, Jack Lindsay, and Kenneth Slessor, it struck a pose against both the populist balladeers of the *Bulletin* and European modernism, instead struggling to articulate an aesthetic based on youth and vitality. Decorated with Norman Lindsay's erotic drawings of nymphs and satyrs, its stated aim was to make Australia the centre of a new renaissance. Two *Vision* poets—Slessor himself and R. D. FitzGerald—became major figures, but *Vision*, like so many other journals, folded after a few issues. Lindsay's next magazine venture, *The London Aphrodite* (published by his *Fanfrolico Press, 1928–9), was deliberately planned to cease after six issues. Johnson, at that stage working in *Dymock's bookshop, went on to become a successful *paperback publisher.

In 1939, the Sydney branch of the English Association, based at the University of Sydney, started *Southerly*, now Australia's longest-running literary journal. The Brisbane journalist Clem Christesen established *Meanjin* in the following year. Initially a vehicle for Queensland writers, *Meanjin* had achieved a circulation of 4,000 and a national profile by 1943. Published with the patronage of the University of Melbourne from 1945, *Meanjin* developed during the 1950s and 1960s an increasingly internationalist outlook along with an interest in contemporary political events, as well as in literature and art. Since Christesen's retirement in 1974, it has become predominantly an academic journal.

Angry Penguins (1940–46) promoted surrealist art and writing, making it a target for the 'Ern Malley' hoax perpetrated by the conservative poets James McAuley and Harold Stewart. The duped editor, Max Harris, put up a spirited defence of the poetic quality of the fake author's work, but in the face of withering *tabloid scorn he had little chance of being taken seriously by anyone who was not already sympathetic. It

would be another twenty years before Australian literary editors were comfortable publishing poetry that rejected conventional forms.

5 Since World War II

The end of World War II brought a period of reconstruction. The population boomed—from 7.5 million in 1947 to 10.5 million in 1961. Country towns stagnated, but in the major cities suburban sprawl escalated. Throughout the 1970s and 1980s there was a growing sense of cultural maturity, as writers and artists found it increasingly possible to be based overseas without losing their 'Australianness', or to develop an international profile without leaving Australia.

Higher education expanded dramatically. Until the 1930s, universities were a minor part of the Australian library scene. At that time Australia had just six universities—one in each of the state capitals—and a range of other tertiary colleges. Between 1946 and 1980, thirteen new universities were established. Melbourne's Monash (1958) and La Trobe (1964) were completely new institutions; others, such as the Australian National University (1946) and the University of New England (1954), were developed out of existing regional colleges. A complex series of reconfigurations over the next twenty years saw the number of universities double again, with most having multiple campuses. Many regional centres now have a university campus; some universities have expanded internationally: Monash, for example, has campuses in Malaysia, South Africa, and Italy. The number of students as a proportion of the total population has grown from a few thousand out of 3.7 million in 1901 to around half a million students in a population of 20 million at the end of the century.

The growth of higher education was a major factor in the development of Australian publishing, in particular during the 1960s and 1970s, as income from textbooks gave publishers scope to risk promoting less commercial works—poetry in particular—that they considered culturally important. A precondition for the growth of tertiary education was increasing retention rates in secondary schools. F. W. Cheshire in Melbourne and the Jacaranda Press in Brisbane specialized in secondary-school publishing. Melbourne University Press (which concentrated on non-fiction, including key reference works such as the *Australian Dictionary of Biography*) and the University of Queensland Press (which played a leading role in promoting the work of new poets and novelists, most famously Peter Carey, David Malouf, and Michael

Dransfield) became major players in both the general and education markets. Angus & Robertson continued to produce important reference works, notably the ten-volume second edition of the *Australian Encyclopedia* (1958), and Ferguson's *Bibliography of Australia*, the seventh volume of which appeared in 1969.

The Australian branches of *Oxford and *Cambridge university presses seemed intent on outdoing each other with guides and companions to all aspects of Australian history and culture. Oxford argued, with some justification, that the Australian edition of its *Concise English Dictionary* was a more genuine Australian production than its locally named but American-sponsored competitor the *Macquarie Dictionary*. Cambridge picked up the *Encyclopedia of Melbourne* (2005) when it was abandoned by Melbourne University Press. The small publisher Currency matched the academic presses with its *Companion to the Theatre in Australia* (1985) and *Companion to Music and Dance in Australia* (2003). Another minnow, Australian Scholarly Publishing, produced the first volume of John Arnold *et al*'s *Bibliography of Australian Literature* (2001); subsequent volumes were published by the University of Queensland Press. Melbourne University Press added to its stable of reference works with Marcie Muir and Kerry White's *Australian Children's Books: A Bibliography* (1992–2004).

The pace of postwar change and the structures adopted for the expansion of public library services differed from state to state: in Victoria, for example, local lending libraries were run by municipalities, with the State Library completely separate; in Tasmania, local lending libraries became branches of the State Library. However, the broad principle of public funding for library services—a radical innovation when it was proposed by Munn and Pitt in 1935—had become the accepted norm. Professional qualifications for librarians and archivists shifted from a workplace training model to graduate qualifications. Melbourne Teachers' College introduced a programme for school librarians in 1955. *Metcalfe initiated a postgraduate diploma course at the University of New South Wales in 1960; a master's programme began in 1972. Jean P. Whyte, a Master in Library Studies graduate of the University of Chicago, started a master's programme at Monash University in 1976. By the 1990s, graduate professional qualifications were also becoming a requirement for editors and publishers.

Libraries were becoming conscious, too, of rare or 'heritage' materials, and specialist rare book librarians were beginning to be appointed in the larger institutions. During the 1960s and 1970s, increasing numbers of private individuals gave their collections to them. Among the more significant were: Henry Allport and Sir William Crowther to the State Library of Tasmania; *McLaren and Orde Poynton to the University of Melbourne; J. K. Moir to the State Library of Victoria; Father Leo Hayes to the University of Queensland; and Sir Rex Nan Kivell to the National Library.

A Commonwealth Literary Fund had been established in 1908, essentially as a pension scheme for writers and their dependants. In 1973 its functions were taken over by the Literature Board of the Australia Council, which, with a dramatically increased budget, moved to provide fellowships to support writers during their working lives. The Miles *Franklin Award, for a published novel portraying some aspect of Australian life, was initiated in 1957; other literary prizes proliferated during the 1970s and 1980s.

The award of the 1973 *Nobel Prize for Literature to Patrick White brought international attention to Australian literature. In the decade leading up to the award, a generation of writers that included Randolph Stow, Thea Astley, and Christopher Koch followed White's lead in rejecting 'dun-coloured realism'. However, White was only able to produce the sort of work he did because he was independently wealthy and did not need to earn money from his writing. In contrast to White was the prolific pulp writer 'Carter Brown' (Alan Yates), who wrote several hundred thrillers during his 30-year career. His early successes in the Australian market enabled him to leave his day-job as an airline publicist, and huge American sales brought him wealth and (at least *pseudonymously) fame. The detective novelist Arthur Upfield and the *romance writer Lucy Walker were hailed overseas but disdained in Australia—Upfield sought his revenge by casting one of his detractors, the novelist Vance Palmer, as the murder victim in *An Author Bites the Dust* (1948). It was only with Peter Corris's Chandleresque Cliff Hardy in the 1980s that crime writing acquired local critical respectability.

Penguin established a Melbourne office in 1946 and immediately became a major publishing force, selling some half-million books in their first year. George Allen & Unwin established a Sydney branch in 1976; this became the Australian-owned Allen & Unwin in 1990. Meanwhile, small Australian publishers such as Outback Press (1973–80), McPhee Gribble (1975–89), and Fremantle Arts Centre Press (1976–) were discovering writers as diverse as 'B. Wongar', Helen Garner, and Elizabeth Jolley. The arrival of significant numbers of Vietnamese refugees in the late 1970s, along with the Australian government's shift from 'White Australia' to a commitment to multiculturalism, was followed by the flowering of a non-English language press; by the 1990s leading non-English newspapers such as the Greek *Neos Kosmos* and the Italian *Il Globo* were commonly available in metropolitan newsagents. Aboriginal people were recognized as citizens after a referendum in 1967; movements for land rights and reconciliation followed. Magabala Books (established 1974, wholly Aboriginal-owned since 1990) took the lead in promoting indigenous writers; IAD (Institute for Aboriginal Development) Press and the Aboriginal Studies Press soon followed. The mainstream success achieved by the feminist cooperative Sisters (1979–83) encouraged the development of other feminist presses. Gay and lesbian writing began to enter the mainstream commercial market in the 1990s.

The Children's Book of the Year awards instituted by the Children's Book Council in 1946 encouraged the development of critical standards in evaluating writing for children and young adults, although its awards have been frequently criticized for favouring worthy, issues-based books over material that attracts and engages young readers. The Yabba awards (instituted 1985) are selected by children and invariably produce a very different list from the CBC awards.

*Creative writing programmes began to proliferate during the 1990s, just as publishers moved away from cross-subsidization and became increasingly reluctant to risk publishing anything that would not pay its own way. Whether in spite of or because of this, a new professionalism in publishing emerged, and a cultural maturity capable of accepting that for most readers of fiction the tag 'Australian literature' is not in itself sufficient reason to buy or read a book. At the beginning of the 21st century, Australian crime, romance, and speculative-fiction writers are finding commercial and critical success both at home and abroad. A generation that includes Shane Maloney, Kerry Greenwood, Garth Nix, and Glenda Larke seems at last to have found forms of expression for an Australianness that needs neither assertion nor concealment.

BIBLIOGRAPHY

D. Carter and A. Galligan, eds., *Making Books: Contemporary Australian Publishing* (2007)

W. Kirsop *et al.*, eds., *A History of the Book in Australia*, vol. 1: *To 1890* (forthcoming)

M. Lyons and J. Arnold, eds., *A National Culture in a Colonised Market, A History of the Book in Australia*, vol. 2: *1891–1945* (2001)

C. Munro and R. Sheahan-Bright, eds., *Paper Empires, A History of the Book in Australia*, vol. 3: *1946–2005* (2006)

A National Survey of Reading, Buying and Borrowing Books for Pleasure, Conducted for Books Alive by A. C. Nielsen (2001)

P. van Toorn, *Writing Never Arrives Naked* (2006)

E. Webby, ed., *The Cambridge Companion to Australian Literature* (2000)

45 The History of the Book in New Zealand

SHEF ROGERS

1 Missionaries and colonies

A narrow, mountainous pair of islands stretching almost 800 miles through the South Pacific, New Zealand possesses a rich and well-documented print heritage despite its geographic isolation. From 1848, would-be colonists could peruse E. J. Wakefield's *Hand-Book for New Zealand* for a recommended list of books on practical topics such as cooking, ornithology, and astronomy. Early settlers, conscious of a non-literate aboriginal population far larger than their own, deliberately recorded their efforts to establish a local *print culture. Jim Traue, a former chief librarian of the *Turnbull Library, has argued for two histories (aboriginal and colonial) of New Zealand print culture and notes that the country's settler history is typical of other 19th-century colonies: its print history begins with *newspapers and *periodicals, then only gradually moves to books.

New Zealand's book history is, therefore, very much a history of importation, even for books in Maori. Numerous Europeans (particularly whalers, sealers, and traders from New South Wales) visited in the late 18th and early 19th centuries. Christian missionaries brought books and printing presses to provide religious works for the Maori; they made strenuous efforts to establish a written form of the Maori language and to record Maori oral culture in print (*see* **9**). By 1815, the Church Missionary Society (CMS) had produced a Maori *grammar and Maori *primers, printed in London and Sydney. In 1830, at the Kerikeri Wesleyan settlement, the Revd William Yate printed Maori hymn sheets and a six-page Maori *catechism. The CMS further established the printed word in New Zealand when William Colenso arrived with a *Stanhope press in 1834. Colenso overcame numerous technical problems to produce the New Testament in Maori in 1837 (the Old Testament was not fully translated until 1868) and remained active as a printer in both Maori and English until 1840, one of his last publications being the printed version of the Treaty of *Waitangi, New Zealand's founding constitutional document. His ledgers survive in the Alexander *Turnbull Library in Wellington, making New Zealand one of the few nations able to produce the *account books of its first significant printer.

Nine months after the Treaty of Waitangi, Queen Victoria established New Zealand as a separate Crown colony; organized settlement soon followed. In almost every New Zealand Company community, colonists established printing presses within a year of arrival: sixteen newspapers were founded by 1851, 28 by 1858. The Government created an official Printing Office in Auckland in 1842–7, and in Wellington from 1864, until its privatization in 1989. For many years it was the country's most technically advanced printer, producing parliamentary material, along with numerous major reference works and New Zealand's largest publication, the *telephone directory.

2 Newspapers

Population grew rapidly with the discovery of gold in the South Island in 1861. Each new strike seemed as likely to yield a newspaper as a nugget, with 181 newspapers founded 1860–79. These mainly English-language newspapers depended heavily upon reprinting material from overseas publications, eagerly resetting stories from newspapers and *magazines as soon as a ship berthed. Although it was often cheaper and easier for a newspaper to serialize a syndicated British work, original local writing was also published, especially accounts of inland exploration and of native flora and fauna. This local interest was reflected in the scientific nature of many of the 19th-century *pamphlets printed for exchange via the postal services with colleagues internationally. The third governor-general, Sir George *Grey, was especially active in collecting and translating Maori songs, while fictional and semi-fictional accounts of settlers' experiences provided popular topics for early literary efforts.

Newspapers were also the main publishers of printed Maori, other than the religious books imported and printed by missionaries. Although the largest book produced in 19th-century New Zealand was the Maori Bible, most other printed books were in English. The Government Printer continued to produce some works in Maori, but after publication of *The Native School Reader for Standards II and III* in 1886, government policy shifted toward teaching the Maori to read in English, a focus retained in schools until the beginnings of Maori language immersion schools in the late 1970s. Maori only became an official language of New Zealand in 1987, and the first New Zealand publisher specializing in Maori, Huia, was not established until 1991.

3 Publishers commercial and educational

English-language printing and publishing expanded significantly from the 1880s. Distribution improved with the coming of railways between most of the main centres; the new telegraph cable to Australia in 1876 improved the speed of international communication. The major Australian periodical distributor, Gordon & Gotch, gradually expanded from Victoria throughout Australia and into New Zealand at the turn of century, and remained a major periodical supplier (although a subsidiary of PMP Communications since 1992). Booksellers continued to order books independently, under various legal arrangements intended to maintain Britain's dominance over Commonwealth markets. Until World War II, there were no European or American *wholesale booksellers in New Zealand; many publishers still find the country too small a market to merit the presence of a wholesaler, locating Australasian offices in Sydney or Melbourne.

Within the country, however, the end of the 19th and the first half of the 20th centuries saw the development of significant bookselling chains that also became successful publishers. First and foremost was *Whitcombe & Tombs. The bookseller George Whitcombe and the printer George Tombs, both of Christchurch, merged their businesses in 1882, expanding to Dunedin in 1890, then throughout the country and ultimately overseas to Australia and England. Deriving early success from its educational publishing, Whitcombe & Tombs merged with the Dunedin printing firm *Coulls Somerville Wilkie to form Whitcoulls in 1973. The new company dominated publishing until the mid-1980s and remains the country's most significant retail bookselling chain.

Educational publishing continues to dominate New Zealand book production, with millions of copies sold. From 1877, the New Zealand government required all regional authorities to provide public schools, but not books; those remained a cost to students' families. Seeing an opportunity in the market because of the high prices of imported texts, Whitcombe & Tombs began selling, then publishing, school textbooks. The first challenge to the firm's dominance came in 1907, when the government established the *School Journal*, distributed free to primary schools. Only after World War II, however, did the newly formed School Publications Branch of the Education Department begin producing a regular series of publications that gradually eroded Whitcombe & Tombs's textbook market.

Although the average *press run for a textbook exceeded 5,000 copies, print runs for more literary works could be as small as a few hundred. Nonetheless, New Zealand's most successful literary publisher, Caxton Press, managed to sustain quite a strong list in this small market. Begun by several like-minded friends from Canterbury University between 1933 and 1935, Caxton quickly established a reputation for high-quality printing of well-regarded writers; but as other literary publishers came on the scene, Caxton returned to its roots as a printer. Similarly, the Dunedin printing firm McIndoe (established 1890) was, under John McIndoe III, a notable publisher from 1956 until the mid-1980s, but then reverted solely to printing. In 2002 it merged with a complementary printing firm to create Rogan McIndoe. Another significant literary publisher, Pegasus Press (1947–86), issued more than 100 volumes of poetry, as well as seven of Janet Frame's novels, and was one of the first New Zealand firms to secure international joint publication agreements and translation *rights for its authors. Four university presses, all established since 1960, have developed, in addition to their academic titles, specializations in New Zealand poetry, fiction, history, or natural history. They all subsidize these academic and New Zealand-centred ventures with revenues from traditionally lucrative textbook titles.

Children's publishing, predominantly in English but with a consistent Maori presence, has long been an important part of New Zealand publishing. Edward Tregear's *Fairy Tales and Folk Lore of New Zealand and the South Sea* (Wellington: Lyon & Blair, 1891) is considered the first New Zealand children's book (*see* **15**). Whitcombe & Tombs entered the market with Johannes Andersen's *Maori Fairy Tales* in 1908 and developed a series, *Whitcombe's Story Books* (1904–56), with *c.*450 titles—the largest children's book series in the world. With its research into literacy and methods of reading instruction, and the talents of such witty authors as Joy Cowley, Margaret Mahy, and Lynley Dodd (not to mention many captivating illustrators), New Zealand has become a leader in early reading series. Publishers such as Nelson Price Milburn (now an *imprint of *Thomson), Wendy Pye, and Mallinson Rendel maintain New Zealand's reputation in this field.

The New Zealand publisher best known internationally is undoubtedly *Reed. Like Whitcombe & Tombs, A. H. Reed found a niche market—religious publications. From the mid-1930s, he became a leading figure in the New Zealand trade, with historical booklets for general and educational markets, sports books, and other popular works on local topics. He was joined by his nephew A. W. Reed in 1925; together, they wrote more than 100 of the approximately 1,000 titles published by the firm.

Such local successes dwindled in the face of faster transport and a global media. By the end of the 20th century, there were no longer any major New Zealand-owned printing companies or bookselling chains. This shift away from local ownership began with the arrival of firms like Collins, *Random House, and *Longman in the 1960s, though the pace of mergers quickened at the end of the 20th and start of the 21st centuries. Whitcoulls absorbed the Government Printer and was, in turn, taken over by U.S. Office Products; London Books is owned by the Blue Star Conglomerate, owner of U.S. Office Products; and Reed, having changed names and hands at least six times, became part of Reed Elsevier. Smaller independent booksellers and publishers survived, but faced tough competition from the chains' discounts and from increasing use of the *World Wide Web for individual orders of less readily available titles. *Borders Bookstores opened its first New Zealand branch in Auckland in 1999 and, by 2007, had expanded to Wellington and Christchurch, with a second store planned for Auckland.

Despite the dominance of multinationals in its domestic market, New Zealand retains a strong international presence in intellectual publishing. The Royal Society of New Zealand (established in 1867 as the New Zealand Institute) has fostered a range of specialist scientific journals and research programmes. In association with the Government Printer, the Royal Society developed the world's first computer typesetting system in the mid-1970s. Developments in digital printing have further transformed the publishing industry and reduced costs for shorter runs of books. Government support for an upgraded Internet feed has eased electronic exchange of published material in print and film media.

4 Libraries

Although New Zealanders have always purchased relatively large numbers of books, they have also been eager borrowers. The Otago region on the lower South Island supported 116 *public libraries and *athenaeums between 1872 and 1884 (for an 1881 population of 135,023); the province of Nelson at the top of the South Island sustained eleven institutions holding collectively some 12,000 books in 1874 (for a population of 22,558). The novelist Anthony Trollope, visiting in 1872, commented: 'In all these towns are libraries, and the books are strongly bound and well thumbed. Carlyle, Macaulay and Dickens are certainly better known to small communities in New Zealand than they are to similar congregations of men and women at home' (Rogers and Rogers, 3). British publishers' *colonial editions made many current works of fiction available in the colony more cheaply than in London, although booksellers and libraries sometimes had to settle for what arrived rather than precisely what they wanted. Australia provided alternative import sources, predominantly through the *New South Wales Bookstall Co. and later *Angus & Robertson.

Within two decades of settlement, readers could select from a good range of books and, in the larger towns, from an assortment of *subscription libraries. George Chapman's lending library in Auckland held more than 4,000 titles in 1863. Traue has shown, through comparisons with Australia and Britain, that 'within 40 years of settlement New Zealand had more public lending libraries per head of population than any other country in the world' (Traue, 'Fiction, Public Libraries', 86). As with all such comparative statistics, the per capita qualification is crucial; New Zealand's high figures result, in part, from a fairly sparse and dispersed population. Nonetheless, demand was strong and reading widely valued. One reason that colonial New Zealand enjoyed so many libraries was that provincial, and later central, government education boards offered institutions with libraries an annual subsidy of up to £100 to purchase books. From 1877 to 1902, however, this subsidy was made available only if an institution imposed an annual borrowing fee of at least 5s., although most permitted free on-site reading. This stricture discouraged the establishment of free municipal libraries. It also reinforced a Protestant sense of propriety that regarded the reading of fiction as entertainment, and therefore a personal luxury. Later, the influence of the Carnegie Corporation encouraged a move away from lending fees; eighteen institutions benefited from its support, as did universities and other specialist libraries when the Corporation funded overseas training for librarians in the 1930s and 1940s. Even free institutions, however, retain a semblance of the older view, with modest fees ranging from 50¢ to $5 rental for the most popular items, such as *detective fiction or current bestsellers. Such fees permit libraries to collect a much broader range of works and still meet the demand for current fiction.

In a country so dependent on importation for the availability of books, libraries play a major role in providing access to them, and few towns of any size lack a public library. The Library and Information Association of New Zealand boasted 459 institutional members in 2006, for a country with only five main cities. Public libraries (as opposed to the earlier subscription services) first came to most small towns in the form of *mobile libraries (book vans) operated by the Country Library Service set up by G. T. Alley in 1938. The service continued until 1988, when it was replaced briefly by a mail service, until overtaken by the Internet. In 1942, the government formed the School Library Service, a programme that amalgamated with the Country Library Service to form the first National Library Service in 1945. Meanwhile, copyright *legal deposit requirements fed continual growth of the General Assembly Library in Wellington, which, together with the National Library Service, formed the basis of the National Library established in 1965.

The National Library houses the Turnbull Library, one of New Zealand's three most significant heritage collections; the others are the Grey Collection (*Auckland City Libraries) and the *Hocken Collections (Dunedin). All three—gifts from dedicated collectors interested in the early history of New Zealand—were established between 1882 and 1920, but have been continually expanded by further gifts and bequests to ensure that the country's print heritage is well preserved.

5 Current trends

The small publisher remains the norm in New Zealand: a 2003 report found that only a few multinational publishers, such as *Penguin, successfully exported New Zealand titles, while three-quarters of New Zealand publishers together generated just 2 per cent of the total revenue from book exports. Thus, the majority of New Zealand books are just that— books written by New Zealanders for New Zealanders. International distribution, where it occurs, is most likely to be carried out by a multinational publisher, while book production may take place either in New Zealand or overseas, primarily in Asia. Fortunately, New Zealanders continue to borrow and buy books in healthy numbers, and the number of publishers and titles continues to rise, although the average size of print runs is probably dropping.

A small country of slightly more than 4 million people, New Zealand has always been self-conscious about documenting itself. This has resulted in the creation and preservation of much material. Yet, this abundance of sources, the bifurcated strands of New Zealand print history, and uncertainties about the social status of print have also produced, problematically, a certain hesitancy about composing a national history of the book. The exemplary selected studies of aspects of print history in *Book & Print in New Zealand* have sketched out what is known of many aspects of New Zealand print culture, and recent investigations have added greatly to knowledge of Maori newspapers. More detailed bibliographies, such as George Griffiths' *Books and Pamphlets on Southern New Zealand* (2006), acknowledge the significance of the local even as they enumerate a daunting number of potential new sources. Teasing out the strands of local, national, and international history remains a desideratum, one that will probably await the completion of histories in other former colonies, including Australia and Canada. Allen Curnow, New Zealand's most famous poet, memorably characterized New Zealand as a 'small room with large windows', and the publishers, readers, and writers of New Zealand will undoubtedly maintain their tradition of a strong local sense of place mediated by a broad international perspective.

BIBLIOGRAPHY
A. G. Bagnall, *New Zealand National Bibliography to the Year 1960* (5 vols in 6, 1969–85)
J. Curnow *et al.*, eds., *Rere Atu, Taku Manu: Discovering History, Language and Politics in the Maori Language Newspapers* (2002)

Exports of New Zealand Published Books, report for the Ministry of Culture and Heritage (2003), www.mch.govt.nz/publications/book-export/export-nz-books-report.pdf, consulted Mar. 2007

P. Griffith *et al.*, eds., *Book & Print in New Zealand* (1997); online at the New Zealand Etext Centre, www.nzetc.org/tm/scholarly/tei-GriBook.html, consulted Sept. 2007

P. Parkinson and P. Griffith, *Books in Maori, 1815–1900* (2004)

L. Paterson, *Colonial Discourses: Niupepa Maori, 1855–1863* (2006)

H. Price, *School Books Published in New Zealand to 1960* (1992)

A. Rogers and M. Rogers, *Turning the Pages* (1993)

J. Traue, 'The Two Histories of the Book in New Zealand', *BSANZ Bulletin*, 25:1–2 (2001), 8–16

— 'Fiction, Public Libraries and the Reading Public', *BSANZ Bulletin*, 28 (2004), 84–91

46 The History of the Book in Latin America (including Incas, Aztecs, and the Caribbean)

EUGENIA ROLDÁN VERA

1 Pictorial MSS

Before the Spanish conquest, the people of the Americas had a wide range of systems for recording dates, astronomical information, and numerical data. Writing, in the form of pictograms that represent meanings with no relation to sounds, was used by virtually all indigenous groups throughout the continent. Good examples are known from the Olmecs, Zapotecs, Mixtecs, Purépechas, and Aztecs in Mexico, and the Incas in Andean South America. Although these people did use some developing phonetic signs, only the Mayas in Mesoamerica (the region comprising today's Central America, southern Mexico, and central Mexico) developed a method of writing that represents phonetic language, from the 3rd century BC. Theirs was a system that combined logograms, phonetic syllables, and ideograms, and it was significantly more complex than the writing systems of later Mesoamerican civilizations. Both pictographic and phonetic scripts were carved in stones or bones, engraved in metal, and painted on ceramics; some scholars suggest that the still not fully deciphered Inca quipu computing system, consisting in assemblages of knotted strings, was a form of writing in its own right (*see* **1**).

In Mesoamerica, information was also recorded on long strips of paper (made of the bark of the amate tree, a variety of the genus *Ficus*), agave fibres, or animal hides, which were folded like an accordion for storage and protected by wooden covers. These were the so-called codices (*see* CODEX) or pictorial MSS, for many the Americas' first proper 'books', which must have existed at least since the Classical Period (AD 3rd–8th centuries). Codices recorded astrological

information, religious and astronomical calendars, knowledge about the Indian gods, peoples' histories, genealogies of rulers, cartographic information (land boundaries, migration routes), and tribute collection. They were stored in temples and schools, and reading them was an activity that combined individual visual decoding with an oral explanation provided by priests or teachers. Other codices seem to have been used as visual mnemonic supports for traditional oral poetry, storytelling, and moral teachings given by parents to their children. Although most of these codices were burnt by the Spanish conquerors and missionaries after 1521, fifteen have been preserved, among them the codices Borgia, Fejérváry-Mayer, Laud, Vindobonensis, Nuttall, Bodley, Vatican B, Dresden, and Tro-Cortesiano. They all date from the 14th–16th centuries and belong to the Maya, Mixtec, Aztec, and other peoples from the Nahua group.

In spite of the large-scale destruction of indigenous culture caused by the Spanish conquest and colonization (16th–early 19th centuries), pictorial MSS remained a widespread form of recording information in Mesoamerica during much of the colonial period. Apart from the introduction of Western painting styles and the use of Spanish paper and cloth in addition to the indigenous amate, the most significant change in the post-conquest codices was the combination of painting with text written in the roman alphabet, which was introduced by the Spaniards. Most of these MSS were used for administrative purposes—they were made by indigenous local authorities as registers of tribute for the colonial rulers and proof of land titles in the context of litigation. Others were commissioned from indigenous scribes—or indigenous students trained in Spanish schools—in the first decades of

Spanish rule by missionaries or colonial authorities interested in pre-Columbian thinking and traditions, history, and knowledge about the natural world. Whereas for the Spanish these codices were seen as a means to facilitate Christianization or colonial administration, for the Indians they constituted a way to preserve the memory of their culture. Nearly 430 codices of this sort have been preserved, the most comprehensive inventory of which was produced by Cline (Cline, 81–252). Some paradigmatic examples include: the *Tira de la Peregrinación*, the Codex Xólotl, the *Matrícula de Tributos* (which showed the tribute system of the Mexica empire), the Codex Bourbon and the *Tonalámatl Aubin* (divinatory almanacs), the Codex Mendoza (commissioned by the first viceroy of New Spain, Antonio de Mendoza, to inform the emperor Charles V (King Charles I of Spain) about the history, administration system, and everyday life of the ancient Mexicas), the Codex Badiano (an inventory of medicinal plants), and the Codex Florentino (a compilation of testimonies of the elderly about the divine, human, and natural world of the pre-Columbian Mexicans).

Spanish missionaries drew on the tradition of codices in their effort to convert the indigenous population to Catholicism. They created the genre of pictorial *catechisms—known as 'Testerian MSS'—which were small volumes of religious doctrine drawn with mnemonic figures, each of which represents a phrase, word, or syllable of the Christian text in indigenous language. Through them, the Indians were to memorize the dogmas, prayers, and commandments of the new religion, and by means of the images they would be able to communicate to the priests the sins they had committed. On the other hand, Indians also chose to use the roman alphabet to put down in indigenous languages information that had been previously orally transmitted in their cultures; the best examples of such texts come from the Maya region. The *Popol Vuh*, a history of the Mayan people (allegedly based on ancient codices and oral tradition), was secretly recorded (*c.*1550) in Mayan language but in roman alphabet by Indians who had attended Spanish missionary schools. Mayan priests followed a similar strategy in their writing of at least eighteen *Chilam Balam* books, in which they recorded the past, described the present, and stated prophecies for the future. These were collectively written MSS—with the main body of the text in Mayan language, often accompanied by drawings—copied and enlarged during the 16th–18th centuries, and passed down through the generations. This new arrangement epitomized

Notes on astronomy from the MS *Chilam Balam de Chumayel* (c.1775–1800). The MS relates the Spaniards' conquest of the Yucatán.

the semantic transformation that took place with the introduction of new writing and reading practices in the colonial period: images, which in pre-Columbian codices were the powerful support for a predominantly oral culture, became a device meant to assist the understanding of written texts.

The persistence of the codex as a form for recording information in later stages of the colonial period is exemplified by the so called *Techialoyan* codices or 'fake' pictorial MSS, produced by some indigenous communities by the end of the 17th and the early 18th centuries. These were the communities' property titles intended to prove their ancient possession of the land; they were drawn in a way that made them appear pre-Columbian and were used in litigation (*see* FORGERIES AND HOAXES).

2 Book restrictions under colonial rule

The Spanish and Portuguese conquerors brought with them not only the alphabet but also the printed book and, at least to some places, the printing press. The first books to arrive in America were the *books of hours taken by Columbus's men to the Caribbean islands, together with chivalric *romances—such as the *Amadís de Gaula*, *Cid Ruy Díaz*, or *Clarián de Landanis*—and other fictional literature which contributed so much to feeding the conquerors' imagination and their dreams of glory. Although the Spanish Crown attempted to prohibit the export of non-religious popular literature (of which more than 50 titles in at least 316 editions were printed in Spain during the 16th century) to the New World, its flow was steady throughout the first century of colonial rule.

Spain and Portugal attempted to control the production and reading of books in their colonies, both by issuing exclusive printing and trade rights and through the vigilance of the *Inquisition. In 1525, the Spanish Crown gave the Seville-based publisher Jakob *Cromberger absolute control over the book trade with New Spain (today's Mexico, parts of the southwestern US, and Central America), a monopoly that was later transferred to his son Johann (Juan). Subsequently, the Spanish Crown granted exclusive publishing rights to selected printers in the colonies, especially for the publication of popular religious books; the rights also tended to inhibit the expansion of print in those territories. The Inquisition was meant to see that none of the books listed in the *Index Librorum Prohibitorum*—mainly heretical works, books of magic and divination and, in the 18th century, works of the French *philosophes*—made its way into the Americas. Yet this form of control was not very strict, and smuggling from Britain and France was common, especially in the last decades of Spanish rule. Furthermore, every book printed in Spanish America had theoretically to be examined by the Inquisition, the *Consejo de Indias*, or the *Real Audiencia* before publication, but this form of *censorship was less effective in the control of print than the granting of exclusive printing rights. Portugal's monopoly over Brazil was even stricter, for the colony was treated largely as an agricultural producer, and the production of manufactured goods, including print, was prevented by a series of laws until the mid-18th century.

Nevertheless, during colonial times c.30,000 titles were printed in Latin America, the most comprehensive accounts of which can be found in the bibliographies compiled by *Medina. Of all those titles, 12,000 were produced in New Spain. Indeed, during the 16th and 17th centuries, only the viceroyalties of New Spain and Peru, the richest colonies of the Spanish empire, possessed printing presses. The first printing press of the Americas was established in Mexico City in 1539, by *Pablos, a contractor of Johann Cromberger. In Lima, the first printing press was established in 1581, in the charge of the typographer *Ricardo. With the exception of Puebla, in New Spain, and Guatemala City, which acquired their first printing presses in the 17th century (1640 and 1660 respectively), the rest of the Spanish and Portuguese colonial cities had to wait until the 18th or even until the 19th century to acquire a press: La Habana in 1701, Oaxaca in 1720, Bogotá in c.1738, Rio de Janeiro in 1747, Quito in 1760, Cordoba (Rio de la Plata) in 1765, Buenos Aires in 1780, Santiago de Chile in c.1780, Guadalajara and Veracruz in 1794, San José de Puerto Rico in c.1806, Caracas in 1808, La Paz in 1822, and Tegucigalpa in c.1829. In their South American reductions or settlements, the Jesuits attempted to make their own manual printing presses; but they managed this only in some cases. In Paraguay (a territory that comprises today's Paraguay and parts of Brazil and Argentina), they put together a rudimentary hand-made press towards 1705, with which they printed works in Spanish and in the Guarani language.

Peruvian and Mexican publishing in the 16th century was largely dominated by material used for the religious conversion of the Indians—catechisms, doctrines, and *primers, as well as dictionaries and grammars of indigenous languages; prayer books and liturgical works, alongside compilations of laws, were also published from an early date. But none of the *chronicles of the conquest or of the works of the missionaries about the history and traditions of the indigenous peoples was published in the Americas. Neither was a single chivalric romance published in the colonies, in spite of the genre's popularity in those territories, thus indicating the efficiency of the Spanish publishers' monopoly over certain kinds of works. In the 17th century, book production increased considerably; in New Spain alone 1,228 titles were published, in contrast with the 179 of the previous century. New genres were added to the works used regularly in Christianization: books about natural history and astrology such as the *Repertorio* by Henrico Martínez (Mexico City, 1606), chronicles of the activities of the religious orders in the respective colonies, and even literary works by authors such as Bernardo de Balbuena, the Mexican nun Sor Juana Inés de la Cruz, and the Peruvian Juan de Espinosa Medrano ('El Lunarejo'). The books imported from Spain were largely literary, with the dominant romances giving way to *plays. Most of the books of this period, given their scarcity, high cost, and the low level of the general population's literacy, ended up in the libraries of the universities of Mexico City, Lima, and Santo

A bilingual book for the conversion of the Indians in the New Spain: the Franciscan priest Alonso de Molina's *Confesionario Mayor en la lingua Mexicana y Castellana* (Mexico, 1569).

Domingo, in convents, or in the private libraries of members of the upper-level clergy and government officials.

In the 18th century, the production of print in Latin America increased threefold compared to the previous century (in New Spain at least 3,481 titles were published), partly thanks to the establishment of *printing offices in other colonies. Works of religious doctrine and religious instruction continued to dominate, alongside religious chronicles and some historical and literary works. The main novelty of this century, however, was the emergence of the periodical, in the form of the monthly or weekly *Gacetas*. These publications contained news from the Crown; events in Europe and in the different colonies; notices about the arrival and departure of ships; edicts; and information about deaths, feasts, and lost objects. They became common in the second half of the 18th century and in the first decade of the 19th. The following titles exemplify this trend: *Diarios y memorias de los sucesos principales* (Lima, 1700–1711), *Gaceta de México* (1722, 1728–42), *Gaceta de Guatemala* (1729–31), *Gaceta de Lima* (1739–76), *Mercurio de México* (1741–2, 1764), *Gaceta de La Habana* (1764), *Papel Periódico de La Habana* (1789), *Papel Periódico de la Ciudad de Santafé de Bogotá* (1791–7), and the *Gaceta de Buenos Aires* (1810–21). Some *gacetas* focused specifically on scientific and learned matters, such as the *Mercurio volante* (Mexico City, 1772–3), by José Ignacio Bartolache; the *Gaceta de literatura de México* (1788–95), by José Alzate; and the *Mercurio peruano* (1791–4); these were intended not only for the scientific community but also for the enlightened general reader. A few daily newspapers such as the *Telégrafo mercantil del Río de la Plata* (1801–5) and the *Diario de México* (1805–17) appeared at the turn of the century. It is generally assumed that these periodicals helped form an incipient public sphere: communities of readers were created and provided with a space in which awareness of their own country and of the situation within the Spanish empire was moulded on a daily basis. Such writings also gave shape to a feeling of American (or creole) identity, which was reinforced by another kind of literature imported from abroad: works published by a handful of exiled Jesuits (expelled from the Spanish empire in 1767) about the history, the natural world, and the geography of individual Spanish-American countries. José Gumilla's *El Orinoco ilustrado* (1741–4), Juan José de Eguiara y Eguren's *Bibliotheca Mexicana* (1755), or Francisco Xavier Clavijero's *Historia antigua de México* (1780) are the best examples of this kind of works.

In addition to such developments, educational reforms carried out in the Spanish empire in the last decades of the 18th century resulted in an expansion of basic literacy, thus expanding the market for print. Moreover, changes in maritime trade brought about by the French Revolution and the Napoleonic wars led the Spanish and Portuguese empires to lose some of their monopoly over the Americas. This facilitated the smuggling of French and British books to the colonies, which enlarged the libraries of Spanish-American creole elites and gradually made them more cosmopolitan.

3 Independence and the print revolution

The French invasion of the Iberian Peninsula in 1808 unleashed a political crisis throughout the Spanish and the Portuguese empires that, between 1808 and 1824, eventually led to the independence of all their colonies in America (except Cuba and Puerto Rico). These events were accompanied by a print revolution. The Spanish king's abdication and the dissolution of his empire resulted in the virtual disappearance of the printing monopolies, the end of the Inquisition, and the lifting of restrictions on the import of foreign books and printing presses. The need for rapid information about events in Europe and about the independence movements' development stimulated the publication of periodicals, the appearance of new genres such as flyers and *pamphlets, and the opening up of new spaces for public discussion and collective reading. The armies fighting for independence began to use portable printing presses, as they were advancing, to promulgate their manifestos and war reports. Moreover, the liberal 1812 Spanish constitution (endorsed by the colonies that had not yet become independent) established *freedom of the press, a measure which was later incorporated into the liberal constitutions of all the newly independent countries— most of them republics. As a result of these developments, a total of 2,457 books and pamphlets were printed in Mexico alone between 1804 and 1820, and over that period the ratio of religious to political titles was inverted from around 80 per cent over 5 per cent in 1804–7, shifting to 17 per cent over 75 per cent in 1820 (Guerra, 288–90). In Venezuela, where the first printing press was introduced in 1808, 71 periodicals were published between 1808 and 1830.

In Brazil, the print revolution corresponded to Rio de Janeiro's rise between 1808 and 1821 as the metropolis of the Portuguese empire. When the royal family fled Lisbon and settled in Rio de Janeiro, the king lifted the ban on printing and established the official *Impressão Régia* (Royal Press) there, which opened with a few presses imported from England. The Royal Press produced roughly 1,200 titles on a variety of subjects over the course of thirteen years. When Brazil declared its independence in 1821 and constituted itself as a liberal parliamentary monarchy (with Dom Pedro, the son of the Portuguese king, as its head), press freedom was declared. As a result, the official printing house's monopoly ended; the number of printing presses grew exponentially; books could be imported without restriction; and local publishing flourished. Haiti, which had obtained its independence from France earlier, in 1804, experienced a similar expansion of print during the liberal regimes of the first two decades of the 19th century. The South American Liberator Simón Bolívar was reportedly provided with a printing press for military use by the Haitian President Alexandre Pétion in 1815.

During the early years of independence, the expansion of print with a more or less free press and a system without exclusive printing rights led to the formation of a rudimentary public sphere. In the painful process of nation-building, the publication of periodicals and pamphlets, the prime genres of the first half of the century, contributed to the circulation of opinion; some 6,000 titles, for example, were published in Mexico between 1821 and 1850. Throughout the continent, a cosmopolitan liberal elite of men of letters who combined political activity, legislation, and literary work played a disproportionate role in shaping local book production. Among the new types of publication were accounts of the wars of independence, personal apologias for political histories, discussions about the best way to organize the new countries, and literary works about the nature of America and about the ideal of pan-American unity. A Mexican, Fray Servando Teresa de Mier, a Cuban, José María de Heredia, and a Chilean, Andrés Bello, were among the prominent members of a group of writers who produced these sorts of work. The first national libraries, sponsored with public funds, were founded in the 1810s and 1820s (of *Brazil and of *Argentina in 1810, of *Chile in 1813, of Uruguay in 1816, and of Colombia in 1823), largely on the basis of the collections of books confiscated from the Jesuits after their expulsion from the Spanish empire in 1767; but these institutions' existence was interrupted throughout the century. However, political instability and economic grievances, as well as the high price of imported paper, hampered the development of profitable and long-lasting publishing industries, and only the so-called 'state presses', funded directly by governments for the publication of official periodicals, were able to survive continuously. Imported books, mainly Spanish editions printed in France or England, largely dominated the newly opened reading markets. These books were sold in different kinds of places (groceries, stalls in the marketplace, haberdashery shops, sugar depots, ironmongers, butchers, or post offices) and in a handful of bookshops, some of which were branches of well-established French booksellers— such as Bossange, *Didot, *Garnier—or of the London publisher and bookseller *Ackermann. British and French novels, together with treatises by European writers (mostly by Jeremy Bentham, Benjamin Constant, Destutt de Tracy, and Montesquieu), formed the majority of imported books. The reprinting of successful foreign works by local printers was also a common practice throughout much of the 19th century; before the *Berne Convention on copyright in 1886, there were no bilateral agreements for the protection of publishers' rights between France, Britain, or the US and any Spanish-American country (although some countries signed sporadic individual agreements on an individual basis).

From the 1840s to the 1860s, a handful of local printer-publishers achieved a degree of commercial success thanks to a combination of factors: the beginning of local paper production (in Chile, Brazil, and Mexico); a strategy of market diversification (periodicals, *tracts, and *coffee-table books), with publications for specific groups, such as women or children; and a policy of securing agreements with foreign publishers. The printer-publishers *Cumplido, Mariano Galván Rivera, and Vicente García Torres in Mexico and Santos Tornero in Chile are examples of such successful local publishing ventures. Moreover, the emergence of the popular serial novel (*feuilleton*) in newspapers towards the middle of the century changed the reading habits of large parts of the population (*see* NUMBER; **14**). Historians maintain that Brazilian and Mexican serial novels, such as Manuel Antônio de Almeida's *Memórias de um sargento de milícias*, published in the *Correio Mercantil* (1852–3), and Manuel Payno's *El fistol del diablo*, in *Revista científica y literaria* (1845–6), contributed significantly to the growth of the reading public in their countries.

The consolidation of nation-states in the second half of the 19th century, together with gradual economic expansion, gave a new impetus to the publishing industry and shaped the emergence of new genres. This growth was reflected in the increased production of national histories and geographies, the foundation of more national libraries (of Puerto Rico in 1843, of Nicaragua in 1882, and of *Mexico in 1867), and the quest for national literatures. Under the influence of romanticism, local book production was dominated by national themes, local landscapes, and regional human types; the colonial past became the subject of the increasingly popular historical novel. José Hernández's *Martín Fierro* (Argentina, 1872–9), which became a bestseller, Jorge Isaacs's *María*, a Cuban anti-slavery novel, (Colombia, 1867), and Ricardo Palma's *Tradiciones peruanas* (1872–1910) are only a few examples of this nationalistic approach.

Moreover, although universal education was made a legal requirement from the early period of independence, considerable expansion of the educational system in most Latin American countries only began in the second half of the century. The growth in numbers of students had the double result of enlarging the reading public and of making *textbooks a secure and fast-growing business after 1850—a business that was dominated by foreign publishing houses with branches in Spanish- and Portuguese-speaking countries. Indeed, the incursion of foreign publishers in the Latin American textbook market had started in the 1820s, when Ackermann exported, with limited success, large numbers of secular 'catechisms' of general knowledge (meant for both school and non-school audiences) to all Spanish-American countries. Later in the century, in the 1860s and 1870s, the American D. *Appleton & Co. was more successful with exports of books to South America. But it was the French publishing houses Bouret, Garnier, and *Hachette with branches for the printing and selling of their publications in Spanish-American countries and Brazil, that became the most important textbook suppliers in the second half of the 19th century and the beginning of the 20th. The expansion in schooling was accompanied by the creation of larger numbers of *public libraries (the prime example was in Argentina, where the reformer Domingo Faustino Sarmiento founded more than 100 public libraries after 1868). Toward the last decades of the 19th century, the influence of positivism encouraged the production of national bibliographies—of which the works by the Chilean Medina about all the Spanish-American countries are the foremost examples—and monumental national histories, such as the five-volume work coordinated by Vicente Riva Palacio entitled *México a través de los siglos* (1880), the ten volumes of Vicente Fidel López's *Historia de la República Argentina* (1883–93), and Diego Barros Arana's sixteen-volume *Historia general de Chile* (1894–1902). In terms of literature, the economic stability and relative prosperity of the last two decades of the 19th century favoured the development of modernism, a trend that was influenced by European cosmopolitanism and fascination for the 'Orient'. Most of the works of Rubén Darío of Nicaragua, José Martí of Cuba, José Asunción Silva of Colombia, and Manuel Gutiérrez Nájera and Amado Nervo of Mexico were also published in Latin American countries other than their own, indicating that their movement's cosmopolitanism was paralleled by the internationalization of the literary market. This broadening of the marketplace coincided with a trend across the region toward the professionalization of publishing, which became a separate business from printing and bookselling.

4 The development of the publishing industries in the 20th century

By the early 20th century, the growing Latin American book market was still dominated by French publishing houses—Garnier, Bouret, Ollendorff, Armand

Colin, Hachette, Michaud, and Editorial Franco-Iberoamericana—plus some German (Herder), English (*Nelson) and American (Appleton) houses. They all specialized not only in translations but in original publications in Spanish and Portuguese, and their superior technology and commercial policies allowed them to make large profits. However, after the outbreak of World War I French book exports to Latin America declined considerably, and Spain began taking over as an important supplier of books to the region. In fact, a few years after the 1898 Spanish-American war, when Spain lost Cuba and Puerto Rico, its last colonies in the continent, the former power tried to deepen its cultural ties with its past colonies, and successive Spanish governments saw in the book trade a vehicle for this. Thus, new international involvement, and the implementation of a fiscal regime more or less favourable for book exports to the region from the late 1910s to the 1930s, led Spain to become a power in Spanish-language publishing. By 1932, Spain's book exports had reached US $1,214,000 (Subercaseaux, 148). Similarly, French involvement in World War I also resulted in a decrease of book exports to Brazil, which in turn favoured Portuguese exports to its former American colony.

On the other hand, the Mexican revolution (lasting from 1910 to c.1920) and the repercussions of World War I generated new intellectual trends across the continent; many thinkers were led to reconsider the cultural uniqueness of Latin America as a region in relation to other parts of the world. In the wake of nationalism and pan-Americanism, new genres flourished, especially novels with a social content and provocative essays. Intellectuals with political positions such as the Uruguayan José Enrique Rodó, the Peruvian José Carlos Mariátegui, the Mexicans José Vasconcelos and Alfonso Reyes, the Dominican Pedro Henríquez Ureña, and the Colombian Germán Arciniegas wrote extensively on the conceptualization of Latin America as a geographic, cultural, and spiritual unity. In parallel with intellectual debate, social reform—the attempt to integrate marginal sectors of the population, including Indians and Africans, into the new idea of the nation—resulted in creating a huge reading public for the first time in the history of those countries.

Although the 1930s were affected badly by the world economic depression, the outbreak of World War II in Europe coincided with the start of industrialization in most Latin American countries, with positive repercussions for the publishing industry. Indeed, the Spanish Civil War (1936–9) and World War II gave the emerging publishing industries of many Latin American countries an unexpected boost. A decrease in European book exports allowed domestic book production to increase, resulting in the creation of new publishing houses throughout the region. After 1945, the book industry followed the rapid pace of economic growth and industrialization, aided by strong government incentives.

In an era of state expansion and support for nationalism, culture was seen to be a government responsibility. In Argentina, Brazil, Colombia, and Mexico, favourable tax regimes for publishers (but not necessarily for booksellers) were inaugurated; in many cases, levies on imported materials for book production were lifted; the budget for public universities—which had their own publishing departments—increased, and the state itself even became the *patron of some publishing houses. Prominent examples of state-sponsored publishers include: the *Fondo de Cultura Económica, created as a government holding in Mexico in 1934; the National Book Institute in Brazil (1937); and the Mexican Comisión Nacional de Libros de Texto Gratuito (1959), established to publish set works for primary schools in the whole country. In addition, those countries' publishing industries began to acquire the structure of modern enterprises, ruled by market forces: low production costs were achieved through high *press runs (especially for pocket books and textbooks), which could be sold in Latin American countries with less developed publishing industries such as Chile, Uruguay, Ecuador, Peru, Bolivia, and the Central American republics. As a result, Mexican book exports grew threefold between 1945 and 1955; by 1967 export levels reached US $11.5 million. Yet the most spectacular growth was experienced by the Argentinian publishing industry, for which the period 1938–55 is known as 'the golden years': its exports went from US $20,000 in the 1940s to nearly US $200 million in the 1960s (Subercaseaux, 147). By 1960 Argentina had some 160 publishing houses, not counting the printing departments of ministries, universities, and public cultural institutions. Brazil, which had started exporting books to Portugal in the late 1920s (mainly through the publishing house *Civilização Brasileira), also saw a great increase in that trade between 1958 and 1970, from US $54,000 to US $2.4 million (Hallewell, 208).

By the 1960s, Latin American publishers also helped to expand the population's reading habits by diversifying distribution. Instead of relying only on bookshops (which were still limited in number), they reached out to *stationers, post offices, corner shops, and other kinds of popular outlets. This strategy, which was initiated successfully by *Monteiro Lobato of Brazil in the 1910s and 1920s, was later put into practice by the Argentinian Editorial Universitaria de Buenos Aires (EUDEBA) and the Centro Editor de América Latina. Among other factors, these measures contributed to the consolidation of the internal market from the 1950s through to the 1970s.

State support came later (reaching its peak in communist Cuba, where all publishing houses were state-related and publishing was controlled by the government) or was limited in other Latin American countries; but on the whole the entire region experienced a growth in book production and consumption during the mid-20th century. It was precisely at this time of the Latin American publishing industry's expansion that literary production grew and came to be recognized internationally as original and characteristically 'Latin American'. With a combination of influences from early 20th-century surrealism, an interest in social topics, and the consciousness of a distinct Latin American cultural identity, poetry and fiction created new kinds of realism, in particular 'magical realism', metaphysical tales, and other kinds of fantastic literature. Pablo Neruda, Octavio Paz, Gabriel García Márquez (all of whom won the *Nobel Prize for Literature), Miguel Angel Asturias, Julio Cortázar, Jorge Luis Borges—to mention only the best-known authors—produced their most important works between the 1940s and the 1960s. Their rapid rise to international fame was assisted by the peak in production and international trade reached by Latin American publishing in the period.

Complementing state support for the production and reading of books, *UNESCO in 1971 created a Regional Centre for the Promotion of the Book in Latin America and the Caribbean (CERLALC), situated in Bogotá; members of the centre were Argentina, Bolivia, Brazil, Colombia, Costa Rica, Chile, Cuba, Dominican Republic, Ecuador, Guatemala, Nicaragua, Panama, Paraguay, Peru, Spain, Uruguay, and Venezuela. CERLALC's aim was and is to promote the production, circulation, distribution, and reading of books in Latin America. Its design incorporates legal frameworks for free trade in books; it encourages regional governments to sign international conventions concerning copyright and against *piracy; it initiates reading campaigns and training for professionals in the book industry. CERLALC also monitors aspects of book production and circulation in most Latin American countries, about which it publishes quantitative material and qualitative essays

on its website, and in books, newsletters, and journals. As a result of CERLALC's efforts, a number of Latin American countries issued so-called 'Book Laws' from the 1970s to the 1990s, which (taking as a model the Spanish book law of 1967) attempt to create legal and fiscal frameworks favourable for the production and circulation of books, as well as for the protection of authors' rights. Yet these laws, while tending to privilege author's and publishers' rights, have done little to help booksellers.

Despite such legal measures, in the second half of the 20th century the Latin American publishing industry developed unevenly and suffered important setbacks. Argentina's and Mexico's primacy in the Spanish book trade were somewhat curtailed by Spain's renewal in the 1950s and 1960s; indeed, by 1974 Spanish book exports had reached US $120 million (Subercaseaux, 148). The bloody military dictatorships of the 1950s–1980s that quashed vigorous social movements in Nicaragua, Paraguay, Guatemala, Haiti, Bolivia, Uruguay, Chile, and Argentina imposed tight censorship and control over the importing, production, and reading of a large number of books. Ill-considered policies in other countries ended up affecting the book industry or the business of bookselling: for example, a protectionist national policy toward papermaking in Mexico resulted in higher production costs for books. In addition, the fall in oil prices, precipitating a financial crisis that led to cycles of hyperinflation, devaluation, and economic recession in most of the region during the 1980s actually reduced the population's income, increased book production costs, and led to declining book sales. From 1984 to 1990, for example, Argentina produced 18 per cent fewer titles.

By the mid-1990s, the return of democracy in most Latin American countries and trade liberalization stimulated the circulation of books throughout the region, but it took away some of the direct state support of the publishing sector; in some countries, this resulted in increased retail prices for books. An imported book in Peru in the 1990s, for example, cost 40 per cent more than in its country of origin, because of the high taxes imposed by a government needing to increase its revenues. By 1999, Brazil was publishing 54 per cent of the total number of books in Latin America, Argentina 33 per cent (11,900 titles), Mexico 29 per cent (6,000 titles), and Colombia 11 per cent (2,275 titles) (UNESCO). With the exception of Argentina and Chile, school textbooks were the dominant genre in all Latin American countries.

National unity was now no longer a reliable guide for understanding the publishing industry. A new phenomenon, the result of globalization, was the merging of transnational publishing groups and the integration of Latin American and European publishing houses. Groups such as *Planeta, Santillana, Norma, *Random House, *Mondadori, and Hachette absorbed the most successful publishing houses and operated with branches in six or more countries. Such consolidation led to a reduction in the number of independent publishers, and of publishers with a specific cultural agenda. Most of the conglomerates made their money in the secure textbook market; reduced costs by producing in countries where materials and labour were cheap; published large numbers of editions of established authors and relatively few editions of new works; and aided their distribution by using mass media they also owned. For its part, the Mexican Fondo de Cultura Económica, which still enjoyed government subsidies, became one of the strongest non-textbook publishing houses by opening branches in Argentina, Colombia, Brazil, Peru, Guatemala, Chile, and Spain.

5 Trends and perspectives for the 21ˢᵗ century

In the first decade of the 21ˢᵗ century, the trend toward the transnational merging of large publishing houses has persisted. Spain recovered its dominant position as provider of Spanish-language books: by 2005 it produced 39.7 per cent of all Spanish books sold in Latin America, whereas Spanish-American countries accounted for 40.2 per cent of sales. The biggest Latin American publishers of books in Spanish continued to be Argentina (27.1 per cent), Mexico (19 per cent), and Colombia (16.3 per cent), followed by Peru (6.1 per cent), Venezuela (5.9 per cent), Chile (5.6 per cent), Ecuador (4.3 per cent), Costa Rica (3.8 per cent), and Cuba (2.8 per cent) (SIER). Given that school textbooks were still dominant—with the significant exceptions of Argentina and Chile, where general-interest books still prevailed—and considering that the school population remained stable, the region's book industries continued to thrive. However, the main problem appeared to be distribution: large numbers of books remained unsold, booksellers had few incentives to innovate, and the big publishing groups relied on discount bookshops or supermarkets to sell their products.

Finally, the numerical domination of textbooks in book production was also suggestive of the poor reading habits of the adult Latin American population—a subject that has become a major concern in studies carried out since 2000. Although varied in scope and methodology, these investigations seem to suggest that, in spite of relatively high levels of basic literacy, the number of books read per capita in Latin American countries is very small. According to UNESCO, Mexicans read on average less than 1 book per year (although a government study from 2003 raised that number to 2.9), and only 2 per cent of citizens regularly bought a newspaper; Colombians read an average of 1.6 books, Brazilians 1.8, and Argentinians 4. In countries such as Mexico and Brazil, where there were wide social divisions, there has been a persistent pattern of polarization between groups of the population who read many books each year and groups who read nothing. A study carried out in Mexico in 2001 about the population's reading habits revealed that the most widely read 'book' was the weekly adult comic *El libro vaquero* (The Cowboy Book), of which 41 million copies were bought each year—18 million copies fewer than in 1985. Whether such a decrease indicates a change towards more sophisticated reading habits, declining enthusiasm for what popular adult comics offer, or a decrease in reading altogether awaits further determination.

BIBLIOGRAPHY

Centro Regional para el Fomento del Libro en América Latina y el Caribe (CERLALC), www.cerlalc.org, consulted Aug. 2007

CERLALC, *Producción y comercio internacional del libro en América Latina* (2003)

H. F. Cline, ed., *Guide to Ethnohistorical Sources, Handbook of Middle American Indians*, vol. 14, part 3 (1975)

J. G. Cobo Borda, ed., *Historia de las empresas editoriales en América Latina* (2000)

R. L. Dávila Castañeda, 'El libro en América Latina', *Boletín GC*, 13 (Sept. 2005), www.sic.conaculta.gob.mx/documentos/905.pdf, consulted Aug. 2007

V. M. Díaz, *Historia de la imprenta en Guatemala* (1930)

J. L. de Diego, *Editores y políticas editoriales en Argentina* (2007)

Facultad de Filosofía (UNAM), *Imprenta en México*, www.mmh.ahaw.net/imprenta/index.php, consulted Aug. 2007

A. Fornet, *El libro en Cuba* (1994)

M. A. García, *La imprenta en Honduras* (1988)

F. X. Guerra, *Modernidad e independencias* (1993)

L. Hallewell, *Books in Brazil* (1982)

T. Hampe Martínez, 'Fuentes y perspectivas para la historia del libro en el virreinato del Perú', *Boletín de la Academia Nacional de la Historia* (Venezuela), 83.320 (1997), 37–54

I. A. Leonard, *Books of the Brave*, 2e (1992)

M. León Portilla, *Códices* (2003)

J. L. Martínez, *El libro en Hispanoamérica*, 2e (1984)

A. Martínez Rus, 'La industria editorial española ante los mercados americanos del libro', *Hispania*, 62.212 (2002), 1021–58

J. T. Medina, *Biblioteca hispano-americana (1493–1810)* (7 vols, 1898–1907)

I. Molina Jiménez, *El que quiera divertirse* (1995)

E. Roldán Vera, *The British Book Trade and Spanish American Independence* (2003)

D. Sánchez Lihón, *El libro y la lectura en el Perú* (1978)

SIER (Servicio de Información Estadística Regional), *Libro y desarrollo* (2005), www.cerlalc.org/secciones/libro_desarrollo/sier.htm, consulted Aug. 2007

L. B. Suárez de la Torre, ed., *Empresa y cultura en tinta y papel* (2001)

B. Subercaseaux, *Historia del libro en Chile* (1993)

E. de la Torre Villar, *Breve historia del libro en México*, 2e (1990)

UNESCO Institute for Statistics, 'Book Production: Number of Titles by UDC Classes' (2007), www.stats.uis.unesco.org/unesco/TableViewer/tableView.aspx, consulted Aug. 2007

H. C. Woodbridge and L. S. Thompson, *Printing in Colonial Spanish America* (1976)

G. Zaid, *Los demasiados libros* (1996)

47 The History of the Book in Canada

PATRICIA LOCKHART FLEMING

1 Before printing

Since printing came late to Canada, book historians turn to anthropologists and other scholars to understand its antecedents, the Aboriginal systems of cultural transmission described by European newcomers. These scholars have observed that Native peoples created pictorial records of hunts, warfare, and spiritual life on rock by painting and carving, drew on bark scrolls and animal hides, and kept tallies on wooden slabs and notched sticks. Native allies of the French helped explorers such as Samuel de Champlain to draft maps. On the Pacific shore, cedar totem poles carved with crests announced the ancestry of family or clan, while in eastern North America *wampum strings or belts made of shell beads documented events by means of symbols that were read in public performance.

Beginning with Jacques Cartier's voyage up the St Lawrence River in 1534, France claimed the Atlantic region and Quebec, as well as territories around the Great Lakes and further inland. Founded by Champlain in 1608, the city of Quebec was the capital of New France and a centre for trade, civil administration, and missionary activities. Although several of the governors requested equipment for the production of official documents, their proposals failed, leaving New France without a printing press. Forms and bills of exchange were ordered from France or copied locally; proclamations were published orally and circulated in MS. A Huron *catechism was printed in Rouen in 1630; a book of ritual for the diocese of Quebec bore a Paris imprint of 1703. It was not until after the conquest of New France, when France ceded the colony to Britain in 1763, that a press was finally set up in Quebec. By that time printing had already begun at Halifax, an Atlantic port founded by the British in 1749 to counter the French, established at Louisbourg on Cape Breton Island.

2 1752–1840

The first press belonged to Bartholomew Green, a Boston printer who died soon after coming to Nova Scotia in 1751. His partner, *Bushell, succeeded him, launching the *Halifax Gazette* on 23 March 1752. Bushell's output was typical of a colonial office: a weekly newspaper, government orders, *jobbing printing, and *pamphlets such as the rules of a local club of firemen. He printed in English and occasionally in French. His successor, Anthony Henry—who worked at the press in Halifax for more than 40 years—launched two durable *almanac series, the second in German to compete with imports from Pennsylvania favoured by the 'foreign Protestants' settled in Nova Scotia by the British. When the *Stamp Act of 1765 required newspaper printers to use paper marked with a British tax stamp, Henry first complied but then showed opposition by framing the text with thick black mourning rules, a mockery he may have copied from the New England press. Quebec's first printers, William *Brown and Thomas Gilmore, who had come from Philadelphia and founded the *Quebec Gazette/La Gazette de Québec* in June 1764, suspended it for seven months in 1765–6 when the Stamp Act drove up paper prices. Brown, his Neilson nephews, and John *Neilson's sons went on to dominate the trade in Quebec for decades. Although their earliest translations have been criticized, their French improved and they ventured into Native languages, completing 2,000 copies of a Montagnais prayer book in 1767. Montreal's first printer, who also came to Canada from Philadelphia,

Quebec's first press—founded in 1764 by William *Brown and Thomas Gilmore—printed a Montagnais prayer book, *Nehiro-Iriniui* by Jean-Baptiste de La Brosse, in 1767.

was *Mesplet, a native of Marseilles. As French printer for the Continental Congress, he had printed three letters encouraging the inhabitants of Quebec to join the Americans in rebellion. He packed his press and set off for Montreal in 1776 while the city was occupied by the American army, but when the troops withdrew he was detained. The political turmoil that brought Mesplet to Montreal drove other printers, Loyalists, from a newly independent US. John Howe came from Boston to Halifax, while Shelburne, on Nova Scotia's south shore, attracted printers from New York and Philadelphia. New Brunswick's first printers were Loyalists; its first *King's Printer was Christopher Sower III, member of a distinguished printing family in Germantown, Pennsylvania. The first presses on Prince Edward Island and Newfoundland were also Loyalist in allegiance. However, when the province of Upper Canada was created in 1791 to extend British laws and customs to the Loyalists settling present-day Ontario, the first printer at Niagara

was not a Loyalist but a native of Quebec, trained there by William Brown. The lieutenant-governor's wife noted in her diary that the French printer Louis Roy did not write good English.

Canada's founding printers shared similar patterns of diversification as booksellers, binders, and stationers. The spread of the press can be mapped by the establishment of newspapers, because most printers in the years before 1840 were also newspaper publishers. Many papers were partisan, some openly political, others allied to a denomination or faction. Government supporters won printing contracts; opponents could face prosecution. In Montreal, Mesplet and the editor of his first newspaper were detained without charge for three years. A Scottish reformer, found guilty of seditious libel at Niagara in 1821, was banned from the province; his publisher was sentenced to a lengthy prison term. At Toronto, Francis Collins served 45 weeks for libel, although he continued to edit the *Canadian Freeman* from his cell. In 1835, Joseph *Howe overwhelmed and convinced a Halifax jury with a speech of more than six hours in his own defence against a charge of seditious libel.

Two of the most prominent printers who voiced public demands for government reform in the 1830s were *Mackenzie of Toronto and *Duvernay of Montreal. The office of Mackenzie's *Colonial Advocate* was vandalized in 1826, but compensation awarded by the court kept him in business. Elected to the House of Assembly in 1828, he continued to attack the government and was expelled then re-elected several times. In 1834 he was Toronto's first mayor; in 1837 he led the rebels who marched on the city but were easily put to rout. Mackenzie escaped to the US, returning in 1849 after an amnesty. Between 1828 and 1836, Duvernay was jailed three times and wounded in a duel because of articles in *La Minerve*. Warned that he was on a list of Patriote leaders about to be arrested in 1837, he left Montreal and lived in the US until 1842. Duvernay was more fortunate than many of his colleagues in Quebec and Montreal—journalists, printers, publishers, and booksellers were jailed or exiled after the Rebellions of 1837 and 1838.

The English writer Anna Jameson declared, during an unhappy visit to Toronto in 1837, that in the absence of books, newspapers were the principal medium of knowledge and communication in the province. Yet books too played an essential role in early Canada. Books were written, published, advertised, reviewed, imported, sold, serialized, bought, borrowed, collected, recited, and read. Ambitious authors writing in English usually looked abroad for publication, since the domestic market for literature was narrow. At home, they circulated poems in MS and tried to find an audience in newspapers and magazines. *Subscription publishing brought some books to press, others were subsidized by the author. One bestselling work offered a warning to Canadian publishers whose original editions—not registered in Britain prior to publication, or produced within American jurisdiction by an American citizen—were not protected by *copyright. Howe first published Thomas Chandler Haliburton's sketches for *The Clockmaker* in his *Novascotian* in 1835–6. Their positive reception prompted him to issue the series in book form. Within the year, editions published in London, Philadelphia, and Boston were competing for sales, even in Halifax. Haliburton thrived on international success, but Howe suffered professional and financial losses. Estimates of the output of Canadian presses show that most printers minimized risk by printing for government (nearly 40 per cent of imprints before 1821) and by relying on safe religious publication (22 per cent, in 1821–40). Almanacs were steady sellers throughout the period while *cookbooks, a genre that would support the publishing ambitions of some small houses in the 20th century, first appeared in French and English in 1840.

On the shelves of bookshops in town or general merchants in the country, modest local imprints were outnumbered by books imported from the US, Britain, and France. Newspaper publishers filled columns with lists of new books for sale at their printing offices. Leading figures such as Neilson and Mackenzie travelled abroad to deal directly with wholesalers, while from the 1830s *Fabre, a Montreal bookseller who had learned his trade in Paris, published catalogues of imported stock. Although lists of books on offer provide some indication of what was available for purchase, the published catalogues of *subscription and garrison libraries and the first *mechanics' institutes bring us closer to the eager readers of novels, memoirs, travel, science, and history.

Recent studies of the book in Canada have taken the year 1840 as the end of the pioneer period. By that date, printers were organizing and their first strike in Toronto had failed; power presses were speeding production; the first major literary magazine was thriving in Montreal, novels had been published in French and English; and Ontario and Quebec were joined in political union. In that year, James *Evans, a Wesleyan Methodist missionary in the Northwest, began to print in Cree using a syllabic system that the Aboriginal peoples adopted and still use today.

3 1840–1918

Between 1840 and 1918 Canada settled into its modern borders, lacking only Newfoundland, which joined Confederation in 1949. The population grew from 2.4 million in 1850, 3.7 in 1871, and 4.8 in 1891 to 8.8 million by 1921. Political change was negotiated in print, from responsible government in 1848 to Confederation of the provinces between 1867 and 1905, and the enfranchisement of women starting in 1918. In World War I Canada outgrew colonial status, but the monetary burden was heavy and social division severe when many in Quebec opposed conscription, and suspicion of immigrants spread. Starting in the 1870s, the federal government promoted immigration and settlement of the West. An energetic programme in which print played a central role addressed both the repatriation of Canadians who had moved on to a more prosperous US and the recruitment of newcomers from Britain and the Continent. The Dominion Lands Act of 1872 offered free land to homesteaders lured by thousands of newspaper notices and millions of pamphlets and posters published in more than a dozen languages. Completion of the transcontinental railway from Halifax to Quebec in 1876, and Montreal to Vancouver in 1885, ensured transportation and communication from Atlantic to Pacific. Block settlements were set aside for Mennonites, Icelanders, Doukhobors, and Hutterites. Other communities (such as Ukrainians) took up lands together in certain districts. The railway brought thousands of immigrants to the West—more than 100,000 in 1882, 1883, 1884, and 1903; more than 200,000 in 1907; and 400,000 in 1913.

Although some groups read American newspapers published in their own languages, most were eager to establish a local press. Like the Loyalists in Atlantic Canada a century before, they usually started with a four-page (one-sheet) weekly. An Icelandic paper in 1877 was the earliest in that language in North America. German printing, which began in Nova Scotia in 1787 and continued in Ontario from the early 19th century, dates from 1889 at Winnipeg, a printing centre for many immigrant groups. A Swedish press was established there in 1887, and the first of a flurry of competing Ukrainian newspapers appeared in 1903. A pioneer Yiddish weekly, published in Winnipeg from 1906, was soon joined by others in Montreal and Toronto. Immigrants who settled in urban centres established printing offices: Chinese and Japanese in Vancouver in 1903 and 1907, Arabic speakers in Montreal in 1908, and Italians and Bulgarians in

Toronto in 1908 and 1912. In its programme to settle sturdy farmers in the West and to recruit workers for central Canada, the government preferred immigrants from Britain, Germany, and Scandinavia. After the British empire, including Canada, entered the war in 1914, however, Germans and some eastern Europeans were declared enemy aliens. Bilingual schools were closed, recent immigrants interned, and publication, even possession, of printed material in enemy languages was banned until the lifting of restrictions in 1919.

The pockets of ethnic publishing that grew up among mission and commercial presses already established in the West strengthened the regional nature of Canada's trade during the 19th century. While publishers in Montreal and Toronto defined their ambitions nationally and imagined international success, regional publishers supplied their markets with newspapers, almanacs, *textbooks, as well as verse, sermons, history, and politics, of local composition or interest. The westward expansion of the press saw newspapers established at Victoria in 1858; Winnipeg in 1859 (with a French paper across the river in St Boniface in 1871); Battleford, Saskatchewan in 1878; and Edmonton in 1880. In the North, the first gold-rush press at Dawson City, Yukon, in 1898 was preceded by *Arctic printing on board the flagships of five expeditions engaged in the search for Sir John Franklin and his crew between 1850 and 1854. Although the mission of shipboard printers was to produce rescue information on coloured paper and silk for release as balloon messages, they amused their isolated readers with an almanac, a weekly newspaper, song sheets, and playbills.

Two firms established in the Atlantic region in the 1820s as booksellers, and conducted within the family for more than a century, exemplify adaptability in the trades. J. and A. McMillan of Saint John, New Brunswick, published poetry and local history, and printed for temperance, religious, and business interests. They operated a bindery, acted as wholesalers, and sold books and *stationery. In Halifax, A. and W. MacKinlay's list was similar to McMillan's, with a particularly strong line of textbooks reprinted from Irish and Scottish series. On Prince Edward Island, three generations of the Haszard family sold books and stationery, served as King's and Queen's Printers, and published newspapers, textbooks, an important almanac, and other books of local interest. At its landmark 'Sign of the Book' in downtown St John's, Newfoundland, Dicks & Company, binders and stationers from the 1850s, expanded for the 20th century into printing

and publishing. An early venture, *Through Newfoundland with the Camera* (1905), was directed towards an expanding tourist market for guidebooks and souvenirs of spectacular Canadian scenes.

A popular destination for visitors, the city of Quebec was also Canada's most important printing centre before 1840, although Montreal's share increased after 1820. At mid-century, Montreal's population exceeded that of Quebec; as growth slowed in the capital, Montreal boomed, emerging as a national leader in trade, industry, and transportation. Shifts within the population of both cities altered the composition and ambitions of the book trades, narrowing the market at Quebec as English speakers declined from 40 per cent in 1861 to 15 per cent by 1901. In contrast, Montreal francophones were outnumbered by British and Irish immigrants between the 1830s and the 1860s. Both markets were courted by entrepreneurs such as *Beauchemin and John *Lovell. French readers could browse catalogues of Beauchemin's stock or shop at Beauchemin et Valois. He published popular fiction and literary work by contemporaries; children studied Beauchemin textbooks and set off for school with his colourful notebooks. A marker of daily life, the *Almanac du peuple* was owned by Beauchemin from 1855 to 1982, and is still published today.

The founding Beauchemin, Charles-Odilon, began his career in the shop of John Lovell, arguably the most important figure in the book trades in 19th-century Canada. Apprenticed to a printer in 1823, he died 70 years later at the head of a prosperous Montreal firm. An early venture was the *Literary Garland* (1838–51), the first successful literary magazine in Canada as well as the first to pay contributors. In addition to publishing a wide range of trade books in English and French, Lovell was a pioneer printer of Canadian music. His series of textbooks was the first written by Canadians for Canadian schools. He took on lucrative contracts for government printing, and lost money on the massive *Lovell's Canadian Dominion Directory* (1871). As an active reprinter of popular British and American books, he tried to negotiate local and imperial copyright laws. He occasionally resorted to *piracy, and shocked the trade in 1871 by building a plant just over the New York state border to print British works for import into Canada as foreign reprints, which had to pay far lower duties to British copyright holders than did Canadian editions.

Around mid-century in Toronto, the book trades grew out of newspaper offices when successful printers and publishers built companies that would remain in business throughout the next century and beyond.

Copp Clark, tracing its origins back to the founder's apprenticeship in 1842, took over the *Canadian Almanac* (1848–) and produced maps and scientific works. The firm competed in the lucrative textbook market that expanded in Ontario after the passage of the 1871 School Act. Books authorized for the Ontario system (shaped from 1844 to 1876 by Egerton Ryerson, a Methodist of Loyalist descent) were readily adopted for use in classrooms across Canada. By the 1880s, Copp Clark was one of three publishers sharing a school reader contract that would earn profits for the next twenty years. The others were Gage and the *Methodist Book and Publishing House. Finally sold to a multinational in 2003, Gage had opened as the Toronto branch of a Montreal partnership in 1860. In addition to printing, publishing, and bookselling, W. J. Gage operated a paper mill and made a speciality of school notebooks: for the 1898 school season, he had two dozen workers filling orders from all parts of the country. Established by Ryerson in 1829 to publish a denominational paper and sell religious works, the Methodist Book and Publishing House expanded its publishing mandate after the election of William Briggs as book steward in 1878; by the 1890s, it was probably Canada's largest printing and publishing enterprise.

In the 1870s, Toronto's reprint publishers earned a reputation as pirates by exploiting weaknesses in the international copyright system to pick off popular titles for unauthorized reprinting. Under various imprints and at different presses, the Belfords pirated books by the expatriate New Brunswicker May Agnes Fleming, as well as by Trollope, Mark Twain, and others. John Ross Robertson, a prominent newspaper publisher and advocate for copyright reform in parliament in the 1890s, is said to have pirated hundreds of titles for his cheap series in the 1870s and 1880s. Of course, Canadians were not alone in the scramble to supply an expanding market with cheap reading in book and serial form. One of the first local books to attract an international readership was *Black Rock* by Ralph Connor, the pen name of Charles Gordon, a young Presbyterian minister living in Winnipeg. Serialized in 1897 in a denominational paper, the novel was published the following year by Westminster in Toronto and by *Hodder & Stoughton in London. Since simultaneous American publication had not been arranged, the book was widely pirated in that country. Gordon remained in Winnipeg, while most of his later works were printed in the US or *stereotyped there for the Toronto publisher.

Other Canadian authors followed a similar path, selling verse and stories to American serials and trying to place their fiction in the more lucrative American markets. Marshall Saunders's *Beautiful Joe* appeared in Philadelphia in 1894, while L. M. Montgomery's fifth attempt to find an American publisher for *Anne of Green Gables* (1908) succeeded with Page of Boston. *The White Wampum* (1895) by the Native poet and performer Pauline Johnson was accepted in London by John *Lane, and Louis Hémon's *Maria Chapdelaine* appeared in a Paris serial in 1914, two years before the illustrated Montreal edition. Because the French-born Hémon had already published in *Le Temps*, his situation differed from other authors writing in Quebec, whose principal markets remained local serials, almanacs, and school prize books. A notable exception was *Les Anciens Canadiens*, a novel by Philippe-Joseph Aubert de Gaspé published at Quebec by *Desbarats in French (1863) and English (1864), and frequently reprinted. Outside government printing offices, translation between the two languages was not common at this time, although Pamphile Le May translated two works into French for Quebec readers: Longfellow's *Evangeline* in 1865 and William Kirby's *The Golden Dog* in 1884.

At the end of the century, a certain stability prevailed in Toronto. Britain had joined the *Berne Convention for international copyright in 1886; new copyright laws were in force in Canada and the US, and a reciprocal Anglo-American agreement for the protection of copyrights was signed in 1891. Books took their place among other important commodities such as groceries, hardware, and dry goods in the expanding trade journal empire of *Maclean-Hunter with the launch of *Canadian Printer and Publisher* in 1892. *Books and Notions*, published since 1884, became *Bookseller and Stationer* in 1896. New directions at the Methodist Book and Publishing House included publishing Canadian authors and strengthening the agency system. The firm moved cautiously with the Canadian list, publishing at the risk more often of the author than of the house. Robert Service sent $100 to have *Songs of a Sourdough* (1907) printed, and at the age of 92, the widely published Catharine Parr Traill was expected to find 200 subscribers for her new work of natural history. Other books were not accepted until the MS had been placed with a British or American firm. Under the agency system—which prevailed through much of the 20th century—Canadian houses were named exclusive agents for foreign publishers. In some instances they distributed bound books, in others they imported printed sheets, or bought or rented stereotype *plates for a Canadian issue, possibly under a local imprint. As the trade developed, foreign firms opened branches in Toronto: *Oxford University Press came in 1904; *Macmillan opened in 1906. Young entrepreneurs, such as the founders of *McClelland & Stewart, left established houses to set up their own companies in the early decades of the new century.

By this time public libraries were an important market for wholesalers and publishers. Starting in the 1880s, the patchwork of subscription, *circulating, parish, and mechanics' institutes libraries gave way to tax-supported *public libraries. Ontario set the pattern with enabling legislation in 1882. Voted into existence by a majority of citizens, the *Toronto Public Library opened in 1884. By 1901, Ontario had 132 free public library boards; by 1921, there were 111 new libraries built with support from the Carnegie Foundation. Thirteen *Carnegie libraries in the west included landmark buildings in Victoria, Vancouver, Edmonton, Calgary, Regina, and Winnipeg. Readers living at a distance from libraries and booksellers could supplement the offerings of the local general store by mail order. Eaton's department store, circulating 1.3 million catalogues annually by 1901, began to offer books in the 1880s. With cut-rate prices and low, even free, postage, department stores offered stiff competition to the retail trade. Rural readers could also anticipate visits from pedlars, Bible and tract society volunteers, and agents of subscription publishers. Particularly in southwestern Ontario, local firms and branches of American houses outfitted travelling agents with samples of elaborate binding styles available to subscribers who signed up for a religious or topical volume. For everyday reading, almanacs—particularly Quebec's literary and historical series—remained popular. The circulation of daily and weekly newspapers exceeded 1 million copies before the end of the 19th century; and despite an abundance of imported titles, domestic publishers supplied religious and agricultural serials as well as illustrated magazines. The postal rate, reduced to a penny per pound by the end of the century, encouraged the publication and circulation of Canadian periodicals.

4 1918–2000

In the prosperous postwar years, Montreal and Toronto remained the publishing centres for French and English. Although Canada had fought free of its colonial past, the future was in question. Lingering bitterness over conscription, and limits on the teaching of French in schools in Ontario and the West, isolated Quebec from the rest of Canada. New publishing houses in Montreal were largely nationalist,

offering popular and patriotic works by French Canadians. In 1920s Toronto, three publishers were investing in books by Canadian authors: McClelland & Stewart; *Ryerson Press, established in 1919 to continue the trade list of the Methodist Book and Publishing House; and Macmillan of Canada. The Great Depression, which lingered through much of the 1930s, hit Canada hard, particularly in the West and among immigrants and blue-collar workers. Publishers became more cautious about Canadian MSS, although textbooks and agency sales continued to return a profit. There was fresh competition from *book clubs, department stores, and cheap imports—so much activity that a new book trade journal, *Quill & Quire (1935–), was launched. The establishment by the federal government in 1932 of a public broadcaster, the *Canadian Broadcasting Corporation since 1936, was a turning point for book culture in Canada. On radio, and television from 1952, authors found both a market and an audience. After Canada entered the war in 1939, the Canadian Broadcasting Corporation, the new National Film Board, and print in every form from ration books to posters were mobilized.

The occupation of France by the German army in 1940 transformed Quebec into an international centre for French publishing, with Europeans writing in exile and the authorized reprinting of French books. *Fides and other major houses were established in Montreal during this period. After the war, when restrictions on paper and other materials were lifted, the publishing trade was ready for change. The great Jack McClelland entered his father's firm in 1946; a year later, the University of *Toronto Press issued a catalogue reflecting its new programme; the bookseller Jack *Cole published the first Coles Notes in 1948; and the imprint 'A *Harlequin Book' was initiated by a Winnipeg publisher in 1949. Canadian librarians formed their national association in 1946, the same year that the Bibliographical Society of *Canada was organized. A doubling of university enrolment from 1944 to 1948 spurred the growth of collections and the construction of new libraries for *McGill, the *University of Toronto, and other institutions.

At the end of the decade, the federal government appointed the Royal Commission on National Development in the Arts, Letters and Sciences, which reported in 1951. Taking a strongly nationalist stance—particularly in 'The Forces of Geography', an introductory chapter documenting the powerful influence of American institutions, media, and books—the commissioners argued for a distinct Canadian culture that would be supported by public funds. They recognized the insecurity of domestic publishing, noting that the fourteen works of fiction in English published in Canada in 1948 competed with some 3,000 from Britain and the US. In addition to funding for media and the arts, they recommended scholarships and aid to universities, and chided the government about the absence of a national library. A key recommendation was the establishment of an arts funding board, the *Canada Council, created in 1957. Together with the *Social Sciences and Humanities Research Council of Canada (1978), it continues to play a central role in support of authors and publishers. The National Library, now *Library and Archives Canada, was established in 1953 but waited until 1967 for a new building. In that same year, the Bibliothèque nationale du Québec, now Bibliothèque et Archives nationales du *Québec, was formed.

The celebration in print of the Centennial of Confederation in 1967 was marked by *Dair's gift to the nation of Cartier, the first roman fount designed in Canada. *Tundra Books began modestly in Montreal with paperback guides to Expo '67. House of *Anansi, still a major literary publisher, issued its first title in 1967. In Quebec, writers, and publishers such as *Éditions de l'Homme were leaders in the Quiet Revolution that transformed political, social, and cultural life as power shifted in the 1960s from Church to state. This extraordinary decade ended badly in Toronto when major publishers began to fail. As the textbook market, which had sustained the industry for more than a century, was weakened by pedagogical change and increasing competition from foreign branch plants, Gage sold its publishing division to an American educational publisher and Ryerson was bought by *McGraw-Hill.

The Ontario government, which had established a Royal Commission on Book Publishing, acted promptly when Jack McClelland offered his company for sale in 1971, loaning almost $1 million and setting up a system for loan guarantees. In 1972, the federal government initiated block grants and translation subsidies; other measures followed, including controls on foreign takeovers, assistance with promotion and distribution, and, in 1979, a programme to award funds on the basis of sales. Still crucial to the Canadian-controlled sector, it continues as the Book Publishing Industry Development Program. Other federal grants targeting youth employment and local initiatives supported writers and new presses, including specialists in alternative and feminist materials. *Kids Can Press, a leader in the children's industry, began as one of the collectives in 1973. In the West, two seasoned bookmen ventured into publishing: *Hurtig, an Edmonton bookseller since 1956, and J. J. Douglas, later *Douglas & McIntyre of Vancouver. A publishing renaissance in the Atlantic region took shape around new presses and in scholarly, literary, and popular periodicals.

By the 1980s, every province but Prince Edward Island was funding its writers and publishers. Quebec went further, with a policy giving bookshops wholly owned by Canadians resident in the province the exclusive right to sell to institutions. Together with federal and provincial support programmes, this realignment of the trade led to growth and prosperity in the 1980s and 1990s. In contrast, the closing decades of the century were treacherous for the English sector when recessions choked the market and the federal government imposed a tax on the sale of books in 1991. The budgets of granting agencies fluctuated with changes in government, and mergers and takeovers of Canadian-owned firms increased. Concentration on retail bookselling left publishers and distributors vulnerable when the superstore *Chapters, having bought up other national chains and squeezed out many independents, demanded stiff discounts and returned books in unprecedented numbers.

In the early years of the 21st century, publishing in English Canada is dominated by a handful of multinationals sharing the market with smaller, Canadian-owned presses from every region of the country. New Canadian titles in English, some 12,000 a year, now enter the market with 150,000 from Britain and the US.

BIBLIOGRAPHY
HBC
R. MacSkimming, *The Perilous Trade*, 2e (2007)

48 The History of the Book in America

Scott E. Casper and Joan Shelley Rubin

1 General

For nearly four centuries, the production and distribution of books has occurred within broader transformations of the American economy. Colonists in British North America depended on London for their bibles and much other reading matter, even as local printers produced many of the secular staples of everyday life. Those colonial printers and their successors in the new United States worked within the craft economy that typified most early American manufacturing. During the nation's industrial revolution of the 19th century, capitalist publishing firms came to dominate an increasingly sophisticated trade that encompassed sometimes complex author–publisher relations, mechanized production processes, and nationwide networks of distribution and credit. Modern business methods and the ascendancy of *advertising reshaped publishing and bookselling in the first half of the 20th century, even as publishers sought to preserve the notion of books and literature as a realm apart from the marketplace. Since World War II, American books have more and more become the products of a global economy, where publishing conglomerates and, more recently, the *World Wide Web blur the boundaries between nations.

Because the book has never been like most economic commodities, which are utilitarian and for which equivalent substitutes can be found, its meaning has always been linked to the central tensions in American culture. The capitalist market for books has simultaneously promoted broad access to diverse publications and fuelled a persistent concern about the welfare of the nation's literary and spiritual life. Cultural mediators have sought to exert centripetal force on Americans' choices for and their practices of reading from the 17th century to the present day. From Puritan authorities who attempted to guard early New Englanders from worldly publications, to 20th-century cultural figures who hoped to restore the place of 'great books' in America's schools and homes, individuals and institutions have seen the book as a bulwark against spiritual decline and secular democracy. Yet American history has witnessed an ever-expanding array of religious, ethnic, occupational, political, and regional ties, which complicate any unitary definition of national culture. That multiplicity of collective identities, as well as the differences among the intermediaries themselves, has worked to foster a wider range of meanings, purposes, and settings for reading.

2 The colonial period: a transatlantic world of books

2.1 17th-century printing

Printing in America before 1700 was a colonial endeavour in most respects. The first printers were immigrants, some of whose families would remain in the trade for generations, such as the Greens of New England and the Bradfords of Pennsylvania and New York. For lack of manufacturing in the colonies, they imported their capital goods (presses, *type, *composing sticks, and other materials) and even their paper, until the establishment of America's first *paper mill outside Philadelphia in 1690. Far from London, some Boston and Cambridge printers produced their own *almanacs and other cheap books as early as 1640, when the *Bay Psalm Book became the first book

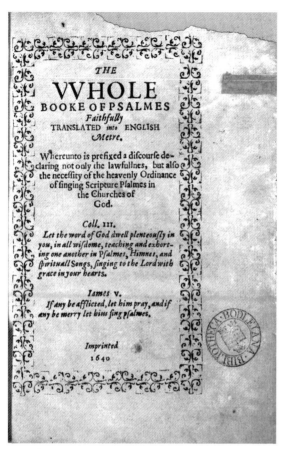

One of the eleven known surviving copies of the *Bay Psalm Book, printed by Stephen *Day at Cambridge, Massachusetts, in 1640.

printed in British North America. The Licensing Act (*see* PRINTING ACT) of 1662, however, gave the London *Stationers' Company a royal *patent on most of the significant works and genres, including bibles, *psalters, *textbooks, almanacs, and *law books. Long after that Act expired in 1695, economic factors posed still greater barriers to indigenous colonial production. Except for identifiably strong sellers, particularly annual almanacs and schoolbooks such as the *New England Primer, few books justified the risk required for a sufficient *press run to meet the costs of capitalization. Importing small quantities of works from England was much more profitable for colonial booksellers.

American printing in the 17th century depended heavily on governmental and clerical *imprimatur and *patronage. The earliest press was at Cambridge, brought from England in 1638 to serve the needs of Harvard College, the General Court (colony government), and John Eliot's mission to the Massachusett Indians. It was not until after the publication of Eliot's

Indian Bible (1661–3) that the Cambridge printers Marmaduke Johnson and Samuel *Green began reprinting London *pamphlets, a short-lived commercial endeavour that the colonial magistrates may have closed. In 1674, the General Court granted Johnson permission to operate a press in Boston, where printing quickly assumed a different character. While Cambridge imprints were local and ecclesiastical, Boston's diverse productions included histories and biographies, almanacs, practical *medical texts, and other works catering to an incipient commercial market.

Printing was slower to originate in Virginia. In 1671, more than six decades after the colony's founding, Governor William Berkeley wrote to the English government about the potentially destabilizing effects of printing and schools: 'But I thank God, there are no free schools or printing [in Virginia], and I hope we shall not have these [for a] hundred years, for learning has brought disobedience, and heresy, and sects into the world, and printing has divulged them, and libels against the best government. God keep us from both!' (Hening, 2. 517). Virginia's laws were published *scribally until the early 1680s, when a member of the House of Burgesses imported a press and a skilled printer, *Nuthead, to print them. The governor and council quickly ordered the process to be stopped for lack of authorization, and Nuthead departed for Maryland, becoming that colony's first printer. Pennsylvania's proprietor, William Penn, brought its earliest printer, William *Bradford, to the colony to produce Quaker materials. After various disputes with the authorities, Bradford left to become New York's first official printer.

2.2 The 18th-century book trade

If colonial printing began and sometimes ended at the whim of governmental authority, the 18th-century rise of printers in the northern seaport cities betokened a new era of commercial, competitive *print culture. Philadelphia, where Benjamin *Franklin made his way in 1723, is illustrative. Andrew Bradford, son of William, became Pennsylvania's government printer in the 1710s, but his output remained the typical mix of laws, almanacs, and religious publications. A London emigrant and failed printer, Samuel Keimer, arrived the same year as Franklin, established a competing press, and hired the seventeen-year-old Bostonian as his pressman. Soon Bradford and Keimer were printing rival political pamphlets and almanacs and vying for the most lucrative contracts, from the Society of Friends and the government. After an eighteen-month sojourn in London, Franklin entered the fray. With press and type ordered from London, he and Hugh Meredith opened their own *printing office in 1728 and won a Quaker commission that had languished in Keimer's hands. His ambition to publish a rival newspaper to Bradford's *American Weekly Mercury* foiled by Keimer's launch of the *Pennsylvania Gazette*, Franklin satirized Keimer's paper in articles for Bradford's, then bought the *Gazette* when its circulation plummeted. By 1730, Pennsylvania's political wars had cooled and Keimer had departed for Barbados, leaving Franklin indisputably Philadelphia's second printer. *Zenger played the same role in New York, setting up shop in competition with his former master, William Bradford. However, where Franklin printed contributions from all sides of the political debate, Zenger allied his *New-York Weekly Journal* with the council and against the governor— leading to the libel trial that would eventually make his name a staple of journalistic history.

Franklin built his reputation by capitalizing on nearly every niche in an increasingly intercolonial print culture. In addition to the *Gazette* and his *Poor Richard's Almanack*, he published books occasionally at his own risk, generally English works of proven appeal. More often, he printed books and pamphlets for other individuals or for corporate bodies such as the Presbyterian synod or the *Library Company of Philadelphia, which he founded in 1731. A significant portion of his business was in the *jobbing printing of legal *forms and other *ephemera. He procured lucrative government contracts to print the laws and proceedings of the Pennsylvania assembly and issues of paper money for Pennsylvania, Delaware, and New Jersey, and he won Pennsylvania's postmastership in 1737. Through partnership arrangements, Franklin helped establish printing offices across the colonies, including his former *journeyman *Timothy's office in Charleston, South Carolina. He also set up paper mills (including Virginia's first) to control the supply for his own printing and to assist printers elsewhere. By the 1750s, he was the colonies' largest paper merchant as well as Philadelphia's leading book importer and bookseller. Remarkable both in its own time and in the perspective of his subsequent scientific, political, and diplomatic career, Franklin's life as a printer was an unusually diverse variation on the 18th-century norm. Colonial printers made a living by combining printing and bookselling and by emphasizing jobbing printing and *government printing over work on their own account. Only in Boston did a distinctive bookselling trade develop in imports from London and in

locally sponsored works. By the 1740s, with the growth of commerce between the colonies, the distribution of domestically printed works went beyond their place of production as men like Franklin and his network of printer-booksellers exchanged works from New England to South Carolina.

The 18th century also witnessed an expanding transatlantic book trade, for imports of British books far outpaced population growth in British North America. It has been estimated that 'America-bound shipments between 1771 and 1774 (inclusive) comprised some 60 per cent of all English book exports' (Raven, 185). New England absorbed the greatest share of these imports in the first half of the century; from 1751 to 1780, other colonies (particularly Virginia and Maryland) accounted for a rising proportion. London wholesalers sent large shipments to colonial traders, including to small general merchants as well as dedicated booksellers and printer-booksellers. The bookshop in Williamsburg, Virginia, for example, counted more imported books than domestically produced ones in its inventory. Booksellers' newspaper advertisements proliferated throughout the colonies. Colonial retailers, such as Williamsburg's William Hunter and Joseph Royle, cultivated relationships with London traders and agents in order to acquire information about new publications and to improve their terms of payment and credit. Distance often led to strained relations, and delayed shipments—and payments— were common. American retailers complained that wholesalers dumped unsaleable London books on the colonial market, or sent books they had not ordered. London wholesalers, moreover, did not typically give American printer-booksellers the same credit terms and discounts that English metropolitan and provincial retailers received. For all the American booksellers' complaints, imports diversified their stock and connected colonists to the cosmopolitan and intellectual worlds of the imperial capital.

2.3 Reading communities and practices

*Literacy rates increased in most sections of the colonies during the 18th century, although book ownership (except for almanacs and other cheap books) remained primarily the province of the affluent and the learned. Studies of signature literacy—an imprecise measure of writing ability, which lagged behind reading ability in a society where reading was taught earlier in life—offer several conclusions. Colonists arrived in America with high levels of literacy, compared with contemporary European rates. For example, 69 per cent of male indentured servants emigrating from London between 1718 and 1759 signed their contracts, as did 34 per cent of female indentured servants. Among male German immigrants, required to take loyalty oaths in Philadelphia, 60 per cent signed their names in the 1730s, a rate that rose above 80 per cent after 1760. Increasing literacy rates were the predominant pattern. This was most evident in New England, where 60 per cent of men could sign their names in 1660, 70 per cent by 1710, 85 per cent by 1760, and 90 per cent by 1790. Women's literacy rates began significantly lower (45 per cent in the early 18th century), but narrowed the gap with men's by the 1780s. Elsewhere in the colonies, literacy rates were lower, but increased during the century. Anticipating laws that would become more prevalent in the 19th century, several colonies began to proscribe instruction in writing for African-American slaves, fearing insurrection or escape: South Carolina after 1740, Georgia fifteen years later.

Estate inventories suggest that the typical household library was tiny, containing only a bible or psalter and occasionally a few other books. Bookshops' most frequent customers, learned and wealthy men, purchased mostly British imprints in an era when the financial risk of reprinting London books dwarfed that of importing a few copies. Cheap books—almanacs, *chapbooks, primers, psalters, and pamphlets—were the exception, produced locally and vended in large quantities even in the colonial hinterlands. The bookshop at Williamsburg sold 4,000 to 6,000 almanacs a year in the 1750s and 1760s, and Franklin estimated that 10,000 copies of *Poor Richard's Almanack* sold annually around the mid-century. Franklin's Philadelphia partner David Hall calculated that the firm printed 141,257 copies of the almanac and 25,735 more in a pocket size, between 1752 and 1765. Such cheap publications were disseminated not only (or not even primarily) by printers and bookshops, but by *chapmen or *colporteurs and through general stores. *Subscription and *circulating libraries also originated in the mid-1700s, offering access to books to members without the cost of purchase.

Especially in emerging colonial cities and towns, reading communities took shape in a variety of social milieus that had English antecedents. In literary salons organized by elite women such as Annis Boudinot Stockton in Princeton, New Jersey, and Hannah Simons Dale in Charleston, South Carolina, women and men circulated their poetry and prose in MS. *Coffee houses became centres for the exchange of news among men, as well as meeting places for private societies that practised cosmopolitan ideals

of witty writing and conversation. Like the salons, coteries such as the Tuesday Club of Annapolis, Maryland, and the Schuylkill Fishing Club of Philadelphia fostered the emergence of a 'public sphere' separate from official government and religious discourse. Learned institutions also fostered intellectual connections. Colonial America had three colleges (*Harvard, William and Mary, and *Yale) by the early 18th century and five more by 1770. Pioneering learned and scientific societies included the American Philosophical Society for the Promotion of Useful Knowledge, created in 1769 by the merger of two existing societies. Such institutions subscribed to the transatlantic notion of a 'republic of letters', in which free inquiry would counteract the long-standing effects of church and state control. At the same time, evangelicals, influenced by the mid-century Great Awakening, developed their own reading communities, often based in the libraries and homes of local ministers and fuelled by opposition to worldly urban elites and self-consciously polite culture.

Reading practices differed according to the nature of the work and the purposes that Americans brought to their books. Cheap and ephemeral texts, such as almanacs, newspapers, and pamphlets, might be 'read to death'. For books, the oldest and still strongest meanings were spiritual: whether the Bible, Bunyan's *Pilgrim's Progress*, or Christian biographies, printed works possessed the power to transform the reader's inner self. An alternative, newer mode of reading emphasized secular rationalism, generally against the perceived excesses of evangelical enthusiasm. By the mid-18th century, literary sentimentalism offered a semblance of common ground between the evangelical and rationalist models, blending their shared emphasis on moral formation. The popularity of Samuel *Richardson's *Pamela* suggested the emergent power of this model, even as it engendered enduring debates about the potentially pernicious effects of novel-reading.

The Revolution did not immediately transform Americans' reading, although it inspired the first indigenous bestseller, Thomas Paine's *Common Sense* (1776), and helped swell the number of American newspapers from 23 to 58. The war suspended the transatlantic trade in books and most other commodities. Printers struggled to survive, and membership in the trade was marked by high turnover. An emergent colonial reprint business, begun by the Scottish-born Philadelphia printer Robert *Bell in the 1760s, collapsed. Instead, the war politicized printers, whose circumscribed output still included newspapers, pamphlets, government documents, and *broadsides. Independence freed printers from the royal *copyright on bible publication: petitioned by Presbyterian clergymen, a committee of the Continental Congress recommended the publication of an American edition of the Bible. After Congress fled from Philadelphia, the Scottish émigré printer *Aitken undertook the venture on his own, producing five successful editions of the New Testament. Unfortunately for Aitken, he decided to print the entire Bible just before the war ended—and the resumption of British imports undercut his initiative with cheaper bibles. As they had a century earlier, economic realities proved more powerful than either political restrictions or their demise.

3 The 19th century: print cultures in the expanding nation

3.1 The emergence of American publishing

In the aftermath of the Revolution, the new nation's publishing trade originated primarily in reprints of familiar works, not in the production of new books written by Americans. Aitken's failure did not deter other printers from attempting American imprints of British books. Thomas Dobson, an Edinburgh clerk, was sent by his bookseller employer to Philadelphia to open a bookshop for imported stock. Dobson diverted much of the proceeds to creating his own publishing enterprise, which included American editions of Adam Smith's *Wealth of Nations* (1788) and the eighteen-volume *Encyclopaedia Britannica* (1789–98). Isaiah *Thomas, a Worcester, Massachusetts, newspaper printer, began his publishing career with reprints of small *children's books (*see* **15**), then turned to the project that had bedevilled Aitken. Indeed, in the 1790s numerous American printers worked on editions of the Bible. The profusion of bibles, in a variety of *formats from *folio to *duodecimo with market niches for diverse customers, provided the first evidence that American reprints could supplant British imports.

That recognition became the genesis of a publishing trade in the US. Some publishers, such as Dobson, had begun as importer-booksellers. Others, such as the Irish émigré Mathew *Carey, started as printers, went into bookselling, and parlayed their capital into publishing (assuming the financial risks of production). Between the 1790s and the 1820s, these publishers devised a variety of mechanisms to address the common challenges of financing, distribution, and competition. At a series of *book fairs following the *Frankfurt and *Leipzig models, held from 1802 to 1806, publishers gathered from around the nation to exchange and sell unbound stock to one another in larger quantities and at greater discounts than ordinary retailers received. Publishing by *subscription, a method that in the US dated back to the 18th century, helped ensure sales in advance of production, especially for expensive illustrated or multi-volume works. In collaboration with the itinerant bookseller Mason Locke Weems, Carey used this method to redirect the southern and western markets for such works away from British imports and towards his own productions. Weems's contacts with local retail booksellers in these regions also provided Carey with a network of 'adjutants' for his cheaper books. Co-publication, an arrangement whereby multiple publishers jointly assumed the risks by purchasing a percentage of an edition in *sheets, offered an alternative in the 1820s to cut-throat competition for popular British works. Beginning in 1824, publishers promoted *trade sales, at which booksellers purchased works at auction. Trade sales helped establish uniform wholesale prices for books, encouraging differentiation within the book trades, with wholesaling and distribution distinct from publishing.

Meanwhile, religious publishers pioneered new forms of mass production and distribution. Non-denominational, evangelical organizations such as the Society for Propagating the Gospel Among the Indians and Others in North-America (founded in 1787) and the Massachusetts Society for Promoting Christian Knowledge (1803) contracted with printers to produce books and *tracts, to be distributed to the worthy poor by volunteer travelling agents. The Philadelphia Bible Society (1808) and the New England Tract Society (1814) went a step further, becoming large-scale publishers as well as distributors. Their business model combined economy of scale in production with decentralized, local distribution. Taking advantage of the new technology of *stereotyping, the Philadelphia society produced bibles in the tens of thousands; a network of auxiliary societies distributed them across Pennsylvania. The national evangelical publishing concerns founded over the next two decades—the *American Bible Society (1815), the *American Sunday-School Union (1824), and the *American Tract Society (1825)—employed similar methods. These religious publishers stood at the forefront of technological change and mass communication in the US. To produce their huge print runs, they relied upon stereotyping before the commercial publishers did; moreover, by the 1820s the American Bible Society had also invested heavily in steam-powered printing (using the new Treadwell press) and mechanized papermaking (with *Fourdrinier machines) (*see* **10, 11**). Even as the societies' nationwide distribution networks launched what would later be recognized as modern communications, their message was explicitly anti-commercial. The book market, they argued, spread the gospel of greed and immorality in the form of vicious literature, which only an equally vigorous programme of religious publishing could combat. The religious societies' early business model proved difficult to sustain. As local auxiliaries lost their energy by the 1840s, the American Tract Society and the American Bible Society employed colporteurs to distribute their books. Although the major national societies continued to prosper throughout the century, their centralized dominance of the field gave way to smaller, denominational publishing concerns.

By the 1830s, commercial firms such as Philadelphia's *Carey & Lea and New York's *Harper & Brothers exemplified a new mode of publishing. Some of the publishers, including the four Harper brothers, had trained as printers, but most—including New York's G. P. *Putnam, Boston's W. D. Ticknor and J. T. Fields, and Philadelphia's J. B. *Lippincott—had never been printers but came to publishing from other businesses. These publishers became book-trade entrepreneurs, coordinating the supply of raw materials and the physical production of printed, bound works. A few publishers conducted most of these operations themselves; most famously, the Harpers erected a seven-storey factory in 1853 after fire destroyed their earlier, more modest operation. Others, such as *Ticknor & Fields, built relationships with local firms specializing in papermaking, *composition, stereotyping, printing, and *bookbinding. By the 1850s, American book publishing was increasingly centralized in New York, Philadelphia, and Boston; Cincinnati had a brief heyday as a western publishing hub. Firms elsewhere were associated with particular genres; for example, Chicago's *Rand McNally became America's leading *map publisher late in the century. Yet the eastern cities that gained predominance by the mid-19th century remained the nation's publishing centres through the 20th.

New technologies facilitated the publishers' ascendancy and fostered their distinctive identities in the literary marketplace. Stereotype plates became capital, signifying the right to publish a work and discouraging competitors from the expense of producing their own editions. As *case bindings replaced unbound sheets or unadorned *boards, publishers

created *house styles to promote brand identification. Among the first to seize this opportunity, the Harpers produced series such as 'Harper's Family Library', intended for wholesome domestic reading, and 'Harper's School District Library', designed to capitalize on the burgeoning public school movement. Both 'Libraries' were composed of diverse works, mostly by British authors, unified by a common series name and binding. As promoters of American authorship drew upon the 1840s rhetoric of Manifest Destiny, *Wiley & Putnam advertised native productions in its *'Library of American Books' series, which included Melville's *Typee*, Hawthorne's *Mosses from an Old Manse*, and works by Margaret Fuller, Edgar Allan Poe, John Greenleaf Whittier, and William Gilmore Simms. Soon thereafter, 'blue and gold' clothbound editions of British and American authors helped Ticknor & Fields create a reputation as America's premier publisher of transatlantic 'high' literature.

At the same time that they were organizing the processes of book production, publishers worked to manage their trade and subvert the potential for ruinous competition. In the absence of international copyright treaties, rival editions of popular British authors could lead to falling book prices as publishers sought to undersell one another. This concern led to the extra-legal but widely understood conventions known as 'the courtesy of the trade'. The primary tenet of trade courtesy stipulated that the first American publisher to announce that it had a foreign work 'in press' won the rights to its publication; other publishers were expected to relinquish any plans to publish it. By a second principle, the 'rule of association', the publisher that initially reprinted a foreign author's work could stake a claim to that author's subsequent works. The system was far from perfect, and participating publishers routinely complained about trade *pirates who failed to obey these unwritten rules, such as the publishers of 'mammoth weeklies' in the 1840s and of 'cheap libraries' 40 years later. A boom-and-bust economy exacerbated the precariousness of publishing. J. P. *Jewett published the century's best seller, Stowe's *Uncle Tom's Cabin*, in 1852, but suspended payments and went out of business during a nationwide depression five years later. Ticknor & Fields experienced a series of reorganizations over three decades, over-extended its resources in the 1860s and 1870s, and ultimately merged in 1878 with another publisher to form what would become *Houghton Mifflin Co.

Attempts to organize were more successful in niche publishing markets than in the general trade. The short-lived *American Book Trade Association of the 1870s, which included most of the leading publishers as well as dozens of smaller ones, sought to establish uniform discounts to vendors in an effort to regulate prices and combat 'underselling' by agents and retailers. In more specialized areas, consolidation reigned by the end of the century. Schoolbook publishers formed their own Board of Trade in 1870; after its collapse, the four largest firms created a syndicate and eventually merged into the *American Book Company, which contemporaries believed controlled 50–90 per cent of the textbook market. *Music publishers, who flourished in large and small cities across the nation, formed a Board of Music Trade in 1855 to curtail their own tendencies towards ruthless price-cutting and discounting. By 1890, Boston's *Ditson & Co. had swallowed most of the other leading firms from Philadelphia to San Francisco, achieving a measure of industry-wide control unparalleled in any other part of American publishing.

3.2 Disseminating the industrial book

No matter how effectively they centralized book production, American trade publishers needed to distribute their wares to far-flung customers across a geographically expanding nation. To accomplish this, they created networks to exchange information, goods, and credit. The traditional means of sharing information by letters was supplemented by specialized periodicals, notably the magazine that began as *Norton's Literary Advertiser* (1851) and became *Publishers Weekly* (1873). Advertising was promoted through *publisher's lists and catalogues, with *posters and flyers for new books, and in newspapers and periodicals. From the 1850s, the major firms' own general-interest magazines (such as *Harper's New Monthly Magazine* and *Putnam's Monthly*) became important venues for reviewing and advertising their books. Books were distributed by express companies and the US postal system, which maintained special rates for printed matter. To coordinate both supply and credit, publishers relied increasingly on wholesale book dealers, known as jobbers. These dealers, such as the *American News Company and *McClurg & Co., distributed publishers' books to booksellers, who received a discount on the stated retail price. Trade sales, which persisted as a forum for auctioning stock, declined in importance by the 1870s as the larger publishing houses and jobbers dispatched travelling agents ('commercial travellers') to visit local retailers. Publishers in specialized areas developed distinct distribution systems: for instance, *sheet music and scores were sold primarily in music shops, and

schoolbook publishers hired sales agents to secure adoptions by county and state school districts. Especially after the Civil War, subscription publishing firms sent sales agents across the nation and even into remote towns and mining camps to vend their wares. In rural areas where bookshops were few, customers purchased books in general stores, ordered them by mail or by subscription, or borrowed them from libraries and other associations devoted to collective ownership. None of these modes of book distribution offered what bookshops in cities and towns made available: the fullest range of trade publishers' titles. However, unlike 20th-century bookshops, these urban shops were not places for browsing; organized by publisher rather than by subject, the stock was shelved behind the counter, with sales clerks serving and advising readers.

As Americans embraced the pleasures of reading many books just once (what scholars have termed 'extensive reading') alongside the familiar custom of studying the same ones (such as the Bible) again and again ('intensive reading'), the collective ownership of books remained an attractive alternative to individual purchase. Social libraries—voluntary associations founded by members' purchase of shares—blossomed after the Revolution, flourishing until the 1830s. More than 2,100 such libraries were created between 1786 and 1840, but many did not survive their first decade as their collections stagnated and members sought new books elsewhere. Created to shape appropriate reading tastes, social libraries generally did not collect the *novels and *romance fiction that readers most desired. Commercial circulating libraries, often operated by booksellers, filled that gap, offering readers the opportunity to borrow recent, popular fiction for a fee. Other sorts of libraries, founded for specific segments of urban society such as *apprentices, mechanics, and merchants, were torn between their founders' mission to provide morally and socially edifying fare and their fee-paying members' wishes for popular literature. By 1875 the largest of these, the New York Mercantile Library, boasted 160,000 books to cater to its members' tastes. The crusade for 'proper' reading persisted in Sunday school libraries, which increased in number from 2,000 in 1850 to more than 34,000 two decades later, and in the tax-supported school district libraries that began in Massachusetts and New York in the 1830s and 1840s.

Local governments launched the movement for tax-supported public libraries, the first being the *Boston Public Library (1854). The movement spread slowly, but by 1894, according to one study, there were 566 free public libraries with collections of 1,000 books or more. The earliest professional librarians were men associated with learned libraries, such as Joseph Green Cogswell of New York's *Astor Library. Although the *Smithsonian Institution's C. C. *Jewett first imagined the possibility of a *national union catalogue based on the published catalogues of many American libraries as early as the 1850s, standardization in *cataloguing and collection practices proved elusive. The *American Library Association and the *American Library Journal* were founded in 1876, but professional librarianship took several more decades to catch up with the spread of public libraries across the nation.

American learned culture in the first half of the 19th century relied heavily on its better-developed European counterparts. Aspiring scholars studied in German universities; and scholarly books continued overwhelmingly to be imported from Europe, even as American publishers reprinted European works in most other genres. The transatlantic moorings of learned culture gradually shifted as the US developed its own sites for the production and dissemination of knowledge: discipline-specific scholarly periodicals, colleges, seminaries, and research universities along the German model. The US government played a significant role in publishing the fruits of American science and exploration, in such works as the *Smithsonian Contributions to Knowledge* (1848–1916), the seven-volume geological surveys of the 40th parallel (1870–80), and John Wesley Powell's geological and ethnographic studies of the American west. At the same time, commercial publishers created niches by catering to the learned professions: *Little, Brown, & Co., and Baker, Voorhis, & Co. in law books; Lea & Blanchard (successors to Mathew Carey's firm), William Wood & Co., and P. Blakiston's Sons in medical books.

3.3 Literacy and modes of reading

Across the century, literacy rates rose in tandem with the spread of public schooling, especially in the northeast and northwest (today's midwest). Tax-supported schools dated from the 17th century in Massachusetts because individuals' ability to read the Bible had been central to Puritan theology, but their operation had been sporadic and decentralized. After the Revolution, proponents of education added a republican argument (the need for an educated citizenry) to the older religious one, and reformers such as Henry Barnard and Horace Mann proposed statewide school systems to coordinate teacher training and ensure educational standards across economically and ethnically diverse

populations. The number of public schools grew rapidly in New England and western states (such as Ohio) populated by New England emigrants. Few southern states or localities established public schooling before the Civil War, both because wealthy planters resisted paying to educate poorer white farmers' children and because populations were widely dispersed. In 1840, the first time the US census enumerated school attendance, 38.4 per cent of white children aged 5–19 went to public or private school for some portion of the year; by 1860, attendance had increased to 58.6 per cent. Beneath these aggregate numbers lay significant regional variation: more than four-fifths of children in New England attended school in 1840, but fewer than one-fifth of children in the south did. Similarly, although literacy was nearly universal in New England, nearly 20 per cent of white southerners reported an inability to read or write. Most southern states proscribed teaching enslaved African-Americans to read or write; an estimated 5–10 per cent of slaves were literate. After the Civil War, when southern states created public school systems and former slaves sought education for themselves and their children, the ability of African Americans to write (and, hence, presumably to read) increased rapidly: from 30 per cent in 1880 to 55 per cent two decades later.

By the mid-19th century, several conceptions about reading predominated in the US. The oldest, grounded in evangelical Protestantism, gained new energy with the Second Great Awakening, the rise of reform movements such as temperance and abolition, and the tract societies' and religious publishers' prodigious output. Evangelicals argued for literacy and reading, but against reading the wrong books: fiction, adventure stories, and irreligious material. A second ideology, linked to the public-school movement, emphasized the civic value of literacy. Equally, mass immigration led educators and civic leaders to proclaim the need to Americanize the 'foreign element'. A third mode—reading for 'self-culture', to use William Ellery Channing's term—sprang from the middle-class emphasis on self-improvement and character development. In such institutions as lyceums, lecture series, and debating societies, women and men sought intellectual and moral improvement from one another and from lecturers and authors such as Emerson. A fourth mode increasingly separated self-improvement from its earlier religious foundation: it had a transatlantic, cosmopolitan vision that developed primarily after the Civil War and prefigured 20th-century literary publishers and book clubs. Books and learning in this model implied or conferred a social and cultural cachet as well as knowledge. Against all these models stood reading purely for pleasure, which expanded with the proliferation of inexpensive books and the spread of libraries. However, commentators continued to lament the corrupting or subversive potential of entertaining reading, especially on impressionable segments of society such as women and the young.

Americans read in a variety of settings and for diverse purposes, connected to individual and collective identities. The widening availability of books, more leisure time (at least within and above the middling classes), and enhanced lighting (oil lamps and, later, electric lights) all increased the opportunities for home reading at night as well as by day. Although elementary instruction moved from households into schools, Americans still probably read more at home than anywhere else. Publishers capitalized on that transformation by marketing books in editions designed for parlour display as well as for everyday perusal. Shared reading experiences, whether the Bible on Sundays or secular works read aloud, reinforced family bonds. In schools and colleges, especially those for young women, reading contributed to the intellectual and political formation of individuals who challenged conventional constraints. Biographies of learned and eminent women encouraged their readers to imagine intellectual and social possibilities outside 'women's sphere', and so did many other genres: belles-lettres, history, travel literature, even fiction. In the last quarter of the century, the home-study programme of the Chautauqua movement sponsored or inspired thousands of reading circles and study clubs. In these settings, women enjoyed the sorts of opportunities for self-improvement that men had long found in debating societies and mercantile associations.

Depending on the books and the circumstances, reading could strengthen national identity or promote other collective sentiments. For example, reading societies in the north before and after the Civil War instilled a sense of racial and social pride among middle-class African-Americans, who sought at once to assert their membership in the national mainstream and to challenge its assumptions about black people's capacity for education. Foreign-language publications always played a similar, dual role for their first- and second-generation American readers. From their origins in colonial Pennsylvania, German-language presses followed German-speaking Americans as far west as St Louis. Rather than form a unified German-American identity, these presses promoted various senses of belonging such as to religious, literary, and learned groups, as well as to a vernacular culture. For other immigrants, reading promoted both Americanization and home ties. The Yiddish press published editions of European and American books, and America's 23 Yiddish periodicals had a circulation of 808,000 by 1910. For immigrant central and eastern European Jews, as for newly arrived Italians and many others, access to American printed works in their native languages became a tool for creating ethnic identity and community.

4 1890–1950: modern business and cultural capital

4.1 Trends in publishing and marketing

In some respects, the history of book production, distribution, and consumption between 1890 and 1950 is one of continuity with the previous period: the processes of urbanization, industrialization, and technological change that confronted publishers with opportunities and challenges had been under way for decades, along with the rise in the educational level of American readers. Within those long-term trends, however, particular developments altered conditions for print producers, mediators, and consumers in the first half of the 20th century. The influx of non-English-speaking immigrants, the growth of mass entertainment, the increase in leisure time for some workers as well as for the middle classes, and new forms of advertising and display simultaneously strengthened and threatened the place of print in American life. More books, produced more cheaply and efficiently, were available to more people, but so was a wider array of competing commodities and diversions. Publishers and readers alike responded by negotiating various compromises between acceptance of modern business values and the preservation of a realm for the book that appeared to be above the market.

By the 1890s, the innovations of the preceding 50 years in papermaking (see **10**) and printing (see **11**) had dramatically increased American publishers' output. Of course, the term 'publishers' conceals a range of enterprises, including the *dime novel *paperbacks of *Street & Smith, reprint volumes such as George P. Munro's 'Seaside Library', the mainstream fiction issued by established firms like Harper, and the *collected editions of venerated American writers produced by Houghton Mifflin in variably priced sets. Slim volumes of verse—the products of *self-publishing, or inspired by the Arts and Crafts movement—made poetry available to readers apart from weightier collections from *Macmillan or *Stokes. These various formats in turn created and reinforced differences in the cultural expectations surrounding a given book—whether it seemed ephemeral or permanent, serious or frivolous, entertaining or trashy.

Among the still-powerful trade houses in the first decades of the 20th century were those that had sustained the ethos of the 'gentleman publisher' from their inception: these included *Holt, Charles *Scribner's Sons, Harper & Brothers, Houghton Mifflin, Putnam, and D. *Appleton. They generally remained committed, along with making a profit, to supplying American readers with books that, in the publishers' judgement, possessed literary merit or social utility. Thus, Henry Holt personally oversaw the compilation of *The Home Book of Verse* (1912), edited by Burton E. Stevenson, while putting his resources into such 'serious' authors as Dorothy Canfield Fisher, Robert Frost, John Dewey, and Stuart P. Sherman; Charles Scribner published Henry James, George Santayana, and Edith Wharton, but refused a novel of Arnold Bennett's because of its 'unpleasant sordid details' (Madison, 199). Many of these firms maintained the 'courtesy of the trade' by refusing to lure authors away from their competitors. As had been true for earlier figures such as Fields, however, ideological principles coexisted with, and sometimes served, business priorities. By the turn of the century, the spread of a national market, the volatility of Wall Street, and the aggressive business climate of the late 19th century allowed the book industry to expand, but also heightened the risk that output would fall victim to overproduction, inadequate distribution, or price-cutting at the point of sale. As the older trade publishers, in need of capital, searched urgently for an elusive financial guarantee for their products, they adopted many modern commercial practices they disdained in their role as public servants.

Chief among these was the introduction of professionalization into what had been family-run houses. In 1896 the Harper brothers, out of money, lost control of the company to the financier J. P. *Morgan. Subsequently, the entrepreneur Colonel George Harvey, with Morgan's blessing, took over the firm and reorganized it along lines that had already revolutionized railroad operations and steel production: he introduced separate departments for specialized functions and installed middle-level managers to run them. In 1908, under George Brett, the American branch of Macmillan became the first house in the US to establish a separate higher education division. Capitalizing on the concerns of parents and educators, in 1919

Brett also instituted the first children's book department (*see* **15**). At the same time, publishers sold off unprofitable parts of their business: *Dodd, Mead parted with the firm's bookshop in 1910 and its periodical, *The Bookman*, in 1917. Along with such structural changes, several trade houses vied with cheap reprint libraries by offering their own inexpensive series, such as the 'Modern Student's Library' (Scribner) and *'Everyman's Library' (*Dutton). They also adopted their competitors' distribution methods, selling books through subscription agents or via the mails. The *limited-edition set provided another way in which trade publishers learned to lock customers into a multi-volume purchase—one that carried the promise of literary culture. Such 'gentlemanly' individuals as Holt, Brett, and Houghton Mifflin's Horace Scudder remained committed to fulfilling that promise —hence, their willingness to publish poetry or criticism at a loss—but they did so in part because they understood that distinguishing their firms from reprint houses and producers of cheap fiction had its own marketing value.

In their efforts to rationalize production and distribution, late 19th- and early 20th-century publishers also tried to gain control over the price of books. The imposition of international copyright protection in 1891 and the consequent blow to piracy was one source of price stability. But price-cutting in shops remained a problem for mainstream firms. The usual practice of the period was to offer retail booksellers a 40 per cent discount on trade titles, which they then marked up for sale. By 1900, however, some bookshops and department stores were offering customers a bargain by charging less than the standard markup. To counter that tactic, the American Publishers' Association and the *American Booksellers Association devised a 'net pricing system' (modelled on Britain's *Net Book Agreement) that prohibited publishers from distributing titles to price-cutters. R. H. Macy's legal challenge to net pricing, which the Supreme Court upheld in 1913, required publishers to accept discounting and the uncertain profits it entailed. Subsequent efforts in the 1930s and 1940s to make retailers observe fair trade contracts proved largely unsuccessful.

Modern advertising methods were also used to increase revenues: instead of relying on sober announcements of a firm's new books for the season, some publishers tried promotional campaigns for particular titles. Both *Publishers Weekly* and the monthly magazines affiliated with individual publishing houses were sites for such undertakings, although many publishers before World War I remained convinced that books were different from other commodities and that advertising did not result in greater sales. After the war, that attitude persisted in some quarters, but not in others. Such figures as Albert *Boni and Horace Liveright (of *Boni & Liveright), Richard Simon and Max Schuster (of *Simon & Schuster), Alfred A. *Knopf, Bennett Cerf, Donald Klopfer, Harold Guinzburg, John Farrar and Stanley Rinehart (of *Farrar & Rinehart), and Benjamin *Huebsch—mainly university-educated, Jewish New Yorkers—founded new houses in the 1910s and 1920s or assumed editorial positions that changed the tone of the book business. The relatively prosperous postwar economy and the attendant growth of mass consumer culture fuelled their success. It was also encouraged by the consolidation of a common school curriculum and the rising numbers of high school and university graduates in the same years: a consequent increase in literacy complemented a growing interest in mastering the specialized knowledge that seemed essential for success.

In this climate, new publishers (benefiting from new business methods) had fewer qualms than their predecessors about treating books as consumer goods. When Simon & Schuster started their firm in 1924, they pioneered a number of effective entrepreneurial techniques. The partners sought authors to create MSS they thought would sell; they allocated more money for advertising than other publishers; they developed a recognizable logo and company identity; and they handled each title as if it were 'a separate business venture'. They also surveyed customers by placing return postcards in their books. In 1927, they promoted Will Durant's *The Story of Philosophy*, as *Fortune* magazine noted, with an 'excitement' that was 'impossible to escape' (Rubin, *Middlebrow Culture*, 246, 249). The campaign included sales incentives for bookshops, direct-mail solicitation, a money-back guarantee, and a series of well-placed advertisements that fed readers' desire for knowledge and prestige. Trade publishers like Schuster still thought of themselves as cultural missionaries, but there was a heightened tension between that ideal and the successful marketing of books.

Similarly, Knopf, who founded his own firm in 1915, distinguished it by his commitment to cosmopolitanism, literary quality, and good design. The Knopfs brought the best contemporary writers to American audiences. Insisting that they believed in publishing meritorious works whether or not they would sell, they were particularly hospitable to European literary modernism. Knopf nevertheless was aggressive in marketing books, stamping a recognizable personality

on them: he put men in sandwich boards to publicize Floyd Dell's *Moon-Calf* (1921), was the first publisher to use photographs in testimonial advertisements, and devised slogans that resembled those for household products.

New publishers' openness to modern promotional methods matched a shift in attitude among some typographers and printers. Like their European colleagues, proponents of a streamlined modernist aesthetic hailed machine typesetting as the means to efficiency and beauty. Yet the great American typographers and designers of this period—C. P. *Rollins, *Updike, *Cleland, *Rogers, *Goudy, *Dwiggins—tended to advocate and practise hand-setting and printing as well as machine production to preserve older printing techniques.

The educational mission of scientific publishers dictated both non-profit or subsidized operations and profit-making enterprises. The audience for certain kinds of technical knowledge was necessarily limited; adjudicating the content of books was the task of scientists, not non-specialist editors. By 1919, Van Nostrand and *Wiley & Sons dominated this field with Macmillan and *McGraw-Hill. University presses, founded around the turn of the century as an alternative to commercial houses, accounted for a small share (about 11 per cent) of new scientific titles; over the next twenty years, the proliferation of journals and of publishing programmes sponsored by professional associations furnished additional non-profit outlets for publicizing scientific discoveries. At the same time, both in the interwar years and with greater urgency as the atomic age dawned, trade houses produced volumes of popular science for general audiences.

Similarly, Protestant religious publishing involved a mixture of institutions. Some church-owned publishing firms (e.g. *Methodist Book Concern) issued devotional and inspirational texts. Steady sellers, such as Mary Baker Eddy's *Science and Health*, came from church-related publishers. The market for bibles repackaged in a variety of formats expanded, stimulated by non-profit organizations like the *Gideons. Some commercial, privately owned presses specialized in Protestant subjects, while trade houses maintained religious departments: at Harper's, its masterful editor Eugene Exman took over in 1935. The 1920s saw a surge of interest in religious titles, which poured forth from all these sources, as well as the invention, in 1921, of Religious Book Week, which broke down the distinction between religious and trade books. Yet some of the most popular volumes, such as Mrs Charles E. Cowman's locally published *Streams in the Desert*

(1925), evaded commercial account books, enjoying a kind of hidden life among the devout.

4.2 New mediators for a diverse public

In the interwar period, mediators between producers and consumers of books—book club judges, literary critics and journalists, librarians, and educators—grappled with a set of tensions related to publishers' ambivalence toward commercialism: they sought to juggle a desire to influence large numbers of readers with an awareness that popular appeal would undermine their own stature and the prestige of the book itself.

At the mid-century, publishers distributed directly to readers about half the hardcover books sold in the US. The other half reached purchasers through retail outlets: not only department stores such as Macy's but also large chains like *Doubleday, *Kroch's, and *Brentano's. Independent bookstores such as the *Hampshire Book Shop and Sunwise Turn, whose proprietors offered advice about good reading, particularly flourished near university campuses. At the same time, even before the paperback revolution of the postwar years, the sale of soft-cover books and *remainders at drugstores and newsstands became common practice.

Within the hardcover trade, however, the *book club provided a new method of distribution perfectly attuned to the period's cultural preoccupations. Organizations such as the *Book-of-the-Month Club, founded in 1926, sought to satisfy social as well as intellectual aspirations, mediating between 'high' culture and consumer desires. Henry Seidel Canby, the longtime head of the Club's Selecting Committee, undertook a similar role as editor of the *Saturday Review of Literature*, a periodical he helped found in 1924. As part of an effort to widen and to guide the audience for 'serious' novels and non-fiction, Canby and Stuart P. Sherman, his counterpart at the *New York Herald Tribune's Books*, sustained a concern for the craft of writing, taking a dim view of modernist experimentation while adapting literary criticism to the consumer-friendly format of a weekly *tabloid.

Librarians, too, balanced acting as cultural authorities against their interest in building systems and institutions that would serve diverse populations and varying standards of taste. At the close of the 19th century, the leaders of the American Library Association felt that they were responsible for stocking their shelves with the 'best' reading. The reformer Melvil *Dewey ardently promoted that principle, which implicitly relegated most fiction to an inferior status.

The rapid proliferation of local libraries between 1900 and 1920 (thanks in large part to *Carnegie's philanthropy), however, heightened librarians' concern with library science (*see* INFORMATION SCIENCE). The ALA's *Booklist*, created in 1905, was designed to help library professionals systematically identify good books for their growing numbers of patrons. In the 1920s and 1930s, library leaders such as Douglas L. Waples sought to establish their authority on civic grounds, arguing that democracy required the nurturing of 'enlightened public opinion'. The ALA's 'Reading with a Purpose' campaign reflected that concern, along with anxieties about mass media and materialism; yet its proponents adopted modern advertising techniques to get across their message. Progressive educators, aware of the 'large foreign element' in schools, joined library professionals in the belief that inculcating good reading habits would prepare the nation's children for adult citizenship. Yet librarians continued to struggle among themselves about how much to oppose the public's overwhelming preference for novels. Despite the official emphasis on 'purpose', that preference led most ordinary working librarians to concentrate on providing information rather than shaping taste.

The individuals who developed the nation's great research libraries after 1900 experienced fewer tensions, because they saw themselves as contributing to the modern advancement of knowledge. That outlook led the Library of *Congress in 1901 to create its own classification system, which promised to accommodate new subject areas more flexibly than *Dewey decimal classification. The standardization of interlibrary loans in 1917 allowed higher education institutions to share materials readily. Two commercial publishers, R. R. *Bowker and H. W. *Wilson, produced bibliographies, the *Reader's Guide to Periodical Literature*, and other indices for the library market. Under the administration of Herbert *Putnam, the Library of Congress joined in this activity, developing the National Union Catalog in the early 1900s; its publication in the mid-1940s of volumes reproducing its printed catalogue cards was another landmark in LC's nationalization of support to scholars. At roughly the same time, the *New York Public Library (second in its holdings only to the Library of Congress) embarked on wide-ranging collection-building. Relatively free of the ideological constraints that animated their less cosmopolitan colleagues, the librarians who built the NYPL (especially its Reference Department, which became the Research Libraries in 1966) were committed to acquisitions that reflected the multiplicity of human experience and the unpredictable needs of future scholars. Their democratic outlook and their devotion to wide collecting distinguished them from their European counterparts. A dedication to comprehensiveness also characterized the major academic libraries (e.g. at Harvard, Yale, *Columbia, *Cornell, and the University of *Chicago); by 1939, each of those had amassed more than a million volumes. In the same years, several individuals—among them Henry E. *Huntington, J. P. *Morgan, Jr., and H. C. *Folger—enriched the possibilities for scholarship by founding repositories (the *Huntington Library, the Pierpont Morgan Library, the *Folger Shakespeare Library) to house and build upon great private collections.

4.3 Continuity and community in reading

As producers and mediators of books adapted to the burgeoning, diverse consumer culture of the 20ᵗʰ century, their audiences perpetuated established reading practices while simultaneously endowing print with new significance. In the 1930s, the Civilian Conservation Corps popularized the term 'functional literacy' to denote the skill necessary to read the materials pertinent to daily life. By 1947, when the Census Bureau defined 'functional illiterates' as those with fewer than five years of schooling, only 6 per cent of Americans fell into that category, in contrast with 24 per cent in 1910. Book readers were more likely to be from the middle or upper classes than from the working class, and before World War II most people, regardless of income, preferred newspapers and magazines. As Waples and other social scientists had shown in the preceding two decades, a minority of Americans turned to books for self-improvement, pleasure, and (especially during the Great Depression) diversion from daily life. They made meaning by connecting eclectic texts to their experiences within families, religious settings, and classrooms. Although silent reading largely displaced reading aloud as an instructional mode and leisure activity, the social dimension of reading persisted in the 'literary evening' and the book group. For both white and African-American women, literary clubs fostered a sense of identity and empowerment, as well as political activism.

5 1950 to the present: the American book in a global economy

5.1 Consolidating the publishing industry

Although technological innovation, ever-proliferating leisure activities, and a more highly educated population remained part of the book's social environment in the US following World War II, a distinguishing feature of the second half of the 20ᵗʰ century was the repositioning of the book business within a global economy. The war itself contributed to internationalization by involving publishers in efforts to supply American troops abroad with reading material: beginning in 1943, the Council on Books in Wartime, an industry consortium, brought out more than 13,000 titles in lightweight, pocket-size *Armed Services Editions. It also oversaw the issuing of Overseas Editions—volumes aimed at building understanding of the US among Europeans. The project stimulated and prefigured the expansion of American publishing into foreign markets in the immediate postwar period. *Textbooks and works on scientific and technical subjects dominated the vigorous export trade in the 1950s and 1960s, and the sale of translation rights also increased dramatically. American firms subsequently developed independent subsidiaries abroad—32 by the 1980s. At the same time, European publishers such as *Oxford University Press, *Elsevier, and *Springer opened offices in the US.

The impetus for the internationalization of American publishing was partly political, given the Cold War perception that America needed to strengthen its cultural presence around the world. For the most part, however, the US book industry's global expansion was the result of a quest for greater profits—a fact that underscored its similarity to other businesses. Still, many of the dominant figures in 1950s and 1960s trade publishing maintained a sense of obligation to turn out good books—even though initial printings of non-fiction volumes tended not to make money—and cultivated a personal tone with authors and employees.

The relationship between books and other means of communication changed after 1950. Whereas many publishers had sought to maintain the book's position on higher cultural ground than that occupied by film, radio, and recorded music, the sale of *Random House to the Radio Corporation of America in 1965 symbolically recast print as simply one of several forms of entertainment available to the American public. Moreover, by the 1970s the sale of *subsidiary rights—not only to *book clubs or to the booming *paperback houses, but also to Hollywood or television—had become the major source of some firms' revenue, so that, far from fearing competition from other leisure activities, many publishing executives now depended on those activities for their survival.

In the last decades of the 20ᵗʰ century, media conglomerates—several based in Europe—continued to absorb formerly independent publishers, both exclusively trade operations and those houses with mass-market paperback divisions. Scribner merged in 1984 with Macmillan, which was in turn bought by Paramount nine years later; *Bertelsmann purchased *Bantam, Doubleday, and *Dell in 1986; Rupert Murdoch acquired Harper in 1987. Christian publishing was not exempt from this pattern: *Zondervan became part of HarperCollins in 1988. More recent industry mergers include Viacom's purchase of Paramount in 1994, the amalgamation of its publishing interests under the name of Simon & Schuster, and Simon & Schuster's reorganization as part of CBS Corporation in 2006. In 2002, the eight largest firms controlled more than half of American book sales. At the same time, the production of new titles, especially in categories such as religion and fiction, increased sharply: between 1992 and 1997 the book industry grew at a rate of 34 per cent.

The industry's volatility increased the pressure on editors to sign up titles that would make money, with a corresponding expansion of the role of the *literary agent. Owners of the new conglomerates, indifferent to editorial freedom and cultural ideals, required high profits from each book and a concentration on big sellers. Paperback publishers, who in the 1970s and 1980s had discovered the lucrativeness of issuing original titles in such genres as romance fiction, contributed to the competitive atmosphere by bidding up the cost of reprint rights as well. The rise of media conglomerates has been blamed for a marked decline in American publishing, measured by the quality of the industry's product. The complaint echoed the lament of designers and typographers, adjusting to the development in the 1970s of *photocomposition and *offset printing, that labour-saving automation was destroying aesthetic standards.

Some observers have challenged those assumptions, arguing that the book business needed to overcome inefficiencies. Moreover, independent publishers have retained a significant economic and cultural role into the 21st century. According to the Book Industry Study Group, the number of small firms in 2005 was higher than ever. There is room, still, for the limited edition of poetry and for *fine printing, typified by the Black Sparrow and the Arion presses; even within the trade, houses such as Knopf strive for excellence in design. The spread of identity politics in the 1960s created niche markets for houses publishing Hispanic and African-American literature (such as Arte Publico and Broadside Press). Evangelical publishers market works in Spanish to reach their multicultural followers. Outside the commercial sector, university presses and other entities such as the New Press, which André Schiffrin founded in 1990, uphold their mandate to bring new knowledge to the reading public. Even the disaffected former Random House editor Jason Epstein conceded in 2001 that, in absolute numbers (rather than as a percentage of total output), more 'valuable' books were being published than ever before. Yet these trends and the diversity they preserve do not counteract the disproportionate influence of the media giants on the choices available to American readers.

Although internationalization and mergers also affected scientific and educational publishing, the nature of the subjects and their exponents exerted a visible effect on the content of books. In the 1980s many smaller companies disappeared; by the end of the decade, *Macmillan, *Harcourt, and Simon & Schuster owned close to half of the textbook trade. Subsequently, the British conglomerate *Pearson, which acquired Simon & Schuster's educational operation in 1998, controlled more than one quarter of American textbook production. Yet the stifling of variety has resulted as much from local as from global forces. State-wide adoption committees, especially those in Texas and California, have long wielded power over publishers by requiring that they comply with rules about representations of race, gender, environmental issues, 'lifestyles', and similar matters. The most controversial of such stipulations has concerned the presentation of evolution versus creationism. In the 1960s and 1970s, federally funded innovative books for use in biology, physics, and social studies courses provoked attacks from conservative groups because of their ostensible 'humanism' and cultural relativism. Left-wing critics, often at odds with one another, have likewise been vocal in assailing the depiction of African-Americans as either idealized or too realistic, too separate or too integrated. The result, some educators charge, is a reduction of the average American textbook to a bland, inoffensive, lowest common denominator calculated to win the biggest market. However, scientific thought has also produced books that serve and reflect the priorities of scientists themselves: reference works such as the *Science Citation Index* (now online and part of *Thomson Publishing); texts for advanced study synthesizing new research (e.g. James Watson's *Molecular Biology of the Gene*, 1965); and trade books such as James Gleick's *Chaos* (1987) and Stephen Hawking's *A Brief History of Time* (1988), popularizing the activities of the scientific community for lay readers. Even as the scholarly journal, in *digitized form, became entrenched, by the 1990s, as the primary means for the circulation of scientific knowledge, the science book had its place in laboratories and living rooms alike.

5.2 Transforming bookselling and libraries

In the postwar period, the forces of consolidation were also at work within institutions disseminating books to readers. The Book-of-the-Month Club became part of Time Inc. in 1977 (later *Time Warner); Bertelsmann became its sole owner in 2007. At the same time, the Selecting Committee virtually vanished from club advertising and was disbanded in 1994. With it went the idea that distance from commercialism was worth maintaining. Yet the Club's reorganization as part of a conglomerate arguably led to less homogenization as its executives, aiming to reverse declining membership, gave up the pretence of choosing the 'best' books for all in favour of targeting particular type of volumes at niche markets.

Retail bookselling developed against the backdrop of postwar suburbanization, evolving from a mix of department store, drugstore, independent, and chain outlets to a business dominated by a few national chains. In the 1960s and 1970s, *Waldenbooks and B. Dalton opened in suburban shopping centres throughout the country. The distinguishing feature of those shops was that their proprietors believed they could sell books in the same way that Kmart, which bought Waldenbooks in 1984, sold socks. Using computer technology, they centralized inventory control. After Crown Books introduced consistent discounting in 1977, both Waldenbooks and B. Dalton followed suit. Independent bookshops responded by imitating the informal atmosphere the chains were creating. At the same time, some stores cultivated specialized clienteles: political activists, children, New Age believers. In the 1990s, the superstore chains (*Barnes & Noble and *Borders were the largest) supplanted mall shops and dealt a fatal blow to many independents. Operating in huge spaces, the superstores welcomed readers with cafes, book talks, discounts, and vast selection. In 1997 the two biggest chains had 43.3 per cent of bookshop sales: by then both publicly traded companies, they wielded unprecedented power over publishers in matters such as pricing and display.

In cultural terms, the consolidations in the book business entailed a repudiation of the genteel aura that had once surrounded Brentano's or Scribner's. The function of the bookseller as supplier of literary guidance was largely a casualty of this process; the connection between buying a book and affirming one's 'literariness' grew weaker as well. Arguably, however, the rise of superstores was less detrimental to American culture than was the wave of mergers among publishers: purchasing books became unintimidating and the bookshop a more prominent feature of the retail landscape, encouraging buying of and conversation about books, if not more reading.

Other mediators emerged to guide readers in choosing books. The relocation of literary critics to academia in the 1950s and 1960s reduced the role of the generalist 'man of letters'. Yet, the more educated readers leaving the nation's burgeoning universities expanded the audience for the purveyors of expertise in the *New York Review of Books (founded in 1963) and other specialized journals. The creation of *amazon.com in 1995, which inaugurated large-scale Internet retailing, seemed to transfer authority from the critic to the ordinary reader. Despite the loss of face-to-face contact, those who ventured to explore Amazon's website found personalized recommendations and customer reviews to guide their purchases. In 1996, Oprah Winfrey (the ordinary reader writ large) created bestsellers and revived older titles by choosing them for *Oprah's Book Club on her television talk show. The American Library Association joined with Winfrey and the publishing industry to donate the club's selections to community libraries nationwide.

That intervention on the part of librarians to shape America's reading habits, however, was something of an anomaly by the 1990s. In the years following World War II, library professionals moved even further away from their commitment early in the century to influence readers. The proponents of libraries as information centres rather than book repositories began to be heard. An infusion of federal money, much of which went into computerization, enhanced the emphasis on librarianship as *information science. Although libraries continued to acquire books, in the political climate of the 1960s and 1970s the predominant vision of the institution was of an organization providing its 'customers' with knowledge leading to jobs, justice, or a good used car; it also served as a meeting place. The affinities with postwar consumer culture (and hence with the ethos of publishing and bookselling) were clear: the new public library accommodated users looking for a particular item of information, not necessarily for self-cultivation. As with bookshops, this trend did not necessarily signal cultural decline: it got more people into the building, fostered community, and increased book circulation. Within research libraries, the picture was gloomier: budget crises curtailed book purchases in the 1970s. Throughout the succeeding decades, the growth of online databases and inter-library loans continued to reduce the place of periodicals and scholarly monographs in university collections. Undergraduates had to be reminded that the stacks—not just the Internet—contained resources for their work.

5.3 Modern American reading

Greater knowledge and pleasure remained among the chief goals of reading in the postwar period, but the political and cultural developments of those years created opportunities for readers to use books in historically specific ways. The growth of '*speed-reading' among managers and executives testified that the mastery of voluminous printed information seemed increasingly necessary for success in the corporate sector. Conversely, in the 1960s the spirit of the New Left, itself a product, in part, of its participants' youthful brush with existentialist writers, found expression in reading groups devoted to explorations of radical thought. Similarly, women activists in the 1960s and 1970s drew support from feminist works that, if not necessarily discussed collectively, nevertheless sustained social connections by assuring individuals that they were not alone in their discontent. By the 1980s, women's literary clubs typically stood aloof from reform agendas; like their predecessors, however, club members derived a sense of community from reading with others.

As the imperatives of personal growth and self-help became more pervasive in American culture, therapeutic language became a hallmark of readers' remarks about the role of books in their lives. Among the thousands of respondents to the former *poet laureate Robert Pinsky's invitation to reflect on their 'favorite poem', for example, many people spoke of works as wellsprings of insight and healing. Yet encounters with the book still led readers outside the self, into what one subscriber to the Book-of-the-Month Club called 'enhanced intellectual or spiritual understanding of the meaning of life' ([Library of Congress,] *Survey of Lifetime Readers*, 6).

Throughout the second half of the 20th century, investigators (building on librarians' and sociologists' studies in the interwar period) conducted periodic surveys to determine Americans' reading habits. Animated by concerns over the teaching of reading in public schools, and worried about the nation's future prosperity, researchers repeatedly raised alarms about the fall in the number of citizens who regularly read books. The *National Endowment for the Arts reported that literary reading had dropped in almost

every demographic category between 1982 and 1992; in 2004 and again in 2007, the NEA declared that even more precipitate declines jeopardized the prospects for a rich civic life. Yet those who do read books continue to remake texts in the light of their own needs, aspirations, and locations, and to enrich American culture in the process.

5.4 The future of the book

The impact of digitization on the processes of production, distribution, and reading are easy enough to specify in broad outline. In the 1980s and 1990s, the development of editing and design software transformed the preparation of MSS for publication. In the same period, the birth of *desktop publishing and the use of lasers rather than film to reproduce images, followed in the early 1990s by the introduction of digital printing presses, enabled producers to tailor press runs and books themselves to specific markets. This new world of *print-on-demand promises to eliminate the costs of overproduction and overstocking; ordering a book can mean requesting not merely that it be sent to a retailer but, rather, that it be moved from screen to page. The digital revolution has also allowed publishers of conventional books to construct web sites featuring 'podcasts' with their authors, distribute textbook supplements electronically, and streamline office and inventory operations. Similarly, the advent of online reference works and electronic catalogues, together with the creation of digitized databases and document collections, enlarged the scope of library holdings and offered patrons greater access and convenience. As already noted, Internet bookselling, complete with its mechanisms for customer feedback, simplified distribution and facilitated direct contact between author, publisher, distributor, and reader.

The rapidity of these changes led publishers and entrepreneurs in the 1990s to predict—and to invest money in—the dominance of the ebook (*see* **19**), especially for scholarly monographs. The prospect was particularly appealing to academic presses because, by 2000, university libraries, faced with the rising costs of periodicals, were buying only about a quarter as many volumes as they had in the 1970s. Commercial publishers—notably Simon & Schuster and Random House—put sizeable funds into ebook development. The bestselling novelist Stephen King tested the waters in 2000 by arranging to sell a novella exclusively to readers who paid $2.50 to download it over the Internet; there were 400,000 requests for it on the first day alone. Yet, in its 2001 report, the *Bowker Annual* declared that hopes for electronic publishing had given way to 'business realities': consumers were not rushing to curl up with hand-held screens in place of physical books (*Bowker Annual*, 2002, 18). By the same token, the non-profit History Ebook project, an attempt to issue new and out-of-print scholarship electronically along with university presses' publication of print versions, struggled to secure sufficient subscriptions from libraries to sustain itself, although it has subsequently achieved stability under the auspices of the American Council of Learned Societies. Nevertheless publication of books in conventional printed form (at least initially) remains the widely shared preference of academic historians. They are much more enthusiastic about the research possibilities digitization has generated, including the *Google Book Project, which is scanning thousands of works in university libraries and making some entire texts available for online searching.

If the future of the book does not lie exclusively in the electronic format, perhaps the advent of the digital age will ensure the preservation of diversity in American publishing. Epstein's reflections on the triumph of commercial over literary values in the current book industry end with that hope; he envisions the Internet and related technologies as forces liberating authors and readers from the tyranny of profit-minded publishers and booksellers. Whether or not Epstein's prophecy proves true, the book is sure to remain connected, as it has always been, to the tensions between democracy and refinement, materialism and spirituality, at the heart of American culture.

BIBLIOGRAPHY

T. Augst and K. Carpenter, eds., *Institutions of Reading* (2007)

B. Bailyn and J. B. Hench, eds., *The Press and the American Revolution* (1981)

R. W. Beales and E. J. Monaghan, 'Literacy and Schoolbooks', in *HBA* 1 (2000)

M. Benton, *Beauty and the Book* (2000)

Bowker Annual of Library and Book Trade Information (1991, 2002)

R. H. Brodhead, *Cultures of Letters* (1993)

R. D. Brown, *Knowledge Is Power* (1989)

K. E. Carpenter, 'American Libraries', in *HBA* 2

— 'Libraries', in *HBA* 3

S. E. Casper, *Constructing American Lives* (1999)

— *et al.*, eds., *Perspectives on American Book History* (2002)

W. Charvat, *The Profession of Authorship in America*, ed. M. J. Bruccoli (1968)

J. D. Cornelius, *'When I Can Read My Title Clear'* (1991)

L. A. Coser *et al.*, *Books: The Culture and Commerce of Publishing* (1982)

P. Dain, 'The Great Libraries', in *HBA* 4

J. P. Danky and W. A. Wiegand, eds., *Print Culture in a Diverse America* (1998)

C. N. Davidson, ed., *Reading in America* (1989)

K. C. Davis, *Two-Bit Culture* (1984)

DLB 46, 49

J. Eddy, *Bookwomen* (2006)

J. Epstein, *Book Business* (2001)

S. Fink and S. S. Williams, eds., *Reciprocal Influences* (1999)

J. Gilreath, 'American Book Distribution', *PAAS* 95 (1985–6), 501–83

J. N. Green, 'The Book Trade in the Middle Colonies', in *HBA* 1

— 'English Books and Printing in the Age of Franklin', in *HBA* 1

— and P. Stallybrass, *Benjamin Franklin, Writer and Printer* (2006)

P. C. Gutjahr, *An American Bible* (1999)

— 'The Perseverance of Print-Bound Saints', in *HBA* 5

M. Hackenberg, ed., *Getting the Books Out* (1987)

D. D. Hall, *Worlds of Wonder, Days of Judgment* (1989)

— *Cultures of Print* (1996)

— ed., *A History of the Book in America* (5 vols, 2000–2010)

W. W. Hening, *The Statutes at Large; Being a Collection of all the Laws of Virginia* (13 vols, 1819–23)

B. Hochman, *Getting at the Author* (2001)

W. L. Joyce *et al.*, eds., *Printing and Society in Early America* (1983)

C. F. Kaestle *et al.*, *Literacy in the United States* (1991)

M. Kelley, *Learning to Stand and Speak* (2006)

H. Lehmann-Haupt *et al.*, *The Book in America*, 2e (1951)

[Library of Congress, Center for the Book and Book-of-the-Month Club,] *Survey of Lifetime Readers* (1990)

E. Long, *Book Clubs* (2003)

B. Luey, 'The Organization of the Book Publishing Industry', in *HBA* 5

E. McHenry, *Forgotten Readers* (2002)

C. A. Madison, *Book Publishing in America* (1966)

L. J. Miller, *Reluctant Capitalists* (2006)

E. J. Monaghan, *Learning to Read and Write in Colonial America* (2005)

G. F. Moran and M. A. Vinovskis, 'Schooling, Literacy, and Textbooks', in *HBA* 2

M. Moylan and L. Stiles, eds., *Reading Books* (1996)

D. P. Nord, *Faith in Reading* (2004)

C. Pawley, *Reading on the Middle Border* (2001)

J. A. Radway, *Reading the Romance* (1989)

— *A Feeling for Books* (1997)

J. Raven, 'The Importation of Books in the Eighteenth Century', in *HBA* 1

E. C. Reilly and D. D. Hall, 'Customers and the Market for Print', in *HBA* 1

R. Remer, *Printers and Men of Capital* (1996)

A. G. Roeber, 'Readers and Writers of German in the Early United States', in *HBA* 2

J. S. Rubin, *The Making of Middlebrow Culture* (1992)

— *Songs of Ourselves* (2007)

B. Ryan and A. M. Thomas, eds., *Reading Acts* (2002)

J. Satterfield, *The World's Best Books* (2002)

A. Schiffrin, *The Business of Books* (2000)

D. Sheehan, *This Was Publishing* (1952)

J. H. Shera, *Foundations of the Public Library* (1949)

D. S. Shields, *Civil Tongues and Polite Letters in British America* (1997)

B. Sicherman, 'Ideologies and Practices of Reading', in *HBA* 3

L. Soltow and E. Stevens, *The Rise of Literacy and the Common School in the United States* (1981)

C. Z. Stiverson and G. A. Stiverson, 'The Colonial Retail Book Trade', in *Printing and Society in Early America*, ed. W. L. Joyce *et al.* (1983)

L. I. Sweet, ed., *Communication and Change in American Religious History* (1993)

G. T. Tanselle, *Guide to the Study of United States Imprints* (2 vols, 1971)

J. Tebbel, *A History of Book Publishing in the United States* (4 vols, 1971–81)

I. Thomas, *History of Printing in America* (2 vols, 1810)

J. B. Thompson, *Books in the Digital Age* (2005)

C. Turner, *Marketing Modernism* (2003)

J. L. W. West III, *American Authors and the Literary Marketplace since 1900* (1988)

W. A. Wiegand, *The Politics of an Emerging Profession* (1986)

M. Winship, *American Literary Publishing in the Mid-Nineteenth Century* (1995)

— 'The Rise of a National Book Trade System in the United States, 1880–1920', in *HBA* 4

E. Wolf, 2nd, *The Book Culture of a Colonial American City* (1988)

L. C. Wroth, *The Colonial Printer* (1931)

R. J. Zboray, *A Fictive People* (1993)

N. Zill and M. Wingler, *Who Reads Literature?* (1990)

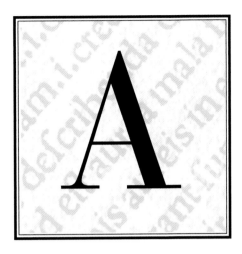

Aa, Pieter van der (1659–1733) Leiden bookseller and publisher. The son of a German stonecutter from Holstein, van der Aa began his career at Leiden in 1683 as a Latin trade publisher, specializing in classical texts and academic books on medicine and science. Gradually he widened his scope, producing pirate editions of foreign bestsellers as well as luxuriously illustrated works, geographical descriptions, *atlases, and travel accounts in French and Dutch for a non-scholarly public. In 1713 he moved his establishment to the location of the former *Elzevier printing office, next to the main building of the university. His ambition to become Leiden's leading book trade entrepreneur was fulfilled two years later, when he was appointed printer to the university and city. Among his most notable publications are the *Opera Omnia* of Erasmus (10 vols, 1703–6), the three multi-volume thesauruses of Roman, Greek, and Italian antiquities, and the megalomaniac *Galérie Agréable du Monde* (66 vols, 1729). He was also active as an auctioneer. His own library of some 20,000 books was auctioned in two instalments in 1729 and 1735. PGH

P. G. Hoftijzer, *Pieter van der Aa (1659–1733)* (1999)

Aarflot, Sivert Knudssøn (1759–1817) Farmer, schoolteacher, and pioneer printer on Norway's west coast. Inspired by Enlightenment ideas, he converted his private library into a public *lending library (in 1797, it had 84 books; at his death, 550). To spread information about history, farming, and natural sciences, he established a local *printing office in Ekset, Volda (1809), publishing the rurally based weekly magazine *Norsk Landboeblad*, various books, and *ephemera. EEi

Abagar The first Bulgarian printed book. A Roman Catholic *breviary, it includes the apocryphal story of King Abgar, accompanied by other apocrypha and prayers according to the Catholic rite. Filip Stanislavov edited it in Rome in 1651, when Catholicism started penetrating Bulgaria. The language is Church Slavonic with elements of modern Bulgarian and Serbo-Croatian. Printed on the *rectos of five *leaves, the text is illustrated by nine woodcuts. Fifteen copies are known. RK

Abbey, John Roland (1894–1969) English book collector. He amassed important collections of bindings, fine press volumes, and *colour-plate books before turning to *illuminated MSS. He acquired the C. H. St John Hornby collection in 1946 en bloc for £40,000 and added to it extensively. After his death, 184 of his medieval and Renaissance MSS were dispersed at auction sales (*see* BOOK AUCTIONS) at *Sotheby's between 1970 and 1989. ASGE

ODNB

abbreviations and **contractions** Abbreviations omit some or all letters of a word after the first, or they replace words with symbols, such as the *ampersand. They include contractions, which omit letters of words, and acronyms. Abbreviations have been used since antiquity to save space (especially in MSS) and/or time; until the 16th century, they also served to avoid word division at line endings and in *justification. Sacred names (*nomina sacra*) were abbreviated from a sense of reverence, but sacred texts otherwise generally avoided abbreviations. Latin and technical (e.g. legal) texts were more heavily abbreviated than vernacular and general ones. Vernacular abbreviations followed the commonest Latin practice. Although some individual words were generally abbreviated in the same way, many marks of abbreviation in MSS and early printed books were used in any word: such as a macron or tilde over a vowel to indicate omission of a following (or occasionally preceding) 'm' or 'n'; a mark like ^{9} for a missing terminal '-*us*'; a mark like $_9$ for '*com*' or '*con*'; a final figure like 4 for '*rum*'; a ^{2} for omitted '*ur*'; q for '*que*'; and marks through the descender of p for '*per*', '*pro*', '*pre*', and '*prae*'. Square brackets or italics indicate

the expansion of abbreviations in transcription. Abbreviations used in modern texts should be listed, normally in the *preliminaries. *See also* INITIAL (1).   KEA
Butcher
A. Cappelli, *Lexicon Abbreviaturarum*, 3e (1929)
McKerrow, *Introduction*

ABC The first texts to teach children to read, also known as 'absey', 'abcie' or 'abcee books', 'alphabet books', and 'abecedaria'. Although the term has been used interchangeably with *primer and some overlap of content may be present, alphabet books are more elementary and are substantially shorter than primers. ABC books are the successors of *hornbooks. They appeared in various European languages and countries in the 16th century—in Germany in 1524 (*Enchiridion Elementarum Puerilium*); in Sweden (in Finnish, Mikael Agricola's *Abc-kiria*) in 1543; in Belgium (in French, *L'ABC ou Instruction pour les petis enfans*) in 1564; in Ireland (*Aibidil Gaeidheilge & Caiticiosma*) in 1571; and in Denmark (in Low German, by Vingaard) in 1591. Originally, they combined teaching children the letters with religious instruction, an aim that remained predominant until the end of the 17th century. The first English ABC, dated to 1538, is Thomas Petyt's *The BAC [sic] Bothe in Latyn and in Englysshe*. A 16-page *octavo black-letter book with 21 lines per page, standard contractions, and no illustrations, it comprises the alphabet (two lines), vowels (one line), syllabic exercises (five lines); the Lord's Prayer, Hail Mary, and Apostles' Creed (all three in Latin and English); graces and prayers; and an abbreviated, rhymed form of the ten commandments. Petyt set the pattern for subsequent ABC books, although the particular prayers and graces varied between publications, which sometimes included the litany and catechism; later alphabet books were monolingual. By 1545, ABC books were published by public authority, although unauthorized texts flourished simultaneously. They were extremely popular, with 10,000 ABCs printed within eight months of 1584–5 alone. Their religious slant was sometimes polemical, as in *The Protestant Tutor* with its anti-Catholic catechism (1679), ancestor of America's enduring ABC, *The *New England Primer* (1686).

In John Hart's *Methode or Comfortable Beginning for all Unlearned to Read English* (1570), thought to be the first picture alphabet printed in England, small cuts illustrate letters by representing objects. Comenius' (*see* KOMENSKÝ, JAN AMOS) Latin picture-book *Orbis Sensualium Pictus* (1658), rapidly translated into vernacular languages, influenced later ABCs with its alphabets of upper- and lower-case letters accompanied by woodcuts of animals: the animal is used to explain the name of the letter, for example g, 'The *Goose* gagleth, gá gá'.

The 18th century saw more attractive and more entertaining ABC books besides those preserving a strong Christian flavour, commencing with T. W.'s reading and spelling book, *A Little Book for Little Children* (c.1702); this had a picture for each letter, interpreted in a two-line verse, and included the jingle beginning: 'A was an Archer

and shot at a frog / B was a Butcher and kept a great dog'. By this time 'A Apple Pie' ('B bak'd it, C cut it', etc.), of which the *Opies list approximately 25 editions or versions between 1743 and 1900, was also known. Pictures and letters were not always related, as is clear from *Newbery's *A Little Pretty Pocket-Book* (1744). Illustration predominated in *Bewick's extremely popular, frequently reprinted series of 24 miniature cuts (each under one inch square) to illustrate letters of the alphabet, which first appeared in the early 1770s; these simply gave the name of the creature and the picture. (Some later editions added the letters in upper and lower case.)

A stream of pictorial alphabets was published in the 19th century (pictures, letters, sometimes rhymes), sometimes themed (e.g. military, peace, railway, animals). Renowned illustrators of ABCs were *Greenaway and W. *Nicholson. Nonsense writers of ABCs included *Lear and, in the 20th century, Dr Seuss. The 20th century also saw some ABCs intended for a more advanced audience, either on account of their sophisticated illustration, or for the subjects on which the books are based (e.g. Cassen Mayers's ABCs based on the collections of various renowned museums, 1988).   KEA
H. Anders, 'The Elizabethan ABC with the Catechism', *Library*, 4/16 (1936), 32–48
C. C. Rostankowski, 'A is for Aesthetics: Alphabet Books and the Development of the Aesthetic in Children', *Journal of Aesthetic Education*, 28 (1994), 117–27
M. F. Thwaite, *From Primer to Pleasure in Reading*, 2e (1972)
I. Willke, *ABC-Bücher in Schweden* (1965)

'Abd al-Rahīm 'Anbarīn-Qalam (late 16th–early 17th century) One of the many Iranian calligraphers and artists who emigrated to India during the Mughal era, especially during the 17th century. 'Abd al-Rahīm was from Herat and worked at the court of the emperor Akbar (r. 1556–1605). After the latter's death, he worked for his successor, Jahāngīr (r. 1605–27). He was a specialist in *nasta'līq* *calligraphy, greatly appreciated by the emperor. In 1610 he produced a copy of the *Khamsah* of Nizāmī (BL Or.12208), which has his portrait painted after the colophon.   DLJ
A. Schimmel, *Calligraphy and Islamic Culture*, 2e (1990)

Ābdul Karim, Sāhityabiśārad (1869–1953) Born in Chattagram (now in Bangladesh), Ābdul Karim collected nearly 2,000 MSS from East Bengal, now held by Barendra Research Institute in Rajshahi and Dhaka University. Given the title 'Sāhityabiśārad' by Chattagram Sāhitya Samiti, Karim edited MSS and wrote *Bānglā prāchīn pu·thir bibaran* (1914), a study of old Bengali MSS.   SKC

AbeBooks Currently, the largest online seller (*see* WORLD WIDE WEB) of second-hand and rare books. Based in Vancouver, Canada, the company was founded in 1996 as 'Advanced Book Exchange' by Keith Waters. Waters turned the concept behind the long-established *AB Bookman's Weekly* into an online warehouse. Dealers pay monthly fees to list their books on the service, which enables shoppers to find books worldwide and compare prices and quality. By mid-2006, AbeBooks listed 80 million volumes. Rare books constituted 30 per cent of sales, new titles 10–15 per cent, second-hand books and textbooks 55 per cent. In 2006, AbeBooks became linked to *Amazon.com. DE

www.abebooks.co.uk, consulted July 2008

Aberdeen University Library Formed out of the merging in 1860 of two earlier foundations: King's College Library (originally St Mary's, founded in 1495) and Marischal College (founded in 1593). King's retained the general collections, while Marischal housed medical, legal, and scientific material. The library currently contains some one million items. RAE

C. A. McLaren, *Rare and Fair: A Visitor's History of Aberdeen University Library* (1995)

Åbo Akademis Bibliotek The library of the Swedish-language university in Turku/Åbo, Finland (established 1918–19). The original library of Åbo Academy, founded in 1640, was entirely destroyed by fire in 1827. The present *legal deposit library functions as the (informal) Finland-Swedish national library. Its rich MS collections document Swedish-language culture in Finland. IJM

Abrams, Harry N. New York publisher of art books and reproductions, founded 1949. Each volume in the Library of Great Painters (1950) included 50 pages of high-quality colour plates and sold for $12.50. In 1952, the firm joined *Pocket Books to produce the Pocket Library of Great Art, whose *paperback volumes sold for 50c. Establishing an Amsterdam office in 1953 allowed Abrams to use European colour printing and expand its markets. The firm was sold to *Times-Mirror in 1966 and to La Martinière Groupe in 1997. BEL

C. A. Madison, *Book Publishing in America* (1966)

abridgement Shortened or condensed version of a work. Producing an abridged text usually means editing out material deemed unnecessary for the comprehension of the plot or central argument of a work, as well as removing notes, illustrations, and other *paratextual material. The abridged version of a text is often provided by the publisher, and may be produced with or without the involvement of its author. Such versions are made for several reasons. Works are often abridged for delivery by spoken word (either as *audio books or radio programmes) to reduce the length of time taken to read the text aloud. Printed versions of abridged texts may also be supplied to accompany audio books; to be used as study aids; or to satisfy reader preference. Reference books, such as dictionaries, *thesauruses, and legal or medical works are often abridged to improve portability (e.g. *The Shorter Oxford English Dictionary*). Organizations such as the *Reader's Digest Book Club produce anthologies of abridged (or digested) books which are intended to promote literature and encourage reading. Non-fiction works, such as essay collections, academic readers, collections of letters, or biographies, may be published in an abridged form, consisting of selections or extracts. More controversially, literary works may be abridged by excising supposedly superfluous material in order to produce cheaper editions or to provide condensed versions of long novels that may be more easily tackled by casual readers.

Ideally, an abridged text will retain only words originally supplied by the author and preserve as much as possible of the word order and style of the unabridged version. However, the term is sometimes used to refer to texts that have been simplified or subjected to *censorship or *bowdlerization. Simplified versions of texts may be published for children, for adult education, or for second-language learners. Some simplified abridgements not only reduce the length of the text, but make the language of the original more straightforward by replacing difficult words. Passages deemed inappropriate for a particular age group may also be removed. In some cases, the line between censorship and abridgement may be blurred. After its original private Italian publication in 1928, Lawrence's *Lady Chatterley's Lover* appeared in 'abridged' versions, as well as privately printed and *pirated editions. These abridged editions effectively operated as censored editions, removing contentious words and passages, prior to the publication of the first unexpurgated text by *Penguin in 1960. *See also* ABSTRACT; EXPURGATION. TK

abstract Summary or précis, usually supplied for works of research or other texts that present an argument. An abstract, sometimes called an executive summary, should distil all of the pertinent information regarding the content of a longer work, including its themes, intentions, methodologies, scope, arguments, and conclusions. Abstracts may be part of the *front matter of a book, article, *thesis, or *dissertation; they may be submitted as part of a proposal for a longer piece of work; or they may be incorporated within a piece of criticism. Typically, abstracts are no longer than 10 per cent of a full text, though they may be much shorter. There are three types of abstract: descriptive, informative, and critical. Descriptive abstracts briefly summarize the contents of a work without comment or criticism, sometimes listing associated keywords. Informative abstracts are more substantial and explain intentions and results in greater detail. Critical abstracts are intended to evaluate as well as summarize, and are not provided by the original author of a work.

Abstracts should only present information available in the text—with the exception of evaluations in critical abstracts, no new material should be included. Abstracts are often used to store and retrieve information about academic research—information that is then indexed and made available by dedicated services. In order to facilitate the accurate retrieval of information, an abstract should include all pertinent key terms associated with a given work. Abstract index providers include: the *MLA International Bibliography*, the *Index to Theses with Abstracts Accepted for Higher Degrees by the Universities of Great Britain and Northern Ireland and the Council for*

National Academic Awards, and *Dissertation Abstracts International*. *See also* ABRIDGEMENT. TK

Academia Early Soviet publishing house founded privately in December 1921 by the Philosophical Society attached to Petrograd University. In 1923, following the rout of the Petrograd philosophical school, it changed its affiliation to the State Institute for the History of the Arts. In 1938 it was incorporated into the State Literature Publishing House in Moscow. Its output of more than 1,000 books comprised scholarly works (mainly in the humanities) and world classics. Academia was renowned for its high standards of editing and graphic design.

SLo

V. V. Krylova and E. V. Kichatova, *Izdatel'stvo 'Academia'* (2004)

Académie française Oldest of the five academies composing the *Institut de France, it was founded in 1635 by Cardinal Richelieu. Membership, limited to 40, has traditionally included writers, scientists, clergymen, generals, and politicians, but excluded visual artists and musicians. The first woman elected was Marguerite Yourcenar (1980), the first francophone African Léopold Sédar Senghor (1983). The Académie's original mission, in keeping with Richelieu's policies, was to regulate the French language and make it common and understandable to all. The first edition of its dictionary appeared in 1694; others followed in 1718, 1740, 1762, 1798, 1835, 1878, 1932–5, and 1992. VAG

accents *Diacritical signs placed under or over letters to signify ways in which they should be stressed or pronounced when spoken. Familiar examples include the acute, grave, and circumflex accents used in French, or the umlaut used in German, but many languages use a wide variety of accents; English is unusual in generally restricting their use to loanwords from other languages. Accents associated with letters are sometimes considered to create separate, additional letters within their native alphabet. Diacritical marks have a long history and are known in Greek texts from at least the 2nd century AD. For some languages, the challenges of typecasting heavily accented *founts—and, especially, the complexities involved in composition and distribution with so many closely related but distinct *sorts—led to the use of *types that were simpler than their written *letterforms. Types for *lower-case letters with accents are cast as a single unit, as are most *upper-case letters, but for the large upper-case sorts used for *display type it is sometimes necessary to use separately cast accents (sometimes called 'floating accents'), whose position must be carefully adjusted with leads. Sorts for letters with non-standard accents are sometimes known as 'special sorts' or 'peculiars'. DRSP

Access to Archives (A2A) Launched in 2001, this regularly updated and expanding online database of catalogues—searchable by person, place, and subject—describes archives from the 8th century onwards held in England and Wales. In October 2007 it contained records of more than 10 million items in 414 repositories, located via the ARCHON directory, also online and housed at the *National Archives. VML

www.a2a.org.uk, consulted Sept. 2007
www.nationalarchives.archon, consulted Sept. 2007

accidentals and **substantives** Terms first used by *Greg in his 'Rationale of Copy-Text' to distinguish between two categories of textual expression: 'substantives' ('those … that affect the author's meaning or the essence of his expression', usually interpreted as the actual words used) and 'accidentals' ('spelling, punctuation, word-division, and the like, affecting mainly its formal presentation'). This distinction, however, was 'practical, not philosophic'. Greg believed that 16th- and 17th-century scribes and compositors treated substantives and accidentals differently, a point (at least partially) supported by J. *Moxon: '*the carelessness of some good Authors, and the ignorance of other Authors, has forc'd* Printers *to introduce a Custom, which among them is look'd upon as a task and duty incumbent on the* Compositor, *viz. to discern and amend the bad* Spelling *and* Pointing *of his* Copy.' Greg was countering the prevailing view that editors should follow their chosen *copy-text in all features of the text (what he described as the 'tyranny of the copy-text') by positing a 'divided' authority in which one copy-text was used for accidentals and one or more copy-texts were used for substantives. Because scribes and compositors were more likely to change accidentals rather than substantives, and because authors themselves might change substantives in later editions but leave the accidentals untouched, the copy-text for the accidentals of a work was, ideally, an authorial MS (or, failing that, the first edition); however, it was permissible for an editor to import *variant substantives from later editions that he or she believed to be authorial. (Greg also allowed the incorporation of later accidental variants for the same reason.) Such editorial practice produced what were later described as *eclectic editions.

IG

W. W. Greg, 'The Rationale of Copy-Text', *SB* 3 (1950–51), 19–36

accordion book Book format in which the individual leaves are conjoined sequentially to fold out, rather than the more conventional structure, in which leaves are hinged around a single joint. Pages with text or illustrations are protected by stiff board covers, to which the first and sometimes last leaves in the sequence are joined. Often used for the production of children's books (*see* 15), this format was also adopted for illustrated books, such as travel guides and other books aimed at tourists. High-quality photographic books have sometimes been made as accordion books, notably *Richard Avedon Portraits* (2002). *See also* PLEATED BINDING, EAST ASIA. RWO

account book A book for recording monetary dealings. Single-entry accounting records transactions once in the account book. Double-entry accounting records every

A pre-Columbian 'leporello' or **accordion book**, the Codex Dresden: written on both sides of 39 leaves, by 1739 it had reached Vienna. Reproduced here from a 1975 *facsimile, ed. H. Deckert and F. Anders.

transaction twice—the total of debit transactions must equal the total of credit transactions. For example, a record of an item sold is documented as an item gone from the inventory, while the cash received for it is recorded as a credit. Double-entry accounting was widely used by 15th-century Venetian merchants and may date to the 12th century. Although such materials are highly ephemeral, it appears that specially *ruled accounting ledgers were sold, first in MS and, later, as printed books from early times. Commonly, an account book is part of an accounting system, or series of books, in which a merchant reckons capital, income, and expenditure. Account books can be divided into journals or *daybooks, which record daily transactions, and ledgers, which record creditors and debtors. Entries from journals are posted (copied) into ledgers. Separate ledger series are kept for sales and purchases, wages, and inventory. Some books will be specific to the merchant's trade: printers record paper inventories, publishers record payments to authors, and booksellers record customers' purchases.   AAW

Ackermann, Rudolph (1764–1835) Printer and publisher who bankrupted himself in early attempts to invent *lithography as a cheap alternative to *letterpress. Born in Germany, he came to England in 1787, establishing a publishing company and shop in the Strand for *aquatints and fine illustrations (*see* **16**), and publishing an English translation of *Senefelder's *A Complete Course of Lithography* (1819). Ackermann is credited with introducing the first successful use of lithography to Britain, and was famous for his printed colour illustrations in *annuals and books such as *The Microcosm of London* (1808–10) and architectural histories illustrating Westminster Abbey, Oxford, Cambridge, and public schools. He published illustrations by *Rowlandson and Auguste Charles Pugin. Ackermann's inventive genius extended to waterproofing and bicycle steering mechanisms, as well as innovations in *colour printing. He supplied Spanish language books in the period following the fall of constitutional government in Spain in 1823.   PLS
ODNB

Ackers, Charles (1702/3–59) English printer. While serving his apprenticeship with S. *Palmer, he began an important lifelong collaboration with the typefounder W. *Caslon. His business included printing *textbooks, *almanacks, and a weekly newspaper. His interest in periodicals led to the *London Magazine*, for which Ackers was both printer and shareholder. It was a significant rival to the *Gentleman's Magazine*, reaching a circulation of *c*.8,000. Ackers's success can be measured in other ways: he took seventeen *apprentices, worked up to five printing presses, and, in some years, produced more than a million printed sheets. His son John (*c.*1726–56) was partner from 1749 until his early death. CYF

D. F. McKenzie and J. C. Ross, eds., *A Ledger of Charles Ackers*, OBS, NS 15 (1968)

Acta Medica et Philosophica Hafniensia Danish scientific journal published at Copenhagen, 1673–80. Founded and edited by Thomas Bartholin, it was among the first such European journals. Mainly concerned with medicine, it covered other scientific disciplines. Most contributors were Danish or Norwegian; it was conducted in Latin for a European audience. CA, KSP

Actes Sud Publishing house founded in 1978 in Provence by the Belgian writer Hubert Nyssen. A successful pioneer of French cultural decentralization, with its seat in Arles since 1983, the firm is particularly active in literary translation. Its authors include Nina Berberova (rediscovered in 1985, at 84, with *The Accompanist*), Paul Auster, and Imre Kertész (2002 *Nobel Prize in Literature). By 2004, when it won its first *Goncourt, Actes Sud's catalogue comprised some 5,000 titles. VAG

Act for the Encouragement of Learning, An (also known as 'The Statute of Anne' or 'The Copyright Act') The world's earliest *copyright statute, passed by Parliament in 1709 to take effect in 1710. In England, the final lapse of pre-publication *licensing in 1695 eventually led to the passage of 'An act for the encouragement of learning, by vesting the copies of printed books in the authors or purchasers of such copies, during the times therein mentioned' (8 Anne c. 19), which became the dominant legal framework for the conduct of the book trade, the understanding of literary property, and the construction of *authorship throughout most of the 18th century.

Under the licensing regime, a *stationer established his right to publish a work by entering it as his '*copy' in the *Stationers' Company register. This copy, or right of ownership, could subsequently be divided into shares and sold (*see* TRADE SALES), but only members of the Stationers' Company could own copies, a provision that excluded most authors. The Act, modelled in part on the provisions regarding patents in the Jacobean Statute of Monopolies (21 Jac. I c. 3), established a regulatory system reflecting long-standing Stationers' Company protocols, but was innovative in specifying that copyright was a limited privilege, rather than a perpetual right—a principle definitively established in *Donaldson vs Becket (1774). The Act stipulated that the owner of a newly published work was entitled to fourteen years of copyright protection; a second, fourteen-year term took effect if the author were still living at the end of the first. The owner of a copy already in print was entitled to twenty-one years of protection, with no possibility of renewal. (Despite these provisions, many members of the London trade conducted business as if copyright were perpetual.) Authors owned the copyrights of their works, which they were free to sell or retain.

The Act for the Encouragement of Learning is one of the threshold moments in the history of intellectual property: its very title established that there is a public good to be considered in regulating copyright; it recognized the author's legal right of ownership and established that ownership was temporally limited. Perhaps most importantly of all, it set the legislative precedent that issues pertaining to literary property should be determined not by the Stationers' Company, nor by the monarch, but by Parliament and the judiciary. MFS

J. P. Feather, *Publishing, Piracy and Politics* (1994)
J. Loewenstein, *The Author's Due* (2002)
L. R. Patterson, *Copyright in Historical Perspective* (1968)
M. Rose, *Authors and Owners* (1993)
— 'Copyright, Authors, and Censorship 1695–1830', in *CHBB* 5

Adam, Robert B. (1863–1940) American book collector. After creating collections of Ruskin and James Hogg (both of which he gave to *Yale) and of Robert Burns (which he sold), Adam assembled the finest private collection of the works of S. *Johnson. In 1948, he sold it to Donald and Mary *Hyde. ASGE

M. H. Eccles, 'Adam, Tinker, and Newton', in *Mary Hyde Eccles: A Miscellany of her Essays and Addresses* (2002)

Adams, Katharine (1862–1952) English bookbinder. She learned binding from S. *Prideaux and D. *Cockerell and set up her own bindery; her work was supported within the *private press and Arts and Crafts circles. Many of her more than 300 bindings are preserved in major collections. She also carried out conservation work on early books and MSS, and taught binding to the nuns of *Stanbrook Abbey. DRSP

M. Tidcombe, *Women Bookbinders 1880–1920* (1996)

adaptation The transformation of a source work into a new form, commonly a *novel rewritten as a *play (theatrical adaptation) or as a film (film adaptation). Adaptation is sometimes associated with postmodernist notions of intertextuality and hybridity and the study of the interweaving of different texts and textual traditions in literature, art, film, and music. Literary adaptations refer to a written text, story, or characters recast to suit a new form, often with the purpose of offering a commentary on the source. The Bible, *Homer's *Iliad* and *Odyssey*, *Shakespeare, and folk tales have been frequently adapted, their well-known stories reworked for different audiences and reinterpreted for different social and political contexts.

Adaptations are often described in two ways: 'faithful', indicating that they are close to the original text (e.g. in storyline, setting, or dialogue); or 'interpretative', indicating that the original has been significantly altered in order to emphasize a particular aspect (e.g. to modernize the characters, setting, or language of a Shakespeare play, or to parody or reflect on the source text). Adaptations may change the source text through versification, dramatization, fictionalization, or other transformative processes. Adaptation can also take the form of transferring a source text to a different medium: the retelling of tales in pictures through illustrated books, films, and television are common forms. This may involve the shifting of genres, the *abridgement and condensation of the source text, the elision of storylines, the addition of material (e.g. the interpolation of characters), and the resequencing or fragmentation of the narrative. Adaptation results in the circulation of varying versions of a text or story in different historical periods.

Examples of adaptation include Charles and Mary Lamb's *Tales from Shakespeare* (1807) and *My Fair Lady* (1956), a musical version of George Bernard Shaw's *Pygmalion* (1913), whose title is from Ovid's *Metamorphoses. The Water Margin* (1977) was an adaptation for television of one of the four classical novels of Chinese literature. In reverse adaptation, a script forms the basis of a novelization of the story; Douglas Adams's *The Hitch Hiker's Guide to the Galaxy*, for example, was initially a radio play (1978). Authors' and adapters' conflicting claims to creative ownership of the source and adapted text have given rise to debates over the rights of each. British *copyright law, the model for copyright in many countries, has long defined adaptations separately for literary, artistic, dramatic, and musical works.

AAW

J. Sanders, *Adaptation and Appropriation* (2006)

addendum Material at the end of a book, such as extra entries in a *dictionary, typically added when their need is discovered after typesetting the main text.

Addison-Wesley American *textbook publisher based in Reading, Mass. Founded in 1942 by the printers Lew Addison Cummings and Melbourne Wesley Cummings (who were not related), it began by publishing college science texts, adding elementary and high school science and mathematics books in 1957. After World War II, international sales became a significant part of its business, and a London office opened in 1959. The firm publishes in many languages. Addison-Wesley began publishing children's books (*see* **15**) in 1969, selling that list to *Harper & Row in 1984. Its trade division was established in 1974. The *Pearson Group purchased Addison-Wesley in 1988, and in 1995 Addison-Wesley merged with *Longman. The merged firm purchased *HarperCollins Educational Publishing in 1996 and, in that year, joined with *Scott, Foresman to form Scott Foresman–Addison Wesley School Publishing. BEL
www.aw-bc.com/aboutus/history.html, consulted Sept. 2007

address book Personal book that typically includes spaces for friends' and contacts' names, addresses, telephone numbers, email addresses, and birthdays. Address books may be soft-, hard-, or spiral-bound or offer page refills to facilitate editing or appending information. Software applications are available for computerized address books. EDG

Adelphi Milan publishing house founded in 1962 by Luciano Foà and directed from the early 1970s by the intellectual and novelist Roberto Calasso. Although it originally sought to publish writers ignored in the prevailing intellectual climate, its success stems chiefly from publishing modern writing. Its harmonious pastel-colour graphics provide a distinct bookshelf identity. NH

Adler, Elkan Nathan (1861–1946) Lawyer, scholar, and travelling collector. Born into a leading Anglo-Jewish family, he amassed a vast collection of Hebrew books. In 1923, the *Jewish Theological Seminary of America in New York purchased his collection of 4,200 MSS and 30,000 printed books of all periods. His library also contained 30,000 documents from the *Genizah of Cairo, bought privately in Egypt. EGLS
S. Liberman Mintz and E. Deitsch, *Great Books from Great Collectors* (1993)

Adler, Elmer (1884–1962) New York fine press printer, publisher, book collector, and educator. Although not prolific and rarely successful financially, Adler's Pynson Printers (1922–40) influenced printers, designers, collectors, and librarians, most notably through its periodical the *Colophon (1930–40) and its work for the *Limited Editions Club. Adler closed the press in 1940 to teach at Princeton University, to which he donated his extensive book collection and personal papers. Retiring from teaching in 1952, he founded La Casa del Libro in San Juan, Puerto Rico. PWR
P. A. Bennett, ed., *Elmer Adler in the World of Books* (1964)

adult magazine Affordable, glossy, softcover, picture magazine containing photographic sexual imagery aiming to stimulate erotic responses. Such publications are also called 'sex magazines', 'blue books', 'top-shelf magazines', 'pornoblads', or simply 'pornographic magazines'. They are sometimes euphemistically called 'lifestyle magazines' or conflated with the less sexually explicit men's magazines. The best-known and most successful adult magazines are *Playboy*, *Penthouse*, and *Hustler*, all American, softcore magazines for heterosexual men.

The expansive history of ephemeral, underground pornographic publications, dating from the beginnings of the printing press, forms the pre-history of the adult magazine, although many credit advances in colour printing after World War II with the rise of adult magazines in their current form (*see* PHOTOLITHOGRAPHY; PHOTO-OFFSET). Other precursors include the pin-up and US comics in the genre of 'Tijuana Bibles', softcover publications of cartoons with erotic or obscene content, circulating underground during the 1930s and 1940s.

Playboy's first issue, in December 1953, featured a nude centrefold of Marilyn Monroe, and sold more than 54,000 copies (at 50c.). Hugh Heffner, Playboy's founder, cited the Kinsey report in the first editorial; indeed, the liberalization of American public discussion about sex in the wake of that report is another crucial context. This liberal reading background was not wholly exported to Anglophone countries such as Australia, however, where *Playboy* was first systematically and then sporadically banned until the 1960s. Publications like it were transforming newsstands (newsagents) around the world, and competition to show more explicit images intensified as the reading market expanded throughout the 1960s and 1970s. Playboy Enterprises now circulates 4.5 million copies of its magazine a month, and has 23 television and film networks around the world. Some countries with large majority Muslim populations (including Indonesia and Iran) effectively ban adult magazines, or produce local variants with quite different standards of explicitness.

Although heterosexual, middle-class, 'westernized' men are the predominant consumers, adult magazines are also produced for specialized markets catering to groups interested in, for example, fetishes and sadomasochism. Gay and lesbian adult magazines also have a place in the market. Small, independently owned magazines such as *On Our Backs*, a US feminist magazine of lesbian erotica with a title satirizing the sometimes anti-pornography feminist magazine *Off Our Backs*, publish content challenging the conventions of erotic representation. *See also* CENSORSHIP; OZ SCHOOL KIDS ISSUE; PORNOGRAPHY. NRM

Advaita Ashram The most active publishing wing of the Ramakrishna Math, a monastic order established by Swāmī Vivekānanda in Kolkata in 1897. Along with the Ramakrishna Math of Chennai, the two centres have published nearly 1,300 titles on religion and spirituality. One of its earliest publications was *The Atman* (1905). AG

advance System of author payment, whereby money is given in anticipation of future *royalties. Royalties are offset against the advance, and are not paid until the advance is 'earned out'. Publishers rarely demand the return of advances, unless the delivered MS is deemed unpublishable. *See also* AUTHOR–PUBLISHER AGREEMENTS. CMS

advance copy Copy available before publication once a book has been printed. The first copies sent from the printer will be scrutinized for any printing errors. When an important title is embargoed before publication, advance copies are kept secure to prevent their contents being leaked to the press. AGP

Advani, Ram (b. 1920s) Originally from Karachi, he graduated from Lucknow University and joined the family bookshop in Lahore in 1945. He migrated to Shimla (1947), then to Lucknow (1948) to become an academic bookseller at the centre of Lucknow's intellectual life. His son, Rukun Advani, runs Permanent Black publishers. RBC

adversaria [Lat. *adversaria scripta*, 'things written on one side of the paper'] Notes, collections of miscellaneous remarks or observations. The term, often used for MS miscellanies, also figured in titles of controversial works by scholars and theologians: its earliest occurrence is probably in Bartolomaeus Latomus's *Scripta Duo Adver-*

saria (Strasbourg, 1544), an example soon followed by the French Hellenist Adrianus Turnebus in 1564, and by many other scholars until the end of the 19th century. NGW

advertisement Advertisements have two main functions: conveying general information through the public notice (formerly achieved through street criers), and conveying commercial information, the second being the more common usage. The origins of the advertisement in antiquity are ill defined. In England, the earliest known printed advertisement (and, arguably, the earliest surviving *clap or *broadside, as the reader is requested not to remove it) dates from 1476–7 and advertises *Caxton's edition of the Sarum *Ordinal* or *Pye*. The 17th century saw the creation of *pamphlets or broadsheets devoted to advertising, e.g. *The Publick Adviser* (1657) and various city *Mercuries (from 1667). Advertisements could be separately printed as single or folded sheets or incorporated into the text of newspapers, magazines, or other publications. Magazine wrappers frequently included advertising, and separately printed advertisements could be bound into periodicals as inserts.

Broadly speaking, two of the major developments in the history of print advertising were: the effect of English taxes on press advertisements (1712–1853) and newspaper printing (1712–1855); and, worldwide, the development of colour printing, especially *chromolithography, from *c.*1860. The latter brought a blaze of colour into homes and to hoardings. Thereafter, advertisements tended to make their impact visually (with less text than 18th-century advertisements). In the 20th and 21st centuries, advertisements spread to non-printed media, such as film, radio, television, and the *World Wide Web. *See also* ADVERTISING IN BOOKS; ADVERTISING, MARKETING, AND PUBLICITY FOR BOOKS. JALa

B. B. Elliott, *A History of English Advertising* (1962)
E. S. Turner, *The Shocking History of Advertising* (1952)

advertising in books Advertising in books has existed in some form since printed books became a marketable commodity in the *Gutenberg era. *Printers' devices served as early forms of trademark, giving printers a commercial identity. With the advent of modern advertising techniques in the 18th century, publishing booksellers developed early forms of commercial publicity by including at the end of their books lists of other works available for sale. It was not until production techniques were industrialized in the 19th century, however, that books entered the mass market and began to interest advertisers of other commodities. This development was encouraged by the 19th-century practice of publishing novels serially in instalments (sometimes called '*numbers' or 'parts') in magazines financed by *advertisements. These advertisements stayed with the text when it was published in volume form: one Victorian edition of *Pepys' diaries contained 56 pages of advertisements.

The 20th century saw several attempts to use books as advertising vehicles, with manufacturers identifying potential clients through their reading habits. Thus, a romance novel might include a card insert advertising scent. It is presumed that such experiments were generally unsuccessful, as the practice was discontinued in novels by the late 20th century. However, advertising remains a feature of some non-fiction genres such as travel guides. Advertising has also made the leap from the *paratext to product placement in the text itself: the novelist Fay Weldon signed a contract with the jewellers Bulgari to mention their products in her novel *The Bulgari Connection* (2000). This example does not appear to have been widely followed, however, perhaps because books are not an efficient medium for advertisers. In addition, there is the issue of hostility by readers, for whom books retain an aura of cultural prestige perceived, perhaps naively, to be tainted by the commercial concerns of advertising. *See also* **14**.   SLP

advertising, marketing, and publicity for books

1. Publicity and advertising
2. Marketing
3. Market research

1. Publicity and advertising

Publishers rely heavily on word of mouth to promote their books. Successful word-of-mouth titles include Kenneth Grahame's *The Wind in the Willows* (1908) and Louis de Bernières' *Captain Corelli's Mandolin* (1994). To encourage the effect, publishers sometimes give away copies. But W. *Tinsley, who published Hardy's second novel, *Under the Greenwood Tree* (1872), wrote: 'I almost raved about the book, and gave it away wholesale to Pressmen and anyone I knew interested in good fiction. But ... it would not sell' (127). The growth of *reading groups, recommendations on websites such as *Amazon, and blogging have added to the readers' potential for promoting books. Another form of promotion is securing *reviews in the media. Before the advent of marketing departments, publishers employed publicity staff, who cultivated newspapers' and magazines' literary editors. From the early days of printing, publishers have used title-pages as promotional handbills. J. *Lackington must be counted as an early master of publicity.

Authors are often called upon to help with promotion. They may send out flyers, post adverts in their email signature, attend literary festivals, appear on radio and television, and do press interviews. For some, the trail of appearances and book signings has become onerous; in 2006, Margaret Atwood devised a machine enabling her to sign books remotely. The influence of the media on a book's fortunes is very strong. Television book clubs such as *Oprah and *Richard and Judy have enormous impact. Similarly, winning a major literary prize, such as the *Booker, can transform a novel's sales. Publishers and booksellers advertise little on television due to the high cost, but film or television tie-ins (using production stills on a book's cover) increase sales. Publishers have long advertised in the press, as well as on billboards, buses, and trains. In 1920s New York, *Knopf used men wearing sandwich boards, with books attached to their boards for potential purchasers to browse.

2. Marketing

A broader activity than publicity, marketing for individual titles and series involves the preparation of extensive plans. Publishers' sales representatives continue to visit bookshops in the 21st century, but with the growth of large chains, buying decisions have become more centralized. Sales representatives develop relationships with key decision-makers in retailers, including supermarkets. They show new titles, cover designs, and proofs to head office buyers ahead of publication, and hold discussions about quantities, discount, and in-store promotion. Budgets remain low by comparison with the expenditure on marketing popular consumer items, but the promise of a sizeable marketing spend helps to obtain a decent order. In-store promotions such as 3-for-2 offers, Christmas catalogues, and wider exposure in supermarkets are important ways of promoting sales. Perhaps the most influential marketing tool is the book cover: research suggests that once browsers pick up a book, they are five times more likely to buy. In *educational publishing, the aim of marketing is to influence teachers, lecturers, and librarians. Free inspection copies are given to lecturers in the hope that they will adopt a *textbook for their courses.

With some notable exceptions, such as *Penguin, few company brands are well known among consumers. Instead, familiarity with the author is key to a consumer's decision to buy. Thus, writers such as Stephen King and Danielle Steel are developed as brands, and readers are encouraged to buy new titles from their favourite names.

Pricing has become increasingly sophisticated, moving away from cost-based approaches, which lowered the unit cost and published price but encouraged overprinting. Books are priced to market and, in countries without fixed prices, bestsellers are heavily discounted. In 1930s England, books were given away at reduced prices on receipt of coupons from newspapers or cigarette packets. Today, books may be included in cereal packets or as cover mounts on magazines. Direct mail is used by book clubs and for sales to academics or professionals. Door-to-door or subscription selling, widespread in the 19th-century US, still exists in countries without full bookshop networks. Some companies run innovative direct sales operations, and books are sold at school fairs, in offices, and at academic and professional conferences. Generic initiatives to encourage reading and the purchase of books include *book tokens, introduced in the UK in 1932; *World Book and Copyright Day; and City Reads, a programme begun in Seattle in 1998 that encourages all adults in a city to read the same book.

The *World Wide Web has enabled publishers and booksellers to keep in touch with customers and recommend suitable titles. Websites for books and authors, run by publishers or authors, feature related content such as games and e-cards. For publishers of all sizes, the Internet offers a cost-effective method of promotion. Free downloads of chapters and even of whole books may encourage sales of the printed work, and initiatives such as *Google Book Search allow readers to browse online before purchase.

3. Market research

As the book industry has become more sophisticated, market research has grown in importance. Point-of-sale data is used by bookshops to inform their stock purchasing. Publishers can access this data, as well as reports on book-buying habits and on changing purchaser demographics. Book purchasing tends to correlate with income and educational level, but consumption differs among age groups and the sexes. Bookshop chains have distinct demographics, and publishers may view some books as more suited to one chain than another. The temptation is to market to regular book buyers, rather than to infrequent purchasers, who are harder to reach and influence. The success of *Harry Potter has encouraged publishers to look for new 'crossover' titles, books read by both children and adults. A UK marketing campaign, 'Good Booking', run by Penguin Books in 2004, was based on research that women are attracted to men who read books.   AGP

A. Baverstock, *How to Market Books*, 3e (1999)
Norrie
J. Tebbel, *Between Covers* (1987)
W. Tinsley, *Random Recollections of an Old Publisher* (1900)

aerial leafletting Air-dropped leaflets have been an instrument of war *propaganda since 1806, when a British Royal Navy officer used kites to land proclamations from his ships into France. By the mid-19th century, balloons were employed, but it was not until World War I that air-disseminated leaflets were used on a large scale. Since then, they have featured in nearly every theatre of war and been used for peaceful (sometimes artistic) purposes.   MFS

www.psywarsoc.org/FallingLeaf, consulted July 2008

African Bookman First South African oppositional publishing house. Founded by Julian Rollnick in 1943 and active until 1948, it aimed to make available literature suitable in language, content, and price for African readers. Notable series included 'Sixpenny Library', 'Pro and Con Pamphlets', and 'AB Adult Readers'.   FCG

African Book Publishing Record A current *bibliography that provides extensive coverage of new and forthcoming books in sub-Saharan African countries. It has appeared quarterly since 1975, each issue containing full bibliographical information, prices, a directory of publishers, and a key to currency abbreviations. Material published in English and French, and important titles in various African languages, are included. Arrangement is by subject, country of publication, and author; this information is collected every four to five years to update *African Books in Print*. Other features include an extensive reviews section for books and new African magazines, and occasional articles, interviews, and reports on activities and developments in the African publishing and book trade. The second issue of each volume contains 'Africana Reference Works', an annual list of reference works published in the preceding year.   ALD

H. Zell and C. Lomer, *The African Studies Companion*, 2e (1997)

African Books Collective (ABC) A non-profit-making organization founded, owned, and governed by African publishers, ABC seeks 'to strengthen indigenous African publishing through collective action and to increase the visibility and accessibility of the wealth of African scholarship and culture'. Beginning in 1985, ABC has, with the support of international funds, grown to represent over 100 African publishers. Currently operating from Oxford and from Michigan State University Press, ABC promotes, markets, and distributes African-published books internationally. Its *Annual Reports* record its training projects, promotion of new technology (159 available *print-on-demand titles), and book distribution schemes. *See also* AFRICAN PUBLISHERS NETWORK.   JMG

www.africanbookscollective.com, consulted Mar. 2008

African libraries, East and West Modern African library development is associated with the colonial and post-independence periods. History, geography, and politics account for similarities and differences across and within the eastern and western regions of Africa. Libraries in British-influenced East and West Africa and French-influenced West Africa share some characteristics, but there are wide differences, for example, between Eritrea and Uganda.

The West African (1953) and East African (1956) Library Associations were founded to nurture regional library development, but dissolved during the 1960s and 1970s to make way for national associations. Today, regional groupings—such as the Standing Conference of Eastern Central and Southern African Library and Information Professionals (SCECSAL) and the Standing Conference of African University Libraries in West Africa (SCAULWA)—also provide librarians with opportunities for professional development.

Special libraries and documentation centres related to government administration, agriculture, and geology (for example), as well as those associated with non-government and semi-state organizations, were among the first to be established. Academic libraries have had to face the severe financial difficulties of their countries; prohibitive book prices and weak currencies have led to deteriorating collections and, in some instances, have necessitated efforts to share resources and seek solutions through electronic means. National libraries often serve multiple purposes as public and school libraries, and as central headquarters to assist branches around the country. *See also* **37**.   ALD

A. Olden, *Libraries in Africa* (1995)

African Publishers Network (APNET) A non-profit organization established in 1992, uniting national publishers' associations and communities to strengthen indigenous publishing throughout Africa. It aspires, through networking, training, and trade promotion, to meet local needs for quality books relevant to socioeconomic, political, and cultural realities. APNET's highest authority is a General Council, and decisions are implemented by a Board aiming to reflect some of the linguistic diversity of Africa. Executive action may be entrusted to the Secretariat, currently located in Abidjan, or to Project Committees which oversee activities including science education programmes, research, and documentation. *See also* AFRICAN BOOKS COLLECTIVE. JMG

African Universities Press Erstwhile Nigerian firm established by André *Deutsch in Lagos in 1962. Numerous university presses now exist in Nigeria; the first was *Ibadan University's, established in 1951, the first outside South Africa, whose University of the Witwatersrand Press, founded 1922, is reputedly the continent's oldest and largest. AEV

A. Darko-Ampem, 'A University Press Publishing Consortium for Africa: Lessons from Academic Libraries', *Journal of Scholarly Publishing*, 36 (2005), 89–114

C. Davis, 'The Politics of Postcolonial Publishing: Oxford University Press's Three Crowns Series 1962–1976', *BH* 8 (2005), 227–44

Afrikaans Literary Museum and Documentation Centre, National Founded in 1973 and based in Bloemfontein, South Africa, it is a repository of MSS, books, and other items relating to Afrikaans-language writers. Its special collections and archival material are accessible through catalogues, exhibitions, a bibliography, and an electronic database called Knipkat. ALD

Afshār, Īraj (1925–) Iranian literary scholar, bibliographer, and codicologist. He has made notable contributions to the study of Persian MSS and to editing Persian texts. Also active in recording Iranian printed publications, he has been editor of several bibliographical periodicals. GJR

K. Eslami, ed., *Iran and Iranian Studies* (1998)

afterword A relatively brief, unnumbered epilogue or postscript in a book, not necessarily by the book's author. Typographically, it is usually treated like a *foreword.

Agard, Arthur (1535/6–1615) English archivist and antiquary. He became deputy chamberlain of the exchequer in 1570, a position he held for 45 years; this gave him responsibility for the preservation of royal records. He made numerous abstracts and inventories of documents under his care and also sought to make them physically secure. Agard was a close friend of *Cotton, to whom he bequeathed a number of MSS. ASGE

ODNB

agenda format [Lat. *agenda*, 'things to be done'] Term originally describing pocket books, often printed with the days of the week, employed in the 18ᵗʰ and 19ᵗʰ centuries as *diaries; by analogy, any small, narrow book. NH

D. Foxon, 'Some Notes on Agenda Format', *Library*, 5/8 (1953), 163–73

Agricola, Mikael (1507?–57) Bishop of Turku/Åbo, reformer, publisher, translator, and creator of the Finnish literary language. He published the first books printed in Finnish: the smaller *catechism [1543], a prayer book, the New Testament (1548), Old Testament texts, and liturgical works; all were printed in Stockholm, Sweden. APä

Aguilar, Editorial Spanish publisher. Based in Madrid, the firm was founded in 1923 by Manuel Aguilar (b. 1888). Although its output has been very diverse, Aguilar is best known for issuing the complete works of classic authors in compact, well-printed *India paper *editions bound in flexible *leather. DRW

Aḥmad Bābā Library A major public repository of Islamic MSS in Timbuktu, Mali. It has collected more than 18,000 MSS, mainly in Arabic, from the private libraries that form the area's rich literary and scholarly heritage. Its conservation, cataloguing, and *digitization projects are supported by *UNESCO and Arab donors. GJR

airport novel Like the French *roman du gare* (railway station novel), an engrossing but not particularly weighty work of fiction intended to divert travellers flying from one city to another. Sold at airport terminal newsstands and always in *paperback format not meant to withstand

The apotheosis of the **airport novel**: an automatic book-vending machine by Novel Idea Vending. The Irish firm was launched in 2005 with a contract to supply machines at British airports.

multiple readings, it is usually a long, winding tale involving political or military intrigue, business machinations, technological wizardry, multigenerational joys and sorrows, and, often, a great deal of heated romance and sex. The term has been around since the late 1960s, and, like 'potboiler' or 'schlockbuster', is invariably derogatory.

EDG

Aitken, Robert (1735–1802) Philadelphia printer. Apprenticed in Edinburgh, he became a binder and bookseller in Paisley, Scotland. Emigrating to Pennsylvania in 1771, he opened a *stationer's shop, launched the *Pennsylvania Magazine* (1775–6), and became printer to the Continental Congress. When English bibles (*see* **2**) (production of which was restricted by royal patent) were embargoed during the Revolution, Aitken published five editions of the New Testament. After the war, he printed the first complete English Bible with an American imprint (1782). After Aitken died, his daughter Jane continued his business until 1814.

SEC

ANB

Ajuda, Biblioteca da The Portuguese royal library, incorporating the outstanding music collection formed by João IV, was destroyed in the 1755 Lisbon earthquake. Its succeeding collection, sent to Rio de Janeiro in 1810, is now the highlight of the National Library of *Brazil. A third library, begun on João VI's return to Portugal in 1821, is housed in the Ajuda Palace, Lisbon. It numbers more than 100,000 volumes, including 60,000 pre-1800 books; 2,300 MS volumes; and important holdings of *maps, *atlases, and music. Perhaps its greatest treasure is the 13th-century Cancioneiro da Ajuda, a MS compilation of Portuguese poetry.

DRW

Akademická tlačiareň Set up by the Jesuit University in Trnava, Slovakia, in 1640, the press continued the printing activity started by Miklós Telegdi in 1577. It developed into the most productive *printing office in Slovakia, maintaining six presses, its own typefoundry, *paper mill, and bindery. It printed in Greek, Hebrew, and Cyrillic, and published *c*.5,000 titles until its move to Buda, Hungary, in 1777.

DP

V. Breza, *Tlačiarne na Slovensku* (1997)

Akbar-nāmah MSS The official history of the reign of the Mughal emperor Akbar (1556–1605). The first volume was finished in 1596, and the third in 1598. There were two illustrated versions. The earlier (V&A IS2(55-93)-1896) was completed in the 1590s, while the other (BL Or. 12988; Chester Beatty Library MS 3) was finished around 1604. The MSS were profusely illustrated by a team of artists, both Muslim and Hindu. Detached leaves are to be found in various public and private collections.

DLJ

L. Leach, *Mughal and Other Indian Paintings from the Chester Beatty Library* (1995)

Akitaya Ichibei Osaka publisher. The firm's earliest publications were two popular reference works appearing in 1691; in 1698, it was one of the 24 publishing concerns belonging to the unofficial publishers' guild of Osaka. It produced a pictorial guide to China in 1715, but mostly published sinology, fiction, and educational books, often in conjunction with other publishers. It was still operating as late as 1879, but closed not long thereafter.   PFK

Akutagawa Prize Japan's foremost literary prize, the Akutagawa Ryūnosuke Shō is the only leading national literary prize routinely awarded for short fiction. Founded in 1935, in memory of the writer Akutagawa Ryūnosuke, the prize is awarded semi-annually for the best story published in the periodical press by a promising writer.

JFE

'Ālam al-Kutub (**The World of Books**) Arabic bibliographical periodical, published in Saudi Arabia since 1980. It carries scholarly articles on MSS and textual editing, historical bibliography, librarianship, and digitization, as well as book reviews, systematic bibliographies of theses and periodical articles, and discussion and commentaries on bibliographical matters.   GJR

À la recherche du temps perdu Published as seven separately titled novels, Marcel Proust's masterpiece was nevertheless conceived as a single work, first drafted in two parts in 1910–11. The unfinished autobiographical novel *Jean Santeuil* (1895–9), published only in 1952, was a preparation for it, the fragments published in 1954 as *Contre Sainte-Beuve* (composed 1908) a preliminary version. Turned down by three publishers (including *Gallimard), the first part, *Du côté de chez Swann*, was issued in November 1913 (in 1,750 copies) by *Grasset, who, however, cut the volume by a fifth, the excised text afterwards reworked into the opening of *À l'ombre des jeunes filles en fleurs*. Gallimard, having bought the rights, published it, and the book won the 1919 *Goncourt. By then, the second and third parts announced in 1913 had grown to four and eventually to six. *Le Côté de Guermantes I* appeared in 1920, *Guermantes II* and *Sodome et Gomorrhe I* in April 1921, and *Sodome et Gomorrhe II* in April 1922. After Proust's death (18 November 1922), his brother Robert oversaw the publication of the last three parts, assisted at Gallimard by Jacques Rivière (1886–1925) and Jean Paulhan. For *La Prisonnière* (1923), they used as *copy-text one of three partially corrected typescripts; for *Albertine disparue* (1925), a typescript of the fair copy; and for *Le Temps retrouvé* (1927), an unauthoritative typed copy of the MS. The whole *Recherche*, edited by P. Clarac and A. Ferré, came out in three volumes in the *Pléiade collection in 1954 (*Albertine disparue* retitled *La Fugitive*, an alternative considered by Proust). For the next three decades, this version, though based on incomplete sources, superseded the often faulty text of 1913–27. Meanwhile, most of the surviving Proust MSS (drafts, notebooks, corrected typescripts with extensive MS additions, galleys) had remained with the family. After initial negotiations with Harvard University, they were acquired by the *Bibliothèque nationale in 1962 (with subsequent additions). A new, four-volume Pléiade edition, edited by J.-Y. Tadié (and reverting to the title *Albertine disparue*), came out in 1987–9, based principally on MS sources, its appendices comprising a generous selection from the BnF materials. Other editions in the 1980s and 1990s, made possible when Proust's work entered the public domain, all present textual differences, particularly in the last three parts, for which it is impossible to establish a definitive text. VAG

M. Proust, *À la recherche du temps perdu*, ed. J.-Y. Tadié (4 vols, 1987–9)

Albania, National Library of (Biblioteka Kombëtare) Established in Tirana in 1917, it became a national library in 1922 with a collection of 6,000 volumes. The library receives Albanian *legal deposit material and functions as the national bibliographical centre, the main national institution for book preservation, and the centre for professional training in librarianship. The library holds about 1 million items, including collections of MSS, old and rare books in Albanian, and books in other languages about Albania, published before 1799. The special collections consist of 2,050 volumes, including seven *incunabula. MVG

Albatross Verlag German publishing house. The company, located in Hamburg and later also in Paris, was founded in 1932 to publish one of the earliest series of modern paperbacks. The 'Albatross Modern Continental Library', its first volumes designed and printed by G. *Mardersteig, rivalled *Tauchnitz's publications and set standards for subsequent paperback series (especially for *Penguin Books)—most notably in its colour system for different genres and the Albatross logo. Rapid success made a takeover of Tauchnitz possible in 1936, but the beginning of World War II precipitated its decline. US

A. McCleery, 'Tauchnitz and Albatross: A "Community of Interests" in English-Language Paperback Publishing, 1934–51', *Library*, 7/7 (2006), 297–316

Albin Michel Established in Paris in 1900 (and named after its founder), the firm became successful by publishing Henri Barbusse and Romain Rolland (1915 *Nobel Prize) and Pierre Benoît's best-selling *L'Atlantide* (1919). It grew in the 1920s and 1930s, purchasing Ollendorf's book list in 1924, while its foreign authors included Tagore, Kipling, Thomas Mann, and Wells. By 2000 it was the fourth largest French publishing group, combining a prestigious literary list with detective and popular fiction. VAG

Albion press An iron hand press, invented by Richard Whittaker Cope in London *c*.1820; it worked by a toggle action (unlike the *Columbian). The workhorses of British printing for some 30 years, Albions were thereafter favoured by *private presses and used for *proofing and *jobbing. *See also* COLUMBIAN PRESS; STANHOPE PRESS. PWN

R. Stone, *The Albion Press* (2005)

album [Lat. *album*, 'white'] A book for collecting autographs, verses, drawings, and souvenirs. In the 1540s, German students travelling between universities began keeping books for friends and teachers to record their names, testimonials, and other memorial texts. The *album amicorum* (Lat.) or *Stammbuch* (Ger.) ('album of friends') adapted the *album* or whitened tablet, which displayed public notices in ancient Rome, to a more personal function. The earliest examples were interleaved textbooks and *emblem books, chosen to demonstrate the owner's taste. The first specially designed album appeared in 1558, and the fashion spread to universities and royal courts in the Low Countries, France, and Italy. By 1600 the small, oblong, *blank pocket album was in general use. Classical or scriptural quotations displayed contributors' erudition or piety, and pages were embellished with coats of arms, portraits, and other decorations.

Although claims were made for albums' moral value, satire against self-serving album-owners who solicited strangers for compliments was more common. Collectors' taste for contemporary autographs quickly expanded to include those of the celebrated dead, however, and antiquaries also saw the form's potential to archive historical documents. From the late 17th century, 'album' also refers to substantial large-format volumes of autograph and *facsimile documents and art prints.

The album remained a predominantly masculine genre until the 18th century, when it was imported into the UK (English commentators still sometimes characterize it as a German or 'foreign' import). Men's contributions to rare early examples kept by high-ranking women translated flattery into a courtly idiom; this convention continued as album-keeping was domesticated in the late 18th century, becoming as popular as novel-reading among upper- and middle-class women. Romantic-period women's albums were often elaborate productions containing watercolour sketches, transcriptions of favourite texts (as in *commonplace books), original *poetry solicited from authors (including Byron, Wordsworth, and Lamb), pressed flowers, and locks of hair. The album's feminization, and its early 19th-century association with the *gift book, *keepsake, *annual, and slight 'album verse', led to concerns that album-keeping was trivial or pernicious.

In the mid-19th century, the album metamorphosed into the printed *autograph book and the *visitors' book. The large-format album continues as a flexible vehicle for miscellaneous domestic collections—including postage stamps, photographs, and newspaper cuttings—closely related to the more ephemeral *scrapbook. SM

M. A. E. Nickson, *Early Autograph Albums in the British Museum* (1970)

alchemical books A philosophical and practical tradition, alchemy was esoteric, accessible only to the initiated. Its books concealed the secrets they disclosed regarding the philosophers' stone, a substance to transmute base metals into gold or to produce an elixir restoring health and prolonging life. Alchemist authors guarded their secrets with arcane paradoxes, digressions, erroneous quantities, numerical encodings, or anagrams. Substances and processes were recorded in specialized symbols, and illustrations might include alembics, diagrams, scenes of the alchemist's laboratory, or depictions of the kings, queens, dragons, and toads that populated the allegories.

Arriving in Europe with the mid-12th-century influx of Arabic works, alchemical texts circulated in Latin, often under mythical names such as Hermes Trismegistus, or with spurious attributions to Thomas Aquinas, Ramon Lull, and other great scholars. Vernacular works began appearing in the 15th century. In the 16th century, alchemical works first appeared in print, but MSS preserving ancient knowledge remained highly valued. From the 1520s, Paracelsus (1493–1541) called for medical reform using alchemical expertise. Writing in the vernacular, he replaced the Galenic system with a 'doctrine of signatures' in which like cured like. Alchemical publications in the later 16th century encompassed the corpus of reputedly ancient and medical sources, and an increased range of genres. Practical works on metallurgy and distillation became systematic textbooks, beginning with Andreas Libavius's *Alchemica* (1597).

In the 17th century, alchemical expertise moved from courts and universities to urban centres. The American George Starkey (1628–65) challenged the Paracelsian emphasis on the art's medicinal virtues, becoming the century's most important alchemist and influencing Robert Boyle (1627–91). Starkey's many works under the name Eirenaeus Philalethes circulated throughout Europe in MS; by the end of the 17th century, most of them were printed. Bibliographical collections of this period—Pierre Borel's *Bibliotheca Chimica* (Paris, 1654), William Cooper's *A Catalogue of Chymical Books* (London, 1673, 1675, 1688), and Jean-Jacques Manget's *Bibliotheca Chemica Curiosa* (Geneva, 1702)—document the elasticity of alchemical definitions, recording medieval allegories along with works of natural history and matter theory.

Alchemical books continued to be printed in the 18th century and beyond, but by then they had become theosophical rhapsodies, collections of medical preparations, and chemical textbooks. LK

W. Eamon, *Science and the Secrets of Nature* (1994)
P. O. Long, *Openness, Secrecy, Authorship* (2001)
B. T. Moran, *Distilling Knowledge* (2005)
C. Webster, 'Alchemical and Paracelsian Medicine', in *Health, Medicine and Mortality in the Sixteenth Century*, ed. C. Webster (1979)

Alcoholics Anonymous (AA) Mutual aid organization founded in 1935 for alcoholics seeking to stay sober. It has developed a large private publishing programme which creates and distributes literature for an estimated 2 million members in more than 150 countries. AA's publishing arm, AA World Services, Inc., currently publishes seven books, two magazines, and 48 pamphlets. Although few of these circulate through traditional retail outlets, net sales of literature in 2000 were just over $9 million. Reflecting AA's roots in evangelical Christianity, the organization promotes (but does not require) daily devotional reading as a key aid to continuing sobriety. The fourth edition of *Alcoholics Anonymous*, AA's central

philosophical text, commonly known as 'the Big Book', appeared in 2004; an estimated 25 million copies had been sold by 2005. TT

www.aa.org/en_information_aa.cfm, consulted Sept. 2007

Aldus Manutius (*c*.1451–1515) and **Manutius family** Born at Bassiano, near Rome, Aldus (Aldo Manuzio) founded a publishing dynasty active at Venice, and latterly at Rome, from 1495 to 1597. Although the character of the firm's products changed over the years, it never lost the prestige and even glamour that the elder Aldus provided through his novel programme of publication of the Greek classics in the original language. Aldus had a humanist education at Rome and Ferrara before entering the circle of Giovanni Pico della Mirandola, whose nephews, princes of Carpi, he tutored in the 1480s. By 1490 he had moved to Venice, and began accumulating MSS, *types, and capital for a press there, supported by financing from a Venetian patrician and technical expertise from the established printer *Torresani, whose daughter he married in 1505.

His first publication, the Greek *grammar of Constantine Lascaris, is dated February–March 1495; however, the real business of the partnership was to produce the 'Aldine Aristotle', whose five volumes and 3,700 folio pages appeared from 1495 to 1498. Aristotle and the other early Greek books (Aristophanes, Theocritus, scientific and ecclesiastical works, plentiful aids for learning the language) were accompanied by a sprinkling of Latin texts, largely private-press work, but some making serious contributions to learning, as with Perotti's *Cornucopiae* and Poliziano's formidable philological works (1498–9). Books printed on commission include two in Italian: the *Hypnerotomachia Poliphili* (1499) and the letters of St Catherine of Siena (1500). The latter has set, in a woodcut, the first example of *italic type; all Aldus' types, including the fine *romans and the *Greeks modelled on contemporary *cursive script, were cut by *Griffo. The Aldine italic types were a revelation to contemporaries, Erasmus calling them the 'neatest types in the world'.

The italic was used as the text type for the innovative series of pocket editions of the Latin classics, beginning with the *Virgil of April 1501. The innovation lay not in the *octavo *format, often used by printers for devotional texts, but in applying it to a class of literature hitherto printed in imposing *folios or *quartos, often drowning in a sea of commentary. *Press runs were large—up to 3,000—and supplied plain texts for a new class of educated readers. They were soon imitated, especially at Lyons, against whose publishers Aldus issued a printed warning. From 1502 onwards, promotion of the Aldine brand was further enhanced by his 'dolphin and anchor' *printer's device. Along with the octavos, which came to include the Greek and Italian classics (Homer, the tragedians, Dante (*see* DIVINA COMMEDIA, LA), *Petrarca), Aldus continued to print major editions of the classical Greek authors (e.g. Herodotus, Thucydides, and Plato) and the occasional work of modern erudition (e.g. Erasmus' amplified *Adagia*, 1508). For much of his career, Aldus was the only source of these Greek texts; only one canonical Greek writer, Aeschylus, remained unprinted before the publisher's death in February 1515.

Torresani assumed direction of the firm with his sons from 1515, remaining largely true to Aldus' vision: an Aeschylus appeared in 1518, a vast Greek Galen in 1525. Initially working with his uncles, Aldus' youngest son, **Paulus** (1512–74), eventually asserted his family's right to possession of the Aldine types and name, printing books as 'The Sons of Aldus' from 1539 onwards. Greek took a secondary place in Paulus' publishing policy, Latin being very much to the fore—above all, works of Cicero, to whose text and interpretation he made signal contributions. His own letters and his handbooks of Roman antiquities found enduring success with the public. Paulus had two successive spells as an official printer: for the Accademia Veneta (1558–61) and for the pope in Rome (1561–70), the latter to produce Tridentine Counter-Reformation material at a handsome salary. The commissioned work palled, however, and he retired some years before his death. Paulus' son, **Aldus the Younger** (1547–97), an infant prodigy who wavered between publishing and the academic life, moved further again from his grandfather's vision to the total exclusion of Greek books. At Venice, he published much classical and humanist Latin, mingled with vernacular texts, notably early editions of Tasso.   MCD

DBI (*s.n.* Manuzio)
Lowry

Aldus Society Founded in 2000, this bibliophilic organization, based in Columbus, Ohio, offers lectures and workshops on the history of printing, publishing, and other aspects of book history. An affiliate of the *Fellowship of American Bibliophilic Societies, the Aldus Society produces its own quarterly newsletter.   MDB

www.aldussociety.com/home.htm, consulted Nov. 2007

Aleppo Codex ('Keter Aram Tzova') One of the earliest MSS of the Hebrew Bible, now in the Ben Zvi Institute in Jerusalem. Copied more than a millennium ago by Solomon ben Buya'a and probably vocalized by Aaron ben Asher, it was held for centuries in a synagogue in Aleppo, Syria, which burned down in 1947; about one third of the MS was lost. It was smuggled to Israel a few years later. *See also* **2**.   EGLS

Alexandrian Library Ptolemy I Soter (367/6–282 BC) founded the universal library in Alexandria, but the idea was originally conceived by Alexander the Great, who intended to store in one library all the literature of all the peoples in his empire, translated into Greek. Ptolemy, wishing to link the library with Aristotle's Lyceum, invited Theophrastus to run it, but he refused; Demetrius of Phaleron was appointed instead. The only extant document referring to the purpose of the Library is the so-called *Letter of Aristeas*, probably written *c.*160 BC, which cites a conversation between Ptolemy II and Demetrius about the Greek translation of the Bible (the Septuagint) and the policy of acquiring all kinds of literary and other work. Demetrius estimated that the Serapeum Library

had 42,800 books and the Imperial Library 400,000 'composite' and 90,000 'unmixed' scrolls. According to one of the Oxyrrhynchus papyri, the directors of the library were Zenodotus, Apollonius Rhodius, Eratosthenes, Aristophanes of Byzantium, Apollonius Eidographus, Aristarchus, Cydas, and perhaps a certain Onesander.

Distinguished Alexandrian literary scholars completed extensive editorial work on the classics, especially poetry. Callimachus made another major contribution by compiling the *Pinakes*. The contents of the library can be divided into three categories: all works representing the Greek literary tradition, books supplying material for the biographical notes on writers listed in the *Pinakes*, and foreign books. Two main legends surround the destruction of the library: that it was accidentally burnt down when Julius Caesar was under siege in Alexandria, or that it was destroyed on the orders of Caliph Omar. The original source for the conflagration story is Livy, but he, according to Seneca, states only that 40,000 books 'of excellent quality' were destroyed; presumably, these were blank rolls destined for export to Rome. According to the second legend, Caliph Omar, in AD 642, instructed Emir 'Amr that if the contents of the books accorded with the Qur'ān, they were not needed; if they did not, again they were not needed. In either case, then, he was to destroy them. The likely truth is that interest in the library waned after the Ptolemaic era and that looting, natural disasters, and the inexorable ravages of time led eventually to its disappearance.   KS

L. Canfora, *La biblioteca scomparsa* (1986)
E. A. Parsons, *The Alexandrian Library*, 3e (1967)

Alexandrina, Bibliotheca New library in Alexandria, Egypt, opened in 2002. Built, with *UNESCO involvement, to evoke the ancient *Alexandrian Library, it occupies a dramatic dish-shaped building near the Eastern Harbour. It contains current and rare books and MSS, specialized libraries for children and the visually impaired, and extensive audiovisual and electronic resources.
                                          GJR

Alexandrinus, Codex BL Royal MS I D.V–VIII, so called because it was discovered in Alexandria, from where it was brought in the 17th century and presented to Charles I. The MS dates from the 5th century and is written in Greek *uncial script. It is an important early MS witness to the texts of both the Old and New Testaments, and is also one of the first Bible MSS to attempt consistent decoration, here as a means of indicating the end of each book.   ASGE

W. H. P. Hatch, *The Principal Uncial Manuscripts of the New Testament* (1939)

Alfaguara Spanish publisher. Founded in 1964 by the author (and future Nobel laureate) Camilo José Cela, Alfaguara is one of Spain's leading literary publishers. Its specialities are modern fiction by Hispanic authors—including J. Cortázar, M. Vargas Llosa, and A. Pérez-Reverte—and foreign literature in Spanish *translation.
                                          DRW

Alfonso de Zamora (*c*.1474–1530) A convert from Judaism, and author of a number of works in Hebrew and Latin, he taught Hebrew at Salamanca. For the *Complutensian Polyglot Bible, he revised the Hebrew text and prepared a text and Latin translation of the Aramaic Targum to the entire Hebrew Bible; only the Targum of Onkelos on the Pentateuch was printed.   BT
J. P. R. Lyell, *Cardinal Ximenes* (1917)

Alken, Henry (**Ben Tally Ho**) (1785–1851) English sporting artist, illustrator, and caricaturist. Alken's best-known work, *The National Sports of Great Britain* (1821), consisted of 50 *aquatints depicting a wide range of sports. His *Sketchbook* (1823) and *Sporting Scrapbook* (1824) were also influential.   MMS
ODNB

all-along sewing In bookbinding, the most thorough form of *flexible sewing, in which the thread is passed around every sewing support as it is run up and down the *quires (*see* **17**). An alternative is to take shortcuts by moving between quires to generate skip-station sewing, sometimes called two-on, three-on, etc.   DRSP
Middleton

Allan Wingate British publisher founded by *Deutsch in 1944. After disagreements with the directors, Deutsch departed, founding his eponymous company in 1951. Allan Wingate continued, becoming a *Hamlyn subsidiary in 1960.   CMS
DLB 112

Allde family English booksellers and printers. **John** (*c*.1531–84), printed and published ballads in particular, as well as *almanacs and popular books. The large number of *apprentices he took on is a measure of his success. His widow, **Margaret** (*fl.* 1584–*c*.1603), continued the business, including binding apprentices, until at least 1603. **Edward Allde** (1555×63–1627), their son, was freed by patrimony in 1584 and played an active role in the *Stationers' Company. Late in 1588 he left the family business to work as a trade printer, producing ballads and music, pamphlets and books, including Shakespeare play *quartos.   KMQ
ODNB

Allen, Thomas (1540–1632) English collector of medieval MSS. Nearly 300 survive that bear evidence of his ownership, the majority of which are now in the Digby collection in the *Bodleian; a number of these seem to have come from monastic houses or from Oxford colleges.   ASGE
G. Watson, 'Thomas Allen of Oxford and his Books', in *Medieval Scribes, Manuscripts and Libraries*, ed. M. B. Parkes and A. G. Watson (1978)

Allen & Unwin, George British publishing firm, founded in 1914 when Stanley Unwin bought the bankrupt firm of George Allen & Co. Allen, known primarily as the publisher of Ruskin's work, had merged in 1911 with Swan *Sonnenschein, whose list included Marx, Shaw, and Freud. Unwin published many important thinkers, including Bertrand Russell and R. H. Tawney, and also enjoyed more popular successes with works by J. R. R. Tolkien and Thor Heyerdahl.   CL
ODNB

Allen Press Lewis and Dorothy Allen produced over 50 classic texts in hand-printed editions (1939–80) in the style of *artists' books at their *private press north of San Francisco. *Printing with the Handpress* (1969) is their manual of hand press production.   KAW
L. and D. Allen, *The Allen Press Bibliography* (1981)

Allestree, Richard (1619–81) English theological author, and book collector. Educated at *Christ Church, Oxford, he became Regius Professor of Divinity there. His personal library formed the Allestree Library, now housed in an annexe of Christ Church. The library comprises largely 17th-century books.   ASGE
M. Purcell, '"Useful Weapons for the Defence of That Cause": Richard Allestree, John Fell and the Foundation of the Allestree Library', *Library*, 6/21 (1999), 124–47

Alliance & Co. Established in 1901 by the bookseller Kuppuswamy Iyer, Alliance published patriotic books in the 1930s and 1940s, Tamil short-story anthologies, and translations from Bengali. The firm suffered a setback with the founder's death in 1949, but revived in the 1980s under his grandson V. Srinivasan.   ARV

Allibone, Samuel Austin (1816–89) Philadelphia-born American bibliographer. A businessman by profession, and largely self-taught, he compiled a three-volume *Critical Dictionary of British Literature and British and American Authors* (1855–71)—to which a two-volume supplement, edited by John Foster Kirk, appeared in 1891—and two huge anthologies of verse and prose quotations (1873–6). Allibone served as librarian of the *Lenox Library in New York from 1879 to 1888.   VAG

Allied Publishers Born out of a small bookshop set up in 1934 by M. Graham Brash, a former employee of *Macmillan. The firm was taken over in 1947 by R. N. Sachdeva, who nurtured it into one of the largest book wholesalers in India, with its headquarters in Delhi.   RBC

all published Term indicating that a book or series (whatever the original intent or the appearances to the contrary) was never completed; no further portions appeared.

All Souls College Library, Oxford The original library of the college, founded in 1438, was in a Tudor room that still survives. It was replaced by the magnificent Codrington Library, built from 1716 to designs by Nicholas Hawksmoor with funds bequeathed by Christopher Codrington, a former fellow, together with a 10,000-volume library. The collections include medieval

MSS, some from founders' gifts, college *archives, and a large printed book collection strong in theology, law, and history. Later MSS include those of N. *Luttrell and over 400 Wren drawings.   ASB

H. H. E. Craster, *The History of All Souls College Library* (1971)

Allyn & Bacon Boston *textbook publishers, founded in 1888 by John Allyn and George A. Bacon. Allyn, a classical scholar, had owned a bookshop in Cambridge, Mass., since 1868 and published his first Latin text in 1880. Bacon, a high school principal, joined him in 1888. The firm's books were known for the creativity and technical quality of their illustrations. The company, which publishes textbooks in a wide range of subjects for elementary school to college markets, was sold in 1952 to *Prentice Hall, but spun off in 1957 and went public as an independent firm. In 1965, it was acquired by CBS, and sold in 1981 to Esquire, Inc. *Simon & Schuster acquired the company in 1984 and sold it to *Pearson Education in 1998.   BEL

almanac (almanack) [Arabic *al-manaakh*, 'the climate'] An annual publication containing astronomical data, dates of fixed and movable holidays, and other practical information, including predictions of the weather.

1. Origins and early history
2. The 17th century and beyond

1. Origins and early history

Almanacs were known in England at least from the time of Roger Bacon, and were evidently produced in several formats. BL Harleian MS 937 is an almanac for 1431, designed to be attached to a girdle or belt for handy reference. Others were made for public display, and were written (later stamped or *woodblock printed) on *folio sheets or *broadsides. They are likely to have been among the mainstays of the printer's trade from the beginning, and there would have been a large demand for them; but as there is little reason to retain an out-of-date almanac, scarcely more than a few fragments remain from before 1500. However, two copies of the *Almanacke for xii. yere*, printed in 1508 by de *Worde, do survive. Evidently intended for the pocket, its minute format (*thirty-twomo) would have increased the likelihood of its being lost or quickly worn out. These copies must have been preserved carefully by frugal owners, aware of the fact that the almanac was valid until 1520.

The *daybook of the Oxford bookseller *Dorne discloses the various kinds of almanacs offered in the 1520s. What he calls the 'ciclus vel almanck [*sic*]' was evidently a broadside—giving the cycle of the year and its movable feasts—which sold separately for 2*d*. No example of this popular almanac, published annually at least till the Reformation, now survives. *Stella Clericorum* was another kind of almanac (such as is still prefixed to editions of the Book of Common Prayer), based on the ecclesiastical calendar and giving only basic astronomical information. Dorne also sold copies of a 'perpetual' almanac valid for 30 years at the very high price of 4*s*. 8*d*. Finally, there

were what he records as prognostications, evidently among his bestsellers. Their prices ranged from 1*d*. to 3½*d*., suggesting considerable variation in size. Most were English translations of continental originals. The 1508 Almanac claims to be calculated specifically for Oxford, and later in the century publication of separate almanacs for York, Dublin, and Salisbury was, apparently, commercially viable.

Although Dorne often sold almanacs and prognostications together, they were always published separately; the former were respectable, the latter not. The annual predictions of the Laet family of Antwerp appeared for many years in English (from 1493, according to *Bagford), but their astrological matrix made them ecclesiastically suspect. From time to time, laws 'against sorcery' (actually intended to suppress religious or political dissent) penalized the publication of prognostications; publication was always strictly controlled. Two godly supporters of the Elizabethan Settlement, Richard Watkins and James Roberts, received royal patents for printing combined pocket almanacs and prognostications between 1571 and 1599. So valuable was their monopoly that they declined to print the cheaper sheet almanacs, leaving them to the poorer members of the *Stationers' Company. The compiler of their prognostications was John Dade, under whose surname almanacs continued to appear until 1707.

A long-lived almanac on a much larger scale was the Shepherds' Calendar. *Le Compost et grand kalendrier des bergiers* first appeared in 1493, offering to mostly humble and rustic readers a compendium of basic religious teaching on virtues and vices, hints on the preservation of health, and an introduction to astrology and physiognomy, in addition to the usual astronomical information. A translation into Lowland Scots published in Paris in 1503 was followed by many versions in English from 1506 onwards. Copies from nineteen editions survive; the text was conservatively modified from time to time in deference to religious orthodoxy, but the woodcuts derived from the first edition continued in use to the last edition of 1656, largely determining its content. The Protestant reformers greatly disliked the Shepherds' Calendar for its spiritual element as much as for its reliance on pre-Christian authors. The Bible translator Miles Coverdale published *A Faythfull and True Pronosticacion* [1545?], composed 'not after the doctrine of the Papistes, not after the lernynge of Ptolomy' and said to be perpetually accurate until the Second Coming. This radical alternative did not reach a second edition.

2. The 17th century and beyond

The Stationers' Company continued to impose stringent controls on the publication of almanacs in the first part of the 17th century, and it seems likely that a growing Puritanism among townspeople, making them suspicious of all but Biblical prognostication, reduced the market considerably. Restraints were lifted with the Restoration of the monarchy in 1660 and a number of very long-lived almanacs began life thereafter. John Partridge's *Merlinus Liberatus* long survived its author's death in 1715 (as well as his fictitious 'death' announced by Swift). Very often, the name of the original almanac-maker rather than the actual compiler appeared as a guarantee of 'old-fashioned' reliability. Even the name of the Shepherds' Calendar was briefly revived in the 1670s to help sell a new almanac. Those who bought almanacs did not care for novelty.

The post-1660 market for almanacs was vast (it has been said that enough were published to supply one in every three English families), and many compilers competed for it. As many as a dozen almanacs for the same year of the 18th century can often be found bound together in a contemporary and sometimes expensive binding, perhaps so that rival predictions could be compared. Almanac makers vied to outdo one another in sensationalism, but ridicule finally forced them to decline into the anodyne imprecision of *Old Moore's Almanac* and other current survivors of the genre.

*Franklin's *Poor Richard's Almanac* (from 1732) is remembered for being the first American bestseller, and for the author's maxims and aphorisms that adorn the text. The Bible and an almanac were the only books required by a settler breaking new ground, and the genre flourished in America late into the 19th century, often charting the spread of the press in the newly opened-up country. Not all were ephemeral: Gruber's *Hagerstown Town and Country Almanac* has appeared annually since 1797. In Victorian England there was a vogue for local and provincial almanacs, often in laboriously transcribed 'dialect', which lingered longest in the north.

As the desire for prognostication declined, the 'useful information' contained in almanacs expanded. More and more were produced for specialist markets (attorneys, freemasons, theatregoers, gourmands), leading ultimately to the very large compendia of political, statistical, and other factual matter of which *Whitaker's Almanack* (from 1868) and *The New York Times Almanac* are prominent contemporary examples.

That poor relation, the sheet almanac, has had a continuous and not entirely inglorious career. The University of Oxford has for over 330 years published its annual *broadside *Almanack*, on which the Heads of Houses and the phases of the moon were latterly given equal prominence. Many copies will have been preserved because of the excellence of the illustrations. Nowadays, the sheet calendars given away by old-fashioned shops and businesses at Christmas keep the genre alive. Their illustrations, alas, fall into another category. **BJF**

E. F. Bosanquet, *English Printed Almanacs and Prognostications* (1917)

B. S. Capp, *Astrology and the Popular Press* (1979)

M. Harris, 'Astrology, Almanacks, and Booksellers', *PH* 8 (1980), 87–104

S. K. Heninger, Jr., ed., *The Kalendar of Sheepehards* (facsimile) (1979)

C. W. Miller, 'Franklin's Poor Richard's Almanacks: Their Printing and Publication', *SB* 14 (1961), 97–115

M. B. Stowell, *Early American Almanacs* (1977)

Almanach de Gotha Genealogical handbook. In 1763 the Gotha publisher J. C. Dieterich issued the first *Gothaischer Hofkalender*, an almanac that included a genealogy of European rulers. C. W. Ettinger took it over in 1776, and was succeeded by his former apprentice J. Perthes in 1817. Although it began as a diverting publication—often embellished with engravings by *Chodowiecki and others—the yearly, and its French equivalent *Almanach de Gotha* (from 1770), slowly became a reference tool of international renown about European aristocracy. The aim of exhaustive coverage, especially of German nobility, gave rise to four additional series: the almanac, concentrating on princely houses, was joined by *Gräfliche Häuser* (1825), *Freiherrliche Häuser* (1848), and finally *Adelige Häuser*, subdivided into *A: Uradel* (1900) and *B: Alter Adel und Briefadel* (1907). From 1926, the statistical section, *Diplomatisch-statistisches Jahrbuch*, was published separately. The *Gotha*, a treasure trove of facts, ceased to exist in 1942 (the last *Almanach* was issued for 1944); in 1945, Soviet occupation forces set fire to the Gotha archive. Since 1951, the *Genealogisches Handbuch des Adels* has continued the tradition. A two-part English *Almanach de Gotha* on princely families was begun in London in 1998. **JWUS**

T. von Fritsch, *Die Gothaischen Taschenbücher, Hofkalender und Almanache* (1968)

Almanzi, Giuseppe (1801–60) Collector of Jewish books. His collection was built on the foundation laid by his father, who had bought part of the library of Hayyim Joseph David Azulai (1724–1806) in 1816. Almanzi's collection, then including 332 MSS, was sold to the British Museum in 1865 by A. Asher & Co. of Berlin. It is one of the foundations of the *British Library's collection of Jewish MSS and printed books. **EGLS**

Almon, John (1737–1805) London bookseller and political journalist. Almon's journalism was passionately radical and his Piccadilly bookshop became a Whig focal point. He fought alongside his friend John Wilkes for parliamentary proceedings to be published, and was charged with seditious libel in 1770 for publishing debates illegally. Accused of libel again in 1786, he fled to France, but was imprisoned for a year on returning to England. Almon founded the monthly *Parliamentary Register* in 1774. **JH**
ODNB

alphabet, printer's Set of types kept in *upper case, *lower case, and small capitals within a *fount. It originally excluded j (represented by i), u (represented by v), and w (represented by vv), but included accented letters and *ligatures. The quantities of each letter depended on their frequency of use. **KEA**

alphabet book *See* ABC.

ALS (Autograph Letter Signed) A standard abbreviation used in catalogues to denote a letter both written in the hand of, and signed by, its author.

Alsop, Benjamin (*c*.1658–1703) English bookseller. Apprenticed to *Ponder in 1672, Alsop was made free of the *Stationers' Company in 1679. He was involved in the publishing of Nonconformist authors such as Bunyan, during a career which was also notable for his involvement in *subscription publishing.　　　　　KMQ
ODNB

Alston, Robin (1933–) Trinidad-born bibliographer, librarian, publisher, scholar. Starting his career as an academic, Alston was later appointed consultant to the Director General of the British Library (1975–95), editor of the *ESTC (1978–89), and Professor of Library Studies, University of London (1990–98). In addition to a bibliography of the English language to 1800 (1965–), he founded the Scolar Press, which in its original incarnation (1966–72) produced over 1,000 affordable *facsimile editions of early modern English literary, linguistic, and recusant texts.　　　　　MW

Altschul, Frank (1887–1981) American book collector. A prominent banker, who had been influenced as a student at Yale by C. B. *Tinker, Altschul initially collected English novelists (particularly George Meredith) and French illustrated books. Later, he was a generous donor of early printed books, fine-press books, and French literature to his alma mater.　　　　　ASGE
DABC

Alves, Francisco Brazilian publisher. Founded in Rio de Janeiro in 1854, and managed from 1882 to 1917 by Francisco Alves, it is Brazil's oldest active publishing house. After winning control of the textbook market, it moved increasingly into literary publishing, absorbing several smaller houses and purchasing the *Laemmert firm's copyrights.　　　　　DRW

Amānat Khān (d. 1642) Master calligrapher, whose full name was ʿAbd al-Ḥaqq Amānat Khān Shīrāzī. From Iran he went to Mughal India in around 1608, following his brother Afḍal Khān to the imperial court. He completed the inscriptions for Akbar's tomb in 1613–14 and those for the Tāj Mahal *c*.1632. He served in the royal library of Jahāngīr and Shāh Jihān, possibly as librarian. Several imperial MSS bear his seal of inspection. His final years were spent in Lahore, where in 1642 he copied a Qurʾān, now in London.　　　　　DLJ
M. Bayani *et al.*, *The Decorated Word* (1999)

Amar Chitra Katha India's longest-running series of *comic books. Started in 1967 by Anant Pai, it is published by India Book House (*see* OXFORD & IBH). Issued in almost 20 Indian and foreign languages, most of its 436 titles are on Indian history and mythology. The first title in the series was *Krishna*. Most are single issues, with the exception of the 42-part issue of *Mahābhārata* and a nine-part issue of the *Bhāgavata purāṇa*.　　　　　AG

amazon.com Pioneering online bookseller, founded in 1994 by Jeff Bezos. Although Amazon now sells a wide range of consumer products and services via the *World Wide Web, the company began with books, selling its first volume in 1995. Within a month, it had shipped books to all 50 of the states in the US and to more than 40 other countries. In 2007, it also had operations in the UK, Germany, France, Japan, and Canada. Amazon sells new, second-hand, *electronic, and *print-on-demand books directly and through services for outside vendors. Its site offers information about books provided by publishers, excerpts from published reviews, and reviews posted by readers. Some listings permit readers to browse books, search them, examine tables of contents, or read chapters. The site also recommends books to customers based on their previous purchases and on the purchases of others who have bought the same books. Using a proprietary algorithm, Amazon ranks the books it sells on the basis of their sales on the site; authors have been known to follow these rankings closely, although no one has yet learned to translate the rankings into sales estimates.　　　　　BEL

www.amazon.com, consulted June 2007

Ambrosiana Library, Milan Intended as a weapon in the Catholic response to Protestant supremacy in theology and biblical scholarship, the library opened to the public by statute in 1609. It was established by Cardinal Federico Borromeo (1564–1631)—together with a college, an academy of fine arts, and an art gallery—and is famous for its MS holdings, which include Leonardo da Vinci's Atlantic *codex. Severely damaged in World War II, when its reading room was destroyed, it remains the property of the Catholic Church.　　　　　NH

Ameno, Francisco Luis (1713–93) Portuguese printer. A sometime schoolteacher, minor literary talent, editor, and translator of Italian opera libretti, Ameno opened a Lisbon printing office in 1748. Following the 1755 earthquake, he quickly recovered and, save for a hiatus *c*.1767–78, remained a prominent printer until his death.　　　　　DRW

Amerbach, Johann (1440/45–1513) Born in Amerbach, Lower Franconia, he became the leading printer in Basel, Switzerland. He studied in Paris—where he met Johann Heynlin de Lapide and German printers—gaining an MA at the Sorbonne in 1464. After an educational sojourn in Venice 1462–5, he established a printing press in Basel 1475–7, close to the charterhouse, whose MSS he used for his editions. He worked with the scholars Johann Heynlin, *Reuchlin, and *Rhenanus; his business partners were *Koberger in Nuremberg, and J. *Froben and *Petri in Basel. The first printer north of the Alps to use *roman type for an entire *volume, Amerbach printed classical and humanist authors, Latin bibles, and some scholastic works. His main scholarly contribution is the complete edition of the writings of St Augustine (1506). After his death in 1513, the printing office was continued by his sons Bruno and Basilius in association with Froben, who completed Amerbach's edition of St Jerome with the help of *Erasmus.　　　　　CS
LGB

461

American Academy of Arts and Letters An organization of members elected for life from the ranks of distinguished writers, composers, artists, and architects. It was founded in 1898 as the National Institute of Arts and Letters, with membership limited to 150 (raised to 250 in 1907). In 1904 a smaller group was selected from Institute members as the American Academy, with membership limited to 30 people and, later, 50. The two groups merged in 1976, but retained two levels of membership. In 1992 the Institute was dissolved, and the Academy now has 250 members at a single level. The Academy is housed in two *beaux arts* buildings on the upper West Side of New York City. It gives awards and prizes; sponsors exhibitions, readings, and performances; and purchases art for museums. Its art, book, and MS collections are open to accredited scholars. BEL

www.artsandletters.org, consulted July 2008

American Antiquarian Society (AAS) A learned society and independent research library in Worcester, Massachusetts, founded by I. *Thomas in 1812. By donating his own large collection and by writing the first history of printing in America (1810), Thomas put AAS on course not only to build one of the major repositories of American *imprints to 1876 but to become an important centre for scholarly research and publication in American book history. The collections, which include MSS and graphic arts, support advanced research on almost any topic within AAS's scope, the *history of the book above all. Thomas's successors have strengthened the library holdings and developed numerous programmes to support and disseminate research. These include publication of a scholarly journal, the *Proceedings of the American Antiquarian Society*, as well as books, several of which are the definitive bibliographies of various genres. The Program in the History of the Book in American Culture sponsors seminars, lectures, and publications, most notably *A History of the Book in America* (5 vols, 2000–2010). The Society's fellowship programme has helped produce important scholarly research. AAS is actively *digitizing parts of its collections. JBH

www.americanantiquarian.org/history.htm, consulted Nov. 2006

American Art Association (AAA) New York auction house, founded in 1883 by Thomas E. Kirby, James F. Sutton, and R. Austin Robertson as an art gallery and art retail business. Under Kirby's sole proprietorship (1895–1923), it became the premier American art auction firm. Cortlandt F. Bishop acquired the company in 1923; in 1929 it merged with the *Anderson Galleries, adding rare books to its business. After Bishop's death in 1935, the firm was run by Hiram Parke and Otto Bernet, who left in 1937 to form *Parke-Bernet Galleries. Bankrupt in 1940, the AAA was bought by Parke-Bernet. DBW

F. Herrmann, *Sotheby's* (1980)

American Bible Society (ABS) Formed in New York City in 1816 to produce and distribute the Bible in the US and around the world. Committed to publishing the Bible 'without note or comment', by the 1820s the ABS stood at the forefront of innovations in American mass publishing. By integrating the use of power presses, multi-language *translation work, *stereotype plates, complex networks of distribution, and *edition binding, the ABS issued as many as 350,000 bibles and New Testaments annually. The ABS continues to be one of the largest producers of bibles in the US, as well as an innovator in biblical translation. PCG

P. C. Gutjahr, *An American Bible* (1999)
C. Lacy, *The Word Carrying Giant* (1977)
P. Wosh, *Spreading the Word* (1994)

American Book Co. In April 1890, during the era of trusts in the US, four leading *textbook publishers attempted to dominate a crowded market by merging their textbook lists to form the American Book Co. The companies, in order of contributed assets, were Van Antwerp Bragg; Ivison, Blakeman, Taylor; A. S. Barnes; and D. *Appleton. In June, the company bought the large textbook list of *Harper & Brothers. Over the next decade, the trust acquired more than a dozen other firms. Titles owned by the new organization included the Eclectic Readers of William Holmes *McGuffey (which went on to sell 130 million copies), Joseph Ray's arithmetics (more than 100 million), and the penmanship books of Platt Rogers *Spencer and his sons, which taught three generations to write. The company's records are at Syracuse University. CM

W. W. Livengood, *Our Heritage: Being a Brief History of the American Book Company* (1947)

American Book Collector A periodical for *bibliophiles. It began in 1932 as a monthly published in Metuchen, New Jersey, edited by Charles Frederick Heartman and Harry Bischoff Weiss. In 1950, it moved to Chicago, under the editorship of W. B. Thorsen, and was published bimonthly. Beginning in 1980, it was published in New York by the Moretus Press. It is now published as *Book Collector's Market*. BEL

American Book Publishers Council (ABPC) Founded 1945 as the US Book Publishers Association, the organization became the ABPC in 1946. Coordinating business practices and promoting American books at home and abroad, ABPC oversaw *National Book Awards and created its Committee on Reading Development (1950) and *National Book Committee (1954). In 1970 it merged with the American Educational Publishers Institute to become the *Association of American Publishers. TT

American Booksellers Association (ABA) A nonprofit organization with headquarters in Tarrytown, New York. Founded in 1900, it acts as an advocacy group for the interests of independently owned bookshops. The ABA promotes the protection of free speech, especially in print, and encourages literacy and reading. It holds an annual convention and has a website that circulates relevant trade news to its membership. ASGE

www.bookweb.org/index.html, consulted July 2008

American Book Trade Association (ABTA) Founded in 1874 as the American Book Trade Union, this group of publishers, wholesalers, and retailers became an association later that year to emphasize its professional, reformist agenda and avoid the taint of radicalism. ABTA aimed to stabilize the erratic pricing practices that characterized the post-bellum book trade. Member organizations proposed a uniform discount for all sales to allow for improved *inventory control, cash flow, and predictability, but soon slid back into making separate deals advantageous to their individual profits. Painted by the press as a price-fixing scheme, ABTA dissolved in 1877. TT

American Heritage Publisher of books and magazines about history, founded in 1954 by Courtlandt Canby and Allan Nevins. The firm began by publishing *American Heritage*, a hardcover, heavily illustrated bimonthly magazine edited by a series of distinguished historians and sponsored jointly by the American Association for State and Local History and the Organization of American Historians. It published its first book in 1957, and sold books by mail order and through retail booksellers. In 1959, it added children's books (*see* 15), sold by *subscription, to the list. Its bestselling books were Bruce Catton's *The Civil War* and *Four Days*, an account of John F. Kennedy's assassination and funeral, which sold 2.5 million copies. (The *American Heritage Dictionary* is published by *Houghton Mifflin.) The firm was owned briefly by *McGraw-Hill and went independent *c.*1980 (as American Heritage, Inc.); the magazine was subsequently published by Forbes, but was bought in 2007 by Edwin S. Grosvenor. BEL
www.AmericanHeritage.com, consulted Dec. 2007

American Institute of Graphic Arts The professional association for graphic designers in the US, founded 1914 in New York City. With more than 19,000 members, the AIGA offers members services, such as job listings, and sponsors conferences, exhibitions, competitions, periodicals, and educational programmes. BEL
www.aiga.org, consulted July 2008

American Library Association (ALA) The world's first and largest library association (67,000 members in 2006). Organized in 1876, the ALA initially concentrated on the standardization of library practices (e.g. cataloguing and classification), inter-library cooperation, and promoting the reading of 'good books'. In subsequent decades, it established permanent headquarters in Chicago and became a national and international voice for library interests through its professional activities as an opponent of *censorship and an advocate for *reading. Its publications and professional practices have influenced book collections in hundreds of thousands of libraries. WAW
W. Wiegand, *Politics of an Emerging Profession* (1986)

American Mission Press Founded 1820 in Madras (Chennai). Its most important publication was *A Com-* prehensive *Tamil and English Dictionary* (1862) by the Revd Miron Winslow, a member of the American Ceylon Mission. The *types for the book, cut by P. R. Hunt, remain a high-water mark of Tamil *typography. *See also* 39. AG

American News Co. American periodical and book wholesaler. Formed in 1864 by the merger of two major New York newsagents under the direction of Sinclair Tousey, the firm was for a century the largest US wholesale distributor of newspapers, periodicals, stationery, and books. Unique among American book wholesalers, the firm's periodical business required it to establish branch offices in major cities across the nation. The firm was particularly important for the distribution of cheap, paper-covered books to newsagents, department stores, and other non-trade outlets. It ceased book distribution operations in 1969 after becoming part of Ancorp National Services, Inc. MBW

American Printing History Association (APHA) A scholarly, educational, and charitable organization fostering the study of printing history (especially American) and the book arts. Established in 1974 with offices in New York City, the association has more than 700 members worldwide. Regional chapters on the east and west coasts offer lectures and field trips. The APHA publishes its journal, *Printing History*, twice a year, holds an annual conference in different US cities, and sponsors the annual Lieberman Memorial Lecture. Since 2003 the APHA has awarded an annual $2,000 research Fellowship in Printing History. BLF
www.printinghistory.org, consulted Sept. 2007

American Printing House for the Blind (APH) Founded in 1858, it ranks among the world's largest nonprofit organizations dedicated to educating people with visual impairments. The APH adopted Standard English Braille in 1932 and added Large Type in 1946. By 1964, its partner, IBM, donated equipment to computerize text-to-braille translations. More recently, the APH digitized the *'Talking Book' series, and added Book Port downloadable audio text files in 2003. MDB
www.aph.org/about/highlite.htm, consulted Dec. 2007

American Publishing Co. Nineteenth-century *subscription publisher based in Hartford, Connecticut, best known for publishing books by Mark Twain. In 1867 the company president Elisha Bliss invited Twain, then a newspaper journalist, to write *The Innocents Abroad*, which became a major success thanks to Bliss's aggressive marketing. The firm went on to publish Twain's *Roughing It* (1862), *The Gilded Age* (1873), *Sketches Old and New* (1875), and *Tom Sawyer* (1876). Twain would later claim that he was swindled by the company. EDG
H. Hill, *Mark Twain and Elisha Bliss* (1964)

American Standard Code for Information Interchange (ASCII) A computing standard defining an alphanumeric set of characters storable within seven bits. Due to its universal readability, ASCII is the predominant computing standard. Although texts can be created and read in other formats—such as page-makeup, *hypertext, and *word-processing programs—ASCII does not require any proprietary software. Its chief competitor is Unicode. MFS

American Sunday-School Union (ASSU) In 1824, the Philadelphia Sunday and Adult School Union, created to supply books and curricular material to local Sunday school teachers, renamed itself the American Sunday-School Union. The ASSU soon launched a missionary network, auxiliaries in nineteen states and Washington, DC, and a publishing enterprise and book depository. A leader in disseminating American children's literature, it produced several of the earliest magazines for children. In an era of numerous sectarian publishing programmes, the ASSU (like the *American Tract Society) rejected denominational affiliation in favour of broad-ranging evangelical and cultural influence. *See also* **15**; SUNDAY SCHOOL LIBRARIES. SEC
A. M. Boylan, *Sunday School* (1988)

American Tract Society (ATS) Established in 1825, becoming one of the most important producers of mass literature in the US. Using innovations in steam-powered presses, paper production, *woodblock and *lithographic illustration technologies (*see* **16**), and *stereotyping, by 1830 the ATS produced more than 5 million *tracts a year, as well as numerous books, *almanacs, and magazines. The ATS distributed tracts through a vast *colporteur system in which agents canvassed locations door-to-door. The ATS remained an important American religious publisher until the 1870s, when it increasingly published for international markets. In the 1940s, it once again turned its attention to the publication of English-language material. PCG
D. Morgan, *Protestants and Pictures* (1999)
D. P. Nord, *Faith in Reading* (2004)
L. Thompson, 'The Printing and Publishing Activities of the American Tract Society from 1825 to 1850', *PBSA* 35 (1941), 81–114

American Type Founders Co. (ATF) In response to competition from *Linotype and *Monotype and their *hot-metal composition methods, 23 *typefoundries established the American Type Founders Co. in 1892. It acquired rights to a large number of *typeface designs, employing M. F. Benton as its principal designer (1900–1937), and issuing an important series of *type specimen books. The dominant manufacturer of metal type in America until the 1940s, it also sold printing equipment. Technological changes led to mergers; it was acquired by Kingsley in 1986, closing in 1993. Kingsley/ATF still owns registered trademarks of some typefaces sold by Adobe and Bitstream. The ATF *phototypesetter and *digital type *founts were among the firm's responses to the trend toward modernization. Its library, established by H. L. *Bullen, and *archives are now at Columbia University. MMS
P. A. Cost, 'Linn Boyd Benton, Morris Fuller Benton, and Typemaking at ATF', *Printing History*, 16 (1994), 27–44

Ames, Joseph (1687–1759) English bibliographer and first secretary of the Society of *Antiquaries (1741–59). His pioneering account of English printing to 1600, *Typographical Antiquities* (1749), was the first to try to date books by identifying their *types: the work was revised and enlarged in three volumes by *Herbert (1785–96). Ames's vast collection of early *title-pages, taken from imperfect and damaged books, is now in the *British Library. RM
ODNB

Amherst, William Amhurst Tyssen-, 1st Baron Amherst of Hackney (1835–1909) English book collector. Educated at *Christ Church, Oxford, he collected *incunabula, including seventeen *Caxtons, bindings, English bibles, ecclesiastical history, and Egyptian *papyri. Much of his collection was sold at auction (*see* BOOK AUCTIONS) just before and just after his death at *Sotheby's between 3 December 1908 and 24 March 1909 for £32,592. His Caxtons were sold privately to J. P. *Morgan for £24,000. ASGE
ODNB

Amiatinus, Codex The oldest surviving complete copy of the Latin Bible, held in the Laurentian Library, Florence (cod. Amiat. 1). A *pandect, it was made in the early 8th century at either Wearmouth or Jarrow, in Northumbria, where it was copied from the Codex Grandior of Cassiodorus at the behest of Abbot Ceolfrith (642–716). Ceolfrith had intended to take it to Rome to present to the pope, but he died on the way there. The MS was subsequently in the abbey of Monte Amiata, in Tuscany. Its origins were not established until the 19th century. ASGE

Amman, Jost (*c*.1539–91) Swiss illustrator in *woodcut and copper *engraving. Working in Nuremberg, principally for the Frankfurt publisher *Feyerabend, Amman was a prolific artist, mostly in woodcut, producing portraits, coats of arms, and many prints, as well as illustrating more than 75 books, including bibles, *chronicles, classics, *costume books, *medical books, and literature. His most famous illustrations (*see* **16**) are for the book of trades, *Eygentliche Beschreibung aller Stände* (1568): among its images are a papermaker (*see* **10**), a printer, and a *bookbinder. His 1588 book of playing cards has suits of printer's *ink balls and of books. MMS

Amory, Hugh (1930–2001) American bibliographer and historian of the book, senior cataloguer at the *Houghton Library at Harvard (1972–95), and a scholar of wide-ranging interests, notably Henry Fielding and the 18th-century book trade. He edited, with W. H. Bond, *The Printed Catalogues of the Harvard College Library, 1723–1790* (1996) and, with D. D. *Hall, *The Colonial Book in the Atlantic World* (2000), volume 1 of *A History of the Book in America*. VAG

ampersand A symbol (&) for 'et'/'and', found alone and in '&c.' for 'etc.' The ampersand developed from a ligature for 'et' found in AD 79 in Roman graffiti; an identifiable ampersand appeared in AD 131, and an 8th-century Merovingian MS contains the earliest ampersand in a familiar roman form. Ampersands are used commonly to join the names of business partners and, in some systems of bibliographical reference, of co-authors. KEA

J. Tschichold, *The Ampersand* (1957)

Amsterdam University Library Founded in 1877, the library is a continuation of the City Library of Amsterdam (founded 1578), which also served the Athenaeum Illustre (since 1632). It holds *c.*4,000,000 volumes, 14,500 current periodicals, 200 medieval and 70,000 modern MSS, 500,000 letters, 145,000 maps, 4,500 atlases, and 130,000 works printed before 1801. The catalogue is *digitized. Special Collections, housed separately, comprises MSS and rare books (including the library of the *Koninklijke Vereniging voor het Boekenvak and the Bibliotheca *Rosenthaliana), maps and atlases (including the library of the Royal Netherlands Geographical Society), and important church historical collections. ARACVU

www.uba.uva.nl, consulted July 2008

Analects The English name for *Lunyu*, the influential collection of philosophical pronouncements attributed to the Chinese sage Confucius (551–479 BC). Brief dialogues between Confucius (Kongzi) and his disciples comprise the text; their repetition and pithiness aid memorization. The interpersonal virtues extolled remain the ethical basis of Chinese society. It is generally accepted that *Lunyu* was not directly composed by Kongzi, but rather represents a later redaction of his teachings by traditional followers. The text has been the subject of comprehensive commentary and scholarship. Since the Song dynasty, the *Lunyu* has been combined with the book of Mencius (*Mengzi*), the Great Learning (*Daxue*), and the Doctrine of the Mean (*Zhongyong*) to form the Four Books (*Sishu*) as part of the Confucian classical canon. JSE

analphabetic A term used for a system of writing or documented communication that is not based on an alphabet (e.g. early pictographic languages or modern phonetic schemes). It may also denote a typographical character used with letters, but without a place in the alphabetic sequence (e.g. punctuation marks and symbols). DRSP

analytical bibliography *See* BIBLIOGRAPHY (1).

Ananda Publishers Founded in Calcutta (Kolkata) in 1957, the firm set high editorial standards and introduced contemporary techniques in Bengali book production and distribution. It belongs to the group of companies that owns *Ānandabājar Patrikā*, the first Bengali daily to have used *Linotype printing (with requisite changes in orthography). SKC

Anansi, House of Toronto publishing house. Launched in 1967 by Dave Godfrey and Dennis Lee, this 'subversive underground publisher'—widely recognized for nurturing new writers—is committed to politics, poetry, and Canadian literature, including translations of French-Canadian works. First sold in 1988, Anansi has been owned by Scott Griffin since 2002. JAD

anastatic printing A short-lived transfer *lithography method for making *facsimiles, a forerunner of photocopying. 'Anastatic', Greek for 'resurrection', indicates the method's reproductive results; its use of paper led to another name, 'papyrography'. An image or text in a greasy medium on paper is transferred by pressure on to a metal (usually zinc) *plate, which is treated, then inked, and printed onto another surface. Cowell's of Ipswich employed it most successfully, into the 20th century. Useful for short runs of documents and drawings, but ruinous to the original, it was superseded by photographic transfer. MMS

G. Wakeman, *Victorian Book Illustration* (1973)

anatomical book Internal anatomy is the subject of a series of nine 'figures of cutting', found first in 12th-century MSS, but possibly going back to the great anatomy school of Alexandria in the 2nd century AD. The first systematic dissections were carried out by Mondino de' Luzzi in Bologna, and his *Anathomia* seems to have been complete by 1316. An attempt to purify the text of Galen led to the most famous illustrated book in the history of anatomy in the West, the *De Humani Corporis Fabrica* of Andreas Vesalius (1543). The *woodcut figures designed by Jan Stephan van Calcar brought a new level of naturalism and technical precision to anatomical illustration (*see* **16**). There was no real advance on Vesalius' work in the 16th and 17th centuries, despite the availability of *engraving. Yet *plates by Gérard de Lairesse, published by Govard Bidloo as illustrations to his *Anatomia Humani Corporis* (Amsterdam, 1685), showed what might be achieved. Surgical anatomy emerged to rival more academic forms. William Hunter's *Anatomia Uteri Humani Gravidi Tabulis Illustrata* (1774), which covered all stages of pregnancy, are exquisitely delicate in their execution. By the 19th century, progress in comparative anatomy, pathology, and cell biology—allied to technical innovations such as *lithography, colour printing, and photography—allowed the concept of the anatomical book as a research tool to expand enormously. In the early 21st century, the Visible Human Project at the *National Library of Medicine marks a new frontier. PMJ

A. Carlino, *Paper Bodies* (1999)

L. Choulant, *History and Bibliography of Anatomic Illustration*, ed. and tr. M. Frank (1920, repr. 1962)

A. Cunningham, *The Anatomical Renaissance* (1997, repr. 2003)

H. Punt, ed., *Bernard Siegfried Albinus (1697–1770) on 'Human Nature'* (1983)

K. Russell, *British Anatomy 1525–1800* (1987)

J. Thornton, *Jan Van Rymsdyk* (1982)

Anaya Spanish publishing conglomerate. Founded in 1959 by Germán Sánchez Ruipérez, Grupo Anaya specializes in *educational publishing. It absorbed Alianza Editorial in 1989 and was acquired by *Hachette in 2004. The Fundación Germán Sánchez Ruipérez, established by Anaya's founder in 1981, is a leading book-history publisher in Spain. DRW

Andere Bibliothek Monthly series, established in 1985 by the German author H. M. Enzensberger and the printer F. Greno, who produced the first issue in *hot-metal type. The series—comprising fictional and non-fictional literature, original and reprinted works—is an outstanding example of contemporary book design. Since 1989 the series has been published by Eichborn Verlag. In 1999, the Lesegesellschaft der Anderen Bibliothek was founded to promote communication among its readers. US

H. Boehncke, 'Die Andere Bibliothek', *Imprimatur*, NS 20 (2007), 215–38

Anderson, Alexander (1775–1870) American engraver and illustrator. The 'father of American wood engraving', Anderson was its pre-eminent exponent until about 1840, producing the first American wood-engraved volume, *Looking-Glass for the Mind* (1795). During his long career, he illustrated more than 2,000 books, including several children's books for New York and Boston publishers (*see* **15**). Inspired by *Bewick, whose techniques and images he initially copied, Anderson produced work with distinctive and vigorous lines and a telling black-and-white contrast; his engravings of children are fresh, sometimes with mild caricatures. MMS

J. R. Pomeroy, *Alexander Anderson* (2005)

Anderson, H. C. L. (Henry Charles Lennox) (1853–1924) Head of the State Library of *New South Wales (1893–1906), Anderson oversaw an enormous expansion of library services, particularly for rural readers and for businesses. His most lasting achievement was securing the bequest of D. S. *Mitchell. IM
ADB

Anderson Auction Co. *See* ANDERSON GALLERIES.

Anderson Galleries New York auction firm. John Anderson, Jr. founded the company in 1900, and, in 1903, he acquired *Bangs & Co., the oldest auction house in the US. Mitchell Kennerley became president of the Anderson Galleries in 1915 and made it the most important book auction business during a golden age of *bibliophily in America. The Anderson Galleries merged with the *American Art Association after Kennerley resigned in 1929. Famous sales include those of R. *Hoe (1911–12), Herschel V. Jones (1918–19), Beverly Chew (1924–5), and J. *Kern (1929). DBW

M. J. Bruccoli, *The Fortunes of Mitchell Kennerley, Bookman* (1986)

Andreae, Hieronymus (Enderlin, Hieronymus; Formschneider, Hieronymus) (*c*.1485–1556) German block-cutter and printer in Nuremberg. He worked for Emperor *Maximilian I and *Dürer, and, after 1525, ran a printing shop. CHR

C. Reske, *Die Buchdrucker des 16. und 17. Jahrhunderts im deutschen Sprachgebiet* (2007)

Andrews, William Loring (1837–1920) American writer and book collector. Andrews collected medieval MSS and early printed books, as well as *maps and prints. A founding member of the *Grolier Club, he wrote widely about *bibliography and collecting. Andrews gave his early printed books to Yale in 1894. Other parts of his library were sold at auction after his death. ASGE

R. Nikirk, 'Two American Book Collectors of the Nineteenth Century: William Loring Andrews and Beverly Chew', in *Book Selling and Book Buying*, ed. R. G. Landon (1978)

Angeli, Franco (1930–2007) Founder of the Milan publishing house of the same name (1955), which exploited a gap in the market for management studies; subsequently, it fed on the expansion of the university system, combining small-scale subsidies with large-scale series, so that in 2007 it had 12,000 titles in its catalogue. NH

Angelica Library, Rome Founded by Bishop Angelo Rocca (1545–1620). Traditionally, the opening of the library is dated to 1614, when it was gifted to the Augustine order; however, on the basis of an inscription, recent claims have been made for 1604–5. Its importance as a public library won it a mention, together with the *Bodleian and the *Ambrosiana, in *Naudé's 1627 *Advis*. In 1873, with the suppression of the religious orders, ownership passed to the Italian state. NH

A. Serrai, *Angelo Rocca, fondatore della prima biblioteca pubblica europea* (2004)

Angelushev, Boris (1902–66) Bulgarian artist and illustrator. Graduating from the Academy of Art, Berlin (1928), he developed a realistic style with a strong, expressive manner. His work in book illustration (*see* **16**), book design, hand lettering, political *posters, and caricature established a new trend in contemporary Bulgarian printed graphics. EVM

Anglo-Saxon Chronicle A set of annals that together constitute a primary source for Anglo-Saxon history. The surviving versions (most of which are in Old English) vary, including events of local interest not found elsewhere. Behind them lies the 'common stock' of shared narrative, the compilation of which is associated with the late 9th-century court of King Alfred at Winchester. The text considered closest to the original is the Parker Chronicle (Cambridge, *Corpus Christi College 173); the Peterborough Chronicle (Bodleian Laud misc. 636) contains continuations to 1154. KAL

The Anglo-Saxon Chronicle, ed. S. Keynes and D. Dumville (1983–)

Anglo-Saxon type The type's history exemplifies the political aspect of *letterforms. The original impetus for Anglo-Saxon type came as part of M. *Parker's campaign to establish an English Church on the basis of ecclesiastical and theological precedents, which he wanted to publish using a type that authoritatively reflected their origins. The first book printed in the type designed for him was *A Testimonie of Antiquitie* (J. *Day, *c.*1566). Later, when James I and Charles I published Anglo-Saxon documents to prove their right to rule, they also employed Anglo-Saxon type—principally for quotations—to help establish the antiquity and authority of their claims. Somewhat later, scholars of linguistics and literature needed Anglo-Saxon type for whole texts in Old English, such as the *Anglo-Saxon Chronicle, **Beowulf,* *grammars, and *dictionaries. The type was usually a hybrid, combining an essentially *roman alphabet with the necessary additional special *sorts for Anglo-Saxon characters and *abbreviations. There were three sets of 16th-century Anglo-Saxon types and another four in the 17th century; interest continued in succeeding centuries, especially in the scholarly community. MMS

R. W. Clement, 'The Beginnings of Printing in Anglo-Saxon, 1565–1630', *PBSA* 91 (1997), 192–244

P. J. Lucas, 'Parker, Lambarde, and the Provision of Special Sorts for Printing Anglo-Saxon in the Sixteenth Century', *JPHS* 28 (1999), 41–69

— 'From Politics to Practicalities: Printing Anglo-Saxon in the Context of Seventeenth-Century Scholarship', *Library*, 7/4 (2003), 28–48

T. B. Reed, *History of the Old English Letter Foundries*, 2e, ed. A. F. Johnson (1952)

Angus & Robertson Australian publisher and book-seller. D. M. Angus started in business as a bookseller in Sydney in 1884, and was joined by George Robertson (unrelated to G. *Robertson the Melbourne bookseller) in 1886. A&R soon became a leading publisher, fostering such canonical figures as C. J. Dennis, Henry Lawson, A. B. 'Banjo' Paterson, and the children's fantasist May Gibbs. The firm also published Norman Lindsay's immediate classic *The Magic Pudding* (1918), while its non-fiction publishing included such core works as the *Australian Encyclopedia* (1925–6; 2e, 1958), the *Official History of Australia in the War of 1914–18* (1921–42), and J. A. *Ferguson's *Bibliography of Australia 1784–1900* (1941–69). From the 1960s, despite occasional revivals, A&R's publishing activities declined. Their bookselling continued to grow, however, especially after introducing franchising in 1977. Now boasting 170 outlets, A&R is the largest bookseller in Australia. IM

ADB

aniconic initial A letter that embodies some non-human object or image as a symbolic representation of a deity, typically in a MS illustration (*see* **16**).

Annenberg, Walter (1908–2002) American media executive. In 1953, Annenberg founded *TV Guide*, the world's largest-selling serial publication, reaching 20 million weekly subscribers during the 1970s. Rupert Murdoch purchased it in 1988 for $3 billion, the most ever paid for a publishing property. MDB

www.museum.tv/archives/etv/A/htmlA/annenbergwa/ annenbergwa.htm, consulted Nov. 2007

annotation Marks written in books by owners or others through whose hands they pass. Annotations may be comments on the text, noting corrections, highlighting passages which the reader is likely to wish to refer to again, agreeing or disagreeing with views expressed by the author, or providing translations into native language. They are often written in *margins, adjacent to the relevant text (in which case they may be termed *marginalia), or they may be written on *endleaves or other blank spaces. Annotations in books are not always text-related; people have used free space in books to write occasional jottings, accounts, library lists, poems, and other kinds of content, and they have sometimes included pictures as well as words. Bibles and devotional books have often been annotated with lists of births, marriages, and deaths so as to create biographical registers for the families through whose generations they passed.

Annotating books has a long history; expository glosses (*scholia) were added to texts in the ancient world. Although the annotations of respected scholars have typically been valued, there is also a long tradition of ambivalence as to whether it is acceptable to write in books; some people regard this as defacement, and this view prevailed among many book dealers and collectors until recently. Modern book historians increasingly recognize that annotations, of all sorts, can offer a window on to the relationship between texts and their readers, or show how books were being used. Hence, annotations are increasingly perceived as valuable to the study of books. DRSP

H. J. Jackson, *Marginalia* (2001)

R. Myers *et al.*, eds., *Owners, Annotators and the Signs of Reading* (2005)

D. Pearson, *Books as History* (2008)

W. Sherman, *Used Books* (2008)

annual For Victorians, the word 'annual' generally meant not just any work published on an annual basis but, more particularly, a literary annual or Christmas book of the sort originally published in October 1822 by *Ackermann. That year, he launched the first *Forget Me Not* (dated 1823), ushering in what an anonymous writer in the *Bookseller* described as a 'class of highly illustrated books which formed … so striking a feature of the literature and fine arts of the United Kingdom, under the designation of "Annuals;" and which, besides the services they rendered in diffusing a taste for elegant pursuits among the middle classes, were the means of affording profitable employment to a larger body of persons connected with the executive departments of literature and the fine and useful arts, than any other order of publications whatsoever'. Ackermann may have been imitating the German style of *Taschenbuch*, to which even Goethe and Schiller contributed, or his idea may have grown naturally from his women's magazine the *Repository of*

Arts. The *Forget Me Not*s were so successful as illustrated compendia of poems and sketches that imitations soon crowded the Christmas market with titles such as *Keepsake, Souvenir, The Graces, Literary Souvenir, Friendship's Offering, Book of Beauty, Pictorial Annual, Turner's Annual*, and *Amulet* to name some of the better known. Annuals for young people include *The Juvenile Forget Me Not* and *The Boy's Own Book*. There was at least one *Comic Offering* and a variety of religious publications like *The Missionary Annual*. The seemingly universal characteristics were an elegant binding (often of silk or velvet), engraved plates, publication near Christmas, and sentimentality within the bounds of propriety.

The *Bookseller* writer estimated that by 1829 the annuals constituted an industry worth £90,000 per year. This sum was based on expenses paid by the publisher to authors and editors, painters of pictures, owners of *copyrights, engravers, copper-plate (*see* ENGRAVING) printers, letterpress printers, paper manufacturers, bookbinders, silk manufacturers, and leather sellers, as well as for *advertisements and incidental expenses; despite this outlay, publisher's profits and retail booksellers' profits accounted for one third of the total.

Victorians bought annuals at a tremendous rate, but tended also to be apologetic about their literary or artistic value; indeed, in the early years their quality was uneven at best and, with popularity, many annuals of inferior quality crowded the market. However, reviews in the *Athenaeum, Spectator, Examiner*, and *Art Journal* are reported to have 'protested against the injustice of which these works have been the objects, and have borne cordial testimony, as they might fairly do, to their merits, literary and artistical' (*Bookseller*). It is clear that many a writer found a much larger audience in this form than in others. The best annuals employed the services of well-known artists and paid top prices for the craftsmanship required for illustrations (*see* **16**). Tennyson, the Brownings, Thackeray, and other elite writers can be found in annuals, though their contributions may not have represented their finest work. The genre clearly developed its own aesthetic and authors wrote to it. W. *Scott is said to have deliberately passed some inferior writings to annuals and then omitted them from his own collected works. Thackeray, on the other hand, describes the start his young hero, Arthur Pendennis, received as a writer contributing to 'a beautiful gilt volume called the Spring Annual, edited by the Lady Violet Lebas … which has since shared the fate of other vernal blossoms, and perished out of the world' (*Pendennis*, vol. I, ch. 32).

The new annual market sharply diminished a previous tendency to give books of poetry by single authors at Christmas. Complaints of lost sales are recorded by Thomas Moore, Southey, Lamb, James Montgomery, and others. John Gibson Lockhart apparently grew bitter over the failure of his own attempt to enter the annuals market with the *Janus*, 'which should depend for its success altogether on its literary merits; for it was coarsely printed, and professed to exclude engravings, upon principle' (*Bookseller*).

A roll call of editors, painters, and writers for the best of the annuals includes some of the most distinguished names of the era. As a genre or class of publication, annuals have never commanded general respect as a vehicle for strong, fine, or enduring art; yet, the annual was certainly considered a lucrative and, hence, commercially important market, exploited with some attention to production standards by the best London publishers, including *Longman and *Smith, Elder. Annuals are frequently grouped with *gift books and *albums. PLS

Anon., 'The Annuals of Former Days', *The Bookseller* (29 Nov. 1858), 493–9

A. Boyle, *An Index to the Annuals*, vol. 1: *The Authors 1820–1850* (1967)

F. Faxon, *Literary Annuals and Gift Books* (1973)

www.orgs.muohio.edu/anthologies/FMN/Bibliography.htm, consulted Sept. 2007

Annual Bibliography of the History of the Book and Libraries (Book History Online)

Published since 1970, *ABHB* is produced with the cooperation of more than 30 countries under the auspices of the Committee on Rare Books and Manuscripts of *IFLA. It seeks to record all scholarly books and articles on the history of the printed book. Since 1989, staff of the *Koninklijke Bibliotheek (The Hague) have formed the editorial board of *ABHB*, building a cumulative database that was launched as Book History Online in 2001. BHO contains all *ABHB* entries from 1990 onwards. PA

www.kb.nl/bho, consulted Jan. 2008

anonymity [Gk, 'namelessness'] An anonymous work, strictly speaking, is one that is circulated, in printed form or in MS, without any author's name upon it. However, this definition can usefully be expanded to include works that have false or mysterious names on them.

1. Definition
2. Prevalence
3. Chronological survey

1. Definition

The definition of anonymity is not always straightforward. Some books have appeared without any author's name upon the title-page, but with a firm indication of authorship elsewhere. The first edition of Robert Burton's *The Anatomy of Melancholy* (1621), for instance, announced itself to be 'by Democritus Junior', but Burton's name appeared at the very end of the book. Others have omitted their authors' names, but found other ways to declare their identity: when Daniel Defoe published any work as 'by the Author of *The True-Born Englishman*' he openly revealed himself. These hardly seem to be cases of anonymity. The convention of a work declaring itself on its title-page (sometimes falsely) to be 'by the author of' another, already published, work became common by the 18th century (in France and Germany, as well as Britain). Sometimes it was a form of anonymity, sometimes not.

Most importantly, anonymity cannot be wholly distinguished from pseudonymity. Pseudonymity amounts to anonymity when it provokes uncertainty (and speculation) about authorship. Some *pseudonyms are generic: many works in English (sometimes written by men) have been published as by 'a Lady' or some version of this designation. Other countries have had their equivalents, with German books announcing themselves to be 'Von einer Dame von Stande', for example. Other pseudonyms have been so evidently fictional as to indicate that the true name of the author was being withheld. When the first edition of Swift's *Gulliver's Travels* appeared in 1726, its title-page called it *Travels into Several Remote Nations of the World* and announced it to be 'by Lemuel Gulliver'. By using the pseudonym Michael Angelo Titmarsh on a title-page, Thackeray was advertising his disguise to his readers. Many pseudonyms, such as Stendhal, or Mark Twain, or George Eliot, began as disguises and became eventually the literary names of widely acknowledged authors.

Anonymity has often been temporary: a work is first published anonymously but has its true author's name printed in later editions. A sizeable proportion of what has come to be regarded as English literature was first published without the true author's name upon it. Even in library catalogues, the marking of anonymity (conventionally indicated by giving the author's name in square brackets) is inconsistent and unreliable. The needs of library cataloguers in the 19th and early 20th centuries occasioned many national dictionaries of anonyma and pseudonyma. Sometimes, anonymity is more policy than fact: Tennyson ensured that *In Memoriam* never appeared with his name during his lifetime, even though he was universally known to be its author. It would be wrong to suppose that anonymous authors have always intended to conceal themselves.

2. Prevalence

In certain types of publication—*broadsides, *chapbooks, occasional *pamphlets, and works of controversy—anonymity has been more common during some periods than others. Most novels published in the 18th and early 19th centuries were anonymous. In booksellers' lists of their novels, or in the catalogues of *circulating libraries, works were typically itemized alphabetically by title; rarely were authors' names given. So too, most writing that appeared in periodicals before the 20th century was anonymous. This included such elevated examples as the essays of the *Tatler* and *Spectator* in the 18th century, and the great reviews of the 19th century such as the *Edinburgh* and the *Quarterly*. Book reviews were invariably anonymous until the late 19th century, though arguments against anonymity were growing. Most reviews printed in the *Times Literary Supplement* were unattributed until 1974, when the journal abandoned its official policy of anonymity.

3. Chronological survey

Anonymity precedes print. The author of *Beowulf* is nameless. So is the poet who wrote *Sir Gawain and the Green Knight*. In fact, most medieval European literature is anonymous, and scholars tend to argue that, before the arrival of print, *authorship had none of the status that it would later acquire. An emerging *print culture gave new significance to the author's name, or to its absence. From the mid-16th century, *title-pages became common. They usually advertised the names of those publishing, printing, and selling a book, and sometimes its author. The absence of an author's name was now a potentially significant omission.

The word *anonymous*, imported from Greek, first began to be used in English late in the 16th century, particularly in printed works such as poetical *miscellanies. In the 16th and 17th centuries, it was typically considered improper for men of rank to appear in print—the so-called 'stigma of print'. Ambitious writers who did allow their work to be printed often exhibited reluctance. Anonymity could be synonymous with modesty. An example of this was Spenser's *The Shepheardes Calender* (1579). Like other works of the period, it withheld its author's name but blazoned that of his patron, Philip Sidney. The poet called himself 'Immerito', yet was certainly seeking recognition and advancement.

As well as gentlemanly reluctance, there was sometimes real caution or fear about the consequences of being identified. Before the 18th century, works of religious or political controversy were frequently anonymous in order to protect their authors, especially when *censorship was enforced. Unsurprisingly, anonymity was often seen as a threat by those in power and sometimes outlawed. In 1546, Henry VIII issued a proclamation requiring printers to include their own name and that of the author on every copy of a work. During the 17th century, there were periods when an author was also legally bound to declare him- or herself on the title-page: a Star Chamber Decree of 1637 ordered that the author's name be printed on any book or pamphlet. In 1642, Parliament required the *Stationers' Company to ensure that printers did not print anything 'without the Name and Consent of the Author'. If a printer did not identify an author, he would be treated as if he were the author. Further Acts of the 1640s and 1650s outlawed anonymous publications. However, after the Restoration, the *Printing Act of 1662 included no stipulation that an author's name be prefixed to any publication.

From the 18th century, professional writers, who sold their books in part on the strength of their names, still published anonymously on occasion. *Pope, a man who became wealthy from the sale of his poetry and was proud of his independence from any patron, felt no embarrassment about the business of publishing his work, yet still exploited anonymity for the first editions of *The Rape of the Lock*, *An Essay on Man*, and *The Dunciad*. In such cases, anonymity seems to have been intended to arouse curiosity rather than maintain secrecy. Satirists, such as Swift and Byron, have had a particular liking for anonymity.

It remained common until the late 19th century for an author to publish his or her first work anonymously. This was the case in many European countries: in Germany, for instance, *Erstlingswerke* were commonly anonymous, even if their authors later made names for themselves.

There are also many remarkable cases of authors who maintained anonymity for playful or provoking purposes. Writers have gone to great lengths to conceal their authorship, while not really wanting to remain hidden. In the early 19th century, for instance, Sir W. *Scott became the bestselling novelist writing in English while resolutely maintaining his official anonymity. The attribution of anonymous books was for centuries the common habit of readers, a habit that writers could foresee and excite.

Although a chronological survey is possible, there can be no simple narrative of the changing conventions of anonymous and pseudonymous publication. At any given time, there have been different reasons for anonymity. Particular authors have sometimes published anonymously, and sometimes not. However, it is clear that anonymity became much less common in the 20th century, and few literary authors made much use of it. One reason is that the convention of genteel reticence about making one's name public had been eroded; another is that the business of selling authors had become inextricable from the business of selling books. There have been exceptions. When the roman-à-clef *Primary Colors, 'By Anonymous', became a bestseller in the US in 1996, its anonymity was widely treated as a great novelty. Speculation about the identity of its author (in fact, the political journalist Joe Klein) clearly fuelled the interest of readers. Authors and readers of earlier ages would have recognized the pattern. See also ATTRIBUTION.   JDM

R. J. Griffin, ed., *The Faces of Anonymity* (2003)
S. Halkett and J. Laing, *A Dictionary of the Anonymous and Pseudonymous Literature of Great Britain*, rev. J. Kennedy, 2e (9 vols, 1926–62); vol. 1: 1475–1640 (3e, 1980)
J. Mullan, *Anonymity* (2007)
A. Taylor and F. J. Mosher, *The Bibliographical History of Anonyma and Pseudonyma* (1951)

Antériorité des civilisations nègres Forming the centrepiece to Cheikh Anta Diop's extensive and still highly controversial corpus of work, *Antériorité des civilisations nègres: mythe ou vérité historique?* (1967; reissued 1992) marks a high point in the career of a Senegalese scholar whose writing remains an influential point of reference for the study of African history and historiography, and particularly its 'decolonization'. Following his *Nations nègres et culture* (1954) and *L'Unité culturelle de l'Afrique noire* (1959), and anticipating his last major work, *Civilisation ou barbarie* (1981), *Antériorité* displays the ability to marshal historical, anthropological, linguistic, political, philosophical, and sociological arguments that made Diop something of a national hero in Senegal, and led to the University of Dakar being renamed the Université Cheikh Anta Diop de Dakar in 1987. It is, however, precisely Diop's range and methodology that attracted criticism; his central thesis that ancient Egypt was essentially a black civilization is by no means widely accepted. Furthermore, his undoubted political commitment to the emancipation of Africa's intellectual life from colonial influence also left his work open to criticism on the grounds of unscientific partiality, a charge he strenuously denies in this work.

What is not in doubt is its symbolic value. Published by Présence Africaine—the publisher (and journal) which arguably led the renaissance of African letters during decolonization—Diop's work had a political and psychological impact that cannot be underestimated. The book was republished in 1972 in a co-edition by the leading French publisher *Albin Michel and Le Club du Livre in Abidjan, Ivory Coast, allowing its wider distribution within Africa; a partial English translation followed in 1974. Later, 20th-century postcolonial theory confirmed that the questions raised by the opposition of 'myth' and 'historical truth' in Diop's subtitle remain far from resolved.   AHS

P. Diagne, *Cheikh Anta Diop et l'Afrique dans l'histoire du monde* (1997)
J.-M. Ela, *Cheikh Anta Diop, ou l'honneur de penser* (1989)

anthology [Gk, 'collection of flowers'] A collection of texts, in verse or prose, written by various authors, sometimes synonymous with the related terms *miscellany, *florilegium, *album, *garland, silva, *pratum*, compendium, omnium-gatherum, etc. The most celebrated classical exemplars of this tradition of miscellaneous gatherings of texts include Pliny the Elder's encyclopaedic *Naturalis Historia* and Aulus Gellius' *Noctes Atticae*. Although Pliny gleaned and carefully organized information on all aspects of human knowledge, Gellius depended upon the literary delights of unsystematic dilettantism, simply gathering together texts and his observations on them in a more arbitrary sequence than Pliny, relaying to the reader the easy delight and simple pleasures of sheer literary variety.

More systematic compilations emerged in the medieval tradition of the 'florilegium', or 'book of flowers'. ('Anthology', 'garland', and other related terms for this genre derive linguistically from the metaphorical conceit of picking literary flowers and gathering them together into a single, attractive bouquet.) Largely dedicated to authoritative religious and theological texts, these anthologies were collected to serve as a kind of reference book for preachers and the composers of theological treatises, often emulating the larger anthological character of the Bible—itself a collection of various canonical books by authors from different historical periods. In the following centuries, increasingly sophisticated, highly organized, and encyclopaedic collections of texts on various subjects departed significantly from the more informal, traditional sense of the literary anthology that took shape largely in the 16th century.

During the Renaissance, eclectic collections of literary prose works such as Erasmus's witty *Adagia* (1508–36), Montaigne's *Essais* (1580–95), and Bacon's *Essays* (1597) were wildly popular, though they were single-author collections and not normally thought of or described as anthologies, per se. Scholarly compendia of *annotated and historically *collated and corrected classical texts were also gathered together and published in the manner of anthologies during the period (e.g. the extensive *Miscellanea* (1489) by *Poliziano), or in the form of less scholarly, vernacular collections (e.g. the popular *Silva de* *varia lección* (1540) of Pedro Mexía). Printed *commonplace books of the period also provided readers with compilations of texts, albeit normally in brief excerpted forms classified under specific headings, such as in Melanchthon's theological *Loci Communes Rerum Theologicarum* (1521), which relied heavily on authoritative passages from the New Testament to establish the authority of the major doctrines of Protestantism.

The more significant and most widely recognized literary anthologies of the Renaissance period normally contained a range of works by various authors, and often directly coincided with the emergence and increasing popularity of vernacular literary traditions in Europe. Perhaps the most familiar of these are the Elizabethan anthologies, beginning with *Tottell's *Songs and Sonnets* (1557) (commonly referred to as *Tottell's Miscellany*), which gathered the verses of Surrey, Wyatt, and others. Dozens of subsequent literary anthologies, often endowed with colourful and pleasant-sounding titles, followed Tottell's during the second half of the 16ᵗʰ century, such as *A Handefull of Pleasant Delites* (1595?), *A Gorgious Gallery of Gallant Inventions* (1578), *The Phoenix Nest* (1593), and *Englands Parnassus* (1600). Each of these emphasized, in various ways, Aulus Gellius' classical affection for literary abundance and variety for its own sake. In addition, they also gave increasing form and substance to the conscious development and celebration of national, vernacular literary traditions in the centuries to come.

Hundreds of similar and ever more extensive literary anthologies appeared after the Renaissance. Among English-language collections, the most prominent are R. *Dodsley's *A Collection of Poems* (1748), *Percy's *Reliques of Ancient English Poetry* (1765), and Palgrave's *Golden Treasury* (1861). With the appearance of these and other related anthologies, the more familiar understanding of the nature and function of the anthology—as a compendium of the best available exemplars of prose or verse, gathered together as a representation of the native eloquence and literary genius of a single language and culture—was given greater permanence. Today, the tradition of the anthology is commonly represented in the form of *textbook collections of canonical works, sometimes combined with critical interpretive essays, such as the *Norton Anthologies* and *Oxford Anthologies*. *See also* MISCELLANY.   EAH

J. Csicsila, *Canons by Consensus* (2004)
A. Ferry, *Tradition and the Individual Poem* (2001)
E. Havens, *Commonplace Books* (2001)
J. Leo, ed., *On Anthologies* (2004)
A. Nash, ed., *The Culture of Collected Editions* (2003)
S. Nicols and S. Wenzel, eds., *Whole Book: Cultural Perspectives on the Medieval Miscellany* (1996)
B. Olsen, 'Les Florilèges d'auteurs classiques', in *Les Genres littéraires dans les sources théologiques et philosophiques médiévales* (1982)
B. Taylor, 'Medieval Proverb Collections: The West European Tradition', *JWCI* 55 (1992), 19–35

Antiquarian Book Monthly Review *See* RARE BOOK REVIEW.

Antiquarian Booksellers Association (ABA) Founded in 1906 in London, the ABA is the senior trade association for dealers in rare books and allied materials. Membership is gained through a combination of experience, expertise, and integrity, and its Code of Good Practice is stringent. It is overseen by an elected council and, although wary of becoming a fully fledged professional body through formal systems of qualification, it has proved a significant force for good in the governance of the trade. The annual ABA international *book fairs at Olympia and Chelsea are highlights of the rare book year.   LJW
www.aba.org.uk, consulted Apr. 2008

Antiquarian Booksellers' Association of America (**ABAA**) Founded in 1949 to form a counterpart in the US to other national associations linked to the *International League of Antiquarian Booksellers. Its aims were to promote the rare book trade and to maintain standards within it. A pioneering Code of Ethics was soon adopted—a code later bravely enforced in a fraught court case over the expulsion of a member. Controlled by an elected Board of Governors giving representation to its various regional chapters, the ABAA remains the public face of the serious rare book trade in the US.   LJW

Antiquaries, Society of The principal British society for the study of antiquarian subjects. Instituted in 1717 after developing from less formal groups, the Society acquired a permanent home and started a library in 1753. It currently has *c*.2,500 Fellows. It has been at Burlington House, Piccadilly, London, since 1875, and has valuable collections on archaeology and antiquities. The British collections are of major importance, and include *broadsides, proclamations, MSS, *incunabula, and material relating to prominent antiquaries, such as W. *Morris.   ASB
J. Evans, *A History of the Society of Antiquaries* (1956)

Antonio, Nicolás (1617–84) Spanish bibliographer and critic, Philip IV's agent-general in Italy. In Rome he amassed a personal library of 30,000 volumes. His *Bibliotheca Hispana Vetus* catalogued Spanish authors who wrote in any language from the time of Augustus to 1500 (1696; rev. by Pérez Bayer, 1788; *facsimile repr. with study by V. Infantes, 1996); the *Bibliotheca Hispana Nova* (1672) continued to 1670; it was revised in 1783.   BT

Antwerpsche Bibliophielen, Vereniging van Pre-eminent society of bibliophiles and scholars in Belgium, based in the *Plantin-Moretus Museum. Since its inception in 1877, the society has published on the pre-1800 book history of Antwerp through monographs (50 vols to date, in three series) and a journal, the ephemeral *Bulletijn* (2 vols, 1878–86), replaced in 1923 by *De *Gulden Passer*. In 1941, the society's scope was explicitly widened to book history and humanism in the Low Countries, including, from 2003, the 19ᵗʰ- and 20ᵗʰ-century book.   GPr
L. Voet, '"Vereeniging der Antwerpsche Bibliophielen" honderd jaar 1877–1977', *GP* 56 (1978), 8–20

apartheid, censorship under A highly efficient, bureaucratic system of *censorship operated in South Africa under the National Party government (1948–94). Numerous repressive Acts of Parliament allowed for the proscription of writers and activists, preventing publication of their writing or speech. In 1963, the Publications and Entertainments Act superseded the 1930 Censorship Act, replacing the Board of Censors with a euphemistically named Publications Control Board empowered to ban material judged indecent or obscene, blasphemous or offensive to any faith community, ridiculing members of any race, or threatening state security. Books, films, and newspapers seized by customs officials or the police, or submitted by publishers, librarians, or members of the public, were subjected to rigorous scrutiny by committees of readers (including retired bureaucrats, literary academics, and writers), who could recommend banning. The work of many anti-apartheid authors (including Alex La Guma, Dennis Brutus, Lewis Nkosi, and Mazisi Kunene), some of whom could (also) not be quoted under anti-Communism legislation, was banned as a result, as were anti-apartheid newspapers.

The right to challenge bans in court was removed by a new Publications Act in 1974, which created a Publications Appeals Board. Several appeals—including against the banning of André Brink's *'n Droë Wit Seisoen* (*A Dry White Season*) and Nadine Gordimer's *Burger's Daughter*, both in 1979—led to nuanced criteria for undesirability, including the substitution of the standard of the reasonable (later probable or likely) reader for that of the average person, and preventing consideration of the motives or the record of author, publisher, or distributor. The 1977 banning of the Afrikaans novelist Etienne Leroux's *Magersfontein, O Magersfontein!* was a cause célèbre in Afrikaner intellectual circles; several of J. M. Coetzee's novels were read by the censors, but none banned. Political control of publication continued into the 1990s. Today, censors in democratic South Africa are chiefly concerned with violence and *pornography.   AEV

M. De Lange, *The Muzzled Muse* (1997)
P. D. McDonald, *The Literature Police* (2009)
C. Merrett, *A Culture of Censorship* (1994)

Apocalypse St John of Patmos' visions known as the Book of Revelation, the last canonical book of the New Testament, were from early Christianity a rich source for iconographical themes. Scenes from the text had become familiar to many Christians through architectural ornament and mosaics. From Carolingian times they appeared in *codices. In England, spectacular codices were produced from the 12th century—the richly illuminated *Apocalypse* in Trinity College, Cambridge, dated c.1255–60, being the most famous of all. The images in such MSS, also produced in Germany and the Low Countries, incorporate small sections of text, mainly relating image to the original Bible text. These representations in MS became the model for blockbooks (*see* BLOCK PRINTING) that appeared from the middle of the 15th century. Six editions of *Apocalypse* blockbooks can be identified, the earliest produced c.1451–2 in The Netherlands, the three later ones in Germany in the Rhine valley, representing two distinct iconographical traditions. Within the editions, variations in the use of paper allow scholars to distinguish impressions.   LH

G. Bing, 'The Apocalypse Block-Books and their Manuscript Models', *JWCI* 5 (1942), 143–58
Blockbücher des Mittelalters: Bilderfolgen als Lektüre, ed. S. Mertens and C. Schneider, Gutenberg-Museum (1991)
BMC 1, 3
W. L. Schreiber, *Manuel de l'amateur de la gravure sur bois et sur metal au XVe siècle*, vol. 4 (1902; repr. ed. H. T. Musper 1969)
A. Stevenson, 'The Quincentennial of Netherlandish Blockbooks', *BMQ* 31 (1967), 83–7
The Trinity Apocalypse, ed. D. McKitterick (2005)

apocrypha [Gk, 'hidden [things]'] Of unknown authorship, hence, inauthentic, spurious, or uncanonical. More specifically, 'Apocrypha' refers to the biblical books received by the early Christian Church as part of the Greek version of the Old Testament, but not included in the Hebrew Bible and hence excluded by non-Hellenistic Jews. Early Christians received these books from Hellenistic (especially Alexandrian) Judaism. At the Reformation, Protestant leaders rejected the inspired status of all books of the Vulgate not found in the Hebrew canon. *See also* **2.**   MFS

L. H. Brockington, *A Critical Introduction to the Apocrypha* (1961)
B. M. Metzger, *Introduction to the Apocrypha* (1957)

apparatus A formal presentation of a work's textual history, with an emphasis on a list of *variants. A comprehensive apparatus allows a reader to reconstruct a work's entire textual tradition—it is therefore essential to a *critical edition. The standard format of an apparatus contains: the position of the variant (line number, page number); the reading in the present text (*lemma), usually followed by a closing square bracket; and all other readings, along with an abbreviated reference (*siglum) for each source that contains those readings.   SK

G. T. Tanselle, 'Some Principles for Editorial Apparatus', *SB* 25 (1972), 41–88

appendix (app.) Supplement to a volume containing material that supports content in the main text. Appendices may comprise tables, lists of entities or events, charts, questionnaires, texts or translations of documents discussed, or explanations and elaborations judged to be too long for *footnotes or endnotes. Appendices are usually the first element of *endmatter, preceding *endnotes and bibliography (*see* BIBLIOGRAPHY (2)); for books with multiple *authorship and those requiring *offprints of individual *chapters, appendices precede the references to each chapter. Unless they contain complicated mathematics, long quotations, or other displayed material, appendices are often in smaller type than the text. In books with divisional *title-pages, a title leaf precedes the appendices to indicate that they pertain to the entire work, not just the final part. Where more than one appendix is present, appendices are numbered or lettered and given titles. Appendices to journal articles, and appendices containing information supplementary to a text, should be indexed; those reproducing documents discussed in a text are not. KEA

Butcher

The Chicago Manual of Style, 15e (2003)

Appleton & Co., D. (Appleton-Century-Crofts) In 1831, Daniel Appleton converted his New York dry-goods store into a bookshop and issued his first volume as a publisher, *Crumbs from the Master's Table*, a miniature book of religious instruction. His publishing efforts remained modest until his son, W. H. Appleton, became a partner in 1838. The firm, renamed D. Appleton & Co., did a brisk business in school texts, medical books, travel literature, and encyclopaedias. Its science list included Darwin's *Origin of Species and Spencer's First Principles. By 1865, Appleton ranked second in size and influence (behind *Harper & Brothers) in the US.

Appleton published a strong fiction list during the late 19th century, including Joel Chandler Harris's Uncle Remus tales, Arthur Conan Doyle's Sherlock Holmes stories, and Stephen Crane's fiction. Yet, in 1900, plagued by slow payments on *de luxe *subscription volumes, the firm went bankrupt; when reorganized it was no longer a family business. Appletons subsequently merged with the Century Company in 1933 to form D. Appleton-Century. This imprint prospered after World War II, especially upon acquiring F. S. Crofts & Co. (1947) to form Appleton-Century-Crofts, which dominated US textbook publishing for several decades after 1950. JLWW

C. A. Madison, *Book Publishing in America* (1966)

G. Overton, *Portrait of a Publisher* (1925)

appointment book Personal *blank book or software application that breaks each day into blocks of time in which to enter meetings, appointments, tasks, and errands. Appointment books come in a range of sizes, from pocket-size to full-page, with scheduling times available in hourly, half-hourly, quarter-hourly, or open, untimed sections. EDG

apprentices and apprenticeship Within the book trades, the problem of recruiting and training new entrants was met by the custom of apprenticeship, which was widespread among many different kinds of trade, and whose roots lay in the medieval guild system. Apprenticeship was a common career path until the late 19th century; thereafter, some of the training became the work of the technical schools. In theory, an apprenticeship was a legal contract embodied in a written indenture, between a boy, his parents, and a master printer (for example), for seven years. The boy would be trained in the trade, but would receive no payment for his work; instead, the master would provide his food and lodging. At the end, the apprentice would become a *journeyman (i.e. able to receive wages for each day's work), and eventually he could become a master, himself taking on apprentices.

In practice, the contract did not always fulfil these expectations: the boy might be ill-prepared for his work or ill-suited to the trade, or the master happier to exploit the boy as cheap labour than to train him thoroughly. A great many apprentices never completed their seven-year terms; only a small proportion became masters. The practice of freeing by patrimony allowed individuals to be freed from their apprenticeship by virtue of their fathers being members of the *Stationers' Company. In England, the 16th century saw the advent of statutory regulation concerning apprentices and guilds more generally. In the print trade, journeymen and masters had to belong to the Stationers' Company. The Company regulated apprenticeship, attempting to control numbers entering the trade by establishing ratios of apprentices to journeymen according to the number of presses, which was fixed by law. The Statute of Artificers (1563), and statutes of Parish Apprenticeship (1536, 1601) also sought to regulate the apprenticeship system. 'Indoor' apprenticeship had apprentices living in the master's house, which kept their numbers relatively low, but by the mid-18th century 'outdoor' apprenticeships had become common. The struggle between the journeymen, who sought to limit numbers of apprentices, and the master printers, who hoped to increase them, was, according to Child, a force behind the industry's development of formal labour relations. Statutory apprenticeship was abolished in 1814, although in the printing industry the 'apprentice question' remained lively throughout the century. Skingsley points to the increasing volume of manufacturing and the need for technical specialization as important factors in the failure of the system. In lieu of the training that apprenticeships provided, the London Technical Education Board began in the 1890s to support both the Bolt Court School of Photo-engraving and Lithography, and the St Bride Foundation Institute Printing School. MMS

C. Blagden, *The Stationers' Company* (1960)

J. Child, *Industrial Relations in the British Printing Industry* (1967)

C. Y. Ferdinand, 'Towards a Demography of the Stationers' Company 1600–1700', *JPHS* 21 (1992), 51–69

E. Howe, *The London Compositor 1785–1900* (1947)

— *The British Federation of Master Printers 1900–1950* (1950)

T. A. Skingsley, 'Technical Training and Education in the English Printing Industry: A Study in Late Nineteenth-Century Attitudes', *JPHS* 13 (1978–9), 1–25; 14 (1979–80), 1–58

aquatint An *intaglio printing process that, like *etching, uses acid to bite the design into a metal *plate. A powdered, acid-resistant resin ground—shaken onto the plate and fused by heat—creates a surface whose grainy texture is particularly suited to imitating the tonal effects of wash drawings. Shading is achieved by controlled biting (the frequency and timing of the plate's immersion in the acid bath); linear details can be added using etching needles and other tools. J. R. *Abbey's catalogues of aquatints and *lithographs provide an indispensable guide to the study of 18th- and 19th-century illustrated topographical publications. JCI

Arabian Nights *See* THOUSAND AND ONE NIGHTS, THE.

Arabic script Having its origin in Nabataean (an off-shoot of Aramaic), Arabic script began as a very imperfect means of communication. In its original form the Arabic alphabet consisted of only seventeen basic letter shapes (graphemes), which included a number of similar-looking forms (homographs) but no vowels. In order to distinguish the various homographs, a system of diacritical marks was gradually introduced. Vocalization and some orthographic signs in early Qur'ānic MSS were indicated by means of multi-coloured dots, while the current vocalization system was probably introduced only towards the end of the 9ᵗʰ century. Today, the Arabic alphabet consists of 28 letters, all consonants, as is characteristic of Semitic scripts, and all having numerical values—similarly characteristic of Semitic and Greek alphabets.

For most of the first Muslim century (until after 690), there was very little standardization of the script. A greater effort to achieve this came only in the early 8ᵗʰ century, especially towards the end of the Umayyad period and the beginning of the Abbasid rule (*c*.750), the era which later produced some of the greatest examples of 'Kufic' *calligraphy. From then on Arabic script was transformed into a great variety of calligraphic styles, most of which became extinct by the middle of the 10ᵗʰ century, however, when a new set of so-called 'proportioned' scripts was developed. From the 11ᵗʰ century onward, six scripts—*thulth*, *tawqī'*, *riqā'*, *muḥaqqaq*, *rayḥān*, and *naskh*—established themselves as dominant in the eastern part of the Islamic world, while *Maghribī* came to be preferred in the western part. Other regional scripts also emerged from the 13ᵗʰ century onwards, among them: *Bihārī*, *nasta'līq*, *dīwānī*, and in the late 18ᵗʰ century, *ruq'a* (Turkish *rık'a*). *See also* CALLIGRAPHY, MUSLIM. AGa

F. Déroche *et al.*, *Islamic Codicology* (2006)

Arabic type Arabic script is essentially cursive, with most letters of the alphabet joined to the preceding letter in a word, and many to the following one as well. This often involves distinctive *ligatures of two or more letters. There are also different initial, medial, final, and isolated forms of most letters. Since Arabic has never developed a separate system of discrete *letterforms, it presents problems quite unlike those of European-language typography. A higher degree of *punchcutting skill is required—especially if calligraphic norms are adopted—and *matrices must be *justified minutely if the breaks between adjacent *sorts are to be disguised. *Compositors must constantly ensure that the right letterforms and ligatures are used. If vowel-signs (*ḥarakāt*) are required—i.e. for Qur'anic and certain other texts—then even more sorts are needed, along with many *quads and leads to be interspersed between the vowel-strokes. A full Arabic *fount can therefore contain more than 600 sorts. Although some simplification was introduced in later periods, the Arabic script has never really acquired the separate typographic norms, either aesthetic or practical, that could permit a decisive breach with its scribal past.

The first Arabic movable types were created in Italy in the early 16ᵗʰ century. They were of an inelegant and clumsy design, as were those that followed. In the 1580s, *Granjon produced his elegant Arabic types, which for the first time achieved calligraphic quality with their liberal use of ligatures and letterforms derived from the best scribal models. They set the standard for most subsequent European Arabic types designed by *Le Bé, *Raphelengius, *Erpenius, *Savary de Brèves, *Caslon, *Bodoni, W. *Martin, and others down to the 19ᵗʰ century.

Arabic typography was not used in the Muslim world until the 18ᵗʰ century. From 1706 onwards, Syrian and Lebanese Christians used types cut and cast locally, modelled partly on local Christian bookhands, but also influenced by the European tradition. Muslim typography started at the *Müteferrika press in Istanbul in the 1720s, using Arabic types based on indigenous *naskhī* hands, but somewhat cramped and utilitarian, rather than calligraphic. This was true also at the *Būlāq Press in Egypt from 1822 onwards, and such styles set the norm for Arabic typography at most Muslim Arabic and Turkish presses until the late 19ᵗʰ century. *Nasta'līq* and Maghribī types were also occasionally employed, but *lithography soon superseded them for book production in those script styles.

In the 19ᵗʰ century, many Arabic books were printed at Christian missionary presses (*see* 9). Because of resistance to the European typefaces initially used, these presses designed new founts from calligraphic models, which helped to raise the standards of Arabic typography in that period. The requirements of newspapers also played a part in the considerable improvements in typefaces of the late 19ᵗʰ and early 20ᵗʰ centuries. In Egypt, *Dār al-Ma'ārif and Būlāq (from 1902 onwards) set higher standards of clarity and elegance. In 1914, the new fount designed at Būlāq for Aḥmad Zakī Pasha halved the number of sorts by eliminating many ligatures, while retaining some of the features of the older Būlāq types. Later, the introduction of *Linotype machines further simplified the setting of Arabic-script texts, while inevitably moving further from traditional *calligraphy and bookhands. However, with the decline of metal and the introduction of *digital type design, the way has been opened both for a return to calligraphic norms and for new experiments in lettering. *See also* LITHOGRAPHY IN THE MUSLIM WORLD. GJR

E. Hanebutt-Benz *et al.*, eds., *Middle Eastern Languages and the Print Revolution* (2002)

H. Smitshuijzen AbiFarès, *Arabic Typography* (2001)

Arbeiderspers Dutch publisher. Founded in 1929, the Arbeiderspers (Workers' Press) combined a number of existing socialist bookselling and publishing enterprises, including various newspapers and other periodicals. In 1938, it helped launch 'ABC-romans', fiction published at unprecedentedly low prices. From its original emphasis on working-class education, Arbeiderspers became a

The *lay of an **Arabic type** case: the case, designed by the Stempel typefoundry in Frankfurt, contains extra Turkish *sorts.

prominent general publisher after World War II, with a strong presence in literary fiction, both in Dutch and in *translation. Notable book series include 'Privé-domein' (autobiographies, from 1966) and 'Synopsis' (essays, from 1972). AHVDW

S. Hubregtse, 'Uitgeverij De Arbeiderspers', *Jaarboek voor het democratisch socialisme*, 7 (1986), 132–67

Arber, Edward (1836–1912) First professor of English literature at Birmingham University. His most enduring monuments were the privately printed five-volume *Transcript of the Registers of the Worshipful Company of Stationers* (1875–94) and three-volume *Term Catalogues, 1668–1709* (1903–6). He edited and published, mostly at his own expense, 30 volumes of an inexpensive series of *English Reprints* (1868–71), followed by five further series (1877–1907), totalling some 70 volumes. RM
ODNB

archetype The MS or text posited at the head of the tree or stemma, after *recension. The archetype is the source from which all other witnesses descend; being usually not extant, it is the focus of editorial attempts hypothetically to reconstruct its details, using the surviving witnesses. *See also* EMENDATION; LACHMANN METHOD. ASR

architectural book A conventional history of architecture publishing sees a text-orientated progress from the recovery of Vitruvius in the Italian Renaissance, through its celebration and elaboration in Mannerism and Baroque, down to today's urban planning and interior design. On the other hand, the genre is a child of print culture, and developments therein relate directly to parallel advances in printing methods, especially in reproducing illustrations (*see* **16**).

1. Early history
2. Later history

1. Early history

In MS culture, the chief obstacle to the transmission of architectural literature was the impossibility of accurately reproducing hand-drawn images and diagrams.

It is significant, for instance, how the marvellously illustrated 15th-century treatises by Antonio Averlino, known as Filarete (written 1451–64, published 1972), and Francesco di Giorgio Martini (written after 1482, published 1841) found no outlet in their day. The invention of printing provided architects, first through *woodblocks, subsequently through copper-plate *engraving and *lithography, with a technology for uniform visual communication.

Rediscovered by *Bracciolini in 1414, the text of Vitruvius' *De Architectura* (Ten Books of Architecture) was first published in an unsigned edition, now attributed to Silber in Rome, some time before 16 August 1487 (date of a purchase note in a copy now at Oxford). The author was an architect and engineer, who probably served in the Roman army in Gaul under Julius Caesar. His treatise, dedicated to the emperor Augustus, codifies the Greek influence on Roman architecture, especially in its insistence that a building should unite strength (*firmitas*), usefulness (*utilitas*), and elegance (*venustas*). In the *editio princeps*, the text is devoid of illustrations (*see* **16**), although it refers to nine or ten *formae*, probably simple geometric diagrams. The earliest reprint, which curiously displays two *colophons, one dated Florence 1496 and the other Venice 1497, is also image-free. In 1511, however, a version was published in Venice, edited by the contemporary architect, draughtsman, and Dominican monk, Giovanni Giocondo, containing 136 woodcut illustrations. It was followed by the remarkable Italian paraphrase, published in Como in 1521 by the architect Cesare Cesariano, also with 119 splendid images. A closer Italian *translation by Daniele Barbaro appeared in Venice in 1556, in which the figures were drawn by Palladio. Very much in the Vitruvian vein, and in some ways a commentary, was Alberti's *De Re Aedificatoria*, first published posthumously in Florence in 1485; the *printer's copy was recognized in 2005 in a MS in the *Laurentian Library. Again, the *princeps* was devoid of illustrations, so that when they were first added to the Italian translation by Cosimo Bartoli (1550), they were not authorial. Nevertheless, Vitruvius and Alberti held sway over architectural theory and practice until the 18th century.

The influence of printing on architecture inevitably involves other publishing genres. Classical antiquity was extolled in *guide books such as the *Mirabilia Romae*, which contained images of monuments like the Coliseum and which, from 1563, included a text originally published by Palladio in 1554. Equally significant were the cityscapes cut for travelogues, such as *Breydenbach's *Peregrinatio in Terram Sanctam*, in which the images were impressed by woodblock on separate *sheets glued together to form a folding *insert, while *Schedel's *Nuremberg Chronicle pictures urban landscapes, some authentic, others pure fantasy. Mid-16th-century theory otherwise was dominated by the Mannerist architect Sebastiano Serlio, whose *Seven Books of Architecture* have a complex publishing history: Book IV came out at Venice in 1537 and III in 1540; Books I and II were published in Paris in 1545, followed by V in 1547 (a collected version of I–V duly appeared in Venice in 1566); a *Livre extraordinaire* (not in the series) was printed at Lyons in 1551; Book VII was issued posthumously in 1575 at Frankfurt; and VI remained in MS (its contents were made known in 1978). Their efficacy derived from the alliance of text and image. For instance, the labelling of the five orders of architecture, given in the title of the 1537 instalment as Tuscan, Doric, Ionic, Corinthian, and Composite, would have been meaningless had it not been accompanied by the picture of five different columns. In the event, this labelling entered the lexis of architecture, just as Serlio's image of a church façade crystallized a format that was reiterated for another two centuries. His formula meant that architects no longer travelled to see the design of a building. Its essence was captured and communicated instead through print, while Serlio's models presented themselves explicitly as a design blueprint that was to be copied and adapted. The recipe undoubtedly encouraged imitation and uniformity, especially in northern Europe. In his native Italy, on the other hand, it was attacked in 1584 by Giovan Paolo Lomazzo for inducing mediocrity and repetitiveness.

The publication in 1550 (rev. edn 1568) of Vasari's *Lives of the Artists*, with its biographies of architects such as Brunelleschi and Michelangelo, paved the way for changes in social and professional status. The process was enhanced by large-scale building projects, such as St Peter's, in which classical precepts were reworked in a Renaissance idiom. Virtually all significant activity was Italian, with (besides Serlio) writings from major architects such as Vignola (*Regole delli Cinque Ordini dell'Architettura* [1562]) and Scamozzi (*Idea dell'Architettura Universale*, 1615). The latter name calls to mind books on military architecture, which were also the first to raise the modern issue of city planning. Scamozzi reproduced the plan of the city-fortress of Palmanova in Friuli, built in 1593 on a design by Giulio Savorgnan. The dominant figure of the period, however, both as an example and as a theorist, was Andrea Palladio, whose *Four Books of Architecture* (*I Quattro Libri dell'Architettura*, 1570) were translated into English in 1715–20, but before then had inspired Inigo Jones. In colonial America, its *formulae* were applied by Thomas Jefferson, who referred to it as 'the Bible' of architecture. The launch of architecture studies as an academic discipline, beginning with the foundation of the French Academy at Rome in 1666, saw a further professionalization; educational tools, such as its first president François Blondel's *Cours d'Architecture* (1675–83), became commonplace. At the same time, the triumph of copper-plate printing as the prime means of visual communication shifted the emphasis to the representation of architecture in a landscape. Here the master and model was Piranesi, whose views of the remnants of Rome's civilization swelled the mania for ruins and follies elsewhere in Europe. In particular, the sequence known as *Imaginary Prisons* (*Carceri d'invenzione*, 1st state of 14 prints, 1745; 2nd state with 2 additions, 1761)—showing vast subterranean vaults and infinite, labyrinthine stairways—profoundly influenced Romantic imaginings and probably inspired architects of Victorian railway stations.

2. Later history

The 19th century saw further developments in the profession, with the foundation of the Royal Institute of British Architects in 1834, its American counterpart in 1857, and analogous organizations in other countries. Professional requirements increased the learning aids and practical manuals in a field that was becoming ever more complex, with changes wrought by the transport revolution and rapid urban growth. In printing terms, *lithography facilitated the use of colour and simplified the impression of complex designs, since a draughtsman could either transfer an image by lithographic paper or draw directly on the stone. The century's dominant figure was the French architect Eugène Viollet-le-Duc, whose extensive restorations of medieval buildings helped launch the Gothic revival. His books—in particular the *Dictionnaire raisonné* of French architecture (1854–68) and its companion (1858–75), devoted to furnishings—reached a huge readership when issued in *serial form.

The 20th century, on the other hand, has been governed by photography's ability to reproduce an extant building or interior without the mediation of an artist-engraver. The camera has inspired numerous monographs illustrating the corpus of architects both ancient and modern, as well as the publication of manifestos. Examples are the Gropius-inspired *Bauhausbücher* (1925–32) and Frank Lloyd Wright's statements in *An Organic Architecture* (1939) and *A Testament* (1957). In the Francophone world, the writings of Le Corbusier, beginning with *Vers une architecture* (1923), have likewise been influential. Yet the dominant form of publication has been the illustrated magazine, beginning in 1896 with the *Architectural Review* and its more gossipy counterpart, the *Architect's Journal*. Aimed at a non-professional public, and also a glossy advertising vehicle, is the American *Architectural Digest* (1920), whose best-known European counterpart is the Italian *Casabella* (1928). Journals expounding the viewpoints of particular groups or of university schools of architecture are also numerous. The link between these trends and the rise of *offset printing and phototypesetting after World War II is evident. Last but not least, the *World Wide Web, in which images and text are easily married and multiplied, is proving a new forum for the present and future of the architectural book.   NH

M. Carpo, *Architecture in the Age of Printing* (2001)

K. Hafertepe and J. F. O'Gorman, eds., *American Architects and their Books to 1848* (2001)

N. Savage *et al.*, ed., *Early Printed Books, 1478–1840: Catalogue of the British Architectural Library Early Imprints Collection* (5 vols, 1994–2003)

archives and archivists Collections of documents produced by institutions or persons. Archives are almost as old as writing itself: Mesopotamian archives on clay *tablets remarkably survive. Modern archives may contain sound recordings, still and moving visual materials, and electronic files. Archival organization, practice, and description flow from the fundamental feature of the documents involved: *respect du fonds*, i.e. the administration, arrangement, and conservation follow from the original arrangement of the materials, as determined by the agents responsible for their production and collection. An emphasis on provenance and the size of collections means that individual pieces frequently are not described. Archives are usually arranged in a descending order of fonds or groups, subgroups (subfonds), classes (series), items (files), and pieces. Finding aids (paper or electronic) describe the nature, history, and arrangement of a collection, restrictions on access to it, and often a list of files in a given fond. Such aids facilitate the administration of and access to a collection.

The modern archival profession dates from the mid-19th century, when many nations began to organize and catalogue the vast number of older records produced in pre-Napoleonic Europe. Some industrialized states, seeking closer control of their citizens, needed access to modern records. Early archivists emphasized the study of older documents as historical tools, and their training stressed the importance of *palaeography and *diplomatic. Modern archivists have emphasized the study of the recent past, including local, family, and business history, and paid more attention to such topics as preservation, security, and *digitization.

International cooperation among archivists began in the late 19th century, but the practices of individual archives remained quite separate until the late 20th century, when standards were developed for the description of archival collections. The growth of the *World Wide Web allowed archives to provide remote access to their finding aids and to the digitization of portions of their collections. This development spurred more cooperation and led to such widely adopted standards as the International Standard Archival Description (General). The widespread use of Encoded Archival Description meant that finding aids, even older ones, could be made available and searchable through the Internet.

The archive is both a physical, institutional space housing material traces of the past and a conceptual space in which the nature and purpose of discourse and cultural work are debated and re-imagined. A catalyst for rethinking the archive in the later 20th-century was Foucault's *The Archaeology of Knowledge* (1969), in which he redefined the archive as 'the general system of the formation and transformation of statements' (Foucault, 130). Gilles Deleuze expanded upon the possibilities of this theoretical archive in *The New Archivist* (1972); *Derrida offered a deconstructionist approach in *Archive Fever: A Freudian Impression* (1996).   LSC

J. G. Bradshear, ed., *Managing Archives and Archival Institutions* (1991)

M. F. Daniels and T. Walch, eds., *A Modern Archives Reader* (1984)

M. Foucault, *L'Archéologie du savoir* (1969; Eng. tr. *The Archaeology of Knowledge*, 1972)

International Council on Archives, www.ica.org/en/about, consulted Apr. 2008

[Society of American Archivists,] *Describing Archives: A Content Standard* (2004)

Archiv für Geschichte des Buchwesens (Archive for the History of Book Matters) Edited since 1956 by the

Historical Commission of the Börsenverein des Deutschen Buchhandels in Frankfurt, *Archiv* publishes original studies on book-historical themes dealing with book production, distribution, and reception. Since 1998, some titles have also been published as separate books in a Studies series. To date, 62 volumes have appeared. The spectrum of their themes mirrors the research interests of the last 50 years: from descriptive bibliographies of *incunables, to research about readers in the 18th and 19th centuries, to studies of modernist publishing. During recent decades, *Archiv* has increasingly dealt with questions about the history of the book trade, and is currently preparing a history of the German book trade during the 19th and 20th centuries, also edited by the Historical Commission.   ME

Arctic shipboard printing Undertaken by the British Admiralty searching Canadian waters for Sir John Franklin and his crew, lost in 1847 seeking the Northwest Passage. Rescue information, printed on paper and silk, was released from balloons or buried under cairns. PLF
E. Hoag, 'Caxtons of the North', *BH* 4 (2001), 81–114

Ardizzone, Edward (1900–1979) English painter, graphic artist, and author. He is best known for writing and illustrating the 'Tim' picture books (1936–72), based upon stories told to his children. The most famous, *Tim All Alone*, won the Kate *Greenaway Medal for illustration (1956). An official war artist during World War II, he based *Baggage to the Enemy* (1940) and *Diary of a War Artist* (1976) on his experiences. Throughout his 50-year career, Ardizzone contributed illustrations to nearly 200 publications—including works by Dickens, Anthony Trollope, and R. L. Stevenson—and drew for the *Radio Times* and *Punch*.   KES
ODNB

Arents, George Astor (1885–1960) American collector and businessman. Having worked at the American Tobacco Company (then the International Cigar Company), he developed a collection on tobacco, described in *Tobacco, Its History Illustrated by the Books, Manuscripts, and Engravings in the Library of George Arents, Jr.* (1937–52). In 1943 he gave it to the *New York Public Library, with his collection of 'books in parts', primarily literary works in their original *serial appearances.
MEK

Areopagitica Tract by Milton in the form of a classical oration addressed to Parliament, arguing against *censorship of the press: a hill in ancient Athens, the Areopagus was the seat of the city's highest judicial court. Licensing had ended with the Star Chamber's abolition in 1641, but on 14 June 1643, the 'Ordinance for Regulating the Abuses in Printing' reinstated the measures. Milton was pursued in 1644 under the Ordinance for his publication of divorce tracts, and the appearance of *Areopagitica*, unlicensed and without the name of its printer or publisher, on 23 November, was his response. By printing his name on the *title-page, Milton directly challenged the Ordinance, accusing Parliament of reviving the Star Chamber's censorship. Although *Areopagitica* was unsuccessful, it is still valued for its eloquent appeal for the abolition of pre-publication censorship. Milton did not, however, advocate a completely free press, and he excluded Catholic works from toleration. Nor was this the first *pamphlet to argue for *freedom of the press: on 24 March 1644, Henry Robinson had published anonymously his unlicensed *Liberty of Conscience, or the Sole Means to Obtaine Peace and Truth*, which argued for freedom of speech and the press on the basis of laissez-faire economics. *See also* **7**.   MB

Aretino, Pietro (1492–1556) Italian author of *Sonnets on the 'XVI modi'*. In Rome in 1524, Marcantonio Raimondi engraved plates, inspired by Giulio Romano's erotic paintings for the Palazzo del Té in Mantua, which illustrated sixteen *modi*, or ways, of copulation. An infuriated Pope Clement VII imprisoned Raimondi and had copies destroyed (only fragments survive). Shortly afterwards, probably in 1525, Aretino wrote sixteen caudate sonnets (i.e. the standard 14-line structure with the addition of a 2½-line tail) and published them with the *engravings, thus founding modern *pornography. The bibliographical history of the book remains obscure, since the early editions were destroyed by *censorship or by use. One of Aretino's letters shows that it was printed in Venice by 1527. Today, only one incomplete copy is known in a private collection; it most likely was a later reprint, containing clumsy woodcut versions of the copper-plate originals. The disappearance of its opening leaf also means that the Renaissance title of the work is lost: its usual designation, the *Sonetti lussuriosi*, first surfaced during the 18th century in clandestine editions. The modern critical text and title were established by Aquilecchia in 1992.   NH

Argenteus, Codex The 'Silver Bible', now in the *Uppsala University Library, was written in Ravenna *c*.520 from the Gothic version of Bishop Ulfilas. The MS is a gospel book that now survives only in part (188 out of 336 leaves remain, including a single leaf in Speyer Cathedral in Germany). Remarkably sumptuous, the MS is copied in silver and gold on purple-coloured *vellum. The MS entered Queen *Christina's library as war booty from Prague; after some time in Holland, it was brought back to Sweden by *De la Gardie and given to Uppsala University in 1669.   ASGE, PSR
T. Kleberg, *Codex Argenteus*, 6e (1984)

Argentina, National Library of the Republic of (**Biblioteca Nacional de la República Argentina**) Founded in 1810 as a public library for Buenos Aires, it was designated the national library in 1884. Paul Groussac (director, 1887–1929) greatly expanded the collections and secured a new building in 1901. Following Perón's downfall, the directorship passed to the great writer Jorge Luis Borges, during whose tenure (1955–72) ground was broken for a new building, which opened in 1992. Despite chronic political, financial, and space problems, the collection now numbers two million volumes, and services are expanding. Since 1956, the national *library school has had its headquarters there.   DRW

Arias Montano, Benito (1527–98) Hebraist. In 1568, Philip II sent him to Antwerp to direct the edition of the *Plantin *Polyglot Bible (8 vols, 1569–73), intended to outshine the *Complutensian Bible. He revised the texts and wrote prefatory material. He was also the author of Latin works and some poetry in Spanish.   BT

A. V. Bécares Botas, *Arias Montano y Plantino* (1999)

Arion Press Founded in San Francisco by Andrew Hoyem in 1974 with the type and equipment of the *Grabhorn Press (later Grabhorn-Hoyem), where Hoyem had earlier been an apprentice. In 1976, Arion Press issued a monumental edition of *Moby Dick* using handset type and original wood engravings, setting the standard for a series of *artists' books of mostly classic texts with original work by such major artists as Robert Motherwell and Jim Dine. The Press averages two titles per year. Since 1989, Arion Press has been housed with M & H Type, the largest surviving typefoundry in America.   KAW

arm In type design, the horizontal *stroke in E, F, or L. The horizontals of e, A, and H are called 'bars'. *See also* CROSS-STROKE.

Armagh, Book of (Liber Ardmachanus) *Trinity College Dublin (MS 52), the earliest document surviving in Irish *minuscule script. It was written by the scribe Ferdomnach of Armagh (d. 845–6), who appears to have produced the first part of the Book in 807–8. The manuscript includes the earliest lives of St Patrick and other biographical materials related to him, as well as parts of the New Testament. It is one of the earliest surviving documents in Old Irish and one of the earliest prose narratives in that language.   ASGE

J. Gwynn, ed., *Liber Ardmachanus* (1913)

armed forces libraries Also referred to as military libraries, they date back to the late 1700s in Western culture and include collections at national ministries of defence, war college libraries, technical libraries for specialized units, and general purpose libraries on military bases and ships. During World War II—considered the 'golden age' of armed forces libraries—more than 1,000 American military libraries were established around the world, and *Armed Services Editions of technical and popular books were sent to every fighting front. Examples of armed forces libraries today include the Military History Institute, the Naval Operational Medicine Institute Library, the Pentagon Library, the Naval Oceanographic Office, and the Air Force Research Laboratory Research Library, which focuses on such scientific disciplines as geophysics, astronomy, astrophysics, physics, and chemistry.   EDG

Federal Armed Forces Libraries Round Table, www.ala.org/ala/faflrt/aboutfaflrt/aboutfaflrt.htm, consulted June 2007

J. A. Jamieson, *Books for the Army* (1950)

Armed Services Editions American forces overseas during World War II needed books, but second-hand books, donated by the million in 1941–3, were not very appealing to GIs. In early 1943 the Council on Books in Wartime, a non-profit organization established by the publishing trade, solved the problem through this purpose-made series. From 1943 until 1947, when troops still occupied Germany and Japan, nearly 123 million pocket-sized *paperback copies of 1,322 titles were issued. The list included classics and serious contemporary books, but most provided light reading (*mysteries, westerns, humour). Publishers sold rights for next to nothing, in return for a promise that the Armed Services Editions would never enter the domestic market. The series is widely credited with creating a new generation of book readers and fuelling the postwar paperback boom.   JBH

J. Y. Cole, ed., *Books in Action* (1984)

J. A. Jamieson, *Books for the Army* (1950)

Armenian MS book Armenia accepted Christianity as its state religion around 314, but Greek and Syriac were used as the languages of instruction and the liturgy until Mesrop Mashtots' invented the Armenian alphabet *c*.405. Three main types of writing occur, each with transitional forms. The first, *yerkat'agir* ('ironscript'), is a monumental *uncial, not separating words, requiring much space, used in inscriptions on stone and in early MSS; a mixed *erkat'agir-bolorgir* ('roundscript'), attested from 981 (on the earliest Armenian paper; Yerevan, Matenadaran MS 2679) to 1304; it combines uncial with *minuscule. The second, *bolorgir*, is a minuscule used from the end of the 12th until the beginning of the 19th centuries. Words are separated when this *script is used. The third main type is *notrgir* ('notaryscript'), attested from the 14th to the 19th centuries. It is a late minuscule, almost *cursive, and smaller than *bolorgir*. *Sghagir*, a *ligatured cursive, is attested from the second half of the 19th century onwards.

Separate *leaves from before the 8th century have been preserved, mostly as *endleaves in later MSS. The earliest dated MS is from 862 (Venice, Mekhitarist Brotherhood, MS 1144/86); MS publication remained important into the 18th and even 19th centuries (*see* **13**). The earliest illuminations date from before 640, and occur in the Etchmiadzin Gospel (Yerevan, Matenadaran MS 2374; dated 989), whose binding has a 6th-century ivory decoration.

The distribution of *scriptoria reflects the vicissitudes of Armenian history: in the 10th and 11th centuries, the kingdoms of Ani and Vaspurakan were predominant; Sebastia and Melitene, centres of Armenian emigration, produced several *illuminated MSS in the 11th century. After 1080, with Armenian migration to Cilicia and its elevation to a kingdom in 1198, new scriptoria flourished. In 1173, at Skewŕa, Bishop Nersēs Lambronats'i commissioned the oldest known copy of Grigor Narekats'i's *Book of Lamentation* (1002) (Yerevan, Matenadaran MS 1568); between 1256 and 1268, Armenia's most famous artist, T'oros Ŕoslin, illuminated MSS for Church and Crown at Hŕomklay. In Greater Armenia, several centres flourished: Erznka, the renowned monastic schools of Gladzor and Tat'ew, and the Van region, with Khach'atur and Minas as prominent illuminators (15th century). Cilician traditions prospered in Armenian monasteries in the Crimea from the 14th century, and in Constantinople from the 16th century onwards. In the 17th century, New Julfa (Isfahan)—where Shah Abbas I deported Armenians in 1604—became a centre of MS production and illumination, continuing traditions from Greater Armenia.

Armenian MSS often include extended *colophons, typically providing information on date, location, *patron, and producers. Bookmaking was closely related to Greek and Syrian traditions, evolving into a specifically Armenian type of *codex. Until the 13th century, paper (probably not manufactured locally) did not significantly replace *vellum, which remained in use until the 17th century. Sometimes a ruling frame was used (Arabic *mastara*; Armenian *toghashar*). *Ink usually was of a carbon type; later iron-gall ink was used, which could damage the substrate. Pigment analysis allows scholars to distinguish the Armenian palette from Byzantine and Islamic ones, and to observe local and even individual differences.

Notches, usually v-shaped, cut out in the *gatherings provided space for the thread to sew them together, allowing flat spines (*see* **17**). Thin wooden *boards were used, identical in size to the *text block. The grain ran horizontally, preventing the board breaking at the drill holes on the *spine side opposite the notches, allowing supported sewing, a highly unusual feature in Middle Eastern bookbinding. Raised endbands consisted of a cord providing additional support for the *text block, and functioned as base for a further, decorative silk cord. At the board's *fore-edge, a *leather flap was added for decoration and protection.

Edge colouring extends only to about one centimetre from the spine. *Tooling may feature a Calvary cross on the upper cover, or rosettes. *Fastenings were usually attached. Silver and jewelled plaques or crosses decorate the covers of some MSS from the Cilician period onwards, some of which are inscribed, as are the leather covers of some MSS from 17th- and 18th-century New Julfa.

About 30,000 MSS are known to exist. The largest collection is held in the Matenadaran in Yerevan, with 13,000 MSS. The Armenian Patriarchate in Jerusalem and the Mekhitarist Brotherhood in Venice each hold 4,000, the Mekhitarists in Vienna 1,200. Further significant collections are in New Julfa, the Catholic Armenian Catholicosate in Bzommar, the Armenian Catholicosate in Antelias, at the Mother See in Etchmiadzin, the *Bibliothèque nationale de France, the *British Library, and elsewhere.   TMVL

R. H. Hewsen, *Armenia: A Historical Atlas* (2001)
D. Kouymjian, 'Les Reliures de manuscrits arméniens à inscriptions', in *Recherches de codicologie comparée*, ed. P. Hoffmann and C. Hunzinger (1998)
T. F. Mathews and A. K. Sanjian, *Armenian Gospel Iconography: The Tradition of the Gladzor Gospel* (1991)
T. F. Mathews and R. S. Wieck, eds., *Treasures in Heaven: Armenian Illuminated Manuscripts* (1994)
S. L. Merian, 'The Structure of Armenian Bookbinding and Its Relation to Near Eastern Bookbinding Traditions', Ph.D. thesis, (Columbia University, 1993)
— 'From Venice to Isfahan and Back: The Making of an Armenian Manuscript in Early Eighteenth Century Persia', in *Roger Powell*, ed. J. L. Sharpe, *Bibliologia*, 14 (1996)
M. E. Stone *et al.*, *Album of Armenian Paleography* (2002)

Armenian type Woodcut Armenian letters appeared in *Breydenbach's *Peregrinatio in Terram Sanctam* (1486). The pioneer Armenian printer, Yakob Meghapart, created the first movable types, publishing five books in Venice between 1511 and 1513, under the enigmatic *imprint D.I.Z.A. Orientalists such as Guillaume Postel (Paris, 1538) had books printed containing Armenian, and the Italian Teseo Ambrogio cut new types for his *Introductio* (Pavia, 1539). The second Armenian printer, Abgar Tokhatetsi, introduced Armenian typography in the Orient (Constantinople, 1567). *Granjon created types for Armenian publications in Rome (1579), and the Congregatio de *Propaganda Fide started printing Armenian books there in 1584. The Armenian Apostolic bishop Oskan Erevants'i published the Armenian Bible in Amsterdam in 1666, at the Surb Etchmiadzin and Surb Sargis Zorawar press, which subsequently moved to Livorno (1669), Marseilles (1672), and Constantinople (1695–1718). In Amsterdam, the Vanandetsi family were active in Armenian typography from 1685 until 1718. The Armenian Church in New Julfa inaugurated printing in Persia in 1636. Printers used the three main Armenian types, usually ranging in point sizes (*see* POINT, TYPOGRAPHIC) from 10 to 14, while binding techniques followed MS practice.   MP, TMVL

R. H. Kévorkian, *Catalogue des "incunables" arméniens (1511/1695)* (1986)
M. Pehlivanian, 'Mesro's Heirs', in *Middle Eastern Languages and the Print Revolution*, ed. E. Hanebutt-Benz *et al.* (2002)

armorial A compendium of the coats of arms of a set of people or institutions, covering a particular family, place (e.g. a county or country), or other defined grouping, such as the Knights of the Garter. An armorial will typically include both blazons (descriptions of armorial bearings in technical heraldic language) and pictorial representations. Rolls of arms like this (typically written and painted on *parchment *scrolls) began to be created in England in the 13th century and many survive from the later medieval centuries. Heraldry was important in the early modern period, when the right to a coat of arms was a mark of family status, and much effort was directed towards the granting, checking, and claiming of arms. Between 1530 and 1688 the English heralds—the officers of the *College of Arms, who governed the use of armorial bearings—carried out regular visitations across the counties to record the arms in use, often accompanied by professional arms painters. This led to the creation of many armorials which are valuable today as chronicles and family records, as well as for their interest to antiquaries and heraldic historians. Armorial bearings (often woodcuts or engravings) continued to be displayed in later genealogical reference works, such as *Debrett's Peerage and the *Almanach de Gotha. The term 'armorial' is also used to signify a binding or *bookplate bearing a coat of arms (see ARMORIAL BINDINGS).　　DRSP

A. Wagner, A Catalogue of English Mediaeval Rolls of Arms (1950)
T. Woodcock and J. M. Robinson, The Oxford Guide to Heraldry (1988)

armorial bindings A binding decorated with a coat of arms or other heraldic insignia, usually indicating ownership by a person or institution. This form of decoration began in continental Europe in the late 15th century, initially for royalty, and was commonly used by many classes of book owners between the 16th and 19th centuries. The earliest English non-royal armorial binding dates from c.1555; many hundreds of armorial tools were created for the aristocracy and gentry during the succeeding centuries.

Armorial bindings were most commonly made by applying an engraved tool representing a coat of arms to the centres of the *covers. Instead of the full armorial, a crest, badge, or other heraldic symbol may have been used. Small heraldic tools (particularly crests) were often used on spines. Armorial decoration was typically tooled in gold, without attempting to represent the true heraldic colours (tinctures), although there are exceptions to this. Other ways of representing coats of arms on bindings are occasionally found, e.g. in needlework or by using small tools to build up armorial patterns.

Armorial tools were sometimes applied to bindings for their first owners, and sometimes for later ones; they are not necessarily contemporary with the books. Institutions (e.g. cathedrals and colleges) used them, as well as individuals, and they are a common feature of *prize bindings. Armorials are not invariably a sign of ownership; in institutional collections, they were sometimes used to mark books purchased with donated money. Royal arms were also used as a purely decorative device on books that were never in royal ownership.

Identifying armorials relies on deciphering their heraldry and pinpointing the particular family member, although this can be difficult. Armorial tools, like *bookplates, were sometimes used by successive generations within a family. There is a range of standard reference works available, but these are mostly out of date.　DRSP

J. Guigard, Nouvel Armorial du bibliophile (1890)
J. Harthan, 'Armorial Bookbindings from the Clements Collection', Apollo (Dec. 1960), 179–83; (Jun. 1961), 186–91; (Dec. 1961), 165–71
E. Olivier et al., Manuel de l'amateur de reliures armoriées françaises (30 vols in 29, 1924–38)
Pearson, Bookbinding

Armstrong, Margaret Neilson (1867–1944) Book designer and author, born in New York, where she spent most of her life. She began designing publishers' book covers in 1890 and subsequently produced over 300 binding designs, principally for *Scribner's and G. P. *Putnam. In later life, she turned to writing and published numerous books, most notably a Field Book of Western Wild Flowers (1915).　　DRSP

C. Gullans, Margaret Armstrong and American Trade Bindings (1991)

Arnold, Edward (1857–1942) British publisher. Grandson of Thomas and nephew to Matthew Arnold, Edward joined the firm of Richard *Bentley (1794–1871) in 1883 as a magazine editor before editing Murray's Magazine (1887) for J. *Murray. Arnold famously declined Hardy's Tess on Murray's behalf. Publishing in his own name from 1890, he specialized in educational books, Egyptology, exploration, and mountaineering. The firm published 1,500 titles before his retirement in 1930. Arnold's most notable author was E. M. Forster.　　PLS
ODNB

Arrighi, Ludovico (Vicentino) **degli** (fl. 1510–27) Italian scribe. After perhaps studying under Tagliente in Venice, Arrighi worked as a publisher in Rome (1510), a leading calligrapher for private patrons (1514), and then as copyist in the papal chancery, probably until 1521. He followed his woodblock writing book (1522)—the first to display the formal chancery hand—with one partly set in type (1523): the first chancery italic. His second italic (1524) introduced *swash capitals. These italics, more elegant than that of *Aldus, found successors in Italy, but contributed to the typographical mainstream primarily when Peter *Schoeffer II, *Granjon, and others blended them with the Aldine (1537–1540s). They served as models for new types in the 1920s.　　JAL

A. S. Osley, Scribes and Sources (1980)

Arrivabene family Printers in Venice. **Giorgio** (active 1483/4–1515) printed legal and theological works; his successor was **Cesare** (active 1517–28). Also attested are **Andrea** (active 1534–70), whose religious heterodoxy was notable, his brother **Antonio Francesco** (dates unknown), and **Cornelio** (active 1577–98).　　CWK
DBI
DTEI

Arrowsmith family Bristol publishers, father (**Isaac**) and son (**James William**). In partnership with H. C. Evans until 1857, Isaac's business was mainly as a *bookseller and *jobbing printer, though he also published *railway timetables and works of local interest. The son joined well before Isaac's death in 1871, though there were few changes until the firm rose to national prominence in the mid-1880s, as a result of the startling success of Hugh Conway's short thriller Called Back. It was first issued as Arrowsmith's Christmas *Annual for 1883 and was endlessly reprinted as a paperback volume in the new Bristol Library. The profits kept both series thriving with contributions from up-and-coming metropolitan authors, including Conan Doyle and Rider Haggard. With over 100 titles before his death in 1913, J. W. Arrowsmith proved himself one of the most innovative purveyors of popular fiction in Britain.　　GL
DLB 106

Arsenal, Bibliothèque de l' Parisian library, named after its location since 1756. It began as the private collection of the marquis de Paulmy. Sold in 1785 to the comte d'Artois, Louis XVI's youngest brother, it was spared by the Revolution and became a state institution on its owner's accession as Charles X (1824), acquiring particular prestige under *Nodier's librarianship. An autonomous part of the *Bibliothèque nationale de France since 1934 (plans for outright absorption were dropped following a heated public campaign in the 1990s), it is strong in the 17th and 18th centuries and French literature, especially theatre.   VAG

art book Art and the book have a long common history, from *books of hours to modern *artists' books. A new type of book, however, appeared once the history of art, in the late 19th century, began to be identified as an academic subject. Indeed, the notion of the art book is inseparable from a didactic or documentary purpose. Although there is no universal agreement on what constitutes an art book, a generally acceptable definition is a book relating to any aspect of the fine or decorative arts, including architecture and photography, illustrated with photographic reproductions. The notion thus encompasses, at one extreme, the most authoritative scholarly works and, at the other, lavish publications—bordering on *coffee-table books—in which the text is distinctly subservient to the pictures.

1. Origins and development
2. Publishing art books after World War II
3. Technical and editorial innovations
4. Publishers and pricing
5. Exhibition catalogues

1. Origins and development
Publication of the first art books was made possible by the invention of *heliogravure, the process of photographic reproduction discovered by Karel Klíč in the late 1870s. The production of art books, however, began seriously only in the 1920s and 1930s, under the impulse of leading art historians, such as Henri Focillon, Roger Fry, and the German-born scholars associated with the Warburg Institute, first in Hamburg, then in London, and under whose auspices, for example, the catalogue raisonné of Poussin drawings began to be issued in 1939. Yet art books were also prompted by dealers, auction houses, and art collectors. Some of those early art books were *limited editions, such as Fry's monograph on *Matisse (1930), but popular monographic series of *paperbacks intended for a broader readership of students and amateurs also date from that period. In France, Beaux-Arts issued 'L'Art français'; Rieder issued 'Maîtres de l'art moderne'; and Floury (publisher of Toulouse-Lautrec's famous 1898 album *Au pied du Sinaï*) issued 'Anciens et nouveaux', in which Gertrude Stein's *Picasso* came out in 1938. Mainstream publishers showed an early interest in art books as well. *Faber & Faber published the first catalogue raisonné of Velázquez (1935) and Armand Colin published Émile Mâle's popular volumes on church

architecture, while Gallimard's collections—'Les Peintres nouveaux' and 'Les Maîtres nouveaux'—popularized contemporary painters. The period also saw the appearance of art *encyclopaedias, such as Hachette's *Encyclopédie des Beaux-Arts* (1925), Larousse's *L'Art des origines à nos jours* (1932), or the bilingual, five-volume *Photographic Encylopaedia of Art* (1935–49) published by Tel with photographs by André Vigneau.

2. Publishing art books after World War II
The nature of art books was profoundly modified by the dissemination, after 1945, of colour photography, which, though invented in 1898, remained rare and expensive until the invention of the Kodachrome process in 1938. Colour printing suddenly made art books attractive to much broader audiences. New specialist publishers appeared in the 1940s: the Éditions du Chêne, founded in Paris (1941) by Maurice Girodias of *Olympia Press; Fernand Hazan in Paris (1946); *Electa, under the tutelage of Bernard Berenson, in Florence (1944); Fabbri in Milan (1944); *Thames & Hudson in London (1949); *Abrams in New York (1949); the Fribourg Office du Livre in Switzerland (1946); and Mazenod in Switzerland (1947), subsequently Citadelles & Mazenod. The Piedmontese De Agostini, previously focusing on cartography, became an art book publisher when the founder's son took over in 1942. So too, *Skira, previously Paris-based and focusing on *livres d'artistes*, relocated to Geneva and, as of the 1950s, became a European leader in the field.

3. Technical and editorial innovations
Art books are, by their nature, expensive to produce, with high fixed costs that do not diminish with a higher *press run. To make production viable, various strategies have been successfully tried over the years. Some were technical, such as the generalization of *offset reproduction beginning in the 1960s. (Zodiaque—based in the Burgundian Benedictine monastery of La-Pierre-Qui-Vire and a producer, from 1951 through the 1990s, of handsome volumes on Romanesque architecture and art—was one of the last to use heliogravure.) More recently, one solution has been to outsource printing or photographic reproduction to South East Asia. In 1983, the 22-year-old Benedikt Taschen launched his own art book publishing venture in Cologne, issuing titles in several languages at moderate prices thanks to innovative marketing techniques—a model subsequently imitated in other countries. Since the 1950s, however, the most constant and successful feature of art book publishing has been *co-editing, a more widespread practice in this than in any other branch. Many titles published in Abrams's 'Pocket Library of Great Art' were thus issued under the heading 'Le Grand Art' by *Flammarion—by then a leading French art book publisher—and by Kurt Desch in Munich. Similar partnerships have involved Flammarion and *Rizzoli, Larousse, and De Agostini. Electa alone has been involved in co-editions with *Aguilar, DuMont, Flammarion, Gallimard, *Phaidon, *Praeger, and Thames & Hudson, among others. In Fribourg, the Office du

Livre, under its dynamic director, Jean Hirschen, has issued art books for more than three decades in English, French, and German in co-editions with such diverse publishers and institutions as the Bibliothèque des Arts and the Société française du livre in Paris, the National Trust in London, DuMont in Cologne, Hirmer in Munich, Rizzoli in New York, and Harvard University Press. Co-editions can also be spearheaded by specialized institutions such as the Canadian Centre for Architecture, the International Center of Photography, or the Getty.

4. Publishers and pricing

Given the high investment art book publishing requires, the field has been dominated since World War II by firms established in a handful of countries: Britain, France, Germany, Italy, Switzerland, and the US. It has involved publishing giants such as *Hachette, *Mondadori, *Penguin (and its subsidiary *Dorling Kindersley), *Random House, Rizzoli, and *Viking, as well as large and small traditional independent publishers, such as *Braziller and Gallimard, and academic publishers, especially *Oxford University Press and Yale University Press. In the English-speaking world, the leading specialized houses are the London-based Phaidon and Thames & Hudson, and the New York-based Harry N. *Abrams and Abbeville Press (founded in 1977). In Germany, they include Belser in Stuttgart and Prestel in Munich (both notable for their *facsimile editions of medieval MSS), DuMont (founded in 1956 as a department of the long-standing press publisher DuMont Schauberg), and Hatje Cantz Verlag, based in Ostfildern near Stuttgart. Notable Parisian houses are Arthena, particularly active as publisher of catalogues raisonnés, and Hermann, originally a science publisher, acquired in 1956 by the distinguished antiquarian bookdealer Pierre Berès, who, advised by the art historian André Chastel, created the collection 'Arts de France' in 1960.

One of the paradoxical elements of art book economics is that—despite the vitality of affordable, academically oriented paperback or pocket book collections (Hazan's 'Petite Encyclopédie de l'art' being one of the longer-lasting and more successful)—the price of high-end art books has seldom been a disincentive to their production or sale. Indeed, notwithstanding a slump (possibly a consequence of overproduction) in the 1990s, the average book buyer appears ready and willing to spend more on an art book than on any other kind of book (except possibly reference works), making art books, as it were, the champagne of the book industry.

5. Exhibition catalogues

The most important development in the field of art books in the recent decades—one that has altered both its nature and its economics—has been the success, beginning in the 1970s, of large-scale exhibitions organized by major museums. ('The Treasures of Tutankhamun', first seen at the British Museum, drew a record 1.6 million visitors in 1972 and was comparably successful in other countries.) Once modest in size, exhibition catalogues have become massive, lavish publications, not uncom-

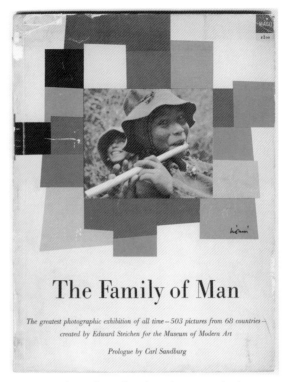

The **art book** as a bestseller: the various *paperback versions of this exhibition catalogue sold more than 4 million copies. This first edition was published by Maco, the Magazine Corporation, in 1955.

monly selling more than 100,000 copies. The catalogues of the Paris–Moscow, Paris–Berlin, Paris–New York, and Paris–Paris exhibitions held at the Centre Pompidou between 1977 and 1982 were even reissued by Gallimard ten years later. Such publications require years of research and meticulous editing; costs are not only shared by participating institutions, but are also largely absorbed by the museums' regular curatorial expenses, while publicity is covered by the exhibition's budget. Major art publishers (Electa, Gallimard, Yale) are frequently involved, but they are not the driving forces behind such ventures, even though their own art publications related to the theme of an exhibition may benefit from its success. In fact, museums, rather than art publishers, have become the engines of art book publishing. They have also turned into its largest distributors: the once modest bookstands selling catalogues and postcards are now large bookshops (and important museums have several), offering not only the museum's own publications but a vast selection of books on all subjects connected to the arts. Unlike regular bookshops, museum bookshops have not suffered from the competition posed by the *World Wide Web and, indeed, are expanding, opening branches outside their premises and even in airports. As things now stand, it would appear that art books are unlikely, for the time being, to be threatened by online publishing.   VAG

'Art, livre d'', in DEL
P. Fouché, L'édition française depuis 1945 (1998)
Storia dell'editoria d'Europa, vol. 2: Italia (1995)

artist's book A medium of expression that creatively engages with the book, as both object and concept.

1. Disputed definitions
2. A brief historical sketch
3. The 1960s
4. Artists' books and presses

1. Disputed definitions

Artists' books constitute a highly heterogeneous and malleable genre, which has so far resisted any straightforward categorization and classification. The absence of a workable and readily accepted definition of an artist's book stems partly from its variety and from its propensity to cross various boundaries and to intersect different disciplines. Certainly, artists' books often use several modes of creation and exploit various (usually inexpensive) materials and media. Some artists' books may contain a text (or at least, some words); others do not. Similarly, some artists' books may include some pictures or illustrations (*see* **16**); others may not. Although many artists experiment with the conventional form of the book (i.e. the *codex), there are numerous examples of artists' books that engage with other traditions of book shapes, including the blind book, the fan book, the *accordion book, and/or the *scroll. Other models of artists' books do not allude to any traditional book forms, but take on the anatomy of whatever the artist believes a book might be or become. Although some artists' books are produced as multiples, others are created in *limited editions. There are also examples of artists' books that are produced as unique objects.

Despite their formal and conceptual differences, however, most creators of artists' books unite in their attempt and desire to take the book—and the experience arising from holding and reading or looking at a book—beyond everyday expectations. Readers often have to suspend their anticipations of reading a text sequentially, from the beginning to the end, and go along with different—sometimes humorous, sometimes disturbing, often surprising—ways of interacting and engaging with the book as a communicative vehicle. As such, artists' books must be contrasted with *art books as well as with *livres d'artistes*, illustrated books, and painters' books. In English, these last three terms are usually used synonymously to designate de luxe editions of books containing original graphic material by an artist (in French, confusingly, a 'livre d'artiste' corresponds to the English artist's book). However, unlike artists' books, *livres d'artistes* are usually conceived and produced by editors or entrepreneurs and are, hence, not free from the pressures of the art market. Conceptually, they are also different because 'they are productions rather than creations, products rather than visions, examples of a form, not interrogations of its conceptual or formal or metaphysical potential' (Drucker, 5). In contrast to these *livres d'artistes*, artists' books are typically envisioned and created by the artist who explores the structural, typographical, and conceptual possibilities of the book from its very inception.

2. A brief historical sketch

The origins and the history of artists' books are as disputed as their definitions. Although most scholars agree that artists' books came to maturity during the second half of the 20th century, some critics (including Drucker) are more willing than others to recognize that the genre had influential precedents. *Blake, for instance, is often named as having significantly contributed to the conceptual history of artists' books. Like late 19th-century and 20th-century creators of artists' books, Blake explored the formal and structural potential of the book in order to express his unique creative imagination. Through innovative printing techniques and the marriage of image and text, Blake produced a distinctive vision of the book—one that embodied his own ideas of the arts and of the world. Moreover, because he was *self-published, Blake had full control over the realization and materialization of his ideas. Another artist frequently mentioned as a contributor to the intellectual and material history of artists' books is the 19th-century French Symbolist poet *Mallarmé. His *Coup de dés*, first published in 1897, is a typical instance of the layout of the book being put at the service of the poet's imagination. The work by Sonia Delaunay-Terk entitled *La Prose du Transsibérien et de la petite Jehanne de France* (1913), published by Blaise Cendrars, is another often-cited example. Unlike most earlier artists' books, the piece deliberately abandoned the codex form and creatively explored new ways of articulating the relationship between the book's content and its structure. Many other important examples could be mentioned. Indeed, since the early 20th century, it is hard to find an art movement that has not engaged with some components of artists' books: Cubism, Dada, Futurism, Expressionism, Surrealism, Postmodernism, Conceptualism, Minimalism, Performance Art, and Fluxus have all experimented with the book as an art form.

3. The 1960s

The 1960s saw a surge of artists' books, in Europe as well as in the US. For most scholars, it is in the early 1960s that the artist's book was born as a distinct genre. Anne Moeglin-Delcroix, for instance, specifically sees the origins of artists' books in the works of the American Edward Ruscha and the Swiss-German Dieter Roth (Moeglin-Delcroix, 1997, 24–5). Certainly, the work of these two artists—including Ruscha's famous *26 Gasoline Stations* (1963) and Roth's *Daily Mirror* book (1961)—stand as models for many book artists. Several factors explain the increase of artists' books during these years. The improvement in technology (mainly photocopying and *offset printing) rendered the production and distribution of artists' books increasingly inexpensive. Moreover, the ability to produce and provide such inexpensive multiples played right into the idea of the book as a democratic form of art—an idea fundamental to the concept of artists' books at a time when social and political activism were particularly fertile. Certainly, in the 1960s, artists' books aimed to subvert the establishment and counter the culture of *fine printing and of the art market. Artists' books became a way to reach a wider audience, providing 'a critique and an alternative to the system whereby a work of art is unique, revered, inaccessible to any but an elite, and bought and sold as investments and as highly prestigious objects of private property' (Guest, 8).

However, the myth of the democratic multiples has since been questioned by a number of scholars. In fact, many of the principles guiding and characterizing the production of artists' books in the 1960s have gradually eroded. Since the late 1970s, for instance, more and more artists' books have become book-like objects. A typical example of such book-sculptures is Miriam Schaer's *With In My Reach I* (2004). In the 1980s, artists' books often developed into installation pieces. However, some—but not all—critics believe that such book sculptures and book installations cannot be defined as artists' books but move into another art form.

4. Artists' books and presses

Since a surge in the production of artists' books in the 1960s and 1970s, many presses have specialized in their publication, including Granary Books in New York City, Brighton Press in San Diego, Coracle Press in London, and In-Out Productions in Amsterdam. The development of artists' books has also been closely tied to the establishment of other major centres of production and distribution. Art Metropole (set up by the group General Idea in 1974 in Toronto), Other Books and So (a gallery/bookshop established by the Mexican Ulises Carrión in 1975 in Amsterdam), and Printed Matter (started by Sol LeWitt, Lucy Lippard, and other artists in 1976 in New York City) were among the first to be founded. Since then, many other institutional sites, including museums, universities, and libraries in Europe and America, have become instrumental in encouraging the production, distribution, and *conservation of artists' books.   KJ

S. Bodman, *Creating Artists' Books* (2005)
B. Bright, *No Longer Innocent: Book Art in America 1960–1980* (2005)
S. Bury, *Artists' Books: The Book as a Work of Art, 1963–1995* (1995)
R. Castleman, *A Century of Artists Books* (1994)
S. Clay, ed., *When Will the Book Be Done?* (2001)
— and J. Rothenberg, eds., *A Book of the Book* (2000)
J. Drucker, *The Century of Artists' Books*, 2e (2004)
T. Guest, 'An Introduction to Books by Artists', in *Books by Artists*, ed. T. Guest (1981)
R. R. Hubery and J. D. Hubert, *The Cutting Edge of Reading* (1999)
S. Klima, *Artists Books* (1998)
C. Lauf and C. Phillpot, *Artist/Author* (1998)
J. Lyons, ed., *Artists' Books* (1985)
A. Moeglin-Delcroix, 'Bibliophilisms: The Multiple and the Unique', in Rousset-Altounian
— *Esthétique du livre d'artiste* (1997)
J. J. Rossman, 'Artists' Books Information Resource', www.library.yale.edu/~jwilliam/artistsbooks/, consulted June 2006
N. Rousset-Altounian, ed., *Livres d'Artistes: Livres-Objets = Artists' Books: Book-Objects* (1985)

art libraries Libraries whose primary function is to identify, collect, organize, and provide access to documentary material and literature relating to all aspects of the visual arts, including architecture and design. The term 'art library' as currently understood most probably came into use in the second half of the 19th century. Art libraries have continued to flourish ever since, in Europe as well as in the US. In addition to books and periodicals, art libraries may also hold slides (mounted transparencies), photographs, illustrations, prints, *posters, films, *artists' books, and other museum objects. In this regard, the functions and holdings of art libraries may overlap with the collections of other institutions, including art museums, universities, art schools and academies, as well as libraries of independent research institutes. Art libraries are often attached to such other institutions. The most famous art libraries in Europe and the US include London's *National Art Library (part of the Victoria and Albert Museum), the Courtauld Institute, the Kunstbibliothek der Staatlichen Museen zu Berlin, and New York's Frick Art Reference Library, as well as the Ryerson Library and the Burnham Library of Architecture in Chicago.   KJ

T. Fawcett, 'The Compleat Art Librarian', *ARLIS Newsletter* (UK), 22 (1975), 7–9
IEILS
P. Pacey, *A Reader in Art Librarianship* (1985)

Arts Council of Great Britain (ACGB) A public body dedicated to the promotion of the fine arts in Britain, originally set up in 1940 as the Council for the Encouragement of Music and the Arts (CEMA). The Arts Council of Great Britain was established in 1946 as its successor. With the establishment of ACGB came an additional responsibility: promoting access to the arts. Although CEMA had directly funded productions and performances, ACGB's role was to encourage arts organizations to produce high-quality work that a wider public could enjoy.

During the 1960s, there was some devolution with the establishment of regional offices of the ACGB, including a Scottish office. By 1994, anticipating the arrival of the new National Lottery, ACGB was abolished, and its functions transferred to three new bodies: the Arts Council of England, the Arts Council of Wales, and the Scottish Arts Council.   SD

www.artscouncil.org.uk
www.artswales.org.uk
www.scottisharts.org.uk, all consulted June 2006

artwork Illustrations (*see* **16**) prepared for printed reproduction. Often used synonymously with *camera-ready copy to refer to material supplied to a printer for *offset printing.

Arvon Foundation Founded in 1968 by John Moat and John Fairfax, with early support from Ted Hughes, it is a charity running residential writing courses at centres around Britain. In an informal atmosphere, novice writers have the opportunity to be mentored by experienced, published authors.   SD

J. Moat, *The Founding of Arvon* (2005)

Asad National Library The national library of Syria in Damascus, inaugurated in 1984 under the auspices of then President Ḥāfiẓ al-Asad. It holds approximately 200,000 printed volumes. Its impressive MS collections, numbering some 40,000 texts, mainly in Arabic, were gathered from the old Ẓāhirīya Library in Damascus, the Awqāf (religious endowments) and the Aḥmadīya libraries in Aleppo, as well as others throughout the country. The library is in the process of automating its catalogue. It has been responsible for preparing the Syrian National Bibliography since its inception and has also organized an annual *book fair since 1985.   DGH

ascender The part of a lower-case letter that extends above the *x-height; by transference, sometimes used of the letter itself, as in 'b' and 'h'. Counterpart to *descender.

Aschehoug Norwegian publishing house, founded 1872 in Oslo. With William Nygaard as director from 1888, it expanded rapidly. Nygaard strongly encouraged Norwegian authors to stop publishing in Denmark; through his endeavours, such well-known Norwegian authors as Sigrid Undset and Fridtjof Nansen published with Aschehoug. Today, Aschehoug covers fiction for all generations and scholarly works, including *encyclopaedias, and *textbooks.   EEi

ASCII *See* AMERICAN STANDARD CODE FOR INFORMATION INTERCHANGE.

Ashbee, Henry Spencer (1834–1900) Successful English businessman, book collector, and bibliographer. His collecting and bibliographical interests had two aspects: Cervantes and *erotica. *An Iconography of Don Quixote 1605–1895* (1895) was largely based on his own library. Under the *pseudonym Pisanus Fraxi, he published three volumes of erotic bibliography: *Index Librorum Prohibitorum* (1877), *Centuria Librorum Absconditorum* (1879), and *Catena Librorum Tacendorum* (1885), all based on his own collections. On his death, Ashbee's collections were bequeathed to the British Museum (*see* BRITISH LIBRARY). The erotica (*c.*1,600 books) formed the most substantial part of the restricted *Private Case there. He is often identified as the author of *My Secret Life*, published under the name of Walter.   ASGE
P. Mendes, *Clandestine Erotic Fiction in English, 1800–1930* (1993)
ODNB

Ashburnham, Bertram, 4ᵗʰ earl of (1797–1878) Collecting *incunabula in his youth and, subsequently, MSS, he formed one of the most important private libraries in England. He purchased en bloc the *Libri collection (1847) and the *Stowe and Barrois libraries (1849). Between 1844 and 1877, he also bought about 250 other MSS—many of them medieval—later sold to H. Y. *Thompson.   ASGE
A. N. L. Munby, *Connoisseurs and Medieval Miniatures* (1972)

Ashendene Press A *private press run by Charles Harry St John Hornby. After a printing apprenticeship at

W. H. *Smith, he set up a press in the summer-house of his father's home at Ashendene, Hertfordshire, in 1895, inspired in part by the printing revival begun by W. *Morris. In 1899, he moved to Shelley House, London, where the Press remained until its closure in 1935. Printing purely for pleasure, Hornby was interested chiefly in typography, although Ashendene books were occasionally illustrated and often decorated, sometimes with calligraphy by Graily Hewitt. Hornby became a director of W. H. Smith, and the firm's bindery, under D. *Cockerell, bound many later Ashendene publications. Hornby's books achieved a fine reputation, his folio Dante (1909) and *Descriptive Bibliography* (1935) being among the most highly regarded. He commissioned two typefaces for the Press: 'Subiaco' (1902) was designed by E. *Walker and Sydney *Cockerell (1906–87) after the first roman type used by *Sweynheym and Pannartz, and Walker designed 'Ptolemy' (1927) after another 15ᵗʰ-century face. Both types now belong to *Cambridge University Press.   PWN
C. Franklin, *The Ashendene Press* (1986)
C. St J. Hornby, *Descriptive Bibliography of the Ashendene Press* (1935; repr. 1976)

Ashmole, Elias (1617–92) English antiquary, book collector, benefactor. Most of his books and MSS, collected over a period of more than 50 years, came to the Ashmolean Museum, Oxford, in 1692; others were sold at auction in London in February 1694. The Ashmolean library, transferred to the *Bodleian Library in 1860, includes *incunabula and more than 700 primarily medieval or early modern MSS. Ashmole's collecting was closely related to his antiquarian interests in alchemy, astrology, and heraldry, particularly the history of the Order of the Garter. More than half of his MSS are, in the broadest sense, scientific and just under a quarter are concerned with heraldry. The Ashmolean Museum, opened in 1683, was founded on Ashmole's antiquarian collections, which he presented to Oxford University.   ASGE
W. H. Black, *A Descriptive, Analytical and Critical Catalogue of the Manuscripts Bequeathed unto the University of Oxford by Elias Ashmole* (2 vols, 1845–66)
ODNB

Ashurbanipal's library Wishing to raise cultural standards, Ashurbanipal, king of Assyria (668–628 BC), decided to establish a library at Nineveh. He therefore sent agents out to every corner of the empire to gather copies of Babylonian and Assyrian literary works from public and private libraries. Containing more than 25,000 *tablets, Ashurbanipal's library was divided into two sections, with *archival material in one and literature in the other. He boasted that he had 'obtained the hidden treasures of the sum of the *scribes' knowledge'.   KS
O. Pedersen, *Archives and Libraries in the Ancient Near East 1500–300 B.C.* (1998)

Asia Publishing House Founded in 1943 by Peter Jayasinghe, it became one of India's leading publishers of scholarly books. The first Indian-owned publishing house to be organized along professional lines with specially trained staff, it published more than 4,000 titles. In the 1970s, it experienced a sharp decline.　　　AG

Asiatic Society Library, Calcutta (Kolkata) Founded in 1784, when the Society received seven Persian MSS from Henri Richardson; the library opened to the public in 1808. One of its first accessions was a selection from the library of Tipu Sultan in 1808. The library holds *c.*149,000 volumes and is noted for its extensive Indic and Asiatic collections, including the library of the College of *Fort William. Important holdings include a MS of the *Pādshāhnāmah* bearing an autograph of the Emperor Shāh Jihān, N. B. Halhed's *A Grammar of the Bengal Language* (1778), and a 1614 edition of *Purchas: His Pilgrimage*.　　　AG
www.asiaticsocietycal.com, consulted June 2008

Asiatic Society of Bombay (Mumbai) Founded in 1804 by Sir James Mackintosh under the name 'Literary Society of Bombay'. The acquisition of the library of the Medical and Literary Society of Bombay (founded 1789), formed the nucleus of the Society's library. In 1833, the collection was moved to the newly built town hall, where it has since stayed. Its holdings include a valuable 14th-century illuminated MS of Dante's *Divina Commedia*, which was donated to the society by Mountstuart Elphinstone, governor of Bombay. The library holds more than 3,000 ancient MSS in Persian, Sanskrit, and Prakrit.　AG
www.asiaticsociety.org, consulted June 2008

A sizes, paper Series of trimmed rectangular paper sheet sizes—ranging from A0 (largest, area 1 square metre) to A10—used for general commercial and printing purposes. They are defined according to metric measurements, with the area of each successive size being exactly half that of the preceding size. Sheets are therefore geometrically similar to each other, with the ratio of short and long edges constant, being that of the ratio of a square edge to its diagonal ($1:\sqrt{2}$). Originally proposed in 1917, the sizes were adopted as a German standard in 1923 and as an International Standard in 1930, although their adoption by many countries, including England, only started *c.*1950s. Two further complementary sizes exist: Series B and Series C. The first is used for printing applications; sheets have the same ratio of edge dimensions as the A series, but lateral dimensions are intermediate between the different A series sheets. Series C is used for envelopes and special applications.　　DCC
Labarre

as new Term used to describe a book in immaculate condition, rather better than most new books are after initial bookshop delivery and shelving.

Assemanianus, Codex A short gospel *lectionary (*Vatican Library, cod. slav. 3), named after Giuseppe Simone Assemanin, who acquired it for the Vatican. Probably written in the 11th century in Western Bulgaria, and one of the classical Old Church Slavonic MSS, it is of great importance as an early witness to the Slavonic

Gospel text, with some readings that were eliminated in later revisions. A high-quality MS, it is written in a fine round Glagolitic hand with numerous large decorative *initials; their style is somewhat inconsistent, reflecting varieties of provincial Byzantine illumination of the period (*see* **4**).　　　RMC
V. Ivanova-Mavrodinova and A. Džurova, eds., *Il Vangelo Assemani* (1981)

association copy A copy of a book (normally a printed book) that has been formerly owned or identifiably used by someone associated with the book's production, *authorship, or subject. Occasionally, such as with Keats's copy of *Shakespeare, a book may be described as an association copy if the person associated has no particular connection with the production or authorship of the book, but is someone of interest or significance in his or her own right. The term is most commonly used in the antiquarian book trade and often indicates an opportunity to increase the market value of a book. Association copies are identifiable through marks of *provenance and may contain additional, related material such as letters, proofs, advertisements, etc.　　RWO
J. Carter and N. Barker, *ABC for Book Collectors*, 8e (2004)
J. Sparrow, *Association Copies* (1978)

Association of American Publishers Public education and lobbying organization representing trade and *textbook publishers, founded in 1970 from the merger of the *American Book Publishers Council and American Textbook Publishers Institute. It advocates press freedom, the importance of reading in America, and an improved flow of American books abroad.　　TT

Association of American University Presses The AAUP, which has its headquarters in New York, represents more than 125 non-profit publishers (including university presses, museums, professional associations). Founded in 1937, it promotes *scholarly publishing and provides services through its American University Press Services subsidiary.　　BEL
G. Hawes, *To Advance Knowledge* (1967)

Association of Little Presses (ALP) Established in 1966 by Bob Cobbing, the Writers Forum, and Stuart Montgomery (Fulcrum Press) to promote small presses in Britain and Ireland, it publishes a newsletter including publication lists and trade information. The ALP organized regular book fairs, but activities decreased in the mid-1990s.　　AMS

Association Typographique Internationale (ATypI) Association for type designers and manufacturers, founded in 1957. The first members were drawn from several type foundries, and intended to agree upon a common procedure for licensing *typefaces, setting out the principles of the organization in a 'Moral Code'. ATypI still provides a place to discuss *copyright, licensing, and legal matters about type. Beyond this objective, the Association provides a focus for discussion about type and *typography, whether concerned with education, industrial practice, history, or aesthetics. The characteristics of ATypI's membership have changed considerably since *computerized typesetting became widespread. Typically, type 'foundries' producing *founts—computer files describing a typeface—may consist of only one or two people. The largest corporate members are software companies, designing office or *desktop publishing applications. ATypI provides a place where they can discuss typographic technology with type designers and typographers.   ABRW

www.atypi.org, consulted June 2008

Āstān-i Quds-i Razavī Library, Mashhad, Iran
Among the oldest public endowed libraries in Iran (and the Islamic world), well known for its collection of nearly 47,000 MSS and 247,000 printed volumes. These include several fine and early Qur'āns, notably one dated 1003. The library was in use as early as 1456, but was severely looted in 1590. Safavid and later rulers restored some of the looted items and bequeathed some of their own valuable MSS, as did several scholars and benefactors. Systematic cataloguing began in the early 1920s and has continued to the present.   KE

R. 'A. Shākirī, *Ganj-i hizār sālah* (1989)

asterisk (*) Symbol used in writing and printing to sign *preliminaries, to obscure identity or obscenity, or to indicate footnotes, cross-references, hiatus, or conjecture.

Astle, Thomas (1735–1803) English collector of books and MSS, best known for assembling the mainly medieval MSS that became the Stowe collection in the *British Library. This collection—bought by George Grenville, 1st marquess of Buckingham and lodged at *Stowe House, Buckinghamshire—was purchased by Bertram, 4th earl of *Ashburnham in 1849. In 1879, Ashburnham's son, the 5th earl, sold most of the holdings to the British Museum.   ASGE

ODNB

Astor, John Jacob (1763–1848) German immigrant, fur trader, and capitalist. The wealthiest man in America at the time of his death, he left $400,000 (of an estate conservatively valued at $20 million) to establish a reference library in New York City that opened in 1849. In 1895, the reference and research collection of the Astor Library was combined with the *Lenox Library and the *Tilden Trust to form the *New York Public Library.   MEK

Athenaeum British periodical. Founded in 1828, it soon became the bestselling weekly of the 19th century—liberal, serious, and imaginative. It attracted readers through the variety and intelligent treatment of its material: from literature and the arts, through politics and current affairs, to technology and science (including work-in-progress, and very full reports on the meetings of the *Royal Society and other learned institutions). Its *reviews were influential (*see* REVIEWING IN RELATION TO CONSUMPTION), and its obituaries were an important source for the *Dictionary of National Biography*. In 1921 it merged with *The Nation*; it closed in 1923.   SJG

L. Marchand, *The Athenaeum* (1941)

Atheneum A New York trade house founded in 1959 by three senior editors: Simon Michael Bessie of *Harper & Brothers, Hiram Haydn of *Random House, and Alfred *Knopf, Jr., of the firm founded by his parents. Haydn left the firm in 1964, followed shortly by Bessie. Atheneum focused on books of literary value for adults and children. Its authors included Ignazio Silone, Loren Eiseley, Wright Morris, Randall Jarrell, Daniel Boorstin, Isabel Allende, Edward Albee, and Theodore H. White, author of the bestselling *Making of the President* series. It began publishing children's books (*see* **15**) and *trade paperbacks in 1961. *Scribner acquired Atheneum in 1978. Since 1994, it has been part of the Scribner division of *Simon & Schuster. Although some fiction appears with the Atheneum *imprint, today the firm is associated mostly with children's books, including Ian Falconer's 'Olivia' series, the 'Bunnicula' books, and Judith Viorst's many titles.   BEL

Athias, Joseph (1634/5–1700) Jewish printer at Amsterdam. A Sephardic immigrant, Athias began printing books in Hebrew and other languages in 1654. In 1661, he produced the first Hebrew Bible with numbered verses, which earned the esteem of the Dutch States General. He was engaged in the large-scale printing of English export bibles, in which he appears to have experimented with *stereotyping. In 1681, he acquired Daniel *Elzevier's *matrices.   AKO

H. Carter and G. Buday, 'Stereotyping by Joseph Athias', *Quaerendo*, 5 (1975), 312–20

L. Fuks and R. G. Fuks-Mansfeld, *Hebrew Typography in the Northern Netherlands 1585–1815*, vol. 2 (1987)

Athlone Press UK publisher founded in 1948 as the press of the University of London. The company was acquired, in turn, by the printers *Bemrose in 1979, Brian Southam in 1981, and the Continuum Publishing Group in 2001.   AGP

Athos, monastic libraries of Mount The libraries on Mount Athos possess a particularly rich collection of Christian MSS and printed books. Dispersed among the twenty main monasteries, the Protaton Church, the larger hermitages, and even anchorites' isolated cells, they contain more than 16,000 MSS, many printed works, and *archival records. Outstanding among them are *codices written in the *scriptoria of Constantinople and donated by Byzantine emperors. The oldest monastery is Great Lavra, founded in 963, which has the richest library. Also very important are the libraries of the Vatopedi and Iviron monasteries, both founded in the 10th century. Many valuable MSS were spirited away from Mount Athos after the fall of Constantinople (1453) and are now in Europe's larger libraries. The numerous agents responsible for their removal include Janus Lascaris (for the Medici), Nikolaos Sofianos (for Hurtado de Mendoza), and Porphyrius Uspensky (for the Russian Church).   KS

Ática, Edições (**Nova Ática**) Portuguese publisher. Established *c*.1929 in Lisbon, Ática (since 2001, Nova Ática) is one of Portugal's leading publishing houses. It has issued many important *editions of Portuguese literature, most notably the poems of Fernando Pessoa (1888–1935), and was instrumental in building Pessoa's worldwide reputation.   DRW

Ática, Editora Brazilian publisher based in São Paulo. Founded in 1965 by Anderson Fernandes Dias (d. 1988), Ática is an innovative leader in the juvenile and educational markets. It introduced teachers' manuals to Brazil and provides *textbooks at all educational levels. Ática has also published many general interest titles.   DRW

Atlântida Portuguese publisher. Active for 60 years (*c*.1926–85), Atlântida had close ties with academics at the nearby University of Coimbra. It issued many works on law, political science, anthropology, and history, along with some significant literary titles, such as the poems of Miguel Torga (1907–95).   DRW

atlas A collection of *maps, issued together, and bound in one or more volumes. By extension, a collection of plates illustrating a complex subject, e.g. an anatomical atlas.

1. Early atlases
2. 'Modern' maps: Ortelius and Mercator
3. The Hondius family, Blaeu, and their legacy
4. Sea atlases and nautical charts
5. Production and consumption

1. Early atlases

The term derives from a collection of maps by *Mercator published posthumously in 1595: *Atlas, sive Cosmographicae Meditationes de Fabrica Mundi et Fabricati Figura* (*Atlas, or Cosmographical Reflections on the Creation of the World and its Visible Forms*). The engraved *title-page shows Atlas, the Titan of Greek mythology, measuring the globe with compasses rather than carrying it on his shoulders. The earliest atlases, dating from the 14th century, were *portolans, collections of coastal charts of the navigable world. Collections of land maps first appeared in western Europe by 1400 as supplements to MSS of Ptolemy's *Geographia*. These generally contained a world map and 26 regional maps corresponding to Ptolemy's division of the world, and were drawn from his tables of co-ordinates. These 27 maps, *engraved on copper plates, appeared with the first printing of a Latin translation of the *Geographia* (1477). The maps of the 1482 edition were woodcuts, however, perhaps because more impressions could be taken from them, and five *tabulae modernae*, maps of contemporary Europe and the Holy Land, were added. In 1528, the geographer *Münster published a request for the cooperation of local surveyors and amateurs in creating 'a mirror of all Germany, with its villages, towns, and trades'. The projected national atlas was never completed, but detailed German maps were included in Münster's edition of Ptolemy (1540).

2. 'Modern' maps: Ortelius and Mercator

Although Ptolemy remained the standard geographical text, the production of 'modern' maps, based on contemporary observation and measurement, proliferated; Rome and Venice became the chief centres for their engraving and sale. Maps were normally sold separately, but the engraver and map-seller Antonio Lafreri, who worked at Rome (1544–77), specialized in gathering collections to suit individual needs. The general title-page that he engraved for these ad hoc volumes is the first to show the familiar figure of Atlas bearing the world on his shoulders. The Antwerp mapseller *Ortelius seems to have been the first to perceive the advantages to both publisher and user of a standard collection of maps. For the first edition of his *Theatrum Orbis Terrarum* (1570), 70 older maps were re-engraved on 53 plates of a uniform size and published with *letterpress text and a *catalogus auctorum* acknowledging the cartographers whose work he had included. Some 30 further editions, with growing numbers of maps, followed; the edition of 1612 contained 167. The letterpress of the later editions included translations into three modern languages; an edition with English text appeared in 1606, after Ortelius' death. Several editions of an *Epitome* were also published at a reduced cost, containing fewer maps; this too ultimately appeared in English (?1601).

The geographer Mercator, characterized by Ortelius as 'the Ptolemy of our age', projected as early as the 1540s an encyclopaedic study of the entire creation, to include a series of maps surpassing anything hitherto published. They would be not only uniform in size, but on a uniform projection, and based on a single surveying method, for he envisaged each sheet of his atlas as a section of a unified world map. (Ortelius, a practical man with a shrewder knowledge of the market, was content simply to offer the best available maps, although recognizing that all the maps of a particular country should be the work of one cartographer.) Mercator, a skilful draughtsman and engraver, applied himself vigorously to the fulfilment of his magnificent scheme, but its vast scale and his painstaking attention to detail meant that work was slow. By the time of his death in 1594, he had (with the assistance of his son and grandsons) finished 107 maps, almost entirely of Europe. These, together with a treatise on the creation of the world, were published the following year. Although only a fragment of his projected life's work, Mercator's *Atlas* and edition of Ptolemy (1578) set the highest standards of geographical accuracy.

A complete national atlas, the first of its kind and perhaps inspired by the work of Ortelius, was realized by the Yorkshireman Christopher Saxton (1542×4–1610/11). His survey of England and Wales began in 1570, and maps were engraved as each county was completed, being sold (uncoloured) for four pence a sheet. Of the maps which are signed, sixteen were engraved by Flemish craftsmen and seven by Englishmen. The complete work was published at 15*s.* in 1579; a smaller atlas with twenty sheets of maps, presumably less expensive, was published in 1583.

3. The Hondius family, Blaeu, and their legacy

Mercator's successor was the Amsterdam engraver *Hondius, who bought the plates of the *Atlas* from Mercator's heirs in 1604 and published an enlarged edition two years later. Hondius' 36 new maps were derived from a variety of sources, and did not match Mercator's in quality or style; nevertheless, he had judged the market well, and the reissue was commercially very successful. His son Henricus and son-in-law Johannes *Janssonius continued his business after his death in 1611, publishing several further editions of his *Atlas Novus*. The last included over 500 maps bound in ten volumes, with a printed text in Latin and four other languages. Hondius' shop also produced work for other publishers, notably the maps for John Speed's *Theatre of the Empire of Great Britain* (1611–12).

The principal rival to the Hondius family (although they were not above buying in maps from each other) was Willem Janszoon *Blaeu. A pupil of the Danish astronomer Tycho Brahe and an accomplished engraver, he was well qualified to oversee and control every stage of the production of his maps. The States of Holland and the Dutch East India Company appointed him their official cartographer, and through these privileged connections he obtained early and reliable information about recent discoveries. The titles of Blaeu's publications acknowledge the achievements of his predecessors. His first publication was *Atlantis Appendix* (1630), with 60 maps (including some of Hondius'), a supplement to Mercator's *Atlas* of 1595. His *Appendix Theatri A. Ortelii et Atlantis G. Mercatoris* appeared in the following year, containing 99 new maps, and in 1635, *Theatrum Orbis Terrarum sive Atlas Novus*, in two volumes with 207 maps. His sons continued to expand the scope of this work, culminating in the *Atlas Major sive Cosmographia Blaviana* of 1662, in eleven volumes with nearly 600 maps. Like their father, they were successful in obtaining reliable surveys of obscure places: the 1655 edition of *Atlas Novus* included a volume each of Scottish and Chinese maps.

The Hondius and Blaeu establishments made Amsterdam the unrivalled centre of European commercial map and atlas production for the whole of the 17th century. The ambitious *English Atlas* (1680–3) of Moses Pitt, for example, contained no original maps but only reworkings purchased from the 'heirs of Janzson'. The Blaeus' printing house became one of the wonders of the city, with its nine letter presses (each named after one of the Muses) and six *rolling presses for copper-plate printing. The Blaeus had also their own *typefoundry, bindery, *paper mill, and colouring shop; finished copies of the late atlases—lavishly coloured and gilded, and bound in fine *vellum—are among the choicest artefacts of 17th-century book production. Beyond the commercial world, the publication of atlases depended entirely on patronage.

In 17th-century France, the maps of Nicolas Sanson d'Abbeville and his sons were commissioned by the Crown; only at the end of the century were they 'edited', re-engraved by Jaillot, and published as highly decorative atlases. The polymath Franciscan friar Vincenzo Coronelli obtained the post of Cosmographer to the Republic of Venice, which underwrote the production costs of his enormous *Atlante Veneto* (1697).

4. Sea atlases and nautical charts

The printed sea atlas did not begin to appear until the late 16th century, MS pilot-books and descendants of the portolan having sufficed until then. In 1583–6, Lucas Janszoon Waghenaer published (with *Plantin of Antwerp) *De Spiegel der Zeevaerdt*, a collection of engraved charts with sailing directions. Rival sea atlases soon appeared (including two by Blaeu), but Waghenaer's name was widely applied to all books of this kind; English seamen called them 'wagoners'. Increasing maritime activity both in war and peace called for more detailed and accurate cartography than Waghenaer's. The first printed sea atlas to cover the known world, and the first to use Mercator's projection, was Sir Robert Dudley's *Del l'arcano del mare*, first published at Florence in 1645 under the patronage of the Grand Duke of Tuscany, and subsequently enlarged to include 130 charts and maps. All are entirely original, and represent the acme of naval knowledge at the time; Dudley included even the Australasian discoveries made by Tasman in 1642. The maps form only a part of what Dudley had projected as a maritime encyclopaedia covering practical astronomy, shipbuilding, and navigation. They were engraved over twelve years by Antonio Lucini, in a highly personal style which has little in common with the artists of the Low Countries.

A more accurate determination of latitude and longitude was undertaken by astronomers of the Académie Royale des Sciences (founded 1671). Their work enabled the publication in 1693 of *Le Neptune françois*, in which the coasts of western Europe were accurately mapped on Mercator's projection. Throughout the 18th century, voyages of discovery surveyed and charted more and more coasts and sea routes. The Académie continued to produce charts of great accuracy, finally collected in *L'Hydrographie française* of 1756; the British Admiralty commissioned charts of more than 1,000 miles of American coasts, both before and after Independence, and sent one of the best hydrographers of his day, Captain Cook, to chart the islands of the Pacific. According to L. Bagrow, the result of this great expansion of cartography was that 'craftsmanship was finally superseded by specialised science and the machine'. Perhaps it is truer to say that the map now became essentially a precision tool, without necessarily ceasing to be a work of art.

5. Production and consumption

In order to accommodate as much detail as possible, atlas maps and charts were usually engraved on *folio copper-plates. At its best, copper-engraving is clear, precise, and capable of much integral decoration. However, the number of sharp impressions from a copper-plate is limited, and colouring has to be applied by hand. The atlases of the Blaeus were greatly admired, but always costly. From the early 17th century, smaller and cheaper atlases began to appear. Detail was necessarily reduced, but accuracy and handsome appearance were not sacrificed, even in *duodecimos. Later in the century, 'classical atlases' of the ancient world were regularly published in *quarto or smaller *formats as reference books for students. An inexpensive alternative to the atlas for the schoolroom or study was the globe. World maps were engraved in many sizes to cover globes from a few inches to several feet in diameter, but the sections or 'gores' were not published as an atlas.

If the 17th century was the era of the artistic atlas, the 19th was that of the popular atlas. Steel engraving allowed for longer print runs, although colouring still had to be done by hand; *lithography made colour printing possible, but was adopted rather slowly by map printers. Stieler's *Handatlas*, in print between 1817 and 1944, was a pioneer in offering an attractive and reasonably detailed atlas at a moderate price; there were many imitators and rivals, and by the middle of the 19th century the cheap 'school atlas', limited in detail and not always up-to-date, provided the bread and butter of many map publishers. Folio 'library atlases', drawing on the results of exploration and refined methods of surveying and measurement, appeared in most languages. Among the last of the 'artistic' atlases is that originally published by the Society for the Diffusion of Useful Knowledge (Peacock's 'Steam Intellect Society') in 1844. Elegantly engraved and coloured, it is unusual in including star maps and plans of major cities.   BJF

L. Bagrow, *History of Cartography*, 2e (1985)
R. V. Tooley, *Dictionary of Mapmakers* (1965)
— *History of Cartography* (1969)

Atmaram Sagoon Started in Bombay (Mumbai), this publishing firm appears to have been inherited by Mrs Radhabai Atmaram Sagoon *c*.1889. Under her, the firm both published and sold books, mainly on Indological and antiquarian subjects, until *c*.1920.   RBC

attribution The theory and practice of determining *authorship. Attributions are made on the basis of internal evidence, external evidence, or a combination of both.

Internal evidence refers to various stylistic and thematic aspects: metrical and syntactical habits, word frequencies, and verbal and thematic parallels to other works by the same author. Such evidence alone is rarely sufficient to make a convincing attribution, because one needs to show (for example) that a certain pattern of imagery is distinctive to a particular author and no other. Because language is a social medium, internal evidence of this nature will always remain suggestive rather than definitive. The history of attribution contains many instances in which claims of authorship based primarily on internal evidence were later rejected. One of the best-known recent examples is the attribution of W. S.'s *A Funeral Elegy* (1612) to *Shakespeare; John Ford is now

accepted as the poem's likely author. Byrne's useful discussion of the use and abuse of verbal and thematic parallels in attribution may be supplemented by Schoenbaum.

Internal evidence nonetheless has its value, and is especially effective in the effort to de-attribute a work, i.e. to show that a particular author almost certainly did *not* write the work. Internal evidence is also useful when external evidence has significantly limited the pool of likely authors. In such a situation, internal evidence need only demonstrate that certain features are distinctive to one author compared to the few other candidates. A famous example of attributing authorship in this situation is Mosteller and Wallace's work on the twelve disputed *Federalist* papers.

Their study was also notable for using advanced statistical techniques to marshal the relevant internal evidence, and this approach—also known as *stylometry—has become influential in an era when computer technology is ubiquitous and many texts are available electronically. *Morton was an early advocate of stylometry, and many others have since pursued various quantitative approaches, though no single method has yet gained widespread acceptance. Indeed, many scholars working on particular attribution problems are sceptical about these quantitative methods, which are surveyed by *Love.

External evidence includes letters and diaries, handwriting, a work's publishing history, attributions made by the author's contemporaries as well as by later investigators, and other biographical information. In cases of disputed authorship, this kind of evidence rarely offers direct and unambiguous proof, but the accumulation of significant external evidence can often show that a particular author did or did not write the work in question. Quite often, the dearth of available evidence is itself the problem, and in those instances, the importance of one particular piece of evidence is sometimes exaggerated. The emergence of searchable databases is likely to result in the discovery of previously unknown external evidence relevant to particular problems concerning authorship.

One particularly vexing problem involved in studying attribution concerns what may be termed 'the centripetal force of the major author'. Those who present claims of attribution—whether long ago or in the present—often do so to augment a major author's canon. (The swelling of the Defoe canon long after his death is a good case in point.) This situation occurs for various reasons: the discovery of a 'new' work by a major author is viewed as more significant than one by a minor author; the survival of other works by the major author permits comparisons not otherwise available for minor authors; and a major author is often viewed as possessing a distinctive style. However, scholars who offer claims of attribution would do well to remember that the vast majority of works are written by minor authors, including authors whose identities have long vanished from historical memory. This situation especially pertains to more ephemeral genres, such as journalism.

Because attribution depends on highly particularized knowledge concerning authors themselves, their milieu, their language habits, and their historical and cultural contexts, 'rules of attribution' are difficult to formulate and frequently disputed. *See also* ANONYMITY. SK

M. St C. Byrne, 'Bibliographical Clues in Collaborate Plays', *Library*, 4/13 (1932–3), 21–48

D. V. Erdman and E. G. Fogel, eds., *Evidence for Authorship* (1966)

H. Love, *Attributing Authorship* (2002)

F. Mosteller and D. L. Wallace, *Inference and Disputed Authorship* (1964)

S. Schoenbaum, *Internal Evidence and Elizabethan Dramatic Authorship* (1966)

Atuagagdliutit (**Something to Read**) Greenlandic-language periodical, published in Nuuk since 1861, with twelve issues appearing yearly from 1874. The periodical's artistic merit and technical production values were extremely high, thanks to Lars Møller (1842–1926), a hero of Greenlandic printing. Until the 1930s, it was freely distributed to all households. Today, after a merger with a Danish-language paper, it is bilingual and published twice weekly. TKj

Aubert, David (*fl.* 1458–75) Prolific 15ᵗʰ-century *scribe in Burgundy. He copied, in part or in whole, more than 40 MSS, chiefly *de luxe ones for royalty or members of the nobility in France and England, including Edward IV and Margaret, duchess of Burgundy. He was mainly employed in the household of Philip the Good. ASGE

R. E. F. Straub, *David Aubert, escripvain et clerc* (1995)

Auckland City Libraries Founded in 1880 as Auckland Public Library, ACL is New Zealand's largest *public library system. It includes one of New Zealand's most significant research collections of rare books and *archives, originating in *Grey's donation in 1882 of rare New Zealand publications and documents, medieval MSS, *incunabula, and highlights of European printing. Grey's donation stimulated others, such as Henry Shaw's gift of medieval and illustrated books, and Frank Reed's collection of Alexandre Dumas *père*. The special collections have since grown to reflect both New Zealand's indigenous history and its European heritage. GP

www.aucklandcitylibraries.com, consulted June 2008

Auct. Bible *Bodleian Library MS Auct. E. inf. 1–2 was produced at Winchester, in two stages, *c.*1160 and *c.*1170–80. One of a number of highly decorated, two-volume, *lectern bibles produced in England in this period, it has a particularly close textual and decorative relationship to the *Winchester Bible. The Auct. *scribe copied several *leaves in the Winchester MS and the text of Winchester was corrected against it; one of the artists of that Bible also contributed to this MS. *See also* MANUSCRIPT CORRECTION. ASGE

W. Oakeshott, 'The Origin of the "Auct." Bible', *BLR* 11 (1982–5), 401–6

auction *See* BOOK AUCTIONS.

auction catalogues Perhaps the most enticing documents of the antiquarian book trade, filled with possibility when new and replete with interest when old, especially if marked up with purchasers and prices. The first English book auction catalogues date from the 17ᵗʰ century; by 1686, two individual lots in the Anglesey sale comprised groups of earlier (and evidently already collectible) catalogues. The arrangement of the Anglesey catalogue, divided between foreign and English books, then under broad subject headings (in Latin), and by *format, is typical of the time. Beyond the occasional note of '*editio optima*', a reference to 'black letter', or mention of a 'curious' or '*corio turcico*' binding, there is little by way of additional bibliographical information in catalogues of this period. Notes on condition are cursory or non-existent, which broadly remained the case until the 20ᵗʰ century. Individual books of importance gradually attracted more detailed attention from cataloguers (this work was often contracted out to booksellers, auctioneers rarely having in-house expertise); but most books were no more than briefly identified.

It was only with the introduction of the controversial buyer's premium in 1975 that truly major change occurred. A profound shift in the balance of the trade ensued, with auctioneers becoming not wholesalers to a knowledgeable coterie of well-informed dealers, but assertive self-publicists retailing directly to the public. Emerging to reflect and promote this change was the glossy modern catalogue, filled with extensive notes, heavily illustrated, and—in a new and significant departure—supplied with price estimates. What did not change were the intricacies of the small print—the exclusions, reservations, and lack of warranties—that still adorn auction catalogues and contrast so markedly with the plain-language guarantees of the booksellers' codes of the *American Booksellers' Association and the *Antiquarian Booksellers' Association of America. *See also* BOOKSELLERS' CATALOGUES. LJW

Pearson, *Provenance*

Audin, Marius (1872–1951) French Beaujolais-born printer and publisher. He opened his *private press, the Maison des Deux Collines, in Lyons in 1919. S. *Morison contributed to his *Causeries typographiques* (1921–5). Only two volumes appeared of the twenty planned for his *Somme typographique* (1948–9). His son Maurice continued his work. VAG

audio book On 22 February 1952, the poet Dylan Thomas read a selection of his poetry into the recording microphone of Peter Bartok, the composer's son, to an empty hall in New York City. The impetus for this recording came from two recent college graduates who offered Thomas $500, plus a 10 per cent *royalty, for his efforts. With this recording, Barbara Cohen and Marianne Roney launched Caedmon Records, and the era of the modern audio book. Other early writers whose voices were recorded on Caedmon included T. S. *Eliot, Robert Frost, and F. Scott Fitzgerald.

The initial technology for spoken-word recordings was the aluminum disk, used in the 1930s by the anthropologist J. P. Harrington to record oral histories of Native

Americans. Thomas recorded his poetry onto a vinyl record, which held approximately 45 minutes of material; his inclusion of 'A Child's Christmas in Wales' for side two supposedly occurred because he did not carry enough poetry with him to Steinway Hall to fill both sides of the record, and someone was dispatched to find a copy of a year-old *Harper's Bazaar in which the story had first appeared, the bookshops being closed for a holiday.

The late 1970s saw an increased interest in audio books as the technology turned to the more portable cassette tape. In America, Recorded Books (1979) and, in Britain, Chivers Audio Books (1980) worked with professional actors to produce their recordings. Chivers saw the potential for libraries as part of their market, and consulted librarians about everything from titles to packaging. Abridged audio books also became more prevalent at this time.

As the population of the developed world ages, audio book use is increasing sharply, although the average age of listeners is dipping slightly due to the number of children and young people who are using spoken-word materials. Other demographic trends include higher household incomes of users and their tendency to read a greater number of printed books. Library statistics in Europe and America indicate that growth in audio book circulation is outpacing that of other materials. Increased commuting times and the prevalence of book clubs have also contributed to audio books' popularity. According to the Audio Publishers Association, the size of the audio book market in the 2001–3 fiscal year was more than $800 million, making it a significant aspect of late-20th-century publishing.

Although cassette tapes are still usually available in libraries, both CD and, increasingly, downloadable digital formats are widely available for individual rental and purchase. Virtually all top-selling book titles are formatted as audio books in abridged and unabridged versions. In 2006, the first audio-only novel, Brian Luff's *Sex on Legs*, a 75,000-word, six-hour-long science fiction story, was recorded in England. *See also* BLIND, BOOKS FOR THE; TALKING BOOK. KAW

Aufbau-Verlag German publishing house founded in 1945 in East Berlin. It became a famous publisher of exiled authors (e.g. Brecht) and of contemporary fiction in the GDR. In 1990 it passed into private hands. US
C. Wurm, *Jeden Tag ein Buch. 50 Jahre Aufbau-Verlag 1945–1995* (1995)

Augereau, Antoine (*c.*1485–1534) Protestant Parisian printer and punchcutter, born in Fontenay-le Comte (Poitou). *Garamont's teacher, he printed three editions of *Marguerite de Navarre's *Miroir de l'âme pécheresse*. Arrested in connection with the publication of anti-Catholic pamphlets, he was hanged at Place Maubert on Christmas Eve 1534. VAG

Augsburg, Stadtbibliothek Founded in 1537 as a reformed city library with collections from dissolved monasteries, its first catalogue was printed in 1600. After Augsburg became part of Bavaria (1805–6), the library (renamed Staats- und Stadtbibliothek) acquired collections from other dissolved monastic houses. Today, the collections comprise 3,762 MSS and 2,797 *incunables. BW

August the Younger, duke of Braunschweig-Lüneburg (1579–1666) Collector and founder of the *Wolfenbüttel Library. Inspired by the Baroque ideal of universal learning, the scholarly prince, interested in theology and history, started a 'Bibliotheca Selenica' at Hitzacker in 1604, employing a network of correspondents. After his succession to the dukedom (1635), the newly named 'Bibliotheca Augusta' was transferred to the see of Wolfenbüttel in 1644. At his death it consisted of 135,000 titles in 40,000 uniform volumes that form the core of the present research library, including a catalogue in six folio volumes compiled by himself. JWUS
LGB

Augustus Frederick, Prince, duke of Sussex (1773–1843) Sixth son of George III, book collector. With the assistance of his surgeon and librarian Thomas Pettigrew (1791–1865) he assembled a library of over 50,000 books and MSS. It included large collections of bibles, *incunabula, history, and topography. His books were sold by Evans between July 1844 and August 1845 and realized over £19,000. ASGE
de Ricci

Aureus, Codex Stockholm, Royal Library MS A. 135 is a *gospel book in *uncial script that was probably produced at St Augustine's Abbey, Canterbury in the mid-8th century and has stylistic links to other MSS produced there, such as the *Vespasian Psalter. Its sumptuous decoration probably led to it being looted by Norse raiders in the 8th century and later ransomed, and donated to Christ Church, Canterbury. Post-Dissolution the MS reached Spain where, in 1690, it was purchased for the Swedish royal family. ASGE
J. J. G. Alexander, *Insular Manuscripts, 6th to the 9th Century* (1978)

Aureus of St Emmeram, Codex Munich, Bayerische Staatsbibliothek, MS clm. 14000 is a large *gospel book made for Charlemagne's grandson, the emperor Charles the Bald. Copied by two named *scribes, it was completed in 870 and later presented to the monastery of *St Emmeram in Regensburg. It is one of the most elaborate surviving books of this kind, particularly notable for the high quality of its full-page miniatures (*see* MINIATURE (1)) and its extensive use of *gold leaf and purple *vellum. The MS is bound in a sumptuous gold and jewelled *treasure binding. ASGE
R. Calkins, *Illuminated Books of the Middle Ages* (1983)

Aurispa, Giovanni (1376–1459) Sicilian humanist. He was (with Poggio *Bracciolini) the most fortunate Renaissance discoverer of literature, in his case chiefly of Greek texts. Several trips to the East allowed him to introduce to Italy: Aeschylus, Sophocles, Euripides, Aristophanes, Plutarch, Thucydides, Plato entire, and apparently the poems of the pre-Socratic philosopher Empedocles, now lost again. To his contemporaries, he was more a merchant in MSS than a reader of them.

MCD

Austin, Richard (1756–1832) English *punchcutter, *engraver, and from 1815 *typefounder. When the publisher J. *Bell established a typefoundry for his new press in 1787, he issued specimens of Austin's type (1788) 'cut upon new, and … very improved principles' reflecting not only *Baskerville, but for the first time in England also the *Didots. Austin cut *Porson's *Greek (1806–8), and *modern face types for Miller (c.1809), A. *Wilson (c.1812), and his own foundry. Three sons worked in the field, George (1783?–1834) as Richard's partner (1821) and successor.

JAL

A. Johnston, *Transitional Faces* (forthcoming)

Australia, National Library of (Canberra, Australia) NLA's origins date from the federation of the Australian colonies in 1901. The Commonwealth Parliamentary Library fulfilled the functions of a national library (intended to emulate the Library of *Congress) until 1960, when NLA was established as an autonomous entity. In addition to its *legal deposit role, provision of reference services from its own collections (now totalling around 6 million items), and an active publishing programme, NLA's operations include management of Libraries Australia (the national bibliographic database), and coordination of other national projects such as Picture Australia, and Pandora (Australia's Internet archive).

IM

ALIAS

Australian Book Review (*ABR*) Edited by Max Harris, Geoffrey Dutton, and Rosemary Wighton 1961–73; resumed with National Book Council support in 1978, and now established as Australia's premier reviewing journal. *ABR*'s longest-serving recent editors have been John McLaren (1978–86), Rosemary Sorensen (1989–94), Helen Daniel (1994–2000), and Peter Rose (from 2001).

IM

Australian Scholarly Editions Centre Established in 1993 at the University of New South Wales to coordinate, on behalf of the Australian Academy of the Humanities, the Academy Editions of Australian Literature project (ten scholarly editions, 1996–2007). Directed by the project's general editor, Paul Eggert, the Centre was the first of its kind in Australia, involving scholars from many universities and, for thirteen years, facilitating editorial and bibliographical scholarship: the final five scholarly editions in the 'Colonial Texts' series (1988–2004); an Australian literary bibliography series; an 'Occasional Papers' series; conferences, workshops, and developmental work on electronic editions.

PE

www.unsw.adfa.edu.au/ASEC/index.html, consulted July 2007

Austrian National Library (Österreichische Nationalbibliothek) One of the great libraries of the world, the OeNB is international in scope. Founded in the second half of the 14ᵗʰ century as the heir to the Habsburg Imperial Court Library, the library now houses 8.7 million objects in ten collections, including *papyri and MSS, books and periodicals, *broadsides and posters, music, portraits and photographs, electronic media, and globes, as well as 4,000 *incunabula. During the Nazi era (1938–45), approximately 400–500,000 objects looted from Jewish and other libraries came to the OeNB. Some of them were given to other libraries, but some 52,000 objects have been, or are being, returned. The monumental Baroque library was built by J. B. Fischer von Erlach in 1723–6. The library of Prince *Eugene of Savoy is now housed in the State Hall. The rich private library of the Habsburgs (Fideikommiss-Bibliothek) was added in 1921, and an Austrian Literary Archive established in 1989. Since 1946, the OeNB has compiled the *Österreichische Bibliographie*.

PRF

M. G. Hall and C. Köstner, '… *allerlei für die Nationalbibliothek zu ergattern* … ': *Eine österreichische Institution in der NS-Zeit* (2006)

H. W. Lang, ed., *Handbuch der historischen Buchbestände in Österreich*, vol. 1 (1994)

Austrian State Printing Office (Österreichische Staatsdruckerei, Vienna) Established by V. Degen in 1804 as the Hof- und Staatsdruckerei, to produce official documents. Under von Welsbach's direction, it acquired many foreign *founts and added a publishing branch. Specializing in bank notes and stamps, it has been Print Media AG since 1999.

PRF

A. Durstmüller, *500 Jahre Druck in Österreich* (3 vols, 1982–8)

authorial intention Before the later 20ᵗʰ century, the idea that an editor aimed to present a text that embodied the intentions of its author was generally accepted implicitly, and was usually stated only rhetorically, if at all (though there were always complications, such as final intention, and authorial revision). Such a consensus has been harder to find since the 1980s. Questioning the notion of authorial intention has been a concomitant of the recent development of criticism interested in the sociology of texts, led by the writings of *McKenzie and *McGann. Specifically, the editing of texts that are meant to represent or reconstruct an authorially intended version has been criticized for idealism, and for working against the endemic nature of textual instability. Such criticism, perceiving the creation of texts as fundamentally a social action by collaborative forces in production—book designers, compositors and printers, binders (and, according to some scholars, readers)—views the pursuit of authorial intention as an ultimate impossibility, or just one factor among many. The most extensive response to this general critique has been provided by *Tanselle, who finds its premises exaggerated, arguing that the pursuit of an author's intention aims to discover not a perfect and ahistorical ideal text, but rather a contingent contribution towards understanding a work at one historical moment. Moreover, he suggests, critical editions have always acknowledged both their own subjectivity and the instability of texts, by the very fact of their textual reconstruction from different stages. The debate continues between those who see the investigation of authorial intent as a pragmatic editorial function and those who question its rationale. ASR

J. J. McGann, *A Critique of Modern Textual Criticism* (1983)
G. T. Tanselle, 'The Editorial Problem of Final Authorial Intention', *SB* 29 (1976), 167–211
— 'Textual Criticism and Literary Sociology', *SB* 44 (1991), 83–143

Authorized Version of the Bible At the beginning of the 17th century, two English versions of the Bible were current: the official Bishops' Bible, first published in 1568 and nearly always a *black-letter *folio; and the Geneva Bible, a handier volume first published in 1560, printed in *roman type, aimed at the popular market, and including distinctively Puritan notes. The translation produced by Roman Catholic scholars at Douai and Rheims circulated little in England.

A revised *translation of the Scriptures was mooted at a conference convened by James I in 1604. Fifty-four scholars were chosen; the 47 actual participants formed six subcommittees, meeting at Oxford, Cambridge, and Westminster. Each group was assigned certain books of the Bible; their first drafts were sent to the other groups for criticism, and a final text was edited by a revision committee, convened at Stationers' Hall.

As the 'Preface of the Translators' states, their task was not to produce a translation *de novo*, but to revise the Bishops' Bible (itself heavily dependent on Tyndale's version) in the light of the original Hebrew and Greek. They adopted some better renderings from Geneva and Douai while avoiding those versions' sectarian terminology, confining their notes to *glosses on Hebrew and Greek names and technical terms. Most of the translators were already beneficed with Church and university posts, and appear to have worked unpaid; the members of the revision committee, however, were generously rewarded for their work, partly at least by the *Stationers' Company.

The final text (the MS of which seems to have survived until the Great Fire of London) was published in 1611 by R. Barker, the *King's Printer, who paid £3,500 for the patent. The two *issues (or perhaps *impressions) of 1611—known after a key textual divergence as 'He' and 'She'—suggest that two establishments cooperated in the printing. The handsome engraved title of this substantial black-letter *lectern bible proclaims (inaccurately) that it had been 'newly translated out of the originall tongues', and that it was 'appointed to be read in churches'. A *duodecimo edition of the New Testament alone appeared in the same year. *Quarto and *octavo editions of the entire Bible printed wholly in roman appeared in 1612; a folio edition of 1616 containing some revisions to the text was also printed in roman, as were most subsequent editions.

The Authorized Version was never formally authorized by king, Church, or Parliament; it nevertheless immediately superseded the Bishops' Bible in public worship. It has often been described as a masterpiece of classical English prose, even though the translators (except Lancelot Andrewes) were not notable stylists. Although its prose rhythms, tone, and much of its vocabulary descend from Tyndale's version of 80 years earlier, its language would not have seemed self-consciously archaic in 1611. It had to compete for pre-eminence with the Geneva Bible, which continued to be preferred in Puritan circles, until the Restoration swept that 'disloyal' version out of print and (surprisingly soon) out of memory.

Although the modern reader may find its archaisms of language and syntax a hindrance, the Authorized Version is still often preferred for declamation on formal occasions. By certain fundamentalist Christians in America (where it is usually called the King James Version) it is regarded as the sole authentic record in English of the utterances of God. Its English *copyright is still a Crown possession; only the Queen's Printer (currently *Cambridge University Press) and other patentees have the right to print it, although its reduced share of the market has made this privilege no longer lucrative. BJF

The Bible: King James Version, ed. D. Norton (2006)
CHB

author–publisher agreements Contractual agreements between authors of books and publishers of those books have been and remain an essential instrument for an orderly market in commercial book publishing.

1. Contract and copyright
2. Terms of agreement
3. Rights and obligations
4. Historical practices

1. Contract and copyright

As with contracts more generally, agreements between authors and publishers aim to establish a relationship of confidence between the contracting parties, to their mutual benefit. In theory, author–publisher agreements manifest the freedom that is held to ground the liberal, free-market economy by securing the rights of the contracting parties in a manner that can be tested at law. In practical terms, such agreements impose a high degree of legal formalization on an activity of intellectual creation and cultural dissemination. Author–publisher contracts now constitute a routine but indispensable component in the juridical governance of the book trade. They operate alongside other bodies of law, notably *copyright. Contract and copyright are complementary but not coterminous instruments. Each has its own existence and area of operation, although in the more completely codified context of French law, the statutory conditions for author–publisher agreements (*le contrat d'édition*) are detailed in Articles L132–1 to L132–17 of the Intellectual Property Code.

2. Terms of agreement

The author–publisher agreement defines the terms of a basic exchange: from the author, the publisher acquires the exclusive entitlement to publish, market, and distribute the work and, in turn, incurs an obligation to provide a measure of remuneration to compensate the creator of the work. In short, the agreement confers on the publisher a licence to exploit the author's creation. Athough varying in detail from publisher to publisher, the essential terms of this contractual exchange display a generic resemblance. They establish agreement between author and publisher on the length and nature of the work, the form and date of delivery of the completed MS, and the format or formats of publication. The nature and amount of the publisher's remuneration to the author are specified, in the form either of a one-off payment or of a *royalty or percentage of income from sales, on which an *advance payment may be offered. A schedule of royalty payments is conventionally included. As their part of the agreement, authors undertake to guarantee that the work does not infringe an existing copyright. The author is also required to confirm that the work does not contain defamatory, obscene, or privacy-invading matter that might render the publisher liable to legal action. In some contracts, the author undertakes to indemnify the publisher's costs in the event of such legal action. The agreement becomes binding only when signed by both parties.

3. Rights and obligations

Each side thus incurs a number of definite legal obligations. Yet it remains a moot point whether such agreements emerge from a negotiation between author and publisher as equals, free of all undue influence. Inequality might be blatant where the author's status is that of a novice. Here, the publisher proposes, the author accepts. Yet an established author, armed with *literary agent and lawyer, is not without trumps, as manifested in the 21st century in the form of spectacular advance payments on the scale of *Bloomsbury's *Harry Potter. It is important to recognize that—for the author—*rights are multiple. Copyright now comports a veritable 'bundle' of positive rights, each assignable to different persons and for different periods. In addition to the primary rights of reproduction, publication, distribution, and sale, the rights owner enjoys a proliferating array of secondary or subsidiary rights to license *adaptations, *serializations, reprints, *translations, broadcasts, *digitizations, and so on. As economic rights, these attach to the work and to whoever owns its copyright, unlike the subjective *moral rights of attribution and integrity that attach to the person of the work's creator.

4. Historical practices

The very existence of this panoply of rights differentiates today's author–publisher agreement from the simple 'registration of sale of property' agreements whereby members of the early modern *Stationers' Company purchased an author's MS, acquiring thereby perpetual title and exclusive right of property in the work. An anachronistic outrage might now be professed at the act of 'dispossession' that, in 1667, saw a blind Milton sell the right to copy *Paradise Lost* to the Stationer, Samuel Simmons, for just £10 (with an additional £5 each for the second and third editions). Yet outright sale remained normal through the following century. In 1730 James Thomson received £150 for his *Seasons*, and in 1749 Henry Fielding £700 for *Tom Jones*, each author selling his copyright to the publisher A. *Millar, subsequently a litigant in the landmark copyright case of *Millar vs Taylor (1769). By 1855, however, Elizabeth Gaskell was contracting with her publisher, *Chapman & Hall, for what some have called the earliest royalty agreement in publishing history. In the same year, Charles Reade indicated to the American publisher *Ticknor & Fields that he favoured the American royalty system over the British joint-profit agreement. Hence, the slogan of the Victorian *Society of Authors' accountability campaign against exploitative English publishers: 'No Secret Profits.' Meanwhile, the American publishers profited by not paying royalties to foreigners.

In the 21st century, a functioning publishing market has to provide publishers with a fair return on investment and authors an adequate incentive to produce future works. The administration of an author–publisher agreement can involve actors other than the two protagonists. In addition to literary agents, the British publishing scene since 2006 has been administered in part by a Collective Rights Management Agreement reached between the Publishers Licensing Society and the Authors' Licensing and Collecting Society. This development marks a 'collectivization' of what had been—or was often imagined to be—an exemplary personal, even private relation between publisher and author. This agreement is intended to contribute to the more effective administration of rights—for both authors and publishers—in the 'information age' of digitized print. DS

J. P. Feather, *Publishing, Piracy and Politics* (1994)
J. A. Sutherland, *Victorian Novelists and Publishers* (1976)

Authors Guild The oldest and largest US association of published authors. The Guild, which began as the Authors' League of America in 1912, has its headquarters in New York and has 78,000 members, all of whom have published at least one book or several articles not at their own expense. The Guild lobbies for authors' interests in such matters as copyright, taxation, and freedom of expression. It files suit on behalf of authors, sometimes together with publishers' organizations and sometimes in opposition, and it frequently files *amicus curiae* briefs. The Guild provides numerous resources for members: legal services, including contract review; the 'Model Trade Book Contract and Guide'; a republication service for members' out-of-print books; seminars on subjects such as marketing, contracts, and web pages; webhosting and design services; symposia on topics of interest to members; and access to health insurance. It publishes the quarterly *Authors Guild Bulletin*. BEL
www.authorsguild.org, consulted July 2008

authorship In early modern English 'author' signified a writer who was regarded as an authority. Today, the word suggests a different definition: 'the originator or inventor of anything', or 'one who sets forth written statements; the composer or writer of a treatise or book'. Authorship thus relates chiefly to those who write for the attention of a reading public. Such a definition underlies the law of *copyright and the notion of intellectual property. The writer of an original work may assert his *moral rights as its author; as the legal owner of copyright, he has exclusive control over the publication and distribution of his work until he assigns or sells those *rights.

Originality is generally considered a condition of authorship, although some modern literary theory has denied that there is such a thing. According to Roland Barthes, all texts (however 'original' in the mind of their writers) are 'tissues of quotations from innumerable centres of culture'. His object was to undermine the received notion that the only valid meaning of a text is that which its author intended, and that the reader's task is to discover what that intention is. However, it would be absurd to apply this analysis to all forms of writing. In most academic subjects, for example, knowledge is advanced largely by the publication of genuinely ground-breaking discoveries. This is of course an area in which questions of *plagiarism (Lat., *plagiarius*, 'a kidnapper') arise most acutely—the crime of stealing not the legal rights created by publication, but an author's words and ideas. Academic plagiarists (a rare breed, despite the pressing need to publish or perish) would be ill-advised to excuse their frauds by appealing to the doctrines of Barthes and his followers. *Love more fruitfully describes literary authorship as 'a repertoire of practices [and] techniques … whose nature has varied considerably across the centuries'. It is not a single coherent activity, but 'a series of functions performed during the creation of a work', which may include being influenced by conversations, by literary and historical sources, by the Zeitgeist, and even by divine inspiration. Authors may consciously or unconsciously absorb the work of earlier writers; they may also choose to create a kind of mosaic, embedding in their writing striking images and phrases culled from their reading.

From this perspective, it is virtually impossible to write without borrowing from others; if no author can be wholly original, every author must to some extent be a plagiarist. Proust's cork-lined room may have been a powerful symbol of his desire to exclude all external influences from his writing, but (as Love suggests) even an introspective magnum opus needs 'a long roll-out of credits at the end'. Against this view can be set Coleridge's classic distinction between the 'talented author, who knows well how to apply the knowledge of others', and the author of 'real genius'. It is probable that entirely original voices may still be heard, for there are evidently many kinds of authorship, not all of them amenable to literary theory.

It is often said that the concept of authorship came into existence only in the 18th century; indeed, the word is cited in the *OED* (*see* NEW [OXFORD] ENGLISH DICTIONARY) only after 1710. Forty years earlier, Dryden had distinguished between gentlemen who write merely for pleasure (and perhaps circulate their writing only in MS

among friends) and those who get their bread by writing (and hope to sell as many copies of their work as possible). The latter had emerged in England at least by the later 16th century, as pamphleteers and 'hack' playwrights. However, it is anachronistic to describe them as 'professional' authors; even in 18th-century usage, a 'professed author' (unlike a 'professed cook') was merely one whose name appeared on the *title-page of his book.

It has also been suggested that the use of 'author' (rather than 'writer') might indicate a higher degree of seriousness or ambition; but evidence for this is neither abundant nor conclusive. Milton's English works, for example, mostly bear 'The Author *J. Milton*' (or a close variation) on the title. If this idiosyncratic formula was the author's own preference, he clearly did not reserve it exclusively for his 'serious' works of epic poetry.

The 18th century nevertheless merits S. *Johnson's description as 'the age of authors', a time when writing was becoming recognized as a potentially respectable as well as rewarding means of earning a living. Under no illusions about his own or other authors' practical motives for writing, Johnson declared in the Preface to his *Dictionary* that the 'chief glory of every people arises from its authours'. He regarded authorship as an index of the intellectual life and vigour of society, deserving (at its best) dignity, respect, and authority.

By *c*.1800, authorship could plausibly be claimed as one of the professions, although Coleridge, perhaps ironically, equates 'the profession of literature' with 'the trade of authorship'. Successful authors of the ensuing century were often dignified as 'men of letters', distancing them from the 'unfledged MS authors' who besieged the publisher *Murray, and from the whole tribe of commercial wordsmiths.

Not all authors wish to be identified: since the time of Xenophon, they have sometimes found it prudent to resort to *anonymity or *pseudonymity. A named author can be held legally responsible for his opinions; when these are judged offensive, libellous, or heretical, his imprisonment, exile, or execution may result. Much 16th- and 17th-century theological polemic was pseudonymous, with the hope of protecting the authors from personal abuse or ecclesiastical censure. Well into the 19th century, 'gentlemen' authors, when coaxed into print, could still shrink from the publicity thought to be inconsistent with their station. 'Lewis Carroll' begged to be excluded from the first edition of *Halkett and Laing's *Dictionary of Anonymous and Pseudonymous Literature*, fearing the 'notoriety' of being identified; many less sensitive dons have resorted to a pen name for their detective stories and other parerga.   BJF

D. Griffin, 'The Rise of the Professional Author?', in *CHBB* 5
H. Love, *Attributing Authorship* (2002)

Authors' League of America A membership organization, founded in 1912, that represents the interests of authors and playwrights. It is composed of two guilds. The *Authors Guild represents writers of poetry and prose fiction and non-fiction. The Dramatists Guild represents approximately 6,000 playwrights, composers, and lyricists writing for the stage. It provides model contracts; acts as an advocate for its members in matters of *copyright, freedom of expression, and taxation; and provides educational programmes. The Authors League Fund makes interest-free loans to professional writers in times of financial crisis.   BEL

author's proof A corrected, 'clean' first proof, sent to the author for checking. *See also* FIRST PROOF; GALLEY PROOF; PROOFS AND PROOFREADING.

authors' societies and communities Organizations whose mission is to advance the rights and careers of authors, freedom of expression, and the appreciation of the written word. Membership organizations include large, influential international societies (e.g. *PEN) and, in the US, for example, regional, state, and local organizations; unions (the Writers' Guild, representing those who write for films); well-organized advocacy and educational groups (the *Authors Guild); and informal gatherings. Some are confined to a single genre (the Academy of American Poets, Mystery Writers of America, National Association of Science Writers). Some are highly specialized (the Cat Writers' Association, the Dog Writers' Association). Membership qualifications also vary, from the exclusive *American Academy of Arts and Letters to amateur poetry societies that welcome anyone who wishes to participate. Many give prizes.

Authors' communities are residential facilities that offer fellowships to writers so that they can focus on their work with little distraction, in the company of other creative artists. There are roughly 200 such communities in the US, scattered across the country. The most famous are Yaddo, in Saratoga Springs, New York, founded in 1900, and the MacDowell Colony, founded in New Hampshire in 1907.   BEL

Autobiography of Malcolm X, The A classic of the mid-20th century American Civil Rights era, *The Autobiography of Malcolm X* extended the black narrative tradition of radical self-invention in Frederick Douglass and Ralph Ellison. It also marked itself as part of a new media genre—the 'as told to' celebrity book. With a father killed by vigilantes and a mother plunged into insanity, Malcolm Little (1925–65) moves from life as a petty criminal and jailbird to celebrity in the Black Muslim movement and spokesperson for Black Power. The work ends with the protagonist's assassination.

The *Autobiography*, published by *Grove Press (where Gilbert Sorrentino was the book's in-house editor), became a bestseller and, then, a book routinely assigned in US classrooms. Its ghostwriter, Alex Haley, went on to write *Roots* (1976), a book and media event that did as much for African-American identity as any production of the era. The *Autobiography* was published in England by Hutchinson (1966) and by *Penguin in 1968, and was the basis of a successful 1992 film, directed by Spike Lee. *Time Magazine* hailed the book as one of the ten most important non-fiction works of the 20th century.   PDB
www.brothermalcolm.net/introduction.html, consulted July 2008

autograph Any kind of MS containing the handwriting of the composer of the work or document in which it appears. The term can apply to a document that includes a signature, or can describe the whole MS. In the former case, it may signify no more than ownership or identity. In the latter instance, it is synonymous with *holograph. Autographs of either kind are often the focus of collectors or scholars interested in authorial documents. The oldest autograph literary MS in English is the 12th-century *Ormulum*.   ASGE
A. N. L. Munby, *The Cult of the Autograph Letter* (1962)

autograph book (album) A printed or *blank book for collecting *autographs and other occasional texts by celebrities and friends. It originates in the 16th-century German *album amicorum*, in which male students collected memorial contributions from mentors and peers. This association with immaturity continued when the genre was feminized in the late 18th century; it was identified with children and adolescents from the mid-19th century. Well-connected collectors carried *albums when travelling or socializing to secure prestigious contributions (what Charles Lamb called the 'albumean persecution'). Until *c*.1850, autographs were recorded in elegantly bound blank books. True autograph books contain personal *inscriptions by their owners' peers; by contrast, the album or *scrapbook (stigmatized as a commercially motivated form) is characterized by autographs of historical and contemporary notables cut and pasted from MSS, explaining the many signatures missing from archival documents.

Advances in printing technology, allowing images, decoration, and *letterpress to be printed affordably on the same page, encouraged a competitive market in novelty printed autograph books, a specialized branch of the flourishing late Victorian *gift book and stationery industry. The characteristic 16mo *landscape format book with coloured pages (still the most common format) was established *c*.1870.

Victorian special-interest groups exploited the popularity of autograph collecting, adapting the concept to a domestic context and instructive content, as with the autographic and scriptural *birthday books published by *Bagster. The genre's democratization is graphically expressed in this transferred responsibility for wise or witty sayings from the signer to the compiler; many Victorian autograph books are also anthologies of epigraphs.

The confession album or 'character book' is a significant subgenre: it contains multiple copies of a questionnaire that contributors completed to create miniature autobiographies. Originating in courtship rituals and parlour games, the confession album was unusual in being popular with both men and women. Literary biographers use 'confessions' as sources for lives (Oscar Wilde, Marcel Proust), but such documents also provide valuable information about reading practices and cultural history.

The production values and ingenuity of autograph books declined in the early-20th century, but a strong folk tradition continued among children and adolescents: American anthropologists have used 20th-century autograph verses to map regional cultural practices. From the 1960s, printed albums became more overtly commercial, as themed albums were aimed at fans of film stars, footballers, and television series. However, the decline of handwriting in the digital age is reviving interest in the unique qualities of personal and handmade albums. SM

M. A. E. Nickson, *Early Autograph Albums in the British Museum* (1970)

Auvergne French region, among the first in the country to develop papermaking; a mill reputedly founded there in 1326 still operates as a working museum.

Avery, Samuel Putnam (1822–1904) American book collector. Avery was a prominent art dealer who was an important figure in the development of the *New York Public and *Columbia University libraries. To the former, he donated, in 1900, his collection of nearly 18,000 prints. To Columbia, he gave his books on architecture, now housed in the Avery Architectural Library, which also holds his collection of works on the history of bookbinding. ASGE
DABC

aviary [Lat. *avis*, 'bird'] A discursive and descriptive catalogue, typically illustrated, about birds, their habits, and habitats. In their most developed form, they are arguably among the world's most beautiful books. Books about birds can be traced to Pliny the Elder's 1st-century AD *Naturalis Historia*, through Pierre Belon's *L'Histoire de la nature des oyseaux* (1555), to Francis Willughby's and John Ray's *Ornithologia* (1676). The 18th century witnessed the maturation of the genre, one increasingly delimited by regional or national boundaries, in works such as Mark Catesby's *Natural History of Carolina* (1731–43) or *Bewick's *British Birds* (1797–1804). Illustrations became more commonplace in aviary books to enhance reports of new species from European exploring expeditions and from colonials around the world; notable examples include John Latham's *A General Synopsis of Birds* (1781–5), an ornithology of Australian birds, and François Le Vaillant's *Histoire naturelle des oiseaux d'Afrique* (1796–1808). Aviary books reached their apotheosis in the 19th century with the publication of Audubon's monumental *Birds of America* (1827–38) and the British naturalist John Gould's magnificent *Birds of Australia* (1840–48) and *Monograph of Trochilidae* (1861–7). Aviary books and the *plates of these volumes (Gould and Audubon particularly) are sought after by collectors and command extraordinary prices for well-preserved examples.

Audubon's and Gould's books are distinguished from previous ornithological works by their hand-coloured etched and lithographic plates, which represent birds alone or in same-species groups in true-to-life poses and habitats. Their books, and those that followed, depart from previous authors who arranged birds randomly, alphabetically, or taxonomically using a system other than that of Linnaeus. Additionally, many previous authors tended to represent birds in interspecies groups—such as are found in Alexander Wilson's *American Ornithology* (1801–14)—rather than singly or in male–female pairs. Beginning in the early 19th century, authors worked to capture birds' vibrancy of life and colour in their natural habitats, eschewing artificial poses and taxidermic qualities. Such changes in aviary books are attributable to the embrace of *lithography over *etching and *engraving and to authors working from preserved skins or freshly killed field specimens.

Until the early 20th century, most aviary books appeared in multi-*volume sets, many of them printed in *folio or larger *formats, making them extraordinarily expensive and difficult (if not impossible) to consult in the field. Owing to the popularity of bird identification, working ornithologists began in the early 20th century to organize field guides arranged taxonomically, with descriptions of species size, distribution, and habits. In 1934 Roger Tory Peterson, an American naturalist, published his *Guide to Birds*, a pocket-sized volume that employed paintings of similar species together with arrows indicating distinguishing features to facilitate quick identification. With the rise of inexpensive field guides and scientific specialization, the publication of large-format aviary books has largely ceased. AJL

J. Anker, *Bird Books and Bird Art* (1938)
L. Barber, *The Heyday of Natural History, 1820–1870* (1980)
M. Cocker and R. Mabey, *Birds Britannica* (2005)
P. L. Farber, *Discovering Birds: The Emergence of Ornithology as a Scientific Discipline, 1760–1850* (1996)
M. Walters, *A Concise History of Ornithology* (2003)

Avignon, Bibliothèque municipale Seat of the papacy from 1305 to 1378, Avignon became French during the Revolution and the 25,000 books and 610 MSS confiscated at that time constituted the nucleus of the public library, which opened in 1806. In 1826 it merged with the Museum Calvet (formed by Esprit Calvet's 1810 donation of his art and book collection). Enriched by gifts such as the collection of the Félibre (Provençal writer) Paul Mariéton in 1911, the library was moved from the museum building in 1982 to impressive new premises (a restored 14th-century cardinal's palace), which by 2000 housed nearly 300,000 volumes. VAG

Avon Books *Paperback publisher founded in 1941 by the *American News Co. when it lost its distribution contract for *Pocket Books. Avon published *mysteries, westerns, and other genre fiction. In 1959, it was bought by the *Hearst Corporation, which provided the capital the firm needed to improve its list. Its first bestseller, a reprint of Henry Roth's 1934 novel, *Call It Sleep*, sold more than a million copies. In the 1960s and 1970s, its bestsellers included Robin Moore's *The Green Berets*, Bel Kaufman's *Up the Down Staircase*, Thomas Harris's *I'm OK—You're OK*, Richard Adams's *Watership Down*, and Richard Bach's *Jonathan Livingston Seagull*. Avon also began publishing paperback originals. In the

1970s, Avon revived its 'Bard' series of literary fiction and launched the Camelot young adult series. Its biggest enterprise of the 1970s, however, was venturing into *romance fiction. The firm quickly became dominant in historical romances, a field that it still promotes heavily. In 1999, when the News Corporation bought Hearst's book division, Avon became an *imprint of *HarperCollins, under whose umbrella it has added imprints publishing erotica and contemporary women's fiction. BEL

K. C. Davis, *Two-Bit Culture* (1984)

Awqāf Library, Baghdad The Central Library of Religious Endowments (*Awqāf*) was created in 1928 from separate endowed MSS and rare book collections of the Ottoman period; others were added later. In 2003, following the US invasion, the library was sacked and many of its old and rare Arabic books burnt. GJR

'Awwād, Kurkīs (1908–92) Iraqi bibliographer and codicologist. In the course of his long career he produced, to high scholarly standards, a large number of Arabic and other MS catalogues and surveys, as well as systematic enumerative bibliographies of the writings of Iraqis and other Arabs. GJR

Ayer, Edward E. (1841–1927) American book collector. Ayer collected books and MSS on American Indians. In 1911, his library became part of the *Newberry Library, of which he was a trustee; it has continued to be enlarged through his endowment and is one of the foremost collections on Native Americans. His substantial ornithological collection was donated to the Field Museum in Chicago. ASGE

F. Lockwood, *The Life of Edward E. Ayer* (1929)

Aylmer, Brabazon (1645–*c*.1719) London bookseller. A leading publisher of religious literature, Aylmer included amongst his authors his friend Milton, the Calvinist Isaac Barrow, Bishop John Tillotson, and the anti-Quaker George Keith. He purchased the *copyright of *Paradise Lost* from Samuel Simmons, but did not publish it. CYF

ODNB

Ayres, John (d. 1704×9) English *writing-master, and author of a number of copybooks. Although not opposed to calligraphic elaboration in *letterforms, Ayres was best known for his clear 'round', Italian-derived hand. His views on *calligraphy, and fellow calligraphers, were expressed in various *editions of *The Accomplish'd Clerk or Accurate Penman* (first published *c*.1683) and in other *volumes printed in the late 17th century. Samples

of his writing were included in *Bickham's *Universal Penman*. ASGE

Heal
ODNB

Ayscough, Samuel (1745–1804) English librarian and antiquary. Ayscough spent most of his working life in the British Museum (*see* BRITISH LIBRARY), where he undertook some prodigious feats of cataloguing. In 1782 his catalogue of the institution's undescribed MSS (some 5,000) appeared, and in 1787 a similar work on the printed books. He later compiled *indexes to the *Monthly Magazine* and the *Gentleman's Magazine*, as well as the earliest *concordance to the plays of *Shakespeare. ASGE

ODNB

A–Z London street atlas, created by Phyllis Isobel Pearsall (1906–96) in 1936. Finding herself lost in the capital, and that its last street map was made in 1919, she became determined to produce her own. Using Ordnance Survey sheets, she walked the capital eighteen hours a day to compile 23,000 index cards. The result was the *London A–Z Street Atlas*, published in 1936. That same year, Pearsall founded the Geographers' Map Company Ltd, which produced maps of the war fronts during the World War II and overcame later paper shortages by printing the A–Z in Holland. During the 1950s and 1960s, UK road atlases and 'premier' maps of cities such as Birmingham, Manchester, and Glasgow were introduced. In 1965 Pearsall founded Geographers' Map Trust, transferring all her shares into the trust in order to protect her loyal employees' jobs and the company's assets from takeover. The A–Z insignia was incorporated into the company title in 1972. After Pearsall's death, the firm continued to publish maps and street atlases in a variety of formats and bindings; it also introduced electronic versions for PCs, GPS devices, and mobile phones. JEP

ODNB

Azbukovnik Medieval Russian reference book, arranged according to the alphabet (*azbuka*). Azbukovniki evidently originated as glossaries to the Scriptures and were apparently compiled from earlier *glosses and *commentaries. They include not only foreign words (e.g. Greek and Hebrew) but also archaic or regional Slavonic words unfamiliar to the Russian reader. They also cover a much wider range of sources than the Bible, becoming more comprehensive with the passage of time. Definitions range from a single word to lengthy articles. They are usually found with other texts as part of a *miscellany. RMC

L. S. Kovtun, *Azbukovniki XVI–XVII vv.* (1999)

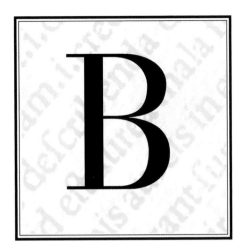

Baby and Child Care The paediatrician Benjamin Spock's *Commonsense Book of Baby and Child Care* was first published by *Pocket Books in 1946. In the same year, the 25c. paperback edition was published as *The Pocket Book of Baby and Child Care*. With seven revised editions between 1957 and 2004, it became an international *bestseller, second only to the Bible in American sales, with more than 50 million copies sold by the time of Spock's death in 1998. Translated into 39 languages, it continues to be *reissued and is currently in its eighth edition, having been updated and revised by Robert Needlman.

Written in cheerful, non-technical prose, *Baby and Child Care* gives advice in a tone expressing confidence in individual patterns of development as well as motherly instincts ('Trust Yourself: You Know More Than You Think You Do'). Many parents of the 'baby boom' generation abandoned rigid feeding, sleep, and toilet-training schedules to follow Spock's more responsive, child-centred approach. During the Vietnam War, when he aided the anti-war effort, Spock was sometimes criticized for promoting the permissiveness that nurtured an undisciplined generation; yet *Baby and Child Care* recommended firmness and consistency as well as affection. In the 1970s and 1980s, the book came under fire for its assumption that the child's welfare was entirely the mother's job. The fourth edition, published in 1976, gave expanded attention to the father's role, and later editions covered divorce and single-parent families. BH

back *See* SPINE.

backing *See* ROUNDING AND BACKING.

back in sections *See* COMPARTMENT.

backlist, publisher's Established titles in a publisher's list. Once the initial costs of publication have been recouped, backlist titles are usually more profitable than new books (the frontlist), although their unit sales may be lower. Publishers with secure backlist sales can count on a reliable source of income. Titles in the backlist have the potential to be revitalized with new covers or through new editions. If authors move publishing houses, their backlist may move with them, so that all their titles can be promoted together. A strong backlist will make a publisher more attractive for purchase by another publisher. AGP

backstrip *See* SPINE.

Badger & Co., Richard G. Boston-based *vanity press of the late 19th and early 20th centuries. Badger specialized in poetry and in works related to sex and psychoanalysis. The firm also published the magazine *Poet Lore*. Its most famous author was Edwin Arlington Robinson: in 1897, Badger issued 550 copies of *The Children of the Night*, a friend of Robinson's paying the publishing costs. Around 1917, Badger became proprietor of the Gorham Press, also a vanity undertaking. In 1929, the company absorbed the New York firm of Harold Vinal. JSR

Badier, Florimond (*fl.* 1630–60) Parisian bookbinder, noted for producing high-quality luxury bindings, characterized by the use of then-fashionable *pointillé tools. He began his apprenticeship in 1630 and became a master binder in 1645; little is known about his life. Attributions should be treated with caution, as numerous contemporary workshops produced similar bindings. DRSP

[Baltimore Museum of Art,] *The History of Bookbinding, 525–1950 A.D.* (1957)
R. Devauchelle, *La Reliure* (1995)

Badische Landesbibliothek Karlsruhe *See* WÜRTTEMBERG STATE LIBRARY.

Badius Ascensius, Jodocus (*c*.1461–1535) Paris printer and scholar of Flemish origin (Joost van Asshe), who began his career as corrector to Trechsel's *printing office in Lyons. He established his own in Paris in 1503, employing as his *printer's device the famous image of a press. His numerous editions of classical texts were often furnished with his own commentaries. Of his original works, the best-known is the *Stultiferae Naves* ('The Ships of Foolish Women'). FS

'bad' quartos of Shakespeare's plays A group of play texts by Shakespeare, printed in *quarto format during his lifetime, notable for their textual differences from, and perceived inferiority to, the longer and better-known versions of Shakespeare's plays. In 1909 A. W. *Pollard first identified a category of play texts he labelled 'bad' quartos, which came to include the first quartos of *2 Henry VI* (1594), *3 Henry VI* (1595), *Romeo and Juliet* (1597), *Henry V* (1600), *The Merry Wives of Windsor* (1602), and *Hamlet* (1603). Recent scholarship increasingly resists the long-dominant view according to which the 'bad' quartos are the result of memorial reconstruction by rogue actors and surreptitious publication by corrupt *stationers. Now believed to be legitimate publications that contain important information about how Shakespeare's plays were originally performed, the 'bad' quartos are often relabelled as 'early quartos' or 'short quartos'. LE
L. E. Maguire, *Shakespearean Suspect Texts* (1996)

Baedeker, Karl (1801–59) German publisher. In 1827, he founded a bookshop and publishing house in Koblenz (Rhineland). The rise of international tourism made his idea of publishing *travel guides for a new market successful. From 1832 the company published German, English, and French guides written by specialists for mass circulation. The popular small book series with redbound covers and the name 'Baedeker' became a model for subsequent travel manuals. In 1872 Baedeker's son Fritz relocated the expanding company in Leipzig. Destroyed in 1943, the publishing house was reopened in 1948 in Hamburg, and later based in Freiburg. In 1984 Baedeker became part of the MairDuMont group. US
D. Bessen, 'Karl Baedeker und die Reiseliteratur', in *Buchkultur inmitten der Industrie*, ed. D. Bessen and K. Wisotzky (2000)
A. W. Hinrichsen, *Baedekers Reisehandbücher 1832–1944* (1981)

Baer German antiquarian bookshop in Frankfurt, founded in 1785 by Joseph Baer. In the 19th and early 20th centuries, Baer was a modern, international company, specializing in autographs, *incunabula, German literature, and academic books. It was closed in 1944. US
F. H. Schwarz, 'Zur Geschichte des Firma Joseph Baer & Co. (1785–1944)', *Aus dem Antiquariat*, 29 (1973), A415–18

Bagford, John (1650/51–1716) London bookseller and antiquary. Trained as a shoemaker, Bagford was active as a bookseller from 1686. He served some of the greatest collectors of the day—including *Pepys, the *Harleys, *Sloane, and Moore—and earned the respect of such distinguished antiquaries and bibliographers as *Hearne and *Wanley. He is chiefly remembered for his collections (now in the *British Library) of English Restoration *ballads, and of fragments of early printed books and medieval MSS. The latter collections were intended to support his bibliographical research, particularly his account of the history of printing—an undertaking that was never fully published. He was vilified in the 19th century as a biblioclast, but is now better understood as a pioneering preserver of binding fragments, both MS and printed, that would otherwise have been lost. RAL
ODNB

Bagster, Samuel (1772–1851) London bible publisher. Since royal *privilege only covered unannotated bibles, Bagster published annotated *parallel texts: the *English *Polyglot* (1816), *Biblia Sacra Polyglotta Bagsteriana* (1817), and the *English Hexapla* (1841). He also compiled the popular religious *textbook *Daily Light on the Daily Path* (1841). PGS
ODNB

Bailey, Francis (1735?–1815) Pennsylvania publisher, printer, and bookseller. Taught by Peter Miller, at Ephrata, Bailey published the *Pennsylvanische Zeitungs-Blat* (1778), *United States Magazine* (1779), and *Freeman's Journal* (1781–92); he printed the *Supporter* (1800) for John Nicholson. Lydia Bailey, married to Bailey's son Robert, took over his Philadelphia printing business in 1808, continuing until 1861. SJW
ANB

Baine, John (1712/13–1790) Scottish typefounder. Partner and perhaps *punchcutter to A. *Wilson from 1742, in Dublin from 1747, leaving the partnership in 1749. After issuing a type specimen perhaps at London, he opened an Edinburgh typefoundry (1764), producing novel, *bold *romans and supplying printers in America. In 1787, he and his grandson moved to Philadelphia, establishing the first major American typefoundry, dissolved *c*.1799. JAL
SBTI
R. Silver, *Typefounding in America* (1965)

Bakalár, Mikuláš Štetina (*fl.* 1498–1513) Printer, editor, and translator of Slovak origin. He studied in Cracow and established a printing press in Pilsen, Western Bohemia, printing in the Czech language using the Schwabacher *type. His pre-1500 *imprints represent one quarter of all Czech-language *incunabula. DP

Baker, Thomas (1656–1740) Educated at St John's College, Cambridge, of which he became a fellow, Baker, a keen antiquary, amassed a library of more than 5,000 books and MSS. He collected material relating to his college and university, bibliographical works, early printing, and 16th-century theology. Much of his library survives in St John's and *Cambridge University Library. Deprived of his fellowship as a nonjuror, he inscribed his books 'Thomas Baker Collegii Johannis Socius Ejectus'.   ASGE

F. Korsten, *A Catalogue of the Library of Thomas Baker* (1990)
ODNB

Baker & Taylor   New York book wholesaler. Tracing its origins to 1828 and the Hartford binding and publishing firm D. F. Robinson & Co., the firm relocated to New York in 1835. From the 1870s it specialized in the wholesale distribution of books and *stationery, with a particular focus on the library trade. It has operated as Baker & Taylor since 1885, and remains one of the major American wholesale distributors.   MBW

Baldung, Hans, called **Grien** (1484/5–1545) German painter, printmaker, and illustrator. In 1503–*c*.1507 he probably worked with *Dürer in Nuremburg, designing woodcuts for Pinder's *Der beschlossen Gart des Rosenkrantz Marie* (1505) and *Speculum Passionis* (*c*.1507). Undoubtedly Dürer's most brilliant pupil, he produced slightly more than 400 *woodcuts for book illustration (*see* **16**) and about 150 single-sheet woodcuts. In Strassburg from 1509, he worked for several publishers, and in 1510–11 was among the first to produce prints using the recently invented technique of printing in colour from two or more blocks.   PHJG

G. Bartrum, *German Renaissance Prints 1490–1550* (1995)

Baldwin, Jr., Richard (1724–70) English bookseller. Son of a London bookseller, he was apprenticed to B. *Collins in Salisbury. Capitalizing on experience and contacts gained through Collins, he launched a successful career that included shareholding in the *London Magazine*.   CYF

C. Y. Ferdinand, 'Richard Baldwin Junior, Bookseller', *SB* 42 (1989), 254–64

Bale, John (1495–1563) English bibliographer. A Carmelite friar who turned Protestant polemicist, Bale also saw himself as *Leland's protégé. He brought into print the short work by Leland known as *The New Year's Gift* (1546) and produced his own listings of British authors, including the *Scriptorum Illustrium Maioris Brytannie … Catalogus* (1557–9). His fullest work, a *notebook comprising *Index Britanniae Scriptorum*, remained unpublished until 1902.   DGR
ODNB

Bales, Peter (1547–1610?) English *writing-master and calligrapher. Bales taught *calligraphy, made fair copies of documents, and later became tutor to Henry, Prince of Wales. His skill in 'micrographical' writing was so great that he copied a complete bible which could fit into a walnut shell. In 1590 he published *The Writing Schoolemaster*, one of the first engraved copybooks, which contained an early form of *shorthand.   ASGE
Heal
ODNB

Balfour, John (1715–95) Scottish bookseller and printer. Balfour began as a clerk in his brother-in-law Gavin Hamilton's bookshop, joining him for a time in partnership. With the printer Patrick Neill, their academic press published student texts and reprinted classics, including Scotland's first edition of *Shakespeare's works. They mentored *Smellie, with whom Balfour subsequently collaborated on the first Gaelic New Testament. While promoting Scottish literature, Balfour also became Scotland's foremost importer of French books.   KAM
ODNB

Balkema, A. A. (**August Aimé**) (1906–96) Dutch publisher who established his company in South Africa in 1946. His list included belles-lettres (sold to Human & Rousseau in 1962) and non-fiction (natural and cultural heritage). The books were elegantly designed, influenced by the Dutch typographer van *Krimpen.   FCG

Ball, Elizabeth (1897–1982) American book collector. Inheriting a collection of children's books (*see* **15**) from her father, she augmented it extensively. She gave part of it to the *Pierpont Morgan Library (1964); the rest was sold, after her death, to the *Lilly Library of the University of Indiana. She formed other collections that she either donated or sold, including *hornbooks (to the *Free Library of Philadelphia) and American *imprints (to the *American Antiquarian Society).   ASGE
DABC

ballads   The ballad is in origin a song, composed or improvised, to accompany dancing.

1. Early ballads
2. Production and consumption
3. Collecting and collections
4. The trade in the 18th and 19th centuries

1. Early ballads

In the later Middle Ages, the term came to be used of any lengthy song in which a story is narrated. The traditional ballads are all anonymous, and were orally transmitted long before they were first printed. Successive generations modified or modernized their language, increased or decreased the number of stanzas, and probably reworked ballads that glorified pagan and heroic rather than Christian values. It seems likely that the form in which most traditional ballads are now known belongs to the later 16th century.

The earliest surviving printed English ballad is *A Lytel Geste of Robyne Hood*, printed in 1506 by de *Worde. Newly composed ballads began to appear soon afterwards; the laureate John Skelton's *Ballade of the Scottysshe Kynge* (1513) is perhaps the earliest example of an acknowledged poem narrating contemporary events in traditional ballad form and style. Such topical ballads soon became a very important portion of the genre; a large part of the population would have learnt the news of the 'great world' from hearing or reading them. Although most are by anonymous members of the 'uncountable rable of ryming Ballet makers' sneered at by William Webbe in his *Discourse of English Poetrie* (1586), three on the defeat of the Armada are known to be by Thomas Deloney, the leading delineator of Elizabethan artisan life.

2. Production and consumption

Most printed ballads filled only one side of a single sheet (the *broadside). Shorter pieces could be *imposed twice or more on a sheet from one setting of type, the separated copies forming long strips. The *press run must often have been much larger than that of most books: possibly a third of the population of London was literate by 1600, and the demand for halfpenny and penny ballads there and in rural England was apparently insatiable. Shakespeare's rogue Autolycus in *The Winter's Tale* typifies the pedlars and *chapmen who did a brisk trade in romantic ballads among those who can have been only barely literate (and credulous into the bargain, thinking that anything printed must be 'true'). Nor were ballads enjoyed only by the least sophisticated. The *daybook of the Oxford bookseller *Dorne (1520) shows that although the value of his turnover was made up chiefly of academic books, its volume consisted much more of ballads and other ephemera (*see* **14**). Later in the century, the popularity of the ballad explains why its 'common' metre (iambic lines, alternating eight and seven syllables) was widely used in metrical translations of the psalms for congregational singing in church, even though many of the older Protestant tunes were in other metres.

The *Stationers' Company, which began to regulate printing in 1557, charged four pence for each entry of a ballad. Many thousands were so registered, but vast numbers were not. The various collections of ballads now in the *Bodleian total some 30,000 items, but the majority of those printed no longer survive. The ballad's fate was often to be posted on walls and doors, and to be discarded as waste paper when no longer topical. Printed ballads were not considered worthy of preservation until the mid-17th century; indeed, even R. *Burton, an enthusiastic collector of popular literature, does not seem to have bothered with them. An idea of the sheer volume of the 17th-century trade is given by a probate inventory of 1664 of the stock of Charles Tias of London Bridge (the great centre of cheap publishing before the Fire of London). It includes 37,500 ballad sheets, as well as other ephemera; and Tias was but one of many wholesalers.

3. Collecting and collections

The first collectors of printed ballads valued them chiefly as evidence for social and political history. *Pepys had his collection of ballads bound into ten volumes, classified as follows: Devotion and Morality; History True and Fabulous; Tragedy *vizt* Murders, Executions, Judgements of God &c; State and Times; Love Pleasant; Love Unfortunate; Marriage, Cuckoldry, &c; the Sea, Love, Gallantry, & Actions; Drinking and Good Fellowship; Humour, Frollicks &c, mixt. Pepys evidently had an eye for the 'curious' and unusual in both 'merry' and 'godly' ballads, and his collection tells us as much about him as about his times. The *bookrunner *Bagford had a good eye for detail; he assembled for *Harley a collection of ballads illustrating the political commotions of the late 17th century, which was subsequently acquired by J. *Ker, the duke of Roxburghe, and is now (together with the rest of his very large collection) in the *British Library.

The first serious attempt to assemble a corpus of popular and traditional, rather than topical, ballads was made in *A Collection of Old Ballads* (1723–5). The editorship is ascribed, possibly jestingly, to the poet Ambrose Philips ('Namby-Pamby'). The *Collection* sold remarkably well, and was twice reprinted by 1727. The text is said to have been 'corrected from the best and most ancient copies extant', but the sources are unidentifiable, and the extent of the editor's 'corrections' can only be guessed at. A more famous collection, although not exclusively of traditional ballads, is Thomas *Percy's *Reliques of Ancient English Poetry* (1765). Of its 180 items, 45 derive from a single 17th-century MS collection (BL Add. MS 27879), now called the Percy Folio. S. *Johnson, who characterized *Chevy Chase* as 'a masterpiece of chill and lifeless imbecility', nevertheless drew Percy's attention to those ballads he did admire, and many unnamed contributors (including 'ladies') are thanked by the editor. Perhaps to emphasize his slender connection with the dukes of Northumberland (the *Reliques* are dedicated to the Duchess), Percy took special pains to present ballads from the Scottish Border country, a body of traditional poetry hitherto unknown to southerners. The supernatural element that permeates many of these ballads was much admired, and inspired a great deal of 'gothick' imitation. Percy's editorial methods leave much to be desired, but his chief source still survives—now bearing his intrusive annotations and editorial marks, but lacking the leaves he appears to have removed, as well as those used by its previous owner for lighting the fire. (Some songs in the Folio, judged too 'loose and humorous' for publication, were published only in 1868.) Percy made no attempt to discriminate between genuinely ancient ballads and quite recent ones, partly perhaps because he wished to demonstrate the continuing vitality of a native pre-classical form, and to encourage others to perpetuate it. Imperfect though it was, Percy's collection inspired a new taste for the English and Scottish ballad, inspired many imitations, and encouraged greater respect for such evidences of popular culture far beyond the British Isles.

The antiquary and bookseller Thomas Evans sought to improve on Percy in *Old Ballads, Historical and Narrative, with Some of More Modern Date* (1777–84). The *Reliques* nevertheless continued to be reprinted as the standard work, and W. *Scott conceived his *Minstrelsy of the Scottish Border* (1807) largely as a tribute to Percy for having introduced him to the subject. Meanwhile, several professedly more 'scientific' editors took an interest in the ballad, among them *Ritson, the compiler of several anthologies of 'antient' Scottish (1794) and English (1791) poetry, and of songs relating to Robin Hood (1795); and John Pinkerton, editor of *Scottish Tragic Ballads* (1781) and *Select Scotish Ballads* (1783). Neither was an objective editor, and they quarrelled vigorously in print. John Finlay's *Scottish Historical and Romantic Ballads, Chiefly Ancient* (1808) indicates the beginning of a more nationalistic approach. The *Percy Society was established in 1840 to publish ballads and other popular poetry (the illustrator *Cruikshank sarcastically counter-proposed a *Catnach Society). Twelve years later, 30 volumes had appeared, including *Old Ballads Illustrating the Great Frost of 1683–4*, and *English Naval Ballads*, but the Society was unfortunate in its editors, who included *Halliwell, J. P. *Collier, and E. F. Rimbault. The Ballad Society, whose moving spirit was the experienced editor of 17th-century poetic miscellanies Joseph Woodfall Ebsworth, was active between 1868 and 1896 and published the great collections of the duke of Roxburghe, *The Bagford Ballads* in two volumes (1878), and *The Roxburghe Ballads* in six (1886–9). These editions set a high standard of accuracy and scrupulousness. The American F. J. Child, professor of English at Harvard, was the first to treat the traditional ballad and its analogues as a subject for academic study. He pioneered viva voce collecting and recording; he is said to have acquired a working knowledge of every language in which ballads are known; and he published accurate versions of the tunes proper to many of them. *The English and Scottish Popular Ballads*, published between 1882 and 1898 in five quarto volumes, remains a monument to his scholarship and is still regarded as the definitive corpus, only minor additions having been made since.

4. The trade in the 18th and 19th centuries

Throughout the 18th century, the ballad printers (dominated by the Diceys and Marshalls of Aldermary Church Yard) were as busy as ever. Their typography was often an improvement on their predecessors', and appropriate woodcuts increased the attractiveness of their productions. By the end of the century, however, much of this output was found vulgar, indecent, and politically subversive by the newly influential evangelicals. Hannah More's *Cheap Repository Tracts* and their imitations bombarded the popular market with improving pennyworths, in the hope of weaning readers away from trivial and unworthy literature. A surprisingly large number did turn to this 'serious' alternative, and the production of ballad-sheets seems temporarily to have diminished. In 1802 the Norfolk-born printer John Pitts set up his business in Seven Dials, a somewhat disreputable quarter of London not far from the Strand. He inherited or bought up a large stock of old favourites; it seems that—for sentimental as well as commercial reasons—he preferred to reprint existing ballads rather than commission new ones. (He possessed also a vast collection of woodcuts, some as old as the early 16th century.)

When popular demand revolted against the edifying milk-and-water of the evangelical tract-writers in favour of something more sensational, the broadside publisher Catnach saw his chance. Ballads about disasters, murders and sexual crimes, the dying words of condemned criminals, anti-monarchist and anti-clerical ballads, 'flash' and 'canting' songs about fashionable low-life, were all produced in great numbers by Catnach and, forced into competition, by Pitts and the other ballad printers. *Press runs were sometimes enormous: over a million copies of some bestsellers are said to have been sold, the majority by a somewhat squalid race of 'flying stationers' who bellowed out the latest ballads in the streets and sold copies to passers-by until moved on by the police. An iconic

portrait of a 'long-song seller' offering songs at 'three yards a penny' forms the frontispiece of Charles Hindley's *Curiosities of Street Literature* (1871). The need to cut printing costs to the bone meant using worn-out types and the crudest (what Hindley calls 'anti-*Bewickian') woodblocks; proofreading was minimal, and presswork haphazard. Nevertheless, these ballads, by turns 'comical, tragical, quaint, eccentric, harsh, good-natured, often sinister, and sometimes downright lunatic' (in the words of Shepard), are a vivid index of popular tastes and of a vigorous literary subculture. Before long, improving literature for the poor once again began to cascade from the presses (often given away by would-be philanthropists), and cheaper newspapers provided more sensational news at a low cost. Catnach died in 1843, Pitts in 1844; and popular ballad printing, although lingering on for another 50 years in Seven Dials as well as in the provinces, was moribund. Since then, the street ballad has occasionally undergone a self-conscious revival at the hands of political idealists, as in the peak years of the Campaign for Nuclear Disarmament, when 'protest' song sheets, usually produced on rotary duplicators, were sold in large numbers during demonstrations.   BJF

G. H. Gerould, *The Ballad of Tradition* (1932)
N. Groom, *The Making of Percy's 'Reliques'* (1999)
C. Hindley, *Life and Times of James Catnach* (1878)
H. E. Rollins, *Analytical Index to the Ballad-Entries* (1924)
L. Shepard, *The Broadside Ballad* (1962)
— *John Pitts* (1969)

Ballad Stock A loose consortium of some dozen 17th- and early 18th-century booksellers (including prominent members of the *Stationers' Company) who sold popular, traditional *ballads through a network of *chapmen, operating from a warehouse. *See also* ENGLISH STOCK; LATIN STOCK.   RM

C. Blagden, 'Notes on the Ballad Market in the Second Half of the Seventeenth Century', *SB* 6 (1954), 161–73

Ballantine Books New York *paperback publishing firm founded in 1952 by Ian and Betty Ballantine. Ballantine began controversially by arranging with hardcover publishers to publish books simultaneously in cloth and paper, rather than waiting to reprint in paper after the cloth edition had been on the market for some months. The price of the cloth edition was lower than usual, at $1.50–$2, while the paperbacks were priced higher than usual, at 35–50c. Authors were given higher than normal *royalties on the paperback edition. The firm did not publish exclusively under this arrangement, however. Ballantine published in all genres but specialized in *fantasy and *science fiction, including J. R. R. Tolkien's *The Hobbit* (1966) and Ray Bradbury's *Fahrenheit 451* (1953). The firm also published paperback editions of some *Sierra Club publications. Ballantine was purchased by *Random House in 1973.   BEL

K. C. Davis, *Two-Bit Culture* (1984)

Ballantyne, James (1772–1833) Edinburgh printer and newspaper editor. Ballantyne published W. *Scott's early poetry, printed Scott's *novels, corrected his *proofs, and advised on style. His excellent layout (*see* MISE-EN-PAGE), *typography, and printing became a model for the British industry. Scott and Ballantyne, with his brother John *Ballantyne, contracted ill-fated printing and publishing partnerships, ruining Scott. DGP

[W. Dobson and W. Carrie,] *The Ballantyne Press and its Founders* (1909)
ODNB
J. Sutherland, *The Life of Walter Scott* (1995)

Ballantyne, John (1774–1821) Edinburgh *literary agent and publisher of *novels and magazines. He was W. *Scott's *literary agent (negotiating handsome terms from the novelist's London publisher) and occasional amanuensis. He joined ill-fated partnerships with Scott and James *Ballantyne, his brother. Scott let John Ballantyne share in the profits of the *Waverley novels. DGP

[W. Dobson and W. Carrie,] *The Ballantyne Press and its Founders* (1909)
ODNB
J. Sutherland, *The Life of Walter Scott* (1995)

Balliol College Library, Oxford The college, founded in 1263, has a notable collections of some 450 medieval MSS, many the gift of William Grey (bishop of Ely, 1454–78). Reformation collections have not survived as well, but its literary and academic holdings are appropriately strong, especially from the 19th century (the period of the college's revival under Benjamin Jowett) onwards. These include books and MSS of alumni, such as Arnold, Clough, and Swinburne, and of Robert Browning (an honorary fellow). ASB

J. Jones, *Balliol College* (1997)
R. A. B. Mynors, *Catalogue of the Manuscripts of Balliol College, Oxford* (1963)

ball-point pen Invented in 1938 by the Hungarian László Biró, who gave his name to it, the pen uses a small ball bearing at its tip to dispense viscous *ink. It reached New York and Europe by 1945, and was called 'the rocket' in the US until the late 1950s. Refillable ball-points are made of metal or plastic; the reservoir is controlled by a spring and button, or a screw. The disposable ball-point, commonly known as a 'Bic' from its manufacturer, is plastic. More recently, rollerball pens use a ball-point design with liquid ink delivered as in *fountain pens. MMS

Balme Library, University of Ghana *See* WEST AFRICAN LIBRARIES.

Balsamo, Luigi (1926–) Italian bibliographer, book historian, and professor at Parma. Director of *La *Bibliofilía* from 1983, he has published books on the Renaissance Milanese printer Scinzenzeler (1959; updated in *LaB*, 1993), the European bibliographical tradition (1984; English translation by W. A. Pettas, 1990), and the Jesuit bibliographer *Possevino (2006). NH

[Istituto di Biblioteconomia e Paleografia, Università degli Studi, Parma,] *Libri tipografi biblioteche: ricerche storiche dedicate a Luigi Balsamo* (2 vols, 1997)

Bamberg, Staatsbibliothek Founded in 1802–3 as a repository for the libraries of the cathedral and bishopric of Bamberg and of dissolved monasteries in Upper Franconia, the Staatsbibliothek holds *c*.6,000 MSS (dating from the beginnings of the bishopric in 1007) and *c*.3,400 *incunables. BW

www.staatsbibliothek-bamberg.de, consulted June 2007

Bamberg Apocalypse One of the finest achievements of Ottonian book production, Staatsbibliothek Bamberg, MS. Bibl. A. 140, comprises the Book of Revelation and a Gospel Lectionary. It was produced between 1000 and 1020 in the *scriptorium at Reichenau, seemingly for the Emperor Otto III, who died before the MS was finished. His successor, Henry II, had it completed and donated it to the collegiate abbey of St Stephan at Bamberg in 1020. Copied in a combination of *uncial and capital lettering, it has 106 leaves containing 57 large miniatures (*see* MINIATURES (1)) and 103 elaborate gold initials. ASGE

E. Harnischfeger. *Die Bamberger Apokalypse* (1981)

Bämler, Johannes (*fl.* 1472–95; d. *c*.1503) Augsburg printer. Of the *c*.120 editions from his press, 94 are German works, often illustrated with woodcuts. With Anton Sorg, Bämler compiled the *Chronik von allen Kaisern und Königen* (1476). BW
Geldner

Bancroft & Co., A. L. Founded in 1856 as H. H. Bancroft & Co., this San Francisco firm specialized in *law books, *textbooks, *subscription books, and guides to and maps of the Pacific Coast. By 1870 the firm had changed its name to A. L. Bancroft & Co., Albert Little Bancroft having assumed management of the business so that his brother, Hubert Howe Bancroft, could devote himself to historical research. After a disastrous fire in 1886, the brothers dissolved their partnership and their firm. JDG

H. R. Wagner, 'Albert Little Bancroft', *California Historical Society Quarterly*, 29 (1950), 97–128, 217–27, 357–67

Bancroft Library, University of California, Berkeley As UC Berkeley's primary special collections library, the Bancroft is one of America's largest and busiest repositories of MSS and rare books. It holds more than 600,000 volumes in addition to 60 million MS items, and it includes the Mark Twain Papers and Project, the Pictorial Collection, the Tebtunis Papyri, and the Bancroft Collection of Western and Latin Americana. MDB

bancroft.berkeley.edu, consulted Nov. 2007

Bandinel, Bulkeley (1781–1861) Under-librarian at the Bodleian Library from 1811 and Librarian 1815–71. His long tenure saw major growth in *legal deposit stock as well as in rare and foreign books and MSS. He was also co-editor of a lavish edition of Dugdale's *Monasticon* (1817–30). ASB
ODNB

bands The sewing supports on which the gatherings of a hand-bound book are sewn, running horizontally across the spine, typically visible as raised bands unless sewn in as recessed bands to create a smooth spine.

Bangīya Sāhitya Pariṣat The Bengal Academy of Literature was established (1893) in Calcutta (Kolkata). Renamed in 1894, it moved to its present location (243/1 Acharya Prafulla Chandra Ray Road) in 1908. Founded and led by the most important figures in 19th-century Bengali culture, it initially aimed to prepare a Bengali *dictionary and *grammar; regularize Bengali technical terms; collect and publish old MSS; translate important works into Bengali; publish a journal; and foster the study of history, philosophy, and science in Bengali. The Pariṣat now houses a library, a collection of MSS, and a museum.   SKC

Bangor Antiphonary Milan, Biblioteca Ambrosiana MS C. 5. inf. The MS was probably written at Bangor, northern Ireland, between 680 and 692. At some point in the early Middle Ages, Irish monks probably brought it to the monastery at Bobbio, which was founded by St Columbanus, an associate of St Comgall (who founded the monastery at Bangor and who is named in the MS). It went from Bobbio to the *Ambrosiana in 1609.   ASGE
F. E. Warren and W. Griggs, eds., *The Antiphonary of Bangor* (2 vols, Henry Bradshaw Society, vols 4, 10, 1893, 1895)

Bangs, Merwin, & Co. (active 1837–1903) New York auction house. The Bangs family managed the longest-lasting book-auction firm of 19th-century New York. Among many important sales were those of John Allan (1864), Thomas W. Field (1875), and William Harris Arnold (1901); *auction catalogues were prepared by William Gowans, *Sabin, and others. From 1837 to 1857, Bangs conducted regular semi-annual *trade sales.
MBW
G. L. McKay, *American Book Auction Catalogues, 1713-1934* (1937)

bank book (passbook) A book for recording the transactions of a deposit account at a bank. Typically, it records the date of the deposit or withdrawal, the amount, and the updated balance. Bank books are typically small and thin—and hence easily inserted into a machine for repeated printing. *See also* CHEQUEBOOK.   AAW

Bantam Books New York *paperback publisher founded in 1945 by Ian Ballantine and financed by *Grosset & Dunlap and Curtis Publishing, a magazine firm that handled Bantam's distribution. From its beginning, Bantam benefited from ties to trade houses. Its board of directors included Cass Canfield (*Harper & Brothers), Charles *Scribner, Bennett Cerf (*Random House), and John O'Connor (Grosset). These connections gave it access to reprint *rights to classic fiction and contemporary novels. Bantam's list ranged from works by Hemingway, Fitzgerald, Twain, Steinbeck, Graham Greene, James Michener, and John O'Hara, to bestsellers by Jacqueline Susann and Judith Krantz. In the 1960s Bantam introduced its 'Extra' series of 'instant' books.

The first was the 1964 Warren Commission report on the Kennedy assassination, which went on sale less than a week after the report's official release. This edition was also unusual in that the paperback edition was followed by a cloth edition (from *McGraw-Hill) and a *Book-of-the-Month Club edition. *The Pentagon Papers*, *The Watergate Hearings*, and *The White House Transcripts* also appeared as 'extras'. In 1968, Bantam was sold to the National General Corporation and, in 1973, to the Italian firm IFI, owned by the Fiat magnate Giovanni Agnelli. In 1977 Agnelli sold a controlling interest in Bantam to the German conglomerate *Bertelsmann, which bought the remaining 49 per cent in 1981.   BEL
K. C. Davis, *Two-Bit Culture* (1984)
C. Petersen, *The Bantam Story* (1975)

bar (lever) The lever of a hand-press which, when pulled, operates the *screw or toggle, applying pressure through the *platen.

Barbédor, Louis (*c.*1589–1670) French *writing-master. A member of the Community of Master Calligraphers, Barbédor developed a form of French round script that was adopted as a writing model by the Parliament of Paris in 1632. He published *Les Écritures financière, et italienne-bastarde … très utile à ceux qui aspirent aux emplois* in Paris in 1647.   ASGE

Barbèra, Gasparo (1818–80) In 1854 this Turin emigrant founded a Florence publishing house that surfed on the patriotic tide leading to unity in 1870, producing series such as the 'Collezione Diamante' (1856) of miniature editions (*see* MINIATURE BOOKS) of Italian classics. The firm passed to his sons, notably Piero (1854–1921), whose *chef d'œuvre* was the *edizione nazionale* of Galileo's works (1890–1909). Under Fascism the firm declined, ending in bankruptcy in 1960, when Giunti purchased it.
NH
DBI
EIDO

Barbi, Michele (1867–1941) Italian textual critic and Dante scholar. His 'new philology'—the title of a 1938 collection of his essays—countered the prevalent *Bédier-inspired textual criticism, arguing that even a good MS requires correction from other sources and through scholarly conjecture. He is also remembered for his work on the final edition of Manzoni's I *Promessi Sposi* (1840–42).   NH
DBI

Barbier-Mueller, Jean-Paul (1930–) Swiss collector and bibliophile. His artistic and ethnographic collections are housed in two museums bearing his name: one for classical antiquity, Africa, Asia, and Oceania in Geneva (inaugurated in 1977), and the other for the Americas in Barcelona (1997). His collection of Italian Renaissance poetry from Petrarch to Chiabrera is at his Geneva foundation, which publishes the scholarly collection *Textes et travaux* and the trilingual annual *Italique*.   VAG

Barbou family French printers, active in Lyons from 1529, then in Paris from 1540. **Hugues Barbou** (1538–1603) subsequently moved to Limoges, where the firm prospered by specializing in *textbooks for Jesuit schools, becoming one of the most flourishing provincial printing establishments in pre-Revolutionary France.   VAG

Barclay, Andrew (1738–1823) American bookseller, bookbinder, and publisher who emigrated from Scotland to Boston *c.*1760, running a business there until the War of Independence, when he joined the Loyalist forces. He moved to New York in 1776 and worked there until moving to Shelburne, Nova Scotia (1783), spending the rest of his life mainly farming. Some of the books he bound in Boston are distinguished by large engraved trade labels.   DRSP

H. French, *Bookbinding in Early America* (1986)

Barker, Christopher (1528/9–99) Printer and publisher. Born in Yorkshire, Barker was trading in London by 1569 at the sign of the Grasshopper in *St Paul's Churchyard. He secured an important and lucrative royal printing patent in 1573, becoming the first in England to print the Geneva New Testament (1575). Barker printed Protestant works, including two by John Foxe. With six presses in 1586, Barker's was the largest *printing office in England.   JH
ODNB

Barker, Nicolas (1932–) English scholar, librarian, and editor (1965–) of the *Book Collector. Following a career in publishing, Barker worked at the *British Library (1976–92), as its first head of conservation, among other roles. Barker's writings extend beyond his major interest in *typography (especially *Aldus and *Greek type) to *forgeries, treasures, and the *Roxburghe Club. He has been *Panizzi lecturer (2001), *Sandars Reader (1999/2000), and president of the *Bibliographical Society (1981–5).   KEA

Barley, William (*fl.* 1587–1614) London bookseller and printer. Completing his apprenticeship as a Draper in 1587, Barley became free of the *Stationers' Company in 1606, when he worked with *Creede at their premises in London, publishing *ballads, *chapbooks, and *music.   KMQ

Barlow, Francis (1626/28–1704) English painter, etcher, and the first native-born book illustrator. Although he designed numerous *frontispieces and *title-pages, his reputation rests on his narrative illustrations (*see* **16**), particularly those he etched after his own designs for Edward Benlowes's *Theophila* (1652) and for *Aesop's Fables* (1666), a volume that gave Barlow, an accomplished animal painter, a suitable showcase for his special talent.   JCI

E. Hodnett, *Francis Barlow* (1978)
ODNB

Barnard, Sir Frederick Augusta (1743–1830) Librarian. Initially employed by George III to develop the King's Library, he became Royal Librarian in 1774. Most of the collection he amassed—including 65,000 printed books—was donated by George IV to the British Museum (*see* BRITISH LIBRARY) in 1823. The catalogue of this collection, *Bibliothecae Regiae Catalogus* (1820–29), was chiefly Barnard's work.   ASGE

J. Brooke, 'The Library of King George III', *YULG* 52 (1977), 33–45
ODNB

Barnes, Warner J. (b. 20th century) American bibliographer and Browning scholar. He compiled the catalogue of the Browning collection at the Harry *Ransom Humanities Research Center at the University of *Texas (1966), and *A Bibliography of Elizabeth Barrett Browning* (1967). He co-edited, with O M Brack, Jr., *Bibliography and Textual Criticism: English and American Literature, 1700 to the Present* (1969), and is one of the editors of the *Complete Works of Robert Browning* published by Ohio University Press.   VAG

Barnes & Noble The largest US bookshop chain in the late 20th century. Originating in New York City in 1917 as a jobber of educational books, it specialized in textbooks until the 1970s. In 1971 it was acquired by Leonard Riggio, who made the flagship New York shop into one of the the country's major bookshops. Riggio greatly expanded the retail business through new outlets and acquisitions, including the 1986 purchase of B. *Dalton, Bookseller. Barnes & Noble also engaged in some book publishing and distribution. With the exception of its college division, it became a publicly traded corporation in 1993. Profoundly influencing retail bookselling in the 1990s, Barnes & Noble refined the concept of the superstore: an emporium carrying more than 100,000 titles that encourages shoppers to spend extended time in its premises by sponsoring book-themed events and providing spaces for reading, eating and drinking, and lounging.   LJM

baroque type *Gaskell's term (*NI*) to group 17th- and 18th-century *roman and *italic types that fall between Renaissance and neoclassical styles; more usually called 'transitional'.

Barreira, João de (*fl.* 1542–90) Portugal's most prolific 16th-century printer. He worked in Coimbra, first with João Álvares (1542–53), then alone (1553–90) as official printer to the University. His *imprints include the second *edition (1553) of the *Exercitia Spiritualia* of St Ignatius of Loyola.   DRW

Bartholomew family Edinburgh cartographic publishers. In business from 1805 to 1986, the firm was founded by the engraver **George Bartholomew** (1784–1871), who followed in the map-making tradition of Richard Cooper and Andrew Bell. Bartholomew worked for the engravers W. H. and Daniel Lizars until establishing his own business. George's son **John** (1805–61) began his own business in 1826 and later shared premises with A. & C. *Black, who frequently used his engravings. John was succeeded by his son **John** (1831–93), and grandson **John George** (1860–1920), who went into partnership with *Nelson and transformed the company into a general publishing firm.   PLS

ODNB

Bartlett, Roger (*c.*1633–1712) English bookbinder, working in London *c.*1654–66, and subsequently in Oxford. He produced high-quality bindings and was employed by a number of Oxford colleges, where many of his bindings survive today.   DRSP

H. Nixon, *English Restoration Bookbindings* (1974)

Barton, Thomas P. (1803–69) American book collector. Barton collected English literature, with a particular emphasis on *Shakespeare—he owned the *First Folio and all three subsequent editions, a number of early *quartos and many ephemera (*see* **14**)—as well as French and German drama and history. His collection amounted to more than 15,000 items, and was sold after his death to the *Boston Public Library.   ASGE

DABC

Baseball Encyclopedia, The First published in 1969 by *Macmillan, this weighty tome (6.5 pounds, or nearly 3 kilos), was based on the work of David Neft and a team of researchers who combed America's newspaper *archives to assemble a work so thorough in its statistical treatment of the game that the book's in-house editor, Robert Markel, likened it to 'volume II' of the King James Bible. Neft's data was recorded on IBM punch cards and formatted to customized design templates to create the right *mise-en-page*. The volume became the first American trade book entirely produced via *computerized typesetting.   MFS

Basel, Public Library of the University The oldest secular library in Switzerland (founded 1460). Its collection of rare books comprises 3,000 *incunabula; MSS of *Luther, *Erasmus, Zwingli, and Melanchthon; and the *Amerbach family collection.   RAK

IDLH

baseline The imaginary line on which the characters in a *typeface rest. The 'x' sits on the baseline; the *descender of 'p' extends below it.

base text A potentially confusing term, in that it is often taken to be (and sometimes used as) a synonym for *copy-text, being the basis of an edition. Yet 'base text' can also refer to that selected as the initial text for comparison at the stage of textual *collation, before a copy-text is chosen. The two may turn out to be the same, of course; but the base text in this sense serves a purpose in the earlier part of the editorial process as the foundational text against which to compare others, required by any system of collation.   ASR

Basic Books New York publisher of advanced college *textbooks and *trade books, focusing on the social and behavioural sciences and social issues. (A house with the same name, headed by Paul Grabbe, had a brief life in the 1930s.) In 1945 the Basic Book Club was organized to distribute books on psychoanalysis. When Arthur Rosenthal took over the club in 1948, he expanded its areas of interests to other social and behavioural sciences. In 1952 Rosenthal began publishing his own list as what is now known as 'Basic Books'. He also developed or acquired a number of other *book clubs, most of which he sold to Crowell-Collier in 1962. Basic's authors included some of the most eminent social and behavioural scientists of the 20th century, including Freud, Ernest Jones (Freud's biographer), Piaget, and Lévi-Strauss. In the 1960s, the firm was led by the neoconservative editors Irving Kristol and Midge Decter. Since that time, its list has become more eclectic and less ideological. The publishing firm was purchased by *Harper & Row in 1969 and is now a member of the Perseus Book Group.   BEL

Basilea, Fadrique de (**Friedrich Biel**) Printer in Burgos, Spain, *c.*1475–1517. One of several itinerant German printers to set up in Spain, he was noted for woodcut illustrations and literary texts, including *La Celestina* (1499) by Fernando de Rojas. He later printed for *Brocar.   DRW

Baskerville, John (1707–75) Birmingham printer and typefounder. Teaching penmanship from *c.*1726 and making gravestone inscriptions, Baskerville inherited his father's estate in 1738 and began manufacturing japanned metal wares, earning a sizeable fortune. He set up a printing office *c.*1750 in the spirit of a *private press, though working with trade booksellers, and oversaw the cutting of his type—by John Handy after Baskerville's own models—experimenting with ink, paper, and the mechanics of the press.

His types reflect the pointed pen and copper-plate *engraving familiar to him as a writing master, fuelling a revolution in conservative English typography. He set new standards of presswork, achieved a splendid effect of black ink on white, hot-pressed paper, and briefly introduced *wove paper (by *Whatman, but only perfected after Baskerville's death). His books show elegant, neoclassical layouts but sloppy editing.

*Bibliophiles worldwide marvelled at Baskerville's 1757 Virgil, and foundries in England and abroad imitated his types. His expensive books found some market among the new industrial middle class, but his perfectionism and over-optimistic press runs consumed much of his fortune. He embraced Voltaire (but never produced his planned edition), disparaged traditional religion, and enjoyed the company of William Shenstone, Mathew Boulton, and B. *Franklin. His types temporarily fell from fashion in England, and his widow sold the punches and matrices to Beaumarchais, who appropriately used them to print Voltaire's banned works outside Strasbourg. Baskerville inspired the *Didots and especially *Bodoni, while *Austin and W. *Martin mixed his influences with their designs.   JAL

ODNB

P. VIRGILII MARONIS

AENEIDOS

LIBER SECUNDUS.

Conticuere omnes, intentique ora tenebant:
   Inde toro pater Aeneas sic orsus ab alto:
Infandum, Regina, jubes renovare dolorem;
   Trojanas ut opes, et lamentabile regnum
5 Eruerint Danai: quæque ipse miserrima vidi,
   Et quorum pars magna fui. quis talia fando,
Myrmidonum, Dolopumve, aut duri miles Ulyssei,
   Temperet a lacrymis? et jam nox humida cœlo
Præcipitat, suadentque cadentia sidera somnos.
10 Sed, si tantus amor casus cognoscere nostros,
   Et breviter Trojæ supremum audire laborem;
Quanquam animus meminisse horret, luctuque refugit,
   Incipiam. Fracti bello, fatisque repulsi
   Ductores Danaum, tot jam labentibus annis,
15 Instar montis equum, divina Palladis arte
   Aedificant; sectaque intexunt abiete costas.
Votum pro reditu simulant: ea fama vagatur.
   Huc delecta virum fortiti corpora furtim
Includunt cæco lateri; penitusque cavernas
20 Ingentes, uterumque armato milite complent.
   Est in conspectu Tenedos, notissima fama
Insula, dives opum, Priami dum regna manebant:
   Nunc tantum sinus, et statio malesida carinis.

Huc

Baskerville's edition of Virgil (Birmingham, 1757): the opening of Book 2 of the *Aeneid*, with *show-through from the end of Book 1. The spacing indicates there is meant to be a *ligature in the work's title.

Baskett, John (1664?–1742) London printer and paper supplier. For most of the 18th century, his family enjoyed a half-share in the bible-printing patent. The handsome *typography of his *folio bibles was vitiated by slipshod proofreading (*see* PROOFS AND PROOFREADING); one 'Baskett-full of printer's errors' is known as the 'Vinegar Bible', after a ludicrous erratum. Baskett opposed the introduction of *stereotyping at Cambridge, perceiving it as a threat to his monopoly. Among his apprentices was W. *Caslon the younger.   BJF
ODNB

Basler Papiermühle The most important museum for paper, writing, and printing in Switzerland, located in the so-called St Alban valley in Basel. In the mid-12th century, the Cluniac monastery of St Alban built a canal to provide water power via water wheels for twelve mills. Ten of these were converted to paper mills in the late Middle Ages. The museum is located in the former mills of the Stegreif and Galliziani families (from Italy). The carefully restored, medieval Gallican mill houses exhibitions relating to the history of paper, writing, and printing.   UBL
P. Tschudin, *Basler Papiermühle* (1975)

Bass, Shabbetai (1641–1718) Jewish bibliographer, book dealer, and author. Born in Kalish, Poland, educated in Prague, he settled in Amsterdam in 1679. In 1680, he published *Sifte yeshenim* (Lips of the Elders), the first Jewish bibliography by a Jew, with approximately 2,200 titles.   EGLS

Bassandyne, Thomas (d. 1577) Bookseller, publisher, and printer. A native of Scotland, Bassandyne probably learnt printing on the Continent. In 1568 he offended

church authorities in Edinburgh by publishing a bawdy song in a *psalter. During the Marian period (1568–73), Bassandyne became heavily involved in a propaganda war, printing on behalf of the queen's supporters. From 1573 he printed books of good quality, including a New Testament with the merchant Alexander Arbuthnet. JH
ODNB

Basson, Thomas, and **Govert Basson** (active *c.*1583–1630) Leiden printers and publishers. English-born Thomas Basson started his business at Leiden in the early 1580s. He produced Dutch translations from English and French authors, did some printing for the town and university, and stocked works connected with the Family of Love. When Govert succeeded his father in 1612, the press's output became more substantial. The publication of the works of the controversial theologian Arminius ultimately led to the firm's dissolution.   TB
T. Bögels, *Govert Basson* (1992)
J. A. van Dorsten, *Thomas Basson* (1961)
— 'Thomas Basson', *Quaerendo*, 15 (1985), 195–224

bastarda type Sub-category of *gothic type, associated with vernacular languages, especially French, English, and German. It is based on *scripts used in chanceries and for luxury MSS, written without many pen lifts and, therefore, called *cursive (running). Bastarda types retained the fluency of this writing hand by some slant-ing, joining of letters, loops on *ascenders, and pointed *descenders for the f and long s. French bastardas (*lettre bâtarde*) are more rounded than the German, including its varieties *Schwabacher, Wittenberg, and the later *Fraktur. German bastardas have a pointed aspect. Early vernacular texts printed in some countries used other types: *roman in Italy; *rotunda in the Iberian Peninsula; *textura or *black letter in England and Scotland. Roman eventually came to predominate.   MMS
BMC 11
H. Carter, *A View of Early Typography*, 2e (2002)
A. F. Johnson, *Type Designs*, 3e (1966)

Basu (Bose), Nandalal (1882–1966) Bengali artist, teacher, and theorist. Widely acclaimed across many media (including watercolour, *woodcut, *lithography), Basu is best known for wash, pen-and-ink, and fresco. He illustrated works by Rabindranath Tagore, a close associate (*Cayanikā, Gītāñjali, Fruit Gathering,* and *Crescent Moon*), and was admired by Gandhi.   MMS

Basumatī Sāhitya Mandir Indian weekly started at Calcutta (Kolkata) in 1896. It printed literary classics and reproductions of artistic works as free supplements, its popularity inspiring the founding of a publishing unit, known for inexpensive editions of classics in (or trans-lated into) Bengali. It is now owned by Basumati Corporation Ltd.   SKC

bath book Waterproof, small-format books, typically made with plastic pages, that provide entertainment and educational opportunities at bath-time for young children. The vinyl (PVC) leaves are filled with polyvinyl foam and heat-sealed so that they float. Subject matter includes, but is not limited to, themes related to the bath, such as fish, oceans, or water play. Contemporary bath books are often *shaped and may include such elements as music module buttons. New technology allows books to be printed on waterproof paper and sold with floatable erasable pens.   KAW

Batsford, B. T. (Bradley Thomas) (1821–1904) British bookseller and publisher, known for illustrated books on architecture and the decorative arts, as well as practical handbooks for professional builders. A pioneer in the use of photographic illustrations (*see* **16**), Batsford and his firm maintained a loyal coterie of authors. His sons, Bradley and Herbert, continued to publish high-quality books on the buildings, topography, and social history of Britain: they were succeeded by their nephew Harry Batsford.   JEP
ODNB

Battala (lit. 'under the banyan tree') The first presses in the Shobhabazar area (north Calcutta (Kolkata)) were established in Battala, which soon became a shorthand term for presses in nearby Garanhata, Ahiritola, and Chitpur. Battala printing is loosely synonymous with inexpensive genres such as farces, ballads, and erotica. Its heyday was from 1840 to 1870.   AG

battledore (battledore book) A piece of cardboard on which was printed the *ABC, a syllabary, and the Lord's Prayer, so called from its usual shape; used as a substitute for the *hornbook.

Battye, J. S. (James Sykes) (1871–1954) Australian librarian and historian. Battye was head of the Public Library in Perth, 1895–1954, and chancellor of the University of Western Australia, 1936–43. His publications include the *Cyclopedia of Western Australia* (1912–13) and *Western Australia: A History* (1924).   IM
ADB

Baudrier, Julien (1860–1915) Compiler of a meticu-lous *Bibliographie lyonnaise* based on notes by his father Henri (1815–84), a prominent Lyons magistrate and collector. Eleven volumes came out between 1895 and 1915; the twelfth (1921) was completed by his brother-in-law H. de Terrebasse.   VAG
DBF

Bauersche Giesserei Frankfurt typefoundry estab-lished by Johann Christian Bauer (1802–67), who learnt punchcutting in Frankfurt, and returned there after eight years in Edinburgh (1839–47). Owned by the Hartmann family from 1898, the foundry flourished between the wars with Futura, Bauer Bodoni, and other *typefaces. After it closed (1972), Neufville (Barcelona) cast its types.   JAL
LGB

Bauhaus typography The creative centre of indus-trial design in Germany, the Bauhaus (1918–33) included typography and advertising in its curriculum. Bauhaus typography is characterized by preference for *sans serif types, bold lines, dots, and diagonals. Among its leading exponents were Herbert Bayer, Joost Schmidt, and *Moholy-Nagy.   WDL

W. Herzogenrath, *50 Jahre Bauhaus* (1968)

Baumgarten, Johann Ernst (d. 1782) Bookbinder, born in Germany, who emigrated to London, probably *c.*1760–65, and established a reputation there as a fine and sought-after craftsman. His apprentice *Kalthoeber became his partner and successor.   DRSP

Nixon and Foot

Bauzonnet, Antoine (d. 1848) Parisian bookbinder. He worked for Jean-Georges Purgold from 1820 and succeeded to his business. Subsequently he was in partnership with Georges Trautz, who began working for him in 1833. The firm was noted as one of the best French binderies of its time.   DRSP

E. Campagnac, 'La Première Reliure signée par Antoine Bauzonnet (1828)', *BB* (1994), 392–400

Bavarian State Library, Munich (Bayerischen Staatsbibliothek) Founded in 1558, when Duke Albrecht V of Bavaria acquired the collection of the orientalist Johann Albrecht Widmanstetter (1506–57) for the court library of the Wittelsbach family. In 1571, the duke purchased the library of the Augsburg merchant Johann Jakob *Fugger, which included the collection of the Nuremberg doctor *Schedel. From 1663, the library has been entitled to *legal deposit of every book published in Bavaria. When Bavarian monasteries were dissolved following the Napoleonic wars (1802–3), their libraries were largely centralized in Munich. Adding to the collection, in 1803–4, the Mannheim library of Elector Carl Theodor was transferred to Munich. *Schrettinger was a central figure in the reorganization of the library. A new building, designed by Friedrich Gärtner, opened in 1843. After the destruction of 500,000 volumes in World War II, the collection was rebuilt and expanded; it now comprises *c.*90,200 MSS, 20,000 *incunables, and more than 9 million printed books.   BW

www.bsb-muenchen.de, consulted July 2008

R. Hacker, ed., *Beiträge zur Geschichte der Bayerischen Staatsbibliothek* (2000)

O. Hartig, *Die Gründung der Münchener Hofbibliothek durch Albrecht V. und Johann Jakob Fugger* (1917)

D. Kudorfer, ed., *Lebendiges Büchererbe* (2003)

Bawden, Edward (1903–89) English painter and designer. After completing a diploma in book illustration (*see* **16**) at the Royal College of Art London, he produced illustrations for *Penguin, *Faber, the *Curwen Press, and others. His work, characterized by its clarity, has drawn comparisons with *Lear.   KES

ODNB

Baybars Qur'ān A superbly produced MS copy of the Qur'ān made in seven volumes, 1304–5, at the request of the Mamluk ruler Baybars al-Jāshnagīr and now BL

Add. MS 22406. It was copied by Muḥammad ibn al-Waḥīd in Cairo and illuminated by three artists whose names are given as Muḥammad ibn Mubādir, Abū Bakr Ṣandal, and Aydughdī ibn 'Abdallāh. The script is gold *tawqī'*, a form rarely employed for Qur'āns. The MS was commissioned by Baybars for a *khānqah* or 'monastery' built at his command in Cairo.   DLJ

D. James, *Manuscripts of the Holy Qur'ān from the Mamlūk Era* (1999)

Bay Psalm Book The earliest book printed in North America, excluding Mexico (where printing had begun a century earlier). Joseph (Josse) Glover, an Anglican minister in Surrey who was interested in the American colony of Massachusetts, contracted with Stephen Day to travel from England to Cambridge, Mass., in 1638 with the necessary equipment to set up a printing press there. Glover died aboard ship, but Day arrived safely and established the first press in the colonies. Day's first job at the press was a broadside entitled *Oath of a Freeman* (1639), of which the text is known but no copies survive. (A forgery of this broadside was produced by M. *Hofmann in the 1980s, but was never acquired by any collector or institution.) The Bay Psalm Book, properly *The Whole Booke of Psalmes Faithfully Translated into English Metre*, was Day's first complete book. It was published in 1640, reportedly in an edition of 1,700 copies, of which eleven survive (*Bodleian Library, *Huntington Library, *Harvard University, Library of *Congress, *New York Public Library, *Yale University, *Boston Public Library (two copies), *American Antiquarian Society, and the *Rosenbach Museum and Library).

The translation of the Psalms as printed in the Bay Psalm Book was a new one, undertaken by three divines then living in New England: Thomas Weld, Richard Mather, and John Eliot, the last of whom was later to translate the Bible into the Massachusett Indian dialect (1661–3). The Psalms are rendered rather mechanically, but the translators were aware of this lack of poetry. At the end of the Preface (sig. **3v) they admit to having attended to 'conscience rather than elegance, fidelity rather than poetry', an aesthetic that resulted in Psalm 23 beginning, 'The Lord to mee a shepheard is, / Want therefore shall not I'. The translation nevertheless found an audience and was reprinted often, well into the 18th century. Day is not known to have been a printer before emigrating to America, and the *typography and presswork of the Bay Psalm Book reveal an amateur in their unevenness and the proliferation of errors. Yet, if he had in fact never served an apprenticeship, Day's production of the Bay Psalm Book is reasonably creditable for a first-time effort.   DBW

Z. Haraszti, *The Enigma of the Bay Psalm Book* (1956)

G. P. Winship, *The Cambridge Press, 1638-1692* (1945)

Beacon Press Non-profit publishing department of the Boston-based Unitarian-Universalist Church. Its list features books for children and adults on gender, race, peace and justice, education and educational reform, nature and ecology, and New England history. The

Unitarian Church established a publishing division in 1854 to disseminate Unitarian literature, thought, and scholarship, and until the early 20th century its focus remained religious. In 1900 its leaders broadened the Church's focus to include 'social justice, education, and civil reform', and the press expanded its list accordingly. It adopted its present name in 1902 and was incorporated in 1914. In the 1950s, the press published both the anti-McCarthy series 'Beacon Studies in Freedom and Power' and the anti-Stalin series 'Beacon Studies in Soviet Tyranny and Power'. It published the complete *Pentagon Papers* in five volumes in 1971–2.   BEL

www.beacon.org, consulted Sept. 2007

Beadle & Co., Irwin P. (**Beadle & Adams**) First publishers of *dime novel series. The brothers Erastus and Irwin Beadle, publishers since 1851 of small periodicals and non-fiction, issued Number 1 of 'Beadle's Dime Novels' in New York in 1860. Cheaply printed in orange *wrappers, with exciting covers, thrilling plots, and shrewd production and distribution methods, this and other Beadle series were highly successful and soon imitated by other firms. Westerns, *detective stories, war stories, and *romances made up much of the Beadle output, along with *song books, biographies, *cookbooks, *self-help books, and periodicals such as *Beadle's Monthly* and *Saturday Journal*. M. J. Ivers & Co. bought Beadle's assets in 1898 and continued some series until 1905, when Arthur Westbrook Co. bought Ivers, keeping some Beadle novels in print for a few more years. MEB
DLB 49

beard On a piece of metal or wooden type, the space above and below the *face defined by the *bevel and the *shoulder; alternatively (USA), the bevel itself.

Beardsley, Aubrey (1872–98) Influential English illustrator. Beardsley developed his unique black-and-white style of illustration, drawing inspiration from the Pre-Raphaelites, including *Burne-Jones, and the French decadents. The most controversial artist of the Art Nouveau era, he created many designs that were grotesque and overtly erotic. In 1893 he was commissioned to illustrate an edition of Malory's *Morte D'Arthur*, and gained notoriety for his illustrations for *Wilde's play *Salomé* (1893). In addition to work for books, he contributed pictures to magazines such as the *Studio* and the *Savoy*, and was the art editor of the *Yellow Book* (issues 1–4). Other book illustrations include those for *Pope's *Rape of the Lock* (1896) and Aristophanes' *Lysistrata* (1896). During this period Beardsley also began work on a version of the *Tannhauserlied*. His unfinished fiction was collected and published in 1903 as *Under the Hill*.   KES

ODNB

bearer type For pages with sizeable blank areas, types were placed in the *forme to bear the *platen's weight. Intended to be blind, they were neither inked nor masked.

Bearers are most frequently observed in *incunabula, although the practice has been reported in some 16th-century books. Lines of text that had already been printed were sometimes used as bearers.   MMS

N. Harris, 'The Blind Impressions in the Aldine *Hypnerotomachia Poliphili*', *GJ* 79 (2004), 93–146
D. Paisey, 'Blind Printing in Continental Books', in *Book Production and Letters in the Western Renaissance*, ed. A. L. Lepschy *et al.* (1986)

beater The press operator responsible for keeping the ink soft by working his *ink balls together, and for inking the *forme (inserting the paper and pulling the *impression being undertaken by a separate 'puller'). The beater was also usually responsible for examining the printed sheet to check for defects.   PWN

Beatty, Sir (Alfred) Chester (1875–1968) Book collector and mining engineer. Born in New York City, Beatty became a British subject in 1933; in 1950 he moved to Ireland. He used his wealth to acquire outstanding collections of Western medieval codices and oriental MSS, the latter now in Dublin's Chester Beatty Library. A number of the Western MSS were sold at *Sotheby's in June 1932. After his death, another 75 were sold at Sotheby's in 1968 and 1969.   ASGE

R. J. Hayes, 'Contemporary Collectors XVIII: The Chester Beatty Library', *BC* 7 (1958), 253–64
ODNB

Beauchemin, Charles-Odilon (1822–87) Trained at J. *Lovell's shop, Beauchemin exemplified the transition from printer to bookseller to publisher. For more than 100 years (1842–1967), Beauchemin et Valois was the most prosperous book trade enterprise in Montreal. YL

F. Landry, *Beauchemin et l'édition au Québec* (1997)

Beauchesne, Jean de (d. 1620) Calligrapher. Little is known of Beauchesne's early life, which seems to have been spent in France. He was in England by 1565, working as a scribe, before publishing the first English writing book, *A Booke Containing Diuers Sortes of Hands* (1570). He later published other manuals in France—*Le Tresor d'escriture* (Lyons, 1580) and *La Clef d'escriture* (c.1595) —before returning to England in 1599 and becoming *writing-master to Charles and Elizabeth, children of James I.   ASGE

A. S. Osley, *Scribes and Sources* (1980)

Beauclair, Gotthard de (1907–92) German book designer and publisher. As producer and subsequently art director at *Insel (1928–62), he turned inexpensive Insel books into collectors' items with excellent *typography. Beauclair established the presses Trajanus (1951), Ars Librorum (1962), and Editions de Beauclair (1966).
          KEA

G. Fischer and H. Richter, eds., *Gotthard de Beauclair* (1996)

Beaufort, Margaret, countess of Richmond and Derby (1443–1509) Patron. Mother of Henry VII, she was a woman of 'singular wisdom and ready wit',

according to her mentor, John Fisher. *Caxton, among others, executed translations at her request, and she bestowed patronage and protection on several English printers, notably de *Worde. Her literary tastes were catholic: the printed books she commissioned include French *romances and the *Ship of Fools*, as well as the *Imitation of Christ* and Hilton's *Ladder of Perfection*. She established Readerships at Oxford and at Cambridge, where she also founded or substantially refounded three colleges. BJF
ODNB

Beaumont Press A British *private press run by Cyril W. Beaumont between 1917 and 1931, with the aim of publishing new poetry and prose. Beaumont printed six of the Press's 26 books on an *Albion in the basement of his bookshop in Charing Cross Road, London, the remainder being printed by commercial firms. PWN
C. W. Beaumont, *The First Score* (1927, repr. 1980)
B. T. Jackson, 'The Beaumont Press', *PL* 2/8(1) (1975), 4–37

Beck, C. H. German publishing house. Founded in 1763 in Nördlingen as a printing office, the company expanded to a bookshop and publishing. Relocated in Munich in 1889, Beck is still family-owned, and one of the leading publishers of law literature in Germany. US
Festschrift zum zweihundertjährigen Bestehen des Verlages C. H. Beck 1763–1963 (1963)

Beckford, William (1760–1844) English author and book collector. A bibliophile of taste and appetite, Beckford purchased *Gibbon's library en bloc in 1796. Additionally, he acquired about 10,000 books and 80 MSS, including *incunabula and other rare books, as well as a magnificent collection of bindings. His library went to his younger daughter, Susan, duchess of Hamilton, and was sold in 1882–4. ASGE
A. R. A. Hobson, 'William Beckford's Library', *The Connoisseur*, 191 (April 1976), 298–305
ODNB

bed The flat surface on which the *forme is supported in a printing press (resisting the pressure of the *platen). In a *common press, the *press stone forms the bed; the beds of later presses were usually of cast iron. In some presses the bed is vertical rather than horizontal. PWN

Bedford, Francis (1799–1883) English bookbinder, who worked for C. *Lewis before entering into partnership with John Clarke (1841–50), then setting up in business independently in 1851. He established a reputation as one of the finest London binders of the 19th century, though noted more for his craftsmanship than his designs, which were typically based on fine-binding styles of earlier centuries. DRSP
Nixon and Foot
ODNB

Bedford, John of Lancaster, duke of (1389–1435) Bedford commissioned at least three fine MSS: the

Bedford Psalter and Hours (signed by the illuminator Herman), a Sarum *breviary, and the Bedford Hours. The latter (BL Add. MS 18850)—produced in a Paris atelier while John was Regent of France for Henry VI—is among the most accomplished of late medieval MSS. 'Personalized' with portraits of John and his wife, it may have been ordered to mark their marriage (1423), although some leaves appear to be later additions, and others may have been already in stock. *See also* BEDFORD MASTER. BJF
ODNB

Bedford Master This highly accomplished French artist, active in Paris in the first quarter of the 15th century, is so named after the MSS commissioned from him by John, duke of *Bedford: the Bedford Hours (BL Add. MS 18850) and the Salisbury Breviary (BnF, ms. lat. 17294). His work has been identified in a number of other MSS now in Britain, Europe, and North America in public and private collections. Because he apparently worked in collaboration with a number of other artists, his oeuvre raises complex questions of *attribution (*see* 5). ASGE
E. König, *The Bedford Hours* (2007)

Bédier, Joseph (1864–1938) French medievalist and textual theorist, born in Paris, where he taught at the Collège de France from 1903. Following his important study *Les Fabliaux* (1893), he turned his attention to the Tristan romances, producing an edition (1902–5) of the poem by the 12th-century Anglo-Norman poet Thomas. He also worked on the *Song of Roland*. His history of French literature (with Paul Hazard) in 1923–4 is still considered a classic. *See also* BEST TEXT. VAG

Beer, Esmond Samuel de (1895–1990) Historian, editor, bibliophile, and benefactor, born in New Zealand. As an academic specializing in the late 17th century, he donated his private collection of books on the period to the University of Otago. His most important contributions to scholarship were as the editor of *Evelyn's diary, (1955), and of the correspondence of *Locke (1976–89). He was a benefactor to the *Bodleian, *British, and *London libraries. RWO
ODNB

Beeton, Samuel O. (1831–77) English publisher of the *English Woman's Domestic Magazine* (1852–77) and the *Boy's Own Magazine* (1855–74). With Charles Clarke, he was the first English publisher of *Uncle Tom's Cabin* (1852). He published Mrs *Beeton's *Book of Household Management* and other books of information. EBL
ODNB

Beeton's Book of Household Management English domestic manual. The mid-19th century witnessed a growing demand from aspirant middle-class readers for affordable sources of factual information. Among the publishers who recognized and met that demand, S. O. *Beeton was a leading pioneer, producing encyclopaedic compilations like *Beeton's Historian* (1860) and *Beeton's*

Dictionary of Universal Information (1862). *Beeton's Book of Household Management*, similarly, was intended to systematize in a cheap, single volume all of the knowledge required by a bourgeois wife to run an efficient home—medical remedies for ailing children, the etiquette of morning calls, the legal obligations of tenants, and, above all, the selection, preparation, and serving of food. *Household Management* was edited by Beeton's wife Isabella (1836–65), who pillaged wholesale and with minimal acknowledgment the works of her predecessors. It first appeared in 24 monthly *part issues (at 3*d*. each) between 1859 and 1861. The single volume edition (at 7*s*. 6*d*.) followed immediately and, according to Beeton himself, sold 60,000 copies in its first year. A second edition (serialized in twelve parts) appeared in 1863, and thereafter Beeton began to issue cheaper *abridgements, like *The Englishwoman's Cookery Book* (1863), focusing on the recipes. This process of repackaging continued after Beeton sold his list to *Ward, Lock, & Tyler in 1866, and titles soon began to incorporate the name 'Mrs Beeton' as a marketing device. Rescensions of *Household Management* appeared at intervals, revised and expanded to conform to changing tastes and conditions, until by the fifth edition (1923), hardly any of the original text survived. *See also* COOKBOOK.   RJD

S. Freeman, *Isabella and Sam* (1977)
K. Healy, *The Short Life and Long Times of Mrs Beeton* (2005)
ODNB

Behmer, Marcus (1879–1958) Illustrator and innovator of 20th-century German book design. Influenced by *Beardsley, he had a predilection for odd and fantastic imagery. He illustrated *Wilde (1903), Balzac (1904), Goethe (1910), and others, and designed bindings and book decoration.   WDL

H. Halbey, *Marcus Behmer als Buchillustrator* (1970)

Behrens, Peter (1868–1940) Architect, designer, and leading figure of the late *Jugendstil* and early-modernist *typography in Darmstadt, Düsseldorf, Berlin, and Vienna. He also co-invented the concept of corporate identity, creating printed materials (for AEG) with a unified design. Behrens designed the famous *types Behrens-Antiqua and Behrens-Mediaeval.   WDL

T. Buddensieg *et al.*, *Industriekultur: Peter Behrens and the AEG*, tr. I. B. Whyte (1978)

Beinecke Library, Yale University Yale's principal repository for early MSS and rare books in literature, theology, history, and the natural sciences. Housed in a building designed by Gordon Bunshaft (completed 1963), the collection includes some 780,000 volumes and more than a million MSS. It also houses the Yale Collections of American Literature, German Literature, Western Americana, and the *Osborn Collection. It encourages interdisciplinary research in medieval, Renaissance, and 18th-century studies, art history, photography, American studies, the history of printing, and artistic and literary

Beeton's Book of Household Management:
the *chromolithographed *frontispiece to the *first edition in book form (1861).

modernism. *See also* STERLING MEMORIAL LIBRARY; YALE UNIVERSITY LIBRARIES.   EDG
www.library.yale.edu/beinecke, consulted Oct. 2007

Beinecke Sr., Edwin J. (1886–1970), and **Frederick W. Beinecke** (1887–1971) American book collectors. The elder Beinecke was, like so many Yale book collectors, influenced as an undergraduate by *Tinker. Initially a collector of R. L. Stevenson, he turned his attention in later years to medieval MSS and *incunabula. These collections were later given to the *Beinecke Rare Book Library at Yale, which he built and endowed. After the library's opening in 1963 until his death, he continued to add a wide range of materials to the collection. From the early 1950s, Beinecke's brother Frederick donated regularly to *Yale University Library, particularly western Americana and materials relating to the Spanish west.
                                            ASGE
DABC

Bel, Matej (1684–1749) Leading Hungarian scholar of Slovak origin. Called 'the Great ornament of Hungary' (*Magnum decus Hungariae*), he organized scholarly research and promoted understanding among the nations of Hungary. His life's work was a historical/geographical account of Hungary (*Notitia Hungariae*, 1735–42). A

515

member of the *Royal Society in London, he edited and published the first regular Hungarian weekly, *Nova Posoniensia* (1721–2).   DP

J. Tibenský, ed., *Matej Bel, doba, život, dielo* (1987)

Belarus, National Library of (Natsional'naia Biblioteka Belarusi) Established in 1922, under the name of the State and University Library, it was separated from the University in 1926. The collection began receiving *legal deposit material from Belorussia and the USSR. In the 1930s, the library opened several branches. Of the two million collection items, only 321,000 survived World War II, although its treasures were safely evacuated; the library re-opened in 1944. When Belarus gained independence in 1991, the Minsk branch became the Presidential Library. The new building opened to the public in 2006.   ER

www.nlb.by/en/default.asp, consulted Oct. 2008

Belgium, Royal Library of, Brussels Founded in 1837, the library comprises several historical libraries, including those of the dukes of Burgundy (later enlarged by Spain's King Philip II), the religious orders abolished in the late 18th century, the private collector Charles Van Hulthem (1764–1832), and the city of Brussels. Since 1966, the library has administered the Belgian *legal deposit system and national bibliography. It holds some 5 million books, 35,000 MSS, 200,000 *maps, and 700,000 prints.   JP

www.kbr.be, consulted Sept. 2007

C. Sorgeloos *et al.*, eds., *Cent trésors de la Bibliothèque royale de Belgique* (2006)

Bell, James Ford (1879–1961) American book collector. A businessman, Bell developed a collection of books, maps, and MSS concerning travel, trade, and exploration between Europe and the non-European world, 1400–1800. Containing more than 20,000 items, it became, in 1953, the James Ford Bell Library in the University of Minnesota Library.   ASGE

[James Ford Bell Library,] *An Annotated Catalog of Original Source Materials Relating to the History of European Expansion, 1400–1800* (1994)

Bell, John (1745–1831) London printer, bookseller, publisher, typefounder, bookbinder, and journalist. He ran Bell's *Circulating Library and the British Library bookshop in the Strand, becoming bookseller to the Prince of Wales in the 1780s. In the later 1770s, Bell published *Bell's British Theatre and Poets of Great Britain*. These popular series were joined by an edition of Shakespeare. Bell was also a leading publisher of newspapers and periodicals, including *The Morning Post* (launched 1772); *The World, or Fashionable Gazette* (1788); *The Oracle* (1789); *Bell's Weekly Messenger* (1796); and *Belle Assemblee, or Court and Fashionable Magazine* (1806), which was 'Addressed Particularly to the Ladies'. As a printer, Bell was a pioneer of type design, commissioning *Caslon to develop a new *fount for the *Morning Post*; in 1788 he started the British Letter Foundry. His

interest in 'modern' *type is credited with the demise of the long 's' (*see* S AND LONG S). Despite his successes in the book trade, Bell was found guilty of *libel in 1792 and twice declared bankrupt (1793, 1797).   JES

T. F. Bonnell, *The Most Disreputable Trade* (2008)

S. Morison, *John Bell* (1930)

L. Werkmeister, *The London Daily Press, 1772–1792* (1963)

Bell, Robert (*c*.1732–84) Auctioneer, bookseller, and printer. Born in Scotland, Bell migrated to Philadelphia in 1768, where he established himself as a successful book auctioneer and reprinter of English books. In January 1776, he printed Thomas Paine's controversial pamphlet *Common Sense*, which established Bell as a major printer of the Revolution, publishing important works for both sides. *See also* RIGHTS OF MAN.   EJL

J. Green, 'English Books and Printing in the Age of Franklin', in *HBA* 1

Bell & Sons, George London educational publisher, founded in 1839 by George Bell, who was in partnership with Frederick Daldy from 1855 to 1873. In 1864 the firm bought H. G. *Bohn's Libraries, adding to them until 1924. The firm published educational and classic series including the 'Bibliotheca Classica' and *Bell's 'Poets of Great Britain'. In 1977, the *publisher's list was sold to Robin Hyman and became Bell & Hyman Ltd.   AAW

ODNB

Bell's British Theatre and ***Poets of Great Britain*** Published by the innovative bookseller and printer John *Bell, *Bell's British Theatre* (21 vols, 1776–8) and *Bell's Poets of Great Britain Complete From Chaucer to Churchill* (109 vols, 1776–83) were among the first cheap reprint series of the late 18th and early 19th centuries. These collections were published and distributed in direct competition with the London printing establishment, and as a result of the House of Lords' 1774 ruling against perpetual *copyright in *Donaldson vs Becket (1774). *Bell's British Theatre*, begun after the initial success of his 'acting' edition of Shakespeare (1773–8), featured carefully produced but inexpensive editions of more than 100 *plays by British dramatists, together with prints of prominent actors in costume and character from those plays. The *Poets of Great Britain*, printed for Bell by Gilbert and John Martin at Edinburgh's Apollo Press in a portable eighteenmo edition, has long been recognized as the impetus behind the competing series of E. *Dilly and his group of London booksellers, which featured biographical and critical sketches of each poet by S. *Johnson. In their popularity and accessibility, both *Bell's British Theatre* and his *Poets of Great Britain* are credited with fostering the concept of a specifically British literary canon among a broad number of popular readers; they were reprinted often, well into the 19th century.   JES

T. F. Bonnell, *The Most Disreputable Trade* (2008)

K. A. Burnim and P. H. Highfill, Jr., *John Bell* (1998)

S. Morison, *John Bell* (1930)

Bembo, Pietro (1470–1547) Cardinal, Venetian patrician, literary theorist, and author. Bembo had enduring relations with *Aldus, who published his dialogues *De Aetna* (1496) and *Gli Asolani* (1505); derivatives of the type cut for *Aetna* by *Griffo are still known by the name 'Bembo'. The epoch-making Aldines of *Petrarca and *Dante (1501–2) were edited by Bembo from his own MSS. Earlier, he helped *Poliziano collate his late-antique *Codex Bembinus* of Terence. Bembo later wrote the *Prose della volgar lingua* (1525), which established a model for the Italian language based on medieval Tuscan.   MCD

Bemporad Florence publishing house specializing in children's books. Established in 1889 by Roberto Bemporad (1842–91)—who married into the Paggi firm—publisher of Collodi's *Pinocchio* (1883). The firm was subsequently built up by his son Enrico (1868–1944). In 1938, the family's Jewish status made it change its name to Marzocco, after the ancient lion symbol of the City of Florence. In 1956, it was bought by Giunti and, in 1960, merged with *Barbèra to form the present-day publishing group.   NH
L. Cappelli, *Le edizioni Bemporad* (2009)
DBI
EIDO

Bemrose & Sons British publisher, founded 1858, from William Bemrose's printing and publishing firm of London and Derby, established 1826–7. Specializing in *railway timetables, local *almanacs, books on applied arts, archaeology, theology, school *stationery, and *textbooks, the company concentrated exclusively on printing from 1909.   JEP
DLB 106

Benedicht, Lorentz (d. *c*.1604) Printer, xylographer, and publisher in Copenhagen. In 1565 a royal *privilege granted him exclusive rights to all printing in Denmark. Although this soon proved untenable, Benedicht retained a dominant position in the trade. He introduced cast music and *black-letter type in the German style to the country. His masterpiece is a magnificent illustrated *folio about the art of war, printed for King Frederik II in only one copy (1578).   CA, KSP
R. Paulli, *Lorentz Benedicht* (1920)

Beneventan script A form of *minuscule script, developed in southern Italy from the mid-8th century by the Benedictine order, initially at their abbey of Monte Cassino. Derived from Roman *cursive script, it was one of the most enduring forms of writing employed in the Middle Ages, continuing in widespread use until the 14th century, and locally beyond that time. It was employed chiefly in liturgical MSS.   ASGE
E. A. Loew [Lowe], *The Beneventan Script*, rev. V. Brown, 2e (2 vols, 1980)

Bengali Family Library An Indian series published by the *Vernacular Literature Society. It aimed to publish titles for a popular collection suitable for both men and women readers. Its first work was a Bengali translation of *Robinson Crusoe: Rabinsan krusor bhramaṇ bṛttānta* (*c*.1852).   SKC

Bening, Simon (*c*.1483–1561) The most famous Flemish illuminator of the 16th century, whose achievements earned the contemporary admiration of Vasari. Bening seems initially to have worked for his father, Alexander (*c*.1469–1518), but by the 1520s he appears to have been running his own very successful workshop. He produced miniatures (*see* MINIATURE (1)) for a large number of religious MSS, all characterized by an extraordinary skill in the creation of dramatic scenes through a naturalism complemented by the deft use of detail.   ASGE
T. Kren, ed., *Renaissance Painting in Manuscripts* (1983)

Benjacob, Isaac (1801–63) Hebrew bibliographer. His *Ozar Ha-Sepharim* (1877–80), edited and published by his son Jacob (1858–1926) in Vilnius, is the last attempt at achieving a comprehensive Hebrew bibliography, including MSS and printed books. Among the *c*.15,000 entries are *c*.3,000 MSS. In 1965, M. M. Slatkine published a supplement.   EGLS

Benn Brothers Ltd London publisher established in 1880 by J. W. Benn. Initially publishing trade journals, the company broadened its range to include mass *paperback publishing under Ernest Benn in the 1920s. It was sold to United Business Media in 1987.   KL
R. Woolley, *The House of Benn* (1980)

Bent, Andrew (1790–1851) Australian printer and publisher. Transported to Tasmania for burglary, Bent became government printer in 1816. He printed the *Hobart Town Gazette* until 1825, when Governor Arthur imprisoned him for seditious *libel. Bent then started his own newspaper, the *Colonial Times* (1825–57). He also published an *almanac, 1824–30. After further libel trials in the 1830s forced him to sell the *Colonial Times*, he moved to Sydney, where he died in poverty.   IM
ADB

Bentley, Richard (1662–1742) English classical scholar and editor; friend of Wren, *Locke, and I. *Newton; Boyle lecturer (1692, 1694); appointed Keeper of the King's Libraries (1694); FRS (1697); Master of Trinity College, Cambridge from 1699; projector and founder of the modern *Cambridge University Press. His first published work was the *Epistola ad Joannem Millium* (1691), a virtuoso scholarly excursus on the writings of the 6th-century chronicler John Malalas. After Sir William Temple founded his argument for the supremacy of the ancients in part on the writings of the Sicilian tyrant *Phalaris, Bentley demonstrated, from literary, etymological, and historical evidence, that Phalaris's extant works were spurious (*Dissertation upon the Epistles of Phalaris*, in W. Wotton, *Reflections upon Ancient and Modern Learning*, 2e 1697; second *Dissertation*, much expanded, 1699). Bentley's edition of Horace (1711; important 2e, Amsterdam 1713) exemplifies his characteristic brilliance in diagnosing error, and willingness to introduce *emendation based on metrical and semantic considerations. In 1720, he proposed an edition of the New Testament, never completed. An edition of *Paradise Lost* (1732) took conjecture to extremes, unsupported by the contextual scholarship which had validated his Horace. Bentley's edition of the *Astronomicon* of Manilius, begun in the 1690s, appeared in 1739. MW

ODNB

Bentley, Richard (1708–82) English designer, draughtsman, and engraver. The classicist Richard *Bentley's son, and one of *Walpole's 'Committee on Taste', he worked on designs for Strawberry Hill, and illustrated *Gray's poetry for publications by R. *Dodsley and the *Strawberry Hill Press. MMS

ODNB

Bentley, Richard (1794–1871) English publisher. Initially in partnership with *Colburn and alone from 1832, Bentley ranks among the leading publishers of 19th-century fiction. In 1834, he had great commercial success with Lytton's *Last Days of Pompeii* and Ainsworth's *Rookwood*, and in 1837 he founded *Bentley's Miscellany* which promptly serialized its first editor's *Oliver Twist*. Although the firm was in difficulties by the 1850s (competition undercut the 'Standard Novels' reprint series and the *Miscellany* was sold in 1854), the publication of Mrs Henry Wood's *East Lynne* (1861) began a revival, and in 1866 Bentley bought the magazine *Temple Bar*, which enlisted a wealth of late Victorian writers from Trollope to Marie Corelli. The business survived Bentley's death under his son George, but its fortunes declined with those of the *three-decker novel; following George's death in 1895, the firm's assets were sold to *Macmillan. RJD

ODNB

Bent's Monthly Literary Advertiser (1805–58) Principal early 19th-century English book trade journal. Founded by the cataloguer William Bent as the *Monthly Literary Advertiser*, on his death in 1823 it was continued by his son Robert, who modified the title in 1829. Initially consisting entirely of publishers' advertisements, it soon carried literary news and notices of book auctions, trade vacancies, etc.; the January issue catalogued all books published the previous year. Originally serving booksellers, printsellers, and libraries, *Bent's*—along with its successor, the *Bookseller*—now represents an invaluable resource for bibliographers. GL

A. Growell, *Three Centuries of English Booktrade Bibliography* (1964)

Benua (Benois), Aleksandr (1870–1960) Russian painter, book illustrator, art historian and critic, theatre designer, and leading figure in the World of Art movement. His innovative ideas on the art of book illustration (*see* **16**) and the problems of graphics were expressed in articles and illustrations for journals such as *World of Art* and *Golden Fleece*. His predilection for fantastic subjects

is evident in his romantic illustrations for E. T. A. Hoffmann's works and for Pushkin's *The Queen of Spades* and *The Bronze Horseman*. PH

M. Etkind, *A. N. Benua i russkaia khudozhestvennaia kul'tura* (1989)

Ben-Yehuda, Eliezer (1858–1922) Hebrew writer and lexicographer, father of modern Hebrew. Born Eliezer Isaac Perlman in Lithuania, he changed his name in Palestine in 1881. His life's work was the revival of Hebrew as the national Jewish language, his chief publication a seventeen-volume *Complete Dictionary of Ancient and Modern Hebrew* (1908–59). EGLS

Benzing, Josef (1904–81) German librarian and bibliographer, employed by the *Prussian State Library (*see* STAATSBIBLIOTHEK ZU BERLIN) (1934–45), and Mainz University Library (1946–66). His special interest was in 16th-century German printing. His publications include: *Ulrich von Hutten und seine Drucker* (1956), *Die Buchdrucker des 16. und 17. Jahrhunderts im deutschen Sprachgebiet* (1963; 2e, 1982; new edn by C. Reske 2007), *Lutherbibliographie* (1966; 2e, 2 vols, 1989–94), *Bibliographie haguenovienne* (1973), *Bibliographie strasbourgeoise* (1981–6), and monographs on individual *printing offices. JLF

Beowulf MS BL Cotton MS Vitellius A. XV., copied in the 10th century, contains the only surviving copy of the longest extant Old English poem, together with other verse and prose from this period. It was owned by *Nowell in the 16th century. In the *Cotton fire of 1731, the MS was damaged and has suffered further loss of text over time. In 1787 an Icelandic scholar, G. J. Thorkelin, prepared two transcripts of *Beowulf*, preserving readings now lost in the original MS. ASGE

K. Malone, ed., *The Nowell Codex* (1963)

Berg, Albert A. (1872–1950) American collector and physician. With his brother Henry Berg (1858–1938), he formed a collection of English and American literature, given in 1940 to the *New York Public Library. In 1941 he added the collections of Owen Young (1874–1962), given jointly, and of W. T. H. Howe (1874–1939), making the Berg collection an exceptionally fine repository of English and American literature. He also bequeathed a generous endowment. MEK

Bergendal Collection The largest collection of medieval MSS in private hands in North America, it was created by Joseph Pope (1921–) in Toronto, and is devoted to religious works. Some of the MSS have been donated to the Pontifical Institute of Medieval Studies. ASGE

Bergendal Collection, www3.sympatico.ca/bergendalcoll, consulted May 2008

J. Pope, *One Hundred and Twenty-Five Manuscripts: Bergendal Collection Catalogue* (1999)

Bergmann, von Olpe, Johann (1455/60–1532) Swiss printer, priest, humanist. In Basel, he printed works by

*Reuchlin, Jakob Wimpfeling, and Sebastian Brant, producing famous editions of Geoffroy de La Tour Landry's *Livre du Chevalier* (German translation, 1493) and Brant's *Narrenschiff* (1494), with woodcuts by *Dürer. CS
Geldner

Bergnes de las Casas, Antonio (1801–79) Spanish publisher. Professor of Greek and sometime rector of the University of Barcelona, he was also a distinguished editor, publisher, and translator. His *c*.300 *imprints—some issued in the series 'Biblioteca Selecta, Portátil y Económica'—included many contemporary European works in Spanish translation. DRW

Berkley Publishing Corporation *Paperback house founded as the Chic News Company in 1954 by Charles Byrne and Frederic Klein, who had worked for *Avon. In 1955 they renamed the firm and started publishing books, specializing in *science fiction and *fantasy. Berkley authors include Robert Heinlein and Frank Herbert. In 1965 Berkley was purchased by *Putnam, whose large science fiction list enhanced its reprint opportunities. Ten years later, Putnam was purchased by MCA. Since 1996, Berkley has been a division of *Penguin Putnam and publishes in all genres, including *mystery and adventure. BEL
K. C. Davis, *Two-Bit Culture* (1984)

Berlin, Deutsche Staatsbibliothek *See* STAATSBIB-LIOTHEK ZU BERLIN.

Berlin, State Library of *See* STAATSBIBLIOTHEK ZU BERLIN.

Berlingske Tidende The oldest Danish newspaper still in existence. It was founded in 1749 by Ernst Heinrich Berling, a member of a German family which established itself as printers in Denmark and Sweden. Berling obtained an exclusive *privilege to distribute his newspaper (originally *Kiøbenhavnske Danske Post-Tidender*) by post. For most of the 19th century it had a semi-official status. Since 1903, *Berlingske Tidende* has been a leading independent, conservative newspaper. CA, KSP

Berne (Bern), **City and University Library of** (StUB) The library's beginnings are linked to the Reformation of 1528, when the University of Bern was founded; accordingly, the libraries of secularized monasteries form the core collection of the present-day 2.2 million holdings. Its most important special collections are the private libraries of the French diplomat and Huguenot Jacques Bongars, donated in 1632, and of the humanist Leonhard Hospinian. In 1951, the newly founded independent Burgerbibliothek (Burger Library) took over the MSS and graphics section of the StUB. RAK
IDLH

Berne Convention The oldest international *copyright agreement. Established in 1886 largely by European nations, the Berne Convention for the Protection of Literary and Artistic Works now has above 150 signatories. A member-state must grant copyright holders of other member-states parity of protection with its nationals. DS
S. Ricketson, *The Berne Convention* (1987)

Berry, Jean, duc de (1340–1416) Son of Jean II of France and greatest *bibliophile of his time. He hired the Lombard illuminator Pietro da Verona as his librarian, and owned historical texts, *romances, and various scientific and astrological works. Among his 59 religious MSS were fifteen *books of hours, purchased or commissioned from the illuminators André Beauneveu, Jacquemart de Hesdin, and, especially, the *Limbourg brothers. These include the *Petites Heures*, the *Grandes Heures* (both *Bibliothèque nationale de France), the *Belles Heures* (Cloisters, New York), the *Très Belles Heures* (Louvre, BnF, and Turin; partly destroyed in 1904), and the *Très Riches Heures* (*Chantilly). *See also* 5. VAG

Bertelsmann World-wide media corporate group located in Gütersloh, Germany now with branches in 63 countries. Shareholders are Bertelsmann Stiftung and the Mohn family. The corporate portfolio includes television and radio, book publishers, magazines and newspapers, music labels, print and media services. Founded in 1835 by Carl Bertelsmann, it originally sought to support the Great Awakening religious movement in Protestant Germany. During the Third Reich, it published volkish-nationalistic and war literature, as well as special Armed Forces editions, but in 1944 the company was closed down. After World War II, Reinhard Mohn refounded the publishing house, which grew into an international company. The 'Bertelsmann Lesering' (book club), founded in 1950, led to similar ventures in many European countries. In 1958 Bertelsmann entered the music market by starting 'Ariola Records'; in 1964 it acquired the 'Ufa Filmproduktionsgesellschaft'. Among Bertelsmann's holdings are German publishing houses such as *Deutsche Verlagsanstalt, the majority of the German newspaper and magazine publishing group Gruner + Jahr (Hamburg), and *Random House Inc. (New York). US
150 Jahre Bertelsmann (1985)
S. Friedländer *et al.*, *Bertelsmann im Dritten Reich* (2002)

Bertelsmann Club Part of the *Bertelsmann group, it is the largest German *book club, with more than 6 million members. The Club offers popular fiction, non-fiction books, and *encyclopaedias, as well as books for children and adolescents. While the Club cooperates with 80 bookshops, it serves its members directly by mail without intermediate trade. It originated from the 'Lesering', founded in 1950: initially Bertelsmann supplied only their own titles because other licences were not yet available. From 1964 onwards, in cooperation with the book trade, the Club established shops alongside the mail order business, while Club Centres sell Bertelsmann offers only. Other media, such as records or DVDs, were soon added to the books. Bertelsmann took over the Deutsche Buchgemeinschaft and, in 1992, Bücherbund, the book club of the Holtzbrinck group. The Club is also active in 24 countries. ME

S. Eckert, *Rentabilitätssteigerung durch Kundenbindung am Beispiel eines Buchclubs* (1994)

Berthelet, Thomas (d. 1555) London printer. Working from *c.*1524, he began printing humanistic authors (Erasmus, Vives, Colet) from his *printing office 'at the sign of the Roman Lucrece' in Fleet Street. He became *King's Printer in 1530 and produced Henry VIII's statutes and proclamations, as well as works such as the *Glasse of Truthe* (1532) and Katherine Parr's *Prayers and Medytacions* (1545). CYF
ODNB

Berthold, Hermann (1831–1904) Typographer. He established an *electrotype firm in Berlin in 1858, and developed the late 19th-century German system for measuring type. The business grew into the world's largest typefoundry, pioneering in the 1950s diatype and diatronic *photocomposition. WDL
100 Jahre Berthold (1958)

Beruni Institute of Oriental Studies Library, Tashkent In the USSR, most Republics' Institutes of Oriental Studies boasted well-resourced research libraries. Uzbekistan's Beruni Library, founded 1943, remains the richest in Arabic, Persian, and Turkic MSS, with more than 25,000 volumes (many from the former State Public Library) containing 45,000 texts. MIW

Bessarion, Cardinal Johannes (*c.*1403–72) Byzantine scholar, Catholic prelate, and book collector who worked (unsuccessfully) to unite the Byzantine and Western Churches. A scholar of Plato and patron of contemporary humanists, he left his splendid library, including many Greek MSS, to the city of Venice. CWK
DBI
G. Fiaccadori, ed., *Bessarione e l'umanesimo* (1994)

Besterman, Theodore (1904–76) Polish-born English bibliographer and editor. His major work, *A World Bibliography of Bibliographies* (1939–40; thrice expanded), listed all bibliographies separately published from 1470 to 1935 in the British Museum (*see* BRITISH LIBRARY) catalogue. He served as founding editor for the *Journal of Documentation*, edited the correspondence of Voltaire, and initiated a new edition of his works as well as a series of 'Studies on Voltaire and the Eighteenth Century'. KEA
ODNB

bestiary A type of book containing descriptions of the physiognomy and behaviour of animals, both fantastical and real, usually with a Christian moralization. Bestiaries also include information on rocks, and in some cases, plants and the Monstrous Races. The majority of bestiaries are English (some 50 MSS are known), though MSS made in other northern European centres (notably France, Flanders, and Germany) also survive.

Bestiary MSS were especially popular in the 12th and 13th centuries.

The medieval Latin bestiary is principally rooted in the 2nd-century AD Greek *Physiologus*, which provided a moral and metaphysical interpretation of nature drawing on the Bible and Church Fathers, as well as on ancient sources including Aristotle, Pliny, and Solinus. *Physiologus* was translated into Latin in the 4th century. Of the early MS witnesses, a 9th-century MS is the earliest illustrated example (Berne, Bürgerbibliothek Lat. 318). The bestiary also borrowed extensively from Isidore of Seville's *Etymologiae* (Book XII), written in the 7th century, which offers an account of animals based on the analysis of their names.

Bestiaries emerged in the 12th century in a distinctive form that combined short texts with images. M. R. *James grouped bestiaries into 'families' on the basis of their texts. The First Family, a group of 12th-century MSS within which there are significant variations, is principally reliant on *Physiologus*, with additional information supplied by Isidore. The Second Family, of which some 25 English MSS survive, developed in the 12th century and is noteworthy for its structural consistency. Only five examples survive of the Third Family, all 13th-century. In these MSS, the text is rearranged and supplemented with additional material—notably on various marvels, including the Monstrous Races, the Fabulous Monsters, and the Seven Wonders of the World. The Westminster Abbey Bestiary (Westminster Abbey, MS 22), made *c.*1275–1300, is the best preserved of these MSS. The Fourth Family consists of a single 15th-century MS (CUL MS Gg 6.5; *c.*1450–75), based on the encyclopaedia of Bartholomaeus Anglicus.

Bestiary images range in technique and quality from relatively simple, sometimes even scruffy MSS to impressively de luxe books. The simplest MSS are illustrated with line drawings, such as Bodleian MS Laud misc. 247 (the earliest surviving English Latin bestiary, *c.*1110–1300) and BL Stowe MS 1067 (*c.*1120–40). The most splendid bestiaries have fully painted and gilded miniatures (*see* MINIATURES (1)); the Worksop Bestiary (New York, Pierpont Morgan MS 81; *c.*1185), the Ashmole Bestiary (Bodleian MS Ashmole 1511; *c.*1200–1210), and the Aberdeen Bestiary (Aberdeen, University Library MS 24; *c.*1200–1210) are among the most luxurious examples.

Typically, each entry in a bestiary begins with an image of the subject of the chapter in question, followed by a description of its appearance and habits, and finally with an allegorical interpretation. The entry for the swan in Oxford, Bodleian MS Bodley 764 (*c.*1240–60), for example, begins with an image of a swan swimming with a fish in its beak. The text describes the meaning of its Latin and Greek names, explaining that the Latin 'cignus' denotes its sweet singing voice. The swan's white feathers concealing black flesh is an analogy for how deceit conceals sin; likewise, its sweet deathbed song is an analogy for the delight taken in worldly things by a proud man even when dying.

Of the English bestiaries with a documented medieval provenance, all but one (Oxford, Bodleian MS Bodley

764) belonged to religious houses. The evidence of institutional book lists demonstrates that bestiaries were categorized as works of theology, grouped together with texts concerning preaching, penance, and moral philosophy, rather than as natural philosophy. Other bestiaries were owned by elite patrons: the first bestiary in French, for example, was dedicated to Henry I's queen. The *Queen Mary Psalter (BL Royal MS 2 B.VII), c.1320, a de luxe MS associated circumstantially with royal *patronage, includes an extensive bas-de-page bestiary cycle.

The relationship between the bestiary and the natural world has attracted much debate. If taken as a work of natural history, the bestiary appears to be strewn with errors, misinformation, and flights of fantasy. For example, according to the bestiary, elephants have no knees; beavers escape from hunters by biting off their own testicles and throwing them at their pursuers; and bears give birth to shapeless foetuses that they lick into cub-shape. Further, bestiaries present real, often quotidian animals (e.g. ants, goats, and dogs) alongside fantastical creatures (e.g. the dragon, the griffin, and the unicorn). Yet the primary aim of the bestiary is manifestly not to function as a zoological tract, but rather as a work of allegory and morality. The pelican, for example, is said to kill its young; three days later the mother pierces her side and lets the blood pour over her dead chicks, which then come back to life. The moralization explains that the pelican signifies Christ: it kills its chicks as the word of God converts unbelievers (killing them to their old lives), and it revives its chicks with its own blood just as Christ saves Christians.

Localizing and dating the production of English bestiaries is notoriously difficult: the evidence is largely circumstantial, and open to conflicting interpretations. Bestiaries seem to have been produced at centres in York and Lincolnshire; it has been argued that the Third Family Bestiary originated at St Augustine's, Canterbury. The dating of bestiary MSS largely relies on evidence of *script, decoration, and *codicology. Production of bestiary MSS slowed in the 14th century, but their influence remained extensive. Iconography apparently derived from (or at least relating to) bestiaries can be found in numerous contexts in the later Middle Ages, including illuminated MSS and misericords.   AB

R. Baxter, *Bestiaries and Their Users in the Middle Ages* (1998)
M. R. James, *The Bestiary* (1928)
F. McCulloch, *Medieval Latin and French Bestiaries* (1960)
X. Muratova, *The Medieval Bestiary* (1984)

bestseller lists The bestseller list has long served as one of journalism's main tools of influence over the book industry. The earliest bestseller lists appeared in the London literary journal *The Bookman* from 1891 to 1901, and in that journal's New York imitator, also called *The Bookman*, from 1895 to 1912. The longest-running American lists are those of *Publishers Weekly* and the *New York Times*. Launched in 1913, *Publishers Weekly* reproduced data available in other journals. In contrast, the *Times* list (launched 1931) followed the *Bookman*

model by soliciting proprietary reports from selected booksellers. Initially focused on sales in New York and other target cities, the *Times* first offered a national summary in 1942, when it began publishing the list in its Sunday Book Review. Since then, the *Times* has expanded and refined its list to indicate separate rankings not only for fiction and non-fiction, but also for hardcover and *paperback, and for such commercially potent but low-status sub-categories as *advice, *how-to, and children's books (*see* **15**).

Other newspapers have established rival lists, ranging from the *Village Voice*'s more selective, narrowly 'literary' list (based on sales at certain independent book stores) to *USA Today*'s more inclusive list (which mixes all genres together and is based on sales figures from c.4,500 shops and online merchants). Many of the other American and British lists, online as well as on paper, are based on data from Nielsen BookScan, which compiles the most complete and rigorous book-sales rankings available.

Despite these proliferating and, in some cases, more accurate alternatives, the *Times* list remains the most powerful. Most American bookstores still post it prominently for customer reference and key their own wholesale purchases to its rankings. It is the list most frequently named on the covers of books seeking to leverage their 'bestseller' status into further sales, and it is the list most often specified in bonus clauses of *author–publisher agreements. Although its sales rankings are strictly national, they have had an increasingly international impact as the 'blockbuster' model of publishing has been extended globally.   JFE

T. J. Bassett and C. M. Walter, 'Booksellers and Bestsellers: British Book Sales as Documented by *The Bookman*, 1891–1906', *Book History*, 4 (2001), 205–36
A. P. Hackett, *70 Years of Best-Sellers: 1895–1965* (1967)
L. J. Miller, 'The Best Seller List as Marketing Tool and Historical Fiction', *BH* 3 (2000), 286–300

best text The single extant witness, MS or print, with the strongest claim to textual authority for a given work. Determining which text is 'best' depends on the criteria employed: some favour the earliest text for its proximity to the author, while others favour the text with the smallest number of errors. Best-text editing, a conservative method of *critical editing derived from *Bédier, employs a single document as the base text and emends only obvious mistakes.   RSG

J. Bédier, 'La Tradition manuscrite du *Lai de l'Ombre*: réflexions sur l'art d'éditer les anciens textes', *Romania*, 54 (1928), 161–96, 321–56

beta radiography Imaging process akin to photography, where a paper sample is interposed between a beta-ray source and a sensitized film or detector, producing a record relating to the areal basis weight density of the sheet. Used for imaging the flocculated 2-D structure of paper, and for recording *watermarks.   DCC

Beughem, Cornelis van (1639–after 1717) Dutch bibliographer. Having worked for J. *Janssonius van

Waesberge and other booksellers in Amsterdam, he started his own bookshop in his birthplace, Emmerich, in 1680. He compiled a series of thematically and systematically arranged bibliographies of outstanding quality, among which is the first *incunable bibliography, *Incunabula Typographiae* (1688). PGH

L. Balsamo, *Bibliography* (1990)

R. Blum, *Bibliographia. Eine wort- und begriffsgeschichtliche Untersuchung* (1969)

Be'ur Bible commentary by one of the founders of the Jewish Enlightenment in Berlin, Moses Mendelssohn (1729–86), with an edition and translation into German (in Hebrew characters). Published in the 1780s and 1790s, the Be'ur reflects a strong ideology. Mendelssohn was the translator and cooperated with Solomon Dubno (1738–1813) on the commentary; others too subsequently collaborated. EGLS

bevel The edge surrounding the *face on a piece of type.

Bewick, Thomas (1753–1828) English wood-engraver. Apprenticed to a metal engraver, Bewick developed the method of using the engraver's burin on the end-grain of wood and largely revived the art of wood engraving (*see* WOODCUT ILLUSTRATION) in Britain. Among his famous early works are his illustrations (*see* **16**) for Gay's *Fables* (1779) and *Select Fables* (1784), and for Ralph Beilby's *A General History of Quadrupeds* (1790). His best-known illustrations are those for *A History of British Birds* (2 vols, 1797–1804). KES

I. Bain, ed., *A Memoir of Thomas Bewick Written by Himself* (1975; rev. ed., 1979) (including chronology and bibliography)

ODNB

Beyazit State Library, Istanbul The first Ottoman state library, opened in 1884 and intended to be a national library. Since 1934, it has served as one of the six *legal deposit libraries in Turkey. Its holdings include private and foundation collections from Ottoman provinces with over 11,000 MSS and 40,000 books, mostly in the Arabic script. SYM

Bezige Bij, De Dutch publisher. It originated in the Dutch resistance during World War II, publishing clandestinely to aid Jewish children. In 1944 it became a cooperative society, albeit still run by its founder, Geert Lubberhuizen (1916–84). Specializing in Dutch and translated literary fiction, it published most of the chief postwar Low Countries authors. Its highly influential *paperback series of 20th-century world classics, 'Literaire Reuzenpockets' (1959), remains in print. The company is now part of Weekbladpers Groep. AHVDW

D. Cartens, ed., *Hoger honing: 60 jaar De Bezige Bij* (2004)

R. Roegholt, *De geschiedenis van De Bezige Bij 1942–1972* (1972)

Bhaghavadgītā Dating from around the 1st century BC, the *Bhagavadgītā* (Sanskrit for 'Song of the Lord') is an important religious text for many Hindus. Appended to the sixth book of the *Mahābhārata*, it has had a long and independent life as one of the foundational texts of Vedantic philosophy. Since the 8th century, it has been the subject of numerous *commentaries, such as those by Śaṃkara, Jñāndeva, Rāmānuja, and Mādhva. Because of its centrality to Vaishnava theology and theistic content, the *Bhagavadgītā* caught the imagination of the West. It was first translated into English by *Wilkins in 1785. Schlegel translated it into Latin in 1823, and Humboldt into German in 1826. A French translation by Burnouf appeared in 1861. It had a significant impact on Gandhi, who read the *Bhagavadgītā* in Edwin Arnold's 1885 translation as a student in London. There have been more than 300 translations of the work into English alone.

The first printed edition of the *Bhagavadgītā* in Sanskrit was issued from Bāburām's Press in Calcutta (Kolkata) in 1808. Robert Nesbit's Marathi translation appeared in 1832; the first version in Bengali was published in 1835. By the last decade of the 19th century, it had also been translated into Spanish. The same period saw a number of commentaries on the *Bhagavadgītā* by Indian thinkers such as Sri Aurobindo, Swāmī Vivekānanda, and Bal Gangadhar Tilak. Currently, the best-known translation of and commentary on the text is by Prabhupada A. C. Bhaktivedanta (1968). *See also* **39**. VBh

Bhaṭṭācārya, Jatīndramohan (1905–90) Compiler of *Mudrita bāṅglā granther panji* (2 vols, 1990–93), the first catalogue of Bengali books printed between 1743 and 1867. He also collected MSS; a substantial part of his collection is now in the National Council of Education, Bengal, in Calcutta (Kolkata). SKC

bibelot Literally, a small curio or collectable item; also, the title of a periodical edited by *Mosher, published in Portland, Maine 1895–1914, containing anthologies of lesser-known works by contemporary authors. It was reprinted in New York in 1924, with a final index volume issued in 1925. DRSP

Bible *See* **2**.

bible paper *See* INDIA PAPER.

Biblia Pauperum A work, consisting mainly of illustrations of scenes from the Bible, which first appeared in the middle of the 13th century and probably originated in Austria or Bavaria. The title, given in a later age, is a misinterpretation of the purpose of the work, which was not primarily intended for teaching the contents of the Bible to those who could not read; rather it delivered a complicated theological message to those who would recognize the biblical scenes. This is the typological notion that events described in the Old Testament ('Types') prefigure the events described in the Gospels ('Antitypes'). 'Prefiguration' is expressed in the words of St Augustine: 'Novum Testamentum in Vetere latet, Vetus in Novo patet' ('The New Testament in the Old lies concealed, the Old in the New is revealed').

In all versions of the *Biblia Pauperum*, openings of *verso and *recto pages are to be viewed in combination. On each page a central image of the life of Christ is flanked by two prefiguring images from the Old Testament. The sequence follows the life of Christ, in some versions extended with the life of the Virgin, and the Last Judgement.

The popularity of the work is evident from some 80 surviving MSS. About 1455–8, the first blockbook (*see* BLOCK PRINTING) edition was printed in Germany, and in this form the work is best known. In the blockbook versions, each opening shows an architectural structure that separates images as if they are sections of a triptych. Above and below the central image are two windows with portraits of prophets. The four spaces above and below the Old Testament images are filled with text identifying the images and Bible texts. After some 200 years of transmission in MS, traditions had diversified, reflected in three distinct versions in the blockbooks, which are known in fourteen editions, represented in almost 130 copies. The earliest, known only as a unique copy in the John *Rylands University Library, was printed in Germany, *c.*1458–60. This was followed by editions printed *c.*1464 in the Low Countries. The last of the blockbooks were printed in 1470 or 1471 in Nuremberg and Nördlingen.

In the same period three editions of the *Biblia Pauperum* (one with Latin, two with German text) were printed in Bamberg by Albrecht Pfister, datable to the early 1460s, with a reduced amount of text, because the only printing type he possessed was very large. A final adaptation appeared early in the 16th century in Paris, in editions where the originally brief textual elements were expanded with an extensive commentary.　　　　LH

U. Baurmeister, 'Das Blockbuch', in *Rationalisierung der Buchherstellung im Mittelalter und in der frühen Neuzeit*, ed. P. Rück *et al.* (1994)

BMC 1

A. Henry, 'The Iconography of the Forty-Page Blockbook Biblia Pauperum: Form and Meaning', in [Gutenberg-Museum, Mainz,] *Blockbücher des Mittelalters: Bilderfolgen als Lektüre* (1991)

G. Schmidt, *Die Armenbibeln des XIV Jahrhunderts* (1959)

A. H. Stevenson, 'The Quincentennial of Netherlandish blockbooks', *BMQ* 31 (1967), 83–7

Bibliofilía, La Launched in 1899 by the antiquarian bookseller *Olschki, it is the most authoritative Italian journal in the field of bibliography and book history. Pioneering in its use of a large format and of high-quality photographic illustrations, it is the flagship of the publishing house of the same name. Under the direction of *Ridolfi (1944–83), it focused attention primarily on *incunabula, but with *Balsamo (1984–), it has broadened its horizons.　　　　NH

L. Balsamo *et al.*, eds., *Cento anni di Bibliofilía* (2001)

bibliographical control The concept of having a comprehensive and searchable listing of the entire published output in a particular field. Universal bibliographical control—a popular later 20th-century idea for which the *International Federation of Library Associations developed a staffed programme (closed 2003)—refers to a unified metadata system covering publications worldwide. C. *Gessner's *Bibliotheca Universalis* (1545) was an early attempt to produce a catalogue of all known books. Major national and international bibliographies, and *union catalogues, have been building-blocks in bibliographic control, but the proliferation of knowledge via the *World Wide Web, and new forms of publication, has increased the complexity of this arena.　　　　DRSP

D. Davidson, *Bibliographic Control*, 2e (1981)

On the Record: Report of the Library of Congress Working Group on the Future of Bibliographic Control (2008)

bibliographical description The description and analysis of the physical characteristics of books. It uses an agreed form of notation, intended to distinguish between *issues and *variants of an *edition, to explain and describe the printing and textual history of an edition, and to arrange it in a correct and logical relationship to other editions. Its chief purpose is to aid textual and literary criticism by providing information about the transmission of texts. Additionally, it helps book collectors and librarians to identify books in their possession, to catalogue them properly, and assess their commercial value.

Bibliographical description aims to describe, not individual copies, but the ideal *copy, based on examination of every available copy of an edition, and to contextualize it. The description falls into five parts: (1) quasi-facsimile *title-page transcription, intended to help the user to visualize the title-page by indicating line breaks and *typefaces as well as reproducing its wording; (2) *format and *collational formula, with statements of signing, number of *leaves, and *pagination; (3) a technical note, listing such features as *signature positions, *catchwords, *press figures, *type, *paper, and *plates or other insets not included in the collation; (4) details of the contents of the book; (5) any other information that will shed light on the book's history, and a list of copies examined.

The emphasis given to each of the five sections depends on the subject unifying the bibliography: for example, contents are extremely important in an author bibliography, while details of type and paper may be less so, and the reverse applies to the bibliography of a printer's output. Mention of catchwords will include their frequency and any errors. Press figures indicate the page and the *forme on which they appear. A brief description of type might include the dimensions of a normal type page (less *headline and *direction line), the kind and 20-line measurement of the text type, the number of lines on a normal page (*page depth), and references to *fleurons, ornaments, and illustrations. Description of hand-made paper should minimally include a note of the *chain-line spacing, the *watermark type if any, and the uncut *sheet size if an uncut copy is available. Details of plates and other insets should include at least the number and position of each plate and the process of production, and might include the subject of each illustration, with dimensions and title transcriptions (*see* **16**). The contents note accounts for each page of the book, including each element of the *preliminaries, *half-titles, end matter (e.g. *advertisements), and blank pages; half-titles and *running titles may be given in quasi-facsimile transcription. The most important elements of 'other information' are notes on the structure of the book which may call for additional comment, such as peculiarities of printing or *gatherings; full details of variant impressions, issues, and states; descriptions of any *trade or *edition bindings that have been identified; and relevant information from external sources, such as printers' and publishers' records, including if possible details of edition quantities and prices. The list of copies examined will identify their locations in libraries and private collections and any distinctive features of individual copies, including evidence of ownership and notes on their binding.

The originator of quasi-facsimile transcription was *Capell in *Prolusions* (1760). *Madan pioneered the concept independently in 1893; it was also Madan who urged using the position of the signatures to identify resetting. The *Bibliographical Society (chiefly A. W. *Pollard, *Greg, and Madan) proposed a uniform system of notation (1906–8). *McKerrow, Arundell Esdaile, Greg, and J. D. Cowley expanded and modified this skeletal form. Bibliographical description today is based on *Bowers, who reproduced and extended this expanded system. A bibliography of works compiled with bibliographical descriptions is called a descriptive bibliography or an analytical bibliography.   KEA

Bowers, *Principles*
D. F. Foxon, *Thoughts on the History and Future of Bibliographical Description* (1970)
Gaskell, *NI*

bibliographical prizes Following an endowment by Eustace Bosanquet, the *Bibliographical Society first awarded a Gold Medal for distinguished work in bibliography in 1929. Since then, numerous prizes in this field have been established around the world, by bibliographical societies and others (e.g. the *International League of Antiquarian Booksellers' Bibliography Prize; Oxford University's Gordon *Duff Prize; and the *Library Association's Walford Award for sustained contribution to bibliography, first awarded 1991).   DRSP

Bibliographical Society The value of a Bibliographical Society in Britain was affirmed in *Notes & Queries* in 1868. Its formation was proposed at a meeting of the *Library Association in 1891. The Bibliographical Society was founded by W. A. Copinger, its first president, encouraged by *MacAlister, on 15 July 1892. Its principal objective was to promote and encourage study and research in historical, analytical, descriptive, and textual bibliography, and in the history of printing, publishing, bookselling, bookbinding, and collecting. Further objectives, intended to fulfil the first, were to print and publish works on bibliography, especially those unlikely to be commercially profitable; to hold meetings at which papers were read and discussed; and to maintain a bibliographical library. In 1929, the Society instigated the award of a gold medal for outstanding services in

bibliography; the five recipients of 1929 included M. R. *James and two of the three early luminaries and long-standing office-holders of the Society, *McKerrow and A. W. *Pollard. The third significant early leading light, *Greg, was awarded the gold medal in 1935. The Society published fifteen volumes in twenty-one parts of *Transactions*, 1893–1920, before taking over the *Library* as its quarterly journal. The Society's single most important monograph was the *Short-Title Catalogue of Books Printed in England, Scotland, & Ireland and of English Books Printed Abroad 1475–1640* (1926; 2e, 1976–91). Other important publications include Greg's *Bibliography of the English Printed Drama to the Restoration* (1939–59), the *Bowyer Ledgers* (1993), and the *Cathedral Libraries Catalogue* (1984–98). Each year the Bibliographical Society organizes six lectures in London and a summer visit to a library.   KEA

Bibliographical Society, www.bibsoc.org.uk, consulted May 2007
[Bibliographical Society, London,] *The Bibliographical Society 1892–1942* (1945)
J. Roberts, 'The Bibliographical Society, 1942–1992', in *The Book Encompassed*, ed. P. Davison (1998)

Bibliographical Society of America (BSA) Incorporated in 1927, the BSA is the oldest scholarly society in North America dedicated to the study of books and MSS as physical objects. It promotes bibliographical research by publishing books through *Oak Knoll Press; issuing the *Papers of the Bibliographical Society of America* (*PBSA*), a leading journal on the subject; and bestowing honours (such as the Mitchell Prize) upon worthy recipients. During the BSA's annual meeting in New York City, members learn of new research by rising academics from its New Scholars Program, which promotes junior scholars, Ph.D. students, and independent researchers working in bibliography. The BSA also funds new research through fellowships. Most are short term and support work in book and publishing history. The Pantzer Senior Fellowship, named after the distinguished bibliographer *Pantzer, provides $6,000 (double the usual amount) for research related to book production during the hand-press period. Finally, the BSA maintains BibSite, a valuable online service (*see* WORLD WIDE WEB) that enables scholars to provide public access to their bibliographic research and freely share their work with each other.   MDB

www.bibsocamer.org, consulted Nov. 2007

Bibliographical Society of Australia and New Zealand (BSANZ) Founded in 1969, modelled on the *Bibliographical Society (UK) and the *Bibliographical Society of America, BSANZ encourages research in physical *bibliography. A journal, the *BSANZ Bulletin*, commenced in 1970; published quarterly since 1981, it was retitled *Script and Print* (2005). Its editors have included *Kirsop (1970), *Love (1970–76), Brian McMullin (1977–82 and 1992–5), Ross Harvey (1987–94), Ian Morrison (1999–2003), Sydney Shep (2003–6), and Patrick Spedding (2006–). BSANZ also publishes occasional monographs, and has collaborated in regional *SHARP conferences in Sydney (2003) and Wellington (2005). **IM**

Bibliographical Society of Canada (Société bibliographique du Canada) Founded in 1946, it has published *Papers/Cahiers* since 1962, with two issues annually from 1991 (available through www.library. utoronto.ca/bsc). The Society sponsors a conference each year, funds fellowships, and awards the Marie Tremaine Medal for excellence in Canadian bibliography. **PLF**

Bibliographical Society of the University of Virginia Scholarly society established in 1947 to promote the study of books and printing. The organization has achieved international influence through its publications, particularly its journal *Studies in Bibliography*, and it has made 'Virginia' a byword for the analysis of books as material objects, the study of the transmission of texts, and the preparation of scholarly editions. The Society has produced some 180 separate publications, including indexes to book trade personnel in the national bibliographies of A. W. *Pollard and G. R. Redgrave, D. *Wing, and C. *Evans. Its journal, founded in 1948 by *Bowers and published annually, has emphasized the study of books and MSS as physical objects. **DLVM**
etext.lib.virginia.edu/bsuva, consulted May 2008
D. L. Vander Meulen, ed., *The Bibliographical Society of the University of Virginia* (1998)

Bibliographie de la France Following sporadic earlier attempts, Napoleon I established in 1811 the weekly *Bibliographie de l'empire français*, listing all new French publications. Renamed *Bibliographie de la France* in 1815, it was administered from 1856 to 1990 by the *Cercle de la Librairie, its bibliographical part (taken over by the *Bibliothèque nationale in 1936) supplemented by news from publishers and discussions of professional issues. (This commercial part, now independent, took the title *Livres hebdo* in 1979.) Renamed *Bibliographie nationale française* in 1990, it stopped appearing in paper form in 2000, becoming freely available instead on the BnF website. **VAG**

bibliography (1) The study of books. Bibliography has five branches that often overlap: enumerative bibliography; analytical bibliography; descriptive bibliography; textual bibliography; historical bibliography.

1. Enumerative bibliography
2. Analytical bibliography
3. Descriptive bibliography
4. Textual bibliography
5. Historical bibliography

1. Enumerative bibliography

In its attempts to synthesize knowledge, enumerative bibliography provides the foundation for scholarship. The basic function of enumerative bibliography (also known as systematic bibliography) is to list all titles of books that fall within specified parameters: geographic,

linguistic, chronological, thematic, or some combination thereof. In its highest form, an enumerative bibliography strives for completeness, although that standard is rarely met. The tradition of enumerative bibliography extends from the *Alexandrian Library to online public-access catalogues (*see* WORLD WIDE WEB), and includes many impressive feats of scholarship: C. *Gessner's *Bibliotheca Universalis* (1545), *Watt's *Bibliotheca Britannica* (1824), the *Dewey decimal system, A. W. *Pollard and G. R. Redgrave's *Short-Title Catalogue* for 1475–1640 (1926), D. *Wing's *Short-Title Catalogue* for 1641–1700 (1945), the *ESTC, and Jacob Blanck's *Bibliography of American Literature* (1955–91). Unlike analytical and descriptive bibliography, enumerative bibliography is not necessarily concerned with the physical makeup of books.

2. Analytical bibliography

Analytical bibliography refers to the practice of reconstructing the physical processes by which printed books came to be produced. (In this respect, the focus of analytical bibliography has a more narrow scope than enumerative bibliography, which may encompass both MSS and printed books.) Analytical bibliographers pursue this historical inquiry for various reasons: to identify a book's printers and publishers; to assign a date to a book; to distinguish between variant *states of the same *edition; and to understand how a book's text was altered in the process of printing. The physical evidence examined by analytical bibliographers includes: *typography, paper (including *watermarks and *chain lines), patterns of *imposition, and the printed marks themselves (including printers' *ornaments, damaged type, *running titles, and *press figures). Although analytical bibliography remains a specialized discipline, it has had and continues to have a profound impact on modern scholarship, as shown by the influence of the '*new bibliography' on how literary texts are edited. In this context, *Hinman's work on the *First Folio of Shakespeare is especially notable. The classic introduction to the field of analytical bibliography is by *McKerrow, and a famous and entertaining study that applies the tools of this field to expose *Wise's literary *forgery was written by J. *Carter and G. *Pollard.

3. Descriptive bibliography

Like analytical bibliography, descriptive bibliography is concerned with books as material objects, and indeed these two branches of bibliography overlap at many points. Yet, while analytical bibliography has various purposes, descriptive bibliography has the single goal of describing the physical structure of books in a clear and concise way. At the heart of a bibliographical description is a statement of *format and a *collational formula. Format is the relationship between the original *sheets of paper and the resultant *leaves after folding and (possibly) cutting. Common formats include *folio, *quarto, *octavo, and *duodecimo. The formula of collation describes how the sheets, bound as *gatherings, were arranged in the final published form of the book, along with any insertions or *cancellations. Anyone familiar with the system of notation used in descriptive bibliography can mentally reconstruct the physical make-up of a book without having it before them. And one can use a bibliographical description to compare a particular copy to the ideal *copy as intended by the publisher. The key work of descriptive bibliography is *Bowers' *Principles of Bibliographical Description* (1949).

In addition to a book's format and collational formula, a descriptive bibliography contains other information, such as the number and priority of the various *states, *issues, and *editions; the paper used; references to known *advertisements; price; *copyright registration; *press runs; binding (*see* **17**); and published responses to the book. A descriptive bibliography may be based on genre and time period (*Greg's *Bibliography of the English Printed Drama to the Restoration*, 1939–59), publisher (*Gaskell's *Bibliography of the Foulis Press* (1964)), or author (J. D. Fleeman's *Bibliography of the Works of Samuel Johnson* (2000)). Regardless of the focus, descriptive bibliography offers a valuable contribution to any historical inquiry concerned with books.

4. Textual bibliography

Textual bibliography refers to any bibliographical endeavour that attempts to reconstruct the transmission of texts, with the possible goal of establishing or editing a specific work. In this respect, textual bibliography is often synonymous with *textual criticism. Yet the term 'textual bibliography' highlights the need for the textual scholar to study how the material forms of texts have affected their transmission. The fields of analytical and descriptive bibliography inform textual bibliography, as do the study of handwriting (*palaeography), linguistic study, and literary scholarship in general.

5. Historical bibliography

Historical bibliography refers to the historical study of books, and as a term it has been displaced by '*history of the book' or *histoire du livre*. Historical bibliography encompasses topics as various as *copyright, *censorship, *authorship, *reading and reception, the technologies of printing (*see* **11**), the economics of publishing (*see* **12**), and the cultural impact of the written word. The overlap between historical bibliography and both analytical and descriptive bibliography should be clear; anyone who studies books as material objects needs to do so with an awareness of particular historical patterns of printing and publishing. Similarly, the physical production of books is very much a part of their history.

Despite the various branches of bibliography and their different methods of inquiry, bibliographers of all types are united around a shared object of study and a desire to understand the cultural and physical conditions that produced books. Ultimately, all the various branches of bibliography intersect, and thorough scholars employ multiple methods and avail themselves of all known forms of evidence. The best theorists of bibliography have sought to push the boundaries of the field beyond the written word. Greg stated that the principles of bibliography 'apply to the transmission of all symbolic representation of speech or other ordered sound or even of logical thought', and

*McKenzie believed that bibliography can 'show the human presence in any recorded text'. Such broad and humanistic perspectives will inform the future of bibliography in the emerging electronic age (*see* **19**).   SK

T. Belanger, 'Descriptive Bibliography', in *Book Collecting*, ed. J. Peters (1977)

Bowers, *Principles*

F. Bowers, 'Bibliography', in *Encyclopaedia Britannica*, vol. 3 (1968)

— 'Bibliography, Pure Bibliography, and Literary Studies', *PBSA* 46 (1952), 186–208

— 'Four Faces of Bibliography', *Papers of the Bibliographical Society of Canada*, 10 (1971), 33–45

J. Carter and G. Pollard, *An Enquiry into the Nature of Certain Nineteenth-Century Pamphlets* (1934)

J. Feather, 'Cross-Channel Currents: Historical Bibliography and *l'histoire du livre*', *Library*, 6/2 (1980), 1–15

Gaskell, *NI*

W. W. Greg, 'What is Bibliography?', *Transactions of the Bibliographical Society*, 12 (1911–13), 39–53, repr. in *Collected Papers*, ed. J. C. Maxwell (1966)

C. Hinman, *The Printing and Proof-Reading of the First Folio of Shakespeare* (2 vols, 1963)

D. F. McKenzie, *Bibliography and the Sociology of Texts* (1986; repr. 1999)

McKerrow, *Introduction*

G. T. Tanselle, 'A Description of Descriptive Bibliography', *SB* 45 (1992), 1–30

— *The History of Books as a Field of Study* (1981)

W. P. Williams and C. S. Abbott, *An Introduction to Bibliographical and Textual Studies*, 4e (2009)

bibliography (2) A list of MSS, books, and articles cited or referred to in a scholarly work, or thought relevant to its subject matter. Such lists are usually printed following the work itself.

bibliomancy [Gk, 'book divination'] An ancient way of resolving a dilemma, in which a book believed to hold truth is taken, balanced on its spine, allowed to fall open, and the undecided person picks a passage with eyes closed. As a method of divination, bibliomancy requires the book to have a *codex structure. It was common in early Christian culture, practitioners using the Bible in part or in whole; thus arose the expression *Sortes Biblicae* (Lat., 'lots, chances'). It was associated also with the beginnings of the Franciscan order; the saint's biographer describes his first followers, who, uncertain what to choose, opened the gospels three times and each time fell on a verse where Christ told his disciples to leave all and follow him. Alternative divinatory texts were Homer and Virgil: hence, the terms *Sortes Homericae* and *Sortes Virgilianae*. One salutary tale narrates how, in the *Bodleian Library, Charles I and Viscount Falkland consulted a finely printed Virgil: the former fell on Dido's invective against Aeneas, the latter on Evander's lament for the death of his son, and both men came to untimely ends. A more random means of questioning the fates is stichomancy, in which a volume is chosen at hazard.

NH

bibliomania A 'rage for collecting and possessing books' (*OED*). The word was first used by *Hearne in

1734, but achieved a wider currency through *Dibdin's *The Bibliomania: or, Book Madness* (1809; 2e, 1811), where it is used to define the characteristics of obsessive book collecting. The most famous example of such obsessive collecting is probably *Phillipps, a self-proclaimed 'vello-Maniac' whose professed aim was 'to have one copy of every Book in the World'; indeed, his appetite to collect early books was so voracious that it consumed virtually the entire space in a large house. Yet, if Phillipps demonstrates the most extreme form of bibliomania, it is a quality to a greater or lesser degree manifested by any serious book collector, one for whom the act of acquisition is not an end but a new beginning. ASGE

N. A. Basbanes, *A Gentle Madness* (1995)
H. Jackson, *The Anatomy of Bibliomania* (2 vols, 1930–31)

bibliophile [Gk, 'lover of books'] Term first used by *Dibdin in his *Library Companion* (1824). It is now generally understood to signify a book collector of refined judgement, the quality of whose library reflects his or her exacting bibliographical standards in respect to such criteria as rarity and *condition within their chosen field(s). Although it may result in bibliolatry, the extravagant admiration of a particular book, bibliophily is to be distinguished from *bibliomania by the degree of discrimination that is exercised in acquiring books. ASGE

J. Carter, *Taste & Technique in Book-Collecting*, 2e (1970)

bibliophobia *OED*'s only citation for this term is in a work of that title by *Dibdin in 1832; it is defined it as a 'Dread of, or aversion to, books'. The state (if it has ever existed) is therefore to be distinguished from the destruction of books for historical and/or political reasons (biblioclasm), as in the burning of works by Jewish and other so-called 'decadent' writers in Nazi Germany during the 1930s (*see* **7**) and the criminal destruction or commercial taking apart by *breakers of certain kinds of book such as *colour-plate volumes or illuminated MSS. ASGE

bibliopole [Gk *bibliopoles*, 'bookseller'] Obsolete term for book dealer (hence 'bibliopoly' meaning the book trade). It was used by S. *Johnson, according to Boswell's testimony.

Bibliopolis Electronic national history of the printed book in The Netherlands, a scholarly, interactive online information system (*see* WORLD WIDE WEB). Bibliopolis offers integrated access to various information sources: a survey of the history of the printed book in The Netherlands written by 40 leading book historians; an image database (including *typefaces, *printers' devices, and *watermarks); reference materials (bibliographical databases, biographical data, book auction catalogues); digitized secondary literature; and retrospective bibliography via online catalogues. Bibliopolis was created (1998–2002) through the *Koninklijke Bibliotheek in cooperation with the universities of Amsterdam, Leiden, Nijmegen, and Utrecht, and the Nederlandse Boekhistorische Vereniging (*see* NBV). MFS

www.bibliopolis.nl, consulted June 2008

Bibliotheck, The A journal that publishes articles, notes, and queries on all aspects of Scottish book history. It has appeared irregularly since 1956; since 2004 it has become semi-annual and is now produced from Napier University. ASGE

Bibliothèque bleue Mid-17th century term to describe a series of cheaply produced, affordable works issued (often in blue wrappers) by the Troyes printer Nicolas Oudot from 1602. Aimed at a broad readership and usually illustrated with crude woodcuts, they included adaptations of chivalric romances, contemporary works, practical handbooks, almanacs, and above all religious literature, often in simplified, censored versions. Oudot's formula, continued by his family, was widely imitated, notably in Caen, Rouen, and Limoges. In its most popular phase, there were about 150 such publishers involved, mostly in northern France. Chiefly available in cities throughout the 17th century, 'blue books' were widely distributed in the countryside by itinerant peddlars after 1700. By the time of the Revolution and the Napoleonic era, new forms of popular literature, especially *lithographic images, started competing with the Bibliothèque bleue. The rise of the popular press in the mid-19th century compounded its decline. It then began to attract the attention of French collectors and social historians, for whom *littérature de colportage* has become an essential source. VAG

G. Bollème, *La Bibliothèque bleue* (1971)
R. Mandrou, *De la culture populaire aux 17e et 18e siècles* (1985)
A. Morin, *Catalogue descriptif de la bibliothèque bleue de Troyes* (1974)

Bibliothèque nationale de France (BnF) Although the 'librairie' of Charles V (1364–80) at the Louvre is traditionally considered its ancestor, the Bibliothèque nationale's real beginnings were under Louis XI (1461–83). The spoils of Charles VIII's Italian campaigns (1495–8) led to the establishment of royal collections in Amboise and Blois, subsequently brought by François I to Fontainebleau to join his Greek MSS under the curatorship of the prominent humanist Guillaume Budé (1468–1540). The library's highly symbolic move to Paris occurred in the 1660s. A MS collection in the mid-17th century, it was radically transformed by J.-B. *Colbert, himself a major book collector, who transplanted it from the Latin Quarter to the Palais Vivienne (near its modern Richelieu site). He made it an authentic copyright library, while the Marolles Collection marked the birth of the Print Department (1667). The Abbé Bignon's librarianship (1719–41) coincided with a period of exceptional growth, witnessed in 1720 by its installation in the former Palais Mazarin (only two galleries remain) and the publication of its first catalogue (1739)—reflecting a new openness to scholars. Enriched by spoils during the Revolution and under Napoleon (some of these last were returned), its holdings doubled, causing crucial space problems. Appointed by Napoleon III in 1854, Labrouste, the architect of *Sainte-Geneviève, designed the landmark new building, which was still unfinished at his death in 1875. In 1897, *administrateur général* Delisle (the position being another Second Empire innovation) launched the publication of the catalogue of printed materials, completed only in 1981. Under Julien Cain, in charge 1930–64 (except for 1940–45 when, being Jewish, he was dismissed, before being deported by the Nazis to Buchenwald), the Bibliothèque nationale took control of the *Arsenal (1934) and the libraries of the Opéra and the Conservatoire (1935). To the traditional departments (Printed Books, MSS, Prints, and Medals, joined by Maps in 1828), his Vichy-appointed replacement, Bernard Faÿ, added Periodicals and Music in 1942. Two more departments, 'Audiovisuel' and 'Arts du Spectacle' (this initially at the Arsenal), followed in 1976. Space becoming critical again, in 1988 President Mitterrand announced the creation of a new library in the recently developed Tolbiac neighbourhood on the left bank. E. Leroy-Ladurie smoothly managed the transition to a two-location institution, renamed in 1994 Bibliothèque nationale de France. Perrault's controversial 'Mitterrand' building, opened to the public in 1996, houses most printed (including an expanded 'Réserve') and audiovisual materials, the other specialized departments remaining at Richelieu.   VAG

Bickham, George (1683/4–1758) English engraver and *writing-master. He is best known for *The Universal Penman*, written with his son or brother John Bickham. Issued in parts between 1733 and 1741, it consisted of copper-plate *engravings of the work of 25 contemporary writing-masters and led to a renewed interest in *calligraphy.   ASGE

P. H. Muir, 'The Bickhams and their *Universal Penman*', *Library*, 4/25 (1944–5), 162–83
ODNB

bifolium A pair of *conjugate leaves, joined at a central fold; the *gatherings of a *text block are made of several bifolia nested together. *See also* DIPLOMA; FOLIO.

Bilibin, Ivan (1876–1942) Russian graphic artist, painter, and theatre designer. He studied at the Academy in St Petersburg under Repin, joined and then exhibited with the World of Art movement (1900–1917). His book illustrations reflect the national romantic trend of the modern graphic style characteristic of the early 20th century. Drawing inspiration from the Russian icon and decorative folk art (the *lubok, peasant embroidery, and wood-carving), his style also shows the influence of German graphic artists and Japanese wood engravers (*see* WOODCUT ILLUSTRATION). Bilibin also paid great attention to the ornamental drawing of letters and created a pastiche antique style by imitating the characteristics of Church Slavonic script (*see* CYRILLIC TYPE). Among the folk stories he illustrated are *The Tale of Ivan the Tsar's Son, the Firebird and the Grey Wolf*, and Pushkin's *The Tale of Tsar Saltan* and *The Tale of the Golden Cockerel*. He also contributed drawings to the journals *Zhupel* (*Bugbear*), *Golden Fleece*, and *Satirikon*. He lived abroad (1930–36), returning to the Soviet Union

to become professor of the Graphic Art Studio of the Leningrad Academy.   PH

S. Golynets, *Ivan Bilibin* (1981)

bilingual dictionary From earliest times, printers had to fulfil the needs of three kinds of bilingual dictionary users: travellers, students, and scholars or translators. In 1480, *Caxton produced a French-English *glossary, for which no *title-page survives, but evidently intended for travellers. In 1499, *Pynson issued a 232-page English-to-Latin *Promptorium Parvulorum sive Clericorum*, signed by 'Galfridus Anglicus'. This was followed by the *Estiennes' great humanist dictionaries: Robert's Latin–French (with occasional Greek) *Dictionarium, seu Latinae Linguae Thesaurus* (1531) and Henri's *Thesaurus Graecae Linguae* (1572–3). Thomas Elyot introduced the term 'Dictionary' into English in his Latin-English glossary of 1538. Reflecting the rise of *translation in the Renaissance, bilingual dictionaries also catered to a growing taste for reading foreign literatures in the vernacular: William Thomas, 'clerk to the council of Edward VI', specified in the subtitle of his 1550 Italian–English dictionary that it was intended 'for the better understandynge of Boccace, Pethrarcha, and Dante'. Richer at first than *monolingual dictionaries, bilingual dictionaries came to rely on them as the monolingual dictionaries improved: Giovanni Torriano, the 1659 editor of John Florio's Italian dictionary (first issued in 1598) made it clear that it had been updated from the 1612 *Vocabolario della Crusca*. A lesser-known characteristic of early bilingual dictionaries, surviving well into the 19th century, is that they occasionally were translations of dictionaries published in other countries: thus I. J. G. Scheller's *Deutsch-lateinisches Lexikon* (1804) was translated by J. E. Riddle as *Lexicon Totius Latinitatis* in 1835. Even if not a translation, a dictionary frequently acknowledged its debt towards a foreign model, as did both Erazm Rykaczewski's (1849–51) and Alexander Chodźko's (1874) Polish–English dictionaries towards Christoph Mrongovius' *Nowy Słownik polsko-niemiecki* (1794).

Like their monolingual counterparts, bilingual dictionaries benefited immeasurably from the progress of philology in the 19th and 20th centuries. In addition, their number and *press runs increased with the development of foreign language teaching, resulting in the proliferation of specialized departments in publishing houses— and, indeed, specialized publishers. A late 20th-century phenomenon is the appearance of so-called 'bilingualized' dictionaries, i.e. bilingual dictionaries based on monolingual dictionaries and incorporating the depth of their lexicographic perspective: the first such dictionary was the *Oxford Student's Dictionary for Hebrew Speakers* (1978), which provided Hebrew and English equivalents, while being modelled on the third edition (1974) of the *Oxford Advanced Learner's Dictionary of Current English*.

One cannot, of course, discuss such works without stressing the difference in longevity between modern-language dictionaries, in constant need of updating— which makes them perfectly suited to electronic publishing—and classical dictionaries, the best of which stand the test of time remarkably well: Félix Gaffiot's Latin–French dictionary, first published in 1934, was still available in 2007, as was Henry George Liddell and Robert Scott's *Greek–English Lexicon*, first issued in 1843, revised by Henry Stuart Jones and Roderick McKenzie in 1929, and never out of print since.   VAG

A. P. Cowie, *English Dictionaries for Foreign Learners* (1999)

H. Van Hoof, *Petite Histoire des dictionnaires* (1994)

billhead A tradesman's or commercial firm's printed bill, typically bearing the concern's name and contact details, most often embellished with an illustration—frequently a shop sign or a depiction of the business premises. An extension of the *trade card, billheads almost invariably bear the words 'Bot of' (bought of) or 'Dr to' (debtor to). With some notable exceptions, contemporary related items of printed commercial stationary—such as the invoice, tradesman's list, order form, and receipt—are most often less ornamental and more utilitarian. Variously printed by copper-plate *engraving, *letterpress alone or with *woodcut or wood engraving, steel engraving, or *lithography, billheads are valued by collectors of ephemera not only for the evidence they provide about business premises and practices but also for the artful ways in which they reflect both technological and stylistic innovations. Outstanding examples of jobbing printing, they were designed to impress customers and attract further patronage. The billhead of the 17th and 18th centuries was usually engraved. Billheads from the 18th and early 19th-centuries typically featured *copperplate script founts, often with shadow and decorated roman capitals. Letterpress billheads commonly manifest the influence of engraved examples and often display a mixed arrangement of *roman and *italic *types. French letterpress billheads of the 19th century are frequently characterized by the use of borders and decorated letters. Lithographic examples most often reflect their engraved forebears, although late 19th-century examples are highly influenced by *security printing. The *Bodleian Library's John *Johnson Collection is an exceptionally fine resource for their study. Over the last decades of the 19th century, the billhead was gradually replaced by the commercial *letterhead. *See also* 14.   MFS

[Bodleian Library, Oxford,] *A Nation of Shopkeepers* (2001)

G. Hudson, *The Design and Printing of Ephemera* (2008)

J. Lewis, *Printed Ephemera* (1962)

M. Rickards, *Encyclopedia of Ephemera* (2000)

M. Twyman, *Printing 1770-1970* (1998)

Billings, Hammatt (1818–74) American artist and architect. Designer of buildings in Boston and at Wellesley College, Billings illustrated more than 225 books, including many mid-19th-century English and American favourites (Hawthorne, Alcott, Goldsmith, Scott, Dickens, and Tennyson). He also drew for the Boston newspaper *Gleason's*. The first edition of Stowe's *Uncle Tom's Cabin* contained seven wood engravings (*see* WOODCUT ILLUSTRATION) based on his designs. His

editions of *Mother Goose* mark him especially as a children's book illustrator (*see* 15).   MMS

Billingsley, Martin (1591-1622) English *writing-master and teacher of calligraphy to Charles I, when Prince of Wales. He wrote *The Pen's Excellencie* (1618), which included a number of engraved plates (by William Hole) and has often been regarded as the first significant English *copy book. It was frequently reprinted. Billingsley's introduction contains classifications of forms of handwriting and instructions for preparing pens and inks. He appears to have published only one other copy book, *The Pen's Paradise* (of which no copy survives), although a number of others have been attributed to him on doubtful authority.   ASGE
ODNB

bill of letter The proportional batch of different *sorts that a *typefounder supplied to a printer, based on each letter's frequency of use.
Gaskell, *NI*

binder's ticket *See* TICKETS.

bindery A workshop or firm whose primary purpose is bookbinding. Before the 19th century, binderies were typically small operations; after that, mechanization and increased book production created large industrial-scale operations. Depictions of early binderies suggest much uniformity of practice and equipment across Europe.
                    DRSP

M. Foot, *Bookbinders at Work* (2006)

binding *See* 17.

Bindley, James (1739-1818) English book collector, was educated at Peterhouse, Cambridge, where he became a fellow; he was also commissioner of the stamp office. Bindley chiefly collected 16th- and 17th-century English books; he owned a number of 17th-century printed pamphlets formerly in *Luttrell's library. *Heber was a major purchaser at the posthumous sales of his books held between 1818 and 1821.   ASGE
ODNB

Bindoni family Venetian printers from the Lago Maggiore. The brothers **Alessandro** (active 1506-22), **Agostino** (active 1523-58), **Benedetto** (active 1520-41), and **Bernardino** (active 1532-62), seem to have operated separately. The most successful venture was by Alessandro's son **Francesco** (active 1518-57), mostly in partnership with Mapheo Pasini, who married his father's widow. Their output consisted of religious, chivalric, and popular editions, many of which have been lost.   CWK
DBI
DTEI

Binny & Ronaldson Philadelphia typefoundry. Archibald Binny (1762-1838) brought *typefounding materials to the US, establishing its first successful typefoundry on 1 November 1796 with his fellow Edinburgh native James Ronaldson (1769–1841). Binny and his son became punchcutters. Ronaldson and his brother ran the foundry 1815–33, then sold it to what became *MacKellar, Smiths, & Jordan. *Type specimens of 1812–22 show *texturas and non-Latins from the Voskens foundry in Amsterdam, brought to New York by Mappa in 1789. The *romans and *italics, cut by Binny or imported, follow recent British designs.   JAL

R. G. Silver, *Typefounding in America* (1965)

biographical dictionary An exception to the modern division of labour, by which dictionaries normally deal with words and *encyclopaedias with things and people, biographical dictionaries—as distinct from reference works including genealogical or biographical components—are essentially a late 18th-century creation. They can be categorized by scope: international, national, or professional.

In the first category, pioneered by Louis-Mayeul Chaudon's *Nouveau dictionnaire historique* (first published in 1766), few projects have matched in size the *Biographie universelle, ancienne et moderne*, published in 85 volumes between 1811 and 1862 by J. F. Michaud (1767–1839) and his brother Louis Gabriel (1773–1858); a second, 45-volume edition came out in 1843–65. Contributors included Balzac, Benjamin Constant, and Sainte-Beuve. Michaud's rival was the 46-volume *Nouvelle biographie générale* of Ferdinand Hoefer (1811–78), issued by Firmin *Didot in 1855–66. Twentieth-century world biographies have had more modest ambitions.

The second category, pioneered as early as 1794–8 by Jeremy Belknap in his *American Biography*, is well represented, with modern national biographies available for nearly all major Western and many non-Western countries. (France here is an odd exception, the *Dictionnaire de biographie française*, planned before 1914, and published in *numbers or *fascicles, beginning in 1933, not having gone beyond the letter 'L' by 2007.) Paradoxically, the most remarkable achievement in this category, the *Dictionary of National Biography*, was originally planned by its publisher, *Smith, Elder & Co., as a universal dictionary. Recruited as its editor, Leslie Stephen (1832–1904) saw the first 26 volumes into production, assisted by Sidney Lee (1859–1926), who succeeded him in 1891. After the 63-volume series was completed in 1900, Lee oversaw the publication of 3 supplements, a reprint in 23 volumes (1908–9), and the 1912 volume covering subjects who had died in the previous decade. In 1992, *Oxford University Press, which had taken over as publisher in 1917 and issued all subsequent supplements (including the 1993 *Missing Persons* for subjects omitted in the original series), began work on a revised *DNB*, edited by H. C. G. Matthew (1941–99) and Brian Harrison. The new *DNB*, called the *Oxford Dictionary of National Biography* (*ODNB*), was published simultaneously in paper (60 volumes) and electronic forms (*see* **19**) in 2004. OUP has also joined forces with the American Council of Learned Societies to produce a new *American National*

Biography (1999) to replace the original *Dictionary of American Biography* published by Scribner's between 1927 and 1936.

The third category—biographical dictionary by discipline or category—was pioneered by the 1733 *Compendioses Gelehrten-lexicon* (Dictionary of Scholars) by Johann Burkhard Mencke (1674–1732), edited and subsequently expanded by Christian Gottlieb Jöcher (1694–1758). One of its early successors is the *Biographie universelle des musiciens* (1835–44) compiled by the Belgian musicologist François-Joseph Fétis (1784–1871).

A rule Fétis did not observe is the traditional exclusion in biographical dictionaries of living persons. These are covered by a fourth category, generically known as 'Who's Who' after the series launched in 1849 by A. & C. *Black, who, it should be noted, subtitled it 'An annual biographical dictionary'.   VAG

biography A written account of a human life thought worthy of memory. Early examples are chiefly didactic in purpose; the influential *Lives* of Plutarch, written before AD 120, parallel the virtues and failings of the great men of Greece and Rome. From the 3rd century onwards, accounts of Christian martyrs and other saints were written to record their heroic fidelity, and to encourage emulation.

The first printed editions of Plutarch (in Latin translation) and of Jacobus de Voragine's *Legenda Aurea*, a popular collection of saints' lives, both appeared in 1470; many further impressions and vernacular translations followed. In England, hagiography remained enormously popular in the Protestant *Foxe's *Actes and Monuments* (1563). The enlarged edition of 1570 was the biggest English publishing project to date. Another highly influential book of the age was Sir Thomas North's translation of Plutarch (1579).

Lives (as distinct from *romances) of secular persons remained uncommon until the 17th century; Izaak Walton's *Lives* (1670; rev. and expanded edn, 1675) was highly influential. 'History plays' then began to have their counterpart in prose and poetic lives of great men. Thomas Fuller's encyclopaedic *Worthies of England* (1662) floated on the surge of Restoration patriotism. *Ballads and *chapbooks about historical persons were always popular, however, and remained in demand well into the 19th century, not least edifying descriptions of the conversion of sinners and deathbed repentances.

A new kind of critical biography, more concerned with the individual's ideas and personality, came to the fore in England with S. *Johnson's *Life of Savage* (1745); Vasari's *Vite dei pittori* (1550) is possibly a remote ancestor. The extensive prefaces of *Johnson's Poets' exemplify his biographical methods. The later 18th-century public also thirsted for anecdotes, *ana*, and 'characteristics', which were amply provided in Boswell's exemplary and very successful *Life of Johnson* (1791). The market for lives of public figures remains buoyant; Michael Holroyd, a most successful practitioner, claims that Britain 'oozes biography, to the incomprehension and amusement of the world'.

The hagiographical style persisted beyond the 18th century with lives of popular preachers and intrepid missionaries. It overlapped somewhat with the 'two-volume tombstone' of life and letters, which immortalized so many prominent (but often insignificant) figures of the 19th century, and has now been succeeded by lives of ephemeral celebrities. *Press runs of the latter are often enormous, for biographies now outsell all other publishing categories but fiction.   BJF

M. Holroyd, 'Our Friends the Dead', *Guardian*, 1 June 2002

birch bark Birch inner bark, cut into strips or rectangles, was commonly used as a writing material (with pen and *ink) in and around north India from at least the 4th century BC until the 18th century AD. Contrary to popular belief, Native Americans did not use birch bark as a writing material, but archaeological digs in Novgorod, Moscow, Belarus, and other sites indicate that peoples in this region did so from at least the early 13th century. *See also* **39**.   DRSP

gramoty.ru, consulted July 2007
www.kotikielenseura.fi/virittaja/hakemistot/jutut/
    vir99laakso.pdf, with English summary, consulted July 2007
J. Losty, *The Art of the Book in India* (1982)

Birckmann family German publishers, booksellers, and printers in Cologne. **Franz** (d. 1530) founded the dynasty in 1513 and supplied the English book market from Antwerp. His brother **Arnold the elder** (d. 1541) succeeded him.   CHR

C. Reske, *Die Buchdrucker des 16. und 17. Jahrhunderts im deutschen Sprachgebiet* (2007)

Birdsall & Son Bookbinding firm based in Northampton, England, founded by William Birdsall (*c*.1750–1826) in 1792 when he bought John Lacy's bookselling and binding business there. The firm was continued by successive family members, specializing more in bookbinding as the 19th century progressed, until it ceased trading in 1961 (under the direction of Anthony Birdsall). Its extensive collection of bookbinding tools, dating back to the 19th century, was acquired by the University of Toronto.   DRSP

E. Evans and R. Grover, *The Birdsall Collection of Bookbinders' Finishing Tools* (1972)

Birds of America John James Audubon's monumental *Birds of America* is arguably one of the most beautiful picture books ever printed and certainly one of the most important *natural history books of the 19th century. Published in 87 parts, *Birds of America* is a collection of life-size hand-coloured *engravings of 489 avian species indigenous to North America. The engravings, based on watercolours by Audubon (1785–1851), were completed in London by Robert Havell, junior, and measured 39×26 inches. The first *edition, known as the double *elephant folio, was extraordinarily expensive when it was completed (after twelve years) in 1838; the *plates (of the volume) remain so today, some images commanding prices in excess of $100,000.

Audubon was born in Saint Domingue, an illegitimate son of a French sea captain, Jean Audubon, and raised near Nantes, France, by his stepmother and father. He was sent to Pennsylvania in 1803 to oversee a farm. Audubon, however, preferred shooting and sketching avian specimens to fulfilling his responsibilities and, through mismanagement and neglect, lost the property. He married Lucy Bakewell in 1808 and the two moved to Kentucky and Ohio before settling in New Orleans, Louisiana, in 1821. There, he began collecting and sketching specimens to supplant Alexander Wilson's *American Ornithology* (1808–14), the first attempt at a comprehensive avian catalogue of North America. Finding little support for his project in Philadelphia, the young nation's leading centre for science, Audubon sailed in 1826 for London, where he discovered both *subscribers and a competent firm to complete the life-sized engravings.

Audubon's engravings depict birds in quotidian activities and in moments of high drama. For readers more familiar with taxidermic-like representations of birds against blank or bland backgrounds, Audubon's engravings of birds shown in vibrant botanical habitats, arranged in groups and male–female pairs, were revelatory. Audubon painted freshly killed specimens posed in ways that mimicked field behaviour, and endowed his birds with action and emotion. His engravings attempted to capture the vitality of avian life and to present a record of uncommon ornithological precision. Audubon was not without his critics, however, who accused him of over-dramatizing his birds and giving them almost human attitudes.

While Audubon was preparing *Birds*, he was recording their characteristics and behaviour for his *Ornithological Biography* (5 vols, 1831–9). The popularity and (in some quarters) notoriety of the first edition of *Birds* prompted a second, smaller, and less expensive edition that substituted *lithographs for engravings and incorporated written descriptions to accompany the images. The success of this second edition (1840–44) cemented Audubon's reputation as one of the finest naturalist artists of his day, his work becoming the standard against which all future avian artists through the 20th century would be judged. *See also* AVIARY.   AJL

J. J. Audubon, *The Audubon Reader*, ed. R. Rhodes (2006)
R. Rhodes, *John James Audubon* (2004)

Birgitta, St (1303–73) Swedish saint who founded the Order of the Most Holy Saviour at Vadstena (1346), and lived in Rome *c*.1350–73. She *dictated her *Revelationes Coelestes* to her confessors, who recorded them in Latin. Exceptionally popular, the *Revelationes* were widely disseminated, and retranslated into Swedish for the use of nuns. The first complete printed edition (816 copies, Bartholomaeus Ghotan, Lübeck 1492) is considered the most impressive of Swedish *incunabula. It was reprinted numerous times in several languages. During the 15th century, the Vadstena monastery became a centre of book culture and housed Sweden's largest library (*c*.1,400 volumes).   MBj

Birmingham Public Library The Central Library, designed by E. M. Barry and William Martin, was opened in 1865; the Reference Library opened a year later. In 1879, a fire destroyed many of the Reference Library's 50,000 books. The library reopened in 1882, funded by donations of money and books. The current building, opened in 1974, is one of the largest public libraries in Europe. Boasting a comprehensive *Shakespeare library (which includes a copy of the *First Folio), it holds more than 8,000 early and fine books printed before 1701. BEF

www.birmingham.gov.uk/centrallibrary.bcc, consulted July 2008

Birnbaum, Solomon A. (1891–1989) Hebrew palaeographer and Yiddish scholar. From 1936 to 1957, Birnbaum lectured on Hebrew *palaeography and *epigraphy at the University of London. His most important palaeographical work is *Hebrew Scripts* (1954–70), incorporating images and descriptions of *scripts of all areas and ages. In 1970 Birnbaum emigrated to Toronto. EGLS

birthday book The term originated in the mid-19th century to denote an *anthology given as a birthday present. The first instance of the term's use occurred in *The Times* of 31 August 1859, which advertised as a new birthday gift *The Boys' Birthday Book*. An illustrated collection of tales, essays, and narratives of adventure by Mrs S. C. Hall and others, it was soon joined by *The Girls' Birthday Book*. By 1876, when *The Shakespeare Birthday Book* appeared, the phrase had taken on its more common meaning of a book in *diary form with space for each day intended for the owner to record birthdays. Birthday books are often illustrated by a particular artist (e.g. Kate *Greenaway's Birthday Book for Children) or using a theme (e.g. cats, forest fairies, Books of Hours, army and navy illustrations). They frequently contain quotations from renowned authors, such as *Shakespeare, Longfellow, and Burns. Among the main Victorian publishers of birthday books were *Routledge and *Warne. KEA

Bishop, William Warner (1871–1955) American librarian. Bishop worked at *Princeton University Libraries (1902–7) and the Library of *Congress (1907–15) before becoming director of libraries at the University of Michigan (1915–41). His numerous writings dealt with cataloguing, reference works, and international cooperation. A leader of the *American Library Association and principal adviser to the *Vatican Library, he founded the *International Federation of Library Associations. JA

C. Sparks, *Doyen of Librarians* (1993)

BL *See* BRITISH LIBRARY.

Black, A. & C. Publishers, founded in 1807 in Edinburgh by Adam Black and his nephew Charles. In 1826, they began publishing the *Encyclopaedia Britannica*; in 1851, they acquired the rights to *Scott's works. They moved to Soho Square, London in 1889, becoming publishers of *Who's Who*. In the first quarter of the 20th century, they issued a highly regarded series of colour-illustrated topographical books. The firm is now owned by *Bloomsbury. SJG

Blackie, John (1782–1874) Scottish publisher. Succeeding in 1807 to the Glasgow publishing business of W. D. and A. Brownlie, Blackie developed a list that included religious, historical, and travel books. Control later passed first to Blackie's son and then to his grandson John Alexander (1850–1918), under whom Blackie & Son became a leading mass-producer of school and children's books (*see* **15**), most notably those of G. A. Henty. RJD

A. Blackie, *Blackie and Son* (1959)
ODNB

black letter Sometimes used popularly as the English equivalent for the whole *gothic type family, both early and more recent; the term also refers to *scripts that developed from the 12th century. Unlike *romans, which were sometimes referred to as 'white letter', gothic types and scripts appear comparatively dense; hence 'black letter'. This density is created principally by the use of short *ascenders and *descenders. A term sometimes proposed for black letter is 'Text', and related to this 'Church Text', but these are rarely used, perhaps chiefly to avoid confusion with the other meanings of the word 'text'; 'English' and 'Old English' are also sometimes employed. Black letter (and gothic) has been sub-categorized variously by *palaeographers and type historians. Most recently, Bain and Shaw proposed the following categories: *textura, *rotunda, *Schwabacher, and *Fraktur; others have divided rotunda into two—rotunda and *gotico-rotunda (or fere-humanistica: *see* GOTICO-ROTUNDA)—and gathered together Schwabacher and Fraktur, along with others, as German *bastardas.

In England, beginning with *Caxton's successors de *Worde and *Pynson, the black-letter design most closely associated with English vernacular works usually refers to the particular gothic category known as textura. Caxton had used some texturas, but about half of his types were bastardas. Texturas from France predominated between about 1490 and 1540, after which Dutch or Flemish copies prevailed for the next 50 years. Certain classes of book still used black letter in the 17th century: the 1611 *Authorized Version, official proclamations, *ABCs published separately and in some school *textbooks, some *chapbooks and *broadside *ballads. Black-letter bibles in English dwindled, but were still in evidence in the early 18th century, as were a few 18th-century *law reports. MMS

P. Bain and P. Shaw, eds., *Blackletter* (1998)
BMC 11
H. Carter, *A View of Early Typography up to about 1600* (1969; 2e, 2002)
CHBB 3
A. F. Johnson, *Type Designs*, 3e (1966)
S. Morison, *Black-Letter Text* (1942)
Vervliet, *Sixteenth-Century*

Black Sparrow Press American publisher. Founded in 1966 by John Martin, it focused on publishing the work of poets and authors outside the cultural mainstream, including Robert Creeley, Theodore Dreiser, and Alfred Chester. In 2002 it became an imprint of David R. *Godine. RSG

www.blacksparrowbooks.com, consulted July 2008

Blackwell Oxford booksellers and publishers. Founded in 1879 by Benjamin Henry Blackwell (1849–1924), it grew from a space of twelve square feet in Broad Street to be one of the largest distributors of academic books in the world. The company started publishing in 1897. Blackwell's son Basil (1889–1984), the first of his family to attend university, joined the firm in 1913 after working briefly at *Oxford University Press. Heading the publishing side of the business, with *Newdigate he revitalized the *Shakespeare Head Press. He launched the 'Oxford Poetry' series, thereby publishing (among others) Auden, Graves, Spender, and Dorothy L. Sayers. On his father's death in 1924, Blackwell took over both sides of the Blackwell business, though he had also begun a separate publishing company, Basil Blackwell & Mott, in 1922. In 1939, he added Blackwell Scientific Publications. Blackwell went on to publish a wide range of authors, including Enid Blyton and Wittgenstein. By mid-century, Blackwell was known the world over as the first choice for academic books and international book buying. It also had a busy antiquarian and second-hand department which sold many academic collections, including that of A. E. *Housman.

Blackwell resigned as chairman of the firm in 1969 (but maintained a close interest in its running), and was succeeded by his son Richard (1918–80). He expanded the business internationally and revitalized its academic publishing. In 1995, Blackwell became the first bookshop in the UK offering online book sales (see WORLD WIDE WEB), and in 1998 added to its other branches by opening a shop in the Charing Cross Road, London. The bookshop chain is still owned by the family; in 2008, the publishing business became Wiley-Blackwell (see WILEY & SONS, JOHN). PLS

R. Rickets, bookshop.blackwell.co.uk/jsp/bobuk_editorial/about_blackwells.jsp, consulted Feb. 2007
Norrie
ODNB

Blackwood & Sons British publisher. William Blackwood (1776–1834), a bookseller's apprentice, began as a rare book dealer (1804), became a publisher (1810), and soon served as Edinburgh agent for J. *Murray. Early connections with James and John *Ballantyne led to Blackwood's and Murray's joint publication of *Scott's *Tales of My Landlord*. An attempt in 1816 to launch a monthly magazine, competing with the *Edinburgh Review*, ended in dismissing the editors (Cleghorn and Pringle) and launching *Blackwood's Edinburgh Magazine* under his own editorship. With J. G. Lockhart, John Wilson, and James Hogg providing editorial advice and contributions, the new magazine pilloried social and literary icons, leading to court cases, temporary exiles, broken ties with conservative businesses, and a challenge to a duel. The *Maga* was a great success, publishing work by William Maginn, De Quincey, Coleridge, and many others. Of Blackwood's seven sons, two (Robert and Alexander) joined the publishing firm in Edinburgh, and a third, John (1818–79), opened the London branch in 1840 following his apprenticeship with the London publisher George Whitaker. After the death of his brother Alexander in 1845, John returned to Edinburgh, taking over the editorship of the *Maga*. Robert died in 1852, leaving John, who took on as his partner a fourth brother, William, recently retired from military service in India. John's London connections and enterprise made Blackwoods a leading literary firm, publishing Elizabeth Barrett Browning, Bulwer-Lytton, Lever, Reade, Blackmore, Hardy, Oliphant, Lewes, and, perhaps most famously, George Eliot. The business also had important lists in travel and science. John's nephew, William (1836–1912), became partner on the death of his father, William, and published a new generation of writers, including Americans (Crane and London), colonials (Henry Lawson, Miles Franklin), and Conrad. By 1910, the business was run by his nephews, George and James. PLS
ODNB

blad [Du. and Swedish, 'leaf'] Sample printed book section, produced to demonstrate layout (see MISE-EN-PAGE), *typography, and illustrations (see **16**). Like the publisher's *dummy, blads are used in book sales and marketing.

Blades, William (1824–90) English printer and bibliographer. Employed by the family firm of *security printers, Blades, East, & Blades, he developed an interest in early printing and travelled widely, collecting material for his *Life and Typography of William Caxton* (1861; 2e 1863), the first serious study of England's prototypographer. His papers and books on printing history formed the foundation of the *St Bride Library. RM

J. Moran, 'William Blades', *Library*, 5/16 (1961), 251–66
ODNB

Blado family Printers in Rome. **Antonio** (1490–1567), active from 1516, official papal printer (1535–67), produced books in eastern and western *founts; music and elaborately illustrated works; and bulls, briefs, indulgences, edicts, etc. His 'heirs', his widow, **Paola** (d. 1588), and his sons, continued the firm until 1590. His second son, **Paolo** (c.1550–94), published separately from 1568, succeeding the firm as papal printer from 1589. CWK
DBI
DTEI

G. Fumagalli *et al.*, *Catalogo delle edizioni romane di Antonio Blado* (4 vols, 1891–1961)

Blaeu family Seventeenth-century Dutch family of publishers, mapmakers, and printers. A pupil of the astronomer Tycho *Brahe, **Willem Jansz Blaeu** (1571–1638; before 1621, also known as Willem Jansz and G. or W. Janssonius) started dealing in globes, maps, and nautical instruments in Amsterdam in 1599. He also ran a copper-plate (*see* ENGRAVING) printing shop, and, from *c*.1614, a letterpress printing establishment. His cartographic productions were famous, particularly his own *Het licht der zee-vaert* (1608; editions in French and English) and the *Theatrum Orbis Terrarum* (1634–5; editions in Dutch, Latin, French, and German). He also published works by prominent Dutch literary and scholarly authors, such as G. J. *Vossius, P. C. Hooft, and H. Grotius. His son **Joan** (1598/9–1673) crowned the firm's cartographic productions through the publication of the *Atlas Major* (11 vols, 1662–72; editions in Latin, French, Dutch, and Spanish (incomplete)). The *printing office was destroyed by fire in 1672. The firm was liquidated in 1708. FAJ

H. de la Fontaine Verwey, 'Dr. Joan Blaeu and his Sons', *Quaerendo*, 11 (1981), 5–23, 83–94, 197–229

J. Keuning, *Willem Jansz Blaeu* (1973)

C. Koeman, *Joan Blaeu and his Grand Atlas* (1970)

[W. J. Blaeu issue,] *Quaerendo*, 3.2 (1973)

Blake, William (1757–1827) English poet, artist, and engraver. Apprenticed to James Basire at 14, Blake was trained in printmaking. He had begun writing poetry at 12, and from 1787 experimented with techniques to print and publish his own 'illuminated' books. Text and illustration were printed from a metal plate created by 'relief *etching', after which Blake or his wife, Catherine, would apply watercolour by hand, making each copy unique. His illustrated books of poetry include *Songs of Innocence* (1789), *The Marriage of Heaven and Hell* (1793), and *Songs of Experience* (1794). His lavishly produced epic *Jerusalem* (1804–20) exists in a unique copy, once owned by *Mellon. Among his other major works are *The Four Zoas* (1795–1804), *Milton* (1804–8), and a series of nineteen watercolours inspired by the Book of Job (1825). His work was highly imaginative, spiritual, and sexually charged. Although largely unrecognized during his lifetime, Blake's books are now greatly prized. His remarkable method of etching has been most ably studied by Joseph Viscomi in *Blake and the Idea of the Book* (1993) and subsequent articles. An electronic *archive of his work has largely set the standard for similar projects. KES

blakearchive.org/blake, consulted June 2008

ODNB

blank book A book, usually with a hard cover, whose pages may be lined or bordered, but in which printed text is limited at most to page numbers and headings. The term thus covers items such as sketch books, *exercise books, *account books, *logbooks, and *scrapbooks. Blank books may be used for any purpose, but they are associated especially with journal-keeping. Although bound blank books were sold by *stationers during the Middle Ages, the form also derives from the blank leaves bound into printed books for handwritten continuation, such as in the *Nuremberg Chronicle (1493), and from 16th- and 17th-century *commonplace books and *miscellanies. Blank books were particularly popular during the early 19th century when paper companies manufactured books designed specifically for illustrative purposes (scrapbooks) and when *albums were in vogue. KEA

E. Havens, *Commonplace Books* (2001)

blasphemy [Gk, 'slander, profane speech'] Scornful, insulting language against God or holy things, in Christian theology distinguished from profanity, which involves careless or inappropriate speech against the same. In blasphemy, the offence is deliberate and therefore malicious; Aquinas defined it as a sin against faith, and in the 6th-century Justinian code it carried the death penalty. While his concept is clear, the definition of a blasphemous act is not. In theocracies, or wherever state and Church form a single established order, it has served often as a nail on which to hang a charge against a political opponent, who is not otherwise guilty. Charges of blasphemy have also been used to justify *censorship. From the Reformation onwards, blasphemy charges possibly carry more weight in Protestant cultures, in part due to a greater familiarity with the Bible as text and object, while in Catholic countries the misdeed was usually compounded in heresy. In Scotland, blasphemy was punishable by death until the 18th century, and it remains on the statute book in England as a common-law offence. The last prison sentence handed down in Britain for blasphemy was in 1921; John William Gott was given nine months' hard labour for his offence. In a famous case brought by the decency campaigner Mary Whitehouse in 1977, the magazine *Gay News* was found guilty of blasphemous libel for publishing James Kirkup's poem, 'The Love that Dares to Speak its Name', describing the homoerotic fantasy of a Roman soldier for the body of the dead Christ. Blasphemy theoretically carries the death sentence in some Islamic regimes, especially Pakistan, and appears synonymous with profanity, at least in Islam's violent clashes with western secular culture. The most notorious episode in this respect is *The *Satanic Verses* by the novelist Salman Rushdie (1988), involving what were regarded as blasphemies against the Qur'ān and the prophet Muḥammad. In 1989 the theocratic ruler of Iran, Ayatollah Khomeini, issued a *fatwā* (religious/legal opinion) condemning the author to death; it has remained in force despite Rushdie's apologies and retractions. This death sentence against Rushdie, a British citizen, not only brought a rupture of diplomatic relations between Iran and Britain but also led to the assassination of the Japanese translator of the novel and to other deaths, as well as fire bombings of bookshops and publishers. NH

D. A. Lawton, *Blasphemy* (1993)

L. W. Levy, *Blasphemy* (1993)

J. Marsh, *Word Crimes* (1998)

Blayney, Peter (1944–) British bibliographer. Blayney began his career with a monumental study of the 1608 *King Lear*, but later widened his focus to the London book trade. An independent scholar since the mid-1980s, he is currently at work on a history of the *Stationers' Company between 1501 and 1616. His meticulousness, perspicacity, and forthright style have established him as perhaps the foremost early modern bibliographer of the post-*Greg era. IG

bleed off An illustration (*see* **16**) or section of text that extends to the edge of the page, leaving no *margin, is said to be bled off.

blind, books for the Of the approximately 100,000 books published in the UK each year, 5 per cent are made available in a format (Braille book, *talking book, *large-print book, or using digital or Web-based technology) accessible to visually impaired readers. However, the embossed paper book remains a fundamental technology giving visually impaired people the opportunity to read.

The main repository for these books is the RNIB (Royal National Institute for the Blind) National Library Service, which holds about 35,000 Braille and Moon books (Moon is a system of embossed reading, invented by Dr William Moon in 1845); 1,000 of these books are despatched within the UK daily. The equivalent library in the US is the National Library Service for the Blind and Physically Handicapped (NLS), part of the Library of Congress.

Several competing systems for producing books for the blind emerged in France, England, and America during the 19th century. All were based on the use of embossed signs read by touch. One of the earliest, and the one currently in most common use, was initially developed in France in 1829 by Louis Braille. Braille, who lost his sight in a childhood injury, based his six-dot cell system on the embossed alphabetic letters created by his teacher Valentin Haüy at the Royal Institute for Blind Youth in Paris, as well as on the sonography (system of raised dots and dashes) created by an army captain, Charles Barbier, to support secret wartime night writing. Of necessity, Braille developed the system itself as well as the means of reproducing books using that system; the technical challenges of reproduction were faced by all the competing systems, and helped lead to later inventions like the *typewriter.

Like Braille, Moon was not born blind. He contracted scarlet fever aged 21; less than a year later he began developing his Moon System for Embossed Reading, and by 1856 had opened a workshop in Brighton to produce Moon books, which use simplified alphabetic letterforms rather than cells—an easier system for newly blind older adults who find reading Braille cells challenging. Moon type is still in use by a small number of readers in the UK, with several hundred titles available. Moon books are rarely read in other parts of the world.

Other systems for embossed reading included, most notably, the New York Point system created by William Bell Wait. Wait also invented two machines to support the production of embossed books, the Keidograph and, later, the Stereograph. Despite the belief of many readers that Wait's point system was less cumbersome than Braille, by Wait's death in 1916 most writing had been standardized to the system most closely resembling British Braille, primarily because of the quantity of material available in that format. In 1932, Standard English Braille was adopted as the uniform system of embossed writing for all English-speaking countries.

Although Braille was unknown in Britain in 1836, the RNIB has at least one 'tactile book' created by that date. These and other early books were typed on various progenitors of the typewriter and are considered unique copies. The RNIB itself was founded in the front room of a London house in 1882 as the Lending Library for the Blind. In America, although the *Boston Public Library established a department for the blind with eight embossed volumes in 1868, most libraries for the blind were founded in the 1890s. The *American Printing House for the Blind, established in Kentucky in 1858, produced its first book in 1866. The NLS was not formally established until 1931.

Contemporary embossed Braille books are produced directly from publishers' files, from scans or typed MSS, or, since 1999, through a digital program called Web-Braille, allowing individual readers to download and print files at home. All of these methods require translation into Braille by expert translators and local embossment on long-fibred paper. Braille needs more space than alphabetic letters: a 400-page novel is issued in five or six ring-bound volumes. Since Braille requires touch, the embossed surface wears down quickly; a typical Braille book lasts for only six to seven readings.

Most Braille books are issued without any alphabetic text, but some books for younger children, the equivalent of *picture books, are printed with both Braille and print letters, thus allowing sighted readers to read the text aloud while the blind reader follows along using touch. *See also* AUDIO BOOK. KAW

National Library Service for the Blind, www.loc.gov/nls, consulted Oct. 2007

Royal National Institute of Blind People, 'reading', www.rnib.org.uk/xpedio/groups/public/documents/code/public_rnib001969.hcsp, consulted Oct. 2007

blind, libraries for the Providers of library services to visually impaired or print-disabled people, namely those unable to read print due to blindness, low vision, or learning or physical disabilities. Material is usually in the form of Braille, *talking books, descriptive videos, electronic books (*see* WORLD WIDE WEB), books combining print and Braille, *large-print books, and other useful alternative formats, such as tactile graphics. Libraries for the blind emerged in the mid-19th century with the charitable work of philanthropists and missionaries. They developed either within a country's mainstream library system or as an extension of charitable agencies whose commitment to the rehabilitation of the blind included the provision of books. Many countries typically established a central library and production system. Access to information for print-disabled people has improved because many library collections have converted to *digital holdings and because of *copyright and licence arrangements. *See also* BLIND, BOOKS FOR THE. ALD

blind tooling The commonest way of decorating a bookbinding, for many centuries, has been by impressing metal tools, carrying a design or picture, into the surface of the *covers so as to leave a permanent mark. If a layer of gold leaf is used, it becomes *gold tooling; more simply, using tools alone, it is blind tooling. The technique works well with most covering materials, including *leather, *bookcloth, and *vellum, and has been regularly practised since the early Middle Ages. Medieval bindings with tawed leather covers were usually not tooled, but the *Romanesque bindings of the 12th century constitute an early group of bindings characterized by their blind-tooled decoration.

Binders' tools of the early modern period were typically made of brass and mounted on wooden handles, either as single stamps or *roll tools. Designs were engraved on the metal surface so as to create a pattern in relief; occasionally, tools might be cast instead. The tools were heated before being applied to the dampened leather covers, in order to achieve a clean and permanent impression; this was usually done by hand, although large tools (e.g. *panels) might be applied using a press. Gauging the right temperature for tools was one of the binders' skills; if too hot, the leather was scorched. Blind-tooled and blind-stamped bindings are sometimes said to be 'decorated in blind'. DRSP

A. W. Johnson, *The Thames and Hudson Manual of Bookbinding* (1978)

M. Lock, *Bookbinding Materials and Techniques 1700–1920* (2003)

Middleton

L. Town, *Bookbinding by Hand*, 2e (1963)

Bliss, Philip (1787–1857) English antiquary and book collector. Educated at St John's College, Oxford, he joined the *Bodleian Library in 1808, held various university offices, including Keeper of the Archives, and was principal of St Mary Hall (1848–57). His editions included John Earle's *Microcosmography* (1811) and Anthony Wood's *Athenae Oxonienses* (1813–20). His personal library, strong in 16th- and 17th-century poetry and MSS fragments, was dispersed through *Sotheby's (1858). ASGE
ODNB

Bliss, Robert Woods (1875–1962), and **Mildred Bliss** (1878–1969) American book collectors. At Dumbarton Oaks in Georgetown, they developed their library of materials relating to medieval Byzantine culture. They gave both house and collection to Harvard University in 1940. The Garden Library, Mrs Bliss's collection of books on gardens and landscape architecture, is also housed there. ASGE

www.doaks.org/about, consulted Nov. 2008
W. M. Whitehill, *Dumbarton Oaks* (1967)

blockbook *See* BLOCK PRINTING.

blocking The application of a large design to the covering of a bookbinding using an engraved metal block and a blocking press.

block printing Printing with wooden blocks or xylography (Gk, 'writing with wood').

1. Asian
2. Arabic
3. Western

1. Asian

Xylography or woodblock printing was the dominant printing technique in East Asia until it was gradually replaced in the late 19th century by *lithography and Western printing presses using Western-style *type. Paradoxically, because it was taken for granted, extant accounts of xylography are fewer and later than those of movable type. The basic steps included preparing the woodblocks (soaking, drying, planing, oiling, and polishing); writing and correcting the copy text; transferring it in reverse to the block (covered with a rice-based paste); carving the mirrored characters in *relief (after carefully removing the paper, leaving the characters behind); polishing and *inking the block; and finally, printing. The blocks were made of wood of various degrees of hardness depending on their purpose, jujube and pear being the most popular, with harder woods used for illustrations. Wood with a straight and close grain was preferred, and usually the woodblocks were cut with the grain. Their shape was mostly rectangular, following the contours of the *text block. The woodblocks were cut on both sides.

In addition to books, xylography was also used for single-sheet illustrations, bank notes, and advertisements; occasionally bronze *plates were also used. Xylography was additionally employed for *colour printing, with techniques ranging from one block printed at one time but inked with multiple colours to one or more blocks or block pieces printed consecutively, each time with a different colour. From high-quality blocks, as many as several tens of thousands of impressions could be taken; yet such high numbers must have been rarely reached. It is thought that seal-carving, rubbings made from stelae, or the printing of textiles may have been predecessors of xylography in China. Xylography also spread to Korea, Japan, and many other Asian countries.

Carved characters ranged from close imitations of *calligraphy to styles with much more pronounced

Medieval Arabic **block printing** (2): passages of the Qur'ān, produced in Egypt in the early 15th century.

cutting characteristics. By the late 16th century the so-called artisans' style (*jiangtizi*), with its advantages for both cutting and readability, had been combined with a grid-like regularized layout. The existence of such standardized styles ensured that a book could present the same style throughout despite being carved by many different artisans, as was usually the case. However, *bibliophiles preferred less craft-like books closer to calligraphy.

The carving of woodblocks was labour-intensive, but movable type was not a realistic alternative in East Asia because the large number of different characters required made production too difficult and expensive for commercial purposes. Moreover, blocks could be easily stored after a first printing and reused later; thus, blocks had advantages that, in the West, would only become available with *stereotyping and *lithography. With xylography, there was also no need for presses or foundries; simple tools sufficed. Average carving and printing did not need much expertise; at the low end, the carving could be done by illiterate women and children, and labour may have constituted a smaller part of a book's price than its paper. Xylography also could respond easily to aesthetic requirements (e.g. individualistic calligraphic styles); *corrections could even take place after carving; and the page layout (*see* MISE-EN-PAGE) was highly versatile (mixing text, illustrations, various sizes and styles of characters, even various scripts). Its technology was also highly portable, contributing to its spread throughout China. It is no accident that, when Westerners in China began printing translations of books on modern science, they used xylography, despite the availability of type and cylinder presses. *See also* CHINESE TYPE; JAPANESE TYPE; KOREAN TYPE. MH

2. Arabic

The existence of medieval Arabic block-printed documents has been known in the West since the 1890s, when they were discovered among a collection of Egyptian *papyri and paper fragments in Vienna. Further examples have since been identified in other collections of preserved and excavated material in Europe, America, and Egypt; but there was little serious study of them until the late 20th century.

Although papyrus and *parchment are known to have been used, all the surviving documents are on paper; most are amulets designed to be worn in lockets, rather than read. The texts are nearly all prayers, invocations, and passages from the Qur'ān. With a few exceptions, they are cramped and difficult to decipher. Three script styles were used: Kufic (sometimes superimposed vertically), *naskh*, and *thulth*. With one exception (possibly from Iran), they are of Egyptian provenance, but their production may have been more widespread. The earliest are attributed, from their archaeological context, to the 10th century, the latest, from its Italian *watermark, to the 15th century. Contemporary Arabic literary evidence for printing is confined to obscure passing references in two or three texts. The technique was apparently not used for book production. GJR

3. Western

Xylography was introduced into western Europe early in the 15th century. Single sheets with devotional scenes combining text and image originated in South Germany and Flanders, the earliest dated 1418. Not until the 1450s was xylography used for blockbooks, formed into *gatherings by folding together multiple sheets. Since they were made with water-based ink, which was absorbed by the paper, most blockbooks are printed on only one side of the sheet. Blockbooks of the *Apocalypse, *Biblia Pauperum*, and *Ars Moriendi* were reprinted many times; typically they were produced on demand in short *press runs once blocks were cut, thus minimizing the publishers' financial risk. The technique, developed in parallel with movable-type printing, initially offered the advantage of combining text and extensive illustration; but in the 1460s some printers began to *compose pages with movable type and *woodcuts. Illustrated blockbooks were rarely printed later than 1472, though the technique was used occasionally until *c*.1500 for *primers and elementary *grammars for young children. Such small, hardwearing books were printed on parchment with the oil-based ink developed for printing with metal type. LH

U. Baurmeister, 'Das Blockbuch', in *Rationalisierung der Buchherstellung im Mittelalter und in der frühen Neuzeit*, ed. P. Rück *et al.* (1994)

K. Schaefer, *Enigmatic Charms* (2006)

Bloomfield, B. C. (Barry) (1931–2002) British librarian and bibliographer. Bloomfield was librarian of the *School of Oriental and African Studies, the *India Office Library, and was keeper of Oriental collections at the *British Library. He compiled bibliographies of Auden (2e, 1972, with E. Mendelson) and of *Larkin (2e, 2002), and was president of the *Bibliographical Society. ASGE

ODNB

Bloomsbury UK publisher. Founded in 1986, Bloomsbury holds the English-language rights to *Harry Potter outside the US. Floated on the stock market (1994), the company chiefly publishes fiction, children's books, and reference. The acquisition of leading titles, e.g. *Who's Who* (with the purchase of A. & C. *Black, 2000) and *Whitaker's Almanack* (2002), broadened the company's range of intellectual property. The 2004 purchase of Walker Publishing expanded its US market presence. AGP

Bloomsbury Auctions (formerly Bloomsbury Book Auctions, Maddox Street, central London) Founded in 1983 by Frank Herrmann, Lord John Kerr, and David Stagg. At that time, it was the sole English auction house selling only books and MSS. It now also sells photography, art, coins, medals, pens, etc. Aiming to offer an alternative outlet to the larger auction houses, it sells more moderately priced materials, and consequently has far more frequent and varied sales than is the case elsewhere. ASGE

Bloomsbury Book Auctions 10th Anniversary (1993)

A page from a *Biblia Pauperum* (The Netherlands, 1470?) showing **block printing** (3): the Resurrection is framed by Samson carrying the doors of Gaza and Jonah and the whale. Reproduced from *Facsimiles from Early Printed Books in the British Museum* (London, 1897).

blotting paper A highly absorbent paper that has not been *sized so it will soak up ink or other liquids. The best quality is made from old cotton rags and may be *watermarked. Lesser qualities may consist of a *furnish of wood pulp or *esparto. Sometimes wool was used. *See also* DRYING PAPER. RLH

Blount, Edward (*c.*1562–1632) English bookseller. Most probably educated at Merchant Taylors' School, he was apprenticed to *Ponsonby 1578–88. Blount's career was notable for his ability to identify literary classics such as the Shakespeare *First Folio (which he published), a skill possibly attributable to his schooling under the humanist Richard Mulcaster. KMQ
ODNB

Blue Book (**1**) Official report of the British Parliament and/or the Privy Council, begun in 1681 and first available publicly by subscription in 1836. Issued in dark-blue paper *wrappers, some—such as Edwin Chadwick's 1842 *Report on the Sanitary Condition of the Labouring Population*—influenced policy and raised social awareness. EBL
R. D. Altick, *The Presence of the Present* (1991)

Blue Book (**2**) (***Biennial Register, Official Federal Register***) From 1816 to 1959 in the US, a biennial compilation of federal employees listing name, station, and salary. After 1907, separate volumes accommodated larger bureaux, e.g. the Post Office. 'Blue Book' or 'Blue Paper' became shorthand for the official listing of federal employees. GR
J. P. Deeben, 'The Official Federal Register of the United States, 1816–1959', *Prologue*, 36.4 (2004), 50–55

Blue Book (**3**) (***Social Register***) Once the *New York Social Register* (1886), the *Blue Book* contains information about the social elite in American cities. In 1976,

538

these editions were consolidated into a single volume, now published by Forbes. GR

www.socialregisteronline.com/history, consulted Nov. 2006

blue book (**4**) (**exam book**) Booklet (7×8.5 in.) used in the US since the 19th century for examinations in secondary and higher education. Since 1977, the booklets have been manufactured by the Pontiac Paper Company. GR

S. Marberg, 'Why Are Blue Books Blue?', *Yale Daily News*, 17 Nov. 2004

Blumenthal, Joseph (1897–1990) New York fine-book printer, publisher, and writer. His Spiral Press (1926–71) was noted for its taste, fine presswork, and association with distinguished artists. Clients included the *Limited Editions Club, *Grolier Club, *Pierpont Morgan Library, and *Random House. The press printed Robert Frost's first collected poems and worked closely with him for many years. After closing the firm in 1971, Blumenthal turned to writing; notable books include his autobiography *Typographic Years* (1982), a biography of *Rogers (1989), and *The Printed Book in America* (1977). PWR

P. N. Cronenwett, *The Spiral Press, 1926–1971* (2002)

blurb A slang term, with an insinuation of hyperbole, for the copy on the *covers and *dust jackets of books. The term is somewhat derogatory, but is used by publishers themselves. The paragraphs of textual summary are descriptive of a book's contents, but also perform the function of advertising the work to a potential reader. Indeed, a good blurb writer should entice a reader's interest without making fallacious claims, or revealing too much of the plot and spoiling the story—a complaint made by *The Times* in 1955 of thriller blurbs. Blurbs can be written by authors themselves, or in-house editors or copy-writers. The term is thought to have originated in 1907 in the satirical guise of Gelett Burgess's 'Miss Blinda Blurb', and has been employed in the ensuing decades to refer both to books' *paratextual marketing copy and, more broadly, to any copy promoting commodities or events. CMS

boards An essential part of any bookbinding, the outer covers used to protect the *text block, usually made of a stiff or semi-stiff material. The term may be employed to refer to the complete, covered, and decorated end product, but more properly means the core material used to make the outer protection before *leather, cloth, or paper is put over it.

Medieval bindings typically had boards made of wood, cut in thin slices from a section of tree trunk, with the grain running parallel to the spine; in England, oak and beech were commonly used. Wood is durable, but also heavy and expensive; in the 16th century, rising book production led to the gradual phasing out of wood in favour of *pasteboard or *pulpboard; around 1700, *millboard was introduced. Various kinds of machine-made board, based on straw, wood chips, or waste paper, have been used since the middle of the 19th century. Other materials, such as *papier mâché, may sometimes be found.

In hand-bound books the boards are attached by passing the sewing supports (on to which the *gatherings are sewn) through holes drilled or punched in the boards (lacing-in). Modern hardback books, since the second quarter of the 19th century, typically have their boards attached to the textblock by *case binding, relying on gluing to hold the elements together. DRSP

M. Lock, *Bookbinding Materials and Techniques 1700–1920* (2003)
Middleton
Pearson, *Bookbinding*

Bobbs-Merrill Co. Indianapolis, Indiana, publisher, which began by issuing *law books and later branched out into *trade and *educational publishing. Originating as a bookshop in the 1820s, the firm began publishing Indiana law books in the 1860s. Its list expanded when it bought *Houghton Mifflin's law list in 1899. In the 1880s, it ventured into general publishing. As a book publisher, it began as Bowen-Stewart & Co. and was reorganized in 1885 as Bowen-Merrill, becoming Bobbs-Merrill in 1903. The firm had an editorial office in New York City for its trade division, whose head during the 1950s was Hiram Haydn. Its best-known fiction authors were Mary Roberts Rinehart, Booth Tarkington, William Styron, and Ayn Rand. Perhaps its most profitable trade book, however, was Irma Rombauer's *The Joy of Cooking*, which remains in print (now published by *Scribner), updated periodically by Rombauer's descendants. The firm issued stock to the public in 1929 and 30 years later was bought by Howard W. Sams & Co. In turn, Sams was acquired in 1966 by ITT, which sold it to *Macmillan in 1985. The *imprint was discontinued during that period. BEL

Bodel Nijenhuis, Johannes Tiberius (1797–1872) Dutch publisher and collector. Following law studies and a thesis on the history of Dutch copyright (1819), Bodel Nijenhuis, whose mother was a descendant of the Leiden *Luchtmans family, became a partner in the family firm in 1821. A collector rather than an entrepreneur, he sold the firm in 1848 to E. J. *Brill. His library and collection of portraits of members of the book trade were sold after his death, but his maps and prints were bequeathed to *Leiden University Library. BPMD

S. van der Veen, *Brill: 325 Years of Scholarly Publishing* (2008)

bodkin A needle or spike mounted in a handle and used in *letterpress printing to remove or manipulate individual pieces of *type in the *forme.

Bodleian Library The original library of Oxford University, established in part of the university church, was founded *c.*1320; after moving, it vanished during the Reformation. Its existence is evoked in parts of its still-extant premises, notably in the room named for the university's benefactor, the 15th-century patron of learning, *Humphrey, duke of Gloucester. The revived institution owes its name, premises, and ethos to Sir T. *Bodley, who made it his mission to reinstate the library for the benefit of his own university and for 'the republic of the learned'.

The refitted premises (still a rare-book reading room) were soon filled with Bodley's own acquisitions and by the first results of a deposit agreement of 1610 with the *Stationers' Company. Other major collections followed in the 17th century, including those of Archbishop William Laud (1573–1645), and the jurist *Selden. Many other collections were added, oriental as well as European, MS as well as printed, confirming the Bodleian's national primacy, including, in the 18th century, the collections of R. and T. *Rawlinson, and in the 19th century *Douce's huge library and, by transfer from the Ashmolean in 1860, *Ashmole's books. Architectural and organizational changes inevitably followed. The magnificent circular Radcliffe Camera was built in the 18th century. Victorian and later developments, in which librarians such as *Bandinel and E. W. B. *Nicholson were prominent, included provision of more reading space and the construction of vast underground storage areas. *Madan started a tradition of bibliographical scholarship that still continues, with projects such as the six-volume catalogue (2005) of the Bodleian's 7,000 *incunabula. Several 'dependent libraries', especially the Radcliffe Science Library, have been created, to meet curricular as well as research needs. The 20th century saw the grossly over-full library expand with the opening of the New Bodleian in 1937. This was also soon filled, as was remote storage in rural Oxfordshire. A much larger repository is currently planned at a reclaimed urban riverside site. The Bodleian, now joined administratively with the many lesser parts of Oxford University Library Services, continues to grow. It serves not only its own academic community but (with major acquisitions as varied as the *Opie Collection of children's literature, Mendelssohn MSS, and the Harding collection of sheet music) the entire *republica literatorum*, as was the founder's intention.   ASB

www.bodley.ox.ac.uk, consulted Aug. 2007

H. H. E. Craster, *History of the Bodleian Library, 1845–1945* (1982)

W. D. Macray, *Annals of the Bodleian Library* (1890)

I. G. Philip, *The Bodleian Library in the Seventeenth and Eigtheenth Centuries* (1983)

Bodley, Sir Thomas (1545–1613) English book collector. Bodley was educated at Magdalen College, Oxford, and, after academic and diplomatic careers, devoted the last fifteen years of his life to the foundation of the *Bodleian Library in Oxford, which opened in November 1602 with a collection of about 2,000 volumes. Bodley continued to enlarge the collection until his death, with the assistance of his first librarian and cataloguer, Thomas *James (1572/3–1629).   ASGE

ODNB

Bodley Head British publisher. Named after the sign on *Mathews's Vigo Street bookshop, the Bodley Head became the most influential literary publisher of the 1890s. Started in 1889 by Mathews and J. *Lane, it succeeded with modern poetry (Le Gallienne, Dowson, the Rhymers' Club) printed at the *Chiswick Press. Lane's publication of the *Yellow Book* (1894) broke the partnership, Mathews continuing under his own name and Lane broadening the Bodley Head *imprint, especially in fiction, with ties to American publishers (*Copeland & Day, *Stone & Kimball) and, from 1896, alone. Lane published Beardsley, Corvo, and Beerbohm, and later Wells, Bennett, and Ford. His successor, A. *Lane, published Stein and Joyce, and the company's strong fiction list included Graham Greene and children's books by *Ardizzone and *Sendak. Its distinctive typographical style was created by *Ryder working for the firm's owner, Max Reinhardt.   PGS

J. W. Lambert, *The Bodley Head, 1887–1987* (1987)

Bodmer, Martin (1899–1971) Swiss book collector. Inspired by Goethe's idea of 'Weltliteratur', he collected MSS and first editions of the great works of world literature from Homer and the Bible to the present. In his own writings (*Eine Bibliothek der Weltliteratur*, 1947; *Variationen zum Thema Weltliteratur*, 1956), he described the aims of his impressive collection, the Bibliotheca *Bodmeriana: depicting the development of the human mind through its written heritage. He also founded the Gottfried Keller Prize for outstanding literary works, and edited the literary review *Corona* (1930–42).   RAK

M. Bircher, 'Verzeichnis der Publikationen von Martin Bodmer', *Corona Nova*, 1/1 (2001), 77–103

Bodmeriana, Bibliotheca *Bodmer's private collection in Cologny, near Geneva, has been open to the public as a museum with permanent and temporary exhibitions since 1971. Its 150,000 items represent the gems of world literature, with one of the finest collections of Shakespeariana. In 2003 the building was enlarged by the famous Swiss architect Mario Botta. The Martin Bodmer Foundation publishes the series *Papyrus Bodmer* (1954–), *Catalogues* (1973–), *Textes* (1975–), and *Corona Nova* (2001–).   RAK

M. Bircher, *Spiegel der Welt* (2000)

— *Fondation Martin Bodmer* (2003)

C. Méla, *Légendes des siècles* (2004)

J. Quentin, *Fleurons de la Bodmeriana* (2005)

Bodoni, Giambattista (1740–1813) Printer, punchcutter, and typefounder at Parma. His grandfather (d. 1723) learned punchcutting in Rome and continued at the Saluzzo (Piedmont) press he inherited and passed on to his son. Giambattista learned typesetting and typefounding there. In 1758 Cardinal Spinelli expanded the printing office of the Congregatio de *Propaganda Fide in Rome, using the Vatican's typefounding materials, and hired Bodoni. He learnt punchcutting, sorted non-Latin types, and admired *Baskerville's books. He left in 1766 for England, but illness and an invitation in 1768 to manage Duke Ferdinand of Parma's Stamperia Reale, kept him in Italy.

Bodoni used *Fournier's types and rococo *fleurons, cutting new materials to match. Baskerville's austere neoclassical layouts would have lost much of their impact with continental types then available, but by 1788 Bodoni developed his own style, winning worldwide acclaim. He set up his own printing office in the Ducal residence in 1791, printed luxurious books for foreign patrons, became printer to the King of Spain, and honoured Napoleon in 1811. He never matched the editorial care or scholarship of the *Didots, but they vied with each other for decades, developing types that dominated the 19th century. Bodoni's workmen cut some of his types. His most mannered non-Latin types bore little fruit, but they appear with splendid *romans and *italics in his sumptuous *Manuale tipografico*, published by his widow in 1818.   JAL

A. Ciavarella, *et al.*, *The "Cimelio" of Bodoni* (1991)

body of type   A type's *size, usually slightly more than the distance from *ascender to *descender. Formerly a measure of the physical rectangular block that formed the 'body' of a piece of *type and determined the distance from *baseline to baseline in unleaded setting, body size is now conventional. Names for bodies were approximately standardized in 16th-century France, ranging from Nonpareil (about 2mm) to Canon (about 14mm). The Paris Académie des sciences *c.*1694, *Fournier in 1737, and F. A. *Didot *c.*1781 introduced units for measuring bodies, known since Fournier as *points.   JAL

Boekenwereld, De (1984–)   Dutch bibliographical journal. Since its foundation, *De Boekenwereld*, 'journal for books and prints', has aimed to publish articles on Dutch book history and the graphic arts for a wide readership including collectors, scholars, and members of the trade. Its regular five issues per year contain reviews, a news section, and book sale reports, as well as special numbers on subjects such as bibliographical journals, *lithography, and *forgeries and frauds in the Dutch world of books.   PGH

www.deboekenwereld.nl, consulted July 2008

Bogeng, Gustav Adolf Erich (1881–1960)   German book scholar and collector. A bibliophile from his youth, he abandoned law to devote his life to the history of collecting, binding, and related topics. His three-volume *Die großen Bibliophilen* (1922) remains a standard reference work.   JWUS

E. Steiner, *G. A. E. Bogeng* (1954)

Bogue, David (1807/8–1856)   English publisher. Bogue's publishing and bookselling business, which he acquired from Charles Tilt in 1843, specialized in issuing children's literature and inexpensive reprints of classic titles (the European Library). He was also the principal publisher of *Cruikshank's illustrated works. Bogue's imprint died with him.   RJD

ODNB

Bohatta, Hans (1864–1947)   Austrian book historian. University of *Vienna Librarian (1890–1922), and from 1928 professor for the history of the book. He published, with Michael Holzmann, the groundbreaking *Deutsches Anonymen-Lexikon* (1902–28) and *Deutsches Pseudonymen-Lexikon* (1906). His *Bibliographie der Breviere 1501–1850* (1937) is similarly unsurpassed.

JWUS

LGB

Bohn, H. G. (Henry George) (1796–1884)   Bookseller, publisher, translator. In 1831 he established an antiquarian bookselling business in London. His famous 'Guinea Catalogue' (published 1841) made his reputation. In the mid-1840s, he began reissuing *remaindered titles in affordable formats in his Standard and European libraries. These were followed by additional series: the 'Scientific' and the 'Antiquarian' (1847), 'Classical' (1848), 'Illustrated' (1849), 'Shilling Series' (1850), 'Ecclesiastical' (1851), 'Philological' (1852), 'British Classics' (1853), and others. These became collectively known as the Bohn Libraries. He contributed to them, editing and indexing new titles and assiduously marketing them in Britain and abroad. In 1864 Bohn semi-retired and sold his Libraries to G. *Bell & Sons. In 1875 he sold the remainder of his publishing business to *Chatto & Windus, retaining only his *Dictionary of Quotations* (1867), containing his own verse and George Gordon's *Pinetum* (1875), which he had enlarged and indexed.   AAW

ODNB

Bohn, J. G. S. B. (James George Stuart Burges) (1803–80)   Son of the bookseller John Henry Martin Bohn (*c.*1757–1843) and brother to the successful translator and publisher H. G. *Bohn, he twice failed as a bookseller (1834–37, 1845–7). However, he attracted bibliographers and scholars to his London shops, his catalogues amounting to bibliographical reference works. He eked out a living as a writer, editor, and compiler of catalogues for other booksellers, notably Nicholas Trübner.   PLS

ODNB

Boitard, François (1667–1719)   French artist, working in London *c.*1709–12. The important—and first illustrated—*edition of *Shakespeare's works, edited by Nicholas Rowe and published by J. *Tonson in 1709, contained 43 *engravings designed by Boitard. He also illustrated Tonson's 1711 edition of Beaumont and Fletcher.   MMS

Boix, Ignacio (d. 1862)   Spanish publisher. Boix opened a Madrid press *c.*1833, soon becoming a leading publisher of drama, history, law, practical guides, and especially illustrated books and magazines. Following a short stint as a publisher and bookseller in Paris, Boix relocated his press to Valencia in 1856.   DRW

bold face   In *type design, the term for a dense and/or large letterform used for advertising, *posters, and, in books, for emphasis and *textual articulation. It replaced earlier terms: *black, *fat, heavy, or Clarendon. *Texturas and large-sized *rotundas had been used from early printing for *headings and emphasis. By the mid-1820s, bold types for *jobbing printing were common, especially for eye-catching posters. Bold designs were based on contemporary *display types, such as fat face, *sans serif, and *slab serif. An early book example is J. Bell's *A View of Universal History* (5e, 1842), which employed 'variegated type' to highlight important people and events. Later that decade, the Fann Street Foundry in London introduced the Clarendon series, specifically for display within books. These were quickly taken up, especially for *textbooks and reference works (e.g. railway *timetables, *dictionaries, *catalogues), and were soon designed to harmonize with the *roman founts they accompanied. They eventually became a standard part of the type family, which includes the further bold varieties, semi-bold and extra-bold (as well as light and extra-light).　MMS

J. Mosley, 'Putting a Bold Face on It: A Note on the Origins of the Related Bold Face', *Linotype Matrix*, 30 (1958), 5

M. L. Twyman, 'The Bold Idea: The Use of Bold-Looking Types in the Nineteenth Century', *JPHS* 22 (1993), 107–43

Bollingen Prize The biennial Bollingen has enjoyed high visibility among America's many poetry book prizes, partially thanks to its scandalous debut in 1949. Established by the Library of *Congress and endowed by the Bollingen Foundation, it was organized by Allen Tate, a member of the Library's Fellows in American Letters, who were enlisted as the jury. When they awarded the first Bollingen to Ezra Pound, avowed anti-Semite and wartime propagandist for Fascism, public outcry led Congress to withdraw support. The prize relocated to *Yale University in 1949. Recipients include Wallace Stevens, e. e. cummings, Richard Wilbur, Mark Strand, and Adrienne Rich.　JFE

Bologna, Archiginnasio Library The library was established in 1801 in the convent of San Domenico in order to cope with the abundance of books left by the suppression of the religious orders. In 1838 the civic library moved to the *studium* constructed in 1562 for the university. Over the years, its librarians have included scholars such as Albano Sorbelli and Carlo Frati; it now runs a city library around Bologna that includes the house and books of the poet and *Nobel prizewinner Giosuè Carducci (1835–1907).　NH

Bologna, University Library The foundation of the university reaches back to 1088, but little is known about its libraries prior to 1712, when the present one was founded by Luigi Ferdinando Marsili. In 1742 it was merged with what was known as the Public Library, received in legacy from the natural-history scholar Ulisse Aldrovandi (1522–1603), and transferred to its new building. In 1869, with the cessation of papal temporal rule, ownership passed to the newborn Italian state.　NH

bolts Threaded rods used to hold or adjust components of printing presses; *common presses have head and nut bolts, *Albions have main and spring bolts.

Bomberghen, Daniel van (b. before 1483–1553) Born into a family of Antwerp merchants with an interest in printing, Bomberghen was the most influential Christian printer of Hebrew books in Venice between 1516 and 1549. Among the more than 200 he produced are first complete editions of the Biblia Rabbinica, the Palestinian and Babylonian Talmuds, and important rabbinic texts. Some of his Hebrew *type, including type by *Le Bé, is still held at the *Plantin-Moretus Museum.　EGLS

Bompiani, Valentino (1898–1992) Founder of the eponymous Milan publishing house (1929). He trained at *Mondadori, and his three volumes of memoirs are an important source for the history of 20th-century Italian publishing. He sold the firm in 1972, and it is now part of the RCS group. Specializing in modern fiction, Bompiani gained huge international success with Eco's *The Name of the Rose* (1980).　NH

Bonet, Paul (1889–1971) French bookbinder and binding designer. After some years in the fashion industry, he began producing bindings in the 1920s. His striking, colourful designs and prolific output led to his becoming one of the leading figures of his generation, widely acclaimed as the natural successor to *Legrain.　DRSP

P. Bonet, *Carnets, 1924–1971* (1971)

A. Duncan and G. de Bartha, *Art Nouveau and Art Deco Bookbinding* (1989)

Bongi, Salvatore (1825–99) Archivist, historian, and bibliographer, who in his youth fought in the cause of Italian unity. In the 1850s he edited several Renaissance texts; from 1860, following his appointment as director of Lucca's state archive, he spent 30 years reorganizing its holdings. From 1890 to 1897 he published, in seven *fascicles, the annals of the *Giolito family, showing a pioneering bibliographical acumen in his description of variant *states and *issues.　NH

DBI

Bonhomme, Pasquier (*fl.* 1453–1501), and **Jean Bonhomme** (*fl.* 1475) Parisian printers. Pasquier issued the first book in French to be printed in Paris, the *Grandes chroniques de France*, the third volume of which is dated January 1476 (i.e. 1477). His relative Jean succeeded him.　VAG

Boni, Albert (1892–1981), and **Charles Boni** (1894–1969) American booksellers and publishers. In 1913, the Bonis opened the Washington Square Book Shop, selling works by political and literary radicals. Later they joined Harry Scherman to create the 'Little Leather Library', a project that spawned the '*Modern Library' at *Boni & Liveright. After a quarrel with Liveright, the Boni brothers formed their own firm, Albert and Charles Boni (1923–39). Upon the firm's dissolution, Albert created the Readex Microprint Corporation.　CCT

'Albert Boni', *Publishers Weekly*, 220 (14 Aug. 1981)

'Charles Boni', *Publishers Weekly*, 195 (3 Mar. 1969)

Boni & Liveright American publishing firm, founded in 1917. It brought together the socialist bookseller Albert *Boni and the stockbroker Horace Liveright. Initially, the firm focused on an inexpensive reprint series of classic and contemporary works, the '*Modern Library'. After less than a year, the partners separated. Liveright continued the firm, creating lists running from controversial political works and spicy bestsellers to avant-garde modernism. Notorious for its public support of obscene works, aggressive advertising, and scandalous office parties, Boni & Liveright provided a training ground for young publishers, especially Bennett Cerf, who left the company in 1925 to found *Random House. In 1928 Liveright changed the firm's name to Horace Liveright, Inc. Despite spectacular success in the late 1920s, he lost control of the business as a result of speculation in stocks and Broadway shows. Arthur Pell, the firm's accountant, removed Liveright in 1930, reorganizing it as Liveright Publishing Corporation after involuntary bankruptcy proceedings in 1933. CCT

T. Dardis, *Firebrand* (1995)
C. Egleston, ed., *The House of Boni and Liveright* (2004)
J. Satterfield, *The World's Best Books* (2002)

Bonnier Sweden's largest publishing house. Adolf Bonnier (1806–67) opened a bookshop in Stockholm 1829 and was soon joined by his brothers, Albert (1820–1900) and David (1822–81). Albert began publishing books in 1837. His son Karl Otto Bonnier (1856–1941) succeeded him, publishing Strindberg, Heidenstam, Lagerlöf, and others. Today, the company has strengthened its leading position in the Swedish book market and branched out as dominant publishers of newspapers (*Dagens Nyheter*, 1903– ; *Expressen*, 1944–) and popular *magazines. The corporation remains a family business. PSR

book (1) A word that has long been used interchangeably and variously to signify any of the many kinds of text that have been circulated in written or printed forms, and the material objects through which those words and images are transmitted. The ancestor of the modern word 'book' is used in both senses in Anglo-Saxon documents. This *Oxford Companion* is a book in the abstract, non-corporeal sense (and can be thus described in its Internet manifestation), and also in the physical sense of a three-dimensional object in *codex format. Books in that first sense have been manifested in the second one in a wide variety of shapes and sizes from ephemera (*see* **14**) to *elephant folios, using many different materials. DRSP

book (2) The word 'book' is often used in the sense of *chapter or part, to signify a subdivision of a whole text, in prose or verse. Milton's *Paradise Lost*, for example, is divided into twelve books; George Eliot's *Middlemarch* is divided into eight, each of which has an individual title to summarize the theme of that part of the whole. The use of the word in this way dates back to antiquity; Virgil's *Aeneid* is divided into twelve books (Liber Primus–Liber Duodecimus). Books, in this sense, are sometimes further subdivided into chapters. The conventions of page layout (*see* MISE-EN-PAGE) and *typography are normally similar to those that apply to chapters. DRSP

book art The idea of the book as a work of visual or tactile art, beyond its textual value, has a long history that can be traced through the many *illuminated or handsomely illustrated books made down the centuries. During the 20th century, the finely produced books of many *private presses would be regarded by many as

exemplars of the book as an art form. Around 1900, there developed the concept of the *livre d'artiste*, or *artist's book, in which visual artists combined with publishers to make works intended as a fusion of images and words within a *codex format, and artistically greater than the sum of their parts. Book art, taking this idea a stage further, covers a variety of artworks based around the form or concept of the book. During the later 20th century, artists worldwide experimented with book art to produce sculptural or conceptual 'books'—which might or might not have words—made from all kinds of material. One of the earliest works in this tradition (sometimes called bookworks) was *La Prose du transsibérien*, by Blaise Cendrars and Sonia Delaunay (1913), mixing words and abstract images on a fold-out sheet. A major collection of book art will be found in the *National Art Library. DRSP

J. Bettley, ed., *The Art of the Book* (2001)
S. Bury, *Artists' Books* (1995)

book auction and sales records The records of auction houses and antiquarian book dealers are of great scholarly importance. They can provide information about the provenance of books and MSS, and often offer what may be the only detailed descriptions of such items, sometimes with illustrations. They also, of course, contain information about prices and the history of the trade. Similarly, auction house and dealers' annotated sets of their own or others' catalogues, where they exist, usually give details of purchasers.

One of the fundamental problems of searching such records is their often unsystematic preservation. Not all libraries preserve sales catalogues or, if they do, catalogue them fully. Not all dealers maintain proper records, and these may not survive in accessible forms. There are some exceptions: *Sotheby's has deposited marked sets of its catalogues in the *British Library. *Christie's maintains its own *archives. Some dealers deposit marked sets of their catalogues in institutional libraries: for example, *Quaritch's archive is in the BL. However, few libraries make systematic efforts to acquire this kind of material. Exceptions include the BL, *Bodleian, *Cambridge University Library, and the *Grolier Club in New York, all of which have large collections of catalogues.

As well as various national bibliographies of sale catalogues, various annual publications provide national records of sales: *Book Auction Records* (1903–94) for the UK; *American Book Prices Current* (1894–), now in CD-ROM format, for the United States; *Jahrbuch der Auktions Preise* (1950–) for Germany. In addition, SCIPIO, an online union catalogue of auctions, gives details of auction catalogues from major North American and European auction houses. ASGE

R. Folter, 'An Annotated Checklist of Catalogue Literature', *PBSA* 89 (1995), 469–74
Pearson, *Provenance*
M. F. Suarez, S.J., 'English Book Sale Catalogues as Bibliographical Evidence', *Library*, 6/21 (1999), 321–60

book auctions Sales of books and MSS, normally to the open market, made to the highest bidder. Books sold by auction were normally second-hand books; new books sold through auctions were normally made through *trade sales restricted to established members of the book trade. The earliest recorded book auctions were in medieval Spain, in Muslim territories, eventually spreading throughout the Mediterranean to Palestine and Turkey. The habit of selling books by auction took longer to become established in northern Europe, but such sales are found in Naples in 1608, where the library of *Pinelli was sold by auction as a single lot, with no catalogue issued. There is archival evidence of auctions in Louvain in the early 16th century. In Britain, the earliest recorded book auction was for the sale of the library of Lazarus Seaman (London, 1676). Despite initial scepticism from within the London trade, auctions soon became an accepted element of the book trade in Britain, with auctions taking place at Cambridge in 1684, and at Oxford and Edinburgh in 1686. The first recorded American colonial book auction was in 1713.

Early auctions took the form of sales by candle, where the duration of bidding was determined by the time taken for a length of candle to burn. Bidding was regulated in later auctions by the auctioneer, marking the close of bidding by the fall of a hammer. The practice of issuing catalogues describing the lots, and governing the order of sale, was largely a 17th-century phenomenon. There is evidence of a printed catalogue having been produced for a sale at Leiden in 1593, but the earliest catalogue to survive is that of the library of Philippe de Marnix de Sainte-Aldegonde, sold at Antwerp on 6 July 1599. The earliest French auction catalogue, compiled by *Naudé, was for the collection of Jean de Cordes, sold in Paris in 1643. The first English printed catalogue was that of the Seaman sale of 1676. Catalogues were generally sold during the 17th century, but could also be provided free, as with the sale of the stock of the bookseller Jonathan Edwin (London, 29 Mar. 1680).

Catalogues served as advertisements for early auction sales, as well as tools for buying books; the advent of newspapers in the late 17th century provided an additional vehicle for advertising book auctions. London and Edinburgh newspapers began advertising auctions that took place in Europe (especially the Low Countries) as well as in Britain from the 1670s and 1680s. Dutch book auctions became especially important mechanisms for distributing books in Europe during the 18th century, with van der *Aa's catalogues for the fictitious collector 'W. Snellonius's' Leiden auction of 1691 distributed in Brussels, Hamburg, London, and Copenhagen. Auction catalogues began to be collected as bibliographical tools from the end of the 17th century, with figures such as Thomas Plume and Thomas Sharp actively accumulating them. Important collections of auction catalogues exist today in the *British Library, the *Bodleian Library, and the *Grolier Club in New York.

The first book auctions tended to deal with hundreds of books, but by the early 18th century auctions had become larger, the 1725 auction of the library of Cardinal du Bois offering for sale more than 30,000 books. Early auctions often took place in the houses where the libraries sold were situated, but could also be conducted in coffeehouses or in booksellers' premises. In the 18th century, specialist auction rooms began to proliferate. Modern book auctions exist in many locations, but for material at the more valuable end of the trade, auctions are dominated by two established houses based in London: *Christie's, which began selling books in 1776; and *Sotheby's, which began its series of book auctions in 1778. Both of these houses have a network of auction rooms throughout the world, but are becoming rivalled by the advent of online auctions, especially those offered through the auction house eBay. RWO

A. N. L. Munby and L. Coral, eds., *British Book Sale Catalogues 1676–1800* (1977)

R. Myers *et al.*, eds., *Under the Hammer: Book Auctions since the Seventeenth Century* (2001)

M. North, ed., *Printed Catalogues of French Book Auctions and Sales by Private Treaty 1643–1830 in the Library of the Grolier Club* (2004)

bookbinding *See* 17.

book burning The ritual destruction of books deemed false, heretical, *blasphemous, indecent, subversive, or simply trivial (distinguished from *library destruction by fire). Whether conducted for or against the prevailing authority, book burning is primarily a form of intellectual intimidation. Indeed, given that the main force that destroys books is not fire but readers' use, the significance of book burning is largely symbolic, albeit powerfully so. Referring to the destruction of the Qur'ān by the Spanish *Inquisition, a character in Heinrich Heine's play *Almansor* (1821) observes, 'where they burn books, they will end in burning men.'

The earliest recorded incendiary campaign occurred in China in 213 BC, where, after taking power, the emperor Qin Shi Huang implemented a ruthless centralization, which included the destruction of all works of philosophy and history not aligned with the regime, and the live burial of scholars and intellectuals who failed to comply —a basic pattern that has presented itself many times since. In Christian culture, much book burning was justified on the basis of Acts 19:19, describing the behaviour of new converts in Ephesus who, having previously practised sorcery, brought out their scrolls and burnt them publicly. After the first Council of Nicaea in 325, the orthodox opponents of Arianism ordained that the books of Arius and his followers should be systematically put to the flame. Likewise in Islam, around 650, the Qur'ān, which had been propagated mostly through oral tradition, was established in a single, authoritative written text on the instruction of the third caliph, 'Uthmān ibn 'Affān, who is said to have ordered that all other versions, whether fragmentary or entire, be destroyed. From the Middle Ages to the Renaissance, the Catholic Church— through its principal instrument the Inquisition— frequently employed book burning as a weapon against dissent (e.g. in the 13th-century crusade against the Cathars). The regular destruction of Hebrew literature by successive popes, beginning with thousands of copies of

Invitation to a Nazi **book burning** in Munich's Königsplatz at 11.30 p.m. on 10 May 1933. The burning of *volkszersetzender Bücher und Zeitschriften* ('books and newspapers that corrupt the *Volk*') was to be accompanied by a series of songs.

the Talmud in Paris in 1243, proved less successful, since Jewish culture was too ramified and too aware of the danger of destruction to suffer permanent loss. Book burning was also employed by secular states, usually with religion as a stalking horse, to subjugate a conquered people and extirpate the memory of their previous civilization. A notorious example is the 1562 destruction of the sacred books of the Maya in the Yucatan.

The advent of the modern age and the printing press shifted the focus in book burning from destruction to public shaming. It is necessary, therefore, to distinguish between actions conducted by those in power—often dictatorships seeking to humiliate their opponents—and pressure groups who target specific texts, such as American fundamentalist sects burning the *Harry Potter books, or Hindu hardliners in Kashmir burning copies of the Qur'ān. In the eschatological fervour of Florence in 1497, the followers of Savonarola ignited a bonfire of the vanities in Piazza Signoria, destroying numerous luxury objects, including paintings, mirrors, gaming tables, and cosmetics, as well as copies of Boccaccio, Ovid, and Pulci. In a tragic turn of the wheel of fortune, Savonarola and two of his disciples were burnt on the same spot a little more than a year later. In 1933, thousands of 'degenerate' books pillaged from the Institut für Sexualwissenschaft were burnt by the Nazis in Berlin's Opernplatz: a plaque there records Heine's premonition of the human holocaust that followed. Well-known depictions of book burning appear in fiction, especially the dystopian future society imagined in Ray Bradbury's *Fahrenheit 451* (1953)—the temperature at which paper spontaneously ignites—of which a film version was made by Truffaut in 1966.   NH

book case A piece of furniture used to store books. Sometimes attached to walls, sometimes freestanding,

book cases necessarily contain *bookshelves, but have a greater degree of construction in order to hold the shelves in place within the case, and books in place on the shelves. Book cases, in their modern form, developed as a result of the shift away from medieval *lecterns and stalls in libraries of the 16th and 17th centuries. During the 17th and 18th centuries they became increasingly decorative as well as functional, particularly for individual book owners such as *Pepys, who stored his books in the earliest extant glass-fronted example. In the 18th century, Chippendale introduced numerous designs for bookcases—among them Gothic, Oriental, or Indian—in *The Gentleman and Cabinet-Maker's Director* (1754), which were then copied by many imitators. Metal bookcases began to appear in the late 19th century, mostly in institutional libraries. In the 1880s, the British Museum (*see* BRITISH LIBRARY) and the *Bodleian libraries became the forerunners of bookcase design when they were fitted with moving cast-iron cases, which use rails to allow multiple book cases on the same track to be rolled together, providing compact storage. *See also* SHELF-MARKS.   RWO

H. Petroski, *The Book on the Bookshelf* (1999)

book chest Wooden chest used by individuals and institutions in the Middle Ages to store books, both permanently and as part of travelling luggage. Chests, which were often carved and had multiple locks to deter thefts, were sometimes set on frames raising them to a convenient height for the top to be used as a desk. Their dimensions varied; surviving chests are between four and seven-and-a-half feet long and between fourteen inches and more than two feet deep, with a width of approximately twenty inches.   KEA

J. W. Clark, *The Care of Books*, 2e (1909)
B. H. Streeter, *The Chained Library* (1931)

One of the twelve **book cases** (no. 4) from *Pepys's library, now at *Magdalene College, Cambridge. The glazed cases—showing Pepys's careful arrangement of volumes by height and double-banking to save space—are 4ft wide, 8ft high, and 18in. deep; they are made of red oak.

bookcloth The fabric used to cover the *boards of a bookbinding. Bookcloth of the kind used today was first developed in the 1820s, although there is a longer history of the use of *textiles as binding materials. It is traditionally a woven cotton cloth, treated ('filled') with starch to give it stiffness and impermeability, allowing it to take and hold impressed designs, and preventing seep-through of the glue with which it is pasted to the boards. It is then *calendered (pressed) to give a smooth finish.

After the earliest experiments of W. *Pickering with dyed, glazed calico in the early 1820s, the use of bookcloth spread rapidly, in tandem with the change in bookbinding technique from laced-in covers to prefabricated (cloth-covered) cases (*see* **17**). During the 1830s, binding cloths began to be embossed with fine all-over patterns or grains; the recognition and classification of these is useful for dating purposes, or for determining the publishing

history of texts that went through multiple editions or issues. The earliest cloths were typically dark or drab in colour, but brighter, more intense colours began to appear during the 1840s and 1850s; striped and marbled cloths were also introduced during these decades. By the time of the Great Exhibition of 1851, seven firms were listed as specializing in bookcloth manufacture. During the 20th century, the Winterbottom Book Cloth Co. (founded 1891) was a dominant supplier in both Europe and America.

Leathercloth, made by coating unstarched cotton cloth with pigmented nitrocellulose to produce a water-proof fabric with leather-like qualities, was invented in the 1880s and came to be used for some kinds of binding work. Rexine, introduced *c.*1900 by the British Leather Cloth Manufacturing Co., was an early example. In the early 20th century, pyroxylin (gelatinized nitrocellulose) was introduced as an alternative to starch for the filling agent, producing a stronger cloth, more resistant to water and insect attack. Later in the century, other synthetic fabrics such as rayon and PVC-coated cloths began to be used as an alternative to cotton.   DRSP

Gaskell, *NI*
M. Lock, *Bookbinding Materials and Techniques 1700–1920* (2003)
M. Roberts and D. Etherington, *Bookbinding and the Conservation of Books* (1982)
G. T. Tanselle, 'The Bibliographical Description of Patterns', *SB* 23 (1970), 72–103
W. Tomlinson and R. Masters, *Bookcloth 1823–1980* (1996)

Book Club of California Founded in 1912 'to advance the study of letters and the promotion of the arts pertaining to the production of books'. Since 1914 it has published books on the book arts and on the history, literature, and *bibliography of California and the West; and since 1933, annual *keepsakes as examples of *fine printing. These have been chiefly printed by presses of the western US, including *Nash, the *Grabhorn Press, and *Marks's Plantin Press. The club sponsors exhibitions, lectures, and grants, and houses the Albert Sperisen Library. SG
J. Larson, 'The Book Club of California', *Bookways*, 2 (1992), 12–17

book clubs (distribution) In the early part of the 20th century, conventional wisdom in trade publishing circles held that there were approximately 200,000 book buyers in the US. Distribution and retailing practices reflected this assumption: in the early 1920s there were fewer than 1,000 bookstores in the country, mostly in large urban areas. The development of book clubs—direct-mail book-selling on a subscription basis—was an attempt to change this inefficient and inegalitarian method of distribution. Typically, clubs relied on panels of experts to select new titles suited to their membership's tastes and needs. For a fixed price (generally well below retail), subscribers received a set number of books per year; most enjoyed some flexibility as to which titles they accepted or declined. Beginning with the *Book-of-the-Month Club (BOMC) in 1926, clubs became enormously popular. Scores of special-interest clubs sprang up during the

1920s, and even more appeared in the prosperous post-World War II era. Their reach and effectiveness changed the landscape of bookselling: to the extent that publishers chose titles hoping that they would be book-club selections, the clubs changed editorial practice as well.

Proponents argued that clubs improved not only the quality of personal life but also the national culture. By separating the wheat from the chaff in a crowded literary marketplace, clubs 'fill[ed] a need long felt by busy and intelligent people', as one BOMC advertisement suggested. At a time when literacy and cultural fluency were increasingly important factors in achieving and sustaining a middle-class existence, clubs helped people to flourish commercially and socially, as well as to enjoy literature. Within the book trade, club supporters argued that their net economic effects benefited everyone: positive responses to books generated among subscribers by word of mouth increased sales of club selections, and of books more generally. To their supporters, clubs seemed a perfect solution to a number of practical and philosophical problems facing the book industry and America as a whole.

The traditional pillars of the literary world tended to disagree. One publisher in the 1920s spoke for many in the trade when he denounced book clubs as 'an octopus which has fastened its tentacles around the throat of the publishers and is sucking away at the vitals of the book business itself'. The trade periodical *The Bookman* adopted a similar stance, suggesting that readers joined clubs because they were 'too feeble-minded, too lazy, or too busy to think much about their choices' in reading materials. The habit of assailing book club members and selections for their lack of individuality and intelligence, and of suggesting that people joined clubs not for the refined intellectual pleasures of reading but simply to obtain a veneer of sophistication, may reflect the anxiety of cultural elites whose monopoly on knowledge was ostensibly threatened by the clubs' democratizing power. This critique of club reading quite possibly reflected both the class and the gender of the critics; they were almost exclusively male, while book club members were predominantly female. Similar cultural dynamics may also have been at work in the Jonathan Franzen–*Oprah's Book Club controversy of 2001.

Book clubs had been created in response to the constricted retail situation of the early 20th century; hence, when chain bookstores with shopping-mall outlets began to spread across the US in the 1970s, the appeal of clubs decreased. Just as publishing houses engaged in aggressive mergers and acquisitions during this period, so too were many speciality clubs absorbed into the BOMC and the *Literary Guild. These two giants were then purchased by the German multimedia conglomerate *Bertelsmann and grouped with other small speciality clubs into an online umbrella entity called Bookspan in 2000. The contemporary electronic manifestation of the book club continues to emphasize streamlined distribution and low prices; but rather than relying on judges, it uses consumer-profiling software to select titles for

subscribers, and offers chat rooms and bulletin boards through which readers can communicate with one another about the books they choose.   TT
J. Rubin, *The Making of Middlebrow Culture* (1992)

book clubs (reading) The tradition of people reading books together is centuries old. Before the era of abundant and inexpensive printed matter, families or groups of friends might take turns reading—perhaps aloud—from one copy of a book, discussing its contents as they went along. In 18th- and 19th-century Britain and the US, private libraries circulated books and provided a community for discussing them, offering subscribers both useful knowledge and social interaction. Access to books and to like-minded readers was an important factor in upward mobility among the working and middle classes, shifting from an agrarian to a knowledge economy. In the US and in Europe, literary societies that read, discussed, and disseminated books were an important feature of middle-class life throughout the 19th century, creating a space for debate over politics and policy as well as for the sharing of imaginative pleasure.

By the mid-20th century, the literary society had been replaced by the book club, sometimes denigrated by elite male critics as a group of suburban matrons content with hearing a summary of a book's content rather than actually reading it. Such clubs did exist, but so did groups—male, female, and mixed—that read for other, more pointed purposes and required more from their members. Feminist scholars have demonstrated that women's mid-century book clubs played a vital role in the lives of college-educated women who had taken up the (often repetitive) job of housekeeping; the experience of the club, in some cases, transferred itself into feminist consciousness-raising in the 1960s and '70s. Book clubs for men seem to have been rarer, and the role of clubs in men's lives has not been studied in depth. Such clubs did exist, however, sometimes as offshoots of colleges, fraternal organizations, or places of worship. During a period of narrowly defined male roles, they may have served as spaces where the era's 'Man in the Grey Flannel Suit' could question the norms of his culture and imagine alternatives to it. Bible study groups have been and remain among the most numerous book clubs in many cultures.

During the 1990s, participation in book clubs hugely expanded, particularly in the US and UK. Sociologists posit that this resulted in part from a growing sense of isolation among urban professionals; book clubs became ways of creating social networks. Changes in the book industry helped to increase club popularity as well: both chain bookshops and independent ones offered groups discount prices, meeting space, and coffee. Publishers interested in increasing sales began to include 'reading group guides' in books that seemed likely to appeal to clubs. At the same time, the Internet made it possible to create online clubs that met in chat rooms, freeing clubs from geographical constraints. The 1990s also saw the launch of community-wide reading initiatives—attempts to bring entire cities, university campuses, or corporations together by reading and discussing a common title.   TT

T. Augst, *The Clerk's Tale* (2002)
E. Long, *Book Clubs* (2003)
E. McHenry, *Forgotten Readers* (2002)

Book Collector, The Founded in 1952 in succession to *The Book Handbook* (1947–51). Its original editorial board included the antiquarian bookseller Percy Muir, the scholar and bibliophile John Hayward, and the novelist Ian Fleming, who provided financial support. From 1966, it was edited by N. *Barker for more than four decades. It publishes articles, notes, and reviews on all aspects of bibliophily, as well as regular series on *bookbinding, library history, and enumerative *bibliography.   ASGE

A. S. G. Edwards, ed., *The Pleasures of Bibliophily* (2002)

Booker Prize Pre-eminent literary *prize, first awarded in 1969, for the best novel by a British or Commonwealth writer. The brainchild of *Maschler, Booker was established by the food company Booker Brothers and the *Publishers Association on the publicity-courting model of the Prix *Goncourt. The Booker soon developed a reputation for quality, controversy, and promotional savvy. John Berger infamously donated half his winnings to the Black Panthers in protest at the sponsor's colonial past. Later, Booker fêted postcolonial writers, including the award of the Booker of Bookers to Salman Rushdie's *Midnight's Children* in 1993. A considerable purse is offered and the award typically has a significant impact on sales. In 2002 the Prize was renamed the Man Booker after its new sponsor (Man Group, PLC). Related awards include the Booker Russian Novel Prize, the Man Booker International Prize, and the Caine Prize for African Writing.   CMS

R. Todd, *Consuming Fictions* (1996)

book fair, antiquarian A cooperative selling exhibition organized by a group of antiquarian booksellers. The first antiquarian book fair was held in London over three weeks in June 1958 under the auspices of the *Antiquarian Booksellers Association and the National Book League (*see* BOOKTRUST), with 24 London and English provincial booksellers participating. Intended as an occasion for creating goodwill, and as a public venue for booksellers who did not operate from a shop, it became thereafter an annual event, whose duration was shortened from three weeks to several days. The English model—which may be regarded as the descendant of much earlier *book fairs, most especially the *Frankfurt Book Fair—was soon followed in other countries, organized by the national antiquarian booksellers' associations: in the US (New York) in 1960, Germany (Stuttgart) in 1962, Japan (Tokyo) in 1966, France (Paris) in 1984, and elsewhere. The fairs quickly became international, in terms of both exhibitors and visitors, as a result of easier air travel and the influence of the *International League of Antiquarian Booksellers (which sponsors regular international antiquarian book fairs following their first held in Amsterdam in 1965). In more recent times, antiquarian book fairs have continued to proliferate.   RAL

book fairs Since the Middle Ages, fairs and markets have provided regular outlets for trading all kinds of goods. From such general fairs, the book fairs at *Frankfurt and *Leipzig evolved; H. Estienne paints a colourful picture of the range of commodities offered at Frankfurt in his *Francofordiense Emporium* (1574). MSS were already being bought at Frankfurt by the 1380s, and printers from Basle were attending the fair at least by 1478. Throughout the 16th century, Frankfurt maintained its position at the centre of the European book trade, until its eclipse in the 17th century by Leipzig. Since the 1880s, books have featured—often in an ancillary role to displays of printing equipment—at the large international commercial exhibitions, such as those held at Amsterdam (1881, 1883–5, 1892, 1913), Chicago (1893), Paris (1900, 1911), St Louis (1904), Antwerp (1904), Brussels (1910), and Leipzig (1914). A Franco-British exhibition was held at the White City, London (1908).

Book fairs in a narrower sense have flourished particularly since World War II, the Frankfurt Book Fair being resuscitated in 1949 after 200 years, while books featured at the Leipzig Spring Fair in 1946. Today, the number of fairs is legion. Those open to the general public often focus on the sale of second-hand or antiquarian books (such as the London fair organized by the *Antiquarian Booksellers Association and the *c.*100 fairs promoted by the *Provincial Booksellers Fairs Association throughout the UK each year). Specialist trade fairs chiefly intended for the publishing industry are primarily concerned with new books and with offering opportunities for the trade to negotiate translation, literary, television, and film rights. Some take place annually or biennially at regular locations; others are only occasional and peripatetic (such as the one organized in conjunction with the annual meeting of the *American Booksellers Association). Some fairs privilege specific types of books, for instance: the Angoulême International Comics Festival (January 2008), the annual Anarchist Book Fair at Montreal, the Small Presses Fair at Mainz (May 2007), and the annual Bologna Children's Book Fair (established 1964). Others are held in conjunction with literary or arts events, such as the week-long festival at Hay-on-Wye (population 1,450, with 39 bookshops), which attracts some 80,000 people each year.

In 2007–8 alone, there were sizeable fairs in Amsterdam, Barcelona, Basle, Belgrade (first held 1956), Brussels, Bucharest ('Bookarest', established 1992), Budapest (1992), Coimbra, Copenhagen, Geneva, Gothenburg, Helsinki, Istanbul (since 1989), Linz, Lisbon (since the 1930s), London, Madrid (since 1933), Moscow (established 1977), Paris (since 1981), Porto, Prague, Riga (since 1998), St Petersburg, Sofia, Tallinn, Thessaloniki, Turin, Vilnius, Warsaw, and Zagreb. Outside Europe, 2007–8 saw fairs in Abu Dhabi, Bangkok, Beijing (founded 1986), Beirut (since 1956), Buenos Aires, Cairo (since 1969, the largest event of its kind in the Arab world), Cape Town, Casablanca, Guadalajara (claimed to be the largest Spanish book event in the world), Havana (established 1991 and lasting two weeks), Hong Kong (since 1990), Jeddah, Jerusalem (biennial since 1963),

Kolkata, Kuala Lumpur (since 1982), Lagos, Montreal, Mumbai (since 2006), New Delhi, New York, Rio De Janeiro (biennial since 1983; 630,000 visitors in 2005), Seoul, Sharjah. Taipei, Tehran (since 1987), Tokyo (since 1994), Toronto, and Washington, DC. Among the most remarkable must be the biennial New Delhi World Book Fair (established 1972), which attracted nearly 1,300 publishers and 1 million visitors in 2006, and the *Kolkata/Calcutta Book Fair, held annually since 1976 in the Maidan, the huge park in the heart of the city, surrounded by some of India's finest colonial-era buildings. In 1997 a fire devastated a third of the fair and caused a stampede; in 1998, torrential rain caused much damage. The chief problem, however, has been the dust raised by the enormous crowds—an estimated 14 million people in 2005—and the concomitant damage to the park and the monuments. This has led to a High Court ban on its being held there in future.

An excellent innovation of the Frankfurt fair was the designation each year of a 'guest of honour'—in this case, a country whose books are specially featured. This practice has since been adopted elsewhere, for example at Bucharest, Paris, and Cairo. Book fairs often also provide the setting for the presentation of prestigious prizes, such as the annual Peace Prize of the German Book Trade (*Friedenspreis des Deutschen Buchhandels), first awarded in 1950 (recipients include Albert Schweitzer, Martin Buber, Carl Jakob Burckhardt, Hermann Hesse, Thornton Wilder, Karl Jaspers, Paul Tillich, Ernst Bloch, Léopold Sédar Senghor, Yehudi Menuhin, Jürgen Habermas, and Wolf Lepenies). Prizewinners at the Jerusalem book fair have included the philosophers Bertrand Russell and Isaiah Berlin and writers such as Max Frisch, Eugene Ionesco, Graham Greene, V. S. Naipaul, Mario Vargas Llosa, and Arthur Miller. JLF

bookhand A formal script used by trained *scribes for the *copying of texts or documents. It may be distinguished from less formal, *cursive hands by its emphasis on the clarity and regularity of the handwriting. During the Middle Ages, however, bookhands also developed out of cursive scripts. ASGE

Book History Annual (1998–) sponsored by *SHARP. It aims to publish articles on every aspect of the history of the book in its social, cultural, and economic dimensions in all fields, methods, and periods. ASGE

book label *See* BOOKPLATE.

booklet A discrete *quire, or set of quires, forming part of a larger MS, identifiable through several factors: wear on the outer leaves; leaves within being different in size from those elsewhere in the MS; *scripts that do not match others in the MS; anomalous numbering of leaves; the presence of 'filler' items in empty spaces in the booklet. Documentary and physical evidence suggests that some booklets circulated independently before being bound within a larger collection. *See also* PAMPHLET; PECIA. CMM
P. R. Robinson, 'The "Booklet"', *Codicologica*, 3 (1980), 46–69

book-louse (lepinotus) A smooth, grey, soft-bodied insect of the order *Psocoptera*, which feeds on paper and is attracted to book-mould. Book-lice are 1–2 mm long with thread-like antennae and scale-like wing pads. They require high humidity for survival. KEA
M.-L. Florian, *Heritage Eaters* (1997)

Book Manufacturers' Institute An association established in 1933 for book producers (printers and bookbinders) in the US. The BMI organizes conferences, seminars, and other activities to discuss issues and developments in the trade, and confers an annual award on a distinguished member. AMS

book marker A device used by a reader to mark a place in a book for future reading. Book markers (also called bookmarks or registers) have been made of many shapes and materials, including paper, *parchment,

A medieval *parchment **book marker**, with line and column indicators: the rotating disc, one of two found in a 13th-century bible from St Augustine's Abbey, Canterbury, may have been used for readings in the refectory.

*leather, textiles, ivory, and precious metals. They are as old as books themselves, although early examples are rare. Parchment strips are found in 3rd-century *codices; Richard *Bury refers to 14th-century readers using straw. Various medieval formats survive, including ribbons with leather or jewels at each end, and cords with sliding, rotating parchment wheels that marked precise points in multi-column texts. C. *Barker presented a fringed silk bookmarker to Queen Elizabeth I in 1584.

Book markers are sometimes made by binding in one or more narrow silk ribbons at the head of the *spine (common particularly in 18th–19th-century devotional books), but are typically separate items not associated with the book's production. Shaped and cut parchment markers that clip to a page exist from at least the 18th century, and this design continues today. Modern markers are more commonly separate rectangular strips of material placed loosely between pages. Woven silk markers of this shape, manufactured commercially, became popular in England in the 1860s and 1870s (the firm of Thomas Stevens in Coventry was a major producer). In the late 19th century there appeared markers of printed card stock, carrying advertisements. The idea quickly caught on, and since then countless thousands of such printed markers have been distributed—sometimes with advertising content, sometimes merely pictorial—and have become both collectible and functional.   DRSP

A. W. Coysh, *Collecting Bookmarkers* (1974)

R. Emms, 'Medieval Rotating Column-Indicators', *TCBS* 12 (2000–2003), 179–84

J. A. Szirmai, *The Archaeology of Medieval Bookbinding* (2000)

bookmobile In 1905 Mary Titcomb, a Maryland librarian, employed a horse-drawn wagon as the first 'library on wheels'. Subsequently, specially fitted buses brought library services to rural areas, schools, hospitals, retirement homes, and homebound individuals. Modern vehicles may carry computers, in addition to videotapes, compact discs, and other materials.   CJP

Book of Common Prayer (*BCP*) The service book of the Church of England is one of the most frequently reprinted works in the world. With two notable interruptions (1553–8 and 1645–60), barely a year went by between the first Edwardian edition of 1549 and the *Alternative Service Book* of 1980 without some new printing. The 1549 editions were produced in *folio by the *King's Printer *Grafton and his former partner Edward Whitchurch; a *quarto was also produced from Worcester by John Oswen, who was given a *royal licence to produce prayer books for Wales and the Marches. Prayer Books for Scotland were first produced in Edinburgh under Charles I in the 1630s. From 1629, the press at *Cambridge University was granted permission to print prayer books, but only when bound with bibles in *formats smaller than folio. *Oxford University gained the same rights in 1636, but only exercised them from 1675. Small formats for the pew or private devotion became increasingly common from the mid-Elizabethan period onwards.

The first prayer book of 1549 shocked traditional Catholics by putting the Mass into English, bringing with it riots and incipient rebellion in some parts of the country. The revised edition of 1552 in turn shocked reformers through its Puritanized revisions of the Eucharistic sacrament and other ritual elements. From the newly revised Elizabethan edition of 1559 onwards, the prayer book was the focus for dispute between religious parties over sacraments, the priesthood, ceremonies, vestments, and doctrines. A highly political as well as religious book, its standing as the most visible sign of state (and specifically royal) control of religion was confirmed by the fanfare accompanying its restoration and reinvention in 1662.

Printing of the new prayer book was initially undertaken by the Royal Printers John Bill and Christopher Barker and, in *octavo, by John Field at Cambridge; but in the early 18th century *Baskett began to transform the trade. *Roman type had been employed as an alternative to *black letter since Elizabethan times; Baskett championed its use and made other reforms of orthography and style. Later in the century, *Baskerville was similarly influential as an innovator in Cambridge prayer books. In the 19th century, the royal printers gave over to *Eyre & Spottiswoode, who with the university presses dominated the industry down to modern times.

The *BCP* was disseminated remarkably widely. Colonial use began in 1551 with the first-ever printed book in Dublin; the first independent American edition dates from 1710. An edition appeared in Welsh in 1567 and in Irish in 1608; in French (for use in Calais) in 1553 and in Mohawk in North America in 1715; in Tamil in 1802, Urdu in 1814, Bengali in 1840; in Maori in 1830, Cantonese in 1855, Malay in 1856, and a southern dialect of Swahili in 1876. In all, there are about 1,200 translations into some 200 languages and dialects.   BAC

D. Griffiths, *The Bibliography of the Book of Common Prayer, 1549–1999* (2002)

book of hours A devotional book centred on the Hours of the Virgin, a series of prayers to be said at the eight canonical hours (Matins, Lauds, Prime, Terce, Sext, Nones, Vespers, and Compline). Its core text, the Hours of the Virgin (known also as the Little Office of the Blessed Virgin), was modelled on the Divine Office, the cycle of prayers said at the eight appointed hours throughout the day and night by clergy and members of religious orders.

1. Origins and development
2. Centres of production and 'Use'
3. Illumination, miniatures, and other decoration
4. Women owners and indications of reading
5. From bespoke MSS to mass circulation

1. Origins and development

The Hours of the Virgin perhaps originated as early as the mid-8th century, and was established by the 10th century as an abbreviated version of the Divine Office for monks and canons. During the 12th century the text gained popularity with a broader audience, including lay men and women, when it was often attached to the *psalter, then the most popular type of book for lay devotions. In the 13th century the book of hours (known in Latin as Horae, and in English as Primer) emerged as a stand-alone book, and by the mid-13th century it exceeded the psalter in popularity among elite lay *patrons. It gained prevalence throughout Europe, but particularly in northern regions. Most books of hours are in Latin, but examples written in vernacular languages, either whole or in part, also survive.

In addition to the Hours of the Virgin, books of hours normally included additional texts, which could include a *calendar of saints' days; extracts from the Gospels; prayers to the Virgin (especially 'Obsecro te' and 'O intemerata'); Hours of the Cross, the Holy Spirit, the Trinity and the Passion; the Seven Penitental Psalms (Pss. 6, 31, 50, 101, 129, and 142); a litany of saints; the Office of the Dead; and memorials to saints known as Suffrages. The earliest surviving stand-alone English Hours MS is the De Brailes Hours (BL Add. MS 49,999), *illuminated by the Oxford limner W. de *Brailes for an unknown female patron c.1240.

2. Centres of production and 'Use'

The origin, or more often the destination, for a book of hours is often indicated by variations in its calendar, litany, and the text itself. This liturgical orientation of the hours' texts is known as its 'Use'; the most common Use in England was 'Sarum' (which originated at Salisbury). Uses of Bangor, Hereford, Lincoln, and York were also known in England and Wales. Other common Uses were Rome, Paris, and those of particular religious orders, particularly of the mendicants. Books of hours were often produced in one place for use in another. For example, many Sarum hours were made in Paris, Rouen, and Flanders for English patrons. Some of these MSS were de luxe bespoke copies, while others were made speculatively for export or for the domestic market. One such book is a richly illuminated Sarum hours made in northern France c.1430 and owned by Sir William Oldhall of Naford (BL Harley MS 2900).

The book of hours appealed to owners on a number of grounds. Most significant of these was its devotional focus on the Virgin Mary, whose cult attracted ever-greater fervour during the Middle Ages, and especially from the 12th century. The book of hours can be seen as both a cause and a consequence of the intensity of Marian devotion, with its rise to popularity reinforcing the Virgin's central position in the devotional culture of the later Middle Ages. Additionally, books of hours offered a range of adaptable texts, and very often images, that could structure and support their owners' devotions every day of the year. Contents were modified to reflect the liturgical orientation, aesthetic preferences, and wealth of their owners.

3. Illumination, miniatures, and other decoration

Books of hours range in visual embellishment, from plain, workaday copies to super-de luxe volumes illuminated by the greatest artists of the period. The quality and quantity

of illuminated books of hours make them an essential source for the history of painting in Europe from the 13th century through the 16th century. In illuminated books of hours, the calendars frequently included images of the signs of the zodiac and the labours of the month, the latter depicting seasonally appropriate activities (e.g. feasting in January, warming by the fire in February, pruning in March). Each of the eight Hours of the Virgin is normally prefaced with a narrative scene, either relating the Infancy or the Passion of Christ. Fully painted and gilded borders enriched many, and sometimes even all, of the pages of the most luxurious volumes. Other texts could be prefaced with an appropriate image, ranging in scale from a *historiated initial to a full-page miniature (see MINIATURE (1)). Such images helped readers to navigate their books, but more importantly offered their owners a meditational focus. The remarkable miniature in the Hours of Mary of Burgundy (Österreichische Nationalbibliothek, Vienna, Codex Vindobonensis 1857, fo. 14v), made c.1470–75, reveals the transcendental possibilities of the hours' combination of text and image. The miniature shows a woman (possibly Mary of Burgundy) absorbed in the pages of her hours in an intimate, probably domestic setting; through the window behind her, she is seen having a visionary encounter with the Virgin and Child under the soaring vaults of a Gothic cathedral.

The margins or *borders of books of hours, particularly those made in France, England, and the Low Countries, were also often embellished with playful or even mildly subversive imagery (see BORDER DECORATION). A small hours (BL Stowe MS 17, fo. 38r), measuring no more than 9.5×7cm, made in Liège c.1310–20, includes numerous such images, including one satirical portrayal of a barefoot nun dancing wantonly to the cacophony produced by a friar sawing away at a bellows with a distaff. The margins of a French book of hours of the 1320s, now divided between New York and London (Pierpont Morgan Library, MS M 754 and BL Add. MS 36,684), teems with apes, birds, skeletons, and hybrids parodying the solemn devotional imagery in the accompanying miniatures.

4. Women owners and indications of reading

Books of hours range in size from minute to substantial, but most are about the size of a paperback novel, suited to personal use and quite portable. Both men and women owned books of hours, but their place in female devotion is particularly noteworthy. Collectively, they offer an indication of the development and character of female literacy and piety. Portraits of women in these MSS, and in other contexts as well, often show them holding or using books of hours.

The image of a queen (possibly Queen Isabella) watching the elevation of the host under a canopy in the Taymouth Hours, c.1325 (BL Yates Thompson MS 13, fo. 7r), includes a depiction of a book of hours resting on a prayer bench before her; this image hints at the difficulty of distinguishing between public and private devotions in the role of a book of hours. Although many aspects of the book of hours were devised for private, even solitary use, some standard elements (such as the Office of the Dead) could also function in a more public context. A note-worthy example of the longevity of the hours as a symbol of elite piety is the austere portrait in oil on panel of Lady Margaret Beaufort (1443–1509), mother of King Henry VII of England, in the dress of a chaste widow and holding an open hours MS (Christ's College, Cambridge). Books of hours often contained the portraits and heraldry of their patrons; such images were frequently placed in the Hours of the Virgin at Matins, the first canonical hour of the day. Through the use of such imagery, books of hours served to record and promote the identity of their patron(s) and their dynastic allegiances.

Many hours MSS include evidence of use, including inscriptions, additions, removals, and alterations. The most common additions were notes of the obits of family members, which were inscribed in the calendar, presumably with the intention that the deceased be remembered in the prayers of the living on the appropriate date, perhaps with a recitation of the Office of the Dead. The book of hours was thus a point of connection between the living and the dead, lessening the agonies of purgatory for both. Books of hours were sometimes refurbished to a greater or lesser extent as they passed from one owner to the next. The complex history of the *Sforza Hours, for example, begins in c.1490, when the MS was started for Bona Sforza, duchess of Milan. Following the theft of many of its pages from the workshop of its illuminator, Giovanni Pietro Birago, and Bona's death in 1503, the book remained in an unfinished state for nearly 30 years. In 1517 Margaret of Austria, who had inherited the book in 1504, commissioned scribes and the Netherlandish illuminator Gerard Horenbout to complete it. Other changes to books of hours may be the result of post-medieval interventions. For example, as part of the suppression of the cult of St Thomas Becket by Henry VIII in 1538, it was ordered that images of and prayers to the saint be destroyed; the subtle scratches across images of Becket in many books of hours show signs that, in England, this injunction was obeyed in practice, if not always in spirit.

5. From bespoke MSS to mass circulation

The most celebrated book of hours is undoubtedly a MS illuminated for Jean, duc de *Berry by the *Limbourg brothers, who devised a programme of illustration of unprecedented scale and invention. Left unfinished at the death of Jean and at least two of the brothers in 1416, the book is known to posterity by its apposite inventory description, the *Très Riches Heures* (Chantilly, Musée Condé, ms. 65). The vast majority of books of hours, however, were at the lower end of the scale. From the early 15th-century, hours MSS were produced on a mass scale that prefigured, or even ushered in, the age of print. These printed hours were sometimes enhanced with *woodcuts, pasted in and often coloured; especially in the early years of the printing press, devotional prints were sometimes also included in MS hours. Owners could thereby adapt their hours books for their own purposes.

The printing press made books of hours accessible to those of relatively modest means from the second half of the 15th century; nonetheless, elite patrons continued to commission de luxe illuminated MS copies. Not merely a focus for devotion, books of hours could also function as expressions of fashion, wealth, social status, and conspicuous piety. Although the early bindings of most books of hours no longer survive, some of those that do reveal that the outside of a high-quality book of hours could be a sumptuous declaration of the book's value. The book of hours of Bonaparte Ghislieri (BL Yates Thompson MS 29)—which includes miniatures by a number of the most prominent Italian artists of c.1500, including Perugino and Amico Aspertini—has an especially elaborate later binding of cut *leather over *silk, with miniatures and medallions on the upper and lower boards.

While elite patrons indulged their taste for MS Hours, enterprising publishers capitalized on the widespread demand for these books. MS and *incunable books of hours survive in great numbers; indeed, the total amount of surviving copies in public and private libraries has never been calculated. In the aftermath of the Reformation, the de luxe book of hours became an object of desire for collectors, and in some instances an assertion of Roman Catholic faith. AB

J. Backhouse, *Books of Hours* (1985)
E. Duffy, *Marking the Hours* (2006)
J. Harthan, *Books of Hours and their Owners* (1977)
R. Wieck, *Time Sanctified* (1988)

Book of Mormon Foundational religious text of the Church of Jesus Christ of Latter-day Saints. Its members (commonly called Mormons) believe it was translated by Joseph Smith, Jr. (1805–44) from ancient metal plates, through God's power. First published in March 1830 by Egbert B. Grandin, the c.500-page volume has never been out of print. Used for the Church's worldwide missionary work, members consider it a companion volume to the Bible, not a replacement for it. Translated into more than 100 languages, it reached its 100 millionth copy in 2000.

The first edition, printed in just under 5,000 copies, was set from a copy of the original MS made for the production process. In addition to numerous 19th-century editions, major editions appeared in 1920 and 1981, the latter with new introductory material, new footnotes, and chapter summaries. In 1982, a subtitle was added: 'Another Testament for Jesus Christ'. Royal Skousen's forthcoming critical text project will no doubt encourage yet another edition. DJW

T. L. Givens, *By the Hand of Mormon* (2002)
D. J. Whittaker, '"That Most Important of All Books": A Printing History of the Book of Mormon', *Mormon Historical Studies*, 6 (2005), 101–34

Book-of-the-Month Club (BOMC) American mail-order *book club, founded in 1926 by the advertising copywriters Maxwell Sackheim and Harry Scherman. The BOMC aimed to make popular works of quality fiction and non-fiction available by direct mail to a broad sector of the American public. Armed with insights into consumer psychology from the advertising world, Scherman created a business that played on customers' anxieties. An early BOMC advertisement acknowledged that few people read all the books they intended, and asked: 'Why do you disappoint yourself?' Scherman's product—Club membership—aimed to assuage this anxiety by providing subscribers with titles selected by a high-powered panel of judges. Club members could also preserve their sense of intellectual autonomy by refusing a selected book and/ or selecting an alternative—exercising what the BOMC called 'the negative option'. Critics of the Club routinely mocked what they believed to be its aesthetically lack-lustre selections, but Club readers clearly disagreed with this judgement. When the BOMC was acquired by Time Inc. in 1977, its subscribers were numbered in the millions. *See also* TIME-WARNER BOOKS. TT

J. Radway, *A Feeling for Books* (1997)

J. Rubin, *The Making of Middlebrow Culture* (1992)

bookplate A label fixed into a book, for recording its ownership. Bookplates normally take the form of paper labels (sometimes *leather or *vellum) attached to the upper pastedown of a book (*see* ENDLEAVES), or to one of the upper endleaves. They are typically printed, but sometimes have an area left for an owner's name to be inserted by hand. Bookplates were first used in late 15th-century Germany, recording the gift of books to the Carthusian monastery in *Buxheim. The earliest recorded British bookplate is that of Nicholas Bacon, dated 1574, cut to record the gift of books to *Cambridge University Library. They were employed only occasionally by 17th-century British book owners, but their popularity increased *c*.1680–1700; they have been used extensively since then.

Early bookplates commonly include the heraldic device of the owner in the form of an *armorial; when the name is not printed, a knowledge of heraldry is required to determine the owner's identity. Bookplates also frequently record institutional ownership. Bookplate design in England went through a series of clearly identifiable periods whose distinctive styles have been given names, from simple armorial styles of the 16th and 17th centuries (Tudoresque and Carolian), through the Early Armorial, Chippendale, and Die-sinker styles typical of the 18th century, to the more varied ones of the 19th century. Landscape as a pictorial feature of the bookplate de-veloped from the mid-18th century. Bookplates gradually became a vehicle for individual expression beyond the formality of the armorial, with artists, engravers, typo-graphers, and calligraphers being employed to design and occasionally print them. Artists such as *Hollar, Loggan, Vertue, *Hogarth, *Bewick, *Beardsley, E. *Gill, *Kent, R. *Stone, and *Kindersley all designed and some-times printed bookplates as part of their commercial activities. Artistic and design periods and genres such as Baroque, Rococo, Gothic Revival, Pictorialism, Art Deco, Cubism, and Modernism have all influenced the design of bookplates, and have fostered collecting genres of their own. Individuals who collected books over long periods often used a number of bookplates in succession—or occasionally simultaneously, either for books kept

in different locations, or for books of different types. The ease with which bookplates can be removed and replaced has encouraged *forgers falsely to suggest ownership by placing genuine bookplates inside books that were not owned by the individual or institution associated with the bookplate. Bookplates have also been forged.

Genuine bookplates became collectable items in their own right (often separated from the books for which they were originally intended) in the 19th century, developing into a specialized collecting genre with societies and journals supporting the activity. The first books about bookplates appeared in France in the late 19th century, reflecting a growing passion for collecting there. In addi-tion to collecting bookplates based on nationality—a tradition which the French were the first to establish—acquiring bookplates according to type (such as erotic, medical, or royal bookplates) has also become a signi-ficant aspect of bookplate collecting. The Bookplate Society, founded in 1972, is the leading UK organization in this field. The Franks Collection in the British Museum is the most important of the numerous institutional col-lections of bookplates in Britain.

The term 'book label', typically applied to pasted-in labels that are smaller and simpler than bookplates, with-out any pictorial or heraldic content, is also common. *See also* ASSOCIATION COPY; PROVENANCE. RWO

www.bookplatesociety.org, consulted Sept. 2007

E. R. J. Gambier Howe, *Catalogue of British and American Book Plates bequeathed to the British Museum by Sir Augustus Wollaston Franks* (3 vols, 1903–4)

B. N. Lee, *British Bookplates* (1979)

— *Early Printed Book Labels* (1976)

Pearson, *Provenance*

book press (**armarium**) A wooden cupboard with doors, shelves, and vertical divisions, free-standing or within recesses in walls, used from antiquity through-out the Middle Ages to store books. Book presses were lined with wood, and resembled presses used for other purposes. *See also* BOOKSHELVES; SHELFMARKS. KEA

J. W. Clark, *The Care of Books*, 2e (1909)

bookrunner (**book scout**) The runner belongs to a dying breed of peripatetic second-hand bookseller, usu-ally holding virtually no residual stock, but flitting from shop to shop, buying in one and selling in another. The successful runner's knowledge not only of books, but also of booksellers, is rarely surpassed. LJW

bookseller A vendor and, until around 1800, a pub-lisher of books. The medieval trade of selling MSS developed during the early modern period into that of selling printed books. Early booksellers, often selling both MS and printed texts, sometimes styled themselves *stationers; the London livery company to which some of them belonged was the *Stationers' Company. London and Edinburgh were the focal points of the early British book trade, although provincial booksellers gradually emerged during the late 16th and 17th centuries. By the

mid-18th century, most towns of any importance had at least one bookseller, who was often also a printer and publisher and sometimes a newspaper proprietor. Booksellers, especially in the provinces, typically sold a wide range of goods, such as patent medicines, in addition to books. The retail trade in imported scholarly books, mostly in Latin, remained very important up to the 17th century. Bibles, the *Book of Common Prayer*, *psalters, books of sermons, *ABCs, and school books were staples of the bookselling trade; popular *ballads, *chapbooks, and other ephemeral texts were also sold by itinerant *chapmen or *colporteurs. See also PUBLISHER.
JH

J. Feather, *A History of British Publishing*, 2e (2006)

J. Fergus, *Provincial Readers in Eighteenth-Century England* (2007)

Bookseller, The UK trade magazine founded in 1858 by J. *Whitaker. It carries news and features about publishing and bookselling, and many senior industry figures have appeared in its correspondence columns. Its online site (*see* WORLD WIDE WEB) has a newsfeed to subscribers. Editors have included Edmond Segrave, David Whitaker, and Louis Baum. Since 1999 it has been owned by VNU Entertainment Media UK Ltd. Each year, the *Bookseller's* Diagram Prize is awarded to the oddest book title: winners have included *Reusing Old Graves*, *Greek Rural Postmen and their Cancellation Numbers*, and *The Joy of Chickens*.
AGP

www.thebookseller.com, consulted June 2008

Booksellers Association of Great Britain and Ireland Trade body representing 95 per cent of booksellers in the UK and Ireland. Originally the Associated Booksellers of Great Britain and Ireland (1895), it adopted its present name in 1948. The Association had 877 members in 1925 and 2,400 by 1945. By 2006, it represented the interests of more than 4,000 retail outlets. The Booksellers Association has been responsible for important trade initiatives, including *book tokens, and is one of the organizers of *World Book and Copyright Day in the UK.
AGP

www.booksellers.org.uk, consulted June 2008

Norrie

booksellers' catalogues Such catalogues have traditionally been the most common means by which booksellers offer their stock for sale, whether of new, *remaindered, second-hand, rare, or antiquarian works. Although many are still issued in printed form, they are increasingly disseminated through the Internet (*see* WORLD WIDE WEB). Such catalogues vary markedly in the level of detail they may contain, but they all provide a description of the book that includes author, title, date, price, and some indication of its contents. Other elements will vary according to the competence and/or scholarly resources of the individual bookseller and the significance of the work being catalogued; the more thorough descriptions are most likely to be found in listings of rare or antiquarian books. These elements can extend to detailed physical descriptions, including an account of the *collation and binding (*see* **17**), a general discussion of the work in question, and/or an analysis of the specific copy being offered for sale. Such discussion may involve questions of rarity and *provenance. There may also be illustrations (*see* **16**) and references to appropriate bibliographical and other reference works. Booksellers' catalogues can in themselves become important reference works when they contain well-catalogued collections of works devoted to a particular author, collector, or subject. Booksellers' catalogues are distinct from publishers' or *auction catalogues. The former are concerned with the marketing of a single *imprint or group of imprints. Auction catalogues have much in common with antiquarian booksellers' catalogues, but differ chiefly by their lack of a fixed price for each item being sold, offering instead an estimated price range that may reflect a reserve price.
ASGE

M. F. Suarez, S.J., 'English Book Sale Catalogues as Bibliographical Evidence', *Library*, 6/21 (1999), 321–60

H. R. Woudhuysen, 'Catalogues', in *Out of Print and into Profit*, ed. G. Mandelbrote (2006)

booksellers' price code Coded markings in old or rare books serve as a reminder to the bookseller of the original price paid (and sometimes the date or place of purchase). This most often takes the form of a simple substitution code, where a ten-letter word such as 'Cumberland' (in which each letter is used once only) is made to stand for the ten digits: C=1, U=2. More complex formulations are sometimes found. Codes can often be seen in 17th-century books, where prices may be written on the *title-page in ink; more modern dealers tend to add them in pencil at the volume's end. When the value of a book often exceeds its original price, some hard-nosed buyers seek an advantage from the system of coded markings.
LJW

Pearson, *Provenance*

bookshelves Storage and display supports for books, normally made of wood. Bookshelves developed with the *codex, from the storage mechanisms designed for *scrolls. The earliest depiction of bookshelves, in the 8th-century Codex *Amiatinus, shows books placed horizontally on wooden shelves in a book cupboard. During the Middle Ages, many institutional libraries stored books on shelves that formed part of substantial desks (*distinctiones*), to which a few books could be *chained. As the Middle Ages progressed, these desks became larger, and smaller-format books could be shelved vertically. The interior walls of cloisters sometimes contained book cupboards (*armariolae*), the remains of which can be seen at locations such as Dryburgh Abbey, Scotland. During the later Middle Ages and the 16th century in England, institutional libraries operated a 'stall' system with two or more shelves per stall, which project out from walls (as in *Merton College, Oxford, perhaps the first stall system used in England). The creation of Arts End at the *Bodleian Library in 1609 introduced multi-layered shelving arranged against the wall. By the end of the 17th century, bookshelves in private and some institutional collections were increasingly being replaced by

An early stall library in Oxford, at *St John's College, built in 1598. The **book shelves** form bays of about 6ft 3in., with windows between them: the benches facing the desks are probably older than the shelves.

free-standing *book cases. The fashion for recessed niches fitted with shelves, as at Stourhead, returned by the 19th century. The strength of hardwoods made them ideal for bookshelves; 16th-century accounts from Oxford suggest that oak was then a common material. After the mid-19th century, metal was used for bookshelves, generally within fitted book cases, with cast iron being used in both the *British Museum and the Bodleian libraries from the 1880s. RWO

J. W. Clark, *The Care of Books*, 2e (1909)
P. D. Clarke and R. Lovatt, eds., *The University and College Libraries of Cambridge* (2002)
H. Petroski, *The Book on the Bookshelf* (1999)

Bookshop for Boys and Girls Opened in Boston in 1916 with funds from the Women's Educational and Industrial Union, the Bookshop gained significance primarily because of Bertha Everett Mahony, its manager and driving force. The shop's booklist developed into *The Horn Book*, a prominent periodical dedicated to children's reading. In 1936, after Mahony decided to focus exclusively on *The Hornbook*, the shop was sold to the *Old Corner Bookstore. *See also* **15**. JE

J. Eddy, *Bookwomen* (2006)

Books in English Bibliographic record published bi-monthly by the *British Library from 1971 to 2003.

Records were produced on microfiche and consisted of a cumulating list of all titles from the *British National Bibliography, in addition to those catalogued by the Library of *Congress. CMS

Books in Print Reference work listing currently available book titles and *editions in the US. It began as an *annual published in 1948 by *Bowker, and eventually became an electronic resource. Related *serials were later produced, including guides to *paperback, children's, and forthcoming books and to out-of-print books. *Books in Print* was important for librarians and retailers, who used it for ordering and bibliographical information. Although only books with an *International Standard Book Number were included, it was the only comprehensive source of its kind until other electronic databases began to offer competition in the 1980s. LJM

Book Society British book club, founded 1929. Like its American counterpart the *Book-of-the-Month Club, the Book Society used a panel of experts—including J. B. Priestley and Hugh Walpole—to select books. Titles were then sold (not republished, as with some other clubs) at full price by mail order, reaching remote corners of Britain and the empire. Publishers welcomed the Club, but booksellers feared it would threaten their business. Other clubs followed the Society's success, including

A revolving **book stand** with *book cases, table, and stools occupy a bay in the library of *Trinity College, Cambridge: all were designed by Wren, who called these compartments 'cells'. The book cases are 11ft 10in. high.

V. *Gollancz's *Left Book Club. The *paperback *imprint *Pan began as a members-only offshoot of the Book Society. CMS

book stand A sloping stand to prop books upright, usually on a desk, with a ledge at the bottom on which to rest the book, and a support at the back. Book stands are usually wooden, adjustable, and sometimes collapsible. Although stationary stands for single books are the norm, stands may rotate and may have two or more sides. Book stands can be traced back to the Renaissance or earlier: in some Renaissance MSS and pictures scribes are shown copying, with their *exemplar on a book stand placed above their desk. *See also* BOOK WHEEL. KEA

book tokens Gift certificates for books; also a system for selling, marketing, or giving away generally unspecified books. Book tokens are used to encourage book sales, either by a country or a local body promoting reading in general or by a company hoping to increase sales. The token is a voucher (generally a card) that bears stamps, or otherwise indicates a monetary value or a number of books, entitling the recipient to exchange the token for a book or books in any participating bookshop, or (as is sometimes the case) through a particular book club or in chain stores. In Britain, a widely organized system of book tokens was initiated in 1932 through Book Tokens Ltd by Harold Raymond, then director of *Chatto & Windus. It was managed for the trade by the National Book Council, and, after 1943, by the National Book League (*see* BOOKTRUST). AMS

Booktrust An independent national charity that encourages people of all ages and cultures to discover and enjoy reading. Booktrust grew out of the National Book Council (NBC), founded in 1924 by Stanley *Unwin as an organization to foster cooperation between publishers. That group then became the National Book League (NBL) in 1944, aiming 'to promote the habit of reading and the wider distribution of books'. Booktrust was registered as a charity in 1963 and is based in Book House, south London. An independent educational organization, working to bring books and people together, Booktrust provides information for the public about books, writers and publishers; produces resources for schools and for reading groups; and runs a number of literature programmes.

Book Trust Scotland was first established as an outpost of the London office of the NBL in 1961 and became a fully independent organization (renamed Scottish Book Trust) in 1998. The two organizations work together on projects such as Story, the national campaign to celebrate the short story, which includes the National Short Story Prize.

Booktrust administers book prizes including the *Orange Prize, Nestlé Children's Book Prize, and the Early Years Awards, and for some years the *Booker Prize, as well as a number of projects including Bookstart (the national 'books for babies' scheme), and the *Children's Laureate award. SD

www.booktrust.org.uk, consulted Oct. 2008
www.scottishbooktrust.com/cocoon/sbt, consulted June 2006
The Times, 22 Mar. 1944

book weights Weights designed to keep pages open when reading (often on a *book stand)—for convenience and to avoid contact between human skin (perspiration) and the paper or membrane. The main kinds are snakes (i.e. chains of cloth-covered beads) and flat, circular leather-covered weights. They have been known since the Middle Ages: a book held open by two strings extending from the top of a *lectern with a weight attached to each string appears in a mid-15th-century MS illustration of a scholar in his private study and in a Flemish MS made for Henry VII. KEA

book wheel (wheel desk) A revolving sloping desk, usually circular, used in the Middle Ages and subsequently to accommodate several open books simultaneously; the reader pressed a lever at his foot to rotate the books. The surface sloped, with a ledge at the bottom to rest the books. The desk could be raised or lowered like a music stool by a large central screw. Agostino Ramelli famously published a design for a more elaborate device—looking like a miniature Ferris wheel for books—in 1588; it was much copied, but rarely built. KEA

J. W. Clark, *The Care of Books*, 2e (1909)

bookwork The term used to indicate that a printing firm undertakes the printing of whole books, almost always interspersed with some *jobbing printing.

bookworks *See* BOOK ART.

bookworms Not 'worms' at all, but the larvae of beetles (more than 150 species). The mature female lays eggs on the edges of books, or in bookshelves; the larvae, when hatched, burrow into the books, or shelves, creating miniature tunnels. They are known to cause extensive damage to books and libraries, requiring fumigation, but may also supply valuable bibliographical evidence. *See also* BOOK-LOUSE. MFS
M.-L. Florian, *Heritage Eaters* (1997)
W. W. Greg, 'A Study of Wormholes', *Library*, 4/3 (1922–3), 53–4
N. Hickin, *Bookworms* (1985)
F. B. Williams, Jr., 'Wormholes in Stored Sheets', *Library*, 4/18 (1937–8), 463–4

Boosey & Hawkes One of the world's leading music publishers, founded in 1930 with the merger of two well-established English family businesses, Boosey & Co. and Hawkes & Son. The company pioneered inexpensive music editions and—by acquiring the agencies of Belaieff, Editions Russes de Musique, Gutheil, and *Universal Edition—expanded rapidly, securing many of the most important 20th-century music *copyrights. It has corporate representatives in more than twenty countries. KL

Bordas French publisher founded in 1946 by two brothers and best known for textbooks, atlases, and dictionaries. Its six-volume Lagarde et Michard survey of French literature from the Middle Ages to the 20th century, first issued in 1948, was still in print in 2004. Bordas merged with Larousse in 1996. VAG

Bordeaux municipal library (**Bibliothèque municipale centrale de Bordeaux**) Bordeaux had a public library as early as 1740, founded by the Bordeaux Academy. Revolutionary confiscations constituted the bulk of the collections of the Bibliothèque municipale, officially established in 1803. Its nine-volume catalogue was published 1830–56. Moved in 1891 to a disused Dominican monastery, the library was then the largest in the French provinces. Opened in 1991, its new premises now make it one of the most modern. Its rare book department features distinguished holdings for the three greatest Bordelais writers, Montaigne (including the *Essais* MS known as the Exemplaire de Bordeaux), Montesquieu, and Mauriac. VAG

border A form of painted decoration added to one or more of the four *margins of the page of a book, usually, but not invariably, a MS. Such borders often have a substantial floral element, although they can include illustration (*see* **16**) and (usually on the first page of text) may bear the owner's coat of arms. Floral borders are not uncommon in *incunabula. In certain kinds of mass-produced MSS (e.g. *books of hours), borders may be produced from stencils. They often served, particularly in MSS, as a way of marking off significant textual divisions. In later periods, *woodcut or engraved borders were sometimes added to the margins of printed books. *See also* BORDER DECORATION. ASGE
K. L. Scott, *Dated and Datable English Manuscript Borders c.1395–1499* (2002)
— 'Design, Decoration and Illustration', in *BPPB*

border decoration The practice of embellishing, by hand, the blank marginal spaces found in pages of MSS and printed books. Generally regarded as a feature of MS illumination, it has received comparatively little scholarly study in comparison to set-piece *illumination. Border decoration usually surrounded the textual elements of an individual page, often being employed as a device to indicate to the reader where significant divisions of texts were to be found, such as the start of a new *chapter. Occasionally, where multiple texts were copied into a single volume, each individual text might have its own distinguishing border decoration. Stylistic elements—such as animals, heraldic devices, and sometimes human beings—were often incorporated into border decorations, as in the *Luttrell Psalter, but the most common motifs are flowers and foliage. The combination of general artistic style, the incorporation of specific design elements, and the use of colours in combination is sometimes used to help localize and date the books in which they are found. This kind of individual decoration by hand of page borders is sometimes found in luxury copies of printed books from the 15th and early 16th centuries, but rarely thereafter. RWO
M. Camille, *Image on the Edge* (1992)
K. L. Scott, *Dated and Datable English Manuscript Borders c.1395–1499* (2002)

Borders Ann Arbor, Michigan bookshop that grew into the second-largest bookshop chain (after *Barnes & Noble) in the US. Started as an antiquarian bookshop by the brothers Louis and Thomas Borders, it became a general bookshop in 1973. Catering to a university clientele, Borders was recognized for its knowledgeable staff and wide selection. In 1985 it began to establish branch outlets, providing a model for the book superstore that flourished in the 1990s. It was purchased in 1992 by Kmart, owner of *Waldenbooks. Becoming a publicly traded corporation in 1995, Borders then helped spread the superstore model globally by establishing international outlets, before declining precipitately in 2008. LJM

Börsenverein des Deutschen Buchhandels German association of all branches of the book production and distribution trade. Currently, 4,326 retail booksellers, 1,823 publishers, 83 wholesale booksellers, and 33 publishers' agents belong to the Börsenverein, which represents members' interests regarding trade policies and services. The association was founded in 1825 in Leipzig; since 1991, it has been based in Frankfurt. From 1834 it has published the *Börsenblatt* (magazine for the German book trade). In 1950 it began issuing the *Friedenspreis des Deutschen Buchhandels (Peace Prize of the German Book Trade). ME

Der Börsenverein des Deutschen Buchhandels, 1825–2000 (2000)

Borso d'Este, Bible of One of the most magnificent *illuminated MSS of the Renaissance, densely decorated and illustrated, made for Borso d'Este, duke of Urbino (1413–71) in Ferrara. A contract dated 1455 with the illuminators Taddeo Crivelli and Franco dei Russi specified that work was to be completed within six years. Other illuminators employed included Girolamo da Cremona and Giorgio d'Alemagna. RWa

J. J. G. Alexander, ed., *The Painted Page* (1994)
La Bibbia di Borso d'Este (2 vols, 1997)
C. M. Rosenberg, 'The Bible of Borso d'Este', in *Cultura figurativa ferrarese tra XV e XVI secolo* (1981)

Bosnia and Herzegovina, National and University Library of (Nacionalna i univerzitetska biblioteka Bosne i Hercegovine) Established in Sarajevo in 1945, the library was, until 1992, one of eight *legal deposit libraries in the former Yugoslavia. During the war (1992–5), the library was burnt to the ground, and 90 per cent of the 3 million-item collection was destroyed. The reconstruction of the library began after the war in the buildings of the former military barracks. The library holds various MSS in oriental, *Cyrillic and *Latin *scripts, and the rare book collection numbers 3,900 volumes, including four *incunabula. MVG

bosses Large metal studs added to the boards of bookbindings for protection or decoration. Typically associated with medieval bindings and wooden boards, they are uncommon after 1600.

Boston Athenæum Independent membership library. Founded in 1807 by the Anthology Society, editors of *The Monthly Anthology and Boston Review* (1804–11), it was modelled on England's private (public) libraries, becoming by 1851 one of the five largest libraries in the US. Today, its collections exceed 500,000 volumes, primarily in Boston and New England history, abolitionist literature, biography, English and American literature, and the fine and decorative arts. The current building, constructed 1847–9, was enlarged 1913–14. PMW

[Boston Athenæum,] *The Athenæum Centenary* (1907)
R. Story, 'Class and Culture in Boston: The Athenaeum, 1807–1860', *American Quarterly*, 27 (1975), 178–99

Boston Public Library America's first publicly funded free library. Opened in 1854 with 16,000 volumes, it is currently among the world's largest public collections, with 6.1 million circulating books and 1.2 million rare books and MSS. The Italianate building, designed by Charles McKim as a 'palace for the people', opened in 1895; a modern addition opened in 1972. Its 27 branch libraries serve the city's diverse neighbourhoods. PMW

[Trustees of the Public Library of the City of Boston,] *Upon the Objects to be Attained by the Establishment of a Public Library* (1852; reprinted 1975)
W. M. Whitehill, *Boston Public Library* (1956)

Bostwick, Arthur (1860–1942) American librarian. Bostwick spent most of his career as head of the St Louis Public Library. He championed public libraries as institutions for popular education through his writings, including a widely used *textbook, *The American Public Library* (1910). In 1925, he travelled to China as a representative of the *American Library Association, later serving as honorary director of the Library Association of China. MAK

A. Bostwick, *A Life With Men and Books* (1939)

botanical book No category of natural history has proved as popular and enduring for producers and consumers of books as botany, the scientific study of plants. Whether descriptive lists of plants or illustrated catalogues of individual species, books on botany are some of the earliest writings devoted to a scientific subject and are among the most actively sought by collectors. The inexpensive *plates of these books are standard fare for interior decorators and are ubiquitous in antiquarian book shops; copies of prized volumes and series are the core of many impressive book collections and command extraordinary prices.

1. Early history
2. Linnaeus and after

1. Early history

The history of botanical books can be traced to the Greek scholar Theophrastus (372/1 or 371/70–288/7 or 287/6 BC), a contemporary of Aristotle and author of *Historia de Plantis* and *De Causis Plantarum*. In contrast to other writers of his time, Theophrastus offered natural explanations, rather than supernatural ones, for the physiological changes in plants. The writings of Theophrastus were joined by those of the Greek physician Dioscorides, author of *De Materia Medica* (*c.*65 AD), a medical catalogue of some 600 plants. These works formed the core of the ancient world's botanical writings and of botanical practice during the early modern era.

Until the 16th century, most botanical writings were *herbals—lists and recipes for plant-based medical remedies—and *translations and elaborations of earlier works. Notable exceptions include Albertus Magnus' 13th-century *De Vegetabilibus*, a widely read treatise on plants and vegetables, and Konrad von Megenberg's 15th-century *Das Buch der Natur*, a translation of Thomas de Cantimpré's 13th-century *De Natura Rerum*. Von Megenberg's volume contains some of the first printed natural history illustrations (*see* **16**), and *Das Buch*, some scholars argue, became a model for illustrated printed books, passing through five *editions by 1500.

The 16th century witnessed the beginning of modern botanical book publication, with greater attention paid to accuracy of illustration, accounts based on eyewitness observation, attempts at a comprehensive classificatory scheme, and the listing of plants both in Latin and the vernacular. In this regard, the works of Otto Brunfels, Hieronymus Bock (Tragus), and Leonhart Fuchs are exemplary. Some scholars argue that Brunfels, a

Carthusian monk and Lutheran convert, may be considered the link between ancient and modern botany. His most important work, *Herbarum Vivae Eicones* (1530), adopted the ancient classification of plants as woody and herbaceous, but substituted an arrangement based on medicinal value rather than an alphabetical list. His *woodcuts, much improved over previous herbals, were original and not copies. Bock's *Kreuterbuch* (1539)—which ordered plants by their outward appearance rather than their medicinal qualities—offered greater coherence of taxonomic arrangement. Bock employed the woodcuts of the artist David Kandel, who completed some 550 new images, perhaps Kandel's crowning artistic achievement. Fuchs's *De Historia Stirpium* (1542) included woodcuts drawn from nature, each genus occupying a full page. Of equal importance, however, was the publication of an edition in German to assist local people in identifying useful plants. Fuchs's herbal contained images and descriptions of 400 plants native to Germany, as well as 100 species from abroad, including the first known European images of pumpkins and Indian corn from the New World.

By the end of the 16th century, botanical books began to divide into permeable but distinct categories. The herbalist tradition remained vibrant (though waning) as authors throughout Europe recorded plant-derived recipes and depicted specimens. However, the taxonomic variety posed by New World species and exotics from the around the world challenged those interested in plants to account for them more scientifically, forcing the development of new systems of nomenclature and works devoted to defending an organizational theory for all plants. Additionally, a growing interest in exotic, landscape, and pleasure gardens led to the new genre of garden books, offering recommendations and theories for particular plantings, strategies for mixing species, and thoughts on general garden and landscape design. Among English-speaking authors, the diarist *Evelyn looms largest in the 17th century. Evelyn translated Jean de la Quintinie's *Instruction pour les jardins fruitiers et potagers*, publishing it in 1693 as *The Compleat Gard'ner*, a guide to fruit and kitchen gardens along with a calendar for planting, a supplement that became more popular in the 18th century. Increasingly, garden books were written in the vernacular and were chiefly aimed at the practical gardener. Evelyn also published *Acetaria, A Discourse of Sallets* (1699), his own gardening manual, and *Sylva, or a Discourse of Forest Trees* (1664), a practical guide to forest and orchard management.

2. Linnaeus and after

Throughout the 18th century, disputes over the virtues and drawbacks of rival taxonomic systems underlay many of the century's botany books. Yet Carolus Linnaeus' binomial system, outlined in *Systema Naturae* (1735), became the most celebrated and widely adopted, though his was by no means the only coherent system. Augustin Pyramus De Candolle elaborated upon and refined Linnaeus in his two-volume *Natural System of the Vegetable Kingdom* (1817–21). Darwin's *On the *Origin of Species* (1859)

offered natural selection as the means by which new species arise, and Gregor Mendel's observations of peas, 'Versuch über Pflanzenhybriden' (1866), laid the foundation of modern genetics.

These scientific achievements were concurrent with an explosion in botanical book publishing as the 19th century became the great century of botanizing. Less expensive *engraving technologies (including hand- and mechanical-colouring), developments in *lithography, an ever-growing collection of plants described and drawn, and an increased number of talented artists made botany books some of most celebrated publishing achievements of the era. Of equal importance to these technological changes was the fact that authors began to write, and publishers began to direct, manuals and treatises on gardening and flowers to women readers. Noteworthy publications include John Loudon's *Arboretum et Fruticetum Britannicum* (1838), an exhaustive account of all species of trees and shrubs in Great Britain accompanied by hand-coloured plates drawn from life. Loudon's wife, Jane, author of the frequently reprinted *Gardening for Ladies* (1838), became a prolific and accomplished author, writing at least five different titles on gardening and flowers for women.

The 20th century saw increasingly specialized scientific writings on botany, which were distinct from works for the general public. Moreover, the audience for richly illustrated botanical works diminished as engravings and lithographs were superseded by less expensive photography, and as gardening and botanizing were replaced by other pastimes and amusements. Nevertheless, artists' botanical books remain moderately popular, and botanical photography books appear more frequently. Pocket-sized field guides to nearly every conceivable class of plant now occupy the place formerly held by cloth-bound botany manuals, except among the specialist and collector.   AJL

A. Arber, *Herbals*, 3e (1986)
W. Blunt, *The Art of Botanical Illustration* (1951)
A. Coats, *The Book of Flowers* (1973)
L. DeBray, *The Art of Botanical Illustration* (1989)
R. H. Grove, *Green Imperialism* (1995)
N. Jardine *et al.*, eds., *Cultures of Natural History* (1996)
E. Kenney, *The Botanizers* (1992)
H. Lack, *Garden Eden*, tr. M. Walters (2001)
A. G. Morton, *History of Botanical Science* (1981)
K. Reeds, *Botany in Medieval and Renaissance Universities* (1992)
J. L. Reveal, *Gentle Conquest: The Botanical Discovery of North America* (1992)
G. Saunders, *Picturing Plants* (1995)
L. Schiebinger and C. Swan, eds., *Colonial Botany* (2005)
S. Sitwell and W. Blunt, *Great Flower Books, 1700–1900* (1990)
A. Stroup, *A Company of Scientists* (1990)

Botfield, Beriah (1807–63) English antiquary and book collector. Botfield was educated at *Christ Church, Oxford, and became a successful industrialist. He produced a number of editions and catalogues connected with medieval Britain, and collected *Caxtons and other *incunabula. On his death, his books were bequeathed

to the *Thynne family, at Longleat. These were dispersed in *book auctions at *Sotheby's (1979) and *Christie's (1994 and 2002). ASGE
ODNB

Boucicaut Master Anonymous Parisian illuminator of the first two decades of the 15th century known after his major work, the Hours of the Maréchal de Boucicaut, (Paris, Musée Jacquemart-André, ms. 2). He chiefly painted *books of hours and historical MSS. His style is characterized by miniatures of exceptional quality (*see* MINIATURES (1)), depicting graceful figures in elegant interiors and extensive landscapes, often from an aerial perspective. He ran a prolific workshop, collaborating with leading Parisian artists of the day, including the *Bedford Master. FL-T
M. Meiss *et al.*, *French Painting in the Time of Jean de Berry: The Boucicaut Master* (1968)

bound proof *See* PROOF COPY.

Bourdieu, Pierre (1930–2002) French sociologist, widely influential in modern book history for his theory of 'the field of cultural production', which he identifies as a site of struggles for the right 'to impose the dominant definition of the writer'. Bourdieu's analysis is France-focused, and sees the field of cultural production as a bipolar power relation between dominated 'autonomous' (independent, artist-led) and dominant 'heteronomous' (market, society-led) models of production, pitting the poor, select market, intellectual or Bohemian, and young against the rich, mass market, bourgeois, and old. MW
P. Bourdieu, *The Field of Cultural Production*, ed. R. Johnson (1993)

boustrophedon [Gk, 'ox-turning'] Text written in lines running alternately left to right, and right to left, a style used in several ancient civilizations.

Bowater, Eric (1895–1962) British papermaker and industrialist. He became managing director of the family firm of paper merchants in 1924, transforming it into a manufacturing business. The first Bowater *paper mill opened at Northfleet, Kent, in 1926; further mills followed, and by the mid-1950s Bowaters became the world's largest *newsprint manufacturer. DCC
ODNB

Bowdler, Thomas (1754–1825), and **Henrietta Maria Bowdler** (1750–1830) English Shakespearean editors. They wrote and produced medical and travel books, sermons, editions of devotional writings, and a novel, but their lasting impact was in expurgating and shortening Shakespeare's plays for family reading. Maria's twenty-play version appeared anonymously in Bath in 1807, and Thomas's full 10-volume *Family Shakespeare* from *Longman in 1818, replacing some scenes Maria had deleted but cutting further words and phrases. An 1821 attack in *Blackwood's* and a defence by Francis Jeffrey in the *Edinburgh* brought increased sales, with reprints continuing into the 1860s. In the

1870s, Swinburne praised Bowdler for giving 'intelligent and imaginative children' access to Shakespeare. The term 'Bowdlerize' for prudish cutting is first noted in 1836, and 'Bowdlerized' in 1879. PGS
C. Franklin, 'The Bowdlers and Their Family Shakespeare,' *BC* 49 (2000), 227–43
ODNB

Bowers, F. T. (Fredson Thayer) (1905–91) American literary scholar, bibliographer, and textual critic. His awareness of what the physical features of books could tell about their production history led to his *Principles of Bibliographical Description* (1949) and to the application of such analysis in editions of some 60 volumes of writings by authors from five centuries. Building on the insights of *Greg, he emphasized the importance of the scholar's critical judgement in reconstructing *authorial intentions for a work. The ideas about the relationship of literary criticism, *textual criticism, and analytical bibliography that he developed in three major lecture series (*Rosenbach, *Sandars, and *Lyell) became important books: *On Editing Shakespeare and the Elizabethan Dramatists* (1955), *Textual and Literary Criticism* (1959), and *Bibliography and Textual Criticism* (1964). In 1947, he helped to found the Bibliographical Society of the University of *Virginia, and he edited the society's journal, *Studies in Bibliography*, from its inception in 1948 until his death. His *Elizabethan Revenge Tragedy, 1587–1642* (1940) remains a standard treatment of its subject. As chair of the English Department of the University of Virginia from 1961 to 1968, he raised that department to prominence. DLVM
G. T. Tanselle, *The Life and Work of Fredson Bowers* (1993)

Bowes & Bowes British bookseller and publisher. Robert Bowes joined the family company *Macmillan in 1846, taking charge of the Cambridge bookshop in 1863. In 1899 Bowes went into partnership with his son, forming Bowes & Bowes in 1907. The company was sold to W. H. *Smith in 1953, but continued to trade under its original name—and acquire other bookshops—until 1986. CMS
Norrie

Bowker, R. R. New York-based publisher of reference books and periodicals for *publishers, *booksellers, book manufacturers, and librarians; US ISBN (*see* INTERNATIONAL STANDARD BOOK NUMBER) agent. Bowker's publications include *Publishers Weekly* (1873–), *Library Journal* (1876–), *Ulrich's International Periodicals Directory* (1932–), *Literary Market Place* (1943–), and *Books in Print* (1948–). *PW* and *LJ* were founded by *Leypoldt but taken over by Richard Rogers Bowker, a member of the editorial staff, in 1884. The firm was purchased by Xerox in 1967, by *Reed International in 1985, and by the Cambridge Information Group in 2001. BEL

HBPUS

bowl The round or elliptical shape that forms the basic body of letters such as C, G, O, and b, c, e, o, and p.

Bowyer, William (1663–1737), and **William Bowyer** (1699–1777) London printers, best known for producing scholarly books. William senior, who served his apprenticeship under Miles Flesher, was in business by 1699. His son was educated at Cambridge, where he learned Latin, Greek, and Hebrew, but did not take a degree, probably because of the family's nonjuring inclinations. Thus, the unusually learned William junior took over the job of *proofreading when he joined the firm in 1722. The Bowyers printed the votes of the House of Commons from 1729, and bought, with the cooperation of *Faulkner, significant *copyrights of Irish writers such as *Swift. William junior formed a partnership with his overseer James Emonson in 1754, but Bowyer's unwillingness to share control meant that it was short-lived. He secured the right to print for the *Royal Society in 1761, and in 1765 made a joint bid for the Cambridge University printing *privileges. His former apprentice *Nichols became junior partner the following year (equal partner in 1773). His *Literary Anecdotes*, along with the Bowyer *archive, chart the history of this important printing firm.   CYF

K. Maslen and J. Lancaster, eds., *The Bowyer Ledgers* (1991)
ODNB

Boydell, John (1720–1804) English engraver, publisher, and printseller. After studying *engraving in London, Boydell earned his living by publishing his engravings of English and Welsh landscapes. Yet his renown was for publishing the engravings of others. His printselling business was fully established by 1751; shortly thereafter, he launched his collections of engravings after famous English paintings. In 1786, he began publishing a series of prints illustrating Shakespeare. Paintings were commissioned from leading artists and a gallery was built in Pall Mall to house the works. Financial pressures led to the sale of the collection by lottery in 1804.   KES
ODNB

Bozérian, Jean-Claude (1762–1840) Parisian bookbinder, in business *c*.1795–1810. Like his brother Bozérian le jeune (*fl.* 1802–18), he ran a large and successful bindery producing both ordinary and luxury work. The Bozérian firms are generally recognized as helping to restore a tradition of fine binding in Paris after the French Revolution, although their designs have been criticized as uninspired.   DRSP

P. Culot, *Jean-Claude Bozérian* (1979)
C. Ramsden, *French Bookbinders, 1789–1848* (1950)

Božidar, Vuković *See* VUKOVIĆ, BOŽIDAR.

Bracciolini, Poggio (1380–1459) Florentine humanist. He was a papal bureaucrat for 50 years, and latterly chancellor and historian of Florence. His fame rests on a series of rediscoveries of Latin classics made while attending the Council of Constance, 1414–18. Forays to Cluny, Langres, Cologne, Fulda, and, most fruitfully, *St Gall, brought to light Lucretius, Ammianus, Quintilian (hitherto mutilated) complete, and new Ciceronian speeches. From a stay in England and another trip to Cologne, he

recovered both the excerpts and the *Cena Trimalchionis* of Petronius. All of these were unknown to Italians and to the Middle Ages at large; Poggio had a hand in shaping nearly all Latin textual traditions that saw renewed life in the 15th century. He also created the 'humanistic' script that is the direct ancestor of modern *roman type. His 600-odd surviving letters give a sparkling insight into early humanism at work.   MCD
DBI

bracketed In type design, a join between two elements (e.g. stem (*see* STROKE) and *serif) that uses a concave curve, rather than a stark right angle.

Bradbury & Evans William Bradbury (1800–1869) and Frederick Mullet Evans (1803–70), English printers from 1830, took over from Bradbury's failed partnership with William Dent. Initially printers of legal work, they soon printed for newspapers and periodicals, installing the biggest and best equipment available. Much of their book printing was for publishers such as *Moxon; Alexander Smith; *Smith, Elder; *Chapman & Hall; and the Edinburgh publishers *Chambers, for whom they printed *Chambers Cyclopedia*. They became publishers themselves in 1841 when they launched *Punch* (1841–1992). They published Dickens, *Thackeray, R. S. Surtees, and many other *serial novelists from the late 1840s until they retired in 1865, merging with the Agnews of Manchester, into whose family Bradbury's son Henry and daughter Edith had married.   PLS
ODNB

Bradfer-Lawrence, Harry (1887–1965) English antiquary and collector of medieval and Renaissance MSS. He edited various volumes for the Norfolk Record and Archaeological Societies. Most of his MS collecting was undertaken after World War II; some items came from the *Lyell collection. After his death, his MSS were deposited in the *Fitzwilliam Museum, Cambridge. Subsequently, they were acquired by *Quaritch and dispersed.   ASGE

A. S. G. Edwards, 'The Bradfer-Lawrence Collection of Medieval Manuscripts', *BC* 53 (2004), 64–9

Bradford, William (1663–1752) Colonial printer in Philadelphia and New York. In 1682, the apprentice Bradford sailed with William Penn; by 1685 he had left London again, with his freedom, a spouse, and press equipment. Bradford struggled to generate trade while also printing for the Quakers and civil government. Bradford founded British North America's first *paper mill in 1690. By 1692, he had published the controversialist George Keith, thus upsetting the Philadelphia Meeting. Briefly imprisoned, he agreed in 1693 to become New York's printer. In Pennsylvania, Bradford had taken the riskier option of speculative publishing, but in New York he was ensured stability by his status as government printer and his colony-funded salary. *Zenger's competition in 1733 made Bradford's *New-York Gazette* (New York's first newspaper) partisan, but Bradford fared

better in the long term. He stayed active in New Jersey and in Philadelphia, through his son's and grandson's business.   MPB
ODNB

Bradley, Benjamin (d. 1862) Bookbinder in Boston, Massachusetts, noteworthy as the first known binder in America to specialize in *edition binding in *bookcloth. He trained with Simri Whitney before establishing his own bindery in 1832, and began making cloth bindings for several publishers during the 1830s. After Bradley's death, the business was continued by his former partner Thomas Crowell; it moved to New York in 1900 and was closed after a fire in 1919.   DRSP
H. Lehmann-Haupt, ed., *Bookbinding in America* (1941)

Bradley, Will (1868–1962) American graphic artist. As a young illustrator in Chicago, Bradley discovered the designs of *Beardsley, whose art nouveau style heavily influenced his early commercial work. In 1895 he founded the Wayside Press in Springfield, Massachusetts, where he published a literary and arts magazine, *Bradley: His Book*, in the style of the *Kelmscott Press. Later he moved to Cambridge and then New York, where he was art director for various manufacturers and publishers, including the *American Type Founders Company, Collier's, and *Hearst, designing magazine covers and advertising brochures in a characteristic 'American Colonial' *chapbook style.   MA
R. Koch, *Will H. Bradley* (2002)

Bradshaw, Henry (1831–86) English scholar, librarian, and bibliographer. Bradshaw was a leading British authority who brought together *bibliography and *codicology, establishing the foundations of modern bibliographical method, in particular by devising the *collational formula. Bradshaw advanced knowledge of early *typography, his particular interest, by identifying *founts with individual presses. He devised the order of arrangement for early presses subsequently developed by *Proctor as 'Proctor order'. Bradshaw's studies of Chaucer were incorporated into *Furnivall's and *Skeat's editions. He rediscovered MSS in *Cambridge University Library, including the Book of Deer, and, as librarian (1867–86), developed its incunabular holdings; he also gave the library his own collections of *incunabula and of Irish books.   KEA
ODNB
G. W. Prothero, *A Memoir of Henry Bradshaw* (1888)

Brahe, Tycho (1546–1601) Danish astronomer and nobleman. In 1576 he established a veritable research centre on the island of Hven in Øresund, north of Copenhagen, where he acted as a patron to a large number of students and assistants. In order to secure control over the technical and aesthetic quality of his scientific works, he established his own printing press and paper mill on Hven. Among his published works is a collection of his correspondence with many leading European scholars, a forerunner to the scientific journal.   CA, KSP

Brailes, William de (*fl. c.*1230–1260) The earliest surviving *book of hours in England (BL Add. MS 49,999), made for a laywoman, contains a painted *initial showing a tonsured man in prayer with the inscription 'w. de brail' qui me depeint'. This artist has been identified with a man whose name occurs in a number of Oxford documents of *c.*1230–50: de Brailes was connected with the thriving book trade in the city. His hand can be identified elsewhere, and his signature also appears on fo. 3r of *Fitzwilliam Museum, MS 330.   CMM
C. Donovan, *The de Brailes Hours* (1991)
ODNB

Brasiliense Brazilian publisher. Progressive in outlook, Brasiliense was founded in 1943 by Arthur Heládio Neves of *Companhia Editora Nacional, with support from *Monteiro Lobato and Caio Prado Júnior. Now a leading publisher, it specializes in social sciences and popular series such as *Primeiros passos* and *Tudo é história*.
                                                            DRW

Braun + Schneider German publishing house, founded in 1843 in Munich, famous for its illustrated periodicals (*Fliegende Blätter, Münchner Bilderbogen*) and humorous books. Its children's books, such as W. Buschs's *Max und Moritz*, were a forerunner of modern *comics. The company was liquidated in the 1980s.   US

Braunerová, Zdenka (1858–1934) Czech painter and graphic artist. She was a pioneering figure in the Czech movement promoting the book as a beautiful artefact in the 1890s. Impressed by the work of W. *Morris and the English *private presses, she turned for inspiration to Czech Renaissance and Baroque printing. Her most distinctive creations were rich decorative *borders, *headpieces, and *initials. Braunerová sought perfection in her designs both in her choice of materials and of workmanship; her books masterfully unify graphic design and *typography.   DP
P. H. Toman, *Zdenka Braunerová* (1963)

Brazil, National Library of (Biblioteca Nacional) The library's nucleus was the 60,000-volume Portuguese royal collection, reconstituted after the 1755 Lisbon earthquake, shipped in 1810 to Brazil, and augmented by en bloc acquisitions and *legal deposit. The library's collections are not large, but its rare-book and MS holdings are perhaps the richest in Latin America. Strong in Portuguese and Brazilian history, its treasures include the library of *Machado and the 50,000 volumes ceded by the exiled Emperor Pedro II, as well as vast holdings of *prints, music scores, and Brazilian MSS. The library's present building in Rio de Janeiro opened in 1910.
                                                            DRW

Braziller, George (1916–) American *publisher and *book club founder. Working as a clerk for a *remainder company, Braziller conceived the idea for Book Find Club, which he launched in 1942 by asking his immediate family to join. Braziller's personal interest in art led to the founding of the Seven Arts Book Society. The clubs reached the peak of their popularity before the House Un-American Activities Committee listed Book Find Club as a subversive organization (1953), but they continued to contribute to Braziller's publishing business until Time, Inc. purchased them (1969). In 1954, Braziller began publishing literature and quality non-fiction under his own *imprint. George Braziller Inc. became an important source of foreign literature in *translation for the American market, giving particular support to the French *nouveau roman*; it also introduced several series of books on art, architecture, American culture, and religion. With the success of *facsimile editions of *illuminated medieval *books of hours and art books such as *Matisse's *Jazz*, Braziller maintained his firm's independence and published books others avoided, including a 1994 collection of essays by Muslim authors in support of Salman Rushdie.   HSS

Columbia University Oral History Collection, 'The Reminiscences of George Braziller' (1980)

breaker A breaker or breaking copy is a book destined, with the tacit consent of buyer and seller, to be dismembered and its component parts sold individually. This usually applies to plates, illustrations, or maps, but sometimes individual leaves from early printed books, individual plays, or discrete sections of early collections will also be treated in this way. Breaking is occasionally done purely for profit, but it is generally reserved for incomplete or otherwise badly damaged books. The term 'breaker' also occasionally refers to a bookseller who habitually breaks such books. The Code of Good Practice of the *Antiquarian Booksellers Association expressly commits its members to the preservation of historical materials and precludes the breaking of complete and intact copies. The practice of breaking and of creating *made-up copies (including the transference of *dust jackets) destroys the bibliographical integrity of items. *See also* LEAF BOOK.   LJW

Breitkopf & Härtel Leipzig publishers, printers, and typefounders, best known for their *sheet music. Bernard Christoph Breitkopf, who established the business, married the widow of a printer and typefounder (1719). His son Johann Gottlob Immanuel Breitkopf (1719–94), the best-known pioneer of type for polyphonic music (1750s), was head of the firm from 1762, becoming a leading scholar-printer. His music *type, with notes and staff built up from small units, competed with copper-plate *engraving and punched pewter *plates; he applied the same technique to *map printing. His foundry and *printing office also had a wide assortment of non-Latin types. Gottfried Christoph Härtel (1763–1827), partner (1795) and sole owner from 1796, began printing music *lithographically (1806), a technique that soon dominated all others. The firm still publishes music.   JAL
LGB

Bremer Presse German *private press, founded in 1911 by Willy Wiegand and Ludwig Wolde. Well advised by H. v. Hofmannsthal and R. Borchardt, they produced excellent contemporary German works as well as classical texts. In 1921 Bremer moved to Munich, where Wiegand founded a publishing house of the same name. Bremer Presse's masterful edition of *Luther's Bible (*Biblia teutsch*, 1926–8) was set in specially cut *gothic type. The 'queen of German private presses' was closed in 1935.   US

J. Lehnacker, *Die Bremer Presse* (1964)

Brent, Stuart (*c*.1915–) Chicago bookseller from 1946 to 1996. Located first on North Rush, his shop moved to Michigan Avenue in 1951. Brent was known for close relationships with authors who visited the store, for personal service, and for strong opinions about his wares. A pioneer in selling books and music under one roof, Brent also hosted a television show, ran a *book club, and wrote children's books (*see* 15).   BEL

S. Brent, *The Seven Stairs* (1962)

Brentano's Longest-lived bookshop chain in the US. It began when August Brentano, an Austrian immigrant, started a newsstand in New York City in 1853; the business was moved to an enclosed shop in 1860. The firm established branches in several other cities, including Paris. The flagship Brentano's in Manhattan's Union Square, and later on Fifth Avenue, was one of the largest and best-known bookshops in the country. It helped to create Americans' image of the fine bookshop catering to the carriage trade. Until 1933, Brentano's also engaged in some publishing. However, it experienced financial difficulties and, after the family sold the firm in 1933, had a succession of owners. In 1982 it filed for bankruptcy, and was acquired in 1983 by *Waldenbooks, which developed Brentano's as a more upmarket alternative to Waldenbooks outlets. By the early 2000s, with the superstore format dominant, most branches of Brentano's were converted or closed.   LJM

Brenthurst The Brenthurst Library in Houghton, Johannnesburg, houses the Africana collection of the *Oppenheimer family. Sir Ernest Oppenheimer started collecting Africana in Kimberley after the Anglo-Boer War (1899–1902), before coming to Johannesburg and establishing the Anglo American Corporation in 1917. His son, Harry Oppenheimer, developed the library into South Africa's largest and most valuable private Africana collection. It contains MSS, artworks, maps, rare books, and *pamphlets. The Brenthurst Press was founded in 1974 to publish limited editions related to the library's MSS and art works. A well-equipped bindery contributes to the preservation and enhancement of the collection.   ALD

Brepols Belgian publishing house, founded 1796. P. J. Brepols's printing office in Turnhout specialized in prayer books during the 19th and early 20th centuries. An academic publisher since 1949, Brepols placed the patristic series *Corpus Christianorum* at the core of its activities.   PD

R. Baetens, *Brepols drukkers en uitgevers* (1996)

Brera Library, Milan (Biblioteca Nazionale Braidense) With Milan under Austrian rule, the Empress Maria Theresa established a public library in 1770 as a counterpoise to the church-owned *Ambrosiana. The suppression of the Jesuit house in 1773 provided the building, in a complex including the Academy of Fine Arts and the Brera Gallery. The foundation collection—from Carlo Pertusati (d. 1755)—was acquired in 1768, and the library opened in 1786. In 1859, with the annexation of Lombardy, ownership passed to the fledgling Italian state.   NH

Breslauer, Martin (1871–1940) Antiquarian book-seller in Berlin from 1898. His superb catalogues included modern *bibliophilic editions, antiquarian German literature, *incunabula, Renaissance, and 18th-century French books. He also organized important book auctions (e.g. Stolberg-Wernigerode, Empress Marie Louise). Forced to emigrate in 1937, he died in a German bomb attack on London.   RW
M. Breslauer, *Erinnerungen, Aufsätze, Widmungen* (1966)

breviary A liturgical book, containing the whole text of the Divine Office (Liturgy of the Hours) of the Roman Catholic Church, including 'spoken' and sung items (e.g. psalms, hymns, readings, and prayers) usually, but not always, without musical notation. The Divine Office is the Church's prayer for the sanctification of time, and, in its Western form, can be traced back at least to St Benedict in the 6th century. The Office comprises the recitation of hymns, psalms, and prayers, and readings from Scripture and other Christian texts at prescribed hours of the day and night. In its fullest form, used in monasteries, the Office consists of eight separate services at Canonical Hours known as Matins, Lauds, Prime, Terce, Sext, None, Vespers, and Compline. A simplified form of the Divine Office was celebrated by the secular Church and recited privately by the laity.

In the early Middle Ages, the text of the Divine Office was distributed between several liturgical books. The breviary is similar to the *missal as a compendium drawing together materials from many different sources, including *psalters, *hymnals, and antiphonals (which contained musical items of the Office performed by the choir), along with books of readings such as *lectionaries and hagiographic, biblical, and patristic texts. Much is unclear about the early development of the breviary, but it seems to have evolved in response to the need to standardize liturgical practice, as well as to address a growing demand for liturgical texts from an increasingly literate population. In the late Middle Ages, there was also a growing tendency towards the private recitation of the Divine Office, which required books containing all relevant texts. The breviary became common in the 13th century, but the earliest attempts to produce the whole text of the Office date from the 11th century. The breviary in use by the Roman Curia in the 12th century was adopted by the Franciscan order, and became widely known and employed throughout Europe. The name 'breviary' ('conspectus') appears to derive from the portable compilations that gave only the opening words of texts to be performed at the offices for each day. The full texts for the offices were added later, although in medieval MSS the items were often shortened to a few lines or words.

The breviary is a book intended primarily for use by a cleric or a lay person praying the Divine Office in public or in private. Items in the breviary are organized following the order of the liturgical year, and are subdivided into several main sections, including the Calendar, Psalter, Temporale, Sanctorale, and Common of Saints. In addition, the medieval breviary could contain other liturgical texts, such as 'votive' Offices for special occasions and devotions, most commonly services invoking the aid of the Virgin Mary, or petitioning God's mercy and assistance for the dead. During the Middle Ages, breviaries were often subdivided into two parts (summer being Easter to Advent; winter being Advent to Easter), whereas later breviaries were commonly arranged into four parts corresponding to the four seasons. Some medieval breviaries also contained rubrics with instructions for the conduct of the offices.

Surviving medieval MSS of the breviary vary in appearance and presentation, depending on their intended use. They differ in the number of volumes, size, the order and the choice of textual items, and decoration. Variations in the books' physical form reflect their many functions: there are surviving '*pocket' breviaries, small but very thick, for use when travelling; choir breviaries, with musical notation and a reasonably full text of the sung items; and 'missal-breviaries' (Italian and French in origin), which aimed to combine all liturgical texts for a given day, and had the texts of masses inserted after Terce. Alterations in the form of the breviary throughout the Middle Ages and the modern period reflected the continued development of the Divine Office. In addition, breviaries assumed many local features and mirrored the customs of different religious orders. Breviaries made for various dioceses or monastic establishments can be often identified by the inclusion of locally celebrated feast days and offices in their Calendars and Sanctorale. Attempts to reform and standardize the breviary were undertaken on numerous occasions. An important step was the publication of the Tridentine Breviary in 1568, under Pope Pius V, which was adopted by many dioceses and religious orders and remained in use until the early 20th century. *See also* BOOK OF HOURS.   ES
ODCC
E. Palazzo, *A History of Liturgical Books*, tr. M. Beaumont (1998; French original 1993)
L. C. Sheppard, *The Liturgical Books* (1962)
J. B. L. Tolhurst, *Introduction to the English Monastic Breviaries*, vol. 6 of *The Monastic Breviary of Hyde Abbey, Winchester*, Henry Bradshaw Society, 80 (1942)

brevier *See* SIZE, TYPE.

Breydenbach, Bernhard von (d. 1497) Dean of the cathedral of Mainz. In 1483–4, he undertook a pilgrimage to the Holy Land in the company of the Dominican Martin Roth and the painter Erhard Reuwich of Utrecht, among others. The description of the pilgrimage, first

Hand-coloured *woodcut illustrations from **Breydenbach**'s *Peregrinatio in Terram Sanctam* (Mainz, 1486): above, five figures in various Arabic costumes; below, the Arabic alphabet.

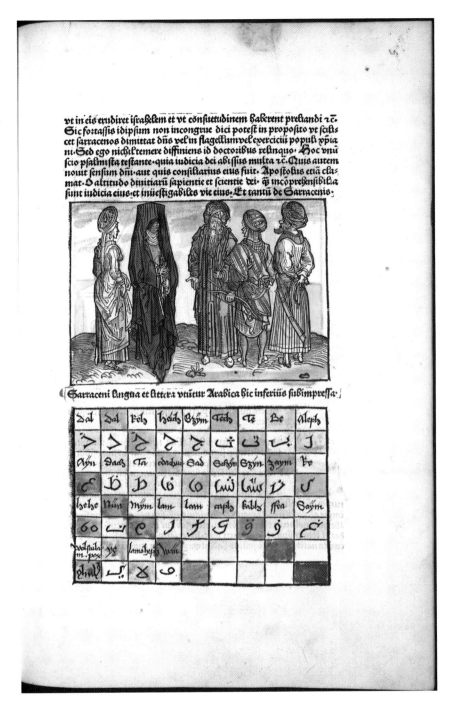

published in Latin with the title *Peregrinatio in Terram Sanctam* (1486), is the earliest printed up-to-date and illustrated travelogue; it also included related theological texts. Roth wrote notes, and Reuwich sketched on the spot. His drawings were the basis for *woodcuts, to which the publication owed much of its success. Seven illustrations (*see* **16**) of locations include spectacular fold-out views of Venice, Candia, and a map of the Holy Land; seventeen smaller woodcuts depict figures such as Saracens, Syrians, and Abyssinians. The work includes woodcut alphabets of Arabic, Hebrew, Greek, Syriac, Coptic, Armenian, and Ethiopic. The first edition (completed in Mainz on 11 February 1486), the *translation into German (21 June 1486), and a Dutch version (24 May 1488) are all printed with Schoeffer's *types, but name Erhard Reuwich as printer.

Although the Latin version of the work was reprinted in 1490 and 1502 in Speyer, the work's main impact was in translations into German (1486, 1488, and *c*.1505), Dutch (1488), Czech (abbreviated, 1498) and Spanish (extended version, 1498). There are two translations into French, the earliest (Lyons, November 1488, with copper engravings) expanded with the itinerary of the translator, Nicolas Le Huen. The second French translation, Lyons (1489), remains close to the original. In 1517 and 1522/3, two more editions in French were published in Paris.

LH

BMC 1, 2, 8, 10
H. Davies, *Bernhard von Breydenbach and his Journey to the Holy Land: A Bibliography* (1911)
GW 5075–82
ISTC

Bridgewater House Located in Cleveland Row, by St James's Palace in London, it contained a library begun by Sir Thomas Egerton, Baron Ellesmere, 1st Viscount Brackley (1540–1617), and developed by later generations of the family. It comprised important collections of MSS (including the *Ellesmere Chaucer and the Bridgewater MS of Milton's *Comus*) and printed books. The literary scholar Henry John Todd acted as librarian and sold duplicates from the collection in 1802 and 1804. J. P. *Collier, who forged material among the MSS, published a catalogue of some of the rarer English printed books (1837). The library was sold en bloc in 1917 and is now part of the *Huntington Library.

ASGE

de Ricci

Brienne, Louis-Henri de Loménie, comte de (1636–98) Eccentric French art and book collector, sometime secretary to Jules Mazarin. Having lost Louis XIV's favour, he joined the Oratory in 1664, eventually giving his son the library on which he had spent a staggering £80,000. Expelled in 1670 on moral grounds, he was judged insane and imprisoned by his family at Saint-Lazare. He remained there eighteen years, collecting on a more modest scale and writing his memoirs.

VAG

Brill, E. J. (Evert Jan) (1811–71) Leiden printer, publisher, bookseller, and auctioneer. From his post as head manager of the Leiden publishing house *Luchtmans, he took over the firm in 1848 and continued it under his own name, specializing in classical studies and oriental languages, and acting as university printer. The company still exists today as an international scholarly publishing house.

BPMD

S. van der Veen, *Brill: 325 Years of Scholarly Publishing* (2008)

Brinley, George (1817–75) American book collector. Brinley was an early, sedulous collector of Americana, amassing a major collection of some 12,000 rare volumes. He also owned a *Gutenberg Bible. He gave a large portion of his collection to *Yale; the dispersal of the rest in New York between March 1879 and April 1893 was perhaps the earliest major American book auction.

ASGE

D. B. Engley, 'George Brinley, Americanist', *PBSA* 60 (1966), 465–72

Briot, Nicolaes (*c*.1585?–1626) Dutch punchcutter and typefounder. A Catholic from Huy (Liège), he was probably apprenticed to a Gouda silversmith whose daughter he married (1609). In 1612 he bought a large house there, opened a typefoundry, and copied van den *Keere's *texturas, adding some baroque curls. Briot's Diamant (4 point) was the world's smallest type. He cut *romans (1620s, subsequently influencing van *Dijck's, *Kis's, and *Caslon's), *Greek, and *Arabic, moving to Amsterdam 1624/5. His *Hebrew for *Menasseh set the style for centuries. In the 1670s, Dirck Voskens united the foundries of Jaques Vallet (Briot's workman and eventual successor) and the *Blaeus (Briot's most important patron).

JAL

J. Briels, *Zuidnederlandse Boekdrukkers* (1974)
J. Lane, 'Nicolaes Briot', in *Bibliotheca Rosenthaliana* (1994; corr. repr. 1996)

Briquet, Charles Moïse (1839–1918) Swiss filigranologist who proposed the potential of using *watermarks to date paper. His four-volume work *Les Filigranes* (1907; 2e, 1923) contains more than 16,000 illustrations, ranging from late 13th- to early 17th-century examples. A standard work for dating early European papers, it is the largest compilation of watermark images ever published. His books were reprinted by the *Paper Publications Society, including a new edition of *Les Filigranes* edited by *Stevenson (1968). *See also* **10**.

DCC

British Academy Established by Royal Charter in 1902, this self-governing fellowship of scholars elected for their academic distinction in the humanities and social sciences supports postdoctoral research, promotes the interests of scholarship, and has an active publications programme, maintaining a publishing partnership with *Oxford University Press.

KL

British and Foreign Bible Society (BFBS) Founded in 1804 and jointly sponsored by Evangelicals and Nonconformists, the BFBS initially provided affordable bibles for Welsh-speakers. Its work expanded during the 19th century to produce and distribute translations and cheap editions of bibles, Testaments, and *psalters in Britain and throughout the world. During its first 50 years, it distributed nearly 16 million bibles and Testaments in English alone, through networks of voluntary 'auxiliary' societies, branches, and associations. With the Society's financial support, translations were undertaken and disseminated by individual missionaries and mission networks. The BFBS continues to operate as the Bible Society, part of the larger United Bible Societies. Its library and *archives, including the collection of bibles catalogued by T. H. Darlow and H. F. Moule (1903–11; English section rev. A. S. Herbert, 1961), are housed in *Cambridge University Library. *See also* **9**, **20**, **37**, **39**.

JES

CHBB 5
G. Browne, *The History of the British and Foreign Bible Society* (2 vols, 1859)

British Book News Bibliographical and book trade *magazine. Published 1940–93, it began as an annotated book listing, produced by the National Book Council (the *National Book League from 1944). The *British Council, which applauded the appearance of this 'Monthly Book List', later become its publisher. The magazine's remit was to inform the world about British books and encourage exports: early issues were subtitled *A Guide to Books Published in the Commonwealth and Empire*. In subsequent decades, it offered lengthier reviews, company profiles, and industry news.   CMS

Anon., 'Thanking the Cat', *British Book News* (1993), 762–3

British Books in Print Bibliographical publication, founded by J. *Whitaker and Sons in 1874 as *The Reference Catalogue of British Literature*. Covering British books and English-language titles published in Europe, it provided comprehensive bibliographical details from information made available by publishers. In the 20th century, microfiche and *CD-ROM versions were published. Over the decades, it documented rising title output as well as the *backlist. With the advent of *EPOS systems, it allowed the continual updating of sales data, which could be categorized, thus improving the accuracy and changing the use of *bestseller lists.   CMS

British Broadcasting Corporation (BBC) The development of television in the 1960s led to the Corporation becoming a commercial publisher. The BBC has published a variety of bestsellers—including Kenneth Clark's *Civilisation* (1969, published jointly with J. *Murray), and Jacob Bronowski's *The Ascent of Man* (1973)—as well as many other books to accompany television series, e.g. titles by Delia Smith and David Attenborough. In 2006 *Random House bought a majority stake in the company.   AGP

British Council The UK's international organization for educational opportunities and cultural relations, founded in 1934 to build mutually beneficial relationships between people in the UK and other countries, and to increase appreciation of the UK's creative ideas and achievements. It is an executive non-departmental public body in the UK, sponsored by the Foreign and Commonwealth Office.

Working in 109 countries around the world, the British Council's main activities are teaching English and exporting British culture by setting up international tours of readings, exhibitions, plays, films, and concerts. It has been accused of producing cultural propaganda and participating in cultural imperialism, but also praised for providing a non-commercially driven view of British culture—particularly to parts of the developing world—and for providing an alternative to the homogenized MTV-culture that might otherwise represent the West.   SD

www.britishcouncil.org/home, consulted June 2006

British Library (BL) Established in London on 1 July 1973. Before this date, the British national collections of MSS and printed books had been part of the British Museum since the foundation of the British Museum library with the purchase of Sir H. *Sloane's collection in 1753 for £20,000. The *Cotton collection of MSS, bequeathed to the nation in 1700, was then brought into the new institution—originally Montagu House, a 17th-century Bloomsbury mansion in Portman Square—and the Harleian collection of MSS was purchased for £10,000 (*see* HARLEY, ROBERT). In 1757, King George II donated the Old Royal Library and conferred on the British Museum the privilege of receiving all copyrighted materials. From the outset, its collections belonged to the nation and were available for consultation by 'all studious and curious Persons'. In 1823, George IV donated the King's Library (a collection of 65,000 printed volumes and other materials that was the library of *George III, now housed in a four-storey glass-walled tower in the middle of the BL), which prompted the construction of the new Museum in Great Russell Street. The British Museum library continued to grow throughout the 19th century, most especially under *Panizzi's visionary and combative leadership. Librarians and scholars who worked on the staff of the British Museum and British Library include *Douce, *Madden, E. M. *Thompson, A. W. *Pollard, *Proctor, *Scholderer, *Nixon, *Alston, Foxon, N. *Barker, and M. *Foot.

The British Library, as established in 1973, included all the library departments of the British Museum library: Printed Books, Manuscripts, Music, and Newspapers, and their separate collections. The Manuscripts Department included all the individual MS collections, those formed by Thomas *Howard, earl of Arundel (the Arundel MSS), *Burney, *Egerton, Francis Hargrave, *Petty (the Lansdowne MSS), *Cotton, the Harleys, Sloane, *Wise (the Ashley MSS), and Yates *Thompson, as well as the Royal, Stowe, and Additional MS collections. Only the Additional and Egerton collections are open MS collections to which additions continue to be made.

The BL also contains the national collections of printed books, including the King's Library and the libraries of *Grenville (originally housed in magnificent purpose-built rooms) and Joseph Banks as well as the printed books bequeathed by Burney and Sloane together with their MSS, the *Private Case, and numerous smaller collections, such as *Garrick's plays. The music collections, both MS and print, are part of Rare Books. Most of the printed books form part of the general collection. As the chief *copyright library in England, the BL is the only one entitled to receive automatically a copy of every printed book and all material in other media. It acquires about 3 million items a year via *legal deposit. The newspaper collections are housed separately, at Colindale, north London.

Since its establishment, the BL has also come to include the former National Reference Library of Science and Invention; the National Central Library; the National Lending Library for Science and Technology; the British National Bibliography; the Asia, Pacific and Africa Collections, formerly the collections of the India Office Library; and the National Philatelic Collections, this last a major research source of over 8 million items. Since

Before the **British Library**: stacks in the British Museum's iron library at Bloomsbury from an 1878 print. The curve of the outside of the Round Reading Room is visible on the left; on the right, the steps and book trolley are part of the *library equipment.

1983, the National Sound Archive has been part of the main library. In total, the contents of the library amount to more than 150 million items in many languages.

In 1997, the BL moved from the British Museum buildings in Great Russell Street to its own purpose-built premises on the Euston Road, St Pancras, designed by Colin St John Wilson. The largest public building built in the UK in the 20th century, it was surrounded by controversy because of delays, cost overruns, criticisms of the design, and a resistence to leaving the Great Russell Street site. Moving from Bloomsbury entailed the loss of a symbol of English intellectual life; the heart of the old British Museum library was the celebrated round reading room (designed by Sydney Smirke and constructed 1854–7) in which many famous figures had studied. In the new building, there are more reading rooms in which specific print materials can be consulted, for Humanities, Social Science, Science, Maps, and Asian and African Studies. As in the old BL library, there are also separate reading rooms for MSS and for Rare Books (the latter is combined with Music, including music MSS). The library, which can accommodate 1,200 readers, also has a major exhibition area, the Sir John Ritblat Gallery, and a Centre for Conservation. There is a public-access online catalogue (*see* WORLD WIDE WEB); in addition, some items from the Library's holdings can also be examined on line. There are also reading rooms at Colindale, for newspapers, including both British and foreign collections, and at Boston Spa in Yorkshire, for reference materials, where there is also the Document Supply Centre.

One of the world's greatest libraries, the BL holds many world heritage and national treasures, including the *Diamond Sutra, the *Beowulf MS, *Magna Carta, the Sultan *Baybars' Qur'ān, the *Lindisfarne Gospels, the *Stonyhurst Gospel, the *Winchester MS of Sir Thomas Malory's Arthurian stories, the Golden Haggadah, a *notebook of Leonardo da Vinci, editions of the *Gutenberg Bible, editions of The *Canterbury Tales printed by *Caxton, multiple copies of the Shakespeare *First Folio, a sumptuous illustrated MS of the Sanskrit epic *Rāmāyaṇa*, the MS of Handel's *Messiah*, and the MS of *Alice's Adventures in Wonderland*.

The BL as currently constituted is in all important respects a great advance over its previous embodiments. The Library provides the world's largest document delivery service, providing millions of items to readers all over the globe, and its website (on which a number of its treasures can be viewed) had some 67 million visitors in 2006; in addition, more than 16,000 people use the library each day. Yet, its existence as a relatively new library on a new site also embodies the huge problems that confront any major research library. Large questions remain concerning such matters as conservation, preservation and storage, access, and security. How these questions are answered will determine the continued success of this institution so central to the intellectual life of Great Britain. ASGE

www.bl.uk, consulted June 2008

P. R. Harris, ed., *A History of the British Museum Library, 1753–1973* (1998)

British Library (**publisher**) Since its creation in 1973, the British Library has published a range of titles under its own *imprint and in association with other publishers, such as *Oak Knoll Press. Largely based on its own collections, the imprint specializes in bibliographies, book history, reference works, and illustrated books, ranging from lavish *facsimiles of medieval MSS to the pocket guides in the 'Treasures in Focus' series.

MHC

British Library Centre for the Book Established in 1990. As its executive secretary, Michael J. Crump, stated in 1992, the Centre was conceived as a means both of promoting 'the significance of the book, in all its forms' and of illustrating the role of the book 'as a vital part of the cultural, academic, scientific and commercial life' of Britain. Additionally, the Centre seeks to promote thinking about the part emerging technologies play in the future of the book. Visiting fellows and an array of educational events—including lecture series, seminars, and an annual conference—are intended to expand the influence of the Centre and of the *British Library, in order to engage the wider community. *See also* LIBRARY OF CONGRESS CENTER FOR THE BOOK.   PDF

M. J. Crump, 'The Centre for the Book', *English Today*, 30 (1992), 3–8

British Museum *See* BRITISH LIBRARY; PRINTS AND DRAWINGS, DEPARTMENT OF (BRITISH MUSEUM).

British National Bibliography (BNB) The national bibliography of the British Isles, begun in 1950 to support library cataloguing, book selection, and reference work. Each issue lists titles—arranged by *Dewey decimal classification and catalogued by Anglo-American cataloguing rules—of books, serials, and (since 2003) electronic publications newly published in the UK and Republic of Ireland received by the *British Library under *legal deposit, and provides information about forthcoming titles. The BNB excludes straightforward reprints, the second and subsequent issues of serials, works published exclusively for a foreign market, research reports and non-trade monographs, some official publications, some local material (e.g. *telephone directories), promotional material, and such forms as *large-print books and ephemera. It is published weekly in print and electronically, with a monthly *CD-ROM and an annual cumulation. The final issue of each month includes a cumulated subject index. The distributor is the British Library, although since 1991 all six legal deposit libraries in the UK and Ireland have shared the cataloguing.   KEA

BL, 'The British National Bibliography', www.bl.uk/services/bibliographic/natbib.html, consulted Aug. 2006

A. Stephens, 'The Establishment of the British National Bibliography', in *Eating the Menus*, ed. R. Bourne (1989)

Brito, Francisco de Paula (1809–61) Brazilian publisher. Self-educated and of mixed race, he worked in Rio de Janeiro 1831–61, becoming Brazil's leading publisher. He was especially supportive of Brazilian authors, offering them every assistance in addition to publication.   DRW

E. R. Gondim, *Vida e Obra de Paula Brito* (1965)

Britwell Court *See* MILLER, WILLIAM HENRY.

broadsheet A newspaper consisting of large, folded sheets ($c.29.5 \times c.23.5$ in.), printed on both sides; often considered to contain more serious journalism than commonly found in a *tabloid. The Berliner format—between these two in size ($c.18.5 \times c.12.5$ in.)—is employed by a number of European newspapers.   MFS

broadside A sheet of paper, printed on one side only. The broadside is the most primitive and immediate application of the printing press: any small amount of matter, such as might be wanted on a poster or public notice, could be printed satisfactorily with a minimum of movable type, and without the skills required in *perfecting a sheet. Because the text of a broadside is usually considered purely ephemeral, its chances of survival are small. Among the earliest broadsides are royal proclamations. Publication had hitherto been achieved viva voce by town criers, but printed copies ensured an accurate publication of the official will in a form that could be consulted when necessary. De *Machlinia, succeeded by de *Worde, was printing English royal proclamations at least from 1486.

Tradesmen and shopkeepers are likely to have ordered printed advertisements wherever a press was established. The remarkable survival of copies of *Caxton's own advertisement for his edition of the Sarum *Ordinale* (1477) shows how fragile such broadsides were. Consisting of merely a few lines in one of his standard book types, poorly justified and making no appeal to the eye, it concludes with a request (in Latin) not to pull the modest fly-bill down. In the greater centres of 15th-century book production, broadside 'publishers' lists' were issued by printers such as *Koberger of Nuremberg.

The needs of the Church and its local representatives accounted for a large part of the output of all early printers. In addition to liturgical books, every church and religious house would require an annual calendar with the dates of the movable feasts (the *ciclus*). The broadside format enabled such a calendar to be pinned or pasted up for easy reference. *Block-printed calendars were probably produced long before those printed from movable types, but not one has survived of either kind. The printing of *indulgences, the trade in which increased greatly during the later 15th and early 16th centuries, kept printers busy from *Gutenberg onwards; examples (mostly fragmentary) are among the earliest surviving *incunabula. They are usually in oblong broadside form; and, perhaps to show that the effect of an indulgence was considered not ephemeral, some were printed on vellum.

The market for popular literature in the 15th and 16th centuries was large and profitable to printers, but prices could be kept low only by reducing paper and printing costs. Some of the earliest printed ballads were substantial pamphlets, and beyond the range of many potential customers. The bestsellers (apart from *almanacs) were broadside *ballads, either the shorter traditional ballads or newly composed poems in ballad style on topical subjects. English broadsides of the 16th century also include verse dialogues encouraging patriotism and reproving sedition and discontent. Some broadsides are versified sermons against slander and cheating; others reflect on the rise and fall of political figures such as Wolsey and Richard Cromwell. Flytings, squabbles in verse between poets and their factions, also appear as broadsheets—

presumably an early form of *vanity publishing. The rich variety of early broadside matter includes advice on diet, health, and how to succeed in business; tables of weights and measures; agreed fares for carters and watermen; notices of lotteries; prayers recommended for use during a national emergency; laments for a king (Edward VI); 'last words' of condemned felons; and handbills advertising performances of a play, with a summary of the plot.

From 1557, the *Stationers' Company had official control over this trade, but fewer than half the surviving broadsides of this period appear to have been registered. Very few could be construed as seditious or even seriously critical of authority, although at least one piece of recusant propaganda appeared (unregistered) as an 'old ballad'. The clandestine presses in any case generally aimed at a more influential audience than the buyers of halfpenny and penny broadsides. After the *censorship of the Star Chamber and the subsequent constraints of the Commonwealth had ended, the publication of political satire (even if obscurely expressed) was possible, and broadside 'squibs' and parodies became common. When a printer set up shop in a provincial centre, his first publications apart from sermons were likely to be broadsides: election addresses, public notices, or verses to celebrate a local event. Of the latter, a few copies were sometimes worked off as an edition *de luxe on silk rather than paper.

The broadside survived strongly into the 19th century, but letterpress *posters and *playbills finally succumbed to *lithography, despite the ingenuity of the letterfounders in producing eye-catching poster types. Those with something to tell the world generally found the *pamphlet a more effective medium than the broadside. The broadside is however far from extinct, and has often been revived by amateur and *private presses as a display of typographical style and skill.   BJF

Brocar, Arnao Guillén de (d. 1523) Spanish printer. Brocar printed at Pamplona (1490), then Logroño (1502), before moving to Alcalá de Henares (1511). There he printed the *Complutensian Bible and various humanist works under the patronage of Cardinal *Jiménez de Cisneros.   DRW

J. Martín Abad, *La Imprenta en Alcalá* (1991)

Brockhaus, F. A. German encyclopaedia publishing house. In 1805, Friedrich Arnold Brockhaus (1772–1823) started publishing in Amsterdam; the company was relocated to Altenburg in 1811, and moved in 1817 to Leipzig, where Brockhaus also established a large, well-equipped printing house. In 1808 he purchased the copyright of the uncompleted *Conversations-Lexikon*, which achieved sustained success in many editions during the 19th century. Besides encyclopaedias, the company published periodicals, historical books, and scientific works. After World War II, a corporate branch was founded in Wiesbaden, but was absorbed into the Leipzig operation in 1992. The firm continues to be a major publisher of encyclopaedias and other reference works.   US

T. Keiderling, ed., *F. A. Brockhaus 1905–2005* (2005)

Brockman, James (1946–) English craft bookbinder and conservator, president of *Designer Bookbinders (1985–7). He studied with I. *Robinson and worked with S. *Cockerell (1906–87) before establishing his own bindery in 1976. His work combines the highest-quality craftsmanship with a penchant for experimenting with structures and visual effects, and will be found in most major collections of contemporary fine bindings.   DRSP

'Fellows of Designer Bookbinders', *New Bookbinder*, 25 (2005), 35

Brokgauz & Efron (active 1889–1930) Founded in St Petersburg by the printer I. A. Efron and the German firm F. A. Brokgauz in order to produce an encyclopaedic dictionary, the multi-volume *Entsiklopedicheskii slovar'* (1890–1907; facsimile, 1990–93), still among Russia's most reputable reference sources. It subsequently published several encyclopaedias, including a sixteen-volume *Jewish Encyclopedia* and a five-volume *Encyclopedia of Practical Medicine*. The firm also published a large-format illustrated series of Russian and foreign classics, popular educational books, and, in the 1920s, illustrated works of literature by distinguished contemporary authors.   CGT

S. V. Belov, 'Brokgauza i Efrona Izdatel'stvo', in *Kniga: entsiklopediia*, ed. V. M. Zharkov (1999)

Brotherton Library, Leeds Named after the university library's outstanding benefactor, the local industrialist Lord Brotherton of Wakefield (1856–1930), the library opened in 1936. It is now one of the largest UK academic libraries, especially important for the arts and humanities; it houses the university library's main arts and social sciences collections, including its rare books, MSS, and *archives. It is most famous for the Brotherton Collection itself, composed of Lord Brotherton's private library, assembled through remarkable collecting activity in the 1920s. Brotherton's endowment ensured the future development of his collection, and in the postwar period, the university concentrated on expanding the already substantial holdings of English poetry and drama, 1600–1750. English literature has continued to dominate collection development in recent years; the holdings of 19th- and 20th-century literary and theatrical archives are now a major strength.   OSP

Bloomfield, *Directory*

Brown, John Carter (1797–1874) American book collector. Brown, who lived in Providence, Rhode Island, particularly collected literature connected with American history and early exploration in the Western world. Since 1901, his library has been an independent research centre at Brown University. The *John Carter Brown Library now contains over 45,000 rare books, chiefly in the fields of its founder's interests.   ASGE

L. Wroth, *The First Century of the John Carter Brown Library* (1946)

Brown, William (c.1737–89) First printer in Quebec, arriving in 1764 from Philadelphia with Thomas Gilmore. Printing in French, English, Latin, and Native languages,

he dominated the trades, as did his nephews and successors, Samuel and John *Neilson, among whose papers Brown's records are held. PLF
DCB

Browne, Hablot Knight (1815–82) English artist famous as 'Phiz', illustrator of the best-known fictional works of Dickens, Charles Lever, and Harrison Ainsworth. Browne took over as illustrator for Dickens's first serial, *The Pickwick Papers* (1836–7), following the suicide of Robert Seymour. Over 23 years, he became Dickens's foremost illustrator and graphic interpreter, his *Hogarthian style a perfect match for Dickens's satire. Of this work, his finest illustrations (*see* **16**) are for *Pickwick, Martin Chuzzlewit* (1843–4), *Dombey and Son* (1846–8), *David Copperfield* (1850), and *Bleak House* (1852–3). The early success of *Pickwick* ensured Browne's reputation, and he was much in demand with book and magazine publishers until he suffered a stroke in 1867. His output numbers more than 3,660 images—mostly steel *etchings and some wood *engravings—ranging from the visual satire of his illustrations for Dickens and Lever to some startlingly sinister experimental compositions for Ainsworth. NG
ODNB

Brown University Library Of the seven facilities that make up the Brown University Library, the John D. Rockefeller, Jr. Library is its primary research centre for the humanities, social sciences, and fine arts. Special Collections, which includes 2.5 million items ranging from Babylonian clay *tablets to Napoleon's hair, are housed at the John Hay Library. The library also holds the world's largest collection of American poetry and plays. MDB
www.brown.edu/Facilities/University_Library/libs/hay/history/hist1.htm, consulted Nov. 2007

Bruccoli, Matthew J. (1931–) American scholar and bibliographer. An expert in 20th-century American literature, he has published extensively on F. Scott Fitzgerald, including a descriptive bibliography (1972), and editions of the notebooks (1978) and correspondence (1980, with Margaret M. Duggan). He has also published bibliographies of John O'Hara (1975), James Gould Cozzens (1981), and James Dickey (1990), and *A Bibliography of American Fiction, 1919–1988* (with Judith S. Baughman, 1991). VAG

Bruce, Jr., David (1802–92) New York *punchcutter and inventor. After working for the typefoundries of his father, David (1770–1857), and uncle George Bruce (1781–1866), and others, he developed the first successful typecasting machines (patented 1838 and 1843). He wrote a history of American typefounding. JAL

Brugalla, Emilio (1902–85) Bookbinder. Paris-trained, he returned to his native Barcelona and became the leading Spanish binder and restorer of the 20th century, making craft bindings that were exhibited and collected

across Europe, and raising the status of binding within Spain. After his death, his son Santiago continued the business. DRSP
E. Brugalla, *El Arte en el Libro y en la Encuadernacion* (1977)
P. Smith, 'Emilio Brugalla', *Designer Bookbinders Newsletter*, 59 (1987), 2–3

Brunei Darussalam The National Library of Brunei Darussalam is still being planned. The Library of the Dewan Bahasa dan Pustaka (Language and Literature Bureau), opened 1970, holds the Bruneiana collection and performs some functions of a national library. The Brunei Museum library acts as the *legal deposit library. HC
www.library.gov.bn, consulted June 2008

Brunet, Jacques-Charles (1780–1867) French bibliographer. The son of a Parisian bookseller, he issued a three-volume *Manuel du libraire et de l'amateur de livres* (1810) which set new standards for bibliographical description and remains a frequently quoted source. His expanded, six-volume 5th edition (1860–65)—incorporating his 1834 *Nouvelles recherches bibliographiques*—is available in several modern reprints and a CD-ROM edition. Brunet's own library was dispersed at auction in 1868. VAG

Bruun Rasmussen Leading Danish auction house, the largest in Scandinavia, founded in 1948 at Copenhagen. Auctions of fine books and MSS are held regularly, and also conducted via the Internet. CA, KSP

Bry, Theodore de (1528–98) Engraver, publisher, and bookseller born in Liège. A Protestant, he moved to Strasbourg (1560–86), then Frankfurt (1589–98). While visiting England (*c.*1586–9), he engraved *maps for *The Mariners Mirrour* (*c.*1590) and *plates (after John White's designs) for Thomas Hariot's *Briefe and True Report of the New Found Land of Virginia* (Frankfurt, 1590). Through these, and similar engravings after J. Le Moyne, de Bry significantly shaped the European view of the costumes and customs of indigenous North Americans. Other work includes plates for topographical and *emblem books. JCI
ODNB

Brydges, Sir (Samuel) **Egerton** (1762–1837) English writer, critic, and genealogist. He revived the memory of forgotten authors, especially Tudor and Caroline poets, by publishing abstracts and criticism. At his *private press at Lee Priory (1813–23), he reprinted more than 30 rare works. He reinstated Aphra Behn and Margaret Cavendish, duchess of Newcastle, among others. Brydges was a founding member of the *Roxburghe Club. KEA
ODNB
M. K. Woodworth, *The Literary Career of Sir Samuel Egerton Brydges* (1935)

bubble-jet printer An *ink-jet printer using heat to make ink bubbles. Expanding air inside the bubbles causes droplets to form and eject from the print-head to make patterns (usually letters) on the page.

Büchergilde Gutenberg German book club founded in Leipzig in 1924 by German printers, who aimed at the distribution of low-priced books of literary and typographic value. During the Third Reich, the left-wing Büchergilde could only work in Switzerland. It was re-founded in 1947 as a subsidiary company of the German Trade Union Congress in Frankfurt. Taking up *book art and craft traditions, it won numerous awards for book design. In 1988 the Büchergilde was sold to its employees, who carry on a sophisticated publication programme. Today, it has about 130,000 members.

ME

U. van Melis, *Buchgemeinschaften in der Weimarer Republik* (2002)

buckram A *bookcloth commonly used to cover book-bindings from the late 19th century onwards, made from cotton or linen, closely woven, and coated with starch or a similar substance. Its durability and ability to take impressed designs led to its widespread use. DRSP

Buildwas The abbey of SS Mary and Chad at Buildwas in Shropshire was founded in 1135. A substantial number of books were produced there in the 12th and 13th centuries; more survive than for any other English Cistercian house. ASGE

J. M. Sheppard, *The Buildwas Books*, OBS 3/2 (1997)

Būlāq Press The state press of Egypt, founded in 1819–20. It was the first major printer and publisher in the Muslim Arab world, and from 1822 onwards produced many important editions of Arabic and Turkish texts. Some were translations of European scientific and historical works, but classical literary and educational texts also appeared, and helped to further the Arab cultural revival. New writers similarly benefited from print publication. Typographic styles long followed traditional MS models, with imitations of *naskh* hands, cramped page layouts with ruled borders, and sometimes marginal commentaries. From the 1890s more modern typographic norms were adopted. GJR

Bulgaria, Central Library of the Academy of Sciences of The origins of the library can be traced to 1869, when the library of the Bulgarian Learned Society in Braila, Romania, was created. Following Bulgaria's independence in 1878, the library moved to Sofia and, in 1911, was renamed the Library of the Bulgarian Academy of Sciences. The library is responsible for managing the network of 47 special libraries of the Bulgarian Academy of Sciences, with total holdings of 2 million items. Of particular significance are the private collections of some 50 prominent individuals, which are held separately.

MVG

Bulgaria, National Library of (Narodna biblioteka 'Sv. Sv. Kiril i Metodii') Named after Saints Cyril and Methodius, it was founded in 1878 (when Bulgaria became an independent state) as the Sofia Public Library. The largest research and *legal deposit library in the country, it holds an estimated 6.8 million items. The collection of Slavonic and Western medieval and modern MSS, which includes 1,700 items, is particularly rich. The collection of rare books, numbering 32,000 volumes, amply represents Bulgarian publishing from 1806 to 1878. The library also holds 1.5 million items of archival material from the Bulgarian National Revival until 1912. MVG

Bulgarska Vuzrozhdenska Knizhnina General term for Bulgarian books and periodicals published between 1806 and 1878 as part of the national revival. Comprising *textbooks, religious books, *translations, and original fiction, the revival literature included contributions by such prominent authors as Neofit Rilski, Joakim Gruev, K. G. *Danov, Khristo Botev, and Ivan Vazov. Important editorial centres were Tsarigrad (Istanbul), Vienna, Belgrade, Braila, and Bucharest. About 100 journal titles appeared in this period, including the first Bulgarian periodical, *Liuboslovie* (founded 1844). RK

Bullen, A. H. (Arthur Henry) (1857–1920) British literary editor and publisher. In the 1880s his modernized editions of lesser-known Elizabethan authors included both dramatists and poets. He published in partnership with H. W. Lawrence from 1891 and under the *imprint of the Shakespeare Head Press from 1904, acquiring a name for the quality of his books, their scholarly value, and his sympathetic treatment of authors such as Gissing and Yeats. GL
ODNB

Bullen, Henry Lewis (1857–1938) Australian-born American printer, scholar, collector, and librarian of the *American Type Founders Company. Credited with successfully promoting the history of important type designers, Lewis wrote about key figures (*Jenson, *Garamont), collected for himself and the ATF Library, and worked with scholars such as *Rogers, *Morison, and B. *Warde. MMS

D. W. Mallison, 'Henry Lewis Bullen and the Typographic Library and Museum of the American Type Founders Company', Doctor of Library Science thesis (Columbia University, 1976)

Bulletin, The Established at Sydney, Australia, in 1880, *The Bulletin* circulated throughout Australia and New Zealand, promoting the bush-balladist 'literary larrikins' of the 1890s as the authentic voice of Australia. Since the 1960s it has been primarily a news magazine. IM

Bulletin du bibliophile Oldest bibliophilic journal still active. The Paris-based review was founded in 1834 by *Nodier and later became the monthly *Bulletin du bibliophile et du bibliothécaire*. Now a quarterly, it is published by the Éditions du *Cercle de la Librairie and has been sponsored since 1965 by the Association internationale de bibliophilie, the organization created in

1963 by Julien Cain and the Friends of the Bibliothèque nationale. It features scholarly articles (in both French and English) on the history of the book in all its aspects, as well as reviews of current events or publications.

VAG

Bulmer, William (1757–1830) English printer. In 1790, Bulmer established the Shakspeare Press. His London company printed in William Martin's *typeface several distinctive *folios, including the works of *Shakespeare and Milton, and *Boydell's *History of the River Thames* with coloured *aquatints (1794–6). Appointed printer to the Royal Society in 1791, Bulmer's productions ranged from sixteen books for the *Roxburghe Club—perhaps the first *book club—to *pamphlets and *auction catalogues.

KAM
ODNB

Bungei Shunjū Tokyo publisher, founded in 1923 by the literary author Kikuchi Hiroshi (1888–1948) with the publication of the monthly journal *Bungei Shunjū*. The firm also publishes general and literary magazines such as *Bungakukai* and *Shokun*. In 1935 the company created the *Akutagawa Prize and the Naoki Prize, which became gateways to success for literary authors. Bungei Shunjū also publishes monographs.

YHM
[Bungei Shunjū,] *Bungei Shunjū Shichijūnenshi* (2 vols, 1991–4)

Burden, Carter (1941–96) American book collector and businessman. Burden assembled a collection of American literature from 1880 to the present, amounting to 80,000 items, including books, MSS, and ephemera (*see* **14**). After his sudden death, the bulk of his collection went to the *Pierpont Morgan Library.

ASGE
C. Burden, 'Collecting Modern American Literature in the 1980s and Beyond', in *Rare Book and Manuscript Libraries in the Twenty-First Century*, ed. R. Wendorf (1993)

Burgkmair, Hans (1473–1531) German painter and designer of *woodcuts. Court painter to Emperor *Maximilian I in Augsburg, Burgkmair may have studied with Martin Schongauer. He learned to design (and perhaps cut woodcuts) in *Ratdolt's workshop, and designed illustrations (*see* **16**) especially for Heinrich Stainer, including biblical images, series depicting the virtues, coats of arms, and *ornaments. He was a principal designer for Maximilian's ambitious programme to preserve his glory, including the unpublished *Genealogy of the House of Habsburg*, the *Theuerdank, Der Weißkunig*, and the *Triumph of Maximilian I* (for which he designed about half of the extant images).

MMS

Burne-Jones, Sir Edward (1833–98) English Pre-Raphaelite artist and decorative arts designer. His reputation as an illustrator rests on his designs for W. *Morris's *Kelmscott Press Chaucer (1896), one of the finest books of the 19th century; it epitomizes the artistic aims of both Morris and Burne-Jones.

JCI
ODNB

Burney, Charles (1757–1817) English book collector, educated at Gonville and Caius College, Cambridge and at King's College, Aberdeen. He became a teacher and later took orders. His library comprised over 13,500 printed books and 500 MSS, mainly of classical works, but also including newspapers and works on the history of the English stage. It was acquired by the British Museum in 1818 for £13,500.

ASGE
ODNB

Burnham Bookstore Boston antiquarian bookseller, established before 1830 by Thomas Burnham and greatly expanded for more than 50 years by his son, Thomas Oliver Hazard Perry Burnham (1813–91). At the younger Burnham's death, three employees purchased his stock at auction. Two of them took over the business, one of whom (Richard Lichtenstein) continued in the trade after the partnership was dissolved in 1908.

SEC
M. B. Stern, *Antiquarian Bookselling in the United States* (1985)

Burns & Oates English publishers. Following his conversion in 1847, the London bookseller James Burns (1808–71) rapidly became a leading publisher of Roman Catholic writers (including J. H. Newman and F. W. Faber). In 1867 he entered partnership with William Oates (d. 1876). Their *imprint, reinvigorated by the creative management (1903–19) of Wilfrid Meynell, has survived several changes of ownership. *See also* MEYNELL, SIR FRANCIS.

RJD
DLB 106

Bursa Library of MSS and Old Printed Works, Turkey Following the 1948 reorganization of dervish convent and foundation libraries in Bursa, the İnebey Medrese was restored to host the Ottoman MSS (over 8,000) and old printed books in Arabic script, including Turkish *incunabula and volumes printed abroad. It is the third biggest library of its kind in Turkey.

SYM

Burt Co., A. L. (active 1883–1937) US publisher of popular fiction. In the 19th century, Burt published inexpensive paperbound library series, including 'Burt's Home Library' (classic texts for family reading) and 'Boy's Home Library' (*dime novels for young readers by authors such as Horatio Alger). In the 20th century, Burt shifted to the hardbound reprint trade, publishing out-of-*copyright and authorized *popular editions of novels by Augusta Evans Wilson, Zane Gray, and Harold Bell Wright, among others.

MJH
C. Grannis, 'A. L. Burt Company', in *Publishers for Mass Entertainment in Nineteenth Century America*, ed. M. B. Stern (1980)

Burton, Sir Richard (1821–90) English explorer, translator, orientalist, travel writer. He left Oxford without a degree, joined the Indian army, visited and wrote about the forbidden cities of Mecca and Herar, discovered Lake Tanganyika while searching for the Nile's source, held consulships at Fernando Po (West Africa), Santos (Brazil), Damascus, and Trieste. He co-founded the Anthropological Society of London (1863). Burton wrote *The Book of the Sword* (1884), translated Luis de Camões's *Lusiads* (2 vols, 1880) and the **Thousand Nights and One Night* (16 vols, 1885–8), and helped found the Kama Shastra Society (of London and, allegedly, Benares (Varanasi)) in 1882 which published the **Kamasutra* (1883; widely pirated) and other books deemed *pornography, such as *Ananga-ranga* (1885) and *The Perfumed Garden of the Cheikh Nefzaoui* (1886).

EBL

J. A. Casada, *Sir Richard F. Burton: A Bibliographical Study* (1990)
ODNB

Burton, Robert (1577–1640) English author and book collector. As his *Anatomy of Melancholy* attests, Burton was a wide-ranging reader. He assembled a large personal library, of which approximately 1,700 titles can now be identified. His will gave first choice of his books to the **Bodleian Library and then to **Christ Church, Oxford, where he had served as librarian. ASGE

N. K. Kiessling, *The Library of Robert Burton*, OBS, NS 22 (1988)
ODNB

Bury, Richard (1287–1345) Bishop of Durham and book collector. Best known as the author of *Philobiblon* (*The Love of Books*)—possibly the earliest study of book collecting—Bury had a large personal library. After his death, five cartloads of his MSS were reportedly sold by his executors. ASGE

R. Bury, *Philobiblon*, ed. and tr. E. C. Thomas (1888)
J. de Ghellinck, 'Un évêque bibliophile au XIVe siècle: Richard d'Aungerville', *Revue d'histoire ecclésiastique*, 18 (1922), 271–312, 482–508
ODNB

Bury Bible Cambridge, Corpus Christi College, MS 2 was originally a two-volume Latin Bible, but only a fragment of the second volume now survives (in private hands). This large and elaborately decorated MS was commissioned *c.*1135 by a sacrist, 'Hervey', of the abbey at Bury St Edmunds, and was illuminated by a versatile artist known only as Master Hugo (*c.*1130–*c.*1150). His illustrations (*see* **16**) are distinguished by the 'damp fold', clinging style of their draperies, a technique that he may have introduced into England. ASGE

R. M. Thomson, *The Bury Bible* (2001)

Busch, Wilhelm (1832–1908) German painter and poet, famous for his satirical tales in rhymed verses with serial cartoons, sometimes believed to be predecessors of 20th-century *comics. He was extremely successful in satirical journals (*Fliegende Blätter, Münchner Bilderbogen*). His most famous book *Max und Moritz* (1865) has been translated into more than 40 languages. Though often considered children's books (*see* **15**), his works, exhibiting deep Schopenhauerian pessimism and agnosticism, also address adults. Public disregard of his paintings fuelled his pessimism, and he often mocked philistine hypocrisy and mendacity. WDL

G. Ueding, *Wilhelm Busch: das 19. Jahrhundert en miniature* (1986)

Bushell, John (1715–61) Nova Scotia printer. He operated the first press in Canada, printing the *Halifax Gazette* no. 1 (23 March 1752), which is considered Canada's earliest *imprint. Bushell cut *ornaments found in Boston printing of the 1730s and 1740s and in his own work. PLF
DCB

business directories General lists of the names, addresses, and occupations of town dwellers, sometimes including topographical or historical information. Directories first appeared in Britain towards the end of the 17th century; many were speculative ventures by publishers responding to increases in the volume of trade. In provincial towns, directories developed from register office lists. The first surviving directory, Samuel Lee's *A Collection of the Names of Merchants Living In and About the City of London* (1677), was arranged alphabetically and dealt largely with the wholesale trade. No more directories are known until 1734; Mortimer's *Universal Director* (1763) organized entries according to trade, but this innovation was only generally adopted after 1820. The first half of the 19th century saw rapid growth in the directory market. The *Post Office Annual Directory* was first published in 1801; other important publishers (William Robson, James Pigot) produced competing works in the 1820s and 30s. Frederic Kelly, then Inspector of Inland Letter Carriers, acquired the copyright of the *Post Office London Directory* in 1837; directories produced by Kelly & Co. dominated the market, especially in London and the Home Counties, into the 20th century. CL

G. Shaw and A. Tipper, *British Directories*, 2e (1997)

business libraries A special branch of librarianship focusing on materials and reference service, supporting research in economics, public administration, business administration and management, commerce and trade, banks and banking, statistics, industry and industrial management, insurance, accounting, and advertising and marketing. The origins of business libraries can be traced to account-keeping by traders in antiquity as they dealt with variations in existing currencies. Colonialism, mercantilism, and the Industrial Revolution further underscored the need for good record-keeping and the archiving of business-related information. Important contemporary business libraries include the Baker Library at Harvard Business School (*see* HARVARD UNIVERSITY LIBRARY) and the Science Industry Business Library of the *New York Public Library. Reference librarians who specialize in business information services are represented by their own section within the *American Library Association. EDG

Business Reference and Services Section (BRASS) of the American Library Association, www.ala.org/ala/rusa/rusaourassoc/rusasections/brass/brass.htm, consulted July 2007

business newspapers The *Economist* is a business periodical, publishing the latest news about matters financial and commercial. It began in 1843 (*Greg's father was closely involved in it) when it joined the long line of serial business publications extending back to at least 1540. Its mix of tables, charts, and words characterizes it as a specialized publication; its history links it to the start of the business press from which all newspapers sprang. Business newspapers antedate general, political newspapers by decades. Business newspapers were the first newspapers.

Born at Antwerp (or possibly even earlier at Venice), the 16th-century business newspaper was simply a two-column table that conveyed the most elemental business information: prices. The commodity price current printed the sale price of goods at the local market; the exchange rate current tracked the local price of bills of exchange drawn for payment elsewhere. By 1600, one or both of these business newspapers was published weekly at Antwerp, Amsterdam, Frankfurt, Hamburg, Middelburg, Rotterdam, and Venice. Before the end of the next century, two new types of business newspaper and many more cities were added to the list. Bills of entry recorded the commodities entered as imported or exported with the local customs authorities; the marine list noted the arrival and departure of vessels at the local port of entry.

Just as London had supplanted Amsterdam as the premier financial and business centre of Europe by 1700, so too had London become the leader in the publication of business newspapers, a position it was to hold until surpassed by New York early in the 20th century. In 1716, a London merchant could subscribe to as many as seven different locally published business newspapers, all of them delivered to his door, at an annual cost of £6 sterling, which, when adjusted for nearly three centuries of inflation, is the equivalent in today's money of roughly £700 sterling. So dynamic was business publishing during the next century that by 1804 the number of different London business newspapers was up to twelve and the subscription cost equal to £1,010.

The business press originated in the early 16th century, grew in the 17th, and reached its maturity in the 18th. Business newspapers increased in size, from mere slips of paper to full pages, sometimes several pages, printed on both sides. They were published more frequently. Monthly and weekly newspapers were replaced by twice-weekly newspapers. What had been simple lists of names and numbers became more complex and, eventually, required some explanatory text. What had been strictly local in its coverage began to be complemented by news from other places. With business publishing spreading to more cities, local editors copied business information from newspapers published elsewhere. Competition for readers drove many of these changes and sometimes assumed a predatory character. More than one publisher of a London business newspaper awoke to find his content copied, his format stolen, his title hijacked. General-interest newspaper editors discovered that they, too, could expand their readership and increase their profitability by including financial and commercial news that they had all too obviously cribbed from the business press. Although the *Financial Times* (founded 1888) and the *Wall Street Journal* (founded 1889) were still decades in the future, much of that future was at least partly to be seen by the early 19th century in the hands of subscribers, for sale in *stationers' shops, and strewn on the tables of *coffee houses.

The history of two of the earliest London business newspapers—still published in the early 21st century—demonstrates both continuity and change. Initially issued from Edward Lloyd's coffee house sometime before January 1692, *Lloyd's List* is, after the official *London Gazette*, the second oldest continually published newspaper of any kind still produced in the world today. It is a marine list in that its primary function, then as now, is to trace the arrival and departure of merchant ships. The *Course of the Exchange*, started by John Castaing in March 1697, runs third in the same race. Castaing's newspaper was essentially an exchange rate current, but, in response to developments in the London marketplace during the explosive 1690s, he enlarged its coverage beyond exchange rates to include the selling prices of company stocks, bank shares, and government securities. It continues to be published today by the London Stock Exchange as the *Stock Exchange Daily Official List*. In October 2003, the exchange launched an electronic edition of the newspaper called the *Daily Official List* (DOL); in December of the same year, it replaced printed publication with electronic publication. The *Economist* appears in both print and electronic modes.　　　　JJM

J. J. McCusker, 'British Commercial and Financial Journalism before 1800,' in *CHBB* 5
— 'The Demise of Distance,' *AHR* 110 (2005), 295–321
— and C. Gravesteijn, *The Beginnings of Commercial and Financial Journalism* (1991)

Bustamante, Juan de (Rodrigues, João) (1536?–88) A Jesuit from Valencia, he pioneered printing in India. His arrival in Goa (1556) with a printing press was accidental, as it was meant for Abyssinia. The first known book to be printed on his press was Francis Xavier's *Doutrina Christã* (1557). *See also* **9, 39.**　　　　AG

Butler, Samuel (1774–1839) English book collector, headmaster of Shrewsbury School (1798–1836), and bishop of Coventry and Lichfield (1836–9). His library was particularly strong in *editions of the Greek and Latin classics, and included an extensive collection of books printed by *Aldus. His books were dispersed in three sales at *Christie's in 1840 and 1841. The MSS were bought for the British Museum library (*see* BRITISH LIBRARY), and are now BL Add. MSS 11828–12117.

　　　　AH

Butter, Nathaniel (1583–1664) English bookseller. Much of Butter's early publishing was ephemeral, but his high points included the first *quarto of *King Lear* (1608). One of the earliest English publishers of periodical news, he used a *newsbook form adapted from Dutch *corantos. The news he published made for a turbulent career (including gaol); he and his partner, Nicholas Bourne,

were satirized by *Jonson in his *Staple of News* (first performed 1626).   CYF
ODNB

butterfly binding, East Asia The first book form to use single *sheets of paper, unlike the *scroll binding or *pleated binding made from a series of connected sheets. With East Asian text arranged vertically in columns from right to left, the butterfly binding was created by folding each sheet in the centre and then pasting along the fold to form the *spine of the book. In the Tang dynasty (618–907), Chinese MSS were written on both sides of thick paper and bound in this way, occasionally aided by internal stitching with silk thread. A column was left blank in the centre of the text to allow for a thin strip of paste. *Leaves of printed books, text on one side only, were folded inward and conveniently pasted along the outside blank fold. In the bound *volume, the page text had upper, lower, and outer *margins. Stiff paper covers were added. The use of butterfly binding increased with the development of *woodblock printing in the Song (960–1279) period, the growth of commercial publishing, and the introduction of new varieties of paper. The open book spread its pages like the wings of a butterfly, hence the name *hudiezhuang* in Chinese. The corresponding term in Korean is *hojŏpchang*. In Japanese, the form is called *kochōsō* or simply *chōsō*. It is also called *detchōsō* in Japan, where related book forms evolved, including *retchōsō*, which uses internal stitching.   JSE
D. Helliwell, 'The Repair and Binding of Old Chinese Books', *East Asian Library Journal*, 8 (1998), 27–149

Butterfly Books *Forgeries of a set of *pamphlets containing poems by distinguished 20th-century poets printed by Frederic Prokosch (1908–89) between 1933 and 1940 in editions of between fewer than ten and 22 copies. Each cover was modelled on a particular butterfly, with a recurrence of veined and metallic patterns. Prokosch himself forged the pamphlets out of mischief 1968–70 and sold them via *Sotheby's 1968–72. After the 1972 sale, A. *Freeman of *Quaritch suspected the forgery from the brightness of the wrappers, whereupon N. *Barker detected anachronistic type and other production materials.   KEA
N. Barker, *The Butterfly Books* (1987)

Butterworths British law publishers. After an apprenticeship with his law-bookseller uncle Joseph (1770–1826), Henry Butterworth (1786–1860) began a rival bookselling and publishing concern at 7 Fleet Street in 1818. He established himself as a major law publisher with H. J. Stephen's *Commentaries on the Laws of England* (1841). His son, Joshua (*c*.1818–95), continued the business, selling it upon retirement to Charles and Richard Bond. It currently trades as Butterworths Tolley.   PLS
ODNB

Buxheim, Imperial Charterhouse of Founded near Memmingen in 1402. Donors like the Augsburg printer *Zainer helped build up its library. After 1803, the monastery fell into private ownership, and the library was auctioned at Munich in 1883.   BW
V. Honemann, 'The Buxheim Collection and its Dispersal', *Renaissance Studies*, 9 (1995), 166–88

Buxtorf, Johannes (1599–1664) Swiss Hebraist, who succeeded his like-named father (1564–1629) as professor of Hebrew at Basel, which gave rise to the witticism *Non ovum ovo similius quam Buxtorf pater et filius*. His own publications included *De Linguae Hebraicae Origine et Antiquitate* (1644) and *Florilegium Hebraicum* (1648), and he completed his father's *Lexicon Chaldaicum, Talmudicum et Rabbinicum* (1639). He was renowned as a collector of Hebrew MSS and printed books.   JLF

Bynneman, Henry (*c*.1542–83) London printer and bookseller. After apprenticeship with Richard Harrison and employment with R. *Wolfe, Bynneman ran one of the largest *printing offfices in London. With the *patronage of Archbishop M. *Parker and Sir Christopher Hatton, he acquired lucrative patents and published titles such as Holinshed's *Chronicles* (1577), but his projects exceeded his means, and he died in debt.   KMQ
J. Barnard and M. Bell, 'The Inventory of Henry Bynneman (1583)', *PH* 29 (1991), 5–46
ODNB

Byrd, William (1674–1744) American diarist and book collector. Byrd, a gentleman farmer in Westover, Virginia, had been educated in Europe. He collected widely but had particular interests in English literature and Americana. His library, amounting to more than 3,000 printed books and MSS, was sold in 1778 for £2,000 and subsequently dispersed at a series of *book auctions in Philadelphia.   ASGE
K. Hayes, *The Library of William Byrd of Westover* (1997)
ODNB

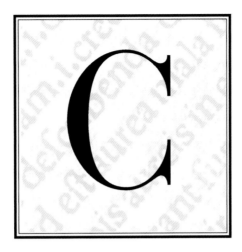

Cadell family Leading London bookseller-publishers from the later 18th century, often operating in tandem with W. *Strahan. Among Cadell's early successes was Gibbon's *Decline and Fall* (1776–88). The firm quickly became known for its generous payments to reputable authors, whether scholars like Hume, novelists like Burney, or poets like Burns.

The son of a Bristol bookseller, Thomas Cadell the elder was apprenticed in 1758 to the London publisher A. *Millar. Entering into partnership with Millar in 1765, he became sole proprietor in 1767, and retired in 1793. He was succeeded by his son Thomas Cadell the younger, in partnership with William Davies. After Davies's death in 1820, the younger Cadell became sole proprietor and the firm was sold on his own demise in 1836.   GL

T. Besterman ed., *The Publishing Firm of Cadell and Davies* (1938)
ODNB

Caflisch, Max (1916–2004) Swiss calligrapher, *type and book designer, teacher, and renowned typographic historian. Caflisch trained as a *compositor, studied with *Tschichold, taught *typography in Basel and Zurich, and was a type-design consultant for several pre-eminent 20th-century firms, including IBM, the Bauer typefoundry (Frankfurt), the Hell Company (Kiel), and Adobe Systems (San Jose). He designed the Columna typeface, and his own *calligraphy was turned into the face Caflisch Script by Robert Slimbach. He wrote on type designers (Tschichold and W. *Morris), and type designs (Bell, Amerigo, *Caslon, Galliard, Minion, and Columbus).

MMS

Calcutta (Kolkata), **Central Reference Library** A subsidiary of the National Library of *India, founded 1955, following the passing of the Delivery of Books (Public Libraries) Act of 1954. Its chief task is to carry out the Indian National Bibliography (INB) project, which began appearing in quarterly instalments from 1958. Although the regularity of its publication has since varied, the INB currently comes out in monthly issues. The library also publishes the *Index Indiana*, an index to selected articles appearing in periodicals.   AG

Calcutta Christian Tract and Book Society Established in 1823 to supply books to missionary-aided vernacular schools. One of its chief publications was a Bengali *translation of The *Pilgrim's Progress* in 1841. Most of its tracts were published from the Bishop's College Press.   AG

Calcutta School-Book Society Founded by Europeans and Indians in Calcutta (Kolkata) in 1817, the Society commissioned and published some of the earliest secular *textbooks in Bengali and English for schools. It also produced *Pasvābali* (*Animal Biography*), a Bengali monthly for young readers, in 1822.   SKC

Caldecott, Randolph (1846–86) English artist and illustrator. Following a brief stint in banking, Caldecott established himself as a news reporter and illustrator for London journals, including *Punch*, the *Graphic*, and the *Illustrated London News*, where his wry, anecdotal humour and spare graphic style brought him an eager following. Professional success came with illustrations (*see* **16**) for Washington Irving's *Old Christmas* (1875) and *Bracebridge Hall* (1877). He is, however, best known for 'Caldecott's Picture Books', a series of illustrated nursery rhymes and stories published by *Routledge, including *The House that Jack Built* (1878) and *Babes in the Wood* (1879).   NG
ODNB

Calder & Boyars British publisher, founded in 1964 after Marion Boyars' earlier investment in John Calder's company. Its influential list included Samuel Beckett,

Eugène Ionesco, and Henry Miller. Successfully prosecuted in 1966 for publishing the 'obscene' *Last Exit to Brooklyn*, the firm subsequently won its appeal (*see* CENSORSHIP). The company was dissolved in 1975, the partners continuing to publish separately as Marion Boyars Ltd and Calder Publications. JEP
ODNB

Calderón family Mexican printing dynasty. In 1631, **Bernardo Calderón** (d. 1641), a Spanish emigrant, started a press that his widow subsequently developed into Mexico City's leading printing establishment. His descendants established several new presses, all of which had closed by the mid-18th century. DRW

calendar [Lat. *calendarium*, 'register'] A book of tables showing a year's subdivision into months, weeks, and days, often including a register of related information; also, a schedule of events specific to a particular institution or profession, usually published annually. The calendar of saints' days and feasts was an important feature in *books of hours that can be used to help localize the book's provenance. Such calendars were often decorated with scenes or occupations suitable to the different months.

Calendars and *almanacs were among the earliest popular printed books, since they made accessible basic knowledge that helped ordinary people to plan their daily lives. The German astronomer Regiomontanus set up a *private press to publish his improved Gregorian *Calendar* (1472), which, in *Ratdolt's decorated version, went through fourteen *editions in several languages during the late 15th century. The calendars produced at Lőcse in Hungary (*see* **31**) included astrological information as well as prognostications. Calendars' usefulness for the semi-literate meant they often rendered key information symbolically, and some pocket calendars could fold out into a single *sheet for display.

Oxford University was the first university to publish an annual calendar of term dates, members, rules, and regulations. In some countries, universities had the exclusive right to sell calendars; the University of Helsinki retained its monopoly on sales of calendars in Finland until the 1990s.

Calendars function best in stable institutions. During frequent periods of political instability in the 18th century, the British court calendar became the butt of jokes: ministries changed so often that it was impossible to keep the list of officials current. The calendar's authoritative status has also been appropriated for polemical or ideological ends. *Evelyn's *Kalendarium Hortense, or Gard'ner's Almanac* (1664) presented a modern theory of gardening, while Edward Burroughs' *The Irish Farmer's Calendar* (1835) was a political intervention in the run-up to the Irish Famine.

As time-keeping became crucial to 19th-century commerce—perhaps best symbolized by the *railway timetable—calendars proliferated in all walks of life. The many calendars dedicated to diverse organizations reflect a concern with social mobility: *The Freemasons' Calendar and Pocket-Book* (1820) typically registers the attempt to forge an exclusive corporate identity while conceding the need to initiate outsiders.

Over the centuries, the trade in such items became more seasonal, with most activity in November and December, when calendars, almanacs, and *diaries were heavily advertised in newspapers. In the 19th century, calendars became associated with periodical as well as annual publication. *Hone's *The Every-day Book* (1825–6)—a *miscellany of useful knowledge, including an almanac, daily readings, saints' days, floral calendar, gardening tips, and historical events—was published in weekly *numbers that could be collected and bound. Racing calendars—a specialized genre of sporting almanac giving details of horse races and other turf lore—were also printed at shorter intervals with sporting *magazines.

From the late 19th century, businesses used calendars as promotional tools, accompanied sometimes by images of the company's products or premises, and sometimes by decorative images that would encourage their prominent display.

The importance of *lithography for the proliferation of such calendars can scarcely be overestimated. This emphasis on visual appeal increased the diversification of *formats, and calendars have lost many of their book-like features. Early 20th-century calendars were typically wall-mounted images on board with tables or a small tear-off pad showing the months and/or days. The collectors' market in vintage calendars is growing as traditional paper calendars, diaries, and *yearbooks lose ground to easily revisable online calendars and electronic scheduling systems. SM

calendar of papers Calendars list the contents of a collection of documents in chronological order, almost always adding a summary of each item. The summaries also frequently include direct or indirect quotations, although the calendar's index may not cover the contents of the summaries. Calendars are commonly made for government papers and historical MSS. Where they include thorough summaries, calendars frequently save the reader from having to consult the original for points of information, or they at least confirm that a document's content is relevant to a topic. Often neglected, they can be treasure troves of historical information. CSR

calender A series of metal rolls within a papermaking machine through which paper is passed to smooth its surface.

calfskin The *leather most commonly used for European bookbindings of the early modern period.

Calleja, Editorial Spanish publisher. Saturnino Calleja Fernández (1853–1915) transformed Editorial Calleja from a Madrid bookshop (founded 1876) into the Hispanic world's leading children's book publisher (*see* **15**), renowned for inexpensive, colourfully illustrated series such as *Cuentos de Calleja* and *Pinocho* (i.e. *Pinocchio*)

Contra Chapete. Its fortunes waned following the Spanish Civil War.   DRW

Callierges, Zacharias (d. *c*.1524) A Cretan, Callierges operated a Greek press in Venice (1499–1500). The *Etymologicum Magnum* (1499), typographically the finest Greek book of the period, was followed by philosophical commentaries and an edition of Galen. His printing (Venice 1509, Rome 1515–23) alternated with work as a *scribe.   MCD

calligraphy [Gk *calligraphia*, 'fine writing'] In classical Greek, the term referred to style of composition, rather than the *script; the early Church Fathers from Basil onwards, preoccupied with the physical form of Holy Writ, gave the word its modern sense.

1. Early fine writing
2. The first manuals and their successors
3. The 17th century
4. The 18th century and after

1. Early fine writing

'Calligraphy' first appears in English in 1613 in the third *edition of Robert Cawdrey's *A Table Alphabeticall of English Wordes*, where it is simply defined as 'faire writing'. *Jonson's *The Magnetick Lady* (1632) enlarges on this: 'I have to commend me … my *Kallygraphy*, a faire hand, | Fit for a Secretary' (3.6.10–13), thus identifying the new role that the invention of printing imposed on the scribe's ancient calling. Fine writing was valued as concomitant with good texts at Alcuin's school at Tours, in the proto-renaissance of the 12th century, and above all by the early humanists, such as Federico da *Montefeltro and *Matthias Corvinus. It was the adoption of their favoured script in the papal chancery in the mid-15th century that defined the new secretarial profession (*see* CHANCERY SCRIPT). The *scrittura* or *littera cancelleresca* in Italy, the 'secretary hand' in England, characterized calligraphy.

2. The first manuals and their successors

Paradoxically, it was printing that set the standard for the approved hands of the new calligraphers. The earliest manuals—in Italian (Sigismondo Fanti, 1514) and German (Johann Neudörffer, 1519)—provided instruction, but those of *Arrighi and Giovanni Antonio Tagliente (1524–5), with samples of script skilfully cut on wood, achieved the greatest popularity. If papal briefs had made the script fashionable all over Europe, it was these books that taught its emulators how to do it. They were reprinted many times until the end of the 16th century, and widely imitated, notably by Giovanni Battista Palatino (1540), who evinced a new interest in ancient and exotic scripts.

In 1560, however, another book emerged that would have a revolutionary effect, the *Essamplare di piu sorti lettere* of Gianfrancesco *Cresci, followed by his *Il perfetto scrittore* (1570). Cresci taught a new *cancelleresca*, as beautiful as the old but distinguished by greater slope

Exuberant **calligraphy**: a specimen sheet by the French *writing-master Jean de *Beauchesne, who came to England in 1565, signed and dated in mirror writing 7 December 1575.

and more current form, with looped *ascenders and *descenders. His specimens were attractive, but, more importantly, this hand could be written fast. Even so, its superiority was not immediately apparent. Conservatively, Cresci had preferred his specimens cut on wood, like his predecessors; but his many imitators, first in Italy, then further afield, produced their specimens engraved on copper, *intaglio instead of *relief. This was to prove an innovation of lasting importance.

The older method of reproducing scripts persisted elsewhere in Europe, in Spain (*Yciar, 1548), Germany (Wolfgang Fugger, 1553), and France (Jacques de la Rue, 1565; Jacques le Moyne, 1568). It reached England in the hand of the Huguenot émigré *Beauchesne in 1570. Like their Italian predecessors, their manuals showed not only the Italian *cancelleresca* but also the different scripts appropriate for different vernacular languages, and for different types of document. Italian merchants had made the *mercantesca*—the script used for commercial transactions (double accounting was another Italian invention that had swept Europe)—widely familiar. Other scripts—for legal and political documents, *charters, indentures, writs, and court records, different in different countries—filled the pages of the *writing-masters' manuals.

3. The 17th century

In 17th-century Holland, engraved writing-books achieved the greatest elegance and force in the depiction of written letters and, thanks to Dutch commerce, the greatest diffusion. The *Spiegel der schrijfkonste* (1605) of Jan van den *Velde, the great engraver, achieved a European reputation and attracted many imitators. Van den Velde produced many books by himself, as well as by other great scribes, including David Roelands and Maria Strick. The first woman to achieve a reputation as a calligrapher, Strick also produced fine books of specimens. The regular sloped and rounded script that they developed became known in England as the 'Dutch *copperplate', losing the first word as it was increasingly imitated in England.

The first English engraved manual was *Billingsley's *The Pen's Excellencie* (1618), and the poet John Davies of Hereford produced another, *The Writing Schoolemaster* (1631), several times reprinted. Yet the most prolific writer was *Cocker, whose many books, often repeating the same *plates in different orders, dominated the later 17th-century market in England.

In France, Guillaume Le Gangneur published a series of influential manuals (1599), as did Robert Vignon and Lucas Materot (1608), and *Barbédor's vast *Les Écritures financière, et italienne-bastarde* (1647) was equally influential. The court of Louis XIV rediscovered the attractions of illuminated MSS of verse or the liturgy. The work of Nicolas Jarry became famous. Louis Senault produced similar books in engraved script, as well as manuals. The French taste was given added currency by its extension to typographic form in the *romain du roi* cut by *Grandjean to celebrate the Sun King's conquests.

The success of British commerce and subsequent colonial expansion encouraged an efflorescence of the art of writing in London. *Pepys took a great interest in it, and collected earlier as well as contemporary manuals. His long connection with Christ's Hospital brought about the appointment of a writing-master as a permanent member of staff. Pepys sponsored other writing-masters, such as *Ayres, who wrote *A Tutor to Penmanship* (1698). There was great rivalry between him and his contemporaries John Seddon, who wrote *The Penman's Paradise* (1695); George Shelley, who wrote *The Penman's Magazine* (1705); and Charles Snell (1705).

Much of this controversy surrounded the desirability or otherwise of 'striking' or 'command of hand', the ability to indite elaborate flourishes or even whole pictures with a single controlled movement of the pen. This derived from earlier Italian models; the works of Giuseppe Segaro (*Dell'idea dello scrivere*, 1608), Giuliano Sellari (*Laberinto di varii caratteri*, 1635), and, last and greatest, Leopardo Antonozzi (*De caratteri*, 1638) are full of them. The decline and fall of calligraphy, at least as published art, in

Italy after the mid-century, is curious. It was not revived until the end of the 18th century.

4. The 18th century and after

It was England that dominated that century; best known are the works of John Sturt, whose engraved editions of the *Book of Common Prayer* became famous, and the names of Robert More, John Clark, William Brooks, John Bland, and Emanuel Austin. Besides their separate manuals, their work was published by the great engravers, who made a fortune from illustrated and music books as well. George *Bickham and his son, also George, were the leaders, and the *folio *Universal Penman* (1733–41) was a great success, later reprinted by the publisher Henry Overton, whose rival Carington Bowles made a living out of writing-manuals. William Massey's *The Origin and Progress of Letters* (1763) is the first history of calligraphy, recording the work of these and earlier masters.

With the 19th century, calligraphy as such was overtaken by that other basic requirement of writing, speed. Only in Spain, notably by José Francisco de Iturzaeta (1788–1853), was writing as an art preserved. In America (and, subsequently, the world), the Spencerian system devised by Platt Rogers Spencer (1800–1864) and its rival, that of Payson, Dunton, and Scribner, came to predominate. But regularity is not necessarily art, and the demon speed extinguished calligraphy until its revival in the 20th century in the hand of E. *Johnston.   NJB

J. I. Whalley and V. C. Kaden, *The Universal Penman* (1980)

calligraphy, Muslim A primitive form of the Arabic alphabet existed prior to the rise of Islam in the 6th–7th century AD, but it was the need to write down the text of the new faith's sacred message, the Qur'ān, that gave the impetus for the full development of the Arabic script and its calligraphic potential (*see* **38**).

A stylized form of script called Kufic was developed as the official *ductus of the new faith and civilization. This was used for public inscriptions, coinage, and, above all, the Qur'anic text. Between the late 7th and late 9th centuries, so many forms of 'classic' Kufic were produced as to defy accurate classification by modern scholars. Between the 9th and late 10th centuries new forms of Kufic, influenced by contemporary cursive book hands, arose. These have been variously designated by modern scholars: Eastern, New Style, etc.

During the 10th century, Qur'āns appear to have been produced for the first time in some of the *cursive hands. These are traditionally divided into two groups: the *khuṭūṭ al-yābisa*, 'dry' or angular forms, and the *khuṭūṭ al-muraṭṭaba*, 'dampened' or cursive forms. The former are *muḥaqqaq* and *rayḥānī*; the latter *thulth* and *naskh*. In each category, the second type is a smaller version of the first, with some minor differences. The cursive group also embraces *tawqī'* and *riqā'*, which are *chancery or diplomatic hands. These form the six classic hands, *al-aqlām al-sittah*, practised in the central Muslim lands: Egypt, Syria, Iraq, Iran, and Turkey.

Iranian calligraphers developed two further forms: *nastaʿlīq* and *shikastah*. In the first the horizontal

CAMBRIDGE UNIVERSITY LIBRARY

elements of the script are exaggerated and the words slope downwards from right to left. In the second, the natural breaks between letters and words are closed up, often in such a way as to defy legibility. The Ottoman Turks devised a further style called *dīvānī*: a form of *tawqī'/nasta'līq* with the spaces between the letters embellished and the text rising to the left at the end of each line. In North Africa and the Iberian peninsula, different forms developed, which are usually grouped together as *Maghribī*, though they can be further divided into four or five sub-types. East and West Africa, India, and Central Asia also developed their own forms, though these have been less studied by scholars.

The letterforms of the Perso-Arabic alphabet can be exaggerated in any direction without the script losing legibility. On this, the art of Arabic calligraphic composition is based. There have always been two forms of calligraphy: one that tries to conform exactly to traditional rules, and another that tries to bend those rules as far as possible. Ottoman and Iranian calligraphy of the second half of the 19th century are good examples of these two different approaches. Today, in all Muslim countries—including Turkey—classical calligraphy is still taught and practised. There is also much experimental work by contemporary artists from those areas combining calligraphy with painting, collage, and even sculpture. *See also* ARABIC SCRIPT. DLJ

S. Blair, *Islamic Calligraphy* (2006)

Calvert, Elizabeth (d. *c*.1675) London bookseller, married to Giles Calvert. They sold Nonconformist, oppositional, and Quaker literature from their shop in *St Paul's Churchyard. Elizabeth played an important role in the production and distribution of radical pamphlets, particularly while her husband was imprisoned, and despite her own imprisonments and interrogations by *L'Estrange. KMQ

ODNB

Cambridge Bibliographical Society The Cambridge Bibliographical Society was founded on 20 January 1949 at the instigation of Bruce Dickins and *Munby. Its aim was to promote and publish bibliographical studies, especially those with some Cambridge connection, such as studies concerning MSS or printed books in Cambridge libraries, books printed at Cambridge, or books written by Cambridge authors. The Society publishes the annual *Transactions of the Cambridge Bibliographical Society* and occasional monographs—the first of which was *Gaskell's *First Editions of William Mason* (1951). The Society presents between two and four lectures a year at *Cambridge University Library and organizes an annual visit. Past presidents include: Sir Roger Mynors (1949), Bruce Dickins (1950–57), *Keynes (1958–71), Munby (1971–4), Edward M. Wilson (1975–7), J. C. T. Oates (1977–81), Frank Stubbings (1981–91) and *McKitterick (1991–). KEA

Cambridge Bibliographical Society, www.lib.cam.ac.uk/cambibsoc, consulted May 2007

Cambridge Press (active 1639–92) First printing press in British North America. In 1638, the Revd Joseph (Josse) Glover sailed to Massachusetts Bay with a press and the would-be printers Stephen and Matthew *Day, a locksmith and his son. Glover died en route, and the press was taken over by Henry Dunster, president of Harvard, who married Glover's widow. With *Green, the Days initially produced *almanacs, laws, a few sermons, the *Bay Psalm Book, and the *Platform of Church Discipline*—titles that were tightly controlled by the magistrates and the college. A second press joined the *printing office for the massive Indian Bible (1661–3), with Marmaduke Johnson and the Algonquin indigene James Wowaus assisting Green. This human and technological operation eventually led to a second, competing Boston printing office in 1674. Green's son Bartholomew was apprenticed to his father at the Cambridge Press, which continued printing until 1692. MPB

Cambridge University Library After hesitant medieval beginnings, in which it was outclassed by some larger college libraries, the university library was settled in the Schools Yard from the mid-15th century. Many of its holdings were lost through the depredations of the Reformation (and later negligence), but the library gradually reconstituted itself. Archbishop M. *Parker's gift in 1574 of several Anglo-Saxon MSS, and the temporary presence during the Civil War of the library of *Lambeth Palace, are evidence of the renewed standing of the university collections. Deposit privileges guaranteed by the Copyright Act of Queen Anne (1710) (*see* ACT FOR THE ENCOURAGEMENT OF LEARNING) greatly increased the quantity of books received. In quality, too, the overall improvement was evidenced by King George I's 1715 donation of the important library—some 29,000 printed books and 2,000 MSS—assembled by Bishop John Moore (1646–1716). In spite of periods of Hanoverian and Georgian torpor, this royal gift foreshadowed many comparable donations. Librarians included the religious controversialist Conyers Middleton (1683–1750), and from 1867 the incunabulist Henry *Bradshaw, whose period in office signalled a new professionalism.

Housed in the Old Schools at the core of the administrative university, the library had become severely constricted by the 19th century, though congestion was relieved in the 1840s by C. R. Cockerell's handsome building nearby (now the library of Gonville and Caius College). This was but a temporary palliative; further major acquisitions, including the historian Lord Acton's library, and the problem of a rapidly expanding library in central Cambridge made an open site urgently necessary. Rockefeller Foundation support enabled construction of a new library on the western edges of the traditional collegiate area. Designed by Sir Giles Gilbert Scott, it was opened in 1934 and has since been several times extended. Much of its stock is open for consultation as well as (following ancient tradition) for loan—thus differing from other British copyright libraries. The stock grows apace, with some holdings (e.g. law and scientific periodicals) housed in satellite institutions. Room has recently been found for the archives of the *British and Foreign Bible Society and the historical library of the Royal Commonwealth Society, along with many other collections emphasizing the importance of Cambridge's research holdings as well as its broad general stock.   ASB

D. J. McKitterick, *Cambridge University Library, A History: The Eighteenth and Nineteen Centuries* (1986)

J. C. T. Oates, *Cambridge University Library, A History: From the Beginnings ot the Copyright Act of Queen Anne* (1986)

Cambridge University Press (CUP) In 1534, Henry VIII issued Letters Patent empowering the university to print, bind, and import 'all manner of books' and to offer them for sale 'in the University or elsewhere within the realm'. The university initially exercised its rights by way of appointed printers, who, for 150 years, made arrangements with the *Stationers' Company in London for control of those rights. Producing CUP's first book in 1584, the university's printer, T. *Thomas, began a printing enterprise that ultimately became one of the largest in the world. His successor, *Legate, recognized the Bible's sales potential (*see* **2**) and, although the Royal Printer's Patent of 1577 seemed to give London's Royal Printer a monopoly, Cambridge printed its first bible in 1591. Puritan and mainstream sectors of the English Church alike appreciated Legate's *octavo edition, featuring the Geneva version in modern *typeface.

Tensions soon arose within the university over how to balance production of scholarly works with the more marketable bibles and *almanacs that made the press financially viable. Related to this issue of profit was the antagonism between the university and its printers—private entrepreneurs motivated by maintaining their monopolies and higher prices. Cambridge responded by founding its own press in 1696, thus wresting control back from London. Richard *Bentley's (1662–1742) 1698 reorganization of the printer's office made it part of the university and imposed on it obligations to print scholarly works, even if they were not necessarily profitable. Licensing, which had controlled printing in England and Wales, lapsed in 1695, thus enabling the Press to meet demand from a steadily growing reading public.

Although the university began its own printing in the 1690s, it did not publish until after 1872, when CUP established its first London office. By that point, the production of bibles had already reached a high of 195,000 copies in 1840, but the *Authorized and Revised Versions would remain staples. Bible sales rose again in the 1960s with the publication of the New English Bible. In the late 20th century, CUP became the Queen's Printer (*see* KING's/ QUEEN's PRINTER) and thus held the patent to publish the 1662 *Book of Common Prayer* within the UK. Other major publications of the century included the *Encyclopaedia Britannica* (11e, 1911), the Cambridge Companion and Cambridge History series, *textbooks, and academic journals. *The Cambridge History of Science* and book series in physics, biology, chemistry, engineering, computer science, and mathematics have made CUP a leader in science publishing. Despite widespread success, bible sales still kept the press afloat and hid substantial financial problems that were only eased with Geoffrey Cass's reforms in the early 1970s. Now fiscally secure, CUP continues to fulfil the university's desire to support the dissemination of knowledge and meet the needs of students around the world. *See also* ROYAL LICENCES.   MDB

www.uk.cambridge.org, consulted Nov. 2007

M. H. Black, *Cambridge University Press, 1584–1984* (1984)

D. F. McKenzie, *The Cambridge University Press 1696–1712* (2 vols, 1966)

D. McKitterick, *A History of Cambridge University Press* (3 vols, 1992–2004)

Camden Society An association founded in 1838 for publishing historical MSS and reprinting early works relating to English history. The society was promoted by John Bowyer Nichols (proprietor of the *Gentleman's Magazine* and parliamentary printer), *Madden, J. P. *Collier, and other prominent antiquaries. Named after the 16th-century historian William Camden, its annual meeting was for many years held on his birthday. By 1845, membership had risen to 1,250 (including the Prince Consort). Two volumes were published in most of the early years, many of them edited by the indefatigable Thomas Wright. The society's fortunes declined as the original generation of gentlemen amateur subscribers died off; membership fell below 200 by 1880. In 1897 it amalgamated with the Royal Historical Society, which continues to publish a Camden Series of edited historical documents; more than 320 volumes have now appeared in five series. Many of the earlier volumes, hastily or inadequately edited, have been superseded; one painstaking early project still of value is Albert Way's edition of the *Promptorium Parvulorum*, completed only in 1865. The Cambridge Camden Society, entirely unconnected, began to publish influential material on church architecture and furnishing in 1839; it was renamed the Ecclesiological Society in 1846.   BJF

camera-ready copy Text and illustrations (*see* **16**) that have been typeset, proofed (*see* PROOFS AND PROOFREADING), and *imposed, and are ready for photographic reproduction on to a *plate for *offset printing.

Cameron, W. J. (William) (1926–89) New Zealand-born bibliographer. As editor of the 1688–97 volume of *Poems on Affairs of State* (1971), Cameron conducted ground-breaking research into 17th-century scribal publication (*see* **13**). He took a leading role in projects to record holdings of pre-1801 books in Australia, New Zealand, and Canada, and to develop education for librarianship in the Caribbean and Latin America.   IM

B. J. McMullin, 'William J. Cameron 1926–1989', *BSANZ Bulletin*, 14 (1990), 15–20

Caminho Portuguese publisher based in Lisbon. Best known as the publisher of Nobel laureate José Saramago, Caminho has been a leading literary house since its founding in 1975. Through its branch offices in Angola

(Editorial Nzila) and Mozambique (Editorial Ndjira), Caminho also specializes in contemporary literature from Portuguese Africa.   DRW

Camões, Premio Literary prize for Lusophone writers, comparable in prestige to the Premio *Cervantes. Jointly established in 1988 and administered by the governments of Portugal and Brazil, the €100,000 prize is awarded annually for a distinguished body of work. Past laureates include Jorge Amado (1994) and José Saramago (1995).
                                                                     DRW

Campbell, M. F. A. G. (Marinus) (1819–90) Dutch librarian and bibliographer. In 1869 he became librarian of the *Koninklijke Bibliotheek, succeeding *Holtrop. Together, they compiled the library's *incunabula catalogue (1856) and the *Monuments typographiques des Pays-Bas au quinzième siècle* (1868). His *Annales de la typographie néerlandaise au quinzième siècle* (1874) is a landmark in Dutch incunabula studies.   MVD
W. G. Hellinga and L. Hellinga-Querido, eds., *Henry Bradshaw's Correspondence on Incunabula with J. W. Holtrop and M. F. A. G. Campbell* (2 vols, 1966–78)

Campbell's decision, Lord In Boosey vs Purday (1849), Lord Campbell ruled that initial publication of their work in England did not entitle non-resident foreign authors to British *copyright protection. British statutory copyright, he opined, promoted intellectual life exclusively for the Queen's subjects.   DS

Campe, Julius (1792–1867) German publisher and bookseller in Hamburg, from 1823 to 1867 owner of Hoffmann & Campe. The publisher of much oppositional and liberal German literature, his most famous author was Heinrich Heine.   US
E. Ziegler, *Julius Campe—der Verleger Heinrich Heines* (1976)

Canada Council for the Arts (Conseil des Arts du Canada) Founded in 1957 as a federal government agency, the Council fosters the arts through grants, services, and awards. It administers the Public Lending Right Commission (see PUBLIC LENDING RIGHT/DROIT DE PRÊT PUBLIC), the *Governor General's Literary Awards, and other prizes. Its Writing and Publishing Section supports writers with grants and travel grants, and funds author residencies, literary readings, and festivals. Programmes for book publishing include author promotion tours, translation grants, emerging publisher grants, and block grants for established publishers to offset the cost of producing Canadian trade books.   PLF

Canada Reads Annual *Canadian Broadcasting Corporation programme (2002). Five celebrities champion a Canadian novel. Publishers then donate copies to libraries and a portion of revenues to literacy causes. Its French counterpart, Le Combat des livres, began in 2004.   JAD

Canadian Broadcasting Corporation (CBC) With its counterpart, Société Radio-Canada, the CBC was established in 1936. Public ownership of broadcasting had been recommended by a royal commission concerned about the intrusion of American radio and convinced that only a national network would serve Canadian interests. Both radio and (from 1952) television have engaged heavily with the written word: employing writers, buying stories, commissioning plays, reviewing books and sponsoring awards, and broadcasting *Canada Reads.   PLF

cancel Best defined as a disturbance in the physical structure of a book, a cancel is usually executed after the completion of the original *press run and sometimes after the distribution of the first copies. From the 15th to the 19th century, compositors worked for the most part with small quantities of *type in the case, so that any *forme, after printing, was immediately *distributed, rather than being kept *standing for a further *impression. Rectifying a mistake, therefore, except through an *erratum or hand-correcting all the *sheets, meant resetting the text concerned. Cancels, as they were known in the trade, went from a tiny piece of paper containing, for example, a single punctuation mark pasted over the error (see PASTED SLIPS) to recomposing one or more sheets of an edition. A single *leaf cancel is recognizable because it is glued to the *stub left by the original, while a double-leaf cancel, folded and sewn in the centre, is often detected by irregularities in the paper structure of the *gathering and by differences in typographical work. A full-sheet cancel, however, can be all but invisible. In principle, early printers sought to conceal such substitutions; therefore, their identification sometimes requires bibliographical expertise, although in the 18th and 19th centuries cancels were often marked with an asterisk in the *direction line. It was also common for the cancelled leaves to be slashed in the *printing office, as an indication to the binder that they were to be removed; at times, though, the instruction was not followed, even when the replacement leaves are also present in the volume.

To avoid ambiguity in describing cancels, bibliographers employ the following terminology, established by R. W. *Chapman: [*folium*] *cancellandum* (Lat., 'that which is to be cancelled'; pl. [*folia*] *cancellanda*) for the cancelled leaf/sheet that has nevertheless survived; and [*folium*] *cancellans* (Lat., 'that which cancels'; pl. [*folia*] *cancellantia*) for the leaf/sheet introduced into the book. There is also a term [*folium*] *cancellatum* (Lat., 'that which has been cancelled'; pl. [*folia*] *cancellata*) for any example of the cancellandum that has been removed but has nonetheless survived, obviously a rare occurrence. In formulas of *collation, where cancellandum and cancellans have the same physical shape, cancels are indicated by combined plus and minus (±) signs.

With modern industrial printing methods, mistakes are rectified by reprinting the whole sheet, or sometimes the entire book; although this is technically a cancel, it is virtually impossible to identify.   NH
R. W. Chapman, *Cancels* (1930)
Gaskell, *NI*

A **cancel**: the slit leaf on the left from Samuel *Johnson's *A Journey to the Western Islands of Scotland* (1775) is the *cancellandum* which was replaced by the *cancellans* on the right, thereby softening a sharp criticism of the Dean and Chapter of Lichfield Cathedral. The MS note is probably by Michael Lort. In the process were added two lines to the *page depth and a *press figure in the *cancellandum's* *direction line.

Candide This most famous of the philosophical tales of Voltaire (François-Marie Arouet, 1694–1778) was published in 1759 as a *duodecimo volume entitled *Candide, ou l'Optimisme, traduit de l'allemand de Mr. le Docteur Ralph*, and without a printer's or publisher's *imprint on the *title-page. It was in fact published in Geneva, by Gabriel and Philibert Cramer, under Voltaire's supervision. The author's identity was an open secret, a fact sufficient to make the work an instant success. Many reprints (about fifteen in all, with or without the author's approval) were immediately published in Paris, London, Lyons, Liège, and other places, amounting to about 20,000 copies. *Candide* was condemned by the authorities in Switzerland, France, and several other countries as anti-religious and immoral, but the distribution and reprinting of the work continued unabated. It remained a bestseller throughout the 18th century, and by the 19th had become a classic. In 1762, and later, Voltaire revised and augmented the text. Modern editions normally reproduce the revised text of the 'encadrée' edition of his *Œuvres* (Geneva, 1775), the last published with his collaboration during his lifetime.   CPC

R. Pomeau, introduction to *Candide*, in Voltaire, *Complete Works*, ed. T. Besterman *et al.*, vol. 48 (1980)

Cannon & Sons, George Q. Until the 1860s, the Church of Jesus Christ of Latter-day Saints generally depended on non-Mormon printers for its publishing needs. In 1866, George Quayle Cannon established a Salt Lake City firm to print for a Mormon clientele. Cannon ran bookshops and published biographies, histories, and juvenile literature. The Church acquired the company just before Cannon's death and renamed it Deseret Book Co. in 1920. In 2007, the operation included 43 retail shops, 26 discount outlets, and four *imprints.   DJW

D. Bitton, *George Q. Cannon* (1999)

E. Knowles, *Deseret Book Company* (1991)

Cano, Benito (*fl.* 1785–1812) Spanish printer. A leading printer in late 18th-century Madrid, Cano was reported

to have 24 presses in operation in 1792. His best work, such as a nineteen-volume illustrated *octavo bible in Spanish (1794–7), rivalled that of *Ibarra and *Sancha.
DRW

Canongate Founded in Edinburgh in 1973 by Stephanie and Angus Wolfe Murray, Canongate published Alasdair Gray's *Lanark* and 'Canongate Classics'. The company went through a series of owners in the early 1990s, culminating in a management buy-out in 1994, led by Jamie Byng. Canongate published Yann Martel's *Life of Pi*, the 2002 Man *Booker Prize winner, and the bestselling book in the prize's history.
SD

A. Billen, 'Loose Canon of Literary Publishing', *The Times*, 10 Jan. 2005

Canterbury Cathedral Library The oldest surviving library in Britain, probably dating from the advent of St Augustine in 597. The library grew to *c*.2,000 books before the Henrician dissolution of Christ Church Priory in 1540. Thereafter, its books were steadily dispersed. From the early 17th century onwards, printed books and some MSS were gradually acquired. In the 20th century, new collections and new buildings were added. The library is now associated with the University of Kent.
ASGE

N. Ramsay, 'The Cathedral Archives and Library', in *A History of Canterbury Cathedral*, ed. P. Collinson *et al.* (1995)

Canterbury School Canterbury was one of the most important centres of English MS production, and especially of illumination, during the Anglo-Saxon and Romanesque periods. During the earlier era, its significance was matched only by Winchester. Canterbury itself was clearly of importance as a religious centre from the end of the 6th century, and its ecclesiastical role was increasingly complemented by its production of high-quality religious MSS. By the 8th century, a *scriptorium existed in St Augustine's Abbey, among the notable MSS of which were the *Vespasian Psalter and the *Codex Aureus. There was also a scriptorium at Christ Church Canterbury; it was influenced in the 10th century by the arrival of the *Utrecht Psalter: it led to the development of techniques of outline drawing that provided the model for several important MSS produced there in the 12th century, including the *Eadwine Psalter and the *Dover Bible. Both institutions remained important sites of MS production after the Norman Conquest.

By the 12th century, Canterbury appears to have been involved in various interchanges of either artists or MS models with other prominent religious houses, such as Bury St Edmunds and St Albans. These subsequent relationships at times make secure attribution to Canterbury problematic. Few later MSS can be confidently localized there.
ASGE

C. R. Dodwell, *The Canterbury School of Illumination, 1066–1200* (1954)

C. M. Kauffmann, *Romanesque Manuscripts, 1066–1190* (1975)

E. Temple, *Anglo-Saxon Manuscripts, 900–1066* (1976)

Canterbury Tales, The The most famous work in the extensive œuvre of Geoffrey Chaucer (*c*.1340–1400), it consists of *c*.17,000 lines, mostly of verse, with two sections in prose. Written largely in the last decade of the author's life, it was left unfinished. The narrative framework—a pilgrimage to Canterbury to visit the shrine of Thomas Becket, during which tales are told by the pilgrims—allowed the author to include previously composed materials. The group of 29 pilgrims from a wide social spectrum meet at the Tabbard Inn at Southwark, where, at an evening meal before setting out, the inn's Host proposes a story-telling competition to be held during the pilgrimage. He joins the pilgrimage and presides over the competition, linking the various tales with his comments and arbitrating over the pilgrims' quarrels. The narrator is 'Geoffrey Chaucer', himself a pilgrim, who, as the group gathers, describes in the General Prologue his first impressions of the appearance, background, and manner of each of the pilgrims. The work is incomplete—the pilgrims do not even reach Canterbury. Of the four tales for each pilgrim proposed by the Host, only 24 are begun, and several are unfinished. The pilgrims are presented as speaking in unmistakably distinctive voices, most famous among them the drunk and bawdy Miller, the excitable Wife of Bath, the solemn Parson, the Nun with her Tale of Chauntecleer, and Chaucer himself telling the Tale of Sir Topas with its hobby-horse trot.

The work was immediately popular, as witnessed by some 80 surviving MSS. The *Hengwrt Manuscript in the National Library of *Wales and the *Ellesmere MS in the *Huntington Library (with its famous marginal illustrations) differ markedly in order and content, although *copied by the same *scribe early in the 15th century. Their divergence reveals traces of editorial intervention that must have taken place after Chaucer's death, when the first attempts were made to assemble the fragments of text he had left into one coherent work. In other MSS, the text was transmitted in different arrangements, and various traditions coexisted. Such diversity presented editorial problems, exacerbated when the work appeared in print. *The Canterbury Tales* was the first substantial work published by *Caxton when he set up a press in Westminster in 1476; a few years later, a different version was brought to his attention, and he amended the text accordingly in his second edition (1483). His successor, de *Worde, introduced further drastic rearrangements on the basis of comparison with yet other versions. Thus began a critical process of analysis of textual sources that has confronted all editors of the *Tales* over the centuries, and continues to the present day. *Tyrwhitt's magnificent four-volume edition (1775; a *glossary constituting vol. 5 was later added) marks another editorial milestone. From the 19th century, scholars (*Bradshaw among them) and editors have divided the surviving narratives into ten numbered groups, which were then arranged in more than one way.

Only three still extant MSS have illustrations, each independently following Chaucer's descriptions of the pilgrims' attire. Caxton's *woodcuts, which appeared in his second edition, were much copied and became the models on which the iconography of Chaucer's Canterbury pilgrimage is based in all editions until 1602.   LH

L. Benson, ed., *The Riverside Chaucer* (1987)

BMC 11

D. Carlson, 'Woodcut Illustrations of the Canterbury Tales, 1483–1602', *Library*, 6/19 (1997), 25–67

E. Hammond, *Chaucer: A Bibliographical Manual* (1908)

J. Manly and E. Rickert, *The Text of the Canterbury Tales* (8 vols, 1940)

ODNB

D. Pearsall, *The Life of Geoffrey Chaucer* (1992)

P. A. Ruggiers, ed., *Editing Chaucer: The Great Tradition* (1984)

canvas A strong plain fabric, made of cotton, linen, or hemp, sometimes used as a covering material for embroidered bookbindings, and also commonly employed, undecorated, for schoolbooks and other cheap books in the late 18ᵗʰ and 19ᵗʰ centuries.   DRSP

caoutchouc binding *See* GUTTA-PERCHA BINDING.

cap Originally the uppermost horizontal member of a *common press, later the topmost part of any press (such as the brass cap of the *Albion).

Cape, Jonathan British publisher. Its founder, Jonathan Cape, began his publishing career as an errand boy for *Hatchards, subsequently working for *Harper & Brothers and *Duckworth. His eponymous company was established in 1921 in partnership with George Wren Howard; Edward Garnett worked as *publisher's reader at the firm until his death in 1937. After acquiring the backlist of A. C. Fifield in 1922, Cape published such authors as T. E. Lawrence, Arthur Ransome, and Ernest Hemingway, and cheap series of quality books, including the 'Travellers' Library'. After World War II, the *James Bond books proved very lucrative for the company. Cape died in 1960, and was succeeded by T. *Maschler. The firm merged with *Chatto (1969), *Bodley Head (1973), and *Virago (1987) to form the CVBC group. One of the foremost British literary publishers, it survives as an imprint of *Random House (since 1987).   CMS

ODNB

Čapek, Josef (1887–1945) Czech writer, art critic, painter, and graphic artist. His interest in the art of advertising led to his bold designs for over 500 book *covers from 1915 until his arrest by the Gestapo in 1939. The strong and contrasting qualities of his favourite technique, the linocut, combined effectively with the coloured papers he employed. Using simple formulae, his covers managed to recreate the personality of the author, convey the atmosphere of the book, and give some idea of its contents.   DP

V. Thiele, *Josef Čapek a Kniha* (1958)

Capell, Edward (1713–81) English literary scholar and Shakespeare editor. Having collected the Shakespearean *folios and many of the *quartos, Capell based his text not on the *textus receptus* transmitted through recent editions, but on his own transcript of a base text, chosen as a result of detailed *collation. The method was trialled in *Prolusions; or, Select Pieces of Antient Poetry* (1760), intended as 'an Example of Care and Fidelity to Persons who take upon them the Publication of our best Authors'. His Shakespeare (10 vols, 1767–8) echoed the *Prolusions* in the chaste elegance of its printing and the paucity of notes on the text page, as well as in textual methodology. Capell's full and learned *apparatus, the *Notes and Various Readings*, appeared in 1774 (vol. 1) and 1783 (vols 1–3).   MW

ODNB

M. Walsh, 'Form and Function in the English Eighteenth-Century Literary Edition: The Case of Edward Capell', *SB* 54 (2001), 225–41

Cape Town International Book Fair Launched in June 2006, it has replaced the Harare event (*see* ZIMBABWE INTERNATIONAL BOOK FAIR) as Africa's leading trade and retail fair. A partnership between the Publishers' Association of South Africa and the *Frankfurt Book Fair, it hosts public lectures and award ceremonies, including for the Alan Paton and *Sunday Times* prizes and the *Noma Award.   AEV

Cape Town Library, University of Founded in 1905 when W. S. Logeman, professor of modern languages, collected in one place books accumulated by departments of the South African College, the university's predecessor. In October 2001, the Chancellor *Oppenheimer Library was opened as the main library building. With eight branch libraries and several special collections, the library houses over 750,000 books and 26,000 journal titles. The library's special collections include the Modern English Poetry collection, the Kipling, *Alice in Wonderland*, and C. Louis Leipoldt collections, and the Bleek-Lloyd collection of Bushman folklore.   ALD

capital, ornamental *See* INITIAL (1).

capital line The imaginary line defining the height of the capitals in a fount, usually below the height of the *ascenders, occasionally the same.

caption title Title above a chapter, section, article, or the title beginning a work without a *title-page; also used for a description beneath an illustration.

carbon paper Originally, paper coated with *lampblack and oil, developed for the Associated Press from 1823 and used for office copying from the late 1860s. It is better suited to *typewriter-generated copy than handwritten. Several copies can be made simultaneously, although those furthest from the typewriter keys are the faintest.   MMS

Carcanet British publisher founded in 1969 by Michael Schmidt and Peter Jones to promote new poetry. The Press moved with Schmidt from Oxford to Manchester, adding fiction to its list. Carcanet's poets include Muriel Spark, Elizabeth Jennings, Edwin Morgan, and Charles Tomlinson.   SD

rylibweb.man.ac.uk/data2/spcoll/carcan, consulted June 2006

cardboard Not a technical term, but one used generally to denote thick paper or light board. The trade uses the term 'board' with a distinguishing word to identify a particular quality. Cardboard normally consists of layers of paper pasted together built up to the correct thickness. The two outer covering layers are better quality than the inferior inner ones. The difference between paper and board is not always clear. Paper may weigh up to 150gm. per sq. metre. A weight of 250–500gm per sq. metre is definitely board. *See also* PASTEBOARD   RLH

J. V. Stirk, *The Last Mills* (2006)

card catalogue The card catalogue developed from the need to provide up-to-date access to the holdings of libraries between editions of printed book catalogues: cards were cheaper than producing a new book every few years. The first card catalogue for public use was created in the 1830s, and the form was common by the middle of the 19th century. Card catalogues had advantages over the printed book catalogue: they were easier to keep current and often easier to browse. There were disadvantages also: cards deteriorated; there was typically only one copy of the catalogue; and significant labour was required to maintain it. The biggest drawbacks resulted from the increasing size of card catalogues as collections grew. Filing rules became so complex that users needed help in finding titles, and the effort involved in changing large files of headings meant that obsolete headings persisted for decades. In large research libraries, the development of electronic catalogues was greeted with relief. Most libraries ceased to add new cards to their catalogues and then gradually eliminated cards for records that were in digital form in the electronic catalogue, which became the Online Public Access Catalogue. In spite of protests, the electronic catalogue had replaced almost all card catalogues in large libraries by the 1990s in the US.
                                                           LSC

Encyclopedia of Library and Information Science 14
C. C. Ryan, ed., *The Card Catalog* (1981)

Carey, Henry Charles (1793–1879) Henry, the son of M. *Carey, succeeded to his father's business in 1822, becoming—in partnership with Isaac Lea—one of the first true *publishers in the US. As general publishers, they are best known for innovations in literary publishing. In the absence of international *copyright, they reprinted British novels by W. *Scott, Dickens, and others. They also made publishing American works a paying proposition for themselves and authors such as James Fenimore Cooper, Washington Irving, John Pendleton Kennedy, and Catharine Sedgwick. In 1825 they created the first American literary *annual, the *Atlantic Souvenir* (sold to Samuel Goodrich in 1832). In 1829 Henry's brother Edward, who had joined the firm in 1827, withdrew, entering into partnership with the printer

Abraham Hart as book retailers and publishers; novels and literary annuals appeared under their *imprint until 1849. William Blanchard joined Carey & Lea in 1833, and the new imprint appeared until 1838, when Henry Carey withdrew in order to pursue his interest in political economy.   MJH

D. Kaser, *Messrs. Carey & Lea of Philadelphia* (1957)
— ed., *Cost Book of Carey & Lea, 1825–1838* (1963)

Carey, Mathew (1760–1839) Philadelphia publisher and bookseller, whose career witnessed a shift from artisanal printing to managerial publishing. An immigrant trained in Dublin and Paris, Carey began creating a national commercial and cultural network with the *American Museum* magazine (1787–92) through correspondence, shipping, travelling, and *subscription publishing. In 1790 he printed a Douay bible, and bible publishing was to be his financial salvation. Although Carey was regularly in debt, his steadily selling *quarto family bible helped him survive economic crises. By 1807 this bible was produced from *standing type, enabling him to print short or long runs without paying for *composition or *proofs and proofreading. By 1792 he was wholesaling books from England for the US; by 1794 he was able to risk the publication of *folio reference works. Carey developed his network through up to 50 agents, including the energetic Mason Weems, and organized national *book fairs from 1802 to 1805. His son H. C. *Carey joined the business by 1817 and Carey retired in 1822, leaving a house that was also America's most important literary publisher to 1840.   MPB

J. N. Green, 'From Printer to Publisher', in *Getting the Books Out*, ed. M. Hackenberg (1987)
ODNB

Carey, William (1761–1834) English missionary who came to India in 1793, he established the *Serampore Mission Press in (1800). Carey oversaw translations of the Bible into Indian languages and Indian epics into English, and compiled Bengali *dictionaries, *grammars, and *textbooks. The publication of the Bengali Matthew's Gospel (1800) is arguably the most significant event in Bengali printing. *See also* **39**; CAREY LIBRARY, SERAMPORE.   AG
ODNB

Carey Library, Serampore Built on the collection of the Serampore Mission library, founded in 1800 by Baptist missionaries, it is named after W. *Carey. The collection merged with the Serampore College library in 1818 and its first librarian was John Fountain. The library contains an unparalleled collection of early missionary publications, including bibles in more than 30 south Asian languages. One of the highlights of the collection is the MS of Carey's unpublished *polyglot dictionary. In recent decades, the library has been nurtured by its long-serving librarian, Sunil Chattopadhyay.   AG

Carlile, Richard (1790–1843) English publisher and writer. Originally a tin worker, Carlile became a radical writer and publisher in 1817, when he started his journal *The Republican* and began reprinting Thomas Paine's banned works. Imprisoned 1819–25 for seditious *libel and again for two years in 1831, Carlile initiated numerous short-lived freethinking journals, but is best remembered for championing press liberty and birth control.

RJD

ODNB

J. H. Weiner, *Radicalism and Freethought* (1983)

Carmelite Missal BL Add. MSS 29704–5, 44892; Glasgow University Library, Euing BD.19–H.9, No. 1875. A late 14th-century MS produced for a Carmelite house in southern England, on which six different artists collaborated. Between 1826 and 1831 the MS was cut into pieces and pasted into *scrapbooks by children. The majority of the fragments were reassembled by Margaret Rickert in the late 1930s. The only surviving Carmelite missal of this period, it is remarkable for the high quality of its decoration and illustration, which involved the collaboration of a number of craftsmen.   ASGE

M. Rickert, *The Reconstructed Carmelite Missal* (1952)

Carnan, Thomas (1737–88) English bookseller and publisher. Carnan is remembered chiefly for destroying the *Stationers' Company *almanac-printing monopoly in 1773. Having printed almanacs for years in flagrant breach of the monopoly, Carnan was prosecuted unsuccessfully by the company, which thus lost its monopoly after a lengthy period of sporadic opposition. Carnan traded for some years with, and then partly succeeded, his stepfather, J. *Newbery.   JH

ODNB

Carnegie, Andrew (1835–1919) Steel magnate and philanthropist. Born in Scotland, the 12-year-old Carnegie moved to Pennsylvania, where he worked as a telegraph operator and borrowed books from Colonel James Anderson's library. His skills and ambition led to increasingly responsible positions at the Pennsylvania Railroad until 1865, when he had sufficient investment income to leave its employment and travel widely. In 1872 he established Carnegie Steel, selling the firm to United States Steel in 1901, thereby realizing an income of $15 million annually. His essay 'Wealth' (*North American Review*, June 1889) argued that rich men should donate money not to charity but to enterprises that encouraged people to raise themselves out of poverty. In 'Wealth', Carnegie outlined his plan to do that by donating library buildings to municipalities that agreed to tax citizens to support the library. It was up to individual citizens to use the collection for self-improvement, just as Carnegie had when borrowing books from Anderson. He formed a foundation, the Carnegie Corporation, and gave grants totalling more than $50 million for 2,811 *public libraries, 1,946 of them in the US. *See also* CARNEGIE LIBRARIES.   CKM

P. Krass, *Andrew Carnegie* (2002)

Carnegie libraries System of 2,500 public and academic libraries in the English-speaking world funded between 1883 and 1919 by A. *Carnegie, Scottish-born steel magnate and philanthropist. Of these, 1,689 were in the US. Initially, Carnegie was personally connected to recipient communities, but in the 1890s the Carnegie Corporation devised a bureaucratic programme to endow

Inside a **Carnegie library**: the Children's Reading Room in the library at Kearney, Nebraska. The library was founded in 1890; the Carnegie building was erected in 1905 and demolished in 1973.

libraries through a standard process administered by its secretary, James Bertram. To receive a grant, a community had to guarantee continuing financial support for the library, since the Carnegie Corporation funded buildings only. Bertram's guidelines stressed function and frugality, but recipients were free to choose whatever architectural style they wished. More than half of the American libraries that the Carnegie Corporation funded were in the top ten recipient states (nine Midwestern states plus California) often in newly settled communities. The libraries proclaimed the values of self-help and independence that civic leaders held to be hallmarks of American democracy. By the end of the 20th century, many Carnegie library buildings retained their original purpose, but others had been converted for different public and private uses, or razed entirely.　　　CJP

A. Van Slyck, *Free to All: Carnegie Libraries and American Culture, 1890–1920* (1995)

Carnegie Medal Britain's leading prize for children's literature, regarded as equivalent to the *Newbery Medal in the US. Named after the great founder and patron of libraries A. *Carnegie, the prize has been administered since 1936 by the UK's Library Association (now CILIP, the Chartered Institute of Library and Information Professionals). A jury of CILIP librarians selects the winner from books written in English and published in the UK the previous year, excluding books first published in other countries. Although there is no cash award, the Carnegie winner typically benefits from publicity and substantially increased sales.　　　JFE

Carolingian (Caroline) **minuscule** A form of compact, rounded *minuscule script that was developed as part of the educational reforms of Charlemagne (*c.*742–814). Spreading through much of western Europe, it was in general use as a book or documentary hand from the late 8th century until the early 12th century.　　　ASGE

Carpentras, Bibliothèque Inguimbertine Named after Joseph Dominique d'Inguimbert (1683–1757), bishop of his native Carpentras from 1735. A Dominican, then a Trappist, he spent 25 years in Italy, where he became archbishop and librarian to Pope Clement XII. The library he brought back from Italy was enriched by additions, most famously the Peiresc collection of early Provençal MSS. It was opened to the public in 1747, and bequeathed to the city with an endowment. Rescued from closure at the Revolution, it was looted in the 1840s by Count *Libri and has been housed in the Hôtel d'Allemand since 1847.　　　VAG

carriage The mechanism of a hand press which allows the *bed to be moved into position beneath the *platen by turning the *rounce.

Carter, Harry (1901–82) English typographer and typographic historian. After an apprenticeship at the *Monotype Corporation, he worked at the Kynoch Press in Birmingham, the *Nonesuch Press in London, and, after the war, HMSO. In 1954, he became archivist to *Oxford University Press, where he stayed until his retirement in 1980. In these later years, he was also involved in scholarship at the *Plantin-Moretus Museum in Antwerp. His major publications include his translated edition of *Fournier on Typefounding: The Text of the Manuel Typographique, 1764–1766* (1930); an edition of J. *Moxon's *Mechanick Exercises*, with *Davis (1958); *Type Specimen Facsimiles* (1963–72); *A View of Early Typography: Up to About 1600* (1969); *A History of the Oxford University Press* (1975); and, assisting *Morison, *John Fell: The University Press and the 'Fell' Types* (1967), a magnificent hand-set volume using the original types.　　　MW

M. Thomas *et al.*, *Harry Carter, Typographer* (2005)

Carter, John (1905–75) English antiquarian bookseller and bibliographer. He entered the book trade with *Scribner's in 1927, and subsequently worked at *Sotheby's. His collaboration with G. *Pollard on *An Enquiry into the Nature of Certain Nineteenth Century Pamphlets* (1934) exposed the *forgeries of T. J. *Wise. Other major publications included *Taste and Technique in Book-Collecting* (1948), *Printing and the Mind of Man* (1963), and the *ABC for Book Collectors* (1952; 8e, 2004).　　　KEA

ODNB

Carter, Matthew (1937–) Type designer, born in London, working in the USA. Son of H. *Carter. His chief designs are Snell Roundhand (1966), the newspaper face Olympian (1970), Bell Centennial, the book face Galliard (both 1978), and the screen fount Verdana (1996). He founded the digital *type company Bitstream in 1981 with Mike Parker.　　　SC

cartonnage A term sometimes applied to the rough plain card used to make simple covers and cheap bindings in several continental European countries from the 16th century onwards.

cartouche Scroll-shaped tablet found primarily on maps to contain the title or ornament; by extension, a round, oval, or decorated label, or a frame-shaped bookbinding tool.

cartulary An archival book containing a collection of muniments (title deeds, privileges) belonging to an individual or institution. During the Middle Ages, the term most frequently applied to a cartulary is *registrum*, and the designation 'cartulary' and 'register' are frequently confused in modern scholarship. A cartulary predominantly contains *charters; although registers may contain charters, other kinds of document (such as memoranda, pleas, pensions, extents, statutes) will predominate. Scholars also identify a form—the chronicle-cartulary— as intermediate between *chronicle and cartulary, with charter transcriptions (sometimes abbreviated) embedded within the narrative structure.

　　The earliest surviving cartularies date from the first half of the 9th century in Europe. The form develops later in England, where the first extant examples are from the beginning of the 11th century. Cartularies assume importance because of the substantial loss of original charters. In Anglo-Saxon England, for example, only around one-fifth of the 1,500 or so known charters survive in contemporary or near-contemporary form; virtually all of the rest exist only in cartulary copies principally dating from the 13th to the 15th centuries. During this period, specialized cartularies relating to particular monastic obedientiaries are frequently compiled in collections concerning larger foundations alongside, or instead of, more general productions. Cartulary scribes necessarily mediated their texts and may not always be relied upon to present them in full: frequently prone to omission or truncation are lengthy witness lists and passages in the vernacular.

Focusing on cartularies' significance as collections of texts, recent historical research has emphasized the evidence they supply about the shifting interests and preoccupations of the individuals and communities for whom they were produced. **KAL**

G. R. C. Davis, *Medieval Cartularies of Great Britain* (1958)

G. Declercq, 'Originals and Cartularies', in *Charters and the Use of the Written Word in Medieval Society*, ed. K. Heidecker (2000)

T. Foulds, 'Medieval Cartularies', *Archives*, 18 (1987), 3–35

J.-P. Genet, 'Cartulaires, registres et histoire: l'exemple anglais', in *Le Métier d'historien au moyen âge*, ed. B. Guenée (1977)

A. J. Kosto and A. Winroth, eds., *Charters, Cartularies and Archives* (2002)

D. Walker, 'The Organization of Material in Medieval Cartularies', in *The Study of Medieval Records*, ed. D. A. Bullough and R. L. Storey (1971)

Casamassima, Emanuele (1916–88) Italian palaeographer and university professor. Working at the National Central Library in *Florence as librarian (from 1949) and director (1965), in 1966 he had to deal with the city's devastating flood. Hindered rather than helped by Roman bureaucracy, he saved the library and its collections, before taking up in 1970 a chair in palaeography. He also produced studies of the first edition of Dante's *Divina Commedia* (Foligno, 1472) and of the calligrapher *Arrighi. **NH**

Casanatense library Established by the legacy of the Dominican cardinal Girolamo Casanate (1620–1700), it opened in 1701 as the order's Rome library and grew rapidly, especially under the direction of Giovanni Battista Audiffredi (1734–94). When religious houses were suppressed in 1873, ownership passed to the Italian state. Today, it holds some 400,000 volumes, including *c*.6,000 MSS, 2,200 *incunables, and 30,000 *engravings. **CWK**

C. Pietrangeli *et al.*, *La Biblioteca Casanatense* (1993)

Casaubon, Isaac (1559–1614) Classical scholar. Born in Geneva to Huguenot parents, he taught Greek at Geneva from 1581 until 1596 (marrying a daughter of H. *Estienne) and in Montpellier (1596–9). Called to Paris by Henri IV, he was appointed sub-librarian of the Royal Library in 1604. After the king's assassination (1610), he settled in England, where he enjoyed James I's

protection. As an editor and commentator, he worked on Aristotle, Athenaeus, Persius, Pliny, Polybius, Strabo, Suetonius, and Theophrastus, among others, while his *Ephemerides* document the daily intellectual life of one of the greatest Renaissance scholars. **VAG**

ODNB

case binding A bookbinding made by gluing the text block into a prefabricated case, using cloth strips or similar material (*see* **17**).

casing machine The production of a modern *case binding typically involves a series of mechanized processes, including folding and sewing the sheets, making the binding cases, and gluing in the *text blocks. The machines to carry out the various stages were mostly developed separately in America during the late 19th century. Case-making machines, first introduced *c*.1891–5, take the boards and covering material, cut them to size, and generate cases ready to take the text block. The associated casing-in machines coat adhesive on the board papers before fitting cases and text blocks together. **DRSP**

J. Peacock, *Book Production* (1989)

Caslon family London punchcutters and typefounders. **William I** (1693–1766), apprenticed to a London gunlock engraver, set up on his own by 1716, also making tools for bookbinders and silver-plate chasers. W. *Bowyer reputedly encouraged him to cut and cast *type, perhaps beginning with a *Hebrew *fount. In 1722 he began work on an *Arabic, then turned to *romans and *italics that soon drove the other English foundries into decline and largely halted the import of Dutch types. His conservative revolution, with romans based on 100-year-old types cut by *Briot in Holland, drove out cruder but more modern English types. From the 1750s, other foundries copied his types and *Baskerville's new style challenged them, but they remained popular to *c*.1800. The first printed edition of the *Declaration of Independence was, for example, produced from Caslon type. The foundry also made many *texturas and non-Latins. In 1763, William and his son issued the first English typefounder's specimen book.

The early work of **William II** (1720–78) is undistinguished, but later he apparently cut good large romans and italics, without attempting to match his father's style. He also introduced excellent large, *sand cast romans (whose cutter remains unidentified). He displayed jealous unkindness toward his talented apprentice J. *Jackson.

William III (1754–1833) left his mother's typefoundry to acquire Jackson's in 1792. He recovered from his 1793 bankruptcy, and **William IV** (1780–1869) succeeded him, while William III's mother, **Elizabeth I** (1730–95), and his brother's widow, **Elizabeth II** (*c*.1755–1809) continued the original foundry—two different Caslon foundries competed for 25 years. William III and IV are not documented as punchcutters. William I's types were among the first historical types to be revived *c*.1840,

spawning new generations of types, including versions that remain popular today. The original typefoundry continued under the Caslon name (with Catherwood and others) until Stephenson Blake (successor to William IV) and *Monotype divided its materials in 1936.　　JAL
ODNB

Cassell & Co. London publishing house founded in 1848 by John Cassell (1817–65), temperance activist and wholesale tea and coffee merchant. During his life, the firm's characteristic publications were cheap, weekly *serials in the 'useful knowledge' tradition associated with C. *Knight—periodicals like the *Working Man's Friend*, and reference works in *parts such as *Cassell's Illustrated History of England*. After his death, the company worked in similar fields on a larger scale, selling syndicated material to hundreds of provincial newspapers and employing canvassers to distribute 50 or more books in parts simultaneously. From the later 19th century, the firm underwent a difficult transition towards business centred on book publication. Despite investing substantially in literary publishing, notably in the 1890s and 1930s, the firm (now part of the Orion group) remains best known for its dictionaries, directories, and other reference works.　　GL
S. Nowell-Smith, *The House of Cassell* (1958)
G. H. Pike, *John Cassell* (1894)

Cassell's National Library Influential series of 'standard works in every branch of literature' with an international reach, issued by *Cassell & Co. in weekly parts priced at 3*d*. in paper covers or 6*d*. in cloth. Beginning in January 1886 with Macaulay's *Warren Hastings*, it was completed in 214 volumes in 1890, the average sale reaching over 30,000 per volume before the end of the century. The editor was Henry Morley, professor of English literature at University College London, who had already overseen 'Cassell's Library of English Literature' (1875–81) and '*Morley's Universal Library' (1883–8) for *Routledge.　　GL

cassie quires The two outside *quires in a *ream of paper. They may consist of sheets already damaged that protect the good paper. *See also* CORDING QUIRE.

Cassirer, Paul (1871–1926) and **Bruno Cassirer** (1872–1941) German publishers and art dealers. In 1898 the cousins jointly founded a publishing house and art gallery in Berlin, but they soon worked independently. Paul established the Pan-Presse in 1908, while Bruno was a successful publisher of contemporary fiction and illustrated books.　　US

casting off copy Estimating a book's length by counting the words in the copy and computing the length of the whole, based on the size of paper, the *format, and the *size of type to be used. This process allows the printer to estimate costs and order the right amount of paper; it also allows permits *composition by formes. Printer's copy that has been cast off sometimes has the ends of

cast-off pages marked. However, a *compositor might similarly mark the copy to indicate the ends of pages as he has finished composing them.　　MMS
Gaskell, *NI*

Catalogue of English Literary Manuscripts 1450–1700 (CELM) Database project, funded by the UK Arts and Humanities Research Council, made freely available on the *World Wide Web in summer 2009. It has been compiled by Peter Beal, on a database designed by John Lavagnino, under the general supervision of H. R. Woudhuysen. Based on Beal's *Index of English Literary Manuscripts, 1450–1700* (2 vols in 4 parts, 1980–93), but extensively revised and expanded from the original coverage of 128 authors, CELM will incorporate some 40,000 entries describing MSS of literary works by more than 200 authors, including *letters, *notebooks, *promptbooks, proof sheets (*see* PROOFS AND PROOFREADING), *annotated books, and other documentary sources. It will be the first stage in creating a MS equivalent to the *Short-Title Catalogue* of printed books.　　PB

catalogues, fixed-price *See* BOOKSELLERS' CATALOGUES.

catalogues of books, MS and print Catalogues record ownership, usually availability, sometimes noting donations or *provenance, and are compiled with the purpose of publicly imparting this information. Catalogues of books, whether in MS or print, require a minimal description of each item for identification. Physical presence at any one place is what distinguishes catalogues from *bibliographies, but the two terms converge when *union catalogues, based on more than one distinct collection, are compiled. Publicizing this information distinguishes catalogues from inventories, which are essentially private records of ownership. A comprehensive listing of locations of copies of distinct editions is called a *census. A catalogue may consist of a single MS sheet with brief titles and shelf-marks, posted on a library wall; it may be published as a multi-volume work, or as an online resource. With databases created by amalgamating sections of large online catalogues, the distinction between catalogue and bibliography typically becomes irrelevant.

Catalogues may be transitory in nature (e.g. auction catalogues, *exhibition catalogues) or more permanent. Yet, as records of physical presence, they are valuable source material for ownership, intellectual history, and the history of book dissemination through the book trade. This record is constantly augmented as books are published. Catalogues are increasingly mined as historical resources by scholars across disciplines who seek to know what texts were available, when and where they were stored, and who had access to them.

1. MSS
2. Printed books

1. MSS

Medieval library catalogues are known from the late 8th century onwards; the earliest include those of the

Benedictine abbeys of Fulda and Bobbio. Medieval catalogues usually listed *volumes, each of which would often include several, even many, distinct works. Towards the end of the period, very substantial catalogues were compiled, for example, in Canterbury's Christ Church and St Augustine's Abbey. Notable examples of medieval union catalogues of monastic libraries include the *Registrum Anglie* (early 14th century, comprising *c*.90 libraries in England, Scotland, and Wales) and, much later in the Low Countries, the *Registrum Rooklooster* (*c*.1535–40). Both are arranged in alphabetical order of author, with *sigla indicating the locations of the listed works. They are primarily finding devices for texts, rather than records of ownership.

2. Printed books

The earliest printed catalogues served the book trade. In *c*.1470, *Schöffer printed a handbill (*see* BROADSIDE) at Mainz listing nineteen works, produced by himself and others, that were available for sale. The thousands of items in the stock catalogues of the 17th-century Dutch booksellers *Blaeu, *Elzevier, *Janssonius, *Leers, and van der *Aa show the range and scope of the international book trade once it was fully developed. In *book fair catalogues, a particular kind of stock catalogue, printers and booksellers listed recent publications for the biannual book fairs in *Frankfurt am Main (published 1564–1750) and *Leipzig (from 1594, continuing until the late 19th century).

MS records of book auctions exist in the Low Countries from the late 15th century onwards, but the first printed *auction catalogue is for a public auction held in Leiden in 1599 by the bookseller Louis Elzevier. In France, this method of sale is known from *c*.1630, in England not until 1676; thereafter, it became a prominent feature of the English book trade. From the 17th century on, printed catalogues of private collections were used as valuable bibliographical tools, although they were often compiled with a view to the books' sale and subsequent dispersal. Consul Joseph *Smith's *Bibliotheca Smithiana* (1755) is exceptional, because it led to purchase en bloc for King *George III, and the collection is preserved virtually intact in the *British Library.

At the turn of the 16th century, the first major institutional library catalogues were published for the university libraries of Leiden (1595), Augsburg (1600), and the *Bodleian (1605), all supplemented in later years. When university and public *lending libraries began to grow more rapidly, *card catalogues were better suited to keep pace. Subject systems for *cataloguing were introduced in the 18th century, first in the University of Göttingen. The consolidation of national libraries in the course of the 19th century brought large cataloguing projects, resulting in printed catalogues of the British Museum Library (from 1881), the *Bibliothèque nationale in Paris (from 1897), and the Library of *Congress (from 1924). In the last decades of the 20th century, many catalogues in major libraries (whether on cards or published) were converted into automated systems. The most recent development is their amalgamation into large national databases, e.g. *COPAC in Britain (www.copac.ac.uk), Catalogue collectif de France (www.ccfr.bnf.fr), and, internationally, the Karlsruhe Virtual Catalogue (www.ubka.uni-karlsruhe.de).

From *c*.1960, major libraries have excelled in mounting exhibitions on selected themes, often accompanied by catalogues compiled by experts, thus producing numerous specialist studies.

Major research libraries have produced numerous catalogues with extensive descriptions of special materials (MSS, maps, *incunabula, 16th-century books). For the enumeration of large quantities of material, the preferred format is a short-title catalogue, the descriptions including standardized forms of author, title, *imprint, and bibliographical *format. This cataloguing schema can well be adapted to conversion into automated databases, for example, the *English Short-Title Catalogue*, or *ESTC, and the *Incunabula Short-Title Catalogue* (ISTC). By combining such databases for access through a single system, the Consortium of European Research Libraries (CERL) has developed the Hand Press Book database, including several millions of records for books published before *c*.1830 in many European and American libraries (www.cerl.org). LH

www.bsc.idcpublishers.info, consulted Oct. 2007
L. E. Boyle OP, *Medieval Latin Palaeography* (1984)
CBMLC
A. Charon *et al.*, eds., *Les Ventes de livres et leurs catalogues XVIIe–XXe siècle* (2000)
B. Fabian, ed., *Die Meßkataloge des sechzehnten Jarhunderts* (5 vols, 1972–2001)
S. Jayne, *Library Catalogues of the English Renaissance*, 2e (1983)
F. G. Kaltwasser, *Die Bibliothek als Museum* (1999)
N. R. Ker, *Medieval Libraries of Great Britain*, 2e (1964); supplement, A. G. Watson (1987)
G. Pollard and A. Ehrman, *The Distribution of Books by Catalogue* (1965)
B. van Selm *et al.*, ed., *Book-Sales Catalogues of the Dutch Republic 1599–1800*
A. Taylor, *Book Catalogues*, rev. W. P. Barlow, 2e (1986)

Cataloguing in Publication (CIP) A publishing

protocol by which the bibliographic record for a work is prepared in advance of publication and is printed in that publication, typically towards the foot of the *copyright page. In many countries, this data—intended primarily to assist libraries in *cataloguing—is produced by the national library, working with publishers. CIP records (created and arranged according to internationally accepted standards regarding information sequence, punctuation, capitalization, and spacing) consequently contribute to the development of national bibliographies. *See also* ISBN; LEGAL DEPOSIT. MFS

BL Bibliographic Services, www.bl.uk/bibliographic/cip.html, consulted Dec. 2008
LC CIP Division, cip.loc.gov, consulted Dec. 2008

cataloguing rules (cataloguing codes) Cataloguing

rules provide guidance for consistent construction of library catalogues, including recording title and publication information, describing the physical item, and choosing and establishing headings. The materials covered have gone from books to non-book materials to e-materials. Only a few codes have addressed subject access. Modern Anglo-American cataloguing rules include the British Museum's 91 rules (1841), C. A. Cutter's rules (1876), the British and American library associations' Joint Rules (1908), ALA rules (2e, 1940), and the Anglo-American Cataloguing Rules (1967; 2e, 1978). Before 1950, most cataloguing codes provided guidance on individual cases, but theorists such as Seymour Lubetzky and S. R. Ranganathan developed rules based more solidly on principles. The Paris Principles of 1961 were an agreement on the choice and form of names and headings; they led to the gradual convergence of catalogue codes worldwide. The Cataloguing Section of IFLA is currently developing a much broader and more solidly grounded set of International Cataloguing Principles.   LSC

M. D. Joachim, ed., *Historical Aspects of Cataloging and Classification* (2003)

E. Svenonius, *The Intellectual Foundations of Information Organization* (2000)

— ed., *The Conceptual Foundations of Descriptive Cataloguing* (1989)

Catalunya, Biblioteca de Founded in Barcelona in 1907 as the Institute of Catalan Studies Library, its mission was to collect the Catalan printed heritage. However, it could not assume the name as well as the role of the Library of Catalonia until 1981. Since 1940, it has occupied the 15th-century Hospital of the Holy Cross, recently renovated in a stunning combination of medieval and modern. Among its 4 million items are excellent holdings of rare Catalan and Spanish *imprints, and a splendid Cervantes collection (*see* DON QUIXOTE). The library maintains *union catalogues of Catalan *imprints and library holdings, and extensive digital collections.   DRW

catchword A word at the end of a page, or *gathering of a MS or printed book, normally in the *direction line, providing the next page's first word. It aided binders in assembling gatherings in the correct order (related to the *signature), printers in the *imposition of pages in the *forme, and readers in anticipating the following page. In MSS it was typically placed near the edge of the page or vertically in the *gutter. Its use declined after the late 18th century. Also related to a *lemma, a text word repeated at the beginning of a note or *gloss.   MMS

catechism The instruction by word of mouth on elementary principles of Christian religion. Such instruction survives in MSS and a few *incunabula, some known as 'abcdaria', which include Latin texts of the creed, the Lord's Prayer, *Ave Maria*, *Nunc Dimittis*, and the *Magnificat*. From early in the 16th century, the oral traditions of religious instruction survive in the form of question and answer in vernacular treatises, many with the title 'Catechism'. One of the earliest to appear in print is the *Cathecismo pequeno da doctrina* by Diogo Ortiz de Villegas (Lisbon, 1504), but in 1502 the term was used in de *Worde's edition of *The ordynarye of crystyanyte or of crysten men*. Printed catechisms were almost immediately instruments for the Reformation. Early Lutheran versions were Luther's *Kleiner* and *Grosser Katechismus* (1529), preceded by Andreas Althamer's *Catechismus in Frag und Antwort* (Nuremberg, 1528). Both were models for many to follow, usually written by known theologians of the Reformation, e.g. Philip Melanchthon, Urbanus Rhegius, Ulrich Zwingli, Theodore Beza, and John Calvin. A few English translations were printed in Antwerp by Martin de Keyser, the widow of Christoffel van Ruremond, and Steven Mierdman (*see STC* 13828.4, 26138, 4797.3). When Protestant printers in Antwerp were prosecuted, other English versions were printed in Emden. During the reign of Edward VI, Dutch versions were printed from 1551 in London by refugees from the Low Countries (*STC* 15260.5, 15260.7, 15263), and in 1561 and 1566 by the English printer J. *Day (*STC* 15261–2). Of the Protestant catechisms, the most widely disseminated was the *Heidelberg Catechismus* (1563), English versions of which were printed from 1572 in London, and from 1591 in Edinburgh and Oxford (*STC* 13023–31.8). The Counter-Reformation adopted the form to produce Catholic versions, the most important of which were the works of Petrus Canisius, SJ (1521–97), who wrote the *Summa Doctrinae* (1555), *Catechismus Minimus* (1556), and the *Parvus Catechismus Catholicorum* (1558). These were followed by the authoritative *Catechismus Romanus* (1566), compiled at the request of the Council of Trent, which remained unchanged until 1969. The catechism has remained an instrument for teaching Christian principles until the present day.   LH

DEL 1

W. Heijting, *The Catechisms and Confessions of Faith in the Dutch Reformation to 1585* (1989)

W. Simon, '"Cathechismus" im Medium Buchdruck', *GJ* 75 (2000), 160–80

Cátedra, Pedro M. (1952–) Bibliographer, historian of the book and of reading, Professor of Spanish at Salamanca, director of the Seminario de Estudios Medievales y Renacentistas, Instituto Biblioteca Hispana (CILENGUA), and Instituto de Historia del Libro y de la Lectura. His methodologically innovative studies include: *Imprenta y lecturas en la Baeza del siglo XVI* (2001); *Nobleza y lectura … la biblioteca de don Alonso Osorio* (2002); and *Bibliotecas y lecturas de mujeres (Siglo XVI)* (2004).   BT

Cathach Psalter Dublin, Royal Irish Academy, S.R.12.R.33. Dating from the 7th century, the Cathach (lit. 'battler') is arguably the earliest surviving Irish MS. It is decorated in a preliminary form of insular art and written in Latin with Irish *glosses. The MS is now imperfect and damaged, with only 58 leaves surviving, containing parts of Psalms 30–105. It is traditionally said to have been written by St Columba (*c*.521–97) and was venerated as part of his cult.   ASGE

M. Herity and A. Breen, *The Cathach of Colum Cille* (2002)

cathedral bindings A style of bookbinding popular in England and France in the first half of the 19th century,

whereby the covers were decorated with designs inspired by the architecture of a medieval cathedral. DRSP
E. Jamieson, *English Embossed Bindings 1825–1850* (1972)

cathedral libraries in Britain Although any important ecclesiastical house in the pre-Reformation period would have owned books, it would not necessarily have had a library. Little is known about the content of libraries in Anglo-Saxon England, but substantial collections existed in Benedictine monasteries and in cathedral priories such as Canterbury and Durham. Exeter Cathedral, for example, had a library to which Bishop Leofric bequeathed his own collection (1072). Benedictine abbeys (and, from the 13th century, the university libraries) were more likely to have significant collections than cathedrals, but catalogues survive for at least seven medieval cathedral chapter libraries: Aberdeen, Exeter, Glasgow, Lichfield, Lincoln, St Paul's, and Rochester. Others, such as Salisbury, had large collections. By the mid-15th century, many had built separate library rooms.

The history of these collections was severely disrupted by the dissolution of the monasteries during the English Reformation and the dispersal of their libraries in 1536–40, when their books no longer seemed to serve any practical ecclesiastical or intellectual purpose. N. R. *Ker has commented that the libraries of cathedrals, of former cathedral monasteries, and of other religious houses that were converted into cathedrals should, in theory, have been more fortunate in retaining their books, since their guardians were not suddenly expelled at the Dissolution. *Durham, he noted, still has more than 300 of its medieval MSS; *Canterbury has only 21, but a further 300 were removed and survive elsewhere. Many books passed into the Royal Library and thence into the British Museum (later *British Library) (e.g. Worcester and Rochester); many of Exeter's are in the *Bodleian. Very little survives from Wells and *York, however.

Thereafter, responsibility for the maintenance of the cathedral libraries passed to the members of the new chapters. Their institutional independence has given the British cathedral libraries their particular character. Although the Henrician statutes of 1540–42 had little immediate impact, there was a slow revival of interest in the libraries during the later 16th century; for example, Bishop Edmund Guest's bequest of his library to Salisbury (1577), new statutes at Hereford (1583), and general signs of recovery by the 1620s (e.g. acquisitions at York and Canterbury). This progress was halted by the destruction and dispersals of the Commonwealth period (1640s and 1650s). Lichfield was burned in 1642, and attempts were made to transfer the larger libraries to depots in London: Durham in 1646, Canterbury in 1650. York was protected by the influence of Thomas Fairfax. The Restoration reversed this process and saw the building of a number of new libraries: Canterbury in 1664, Lincoln in 1675.

Use of cathedral libraries was at first largely confined to the chapters' members, but in the 18th century, their collections were made available not only to the diocesan clergy but to local professional men and even some women—subject to approval by a member of the chapter. Several cathedrals seem to have permitted borrowers in considerable numbers. By the 19th century, the libraries were considered centres for historical research and were often equipped with new buildings, catalogues, and staff. This tendency continued in the 20th century, with an increasing role played by university or other local libraries in supporting the work of the cathedrals. A national forum has been developed in the Cathedral Libraries and Archives Association (1976). A nationally funded project organized by the *Bibliographical Society resulted in the publication of the *Cathedral Libraries Catalogue: Books Printed before 1701 in the Libraries of the Anglican Cathedrals of England and Wales.* DJS

D. Bell, 'Monastic Libraries: 1400–1557', *CHBB 3*
CHLBI
R. Irwin, *The Origins of the English Library* (1958)
P. Kaufman, 'Reading Vogues at English Cathedral Libraries of the Eighteenth Century', *BNYPL* 67–8 (Dec. 1963; Jan., Feb., Mar. 1964)
N. Ker, *Medieval Libraries of Great Britain*, 2e (1964)
M. Lapidge *et al.*, eds., *The Blackwell Encyclopaedia of Anglo-Saxon England* (1999; repr. 2001)
D. Shaw, ed., *Cathedral Libraries Catalogue* (2 vols, 1985–98)
R. Wilson, 'The Contents of the Medieval Library', in *The English Library before 1700*, ed. F. Wormald and C. E. Wright (1958)

Catherine of Cleves, Hours of A *book of hours, Pierpont Morgan Library MSS M 917 and 945, completed in Utrecht, c.1440 for Catherine of Cleves, duchess of Guelders. It is one of the most elaborate 15th-century Flemish MSS, containing over 150 miniatures (*see* MINIATURES (1)) and much other illumination. At some point in its history, it was divided into two parts; however, these were not identified as originating from the same MS until the 1960s. Both parts were acquired by the Morgan Library (in 1963 and 1970). ASGE
J. Plummer, *The Hours of Catherine of Cleves* (rev. edn 1975)

Catnach, James (1792–1841) English *broadside publisher. Using wooden presses in Monmouth Court, Seven Dials, London, Catnach printed cheap broadsides and children's books (*see* **15**) from 1813 to rival John Pitts. Specially commissioned topical ballads, illustrated with lurid or sentimental *woodcuts, concerned murders, hangings, dying confessions, violence, royal scandals, and politics. Sold for a penny by street 'patterers' they sometimes had *press runs exceeding 250,000. Catnach retired in 1839, reportedly worth £10,000. PGS
ODNB

Cave, Edward (1691–1754) English editor, publisher, and printer. Experience with the Post Office and the distribution of news led to Cave's most successful venture, the *Gentleman's Magazine* (1731). Restrictions on parliamentary reporting were behind its famous 'Debates in the Senate of Magna Lilliputia'. He printed or published around 220 titles, including S. *Johnson's *Rambler* (1750–52) and *Adventurer* (1752–4). CYF
ODNB

Caxton, William (*c.*1420–92) England's first printer; mercer, translator, author. When Caxton ventured into printing, he could look back on a career as a successful Mercer, mainly residing in Flanders. He took part in diplomatic missions that brought him into contact with the English court and that of the dukes of Burgundy. From 1462 to *c.*1471 he was governor of the English nation, resident in Bruges. Political turbulence in England in the early 1470s occasioned a period of exile in Cologne. There, Caxton encountered printers who had been established in the city since 1465, and had created a lively centre of printing and the book trade. In Cologne, he published three Latin works with English connections, including Bartholomaeus Anglicus' *De Proprietatibus Rerum*; he also completed a translation from French into English, the *Recuyell of the Histories of Troy* (then a recent work belonging to the pseudo-history of the house of Burgundy).

On returning to Flanders in 1473, he continued printing, beginning with his *Recuyell* (completed in 1473/4), which was *dedicated in extensive prologues to Margaret of York, duchess of Burgundy and sister of King Edward IV. It was followed by his *translation of Jacobus de Cessolis' moralizing allegory on chess, then by four works in French and a Latin *book of hours. The later French works were probably printed in association with Colard Mansion, a *scribe and printer in Bruges.

By the end of 1475, Caxton's diplomatic activities had ended, and he established a *printing office in the precincts of Westminster Abbey. From the middle of 1476 until his death, probably early in 1492, this press produced 98 surviving editions; 90 per cent of these were in English, the remaining 10 per cent mainly Latin works for ecclesiastical use. The first products of the Westminster press include the *editio princeps* of the *Canterbury Tales*, soon followed by English translations from the French, by his *patron A. *Woodville, Earl Rivers, and above all by himself. Almost half of his total output consists of works in translation. These include the *Golden Legend*, translated by him from the French adaptation of Jacobus de Voragine's *Legenda Aurea*, published in 1483/4 under the patronage of the earl of Arundel.

The largest part of his output is literary and historical works. He twice published the *Chronicles of England* (*see* CHRONICLES) with an extension to recent times written by himself, which also appears in his edition of Ranulf Higden's *Polychronicon*. An author of fluent English prose, he is famous for his books' prologues and epilogues, in which he comments on the work and its topicality. His patrons—royal, noble, and mercantile—reflect the connections made in his career as merchant and diplomat. The clientele for his books was not, however, confined to this circle, and he must be considered instrumental in creating new readers for English works appearing in print. LH

N. F. Blake, *William Caxton: A Bibliographical Guide* (1985)
— ed., *Caxton's Own Prose* (1973)
BMC 11
ODNB
G. D. Painter, *William Caxton* (1976)

Caxton Binder The name given to a bookbinding workshop in Westminster, active *c.*1480–1510, associated with *Caxton and his successor, de *Worde. Thirty-nine bindings are known, many on Caxton imprints or including fragments of his printing as binders' *waste. The bindery also bound MSS for *Westminster Abbey.
DRSP
Nixon and Foot

Caxton Club *Bibliophiles' association, founded in 1895 in Chicago, by fifteen bibliophiles who primarily intended to publish high-quality books, chiefly for their own personal libraries. Following four other newly formed book clubs—the *Grolier Club in New York (1884), the *Club of Odd Volumes in Boston (1886), the *Rowfant Club in Cleveland (1892), and the *Philobiblon Club in Philadelphia (1893)—they also began to hold exhibitions and to establish a reference library about books. Some 60 books have been published by the Club, most in *limited editions. Women were first elected to membership in 1976. To mark the club's centenary, Chicago mayor Richard M. Daley declared 1995 'The Year of the Book in Chicago'. Today, its membership, exceeding 300 resident and non-resident members, includes authors, binders, collectors, conservators, dealers, designers, editors, librarians, publishers, and scholars. PTR
F. J. Piehl, *The Caxton Club 1895–1995* (1995)

Caxton Printers Printing and publishing firm in Caldwell, Idaho, since 1903. Established by Albert E. Gipson, the firm remains in the Gipson family. It published Ayn Rand's early novella, *Anthem*, and is renowned as a fine printer and publisher of Western Americana.
SEC

CD-ROM (Compact Disc Read-Only Memory) An optical disc used to store electronic data, including audio, video, and photographic files, as well as computer software and text files. Publishers employ CD-ROMs to deliver scholarly databases, *audio books, and electronic books (*see* 19), including *digitized *facsimiles. The capacity of such discs is enormous: one CD may hold the equivalent of several hundred books. In some markets, it has largely been replaced by the DVD. RSG

CEAA *See* CENTER FOR EDITIONS OF AMERICAN AUTHORS.

Cecil, William, Baron Burghley (1520/21–98) English statesman and book collector. Cecil possessed many works of medieval and later history, as well as a collection of classical literature, largely acquired from the humanist John Cheke. A portion of his collection—comprising more than 3,800 lots of printed books and 400 of MSS—was sold at auction in 1687. Other parts of his library and papers are preserved at *Hatfield House. ASGE
Fletcher
ODNB

cellar book In the wine trade, a utilitarian stock-book of wines purchased, stored, and sold. Among oenophiles, a record of successive tastings, and of the company in which choice bottles were consumed. George Saintsbury's *Notes on a Cellar Book* (1920) may still be read with envious pleasure. BJF

censorship Censorship is generally understood to be the official suppression or prohibition of forms of expression. It has a narrower legal definition—expressly the official inspection of books, journals, theatre, film, music, and popular media to ascertain that they do not offend against legal proscriptions identified by governments. Originally, and increasingly, it has a much broader definition, relating to the supervision by the powerful of public meaning. As old as the public circulation of meaning in civil societies, censorship is exercised in varying forms across the globe.

1. Definitions
2. History of censorship
3. Censorship and governance
4. Beyond the book

1. Definitions

Censorship's formal definition, referring to the inspection of materials before publication, only partially describes it in practice. The chair of the Australian Literature Censorship Board in the 1930s was able to maintain that Australia had no censorship because books were prohibited only after publication, rather than before. Its broadest definition, however, suggests that censorship is the constitutive principle for all speech and meaning. The Roman censors were magistrates responsible for the census, as well as for public morals, and Freud described a necessary, internal, psychological censor, acting to repress the unconscious's disruptive elements. Censorship has been expanded by post-structuralist and sociological approaches to encompass all mechanisms of exclusion by which the speakable is distinguished from the unspeakable, which some view as the constituting norm.

A more functional definition keeps the emphasis on official power. Censorship in this form has itself many varied applications, differentiated often by the nature of the threat identified, present both in the putative meaning and in the communicative abilities and techniques of the media. Censorship is also identifiable in the restriction of forms of expression not only by sanctioned power, but through control over production and distribution exercised by publishers, printers, booksellers, Internet providers, and various media. These agents have, with authors, historically been at the forefront of efforts to resist official censorship and cultural regulation. *Self-censorship is a further category, and a factor in the operations by which censorship becomes, as Sue Curry Jansen has argued, 'the knot that binds power and knowledge'.

2. History of censorship

Exercised in ancient societies such as China and Israel as an essential form of governance to enable both the political and moral control of populations, the presence of censorship through the last 2,000 years of human history is an index of conflicts in organized societies dependent on communication. *Book burnings, the punishment and execution of authors and thinkers, the centralized licensing of production and distribution, with other forms of rigorous or brutal censorship, have become the hallmarks for our modern understanding of medieval dissent. As more books were written and copied, more ideas came into conflict with the aims and teachings of those in power. The introduction of the *Index Librorum Prohibitorum* by the Roman Catholic Church in 1559 heralded the beginning of the modern idea of banned writing, and the Inquisition spread an integrated system of state and church censorship to the colonized Americas, where the burning of Maya codices typifies the ways in which censorship has been a crucial instrument of conquest around the world.

When European printing began to require licensing, systematic governmental control sought to keep pace with the generation of new forms of information. Modern, European bureaucratic censorship is coeval with the development of printing presses, and is arguably a foundational structure of the nation-state. This is not to suggest that this form of censorship is inevitable, necessary, or even always successful, however. *Darnton's work on the relationship between the underground presses and the progress of the French Revolution, emphasizing the importance of seditious and obscene libels both in communicating dissent and in popularizing the new politics, is emblematic of a new attention to the social role of literature outside official censorship. Lynn Hunt's collaborative work on the early modern origins of *pornography has, similarly, emphasized the dynamic relationship between licit and illicit publications, evidencing a *Foucauldian interest in the productive as well as repressive effects of censorship.

3. Censorship and governance

In the modern era, censorship has been exercised by all countries, though with differing aims. A precept of the Enlightenment, the right to 'free speech' as articulated in the constitution of the US has been understood as the corollary to political democracy, but every nation in the 'free' world continues to uphold accepted legal limits on the circulation of meaning to its citizens. The question, then, is what is at stake in that freedom vis-à-vis political, sexual, religious, and other forms of socially contested meaning, especially around so-called 'hate speech' and the rights of minors and differentiated social groupings. The argument of contemporary theorists, such as Michael Holquist, that censorship may be inescapable suggests that 'To be for or against censorship as such is to assume a freedom no one has. Censorship *is*. One can only discriminate among its more and less repressive effects' (Holquist, 16).

The collapse of the Soviet bloc in the late 1980s and 1990s, the same decades in which this argument gained ground, saw the release of a flood of official records from Russia and east European states testifying to the systematic implementation of pre- and post-publication censorship throughout the 20th century, epic in both scope and

In 1940, **censorship** was lifted briefly in Leningrad: Anna Akhmatova was able to publish poems which previously circulated orally. This copy of *Iz shesti knig* (From Six Books) was a *presentation copy from the author, who has written her name beneath its *frontispiece, a 1929 portrait.

ИЗ ШЕСТИ КНИГ

Стихотворения

А Н Н Ы   А Х М А Т О В О Й

1940

Ленинград

СОВЕТСКИЙ ПИСАТЕЛЬ

force, bringing some perspective to this observation about differentiated repression. Continuing political repression—particularly through press censorship—is witnessed by the journal *Index on Censorship*, which exposes the continuing use of censorship by military and religious dictatorships, from Nazi *book-burning spectacles to the 1988 edicts of the Supreme Council of Cultural Revolution in Iran. Military censorship of all kinds has also been a marked feature of both democratic and non-democratic states in times of war—from tariffs on imported publications and paper to the censorship of private correspondence and comprehensive control of the mainstream media.

Nor have all democratic nations enshrined freedom of speech or freedom from censorship as rights for their citizens. The Australian Literature Censorship Board—established in 1933 (precursor to the contemporary Office of Film and Literature Classification), and sharing characteristics with many of the national censorship regimes established in the Anglophone world in the wake of colonial control—was founded as an expert appeal board to mitigate what was seen as the too powerful control of Australian Customs over publications. Because of its small domestic publishing industry, Australian censorship in the 20th century was highly successful; Customs could effectively control and ban imports of all kinds, including books and films. Like Canada, New Zealand, India (for some years), and pre-apartheid South Africa, Australian civil censorship relied on British legislative precedents, investing Customs with the power to prohibit anything considered obscene, blasphemous, or seditious—based on definitions established by the British courts, especially Lord Campbell's 1868 ruling in R. vs Hicklin on the meaning of obscenity.

In the US, the *Comstock ruling of 1873 had a similarly significant impact on the limits of sexual and moral expression, differentiated somewhat by a state-based rather than federal or national approach to the control of publications and films. The power of postal services, vice squads, customs bureaucracies, and, increasingly, what the jurist Julius Stone referred to in 1966 as the proliferation of arbitrary administrative legal powers, effectively counters the idea that Western societies experienced substantive freedom from censorship during the 19th and 20th centuries. The International Convention for the Suppression of the Circulation of and Traffic in Obscene Publications (1923) marked the beginnings of current global regimes of regulation with pornography as their main target. Religious or race-based regimes of moral control in the Catholic Republic of Ireland and apartheid South Africa provided models for more ostensibly liberal countries like Australia, with which Canada shared legislation restricting entry of US comics and pulp fiction. Contemporary forms of censorship continue to vary across the globe, but typically seek to police the incitement of violence and crime, sexualized violence and the exploitation of children, libel, and defamation. In the wake of terrorist threats, national security laws in many countries have increasingly attended to the censorship of seditious materials.

4. Beyond the book

The very category of literature has in many instances been defined by censorship, as much as by taxonomies of reception or institutional and economic imperatives. The mid-20th century saw the success of the defence of literary merit, making available writing that contested the boundaries between popular erotica and serious fiction. In the USSR in the 1960s and 1970s, however, *samizdat was primarily literature, political and serious, although popular literature, comics, and magazines were also banned. Theatre censorship is also older than the book—in many countries influenced by the historical attachments to the courts that saw the *Lord Chamberlain's

Office sustain such control over the British stage—and the same motives continue to influence the censorship of films. Contemporary cultural regulation extends to radio, music, television, all forms of video, the visual arts, popular magazines, advertising, commodity packaging, clothing, and particularly the Internet (*see* WORLD WIDE WEB), where the limits of both the nation state and freedom of expression remain under question. *See also* ADULT MAGAZINE; GAY NEWS; GLAVLIT; OZ SCHOOLKIDS ISSUE; PRESS REGULATION. NRM

Beacon For Freedom, www.beaconforfreedom.org, consulted Oct. 2006
P. S. Boyer, *Purity in Print* (2002)
A. Craig, *The Banned Books of England and Other Countries* (1937; repr. 1962)
R. Darnton, *The Literary Underground of the Old Regime* (1982)
A. de Baets, *Censorship of Historical Thought* (2002)
J. Green and N. J. Karolides, *Encyclopedia of Censorship* (2005)
V. Gregorian, ed., *Censorship: 500 Years of Conflict* (1984)
M. Holquist, 'Corrupt Originals: The Paradox of Censorship', *PMLA* 109 (1994), 14–25
L. Hunt, ed., *The Invention of Pornography* (1993)
W. Kendrick, *The Secret Museum* (1987)
S. Marcus, *The Other Victorians* (1974)
R. C. Post, ed., *Censorship and Silencing* (1998)

censorship, colonial and postcolonial *Censorship in colonial societies has invariably been more severe than in the governing nation. Repressive legislation is often occasioned by concerns about political instability, military security, commercial interests, and religious sensitivities; frequently inherited by postcolonial governments on their independence, such censorship is often maintained or augmented by ideological or religious restrictions. *Index on Censorship*, Reporters without Borders, Amnesty International, and other organs and organizations monitor such censorship, including in regions currently occupied by foreign military forces.

Legal definitions of obscenity were exported to, and subsequently evolved in, European colonies and ex-colonies. The influential British legal test for obscenity framed in R vs Hicklin (1868) long formed the basis of obscenity law in the US, Canada, Australia, New Zealand, India, and South Africa, among other countries. Western Australia adopted the 1857 British Obscene Publications Act in 1876, other states following suit. Around 5,000 books were banned by the late 1930s. Prosecutions for literary obscenity increasingly served to articulate cultural anxieties during a period of developing Australian national identity. Many decisions cemented the applicability of the Hicklin test, although amendments to obscenity laws began to allow for public-good defences of literary, artistic, or scientific merit (as did the British *Obscene Publications Act of 1959).

Independent India has seen tensions between religious conservatism, the demands of public order, and liberalizing tendencies. There is no *blasphemy law, but religious sensitivities are frequently a cause of banning. The constitutional guarantee of freedom of expression is restricted where reasons of national security and prestige, public order, and morality or decency dictate; these restrictions are regulated, inter alia, by the Official Secrets Act (1923), Customs Act (1962), and Indian Penal Code (s292). Items 'kept or used *bona fide* for religious purposes' and representations on or in temples are exempt from indecency prohibitions. The primary consideration in Canadian decisions about publication or broadcast censorship is community standards. In 2000, the Supreme Court ruled that customs authorities could only confiscate material specifically ruled by the courts to breach the Criminal Code. *See also* APARTHEID, CENSORSHIP UNDER. AEV

N. G. Barrier, *Banned* (1974)
D. Jones, ed., *Censorship* (4 vols, 2001)
R. C. Post, ed., *Censorship and Silencing* (1998)

censorship of Jewish books, inquisitional From the second half of the 16th century onwards, Christian censors (many, converted Jews) in Italy checked Hebrew books, signed them, and often expurgated passages considered derogatory about Christianity. Jews usually had to pay for this 'service'. Due to the *ink used, expurgated passages can nowadays often be read. Among the most important censors were Dominico Irosolimitano, Camillo Jaghel, and Hippolitus Ferrarensis. Christian censorship also caused Jewish *self-censorship. EGLS

census of copies Various kinds of book historical study are facilitated by systematically recording surviving copies of a particular book. Bibliographers, seeking to determine authoritative texts, and their historical transmission through successive *editions, use *collation of multiple copies to detect *variants within *issues, and to establish publishing history. Analysis of copy-specific evidence in different copies of a particular book, looking at who owned them, how they were *annotated, and how they were bound, yields insights into that work's circulation and reception over time. Copy censuses may also be useful as finding aids and in assessing relative rarity.

Copy censuses often focus on celebrated or much-studied books; one of the earliest was Sidney Lee's *Census of Extant Copies* of Shakespeare's *First Folio (1902), recently updated by Anthony West. De *Ricci's *Census of Caxtons* (1909) listed all traceable copies of 108 separate works issued by *Caxton. Owen Gingerich's *Annotated Census of Copernicus' 'De *Revolutionibus'* (2002) is a noteworthy model. DRSP

D. Pearson, 'What Can We Learn by Tracking Multiple Copies of Books?', in *Books on the Move*, ed. R. Myers *et al.* (2007)
A. West, *The Shakespeare First Folio: The History of the Book*, vol. 2: *A New Worldwide Census of First Folios* (2003)

Center for Editions of American Authors (CEAA) A committee of the Modern Language Association of America, established in 1963 to produce reliable *scholarly editions of American authors. With funding from the *National Endowment for the Humanities (NEH), the CEAA supported editorial projects and enforced editorial standards for American literature. Initial efforts focused on canonical 19th-century figures: Emerson, Hawthorne, Melville, and Whitman, among others. Editions were to be definitive, clear reading texts, with full annotations and a thorough account of textual variants. CEAA funding was restricted to volumes that followed principles of *critical editing outlined by *Greg and *Bowers. The CEAA's *Statement of Editorial Principles and Procedures* (1972) declared that all texts should be *eclectic, based upon a *copy-text, and follow *authorial intention. Editions meeting these criteria bear their official seal on the copyright page. The organization's efforts were criticized from the beginning, most notoriously by Edmund Wilson in 'Fruits of the MLA' (*New York Review of Books* 11.5 and 6, 26 September and 10 October 1968). More informed critiques challenged the narrowness of the canon and the strict interpretation of editorial principles.

After the NEH ceased funding in 1976, the CEAA was reorganized as the Committee on Scholarly Editions (CSE). The CSE's scope, broader than the CEAA's, encompasses a wider range of authors (more women and writers outside the US) and supports a more diverse range of editorial methodologies. Currently serving in an advisory capacity, the CSE no longer funds editorial projects, but continues to bestow its seal of approval on qualified editions. More than 300 volumes bear CEAA or CSE seals.   RSG

M. Bruccoli, 'What Bowers Wrought: An Assessment of the Center for Editions of American Authors', in *The Culture of Collected Editions*, ed. A. Nash (2003)
Center for Editions of American Authors, *Statement of Editorial Principles and Procedures* (rev. edn, 1972)

Center for Jewish Art (CJA) Established at the Hebrew University of Jerusalem in 1979 to carry out research, documentation, education, and publication on Jewish art. The CJA's Index of Jewish Art is a comprehensive database, including information on Hebrew illuminated MSS. CJA published the periodical (*Journal of*) *Jewish Art*.   EGLS

Centre for Editing Early Canadian Texts (CEECT) Established at Carleton University in Ottawa in 1979. Funded by the *Social Sciences and Humanities Research Council of Canada, and directed by Mary Jane Edwards, the CEECT publishes scholarly editions of eleven major works of 18th- and 19th-century Canadian prose. These include works by Frances Brooke, James De Mille, Thomas Chandler Haliburton, Julia Beckwith Hart, Rosanna Leprohon, Thomas McCulloch, Susanna Moodie, John Richardson, and Catharine Parr Traill.   PLF

centrepiece In bookbinding, a large single tool stamped at the centre of a *cover. Centrepieces of intricate symmetrical design were popular in Islamic binding, and in European binding in the 16th and 17th centuries.   DRSP

D. Pearson, 'English Centre-Piece Bookbindings 1560–1640', in *Eloquent Witnesses*, ed. M. M. Foot (2004)

Century Co. Founded in New York in 1881, when Scribner & Co., the magazine department of Charles *Scribner's Sons, separated from the parent company.

Roswell Smith—who had founded *Scribner's Monthly* in 1870 but left the magazine several years later—took over his successors' share after they retired. He renamed the magazine the *Century Illustrated Monthly Magazine*, and simultaneously renamed the firm. Under Frank Scott's leadership, Century Co. published the bestselling *Battles and Leaders of the Civil War*, which had first appeared *serially in the magazine, as well as John Nicolay and John Hay's ten-volume *Abraham Lincoln: A History* (1890). The company merged with *Appleton in 1933 to become the Appleton-Century Co. and, later, *Appleton-Century-Crofts.   SEC

H. Lehmann-Haupt, *The Book in America*, 2e (1955)

Cercle de la librairie French professional organization, created in 1847, its first president was Ambroise Firmin-*Didot. Involved in all aspects of book production, publication, and distribution, it administered the *Bibliographie de la France* until 1990, and after 1884 played a leading role in the establishment of unions in book professions. It continues to disseminate information on all aspects of the book in France through its magazines (*Livres hebdo, Livres de France*) and databases.   VAG

Cerne, Book of CUL, MS Ll. 1. 10, an early 9th-century collection of devotional and other materials, including extracts from the Gospels, a narrative of the Passion, and devotional writings in Latin and Old English, now bound together with later medieval materials. The Gospels sections are preceded by portraits of the evangelists and abstract designs. Apparently written for Æthelwald, bishop of Lichfield from 818 to 830, the MS appears to be the only surviving illuminated MS from the kingdom of Mercia.   ASGE

M. P. Brown, *The Book of Cerne* (1996)

Cervantes, Premio Literary prize for Spanish-speaking writers, comparable in prestige to the Premio *Camões. Instituted in 1974 by Spain's Ministry of Culture, the €90,000 prize is awarded annually for distinguished literary achievement. Past laureates include Mario Vargas Llosa (1994), Carlos Fuentes (1987), Octavio Paz (1981), and Jorge Guillén (1976).   DRW

Chace Act America's first statutory recognition of international *copyright. The Chace Act (1891), also the International Copyright Act, curtailed American literary *piracy. Foreign authors gained American copyright protection, provided American authors enjoyed reciprocity and the foreign book was manufactured in the US.   DS

S. Nowell-Smith, *International Copyright Law* (1968)

chained books Characteristic of some medieval and post-medieval institutional libraries, chains were used to secure books intended for communal or public use; in modern times, they have acquired a bibliophilic appeal. The earliest evidence for chaining dates from the 13th century (e.g. several Oxford and Cambridge colleges, and the Sorbonne). Most surviving chained books were so fitted in the 16th and 17th centuries; the practice had stopped by the second half of the 18th century. Most of the relevant evidence about this topic comes from the few intact chained libraries, from books showing signs of once having been chained, and from archival records (historical details of chains ordered for library use, or the expenses incurred when chains were later removed). The libraries at Hereford and *Zutphen in the Netherlands are among the most prominent survivals (both were chained in the 16th century); smaller collections of chained books survive with their original *book cases, and there remain numerous individual volumes that were once chained for public access in English parish churches. The style of library shelving dictated the system of chaining: chained books are found lying flat attached to lecterns, attached to one of the shelves or to the lectern in a library employing the stall system, or with their *spines facing inward in a more modern library with wall shelving. The chains are generally made of iron (sometimes originally tinned to prevent rust) and include at least one swivel among the links. They are attached with a brass clip at the *fore-edge of the book's upper or lower cover; at the other end, a ring is secured to the shelf with an iron rod and locking hasp.   RAL

J. W. Clark, *The Care of Books*, 2e (1909)
B. H. Streeter, *The Chained Library* (1931)

chain lines The traditional Western *mould for paper-making had a cover made from parallel bronze laid wires running from left to right. These were bound together by pairs of tying wires spaced widely, running from front to back. These 'chain lines' appear as lighter lines when a *sheet is held up to the light. *See also* WIRE LINES.

RLH

Chalcondyles, Demetrius (1423–1511) Athenian who successively was professor of Greek at Padua, Florence, and Milan. His many pupils included *Poliziano, *Reuchlin, Linacre, and Giovanni de' Medici (Pope Leo X). Chalcondyles's only extant work is a grammatical *Erotemata*, but he was much involved with various Greek presses, editing the first edition of Homer at Florence in 1488, and then Isocrates (1493), and the *Suda* (1499). He inherited the library of his master *Gaza, now lost.

MCD

Chalmers family (active 1736–1876). Aberdeen newspaper proprietors and important regional printers, chiefly remarkable for their long-lasting firm. **James Chalmers II** (1713–64), apprentice and successor to the printer James Nicol, also trained with John Watts in London. His son, **James III** (1742–1810), continued printing newspapers and items for the town council. With the bookseller Alexander Brown, he added papermaking to the business in 1803. On his death, the firm continued under his son **David** (1778–1859).   PLS
ODNB

Chambers, W. & R. Reference, educational, and periodical publishers in Edinburgh, founded by the brothers William and Robert. From 1832 to 1956, the firm published *Chambers's Edinburgh Journal*, a competitor of the *Penny Magazine*. Robert wrote *Vestiges of the Natural History of Creation* (1844) *anonymously, praised by Darwin. From 1860 to 1868, they published *Chambers's Encyclopaedia: A Dictionary of Universal Knowledge* in 520 weekly *numbers at a penny-halfpenny each. In 1955, George Newnes Ltd. revised and reissued a fourth edition. The firm established itself as a leader in the *dictionary market with James Donald's *Chambers's English Dictionary* (1872), adding Chambers's Educational Course (from 1835), adapted to the Scottish educational practice, and later the 'Radiant Way' and 'Radiant Reading' series, which were exported to India and Australia. The firm also published the Nuffield Mathematics Project (1967). In 1989, Chambers was sold to Groupe de la Cité PLC.   AAW
DLB 109
ODNB

chancery Obsolete paper sheet size used specifically in legal establishments, being nominally double *foolscap 26.5×16.5in. (67.3×41.9cm), of a cream colour, and with a wove finish. Known also as judicature.   DCC
Labarre

chancery (chancellery) script A form of handwriting employed in official documentary records of various kinds. In its earlier forms, such *script frequently tended to be a kind of *cursive handwriting, often highly abbreviated to save space. The humanistic cursive script—*italic—used by diplomats, scholars, and others was called *littera cancellarescha* by *Arrighi. In later periods, the various cursive scripts were commonly replaced by national forms of round or *copperplate hand with a considerable emphasis on legibility and ornamentation.
ASGE

T. A. M. Bishop, *Scriptores Regis* (1961)
L. C. Hector, *The Handwriting of English Documents*, 2e (1966)

Changsŏgak Library Library of the Academy of *Korean Studies, taking its name from the royal archive formerly in the Changgyŏng Palace, Seoul. Holding 490 volumes from the royal archive of the Chosŏn dynasty (1392–1910), the Changsŏgak Library constitutes a major research centre for the study of Korean humanities and social sciences. In 2002, it held more than 400,000 books. Changsŏgak actively collects privately owned historic and archival documents, *digitizing them for research and publication.   EDM

Chantilly, Musée Condé Henri d'Orléans, duc d'Aumale (1822–97), the fifth son of Louis-Philippe, bequeathed to the *Institut de France in 1884 the château (restored and rebuilt after 1871) he had inherited from the last duc de Condé, along with his own vast bibliophilic and artistic treasures (including the Standish and Cicongne collections). Acquired largely during his English

An early 19th-century **chapbook**: the *frontispiece and *title-page from James Kendrew's *An Elegy on the Death and Burial of Cock Robin* (c.1815–20). The book consists of a single *gathering of eight leaves.

exile, the Chantilly library houses three of the finest illuminated MSS: the *Très Riches Heures du duc de *Berry* (purchased in Italy in 1856), *Fouquet's *Livre d'heures d'Étienne Chevalier*, and Queen Ingeborg's Psalter. VAG

chapbook A small booklet, usually a single folded sheet, aimed at the popular market, and sold, not by booksellers, but by itinerant pedlars or *chapmen. The majority of chapbooks contained folk tales, historical stories, popular *ballads, moral fables, nursery rhymes, and other juvenile literature. Chapmen did a great deal of business at markets and fairs, but made their living chiefly by carrying a pack of miscellaneous goods from door to door. Frequent demands for the regulation of chapmen from the early 16th century onwards suggest that they were numerous and unruly; the pedlar Autolycus in *The Winter's Tale* is not a particularly lovable rogue. Because anything heavy or bulky would be inconvenient to carry, the chapman's stock of printed matter consisted chiefly of *ballads, *almanacs, and other single-sheet or *broadside publications. Basic literacy was sufficiently common to provide a wide market for such items: in English towns, from a quarter to a third of the population may have been able to read, and in rural places a fair number would be able to make out the words of a ballad, especially if some Autolycus had already sung it for them.

There is little evidence for the chapbook as such in the 16th century. De *Worde, who seems to have had a good eye for the popular market, published a series of thin *quarto books that could have found their way into a pedlar's pack. Many other pamphlets and small books intended for the general public survive from most decades of the 16th century, in England as on the continent, but they would all have cost a good deal more than the halfpenny or penny asked for a ballad or broadside almanac. It is likely that neighbours clubbed together to buy them; a sixpenny *jest book, for example, would remain a good investment until the whole neighbourhood had tired of the jokes, and a rustic community might willingly contribute its farthings towards buying a romance for a 'clerk' to read to them on some holiday occasion. Popular literature was destined to be read to pieces or discarded as ephemeral, and a large part of it is entirely lost. It is sometimes claimed that much influential propaganda for the Protestant Reformation was circulated during the 1530s and 1540s in popular form, but there is very little to show for it beyond some anticlerical ballads, a genre that is perennially popular.

A high proportion of books intended for the popular market may have been unlicensed, although some entries in the *Stationers' Company registers evidently refer to small books now entirely lost. Popular publishing in the earlier 17th century was depressed by the *censorship of the Star Chamber until 1641, and evidence remains sparse. To a considerable extent the trade relied on old favourites, including drastically abridged reprints of fiction published in the 16th century, and condensed versions of traditional tales and romances of chivalry. Robert Greene's *Dorastus and Fawnia* (1588), appropriately enough the source of *The Winter's Tale*, was still being reprinted for sale by chapmen after a century. Richard Johnson's *Seven Champions of Christendom* (1596), pared down to chapbook length, transmitted the legend of St George well into the 19th century; and the romance of Valentine and Orson, printed by de Worde about 1510, remained in print as a chapbook 300 years later. Two more or less contemporary collections of chapbooks are important: the antiquary A. *Wood's, now in the *Bodleian Library, and the rich collection of popular literature in the Pepysian Library at *Magdalene College, Cambridge. *Pepys's chapbooks include practical jokes and magic tricks for boys; others are more practical, of the *Every Man His Own Lawyer* kind; and inevitably there are some fine examples of scatology. Of course, many chapbooks were much more prosaic than these.

The printers of popular literature supplied chapmen directly with their stock, usually on credit. Once established on or near London Bridge, they gravitated towards Little Britain and Aldermary Churchyard near St Paul's after the Great Fire of 1666. The volume of their trade was surprisingly large; probate inventories of the printers Charles Tias (1664) and Josiah Blare (1707) show that their stock-in-hand of 'little books' in *sheets or stitched approached 100,000. The number of titles represented is not known, but a trade list of about 1700 lists more than 100, classified as 'small godly books', 'small merry books', 'histories', and 'double books' (all works of piety). Unlike ballads, chapbooks were rarely illustrated, unless there was room for a battered woodcut on the *title-page.

Until 1750, most English chapbooks were printed in London with depots in the provinces to facilitate distribution. The growing wealth of country towns encouraged printers to set up shop there, and chapbooks, especially for children, were often among their first publications. The standards of provincial presswork were sometimes outstandingly high, as if the printers wished to show the metropolitan trade a thing or two. T. Saint of Newcastle commissioned the earliest work of the wood-engraver *Bewick, and the northeastern market town of Alnwick had the shop of *Catnach (another patron of Bewick), which in 1808 passed into the hands of *Davison. Davison continued to print to a very high standard, and his 'halfpenny chapbooks' are models of thrift and taste. Scotland had many printers of chapbooks in the early 19th century; 4,000 of their booklets are in the collections of the National Library of *Scotland. At Banbury, the Rushers and the Cheneys continued to produce penny chapbooks well into the reign of Queen Victoria; but by then, the proliferation of bookshops and of very cheap printing had made the chapman's trade largely redundant. Since the late 19th century fugitive collections of poetry have often been called chapbooks—notably in the 1920s by the

*Poetry Bookshop, whose very slim volumes were often illustrated 'in the chapbook style' by *Fraser.   BJF

V. E. Neuburg, *Chapbooks* (1972)
R. Schöwerling, *Chapbooks* (1980)
M. Spufford, *Small Books and Pleasant Histories* (1981)

chapel The *journeymen within a *printing office constituted an organization known as the chapel. The origins of the term and the practice are obscure, but there is clear evidence for it from the 17th century, since J. *Moxon describes the chapel as a longstanding practice by his time (1683). He offers a detailed account in 'Ancient Customs used in a Printing-house'—giving evidence for such practices as *copy money, *paper windows, and the *wayzgoose—noting also that workers in *typefoundries were also members of a chapel.

Chapel rules were drawn up locally and were aimed at enforcing the office customs, promoting good conduct, and possibly providing a degree of mutual assistance to the members ('benefit of chapel money'). The principal officer was the Father of the Chapel. 'Solaces' were imposed for mistakes (such as dropping a *composing stick, leaving a candle burning, or allowing type to slip under the *type case), or for contravening office customs (such as swearing, fighting, or being drunk). Solaces were paid by fines, which financed the chapel, or by the offender being beaten with a 'paper-board'. 'Benvenues' were paid by new workers who joined it. Various milestones (such as the birth of a child—more for a son than a daughter) also cost the father's fellow journeymen. The chapel's relationship to earlier guilds and later trade unions is open to debate. Bateman has shown that it became, in part, a social organization. Despite the small number of extant archival records, this aspect of the chapel deserves further study.   MMS

D. Bateman, 'A Bristol Printers' Chapel in the 19th Century', *JPHS* 24 (1995), 107–21
J. Materné, 'Chapel Members in the Workplace: Tension and Teamwork in the Printing Trades of the 17th and 18th Centuries', *International Review of Social History*, 39, Supplement 2 (1994), 53–114
Moxon

Chapin, Alfred C. (1848–1936) American book collector, lawyer, and politician. Collecting *incunabula, English literature, and Americana, Chapin regularly donated his books to his alma mater, Williams College, Mass., where the Chapin Library was formally opened in 1923. By the time of his death, it had received 12,000 volumes from its founder. Since then, the library has increased to more than 50,000 printed volumes and 100,000 other items.   ASGE

L. E. Osborne, *Alfred Clark Chapin* (1937)

chapman An itinerant pedlar of small general wares. The chapman's importance to the book trade is that he supplied printed items to an unsophisticated public who would rarely, if ever, visit a bookseller's shop. When not trading at fairs, he carried a selection of his stock from door to door. This might include *almanacs, *ballads, and *chapbooks, cheap popular books of no more than a *sheet or two. Since *c*.1850, few have made a living as chapmen. Religious booklets are still occasionally sold from door to door, but those who hawk them generally prefer to be called *colporteurs.   BJF

Chapman, Christopher (d. 1756?) London bookbinder. Best known for bindings made for the Harleian Library, he also made high-quality bindings for many others. Apprenticed to William Sparkes in 1704, he became free in 1718, and began binding for *Harley in 1720. His son Nathaniel appears to have taken over the business in the 1750s.   DRSP

H. Nixon, 'Harleian Bindings', in *Studies in the Book Trade in Honour of Graham Pollard*, OBS, NS 18 (1975)

Chapman, John (1821–94) English publisher. Chapman's publishing business (acquired in 1844) provided an important forum for intellectual debate, issuing George Eliot's translations of Strauss and Feuerbach, Harriet Martineau's version of Comte, and works by Herbert Spencer, J. A. Froude, and F. W. Newman. In 1851 he bought the *Westminster Review* but, facing insolvency, sold it and the entire firm in 1860, becoming a physician.   RJD

R. Ashton, *142 Strand* (2006)

Chapman, R. W. (Robert William) (1881–1960) Scottish-born, Oxford-based literary scholar and publisher, known especially for his scholarly editions of Jane Austen's novels (1923) and letters (1932) and S. *Johnson's letters (1952). These involved treating novels and tracing MSS with the systematic textual scrutiny and rigour previously reserved for major dramatists and poets. As Secretary to the Delegates of the Clarendon Press, Chapman significantly advanced the *New (Oxford) English Dictionary*.   KEA

ODNB

Chapman & Hall English publishers. Edward Chapman (1804–80) and William Hall (1800/1–47) set up business in 1830, but it was not until 1836, when they began issuing the monthly parts of *Pickwick Papers*, that the partnership became a major force in 19th-century publishing. They remained (with acrimonious hiatuses) Dickens's publisher for the remainder of his career (and retained reprint rights thereafter), but they also issued works by Thackeray, Mrs Gaskell, Carlyle, Kingsley, and Trollope (who became a director of the firm). In the 1860s they updated their list with sensation fiction—Ouida and Edmund Yates were among their authors—and they were pioneers in the production of cheap reprints (including the *yellowback). The firm was also a leading publisher of children's books (*see* **15**) and initiated annuals for young readers. Chapman & Hall, after a period of decline, merged with *Methuen in 1938.   RJD

A. Waugh, *100 Years of Publishing* (1930)

chapter (Lat. *capitulum*, from *caput* 'head'; hence 'little head'). A subdivision of a prose text, often the largest subdivision of the whole, although some texts are subdivided first into *books or parts, then into chapters. Usually numbered and often given a title, a chapter is typically further subdivided into *paragraphs. Stephen Langton, archbishop of Canterbury (*c*.1150–1228), may have been the first to introduce chapter divisions into the Bible for easier citation of the text. (Verse divisions were a later invention.) A new chapter is generally signalled typographically, often by commencing on a *recto and with its number and/or title prominently displayed at its head. In medieval MSS, the indication of a new chapter was an *initial, possibly *historiated or merely enlarged; in printed books, a *woodcut or a *factotum initial was sometimes used. The chapter title is sometimes repeated in the *headlines of the book. Chapter titles are often listed in the table of *contents, along with their locations. The division of a work into chapters can be authorial or editorial, but is most often an important part of that work's textual *hierarchy.   MMS

Chapter coffee house One of 18th-century London's most famous *coffee houses, established *c*.1710. Situated in Paternoster Row, the Chapter was frequented by booksellers, writers, and men of letters. It became a central venue for the sale of *copyrights by auction and for meetings of *conger associations of booksellers, whose books were originally known as 'Chapter' books. The Chapter was also noted for its supply of *pamphlets and newspapers and—in the later 18th century—for its library and back-files of every London and provincial newspaper, the result of its being a news and advertising agency. The Chapter closed in 1843.   VEMG

Chapters (Indigo) Canada's largest book retail chain, comprising Chapters Inc. (founded 1994 after the merger of Coles (*see* COLE, JACK) and SmithBooks) and Indigo Books & Music (1996), which merged under the latter's corporate name in 2001. The company operates 'big box' Chapters and Indigo stores, and smaller Coles and SmithBooks outlets.   JAD

www.chapters.indigo.ca, consulted July 2008

character book A collection of graphic, witty, and sometimes paradoxical descriptions of human personalities, traits, and foibles, published as a book of essays. The form was practised in 17th-century Europe, especially in England. The genre's chief model is the *Characters* of the moral philosopher Theophrastus (d. *c*.287 BC), where human conduct is presented as an index of personality. Among English imitations, Joseph Hall's *Characters of Virtues and Vices* (1608) is perhaps the most overtly moralizing. Character-writers generally have a light touch, and the best of them display a caricaturist's sharpness and accuracy of observation, as well as a degree of wisdom. Sir Thomas Overbury's *Characters* (1614) and John Earle's *Microcosmographie* (1628) give affectionate and perceptive portraits of relatively humble people often overlooked: 'the plain country fellow', 'the mere fellow of a college', 'the fair and happy milkmaid'. Nicholas Breton's *The Fantasticks* (1626) concentrates on eccentric and ludicrous traits; Richard Brathwaite's

Whimzies (1631) has a more satirical intent. The character is essentially a generalized portrait, although based on individual observation. The satirist Samuel Butler's numerous *Characters* (not published in his lifetime) include thinly veiled personal attacks.   BJF

C. N. Greenough, *A Bibliography of the Theophrastan Character in English* (1947)

Chardron Portuguese publisher. The French bookseller Ernesto Chardron settled in Oporto, branching into publishing in 1869. He gained prominence as publisher to the prolific novelist Camilo Castelo-Branco and other major writers. Livraria Lello e Irmão of Oporto acquired the firm in 1894 and maintained the Chardron imprint until 1988.   DRW

Charleston Library Society Founded in Charleston, South Carolina, 1748 by seventeen young professionals seeking access to Great Britain's latest titles, the Library Society is the third oldest library in the US. Instead of purchasing books from local importers, as did many northern libraries, the society purchased directly from London. It promoted general studies to provide a polite education in law, mathematics, agriculture, and natural history. Using its surviving *letter book (1758–1811) and collections, scholars can investigate the library's purchases, the booksellers with whom it dealt, and details of packing, shipment, and payment.   MDB

J. Raven, *London Booksellers and American Customers* (2002)

charter The term 'charter' covers a wide variety of private, royal, and ecclesiastical documents, including writs, title deeds, wills, leases, settlements of disputes, and other memoranda. In the Middle Ages, charters were known by various terms including *carta, breve,* and *chirographum.* They often survive assembled into a register, in the form of a MS book, known as a *cartulary.

The earliest medieval charters are Merovingian and are written on *papyrus, with wording and formulations closely based on Roman practice. Evidence from later *formularies suggest that they may date as far back as the second quarter of the 5th century, although the earliest surviving original charter is one of 625. In Anglo-Saxon England, the earliest charters date from the 670s, but their reasonably wide distribution across the south of the country implies that they had been introduced some time previously. The vast majority of early charters are royal or ecclesiastical, rather than private. More than two-thirds of the surviving 1,500 or so charters in Anglo-Saxon England are Latin *diplomas, royal grants of land to religious foundations or to individuals. From the 10th century, the inclusion of a vernacular boundary clause providing a circuit of the land unit in question becomes customary.

Diplomas were produced in religious communities until the end of the 9th century, but towards the mid-10th century some kind of centralized production evolved. It remains both unclear and contentious as to whether this was carried out by a type of peripatetic royal chancery or by a less formal grouping of major ecclesiastics from various centres.

By the late 10th century, it became commonplace for kings to convey administrative orders to be read out at shire courts by means of sealed writs. The function of these documents later widened considerably. Writs were composed in the vernacular, as were a small number of wills, which provide a level of socio-historical detail not found in other types of record. Leases, composed in Latin and English, also survive from this period. Those text types involving some kind of contractual obligation (leases and wills) are not infrequently preserved as parts of chirographs or indentures. Here, the text would be written out twice or thrice on the parchment; between each copy of the text, the scribe would write CHIROGRAPHYUM, and copies would be separated by cutting the parchment horizontally through the word.

The majority of early charters do not survive in their original form but are, instead, recorded in cartularies dating in the main from the 13th to the 15th centuries. A notable exception here is the remarkable collection from *St Gall in Switzerland; more than 700 private grants to the abbey and 100 royal diplomas survive there in their original form from the period before AD 1000, providing an unparalleled opportunity for the study of *palaeography and *diplomatic.

By the end of the Norman Conquest, social élites appear to have been accustomed to written documentation, and were aware of the legal advantages that possession of charters to property afforded. The use of the vernacular in documents of particular interest to laymen, such as wills and leases, would no doubt have helped foster the growth of what has been termed a 'literate mentality' (Clanchy). The immediate effect of the Norman Conquest and the replacement of English by Latin in these text types amounted to a setback in that development. However, charter use and production grew exponentially in government circles by the second half of the 13th century, an increase leading to and connected with the development of administrative departments. It had also proliferated down the social scale. Clanchy's summary is telling:

> in the eleventh century laymen of all classes and many monks gave and received tenancies often without any kind of documentary evidence. In the twelfth century magnates used documents occasionally and they and the gentry made gifts for religious houses by charter because the monks wanted this. In the thirteenth century laymen began to convey property to each other by charter; in the latter half of the century this practice extended below the gentry class to some peasants.... By 1300 even serfs, the more prosperous ones at least, were familiar with documents.

Charters constitute primary evidence for scholarly disciplines including, but not restricted to, social, legal, ecclesiastical, administrative and political history, palaeography and diplomatic, onomastics, literacy studies, and language. However, the pitfalls of working with this material require emphasis. It must be remembered that most medieval charters exist today only because of their preservation in religious foundations; others of no lasting interest to such institutions are unlikely to have survived, undoubtedly skewing any understanding of the range and number of documents used. Despite the importance of charters for the study of palaeography, few monastic archives contain the number of single-sheet charters necessary to draw detailed conclusions about *script and script development in specific areas. The practical impossibility of distinguishing between an original and contemporary or near-contemporary copy creates further difficulties in this regard. Although wholesale medieval *forgeries are frequently clumsy, more subtle attempts at 'improvement', such as interpolation, are often difficult to detect, requiring highly specialized knowledge. KAL

N. Brooks, *Anglo-Saxon Myths* (2000)

A. Bruckner *et al.*, *Chartae Latinae Antiquiores*, vols 1–65, 68–70, 72–3, 75–6 (1954–)

M. Clanchy, *From Memory to Written Record*, 2e (1993)

D. Ganz and W. Goffart, 'Charters Earlier than 800 from French Collections', *Speculum*, 65 (1990), 906–32

O. Guyotejeannin *et al.*, *Diplomatique médiévale* (1993)

R. McKitterick, *The Carolingians and the Written Word* (1989)

P. H. Sawyer, *Anglo-Saxon Charters: An Annotated List and Bibliography* (1968); rev. edn available by following links from www.trin.cam.ac.uk/chartwww, consulted Oct. 2007

R. Sharpe, 'Charters, Deeds, and Diplomatics', in *Medieval Latin Studies*, ed. F. A. C. Mantello and A. C. Rigg (1996)

Chartier, Roger (1945–) French book historian and late-generation member of the *Annales* school of social historians. His insistence that the diverse material forms of books produce and change meanings has been especially influential. He has argued for a study of reading practices concerned with religious affiliations, gender, and academic or group traditions as well as with socioprofessional classifications. MW

R. Chartier, *L'Ordre des livres* (1992; tr. L. G. Cochrane as *The Order of Books*, 1994)

— *Forms and Meanings: Texts, Performances, and Audiences from Codex to Computer* (1995)

chase Solid frame of wood or (more commonly) iron into which the type and other matter making up a *forme are locked, usually using *quoins.

Chatsworth House Library Chatsworth, in Derbyshire, is the family seat of the Cavendish family, the dukes of Devonshire, who over five centuries assembled a great private library of *illuminated and other MSS and printed books. Some portions of it were dispersed in the 20th century by sale or gifts to the nation, including such notable MSS as the 10th-century Benedictional of St Aethelwold (now in the British Library) and the Devonshire MS of the *Canterbury Tales* (now *Takamiya MS 24), as well as many *incunabula. Much, however, remains in situ. ASGE

N. Barker, *Five Centuries of Collecting at Chatsworth* (2003)

Chatterton, Thomas (1752–70) English poet and literary forger. The posthumous son of a Bristol *writing-master and antiquary, Chatterton learned to read from illuminated capitals and a *black-letter bible. His father's collection of MS fragments became the basis for an imaginary *archive of a 15th-century monk-poet of Bristol, Thomas Rowley; Chatterton constructed a vocabulary from *glossaries in editions of Chaucer and Spenser, and transcribed the Rowley works in an invented 'antique' script on to *vellum trimmings from documents in the attorney's office where he worked. In 1768, he offered some poems to J. *Dodsley, and in March 1769 he sent a Rowleian treatise on the history of painting to *Walpole; both approaches were unsuccessful. Chatterton went to London in April 1770 and wrote prodigiously for journals. In August he took, perhaps accidentally, a fatal overdose of arsenic. The Rowley poems were edited by *Tyrwhitt in 1777, with an appendix challenging their authenticity on linguistic grounds. *Warton and *Malone concurred, although some contemporaries continued to defend their antiquity. Subsequent attention increasingly shifted to Chatterton's own poetic genius. *See also* FORGERIES AND HOAXES. PTB

The Complete Works of Thomas Chatterton, ed. D. S. Taylor and B. B. Hoover (2 vols, 1971)

ODNB

Chatto & Windus London publishing house established in 1873 on the death of J. C. *Hotten. The driving force was Hotten's chief clerk, Andrew Chatto (1840–1913), who transformed the bohemian house into a respectable business centred on mainstream fiction. Though Chatto continued to publish Hotten poets like Swinburne, his main effort was to attract bestselling novelists such as Wilkie Collins and 'Ouida', not only publishing their new work as triple-deckers (*see* THREE- OR TRIPLE-DECKER), but reprinting the old in various formats, including the *yellowback. R. L Stevenson and Arnold Bennett were among the up-and-coming writers attracted by the firm. Long after Andrew Chatto's departure, it remained respected for its literary lists featuring authors like Aldous Huxley and Iris Murdoch. After absorbing houses such as the *Hogarth Press, it was itself absorbed by *Random House in 1987, though the Chatto & Windus *imprint survives. GL

DLB 106

O. Warner, *Chatto and Windus* (1973)

Chattopadhyay, Sunitikumar (1890–1977) Indian linguist. After studying English at Presidency College, Calcutta (Kolkata), he researched in phonetics, Indo-European and Slavic linguistics, Prakrit, Persian, and other languages at London and Sorbonne universities. He became the first professor of Indian linguistics and phonetics at Calcutta University (1922). His most significant work is the pioneering two-volume *Origin and Development of the Bengali Language* (1926). Appointed national professor in 1966, he became president of the *Indian National Akademi in 1969. AG

Chaucer Society *Furnivall founded the Chaucer Society in 1868 'to do honour to Chaucer' by producing transcripts of his MSS and scholarly studies of his works. Two series of publications were issued. The last volume appeared in 1909 and the society was dissolved in 1912. The New Chaucer Society was established in 1979.

RMa

D. Brewer, 'Furnivall and the Old Chaucer Society', *Chaucer Newsletter*, 1 (1979), 2–3

E. P. Hammond, *Chaucer: A Bibliographical Manual* (1908)

Cheap Repository Tracts A popular serial publication of morally and politically didactic, inexpensive *ballads, tales, dialogues, and *tracts, orchestrated by Hannah More as an antidote to the revolutionary and immoral effects among impoverished readers of the *broadsides and cheap radical *pamphlets circulating in Britain during the French Revolution. During 1795–8, three tracts were published each month for distribution and sale by booksellers, hawkers, private supporters, and ecclesiastics such as the bishops of London and Durham. More wrote approximately 50 of the 114 tracts; the rest were contributed by friends and members of the Bluestocking circle and of the Clapham Sect. In format, style, and tone the tracts imitated cheap ballads, pamphlets, and broadsides; their content stressed conservative morality, piety, and loyalty. Although the series ceased in 1798, individual tracts were reprinted throughout the next century. JES

G. H. Spinney, 'Cheap Repository Tracts: Hazard and Marshall Edition', *Library*, 4/20 (1939–40), 295–340

cheeks The two heavy, upright members of a *common press, which together provide its vertical strength and between which the *carriage passes.

chemise A loose cover for a book, typically made of *leather or cloth, with pockets at each side into which the boards fit. Commonly used in some medieval bindings.

Chen Si (13th century) One of a group of Song commercial publishers and booksellers in Hangzhou (China) surnamed Chen. Also known as Chen Daoren, he was an author. Another, Chen Qi (13th century), was a poet who published many collections by Tang and Song poets. Chen publications are finely printed and most bear *colophons with local addresses. They are called *shupengben*, or bookstall editions, because the shops were located in areas of market stalls. JSE

Chepman, Walter (*c.*1471–1528), and **Andrew Myllar** (*fl.* 1503–8) Printers and merchants in Edinburgh. In 1507, Chepman was granted a patent by James IV to set up a *printing office in Edinburgh, in partnership with Andrew Myllar. They published eleven short works (*c.*1508), mainly literary texts. Chepman, working alone, produced a *Breviarium Aberdonense* in 1509–10.

LH

W. Beattie, *The Chepman and Myllar Prints* (1950)

ODNB

chequebook A book of cheques, which order a bank to pay the sum stated from the depositor's account to the payee. *See also* BANK BOOK.

Cheron, Louis (1660–1725) French painter and illustrator. Settled in London by 1693, Cheron increasingly illustrated books (e.g. for *Lintot and *Tonson). His most influential designs were for Tonson's *Poetical Works of John Milton* (1720) and Plutarch's *Lives* (1727). JCI

H. Hammelmann, *Book Illustrators in Eighteenth-Century England* (1975)

ODNB

Chetham's Library, Manchester Among the oldest surviving public libraries in Britain, it was founded by the will of Humphrey Chetham (1580–1653), a Manchester merchant. Chetham left £1,000 for the purchase of books, which began arriving in 1655, and acquisitions have continued ever since. The library, an independent charity, now holds more than 100,000 printed items (the majority published before 1851) and substantial quantities of MSS and images. Since the mid-19th century, it has concentrated on the arts and humanities, especially the history and topography of north-west England.

OSP

H. Lofthouse, 'Unfamiliar Libraries I: Chetham's Library', *BC* 5 (1956), 323–30

Chevalier, Étienne, Hours of A *book of hours, Chantilly, Musée Condé MS 71, one of the most elaborately illustrated French MSS of the 15th century, was illuminated by *Fouquet between 1452 and 1460 for Étienne Chevalier, the Grand Treasurer of France. Although the main topics of each miniature are biblical (*see* MINIATURES (1)), they are linked to scenes of contemporary places or persons associated with either Fouquet or Chevalier himself. At least 47 miniatures were removed from the MS, probably during the French Revolution, and are now widely dispersed. ASGE

C. Schaefer, *The Hours of Étienne Chevalier*, tr. M. Sinclair (1971)

chi Greek character (χ) used in *collational formulas to denote unsigned *leaves or *gatherings, or (in superscript) duplication of *signatures, except at the beginning of books. *See also* PI.

chiaroscuro A *woodcut illustration technique using a key-block and one or more tone blocks in monochrome shades to achieve a tonal image. Used principally from the early 16th until the late 17th century, at first by *Cranach and *Ugo da Carpi. MMS

W. L. Strauss, *Chiaroscuro* (1973)

Chicago Press, University of Founded in 1891 and operated by the Boston publishing house D. C. *Heath in conjunction with the Chicago printer R. R. *Donnelley, the press was taken over by the university in 1894. Now the US's largest scholarly publisher, it comprises three divisions. Its Books Division publishes *c.*180 new titles and *c.*70 paperback reprints per year—more than 11,000 books since its founding. The Journals Division publishes some 50 peer-reviewed journals and annuals. Distribution Services provides warehousing, distribution, and fulfillment services to 60 publishers at its Chicago Distribution Center, which has on-site digital printing and features BiblioVault, a repository providing university presses with space for digital book files.

The press began publishing books by scholars outside the University of Chicago in 1905, adding a copyediting and proofreading department the same year. This led to the first edition of the *Chicago Manual of Style* in 1906 (*see* STYLEBOOK). It has sold nearly one million copies and is in its 15th edition, but the press's best seller is Kate Turabian's *A Manual for Writers of Research Papers, Theses and Dissertations*, first published in 1937, which has sold several million copies.   MDB

www.press.uchicago.edu/presswide/presshistory.html, consulted July 2008

Chicago Public Library Established in 1873 after the Great Chicago Fire. *Poole, its first Librarian, built the central library's collections and began circulating books. As the library grew and refined its scope (through an 1896 cooperative collection development agreement with the *Newberry Library), it extended services into Chicago's neighbourhoods through delivery stations, branch libraries, and deposit stations. It currently includes one of the world's largest public-library buildings, two regional libraries, and 79 neighbourhood branches. Among its Special Collections are more than 17,000 volumes, 2,000 linear feet of archival material, and 37,000 photographs.   JHBr

Chikchi simch'e yojŏl Popular name for *Paegun hwasang ch'orok pulcho Chikchi simch'e yojŏl* (Essentials of Buddha's Teachings Recorded by the Monk Paegun), printed from metal *types at the Korean Buddhist temple *Hŭngdŏksa in 1377. It is the world's earliest surviving typographic work, dated from its *colophon. The author was the monk Kyŏnghan (1298–1374), known as Paegun, who emphasized harmony between the different doctrinal schools. Only the incomplete second part of this collection survives in the *Bibliothèque nationale de France. The print area measures 202×143 mm. Shapes and sizes of the types are not uniform. The volume was re-covered during the Chosŏn period; a page inserted after the new cover bears the ownership marks of Collin de Plancy (1853–1922) and Henri Vever (1854–1943).   EDM
M. Park, 'A Study on the Type Casting, Setting and Printing Method of "Buljo-Jikji-Simche-Yoyeol"', *GJ* 79 (2004), 32–46

Child, Francis James (1825–96) American scholar. He became Boylston professor at Harvard (1851), and the first professor of English there (1876). Child edited Spenser (5 vols, 1855) and published influentially on Chaucer and Gower, but is best known for his ballad scholarship. *English and Scottish Popular Ballads* (5 vols, 1882–98; originally published 1857–9) remains the standard canonical edition, and contains 305 *ballads and variants still known internationally by their 'Child number'.   NGr

children's books *See* 15.

children's laureate British literary distinction established in 1999 to celebrate writers and illustrators of children's books (*see* 15). Formulated by Ted Hughes (then *poet laureate) and Michael Morpurgo, the *prize carries a bursary and a brief to promote reading and the 'readers of tomorrow'. Administered by *Booktrust and funded by the UK government, corporate sponsors also contribute. Laureates serve two-year terms; holders have included Quentin Blake, Jacqueline Wilson, and Michael Rosen.   CMS

www.booktrusted.co.uk/childrenslaureate, consulted July 2007

children's libraries Although there are early examples of library collections assembled specifically for, or used extensively by, children, it was not until the end of the 19th century that provision for children really began. A number of factors came together to bring this about: the growing maturity of public library movements (*see* LENDING LIBRARIES AND REFERENCE LIBRARIES); the growth of children's *literacy following compulsory education; increased publication of books and magazines aimed at children; and, as children left the workforce due to legislation, rising living standards, changing social attitudes, and a growing recognition of the importance of childhood and child welfare. As early as 1861, Manchester Free Library provided a separate children's room, and in 1882 a 'stand-alone' children's library opened in Nottingham. In Cleveland, Ohio, the city's central library inaugurated a separate children's department in 1895. Children's libraries then spread to countries around the world, including India, South Africa, Russia, and Italy. In the 20th century, children's librarianship was increasingly recognized as legitimate and important. Librarians developed new ways of attracting and retaining young readers: from storytelling and outreach work to the transformation of library space into welcoming environments, latterly with access to audio-visual materials and computers. *See also* 15.   AMB
G. Rees, *Libraries for Children* (1924)

Children's Library, Moscow The collection of more than 500,000 items of material for and about children, the largest in the Russian network of children's libraries, was founded in 1969. The library has strong collections of music scores, audio and video material, software, and sound recordings. Among its fourteen reading rooms are the Fairy Tales Rooms and the Pushkin Room.   ER

Chile, National Library of (Biblioteca Nacional de Chile) Founded in 1813 and opened in 1823, the library has occupied its present building in Santiago since 1925. The collections have grown largely through gift and *legal deposit to over 1.6 million volumes. Its greatest treasure is the library of José Toribio *Medina, whose 22,000 volumes include 60 per cent of all known colonial Latin American *imprints, together with 500 MS volumes. Its first book catalogue was published in 1854. More recently, the library has been a regional leader in automation and

digitization. Since 1963, it has published the journal *Mapocho*.   DRW
S. Martínez Baeza, *Biblioteca Nacional* (1982)

China, National Library of (Zhongguo Guojia Tushuguan) Originally established by the Qing government as the Metropolitan Library in 1909, the library was taken over by the Republican Ministry of Education, and—having become a *legal deposit library in 1916—was in 1928 renamed the National Beiping Library (Guoli Beiping Tushuguan). In 1949, it became the sole national library in China, since 1951 under the name of Beijing Library (Beijing Tushuguan). From 1987, it was called (in English) the National Library of China; in 1998, the Chinese name followed suit. Among its former chief librarians were many noted scholars, including Miao Quansun (1844–1919), Liang Qichao (1873–1929), and *Yuan Tung-li. The library collection comprises more than 24 million items, including 300,000 volumes of rare books, 1.6 million pre-modern works, and 35,000 pieces of oracle bone. Other special collections include *ink-squeeze rubbings, ancient maps, Dunhuang MSS, revolutionary historical documents, and genealogies. The library also has some early European *imprints. As the national library of China, it has been responsible for several large-scale national bibliographies, and has published many specialized catalogues and reprint series of its own holdings.   MH
Beijing tushuguan guanshi ziliao huibian, 1909-1949, 1949-1966 (1992)

Chinese Academy of Sciences, National Library of the (Zhongguo Kexueyuan Guojia Kexue Tushuguan) The national library for natural sciences and technology in China. It was established in Beijing in 1950, and after 1985 was called the Documentation and Information Center of the Chinese Academy of Sciences. Its collections include 500,000 pre-modern items, including Dunhuang and Xixia MSS; Song and Yuan *imprints; local contractual documents and genealogies, as well as noteworthy material from local *gazetteers and Ming and Qing private writings. The ratio of its holdings in natural science to social sciences is 7:3.   MH

Chinese type The world's first description of movable *type refers to type made of baked clay by Bi Sheng in the 1040s (*see* **40**). The oldest surviving works produced with type date to the 1180s, having been printed when the Xixia (or Tangut) government—a state west of China, that had recently developed its own intricate writing system—decided to produce quickly a large number of standardized religious and legal texts. Among these, a Tangut sutra printed using *wood type from the 1180s to 1190s is typically considered the oldest, though other examples, some using clay type, may be earlier. For texts in Uyghur (another language spoken near China), wooden type dating to *c.*1300 is extant. That such type was produced under Chinese influence is not in doubt, and the evidence suggests a continuous use of type in China beginning with the 12th century. Various kinds of Chinese

type were used: wooden type; metal type (bronze, copper, tin, lead), either directly engraved or cast using sand-moulds (*see* SAND CASTING); and occasionally clay type. (Each variety possessed its own price implications.) Metal type was fairly popular during the 15th and 16th centuries; in general, however, wooden type prevailed, especially for such niches as small runs of non-commercial printing.

Type did not replace *block printing until well into the 19th century, however; yet, for some particular circumstances, it simply could not compete economically with xylography. There is, after all, nothing inherently advanced in movable type; given the characteristics of the Chinese writing system (an open-ended set with thousands of different characters), it was more advantageous to use xylography than to produce huge type *founts and to set (and *distribute) type. Theoretically, since wooden type would wear out as fast as (or faster than) woodblocks after x printings, there was little incentive to use type, unless type could be reused more than x times within one book or between several books. In fact, *runs of books printed using type, where known, do not exceed a few hundred copies at most. When faced with unexpected demand, a book set with type was likely to be recut for xylography.

The advent of *electrotype (which could make *matrices out of other kinds of type, usually wooden)—a method first used in the 1850s by William Gamble at the American Presbyterian Mission Press in Shanghai—resulted in the rapid disappearance of the other varieties of type. Even then, it was the need to use metal type for modern high-speed presses that ensured its success, rather than any advantages of its own. By the 20th century, Japan provided most of the newspaper type in China. Although a few Chinese foundries invested in the development of new typefaces before World War II, it was only in the 1960s that a wider variety of type was developed, before type itself gave way to *photocomposition.   MH
X. Zhang and Q. Han, *Zhongguo huozi yinshua shi* (1998)

chirography Handwriting, especially as distinct from typography; sometimes, a person's own handwriting or *autograph handwriting.

Chiswell, Richard (1640–1711) English wholesale bookseller engaged successfully in London and overseas trade. A freeman of the *Stationers' Company, his great innovation was the creation of a joint-stock partnership (known as a *conger) to protect the trade from the proliferation of pirated copies.   CMA
ODNB

Chiswick Press Founded in 1809 by the London printer Charles *Whittingham (1767–1840) at Chiswick. His nephew, also Charles Whittingham (1795–1876), joined the firm in 1824. It worked closely with the publisher and bookseller W. Pickering in the 1830s and 1840s, expanding greatly, printing everything from stationery and ephemera to books. The Press revived the use of *Caslon founts in the 1840s. Basle Roman was created exclusively for it in 1854. George Bell acquired and renamed the firm Charles Whittingham in 1880, but the Chiswick Press name was restored in 1936. W. *Morris's first two books were printed by the press; later he worked with its manager C. T. *Jacobi on various typographic projects before starting the *Kelmscott Press. The firm printed books for several *private presses, including the *Fanfrolico Press, Boar's Head Press, and Golden Hours Press. It took over the business of Sir E. *Walker in 1957, closing in 1962.   JMa

ODNB

Chitalishta Eastern European associations of educated, well-to-do citizens, founded to develop reading in the 18ᵗʰ and 19ᵗʰ centuries. They were initially based on ideas of cultural and scientific cooperation and drew from Western examples: *cabinets de lecture* in France, *subscription and proprietary libraries in England, *Lesegesellschaften* and *Lesekabinetten* in Germany. The Chitalishta movement ultimately played a significant role in the national liberation campaigns in the South Slavonic countries, spreading through Serbia, Croatia, Bosnia and Herzegovina, Macedonia, Montenegro, Slovenia, and Bulgaria. The Chitalishta facilitated easier access to printed materials, organized lectures and performances, and directed relief to war-stricken areas and the underprivileged. Chitalishta were the forerunners of public *lending libraries, which later overshadowed them, except in Bulgaria, where Chitalishta were founded following Serbia's example and still exist.   ABV

D. Stamatović, *Čitališta u Srbiji u 19. veku* (1984)

Chiu, Alfred Kaiming (1898–1977) Chinese library pioneer, also known as Ch'iu K'ai-ming (Qiu Kaiming), who compiled a comprehensive library classification scheme for Chinese books. A graduate of the Boone Library School in China, Chiu began, as a doctoral student at Harvard University in 1927, to catalogue their fledgling collection of Chinese and Japanese books. During a 38-year career, he developed the Harvard-Yenching Library into its pre-eminent status among East Asian research libraries.   JSE

Chodowiecki, Daniel Nikolaus (1726–1801) Polish painter, etcher, and illustrator. Chodowiecki began his career in Berlin in 1754 as a miniature painter and printmaker, but turned increasingly to illustration, etching over 2,000 designs for *almanacs, *calendars, *novels, scientific, religious, educational, and historical works. He was an early illustrator of Goethe. His designs for Johann Kaspar Lavater's writings on physiognomy brought him to the attention of Georg Christoph Lichtenberg, who commissioned several didactic-moral cycles that are, like *Hogarth's, relevant to the development of *comic books or strips.   JCI

A. Griffiths and F. Carey, *German Printmaking in the Age of Goethe* (1994)

Choice A monthly selection tool for academic librarians, published since 1964 by the Association of College and Research Libraries, a division of the *American Library Association. *Choice* evaluates new books, websites, and databases in brief essays (100–250 words), summarizing the new work's purpose, thesis, relationship to key titles in the field, readership level, and recommendations for purchase. Most reviewers are faculty members or academic librarians. Each issue, essential reading for acquisitions librarians, also features a substantial bibliographical essay on a broad topic, discussing background, current controversies, research trends, and key standard and new titles for the topic.   MEB

'Choice of Valentines, The' Known also as 'Nashes Dildo', it is the earliest surviving erotic poem in English. Written by Thomas Nashe (1567–c.1601), it comprises 342 lines, mainly in couplets. Dedicated to 'the right Honorable the lord S', presumably Ferdinando Stanley, Lord Strange, it recounts the visit of the narrator to a London brothel, where a prostitute praises the charms of the dildo. The poem survives in several 17ᵗʰ-century MSS; there is no contemporary printed edition. *See also* PORNOGRAPHY.   ASGE

R. B. McKerrow, ed., *The Works of Thomas Nashe*, rev. F. P. Wilson (5 vols, 1958)

Cholmondeley Award for Poets Founded in 1966 by Sybil Cholmondeley, marchioness of Cholmondeley, and administered by the UK's *Society of Authors, this is the leading lifetime achievement award for British poets. Since 1991, the prize has had four annual recipients, somewhat diluting its symbolic value. Its cash value is £2,000, a fraction of the six-figure sums awarded to winners of the major US poetry prizes, such as the Ruth Lilly Prize of the Modern Poetry Society, the Tanning Prize of the Academy of American Poets, the Lannan Lifetime Achievement Award, and the *Bollingen Prize.   JFE

Ch'ŏn Hye-bong (1926–) Bibliographer and university professor. The pre-eminent scholar of bibliography in Korea, Ch'ŏn has published the survey-history of Korean books *Han'guk sŏjihak* (1997) and many bibliographies, as well as individual studies of the print histories of the Korean dynasties and of movable-type printing in Korea.   EDM

chrestomathy [Gk, 'useful learning'] Collection of choice passages in a single language, intended for use in language acquisition. Chrestomathies may be published independently or with *grammars.

Christ Church Library, Oxford Refounded in 1546, the college's monastic precursors have left little bibliographical record, and the present library owes its distinction to 17ᵗʰ- and 18ᵗʰ-century benefactions, many of them in Hebrew studies, theology, and music. There are, for example, 500 volumes from the library of Robert *Burton; Henry Aldrich (dean, 1689–1710) and the family of Francis Atterbury (dean, 1711–13) left substantial collections. William Wake (archbishop of Canterbury, 1716–37) bequeathed his library (some 5,000 volumes) to his old college; it includes Greek MSS as well as fine copies of contemporary works. An imposing new library was built from 1717 on the south side of the new Peckwater quadrangle, with a handsomely furnished main room on the upper floor. Its ground floor was subsequently adapted to form reading rooms. The *Evelyn books and MSS were formerly on deposit at Christ Church, which still holds collections (including ones deposited by his family and by the family of Alice Liddell) relating to C. L. Dodgson ('Lewis Carroll'), long a resident member of the college.

ASB

W. G. Hiscock, *A Christ Church Miscellany* (1946)
H. R. Trevor-Roper, *Christ Church* (1989)

Christie's Auction house. **James Christie** (1730–1803) founded the London firm in 1766, after serving as an apprentice to and then partner with an auctioneer named Annesley. His first auctions were of vacated estates and tradesmen's stock. In early years, his sales tended toward books, jewels, and especially art, where he gained a reputation for knowledge, elegance, gentility, and success. As part-owner of the *Morning Chronicle* and the *Morning Post*, Christie was assured of advertising space for his auctions. He also introduced the practice of private advance viewings. Brief partnerships developed with Sharpe & Harper, Robert Ansell, and Harry Phillips—this last beginning as his apprentice and splitting off to form the auction house *Phillips (1796). One of Christie's five sons, **James** (1773–1831), succeeded him.

First established in Pall Mall, the firm moved to its present location in St James's Square in 1824, where it attained its dominance in art sales. Upon James's death, his son **George Henry Christie** (d. 1887), in partnership with William Manson, carried on the business; he was followed by his son **James H. B. Christie**. The firm continued for a time as Christie, Manson, & Woods with unimpaired reputation, until the commission-fixing scandals of 2000 and 2001 briefly tarnished the names of both Christie's and *Sotheby's. PLS
ODNB

Christina, queen of Sweden (1626–89, r. 1632–54) One of the greatest book collectors in 17th-century Sweden. Her library (including more than 8,000 MSS) was to a great extent booty from the Thirty Years War, e.g. the Codex *Argenteus. After her abdication, she settled in Rome, continuing to patronize art and philosophy. Parts of her library (*c*.2,000 MSS and 5,500 printed books) are now in the *Vatican. MBj

Christmas book Specially produced cards, *broadsides, leaflets, and books marking the Christmas holiday were sent free as expressions of appreciation from publishers, printers, authors, and book collectors to their friends and colleagues. The tradition probably began in the mid-1880s. These gifts reflected high production values, with fine *type, durable paper, and high-quality bindings. They are greatly valued in the antiquarian book trade, especially those issued during the revival of *fine printing during the Arts and Crafts era, and those published by Cambridge University Press between 1930 and 1974.

Christmas books have taken various forms, including seasonal essays by Washington Irving, original stories of the Nativity, books about the Holy Land, reproductions of Christmas carols, and clever typographical arrangements by designers such as *Rogers. Books about books were also popular; in 1894 *Copeland & Day, one of the first publishers to produce books especially printed for presentation at Christmas, issued *Detached Thoughts on Books and Reading* by Charles Lamb. Luther A. Brewer of the Torch Press began sending Christmas books just before World War I; later, in *The Escape of Alice* (1919), a Christmas Eve setting supplants the fantasy world of Lewis Carroll's Wonderland. In the 1920s, Walter Hill of Chicago printed *The Unique Hamlet*, a parody of Sherlock Holmes dedicated to Sir Arthur Conan Doyle, concerning the theft and detection of a *forged first edition of *Hamlet*. The American book collector A. S. W. *Rosenbach sent *The Earliest Christmas Books* (1927) and *The All-Embracing Dr. Franklin* (1932) to friends and business associates. The New York bookman Philip Duschnes's Christmas books included *The Notorious Jumping Frog of Calaveras County* by Mark Twain (1932) and *A Christmas Salute* by Christopher Morley (1935).

There are, of course, commercial 'Christmas books' about Christmas published for sale to the public, as opposed to Christmas gift books. These are closely associated with Dickens, who wrote five: *A Christmas Carol* (1843), *The Chimes* (1844), *The Cricket on the Hearth* (1845), *The Battle of Life* (1846), and *The Haunted Man* (1848). The original edition of *A Christmas Carol* (also called *Scrooge*) illustrated by *Leech was an instant success, selling over 6,000 copies in one week. Christmas books (either seasonal gifts or commercially sold publications) should not be confused with 'Advent books' of daily readings and prayers preliminary to Christmas.

EDG

W. Klinefelter, *Christmas Books* (1936)
— *A Bibliographical Check-List of Christmas Books* (1937)
— *More Christmas Books* (1938)

chromolithography A major 19th-century *colour printing technique, using several *inks and *lithographic stones or *plates, *overprinted to create a single multicolour image. Patented in 1837 by G. Engelmann in France (and occasionally found before then), chromolithography was used for mass-market colour printing from mid-century. Early practitioners in England included C. Hullmandel and O. *Jones. Unlike later 'trichromatic' or 'process colour' printing—in which colours are separated photographically with standardized filters—chromolithographs typically have between four and twelve colours, selected for their suitability to the *artwork being reproduced. To reduce the time and cost of preparation and printing, a printer might instead use colours from a standard set. Generally, chromolithography was used to print whole books only when colour was needed throughout; publishers occasionally used it to add ornament in the form of illuminated *initials and marginal decoration. By providing a way to print colour images that was both straightforward for artists and suitable for high-speed reproduction, it stimulated the production of elaborate colour *title-pages, colour *plate sections inserted into *letterpress-printed books, and colour illustration (*see* **16**) in popular periodicals.   ABRW

R. M. Burch, *Colour Printing and Colour Printers* (1910; repr. 1983)

chronicles Developed in the early Middle Ages, this historiographical genre remained popular until the late 16th century. In chronicles, historical facts are arranged in chronological order rather than as one coherent narrative. There is some overlap with historical works entitled 'Historia', 'Annales', or their equivalents in vernacular languages. Chronicles may present a universal, a national, or a local history. The late antique histories of the early Christian Church—*Chronicon* and *Historia Ecclesiastica* by Eusebius Caesariensis (*c*.270–339), translated from Greek into Latin respectively by St Jerome and by Rufinus of Aquileia—established the form of universal history divided into 'aetates', or historical periods from the Creation. English church history up to the year 731 was written by Bede in his *Historia Ecclesiastica*. Chronicles based on the lives of popes and emperors, first written by Martinus Polonus (d. 1278), became a popular genre in the 14th century known as 'Chronicon Martinianum'.

From the 1470s, many late medieval works appeared in print; new works were also compiled at this time. In the *Fasciculus Temporum* (Cologne, 1474), the Carthusian author Werner Rolewinck supervised a complicated layout (*see* MISE-EN-PAGE) that graphically positioned the Incarnation of Christ as the central event in world history. The *Fasciculus* was reprinted many times, including translations into German, Dutch, and French. Another large world chronicle, the *Rudimentum Novitiorum* (Lübeck, 1475), appeared in French as *La Mer des histoires*. An even more ambitious work was the richly illustrated *Nuremberg Chronicle, published in 1493 in Latin and in German.

The earliest example of a continuous vernacular history on a national basis is the *Anglo-Saxon Chronicle*, a survey of West Saxon history mainly compiled in the 9th century, with later continuations. Chronicles were frequently extended, often until they found a final form in print. Ranulph Higden's *Polychronicon*, translated into English by John Trevisa in 1387, was continued by *Caxton up to 1460 when he first published it in 1482. So too, the many permutations in the transmission of *Brut's Chronicle* in numerous MSS virtually ended in 1480 with Caxton's publication of a version entitled *The Chronicles of England*, reprinted twelve times until 1528. It was usually issued in combination with Higden's *Description of Britain*, blending history with the geographical description of localities and their most prominent features. Such converging interests became a hallmark of English chroniclers in the 16th century.

A similar process of consolidation in print of MS sources can be observed in other countries, e.g. the first publication of Heinrich Steinhöwel's *Deutsche Chronik* (1473), *Grandes chroniques de France* (1476–7), Diego de Valera's *Crónica de España* (1482), Johannes de Thwrocz's

Chronica Hungarorum (1488), and the *Danske Rimkrønike* (1495). In France, the diplomat Philippe de Commines (1447–1511) chronicled recent political events in his *Mémoires*, which remained in print for centuries as one of the period's most important historical sources. Robert Gaguin (1433–1501) wrote in Latin his *Compendium de Francorum Origine et Gestis*, printed several times from 1495 and valued for its excellent scholarship.

Printed regional chronicles, such as *Holland* (1478), *Wendesche Kroneke* (1485), *Normandie* (1487), and *Brabant* (1497), did not have the same impact. However, one city chronicle, the *Kölnische Kronik* (1499), became a famous book.

In 16th-century England, John Bourchier's translation of Jean Froissart's 14th-century *Chroniques de France, d'Angleterre et des pays voisins* (1523) was reprinted several times. It was preceded by Robert Fabyan's *Cronycles of Englande and of Fraunce*, published posthumously in 1516 and reprinted six times. There was seemingly constant inspiration and appetite for new compilations. Major historical works in English were Edward Halle's *Union of the Two Noble and Illustrate Families of Lancastre & York* (1548–50), which chronicled the reigns from Henry IV to Henry VIII. Richard Grafton's abridged *Chronicle of England* (published from 1563) competed with the ever-revised and expanded *Chronicles* of *Stow (published from 1565). Ralph Holinshed's *Chronicles of England, Scotlande and Irelande* was an extensive compilation by several hands, first published in 1577 and expanded in 1587.

Of the works produced in 16th-century England, William Camden's *Britannia* (1585), surveying the history and antiquities of the British Isles, had the most enduring impact. Camden, who actively participated when antiquaries began to meet in London in the 1580s, heralded the transition from chroniclers to antiquarians who would use chronicles as source material, rather than compiling them.   LH

CHBB 4
DEL 1
ODNB
B. Wagner, Introduction to 'Chronicles and Historiography', in *Incunabula: The Printing Revolution in Europe 1455–1500*, ed. L. Hellinga (1994)

chronogram Phrase or sentence in which the sum of the value in roman numerals of letters distinguished typographically by size or case expresses a date (for books, usually year of publication). Most chronograms are Latin and refer to an event relevant to the date, e.g. 'gVstaVVs aDoLphVs gLorIose pVgnans MorItVr' (1632). The practice was favoured in Catholic states, especially by the Jesuits, and was particularly popular in Austria, Bavaria, Bohemia, and the Netherlands during the 17th and 18th centuries.   KEA

J. Hilton, *Chronograms* (3 vols, 1885–8)
W. H. White, 'Chronograms', *Library*, 4/4 (1923–4), 59–74

chrysography [Gk *chrysographia*, 'writing in gold'] *Gold ink, or sometimes silver, was used in luxury MSS from late Antiquity to the Renaissance in the West and other places, including Byzantium. As early as the 6th century, *parchment stained purple often served as the background for the gold. Many such MSS bear 'golden' names, such as the Codex *Aureus of St Emmeran, made for Charles the Bald c.870. Unsurprisingly, writing in gold is common for religious texts, such as bibles, *psalters, *gospel books, or (in Muslim lands) *Qur'āns. The *Lorsch Gospels prepared in the 9th century in Charlemagne's court is a fine example. The Saint John's Bible, a recent project led by the calligrapher Donald Jackson, has some pages written in gold. Gold printing was used in 15th-century Venice (*Ratdolt's 1482 Euclid); for a 1930s New Testament, De La *Rue applied gold and bronze dust to wet ink.   MMS

Chūō Kōron Shinsha Japanese publisher of *Chūō Kōron* (The Central Review), Japan's oldest general monthly magazine. It was started in 1887 in Kyoto and later moved to Tokyo. In 1944 the company was closed due to its anti-war sentiments. Publication of *Chūō Kōron* was resumed in 1946, and it continues to be influential. The firm also publishes paperback series such as *Chūkō Shinsho* and *Chūkō Bunko*.   YHM
[Chūō Kōronsha,] *Chūō Kōronsha no Hachijūnen* (1965)

Church, Elihu Dwight (1835–1908) American book collector. He assembled a small (c.2,000 volumes) but extremely important collection of books and MSS, which emphasized Americana. In 1905, he bought the Rowfant Library of F. *Locker-Lampson, much of which was subsequently sold to Henry E. *Huntington, who also purchased most of Church's own library in 1911.   ASGE
[Grolier Club,] *Grolier 75* (1959)

Churchill, George Spencer-, 5th duke of Marlborough (1766–1840) English book collector. His purchase of the Valdarfer edition of Boccaccio's *Decameron* (Venice, 1471) for £2,260 in 1812 led to the founding of the *Roxburghe Club. In addition to *incunabula, he collected *Shakespeare. He also owned MSS, including the Bedford Hours (*see* BEDFORD MASTER). His library at White Knights, Reading, was sold by R. H. Evans in June and July 1819.   ASGE
ODNB

Churchill College, Cambridge Churchill College began to collect contemporary *archives in 1965, and opened a dedicated Archives Centre in 1973. Documenting fields of public life in which Sir Winston Churchill was personally involved or interested, the centre houses 570 collections of the private papers of politicians, service chiefs, diplomats, civil servants, scientists, technologists, statesmen, soldiers, sailors, and airmen who have shaped the history of the Churchill era and after. Its most important acquisitions have been the archives of Churchill himself (in 1969 and 1974), and of Margaret Thatcher in 1997.   KEA
www.chu.cam.ac.uk/archives, consulted June 2009

circulating libraries There is evidence that the custom of lending books by subscription in Britain existed as early as the late 17th century, and newspaper advertisements of books for hire are extant as early as 1720. The custom seems to have been most prominent in the provinces before taking hold in cities. By the late 18th century, there were circulating libraries in most provincial towns. Such libraries developed as a result of the rising middle class and the growth in *literacy; many were extensions of literary and philosophical institutions and societies, others were *book clubs. Although a significant number of these libraries were private, the growth of the book industry and the development of a larger reading public created a market throughout the 18th century for book lending as well as sales.

Most circulating libraries were operated by booksellers or publishers. Allan Ramsay, who ran a shop in Edinburgh in 1725, was apparently the first person in Britain to hire books for a fee; the first circulating libraries appeared in London a few decades later. The *OED* cites a reference to an advertisement from 1742, in which Samuel Fancourt proposed a scheme 'for erecting a *Public Circulating Library* in London' as the earliest usage of 'circulating library'. Fancourt specialized in books for the Nonconformist clergy, an ironic twist considering the objections to circulating libraries raised by clerics and critics in the ensuing years.

In the 18th century, circulating libraries were found mostly in provincial seaside resorts and spa towns such as Bath. Their numbers increased in the early 19th century, spurred by the significant increase in the publication of fiction. In 1789 there were six circulating libraries in Bath; by 1830 there were 16, and nationwide the number increased from 1,000 to 6,000 between 1801 and 1820.

Patrons obtained books either by periodic subscriptions or by fixed fees per volume. Initially, subscription prices were prohibitive except for the more affluent in society. Annual subscription rates in Liverpool ranged from a guinea and a half in 1770 to five guineas in 1784. Even though fixed fees per volume were less expensive, patrons in the 1780s might be expected to pay 2s. to 3s. for a novel, a sum equalling the average value of tea and sugar for a month for a family of six. Books were thus generally affordable only by the middle and upper classes; most of the circulating-library clientele were women.

Circulating libraries helped to popularize fiction reading, thus leading critics to claim that the accessibility of novels would lead to the corruption of women and youths. In *The Rivals*, Sheridan has Sir Anthony Absolute declare the circulating library 'an ever-green tree of diabolical knowledge!' (1.2.205). The assault against the light reading supplied by circulating libraries continued throughout the early and mid-19th century. Critics might have targeted Charles Edward Mudie, proprietor of *Mudie's Select Library, the largest and most popular circulating library of its time. However, as the name of the firm suggests, Mudie (a preacher himself) scrupulously selected books for his library, avoiding anything that might appear immoral, thus averting such potential criticism. When Mudie decided against operating bookstalls in railway stations, he opened the way for W. H. *Smith, the largest newsagent in Britain in the second half of the 19th century, to become his main competitor.

Changes in readers' demands, the publishing trade, and *copyright laws, eventually led to the decline of circulating libraries, giving way to the rise of public *lending libraries. SL

Altick

R. Clark, 'Circulating Libraries,' *The Literary Encyclopedia*, www.litencyc.com/php/stopics.php?rec=true&UID=189, consulted Mar. 2007

G. L. Griest, *Mudie's Circulating Library* (1970)

circumtext A term devised by late 20th-century literary theorists to describe content encountered in association with a particular text that is not directly connected with it, but may influence its reception (e.g. the other contents of a journal in which a piece is published).

citron Term commonly used to describe a lemon-yellow colour popular for fine binding work from the 18th century onwards (hence citron *morocco).

City Lights American publisher. Founded in 1953 by Lawrence Ferlinghetti and Peter D. Martin as the first all-*paperback bookshop, City Lights has occupied a building in North Beach, San Francisco, ever since. In 1955, Ferlinghetti launched City Lights Publishers and its 'Pocket Poet' series to publish the work of the Beat poets, including his own poetry. In 1956 Ferlinghetti was arrested and tried (but not convicted) for selling obscene material when he published Allen Ginsberg's *Howl and Other Poems*. Today there are more than a million copies of *Howl* in print. City Lights continues to sell and publish alternative literature. KAW

City or Athenaeum Library, Deventer In 1560, the Dutch Deventer magistrates bought the library of a local priest for the use of the clergy in their struggle against Protestantism. After the Reformation, this now public collection was expanded with books from Catholic churches and monasteries, most importantly that of the Bibliotheca Florentiana, formerly owned by the Brethren of the Common Life. From 1630, the library also served the newly founded Athenaeum Illustre. Although relatively small in size, the City or Athenaeum Library is rich in MS material and early modern printed books. OSL

J. C. Bedaux *et al.*, *Stads- of Athenaeum-bibliotheek Deventer 1560-1985* (1985)

civilité type Type imitating the *gothic handwriting common in northwestern Europe in the 16th and 17th centuries: the first true *script type (as opposed to the semi-cursive *bastarda). *Granjon cut the first civilité (Lyons, 1557), quickly distributing several internationally. *Tavernier's (Antwerp. 1558/9) reflect the handwriting of the Low Countries. Philippe Danfrie's (Paris, 1558) and Van den *Keere's (Ghent, c.1570) are also important. In Scotland (1571) and England (1576), the type was called 'secretary'. More than 30 civilités are known.

Popular for (often Protestant) children's books (*see* **15**), *forms, *dedications, and words accompanying *music, almost always in the vernacular, it saw a broader range of uses in the Low Countries than in France. Though Latin script gradually replaced gothic from the late 16th to the early 18th century, civilités remained in occasional use until their antiquarian revival in the 19th century. JAL

H. G. Carter and H. D. L. Vervliet, *Civilité Types*, OBS, NS 14 (1966)

Civilização Brasileira Brazilian publisher. Founded in 1929, it was initially the *Companhia Editora Nacional's Rio de Janeiro branch (1932–63). Under Ênio Silveira, it specialized in social sciences and Brazilian literature, clashing frequently with the government over its leftist leanings. In the 1960s, its *imprints revolutionized Brazilian book design. DRW

Claesz, Cornelis (*c*.1551–1609) Amsterdam publisher and bookseller. A refugee from the southern Netherlands, he established a bookshop in Amsterdam in 1578. He soon developed into a leading book trade entrepreneur with an extensive *publisher's list, specializing in travel accounts and *atlases. Claesz was very active in the international book trade, as is demonstrated by his stock catalogues, among which is a list of books imported from China. PGH

G. Schilder, *Cornelis Claesz (c.1551–1609)* (2003)

B. van Selm, *Een menighte treffelijcke boecken* (1987)

clandestine publishing Facing *censorship by religious or political authorities, dissident authors have often sought to produce and distribute their writings in exile beyond the reach of authority, or to risk covertly publishing forbidden material, often disguised by *false imprints. During the Reformation, the battle of printers against authority was fought with particular ferocity by the well-developed printing industry in the Low Countries. Formal imperial decrees directed against the works of Luther were issued from 1521, and were soon followed by the suppression of the work of other reformers, and vernacular Bible *translations. Antwerp printers, three of whom were executed between 1542 and 1555, printed Dutch, French, and English works. The Antwerp printer Christoffel van Ruremund died in jail in Westminster; his widow continued working for the English market.

As with materials labelled heretical or seditious, *pornography too was often published clandestinely. Throughout much of the history of print, popular literature, songs, and parodies, especially those satirizing church or state, were also printed in defiance of authority, if not explicitly forbidden in edicts.

A modern instance of clandestine publishing, often in full awareness of parallels with the rebellious printers of the 16th century, can be found during the German occupation of The Netherlands in 1940–45. While highly risky illegal printing took place (e.g. in newssheets with uncensored news), there was simultaneously a surge of small literary publications, issued anonymously and without the required approval of the authorities, and therefore clandestinely. Since their contents often ran counter to National Socialist ideology, publication carried some risk; thus, their imprints were fictitious. Isolated under occupation, there was no influence from imported works produced in exile. This is in contrast to an earlier famous episode concerning the clandestine dissemination of printed works—the decades preceding the French Revolution—in which seditious works were mainly printed outside France and smuggled into the country.

In the former USSR and Soviet bloc countries, *samizdat, the clandestine production and circulation of texts (many of them banned), was an important cultural and political phenomenon. By its very nature covert publication, especially of materials regarded as seditious, is often difficult to detect, and such materials are regularly destroyed because possessing them is a criminal offence. Today, political and social activists circulate forbidden materials via the *World Wide Web, often using computers in 'free' countries to mask their origin. In a different vein, the booming industry of producing *counterfeit books and DVDs, especially in Asia, might be considered the most widespread instance of clandestine publishing.
LH

CHBB 3
R. Darnton, *The Corpus of Clandestine Literature in France 1769–1789* (1995)
L. de Jong, *Het vrije boek in onvrije tijd* (1958)
M. E. Kronenberg, *Verboden boeken en opstandige drukkers in de Hervormingstijd* (1948)
L. Lewin, *Het clandestiene boek 1940–1945* (1983)
A. E. C. Simoni, *Publish and be Free* (1975); C. van Heertum, *Supplement* (1995)

clap Booksellers made 'sticking titles' by printing extra *title-pages which were then posted as advertisements. These title-pages, which often had long descriptive titles and included the name and location of the bookseller (*see* IMPRINT), were sometimes called 'claps', because they were stuck (or 'clapped') on walls and on the wooden 'show-boards' and *rubric posts set out in front of booksellers' shops. *See also* ADVERTISING, MARKETING, AND PUBLICITY FOR BOOKS. MFS

Clarendon Press *See* OXFORD UNIVERSITY PRESS.

Clarke's Bookshop A landmark in Cape Town's Long Street, Clarke's Bookshop was established in 1956. It carries new, second-hand, and out-of-print books on southern Africa. Two catalogues are issued annually. The proprietor traverses southern Africa to buy or barter indigenously published books. FCG

Clark Memorial Library, William Andrews Constructed in Los Angeles between 1924 and 1926, the Clark Library was built by William Andrews Clark, Jr., the son of a wealthy entrepreneur whose fortune came mainly from mining. Clark (1877–1934) began collecting books during World War I. He concentrated on early modern English literature, Oscar Wilde, and *fine printing, particularly the English *private presses. The Clark Library was given to UCLA in 1926, although Clark continued to live on the property until his death. DBW
W. E. Conway and R. Stevenson, *William Andrews Clark, Jr.* (1985)

Clary, William W. (1888–1971) American book collector and lawyer. Clary developed a large collection of books connected with Oxford University, now in Pomona College (a catalogue of the 3,600 items was published in 1968). He also formed substantial collections of Shelley, Andrew Lang, and Milton's *Paradise Lost*, all of which are now in the Claremont Library, California. ASGE
W. W. Clary, *Fifty Years of Book Collecting* (1962)

clasps *See* FASTENINGS.

classification A system of organizing information, typically applied to library books and other materials, both in their arrangement in library catalogues, and in their placement and juxtaposition on the *bookshelves of libraries.

During the Middle Ages, library cataloguers organized their collections according to classes, mirroring their intellectual organization with the physical disposition of books on shelves. Thus, books on theology, music, medicine, and so on were collocated in a hierarchical system of knowledge that ranked bibles and the Church Fathers above all others. As the Middle Ages progressed, these classes were typically mapped on to the university curriculum. Information about early classification systems, gleaned from surviving catalogues and inventory marks in books, shows that practices were far from uniform. In the 14th century, some libraries organized their holdings by subject, others by author, location (and, often, size), and even donor. Around 1389, Br. John Whitfield, librarian at Dover Priory, employed a conventional system of subject classification, marking books by *book press and shelf, a system that dominated library practice from the 16th into the 19th centuries.

As library collections grew during the 19th century, so too did the requirements of large libraries to organize their collections through more sophisticated approaches to classification. Since large libraries, such as the *British Museum Library and the *Bodleian maintained closed stack collections, little emphasis was placed on subject-based arrangement. By the late 19th century, however, librarians such as E. W. B. *Nicholson at the Bodleian began to see the advantage of organizing collections by subject, albeit with fixed locations. Classification schemes truly came into their own as part of the growth of major public and academic libraries in the US, which from the mid-19th century onwards had large parts of their collections accessible to readers, necessitating some organization based on subjects. Thus, *Dewey in the 1870s developed a decimal system of classification by subject which aided both browsing and retrieval of books, based on ten main classes. Dewey was heavily influenced by the thinking of Charles A. Cutter, who developed the Cutter Expansive Classification system. Today the *Dewey Decimal Classification (DDC)—together with its European sister, the Universal Decimal Classification (UDC) developed by the Belgians Paul Otlet and Henri

La Fontaine—is the most widely used system of classification, employed in some 130 countries and dominating the public library sector.

The Library of *Congress Classification scheme was developed between 1899 and 1940 and is still based on 21 major classes, each identified by a single letter of the alphabet. Each class is broken down by sub-class and then by topic, with each topic also broken down by place, time period, format, etc. The LC system—also influenced by Cutter's Expansive Classification—is now dominant in the academic and national library sector throughout the world.　　　　　　　　　　　　　　　RWO

R. M. Brunt, 'Organising Knowledge: Cataloguing, Classification and Indexing in the Modern Library', in *CHLBI* 3

R. Sharpe, 'Accession, Classification, Location: Shelfmarks in Medieval Libraries', *Scriptorium*, 50 (1996), 279–87

Clavell, Robert (*c.*1633–1711) English bookseller. Apprenticed to Richard Royston from 1650, he became a freeman of the *Stationers' Company in 1657. Clavell's name featured as publisher or seller in more than 700 *imprints. He also founded and edited the *term catalogues, and was Master of the Stationers' Company 1698–1700.　　　　　　　　　　　　　　　KMQ
ODNB

Clay, Richard Printing firm in Bungay (Suffolk), London, and New York, established in 1818 by Richard Clay. Printing books and periodicals, it early adopted the stereotyping process. In 1865, Clay's got the commission to print Lewis Carroll's *Alice's Adventures in Wonderland* after Carroll, dissatisfied with the quality of the first printing, had withdrawn the first edition. Clay's purchased Childs of Bungay (which had installed composition machines) in 1876 and renamed it The Chaucer Press. From 1882, the firm printed works for T. J. *Wise, later revealed by J. *Carter and G. *Pollard to be forgeries of first editions and pamphlets. From the 1960s Clay's concentrated its expertise in long-run book work. The firm has printed many of the Harry Potter series.　　AAW
J. Moran, *Clay's of Bungay* (1978)

Cleland, Thomas Maitland (1880–1964) American book designer and illustrator. A 1904 sojourn in Italy led him to reject W. *Crane's and W. *Morris's medievalism. Thereafter he designed in a variety of historicizing, mostly Italianate, styles, eschewing modernism. He drew the typeface 'Della Robbia' for the Bruce Foundry and specialized in book covers as art editor for *McClure's*, 1906–8. Later, as a freelance artist, he successfully straddled the worlds of commercial art, magazine design, trade book publishing, and bibliophile editions, in the latter often collaborating with his friend *Updike.　　　　MA
A. E. Hamill, *The Decorative Work of T. M. Cleland* (1929)

Clements, William L. (1861–1934) American book collector. An industrialist, Clements assembled an important collection of Americana, including books, early newspapers, MSS, and *maps. Clements donated these to the University of *Michigan in 1923, with an endowment for the William L. Clements Library building, and continued to add to the library until his death.　　ASGE
M. F. Maxwell, *Shaping a Library: William L. Clements as Collector* (1973)

Cleverdon, Douglas (1903–87) English radio producer, bookseller, and publisher. His bookshop, open 1926–40 in his native Bristol, specialized in *fine printing and illustration (*see* **16**). He joined the BBC around 1938, retiring in 1969, when he established Clover Hill Editions, using the *Rampant Lions Press as his printer.　　PWN
ODNB

Cleyn, Francis (Clein or Klein, Franz) (1582–1658) German painter, tapestry designer, and illustrator. Established in England by 1625, Cleyn supplemented his income from the Mortlake tapestry factory by designing *frontispieces, *title-pages, *ornaments, and narrative illustrations, several of which he etched himself. His drawings for George Sandys's translation of Ovid's *Metamorphoses* (1632)—coupled with his work for *Ogilby's lavishly illustrated *Fables of Aesop Paraphras'd* (1651) and *Works of Publius Virgilius* (1654; Latin ed. 1658)—are considered early landmarks of 17th-century book illustration in England.　　　　　　　　　　JCI
E. Hodnett, *Francis Barlow* (1978)
ODNB

clicker of a compositors' companionship The foreman of a companionship of *compositors, responsible for distributing the copy, record-keeping, and billing.

clipsheet A single-sheet *offprint of a short article, news item, cartoon, or other matter, usually from a magazine or newspaper, typically printed on one side of the sheet for ease of clipping, often used for promotional purposes. The term is largely confined to North American journalism.　　　　　　　　　　　　PWN

Clique, The British booksellers' trade weekly founded in 1890, in which dealers advertised their desiderata—the 'Medium for the few to communicate their wants to the many'. It ceased publication in 1988, becoming briefly *The Clique Catalogue Bulletin* (1988–9) and the *Book Collector's Bulletin*.　　　　　　ASGE

cloth book (rag book) Brightly coloured picture-book for small children, made of cotton or polyester to allow the book to be washed and to avoid tearing; modern cloth books sometimes include other appliquéd fabrics to enhance their textures. They usually contain nursery rhymes, highly abridged fairy tales, *ABCs, and themed picture-books. Typically between 18 and 22 cm high and often squarish, cloth books are about 8–12 pages long, to facilitate *sewing down the left edge. Cloth books originated in the mid-19th century, the most prolific producer being the Dean Rag Book Co., founded by Henry Samuel Dean (1903).　　　　　　　　　　　　　　KEA

Clowes, William Printers, in Beccles and London, founded by William Clowes in 1803. By 1839, it was the largest printing works in the world, quickly and accurately printing government stationery (*see* LETTERHEAD), periodicals, and books for many publishers. The firm produced catalogues of the Great Exhibition (1851) and *Hymns Ancient and Modern* (1875). It pioneered the use of *Monotype and established a reputation in foreign languages and *music. AAW

A. Weedon, *Victorian Publishing* (2003)

club Term increasingly used from the late 17th century to describe an association of people who 'clubbed' money for social or other activities. In the 18th century, clubs flourished in taverns and *coffee houses across England and the Atlantic world. Literary clubs thrived, including the Augustan satirists' Scriblerus Club, the predominantly female Bluestocking Club, and S. *Johnson's Literary Club. In Edinburgh, David Hume belonged to the Rankenian Club. In the 19th century, these clubs declined in numbers, superseded by voluntary associations and gentlemen's clubs, such as the Athenaeum. VEMG

P. Clark, *British Clubs and Societies 1580–1800* (2000)

Club Bindery A New York bookbinding business created in 1895 by Edwin Holden and other members of the *Grolier Club, prompted by the lack of an American bindery capable of producing luxury bindings to the best European standards. Craftsmen from England and France were recruited, including Léon Maillard from Paris. The bindery was dissolved in 1909, when some of its binders transferred to the Rowfant Bindery in Cleveland, which was in turn dissolved in 1913. DRSP

T. Boss, *Bound to be the Best* (2004)

club libraries These semi-formal, non-profit associations provided members with books, discussion groups, and conviviality (unlike *subscription and *circulating libraries). They were segregated by class, sex, and, occasionally, religion. The great metropolitan clubs (such as the Athenaeum, Reform, etc. in London) have acquired important collections of books and journals over the years. Middle-class clubs charged up to 2 guineas entry and annual subscriptions of up to 31*s.* 6*d.*; they stocked newspapers, novels, history, economics, and politics. Working-class clubs commonly charged 2*s.* 6*d.* entry and weekly subscriptions of 2*d.*; they typically preferred non-fiction. The formation of middle-class clubs peaked *c.*1780–1830. *Mudie's Lending Library competed for the same clientele from 1842. Working-class clubs stemmed from late 18th-century mutual-improvement societies; Chartism and the Co-operative Movement stimulated growth after 1830. Their membership controlled acquisitions, in contrast to *mechanics' institute and workplace libraries, whose middle-class sponsors censored holdings. They produced readers who supported trade unions and Gladstonian Liberalism. DGP

R. Alston, 'The Library History Database', www.r-alston.co.uk, consulted Feb. 2007
C. Baggs, 'Radical Reading?', in *CHLBI* 3
T. Kelly, *Early Public Libraries* (1966)
K. Manley, 'Engines of Literature', in *CHLBI* 2
Rose

Club of Odd Volumes A private club, established 1887 in Boston, of fewer than 150 members, dedicated primarily to the history of books and book collecting. The goals of its eleven founders included promoting 'literary and artistic tastes, establishing and maintaining a place for social meetings and a reference library, occasional exhibits of a special and instructive character and publishing rare prints and books relating to historical and literary matters'. It was the second private club of its kind in the US, founded just three years after New York's *Grolier Club. The Club's inspiration, however, was English, being modelled upon the bookish *Sette of Odd Volumes (established in London, 1878). Meetings are held in the clubhouse at 77 Mt. Vernon Street in Beacon Hill. EAH

A. Williams, *Social History of the Club of Odd Volumes, 1887–1967* (1969)

CNA (**Central News Agency**) Established as a newspaper-selling business in Johannesburg in 1896, it obtained bulk supplies of British magazines through Gordon and Gotch. By the late 1920s, it published most local English newspapers and had outlets throughout South Africa. Over the ensuing decades, it expanded into general publishing. From 1961 to 1996, the CNA Literary Award provided a controversial barometer of local literary development. In 1983 CNA merged with Gallo Africa, but increasing underperformance led to its acquisition by Wooltru in 1997. In 2002, Edcon acquired the bulk of the liquidated business, rebuilding the mass-market chain to 200 shops. FCG

Coach House Books Publishing and printing house founded in 1965 by Stan Bevington, located in a reconfigured stable in downtown Toronto. Shaped by 1960s ideology, CHB first printed draft-dodger pamphlets and menus. Embracing computer technology for design and publishing, it is now known for its high-quality literary and design aesthetics. JAD

co-authorship A process whereby two or more authors jointly produce a work. Co-authorship, whether acknowledged or unacknowledged, can be a controversial issue among critics and scholars. Practically, dealing with more than one author can present difficulties with regard to *copyright and authorial *attribution. More theoretically, claims of co-authorship can undermine ideals of authorial persona and individual creative genius. Consequently, there is considerable debate concerning the dual or multiple authorship of a number of works. A well-known example of overt co-authorship is *Lyrical Ballads* (1798), containing poems by both Wordsworth and Coleridge (although Wordsworth's commentaries on later editions of the collection often played down Coleridge's contribution). An example of a more contentious instance of co-authorship is T. S. Eliot's poem *The Waste Land* (1922). It has been suggested that Ezra Pound and Vivienne Eliot may both deserve some authorial credit for helping rework and edit the poem. Perhaps the most famous co-author in the British canon is Shakespeare. Several plays traditionally attributed to Shakespeare have been reassessed in the light of strong claims of co-authorship, a common practice amongst Elizabethan and Jacobean playwrights. The contested plays include: *Titus Andronicus* (which may have been co-written with George Peele); *Timon of Athens* (with Thomas Middleton); *Pericles* (with George Wilkins); and *Henry VIII* and *The Two Noble Kinsmen* (both with John Fletcher).

Co-authorship remains a relatively marginal literary practice, but it is common within certain branches of academia, especially the sciences and social sciences. Many works of research are co-written, sometimes by staff and research students. In addition to describing co-written literary or academic works, the term 'co-authorship' can also refer to a much broader idea of collaboration between an author and other contributors. In this latter sense, 'co-authorship' has been used by critics in the fields of ethnography, linguistics, literary theory, and creative writing to describe a version of 'authorship' that encompasses all contributors to a work. Under this definition, co-authorship can express a continuing interaction between writer, community, and reader—often implying that there is an authorial imbalance and that some voices may be marginalized or unacknowledged. The concepts of multiple authorship can be further connected to theories of *translation, *ghostwriting, folklore and the oral tradition, and even editing. *See also* AUTHORSHIP.   TK

H. A. Laird, '"A Hand Spills from the Book's Threshold": Coauthorship's Readers', *PMLA* 116 (2001), 344–53

B. Vickers, *Shakespeare, Co-Author* (2004)

Cobden-Sanderson, Thomas James (1840–1922) English bookbinder and printer. He spent much of the early part of his life (including a spell as a barrister) in an unhappy and unfulfilled state before turning to bookbinding, following a suggestion from Jane Morris. After training with Roger de Coverly, he set up his own bindery in 1884; he produced a series of exquisite bindings to his own designs before expanding the business into the Doves Bindery (1893), employing three professional binders. In 1900, in partnership with Sir E. *Walker, he established a *private press, the *Doves Press. Cobden-Sanderson is important not only for the quality of his work, but for his influence in stimulating craftsmanship in the book arts, particularly bookbinding; he is regularly acknowledged as the catalyst for the revival of fine binding in the 20th century.   DRSP

ODNB

M. Tidcombe, *The Bookbindings of T. J. Cobden-Sanderson* (1984)

— *The Doves Bindery* (1991)

Cochin, Charles-Nicolas (1688–1754) With his wife, Magdeleine Horthemeis (1686–1767), and their son Charles-Nicolas (1715–90), Parisian engravers. Protected by Mme de Pompadour and her brother Marigny, the younger Cochin became the most prominent book illustrator of his generation, notably with the 1751–9 edition of La Fontaine's *Fables* with plates after Oudry.   VAG

Cochran, Alexander Smith (1874–1929) American book collector and founder of the *Elizabethan Club of Yale University. Inspired by an undergraduate course on Elizabethan drama, Cochran gathered nearly 200 early English books and MSS, which he donated to the club at its founding. Although yachting soon replaced his interest in book collecting, he went on supporting the club financially.   EAH

Coci, Jorge (d. 1544?) Printer in Zaragoza, Spain, 1499–1537. A native of Germany, Coci enjoyed considerable success as the sole printer in Aragon. His *c*.250 known imprints include much liturgical printing, *books of hours, and the first edition of the chivalric romance *Amadís de Gaula* (1508).   DRW

Cocker, Edward (1631/2–76) An accomplished English calligrapher acclaimed by *Pepys as 'the famous writing-master' (10 August 1664), Cocker produced numerous copybooks. Not all of these survive, but some were frequently reprinted in the 17th century. He also engraved copybooks for fellow calligraphers. He is more widely known for *Cockers Arithmetick*, published posthumously in 1678, from which the phrase 'according to Cocker' (i.e. 'exactly') derives.   ASGE

Heal

ODNB

Cockerell, Douglas (1870–1945) British bookbinder. In 1893 he was apprenticed to *Cobden-Sanderson's *Doves Bindery and set up his own London bindery in 1897. He became an influential voice in the development of bookbinding and conservation standards through his teaching at the Central School of Arts and Crafts and his book on *Bookbinding and the Care of Books* (1901). His son *Sydney joined the firm in 1924 and continued it after Douglas's death.   DRSP

ODNB

Cockerell, Sir Sydney (1867–1962) English museum director and MS collector. Cockerell catalogued W. *Morris's books and MSS, and was secretary to the *Kelmscott Press. As director (1908–37) of the *Fitzwilliam Museum, Cambridge, he rearranged and augmented its collections, including its MSS. Cockerell's descriptions of medieval MSS include two volumes for the *Roxburghe Club (a third discussed *Brailes) and much of the catalogue of the illuminated MSS exhibition at the Burlington Fine Arts Club in 1908.   KEA

ODNB

Cockerell, Sydney (1906–87) British bookbinder, son of D. *Cockerell, who joined his father's firm in 1922 and inherited the business in 1945. He continued the family tradition of binding and conservation work of the highest craftsmanship, carrying out many commissions to repair important MSS for national and university libraries. He developed a distinctive binding style in gold-tooled vellum, often with designs by Joan Rix Tebbutt, and revived the art of *marbling paper.   DRSP

R. Lewis, *Fine Bookbinding in the Twentieth Century* (1984)

ODNB

codex (pl. **codices**; [Lat. 'block of wood', later, a block split into leaves or tablets for writing on]). A book made from hinged *leaves, in contrast to a roll (or *scroll). Developed between the 2nd and 4th centuries AD, the codex was often associated with Christian literature. It initially took the form of writing *tablets, with multiple wax-coated boards *fastened together along one side by thongs or clasps. Wax tablets were eventually replaced in the Roman republic by *parchment leaves folded into *notebooks. Although codices were sometimes made of *papyrus, more durable *vellum became the dominant medium for texts in codex form, before being replaced by paper. RWO

C. H. Roberts and T. C. Skeat, *The Birth of the Codex* (1983)

codicology The study of the *codex or MS book, which gradually supplanted the earlier *papyrus roll in the Mediterranean world from the 1st century AD. The codicologist examines every feature of the book in order to draw out whatever information may be useful for elucidating that book's history, the circumstances of its production, and the purposes for which it was made. Printed books are not normally the business of codicology.

After determining contents and date, studying the book's materials is of first importance. The quality and size of the *vellum or *parchment and its freedom from flaws helps to ascertain the status of the codex; when *paper came to be generally available in the 14th and 15th centuries and grew gradually cheaper, the choice between vellum and paper may mark off the *de luxe from other copies. If it carries a *watermark, paper may provide a date, albeit often approximate, for when the MS was copied (*see* **10**). Books may have vellum bindings, or be bound with more durable and expensive materials for hard wear and for purposes of display (*see* **17**). Few medieval books survive in original bindings (the most noteworthy exception being the *Stonyhurst Gospel).

Using palaeography's techniques, analysis of the work of the *scribe may reveal the book's character, value, and purpose. Different *script styles indicate the approximate date of copying and mark out books for different uses; variations of script within a text often manifest the relative importance attached to different parts of it—for instance, the use of a more formal script for the Latin portions of a vernacular text. The rapid increase in commercial book production in the 13th century led to the development of more *cursive scripts and varieties of professional hands. More informal hands indicate amateur copyists or enthusiasts, usually writing for themselves. Unless copying an *exemplar exactly, scribes (or their supervisors) must make many choices of *ordinatio*, or *format. They must also decide on the size of the *margins (the larger, the more costly the book) and the number of lines to the page (careless or amateur scribes will be less likely to prepare the page by *pricking and ruling). So too, they must determine how explicit the contents of the book and the form of its texts should be, usually by adding more or less elaborate *textual articulation: *incipits and *explicits; *rubrics; *running heads at the top of each page or across the *opening; and book, *chapter, and

*paragraph divisions. They must indicate to decorators with *guide letters which letters to decorate, and leave spaces for illustrators. With books intended for scholars, they can make use of an increasingly elaborate apparatus (first developed in the 13th and 14th centuries); of chapter, verse, and page numbering; marginal finding guides; *indexes; *glossaries; and tables of *contents—all features that are now taken for granted in printed books.

The *illuminator's work, from tinted capitals to full-colour *initials, miniatures (*see* MINIATURE (1)), and *borders, adds to the book's expense and also marks its divisions in strikingly visual ways. Illustrations (*see* **16**) often have significant implications for the interpretation of a text.

The book's makeup or *collation, as it may be deduced from codicological study, reveals much about the circumstances of production. Scribes did not copy into a bound book, but into unbound *quires, typically separated out into *bifolia. Insertion of *catchwords at the bottom of *versos, particularly at the end of quires, was vital to the binder. Completed quires, or groups of quires, might constitute independent book units (*booklets or *fascicles), which could be returned to the *stationer for sale; or for combining with other texts, according to a customer's order; or for making into composite books that contain collections of related texts (*anthologies) or varied contents (*miscellanies). Exemplars were sometimes divided into quires for distribution to different scribes for simultaneous copying. In university towns, quires (*see* PECIA) of scholarly books were loaned out to students for study or copying.

Finally, the margins are a valuable resource of information. They may contain material integral to the text, the scribe's additions, or the comments of later readers, an important aspect of reception history. First and last leaves and flyleaves or *endleaves are often where information about *provenance is to be found. DAP

C. Bezzolo and E. Ornato, *Pour une histoire du livre manuscrit au Moyen Age* (1980)

L. M. J. Delaissé, 'Towards a History of the Medieval Book', *Divinitas*, 11 (1967), 423–36

A. I. Doyle and M. B. Parkes, 'The Production of Copies of the *Canterbury Tales* and the *Confessio Amantis* in the Early Fifteenth Century', in *Medieval Scribes, Manuscripts and Libraries*, ed. M. B. Parkes and A. G. Watson (1978)

M. B. Parkes, 'The Influence of the Concepts of *Ordinatio* and *Compilatio* on the Development of the Book', in *Medieval Learning and Literature*, ed. J. J. G. Alexander and M. T. Gibson (1976)

B. Shailor, *The Medieval Book* (1988)

codicology, Muslim Although there is evidence that medieval authors practised what may be termed primitive codicology, this is, in its broader sense (including *palaeography), a relatively new discipline in the Islamic context. Interest in the study of Arabic MSS in the West is traceable to the late 18th century, and the subsequent 100 years or so show an increase in relevant research and publications. Nevertheless, it seems that the greatest impetus for MS studies came with the first World of Islam Festival organized in London in 1976. This important event, which was responsible for the publication of a number of catalogues, was followed by the first major colloquium on codicology and palaeography in Istanbul in 1986. From then on a number of initiatives, such as conferences, exhibitions, catalogues, and specialized periodicals, have contributed significantly to a more systematic study of Muslim MSS in the West and in the Muslim world.   AGa

F. Déroche *et al.*, *Islamic Codicology* (2006)

A. Gacek, *The Arabic Manuscript Tradition* (2 vols, 2001, 2008)

Cody's Books Berkeley, California bookshop that became a prototype for the community-oriented, independent business carrying many titles. Founded in 1956 by Fred and Pat Cody, the shop became known in the 1980s for hosting author events and for its book selection. Cody's also was a leader in advocating independent bookselling. In 2006, the then owner Andy Ross closed the flagship Telegraph Avenue shop, selling the firm and its remaining two outlets to Yohan, Inc.   LJM

co-edition Run-on edition printed for a separate market. This may be for another English-language market or in another language. Co-edition publishing is common in publishing highly illustrated books, because economies can be achieved by printing different language editions together, simply replacing the text with the relevant translation.   AGP

coffee houses Early modern victualling establishments that provided a new public arena for the exchange and distribution of ideas, news, and intelligence. In 1652 a Turk, Pasqua Rosee, opened the first London coffee house; by 1700 over 500 were trading in the capital. For one penny, the cost of a dish of coffee, anyone was free to enter, read the newspapers (*see* **14**), and socialize with other patrons. Coffee house society promoted the creation of business, political, and cultural institutions, and *clubs. Individual coffee houses attracted particular clienteles. Men of business frequented houses around the Royal Exchange, such as Lloyds and Jonathon's. In Westminster, Tories congregated at the Cocoa Tree, Whigs at the St James's, and lawyers at Alice's. Literary associations flourished within coffee house society. Book trade business was conducted at the *Chapter. Will's in Covent Garden was initially the favourite of poets and men of letters, led by Dryden. Later, Addison and Steele led the move to Button's; their coffee house periodicals, the *Tatler* and the *Spectator*, reinforced the concept of the coffee house as the ideal forum for practising polite sociability. Coffee houses declined in London by the mid-18th century, in part because the associations within them became more formalized: Lloyds created offices; Arthur's became a member's club. They continued in provincial towns, often as newspaper reading rooms, until the early 19th century. *See also* MAGAZINE, ORIGINS OF.   VEMG

B. Cowan, *The Social Life of Coffee* (2005)

M. Ellis, *The Coffee House* (2004)

B. Lillywhite, *London Coffee Houses* (1963)

coffee-table book A large-*format, generally expensive, hardcover book produced on glossy paper, designed to be seen and handled on a flat surface (thus, reminiscent of early books stored face up on *lecterns). With a preponderance of images—photographs or reproductions of artwork—such books are often regarded as suited to casual reading.

Although the precise derivation of the term remains in question, as does the first appearance of the coffee table itself (some time in the late 19th century), early large-format books concentrated on reproductions of artwork. In 1960, David R. Brower, then head of the *Sierra Club in America, introduced a series of large-format books under the title 'Exhibit Format'. The first, *This Is the American Earth*, with photographs by Ansel Adams and text by Nancy Newhall, is often credited as the first coffee-table book to combine fine art photography with a political message. Typical subjects of such books include: history, biography, fashion, art history and contemporary art, cookery and entertaining, interior design, nature, and photography. Their size and often high price have made such books worthy vehicles for book designers to exhibit their art, and for owners to display their cultural consumption.   KAW

F. Dunaway, *Natural Visions* (2005)

coffin The shallow box in which the *press stone of a *common press lies. Appropriately, it is next to the gallows (which supports the *tympan).

Coimbra Editora Portuguese publisher. In 1920, several law professors from the University of Coimbra joined with two local booksellers to establish Coimbra Editora. It has long been Portugal's foremost publisher and distributor of works on all aspects of law and legal history.
                                                                 DRW

Coimbra University Library Portugal's oldest and most prestigious university, founded in Lisbon in 1290, relocated permanently to Coimbra in 1537. Then numbering 130 MS volumes, the library grew steadily, and now contains 2 million volumes. Flush with Brazilian wealth, King João V authorized the construction at Coimbra of the magnificent Bibliotheca Joanina (1717–25), a free-standing building that today houses 200,000 pre-1800 volumes. Coimbra's collections, historically decentralized, have been gradually united, both physically in the central library building (1962) and virtually through a computerized *union catalogue. Library holdings have been described in printed catalogues and the annual *Boletim* (1914–).   DRW

Coke, Thomas, earl of Leicester (1697–1759) Coke's large-scale book buying on the Grand Tour (1712–18) led to the creation of an exceptional library that absorbed and enhanced the legal and literary collections of his ancestor, Sir Edward Coke (1552–1634). Still largely intact at Holkham Hall, Norfolk, the collection embodies the classicizing preoccupations of an early 18th-century virtuoso.   SR

D. P. Mortlock, *A History and Description of the Library at Holkham Hall* (2006)

Colbert family Jean-Baptiste Colbert (1619–83) Louis XIV's minister at Mazarin's death (1661), who shared the cardinal's passion for collecting. Personally overseeing the king's library, he enriched it considerably while supplying his own with royal duplicates and spoils from monastic libraries in difficulty. He purchased de *Thou's library in 1680. Inherited successively by his two sons, Colbert's collections were auctioned in 1728; *c.*7,000 MSS from them were acquired by the royal library in 1732.   VAG

Colburn, Henry (1784/5–1855) Much-vilified London publisher, in business *c.*1806–53, from 1829 to 1832 in bad-tempered partnership with R. *Bentley (1794–1871). Until 1824 Colburn published from his own *circulating library, creating two ground-breaking literary periodicals, the miscellaneous *New Monthly Magazine* and the *Literary Gazette*, a weekly review. From the mid-1820s he led the vogue in 'silver fork' fiction—triple-decker novels with aristocratic settings, often by titled authors— introducing the reading public to Bulwer-Lytton and Disraeli. Colburn's partnership with Bentley produced one more innovation, the '*Standard Novels' series, single volume reprints of recent fiction, which was taken over by Bentley as part of the severance agreement. Colburn eventually re-established himself in London, seeking to rival his ex-partner, notably with the resurrected series '*Colburn's Modern Novelists', but without recapturing his earlier successes.   GL
ODNB
J. Sutherland, 'Henry Colburn Publisher', *PH* 19 (1986), 59–84

Colburn's Modern Novelists Reprint series issued from about 1833 by H. *Colburn, consisting largely of rebound *sheets of earlier editions of fiction. It was initially published by his former partner, R. *Bentley (1794–1871). Retitled 'Colburn's Modern Standard Novelists' in 1839, it was much less innovative and successful than Bentley's 'Standard Novels' series, and seems to have come to an end in 1841.   GL

cold type *Type bought in from an outside *typefounder, as opposed to *hot-metal type, which was usually generated in-house by *machine casting, e.g. *Monotype.

Cole, E. W. (Edward William) (1832–1918) Australian bookseller and publisher. A labourer's son, Cole joined the Victorian gold rush in 1852. Having no success on the diggings, he tried other occupations. In 1865 he hired a stall at Melbourne's Eastern Market, primarily to sell his controversial book, *The Real Place in History of Jesus and Paul*. Flourishing as a general bookseller, he opened a shop in 1873. By the 1890s Cole's Book Arcade dominated an entire city block. Cole remained an active proponent of free thought, both religious and political: he contributed to debates surrounding the Federation of the Australasian colonies by publishing a book proposing *Federation of the Whole World* (1890). He achieved major commercial success with *Cole's Funny Picture Book* (first

Cole's Book Arcade in Melbourne, *c.*1890: taken from an advertisement in *The Victorian Almanac*, in which Cole had a hand and which he later took over.

published 1879, continuously reprinted into the 1960s), and compilations such as *Cole's Fun Doctor* (1886) and *Cole's Intellect Sharpener* (1900).   IM
ADB

Cole, George Watson (1850–1939) American bibliographer and librarian. After producing a bibliography of Bermuda (1907), he compiled the catalogue of the collection of *Church (Americana, 5 vols, 1907; English literature, 2 vols, 1909), which was subsequently acquired by *Huntington. In 1919, he became the first director of the *Huntington Library. He also served as president of the *Bibliographical Society of America.   VAG
D. C. Dickinson, *George Watson Cole* (1990)

Cole, Jack Brothers Jack and Carl Cole opened Coles, a Toronto bookshop in 1940, expanding to 126 Canadian and US locations by 1977. Jack conceived his popular study guides, 'Coles Notes', in 1948, and reissued classics in the 'Coles Canadiana Collection'. Bought by *Chapters in 1995, Coles maintains shops across Canada.   JAD

Colenso, William (1811–99) Printer, missionary, politician. Apprenticed at St Ives in England in 1826, he became Church Missionary Society printer in New Zealand (1834). Within five years he had, with limited resources, produced more than 74,000 copies of mostly religious works and the first New Zealand Government *Gazette*. He also designed a Maori language *lay of the case and printed the Maori text of the Treaty of *Waitangi.   NDW

DNZB

Colines, Simon de (d. 1546) One of the greatest French printers of the Renaissance, Colines established his press in Paris in 1520, after marrying the widow of Henri *Estienne I, by whom he had been employed, probably as a *punchcutter. During his 26-year career, Colines produced about 800 publications, distinguished for the elegance of their typography and design. Thanks to the help of such French book artists and type-designers as *Tory, Oronce Finé, and *Garamont, Colines may be said to have been the first true French Renaissance printer, in that he virtually transformed the French book by wresting it away from its medieval constraints and traditions. In 1528, inspired by the small, handy format of Aldine texts, Colines began to publish reasonably priced *octavo editions of the classics, popularizing *italic types in France. Two years later he initiated an even handier *sixteenmo series.   FS

F. Schreiber, *Simon de Colines* (1995)

Colish, Press of A. (1907–c.1980) Printer and publisher in New York City and Mount Vernon, New York. Abraham Colish (1882–1963) built a reputation for *fine printing, well executed at reasonable cost, through work for the *Limited Editions Club (from the 1930s to the 1980s), and for bibliophile organizations, libraries, and museums. The firm worked closely with a number of prominent American designers, notably *Cleland, *Rogers, and *Kent. On his death, the press was managed by his son Louis, until it finally merged with a *jobbing printer in the late 1980s.   PWR

collateral texts Texts descended from the same origin, but in a different and independent line or tradition of a family tree, with no direct influence upon each other at any stage of transmission (i.e. no lineal connection). It used to be thought that, as collateral texts could not be taken to contain authorial revision, and were often illustrative of different authorities, they could only be encompassed by an *eclectic edition. This has been questioned by editors and theorists interested in the sociology of texts.   ASR

A. Walker, 'Collateral Substantive Texts (with special reference to *Hamlet*)', *SB* 7 (1955), 51–67

collating machines (optical collators) An alternative to manual *collation, such machines optically superimpose two copies of a single page so that differences are more immediately identified. The famous *Hinman Collator was designed in the 1940s; despite its prodigious size and cost, almost 60 were sold. Binocular lenses, mirrors, and lights present alternating images of two pages; differences appear as 'movements'. The Lindstrand Collator, the *McLeod Portable Collator, and Hailey's Comet provide increasingly portable and cheaper options; unlike Hinman's, all rely on stereoscopy in which images from either page are, through angled mirrors, perceived as a single image. Collating machines can only be used to collate copies from the same edition (or, less effectively, different editions with identical lineation).
                                                                IG

S. E. Smith, '"The Eternal Verities Verified": Charlton Hinman and the Roots of Mechanical Collation', *SB* 53 (2000), 129–62
— '"Armadillos of Invention": A Census of Mechanical Collators', *SB* 55 (2002), 133–70

collating sheets The first step in the binding process for a printed book; the *sheets are gathered and checked by their *signature sequence, to ensure completeness and correct order. *See also* GATHERING.

collation Five senses of the word may be distinguished. **1.** The act of checking that the gathered printed sheets are correctly ordered and oriented prior to folding and sewing. J. *Moxon described this as 'Colationing' and observed that it required the use of a special bodkin to move through the sheets with speed and accuracy. From the 1890s, collating marks, often on the spine of the *gatherings, enabled faster verification of the order. **2.** In a related but more modern sense, the construction of a *collational formula: a bibliographical description of the book detailing the *format, the order of gatherings, any inserted or omitted leaves, and the number of leaves. (*OED* cites 1834 for the first usage of 'collation' in this sense.) **3.** The bibliographical comparison of a specific copy of a book with another copy or with a collation formula in a reference work to establish whether the number and order of gatherings is complete. **4.** The editorial comparison of a specific copy of a book with another copy to identify textual *variants; *OED* records its first use by the Chaucer editor, *Thynne, in 1532. Manual collation or the slow and painstaking 'Wimbledon method' of comparing two copies has, since the 1940s, been supplemented by the use of *collating machines. **5.** A list of such variants.   IG

J. Carter and N. Barker, *ABC for Book Collectors*, 8e (2004)
Gaskell, *NI*
Moxon
OED

collational formula A formulaic note of all the *gatherings, individual *leaves, and *cancels as they appear in the ideal *copy of a book, intended to show how the volume was constructed and thus to establish a standard of reference whereby imperfect copies may be detected. Together with the statement of *format, which it follows, it makes up the formula line of a *bibliographical description. The collational formula was devised by *Bradshaw in 1861 and subsequently propounded and expanded by *Greg, who had developed it with the assistance of *McKerrow, in 1934. Greg's formula, expounded by *Bowers, is that used today. The formula is based on the 23-letter Latin alphabet (without *i/j, *u/v, and w (*see* vv/w); any of these letters that appear are listed specially), or an uninterrupted series of numerals used to sign gatherings. *Upper- and *lower-case letters are distinguished, but different *founts are not; it reproduces arbitrary

symbols used as *signatures. Unsigned or duplicated leaves or gatherings are represented by *pi at the beginning of books, by *chi elsewhere. A superscript numeral after signatures indicates the number of leaves in a gathering. The formula allows for duplicated alphabets (e.g. 5B for Bbbbb) and repeated alphabets (2A for the second gathering signed A, with a comma to separate the series) and indicates inserted leaves and subtracted ones (cancels), their positions, when unsigned, and conjugacy (a point indicating conjugacy) within gatherings. It does not describe *plates or engraved *title-pages inserted at the gathering stage. A simple formula may be something like: A-2K8; a more complicated one may read something like: $A4$ B–C4 D4(D3 + χ1) E–G4 H4(H1 + χ1,2) I–M4 N4(N3 + χ1.2). The formula is followed by a statement of signing in square brackets (e.g. [$4]), indicating the point to which gatherings have been signed. **KEA**
Bowers, *Principles*

collected edition An *edition incorporating all the works of a particular author, produced in a uniform format and under the same *imprint. Collected editions, which are also known as collected or complete works, are often the product of extensive scholarship, drawing together previous critical material and representing a full *collation of earlier editions and MS copies in order to produce an authoritative text. Collected editions are often presented as 'definitive' (this contested term is related to other types of edition, including *critical editions, complete editions, standard editions, and final editions, some of which terms are used interchangeably). As such, collected editions often contain extensive critical and editorial material, including textual histories, bibliographies, chronologies, lists of textual *variants, and *indexes. A collected edition may also incorporate juvenilia, correspondence, journalism, criticism, rejected and unfinished works, and other ephemeral items. Collected editions may comprise several volumes and be undertaken by a series of editors over a number of years.

The phenomenon of the collected edition plays a significant part in any understanding of the cultural construction of *authorship. The publication of such an edition demonstrates the significance of an author's works and implies that he or she has achieved a certain canonical status. In the view of some literary theorists, however, collected editions serve to reinforce the exalted status of the author in critical discussion—placing the authorial persona and œuvre at the heart of the critical process and enshrining contentious ideals of individual creative genius. The collected editions of *Chaucer's works, published from the mid-16th century, are among the earliest examples of the practice of bringing together an author's works, along with biographical details and other *paratextual apparatus. Arguably, the publication of collected editions of Chaucer served to invest the figure of the writer with a new authority and helped construct an English secular and vernacular canon. The 1623 *First Folio edition of Shakespeare was similarly important in the construction of the playwright as national poet and pre-eminent English literary figure.

The collected editions of Chaucer and Shakespeare were posthumous, but such collections may also appear during an author's lifetime. Collected editions may be intended to reintroduce early works that may be out of print, to establish new *copyright editions, or to provide a fresh source of revenue for publisher and author. Authors often use the opportunity provided by the publication of a collected edition to revise and *annotate their works and to present themselves and their literary career in a particular light. Besides Henry James's New York edition (1907–9), one notable example of this practice was the publication of W. *Scott's 'Magnum Opus' edition of the Waverley novels (1829–33). In preparation for re-publication and to help re-establish copyright, Scott made significant revisions to his novels, rewriting sections of the text and adding substantial notes and introductory essays. Furthermore, Scott was the first novelist to have a collected edition published during his or her own lifetime, and the first author whose collected works were relatively cheaply priced and aimed at a mass market. Throughout the 19th century, collected editions were extremely popular and appeared in a variety of forms, designed for different markets and often promising their readers fresh textual material or lavish illustrations.

The production of printed collected editions is an important part of modern scholarly research, but such projects often run up against limitations of expense and space. The advent of the electronic book (*see* **19**) has encouraged the development of new strategies for collecting together an author's works. Electronic collected editions have the potential to offer considerably more space than printed editions and consequently may include a greater amount of textual and paratextual material. Hypertext editions and multimedia archives (such as *McGann's Rossetti Archive) can help facilitate the production of collected editions which incorporate full variant editions, MSS, authorial annotations, illustrations and other artwork, and other non-textual material, as well as extensive scholarly *apparatus. Furthermore, electronic collected editions allow readers to engage with works in ways that printed editions cannot. They can bring works to a wider audience, as well as enabling electronic searches, collations, indexes, annotations, and descriptions—all of which expand conceptions of authorship, editorship, and the scope of the collected edition. *See also* UNIFORM EDITION; VARIORUM EDITION. **TK**
A. Nash, ed., *The Culture of Collected Editions* (2003)

College of Arms Library The library of the College of Heralds in London. Since the Middle Ages the Heralds have prepared coats of arms for those of armigerous status. In addition to its numerous armorial records, it has other historical and genealogical MSS including some bequeathed by T. *Howard. **ASGE**
L. Campbell and F. Steer, *A Catalogue of Manuscripts in the College of Arms* (1988)
A. R. Wagner, *The Records and Collections of the College of Arms* (1952)

College Street The centre of the Calcutta (Kolkata) book trade. The *Calcutta School-Book Society set up its retail outlet there in 1826; *Vidyāsāgar established his Sanskrit Press depository at the adjacent College Square in 1847. In the 1880s, S. K. *Lahiri, Gurudas *Chattopadhyay, and *Thacker, Spink moved their businesses there.   AG

Collet's bookshop British bookselling company, established in 1934 by Eva Collet Reckitt, a member of the Communist Party of Great Britain, at the instigation of the party's secretary. Occupying premises on London's Charing Cross Road, the shop sold revolutionary, socialist, and progressive publications, specializing in Russian, Eastern European, and Chinese works. It also stocked *Left Book Club books and *Penguin books, later incorporating a Penguin Bookshop. The business expanded to other sites in London, Glasgow, Manchester, and Cardiff, developed a library supply service, and opened Collet's International Bookshop in 1976.   CMS
ODNB

Collier, John Payne (1789–1883) English literary scholar and forger. Although his first profession was journalism and he was afterwards called to the Bar, Collier's vocation from late adolescence was that of a literary historian. In 1831, his *History of English Dramatic Poetry* brought him widespread recognition and was the first of a series of publications making genuine additions to knowledge of Shakespeare and the literature of his period (he was, for example, the first scholar to publish the description from John Manningham's diary of an early performance of *Twelfth Night*). Following the publication in 1844 of his edition of Shakespeare's *Works* with a prefatory biographical volume, Collier became in 1849 vice-president of the Society of Antiquaries, and in 1850 he received a Civil List pension. In 1853, he published *Notes and Emendations to the Text of Shakespeare's Plays*, containing thousands of variants transcribed from what purported to be a 17th-century hand, and which he claimed to have discovered in the margins of a copy of the Second *Folio bought from a dealer. When these were examined in 1859 by *Madden of the British Museum, however, it rapidly became clear that the annotations of the 'Old Corrector' were of recent date, and subsequent investigation of many of Collier's earlier discoveries revealed that they too had either been fabricated or tampered with. Collier, after a feeble attempt at rebuttal, took refuge in silence.   RJD
A. and J. I. Freeman, *John Payne Collier* (2 vols, 2004)
ODNB
S. Schoenbaum, *Shakespeare's Lives*, 2e (1991)

Collier, Peter Fenelon (1849–1909) Born in Ireland, he emigrated to America in 1869. In 1875, he started his own publishing company, eventually called P. F. Collier & Son. A pioneer in the profitable venture of issuing inexpensive sets of classics by *subscription, he brought out the 50-volume '*Harvard Classics' in 1909, which is still in print. In 1896, he created *Collier's Weekly*, which became one of the premier cultural and political magazines of its time.   PMW
ANB
DLB 49

Collijn, Isak (1875–1949) Swedish librarian and incunabulist. His tenure as head of the Royal Library, now National Library of *Sweden, (1916–40), saw new catalogues and important acquisitions. In 1914, he founded the only Nordic book-history journal, *Nordisk tidskrift för bok- och biblioteksväsen* (*NTBB*). His research on 15th- and 16th-century printing resulted in numerous advanced *incunabula studies and an unsurpassed Swedish bibliography of pre-1600 books. Internationally active, he was chairman of the Gesellschaft für Typenkunde and the first chairman of the *International Federation of Library Associations (1927–31).   PSR

Collins, Benjamin (1715–85) English provincial publisher and banker. Specializing in periodicals, he founded the *Salisbury Journal* and *London Chronicle*. With J. *Newbery, he wrote and published children's books (e.g. the *Royal Battledore*) (*see* **15**). Links with London underwrote his other book investments, including in *Richardson's *Pamela*.   CYF
C. Y. Ferdinand, *Benjamin Collins and the Provincial Newspaper Trade* (1997)
ODNB

Collins, Isaac (1746–1817) Quaker printer, publisher, bookseller. Founder of an early *printing office in New Jersey (1770–96), Collins published the state's first regular newspaper, the *New-Jersey Gazette*. He is best remembered for his 1791 *quarto bible, heralded for its textual accuracy.   JDC
R. Hixson, *Isaac Collins* (1968)

Collins & Sons, William Publishers, printers, and stationers in Glasgow. Founded in 1819 by William Collins, the firm published religious and reference works—including bibles and atlases—and printed stationery. From 1824, it published the Collins Dictionary. In 1900, the business expanded into children's literature and fiction, publishing Agatha Christie. The firm merged with *Harper & Row, New York, in 1989 and became *HarperCollins Ltd.   AAW
D. Keir, *The House of Collins* (1952)

collotype A process of making high-quality reproductions of continuous-tone images from a glass *plate coated with light-sensitive gelatine, exposed through a photographic negative without the use of a screen. The gelatine hardens in proportion to the amount of light transmitted through lighter and darker areas of the image. Harder areas will accept more ink, therefore printing darker. The making and printing of collotype plates is highly skilled, expensive work. The process came into use in the 1870s as a specialist medium for high-quality book illustration (*see* **16**) and fine-art reproductions, but was largely abandoned for commercial purposes in the 1920s.   NG

Cologne, University and City Library University library with the largest historic stock in the German State of North Rhine-Westphalia. Established on the basis of several existing libraries (e.g. City Library of 1602), following the university's foundation in 1919, it has 3.47 million items including 301 MSS and 2,376 *incunabula. PV

Colón, Hernando *See* COLUMBUS, FERDINAND.

colonial editions Editions of books published for distribution at special prices to colonial markets, chiefly Australia and New Zealand, but also India, Canada, South Africa, and elsewhere. Several British firms ran '*Colonial Libraries' series, *Macmillan's enjoying the greatest and longest success, between 1886 and 1960. Some colonial editions were printed in the US, and colonial booksellers occasionally either cooperated with British firms or ran their own *imprints—including A. C. Rowlandson's New South Wales Bookstall Co. Long the leading Canadian importer of colonial editions, Copp Clark also published Canadian authors. Colonial editions were produced in conjunction with 'home' editions, *sheets being sold to different publishers for distinct series. Heavily discounted to colonial booksellers, they supplied the need for recent fiction (90 per cent of titles) in editions substantially cheaper than in Britain (hence, colonial editions frequently being marked 'not for sale' there).

Edward Augustus Petherick, the first to buy sheets from publishers for distinctive colonial editions, is credited with the concept of a constantly up-to-date list of titles. Bankrupted in 1894, his colonial editions were taken over by George *Bell & Sons, who issued some 1,386 titles before 1918. Colonial markets were lucrative—in 1900, c.60 per cent of British book exports were to these markets, with more than 25 per cent of this number for Australia. Such markets were also politically and psychologically significant, contributing to the continuing prominence of British commercial publishing interests in the colonies, and engendering a sense of imperial connection. The importing of cheap print from Britain may have stunted local production, and few colonial authors themselves were published in such inexpensive editions; those who were, however, like Rolf Boldrewood (*Robbery Under Arms*), consequently received wider distribution.

World War I restricted shipping and materials, increasing prices and curtailing *paperback production. Special pricing and lenient credit terms offered to colonial booksellers laid the foundation for longstanding discounting demands in these markets; Trainor and Johanson link the demise of the colonial edition to the end of resale price maintenance in Australia in 1972. AEV

G. Johanson, *Colonial Editions in Australia, 1843-1972* (2000)
P. Joshi, *In Another Country* (2002)
L. Trainor, 'Colonial editions', in *Book & Print in New Zealand: A Guide to Print Culture in Aotearoa* (1997), www.nzetc.org/tm/scholarly/tei-GriBook-_div3-N11A1D.html, consulted June 2007

Colonial Libraries series Series of *colonial editions produced chiefly by British publishers for distribution elsewhere in the Empire (later, Commonwealth). The first, John *Murray's 'Colonial and Home Library' (1843-9), which issued 49 titles in 37 volumes, was available in Britain, unlike most later series—including Murray's 'Imperial Library' (1900-1945). Some, like *Bentley's 'Empire Library' (1878-81; sixteen titles) and 'Colonial Library' (after 1885), were published in conjunction with colonial publishers (the Australian bookseller *Robertson; Sampson *Low also used his *imprint). *Macmillan's series, consecutively the 'Colonial Library' (1886-1913), 'Empire Library' (1913-37), and 'Overseas Library' (1937-60), was the longest-running and most conspicuously successful, with 1,738 titles. Other firms with colonial series included: *Blackwood; John *Lane; *Ward, Lock; *Unwin; *Methuen (providing Kipling editions); and *Blackie & Son, whose reprint editions, issued in India, were not marketed as colonial editions. AEV

www.shl.lon.ac.uk/exhibitions/displays/colonialpostcolonial.pdf, consulted June 2007
J. Spiers, '"Must Not Be Sold Or Imported ...": British Colonial Editions, 1843-1972', in *The Colonial and Postcolonial History of the Book, 1765-2005* (2005)

colophon [Gk, 'summit', 'finishing stroke'] Originally a closing statement written at the end of a text by a *scribe or *rubricator, sometimes providing his name and the date and place of production—i.e. some of what is now in an *imprint. (The related *explicit often closed parts of texts, such as chapters, while the next part opened with an *incipit.) The colophon was retained at the end of the book by some printers of *incunabula, who often placed their *printer's device nearby—for example, in the first printed colophon, found in one copy of the *Mainz Psalter of 1457. The information provided in a colophon gradually migrated to the developing *title-page at the front of the book, which sometimes also acquired the printer's device, or the publisher's. In modern books, the term 'colophon' may refer to the publisher's device itself or to a production statement at the end of a book, a practice revived by the *private press movement of the late 19th century. Today, imprint information is typically distributed between the title-page and the title-page *verso. MMS

A. W. Pollard, *An Essay on Colophons with Specimens and Translations* (1905)

Colophon, The The first issue of the American journal *The Colophon: A Book Collectors' Quarterly* appeared in 1930. With articles on bibliography and the book world in general, it soon became a *bibliophile's treasure for its unusual format: each *gathering of each volume was printed by various distinguished presses in America and in Europe; bound with each volume there was an illustration (*see* **16**), either printed from the original *plates or blocks, or reproduced in *facsimile. The quarterly changed its subtitle twice: *New Series* and *New Graphic Series*, being named *The New Colophon* in its last two years of publication (1948-50). PA

colouring book A book printed with line art, for a reader to colour at will, originally with paint, subsequently with crayons. The earliest known example, *The Little Folks' Painting Book*, appeared in New York in 1879. The genre boomed in the 20th century and was commercialized through links with comic strips, cinema, and television, such as the *Mickey Mouse Colouring Book* (1931). Yet the genre's feel-good, educative features lent themselves to parody and antithesis: the *Black Panther Colouring Book* (1968), probably an FBI forgery, has African-Americans gunning down pig-faced cops, while the *Cunt Colouring Book* (1975) by the lesbian artist Tee Corinne exhibits 42 images of female genitalia.   NH

colour-plate books A rather broad term, strictly applicable to any book with hand-coloured or colour-printed plates, but primarily used to mean the topographical, travel, and natural history books of the late 18th and 19th centuries, distinguished by their lavish *plates in *aquatint or *lithography, and exquisitely hand-coloured (*see* **16**). *Ackermann's topographical publications are prime examples of the genre; J. R. *Abbey's collection is the defining catalogue (at least in a British context and excluding natural history)—a collection, now at *Yale, that captures a whole era of collecting taste.   LJW

colour printing From the beginning of western printing, introducing colour was an important goal. Medieval books had been colourful, due to the *illumination of images and borders and to *rubrication for *textual articulation. The earliest printers experimented in this vein, especially with *red, and sometimes with other colours, including gold printing (*see* CHRYSOGRAPHY). The famous red, blue, and purple initials of the *Mainz Psalter of 1457 were magnificent. However, the extra time and care colour printing demanded made it economically unviable, and it soon became restricted to liturgical, legal, and luxury books, *calendars, and *title-pages. Texts increasingly became monochrome.

For images, the goal to print in colour remained, however, and every process (*relief, *intaglio, *planographic, *stencil, photography, or *digital) eventually led to experiments, many of which were successful, but none completely solving the issue of the cost differential of printing in more than a single colour. For centuries, hand-colouring remained the best method for images, becoming an industry by the 19th. Many books were issued in both coloured and uncoloured copies.

Early in the 16th century, *chiaroscuro printing created tonal variation by means of two or more blocks printed on one sheet. The principle of taking successive impressions—either to lay colours side by side or to *overprint and create additional colours—was applied to the various processes. Printing surfaces could also be inked up in more than one colour, using stump or poupée brushes, but this remained time-consuming and expensive.

From early 18th-century ideas on optics came the techniques of Jakob Christophe Le Blon's three-colour *mezzotint reproductions of paintings, subsequently applied to anatomical works. Yet it was the 19th-century developments of *chromolithography, and chromoxylography (colour woodcut) that genuinely advanced the colour-

printing of images. Charles Hullmandel's *Travels in Ethiopia* (1835) was the first English work using chromolithography, although *Illuminated Books of the Middle Ages* (1844), with O. *Jones's chromolithographs, is better known. Colour in more affordable works was the achievement of such pioneers as *Savage, George Baxter, and C. Knight, who brought chromoxylography to the 'Toy Books' of *Caldecott, W. *Crane, and *Greenaway. *See also* THREE-COLOUR REPRODUCTION.   MMS

[British Printing Machinery Association,] *Catalogue of Exhibitions of British Coloured Books, 1738-1898* (1980)
R. M. Burch, *Colour Printing and Colour Printers* (1910)
B. Gascoigne, *Milestones in Colour Printing 1457-1859* (1997)
M. M. Grasselli, *Colorful Impressions* (2003)
D. Pankow, *Tempting the Palette* (1997)

colporteur [Fr. *col*, 'neck' + *porter*, 'to carry'] Itinerant bookseller, so called because he carried his books in a bag around his neck. From the late 15th century, pedlars in continental Europe sold *almanacs, *ABCs, *ballads, *broadsides, *chapbooks, and *woodcut prints. In the 1540s, colporteurs played an important role in spreading Reformation ideas in France and Germany. In the 19th century, the term came to denote a person employed by a religious society to sell bibles or other religious works. There is an interesting portrait of such a figure in R. M. Ballantyne's novel *Post Haste* (1880), chapter 25.   ASGE

Columbian press An ornate iron hand press, invented by George Clymer of Philadelphia c.1813: it worked by a system of levers (unlike the *Albion). It was popular in America, but was also manufactured and used in Britain. *See also* STANHOPE PRESS.   PWN
J. Moran, 'The Columbian Press', *JPHS* 5 (1969), 1–23

Columbia University Founded 1754 in New York City, Columbia University boasts one of the country's best academic library systems. Its main library is named after the former university president Nicholas Murray Butler (1862-1947). Administrative offices are now housed within the former main library, the architecturally stunning Low Library. The system as a whole contains 8.6 million volumes and 65,650 current serials, along with impressive rare book and MS holdings.   EDG
Nicholas Murray Butler Library, www.columbia.edu/cu/lweb/indiv/butler/index.html, consulted June 2007

Columbus, Ferdinand (Colón, Hernando) (1488-1539) Spanish book collector. Christopher Columbus' illegitimate son Ferdinand formed perhaps the greatest library of his time. Augmenting his father's books with massive purchases made during extensive European travels, Ferdinand acquired more than 16,000 works. He also built Europe's foremost print collection, numbering 3,200 items. All were carefully described and abstracted by a staff of librarians in several innovative MS catalogues (most still extant) intended to comprise a universal bibliography. In 1552 Columbus' heirs ceded the collection,

A **colporteur** depicted by Jost Amman (c.1588): the *broadside print shows a fashionably dressed *hawker selling prints and newspapers; shown behind him are the city of Orleans and the defeat of the Spanish Armada. The verses below refer to the murder of the duke of Guise.

styled the Biblioteca Colombina, to the cathedral library in Seville. More than two-thirds of the books and all of the prints have since vanished.   DRW

[Biblioteca Colombina,] *Catálogo Concordado de la Biblioteca de Hernando Colón*, ed. T. Marín Martínez *et al.* (2 vols, 1993–)

M. P. McDonald, *The Print Collection of Ferdinand Columbus* (2004)

Comédie-Française French state theatre, formed in 1680—by merging *Molière's company with the rival Hôtel de Bourgogne troupe—and continuously in operation since. The large collections of its library-museum make it the foremost resource for French theatrical history, and a unique one for the pre-revolutionary period.

It includes MSS of plays, iconography, actors' files, posters, playbills, music (Offenbach was music director early in his career), and artwork. Officially for the Comédiens-Français' primary use (hence, perhaps, the absence, in 2006, of any publicly accessible online catalogue), it is open by permission to students, scholars, and independent researchers.   VAG

Comenius, Johann Amos *See* KOMENSKÝ, JAN AMOS.

comic books The comic book may be broadly defined as any publication serving as a showcase for comic art (hereafter 'comics') narratives. However, the term especially denotes comic books in the American tradition.

1. Definitions
2. The American comic book

1. Definitions

The comic book may be defined widely, as any book, booklet, or periodical consisting primarily of comics. More specifically, comic books privilege sequential art in multiple *panels, especially sustained, multi-page narratives. In formalist terms, a comic book is simply a publication which showcases extended comics stories, whether magazine, comic paper, album, or *graphic novel. In this sense, the comic book, a global phenomenon, includes many markets, formats, and national traditions as disparate as British tabloid weeklies, Japanese *manga, and Mexican *historietas*.

Historically, the comic book may be more strictly defined as the American comic book, i.e. the roughly half-tabloid-sized comic magazine introduced to US newsstands in the mid-1930s. After 1938 this format enjoyed a period of dramatic growth, initially spurred by the success of so-called costume or superhero comics. The comic-book industry embraced other genres as well, including children's humour and 'funny animal' comics, *Archie*-style 'teen' humour, crime comics, romances, horror, war comics, westerns, and 'classic' literary adaptations. Many of these genres thrived in the postwar era even as superhero comics waned. By 1950, the comic book was a mainstay of American culture.

In sociocultural terms, comic books might be defined as publications of interest to the subculture of fans and collectors that arose in the US in the 1950s. This subculture grew rapidly after 1965, through such institutions as fanzines, amateur press alliances, conventions, and, eventually, by way of comic-book retail stores and trade publications such as collectors' price guides. The centre of this subculture was and is the standard American comic magazine, but collectors have enlarged their focus more recently to include other 'comic books' seen as ancestors of the standard format, such as 19th-century comic albums.

2. The American comic book

Tabloid or odd-sized comic magazines were sporadically sold on US news-stands in the 1920s and early 1930s, without success. Comic books in their definitive form finally emerged from free comics, a genre pioneered in the early 1930s as a means of wringing additional profits from presses. These comics were designed as premiums for other publishing endeavours, and consisted mainly of reprinted newspaper strips rather than original work. Eastern Color, a Connecticut printer, established the standard, half-tabloid-size comic-book format with such a giveaway, *Funnies on Parade* (1933). Eastern then launched the new format as an independent, 10c. commodity with *Famous Funnies* (a single title in 1933, then a series in 1934) which, proving profitable, soon inspired competitors, among them newspaper syndicates reprinting their own strips.

Though new material appeared in *Famous Funnies* from the second issue, early comic books relied overwhelmingly on reprints. Late in 1934, the New York-based National Allied Publications (later DC) launched an exception: a series consisting wholly of original comics, *New Fun Comics* (later *More Fun*). By 1936, the nascent industry had begun to emphasize new material. In early 1938, National launched its famed monthly *Action Comics*, which crystallized the superhero genre with Jerry Siegel and Joe Shuster's seminal Superman. The success of Superman inspired a flood of costumed characters and comic books. The resultant 'Golden Age' propelled the medium through the 1940s. Comic books sold millions, particularly to children and (during wartime) to servicemen.

Postwar, comic books flourished commercially, but came increasingly under attack because of their graphic sensationalism and alleged ill-effects on young readers. Controversial trends included crime comics (which peaked after the war); romance comics (from 1947); and horror comics, popularized by the maverick publisher EC (from 1950). In 1954, the outcry against comic books became a concerted campaign: publication of the psychiatrist Fredric Wertham's incendiary anti-comic book study, *Seduction of the Innocent*, coincided with a series of US Senate hearings investigating the putative link between comic-book reading and delinquency. The anti-comics campaign forced the industry into a defensive posture, so that, late in 1954, most comics publishers adopted a code of *self-censorship. Further troubles, including changes in magazine distribution and growing competition from television, hurt the once-thriving industry.

After this decline, a nostalgic fan culture gradually emerged. A superhero revival, begun late in the 1950s, partially revitalized the industry, more so after the innovations introduced by the publisher Marvel (from 1961). Driving this revival was the rise of an organized fan base in the mid-1960s, as fanzines and comic-book conventions became established. Fans developed their own market, by means of barter, mail order, and speciality shops catering to their interests. At the same time, some cartoonists rejected nostalgia in favour of reinvention, spawning (through the radical press of the day) the so-called underground comics, or 'comix', movement. This trend, typified by the harrowing work of R. Crumb (after 1967), claimed the comic book as an adult medium. Sharply declining after 1973, underground comix nonetheless effectively gave birth to 'alternative' comics and literary graphic novel movements from 1980 onwards.

The allied influences of the underground and the specialty market (which expanded greatly after the mid-1970s) spawned a subculture that, via comic-book shops, spread outward from the US to other English-speaking countries. Since the mid-1990s, cross-pollination among American, European, and, increasingly, Japanese traditions has blurred the definition of 'comic book', to the point that readers are now likely to find the term applied to publications far removed from the model of American periodicals. Although the periodical format is threatened with obsolescence, book-length comics are flourishing.

CWH

I. Gordon, *Comic Strips and Consumer Culture, 1890–1945* (1998)

R. Goulart, *Great American Comic Books* (2001)

C. Hatfield, *Alternative Comics* (2005)

comic weeklies Although Britain has traditionally been a large market for American *comic books, it has its own distinct tradition of comic papers, principally 19th- and 20th-century weeklies. They first developed from 19th-century magazines of topical graphic humour, which trafficked in caricature and placed visuals before text. Foremost amongst these was *Punch* (1841–1992, 1996–2002), which spurred imitations aimed at working-class readers, such as *Fun* (1861–1901) and *Judy* (1867–1907). *Judy* introduced Charles Ross and Marie Duval's feckless 'Ally Sloper'—a scoundrel who became Britain's most merchandized cartoon character since *Rowlandson's Dr Syntax. Ally Sloper was, arguably, the first British comics superstar, graduating (in more gentlemanly duds) to his own title, the penny weekly *Ally Sloper's Half-Holiday* (Gilbert Dalziel, 1884–1923). The conventions of the weekly comic tabloid were soon set: cheap, full of comic strips, and inclined to broad humour, with detailed drawings and dense text. Alfred Harmsworth would undercut *Half-Holiday* with two halfpenny weeklies, *Comic Cuts* and *Illustrated Chips* (both 1890–1953), establishing the pattern for the 20th-century comic weekly.

From the early 1900s, the comics industry catered overwhelmingly for children. The dominance of Harmsworth's Amalgamated Press (AP) was challenged in the late 1930s with D. C. Thomson's oft-imitated *Dandy* (1937–) and *Beano* (1938–). Reportedly selling 2 million copies a week at their peak, these streamlined comics were less text-heavy, with quick pacing and anarchic humour. Further change came in the 1950s, with the rise of more 'serious' comic weeklies adapting conventions of earlier boys' and girls' story papers. The much-imitated *The Eagle* (Hulton Press, 1950–69), featuring Frank Hampson's sumptuous 'Dan Dare, Pilot of the Future', offered adventure with a high moral tone. Many, such as *The School Friend* (AP, 1950–65) and *Girl* (Hulton, 1951–64), echoed girls' story papers, developing genres such as the boarding-school story and—in the modish *Jackie* (D. C. Thomson, 1964–93)—romance.

Comic weeklies declined after the mid-1960s, as shifting social mores, generic overproduction, and competition from television and imported American comics restricted circulation. Their enduring influence is visible, for example, in *2000AD* (IPC/Fleetway, 1977–), a science-fiction weekly with a violent, satirical edge, which became the launching-pad for much of Britain's new comics talent, and *Viz* (originally from Viz/John Brown, 1979–), a punk-inspired adult comic controversial for its viciously satirical, scatological, and sex-oriented humour (yet clearly influenced by *Dandy* and *Beano*) which, while never a weekly, constitutes a gleeful post-mortem on the weekly tradition. CWH

D. Gifford, *The Complete Catalogue of British Comics* (1985)

P. Gravett and P. Stansbury, *Great British Comics* (2007)

R. Sabin, *Adult Comics* (1993)

Comino, Giuseppe (*fl.* 1717–1756) Italian printer. The brothers Gaetano and Giannantonio Volpi entrusted him with the academic press set up in their house in Padua in 1717. Under the name of the *Stamperia Cominiana*, he published some 200 editions up to and including 1756.

NH

DBI

commentary The tradition of adding a commentary to a text is an ancient one. The commentaries of classical antiquity, and the long line of scriptural commentaries, share a number of features that have passed into the modern sense of the term, including paraphrase, allusions to similar or parallel passages (within the author's writing or beyond it), and stating of textual *variants. They are generally (though not always) exegetical. Religious commentaries ranged from the moral to the scholarly; the latter, like commentaries on secular texts, were mainly concerned with the explication of contentious or ambiguous passages, the discussion of textual cruces, and the identification of sources and analogues. Many commentaries (on particular books of the Bible, for instance), were (and continue to be) published as separate works. Within a volume containing both text and commentary, commentary has sometimes run parallel to the text, and sometimes been placed at its end. Following the development of the *footnote at the start of the 18th century (and the gradual reduction in *side notes or marginal *glosses), a commentary would usually be placed either at the end of the text or at the bottom of the page. In modern scholarly editions, textual commentary is often placed apart from discussions of meaning and interpretation; the term itself is most often used now to describe the general structure of editorial content, rather than the more specific *annotation, though the two are frequently used synonymously. ASR

commonplace book A collection of short extracts including elegant turns of phrase, originally formed as an aid to literary composition, from the Lat. *locus communis*, 'something of general application'. More loosely, any miscellany of literary quotations and memoranda, especially if arranged under general headings. The *anthology was well known in antiquity and the Middle Ages, but personal commonplace books were probably rare until cheap paper notebooks became available in the 15th century. When few readers possessed many books of their own to refer to, the value of keeping a record of especially striking, enlightening, or inspiring passages encountered in the course of reading was obvious. The towering authority of classical authors in the Renaissance led students to form collections of 'flowers of speech', *sententiae*, and rhetorical tropes as models for imitation (or wholesale copying) in their own compositions: in *De Copia Verborum* (1512) *Erasmus gave advice on how to do this. The final edition of his *Adagia* assembled nearly 5,000 proverbs, but this was an encyclopaedia of wisdom rather than a commonplace book.

Commonplace books, chiefly or wholly from vernacular sources, were also kept by people with no connection with the world of education and learning. The London grocer Richard Hill's miscellany (Oxford, Balliol College MS 354), which he compiled over a long period up to 1536, is a fascinating record of things that appealed to a practical man of wide interests, rather than a scholar's *florilegium. Alongside songs, poems, and carols (in English, French, and Latin), are memoranda of all sorts: recipes for making rat poison and brewing beer, hints on making one's confession, records of notable events, legal formulas, card tricks, and puzzles. Many commonplace books have survived the death of their makers; those kept by Milton, Berkeley, Thomas Jefferson, Burns, George Eliot, E. M. Forster, and many lesser writers have been published. The choice of *loci communes* and the compiler's comments on them can provide a valuable insight into his or her intellectual development. Francis Meres's *Palladis Tamia* (1598) is evidence of what a late Elizabethan thought worthy of memory, and Jonson's *Timber* (1640) records the 'discoveries [which] flowed out of his daily readings'.

Ready-made books with headings under which to enter commonplaces, following the method of the philosopher John Locke (published posthumously in 1706), appeared in the 18th century and subsequently; many 19th-century educationalists encouraged the habit, as promoting thoughtful reflection. The literary anthology has largely supplanted the commonplace book, however, except perhaps as a record of aphorisms. Such are the published commonplaces of John Julius Norwich (1970ff.), of Geoffrey Madan (1981, but privately printed 1950), and of the publisher John Murray (1996). More in the tradition of Richard Hill's MS, *The Week End Book*, a *miscellany of prose, poetry, song, historical snippets, and eccentric information, has been in print since 1924.

BJF

E. Havens, *Commonplace Books* (2001)

J. M. Lechner, *Renaissance Concepts of the Commonplaces* (1962)

common press The basic design of wooden hand press, used for *letterpress printing throughout Europe and America until the early 19th century. It was so-called to distinguish it from *intaglio or *rolling presses, and later from the iron hand presses that superseded it (such as the *Columbian and *Albion). PWN

Gaskell, *NI*

A **common press**, made from a design attributed to W. J. *Blaeu before 1638 with some later modifications. (*See* **11** for a diagram showing the names of the different parts of the press.)

common reader A term, no doubt to be associated with common sense, popularized by S. *Johnson ('I rejoice to concur with the common reader') in his discussion in the *Lives of the Poets* (1779–81) of Gray's 'Elegy'; it was adopted by Virginia Woolf for her two collections of essays (1925, 1932). Common or ordinary readers may historically constitute the bulk of the literate, book-buying public, but book historians tend to be uneasy about identifying and finding suitable descriptive terms for them for fear of patronizing them as 'middlebrow' or marking them as a cultured elite. HRW

Commonwealth Writers' Prize Founded in 1987 by the Commonwealth Foundation to advance diversity and cultural dialogue in Anglophone literature, the prize consists of eight £1,000 regional awards and two overall awards worth £5,000 and £10,000. Separate juries select a Best Book and Best First Book in each of four designated regions: Africa; the Caribbean and Canada; Europe and South Asia; South-East Asia and the South Pacific. A pan-Commonwealth judging panel then names an overall winner in each category, with the £10,000 grand prize going to the author of the Best Book. Unlike other English-language book-of-the-year awards with global ambitions, the Commonwealth prize is awarded in a different location every year, avoiding the implication that one particular city, such as London or Dublin, is the literary capital or seat of judgement for the entire Anglophone world. JFE

communications circuit First proposed by R. *Darnton in 1982 as 'a general model for analyzing the way books come into being and spread through society', the communications circuit has become one of the defining concepts in the *history of the book. A schematic framework for interpreting information about the 'fate of books', Darnton's model emphasizes the agency of six principal actors: author, publisher, printer, shipper, bookseller, and reader. It has subsequently been refined by Darnton and others. Adams and N. *Barker have proposed a useful alternative model based upon five events in the life of a book: publishing, manufacturing, distribution, reception, and survival. MFS

T. R. Adams and N. Barker, 'A New Model for the Study of the Book', in *A Potencie of Life*, ed. N. Barker (1993)

R. Darnton, 'What is the History of Books?', *Daedalus*, 111 (1982), 65–83

— 'Histoire du livre–Geschichte des Buchwesens: An Agenda for Comparative History', *PH* 22 (1987), 33–41

Companhia Editora Nacional Brazilian publisher. In 1925, *Monteiro Lobato of São Paulo was reorganized as the C.E.N. under Octalles Marcondes Ferreira. It developed into Brazil's largest book publisher, dominating the *textbook and children's book market (*see* **15**) and—through its subsidiary *Civilização Brasileira—much of the adult market. DRW

compartment A term sometimes used to describe the sections into which the *spine of a book is divided by the *bands or the separate parts of the design of the *covers.

Compendium bookshop Counter-cultural London bookshop, established 1968. Concentrating on the radical, the alternative, and the avant-garde, the Camden bookshop was an outpost of late 20th-century bohemia. It closed with the turn of the century, prey to the post-*Net Book Agreement bookselling environment. CMS

www.radicalphilosophy.com/default.asp?channel_id= 2191&editorial_id=9970, consulted Aug. 2007

Complutensian Bible Printed in 606 copies by *Brocar at Alcalá de Henares (Lat. Complutum), Spain, from 1514 to 1517 (but not issued until 1521–2), it was the first polyglot Bible to be published and the *editio princeps* of the Septuagint and Greek New Testament. Cardinal *Jiménez de Cisneros conceived and funded the project, undertaken by leading Spanish scholars. Volumes 1–4 comprise the Old Testament, with Hebrew, Latin Vulgate, and Greek texts in parallel columns, and the Aramaic Targum of Onkelos at their foot; volume 5 contains the Greek and Latin New Testament; volume 6 adds dictionaries, grammars, and *apparatus. DRW

Complutensian University Library Founded in 1499 by Cardinal *Jiménez de Cisneros to support the new university at Alcalá de Henares. The collection initially grew rapidly, but languished during the 18th century. By 1845 the university had moved to Madrid, and the disparate contents of several school libraries were merged into a unified library system. Its present holdings of 2.5 million volumes are divided among more than 30 branch libraries. Rare books and MSS, housed in the Valdecilla Library, number more than 100,000 pre-1800 *imprints, 728 *incunabula (including Spain's second largest collection of Spanish incunabula), and 3,000 MSS. DRW

composing machines Mechanisms for rapid *composition, usually from a keyboard (*see* **11**). Although a design was patented in 1822 by William Church, for more than 50 years no machine could perform all the tasks required. The difficulties included *justification, setting more than one *size of type and line length, and *distribution of the type after use. The Hattersley, Kastenbein, and Thorne machines were employed for newspapers. The successful *hot-metal type machines, *Linotype and *Monotype systems, both cast and set the type, which was then discarded after use. *See also* MACHINE CASTING. ABRW

J. S. Thompson, *History of Composing Machines* (1904)

composing stick A small (often adjustable) hand-held tray, originally of wood (later metal), in which the *compositor arranges *type and spacing material during *composition.

composition The act or process of setting *type. The hand *compositor would stand (or sometimes sit, especially before *c.*1650) at the *type cases, with a *copy-text

An English 19th-century adjustable **composing stick**.

before him (or, rarely, her), sometimes displayed on a *visorum. The *measure would have been decided upon, as would conventions of capitalization and *punctuation. The compositor would normally begin with the main text, leaving until later any *preliminaries (e.g. foreword, *dedication, *title-page). With a *composing stick in his left hand, he would pick the first piece of type, or *sort, from the case with his right hand, and place it, upside-down with the face towards him, at the left end of the stick, holding it there with his left thumb. He might look at the sort as he picked it up, or work largely by feel with his eyes on the copy, knowing which way up to place each sort by the *nick in its body. Equal spaces would be placed between words until the end of the line of type neared the stick's right end. The compositor would then judge whether to break a word (usually using a hyphen), and whether more or less space between words would be needed to *justify the line. When setting verse, or other unjustified text, this last consideration was unnecessary, and the line could be completed with spaces and *quads. In early printing, justification was aided by the free use of contractions and *abbreviations. Careless composition could result in obvious, uneven spacing (*rivers) between words, while the best compositors made word spaces visually uniform (though this could require subtly different spacing between words).

Upon completing one line, the compositor would begin the next, placing the first sort at the left-hand end of the stick, on top of the line already set. A *setting rule might be inserted first, to stabilise the new line and aid the movement of type during justification (the rule was removed once the line was complete). *Leading could be inserted at this stage by laying a strip of type-metal, card, or *reglet atop the first line, before beginning the second. Once the stick was full (a stick might accommodate anything between one and a dozen lines of *pica type), the contents were carefully removed, often into a *galley. Composition would continue with the next stick-full, and so on, until sufficient type had been set to print the first *gathering or *forme. It was not uncommon for two or more compositors to work on different parts of the same book, sometimes even in different *printing offices, when accurate *casting off would be essential, so that each compositor knew where to begin and end.

With the invention of typesetting and *casting machines, such as the Pianotype, *Linotype, and *Monotype, and with later photographic methods, composition changed completely, becoming the process of working a complex keyboard. However, hand composition remained in use for *display and other special matter as long as *letterpress survived, and continues at many *private presses. *See also* HOUSE RULES AND HOUSE STYLE.   PWN

composition by formes A method of *composition in which one *forme (inner or outer) of a *sheet is composed before the other. Standard 16th- and 17th-century practice in some *printing offices, it requires less type than *composition seriatim, and may allow printing to begin and progress more quickly. It demands accurate *casting off, to predict page-breaks. Bibliographers have sometimes detected its use by observing irregular-length pages in one forme, or the *impressions of individual *sorts in both formes of a sheet; the *First Folio of *Shakespeare (1623) is a case in point.   PWN
Gaskell, *NI*

composition seriatim The simplest method of *composition, in which the entire text of a *gathering is composed before *imposition. This has advantages over *composition by formes, because the text can easily be divided into pages with the correct number of lines, and *casting off of copy is not required (unless more than one gathering is being composed seriatim at the same time—'seriatim' is sometimes used to imply that this is not so, but bibliographers should be careful to make this distinction clear). However, it can be slower than working by formes, and requires more type.   PWN

compositorial analysis The painstaking comparison of *spelling, *punctuation, and spacing practices may reveal patterns, enabling scholars to distinguish the individual habits of those setting the type for a book. Such patterns then assist editors in determining the probable source of a particular textual reading. The most reliable studies of compositorial habits rest not merely on idiosyncrasies of spelling or spacing, but on tracking particular (usually damaged) pieces of type across multiple *formes to identify particular *type cases likely to have been used by individual *compositors.

Compositorial analysis has been confined mainly to early modern texts, primarily to Shakespeare's *plays. In his study of the *First Folio, *Hinman explained the procedures for such analysis and methods for recording the particulars. These tasks are facilitated if a single institution possesses many copies of the text (as the *Folger Library does of First Folios). An optical *collating machine is also recommended; although mirror collators can permit comparison between originals and photocopies by adjusting for differing scale, the precision of detail desirable for tracking individual types is difficult to obtain in reproductions.

Since *McKenzie's 'Printers of the Mind', scholars have had to accept that compositorial analysis assumes a more rational and orderly set of practices than was probably ever achieved in an actual printing house. Only *Blayney has fully taken up Hinman's methodology, in his study of *Okes, printer of the first *quarto of *King Lear*. Blayney conceded that the pages of quarto texts of plays are much less textually dense than those of two-column folio texts; there are hence fewer revealing type recurrences or compositorial stylistic tics in each forme upon which to build a case. He abandoned the attempt to achieve a full compositorial analysis of the first quarto of *Lear*, concluding that publishing the play was an anomalous act for Okes.

A related term, 'compositorial practice', refers to the larger sets of conventions such as *signature patterns and symbols, frequency of *catchwords, ornamentation of page numbers, and styles of roman dates that can be used to localize and date printed texts that may have *false or missing *imprints. CSR

C. Hinman, *The Printing and Proof-Reading of the First Folio of Shakespeare* (2 vols, 1963)

D. F. McKenzie, 'Printers of the Mind: Some Notes on Bibliographical Theories and Printing-House Practices', *SB* 22 (1969), 1–75

R. A. Sayce, *Compositorial Practices and the Localization of Printed Books, 1530–1800* OBS, Occasional Publications 13 (1979)

compositors Workers employed, usually within *printing offices, to set type. Compositors ('comps') were responsible also for *distribution, and usually for making *corrections following *proofreading. They normally served an *apprenticeship, lasting at least seven years in England, after which they became *journeymen and would seek employment, often travelling from city to city in the process. Comps were normally paid by piece-work or by the day (the word journeyman being derived from Fr. *journée*), and each would usually possess his own *composing stick (sometimes also *setting rules). Some skilled and/or lucky compositors would find long-term positions within printing offices. Such work was sometimes deemed suitable for women.

The London Society of Compositors was a trade union created around 1845 to protect the profession's interests. With the invention of typesetting and casting machines such as the Pianotype, *Monotype, and *Linotype, compositors felt their jobs were threatened, and took industrial action. Ultimately, many retrained to work at the keyboards of these machines, and such workers may also be called 'compositors'. The term has rarely been transferred to digital technology, where a 'compositor' is normally a person who 'composes' film or audio data, rather than a typesetter. PWN

E. Howe, ed., *The London Compositor* (1947)

computer (digital computer) An electronic device for manipulating digital data. The earliest digital computers, developed during and after World War II, were primarily intended for large-scale numerical calculations. Developments in programming languages in the 1960s and 1970s, however, allowed programmers to devise—and computers to handle—complex data structures, which

offered the possibility of representing many features of the external world. Small computers arrived in type-composing systems at the end of the 1960s, as versatile replacements for the hard-wired controllers that handled the hyphenation and *justification of input text in the *photocomposing machines of the time. Their workload increased, and moved towards the imaging end of the machine, as photographic means of storing character images gave way to *digital and then to numerical techniques. At the same time, computers were being built into the front-end systems that handled the preparation and formatting of copy, particularly in newspaper environments.

This situation changed completely in the mid-1980s. The introduction of personal computers—with interactive graphic displays and pointing devices, *laser printers, and programming languages that dealt with both character images and line and *half-tone graphics on an equal footing—opened the way to the *desktop publishing revolution and the disappearance of traditional reproduction techniques. Every element of book production, except perhaps the very first stage of writing, now depends essentially on computer technology. The text of a new work is almost invariably produced on a personal computer. *Electronic copy is the primary means of communication between collaborating authors, and between authors and publishers. Illustrations (*see* **16**), if they are not prepared directly on a computer using drawing software, are electronically scanned from film or paper originals or photographed with a digital camera. Text and illustrations are assembled using page-makeup software; the results are sent to the typesetter as a set of computer files in a format in which *typefaces, text, and illustrations are all embedded together. The typesetter produces colour separations from the files and passes them to the printer to make *lithographic plates; or perhaps, for short-run work, makes the printing plates directly.

This state of affairs gives author and publisher unprecedented control over every verbal and graphic feature of the finished work; yet it also nullifies the supervisory functions that *editors, *compositors, and printers' readers (*see* PROOFS AND PROOFREADING) traditionally exerted over both the content of the work and its typographic quality. This lack of supervision is even more marked with publication on the *World Wide Web. Here, the printer plays no part; the place of editors and designers in the process is a matter of choice for the author; and, where there is no publisher, no money need change hands. The long-term effects of this democratization of information, which depends on ubiquitous networked computers, are hard to predict. At a minimum, it places on readers—confronted with the mixture of formal and less formal publishing structures that proliferates on the Internet—the responsibility to assess for themselves the reliability of what they find there. RFS

computerized typesetting Techniques for using computer systems to drive type-composing machines. The first steps towards computerized typesetting were taken in the early 1960s, largely in newspaper environments.

Computers received input from multiple keyboards and produced output, initially as punched paper tape, to drive linecasters or *photocomposing machines. This line of development continued throughout the 1960s and 1970s: its end products were large systems for newspaper composition, using visual display terminals for input and driving fast cathode-ray tube photocomposing machines.

At the same time, academic researchers became interested in computerized text handling, increasingly motivated by the cost of conventional typesetting for complex material, such as mathematics. C. J. Duncan at the University of Newcastle upon Tyne published a pioneering study in 1964; in the mid-1970s, workers at Bell Laboratories in New Jersey produced 'troff', a document-formatting language that drove a direct-photography photocomposing machine. However, the real advance in this area was made between 1977 and 1984 by D. E. Knuth at Stanford, with his 'TeX' formatting language for mathematical text and the Metafont system for fount production. TeX is still extensively used in mathematical publishing.

Troff and TeX are batch processing systems. Their input is a file containing the text of the work being composed, interspersed with instructions written in the formatting language. The user has to run the formatting program on the file, and print the result, to see what changes need to be made. The *word-processing and page makeup programs that appeared with the interactive graphical interfaces and *laser printers of the 1980s are quite different. Their users make changes to the content or formatting of text directly on the display, which mimics the appearance of the printed output.

Both approaches have their advantages. In typographically complex material, such as bibliographies, it can be difficult to verify the sequence and spacing of characters on an interactive display, particularly when the characters themselves are small. Such situations are better dealt with by batch-processing systems, where the text editing program that prepares the input file can use large, easily legible characters. Equally, it is hard to construct a piece of *display typography by writing a set of formatting commands; it is far easier to position and modify the text interactively on the display. Their ease of use has now largely swung the balance in favour of interactive programs, except in special situations such as database publishing. RFS

Comstock, Anthony (1844–1915) US reformer against obscenity. After initial crusades against illegal lotteries, fraudulent banks, and rigged racetracks, he turned to advocates of birth control and publishers of 'obscene' literature. In 1873 he founded the New York Society for the Suppression of Vice, and persuaded Congress to pass the so-called Comstock Act, which banned the circulation of salacious literature (including frank writing about sex) and resulted in numerous prosecutions. The mere threat of Comstock's opposition caused many publishers to withdraw books. G. B. Shaw coined the term 'Comstockery'

after Comstock attempted to have *Man and Superman* and *Mrs. Warren's Profession* banned from production. JLWW

H. Broun and M. Leech, *Anthony Comstock* (1927)
G. Trumbull, *Anthony Comstock* (1913)

Conat, Estellina (second half 15th century) Based on the *colophon of a 1474 *edition printed by her husband—Abraham Conat of Mantua (*fl.* 1474–7)—she is the first woman known to be involved in printing, preceding Anna Rueger of Augsburg (mentioned in 1485) by more than a decade. EGLS

concealed edition *See* HIDDEN PRINTING.

concordance An alphabetical list of all the words used by a particular author or in a particular text, usually giving the context for every use of a word. The so-called Dominican concordance to the Vulgate Bible of 1230 was merely a verbal index of biblical references for the use of preachers, but selective quotations were added to subsequent recensions, as in the first printed Vulgate concordance (Strasbourg, *c.*1474). Hebrew and Greek concordances were not published until the 16th century. The widespread dissemination of the Bible among Protestants encouraged the production of vernacular concordances and other helps to study. Perhaps the most famous of all English concordances is that of the erratic Scotsman Alexander Cruden, continuously in print since 1737, and not superseded until the appearance in 1879 of Robert Young's *Analytical Concordance to the Holy Bible*. Here each English word from the Authorized Version is cited in relation to the Hebrew or Greek word it translates, enabling greater precision of meaning. The enormous labour involved (as well as the limited market) discouraged the making of concordances to other works until the 19th century. (Cruden is credited with the verbal index to Milton in Newton's edition of 1769.) Concordances to Shakespeare appeared in 1845, to Milton in 1857, to Chaucer only in 1927. A verbal search of any text held by a computer is now a simple matter, but needs to be refined by the application of human intelligence and discrimination, as in *Howard-Hill's *Oxford Shakespeare Concordances*. BJF

concurrent printing Until the studies of *McKenzie—based on meticulous study of the archives of *Cambridge University Press, and augmented by his 'Printers of the Mind' (1969)—the workflow in a *printing office was assumed to follow a simple pattern of particular *compositors working on specific books, which were then printed in an orderly and predictable fashion on particular presses by particular pressmen. McKenzie's research showed that, on the contrary, several books were produced concurrently at the press, with compositors working on whichever section of any of them needed to be set (*shared setting), and pressmen printing the *formes on whichever press was free. This challenge to bibliographical orthodoxy undermined a number of theories about the meaning of certain observable variations, among them changes in the line length (thought to reflect the different *measures compositors used for their *composing stick) and changes in *skeleton formes (considered significant in the order of presswork and the number of presses in use). In addition to revising theories of transmission, the understanding of concurrent printing and statistics based on the few remaining archival records have, in recent decades, advanced the study of the economics of printing.   MMS

Gaskell, *NI*

D. F. McKenzie, *The Cambridge University Press 1696-1712* (2 vols, 1966); reviewed by P. Gaskell, *JPHS*, 3 (1967), 100–3

— 'Printers of the Mind: Some Notes on Bibliographical Theories and Printing-House Practices', *SB* 22 (1969), 1–75

W. B. Todd, 'Bibliography and the Editorial Problem in the Eighteenth Century', *SB* 4 (1951-2), 41–55

condition Although some booksellers describe the condition of their books in ways that are at best subjective (if not downright fraudulent), the vast majority are perhaps more reliable in this regard than in other aspects of their descriptions. The common terms—'fine', 'very good', 'good', etc.—should be used in ways wholly consonant with their everyday use and should require no special expertise or understanding. 'Good', although it may mean 'merely good' in this context, should still mean 'good' and not 'bad'. Beyond that, there is what used to be called the 'customary allowance for age and format', which is to say that 'fine' describing an antiquarian book will not be the same as 'fine' for a modern book: a book is judged against others of its age and class, not against an absolute standard. The yardstick will be the notional 'average' condition of books of this age and type. Beyond the general descriptive terms, specific individual defects or restorations (certainly where they influence value) should always be mentioned. 'Original condition' is used in a specialized sense of a book wholly unrestored and in its original or first binding.   LJW

J. Carter and N. Barker, *ABC for Book Collectors*, 8e (2004)

conduct book Conduct manuals draw on two traditions. The first defined a moral standard, based on classical ideals of decorum and perpetuated in medieval and Renaissance religious or clerical codes of conduct. A well-controlled body was a precondition for moral and hence spiritual development. Lay religiosity popularized this ideal from the 13th century onwards. The most influential printed conduct manual in this tradition was *Erasmus' De Civilitate* (1530), which prescribed rules of comportment for boys regardless of social rank. The second tradition was conduct at court, which contemporaries deemed conventional rather than morally binding. Manuals describing court behaviour—exemplified by Castiglione's influential *Cortegiano* (1528)—accommodated interaction between the sexes, unlike *De Civilitate* and kindred works. From the 16th century onwards courtesy manuals often combined or confused the two traditions.   DK

D. Knox, 'Gesture and Comportment: Diversity and Uniformity', in *Forging European Identities, 1400-1700*, ed. H. Roodenburg (2007)

conger The original 'wholesale conger' was an association of wholesale *booksellers that purchased *impressions of books (i.e. books in *sheets, already printed) and resold them at an agreed price. Later, 'printing congers' were formed by booksellers who jointly purchased *copyright (or *copies) and organized the printing and sale of new books.

The etymology of the term *conger* is uncertain, possibly originating in some form of *congress* (Fr. *congrès*, Lat. *congruere*). Others suggest that the practice emulates the conger eel, devouring 'the small fry, so this united body overpowers young and single traders'. The *OED* records the first printed definition of *conger* in the *New Dictionary of the Canting Crew* (*c.*1700): 'a Set or Knot of Topping Book-sellers of London, who agree ... that whoever of them Buys a good Copy, the rest are to take off such a particular number ... in *Quires, on easy Terms'. Ten years earlier, however, *Dunton referred obliquely to congers in *A Voyage round the World*.

In fact, the practice began earlier, when booksellers formed groups—sometimes numbering ten or more—to protect their interests during the lapse of the *Printing Act between 1679 and 1685. The earliest documentary evidence for this seems to be the will of the bookseller Richard Royston, dated 3 October 1682, which leaves instructions to reprint his copyright books and 'sell and dispose of the same impressions to six or eight or more Tradeing Booksellers'.

The notebook of the bookseller Thomas Bennet and his successor Henry Clements provides evidence of the early system's workings. The first entry, headed 'Account of What Has Been Done att the Conger', is dated 28 May 1691 and describes how Bennet and his colleagues bought 1,500 copies of *Pharmacopoeia Bateana* from the printer Samuel Smith for 9*d.* each, fixing the partners' price at 1*s.* and the trade price (i.e. to booksellers outside the conger) at 1*s.*4*d.* The retail price is not mentioned. The conger determined the number of copies each member should buy initially, and, if stock remained, would decide how it should be divided amongst the partners. These wholesalers' names do not appear in *imprints; it is only through the fortunate survival of this notebook that the relationship between a book and its 'wholesale conger' can be established.

The 'printing congers' that flourished from the early 18th century are easier to document, for individual members are usually listed in the imprints (after 'printed for') of the books they owned. These were groups of booksellers —essentially joint-stock companies—who bought shares in books, paid printing costs, and divided the profits. Congers, whose members were often the most powerful London booksellers, provided protection against copyright infringement and underselling. As copyright legislation became more effective, however, congers became less useful; the system died out in the mid-18th century.   CYF

N. Hodgson and C. Blagden, *The Notebook of Thomas Bennet and Henry Clements (1686-1719)*, OBS, NS 6 (1956)

Congress, Library of (LC) Established in 1800, the Library of Congress is the world's largest library and research institution. Its collections of more than 132 million items (including 30 million books) are comprehensive in scope, and include *maps, music, MSS, prints, photographs, motion pictures, and research materials in more than 450 languages. The library's three imposing buildings—named after Thomas Jefferson, John Adams, and James Madison—are located near the Capitol in Washington, DC. Each evokes learning, books, and their vital connection to democracy. When it opened in 1897, the ornate Jefferson Building was characterized as the 'book palace of the American people'.

As the oldest US federal cultural agency, the library occupies a unique place in American civilization. From a small legislative library that provided books to the American national legislature, it gradually grew into a national institution. In the 20th century it became an international resource of unparalleled scope and, with support from the US Congress, helped shape American librarianship, scholarship, culture, and public policy. Many Library of Congress administrative units carry out unique national functions or services, including the Congressional Research Service, the Law Library, the US Copyright Office, the National Library Service for the Blind and Physically Handicapped, the American Folklife Center, the Center for the Book, and the National Digital Information Infrastructure and Preservation Program.

The library's national roots were established early. It was created by the national legislature and served as the first library for the entire American government. Its purchase of Thomas Jefferson's wide-ranging personal library in 1815 expanded the scope of its collections. In 1870, all US *legal deposit activities were centralized at the library, ensuring the continued growth of its collections and necessitating the construction of a separate library building. More than 10 million items, mostly from the library's historical collections of American history and culture, are accessible electronically at www.loc.gov. The site also provides access to library exhibitions, catalogue data, legislative, and *copyright information. The library is taking the lead in the creation of a World Digital Library (see DIGITIZATION). Approximately 4 billion transactions were recorded on the library's website in 2005.   JYC

J. Y. Cole and J. Aikin, eds., *Encyclopedia of the Library of Congress* (2004)
J. Y. Cole and H. H. Reed, eds., *The Thomas Jefferson Building* (1997)

Congressional Record Proceedings of the US House of Representatives and Senate. The official House and Senate *Journals* summarize legislative activity and are published at the conclusion of each Congressional session. In contrast, the *Congressional Record* publishes verbatim speeches made on the floor of Congress each day that the House and Senate are in session. Its predecessors include the *Debates and Proceedings in the Congress of the United States* (the *Annals of Congress*) (1789–1824), the *Register of Debates in Congress* (1824–37), and the *Congressional Globe* (1833–73). During its early decades, newspapers and printers summarized

Congress's activities for publication. By the 1850s, developments in *shorthand prompted the *Globe* to provide verbatim reporting of proceedings, for which Congress appropriated public funds. The *Government Printing Office began producing the *Congressional Record* in 1873.

The *Record* includes speeches from the floor of each legislative chamber and additional material inserted by members of Congress. Since 1947, it has included the Daily Digest, a list of the bills introduced, floor actions, votes, and meetings held that day, plus announcements of forthcoming meetings and their purposes. By federal law, the Joint Committee on Printing is responsible for the form of the *Congressional Record* and for providing an *index to it. The House and Senate are responsible for the *Record*'s contents. In the 1990s, the *Record* became available in electronic form; at the GPO Access (www.gpoaccess.gov/crecord/index.html) and Thomas (thomas.loc.gov/home/r110query.html) websites, it can be searched and browsed.   CKM

M. L. Amer, *The 'Congressional Record'* (1993)

Congress of South African Writers (COSAW) Non-racial organization of anti-apartheid writers established in July 1987, with office-bearers including Njabulo Ndebele and Achmat Dangor, and Nadine Gordimer as patron. Informed by Black Consciousness and Maoist ideas about culture and the role of the artist, COSAW ran workshops and peoples' libraries. It launched an *imprint in 1988, and assumed control of the important *Staffrider* journal in 1989.   AEV

P. D. McDonald, *The Literature Police: Apartheid Censorship and its Cultural Consequences* (2009)

Congreve, William (1637–1708) English playwright. Collecting widely, Congreve gathered books in Latin, Greek, French, Italian, and Spanish on subjects including philosophy, medicine, travel, English poetry, drama, and the classics. A MS catalogue (Yorkshire Archaeological Society, Leeds) records the *c.*650 books remaining in his library at his death. As a playwright, Congreve enjoyed a close working relationship with *Tonson. *McKenzie has demonstrated Congreve's editorial attention to the first two editions of his collected works and his implied concern with the way type (especially *accidentals) can present a play text to a reader.   CYF

The Works of William Congreve, ed. D. F. McKenzie (3 vols, 2009)
J. C. Hodges, *The Library of William Congreve* (1955)
D. F. McKenzie, 'Typography and Meaning: The Case of William Congreve', in *Buch und Buchhandel in Europa im achtzehnten Jahrhundert*, ed. G. Barber and B. Fabian (1981)

Coni, Pablo Emilio (1826–1910) Argentinian publisher. A native Parisian, Coni first printed at Corrientes, Argentina (1853–9). In 1863, he moved to Buenos Aires, establishing a press that he and his descendants operated for 90 years. Renowned for its *letterpress printing, the firm specialized in scholarly works and academic journals.   DRW

conjugate leaves Two *leaves of a book that form a single *bifolium. In a *collational formula a point indicates conjugacy, e.g. 'B1.8'. *See also* GATHERING.

Connemara (State Central) **Public Library, Madras** (Chennai) The largest public library in south India. Founded in 1896, it became the chief public library of the state of Tamilnadu in 1950. In 1954, it was made a national deposit library, housing books in all major Indian languages. It is noted for its extensive collection of South Indian Christian missionary writings.   ARV

Conradin Bible Baltimore, Walters Art Gallery MS W. 152 was possibly produced in central Italy or Sicily *c.*1265. It has been traditionally associated with Conradin, king of Jerusalem and Sicily, beheaded at Naples in 1268. This large bible (*see* **2**) is now disordered and incomplete (164 leaves remain, together with other fragments); nonetheless, it is a sumptuously *illuminated MS with 57 large marginal miniatures (*see* MINIATURES (1)), and many more *historiated or illuminated initials. Its programme of decoration reflects in part the diffusion of Byzantine models into high Romanesque art.   ASGE

D. Miner, 'The Conradin Bible: A Masterpiece of Italian Illumination', *Apollo*, 84 (1966), 470–75

conservation The process by which the condition of library materials is stabilized and future damage limited. This involves reducing risks to collections by identifying and controlling the causes of deterioration, as well as treatment-based procedures whereby the conservator works directly on a single object or group of items. These approaches are sometimes distinguished by the terms 'remedial' and 'preventive' conservation. Remedial conservation includes mending tears, cleaning and supporting fragile paper and *parchment, and structural repairs such as *board reattachment. The aim is to give readers better access to the book by making it safer to handle and easier to interpret. Unlike restoration work that can be inappropriate to the age and origin of the object, modern book conservation—which developed in the book repair workshops set up following the Florence floods of 1966—seeks to preserve the historical integrity of an item. In making treatment decisions, conservators apply ethical principles such as minimum intervention and maximum reversibility to ensure their actions do not obscure or destroy bibliographical or palaeographical evidence. Examination to ascertain the original structure, materials, and extent of damage will always precede treatment, and makes use of techniques ranging from simple visual assessment to more sophisticated analytical techniques. This work may be carried out by conservators or by conservation scientists, and often contributes to wider bibliographical research.

Preventive conservation aims to create the optimal conditions for preserving library materials, setting standards of care in a number of overlapping areas. At the core of preventive conservation is storage, which includes boxing as well as monitoring and controlling temperature, humidity, and light levels—all of which influence the deterioration of *leather and paper. Preventive conservation encompasses handling, pest control, and emergency plans to minimize damage from incidents such as fire or flood. Photographic and digital technologies are often used to provide surrogate copies of fragile items and can be extremely effective in reducing damage to originals, but they also highlight the compromise between the continued use of the book and its long-term preservation.   MRS

The Institute of Conservation, www.icon.org.uk, consulted July 2008

J. L. Sharpe, ed., *Roger Powell*, Bibliologia, 14 (1996)

D. Cockerell, *Bookbinding, and the Care of Books* (1901)

The Paper Conservator (1976–)

M. T. Roberts and D. Etherington, *Bookbinding and the Conservation of Books* (1982)

Constable, Archibald (1774–1827) Scottish publisher of Sir W. *Scott, the *Edinburgh Review*, and the *Encyclopaedia Britannica*. Apprenticed to the bookseller Peter Hill, Constable catalogued antiquarian books and private libraries. His 'Scarce Old Books' shop (opened 1795) issued catalogues specializing in Scottish history and literature, and his first publication, *Fragments of Scottish History* (1798), linked his bookselling and publishing interests. Already a well-known publisher of agricultural and scientific journals, Constable started publishing the *Edinburgh Review* in 1802 and purchased the *Encyclopaedia Britannica* in 1812. When Constable went bankrupt in 1826 amid accusations of fiscal mismanagement, his London partner *Longman bought the *Review*. Constable had published Scott's *Marmion* (1808), but the relationship ended following Jeffrey's hostile review of the poem in the *Review* and incivility to Scott from Constable's partner, Alexander Hunter. When Scott's subsequent relations with James and John *Ballantyne ended in disarray, Constable bought Ballantyne's stock.   PLS

ODNB

Constable, Archibald (founded 1890) British publisher. Founded by the grandson of the publisher of the same name, Constable retired from the firm in 1893. Its early reputation and financial stability were based on the sales of George Meredith's work (his son was soon a director of the company). A balanced general list was established, as was an unusual relationship with G. B. Shaw, who undertook all the financial burdens of publication himself and used Constable (as the company became in 1910) as publication agents rather than publishers proper. Constable published Nansen's *Farthest North*, de la Mare, Harold Nicolson, and David Cecil, and began the massive 'Victoria County Histories' project. *Sadleir was a director for many years, but the company did not adapt well to fresh opportunities; it was sold to rivals *Hutchinson in 1962, and the name died after Hutchinson was incorporated into *Random House UK in 1989.   SJG

Constantin (*fl.* 1529–33?) *Punchcutter. One document names 'Me. Constantin' as an early French imitator of *Aldus' romans. He may have cut the fine *romans introduced by R. Estienne in Paris (1529–33): the first

cut in a range of *sizes, and the first cut as large as Canon (41 point) or as small as Nonpareil (6 point).　　　JAL

H. Vervliet, 'The Young Garamont', *Typography Papers*, 7 (2007), 5–60

Constantine, Donation of (*Constitutum domini Constantini imperatoris*) A forged document allegedly written by the emperor Constantine the Great (*c*.272/3– 337) to Pope Sylvester I (r. 314–35), in which Constantine professes his faith and confers on the papacy primacy within the Church, honours equivalent to those of the emperor, and temporal power in the West. The author-ship, date, and primary purpose of the document remain uncertain. In 1440, Valla proved it a forgery by applying the techniques of Renaissance classical scholarship and textual criticism.　　　CWK

L. Valla, *On the Donation of Constantine*, tr. G. W. Bowersock (2007)

contamination In genealogical textual criticism, the blending of MSS that belong to different *stemmatic traditions, resulting in texts that contain readings from conflicting sources. Once it becomes possible or likely that a copyist took readings from different MSS, or cop-ied a witness that had *variants from other sources within it, the copy and its tradition are both seen as contami-nated. In less pejorative terms, contaminated texts have also been referred to as conflated, or as belonging to an 'open tradition'. More generally, contamination is some-times used to denote any form of conflation or corruption in textual transmission.　　　ASR

contents, table of A summary list of a book's constitu-ent elements (*preliminaries, parts, *chapters, illustra-tions, *endmatter, bibliography or list of references, *index, etc.), organized in the order of occurrence within the book. It usually provides the titles of the parts, and indicates the page (*pagination) on which each begins; it may include sub-headings as well as titles. The table is usually located within the preliminaries of a book, some-times as the first *recto following the *title-page. In some regions, for example France, it has traditionally been placed at the back of the book. Occasionally, lists of chap-ter *headings, or capitula, were placed at the head of each part of a MS. A list of headings to be added during *ru-brication, known as a table of *rubrics (or rubrics table) often looks very much like a table of contents. Certain 18th- and 19th-century tables of contents also provided summaries of the contents or occurences within each chapter. An obsolete use of the word 'index' referred to the table of contents.　　　MMS

Continental copyright *Copyright relating to main-land Europe. The term includes two principal concepts: the right to publish a work or translations of a work in European countries, and a tradition of copyright that places emphasis on the statutory moral rights of the au-thor as creator of a work. In the second sense, Continental copyright is often viewed in ideological opposition to the Anglo-American tradition of copyright, which focuses on the entrepreneurial rights of the publisher (but *see* MORAL RIGHTS). Prior to the establishment of the *Berne Convention (1886), copyright laws usually applied only when a book had been formally published and registered in a particular country. Without a system of reciprocal international copyright law, literary *piracy was wide-spread, and until the end of the 19th century, only a few publishers of continental editions, such as *Tauchnitz, paid authors and publishers for the rights to distribute their works.　　　TK

Contini, Gianfranco (1912–90) Italian romance phil-ologist. In his youth, he studied in Paris under *Bédier and was later professor at Freiburg, Florence, and the Scuola Normale in Pisa. Primarily interested in the trans-mission, editing, and apparatus of Italian medieval texts, he also worked on the textual tradition of modern poets such as Montale.　　　NH

G. Breschi, ed., *L'opera di Gianfranco Contini* (2000)

continuous copy The theory that the draft of a Shakespeare play became the *prompt-copy, and was then augmented and rewritten during its theatrical ca-reer by continuous revisions (authorial and otherwise). Coined to describe the textual transmission theories of J. Dover Wilson, it never gained widespread currency or acceptance.　　　ASR

continuous printing In plays, the practice of setting the speech (or its end) of one verse speaker and the speech (or its beginning) of the next on the same line, in order to maintain metrical quantity or to save space; such speeches were more commonly printed on separate lines.　　　ASR

contract *See* AUTHOR–PUBLISHER AGREEMENTS.

Contreras family Peruvian printing dynasty. In 1620, **Jerónimo de Contreras** (d. 1639?) relocated his press from Seville to Lima, thereby founding a dynasty that dominated Lima printing until 1734. From 1686 to 1712, **José de Contreras y Alvarado** (d. 1718?) was Lima's only printer.　　　DRW

Conway, Edward, 2nd Viscount Conway (1594– 1655) Book collector. He owned nearly 15,000 books and MSS, divided between his Irish and his London libraries. His interests were in part literary—he had large collec-tions of romances and of plays—but also included science, mathematics, and works in foreign languages.　　　ASGE

T. Birrell, 'Reading as Pastime', in *Property of a Gentleman*, ed. R. Myers and M. Harris (1991)

A. Freeman and P. Grinke, 'Four New Shakespeare Quartos? Viscount Conway's Lost English Plays', *TLS*, 5 Apr. 2002

cookbook Cookbooks are collections of recipes, in-structions, and information about the preparation and serving of food; they are also important social and his-torical records, offering a fascinating glimpse into an aspect of daily life that is by its very nature ephemeral. They provide information on issues such as the role of

women in the private sphere, social attitudes to hygiene, and even the expansion of international commerce through the availability of ingredients such as spices or coffee.

1. Early cookbooks
2. Printed cookbooks
3. Changing styles of cookbooks
4. Modern cookbooks

1. Early cookbooks

The earliest written recipes are as old as writing itself. Recipes, including some for ale, survive in baked clay *tablets from Sumeria and hieroglyphics from Egypt. The Greeks and Romans compiled cookbooks such as *Hedypatheia*, or *Pleasant Living* (350 BC) by Archestratus and *De Re Coquinaria* by Apicius (AD 14–37), a work that was distributed widely and survives in numerous medieval MSS. The ruins of Pompeii preserved ancient Roman recipes.

Non-Western cultures also produced their own early cookbooks. In China, Huou, the head chef at the 13th-century court of Kublai Khan, wrote a *vade mecum, including a number of soup recipes, called *Important Things to Know about Eating and Drinking*. Ibn Sayyar al-Warraq's *Kitāb al-ṭabīkh* (Book of Dishes), was a 10th-century compilation of earlier Abbasid recipe books.

Despite medieval European cookery's relative lack of sophistication, some cookbooks from the period survive in MS form. One of the earliest in English was the 12th-century *The Forme of Cury*, which consisted of some 200 recipes, many inspired by the French culinary tradition, as recipes such as 'Blank Mang' (*blamanger*) testify. In France, Guillaume Tirel wrote *Le Viander* (*c*.1375), which made heavy use of spices, such as ginger and cloves, to disguise the flavour of ingredients that would frequently have lacked freshness in the era before refrigeration. The Crusades aroused interest in the lively Arabic gastronomic tradition and led to renewed European interest in the art of cookery.

2. Printed cookbooks

Cookery writing was revolutionized by the advent of movable *type. Cookbooks became widely available for the first time. Moreover, beginning in the Italian Renaissance, gastronomy became much more sophisticated, as wealthy merchants vied to outdo each other with the extravagance of their cuisine. The first printed cookbook, *De Honestate Voluptate*, was produced by an Italian, Il *Platina, in 1474. The first English printed cookbook was Richard Pynson's *Boke of Cokery* (1500). During this period, France began its ascendancy in the world of gastronomy. A key event in the history of food publishing was La Varenne's *Le Cuisinier françois* (1651)—planned as a real tool of the chef's trade—which methodically organized the recipes so that the book began with a basic soup stock and became gradually more elaborate. A great success, it was reprinted in some 250 editions until 1815. Publishers thus became aware of the potential of cookbooks as a lucrative market: the expanding middle classes were taking an ever greater interest in food preparation.

In the 17th and 18th centuries, cookbooks were frequently written by women, who compiled recipes along with household management tips in books such as Susannah Carter's *Frugal Housewife* (1765?), published by F. *Newbery. At this time, the first cookbooks were appearing in colonial America. Although handwritten collections of recipes had been circulating for generations, printed cookbooks were exclusively imported from Europe until 1742, when Eliza Smith's popular *Compleat Housewife* was reprinted by W. *Parks. The first original American cookbook was Amelia Simmons's *American Cookery* (1796), which featured typically American ingredients such as cornmeal (ground maize).

3. Changing styles of cookbooks

In the 19th century, as advances in printing technology and education meant that wider sections of the population had access to print, chefs began to produce cheap cookbooks promoting nourishing meals for families on low budgets. In Britain, Alexis Soyer's *Shilling Cookery for the People* (1855), published by *Routledge, sold more than 100,000 copies. Isabella *Beeton's *Book of Household Management* (1861) sold 60,000 copies in its first year of publication. Mrs Beeton's book achieved classic status as a fascinating record of social history, documenting both the role of women in Victorian society and the impact of industrialization in the kitchen at a moment when, for the first time in history, a majority of the population had no direct experience of the rural economy and of growing their own food.

In this period, cookery writers also began to recognize that not all readers would share their expertise. Cookbooks were traditionally written by and for experienced chefs, or by and for women overseeing skilled domestic staff. They were thus often lacking in precise detail regarding quantities and cooking times. A high level of precision was, in any case, impossible in the pre-industrial era. In the US, Fannie Merritt Farmer was the first to introduce standardized level measurements in her recipes, thus guaranteeing reliable results. Over the years, her *Boston Cooking School Cookbook* (1896) became the best-selling *Fannie Farmer Cookbook*, which sold nearly 4 million copies over 70 years.

4. Modern cookbooks

During the 20th century, the cookbook continued to reflect social attitudes to household management. As employing domestic staff became less common, titles increasingly focused on providing recipes that fitted into a busy life. Peg Bracken's *I Hate to Cook Book* (1960) is typical in acknowledging that for many women, cookery was a chore; it provided simple, yet effective recipes, often using processed and packaged foods. In the US, *The Joy of Cooking*, originally privately published in 1931 by a struggling St Louis homemaker, has been continuously in print since 1936, selling more than 18 million copies.

Twentieth-century cookbooks also reflect major historical events and social developments in their use of

equipment and ingredients. During World War II, the British government distributed recipe pamphlets with titles such as *What to Give Them?* using unrationed ingredients—among them, sheep's heart. Postwar prosperity is seen in titles requiring sophisticated kitchen equipment such as the *Mr. and Mrs. Roto-Broil Cookbook* (1955). At the same time, television cookery programmes provided chefs such as Fanny Craddock and Julia Child with instant audiences for their books. After World War II, the increasing availability of international travel led people to discover new and exotic cuisines. Italian and Chinese food was consumed by the public at large, and writers such as Madhur Jaffrey enjoyed success as ambassadors for non-Western cuisines. The need to illustrate unfamiliar techniques and ingredients, together with the emergence of cheap colour printing, led to the widespread use of mouthwatering food photography that is such a feature of modern cookbooks and which has made them characteristic of the *coffee-table book.

In the early years of the 21st century, cookbooks regularly top the bestseller charts for hardback non-fiction. Ingredients recommended in books by popular television chefs such as Delia Smith sometimes would sell out nationwide in days. Publishers have tended to focus either on books by celebrity chefs like Jamie Oliver, or on ever more specialized niches such as Lyndsay Mikanowski's *Uncooked* (2005). Popular as ever, cookbooks remain a staple of the publishing market. SLP

A. Davidson, *The Oxford Companion to Food* (2006)
J. Floyd and L. Forster, eds., *The Recipe Reader* (2003)

Cooper, Thomas (*fl.* 1732–43), and **Mary Cooper** (*fl.* 1736–61) Thomas, London printer and publisher, had premises at Paternoster Row, where he printed the *Daily Courant* in 1735. His widow inherited the business in 1743 (although imprints bear her name from 1736), acting as *trade publisher for *Dodsley, A. *Millar, and others. From 1751 to 1759, she printed *The New Universal Magazine*. KMQ

M. Treadwell, 'London Trade Publishers 1675–1750', *Library*, 6/4 (1982), 99–134

COPAC Freely available online *union catalogue of the Consortium of Research Libraries (CURL) in the UK. It consists of more than 31 million records from 27 member institutions, with items dating from *c.*1100 onwards. Some records include full-text links. CBF

copac.ac.uk, consulted Feb. 2007

Copeland & Day Fine publishers in the arts-and-crafts tradition, active in Boston from 1893 to 1899. Herbert Copeland (1867–1923) was a Harvard aesthete. F. Holland Day (1864–1933) was a noted art photographer. PMW

DLB 49
J. W. Kraus, *Messrs. Copeland & Day* (1979)

Copenhagen, Royal Library (Det Kongelige Bibliotek) Danish national library and the library of the University of Copenhagen, one of two *legal deposit libraries in Denmark (the other being the State and University Library, Aarhus, founded 1902). The Royal Library was established in the 1650s by Frederik III; it grew steadily in the 17th and 18th centuries through the acquisition of such collections as the ducal library of Gottorp and those of O. *Thott and Henrik Hielmstierne. In 1793 access was opened to the public, and in 1849 the library became state property. Founded in 1482, the university library's rich collections of books and MSS were destroyed in the fire of Copenhagen (1728), but the library was soon re-established. The two libraries merged in 1989: in 2004 they contained 188,000 metres of material. In 2005, a further merger with the Danish National Library of Science and Medicine took place. CA, KSP

www.kb.dk/en/index.html, consulted Sept. 2007

Copland, William (*fl.* 1545?–69) English printer. A founding member of the *Stationers' Company, Copland was probably the son of Robert Copland, who was connected to *Caxton's heir, de *Worde. His lineage may thus be traced back to England's first printer; this link was cemented by the material he printed between 1547 and 1567: more than 150 books of a popular nature, largely romances, often first produced by de Worde or Caxton. KMQ

copper facing type To increase the durability of *type, a copper facing can be added to the printing surface by means of electrolysis. *See also* ELECTROTYPING.

copperplate A style of calligraphic script of rounded, *cursive letters. This round hand developed in the 18th century in imitation of the copper-plate *engravings of handwriting models in books by *writing-masters. Sometimes called 'anglaise', or 'English round hand', it established itself as the standard form for copying documents and other records in the 19th and 20th centuries before being rendered obsolete by new technologies and new styles of handwriting, especially italic. Although its alphabet was clear and highly accessible, copperplate's basic calligraphic strokes were commonly ornamented with exuberant flourishes meant to show off the *scribe's 'command of hand'. Thus, 'copperplate hand' connotes a clear, neat, round handwriting, usually slanted and looped, with attractive ornamentation. 'Copperplate' is also a name given to various *typefaces, often bearing no resemblance to the script, but suggesting their clarity and legibility. ASGE

D. Jackson, *Copperplate Calligraphy* (1979)
G. Turner, *The Technique of Copperplate Calligraphy* (1987)

copper-plate engraving *See* ENGRAVING.

Coptic sewing The earliest sewing technique devised for bookbinding, whereby folded *gatherings are sewn together with a chain stitch (*see* **17**). It was abandoned in Europe in favour of *flexible sewing around the 9th century, but continued to be the standard sewing technique used in North Africa and the Near East. DRSP

Coptic type Type for the last form of the ancient Egyptian language, a *script flourishing especially among

Middle Eastern Christians from the 4th century (when it largely superseded demotic) to the 7th century (when the Arabic language and script began to supersede it). Alexander the Great conquered Egypt in 332 BC; the Coptic script emerged about the 2nd century BC from attempts to write the Egyptian demotic phonetically using the *Greek alphabet, supplemented by new characters based on demotic. The language and script declined after the Arabic conquest in 641, but survived as a vernacular into the 17th century. The Coptic Orthodox Church attempted a linguistic revival in the 1890s.

Based on Greek *uncial, the alphabet usually comprises 24 or 25 Greek characters (with or without digamma) and 6 or 7 adapted from demotic. The sahidic dialect dominated until the Church officially adopted the bohairic in the 11th century. The first known Coptic type, used by the Congregatio de *Propaganda Fide in Rome (1630?) may have been cut for the *Tipografia Medicea Orientale c.1598–1600. About 30 types appeared in the metal era, most in the bohairic style, with *majuscule and *minuscule. F. *Didot and his sons produced the first type in the single-case sahidic style (1826) for the Egyptologist Jean-François Champollion, based on early uncial MSS.

Important Coptic MSS of the Bible (especially *gospels and psalms) and Church Fathers encouraged scholarly Coptic editions; biblical and liturgical texts printed for the Egyptian Copts appeared at Rome in the 18th and Cairo in the 19th centuries. The greatest interest in the script today centres on the gnostic and other non-canonical gospels.   JAL

G. Roper and J. Tait, 'Coptic Typography', in *Middle Eastern Languages and the Print Revolution*, ed. E. Hanebutt-Benz *et al.* (2002)

copy 1. The physical original used by a *compositor to set a text in type for printing—typically an author's MS or typescript, or a previous *edition. **2.** A particular exemplum of a printed book. **3.** Shorthand for '*copyright'.

copy, fair The final version of a MS, produced by a copyist (either author or *scribe) after the correction and/or revision of earlier drafts. In early modern England, the fair copy was made from the foul or rough copy, or from *foul papers.   ASGE

copy, ideal '[T]he most perfect state of the book as the printer or publisher finally intended to issue it' (Bowers); 'a historical reconstruction of the form or forms of the copies of an impression or issue as they were released to the public by their producer' (Tanselle). As individual copies from a single *issue, *impression, or *edition might vary (particularly during the hand press era), descriptive bibliographers generalize from the evidence present in surviving copies to reconstruct the intended form of that specific issue, impression, or edition at the moment of publication. Because such evidence may be inconclusive or incomplete, the ideal copy is often conjectural, and it is possible, especially when few copies survive, that no one copy matches the projected ideal copy. Bowers was the first to define the term at length;

Tanselle refined the definition to include 'all the states of each sheet as they were issued'. Ideal copy is usually described using *collational formulas.   IG

Bowers, *Principles*
Gaskell, *NI*
G. T. Tanselle, 'The Concept of *Ideal Copy*', *SB* 33 (1980), 18–53
W. P. Williams and C. S. Abbott, *An Introduction to Bibliographical and Textual Studies*, 4e (2009)

copy book By custom, each workman was allocated one sound copy of every book printed: this could then be sold. Because these books undercut the publisher's price, leading to abuses (e.g. releasing defective copies), *copy money was increasingly substituted.   MMS

F. R. Johnson, 'Printers' "Copy Books" and the Black Market in the Elizabethan Book Trade', *Library*, 5/1 (1946–7), 97–105

copy-book A book in which copies, usually produced by *writing-masters, are written or printed as models for pupils.

copy editor A copy editor works for a publisher, either on the publisher's premises or freelance, with the general aims of removing obstacles between the reader and what the author wishes to convey in the *copy that has been submitted for publication, and saving time and money by resolving problems before typesetting. The editor's responsibilities include production considerations, detailed editing for sense, checking for consistency, and presenting material clearly for the typesetter, resulting in *marked-up copy for the printer. Although *proofs are still generally corrected in paper form, copy editing is now, for the most part, done on-screen, virtually obviating the need for marginal/interlinear marks and making electronic markup an increasingly important feature of copy editing. Copy editors are also known as editors, desk editors, production editors, and sub-editors.   KEA

Butcher

copying The act of seeking to reproduce, either manually or typographically, the content of another document of whatever kind (the *exemplar). The act of copying aims to give an accurate representation of the matter of the original, but it does not necessarily attempt to present an exact representation of the work being copied or to produce a *facsimile of it. Such forms of copying do occur, however. For example, in the later 19th century, copyists such as *Tupper and J. *Harris (1791–1873) made a number of very accomplished hand-copied facsimiles of printed leaves. Some of Harris's copies were made to be inserted into copies of editions of Caxton's works that lacked them. In its most extreme form, unacknowledged facsimile copying amounts to *forgery. *See also* **3, 4, 5, 13**; COPY, FAIR; MANUSCRIPT CORRECTIONS; MANUSCRIPT CULTURE; PALIMPSEST; PECIA; SCRIBE; SCRIPT; SCRIPTORIUM; SCRIVENER.   ASGE

B. Gaines, 'John Harris and the Rylands Copy of Caxton's Malory', *BJRL* 52 (1969–70), 115–28
R. Myers, 'George Isaac Frederick Tupper, Facsimilist', *TCBS* 7 (1977–80), 113–34

copying machines Devices and technologies for multiplying copies, typically from a pre-existing 'original', or a purpose-generated printing or transfer surface. Most copying methods have been based on established printing methods (*intaglio, *relief, *stencilling, *lithography), or newly developed chemical, *photographic, or electrical processes. Many proprietary devices offered quick, cheap, large-volume document duplication, and could be operated by (office) workers with little or no training. Early copying machines include the *pantograph (1603) and the polygraph (mid-17ᵗʰ century), whose linked pens generated duplicate writing. Purely mechanical, these devices usually produced a single copy. Copying presses (1778, possibly earlier), based on the pressure transfer of ink from an original, produced several copies, as did *carbon paper (early 19ᵗʰ century) used in conjunction with writing implements ('manifold' copying) and later *typewriters. Other late 18ᵗʰ-century methods (some devised by *Franklin) combined presses with intaglio or relief surfaces created by novel means. In 1669, Christiaan Huyghens used etched copper stencils and a *rolling press to generate documents in multiple copies, later the basis of 19ᵗʰ-century stencil duplicating. Devices such as the Cyclostyle (Gestetner, 1881) and *mimeograph (1887) differed in stencil makeup, perforation method (eventually performed by typewriters), and printing configuration (rotary or flat-bed). Less efficient copying methods included hectographic printing (1874) and lithography, where printing surfaces were created by a variety of chemical and photographic transfer methods. Printing duplicators (e.g. Multigraph, c.1904) were effectively small-scale rotary relief printing units, while automatic typewriters generated multiple documents from punched paper rolls. Early 20ᵗʰ-century photographic methods made copies in small numbers, but did not typically require a specially configured original. A major innovation was *electrostatic printing (1938), also known as xerography or electrophotography, the basis of most current photocopying. *Laser and *ink-jet printers now duplicate *digital 'originals' but are not generally considered copying machines. ETK

D. Owen, *Copies in Seconds* (2004)
B. J. Rhodes and W. W. Streeter, *Before Photocopying* (1999)

copy money By longstanding custom, one unbound copy of a printed book was the perquisite of each pressman (and often *compositor) who had worked on it. The bookseller Adam Islip (d. 1639) was apparently the first to substitute a cash payment of 4*d.* in lieu of the *copy book, although the *Stationers' Company recommended 3*d.* in 1635. The going rate long remained 4*d.*, and this 'copy money' became a routine part of a *journeyman's wages. BJF

copyright The central purpose of copyright has been to ensure a fair return to the producer of original works, thus encouraging further productions. To this end, copyright accords a capacity to protect a property in an original work, namely the exclusive entitlement to make copies of that work. Where there is property—and

possible profit—there will be dispute, whether over shares in the profit or over the ownership of the property itself. Hence, the emergence of a body of law designed to resolve disputes over copies in works. By the 17ᵗʰ century, this was termed law about 'literary property'. In today's parlance, copyright constitutes one area of 'intellectual property', alongside patents or inventions, designs, trade marks, and logos.

1. Anglo-American jurisdictions
2. Other jurisdictions
3. History

1. Anglo-American jurisdictions

In common conception, the classic copyright dispute lies between authors (has he plagiarized her work?), or between author and publisher (has the market appropriated her work?). In practice, the fact of ownership has proved less contentious than the issue of identity between works: is a subsequent publication substantially identical to an existing copyright work such that it unfairly pre-empts the latter's legitimate market? *Plagiarism is what authors do to one another: I 'pass off' as mine a work that is yours. *Piracy is what publishers do to one another: far from any 'passing off', the whole point is to market a counterfeit of the original. Maintaining the original author's name and the work's title is the essence of a piratical simulacrum.

Law about copyright addresses a tension between ownership and use. Its task is to balance the copyright owner's interest against that of users of copyright materials to create further original works. Talk of 'balance' suggests an ideal equilibrium, but this is misleading. Given shifting commercial, cultural, and technological circumstances, 'balance' refers less to a transcendent principle than to expedient legal settlements. Like other areas of law, to meet its purposes copyright has generated its own technical-normative idiolect. Thus, for a work to count as 'original' for copyright purposes, it does not have to be particularly creative or even new; it simply must be other than a copy of an existing work. An 'expression/idea' dichotomy delimits what is legally protectable from what is not: copyright protects an original expression or representation of an idea, not the idea itself.

Rather, copyright's purpose was and is to settle property disputes by balancing the interests of the parties. The low threshold set for 'originality' makes it relatively easy for owners to claim copyright. Yet the owners' powers are not absolute. Recognized 'exceptions' allow use of copyright material that would otherwise constitute infringement. Some 'exceptions' have a public good rationale: limited copying for educational and library purposes; quotation for purposes of review and criticism. Readers and writers benefit from 'fair dealing' or 'fair use' provisions, allowing for works of parody. These exceptions are always too generous or too parsimonious, depending on whether one's status is owner or user. Current calls for a 'creative commons' would liberalize use of copyright materials for the purpose of creating other original works, a rebalancing in users' favour.

2. Other jurisdictions

Anglo-American copyright is not the only jurisdiction to address the issue of an orderly publishing market. A distinction is conventionally drawn between the copyright regimes that emerged in the common-law systems and regimes of 'author-right' (*droit d'auteur, Uhrheberrecht*) that developed in civil-law jurisdictions. In fact, the jurisdictions have much in common. On both sides, a temporary monopoly protects the holder of *rights, automatically in the first instance the author of an original work. Copyright and the *droit d'auteur* both comprise a 'bundle' of diverse entitlements—rights of first publication, translation, dramatization, serialization, digitization, and so on—that the rights-holder can manage separately. In the global cultural market, the regimes converge. English and American statutes have recently recognized creators' *moral (i.e. personal or non-economic) rights. Many European commentators fear that *droit d'auteur* is succumbing to the copyright norms deployed by American corporate entities bent on worldwide protection of their intellectual property. The point is to recognize but not render absolute the regimes' distinction. Copyright may be seen primarily as a law of property, *droit d'auteur* as a law of personality. Copyright thus provides the rights-holder with remedies against infringement of his or her property. The *droit d'auteur* concerns attributes of a legal subject's personality—honour, integrity, reputation—protected by a positive right. Copyright remains attached to the work, going wherever the work's ownership goes. Conversely, the *droit d'auteur* remains attached indelibly to the author's moral and social self.

3. History

Today's copyright norms have emerged from a piecemeal legal history, marked by the contingencies of centuries of print culture. In England, the early modern origins of law about 'copies' lie in the dual controls exercised by the ecclesiastical censor and the London-based *Stationers' Company. Permission to print required the censors' licence and inscription in the Register Books at Stationers' Hall. Complicity of printer-booksellers' 'copyright' with the exigencies of religious government was not incongruous, given the division of Christian Europe, England's 'swarming sectaries', and the threat of confessional civil war.

By 1710 and the Statute of Anne—the first 'Copyright Act'—the exigencies were geopolitical and commercial: the Act was passed in 1709 and took effect the following year. The 1707 Act of Union created a 'unified' market in books; Scottish reprinters subsequently moved in on the Londoners' monopoly. The 18th-century 'battle of the booksellers' found legal resolution in *Millar vs Taylor (1769) and *Donaldson vs Becket (1774). In the latter of these landmark cases, an anti-monopolistic House of Lords construed the nature of copyright set down in the 1710 legislation: a temporary monopoly, granted under statute to the author or his stationer assigns, in copies of a printed work. With others free to make copies on expiry of the term of monopoly, stationers would not hold perpetual and inheritable property in works, as the *Tonsons had in Shakespeare. Yet the law remained a trade practice matter, constraining unfair competition by granting limited protection to printer-booksellers.

It was for the 19th century to raise the status of the authorial persona as demiurgic creator-owner. In 1842, Parliament responded to the campaigning of Southey, Wordsworth, Dickens, and Scott, extending authors' post-mortem protection. Other artistic media, such as musical compositions, gained protection. Most copyright cases, though, involved illicit replication of works of information, not works of literature.

New geopolitical factors introduced a broader perspective. International relations, previously marginal, now saw copyright agreements fashioned between states. Some were bilateral—the Prussian approach in the 1840s forced the UK government to define what British 'copyright' actually meant. Other treaties were multilateral. The enduring *Berne Convention dates from 1886. The US remained conspicuously aloof, signing this international treaty only in 1989. Indeed, until the Anglo-American agreement (the *Chace Act 1891), American publishers were the century's great 'pirates', piracy being appropriate practice for a country exposed to book imports. Legally speaking, though, since there was no agreement, there was no infringement. Reprinting books by British authors was risk-free, cheap, and efficient. *Harpers and *Putnams could get a large-scale reprint on the bookshelves within 48 hours of advance sheets from England being landed in the US. Dickens described them in less positive terms as 'scoundrel-booksellers'.

The rise of intellectual property is a 20th-century legal commonplace. Given an explosive communications technology, copyright protection extended to new media, at first electrical and analogue—photographic, cinematographic, and phonographic works—and, in the last decades, electronic and digital (promising an 'infinite' number of 'perfect' copies). Battles raged over copyright status for computer software, databases, and graphic morphing. New global bureaucracies—the World Trade Organization, the *World Intellectual Property Organization—emerged as dominant players on an ever-more contested geopolitical scene.

At the time of writing, major publishers are challenging initiatives by an Internet search engine: Google's *digitization of books for its Book Search and Print Library projects. Like 18th-century London stationers confronting Scottish reprinters, they claim a violation of copyright. This fear of what might be done with digital versions of copyright books is just the most recent episode in a multi-dimensional history—commercial and cultural, technical and technological—that should disqualify any view of copyright in terms of philosophical foundations which go deeper than the law's historical conditions and practical purposes. Academic enthusiasts have nonetheless sought noble grounds for copyright in Lockean natural law. Others, inspired by critical theory, have denounced copyright's conceptual deficiency, notably its persistence with notions of 'author' and 'work' in the face of intellectual theories about the death of the author and intertextuality.

Two centuries ago, dismissing as 'undemocratic' notions of a private property in ideas, French revolutionaries imagined a totally free market in books. Existing *Ancien Régime* '*privileges' were annulled, replaced by Revolutionary decrees (1791–3) opening the publishing market up to all. If a work proved profitable, anyone could print copies—a situation Hobbes would have described as a natural right of everyone to everything in a publishing 'state of nature'. Like much of the Jacobin repertoire, this revolutionary deregulation proved catastrophic, rendering book publishing unviable. For books to exist, publishing requires protection.

Today, a technology-saturated view imagines it sees beyond copyright into a revolutionary digital environment for books. As with popular music downloads, individual readers will access works via a contractual payment to the rights-owner. Only one source 'text' will exist, from which an indefinite number of digital copies can be downloaded, on demand. The transparency of contract—between user and owner—will liberate trade in books from the historical opacities of copyright. The revolutionary episode may serve, allegorically, as a response to current visions of transcending the existing legal framework of the complex activity that is book publishing. *See also* COPYRIGHT SYMBOL: ©; ROYALTIES; UNITED BUREAUX FOR THE PROTECTION OF INTELLECTUAL PROPERTY. **DS**

J. P. Feather, *Publishing, Piracy and Politics* (1994)
C. Hesse, *Publishing and Cultural Politics in Revolutionary Paris, 1789–1800* (1991)
J. Loewenstein, *The Author's Due* (2002)
L. R. Patterson, *Copyright in Historical Perspective* (1968)
M. Rose, *Authors and Owners* (1993)

Copyright Act *See* ACT FOR THE ENCOURAGEMENT OF LEARNING.

copyright edition An *edition that establishes *copyright. The term may refer to an edition produced for the express purpose of establishing and safeguarding copyright, or to a later, derivative edition of a work which contains sufficient textual changes to establish a new copyright. A copyright edition often consists of a small number of copies printed prior to the first regular edition, usually withheld from sale or distribution, and which may be registered with a national *stationers' company, copyright library, or other copyright-establishing institution. This procedure may be undertaken because a publisher is anxious to prevent *piracy or because a book is likely to be subject to *censorship.

Before the establishment of international copyright laws in the late 19th century, authors and publishers often attempted to obviate the appearance of pirated copies by publishing editions in multiple countries as soon as possible after the first domestic edition. In some cases, publishers produced only a very limited number of books in one country, which made up the copyright edition. Currently, books produced as part of a copyright edition

may also go on to perform other functions: as review copies, part of the author's allowance, or part of the publisher's *archive. Because of their rarity and unusual provenance, copyright edition works are often highly valuable and prized by collectors. *See also* ADVANCE COPY; BERNE CONVENTION; TRIAL EDITION. **TK**

copyright symbol: © An American legal creation recognized internationally as signifying a work claiming *copyright protection. Until the US Copyright Act (1979), a work required a valid copyright notice if it was to enjoy protection. The word 'Copyright', subsequently shortened to 'copr.' or ©, had to appear in the notice, with the date of first publication and the author's name. Today, copyright is granted without these formalities of legal registration. **DS**

copy-text (**1**) Sometimes used to refer to the original authorial MS from which a *compositor sets a text to be printed.

copy-text (**2**) The particular text chosen as the basis for a *critical edition of a work. It may be an authorial or non-authorial MS, or that printed edition which is thought most closely to reflect *authorial intention, whether the first, or a later (usually in the author's lifetime) edition embodying authorial revision. Editors follow the copy-text in *accidentals (i.e. capitalization, *punctuation, *spelling), with, in the case of a printed edition, the printers' customary normalizations from the MS, according to *house rules and style. Editors may adopt variant authorial readings for substantives (anything that affects the sense), or may provide conjectural emendation where no witnessed reading makes adequate sense. For texts not intended for publication, such as correspondence or diaries, copy-text normally follows the author's accidentals. This is also the case in instances where the author paid particular attention to such matters. Where there are two or more collateral printed texts set from the MS, editors may select one as a copy-text, follow its accidentals, and choose substantive variants from either version. In cases of extensive authorial revision, an editor may choose to ignore one version or to produce a *parallel-text edition. Though the concept of copy-text is much older (*see* *CAPELL, EDWARD), the term itself was devised by *McKerrow in his edition of Nashe (1904; copy-text is further discussed in his 1939 *Prolegomena for the Oxford Shakespeare*). *Greg developed the concept in his influential 'The Rationale of Copy-Text', which introduced the terms 'substantive' and 'accidental'. Later views are based on Greg, either directly or as expounded especially by *Bowers. **KEA**

Gaskell, *NI*
W. W. Greg, 'The Rationale of Copy-Text', *SB* 3 (1950–51), 19–36

coranto [Fr. *courant*, 'running', 'runner'; Du. *krant*, 'gazette', 'newspaper'] Irregular English news serials of the 1620s–30s. Occasional *pamphlet publications translated from Dutch, German, and French had been published in England from the 1590s. In 1622, English booksellers began serial publication, bringing together seriality, translation, a standard three-sheet length, and pamphlet format. They appeared irregularly, sometimes daily, sometimes weekly; news was almost exclusively foreign, owing to conventions restricting the publication of domestic news. Corantos were initially published by a syndicate including *Butter, Nicholas Bourne, Thomas Archer, Bartholomew Downes, and William Sheffard; in 1624, Butter and Bourne took over exclusively. Thomas Gainsford, their first editor, gathered the corantos' diverse sources into a coherent narrative; before and after him, news was presented in discrete sections under the source's location and date. Corantos were widely distributed through carriers and the post, establishing distribution networks for later news publications, and developing a set of typographical conventions, by which news was both organized according to when it arrived in the news office and headed with the location of its source and date of transmission.

In October 1632, Charles I banned corantos. Thereafter, Butter and Bourne published occasional news pamphlets, and from 1638 an irregular series of corantos under royal patent. These were soon superseded by Scottish, then English, news pamphlets that reported on domestic news and by commercial *newsletters. JR

F. Dahl, *Dutch Corantos, 1618–1650* (1946)
— *A Bibliography of English Corantos and Periodical Newsbooks, 1620–1642* (1952)
J. Frank, *The Beginnings of the English Newspaper, 1620–1660* (1961)
J. Raymond, *Pamphlets and Pamphleteering in Early Modern Britain* (2003)

Coray (Korais), Adamantios (1748–1833) Leading figure in the Greek Enlightenment. Born in Smyrna, he encountered mainstream European thought while working as a young trade representative in Amsterdam, and went on to study medicine at Montpelier. In 1788 Coray settled in Paris, where he gained a reputation as an accomplished classical philologist; his French editions of Hippocrates and Strabo and the 'Greek Library' of ancient classics were accompanied by weighty, impassioned prolegomena. AP

cording quire An old term for the outside or top and bottom *quires of a *ream of paper packaged in quires. *See also* CASSIE QUIRE.

Coresi (d. 1583?) Deacon, translator, editor, and printer born in Wallachia. His first *imprints were the Church Slavonic Octoechos, with Logofătul Oprea (Braşov, 1557), and Festal Triodion (Târgovişte, 1557–8). Between 1559 and 1583, his own press in Braşov (Transylvania) produced more than twenty Romanian, Church Slavonic, and bilingual liturgical works. As an editor, Coresi was noted for laying the foundations of the Romanian literary language. BG

D. Simonescu, *Scurtă istorie a cărţii Româneşti* (1994)

Cormellas, Sebastián (d. 1638?) Spanish printer. Cormellas and his son (also named Sebastián) were Barcelona's leading printers, 1591–1654. Their two shops issued nearly 300 works, including the picaresque novel *Guzmán de Alfarache* (1599) and editions of Cervantes, Lope de Vega, Jorge de Montemayor, and Francisco de Quevedo. DRW

Cornell University Library With 7 million volumes in twenty libraries, Cornell University Library is one of the largest in the US. Its Olin and Kroch libraries contain more than half of Cornell's holdings. Strong in national and international documents published by the US government and the UN, Kroch also houses the Division of Rare and Manuscript Collections, which holds 400,000 printed volumes and 70 million MSS. MDB

campusgw.library.cornell.edu/about/about.html, consulted Nov. 2007

Cornelsen German publisher of school books. In 1946, Franz Cornelsen established the company in Berlin; it expanded in the 1960s, combining with Velhagen & Klasing and Schroedel to publish geographical textbooks and atlases. Since 1971, Cornelsen has developed educational media in cooperation with *Oxford University Press. US

S. Damm, *Der Cornelsen Verlag 1946–1996* (1996)

cornerpiece In bookbinding, a large decorative tool, broadly triangular in outline, placed at each corner of a *cover as part of an overall pattern. Cornerpieces are commonly used in designs which also incorporate *centrepieces. The term also refers to metal *furniture nailed on to the corners of bindings with wooden *boards. DRSP

Corpus Christi College, Cambridge A library has existed in the college from its foundation in 1352, and it received some notable early bequests: 75 MSS from Thomas Markaunt, Fellow, in 1439 (of which five remain) and 187 printed books and MSS from Peter Nobys in the 1520s. However, the most significant event in the library's history was the bequest, in 1575, of most of the MSS (400 volumes) and some 800 printed books belonging to Archbishop M. *Parker (1504–75), a former Master. This donation brought to the College more than 40 Old English MSS, as well as significant numbers of other important medieval MSS, particularly of bibles (*see* **2**) and medieval history. Many of these volumes contain Parker's annotations. The Parker Library is now separately housed in the college. Corpus Christi College's MSS were catalogued by M. R. *James (1912) and digitized 2007–9. KEA

B. Dickins, 'The Making of the Parker Library', *TCBS* 6 (1972–6), 19–34
R. I. Page, *Matthew Parker and his Books* (1995)

Corpus *Troilus* Corpus Christi College, Cambridge MS 61 is an early 15th-century MS of Chaucer's *Troilus and Criseyde*. Probably produced in London or at

Westminster, it contains an elaborate *frontispiece miniature (*see* MINIATURES (1)) that depicts a central figure addressing a noble audience. This has been held to be a representation of Chaucer's reading the poem to the court of Richard II, but recent research has questioned this. The MS has about 80 blank spaces for illustrations that were never executed. ASGE

G. Chaucer, *Troilus and Criseyde: A Facsimile of Corpus Christi College Cambridge MS 61*, introd. M. B. Parkes and E. Salter (1978)

correction A revision made to a text to suppress faults of the author, editor, *compositor, printer, or *scribe. The term may also refer to the mark that indicates the error, or that provides the proper text or other insertion. *See also* CANCEL; ERASURE; ERRATA/CORRIGENDA; MANUSCRIPT CORRECTIONS; OVERPRINTING; PROOFS AND PROOFREADING. ETK

corrector (reader) A corrector (of the press) checks the compositor's work against the author's MS or typescript. After the mid-19th century the preferred terms were '(printer's) reader' or 'proofreader'; the *printer's devil who read copy aloud became the reading boy or copyholder. The corrector was responsible for checking *revises, as well as mechanical aspects of printing such as pagination, imposition, and register. Correctors also read copy before it was issued to the compositor for setting in order to rectify errors, mark up layout, or introduce *house rules and house style; hence their role was like that of a modern-day *copy editor. Correctors were considered to be separate from pressmen and compositors, from whose ranks many rose: their pay, hours, and privileges differed as well. *See also* PROOFS AND PROOFREADING. RMR

Gaskell, *NI*

corrigenda *See* ERRATA/CORRIGENDA.

Corser, Thomas (1793–1876) English book collector. He developed his interest in English literature while at Oxford, and amassed a large library, with particular strengths in early English printed books and medieval MSS. His library was sold at *Sotheby's in eight *book auctions between 28 July 1868 and 25 June 1873; another sale took place in Manchester in 1876. These realized more than £20,000. ASGE

Fletcher
ODNB

Corvey German private library. The Fürstliche Bibliothek Corvey is owned by the Dukes of Ratibor and Corvey. Its nucleus was collected in the beginning of the 19th century. It has 74,000 volumes, including an outstanding collection of fiction in German, English, and French, whose contents are being reproduced on microfiche (*see* MICROFORM). PV

Corvinus Press A London-based *private press, run as a hobby by George Dawson-Damer, Viscount Carlow.

Founded in early 1936, the press was important for its original literary output, supplied by Carlow's friends (including T. E. Lawrence, James Joyce, Edmund Blunden, Stefan Zweig, Walter de la Mare and H. E. Bates). It closed in 1945, when the *Dropmore Press acquired its printing equipment. PWN

P. W. Nash and A. J. Flavell, *The Corvinus Press* (1994)

Coster, Laurens Janszoon Legendary inventor of the art of printing at Haarlem in about 1440. The story goes that walking through the local wood, he cut some letters from the bark of a tree; they fell into the sand and made an imprint. This gave him the idea of printing books with movable type. However, during Christmas night of 1441 his servant Johann Faust stole his material, fled to Mainz, and began printing himself. This is in a nutshell the Coster legend, which was first recorded by Hadrianus Junius (*Batavia*, 1588). Coster subsequently became first a local, then a national hero whose honour was widely defended against the claims of *Gutenberg. He became the centre of national celebrations (his statue was unveiled in Haarlem in 1856), music, and plays. In fact, the history of the beginning of printing in the Netherlands is unclear. Before the first dated book (1473) a group of undated, typographically related (but not localized) Netherlandish printings can be distinguished. Formerly called 'Costeriana', they are known nowadays as 'Dutch Prototypography'. CDW

L. Hellinga-Querido and C. de Wolf, *Laurens Janszoon Coster Was Zijn Naam* (1988)

costume book A collection of *woodcuts or *engravings representing the clothing of 16th-century Europeans—and often the dress of Asians, Africans, and inhabitants of the Americas. The genre flourished from 1550 to 1660 in Italy and France, and eventually included books printed in Germany, the Low Countries, and England. The prints were accompanied by captions in up to three languages, often including Latin, which specified the city, rank, and professional or marital status of each figure, and sometimes described local customs. As the genre developed, its purposes expanded to include moralistic, satirical, and patriotic commentary. The popularity of costume books appears to have risen from the assumption that styles of dress captured the character of cities, regions, and nations—and from increased travel and curiosity about discoveries in the Americas. Examples of the genre include François Deserps's *Recueil de la diversité des habits* (Paris, 1562; 121 woodcuts) and Cesare Vecellio's huge *Degli Habiti antichi et moderni di tutto il Mondo* (Venice, 1598). ARJ

U. Ilg, 'The Cultural Significance of Costume Books in Sixteenth-Century Europe', in *Clothing Culture, 1350–1650*, ed. C. Richardson (2004)

C. Vecellio, *The Clothing of the Renaissance World*, tr. M. F. Rosenthal and A. R. Jones (2008)

Cosway bindings Luxury bindings, named after the artist Richard Cosway (1742–1821), made with painted miniatures inlaid in gold-tooled *leather. They were a speciality of the London bookselling firm *Sotheran's and were mostly produced *c.*1902–40. The bindings were often produced by the firm of *Rivière, with the miniatures painted by Miss C. Currie. Sotheran's claimed to have had 900 made by 1930. DRSP

H. Nixon, *Five Centuries of English Bookbinding* (1978)

co-text The words surrounding a particular word or passage within a text that provide context and help to determine meaning.

Cotsen Children's Library, Princeton (CCL) Located within *Princeton University Library's Department of Rare Books, CCL houses items in more than 30 languages from the 15th century to the present, including: an early Coptic Christian schoolbook, medieval MSS, Hans Christian Andersen's *scrapbooks, Beatrix Potter's illustrated letters, drawings by *Lear, American *dime novels, and Soviet Constructivist children's books. It hosts academic programmes on children's book history and distributes Cotsen Occasional Press publications. MDB

www.princeton.edu/cotsen, consulted July 2008

Cotta, Johann Friedrich (1764–1832) German publisher, politician, and entrepreneur. In 1787 Cotta took over the family-owned publishing house in Tübingen. Its rise began in 1794 when Cotta met Schiller; a long period of prosperous cooperation followed. Cotta succeeded in publishing the most famous authors of classical Weimar (Goethe, Herder) and Swabia (Hölderlin, Uhland). Fiction, scientific books, periodicals, and newspapers brought economic success. His *Allgemeine Zeitung* (founded in 1798) became the most influential German daily newspaper of the 19th century, despite being threatened by censorship. Cotta relocated his company in 1806 to Ulm, and in 1810 to Augsburg. In the same year he established a large, modern printing house in Stuttgart; in 1827, he founded the 'Literarisch-Artistische Anstalt' in Munich, producing lithographed geographical, scientific, and other illustrated books. At the Congress of Vienna in 1814, Cotta defended freedom of the press and copyright. Contemporaries called him the 'Bonaparte of the German book trade'. US

B. Fischer, *Der Verleger Johann Friedrich Cotta* (3 vols, 2003)
L. Lohrer, *Cotta* (1959)

cottage roof Name given to a decorative style popular in English bookbinding from *c.*1660 until well into the 18th century; its defining feature is a rectangular panel design whose sloping top and bottom edges resemble a roof or gable. DRSP

Pearson, *Bookbinding*

Cottle, Joseph (1770–1853) English publisher and writer. In 1791, Cottle set up as a bookseller in Bristol. Introduced to Southey and Coleridge in 1794, he became their publisher, issuing Coleridge's journal *The Watchman* (1796) and other works. In 1798, in partnership with Nathaniel Biggs, he published Wordsworth's and Coleridge's *Lyrical Ballads*. However, the investment proved a disaster, and by 1800 Cottle was selling his *copyrights to *Longman. RJD

ODNB

Cotton, Sir Robert Bruce (1571–1631) English politician and collector. From adolescence, Cotton collected English MSS, particularly historical ones, which he lent generously to his circle of fellow collectors and antiquaries. From 1622, his library was kept at Cotton House, Westminster. On Cotton's death, his son, Thomas (1594–1662), inherited 800 MSS, as well as monastic registers, state papers, and other MS materials. Cotton's grandson, John (1621–1702), arranged their purchase by the nation in 1702. Much material was damaged or destroyed in the Ashburnham House fire in 1731. The Cotton MSS became part of the *British Museum collections in 1753. There have been various catalogues: by Thomas Smith (1696), by *Wanley (1705), by David Casley (1734), and by Joseph Planta (1802). Among the treasures in Cotton's library were the *Lindisfarne Gospels, the *Beowulf MS, and two of the earliest surviving MSS of Bede's *Ecclesiastical History*. SP

E. A. Joy, 'Thomas Smith, Humfrey Wanley, and the "Little-Known Country" of the Cotton Library', eBLJ (2005): www.bl.uk/eblj/2005articles/article1.html, consulted Oct. 2008
ODNB
T. Smith, *Catalogue of the Manuscripts in the Cottonian Library 1696*, ed. C. G. C. Tite (1984)
C. G. C. Tite, *The Manuscript Library of Sir Robert Cotton* (1994)
C. Wright, ed., *Sir Robert Cotton as Collector* (1997)

coucher In papermaking, he transfers the newly formed *sheet from the hand *mould on to a felt blanket so that the water can be pressed out. *See also* VATMAN.

coucher book A medieval term that refers to very large volumes, too heavy to be read except when placed on a *lectern. They were designed for use in church services, as in the case of *graduals and some *missals, and for general purposes of edification, as with the *Vernon MS. Often, a coucher book is a large *cartulary or register. Such books were more likely to be owned by institutions than by individuals, in which setting they could be displayed and used for communal readings. CMM

C. Wordsworth and H. Littlehales, *The Old Service-Books of the English Church* (1904)

Coull brothers New Zealand printers, *stationers, and *paper mill proprietors. The Coull brothers—Thomas (1829–1909), William (1831–1917), and James Francis (1835–1909)—settled as printers in Dunedin (1872). In gold rush conditions, and with incoming partners Thomas Culling and the lithographer Joseph Longhurst Gregory, the firm expanded, taking over the Mataura Paper Mill (1884). A Wellington branch followed in 1906. A 1922 merger produced Coulls Somerville Wilkie; another in 1971 with *Whitcombe & Tombs Ltd gave rise to the Whitcoulls Group, keeping the Coull name alive into the next century. KIDM

J. Thomson, ed., *Southern People* (1998)

counter An open space wholly or partly enclosed within a letter. From 'counterpunch', a die used to form a depression in the *punch cut for the type.

counterfeit printing When editions are such close imitations that they may be said to be *forgeries, they are said to be counterfeit—as distinct from editions that are deceitful because they carry *false imprints or *false dates.

Counterfeiting has become increasingly easy since the development of modern scanners and colour printers. The ease with which money can be created has triggered a proliferation of websites with detailed instructions on recreating almost every nation's currency. It has also resulted in added security features embedded in most bank notes and the development of forgery detectors (*see* SECURITY PRINTING).

Some criminals prefer to make money by counterfeiting popular novels, such as the *Harry Potter series, or academic textbooks and selling them for a profit. Publishers say that most illegal copying involves university *textbooks. The *Association of American Publishers maintains that illegal copies of books constitute at least 20 per cent of the market in developing countries, especially China, adding up to some $500 million lost in foreign sales. Expanding economies, increasing enrolments, the widespread use of English in education, a weak tradition of respect for *copyright, and cheap but high-quality printing techniques all contribute to Asia's culture of counterfeiting. Textbooks, which are often expensive required reading, are reproduced either as simple stacks of photocopies or as professionally bound books selling for almost their full market value. British and American publishers offer a lower price in developing regions in order to try to compete, but this often causes more trouble as Western students buy the cheaper copies online (*see* WORLD WIDE WEB) and sell them.

In response to lost sales, publishers have sought the cooperation of foreign governments. Though many administrations show willingness to enforce laws on counterfeit music, films, and computer software, they are less willing to restrict their students' access to textbooks. To support publishers, the Agreement on Trade-Related Aspects of Intellectual Property is being phased in under the authority of the World Trade Organization.

The phenomenon of counterfeit printing is far from new. An early, notorious instance is the case of the *italic type first designed for and used by *Aldus in 1500, which was quickly copied by printers—Barthélemy Trot and Balthazard de Gabiano, among others—in Lyons, who then issued some of the very same works as if they were the Italian originals. *See also* FORGERIES AND HOAXES.

MGB, MMS

B. Bollag, 'Don't Steal This Book', *Chronicle of Higher Education*, 50.30 (2 Apr. 2004)
Lowry

countermark Watermarked image in paper, generally applied to a part of a sheet opposite the main *watermark, or occasionally in the margins or corners, containing identification details relating to the manufacturer or mill, sometimes with date information. Originally such marks were incorporated with the main watermark, but in Venice *c*.1483 the information was separated, and this countermarking practice was slowly adopted elsewhere. In France the use of a countermark opposite the main design was not common until after *c*.1567. By the late 17th century it was established practice to use countermarks to assert a maker's identity, typically using his initials or name; in England after 1816 the Excise mill number was sometimes included.

DCC

Labarre

country-house libraries Country houses have long had book collections for the benefit of their owners, households, and friends, and sometimes a broader public. Before *c*.1700, these were typically kept in studies or in chests scattered throughout the house, but during the 18th century the concept of a library room became increasingly popular. Architecturally, they often either balanced the chapel or were on the main axis of the house; some were private rooms upstairs or converted long galleries. The 19th-century country-house library became a social space, sometimes doubling as a morning or a billiards room. Numerous country-house libraries developed significantly in the 19th century; many such collections have since been dispersed by sale, while others are in the care of the *National Trust.

KEA

S. Jervis, 'The Country House Library: An Architectural History', *Library History*, 18 (2002), 175–90
M. Purcell, 'The Country House Library Reassess'd', *Library History*, 18 (2002), 157–74

Covens & Mortier (active 1685–1866) Book and map publishers in Amsterdam. Covens & Mortier was the most important Dutch publisher of commercial cartography in the 18th and the first half of the 19th century—and possibly the biggest contemporary map-trading house worldwide. The firm was founded by **Pieter Mortier** (1661–1711), who started as a bookseller, but soon began publishing maps and atlases. He was succeeded by his widow and by his brother **David** (1673–1733?). Pieter's son **Cornelis** (1699–1783) ran the business from 1722 with his brother-in-law **Johannes Covens** (1697–1774). Later partners were **Johannes Covens Jr.** (1722–94), **Cornelis Covens** (1764–1825) and **Cornelis Joannes Covens** (1806–90). The company published books, prints, music, games, and general printed matter, but its main focus was on a variety of cartographic material, atlases, (wall) maps, globes, town plans, and city profiles. Although most of the firm's maps were copied after foreign models or printed from older copper plates, the firm acted as a driving force for the popularization of map use in Europe.

MVE

M. van Egmond, *Covens & Mortier* (2005)

covers The upper and lower *boards of a bound book, with whatever covering material (e.g. *leather or cloth) has been put over them.

Covici-Friede New York publisher founded in 1928 by Pascal Covici (partner, Covici-McGee) and Donald Friede (vice-president, *Boni & Liveright). They first specialized in *limited editions, but published commercial fiction during the Depression. The firm was declared bankrupt in 1937. BEL

Covici Papers, www.hrc.utexas.edu/research/fa/covici.html, consulted Sept. 2007

Friede Papers, www.loc.gov/rr.mss/text/friede.html, consulted Sept. 2007

Cowley, Sir Arthur Ernest (1861–1931) Bodley's librarian 1919–31. Cowley joined the *Bodleian staff in 1896, specializing in Sanskrit, Aramaic, and Hebrew MSS, achieving recognition as a leading Semitic scholar. As librarian, he reformed cataloguing procedures and brought several outlying libraries under unified Bodleian control. He saw a solution for serious overcrowding problems in building an extension nearby, but died before it could be started. ASB
ODNB

Coxe, Henry Octavius (1811–81) Bodley's librarian 1860–81. After early work at the *British Museum, he joined the *Bodleian staff as sub-librarian in 1839, devoting much time and *palaeographical skill to the quarto catalogues of classical MSS. He succeeded *Bandinel as librarian, improving accessibility, devising a unified catalogue of printed books, making an additional reading room, improving placing, and incorporating the Radcliffe Library into the Bodleian. ASB
ODNB

Cracherode, Clayton Mordaunt (1730–99) English book collector. Cracherode assembled a library of about 4,500 volumes, particularly strong in early editions of the classics. He greatly valued fine bindings; a number of his books were rebound by R. *Payne. Virtually his entire library was bequeathed to the *British Museum, of which he had been a Trustee. ASGE

A. Davis, 'Portrait of a Bibliophile XVIII', *BC* 23 (1974), 339–54, 489–505
ODNB

Craesbeeck family Portuguese printing dynasty. Having been apprenticed in Antwerp under C. *Plantin, **Pedro Craesbeeck** (1572–1632) established a Lisbon press in 1597. He and his descendants **Lourenço** (1597–1679), **Paulo** (1605–60), and **António Craesbeeck de Mello** (1640–84) dominated Portuguese printing for nearly a century. DRW

H. Bernstein, *Pedro Craesbeeck and Sons* (1987)

craft binding Term sometimes used to describe a bookbinding made by hand, rather than through a mechanized process.

Cranach-Presse German *private press, founded in 1913 by Harry, Graf Kessler in Weimar. His main interest was in printing classical texts of antiquity and modern times. Famous contemporary artists and renowned type-designers such as A. Maillol, E. *Gill, Sir E. *Walker, and E. G. Craig worked closely with the press until it closed in 1933. Its masterpiece is generally thought to be the *Hamlet* of 1928–30. US

J. D. Brinks, ed., *Die Cranach-Presse des Grafen Harry Keßler*, 2e (2005)

Cranach the elder, Lucas (1472–1553) German painter, designer, and *engraver. Mostly working in Wittenberg at the court of the Elector of Saxony, Frederick III (the Wise), Cranach painted portraits (several of his friend *Luther, other Protestant reformers, and humanists), altarpieces, nudes, and mythological subjects. Heavily influenced by his contemporary *Dürer, his most important book work was in designing illustrations (*see* **16**) for Luther's first German New Testament (1522), including 21 anti-Roman Catholic illustrations for the Book of Revelation. With his workshop, including two sons, he produced a series of architectural and decorative woodcut *title-page borders for Luther's sermons and writings in the 1520s, *woodcut illustrations in popular propaganda for the German Reformation, and a *historiated *title-page for the 1541 complete Bible, depicting the fall and redemption of man. MMS

A. F. Johnson, *German Renaissance Title-Borders* (1929)
R. Scribner, *For the Sake of Simple Folk* (1981)
J. Strachan, *Early Bible Illustrations* (1957)

Crane, Ralph (*fl.* 1589–1632) English *scribe, particularly of theatrical MSS, including plays or masques by *Jonson, Middleton, Webster, Fletcher, and Massinger, as well as eight plays in the *First Folio (1623) of *Shakespeare. His characteristic features include regularized layout (*see* MISE-EN-PAGE), distinctive spellings, massed stage directions, and lists of *dramatis personae*. He also made copies of Sir Henry Mainwaring's 'Seaman's Dictionary' and several collections of poetry and devotional works, including verse of his own. PB

T. H. Howard-Hill, 'Ralph Crane: The Life and Works of a Jacobean Scribe in the Next Millenium', *Shakespearean International Yearbook*, 3 (2002), 150–57
ODNB

Crane, Walter (1845–1915) English illustrator, designer, painter, and technical author. Chiefly known for his illustrations for children's books, Crane was inspired by the Pre-Raphaelites, the ideas of *Ruskin, and Japanese prints. In 1865, he began producing designs for a series of colour 'toy' books for children, which were printed from woodblocks by E. *Evans. Crane was a socialist and a founding member of the Arts and Crafts Exhibition Society (established 1888). He also designed decorative items, including tiles, wallpaper, and textiles. *See also* **15**. KES
ODNB

Crane, Zenas (Crane & Co.) Papermaking company founded by Zenas Crane, in partnership with Henry Wiswall and John Willard, in 1801. Investing in cylinder-mould machinery, they ceased hand-papermaking in

1820. By 1842 the company was manufacturing security and banknote papers, and they continued to innovate and expand into other fine paper areas over the coming years. Crane & Co. (incorporated 1922), continue to produce banknotes for the US Treasury, in addition to fine watermarked papers, still made solely from cotton pulp.

DCC

www.crane.com, consulted Oct. 2006
D. C. Smith, *History of Papermaking 1691–1969* (1970)
W. B. Wheelwright, 'Zenas Crane, Pioneer Papermaker', *The Paper Maker*, 20 (1951), 1–7

Cranmer, Thomas (1489–1556) Archbishop and book collector. He owned one of the largest private libraries in mid-Tudor England. After his execution, many of his books passed to *Lumley, subsequently into the Royal Library, and finally into the *British Library. More than 600 printed books from his library survive; these can be recognized by the inscription 'Thomas Cantuarien[sis]' on the title-page.

AH

D. G. Selwyn, *The Library of Thomas Cranmer*, OBS 3/1 (1996)

Crawford, William Horatio (1815–88) Irish philanthropist and book collector. In 1870, he began developing what became a large collection of MSS, *incunabula, and other early books at Lakelands, County Cork. His library made £21,255 when sold over 12 days by *Sotheby's from 12 March 1891. Some of his early charters were bought by the *Bodleian Library.

ASGE

A. S. Napier and W. H. Stevenson, *The Crawford Collection of Early Charters and Documents in the Bodleian Library* (1895)

creative writing programmes Courses of study in literary or artistic production, usually offered at universities. Long established in the US, the oldest and most prestigious Master of Fine Arts (MFA) in an English degree programme is at the University of Iowa, which offered creative writing courses from 1897; its Writers' Workshop, founded in 1936 under the directorship of Wilbur Schramm, claims *poets laureate (US) and *Pulitzer Prize and *National Book Award winners among its alumni. The most notable of hundreds of similar programmes in America are at Columbia University, Cornell, NYU, Brown, Johns Hopkins, Yale, Virginia, Northwestern, and Stanford.

The University of East Anglia pioneered degree courses in creative writing in Britain, its MA being founded in 1970 by Malcolm Bradbury and Angus Wilson. The university has also offered a PhD in Creative and Critical Writing. Its staff have included Angela Carter, Rose Tremain, and Andrew Motion, and early graduates include Ian McEwan and Kazuo Ishiguro. There are numerous other such courses across the UK, including at the universities of Glasgow and Manchester, and a growing number of Anglophone programmes internationally, in Ireland, Australia, New Zealand, and Canada.

Graduate-level creative writing programmes are organized either as MFA courses in fiction or poetry or as MA degrees with a concentration on creative writing. Increasingly, MFA programmes offer dedicated courses in playwriting, screenwriting, children's literature, creative non-fiction, and science writing. Degree programmes are often organized around writing workshops with additional coursework in literature, craft, and theory; they are examined by a book-length creative thesis. Some programmes have affiliated and long-established literary journals and produce *anthologies of students' work.

PDF

University of East Anglia, 'Creative Writing', www.uea.ac.uk/eas/sectors/creative/cwhome.shtml, consulted Sept. 2006
University of Iowa, Writer's Workshop, 'About the Workshop', www.uiowa.edu/~iww/about.htm, consulted Sept. 2006
T. Kealey, *The Creative Writing MFA Handbook* (2005)

Creech, William (1745–1815) Scottish bookseller and magistrate. He was apprenticed to the Royal Printer and then flourished in Edinburgh society by conducting auctions and hosting meetings known as 'Creech's levees'. Creech published nationalist texts for little profit and raised the profile of Scottish literature. He wrote under the *pseudonym 'Theophrastus' for several Scottish newspapers, and in 1791 published a collection of his own satirical writings entitled *Edinburgh Fugitive Pieces*.

CMA

ODNB

Creede, Thomas (c.1554–1616) London printer. Running a small London *printing office, he produced mainly religious and literary books, particularly contemporary dramatic works. Much of his output was self-financed, but by 1600 Creede was increasingly turning to trade printing. This led to a change in his production, with fewer literary works, in favour of political and, especially, religious books.

KMQ

ODNB

A. Yamada, *Thomas Creede, Printer to Shakespeare and his Contemporaries* (1994)

Cresci, Gianfrancesco (**Giovanni Francesco**) (c.1534/5–early 17th century) Milan-born calligrapher and copyist in the *Vatican Library. He published the earliest printed manual of *calligraphy, the *Essemplare* (Rome, 1560), and two later treatises on writing: *Il perfetto scrittore* (Rome, 1570) and *Il perfetto cancellaresco* (Rome, 1579). Cresci consistently questioned the utility of the existing *chancery italic, emphasizing instead earlier book hands and the beauty of Roman inscriptional capitals.

ASGE

A. S. Osley, *Scribes and Sources* (1980)

Crespin, Jean (c.1520–72) A printer's son, educated in Leuven, he began his career in Paris 1541–2 as secretary to the jurist Charles Dumoulin. Condemned for heresy after converting to Protestantism, he settled in Geneva in 1548, where he founded a printing office. Many religious writings in French came from his press. Upon his death, the business was continued by his son-in-law Eustache Vignon.

CS

J.-F. Gilmont, *Jean Crespin* (1981)

Cresset Press A London-based publisher, run between 1927 and 1967 by the wealthy philanthropist Denis Cohen. He initially published illustrated books in *limited editions, including *Gulliver's Travels* (1930), with *pochoir-coloured engravings by *Whistler. After 1932, Cresset issued well-designed trade editions of literary and political works. PWN

J. Dreyfus, 'Dennis Cohen and the Cresset Press', *Matrix*, 12 (1992), 83–93

J. Thompson, 'The Cresset Press', *PL 5/3* (2000), 51–77

Creuzevault, Henri (1905–71) French binding designer and publisher. After training in painting and bookbinding, he specialized in binding design and became one of the leading Parisian exponents of the inter-war years. He joined his brother Louis (d. 1937) in establishing a publishing and bookselling business in 1936, and in 1956 gave up binding to manage an art gallery. DRSP

C. Creuzevault, *Henri Creuzevault 1905–1971* (1987)

A. Duncan and G. de Bartha, *Art Nouveau and Art Deco Bookbinding* (1989)

Crevenna, Pietro Antonio Bolongaro (1736–92) Italian-Dutch book collector. A rich Amsterdam tobacco manufacturer, he amassed an impressive *bibliophile's library, of which he published a catalogue in 1775–6. The main part of the collection was sold in 1790, the remainder three years later. JVH

J. van Heel, 'Bolongaro Crevenna: négociant et bibliophile italien à Amsterdam', in [Association internationale de bibliophilie. XXe congrès, La Haye 1997,] *Actes et communications*, ed. J. Storm van Leeuwen (2004)

crime fiction *See* DETECTIVE FICTION.

critical edition A *scholarly edition that does not replicate the text of one document, but rather presents a corrected text, compiled from one or more source documents, and an *apparatus recording editorial emendations and textual *variants. Most closely associated with *Greg, *Bowers, and *Tanselle, whose numerous writings on textual matters have greatly influenced Anglo-American editing, this methodology holds that editions should fulfil *authorial intention by 'purifying' the text of external corruption. After *collating all relevant documents, critical editors frequently choose one to follow as their *copy-text. Where variant readings exist, they must adjudicate between witnesses. Evaluating the textual evidence to determine the authority of individual *accidentals and substantives, the editor then selects the reading deemed most appropriate. The basis for selecting readings varies according to one's editorial principles (author-centred, reception-centred, etc.), but all editors are duty-bound to follow consistent standards and inform readers of emendations. Rejected variants are documented in the *apparatus, which is occasionally integrated into the text, but more often confined to an appendix or notes. RSG

D. C. Greetham, *Textual Scholarship* (1992)

J. McGann, 'What is Critical Editing?', *Text*, 5 (1991), 15–29

G. T. Tanselle, *A Rationale of Textual Criticism* (1989)

Croatia, National and University Library of (Nacionalna i sveučilišna knjižnica u Zagrebu) Founded in 1607 as the library of the Jesuit College in Zagreb, the library was transferred to the Royal Academy of Sciences in Zagreb in 1776. In 1837, it began to receive *legal deposit copies from the provinces of Croatia and Slavonia in the Austrian empire. It became the University of Zagreb Library when the modern university was established in 1874. In the Yugoslav state (1918–91), it was one of eight legal deposit libraries. The collection consists of 2.5 million volumes, with 3,670 MSS and 10,295 early printed books in *Glagolitic, *Cyrillic, and *Latin *scripts. MVG

Crockford, John (1824/5–1865) English publisher. Crockford began publishing as early as 1843 in association with Edward William Cox, issuing such periodicals as *Law Times*, *Clerical Journal*, *The Critic*, and *The Field*. However, he is best known for publishing the *Clerical Directory*, which appeared in weekly *numbers (beginning 1855) and a full edition (1858). Known as *Crockford's Clerical Directory* from 1860, it was published by *Oxford University Press from 1921 until 1985. PLS
ODNB

Crom, Mattheus (*fl.* 1537–46) Netherlandish printer. In Antwerp, he produced some 80 publications, half of them under anonymous or *false imprints. In 1537, he printed the 'Matthew Bible' for the London publisher *Grafton. His Protestantism prompted his flight to England in 1546. PGH

H. F. Wijnman, 'De Antwerpse hervormingsgezinde drukker Mattheus Crom en zijn naaste omgeving', *GP* 11 (1962), 105–24

Cromberger, Jakob (1472/3–1528), and **Johann Cromberger** (1500–1540) Spanish printers. A German immigrant, Jakob founded Spain's leading 16th-century printing dynasty in 1503. His Seville press, manned in part by slave labour, was renowned for liturgical printing and technical competence. The business expanded under Jakob's son Johann, who exported books to Mexico and in Mexico City established the first New World press, opened in 1539 by *Pablos. DRW

C. Griffin, *The Crombergers of Seville* (1988)

cropped *See* TRIMMED BINDING.

Crossley, James (1800–1883) English book collector and antiquary. Crossley spent most of his life in Manchester, and his library came to include more than 50,000 books and MSS. He had a particular interest in *Defoe, to whose bibliography he made valuable contributions. After his death, parts of his collection were sold in Manchester by Thompson & Son in May 1884; there were further sales at *Sotheby's in London in July 1884 and June 1885. ASGE
ODNB

cross-stroke In *type design, the horizontal *stroke that crosses a vertical stroke on certain letters, such as t or f. A cross-stroke should have at least one end open (not joined to a contiguous letter). Horizontals meeting vertical strokes (as in letters e, A, and H, for instance) are called 'bars'.   MMS

crossword puzzle book The first crossword puzzle was published on 21 December 1913 in the Sunday New York *World*. The 'word-cross'—devised by Arthur Wynne of Liverpool, England, and initially printed without black squares—became an immediate success. In 1924, a new publisher printed the first edition of a crossword puzzle book. *Simon & Schuster, whose publishing house was launched as a consequence of this title, distributed more than 300,000 of these hardcover books, each with a pencil attached. The series continues to the present; the cover of number 256 (2007) declared the firm: 'The Original Crossword Puzzle Publisher'.   KAW

Crouch, Nathaniel (*c*.1640–1725?) London bookseller, publisher, author. Made free of the *Stationers' Company in 1664, Crouch became a successful bookseller and *publisher of a large number of religious and historical books and of popular *miscellanies, as well as being the proprietor of short-lived newspapers. He wrote a number of historical works under the *pseudonym Richard or Robert Burton, as well as books for children. Many of Crouch's books achieved great popularity and success.
                                                                          JH

ODNB

Crown Publishers New York trade house (*see* TRADE PUBLISHER (2)) founded in 1936 by Nat Wartels and Robert Simon, owners of Outlet Book Co., which sold books *remaindered by their *publishers. Crown continued to sell remaindered books, but in 1943 acquired the lists of *Covici-Friede as well as Lothrop, *Lee, & Shepard, whose name they continued to use for their children's books (*see* **15**). (Crown sold Lothrop, Lee, & Shepard to *Scott, Foresman in 1965.) During World War II, remaindered books became scarce, and Crown began publishing new books. Its list was eclectic, including genre fiction (*romance fiction under its Gramercy *imprint, westerns and *mysteries under its Phoenix imprint), *gift books, literary fiction (the works of Sholom Aleichem), and Alex Comfort's *bestseller *The Joy of Sex*. Crown was sold to *Random House in 1988 and has been a division of *Bertelsmann since 1998.   BEL

Cruikshank, George (1792–1878) English caricaturist and illustrator. Self-taught, Cruikshank began his career satirizing political and social situations in humorous cartoons for publications such as the *Scourge*, the *Meteor*, and the *Satirist*. He quickly made his reputation, succeeding Gillray as the most popular caricaturist of the day. Cruikshank continued to publish political cartoons in periodicals until *c*.1825; after 1820, he contributed designs to an estimated 850 books. Among his best-known illustrations are a series of copper-plate *etchings of Grimms' fairytales—*German Popular Stories* (2 vols, 1823–6). Cruikshank also famously illustrated Dickens's

Sketches by 'Boz' (1836) and *Oliver Twist* (1838). Later in his career, his sets of moralizing prints (not unlike those of *Hogarth)—*The Bottle* (1847) and *The Drunkard's Children* (1848)—addressed themes such as the evils of alcohol and of personal excess.   KES
ODNB
R. L. Patten, *George Cruikshank's Life, Times and Art* (2 vols, 1992, 1996)

crushed morocco *Goatskin that has been pressed with polished plates to create a smooth, ungrained surface; popular for luxury bookbinding in the late 19th century.

Crynes, Nathaniel (1685/6–1745) Educated at St John's College, Oxford, of which he became a fellow, Crynes is best known as a book collector. He owned a wide range of English and foreign books and MSS. These were bequeathed variously to the *Bodleian Library, *St John's, *Balliol, and Lincoln colleges, and to his sister Hannah.   ASGE
ODNB

Cuala Press *See* DUN EMER PRESS/CUALA PRESS.

Cuba, National Library of (Biblioteca Nacional 'José Martí') Named after the Cuban national hero José Martí (1853–95) and located in Havana, the library was established in 1901. It did not receive significant government support until the 1940s. Its present building opened in 1958, shortly before the 1959 revolution. Under the Castro regime, its collections have grown to more than 2.3 million volumes, with special strengths in Cuban history and *imprints. The library administers the Cuban public library system, maintains active bibliographical and publication programmes (including the national *Bibliografía Cubana*), and sponsors a network of *book clubs.   DRW

Cuesta, Juan de la (d. 1625?) Spanish printer. In 1604 he took over the Madrid shop of Pedro Madrigal, having worked there from *c*.1599. Until 1625, he was a leading Madrid printer, issuing first editions of Cervantes's *Don Quixote* (1605–15) and *Novelas ejemplares* (1613), and several of Lope de Vega's works.   DRW

cuir ciselé The decoration of leather-covered bookbindings by incising a pattern in the *leather, using a sharp blade (rather than impressed tools). Found on early Coptic bindings, the technique became popular in continental Europe, particularly around Germany and Austria, in the late 14th and early 15th centuries. It was never common in England.   DRSP
M. Foot, *Pictorial Bookbindings* (1986)

cumdach An ornamental box, often richly decorated with jewels or metalwork, made to hold and protect a precious book. The word is Irish in derivation; the first known cumdach was made in Ireland in the late 9th century to hold the Book of *Durrow.   DRSP

Cumplido, Ignacio (1811–87) Mexican printer, publisher, and journalist. Born in Guadalajara, Cumplido published the influential Mexico City newspaper *El Siglo XIX* (1841–96), several periodicals, and much else. His well-equipped printing office—the country's most advanced—acquired Mexico's first *cylinder machine press (1843) and set new standards for Mexican *typography. DRW

Cumulative Book Index (*CBI*) A bibliographical index of English-language books, first published in 1898 by the H. W. *Wilson Co. as a monthly list of books issued in the US. After 1928, *CBI* also included works published in English worldwide. Fiction and non-fiction works at least 50 pages long were included, although some shorter books (including children's books: *see* **15**) were indexed; government documents were not. After 1982, *CBI* was only published as a database, and indexing ceased in 1999. AMS

Curll, Edmund (1675–1747) London bookseller and patent medicine seller. Having been apprenticed to Richard Smith, he set up his own shop in London in 1706. He had several fruitful partnerships during his working life and published the works of some of the most important writers of his time. He earned *Swift's condemnation for publishing some of his writings without permission, and made a lasting adversary of *Pope, calling him a traitor during the Jacobite rebellion of 1715. However, Curll revelled in his reputation as an entrepreneurial, if disreputable, businessman, releasing many indecent works, including the notorious *Eunuchism Display'd* (1718). In 1725, Curll was arrested for producing books of this nature and was accused of *libel. A public apology did not prevent the bookseller from being imprisoned for several months. CMA
P. Baines and P. Rogers, *Edmund Curll, Bookseller* (2007)
ODNB

Currer, Frances Mary Richardson (1785–1861) English book collector. Her library at Eshton Hall in Yorkshire exceeded 20,000 volumes, including printed books in many fields and some MSS. She enjoyed a close friendship with *Heber and was admired by *Dibdin. The bulk of her library was sold at Sotheby's on 30 July 1862 and realized nearly £6,000. Most of the remaining works were sold there on 31 May 1916 and made £3,700. ASGE
ODNB

curses and **anathemas** In the ages of religious faith, the threat of spiritual privation was held to be a more powerful deterrent to stealing or misusing books than chains or electronic tagging (*see* LIBRARY SECURITY). Popes were induced to pronounce formal excommunication *latae sentientiae* on those who despoiled the books of favoured universities such as *Bologna and *Salamanca; lesser institutions had to rely on curses, ranging from the blunt ('He that stealeth this book/shall be hanged on a hook') to picturesquely detailed lists of physical and spiritual penalties, reminiscent of the one that so puzzled Tristram Shandy's Uncle Toby. BJF
M. Drogin, *Anathema!* (1983)

cursive script [Lat. *currere*, 'to run'] The term generally denotes forms of written roman *script copied rapidly without primary concern for clarity and regularity of shape of individual *letterforms. It is written with infrequent lifts of the *pen from the page; hence, individual letters are usually linked and copied at angles. Such a script is used, for example, in correspondence or forms of record keeping, in which emphasis tends to fall on compression, to a degree that is much more pronounced than is the case with formal *bookhands. Yet, the distinction between cursive and other kinds of handwriting is not always a precise one: during the Middle Ages, there developed book hands that employed a number of cursive features, such as the English anglicana and French bastarda scripts.

In antiquity, a Greek cursive (*majuscule cursive, derived from the capital), with the letterforms joined by *ligatures was in common use, especially in administrative *papyri; the more recent *minuscule cursive is found in documents of the 6th and 7th centuries AD. Latin cursive also emphasized rapidity of formation, simplification of letterforms, and the joining of letters. After the 6th century, it is chiefly derived from the minuscule.

Cursive scripts, sometimes called 'running writing' or 'joined-up writing', are also used for everyday writing in a number of modern, non-roman alphabets—e.g. for Hebrew, Russian, Greek, and even Chinese and Japanese. Their common characteristic is that they save the writer time, although they are in some instances considerably less legible than more formal hands. ASGE
M. Parkes, *English Cursive Book Hands 1250–1500*, 2e (1979)
E. Poulle, *Paléographie des écritures cursives en France du 15e au 17e siècle* (1966)
B. Van Hoesen, *Roman Cursive Writing* (1915)
F. Wang, *Introduction to Chinese Cursive Script* (1958)

Curwen Press A printing and publishing firm at Plaistow, founded in 1863 by the music teacher John Curwen. Harold Curwen joined in 1908 and turned the Press from music to general printing. After 1920, when the book designer Oliver Simon joined Curwen, the Press attained a high reputation for *bookwork and *decorated papers, before closing in 1984. PWN
H. Simon, *Song and Words* (1973)

Curzon, Robert, 14th Baron Zouche (1810–73) English book collector. He developed a substantial collection of Western MSS and early printed books. He also owned a number of Greek and Coptic MSS obtained while travelling in the Middle East with his friend and fellow collector Walter Sneyd in the 1830s. His collection was bequeathed to the British Museum. ASGE
A. N. L. Munby, *Connoisseurs and Medieval Miniatures* (1972)
ODNB

Cushing, Harvey (1869–1939) American book collector. An outstanding surgeon, Cushing was influenced by his friend and fellow doctor/collector *Osler (whose biography Cushing wrote). Cushing's collecting interests encompassed medieval and renaissance science and the history of medicine as revealed in both MS and print; he wrote extensively on these subjects. His library was donated to *Yale University. ASGE

Journal of the History of Medicine, 25 (Apr. 1969)

cut A term sometimes used to describe a book illustration (*see* **16**) produced from a *woodcut block, or (less commonly) a metal one.

cylinder machine Papermaking machine characterized by a forming section consisting of a hollow metal cylinder covered with mesh that revolves in a vat of pulp. Water drains through the mesh, leaving a wet fibre mat adhering to the cylinder, which is stripped off and fed through a press and dryer section before reel-up. This design was patented by John Dickinson (1809). Running more slowly than the *Fourdrinier machine, it is used mainly for making speciality papers (notably banknote and *security grades), fine papers, and multi-ply boards. *See also* **10**; MACHINE-MADE PAPER. DCC

Hills
Hunter
Labarre

cylinder press Printing machine in which the *forme is borne on a flat bed under a paper-bearing cylinder, creating an *impression where the two come into contact (*see* **11**). The earliest cylinder press used in Britain was built by Andreas Bauer and Friedrich König in 1812 and sold to *The Times*, which first used the high-speed press to print the newspaper for 29 November 1814. *See also* ROTARY PRESS. MFS

J. Moran, *Printing Presses* (1973)

Cyrillic type Cyrillic movable type was first used in 1491 in Cracow by the German merchant *Fiol to print four liturgical books. It was introduced independently in 1494 in Cetinje by the monk *Makarije, perhaps identical with the Macarie who printed three books in Wallachia in 1508–12. *Skaryna printed two books in 1523–5 in Vilno, which became a major centre after printing was resumed there *c*.1570. Printing began in Moscow in the 1560s, and presses were operating very soon afterwards in Belarus and Ukraine; printing in the Balkans was restricted by Turkish oppression. Among printers whose output was primarily Latin, the earliest to use Cyrillic was Giorgio de Rusconi in Venice in 1512.

The earliest printers were also *typefounders. Established local practice clearly affected printers such as *Vuković in Venice, and Venetian influence is also visible in Skaryna's work, but in general early typefaces resemble the formal Cyrillic hands used to copy the Scriptures and liturgical books in the areas which the presses served. *Fedorov's Moscow typefaces are different from those he later cast in Ukraine. Rusconi and his successors in

Venice and Rome followed the tradition of Western Cyrillic ('bosančica') used by Roman Catholics in the Balkans. In Vilno, the Mamoniči used a style of type resembling Lithuanian chancery hands for some of their books, both secular and sacred.

The modernizing activity of *Peter I of Russia extended to typography. The new Civil *founts designed in 1707–8 imitated Latin antiqua typefaces, with some influence from Russian and Ukrainian chancery hands. It was cast in Amsterdam and Moscow, and after further revision in 1710 became standard for secular printed books. (The Church continues to use the older style of type.) By the end of the century, civil script was being used outside the Russian empire as well.

The gradual end of Ottoman domination in the Balkans in the 19th century led to the expansion of printing there and the development of local styles of type. In Russia, there was a brief flowering of typography in the early 20th century, but in the Soviet period standards declined so seriously that high-quality editions were often printed abroad. With the advent of computer technology it has become much more usual to include several alphabets, including Cyrillic, within a single family of type. RMC

Czech Academy of Sciences, Library of the (**Akademie věd České, Knihovna**) Created in 1952 (together with the academy) by an amalgamation of the existing libraries of the country's principal learned societies. The head of the network of specialist libraries at the individual institutes that have been incorporated into the academy, its significant collections primarily serve members of the academy. The library also supports work in historical *bibliography and is responsible for the compilation of the *union catalogue, *The Bibliography of Foreign Language Bohemica Printed in 1501–1800*. DP

HDHB

Czech Republic, National Library of the (**Národní knihovna České republiky**) The origins of the major Czech library date back to the foundation of the Charles University in Prague in 1348; its library collections were amalgamated in 1777 with the library of the dissolved Jesuit College at the Clementinum building under the name of the Imperial and Royal Public and University Library. The library received government funding and, in 1781, the right of *legal deposit. There were 147,000 volumes. Although collection policies aimed at the universal coverage of subjects, a separate department, 'Bibliotheca nationalis', dedicated to preserving material of Czech interest, was established. Following the creation of Czechoslovakia in 1918, the library was called the Public and University Library, and in 1935 was renamed the National and University Library. Incorporating the Slavonic Library, and becoming the centre of the nationwide library system in 1958, it developed into the State Library; its current name was introduced in the 1990s. In 1992, the library became part of the Czech and Slovak Library Information Network (CASLIN). DP

E. Novotná, ed., *National Library of the Czech Republic* (1997)
P. Oulíková, *The Klementinum* (2006)

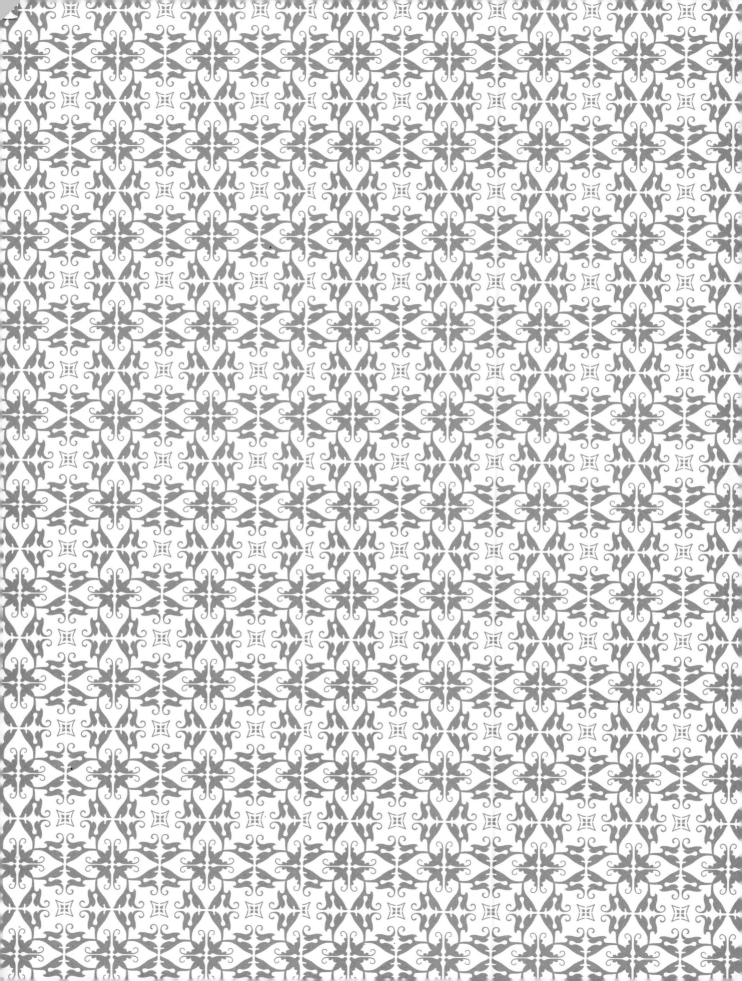